Koren Talmud Bavli

THE NOÉ EDITION

BAVA KAMMA

Steinsaltz Center

KOREN

תלמוד בבלי

KOREN TALMUD BAVLI

THE NOÉ EDITION

בבא קמא

BAVA KAMMA

Daf 62b through Daf 83a

COMMENTARY BY

Rabbi Adin Even-Israel Steinsaltz

EDITOR-IN-CHIEF

Rabbi Dr Tzvi Hersh Weinreb

SENIOR CONTENT EDITOR

Rabbi Dr Shalom Z Berger

EXECUTIVE EDITOR

Rabbi Joshua Schreier

STEINSALTZ CENTER

KOREN PUBLISHERS JERUSALEM

Supported by the Matanel Foundation

Koren Talmud Bavli, The Noe Edition
Vol. 21e: Tractate Bava Kamma, Daf 62b through Daf 83a
Paperback, ISBN, 978-965-7765-98-2

First Hebrew/English paperback edition, 2023

Koren Publishers Jerusalem Ltd.
PO Box 4044, Jerusalem 91040, ISRAEL
PO Box 8531, New Milford, CT 06776, USA
www.korenpub.com

Steinsaltz Center

Steinsaltz Center is the parent organization of institutions established by Rabbi Adin Even-Israel Steinsaltz

PO Box 45187, Jerusalem 91450 ISRAEL
Telephone: +972 2 646 0900, Fax +972 2 624 9454
www.steinsaltz-center.org

Printed in Turkey

הִנֵּה יָמִים בָּאִים, נְאֻם אֲדֹנָי יֱהוִה, וְהִשְׁלַחְתִּי רָעָב בָּאָרֶץ,
לֹא־רָעָב לַלֶּחֶם וְלֹא־צָמָא לַמַּיִם, כִּי אִם־לִשְׁמֹעַ אֵת דִּבְרֵי יהוה.

Behold, days are coming – says the Lord God – I will send a hunger to the land, not a hunger for bread nor a thirst for water, but to hear the words of the Lord. (AMOS 8:11)

The Noé edition of the Koren Talmud Bavli
with the commentary of Rabbi Adin Even-Israel Steinsaltz
is dedicated to all those who open its covers
to quench their thirst for Jewish Knowledge,
in our generation of Torah renaissance.

This beautiful edition is for the young, the aged,
the novice and the savant alike,
as it unites the depth of Torah knowledge
with the best of academic scholarship.

Within its exquisite and vibrant pages,
words become worlds.

It will claim its place in the library of classics,
in the bookcases of the Beit Midrash,
the classrooms of our schools,
and in the offices of professionals and business people
who carve out precious time to grapple with its timeless wisdom.

For the Student and the Scholar

DEDICATED BY LEO AND SUE NOÉ

Steinsaltz Center

Executive Director, Steinsaltz Center

Rabbi Meni Even-Israel

Managing Editor

Rabbi Jason Rappoport

Senior Content Editor

Rabbi Dr. Shalom Z. Berger

Editors

Rabbi Dr. Joshua Amaru, *Coordinating Editor*
Rabbi Avishai Magence, *Content Curator*
Tal Avrahami
Aryeh Bernstein
Menucha Chwat
Rabbi Yoel Domb
Rabbi Yehoshua Duker
Betzalel Philip Edwards
Rabbi Yonatan Shai Freedman
Raphael Friedman
Rabbi Uri Goldstein
Rabbi Alan Haber
Rabbi Tzvi Chaim Kaye
Stephen Lauber
Sholom Licht
Elisha Loewenstern
Rafi Miller
Rabbi Eli Ozarowski
Rabbi David Sedley
Shira Shmidman
Rabbi Michael Siev
Avi Steinhart

Copy Editors

Aliza Israel, *Coordinator*
Bracha Hermon
Ita Olesker
Debbie Ismailoff
Shira Finson
Ilana Sobel
Deena Nataf
Eliana Kurlantzick Yorav
Erica Hirsch Edvi
Nava Wieder
Sara Henna Dahan

Language Consultants

Dr. Stephanie E. Binder, *Greek & Latin*
Rabbi Yaakov Hoffman, *Arabic*
Dr. Shai Secunda, *Persian*
Shira Shmidman, *Aramaic*

KOREN

Design & Typesetting

Dena Landowne Bailey, *Typesetting*
Tani Bayer, *Jacket Design*
Raphaël Freeman, *Design & Typography*

Images

Eliahu Misgav, *Illustration & Image Acquisition*
Daniel Gdalevich, *Illustration & Image Acquisition*

Introduction by the Publisher

The Talmud has sustained and inspired Jews for thousands of years. Throughout Jewish history, an elite cadre of scholars has absorbed its learning and passed it on to succeeding generations. The Talmud has been the fundamental text of our people.

Beginning in the 1960s, Rabbi Adin Even-Israel Steinsaltz שליט״א created a revolution in the history of Talmud study. His translation of the Talmud, first into modern Hebrew and then into other languages, as well the practical learning aids he added to the text, have enabled millions of people around the world to access and master the complexity and context of the world of Talmud.

It is thus a privilege to present the *Koren Talmud Bavli*, an English translation of the talmudic text with the brilliant elucidation of Rabbi Steinsaltz. The depth and breadth of his knowledge are unique in our time. His rootedness in the tradition and his reach into the world beyond it are inspirational.

Working with Rabbi Steinsaltz on this remarkable project has been not only an honor, but a great pleasure. Never shy to express an opinion, with wisdom and humor, Rabbi Steinsaltz sparkles in conversation, demonstrating his knowledge (both sacred and worldly), sharing his wide-ranging interests, and, above all, radiating his passion. I am grateful for the unique opportunity to work closely with him, and I wish him many more years of writing and teaching.

Our intentions in publishing this new edition of the Talmud are threefold. First, we seek to fully clarify the talmudic page to the reader – textually, intellectually, and graphically. Second, we seek to utilize today's most sophisticated technologies, both in print and electronic formats, to provide the reader with a comprehensive set of study tools. And third, we seek to help readers advance in their process of Talmud study.

To achieve these goals, the *Koren Talmud Bavli* is unique in a number of ways:

- The classic *tzurat hadaf* of Vilna, used by scholars since the 1800s, has been reset for great clarity, and opens from the Hebrew "front" of the book. Full *nikkud* has been added to both the talmudic text and Rashi's commentary, allowing for a more fluent reading with the correct pronunciation; the commentaries of *Tosafot* have been punctuated. Upon the advice of many English-speaking teachers of Talmud, we have separated these core pages from the translation, thereby enabling the advanced student to approach the text without the distraction of the translation. This also reduces the number of volumes in the set. At the bottom of each *daf*, there is a reference to the corresponding English pages. In addition, the Vilna edition was read against other manuscripts and older print editions, so that texts which had been removed by non-Jewish censors have been restored to their rightful place.

- The English translation, which starts on the English "front" of the book, reproduces the *menukad* Talmud text alongside the English translation (in bold) and commentary and explanation (in a lighter font). The Hebrew and Aramaic text is presented in logical paragraphs. This allows for a fluent reading of the text for the non-Hebrew or non-Aramaic reader. It also allows for the Hebrew reader to refer easily to the text alongside. Where the original text features dialogue or poetry, the English text is laid out in a manner appropriate to the genre. Each page refers to the relevant *daf*.

- Critical contextual tools surround the text and translation: personality notes, providing short biographies of the Sages; language notes, explaining foreign terms borrowed from Greek, Latin, Persian, or Arabic; and background notes, giving information essential to the understanding of the text, including history, geography, botany, archaeology, zoology, astronomy, and aspects of daily life in the talmudic era.
- Halakhic summaries provide references to the authoritative legal decisions made over the centuries by the rabbis. They explain the reasons behind each halakhic decision as well as the ruling's close connection to the Talmud and its various interpreters.
- Photographs, drawings, and other illustrations have been added throughout the text – in full color in the Standard and Electronic editions, and in black and white in the Daf Yomi edition – to visually elucidate the text.

This is not an exhaustive list of features of this edition, it merely presents an overview for the English-speaking reader who may not be familiar with the "total approach" to Talmud pioneered by Rabbi Steinsaltz.

Several professionals have helped bring this vast collaborative project to fruition. My many colleagues are noted on the Acknowledgments page, and the leadership of this project has been exceptional.

RABBI MENACHEM EVEN-ISRAEL, DIRECTOR OF THE STEINSALTZ CENTER, was the driving force behind this enterprise. With enthusiasm and energy, he formed the happy alliance with Koren and established close relationships among all involved in the work.

RABBI DR. TZVI HERSH WEINREB שליט״א, EDITOR-IN-CHIEF, brought to this project his profound knowledge of Torah, intellectual literacy of Talmud, and erudition of Western literature. It is to him that the text owes its very high standard, both in form and content, and the logical manner in which the beauty of the Talmud is presented.

RABBI JOSHUA SCHREIER, EXECUTIVE EDITOR, assembled an outstanding group of scholars, translators, editors, and proofreaders, whose standards and discipline enabled this project to proceed in a timely and highly professional manner.

RABBI MEIR HANEGBI, EDITOR OF THE HEBREW EDITION OF THE STEINSALTZ TALMUD, lent his invaluable assistance throughout the work process, supervising the reproduction of the Vilna pages.

RAPHAËL FREEMAN, EXECUTIVE EDITOR OF KOREN, created this Talmud's unique typographic design which, true to the Koren approach, is both elegant and user friendly.

It has been an enriching experience for all of us at Koren Publishers Jerusalem to work with the Steinsaltz Center to develop and produce the *Koren Talmud Bavli*. We pray that this publication will be a source of great learning and, ultimately, greater *avodat Hashem* for all Jews.

Matthew Miller, Publisher
Koren Publishers Jerusalem
Jerusalem 5772

Contents

For the vocalized Vilna Shas layout, please open as a Hebrew book.

Introduction to **Perek VII**

If a man steals an ox or a sheep, and slaughters it or sells it, he shall pay five oxen for an ox and four sheep for a sheep.

(Exodus 21:37)

If the theft shall be found in his possession alive whether it is an ox, or a donkey, or a sheep, he shall pay double.

(Exodus 22:3)

If a man gives his neighbor money or vessels to safeguard and it was stolen from the house of the man, if the thief shall be found he shall pay double. If the thief shall not be found, the owner of the house shall approach the judges to determine if he misappropriated his neighbor's goods. For any matter of trespass, from an ox, for a donkey, for a sheep, for a garment, for any lost item about which one shall say: This is it, the claims of both of them shall come before the judges, the one whom the judges convict shall pay double to his neighbor.

(Exodus 22:6–8)

This chapter deals mainly with the fines imposed upon a thief: Double payment in ordinary circumstances, and a fourfold or fivefold payment if the thief steals a sheep or an ox and then slaughters or sells it. Whereas repayment of the principal amount stolen is a simple monetary reimbursement, specific *halakhot* apply to the fines imposed by the Torah, which take effect in a limited set of circumstances.

Several basic questions are addressed, such as: In which precise cases is a thief obligated to pay these fines? What is the relationship between the double payment and the fourfold or fivefold payment?

Other issues discussed in this chapter involve cases in which the thief, during the course of the act of theft, commits a transgression involving a serious punishment. At times this can lead to a cancellation of the monetary obligations incurred through the theft itself. Another question is whether the testimony of two separate sets of witnesses, one concerning the theft of an animal and the other its slaughter or sale, can be combined into a single incriminating testimony. Furthermore, it is necessary to establish the punishment for conspiring witnesses who testify about the theft of an animal, or about its slaughter or sale, or both.

מתני׳ מְרוּבָּה מִדַּת תַּשְׁלוּמֵי כֶפֶל מִמִּדַּת תַּשְׁלוּמֵי אַרְבָּעָה וַחֲמִשָּׁה, שֶׁמִּדַּת תַּשְׁלוּמֵי כֶפֶל נוֹהֶגֶת בֵּין בְּדָבָר שֶׁיֵּשׁ בּוֹ רוּחַ חַיִּים וּבֵין בְּדָבָר שֶׁאֵין בּוֹ רוּחַ חַיִּים, וּמִדַּת תַּשְׁלוּמֵי אַרְבָּעָה וַחֲמִשָּׁה אֵינָהּ נוֹהֶגֶת אֶלָּא בְּשׁוֹר וָשֶׂה בִּלְבַד, שֶׁנֶּאֱמַר: ״כִּי יִגְנֹב אִישׁ שׁוֹר אוֹ שֶׂה וּטְבָחוֹ אוֹ מְכָרוֹ״ וגו׳.

MISHNA **The principle of double payment** applies **more broadly**[NH] **than the principle of fourfold or fivefold payment, as the principle of double payment applies both to** the theft of **something that is alive and to** the theft of **something that is not alive, but the principle of fourfold or fivefold payment applies only to** the theft of **an ox or a sheep, as it is stated: "If a man steal an ox or a sheep, and slaughter it or sell it,** he shall pay five oxen for an ox and four sheep for a sheep" (Exodus 21:37).

אֵין הַגּוֹנֵב אַחַר הַגַּנָּב מְשַׁלֵּם תַּשְׁלוּמֵי כֶפֶל, וְלֹא הַטּוֹבֵחַ וְלֹא הַמּוֹכֵר אַחַר הַגַּנָּב מְשַׁלֵּם תַּשְׁלוּמֵי אַרְבָּעָה וַחֲמִשָּׁה.

Having stated a limitation to the *halakha* of fourfold and fivefold payment, the mishna mentions a further limitation, which applies to all three types of payments. **One who steals** an item **after a thief**[H] has already stolen it, i.e., one who steals a stolen item, **does not pay** the **double payment** to the thief or to the prior owner, **nor does one who slaughters or sells** an ox or a sheep **after a thief** has already stolen it **pay** the **fourfold or fivefold payment.** Rather, he pays only the principal, i.e., the value of the item he stole.

גמ׳ וְאִילּוּ מִדַּת תַּשְׁלוּמֵי כֶפֶל נוֹהֶגֶת בֵּין בְּגַנָּב בֵּין בְּטוֹעֵן טַעֲנַת גַּנָּב, וּמִדַּת תַּשְׁלוּמֵי אַרְבָּעָה וַחֲמִשָּׁה אֵינָהּ נוֹהֶגֶת אֶלָּא בְּגַנָּב בִּלְבַד – לָא קָתָנֵי.

GEMARA The mishna teaches one particular difference between double payment and fourfold or fivefold payment, **while it does not teach** this difference between them: **The principle of double payment applies both in** the case of **a thief and in** the case of a bailee who falsely **states the claim** that **a thief** stole[H] the deposit entrusted to him and who takes an oath to that effect. **But the principle of fourfold or fivefold payment applies only in** the case of **a thief,** not in the case of one who falsely claims that a deposit was stolen.

מְסַיֵּיע לֵיהּ לְרַבִּי חִיָּיא בַּר אַבָּא, דְּאָמַר רַבִּי חִיָּיא בַּר אַבָּא אָמַר רַבִּי יוֹחָנָן: הַטּוֹעֵן טַעֲנַת גַּנָּב בְּפִקָּדוֹן – מְשַׁלֵּם תַּשְׁלוּמֵי כֶפֶל, טָבַח וּמָכַר – מְשַׁלֵּם תַּשְׁלוּמֵי אַרְבָּעָה וַחֲמִשָּׁה.

The fact that the mishna does not teach the latter distinction **supports** the opinion of **Rabbi Ḥiyya bar Abba, as Rabbi Ḥiyya bar Abba says** that **Rabbi Yoḥanan says:** In the case of **one who** falsely **states the claim** that **a thief** stole a **deposit** from him, and it is discovered that he himself is the thief, he **pays double payment.** And if the stolen item is an ox or sheep and **he slaughtered or sold** it, **he pays** the **fourfold or fivefold payment.** According to Rabbi Ḥiyya bar Abba, there is no difference between the applications of double payment and fourfold or fivefold payment in this case.

אִיכָּא דְּאָמְרִי: לֵימָא מְסַיֵּיע לֵיהּ לְרַבִּי חִיָּיא בַּר אַבָּא, דְּאָמַר רַבִּי חִיָּיא בַּר אַבָּא אָמַר רַבִּי יוֹחָנָן: הַטּוֹעֵן טַעֲנַת גַּנָּב בְּפִקָּדוֹן – מְשַׁלֵּם תַּשְׁלוּמֵי כֶפֶל, טָבַח וּמָכַר – מְשַׁלֵּם תַּשְׁלוּמֵי אַרְבָּעָה וַחֲמִשָּׁה?

There are those **who say** a different version of this discussion: **Let us say** that the mishna **supports** the opinion of **Rabbi Ḥiyya bar Abba, as Rabbi Ḥiyya bar Abba says** that **Rabbi Yoḥanan says:** In the case of **one who** falsely **states the claim** that **a thief** stole a **deposit** from him, and it is discovered that he himself is the thief, he **pays double payment.** And if the stolen item is an ox or sheep, and **he slaughtered or sold** it, **he pays** the **fourfold or fivefold payment.**

NOTES

The principle of double payment applies more broadly – **מְרוּבָּה מִדַּת תַּשְׁלוּמֵי כֶפֶל:** Rabbeinu Yehonatan of Lunel writes that after having completed its discussion of the primary categories of damage that are caused by one's property, i.e., the primary categories of Goring, Eating, and Trampling, and the categories of Fire and Pit, the mishna turns its attention to a type of damage caused by a person himself, namely theft. Damage caused by a person was introduced earlier in the tractate, as according to Rav (3b), damage caused by a person is the primary category of *maveh* mentioned in the first mishna of the tractate (2a). Even according to those who disagree with Rav and maintain that damage caused directly by a person is not mentioned in that mishna, it is mentioned in the list of primary categories of damage recorded by Rabbi Ḥiyya and Rabbi Oshaya (4b).

HALAKHA

The principle of double payment applies more broadly – **מְרוּבָּה מִדַּת תַּשְׁלוּמֵי כֶפֶל:** If witnesses testify that an individual stole an item from another person, the thief must pay the victim double the value of the stolen item. Furthermore, if one stole an ox or a sheep and slaughtered or sold it, he must pay four times the value of the sheep or five times the value of the ox (Rambam *Sefer Nezikin, Hilkhot Geneiva* 1:6; *Tur, Ḥoshen Mishpat* 348).

One who steals an item after a thief – **הַגּוֹנֵב אַחַר הַגַּנָּב:** If one steals a stolen item from a thief, he is not required to make double payment to either the first thief or to the prior owner, even if the prior owner of the item has already despaired of recovering it. Similarly, if one steals an ox or sheep from a thief and then slaughters it or sells it, he is not required to pay the fourfold or fivefold payment (Rambam *Sefer Nezikin, Hilkhot Geneiva* 1:17; *Tur, Ḥoshen Mishpat* 350).

A bailee who falsely states the claim that a thief stole – **טוֹעֵן טַעֲנַת גַּנָּב:** In the case of a bailee who takes a false oath claiming that an item entrusted to him has been stolen, and witnesses subsequently testify that his claim was false and the item is in his possession, the bailee is considered a thief and must pay the owner of the item double its value. If he slaughtered or sold an ox or sheep after taking the oath, he pays the fourfold or fivefold payment (Rambam *Sefer Nezikin, Hilkhot Geneiva* 4:1; *Tur, Ḥoshen Mishpat* 352).

מִי קָתָנֵי ״אֵין בֵּין״? ״מְרוּבָּה״ קָתָנֵי, תְּנָא וְשַׁיֵּיר.

The Gemara rejects the inference: **Does** the mishna **teach** that **there is no** difference **between** double payment and fourfold or fivefold payment except for the one mentioned in the mishna? **It teaches** merely that the principle of double payment applies **more broadly** than the principle of fourfold or fivefold payment, and it provides an example of this statement. This does not mean that this is the only difference, and it is possible that the *tanna* **taught** this one case **and omitted** others.

״שֶׁמִּדַּת תַּשְׁלוּמֵי כֶפֶל נוֹהֶגֶת״ כו׳. מְנָא הָנֵי מִילֵּי? דְּתָנוּ רַבָּנַן: ״עַל כָּל דְּבַר פֶּשַׁע״ – כְּלָל, ״עַל שׁוֹר עַל חֲמוֹר עַל שֶׂה וְעַל שַׂלְמָה״ – פְּרָט, ״עַל כָּל אֲבֵדָה״ – חָזַר וְכָלַל,

§ The mishna teaches **that the principle of double payment applies** both to the theft of something that is alive and to the theft of something that is not alive. The Gemara asks: **From where are these matters** derived? It is **as the Sages taught** in a *baraita* with regard to the verse that discusses double payment: "For any matter of trespass, whether it be for an ox, for a donkey, for a sheep, for a garment, or for any manner of lost thing about which one shall say: This is it, the claims of both of them shall come before the judges, the one whom the judges convict shall pay double to his neighbor" (Exodus 22:8). **"For any matter of trespass"** is **a generalization; "whether it be for an ox, for a donkey, for a sheep, for a garment"** is **a detail.** And when the verse states: **"Or for any manner of lost thing," it then generalizes** again.

כְּלָל וּפְרָט וּכְלָל אִי אַתָּה דָּן אֶלָּא כְּעֵין הַפְּרָט, מַה הַפְּרָט מְפוֹרָשׁ דָּבָר הַמִּטַּלְטֵל וְגוּפוֹ מָמוֹן, אַף כָּל דָּבָר הַמִּטַּלְטֵל וְגוּפוֹ מָמוֹן,

Consequently, this verse contains **a generalization, and a detail, and a generalization,**[B] and one of the thirteen rules of exegesis states that in such a case **you may deduce** that the verse is referring **only** to items **similar to the detail.** Therefore, **just as** each of the items mentioned in **the detail** is clearly **defined as an item that is movable property and** has **intrinsic monetary** value, **so too** double payment is practiced with regard to **any item that is movable property and** has **intrinsic monetary** value.

יָצְאוּ קַרְקָעוֹת – שֶׁאֵינָן מִטַּלְטְלִין, יָצְאוּ עֲבָדִים – שֶׁהוּקְשׁוּ לְקַרְקָעוֹת, יָצְאוּ שְׁטָרוֹת – שֶׁאַף עַל פִּי שֶׁמִּטַּלְטְלִין אֵין גּוּפָן מָמוֹן, יָצָא הֶקְדֵּשׁ – ״רֵעֵהוּ״ כְּתִיב.

Land is excluded,[NH] **as it is not movable property.** Canaanite **slaves are excluded, as they are compared to land**[N] in many areas of *halakha*. Financial **documents are excluded, as, although they are movable property, they do not** have **intrinsic monetary** value. The value of the material on which the document is written is negligible; documents are valuable only because they serve as proof for monetary claims. Finally, **consecrated** property **is excluded**[H] because **it is written** in the verse that the one found liable shall pay double to **"his neighbor,"** i.e., to another person, rather than to the Temple treasury.

אִי מַה הַפְּרָט מְפוֹרָשׁ דָּבָר שֶׁנִּבְלָתוֹ מְטַמֵּא בְּמַגָּע וּבְמַשָּׂא, אַף כָּל דָּבָר שֶׁנִּבְלָתוֹ מְטַמֵּא בְּמַגָּע וּבְמַשָּׂא, אֲבָל עוֹפוֹת לָא!

The Gemara asks: **If** the *halakha* of double payment is limited to cases similar to the details mentioned in the verse, it should also be derived that **just as** each of the items mentioned in **the detail** is clearly **defined as an item whose carcass transmits impurity through contact and carrying,**[B] **so too any item whose carcass transmits impurity through contact and carrying** it is subject to double payment. **But birds,** whose carcasses do not transmit impurity through contact or carrying, should **not** be subject to double payment.

וּמִי מָצֵית אָמְרַתְּ הָכִי? וְהָא ״שַׂלְמָה״ כְּתִיב! אָמְרִי: אֲנַן בְּבַעֲלֵי חַיִּים קָאָמְרִינַן, אֵימָא: בְּבַעֲלֵי חַיִּים, דָּבָר שֶׁנִּבְלָתוֹ מְטַמֵּא בְּמַגָּע וּבְמַשָּׂא – אִין, דָּבָר שֶׁאֵין נִבְלָתוֹ מְטַמֵּא בְּמַגָּע וּבְמַשָּׂא – לָא,

The Gemara objects to the question: **But how can you say this? But isn't "garment" written** in the list of specified items (Exodus 22:8)? It is impossible to speak of the impurity of carcasses with regard to clothing. The Gemara responds: **Say,** in response to this objection: **We are speaking** specifically **of animals,** and this is the question that was asked: Why not **say** that **with regard to animals,** an animal **whose carcass transmits impurity through contact and carrying, yes,** it is subject to double payment, whereas an animal **whose carcass does not transmit impurity through contact and carrying,** such as a bird, **no,** a thief would not pay double payment for stealing it?

BACKGROUND

A generalization, and a detail, and a generalization – כְּלָל וּפְרָט וּכְלָל: This method of derivation employs the following logic: If the Torah had intended to include all matters in a particular *halakha* it would have been enough to write the first generalization. If it had intended to exclude all matters except for the details mentioned, it could have written merely the details after the generalization. Since it added a further generalization after the details, it intended to add other matters that are comparable in their characteristics to those mentioned in the Torah.

Transmits impurity through contact and carrying – מְטַמֵּא בְּמַגָּע וּבְמַשָּׂא: Ritual impurity in the Torah typically refers to impurity imparted through contact, i.e., when a person or object comes into direct contact with a source of impurity. If there is an object interposing between the individual and the source of impurity, the interposing object is susceptible to ritual impurity but generally does not transmit the impurity to the person. Yet, there are some sources of ritual impurity, such as most animal carcasses, a *zav*, and a menstruating woman, whose impurity is transmitted by carrying the source of impurity, even if there is no direct contact.

NOTES

Land is excluded – יָצְאוּ קַרְקָעוֹת: *Tosafot* explain how it is possible to steal land: One who owns land extends the boundary markers into the adjacent property of his neighbor, effectively annexing some of it. Another case is where one steals fruits from a tree, as fruit that is attached to the tree is categorized as land.

Canaanite slaves…are compared to land – עֲבָדִים שֶׁהוּקְשׁוּ לְקַרְקָעוֹת: It is explained in the Jerusalem Talmud that slaves are excluded because one benefits only from their labor rather than from their actual bodies. The slave referred to here is a Canaanite slave. The status of a Hebrew slave is like that of any other Jew, and the punishment for kidnapping and selling a fellow Jew is execution. Since monetary fines are not imposed in cases subject to the death penalty, there is no discussion of double payment for one who steals a Hebrew slave.

HALAKHA

Land is excluded, etc. – יָצְאוּ קַרְקָעוֹת וכו׳: One who steals land, Canaanite slaves, or financial documents returns what he stole but does not pay the double payment (Rambam *Sefer Nezikin, Hilkhot Geneiva* 2:2; *Tur, Hoshen Mishpat* 350).

Consecrated property is excluded – יָצָא הֶקְדֵּשׁ: One who steals consecrated property does not have to pay the double payment (Rambam *Sefer Nezikin, Hilkhot Geneiva* 2:1; *Tur, Hoshen Mishpat* 350).

דְּהָא כָּל חַד וְחַד כְּלָל וּפְרָט בְּאַפֵּי נַפְשֵׁיהּ דָּרְשִׁינַן לֵיהּ, אֲבָל עוֹפוֹת לָא!

This line of reasoning is correct, **because we expound each one**[N] of the listed items in the **generalization, and detail,** and generalization **by itself.** Each item is treated individually as representing a category, but the different items are not grouped together into one broad category. Since several animals are listed, it is concluded that if the stolen item is an animal it must resemble the listed animals. **But** since **birds** do not transmit impurity through contact or carrying, they are **not** subject to double payment.

אִם כֵּן, נִכְתּוֹב רַחֲמָנָא חַד פְּרָטָא.

The Gemara rejects this: **If so, let the Merciful One write** just **one detail,** i.e., animal, and that would have been enough to teach that animals are subject to double payment only if they transmit impurity through contact and carrying, so birds are excluded. Since the Torah listed several animals, birds are included.

הֵי נִכְתּוֹב רַחֲמָנָא? אִי כְּתַב רַחֲמָנָא ״שׁוֹר״, הֲוָה אָמִינָא: קָרֵב לְגַבֵּי מִזְבֵּחַ – אִין, שֶׁאֵין קָרֵב לְגַבֵּי מִזְבֵּחַ – לָא, וְאִי כְּתַב רַחֲמָנָא ״חֲמוֹר״, הֲוָה אָמִינָא: קָדוֹשׁ בִּבְכוֹרָה – אִין, שֶׁאֵין קָדוֹשׁ בִּבְכוֹרָה – לָא!

The Gemara questions this assertion: **Which** individual animal **should the Merciful One have written? If the Merciful One had written** only **"ox," I would say** that only an animal that is similar to an ox, in that it **is sacrificed on the altar, yes,** it is subject to double payment. But an animal **that is not sacrificed on the altar, no,** it is not subject to double payment. **And if the Merciful One had written** only **"donkey," I would say** that only an animal that is similar to a donkey, in that its firstborn male offspring is **sacred with** the sanctity of **a firstborn,**[B] **yes,** it is subject to double payment. But an animal that is **not sacred with** the sanctity of **a firstborn, no,** it is not subject to double payment. The principle of double payment would then include cattle, sheep, goats, and donkeys, but not other animals (see Exodus 13:13 and Deuteronomy 15:19).

אָמְרִי: אִם כֵּן, נִכְתּוֹב רַחֲמָנָא ״שׁוֹר״ ״וַחֲמוֹר״, ״שֶׂה״ לָמָּה לִי? שְׁמַע מִינָּהּ: לְאֵתוֹיֵי עוֹפוֹת.

The Gemara responds: **Say** in answer to this question: **If so,** if the Torah had wished to limit double payment to cases where cattle, sheep, goats, or donkeys were stolen, **let the Merciful One write** just **"ox" and "donkey"; why do I** need the verse to mention **"sheep"? Conclude from it** that the Torah intends **to include** even animals that do not meet these criteria, e.g., **birds.**

וְאֵימָא: לְאֵתוֹיֵי עוֹפוֹת טְהוֹרִים, דּוּמְיָא דְּשֶׂה, דִּמְטַמֵּא בְּגָדִים אַבֵּית הַבְּלִיעָה, אֲבָל עוֹפוֹת טְמֵאִים דְּלֵית בְּהוּ טוּמְאָה, דְּלָא מְטַמְּאֵי בְּגָדִים אַבֵּית הַבְּלִיעָה – לָא! ״כָּל״ רִיבּוּיָא הוּא.

The Gemara asks further: **But say** that the verse mentions sheep in order **to include** only **kosher birds,** which are **similar to the sheep**[N] listed in the verse, in **that** a carcass of these birds **renders** both the one who eats it and his **garments** ritually **impure** when it passes through his **esophagus,**[B] as the carcass of a sheep also transmits ritual impurity. **But non-kosher birds,**[B] whose carcasses **do not have ritual impurity** at all, **as they do not render** either the one who eats them or his **garments impure** when they pass through his **esophagus, no,** they are not subject to double payment. The Gemara answers: The word **"any** [*kol*]**,"** in the phrase "for any [*kol*] matter of trespass" is **an amplification,** and serves to include even non-kosher birds in the principle of double payment.

NOTES

Because we expound each one, etc. – **דְּהָא כָּל חַד וְחַד וכו׳**: Rashi explains that as a general rule, in the application of the exegetical method of a generalization, and a detail, and a generalization, when there are many details listed, each detail is expounded individually in the manner of generalization and a detail and a generalization, rather than being expounded as a unified group. *Tosafot*, however, note that there are many instances of a generalization, detail, and generalization in which the items on the detailed list are expounded as a group rather than individually, such as the example of second tithe, cited shortly thereafter. *Tosafot* therefore explain that it is only in the verse pertaining to double payment (Exodus 22:8) that this approach is taken, because the items are not listed in immediate succession but are separated with the word "for [*al*]": "For an ox, for a donkey, for a sheep, for a garment, or for any manner of lost thing." The separation in the sequence of items is what leads the Gemara to expound on each item of the list separately.

Similar to the sheep – **דּוּמְיָא דְּשֶׂה**: "Sheep" is seen as an extraneous item, as the mention of "ox" and "donkey" already includes all animals that are sacrificed on the altar, those for whom the firstborn is sacred, and those whose carcasses transmit impurity through contact or carrying. Consequently, "sheep" is mentioned to include other animals that do not share these characteristics. The Gemara then asks: Granted, "sheep" is representative of a larger category, but it should be sufficient for this category to include kosher birds, which transmit ritual impurity in some manner. Why should the category be expanded so far as to include non-kosher birds, which do not transmit impurity at all and are therefore completely dissimilar to sheep?

BACKGROUND

Sacred with the sanctity of a firstborn – **קָדוֹשׁ בִּבְכוֹרָה**: The Torah commands one to treat with sanctity all firstborn kosher animals born in his flock or herd, as well as his firstborn donkey and his firstborn son. The unblemished kosher animals are sacrificed as offerings and eaten by the priests after their blood has been sprinkled on the altar, while the firstborn donkey and son can be redeemed. The donkey is redeemed with a lamb, while the son is redeemed with five silver coins given to a priest.

Renders one and his garments impure when it passes through his esophagus – **מְטַמֵּא בְּגָדִים אַבֵּית הַבְּלִיעָה**: A special *halakha* applies to the carcass of a kosher bird: Although it is impure, it does not impart ritual impurity through contact or carrying, as does the carcass of a non-avian animal, but only through eating. When a piece of the bird's carcass enters a person's esophagus, he contracts ritual impurity that extends to the clothes he is wearing.

Kosher birds…non-kosher birds – **עוֹפוֹת טְהוֹרִים...עוֹפוֹת טְמֵאִים**: The Torah lists all the non-kosher birds but does not state the indicators that distinguish kosher from non-kosher birds. The Sages provided indicators; the general rule is that a bird of prey cannot be eaten. For a kosher bird the indicators are: It has one digit facing backward, it has a crop, and its gizzard has a membrane that can be peeled off by hand.

BACKGROUND

Amplification and restriction, and generalization and detail – רִבּוּי וּמִיעוּט וּכְלָל וּפְרָט: The methods of amplification and restriction, and those of generalization and detail are two exegetical approaches to biblical verses. They are attributed to Rabbi Akiva and Rabbi Yishmael respectively. Nevertheless, all of the Sages used both of these methods, except in certain circumstances in which each would insist on using his own specific approach.

Both methods are applied to biblical verses in which there is a general statement followed by specific examples of the same *halakha*. Depending on the presentation, there may be an amplification followed by a restricting term, corresponding to a generalization and detail; a restricting term and amplification, corresponding to a detail and generalization; or an amplification and restricting term and amplification, corresponding to a generalization and detail and generalization. According to the principle of generalization and detail, the example mentioned in the verse provides detail through an explanation and definition of the general rule. Consequently, the detail always limits the scope of the generalization, whereas the generalization that follows it is almost always an expansion of the specific example cited.

By contrast, according to the method of amplification and restriction, the specific case mentioned in the verse is not meant as an example but as a defining feature that limits the case by indicating what is not included in the amplification. When an amplification is followed by a restricting term, and these two expressions are followed by another amplification, the only items excluded from the amplification are those that totally differ from the restricting term. Therefore, this method of exegesis tends to be more inclusive than the principle of a generalization and detail and generalization, in which the final generalization expands the detail to include items similar to it.

HALAKHA

Second tithe – מַעֲשֵׂר שֵׁנִי: Second-tithe money must be used to purchase food fit for human consumption. The food must either grow from the ground or be nourished by that which grows from the ground (Rambam *Sefer Zera'im, Hilkhot Ma'aser Sheni* 7:3–5).

וְכָל הֵיכָא דִּכְתַב "כָּל" רִיבּוּיָא הוּא? וְהָא גַּבֵּי מַעֲשֵׂר דִּכְתִיב "כֹּל", וְקָא דָּרְשִׁינַן לֵיהּ בִּכְלָל וּפְרָט!

The Gemara asks: **But** is it so that **anywhere that** the Torah **wrote** the word ***kol* it is an amplification? But isn't it** so that **with regard to** second **tithe,** the word ***kol* is written** in the verse: "And you shall bestow the money for whatever [*bekhol*] your soul desires, for oxen, or for sheep, or for wine, or for strong drink, or for whatever your soul asks of you" (Deuteronomy 14:26)? **And** yet **we expound** that verse **as a generalization, and a detail,** and a generalization.[B]

דְּתַנְיָא: "וְנָתַתָּ הַכֶּסֶף בְּכֹל אֲשֶׁר תְּאַוֶּה נַפְשְׁךָ" – כְּלָל, "בַּבָּקָר וּבַצֹּאן וּבַיַּיִן וּבַשֵּׁכָר" – פְּרָט, "וּבְכֹל אֲשֶׁר תִּשְׁאָלְךָ נַפְשֶׁךָ" – חָזַר וְכָלַל, כְּלָל וּפְרָט וּכְלָל אִי אַתָּה דָּן אֶלָּא כְּעֵין הַפְּרָט, מַה הַפְּרָט מְפוֹרָשׁ פְּרִי מִפְּרִי וְגִידּוּלֵי קַרְקַע, אַף כָּל פְּרִי מִפְּרִי וְגִידּוּלֵי קַרְקַע!

As it is taught in a *baraita*: **"And you shall bestow the money for whatever your soul desires,"** is **a generalization,** as no particular type of food is specified. **"For oxen, or for sheep, or for wine, or for strong drink,"** is **a detail,** as specific types of food are mentioned. When the verse concludes with **"or for whatever your soul asks of you," it has generalized again.** Since the verse is formulated as a **generalization, and a detail, and a generalization, you may deduce** that the verse is referring **only** to items **similar to the detail.** This indicates that **just as** each of the items mentioned in **the detail** is clearly **defined as the produce of produce,** i.e., they grow from a parent organism, e.g., agricultural produce or animals, **and** they are **grown from the ground,** i.e., their sustenance comes from the ground, **so too** the category of items one may purchase with second-tithe money includes **all** items that are **the produce of produce and are grown from the ground.**[H]

אָמְרִי: "בְּכֹל" – כְּלָלָא, "כָּל" – רִיבּוּיָא הוּא. וְאִיבָּעֵית אֵימָא: "כָּל" – כְּלָלָא הוּא, מִיהוּ "כָּל" דְּהָכָא – רִיבּוּיָא הוּא.

The Gemara responds: **Say** in answer to this question that the term *bekhol* is **a generalization,** whereas the term ***kol* is an amplification. And if you wish, say** an alternate answer: The word ***kol*** is usually **a generalization. But** the word ***kol* that** is written **here,** in the verse concerning double payment (Exodus 22:8), is an exception. It is regarded as **an amplification,** as the Gemara will explain.

מִכְּדִי כְּתִיב מֵעִיקָּרָא כְּלָל וּפְרָט וּכְלָל, דִּכְתִיב: "כִּי יִתֵּן אִישׁ אֶל רֵעֵהוּ" – כְּלָל, "כֶּסֶף אוֹ כֵלִים" – פְּרָט, "לִשְׁמֹר" – הֲדַר וְכָלַל,

After all, there is another **generalization, and a detail, and a generalization written at the beginning** of this passage, **as it is written:** "If a man gives his neighbor money or vessels to safeguard and it was stolen from the house of the man, if the thief shall be found he shall pay double" (Exodus 22:6). **"If a man gives his neighbor"** is a **generalization. "Money or vessels" is a detail.** When the verse concludes **"to safeguard," it has generalized again.**

וְאִי סָלְקָא דַּעְתָּךְ הַאי "עַל כָּל דְּבַר פֶּשַׁע" נַמִי לִכְלָל וּפְרָט הוּא דַּאֲתָא, נִכְתּוֹב רַחֲמָנָא לְהָנֵי פְּרָטֵי גַּבֵּי הָאֵיךְ כְּלָל וּפְרָט, "עַל כָּל דְּבַר פֶּשַׁע" לָמָּה לִי? שְׁמַע מִינָּהּ רִיבּוּיָא הוּא.

And if it enters your mind to say that **this** later verse: **"For any matter of trespass"** (Exodus 22:8), **is also coming** to state **a generalization, and a detail,** and a generalization, **let the Merciful One write these details,** i.e., ox, donkey, sheep, and garment, which are cited in the later verse, **together with that** previous **generalization, and detail,** and generalization. **Why do I need** the latter verse beginning with **"for any matter of trespass"? Conclude from it** that the word *kol* **is an amplification** in this instance, and it includes all animals.

הָשְׁתָּא דְּאָמְרַתְּ "כָּל" רִיבּוּיָא, כָּל הָנֵי פְּרָטֵי לָמָּה לִי? חַד לְמַעוּטֵי קַרְקַע, וְחַד לְמַעוּטֵי עֲבָדִים, וְחַד לְמַעוּטֵי שְׁטָרוֹת, "שַׂלְמָה" – לְמַעוּטֵי דָּבָר שֶׁאֵינוֹ מְסוּיָּים, "עַל כָּל אֲבֵדָה" – לְכִדְרַבִּי חִיָּיא בַּר אַבָּא, דְּאָמַר רַבִּי חִיָּיא בַּר אַבָּא אָמַר רַבִּי יוֹחָנָן: הַטּוֹעֵן טַעֲנַת גַּנָּב

The Gemara asks: **Now that you said** that the word ***kol* is an amplification, why do I need all these details** listed in the verse, i.e., ox, donkey, sheep, and garment? The Gemara answers: As for the three animals listed, **one** is mentioned **to exclude land, one to exclude** Canaanite **slaves, and one to exclude** financial **documents.** The example of **a garment** is mentioned **to exclude an item that is not** clearly **delineated** in size or quantity.[N] **"Or for any manner of lost thing"** is written **to** teach that **which Rabbi Ḥiyya bar Abba says, as Rabbi Ḥiyya bar Abba says** that **Rabbi Yoḥanan says:** With regard to **one** who falsely **states the claim** that **a thief** stole

NOTES

To exclude an item that is not clearly delineated in size or quantity – לְמַעוּטֵי דָּבָר שֶׁאֵינוֹ מְסוּיָּים: Rashi explains that an item that is not clearly delineated is one with no distinguishing features. Many early commentaries wonder why the lack of distinguishing features should be a factor with regard to liability for double payment. *Tosafot* provide two explanations. The first is that the Gemara is referring to an item that has no clearly delineated size or quantity. For example, one claims that a roomful or a container of produce was stolen from him, but he cannot delineate precisely how much produce that was. The second explanation of *Tosafot* is that it is referring to an item that is incomplete or broken, e.g., half a pomegranate or a half a nut. The Ra'avad and the Meiri note that the exclusion from double payment of an item that is not clearly delineated is relevant only with regard to double payment in a case where one is obligated to take an oath, e.g., a bailee or one who admits to partial monetary liability. By contrast, the obligation to return stolen items and the obligation to pay double payment in regular cases of theft applies even to such items.

בַּאֲבֵידָה מְשַׁלֵּם תַּשְׁלוּמֵי כֶפֶל, שֶׁנֶּאֱמַר: ״עַל כָּל אֲבֵדָה אֲשֶׁר יֹאמַר״.

a lost item that he had found,[H] which he had been obligated to safeguard until it could be returned to its owner, **he pays double payment, as it is stated: "For any manner of lost thing about which one shall say:** This is it…the one whom the judges convict shall pay double to his neighbor" (Exodus 22:8).

תְּנַן הָתָם: הֵיכָן פִּקְדוֹנִי? אָמַר לֵיהּ: אָבַד. מַשְׁבִּיעֲךָ אֲנִי, וְאָמַר: אָמֵן, וְהָעֵדִים מְעִידִים אוֹתוֹ שֶׁאֲכָלוֹ – מְשַׁלֵּם אֶת הַקֶּרֶן. הוֹדָה עַל פִּי עַצְמוֹ – מְשַׁלֵּם קֶרֶן וְחוֹמֶשׁ וְאָשָׁם.

§ **We learned** in a mishna **elsewhere** (108b) about a case where an owner of an item said to the bailee: **Where is my deposit?** The bailee **said to him: It was lost.**[H] The owner said: **I administer an oath to you** that it was actually lost, **and** the bailee **said: Amen,** thereby accepting the oath; **and** subsequently **the witnesses testify about** the bailee **that he** himself **consumed** the deposit. In this case, the bailee **pays the principal,** i.e., the value of the deposit, to the owner. If the bailee **admitted on his own**[H] that he stole the deposit before any witnesses testified to this effect, **he pays the principal and** an additional **one-fifth** of the principal amount to the owner, **and** he brings **a guilt-offering** to atone for his sin (see Leviticus 5:20–26).

הֵיכָן פִּקְדוֹנִי? אָמַר לוֹ: נִגְנַב. מַשְׁבִּיעֲךָ אֲנִי, וְאָמַר: אָמֵן, וְהָעֵדִים מְעִידִים אוֹתוֹ שֶׁגְּנָבוֹ – מְשַׁלֵּם תַּשְׁלוּמֵי כֶפֶל. הוֹדָה מֵעַצְמוֹ – מְשַׁלֵּם קֶרֶן וְחוֹמֶשׁ וְאָשָׁם.

The mishna continues with another case: The owner said to the bailee: **Where is my deposit?** The bailee **said to him: It was stolen.**[H] The owner said: **I administer an oath to you, and** the bailee **said: Amen; and the witnesses testify about** the bailee **that he stole** the deposit. In this case, the bailee **pays double payment.** If he **admitted** his theft **on his own,**[H] **he pays the principal and** an additional **one-fifth** to the owner, **and** he brings **a guilt-offering** to atone for his sin.

קָתָנֵי מִיהָא בְּטוֹעֵן טַעֲנַת גַּנָּב דִּמְשַׁלֵּם תַּשְׁלוּמֵי כֶפֶל, אֲבָל בְּטוֹעֵן טַעֲנַת אָבַד – לֹא מְשַׁלֵּם תַּשְׁלוּמֵי כֶפֶל. וַאֲפִילּוּ טוֹעֵן טַעֲנַת גַּנָּב, בִּשְׁבוּעָה הוּא דִּמְשַׁלֵּם תַּשְׁלוּמֵי כֶפֶל, אֲבָל שֶׁלֹּא בִּשְׁבוּעָה אֵינוֹ מְשַׁלֵּם תַּשְׁלוּמֵי כֶפֶל.

The Gemara says: **In any event,** the mishna **teaches** that **in the** case of a bailee **who** falsely **states the claim** that **a thief** stole the deposit, **he pays double payment, but in** the case of a bailee **who** falsely **claims that** a deposit **was lost, he does not pay double payment. And** it also teaches that **even** with regard to **one who** falsely **states the claim** that a **thief** stole the deposit, it is only **by taking an oath** to substantiate his claim **that he pays double payment,**[H] **but** for simply lying **without** taking **an oath he does not pay double payment.**

מְנָהָנֵי מִילֵּי? דְּתָנוּ רַבָּנַן: ״אִם יִמָּצֵא הַגַּנָּב״ – בְּטוֹעֵן טַעֲנַת גַּנָּב הַכָּתוּב מְדַבֵּר.

From where are these matters derived? **As the Sages taught** in a *baraita*: The Torah states: "If a man gives his neighbor money or vessels to safeguard and it was stolen from the house of the man, **if the thief shall be found** he shall pay double" (Exodus 22:6). **The verse is speaking of** a bailee **who** falsely **states the claim** that a **thief** stole.

אַתָּה אוֹמֵר: בְּטוֹעֵן טַעֲנַת גַּנָּב, אוֹ אֵינוֹ אֶלָּא בְּגַנָּב עַצְמוֹ? כְּשֶׁהוּא אוֹמֵר: ״אִם לֹא יִמָּצֵא הַגַּנָּב״ – בְּטוֹעֵן טַעֲנַת גַּנָּב הַכָּתוּב מְדַבֵּר.

The *baraita* continues: Do **you say** that the verse is speaking **about one who** falsely **claims that** a deposit **was stolen, or is it** speaking **only about the thief himself,** teaching that if the actual thief is caught he must pay double payment? **When** the Torah **says** in the following verse: **"If the thief shall not be found**…the one whom the judges convict shall pay double to his neighbor" (Exodus 22:7–8), **the verse is speaking of one who** falsely **states the claim** that **a thief** stole the deposit, as it states that no other thief was found. Since the latter verse is speaking of one who falsely claims that a deposit was stolen, it stands to reason that the earlier verse is speaking of this case as well.

תַּנְיָא אִידָךְ: ״אִם יִמָּצֵא הַגַּנָּב״ – בְּגַנָּב עַצְמוֹ הַכָּתוּב מְדַבֵּר. אַתָּה אוֹמֵר: בְּגַנָּב עַצְמוֹ, אוֹ אֵינוֹ אֶלָּא בְּטוֹעֵן טַעֲנַת גַּנָּב? כְּשֶׁהוּא אוֹמֵר: ״אִם לֹא יִמָּצֵא הַגַּנָּב״ – הֲרֵי טוֹעֵן טַעֲנַת גַּנָּב אָמוּר, הָא מָה אֲנִי מְקַיֵּים ״אִם יִמָּצֵא הַגַּנָּב״? בְּגַנָּב עַצְמוֹ הַכָּתוּב מְדַבֵּר.

It is taught in **another** *baraita*: When the Torah states: **"If the thief shall be found** he shall pay double" (Exodus 22:6), **the verse is speaking of the thief himself.** Do **you say** that it is speaking **about the thief himself, or is it** speaking **only about one who** falsely **states the claim** that a **thief** stole? If so, then **when** the verse then **says: "If the thief shall not be found**…the one whom the judges convict shall pay double to his neighbor" (Exodus 22:7–8), the case of **one who** falsely **states the claim** that **a thief** stole the deposit **is** already **stated. How,** then, **do I realize** the first verse about paying double: **"If the thief shall be found,"** so that it not be superfluous? It must be that **the** first **verse is speaking of the thief himself.**

HALAKHA

One who states the claim that a thief stole a lost item he had found, etc. – הַטּוֹעֵן טַעֲנַת גַּנָּב בַּאֲבֵידָה וכו׳: If one took an oath that an item he had found was stolen from him, and then witnesses testified that he himself had stolen the item, he must pay double payment (Rambam *Sefer Nezikin, Hilkhot Geneiva* 4:4).

Where is my deposit, the bailee said to him, it has been lost – הֵיכָן פִּקְדוֹנִי אָמַר לֵיהּ אָבַד: In the case of a bailee who claims that a deposit he has been entrusted with has been lost, and he takes an oath to that effect, and subsequently witnesses testify that the bailee stole the deposit, the bailee pays only the principal amount of the deposit (Rambam *Sefer Nezikin, Hilkhot Geneiva* 4:3; *Tur*, *Ḥoshen Mishpat* 352).

The bailee admitted on his own – הוֹדָה עַל פִּי עַצְמוֹ: If a bailee claims that the deposit entrusted to him has been lost, and takes an oath to that effect, and subsequently admits of his own accord that his claim and his oath were lies, he must pay the principal amount and an additional one-fifth of that amount to the owner of the deposit. He must bring a guilt-offering as well (Rambam *Sefer Hafla'a, Hilkhot Shevuot* 1:8–9).

Where is my deposit, the bailee said to him, it was stolen – הֵיכָן פִּקְדוֹנִי אָמַר לוֹ נִגְנַב: If a bailee takes an oath that the deposit entrusted to him has been stolen from him, and subsequently witnesses testify that the item is in fact still in his possession, then the bailee must pay double payment (Rambam *Sefer Nezikin, Hilkhot Geneiva* 4:1; *Tur*, *Ḥoshen Mishpat* 352).

He admitted his theft on his own – הוֹדָה מֵעַצְמוֹ: If a bailee claims that the item entrusted to him has been stolen from him, and he takes an oath to that effect, and he subsequently admits on his own that his claim and his oath were lies, then he must pay the principal amount plus an additional one-fifth of that amount to the owner of the item. He must also bring a guilt-offering (Rambam *Sefer Hafla'a, Hilkhot Shevuot* 1:8–9).

It is only by taking an oath that he pays double payment – בִּשְׁבוּעָה הוּא דִּמְשַׁלֵּם תַּשְׁלוּמֵי כֶפֶל: If a bailee claims that an item entrusted to him has been stolen, but before he takes an oath to substantiate the claim witnesses come and refute it, he pays only the principal amount of the deposit (Rambam *Sefer Nezikin, Hilkhot Geneiva* 4:1).

NOTES

From where is this interpretation inferred from the verse – מַאי מַשְׁמַע: The plain meaning of the verse cited here is that if no thief is found to corroborate the bailee's claim that the deposit was stolen, the bailee is suspected of having stolen it himself. It is not clear from the verses how this suspicion is substantiated to the extent that the bailee is required to pay double payment. Rava therefore explains that when the verse states: "If the thief shall not be found," it is meant as an absolute negation, meaning that witnesses have testified that the deposit was not stolen from the bailee, as the bailee himself took it for his own use. Consequently, if he has "come before the judges" and taken an oath to corroborate his false claim, he is required to pay double payment.

דְּכוּלֵּי עָלְמָא מִיהַת: ״אִם לֹא יִמָּצֵא הַגַּנָּב״ – בְּטוֹעֵן טַעֲנַת גַּנָּב כְּתִיב, מַאי מַשְׁמַע? אָמַר רָבָא: ״אִם לֹא יִמָּצֵא״ כְּמָה שֶׁאָמַר, אֶלָּא שֶׁהוּא עַצְמוֹ גְּנָבוֹ – יְשַׁלֵּם שְׁנַיִם.

The Gemara comments: Although the two *baraitot* disagree about the meaning of the earlier verse, **in any event everyone** agrees that the latter verse, which states: **"If the thief shall not be not found** [*im lo yimmatze hagannav*]... shall pay double to his neighbor," is referring to a bailee **who** falsely **states the claim** that **a thief** stole the deposit. **From where** is this interpretation **inferred** from the verse?[N] **Rava said** that the verse should be understood as follows: **If it is not found** [*im lo yimmatze*] to be **as he said,** i.e., if his claim that the deposit was stolen is found to be untrue, **but he himself stole it, he shall pay double** to his neighbor.

וּמְנָלַן דְּבִשְׁבוּעָה?

The Gemara turns its attention to another facet of this *halakha*: **And from where do we** derive **that** this double payment of one who falsely claims that the deposit was stolen applies only **when** the bailee has taken **an oath** that it was stolen?

דְּתַנְיָא: ״וְנִקְרַב בַּעַל הַבַּיִת אֶל הָאֱלֹהִים״ – לִשְׁבוּעָה. אַתָּה אוֹמֵר: לִשְׁבוּעָה, אוֹ אֵינוֹ אֶלָּא לְדִין? נֶאֱמַר שְׁלִיחוּת יָד לְמַטָּה וְנֶאֱמַר שְׁלִיחוּת יָד לְמַעְלָה, מָה לְהַלָּן לִשְׁבוּעָה, אַף כָּאן לִשְׁבוּעָה.

The Gemara answers: **As it is taught** in a *baraita* with regard to the verse: "If the thief shall not be found, **the homeowner shall approach the judges** to determine if he laid his hand [*shalaḥ yado*] on his neighbor's goods" (Exodus 22:7). This means that he shall come to court **for** the purpose of taking **an oath. Do you say** he comes to court **for** the purpose of taking **an oath, or is it only for** the purpose of facing **judgment?** The meaning may be determined by means of a verbal analogy. **Laying** the **hand** [*shliḥut yad*], referring to misappropriation, **is stated later,** in the verse: "The oath of the Lord shall be between them both, to see whether he has not laid his hand [*shalaḥ yado*] on his neighbor's goods" (Exodus 22:10), **and laying the hand is stated above,** i.e., Exodus 22:7. **Just as laying** the **hand later** is referring explicitly **to an oath, so too** laying the hand **here** is referring **to an oath.**

בִּשְׁלָמָא לְמַאן דְּאָמַר חַד בְּגַנָּב וְחַד בְּטוֹעֵן טַעֲנַת גַּנָּב – הַיְינוּ דִּכְתִיבִי תְּרֵי קְרָאֵי, אֶלָּא לְמַאן דְּאָמַר תַּרְוַיְיהוּ בְּטוֹעֵן טַעֲנַת גַּנָּב, תְּרֵי קְרָאֵי לָמָּה לִי?

The Gemara analyzes the two *baraitot* cited earlier: **Granted, according to the one who says** in the second *baraita* that **one** verse about double payment is speaking **about** the **thief and one** verse is speaking **about** a bailee **who** falsely **states the claim** that **a thief** stole the deposit, **this is** why **two verses are written,** as each verse teaches a different *halakha*. **But according to the one who says** in the first *baraita* that **both** of the verses **are** speaking **about** a bailee **who** falsely **states the claim** that **a thief** stole the deposit, **why do I** need **two verses?** One verse should be sufficient.

אָמְרִי: חַד לְמַעוּטֵי טַעֲנַת אָבַד.

The Sages **say:** Both verses are necessary because **one** verse serves **to exclude** from double payment the case of one who falsely states **the claim** that the item has been **lost.** Double payment is paid only when the bailee falsely claims that the item under his care was stolen.

וּלְמַאן דְּאָמַר חַד בְּגַנָּב וְחַד בְּטוֹעֵן טַעֲנַת גַּנָּב, דְּלָא מְיַיתַּר, לְמַעוּטֵי טַעֲנַת אָבַד מְנָא לֵיהּ? מִ״גַּנָּב״ ״הַגַּנָּב״.

The Gemara asks: **And according to the one who says** that **one** verse is speaking **about the thief and one** verse is speaking **about** a bailee **who** falsely **states the claim** that **a thief** stole the deposit, so that **there is no superfluous** verse, **from where does he** learn **to exclude** from double payment a bailee who falsely states **the claim** that the item has been **lost?** The Gemara answers: He derives it **from** the fact that the verse could have stated: If **a thief** [*gannav*] shall not be found, but it states instead: "If **the thief** [*hagannav*] shall not be found."

וּלְמַאן דְּאָמַר תַּרְוַיְיהוּ בְּטוֹעֵן טַעֲנַת גַּנָּב, דְּמִיעֵט לֵיהּ טוֹעֵן טַעֲנַת אָבַד, ״גַּנָּב״ ״הַגַּנָּב״ מַאי דָּרֵישׁ בֵּיהּ?

The Gemara asks: **And** since **according to the one who says** that **both** verses are speaking **about** a bailee who falsely **states the claim** that **a thief** stole the deposit one of the verses **excludes** the case of a bailee who falsely **claims that** the deposit **was lost, what does he derive** from the fact that the verse did not state: If **a thief** shall not be found, but it states instead: "If **the thief** shall not be found"?

אָמַר לָךְ: מִבָּעֵי לֵיהּ לִכְדְרַבִּי חִיָּיא בַּר אַבָּא אָמַר רַבִּי יוֹחָנָן, דְּאָמַר רַבִּי חִיָּיא בַּר אַבָּא אָמַר רַבִּי יוֹחָנָן: הַטּוֹעֵן טַעֲנַת גַּנָּב בְּפִקָּדוֹן – מְשַׁלֵּם תַּשְׁלוּמֵי כֶפֶל, טָבַח וּמָכַר – מְשַׁלֵּם תַּשְׁלוּמֵי אַרְבָּעָה וַחֲמִשָּׁה.

The Gemara answers: **He** could have **said to you** that this terminology **is necessary to** teach **what Rabbi Ḥiyya bar Abba says** that **Rabbi Yoḥanan** says, **as Rabbi Ḥiyya bar Abba says** that **Rabbi Yoḥanan says:** One who falsely **states the claim** that **a thief** stole the **deposit pays double payment,** and if the deposit was an ox or sheep and **he slaughtered or sold** it, **he pays** the **fourfold or fivefold payment.**

לְמַאן דְּאָמַר חַד בְּגַנָּב וְחַד בְּטוֹעֵן טַעֲנַת גַּנָּב, דְּהַאי "גַּנָּב" "דְּגַנָּב" אַפְקֵיהּ לְמַעוּטֵי טַעֲנַת אָבַד, דְּרַבִּי חִיָּיא בַּר אַבָּא מְנָא לֵיהּ?

The Gemara notes: **According to the one who says** that **one** verse is speaking **about a thief and one** verse is speaking **about** a bailee **who** falsely **states the claim** that **a thief** stole the deposit, **who employed this** change in terminology, i.e., the fact that the verse could have stated: If **a thief** shall not be found, but states instead: "If **the thief** shall not be found," **to exclude** the case of a bailee who falsely states the **claim that** the deposit was **lost**, there seems to be no source to teach the *halakha* stated by Rabbi Ḥiyya bar Abba. Accordingly, **from where does he** derive the *halakha* taught by **Rabbi Ḥiyya bar Abba,** that if the bailee slaughtered or sold the animal he pays a fourfold or fivefold payment?

אָמַר לָךְ: הֶקֵּישָׁא הוּא, וְאֵין מְשִׁיבִין עַל הֶקֵּישָׁא.

The Gemara answers: He could have **said to you: It is a juxtaposition,**[N] as liability for double payment for a thief and for a bailee who falsely claims that the deposit was stolen are juxtaposed to each other. Therefore, just as a thief pays a fourfold or fivefold payment if he slaughtered or sold the animal, so must the bailee. **And** although these two cases are not entirely comparable, this derivation cannot be refuted on that basis, as there is a principle that **one cannot refute** a derivation based on **juxtaposition**[B] by drawing distinctions between the two juxtaposed cases.

בִּשְׁלָמָא לְמַאן דְּאָמַר חַד בְּגַנָּב וְחַד בְּטוֹעֵן טַעֲנַת גַּנָּב – שַׁפִּיר, אֶלָּא לְמַאן דְּאָמַר תַּרְוַיְיהוּ בְּטוֹעֵן טַעֲנַת גַּנָּב, גַּנָּב עַצְמוֹ מְנָא לֵיהּ?

The Gemara asks further: **Granted, according to the one who says** that **one** verse is speaking **about the thief and one** verse is speaking **about** a bailee who falsely **states the claim** that **a thief** stole the deposit, it is **well. But according to the one who says that both** verses are speaking **about** a bailee who falsely **states the claim** that **a thief** stole the deposit, **from where does he** derive that **a thief himself** must pay double payment for stealing?

וְכִי תֵּימָא: לֵיתֵי בְּקַל וָחוֹמֶר מִטּוֹעֵן טַעֲנַת גַּנָּב – דַּיּוֹ לַבָּא מִן הַדִּין לִהְיוֹת כַּנִּדּוֹן, מַה לְהַלָּן בִּשְׁבוּעָה, אַף כָּאן בִּשְׁבוּעָה!

And if you would say: Let it be derived by an *a fortiori* inference from the case of the bailee who falsely **states the claim** that **a thief** stole the deposit, because if one is obligated to pay double payment for falsely claiming that a deposit was stolen, which constitutes passive theft, all the more so must a thief himself pay double payment, this derivation is not possible. The reason is that **it is sufficient for the** conclusion that **emerges from** an ***a fortiori* inference to be like** its **source.** In other words, a *halakha* derived by means of an *a fortiori* inference cannot be more stringent than the *halakha* of the source from which it is derived. Consequently, on the basis of this *a fortiori* inference, it would have to be concluded that **just as there,** in the source case, the double payment is required only when the guilty party took **an oath, so too here,** when the thief himself pays double, it is only when he took **an oath** that he did not steal it.

נָפְקָא לֵיהּ מִדְּתָנָא דְּבֵי חִזְקִיָּה, דְּתָנָא דְּבֵי חִזְקִיָּה: יֹאמַר שׁוֹר וּגְנֵיבָה, וְהַכֹּל בִּכְלָל!

The Gemara responds: **He derives** the obligation of a thief to pay double payment without having taken an oath from a third verse: "If the theft shall be found in his possession alive, whether it is an ox, or a donkey, or a sheep, he shall pay double" (Exodus 22:3). The double payment in this verse applies to all items, as is derived **from what the school of Ḥizkiyya taught.**[N] **As the school of Ḥizkiyya taught: Let** the verse **state** only **"ox" and "theft," and all** items **would be included.** Why was it necessary to also mention "donkey" and "sheep"?

BACKGROUND

One cannot refute a juxtaposition – אֵין מְשִׁיבִין עַל הֶקֵּישָׁא: A juxtaposition is considered to be the explicit intention of the Torah, and therefore it cannot be refuted by logic alone.

NOTES

It is a juxtaposition [*hekesh*] – הֶקֵּישָׁא הוּא: Rashi cites the opinion that the word *hekesh* here is referring to two cases that are logically comparable, i.e., the case of a thief and the case of a bailee who falsely claims that the deposit was stolen. They are similar in that both the thief and the bailee must pay double payment. Rashi rejects this understanding and claims that the term *hekesh* always refers to two juxtaposed verses. However, it could be argued that the term *hekesh* refers to the broader category of any point of contact between two subject matters, whether through the juxtaposition of two cases in a verse or through a logical affinity between them.

As is derived from what the school of Ḥizkiyya taught – מִדְּתָנָא דְּבֵי חִזְקִיָּה: Rashi notes that the basic answer of the Gemara is that the requirement for a thief to pay double payment is written explicitly in Exodus 22:3. He explains that the Gemara proceeds directly to Ḥizkiyya's analysis of this verse rather than citing the verse itself because the verse mentions only animals and the Gemara wants to prove that the double payment applies to all items, not just animals.

אִילּוּ כָּךְ, הָיִיתִי אוֹמֵר: מָה הַפְּרָט מְפוֹרָשׁ קָרֵב לְגַבֵּי מִזְבֵּחַ, אַף כָּל קָרֵב לְגַבֵּי מִזְבֵּחַ, מָה יֵשׁ לְךָ לְהָבִיא? שֶׂה,

Had the verse had been written **this** way **I would have said: Just as** the item mentioned in **the detail** is clearly **defined as** an item that **is sacrificed on the altar, so too everything that is sacrificed on the altar** is subject to double payment, but other items are not. **What** else **is there for you to include** in this category? **Sheep,** which, like oxen, can be sacrificed on the altar.

Perek **VII**
Daf **64** Amud **a**

כְּשֶׁהוּא אוֹמֵר "שֶׂה" – הֲרֵי שֶׂה אָמוּר, הָא מָה אֲנִי מְקַיֵּים "גְּנֵיבָה"? לְרַבּוֹת כָּל דָּבָר.

When the verse **states "sheep," a sheep is thereby stated** explicitly. Therefore, the detail of "ox" cannot be written to include specifically items that can be sacrificed on the altar, e.g., a sheep. **How** then **do I realize** the meaning of the word **"theft,"** i.e., what is the category of items derived from the detail and generalization? It must be that it serves **to include all** types of **items** in the requirement of double payment.

יֹאמַר "שׁוֹר" "שֶׂה" וּ"גְנֵיבָה", וְהַכֹּל בִּכְלָל! אִילּוּ כָּךְ, הָיִיתִי אוֹמֵר: מָה הַפְּרָט מְפוֹרָשׁ דָּבָר הַקָּדוֹשׁ בִּבְכוֹרָה, אַף כָּל דָּבָר הַקָּדוֹשׁ בִּבְכוֹרָה,

The *baraita* continues to analyze the verse: **Let** the verse **state** only **"ox," "sheep," and "theft," and** in that manner **everything** would be **included.** Why is it necessary to write "donkey"? **Had** the verse been written in **this** manner, without "donkey," **I would have said: Just as** the items mentioned in **the detail,** "ox" and "sheep," are clearly **defined as items that are** subject to being **sacred with** the sanctity of the **firstborn, so too any item that is** subject to being **sacred with** the sanctity of the **firstborn** is subject to double payment, but not other items.

מָה יֵשׁ לְךָ לְהָבִיא? חֲמוֹר, כְּשֶׁהוּא אוֹמֵר "חֲמוֹר" – הֲרֵי חֲמוֹר אָמוּר, הָא מָה אֲנִי מְקַיֵּים "גְּנֵיבָה"? לְרַבּוֹת כָּל דָּבָר.

What is there for you to include in this category? **A donkey. When** the verse **says "donkey," a donkey is thereby stated** explicitly. Therefore, the details of "ox" and "sheep" cannot be written to include specifically items that are subject to being sacred with the sanctity of the firstborn, e.g., a donkey. **How** then **do I realize** the meaning of the word **"theft,"** i.e., what is the category of items derived from the detail and generalization? It must be that it serves **to include all** types of **items** in the requirement of double payment.

יֹאמַר "שׁוֹר" וַ"חֲמוֹר" "שֶׂה" וּ"גְנֵיבָה", וְהַכֹּל בִּכְלָל! אִילּוּ כָּךְ, הָיִיתִי אוֹמֵר: מָה הַפְּרָט מְפוֹרָשׁ בַּעֲלֵי חַיִּים, אַף כָּל בַּעֲלֵי חַיִּים,

The *baraita* continues to analyze the verse: **Let** the verse **state** only **"ox," and "donkey,"** and **"sheep," and "theft," and** in that manner **all** items **would be included.** Why is it necessary to write the word "alive"? **Had** the verse been written in **this** manner, **I would say: Just as** the items mentioned in **the detail,** "ox," "sheep," and "donkey," are clearly **defined as** items that are **animals, so too all animals** are subject to double payment, but not inanimate objects.

מָה יֵשׁ לְךָ לְהָבִיא? שְׁאָר בַּעֲלֵי חַיִּים, כְּשֶׁהוּא אוֹמֵר "חַיִּים" – הֲרֵי חַיִּים אָמוּר, הָא מָה אֲנִי מְקַיֵּים "גְּנֵיבָה"? לְרַבּוֹת כָּל דָּבָר.

What is there for you to include in this category that is not already listed? **Animals other** than oxen, sheep, and donkeys. **When** the verse **states** the term **"alive," animals are thereby stated** explicitly. Therefore, the details of "ox," "sheep," and "donkey" cannot be written to include animals. **How** then **do I realize** the meaning of **"theft,"** i.e., what is the category of items derived from the detail and generalization? It must be that it serves **to include all** types of **items** in the requirement of double payment. This is the end of the *baraita*.

אָמַר מָר: יֹאמַר "שׁוֹר" וּ"גְנֵיבָה". מִי כְּתִיב "שׁוֹר" וּ"גְנֵיבָה"? "גְּנֵיבָה" וְ"שׁוֹר" הוּא דִּכְתִיב!

There are several puzzling elements of the halakhic exposition of the verse in this *baraita*. The Gemara now seeks to explain it in detail. **The Master said** in the *baraita* above: **Let** the verse **state** only **"ox" and "theft."** The Gemara objects: **Are "ox" and "theft" written** in the verse in this order, as a generalization and a detail? No, **it is "theft"** and then **"ox" that is written.** Consequently, the verse contains a generalization and a detail, in which case the generalization is understood to refer only to that which is specified in the detail.

וְכִי תֵּימָא "אִילּוּ נֶאֱמַר" קָאָמַר, אִילּוּ נֶאֱמַר "שׁוֹר" וּ"גְנֵיבָה" – וּמִי מָצֵית אָמְרַתְּ מָה הַפְּרָט מְפוֹרָשׁ? הָוֵה "שׁוֹר" – פְּרָט, וּ"גְנֵיבָה" – כְּלָל, פְּרָט וּכְלָל – נַעֲשָׂה כְּלָל מוֹסִיף עַל הַפְּרָט, וְאִיתְרַבּוּ לְהוּ כׇּל מִילֵּי!

And if you would say that the *baraita* **is saying** that this would be the case **had** the verse **stated** the words in this manner, i.e.: **Had** the verse **stated "ox" and** then **"theft,"** all items would have been included; **how can you** then proceed to **say: Just as** the item mentioned in **the detail,** "ox," is clearly **defined as** an item that can be sacrificed on the altar, so too everything that can be sacrificed on the altar is subject to double payment? **"Ox" is a detail and "theft" is a generalization,** and according to the rules of hermeneutics, in such a case **the generalization adds to the detail, and all items are included,** not just items that resemble the detailed item.

אֶלָּא כִּדְכְתִיב קָאָמַר, "גְּנֵיבָה" וְ"שׁוֹר" – מִי מָצֵית אָמְרַתְּ "הַכֹּל בִּכְלָל" אוֹ "מָה הַפְּרָט מְפוֹרָשׁ"? הָוֵה לֵיהּ "גְּנֵיבָה" – כְּלָל, וְ"שׁוֹר" – פְּרָט, כְּלָל וּפְרָט – אֵין בִּכְלָל אֶלָּא מַה שֶּׁבִּפְרָט, שׁוֹר – אִין, מִידֵּי אַחֲרִינָא – לָא!

Rather, the *baraita* must be **saying** that the verse should be analyzed **as it is** actually **written:** First **"theft" and** then **"ox."** Accordingly, **how can you** then proceed to **say** that **all** items **would be included, or: Just as** the item mentioned in **the detail** is clearly **defined as** an item that can be sacrificed on the altar, as the *baraita* states? This analysis is applicable only when there is a generalization, and a detail, and a generalization. In this verse **"theft" is a generalization and "ox"** is **a detail.** The rules of hermeneutics state that when there is only **a generalization and a detail, there is nothing** included **in the generalization other than what is** listed **in the detail.** In this case, one would necessarily conclude that if one steals **an ox, yes,** he is liable to pay the double payment for stealing it, but if one steals **anything else, no,** there is no double payment.

אָמַר רָבָא: תַּנָּא אַ"חַיִּים" קָא סָמֵיךְ לֵיהּ, וּכְלָל וּפְרָט וּכְלָל קָאָמַר לֵיהּ.

Rava stated an explanation of the *baraita*: When **the *tanna*** suggested: Let the verse say "ox" and "theft," and similar suggestions, **he was relying on** the word **"alive"** at the end of the phrase. He considered this word an additional generalization after the detailed items, and therefore **he was saying** that the phrase is to be treated as **a generalization, and a detail, and a generalization.** Consequently, it should have been sufficient for the verse to state merely "theft," followed by "ox," followed by "alive." Why does the Torah specify further items?

וְהָא לָא דָּמֵי כְּלָלָא בָּתְרָא לִכְלָלָא קַמָּא! הָא תַּנָּא דְּבֵי רַבִּי יִשְׁמָעֵאל הוּא, דִּכְהַאי גַּוְונָא דָּרֵישׁ כְּלָלֵי וּפְרָטֵי.

The Gemara questions this explanation: **But the latter generalization is not similar to the first generalization.** The first generalization, "theft," is so general that it includes all items, whereas the latter generalization, "alive," includes only animals. Consequently, the rule of a generalization, and a detail, and a generalization should not apply. The Gemara responds: **This *tanna*,** the author of this *baraita*, **is of the school of Rabbi Yishmael,**[N] **who expounds generalizations and details in a case like this.** Even if the first generalization and the latter generalization are dissimilar, he interprets the verse as a generalization, and a detail, and a generalization.

וְהָכִי קָא קַשְׁיָא לֵיהּ: "אִם הִמָּצֵא תִמָּצֵא" לָמָּה לִי? יֵאמַר שׁוֹר וּגְנֵיבָה וְחַיִּים, וְהַכֹּל בִּכְלָל!

Rava continues his explanation of the *baraita*: **And this is what** the *tanna* found **difficult** at the end of the *baraita*: **Why do I** need the beginning of the verse to state: **"If the theft shall be found [*himmatze timmatze*],"**[N] with the verb repeated? Rava now explains the entire *baraita*, from the beginning: **Let** the verse **say "ox" and "theft"**[N] **and "alive," and all** items would be **included,** in accordance with the rules of a generalization, and a detail, and a generalization. Why did the verse include other details?

אִילּוּ כֵּן, הָיִיתִי אוֹמֵר: מָה הַפְּרָט מְפוֹרָשׁ – דָּבָר הַקָּרֵב לְגַבֵּי מִזְבֵּחַ, אַף כׇּל הַקָּרֵב לְגַבֵּי מִזְבֵּחַ, מָה יֵשׁ לְהָבִיא? שֶׂה, כְּשֶׁהוּא אוֹמֵר "שֶׂה" – הֲרֵי שֶׂה אָמוּר, הָא מָה אֲנִי מְקַיֵּים "גְּנֵיבָה"? לְרַבּוֹת כׇּל דָּבָר.

The *baraita* answers this by saying: **Had** the verse been written in **this manner, I would have said: Just as** the item mentioned in **the detail,** "ox," is clearly **defined as an item that is sacrificed on the altar, so too everything that is sacrificed on the altar** is subject to double payment, but not other items. **What** else **is there** for you **to include** in this category? **A sheep. When** the verse **states "sheep," a sheep is thereby stated** explicitly. Therefore, the detail of "ox" cannot be written to include specifically items that can be sacrificed on the altar, e.g., a sheep. **How** then **do I realize** the meaning of the word **"theft,"** i.e., what is the category of items derived from the detail and generalization? It must be that it serves **to include all** types of **items** in the requirement of double payment.

NOTES

This *tanna*, the author of this *baraita*, is of the school of Rabbi Yishmael – הָא תַּנָּא דְּבֵי רַבִּי יִשְׁמָעֵאל הוּא: The Meiri cites an example of Rabbi Yishmael's method of exegesis in a case where the final generalization is much broader in scope than the initial generalization. Rabbi Yishmael's opinion is that as long as there is the basic verse structure of generalization, followed by specific details, followed by a final generalization, it is not necessary for the two generalizations to be similar in scope.

Why do I need, if the theft shall be found [*himmatze timmatze*] – אִם הִמָּצֵא תִמָּצֵא לָמָּה לִי: According to Rava's explanation of the *baraita*, and even more so according to the Gemara's final analysis of the verse, the exposition of this verse is based upon the double expression: *Himmatze timmatze*. This is somewhat puzzling, because these words are not mentioned at all in the *baraita* that the Gemara seeks to explain. The Ra'avad explains that it is not unusual for a *tanna* to present only the beginning stages of his exposition of a verse, relying on the individual studying the *baraita* to contemplate the verse and comprehend the rest of the exposition on his own. The *baraita* presented in the Gemara should be seen as only an introductory statement to the halakhic analysis of the verse in accordance with the school of Ḥizkiyya.

Ox and theft – שׁוֹר וּגְנֵיבָה: *Tosafot* note that the word order should be reversed, as the verse first mentions theft and then ox, as stated in the Gemara above. In the text of some manuscript editions of the Talmud, theft is written before ox.

HALAKHA

Item that is sacred with the sanctity of the firstborn – דָּבָר הַקָּדוֹשׁ בִּבְכוֹרָה: The sacred status of the firstborn applies only to firstborn male offspring of Jews, cattle, sheep, goats, and donkeys (Rambam *Sefer Korbanot, Hilkhot Bekhorot* 1:1).

יֹאמַר גְּנֵיבָה וְשׁוֹר וְשֶׂה וְחַיִּים, וְהַכֹּל בִּכְלָל! אִילּוּ כֵּן, הָיִיתִי אוֹמֵר: מָה הַפְּרָט מְפוֹרָשׁ דָּבָר הַקָּדוֹשׁ בִּבְכוֹרָה, אַף כָּל דָּבָר הַקָּדוֹשׁ בִּבְכוֹרָה,

The *baraita* continues: **Let** the verse **say** only **"theft," and "ox" and "sheep" and "alive," and all** items **would be included.** Why is it necessary to write "donkey"? The *baraita* answers: **Had** the verse been written in **this** manner, without "donkey," **I would have said: Just as** the items mentioned in **the detail,** "ox" and "sheep," are clearly **defined as items that are** subject to being **sacred with** the sanctity of the **firstborn, so too any item that is** subject to being **sacred with** the sanctity of the **firstborn**[H] is subject to double payment, but not other items.

מַה יֵּשׁ לְךָ לְהָבִיא? חֲמוֹר, [כְּשֶׁהוּא אוֹמֵר ״חֲמוֹר״] – הֲרֵי חֲמוֹר אָמוּר, הָא מָה אֲנִי מְקַיֵּים ״גְּנֵיבָה״? לְרַבּוֹת כָּל דָּבָר.

What is there for you to include in this category? **A donkey. When** the verse **says "donkey," a donkey is thereby stated** explicitly. Therefore, the details of "ox" and "sheep" cannot be written to include specifically items that are subject to being sacred with the sanctity of the firstborn, e.g., a donkey. **How** then **do I realize** the meaning of the word **"theft,"** i.e., what is the category of items derived from the detail and generalization? It must be that it serves **to include all** types of **items** in the requirement of double payment.

יֹאמַר גְּנֵיבָה וְשׁוֹר וְשֶׂה וַחֲמוֹר וְחַיִּים, וְהַכֹּל בִּכְלָל! אִילּוּ כֵּן, הָיִיתִי אוֹמֵר: מָה הַפְּרָט מְפוֹרָשׁ בַּעֲלֵי חַיִּים, אַף כָּל בַּעֲלֵי חַיִּים,

The *baraita* then asks: **Let** the verse **say** only **"theft," and "ox," and "sheep," and "donkey" and "alive," and** in that manner **all** items would be **included.** The *baraita* answers: **Had** the verse been written in **this** manner, **I would say: Just as** the items mentioned in **the detail,** "ox," "sheep," and "donkey," are clearly **defined as** items that are **animals, so too all animals** are subject to double payment, but not inanimate objects.

מַה יֵּשׁ לְךָ לְהָבִיא? שְׁאָר בַּעֲלֵי חַיִּים, כְּשֶׁהוּא אוֹמֵר ״חַיִּים״ – הֲרֵי חַיִּים אָמוּר, הָא מָה אֲנִי מְקַיֵּים ״גְּנֵיבָה״? לְרַבּוֹת כָּל דָּבָר, ״אִם הִמָּצֵא תִמָּצֵא״ לָמָּה לִי?

What is there for you to include in this category that is not already listed? **Animals other** than oxen, sheep, and donkeys. **When** the verse **states "alive," animals are thereby stated** explicitly. Therefore, the details of "ox," "sheep," and "donkey" cannot be written to include animals. **How** then **do I realize** the meaning of **"theft,"** i.e., what is the category of items derived from the detail and generalization? It must be that it serves **to include all** types of **items** in the requirement of double payment. If so, **why do I** need the phrase **"if the theft shall be found** [*himmatze timmatze*]"? This is the conclusion of the *baraita* as explained by Rava.

Perek **VII**
Daf **64** Amud **b**

אִי הָכִי, שַׁפִּיר קַשְׁיָא לֵיהּ!

The Gemara asks: **If so,** if this is how the *baraita* is to be understood, **the difficulty** it posed **is valid,** as the *baraita* ends with an unanswered question: Why do I need the phrase: "If the theft shall be found"?

מִשּׁוּם דְּאִית לֵיהּ פִּירְכָא: לְרַבּוֹת כָּל דָּבָר מֵהֵיכָא קָמַיְיתֵי לֵיהּ? מִכְּלָל בַּתְרָא. כְּלָלָא גּוּפֵיהּ ״חַיִּים״ כְּתִיב בֵּיהּ,

The Gemara answers: This phrase is necessary **because there is a refutation for** the derivation cited in the *baraita*, as follows: **From where** in the verse **does** the *tanna* **derive** that it means **to include all** types of **items? From the latter generalization** of "alive." But in **the** latter **generalization itself** the word **"alive" is written.**

כְּלָל וּפְרָט וּכְלָל מַאי קָא מְהַנֵּי לֵיהּ? אִי לְאֵתוּיֵי כָּל דָּבָר – הָא ״חַיִּים״ כְּתִיב, בַּעֲלֵי חַיִּים – אִין, מִידֵּי אַחֲרִינָא – לָא! מִשּׁוּם הָכָא אִיצְטְרִיךְ ״אִם הִמָּצֵא״.

What does the principle of **a generalization, and a detail, and a generalization accomplish,** i.e., what does it include in the *halakha* of double payment? **If it is** written **to include all** types of **items,** this cannot be, as the word **"alive" is written** in the verse, indicating that if one steals **animals, yes,** he is liable to pay double payment, but if he steals **something else,** i.e., inanimate objects, **no,** he is not liable to pay double payment. **Due to this** reason, **it was necessary** for the Torah to include the phrase: **"If the theft shall be found** [*himmatze timmatze*]," which includes all items, through the principle of a generalization, and a detail, and a generalization.

אָמְרִי: וְהָא שְׁנֵי כְלָלוֹת דִּסְמִיכִי אַהֲדָדֵי נִינְהוּ! אָמַר רָבִינָא, כִּדְאָמְרִי בְּמַעַרְבָא: כָּל מָקוֹם שֶׁאַתָּה מוֹצֵא שְׁנֵי כְלָלוֹת הַסְּמוּכִים זֶה לָזֶה – הַטֵּל פְּרָט בֵּינֵיהֶם וְדוּנֵם בִּכְלָל וּפְרָט.

The Sages **state** an objection: **But these** repeated verbs **are two generalizations that are adjacent to each other** in the verse, and the details follow both of the generalizations. Consequently, it is not a case of a generalization, a detail, and a generalization, but rather of a generalization, a generalization, and a detail. **Ravina said:** It is **as they say in the West,** Eretz Yisrael: **Any place** in the Torah **where you find two generalizations adjacent to each other, place the detail between them and** then **treat them as a generalization, and a detail,** and a generalization.

שְׁדִי "שׁוֹר" בֵּין "הִמָּצֵא" לְ"תִמָּצֵא", לְאַתּוּיֵי מַאי? אִי לְאַתּוּיֵי בַּעֲלֵי חַיִּים, מֵ"חַיִּים" נָפְקָא! אֶלָּא לְאַתּוּיֵי דָּבָר שֶׁאֵין בַּעֲלֵי חַיִּים, וּדְרוֹשׁ הָכִי: מַה הַפְּרָט מְפוֹרָשׁ – דָּבָר הַמִּטַּלְטֵל וְגוּפוֹ מָמוֹן, אַף כָּל דָּבָר הַמִּטַּלְטֵל וְגוּפוֹ מָמוֹן.

The Gemara applies this principle to the verse: **Place** the first detail, **"ox," between "*himmatze*" and "*timmatze*,"** and treat the verse as a generalization, a detail, and a generalization, so that other items that resemble the detail are included. **To include what? If** it serves **to include animals,** this is not necessary, as animals **are derived from** the word **"alive"** later in the verse. **Rather,** it serves **to include an item that is not an animal,** i.e., inanimate objects, **and this is how you should expound** the verse: **Just as** the items mentioned in **the detail** are clearly **defined as movable property and** are items that have **intrinsic monetary** value, **so too anything that is movable property and has intrinsic monetary** value is included, to the exclusion of land and financial documents.

וְתוּ, שְׁדִי "חֲמוֹר" בֵּין "הִמָּצֵא" לְ"תִמָּצֵא", לְאַתּוּיֵי מַאי? אִי לְאַתּוּיֵי דָּבָר שֶׁאֵין בַּעֲלֵי חַיִּים, מִ"שּׁוֹר" נָפְקָא! אֶלָּא לְאַתּוּיֵי דָּבָר מְסוּיָּים,

And furthermore, following this method, **place** the next detail, **"donkey," between *himmatze* and *timmatze*,** and treat it as a case of a generalization, a detail, and a generalization, so that other items that resemble the detail are included. **To include what? If** it serves **to include an item that is not an animal,** this is not necessary, as it already was **derived from** the word **"ox." Rather,** it serves **to include an object that is** clearly **delineated,**[N] to the exclusion of objects that are not clearly delineated in size or quantity.

אִי הָכִי "שֶׂה" לָמָּה לִי? אֶלָּא, רִיבָּה וּמִיעֵט וְרִיבָּה הוּא, כִּדְתָנָא דְּבֵי רַבִּי יִשְׁמָעֵאל,

The Gemara asks: **If that is so,** if this is the correct way to analyze the verse, **why do I** need the verse to state **"sheep"?** There is nothing left to include. **Rather,** this whole approach must be rejected, and a new method of analysis applied, as follows: It is not treated as a case of a generalization, and a detail, and a generalization; rather, **it is** treated as a verse that **amplified, restricted, and amplified, as the school of Rabbi Yishmael taught.**

דְּתָנָא דְּבֵי רַבִּי יִשְׁמָעֵאל: "בַּמַּיִם" "בַּמַּיִם" שְׁתֵּי פְעָמִים, אֵין זֶה כְּלָל וּפְרָט, אֶלָּא רִיבָּה וּמִיעֵט וְרִיבָּה רִיבָּה הַכֹּל.

As the school of Rabbi Yishmael taught, concerning the verse: "These may you eat of all that are in the waters: Whatever has fins and scales in the waters, in the seas, and in the rivers" (Leviticus 11:9), as follows: The verse states: **"In the waters," "in the waters," two times** and only afterward lists the details of seas and rivers. **This is not** expounded as **a generalization, and a detail,** and a generalization, because the detail does not appear between the generalizations. **Rather,** the verse **amplified, and** then **restricted, and** then **amplified,** and thereby **amplified** the general category "waters" to include **everything** except for "seas" and "rivers," the specific matter excluded in the restriction, Here too, since the two generalizations are written before the details, it is expounded as an amplification, a restriction and an amplification.

מַאי רַבִּי, רַבִּי כָּל מִילֵּי? אִי הָכִי, כָּל הָנֵי פְּרָטֵי לָמָּה לִי? חַד לְמַעוּטֵי קַרְקַע, וְחַד לְמַעוּטֵי עֲבָדִים, וְחַד לְמַעוּטֵי שְׁטָרוֹת, "גְּנֵיבָה" וְ"חַיִּים" – לִכְדְרַב, דְּאָמַר: אַחְיֵיהּ לְקֶרֶן כְּעֵין שֶׁגָּנַב.

What do the generalizations *himmatze* and *timmatze* **include?** Do they **include all items? If so, why do I** need **all these details** of ox, sheep, and donkey? **One** detail serves **to exclude land, and one** serves **to exclude** Canaanite **slaves, and one** serves **to exclude** financial **documents.** The words **"theft" and "alive [*ḥayyim*]"** do not serve to exclude further items from double payment, but **to** indicate the *halakha* taught by **Rav, who says:** If one stole an item, and it deteriorated or its value decreased, he must **revive [*aḥayah*] the principal** to the value it had **as** of the time **when he stole** it, i.e., he must repay the owner according to the value of the item at the time it was stolen.

NOTES

To include an object that is delineated – לְאַתּוּיֵי דָּבָר מְסוּיָּים: Rashi interprets the term delineated to mean that the item has unique, identifying features. Since not all donkeys have such features, he explains that the *halakha* that the item should have this characteristic is not derived by interpreting the verse as referring only to items similar to a donkey. Rather, the word "donkey" is superfluous, since all animals were already included in this *halakha*. Consequently, it is interpreted as qualifying the generalization of: If the theft shall be found, so that this superfluous term serves to include only items that are clearly delineated, as opposed to an item that is not delineated.

וּלְמַאן דְּאָמַר חַד בְּגַנָּב וְחַד בְּטוֹעֵן טַעֲנַת גַּנָּב, וְגַנָּב עַצְמוֹ נָפְקָא לֵיהּ מֵ״אִם יִמָּצֵא הַגַּנָּב״, הַאי ״אִם הִמָּצֵא תִמָּצֵא״ מַאי דָּרֵישׁ בֵּיהּ?

§ Until this point, the Gemara has been discussing the source of the obligation of a thief to pay double payment according to the *baraita* (63b) that maintains that both verses (Exodus 22:6–7) are referring to a bailee who falsely claims that a deposit was stolen from him. The Gemara asks: **And according to the one who says** that **one** of the two verses **is** speaking **about a thief and one** verse **is** speaking **about** a bailee who falsely **states the claim** that **a thief** stole from him, **and he derives** that **a thief himself** must pay double payment **from** the phrase **"if the thief shall be found"** (Exodus 22:6), **what does he derive from this** verse: **"If** the theft **shall be found"** (Exodus 22:3)?

מִבָּעֵי לֵיהּ לְכִדְרָבָא בַּר אֲהִילַאי, דְּאָמַר רָבָא בַּר אֲהִילַאי: מַאי טַעְמָא דְּרַב, דְּאָמַר: מוֹדֶה בִּקְנָס וְאַחַר כָּךְ בָּאוּ עֵדִים פָּטוּר? דִּכְתִיב: ״אִם הִמָּצֵא תִמָּצֵא״, ״אִם הִמָּצֵא״ – בְּעֵדִים, ״תִמָּצֵא״ – בְּדַיָּינִים, פְּרָט לְמַרְשִׁיעַ אֶת עַצְמוֹ.

The Gemara answers: **He requires** this verse **for** the *halakha* **of Rava bar Ahilai, as Rava bar Ahilai says: What is the reason** for the *halakha* **of Rav, who says:** One who **admits** he is liable **to** pay **a fine is exempt,** even if **afterward witnesses come** and testify to his liability? **As it is written: "If** the theft **shall be found** [*himmatze timmatze*]," which indicates that **if it is found** [*himmatze*] **through witnesses** that he is liable to pay the fine of double payment, **it will be found** [*timmatze*] that the fine will be enforced **by judges.** This **excludes** from double payment the case of **one who incriminates himself**[N] by admitting his liability before any witnesses testify concerning him, and the same is applied to all cases that involve fines.

וּלְמַאן דְּאָמַר תַּרְוַיְיהוּ בְּטוֹעֵן טַעֲנַת גַּנָּב, דְּהַאי ״אִם הִמָּצֵא תִמָּצֵא״ מַפֵּיק לֵיהּ לְגַנָּב עַצְמוֹ, מַרְשִׁיעַ עַצְמוֹ מְנָלַן? מֵ״אֲשֶׁר יַרְשִׁיעֻן אֱלֹהִים״, וְלֹא הַמַּרְשִׁיעַ אֶת עַצְמוֹ.

The Gemara asks: **And according to the one who says** that **both** verses are speaking **about** a bailee who falsely **states the claim** that **a thief** stole the deposit, **who applies this** verse: **"If** the theft **shall be found,"** to **the thief himself, from where do we** derive that **one who incriminates himself** is exempt from paying double payment or any other fine? The Gemara answers: He derives it **from** the verse: **"The one whom the judges convict** shall pay double to his neighbor" (Exodus 22:8), which indicates that only one who is convicted by the judges on the basis of testimony must pay double, **but not one who incriminates himself.**

וּלְמַאן דְּאָמַר חַד בְּגַנָּב וְחַד בְּטוֹעֵן טַעֲנַת גַּנָּב, דְּאַיְיתֵי לֵיהּ מֵ״הִמָּצֵא תִמָּצֵא״ לְמַרְשִׁיעַ אֶת עַצְמוֹ, הַאי ״אֲשֶׁר יַרְשִׁיעֻן״ מַאי דָּרֵישׁ בֵּיהּ? אָמַר לָךְ: הַהוּא מִיבָּעֵי לֵיהּ לְמוֹדֶה בִּקְנָס דְּפָטוּר.

The Gemara continues its line of questioning: **And according to the one who says** that **one** verse is speaking **about a thief** himself **and one** verse is speaking **about** a bailee who falsely **states the claim** that **a thief** stole the deposit, **who derives from: "If** the theft **shall be found" that one who incriminates himself** is exempt from payment of the fine, **what does he expound from this** verse: **"The one whom the judges convict** shall pay double to his neighbor"? He could have **said to you: That** verse **is necessary to** teach **that** one who **admits** his liability to pay **a fine** is **exempt** from payment if witnesses never come to testify against him. "If the theft shall be found" indicates that even if witnesses do come after he admitted his liability, he is exempt from paying the fine.

וּמַאן דְּאָמַר תַּרְוַיְיהוּ בְּטוֹעֵן טַעֲנַת גַּנָּב, קָסָבַר: מוֹדֶה בִּקְנָס וְאַחַר כָּךְ בָּאוּ עֵדִים – חַיָּיב.

The Gemara continues: **And the one who says** that **both** verses **are** speaking **about** a bailee who falsely **states the claim** that **a thief** stole the deposit, and, as explained previously, derives from "if the theft shall be found" that a thief is required to pay double payment, **holds** that in the case of one who **admits** that he is liable **to** pay **a fine, and afterward witnesses came** and testified to his liability, he is **obligated** to pay the fine, contrary to the opinion of Rav.

וּלְמַאן דְּאָמַר חַד בְּגַנָּב וְחַד בְּטוֹעֵן טַעֲנַת גַּנָּב, דְּנָפְקָא לֵיהּ גַּנָּב מֵהָתָם, בִּשְׁלָמָא ״אִם הִמָּצֵא תִמָּצֵא״ לְכִדְרָבָא בַּר אֲהִילַאי, אֲבָל כָּל הָנֵי פְּרָטֵי לָמָּה לִי?

The Gemara asks: **And according to the one who says** that **one** verse is speaking **about a thief** himself **and one** verse is speaking **about** a bailee who falsely **states the claim** that **a thief** stole the deposit, **who derives** the *halakha* of double payment for **a thief from there,** i.e., from the verse "if the thief shall be found" (Exodus 22:6), there is a difficulty. **Granted,** the phrase **"if the** theft **shall be found"** is required **for** teaching the *halakha* of **Rava bar Ahilai. But why do I** need **all these details,** "ox," "donkey," "sheep," and "alive"? All the items excluded from double payment, such as land and slaves, are already derived from a different source.

NOTES

This excludes one who incriminates himself – פְּרָט לְמַרְשִׁיעַ אֶת עַצְמוֹ: The Gemara describes two similar cases. One case is where the perpetrator of an act that normally results in a fine admits his liability on his own without the testimony of witnesses. In this case, all agree that the guilty party is exempt from paying the fine. Some explain that the reason for this is that a fine is a judicially imposed punishment rather than an automatic monetary liability. Consequently, if the guilty party admits to his act, the court has done nothing to establish his liability and the judges cannot impose the fine.

In the second case, the perpetrator admits his liability and subsequently witnesses also testify to his liability. The *halakha* here is the subject of a dispute. According to one opinion, once witnesses testify the court can impose the fine, because it is basing its decision solely on the testimony of the witnesses rather than on the admission of the guilty party. Conversely, according to Rav, the exemption of one who admits his liability is not derived by logical analysis but is derived from a verse, as explained by Rava bar Ahilai. Consequently, it applies even if witnesses subsequently testify to the perpetrator's liability.

כִּדְתָנָא דְּבֵי רַבִּי יִשְׁמָעֵאל, דְּתָנָא דְּבֵי רַבִּי יִשְׁמָעֵאל: כׇּל פָּרָשָׁה שֶׁנֶּאֶמְרָה וְנִשְׁנֵית, לֹא נִשְׁנֵית אֶלָּא לְדָבָר שֶׁנִּתְחַדֵּשׁ בָּהּ.

The Gemara answers: This may be explained **in accordance with** what **the school of Rabbi Yishmael taught. As the school of Rabbi Yishmael taught: Any passage that was stated** in the Torah **and was** then **repeated,**[N] **was repeated only for** the sake of **a matter that was introduced** for the first time in the repeated passage. That is, sometimes the Torah repeats an entire passage just for the sake of a single new detail. The single new detail derived from this passage is the *halakha* that one who admits that he is liable to pay a fine is exempt from paying the fine, which is derived from the words: "If the theft shall be found."

וְאֵימָא: גַּנָּב עַצְמוֹ בִּשְׁבוּעָה!

The Gemara asks: **But** since the two cases of a thief and a bailee who falsely claims the deposit was stolen are juxtaposed, as their obligations to pay double payment are expressed in consecutive verses, **say** that **a thief himself** is not obligated to pay double payment unless he falsely confirms his innocence **with an oath,** just as a bailee is liable to pay double payment only under these circumstances.

לָא סָלְקָא דַּעְתָּךְ, דְּתַנְיָא, רַבִּי יַעֲקֹב אוֹמֵר: "שְׁנַיִם יְשַׁלֵּם" – שֶׁלֹּא בִּשְׁבוּעָה; אַתָּה אוֹמֵר: שֶׁלֹּא בִּשְׁבוּעָה, אוֹ אֵינוֹ אֶלָּא בִּשְׁבוּעָה? אָמַרְתָּ: לֹא כָּךְ הָיָה.

The Gemara answers: This **cannot enter your mind, as it is taught** in a *baraita*: **Rabbi Ya'akov says** that the phrase "if the theft shall be found… **he shall pay double**" indicates that a thief pays double even **without** taking **an oath.**[H] Rabbi Ya'akov elaborates: Do **you say** the verse obligates every thief, even **without** his taking **an oath? Or** perhaps **it is** speaking **only** of a thief who falsely confirms his innocence **with an oath? You** must **say: This** second possibility **was not** the Torah's intent.

מַאי "לֹא כָּךְ הָיָה"? אֲמַר אַבָּיֵי: לָא לִכְתּוֹב רַחֲמָנָא "שְׁנַיִם יְשַׁלֵּם" בְּגַנָּב, וְלֵיתֵי בְּקַל וָחוֹמֶר מִטּוֹעֵן טַעֲנַת גַּנָּב: וּמָה טוֹעֵן טַעֲנַת גַּנָּב דְּבְהֶיתֵּירָא אֲתָא לִידֵיהּ – אָמַר קְרָא לִישַׁלֵּם תְּרֵי, גַּנָּב עַצְמוֹ דִּבְאִיסּוּרָא אֲתָא לִידֵיהּ, לֹא כׇּל שֶׁכֵּן?

The Gemara asks: **What** is the meaning of the phrase: **This was not** the Torah's intent? What is the proof that the Torah could not have meant that only a thief who falsely confirms his innocence with an oath pays double payment? **Abaye said:** If this was the Torah's intent, **let the Merciful One not write "he shall pay double" with regard to a thief** at all, **and let it be derived through an** *a fortiori* inference **from** the case of a bailee who falsely **states the claim** that **a thief** stole the deposit, as follows: If, in the case of a bailee who falsely **states the claim** that **a thief** stole the deposit, **for whom the** deposit initially **came into his possession in a permitted** fashion, **the verse states that he must pay double,** then in the case of **a thief himself, for whom** the stolen object **came into his possession in a prohibited manner** from the start, is it **not** clear **all the more so** that he must pay double payment?

אֶלָּא "שְׁנַיִם יְשַׁלֵּם" דִּכְתַב רַחֲמָנָא בְּגַנָּב עַצְמוֹ לָמָּה לִי? דַּאֲפִילּוּ שֶׁלֹּא בִּשְׁבוּעָה.

But then **why do I** need the words **"he shall pay double," which the Merciful One wrote concerning a thief himself?** It must be that the verse adds to the requirement of double payment for a thief and indicates **that** he must pay double **even without** having taken **an oath.**

וְהַאי "אִם הִמָּצֵא" לְהָכִי הוּא דַּאֲתָא? הָא מִיבָּעֵי לֵיהּ לְכִדְתַנְיָא: "יָדוֹ",

The Gemara asks: **And does this** verse, which states "**if the theft shall be found**" and concludes "he shall pay double," **come for this** purpose? **Isn't it required for that which is taught** in a *baraita*: The verse states: "If the theft shall be found in his possession." From the term "in **his possession** [*yado*],"

NOTES

Any passage that was stated and was repeated – כׇּל פָּרָשָׁה שֶׁנֶּאֶמְרָה וְנִשְׁנֵית: It is explained in the *Shita Mekubbetzet* that this is not limited to the interpretation of a passage that was stated previously and is then repeated later in the Torah. In the case addressed here in the Gemara, it is the passage that appears first in the Torah that the Gemara considers repeated for the sake of a single new detail. Rather, the meaning of this rule is that whenever the Torah records two similar passages, one of them, either the first or the second, is written solely for the purpose of the new information found in it.

HALAKHA

He shall pay double even without taking an oath – שְׁנַיִם יְשַׁלֵּם שֶׁלֹּא בִּשְׁבוּעָה: If witnesses testify that a thief stole an item, he must pay double to the owner of the stolen item. Consequently, if he stole a dinar he must pay two dinars, and if he stole an animal he must pay twice the value of that animal (Rambam *Sefer Nezikin*, *Hilkhot Geneiva* 1:4).

אֵין לִי אֶלָּא יָדוֹ, גַּגּוֹ חֲצֵירוֹ וְקַרְפֵּיפוֹ מִנַּיִן? תַּלְמוּד לוֹמַר ״אִם הִמָּצֵא תִמָּצֵא״, מִכׇּל מָקוֹם!

I have derived **only** a case where the stolen item is found in **his hand** [*yado*]. **From where** do I derive that the same *halakha* applies if it is found on **his roof, in his yard, or in his enclosure** [*vekarpeifo*]?[HL] **The verse states** the repetitive phrase **"if the theft shall be found** [*himmatze timmatze*]," to indicate that the same *halakha* applies **in any case,** i.e., in any location that the stolen item is found.

אִם כֵּן, לֵימָא קְרָא אוֹ ״הִמָּצֵא הִמָּצֵא״ אוֹ ״תִּמָּצֵא תִמָּצֵא״, מִדְּשַׁנֵּי קְרָא שְׁמַע מִינָּהּ תַּרְתֵּי.

The Gemara answers: **If so,** if this is all the phrase is coming to teach, **let the verse state** the identical word twice: ***Himmatze himmatze,* or: *Timmatze timmatze.*** **From** the fact that **the verse varied** its wording, one may **conclude two** *halakhot* **from it:** That one is liable to pay double payment regardless of where the stolen item was found, and that a thief pays double payment even if he did not take an oath.

גּוּפָא, אָמַר רַב: קֶרֶן – כְּעֵין שֶׁגָּנַב, תַּשְׁלוּמֵי כֶפֶל וְתַשְׁלוּמֵי אַרְבָּעָה וַחֲמִשָּׁה – כִּשְׁעַת הַעֲמָדָה בַּדִּין.

§ The Gemara returns to **the** matter **itself. Rav says:** When a thief makes his payments, the **principal** is paid **according to** the value as of the time **when he stole it,**[N] whereas the **double payment and** the **fourfold or fivefold payment** are calculated **according to** the value at **the time of standing trial.**[N]

מַאי טַעְמָא דְּרַב? אָמַר קְרָא ״גְּנֵיבָה״ וְ״חַיִּים״, אַמַּאי קָאָמַר רַחֲמָנָא ״חַיִּים״ בִּגְנֵיבָה? אַחֲיֵיהּ לְקֶרֶן כְּעֵין שֶׁגָּנַב.

The Gemara asks: **What is the reason,** i.e., the source, for this ruling **of Rav?** The Gemara answers: **The verse states:** "If the **theft** shall be found in his possession **alive,** whether it is an ox, or a donkey, or a sheep, he shall pay double" (Exodus 22:3). **Why is the Merciful One saying "alive [*ḥayyim*]" in** the context of this **theft?** This juxtaposition serves to teach: When making payment, **revive [*aḥayah*] the principal** to the value it had **as of** the time **when he stole it.**[N]

אָמַר רַב שֵׁשֶׁת, אָמִינָא: כִּי נָיֵים וְשָׁכֵיב רַב אֲמַר לְהָא שְׁמַעְתָּא. דְּתַנְיָא: כְּחוּשָׁה וְהִשְׁמִינָהּ – מְשַׁלֵּם תַּשְׁלוּמֵי כֶפֶל וְתַשְׁלוּמֵי אַרְבָּעָה וַחֲמִשָּׁה כְּעֵין שֶׁגָּנַב!

Rav Sheshet said: I say that **when Rav was sleepy and lying down**[N] to rest, **he said this *halakha*.** Rav Sheshet meant that this is a careless ruling, as it is contrary to a *baraita*. **As it is taught** in a *baraita*: If the animal was stolen when it was **lean and** the thief **fattened it,**[H] **he pays** the **double payment and** the **fourfold or fivefold payment according to** the value of the animal as of the time **when he stole** it. This shows that the double payment and the fourfold and fivefold payment are applied in accordance with the value of the item at the time of the theft, not its value at the time of trial, as claimed by Rav.

אָמְרִי: מִשּׁוּם דְּאָמַר לֵיהּ: אֲנָא פַּטֵּימְתָּא וְאַתְּ שָׁקְלַתְּ?

The Sages **say** in response: This *baraita* is not a refutation of Rav's opinion, **because** the thief **could say to** the owner of the animal: **I fattened** the animal myself, **and will you take** for yourself[N] the added value from its fattening? In this particular case, Rav would agree that all payments are in accordance with the value of the item at the time of the theft.

HALAKHA

His roof, his yard, or his enclosure – **גַּגּוֹ חֲצֵירוֹ וְקַרְפֵּיפוֹ**: One is considered to have stolen an item when he moves it from the property of the owner or lifts it up. If one led another's animal into his property, even leading it to his roof or yard or enclosure, he is liable for theft, despite the fact that he performed no act of acquisition on the animal (*Shulḥan Arukh, Ḥoshen Mishpat* 348:4).

It was lean and he fattened it – **כְּחוּשָׁה וְהִשְׁמִינָהּ**: If one stole a lean animal and fattened it, or he stole a fat animal and caused it to become leaner, he pays the double payment and the fourfold or fivefold payment according to the value of the animal at the time of the theft, as stated in the *baraita*. This *halakha* also applies to the payment of the principal. The *Tur* adds that if the animal grew fatter or leaner on its own after the theft, this is equivalent to the case of appreciation or depreciation in value, discussed on 66a (Rambam *Sefer Nezikin, Hilkhot Geneiva* 1:13; *Tur, Ḥoshen Mishpat* 354; *Shulḥan Arukh, Ḥoshen Mishpat* 354:4).

LANGUAGE

His enclosure [*karpeifo*] – **קַרְפֵּיפוֹ**: The source of this term and its precise meaning are both unclear. Some explain that it is derived from the root *kuf, peh, peh,* similar to the root *gimmel, peh, peh,* with the addition of the letter *reish*. If so, it means an area surrounded by a *gapa*, a fence of some kind. Most commentaries explain that *karpef* means a courtyard positioned behind houses. Such courtyards were used in many ways; sometimes seeds were sown or trees planted in these areas, whereas on other occasions objects were placed there for safekeeping.

Alternatively, *karpef* refers to a slightly raised enclosure located outside urban areas.

NOTES

The principal is paid according to the value as of the time when he stole it – **קֶרֶן כְּעֵין שֶׁגָּנַב**: Many early commentaries address a difficulty raised by *Tosafot*: The *halakha* that a thief pays restitution according to the value of the stolen item at the time of the theft is in fact mentioned in a mishna (93b). What, then, is the novelty of Rav's statement?

Most explain that the key point of Rav's ruling is the second half of his statement, that the double payment and the fourfold and fivefold payments are set in accordance with the value at the time of trial.

Tosafot add that Rav infers from the fact that the verse states that specifically the principal is revived to the value it had as of the time when he stole it that other payments, e.g., the double payment and the fourfold and fivefold payment, are not to be calculated in accordance with the value it had as of the time when he stole it.

The double payment and the fourfold or fivefold payment are according to the value at the time of standing trial – **תַּשְׁלוּמֵי כֶפֶל וְתַשְׁלוּמֵי אַרְבָּעָה וַחֲמִשָּׁה כִּשְׁעַת הַעֲמָדָה בַּדִּין**: Some commentaries distinguish between the double payment, which is based on the item's value at the time of the trial, and the fourfold and fivefold payment, which is calculated in accordance with its value at the time when it became irretrievable, upon its sale or slaughter (Rosh). Others maintain that Rav's statement concerning the time of trial should be interpreted literally with regard to both the double payment and the fourfold and fivefold payment (see *Yam shel Shlomo*).

Revive the principal to the value as of the time when he stole it – **אַחֲיֵיהּ לְקֶרֶן כְּעֵין שֶׁגָּנַב**: The commentaries explain the reason for the difference between the evaluation for the payment of principal and that for the double payment and the fourfold and fivefold payment: The thief's obligation to pay the principal originates from when he took the item. Therefore, he pays according to its value at the time of the theft. By contrast, fines are imposed only by the court, and consequently the obligation to pay the fines of double payment and fourfold or fivefold payment does not start with the act of theft but from the time of judgment (Ra'avad).

When Rav was sleepy and lying down – **כִּי נָיֵים וְשָׁכֵיב רַב**: Although Rav Sheshet's tone is apparently irreverent toward Rav, the *Ḥavvot Ya'ir* (152) explains that this is in fact a compliment to Rav. The statement indicates that he is so great in Torah knowledge that the only way to explain such a mistake is to assume that he was sleeping when he said it.

I fattened the animal myself and will you take for yourself – **אֲנָא פַּטֵּימְתָּא וְאַתְּ שָׁקְלַתְּ**: The commentaries ask: Granted, the thief invested time and money in fattening the animal. Nevertheless, this should not mean that all the increased value should accrue to him. If one improves the property of another without the owner's consent, the *halakha* is that he does not receive all the appreciation in the value of the property, although he is entitled to a certain refund. Why should a thief be more entitled to profit than that individual? Some answer that the standard *halakha* is not applied to a thief because, as in other matters, a special leniency is afforded to thieves in order to encourage them to come forward, repent, and return the stolen property (*Mitzpe Eitan*).

תָּא שְׁמַע: שְׁמֵינָה וְהִכְחִישָׁהּ – מְשַׁלֵּם תַּשְׁלוּמֵי כֶפֶל וְתַשְׁלוּמֵי אַרְבָּעָה וַחֲמִשָּׁה כְּעֵין שֶׁגָּנַב!

The Gemara asks further: **Come and hear** another *baraita* that apparently contradicts Rav's ruling. If the animal was stolen when it was **fat and the thief caused it to become lean,**[N] **he pays** the **double payment and** the **fourfold or fivefold payment according to** the value of the animal as of the time **when he stole** it. The double and fourfold and fivefold payments are not paid in accordance with the value at the time of the trial, as claimed by Rav.

הָתָם נַמִי, מִשּׁוּם דְּאָמְרִינַן לֵיהּ: מַה לִּי קַטְלָהּ כּוּלָּהּ מַה לִּי קַטְלָהּ פַּלְגָא, כִּי קָאָמַר רַב – בְּיוּקְרָא וְזוּלָּא הוּא דְּקָאָמַר.

The Gemara answers: **There too,** there is a reason for this exception, **because we say of** the thief: **What is it to me** if he **killed** the animal **entirely,** and **what is it to me if he killed it partially?** By causing the animal to become lean, the thief is considered to have started to put it to death. Consequently, when he ultimately kills the animal, he pays the fourfold or fivefold payment according to its value when he first began to weaken it, i.e., at the time of the theft. **When Rav says** his ruling, **he is saying** it only **with regard to** cases of **appreciation** in value **and depreciation** in value, not to changes in the animal's physical state.

הֵיכִי דָּמֵי? אִילֵימָא דְּמֵעִיקָּרָא שָׁוְיָא זוּזָא וּלְבַסּוֹף שָׁוְיָא אַרְבָּעָה זוּזֵי, קֶרֶן – כְּעֵין שֶׁגָּנַב; לֵימָא פְּלִיגָא דְּרַב אַדְּרַבָּה, דְּאָמַר רַבָּה: הַאי מַאן דִּגְזַל חָבִיתָא דְּחַמְרָא מֵחַבְרֵיהּ, מֵעִיקָּרָא שָׁוְיָא זוּזָא וּלְבַסּוֹף שָׁוְיָא אַרְבָּעָה זוּזֵי, תַּבְרָהּ אוֹ שַׁתְיָיהּ – מְשַׁלֵּם אַרְבַּע, אִיתְּבַר מִמֵּילָא – מְשַׁלֵּם זוּזָא?

What are the circumstances of the case referred to by Rav? **If we say that initially** the stolen item **was worth one dinar and in the end it was worth four dinars,** and Rav teaches that the thief pays the **principal according to** the value of the animal as of the time **when he stole** it, which is one dinar, **shall we say that Rav disagrees with this ruling of Rabba? As Rabba says:** With regard to **this one who robbed another of a barrel of wine,**[H] if it was **initially worth one dinar and ultimately it was worth four dinars,** and after its appreciation the robber **broke** the barrel **or drank** the wine,[N] **he pays four** dinars. If the barrel **broke by itself, he pays one dinar.** Rabba holds that even the principal is paid according to the time when he broke the barrel.

אָמְרִי: כִּי קָאָמַר רַב, כְּגוֹן דְּמֵעִיקָּרָא שָׁוְיָא אַרְבַּע וּלְבַסּוֹף שָׁוְיָא זוּזָא, קֶרֶן – כְּעֵין שֶׁגָּנַב, תַּשְׁלוּמֵי כֶפֶל וְתַשְׁלוּמֵי אַרְבָּעָה וַחֲמִשָּׁה – כִּשְׁעַת הַעֲמָדָה בַּדִּין.

The Sages **say** in response that Rav agrees with Rabba with regard to the above case. **When Rav says**[H] his *halakha* he is referring to a case where, **for example,** the item was **initially worth four** dinars **and ultimately was worth one dinar.** In this situation, Rav maintains that the thief does not profit from the decrease in the value of the principal. Rather, he pays the **principal according to** its value as of the time **when he stole** it, **and the double payment and** the **fourfold or fivefold payment** are paid **according to** the value at **the time of standing trial.**

תָּנֵי רַבִּי חֲנִינָא לְסַיּוֹעֵיהּ לְרַב: בַּעַל הַבַּיִת שֶׁטָּעַן טַעֲנַת גַּנָּב בְּפִקָּדוֹן, וְנִשְׁבַּע וְהוֹדָה וּבָאוּ עֵדִים, אִם עַד שֶׁלֹּא בָּאוּ עֵדִים הוֹדָה – מְשַׁלֵּם קֶרֶן וְחוֹמֶשׁ וְאָשָׁם, וְאִם מִשֶּׁבָּאוּ עֵדִים הוֹדָה – מְשַׁלֵּם תַּשְׁלוּמֵי כֶפֶל וְאָשָׁם, וְחוּמְשׁוֹ עוֹלֶה לוֹ בִּכְפֵילוֹ, דִּבְרֵי רַבִּי יַעֲקֹב;

Rabbi Ḥanina teaches a *baraita* **in support of Rav:** In the case of **a homeowner** acting as a bailee, **who** falsely **stated the claim** that **a thief** stole the **deposit, and** subsequently **took an oath** as to the truth of his claim, **and** then **admitted** that he was lying and that he in fact took the item himself, **and** at some point **witnesses came** and testified that the bailee himself had the item, **if he admitted** his guilt **before the witnesses came** and testified, **he pays** the **principal and** an additional **one-fifth, and** he must also bring **a guilt-offering.**[H] **But if he admitted** his guilt **after witnesses came** and testified, **he pays** the **double payment and** brings **a guilt-offering, and his** additional **one-fifth is covered by his double payment** that he pays; **this is the statement of Rabbi Ya'akov.**

NOTES

If the animal was stolen when it was fat and the thief caused it to become lean – שְׁמֵינָה וְהִכְחִישָׁהּ: The commentaries note that the Gemara must be speaking of a thief who caused the animal to become lean in such a manner that it cannot regain its previous fattened state (Ra'avad).

Broke the barrel or drank the wine, etc. – תַּבְרָהּ אוֹ שַׁתְיָיהּ וכו׳: The difference between a case where the robber broke the item and a case where it broke by itself is as follows: As long as the stolen item is intact, the appreciation belongs to its owner, as it is supposed to be returned in its current state. When the robber breaks or drinks it, he is considered to have taken it at that moment, and therefore he is liable for its value at that time. By contrast, if it broke by itself, his liability is calculated from when he took the item, at which point it was worth only one dinar (Rashi, citing *Bava Metzia* 43a).

HALAKHA

One who robbed another of a barrel of wine, etc. – מַאן דִּגְזַל חָבִיתָא דְּחַמְרָא מֵחַבְרֵיהּ וכו׳: With regard to one who robbed another of a barrel of wine worth one dinar at the time of the robbery, and it subsequently appreciated in value to four dinars, if the robber himself broke the barrel and drank the wine, sold it, or gave it away as a gift, he pays four dinars, according to its value at the time it left his possession. If the barrel broke by itself or became lost, the robber pays according to its value at the time of the robbery, in accordance with the opinion of Rabba (Rambam *Sefer Nezikin, Hilkhot Gezeila VaAveda* 3:1; *Shulḥan Arukh, Ḥoshen Mishpat* 362:10).

When Rav says, etc. – כִּי קָאָמַר רַב וכו׳: If one stole an animal or item, and at the time of the theft it was worth four dinars but when he stood trial it was worth only one dinar, he pays the principal according to the value of the item at the time of the theft. The fourfold or fivefold payment is paid according to the animal's value at the time of trial, or, more precisely, according to the time of slaughter or sale (*Tur*, citing Rosh).

In a case where the item was worth one dinar at the time of the theft and four dinars at the time of trial, if the thief destroyed the item himself, he pays all payments according to the value at the time of trial. If the animal died or the item broke by itself, he pays its value at the time of the theft (Rambam *Sefer Nezikin, Hilkhot Geneiva* 1:14; *Tur, Ḥoshen Mishpat* 354; *Shulḥan Arukh, Ḥoshen Mishpat* 354:3 and *Beur HaGra* there).

He pays the principal and one-fifth and must bring a guilt-offering – מְשַׁלֵּם קֶרֶן וְחוֹמֶשׁ וְאָשָׁם: In the case of a bailee who was entrusted with an item for safeguarding, and he claimed that it was stolen, and he took an oath to that effect, and afterward he admitted that he was lying and had in fact taken the item for himself, he pays the principal value of the item and an additional one-fifth, and he must also bring a guilt-offering (Rambam *Sefer Hafla'a, Hilkhot Shevuot* 1:9).

וחכמים אומרים ״בראשו וחמשתיו״ – ממון המשתלם בראש מוסיף חומש, ממון שאין משתלם בראש אין מוסיף חומש. רבי שמעון בן יוחאי אומר: אין חומש ואשם משתלם במקום שיש כפל.

And the Rabbis say: It is written concerning a bailee who falsely claims innocence with regard to a deposit entrusted to him: "He shall restore it **according to its principal, and** shall add **its fifth part** to it" (Leviticus 5:24). This verse teaches that with regard to **monetary restitution that is paid** precisely **according to the principal, one adds one-fifth,** but for **monetary restitution that is not paid** precisely **according to the principal,** as is the case here where the bailee pays double the principal value, **one does not add one-fifth. Rabbi Shimon ben Yoḥai says:** Neither the additional **one-fifth nor the guilt-offering is paid**[H] **in a case where there is double payment.** This concludes the *baraita*.

קתני מיהת: חומשו עולה לו בכפילו, דברי רבי יעקב. היכי דמי? אילימא דמעיקרא שויא ארבעה ולבסוף שויא ארבעה, חומשו עולה לו בכפילו?

Rabbi Ḥanina explains: **In any event,** the *baraita* **teaches: His** payment of the additional **one-fifth is covered by his double payment;**[N] this is **the statement of Rabbi Ya'akov.**[P] **What are the circumstances** of this case? **If we say that** the stolen item was **initially worth four** dinars **and ultimately,** at the time of trial, was still **worth four** dinars, how could he say: **His** payment of the additional **one-fifth is covered by his double payment?**

כפילא ארבעה וחומשא זוזא! אלא לאו דמעיקרא שויא ארבעה ולבסוף שויא זוזא, דכפילא זוזא וחומשיה זוזא,

This statement is inaccurate in this case, as **the double payment,** i.e., the penalty included in the double payment, is **four dinars, and the** additional **one-fifth is one dinar.** When the Torah states "fifth" it means one-fifth of the total payment of the one-fifth and the principal together, i.e., one-quarter of the principal. For the additional one-fifth to be covered by the double payment, the two must be exactly equal, which is not the case here. **Rather, is it not** referring to a situation where **initially** it was **worth four** dinars **and at the end** it was **worth one dinar, as the** penalty component of the **double payment is one dinar and the** additional **one-fifth** is also **one dinar?**

אלמא: קרן – כעין שגנב, תשלומי כפל ותשלומי ארבעה וחמשה – כשעת העמדה בדין!

Apparently, the **principal,** as well as the additional one-fifth, is paid **according to** the value as of the time **when he stole,** whereas the **double payment and the fourfold or fivefold payment** is **according to** the value at **the time of standing trial,** as claimed by Rav.

אמר רבא: לעולם דמעיקרא שויא ארבעה והשתא נמי שויא ארבעה, ודקא קשיא: כפילא ארבעה וחומשיה זוזא! הכא במאי עסקינן – כגון שנשבע וחזר ונשבע ארבע פעמים והודה, והתורה אמרה ״וחמשתיו״,

The Gemara refutes this analysis. **Rava said: Actually,** the *baraita* could be referring to a case in which **initially** it was **worth four** dinars **and now,** at the time of trial, it is **also worth four** dinars. **And** as for **what is difficult** with this case, namely that **the double payment is four** dinars **and the** additional **one-fifth** is **one dinar,** this problem can be resolved as follows: **With what are we dealing here?** It is a case **where** the bailee **took an oath** that the deposit was stolen from him, **and he again took** the same **oath,**[N] and so on **four times, and** after each oath **he admitted** afterward that he had lied. **And the Torah said: "And shall add its fifth part** [*ḥamishitav*] to it" (Leviticus 5:24).

HALAKHA

Neither the one-fifth nor the guilt-offering is paid, etc. – אין חומש ואשם משתלם וכו׳: If a bailee claimed that a deposit was stolen from him, and he took an oath to that effect, and afterward witnesses testified that he was lying and that the item was in his possession, he pays the double payment. If the deposit was an animal, and he sold or slaughtered it after the false oath, he pays the fourfold or fivefold payment. He does not bring a guilt-offering in this case, nor is he required to pay the additional one-fifth (Rambam *Sefer Nezikin*, *Hilkhot Geneiva* 4:1).

PERSONALITIES

Rabbi Ya'akov – רבי יעקב: A member of the Sanhedrin at Usha, Rabbi Ya'akov ben Kurshai was appointed by Rabban Shimon ben Gamliel to teach his son Yehuda, later known as Rabbi Yehuda HaNasi. Rabbi Ya'akov's collection of *mishnayot* served as a significant source for the Mishna, complied by Rabbi Yehuda HaNasi. A staunch supporter of Rabban Shimon ben Gamliel, Rabbi Ya'akov prevented Rabbi Meir and Rabbi Natan the Babylonian from deposing him from the position of *Nasi*.

NOTES

His one-fifth is covered by his double payment – חומשו עולה לו בכפילו: From the discussion in the Gemara, it is clear that Rabbi Ya'akov means that if the additional one-fifth happens to correspond exactly to the penalty component of the double payment, in accordance with the change in value of the animal, the payment of the additional one-fifth is canceled out by the double payment.

Rashi explains the reason for this ruling: The payment of the additional one-fifth serves to atone for the false oath. In order for the atonement to be effective, it must be recognizable as a distinct unit. Consequently, the additional one-fifth is canceled only if it coincides exactly with the penalty component of the double payment, as in that case it is evident that he has paid one-fifth for his atonement.

Tosafot raise a difficulty with this assertion, for which there is no apparent biblical source. They explain that the Gemara's inference is based solely on Rabbi Ya'akov's statement itself, which indicates that he is referring to a case where one-fifth is exactly equal to the double payment.

Some interpret Rabbi Ya'akov's opinion in the opposite manner: If one-fifth is equal to the penalty component of the double payment, the bailee pays one-fifth and is excused from paying the double payment (Ra'avad).

The commentaries further ask: According to the interpretation of *Tosafot*, what is the practical difference between the rulings of Rabbi Ya'akov and the Rabbis? After all, Rabbi Ya'akov agrees that he does not pay any more than the double payment. The Maharam Lublin answers that the difference is in a case where one-fifth is more than the penalty component of the double payment. Rabbi Ya'akov requires him to also pay that part of the additional one-fifth that is not subsumed within the double payment, whereas the Rabbis exempt him from the payment of one-fifth entirely, and require him to pay only the double payment (see Ra'avad).

Where he took an oath and he again took the same oath – שנשבע וחזר ונשבע: The commentaries explain that this scenario is possible only in a situation where the bailee was brought to trial each time in a different court. If he returned to the same court, however, the judges would not trust him to take an oath after having admitted to having lied under oath previously (Rashba; Meiri).

הַתּוֹרָה רִיבְּתָה חֲמִישִׁיּוֹת הַרְבֵּה בְּקֶרֶן אַחַת.

Rava continues: The term *ḥamishitav* is in the plural, which indicates that **the Torah included** the possibility of **many** payments of an additional **one-fifth for a single principal.**[H] In other words, each time the bailee takes a false oath he becomes obligated to pay an additional one-fifth, despite the fact that each oath concerns the same item. Since he did so four times, and the one-fifth is actually one-quarter of the principal, the total amount of payments of the additional one-fifth is equal to the principal, which is the same as the penalty component of the double payment.

אָמַר מָר, וַחֲכָמִים אוֹמְרִים: ״בְּרֹאשׁוֹ וַחֲמִשִׁתָיו״ – מָמוֹן הַמִּשְׁתַּלֵּם בְּרֹאשׁ מוֹסִיף חוֹמֶשׁ, מָמוֹן שֶׁאֵין מִשְׁתַּלֵּם בְּרֹאשׁ אֵין מוֹסִיף חוֹמֶשׁ. אֲבָל אָשָׁם מַיְיתֵי.

§ **The Master said** in the *baraita*: **And the Sages say:** "He shall restore it **according to its principal, and** shall add **its fifth** part to it" (Leviticus 5:24). This verse teaches that for **monetary restitution that is paid** precisely **according to the principal, one adds one-fifth.** But for **monetary restitution that is not paid** precisely **according to the principal, one does not add one-fifth.** The Gemara infers: He does not add one-fifth, **but he** is obligated to **bring a guilt-offering.**

מַאי שְׁנָא חוֹמֶשׁ דְּלָא מְשַׁלֵּם – דִּכְתִיב: ״בְּרֹאשׁוֹ וַחֲמִשִׁתָיו״, אָשָׁם נַמִי לָא מְשַׁלֵּם, דְּהָא כְּתִיב: ״בְּרֹאשׁוֹ וַחֲמִשִׁתָיו...וְאֶת אֲשָׁמוֹ״

The Gemara asks: **What is different** about the additional **one-fifth** in that case, **that he does not** have to **pay** it? **As it is written:** "He shall restore it **according to its principal, and** shall add **its fifth part** to it." This indicates that the additional one-fifth is linked to the payment of the precise amount of the principal amount. If so, with regard to the **guilt offering as well,** he should **not** have to **pay,** i.e., bring it, **as it is written:** "He shall restore it **according to its principal, and** shall add **its fifth part** to it … **and his guilt-offering** [*ve'et ashamo*] he shall bring to the Lord" (Leviticus 5:24–25). The verse links the guilt-offering to the payment of the precise amount of the principal, just like it does the additional one-fifth.

אָמְרִי לָךְ רַבָּנַן: ״אֶת״ פַּסְקֵיהּ קְרָא.

The Gemara answers: **The Sages** would **say to you** in response: The superfluous word ***"et"*** in the phrase "and his guilt offering [*ve'et ashamo*]" **divides the verse.** Therefore, only the additional one-fifth payment, but not the guilt-offering, is linked to the payment of the precise amount of the principal.

וְרַבִּי שִׁמְעוֹן בֶּן יוֹחַאי? ״וְאֶת״ עָרְבֵיהּ קְרָא. וְרַבָּנַן אָמְרִי לָךְ: לָא לִיכְתּוֹב רַחֲמָנָא לָא וָי״ו וְלָא ״אֶת״.

The Gemara asks: **And Rabbi Shimon ben Yoḥai,** who maintains that this bailee is exempt from a guilt-offering as well, how would he respond to the Sages' argument concerning *"et"*? He would point out that the term in question is actually ***"ve'et,"*** consisting of the word *et* preceded by the letter *vav*, meaning "and." The conjunction **joins** the clauses of **the verse.** Therefore, both the additional one-fifth payment and the guilt-offering are linked to the payment of the precise amount of the principal. **And the Rabbis** would respond to Rabbi Shimon ben Yoḥai's claim and **say to you:** If the Torah had intended that the two issues should be joined together, **let the Merciful One write neither** the ***vav*** **nor** ***"et."***

וְרַבִּי שִׁמְעוֹן בֶּן יוֹחַאי אָמַר לָךְ: ״אֶת״ לָא סַגְיָא דְּלָא כָּתַב, לְאַפְסוֹקֵי בֵּין מָמוֹן גָּבוֹהַּ לְמָמוֹן הֶדְיוֹט, דִּלְכָּךְ אֲתָא וָי״ו עָרְבֵיהּ קְרָא.

And Rabbi Shimon ben Yoḥai could have **said to you** in response to this argument: It is **not possible** for the verse **to have not written** ***"et,"*** as this term is necessary **to separate between property** belonging to the **Most High,** i.e., the guilt-offering, **and non-sacred property,** i.e., that of a Jew. **Therefore,** as the verse had to use *"et"* to indicate this difference, the ***vav*** **comes** and **joins** the clauses of the **verse.**

אָמַר רַבִּי אִילְעָא: גָּנַב טָלֶה וְנַעֲשָׂה אַיִל, עֵגֶל וְנַעֲשָׂה שׁוֹר – נַעֲשָׂה שִׁינּוּי בְּיָדוֹ וּקְנָאוֹ, טָבַח וּמָכַר – שֶׁלּוֹ הוּא טוֹבֵחַ, שֶׁלּוֹ הוּא מוֹכֵר.

§ The Gemara discusses other cases in which an object undergoes a change after it has been stolen. **Rabbi Ile'a says:** If one **stole a lamb and it** subsequently **became a ram,**[H] or if he stole **a calf and it** subsequently **became a bull,** the stolen item **has undergone a change** while **in** the thief's **possession, and he has** therefore **acquired it** as his own property. Consequently, his obligation of restitution consists of monetary payment rather than giving back the stolen item itself. If he subsequently **slaughtered or sold** the animal, it is in effect **his own** animal that **he slaughters,** or it is **his own** animal that **he sells,** and he is not obligated in the fourfold or fivefold payment.

HALAKHA

The Torah included many payments of one-fifth for a single principal – הַתּוֹרָה רִיבְּתָה חֲמִישִׁיּוֹת הַרְבֵּה בְּקֶרֶן אַחַת: If a bailee claims that a deposit entrusted to him has become lost, or if he altogether denies having received it, and he takes an oath to corroborate his claim of exemption from payment, and subsequently he admits that he was lying, and later he once again claims falsely that the item was lost and again takes an oath to that effect, he must pay the principal amount and add one-fifth for each time that he took a false oath (Rambam *Sefer Hafla'a, Hilkhot Shevuot* 7:15 and *Sefer Nezikin, Hilkhot Gezeila VaAveda* 7:13; *Tur, Ḥoshen Mishpat* 352).

If one stole a lamb and it subsequently became a ram, etc. – גָּנַב טָלֶה וְנַעֲשָׂה אַיִל וכו׳: If one stole a lamb and it grew into a ram, or he stole a calf that grew into a bull, he pays the principal and the double payment, in accordance with the value of the animal at the time of the theft. If he slaughtered or sold the animal after it matured, then since it underwent a change while in the thief's possession, it is considered as though he slaughtered or sold his own animal, and he is consequently exempt from the fourfold or fivefold payment (Rambam *Sefer Nezikin, Hilkhot Geneiva* 1:13 and *Hilkhot Gezeila VaAveda* 2:14; *Shulḥan Arukh, Ḥoshen Mishpat* 353:1, and 360:10, in the comment of Rema).

אֵיתִיבֵיהּ רַבִּי חֲנִינָא לְרַבִּי אֶילְעָא: גָּנַב טָלֶה וְנַעֲשָׂה אַיִל, עֵגֶל וְנַעֲשָׂה שׁוֹר – מְשַׁלֵּם תַּשְׁלוּמֵי כֶפֶל וְתַשְׁלוּמֵי אַרְבָּעָה וַחֲמִשָּׁה כְּעֵין שֶׁגָּנַב. וְאִי סָלְקָא דַּעְתָּךְ קַנְיֵיהּ בְּשִׁינּוּי, אַמַּאי מְשַׁלֵּם? שֶׁלּוֹ הוּא טוֹבֵחַ, שֶׁלּוֹ הוּא מוֹכֵר!

Rabbi Ḥanina raised an objection to Rabbi Ile'a from a *baraita*: If one **stole a lamb and it** subsequently **became a ram,** or if he stole a **calf and it** subsequently **became a bull, he pays** the **double payment and** the **fourfold or fivefold payment according to** the animal's value as of the time **when he stole** it. **And if it enters your mind** that in a case of this kind the thief **has acquired** the animal as his own property **by** virtue of the physical **change** the animal underwent when it matured, **why does he pay** the fourfold or fivefold payment? After all, it is **his own** animal that **he slaughters,** or it is **his own** animal that **he sells.**

אֲמַר לֵיהּ: וְאֶלָּא מַאי, שִׁינּוּי לָא קָנֵי? אַמַּאי מְשַׁלֵּם כְּעֵין שֶׁגָּנַב? לְשַׁלֵּם כִּי הָשְׁתָּא!

Rabbi Ile'a **said to him: Rather, what** would you conclude from the *baraita*? That this physical **change** in the stolen animal **does not** serve to **acquire** it for the thief and render it his property? If so, **why** should he **pay according to** the animal's value as of the time **when he stole** it? **Let him pay according to** the animal's value **now,** i.e., at the time of the slaughter or sale.

אֲמַר לֵיהּ: כִּי הָשְׁתָּא הַיְינוּ טַעֲמָא דְּלָא מְשַׁלֵּם, מִשּׁוּם דְּאָמַר לֵיהּ: תּוֹרָא גְּנַבִי מִמָּךְ?! דִּיכְרָא גְּנַבִי מִמָּךְ?! אֲמַר לֵיהּ: רַחֲמָנָא נִיצְּלַן מֵהַאי דַּעְתָּא! אֲמַר לֵיהּ: אַדְּרַבָּה, רַחֲמָנָא נִיצְּלַן מִדַּעְתָּא דִּידָךְ!

Rabbi Ḥanina **said to him: This is the reason that he does not pay in accordance with** the animal's value **now:** It is **because** the thief can **say to** the animal's owner: **Did I steal a bull from you,** or: **Did I steal a ram from you?** No; I stole only a calf or a lamb, and therefore I will pay you the value of the animal when I stole it. Rabbi Ile'a **said to** Rabbi Ḥanina: **May the Merciful One save us from this opinion** of yours! Rabbi Ḥanina **said** back **to him: On the contrary, may the Merciful One save us from your opinion!**

מַתְקִיף לָהּ רַבִּי זֵירָא: וְנִיקְנִינְהוּ בְּשִׁינּוּי הַשֵּׁם!

Rabbi Zeira objects to this: But even if an animal's natural growth is not considered a physical change, **let the thief acquire** it **through** its **change in name,** i.e., its change of classification, as the animal was originally called a calf or a lamb and now it is considered a bull or ram.

אָמַר רָבָא: שׁוֹר בֶּן יוֹמוֹ קָרוּי שׁוֹר, אַיִל בֶּן יוֹמוֹ קָרוּי אַיִל. שׁוֹר בֶּן יוֹמוֹ קָרוּי שׁוֹר, דִּכְתִיב: "שׁוֹר אוֹ כֶשֶׂב אוֹ עֵז כִּי יִוָּלֵד".

Rava says: There is in fact no change in name here, as even **a day-old bull is called a bull,** and even **a day-old ram is called a ram. A day-old bull is called a bull, as it is written: "When a bull, or a sheep, or a goat is born"** (Leviticus 22:27).

אַיִל בֶּן יוֹמוֹ קָרוּי אַיִל, דִּכְתִיב: "וְאֵילֵי צֹאנְךָ לֹא אָכָלְתִּי", אֵילִים הוּא דְּלָא אֲכַל, כְּבָשִׂים אֲכַל? אֶלָּא לָאו שְׁמַע מִינָּהּ: אַיִל בֶּן יוֹמוֹ קָרוּי אַיִל.

A day-old ram is called a ram, as can be derived from Jacob's statement to Laban, **as it is written: "And the rams of your flock I have not eaten"** (Genesis 31:38). Now, did Jacob mean that **he did not eat** any of Laban's **rams,** but younger **lambs he did eat?** This is certainly not the meaning of this verse, as this would mean he was a thief. **Rather,** must one **not conclude from** this verse that **a day-old ram is called a ram?**

מִכָּל מָקוֹם קַשְׁיָא! אֲמַר רַב שֵׁשֶׁת: הָא מַנִּי? בֵּית שַׁמַּאי הִיא, דְּאָמְרִי: שִׁינּוּי בִּמְקוֹמוֹ עוֹמֶדֶת, וְלָא קָנֵי.

In any case, the *baraita* cited earlier by Rabbi Ḥanina **is difficult** for the opinion of Rabbi Ile'a, as it states that the thief must pay the fourfold or fivefold payment despite the fact that the slaughter or sale of the animal took place after it matured from a calf to a bull or from a lamb to a ram. To resolve the difficulty, **Rav Sheshet said:** In accordance with **whose** opinion **is this** *baraita*? **It is** in accordance with the opinion of **Beit Shammai, who say:** An item, even if it has undergone a physical **change, remains in its place,** i.e., a stolen item remains in the possession of its owner, **and** a thief **does not acquire** it even if it undergoes a change.

דְּתַנְיָא: נָתַן לָהּ בְּאֶתְנַנָּהּ חִיטִּין וַעֲשָׂאָן סוֹלֶת, זֵיתִים וַעֲשָׂאָן שֶׁמֶן, עֲנָבִים וַעֲשָׂאָן יַיִן, תָּנֵי חֲדָא: אָסוּר, וְתָנֵי חֲדָא: מוּתָּר; וְאָמַר רַב יוֹסֵף, תָּנֵי גּוּרְיוֹן דְּמֵאַסְפּוֹרָק: בֵּית שַׁמַּאי אוֹסְרִין, וּבֵית הִלֵּל מַתִּירִין.

As it is taught in a *baraita*: **If one gave wheat** to a prostitute **for her payment,**[H] i.e., the hire of her services, **and** she **made** the wheat into **flour;** or if he gave her **olives and** she **made them** into **oil;** or if he gave her **grapes and** she **made them** into **wine, it is taught in one** *baraita* that it is **prohibited** to bring these products as an offering in the Temple, in accordance with the verse: "You shall not bring the hire of a harlot…into the house of the Lord your God for any vow" (Deuteronomy 23:19). **And it is taught in one** *baraita* that these products are **permitted,** as the physical change renders them into new items. **And Rav Yosef says** that **Guryon of Asporak teaches** in a *baraita*: **Beit Shammai prohibit** these products **and Beit Hillel permit** them. If so, these two *baraitot* reflect a dispute between Beit Shammai and Beit Hillel.

HALAKHA

If one gave wheat for her payment, etc. – **נָתַן לָהּ בְּאֶתְנַנָּהּ חִיטִּין וכו׳**: If one gave wheat to a harlot for her services and she made flour out of it, or if he gave her olives from which she made oil, these products are not prohibited to the altar as the payments of a prostitute, as they have undergone a change, in accordance with the opinion of Beit Hillel (Rambam *Sefer Avoda*, *Hilkhot Issurei Mizbe'aḥ* 4:15).

מַאי טַעֲמָא דְּבֵית שַׁמַּאי? דִּכְתִיב: "גַּם" – לְרַבּוֹת שִׁינּוּיֵיהֶם. וּבֵית הִלֵּל? "הֵם" – וְלֹא שִׁינּוּיֵיהֶם.

The Gemara clarifies the source of these two opinions. **What is the reason of Beit Shammai** for prohibiting these products? **As it is written:** "You shall not bring the hire of a harlot, or the price of a dog, into the house of the Lord your God for any vow; for even both of these are an abomination to the Lord your God" (Deuteronomy 23:19). The apparently superfluous word **"even"** serves **to include their changed** status. **And Beit Hillel,** who permit these items after they have undergone a physical change, maintain that the term **"these"** in the phrase "both of these" teaches that this prohibition applies only to the original items, **but not** to **their changed** form.

וּבֵית שַׁמַּאי? הַהוּא,

And Beit Shammai would reply: **That** term,

Perek **VII**
Daf **66** Amud **a**

"הֵם" וְלֹא וְלָדוֹתֵיהֶם הוּא דַּאֲתָא. וּבֵית הִלֵּל: תַּרְתֵּי שְׁמַעִית מִינָּהּ: "הֵם" – וְלֹא שִׁינּוּיֵיהֶם, "הֵם" – וְלֹא וְלָדוֹתֵיהֶם. וּבֵית הִלֵּל, הָכְתִיב "גַּם"! "גַּם" לְבֵית הִלֵּל קַשְׁיָא.

"these," comes to teach that this *halakha* applies only to the animals given as payment to the prostitute **but not to their offspring.** The Gemara asks: **And** from where do **Beit Hillel** derive this *halakha*? They would say that one should **conclude two** conclusions **from** this term: **"These"** items are disqualified, **but not** when they are in **their changed** form, **and "these"** are disqualified, **but not their offspring.** The Gemara asks: **And** according to the opinion of **Beit Hillel, isn't it written "even"?** Since Beit Hillel reject the *halakha* that Beit Shammai derive from this term, what do they learn from it? The Gemara states: Indeed, the word **"even" is difficult according to** the opinion of **Beit Hillel.**

עַד כָּאן לָא פְּלִיגִי, אֶלָּא דְּמָר סָבַר: שִׁינּוּי קוֹנֶה, וּמָר סָבַר: אֵין שִׁינּוּי קוֹנֶה, אֲבָל לְעִנְיַן שַׁלּוּמֵי – כּוּלֵּי עָלְמָא כִּדְמֵעִיקָּרָא מְשַׁלֵּם, דְּקָתָנֵי: מְשַׁלֵּם תַּשְׁלוּמֵי כֶפֶל וְתַשְׁלוּמֵי אַרְבָּעָה וַחֲמִשָּׁה כְּעֵין שֶׁגָּנַב.

In any event, they **disagree only with regard to** this particular issue: One **Sage,** Beit Hillel, **holds** that a physical **change** in a stolen item causes the thief to **acquire** it, **and** one **Sage,** Beit Shammai, **holds** that a physical **change** in a stolen item **does not** cause the thief to **acquire** it. **But with regard to** the **payment** of the thief, **everyone** agrees that **he pays according to** the **initial** value of the item, at the time of the theft, **as it teaches** in the *baraita* cited above: **He pays** the **double payment and** the **fourfold or fivefold payment according to** the animal's value as of the time **when he stole** it.

לֵימָא, תֶּיהֱוֵי תְּיוּבְתָּא דְּרַב, דְּאָמַר רַב: קֶרֶן – כְּעֵין שֶׁגָּנַב מְשַׁלֵּם, תַּשְׁלוּמֵי כֶפֶל וְתַשְׁלוּמֵי אַרְבָּעָה וַחֲמִשָּׁה – כִּשְׁעַת הַעֲמָדָה בַּדִּין? אָמַר רָבָא: טְלָאִים – כִּדְמֵעִיקָּרָא, דָּמִים – כְּשֶׁל עַכְשָׁיו.

The Gemara suggests: **Shall we say** that this *baraita* constitutes **a conclusive refutation of** the opinion **of Rav? As Rav says:** When a thief makes his payments, **he pays** the **principal according to** the value as of the time **when he stole** it, whereas the **double payment and** the **fourfold or fivefold payment** are calculated **according to** the value at **the time of standing trial. Rava said** in resolution of this difficulty: If one stole **lambs** that subsequently became rams or were fattened, he pays the double payment and the fourfold or fivefold payment according to the **initial** state of the animal, as claimed by both Beit Shammai and Beit Hillel. If there was a change in the animal's value due to fluctuation of the monetary **value** of animals, he pays **according to** the animal's worth **now,**[N] at the time of standing trial.

NOTES

Lambs according to the initial state, monetary value according to the worth now – טְלָאִים כִּדְמֵעִיקָּרָא דָּמִים כְּשֶׁל עַכְשָׁיו: This translation of this phrase follows the interpretation of the Ri, cited by *Tosafot*. According to his opinion, the fundamental distinction Rava is stating is whether the change in value is due to a change in the animal, e.g., a lamb became a ram, or a change in the market value of animals. Accordingly, Rava is stating that if it is a change in the actual animal, the lamb, one pays the double payment and the fourfold or fivefold payment according to the initial state, i.e., the value the animal had when it was a lamb, which is when he stole it. If the change is due to a fluctuation in monetary value and the animal remained the same, he pays the double payment and the fourfold or fivefold payment according to the current market value. The Ri explains the reason for this difference: When the Torah states: "Five oxen for an ox and four sheep for a sheep" (Exodus 21:37), it is referring to the stolen animal. By contrast, the evaluation of the price of the animal, which is not mentioned in the verse, takes place under the auspices of the court, and is consequently based on the animal's value when the court's evaluation is performed (see Rabbeinu Ḥananel, Rashba, and Rid).

Rashi interprets the Gemara differently. In a case where the thief chooses to pay restitution in kind, paying with lambs, he pays in accordance with the value of lambs at the time of the theft; if he pays money, he must pay the value of lambs as they are now.

Yet others explain that if the value of the lambs mentioned in the *baraita* appreciated, whether due to growth, fattening, or price fluctuation, the thief pays in accordance with the original price; if they depreciated in value for any reason he pays according to their worth now (Rabbeinu Tam). Finally, there are those who say that the thief pays the principal value of the stolen item in accordance with the original price, while the double payment and other payments follow the value now (Rav Hai Gaon; Ra'avad).

אמר רבה: שינוי קונה כתיבא ותנינא. כתיבא: "והשיב את הגזלה אשר גזל" – מה תלמוד לומר "אשר גזל"? אם כעין שגזל – יחזיר, ואם לאו – דמים בעלמא בעי שלומי.

§ **Rabba said:** The principle that **a change** in a stolen item causes the thief to **acquire it**[H] **is written** in the Torah, **and we learned** it in a mishna as well. **It is written** in the Torah: "Then it shall be, if he has sinned, and is guilty, **that he shall restore the item that he robbed**" (Leviticus 5:23). **What** is the meaning when **the verse states** the seemingly superfluous phrase **"that he robbed"?** This serves to teach that **if** the item is the same **as** it was **when he stole it, he must return** the stolen item[N] itself. **But if** it is **not** the same as it was then, **he is required** to **pay only money,** while the stolen item remains his to keep.

תנינא: הגוזל עצים ועשאן כלים, צמר ועשאן בגדים – משלם כשעת הגזילה.

We learned this *halakha* in a mishna as well, as it is taught (93b): In the case of **one who robs** another of **wood**[H] **and fashions it** into **vessels,** or one who robs another of **wool and fashions it** into **garments, he pays** the robbery victim **according to** the value of the goods at the **time of the robbery,** and keeps the altered materials for himself.

אי נמי: לא הספיק ליתנו לו עד שצבעו – פטור; אלמא: שינוי קונה.

Alternatively, another mishna can serve as the source for this principle (*Ḥullin* 135a): **If one did not manage to give**[N] the first of the sheared wool of his sheep to a priest[H] **until** after **he dyed it** (see Deuteronomy 18:4), he is **exempt** from giving it to the priest. This mishna indicates that an item that has undergone a change is no longer considered the same item as it had been. **Apparently,** a physical **change** in a stolen item causes the thief to **acquire** it.

יאוש – אמרי רבנן דניקני, מיהו לא ידעינן אי דאורייתא אי דרבנן.

§ Rabba continues to discuss the ways in which a thief acquires ownership of a stolen item: With regard to the owner's **despair**[B] over ever recovering the stolen item, **the Sages say that** this too causes the thief to **acquire** the stolen item. **However, we do not know** if this *halakha* applies **by Torah law or by rabbinic law.**

אי דאורייתא, מידי דהוה אמוצא אבידה, מוצא אבידה לאו כיון דמייאש מרה מינה מקמי דתיתי לידיה קני ליה, האי נמי כיון דמייאש מרה קני ליה, אלמא קני.

Rabba elaborates on the two possibilities he has just mentioned: **If** it applies **by Torah law,** this is **just as it is with regard to one who finds a lost item.** Is it **not** the case with regard to **one who finds a lost item** that **once** the **owner** of the item **despairs** of recovering it, **before** the item **came into** the finder's **possession,** the finder **acquires it** and may keep it for himself? The same principle applies to **this** thief **as well: Once the owner** of the item **despairs** of recovering it, the thief **acquires it** for himself and need no longer return it. **Apparently,** then, the despair of the owner causes the thief to **acquire** the stolen item.

או דלמא לא דמיא לאבידה, אבידה הוא דכי אתאי לידיה – בהתירא אתיא לידיה, אבל האי, כיון דבאיסורא אתאי לידיה – מדרבנן הוא,

Or perhaps the case of a stolen item is **not comparable to** the case **of a lost item,** as **it is** only with regard to **a lost item** that the owner's despair enables the finder to acquire the item, because the item **came into his possession in a permitted** manner. **But in this** case of the thief, **since** the item **came into his possession in a prohibited** manner,[N] this case cannot be derived from the *halakha* of a lost item. If so, the ruling that despair effects acquisition in a case of theft applies not by Torah law but **by rabbinic law.**

דאמור רבנן ניקני מפני תקנת השבים.

Why would this *halakha* have been instituted by rabbinic law? **As, the Sages said that** a thief **should acquire** the stolen item in this manner, **due to an ordinance** instituted **for the penitent.**[B] To encourage thieves to repent and repay their victims, the Sages instituted that they need not return the stolen item after the owner despairs of recovering it. Rather, they can reimburse the owner for the monetary value of the item.

HALAKHA

A change in a stolen item causes the thief to acquire it – שינוי קונה: If one stole an item and it subsequently underwent a permanent physical change, he acquires the item, and he is required to reimburse the owner only with the monetary value of the item he stole. This *halakha* applies even if the owner has not despaired of recovering his stolen item (Rambam *Sefer Nezikin, Hilkhot Geneiva* 1:12 and *Hilkhot Gezeila VaAveda* 2:1; *Shulḥan Arukh, Ḥoshen Mishpat* 353:1, 354:1, 360:1, 360:5, 362:1).

One who robs another of wood, etc. – הגוזל עצים וכו׳: In a case where one robbed another of wood and smoothed it and cut it or chiseled it, rendering it into vessels; or he robbed another of raw wool and dyed, combed, or bleached it, or turned it into felt; if the item can no longer be restored to its prior state, he has thereby acquired it for himself. He must pay the owner the monetary value of the item at the time of the theft (Rambam *Sefer Nezikin, Hilkhot Gezeila* 2:12; *Shulḥan Arukh, Ḥoshen Mishpat* 360:6).

If one did not manage to give the first of the sheared wool of his sheep to a priest – לא הספיק ליתנו לו: One who sheared his flock and dyed the wool before giving a portion to a priest is exempt from giving this gift (Rambam *Sefer Zera'im, Hilkhot Bikkurim* 10:6; *Shulḥan Arukh, Yoreh De'a* 333:3).

NOTES

If the item is the same as it was when he stole it, he must return the stolen item – אם כעין שגזל יחזיר: The commentaries ask: Instead of inferring that if the stolen item is not the same as it was when he stole it he is required to pay only money, why not infer that if it is not the same as it was at that time he is not required to pay any restitution? They answer that the phrase: "He shall restore it" (Leviticus 5:24), indicates that the thief must pay restitution in any event; the only question is whether this consists of returning the stolen item or paying a monetary payment (*Kovetz Shiurim*).

If one did not manage to give, etc. – לא הספיק ליתנו וכו׳: The commentaries explain that this refers to a case where the owner dyed all the wool he sheared, not just the portion intended for the priest. Had undyed wool remained, he would have had to have given that remainder to the priest. Unlike the case of *teruma*, the act of setting aside a specific portion of wool for the priest has no halakhic significance, and the priest is still entitled to any wool that remains (*Tosafot*).

Since it came into his possession in a prohibited manner – כיון דבאיסורא אתאי לידיה: The commentaries infer from this statement that the status of an item after its owner despairs of recovering it is not equivalent to the status of ownerless property, as one can acquire an item that is completely ownerless even if it originally came into his possession in a prohibited manner (*Tosafot*).

Others add that in contrast to the situation when one declares an item ownerless, in which it no longer has any connection to him whatsoever and if he wants to reclaim ownership he has to perform an act of acquisition as would anyone else, in a case where one despairs of recovering a stolen item, it still belongs to its owner as long as no one else has taken it (*Netivot HaMishpat*).

BACKGROUND

Despair – יאוש: Despairing of recovering a stolen item is not merely an emotional state of mind but a legal one as well. According to *halakha*, despair occurs when one who has lost his property gives up on the possibility of recovering it. Once this happens the item is considered abandoned property, and anyone may take it. This concept is relevant to the *halakhot* of returning lost items, as well as the legal status of stolen property. According to some opinions, the owner's despair alone effects acquisition of a stolen item by a thief. Consequently, he is no longer required to return the item itself, but only its monetary value.

Ordinance for the penitent – תקנת השבים: This ordinance is one of many instituted by the Sages to facilitate repentance. They were concerned that were they to enforce the letter of the Torah law, those who otherwise might repent for their theft would refrain from doing so. One of the ordinances the Sages instituted is that one need not return a stolen beam already built into a structure. Instead, the thief can pay the owner of the beam its monetary value.

וְרַב יוֹסֵף אָמַר: יֵאוּשׁ אֵינוֹ קוֹנֶה, וַאֲפִילּוּ מִדְּרַבָּנַן.

And Rav Yosef says: Despair on the part of the owner over the possibility of recovering his item **does not** cause the thief to **acquire**[H] that item at all, **and this is the** *halakha* **even by rabbinic law.**

אֵיתִיבֵיהּ רַב יוֹסֵף לְרַבָּה: גָּזַל חָמֵץ וְעָבַר עָלָיו הַפֶּסַח,

Rav Yosef raised an objection to Rabba from a mishna (96b): If **one robbed** another of **leavened bread and Passover elapsed**[H] in the meantime, so that deriving benefit from it is prohibited,

HALAKHA

Despair of the owner does not cause one to acquire – יֵאוּשׁ אֵינוֹ קוֹנֶה: A thief or a robber does not acquire the stolen item when the rightful owner despairs of recovering it, and he must return the item itself (Rambam *Sefer Nezikin*, *Hilkhot Geneiva* 1:12 and *Hilkhot Gezeila VaAveda* 2:1; *Shulḥan Arukh*, *Ḥoshen Mishpat* 353:2, 361:1).

If one robbed another of leavened bread and Passover elapsed – גָּזַל חָמֵץ וְעָבַר עָלָיו הַפֶּסַח: If one stole leavened bread from another, and Passover elapsed in the meantime, the thief may return the leavened bread as it is and tell the owner: That which is yours is before you (Rambam *Sefer Nezikin*, *Hilkhot Gezeila VaAveda* 3:4; *Shulḥan Arukh*, *Ḥoshen Mishpat* 363:1).

Perek **VII**
Daf **66** Amud **b**

אוֹמֵר לוֹ ״הֲרֵי שֶׁלְּךָ לְפָנֶיךָ״. וְהַאי כֵּיוָן דִּמְטָא עִידַּן אִיסּוּרָא וַדַּאי מִיָּאֵשׁ, וְאִי סָלְקָא דַּעְתָּךְ יֵאוּשׁ קָנֵה, אַמַּאי אוֹמֵר לוֹ ״הֲרֵי שֶׁלְּךָ לְפָנֶיךָ״? דְּמֵי מְעַלְּיָא בָּעֵי שַׁלּוֹמֵי לֵיהּ.

the robber may nonetheless return the worthless bread to the owner and **say to him: That which is yours is before you,** and no compensation is required. Rav Yosef states his objection: **But in this** case, **once the time of** the **prohibition** of leavened bread **arrives,** the owner **certainly despairs** of recovering his now-worthless bread. **And if it enters your mind** to say that the owner's **despair** causes the robber to **acquire** the stolen item, **why can he say to him: That which is yours is before you? He should be required to pay** the owner **full-fledged money** rather than return the worthless food, as the bread now belongs to the robber.

אֲמַר לֵיהּ: כִּי קָאָמִינָא אֲנָא – זֶה מִתְיָאֵשׁ וְזֶה רוֹצֶה לִקְנוֹת, הַאי – זֶה מִתְיָאֵשׁ וְזֶה אֵינוֹ רוֹצֶה לִקְנוֹת.

Rava **said to** him in response: **When I say** that the thief acquires the stolen item upon the owner's despair of recovery it is when **this** owner **despairs, and that** thief **wants to acquire** the item. In **this** case, **this one despairs but that** one **does not wish to acquire**[N] the worthless bread.

אֵיתִיבֵיהּ אַבָּיֵי לְרַבָּה: ״קָרְבָּנוֹ״ – וְלֹא הַגָּזוּל; הֵיכִי דָּמֵי? אִילֵימָא לִפְנֵי יֵאוּשׁ, לָמָּה לִי קְרָא? פְּשִׁיטָא!

Abaye raised an objection to Rabba from a *baraita*. The verse: "If his offering is a burnt-offering of the herd" (Leviticus 1:3), indicates that one's offering must be **"his offering," but not** an animal **stolen**[H] from another. **What are the circumstances** of the case referred to by the *baraita*? **If we say** it is dealing with a stolen animal that the robber consecrates and sacrificed **before** the owner's **despair** of recovery, **why do I need a verse** to teach this? It **is obvious** that this is disqualified, as one cannot even consecrate an animal that does not belong to him.

אֶלָּא לָאו לְאַחַר יֵאוּשׁ, שְׁמַע מִינָּהּ: יֵאוּשׁ לָא קָנֵי!

Rather, is it not referring to one who seeks to consecrate and sacrifice a stolen animal **after** the owner's **despair?** And yet the *baraita* teaches that the animal cannot be consecrated by the thief. **Conclude from** the *baraita* that the owner's **despair** of recovering a stolen item **does not** cause the thief to **acquire**[N] it, as if it belonged to him he would be able to consecrate and sacrifice it.

אֲמַר לֵיהּ רָבָא: וְלִיטַעְמִיךְ, הָא דְּתַנְיָא: ״מִשְׁכָּבוֹ״ – וְלֹא הַגָּזוּל,

Rava said to Abaye in refutation of this proof: **And according to your reasoning,** consider **that which is taught** in a *baraita*: It is written with regard to a *zav*, a man who experiences a gonorrhea-like discharge: "And whoever touches his bedding shall wash his clothes and bathe himself in water and be impure until the evening" (Leviticus 15:5). This indicates that bedding on which a *zav* lies can become ritually impure and impart impurity only if it is **"his bedding,"**[B] **but not** if it is **stolen** bedding.

NOTES

But that one does not wish to acquire – וְזֶה אֵינוֹ רוֹצֶה לִקְנוֹת: Even if the owner's despair of recovery serves to cause the robber or thief to acquire it, this does not occur without the other's consent. This is because despair does not actually cause the robber or thief to acquire the item; at most, it simply removes the owner's possession of it. If the robber or thief is not interested in acquiring the item after the prior owner rendered it ownerless, he does not acquire it.

Conclude from it that despair does not cause him to acquire – שְׁמַע מִינָּהּ יֵאוּשׁ לָא קָנֵי: Abaye assumed that the *baraita* is discussing a robber who stole a non-sacred animal and subsequently consecrated it as an offering. Consequently, if the owner's despair of recovery effects acquisition for the robber, the animal would belong fully to the robber, and there is no reason he could not consecrate the animal and sacrifice it. Although there is a principle that a mitzva that is performed through commission of a transgression is inherently flawed, the commentaries note that this principle is not applicable here, because it applies only to cases where the mitzva itself is performed through commission of a transgression, whereas here the consecration occurred after the animal already belonged to the robber (*Tosafot*).

BACKGROUND

His bedding – מִשְׁכָּבוֹ: By Torah law, a *zav* and *zava* impurify the items upon which they lie or sit during their period of impurity. Those items become primary sources of ritual impurity, as are the *zav* and *zava* themselves.

HALAKHA

His offering but not one stolen – קָרְבָּנוֹ וְלֹא הַגָּזוּל: If one steals the offering of another or takes it by robbery, his sacrifice is invalid and he does not achieve atonement even if he sacrifices that animal. If the owner has despaired of recovering the animal, the sacrifice is valid. Although the owner's despair does not cause a thief or robber to acquire the item, in this particular case the Sages instituted an ordinance that despair effects acquisition (see *Gittin* 55b). Nevertheless, if it is public knowledge that the animal was stolen, the sacrifice does not effect atonement for the one who sacrifices it (Rambam *Sefer Avoda*, *Hilkhot Issurei Mizbe'aḥ* 5:7 and *Kesef Mishne* there; see *Hilkhot Ma'aseh HaKorbanot* 18:14).

הֵיכִי דָּמֵי? אִילֵּימָא דִּגְזַל עַמְרָא וַעֲבַדֵיהּ מִשְׁכָּב, מִי אִיכָּא לְמַאן דְּאָמַר שִׁינּוּי מַעֲשֶׂה לָא קָנֵי? אֶלָּא מַאי אִית לָךְ לְמֵימַר – דִּגְזַל מִשְׁכָּב דְּחַבְרֵיהּ, הָכִי נַמִי דִּגְזַל קָרְבָּן דְּחַבְרֵיהּ.

What are the circumstances of the case discussed in the *baraita*? **If we say that he robbed** another of **wool and made it into bedding, is there anyone who says that** a physical **change** that results from **an action** performed to a stolen item **does not** cause the thief to **acquire it? Rather, what have you to say?** The *baraita* must be speaking of a case in **which** the *zav* **robbed another** of **bedding.**[H] **So too,** the previous *baraita* is dealing with one **who robbed another** of **an offering,** already consecrated.[N] The reason this animal does not atone for the thief is that a consecrated animal cannot be stolen and become the thief's property, as it belongs to the Temple treasury wherever it is located.

אֵיתִיבֵיהּ אַבָּיֵי לְרַב יוֹסֵף: עוֹרוֹת שֶׁל בַּעַל הַבַּיִת – מַחֲשָׁבָה מְטַמְּאָתָן,

Abaye raised an objection to Rav Yosef from a mishna (*Kelim* 26:8): With regard to **hides belonging to a homeowner,**[H] one's **thought renders them susceptible to** contracting **ritual impurity.**[N] Hides and leather are susceptible to contracting impurity only if they are in a finished state. If a private individual uses a piece of hide or leather for a certain purpose, e.g., as a cot or a table top, and decides that this will be its fixed purpose, it is considered a finished product and is susceptible to contracting impurity.

וְשֶׁל עַבְּדָן – אֵין מַחֲשָׁבָה מְטַמְּאָתָן,

But with regard to hides **belonging to a leatherworker, thought does not render them susceptible to ritual impurity.** Since this individual sells leather to others, when he uses a piece of leather for a household purpose and decides that this will be its fixed purpose, this is not considered a finished state, as he is likely to change his mind and sell the leather to one who will process it further and put it to a different use.

שֶׁל גַּנָּב – מַחֲשָׁבָה מְטַמְּאָתָן, שֶׁל גַּזְלָן – אֵין מַחֲשָׁבָה מְטַמְּאָתָן.

The mishna continues: If the hides are those **of a thief,** who has stolen them from another, the thief's **thought renders them susceptible to ritual impurity.** If they are those **of a robber**[H] his **thought does not render them susceptible to ritual impurity,** because he is not considered the owner of the hide. The difference is that unlike the case of a thief, who steals items stealthily, the identity of a robber, who takes the item openly, is known to the owner, and the owner harbors hope of finding the robber and getting the item back. Consequently, he does not despair of recovering his property.

רַבִּי שִׁמְעוֹן אוֹמֵר, חִילּוּף הַדְּבָרִים: שֶׁל גַּזְלָן – מַחֲשָׁבָה מְטַמְּאָתָן, וְשֶׁל גַּנָּב – אֵין מַחֲשָׁבָה מְטַמְּאָתָן, לְפִי שֶׁלֹּא נִתְיָיאֲשׁוּ הַבְּעָלִים.

Rabbi Shimon says that **the matters are reversed:** In the case **of a robber,** the robber's **thought renders them susceptible to ritual impurity.** If the hides are those **of a thief, thought does not render them susceptible to ritual impurity, because the owners have not despaired** of recovering them and the thief has not acquired the hide. Rabbi Shimon's reasoning is that a robber, who seizes items brazenly, is a more difficult criminal to apprehend and bring to justice than a thief.

וּשְׁמַע מִינָּהּ: יֵאוּשׁ קָנֵה! אֲמַר לֵיהּ: הָכָא בְּמַאי עָסְקִינַן – כְּגוֹן שֶׁקִּיצְּעָן.

And although the two *tanna'im* of the mishna disagree as to which situation involves an owner's despair of recovery, whether robbery or theft, in any event one can **conclude from** this mishna that the **despair** of the owner causes the thief or robber to **acquire** the item, as otherwise the perpetrator's thoughts about the hide would have no effect on its status with regard to ritual impurity. Rav Yosef **said to** Abaye in response: **With what are we dealing here** in this mishna? It is a case **where** the thief or robber **trimmed**[B] the leather by cutting it. Although trimming a piece of leather is not a sufficient change to constitute an act of acquisition by itself, it is effective in conjunction with the owner's despair.

מַתְקִיף לַהּ רַבָּה בַּר רַב חָנָן: וַהֲלֹא עִיצְבָּא שָׁנוּ כָּאן, וְעִיצְבָּא אֵין צְרִיכָה קִיצּוּעַ.

Rabba bar Rav Ḥanan objects to this answer: **But is it not** the case that **they taught** this mishna **here** with regard to a leather table **top** [*itzba*]?[L] **And** a leather table **top does not require trimming,** either due to the fact that its edges are not seen or because it is merely ornamental. Since it does not require trimming, this action should not be considered an act of acquisition at all.

HALAKHA

Robbed another of bedding – גְּזַל מִשְׁכָּב דְּחַבְרֵיהּ: A *zav* does not transmit ritual impurity by treading, lying, or riding on an item that does not belong to him. If he stole an item and stepped on it without touching it with his body, he renders it impure only if the owner has already despaired of recovering it (Rambam *Sefer Tahara*, *Hilkhot Kelim* 24:7).

Hides belonging to a homeowner – עוֹרוֹת שֶׁל בַּעַל הַבַּיִת: If a private individual does not intend to finish his hides beyond their present state, and a *zav* lies on them, the *zav* renders them ritually impure. Hides belonging to a leatherworker are generally intended for sale to others, and are consequently not rendered susceptible to ritual impurity through thought alone. They become susceptible to ritual impurity once some action is performed on them that serves to designate them for sitting, lying, or leaning (Rambam *Sefer Tahara*, *Hilkhot Kelim* 24:6).

Hides of a thief…of a robber – שֶׁל גַּנָּב...שֶׁל גַּזְלָן: If a thief steals the hide of another and decides that he will use it for lying upon, the hide will contract ritual impurity if a *zav* treads or lies on it. By contrast, a robber's thought in such a case serves to render the hide susceptible to impurity only if the owner has despaired of recovering it. The *halakha* is in accordance with the opinion of the Rabbis (Rambam *Sefer Tahara*, *Hilkhot Kelim* 24:7).

NOTES

Who robbed another of an offering – דִּגְזַל קָרְבָּן דְּחַבְרֵיהּ: Rashi and the Ra'avad provide two explanations as to how this answers Abaye's question. According to the first explanation, the *baraita* is referring to a case where the owner did not despair of recovering the animal, and it is teaching that not even the owner can sacrifice it at that point because it is not in his possession. According to the second explanation, the *baraita* is speaking about the situation after the owner despairs of recovering the stolen animal. Even if the owner's despair generally effects acquisition for the robber, in this case the robber cannot acquire it because after its consecration the animal is considered to belong to the Temple treasury, not the owner.

Thought renders them susceptible to ritual impurity – מַחֲשָׁבָה מְטַמְּאָתָן: The fundamental *halakha* at the root of this discussion is that only finished products or vessels, not raw materials, are susceptible to ritual impurity. Certain items in various stages of production can be considered either finished or unfinished, depending on the mind-set of the owner. If he intends to improve the item further, it is considered unfinished; if he decides that he will use it in its current state, it is classified as finished. In this way, mere thought is sometimes sufficient to classify an item as a vessel and thereby render it susceptible to ritual impurity.

BACKGROUND

Trimming – קִיצּוּעַ: Trimming is the finishing of a piece of leather by cutting it to an exact size with smooth edges, including the removal of any bulges or external material that may be stuck to the leather. While this process is essential for leather that is to serve a precise function, e.g., shoes, it is not necessary for a piece of leather that will be used as a mere covering.

LANGUAGE

Table top [*itzba*] – עִיצְבָּא: Rashi translates this term as a leather table top. The *ge'onim* say it refers to a leather covering for a saddle. The linguistic source of the word is uncertain. It is possible that it is from the root *ayin*, *tzadi*, *beit*, meaning to fashion.

דִּתְנַן: כָּל מָקוֹם שֶׁאֵין חֶסְרוֹן מְלָאכָה – מַחְשָׁבָה מְטַמְּאָתוֹ, יֵשׁ חֶסְרוֹן מְלָאכָה – אֵין מַחְשָׁבָה מְטַמְּאָתוֹ, חוּץ מִן הָעִיצְבָּא!

As we learned in the previous mishna (*Kelim* 26:7): **Wherever there is no work lacking**[H] for an item to be considered finished, one's **thought renders it susceptible to ritual impurity; when there** is still some **work lacking** for the item to be considered finished, **thought does not render it susceptible to ritual impurity, except for** the case of a leather table **top.**[H] Although further work is required to smooth out the edges, one's thought can render it susceptible to impurity because people do not care if this leather table top has uneven edges. It is with regard to this case of a table top that the mishna distinguishes between a homeowner and a leatherworker. Therefore, Rav Yosef's explanation is rejected.

אֶלָּא אֲמַר רָבָא: הַאי מִילְּתָא קַשְׁיָא בָּהּ רַבָּה לְרַב יוֹסֵף עֶשְׂרִין וְתַרְתֵּין שְׁנִין, וְלָא אִיפְּרְקָה עַד דִּיתֵיב רַב יוֹסֵף בְּרֵישָׁא וּפַרְקַהּ: שִׁינּוּי הַשֵּׁם כְּשִׁינּוּי מַעֲשֶׂה דָּמֵי.

The Gemara suggests a different answer. **Rather, Rava said** that **this matter was a difficulty** posed **by Rabba to Rav Yosef for twenty-two years, and it was not resolved until Rav Yosef sat as the head**[N] of the yeshiva **and resolved it** in the following manner: **A change in name**[H] of an item, representing a change in status, **is similar to a** physical **change** brought about **by an action.**[N]

שִׁינּוּי מַעֲשֶׂה מַאי טַעְמָא? הָתָם מֵעִיקָּרָא עֵצִים וְהַשְׁתָּא כֵּלִים, שִׁינּוּי הַשֵּׁם נַמִּי – מֵעִיקָּרָא קָרוּ לֵיהּ מַשְׁכָּא וְהַשְׁתָּא אַבְרָזִין.

What is the reason that a physical **change** through **an action** causes the thief to acquire the item? It is because **there** the stolen items were **initially** just **wood,** and **now** they are **vessels.** The same can be said for **a change in name as well: Initially they called it a hide, and now** they call it a table **top** [*abrazin*].[L]

וַהֲרֵי מְרִישׁ, דְּאִיכָּא שִׁינּוּי הַשֵּׁם, דְּמֵעִיקָּרָא כְּשׁוּרָא וְהַשְׁתָּא טְלָלָא, וּתְנַן: עַל הַמְּרִישׁ הַגָּזוּל שֶׁבְּנָאוֹ בַּבִּירָה – שֶׁנּוֹטֵל דָּמָיו, מִפְּנֵי תַּקָּנַת הַשָּׁבִים.

The Gemara asks a question with regard to changes in name: **But** what about the case of **a beam,**[N] **where there is a change in name, as initially,** when it was stolen, it was called **a beam, and now,** after it has been placed in a building, it is called **a joist** [*telala*],[L] **and** yet **we learned** in a mishna (*Gittin* 55a): **With regard to a stolen beam**[H] **that** a robber **had built into** a large **building,** the court ruled **that** the owner **should** receive **its** value in **money** rather than demand that the robber demolish the house to return the beam itself, **because of an ordinance** instituted **for the penitent,** i.e., to encourage robbers to admit their crime and reimburse the owner of the stolen item.

טַעְמָא מִפְּנֵי תַּקָּנַת הַשָּׁבִים,

This mishna indicates that **the** only **reason** the robber does not have to return the beam itself is **because of** this **ordinance** instituted **for the penitent.**

LANGUAGE

Table top [*abrazin*] – אַבְרָזִין: Apparently from the Middle Persian word awarzēn, a term that consists of abar, on, and zēn, saddle. Most hold that it refers to a saddle cover.

Joist [*telala*] – טְלָלָא: The source of the word is the Aramaic root *tet, lamed, lamed*, and it is similar to the Hebrew word *tzel*, meaning shade. In this context, it means a central joist of the roof, upon which other, less massive, beams or boards were placed.

HALAKHA

Wherever there is no work lacking, etc. – כָּל מָקוֹם שֶׁאֵין חֶסְרוֹן מְלָאכָה וכו׳: A hide that is processed sufficiently to be used for a purpose is susceptible to ritual impurity through the treading of a *zav* from the moment its owner mentally decides to use it in its current state for that purpose. If the item still requires work for it to be considered finished, one's decision does not serve to make it susceptible to impurity. It is considered susceptible only when the work is completed (Rambam *Sefer Tahara, Hilkhot Kelim* 24:6).

Leather table top – עִיצְבָּא: With regard to a hide that is used to cover a saddle to protect it from dirt, a mental decision to use it in its current state serves to render it susceptible to ritual impurity, despite the fact that it has not been perfected into a finished product (Rambam *Sefer Tahara, Hilkhot Kelim* 24:6).

Change in name – שִׁינּוּי הַשֵּׁם: In the case of a stolen item, if its name has changed, the thief or robber has thereby acquired it, and he does not have to return the item itself. Rather, he must pay the owner its monetary value (*Shulḥan Arukh, Ḥoshen Mishpat* 353:1, and in the comment of Rema on 360:10).

Stolen beam – מְרִישׁ גָּזוּל: If one stole a beam and built it into a building, although strictly speaking he should be obligated to return the beam itself, the Sages instituted an ordinance for the penitent, according to which the thief or robber is not required to dismantle the building to return the beam. He may provide monetary restitution instead (Rambam *Sefer Nezikin, Hilkhot Gezeila VaAveda* 1:5; *Shulḥan Arukh, Ḥoshen Mishpat* 360:1).

NOTES

Until Rav Yosef sat as the head – עַד דִּיתֵיב רַב יוֹסֵף בְּרֵישָׁא: The Gemara in tractate *Horayot* (14a) relates that Rav Yosef was extremely knowledgeable, whereas Rabba had extraordinary analytical skills. Since it was unclear which of them was more suitable to serve as head of the yeshiva of Pumbedita, the issue was referred to the *amora'im* in Eretz Yisrael. They preferred the more knowledgeable scholar. Rav Yosef refused the mantle of leadership and deferred to Rabba, who remained head of the yeshiva for twenty-two years until Rav Yosef assumed leadership.

A change in name is similar to a physical change brought about by an action – שִׁינּוּי הַשֵּׁם כְּשִׁינּוּי מַעֲשֶׂה דָּמֵי: Some commentaries claim that a change in name is not sufficient for a thief to acquire an item. It is effective only when it occurs in conjunction with the owner's despair of recovery, as in the case described in the mishna the owner had despaired of recovery (*Tosafot*). *Tosafot* on 67a state that a change in name is a form of acquisition independent of the owner's despair, and it is entirely equivalent to a physical change brought about by an action (see Rashba).

Beam [*merish*] – מְרִישׁ: The beam mentioned here is intended to be used as a base beam in construction, as opposed to a beam used for roofing, known as a *kora*. Since the removal of a *merish* would require the dismantling of the entire building, the Sages permitted a robber or thief to return the monetary value of the beam in such cases. If he can return a stolen item without causing such a significant loss or expenditure of effort, he must return the item itself (*Divrei Malkiel* 4:138).

הָא לָאו הָכִי – הָדַר בְּעֵינֵיהּ! אֲמַר רַב יוֹסֵף: מְרִישׁ שְׁמוֹ עָלָיו, דְּתַנְיָא: ״צַלְעוֹת הַבַּיִת״ – אֵלּוּ הַמַּלְטְטִין, ״וְהָעֻבִּים״ – אֵלּוּ הַמְּרִישׁוֹת.

One can infer: **But** if were **not** for **this** decree, the beam would have to be **returned** to the owner **as is,** notwithstanding its change in name. **Rav Yosef said:** This is not a genuine change in name, as **a beam retains its name** even after it is inserted into a building. **As it is taught** in a *baraita* with regard to two obscure terms: The verse states: "And there were narrow windows and palm trees on the one side and on the other side, on the sides of the porch; there were also the *tzalot* of the house, and the *ubbim*" (Ezekiel 41:26). **"*Tzalot* of the house"; these are the casings [*hamaltetin*].**[NL] **"And the *ubbim*"; these are the beams [*hamerishot*].** This shows that a beam can retain its name even after it has been built into a house.

רַבִּי זֵירָא אֲמַר: שִׁינּוּי הַחוֹזֵר לִבְרִיָּיתוֹ – בְּשִׁינּוּי הַשֵּׁם לָא הָוֵי שִׁינּוּי.

Rabbi Zeira said a different answer: With regard to **a change in name, a change** in which the item **can revert to its original state**[H] **is not** considered enough of **a change** for the thief to acquire the stolen item. Since the joist can be removed and revert to being called a beam, it is not considered a true change of name.

וְשִׁינּוּי הַשֵּׁם שֶׁאֵינוֹ חוֹזֵר לִבְרִיָּיתוֹ מִי הָוֵי שִׁינּוּי? וַהֲרֵי צִינּוֹר, דְּמֵעִיקָּרָא קְצִיצְתָּא וְהָשְׁתָּא צִינּוֹרָא, וְתַנְיָא: צִינּוֹר שֶׁחֲקָקוֹ וּלְבַסּוֹף קְבָעוֹ – פּוֹסֵל אֶת הַמִּקְוֶה,

The Gemara asks: **And is a change in name** in **which** the item **does not revert to its original state** really considered **a change? But there is** the case of a water **duct,**[N] **where** it was **initially** called **a log** [*ketzitzta*][L] **and now** it is called **a duct, and it is taught** in a *baraita*: **A duct that one hollowed out**[H] **and afterward attached** to the ground or to a building **invalidates a ritual bath** through the water it channels to the bath. The water in a ritual bath must be gathered directly from rain or a stream, not drawn with vessels. If one hollowed out a log and used it to channel water into the bath, this is considered drawn water, as he used a vessel.

קְבָעוֹ וּלְבַסּוֹף חֲקָקוֹ – אֵינוֹ פּוֹסֵל אֶת הַמִּקְוֶה;

By contrast, if **one attached it** first **and afterward hollowed it out, it does not invalidate the ritual bath.** Before the log was hollowed out, it was already attached to and considered part of the ground, and therefore the act of hollowing it out does not turn it into a vessel.

וְאִי אָמְרַתְּ שִׁינּוּי הַשֵּׁם מִילְּתָא הִיא, אֲפִילּוּ קְבָעוֹ וּלְבַסּוֹף חֲקָקוֹ נַמִּי לִיפָּסֵל!

The Gemara states its question: **And if you say that a change in name is** considered **a matter** of significance, i.e., it is considered a real change in the item, then **even if one attached** the log first **and afterward hollowed it out,** the ritual bath **should also be invalid.** Since hollowing out the log leads to a change in name, it should be considered a new vessel at that point.

שָׁאנֵי שְׁאִיבָה, דְּמִדְּרַבָּנַן הִיא. אִי הָכִי, אֲפִילּוּ דְּרֵישָׁא נַמִּי! הָתָם אִיכָּא תּוֹרַת כְּלִי עָלָיו בְּתָלוּשׁ, הָכָא אֵין תּוֹרַת כְּלִי עָלָיו בְּתָלוּשׁ.

The Gemara answers: The *halakha* that **drawn** water may not be used for a ritual bath **is different, as it** applies **by rabbinic law,**[NH] and consequently the Sages were lenient in this case. The Gemara asks: **If so,** then **even in the first clause,** where the log was hollowed out before being attached, it should be permitted **as well.** The Gemara answers: There is a difference between the two cases. **There,** in the first clause, the log **had the status of a vessel while** it was still **detached. Here,** in the second case, it did **not have the status of a vessel while** it was **detached,** but only after it became attached to the ground, and therefore the Sages were lenient.

NOTES

Casings [*maltetin*] – מַלְטְטִין: The *Arukh* has a version of the text which reads *maltusin* instead of *maltetin* and explains that it refers to foundation beams placed along the length of the walls. He adds that the second term, *merishot*, which is translated as beams throughout the Gemara, refers to the secondary boards placed on the aforementioned foundation beams.

Water duct – צִינּוֹר: The pipe is built in such a way that it collects water and is consequently considered a receptacle. Otherwise, it would not be considered a vessel, and the water that ran through it would not disqualify a ritual bath (*Tosafot*). Another possibility mentioned by *Tosafot* is that crevices were made in the bottom of the duct to catch dirt and pebbles. This would also render the duct into a vessel through which water for a ritual bath may not run.

Drawn water is different as it applies by rabbinic law – שָׁאנֵי שְׁאִיבָה דְּמִדְּרַבָּנַן הִיא: Rashi explains that the Gemara is referring to the *halakha* that three or more *log* of drawn water invalidate a ritual bath if they are part of its first forty *log*. There is a range of other opinions as well. Some commentaries maintain that the entire concept of drawn water invalidating a ritual bath is rabbinic in origin, and the various verses brought in the Talmud as sources for this *halakha* are cited as mere supports (Ra'avad). Others state that if a ritual bath contains more than fifty percent drawn water it is invalid. Yet another opinion is that the ritual bath is invalidated only if the water is actually drawn by people using vessels (see *Tosafot* on 66a and Rashba on 66b).

HALAKHA

A change in which the item can revert to its original state – שִׁינּוּי הַחוֹזֵר לִבְרִיָּיתוֹ: A change in which the item can revert to its original state is not considered a valid change for the purpose of a thief acquiring a stolen item. Therefore, if one steals pieces of wood and joins them with nails into a crate, this is not considered a valid change, as it is possible to dismantle the crate so that the original pieces of wood revert to their previous state. In a case where the owner despaired and there was a change in which the item can revert to its original state, some say that this does effect acquisition for the thief; in this case he is not required to return the item itself but can provide monetary compensation instead (Rambam *Sefer Nezikin*, *Hilkhot Gezeila VaAveda* 2:10; *Shulḥan Arukh*, *Ḥoshen Mishpat* 353:2, 360:5, 361:2).

A duct that one hollowed out, etc. – צִינּוֹר שֶׁחֲקָקוֹ וכו׳: With regard to one who carves crevices in a water duct in order to catch loose pebbles and separate them from the water, if it was a wooden duct and he carved a crevice of any size, this invalidates the water that passes through it for use in a ritual bath, because this water is considered to have been drawn in a vessel. Even if one attached the duct to the ground after he carved it in this manner, the water is invalid, as the duct was designated as a vessel while it was still detached. If one attached it to the ground first and afterward carved the crevices, the water that passes through it is valid for a ritual bath (Rambam *Sefer Tahara*, *Hilkhot Mikvaot* 6:6; *Shulḥan Arukh*, *Yoreh De'a* 201:34).

Drawn water is different as it applies by rabbinic law – שָׁאנֵי שְׁאִיבָה דְּמִדְּרַבָּנַן הִיא: By rabbinic law drawn water is invalid for ritual immersion. Moreover, even if there is a body of naturally gathered water of less than forty *se'a*, the minimum amount required for a ritual bath, and three *log* of drawn water fall into it, so that there is more than forty *se'a* of water, the entire bath is invalid for ritual immersion (Rambam *Sefer Tahara*, *Hilkhot Mikvaot* 4:2).

LANGUAGE

Casings [*maltetin*] – מַלְטְטִין: The talmudic words *maltusin*, *maltetin*, *amaltera*, and *maltera* are all apparently derived from the Greek μέλαθρον, *melathron*, meaning a beam in general and specifically a beam used in roofing.

Log [*ketzitzta*] – קְצִיצְתָּא: This refers to wood that one chopped [*katzatz*] into pieces. Only after it has been hollowed out, either by a hole in the middle of it or a channel through which water can pass, would this log be called a duct.

מיתיבי: הגנב, והגזלן, והאנס – הקדישן הקדש, ותרומתן תרומה, ומעשרותן מעשר!

The Gemara **raises an objection** against Rav Yosef's opinion that the owner's despair that he will recover his stolen items does not effect acquisition for the thief, from a *baraita*: With regard to **a thief, a robber, and one who forces** people to sell him items against their will, **their consecration** of the items they obtained in these manners is a valid **consecration;**[N] **and the *teruma* that they separate** from the produce they obtained in these manners is valid ***teruma;***[H] **and the tithes that they separate** from those foods are valid **tithes.** Consecrations, *terumot,* and tithes must be performed by the owner of the item in question. Since there was no physical change in these items, this shows that the thief is considered the new owner merely by virtue of the owner's despair of recovery.

אמרי: התם איכא שינוי השם, דמעיקרא טיבלא והשתא תרומה, הקדש – מעיקרא חולין והשתא הקדש.

The Sages **say,** in answer to this question: **There,** in those cases involving consecrations, *terumot,* and tithes, **there is a change in name**[N] of the stolen item, **as initially** the stolen food was called **untithed produce,**[N] i.e., produce from which *teruma* and tithes have not been separated, **and now** it is called ***teruma***[B] or tithe. With regard to **consecration,** it was **initially** called **non-sacred** property, **and now** it is called **consecrated** property.

אמר רב חסדא אמר רבי יונתן: מניין לשנוי שהוא קונה? שנאמר: "והשיב את הגזלה", מה תלמוד לומר "אשר גזל"? אם כעין שגזל – יחזיר, ואם לאו – דמים בעלמא בעי שלומי.

Rav Ḥisda says that Rabbi Yonatan says: From where is it derived **that a change** in a stolen item causes the thief to **acquire** it? **As it is stated: "And he shall return the stolen item that he took by robbery"** (Leviticus 5:23). **What** is the meaning when **the verse states** the seemingly superfluous phrase **"that he took by robbery"?** It teaches that only **if** the item is in the same state **as when he took it by robbery** it **he must return** it. **But if not, he is required to pay only money;** the stolen item remains his to keep.

האי "אשר גזל" מיבעי למעוטי גזל אביו, שאינו מוסיף חומש על גזל אביו!

The Gemara asks with regard to this derivation: **But this** phrase: **"That he took by robbery," is required to exclude** the case of an item **stolen by one's father,**[H] i.e., **that** when a son returns an item or money that his father had stolen, **he does not add one-fifth to** the principal amount of that which **his father stole.** The passage in question addresses one who stole and took a false oath. This individual is obligated to add one-fifth to the amount he stole (see Leviticus 5:21–24). The apparently redundant phrase "that he took by robbery," teaches that the requirement to add one-fifth applies only to the sinner himself, not to his heirs (see 104b).

אם כן, ניכתוב רחמנא "והשיב את גזילו", "אשר גזל" למה לי למכתב? שמע מינה תרתי.

The Gemara answers: **If so,** if the verse teaches only that *halakha,* **let the Merciful One write** merely: **And he shall return his stolen item,** as from that phrase alone it could be derived that an heir does not have to add one-fifth. **Why do I** need the Torah **to write** the expression **"that he took by robbery"?** One may therefore **conclude two** conclusions **from** this verse: A son need not add one-fifth, and a change in a stolen item effects acquisition for the thief.

BACKGROUND

Untithed produce and *teruma* – טיבלא ותרומה: Untithed produce is produce from which *teruma* and tithes have not been separated. The Torah prohibits the consumption of untithed produce, and one who eats this produce is punished by death at the hand of Heaven. Once the tithes have been separated, the remaining produce no longer has the status of untithed produce and it may be eaten, even before the tithes have been given to those for whom they are designated. The *teruma* is given to a priest, who must eat it in a state of ritual purity. Since priests are not ritually pure nowadays, as there is no red heifer whose ashes can be sprinkled on them to purify them, the *teruma* must be burned. *Teruma* remains the property of the priest and he may derive benefit from it as it is being burned. Nowadays, *teruma* is not given to the priests because they have no definite proof of their priestly lineage. Nevertheless, the obligation to separate *teruma* is in force, although only a small portion of the produce is separated in practice.

NOTES

Their consecration is consecration – הקדישן הקדש: Rashi explains that it is prohibited to derive benefit from an item consecrated by a thief, like any other consecrated item, and the *teruma* separated by him is likewise prohibited for consumption to a non-priest. The commentaries add that an animal consecrated in this manner is not fit to be sacrificed as an offering because that would constitute a mitzva that is performed through commission of a transgression, and it is for this reason that Rashi stresses that it is consecrated only with regard to the prohibition against benefiting from consecrated property (*Penei Yehoshua*).

There is a change in name – איכא שינוי השם: Some early commentaries write that the Gemara specifically mentions a change in name in the case of *teruma,* rather than a second change in possession, which would seemingly occur when the *teruma* is separated, although a second change in possession effects acquisition. This is because *teruma* does not automatically belong to any priest upon being set aside; a priest gains possession of it only when it is actually given to him (see *Tosefot Rid* and Rashba).

By contrast, with regard to consecrated items there is apparently a change in possession from the thief to that of the Temple treasury. *Tosafot* explain that the *baraita* is referring specifically to a type of consecrated item for which the one who consecrates it, the thief in this case, accepts monetary responsibility. In such a case the consecrated item is considered to have not been transferred to the possession of the Temple treasury, although it is consecrated. The Ba'al HaMaor distinguishes between an item consecrated for sacrificial purposes and one dedicated as a monetary contribution to the Temple. There are also those who claim that as consecration does entail a change of possession, the example of consecration should not be mentioned. It is mentioned here only tangentially along with *teruma,* as it is common for these two categories to be paired together (Ramban). There is a discussion along similar lines with regard to tithes (see Rashba).

As initially the stolen food was called untithed produce – דמעיקרא טיבלא: The commentaries suggest that the Gemara could have answered that *teruma* is considered a change in name that can be reversed, as it is possible to retract the separation of *teruma* so that the food once again becomes untithed. The same argument applies to consecrated items. Yet, since retraction of *teruma* and consecration is an unusual occurrence, this is not considered a reversible change (*Tosafot*). Others note that the thief cannot retract the setting aside of the *teruma* and the consecration by himself. He requires a court or a Sage to reverse these actions. For this reason, it is considered an irreversible change in name (Rashba; Meiri).

HALAKHA

Thief…and the *teruma* that they separate is *teruma* – הגנב...ותרומתן תרומה: If a thief, a robber, or one who forces people to sell him items against their will separated as *teruma* produce he obtained in such a manner, the *teruma* is valid, provided that the owner despaired of recovery before the *teruma* was separated. If the owner was still engaged in an effort to recover his produce, it is not valid *teruma* (Rambam *Sefer Zera'im, Hilkhot Terumot* 4:11 and *Kesef Mishne* there; *Shulḥan Arukh, Yoreh De'a* 331:39).

To exclude an item stolen by one's father – למעוטי גזל אביו: If one's father stole an item, robbed another of an item, or owed money to another, and his son and heir has knowledge of this information but denies it under oath, and subsequently admits that he had lied under oath, he repays the principal amount to the rightful owner and is exempt from paying an additional one-fifth (Rambam *Sefer Nezikin, Hilkhot Gezeila VaAveda* 7:3).

NOTES

From where is it derived that a change does not cause the thief to acquire it – **מִנַּיִין לְשִׁנּוּיי שֶׁאֵינוֹ קוֹנֶה**: Rabbeinu Ḥananel has a different version of the text, according to which this question refers specifically to a change in name rather than a physical change: From where is it derived that a change in name of a stolen item does not effect acquisition for the thief? According to his version, this question continues the previous discussion in the Gemara.

וְאִיכָּא דְּאָמְרִי, אָמַר רַב חִסְדָּא אָמַר רַבִּי יוֹנָתָן: מִנַּיִין לְשִׁנּוּיי שֶׁאֵינוֹ קוֹנֶה? שֶׁנֶּאֱמַר: ״וְהֵשִׁיב אֶת הַגְּזֵילָה״, מִכׇּל מָקוֹם. וְהָא כְּתִיב: ״אֲשֶׁר גָּזָל״! הַהוּא מִיבָּעֵי לֵיהּ: עַל גְּזֵילוֹ שֶׁלּוֹ מוֹסִיף חוֹמֶשׁ, וְאֵין מוֹסִיף חוֹמֶשׁ עַל גֶּזֶל אָבִיו.

And there are those who say a different version of the above statement: **Rav Ḥisda says** that **Rabbi Yonatan says: From where** is it derived that **a change** in a stolen item **does not** cause the thief to **acquire** it?[N] **As it is stated: "And he shall return the stolen item that he took by robbery"** (Leviticus 5:23), from which it may be inferred that he must return it **in any case,** even if it has undergone a change. The Gemara asks: **But it is written "that he took by robbery,"** which indicates that, on the contrary, the item need be returned only if it is in a similar state to when it was stolen. The Gemara answers: **That** phrase **is required** to teach another *halakha*: **One adds one-fifth upon** returning **his own stolen** item concerning which he had taken a false oath, **but he does not add one-fifth upon** returning something **stolen by his father.**

אָמַר עוּלָּא: מִנַּיִין לְיֵאוּשׁ שֶׁאֵינוֹ קוֹנֶה? שֶׁנֶּאֱמַר: ״וַהֲבֵאתֶם גָּזוּל אֶת הַפִּסֵּחַ וְאֶת הַחוֹלֶה״, גָּזוּל דּוּמְיָא דְּפִסֵּחַ, מַה פִּסֵּחַ דְּלֵית לֵיהּ תַּקַּנְתָּא כְּלָל,

Ulla says: From where is it derived **that** the owner's **despair** of recovering his stolen item **does not** cause the thief to **acquire** it? **As it is stated** in the criticism of the Jewish people for bringing inferior animals as offerings: **"And you have brought that which is stolen, and the lame, and the sick"** (Malachi 1:13). From the juxtaposition of these cases it may be derived that **a stolen** animal **is similar to a lame** animal: **Just as a lame** animal **has no rectification at all** with regard to its disqualification as an offering,

Perek **VII**
Daf **67** Amud **b**

NOTES

Rav Pappa said one of these statements – **רַב פַּפָּא אֲמָרָהּ**: The Gemara suggests this because it was common for a disciple to cite the statements of his primary teacher without explicitly noting the attribution, as it was widely recognized that his Torah knowledge was obtained from that teacher (see *Yevamot* 96b). It is possible that an unattributed statement made by Rav Pappa was mistakenly attributed to his teacher, Rava.

אַף גָּזוּל דְּלֵית לֵיהּ תַּקַּנְתָּא, לָא שְׁנָא לִפְנֵי יֵאוּשׁ וְלָא שְׁנָא אַחַר יֵאוּשׁ.

so too a stolen animal **has no rectification** for its disqualification. There is **no difference whether** one is dealing with a stolen animal **before** the owner's **despair** of recovering it, **and** there is **no difference** if it is **after** the owner's **despair.** In either case, it is disqualified. This shows that the owner's despair does not effect acquisition for the thief.

רָבָא אָמַר, מֵהָכָא: ״קׇרְבָּנוֹ״ – וְלֹא הַגָּזוּל; אֵימַת? אִילֵימָא לִפְנֵי יֵאוּשׁ, פְּשִׁיטָא, לָמָּה לִי קְרָא?

Rava said: This *halakha* may be derived **from here,** a *baraita*: The verse: "If his offering is a burnt-offering of the herd" (Leviticus 1:3), indicates that one's offering must be **"his offering," but not** an animal **stolen** from another. **When,** i.e., in which circumstances, is it necessary to teach this *halakha*? **If we say** it is dealing with a stolen animal that the robber consecrated and sacrificed **before** the owner's **despair** of recovery, **why do I** need **a verse** to teach this? It **is obvious** that it is disqualified, as one cannot even consecrate an animal that does not belong to him.

אֶלָּא לָאו לְאַחַר יֵאוּשׁ, וּשְׁמַע מִינָּהּ: יֵאוּשׁ לָא קָנֵי, שְׁמַע מִינָּהּ.

Rather, is it not referring to one who seeks to consecrate and sacrifice a stolen animal **after** the owner's **despair?** And yet the *baraita* teaches that the animal cannot be consecrated by the thief. **Conclude from** the *baraita* that the owner's **despair** of recovering a stolen item **does not** cause the thief to **acquire** it, as if it belonged to him he would be able to consecrate and sacrifice it. The Gemara affirms: **Conclude from** the *baraita* that it is so.

וְהָא רָבָא הוּא דַּאֲמַר דִּגְזַל קׇרְבָּן דְּחַבְרֵיהּ! אִיבָּעֵית אֵימָא: הֲדַר בֵּיהּ, וְאִיבָּעֵית אֵימָא: חַד מִינַּיְיהוּ רַב פַּפָּא אֲמָרָהּ.

The Gemara asks: **But Rava was the one who said** that this proof can be refuted, as the *baraita* can be interpreted as dealing with one **who robbed another of an offering** that was already consecrated. Rava apparently contradicts himself. The Gemara answers: **If you wish, say** that Rava **retracted** one of these two statements. **And if you wish, say** instead that **Rav Pappa,** not Rava, **said one of these** two statements.[N]

״וּמִדַּת תַּשְׁלוּמֵי אַרְבָּעָה וַחֲמִשָּׁה״ וכו׳.

§ The Gemara returns to the mishna, which teaches: **But the principle of fourfold or fivefold payment** applies only to the theft of an ox or a sheep, as it is stated: "If a man steal an ox or a sheep, and slaughter it or sell it, he shall pay five oxen for an ox and four sheep for a sheep" (Exodus 21:37).

וְאַמַּאי? נֵילַף "שׁוֹר" "שׁוֹר" מִשַּׁבָּת, מָה לְהַלָּן חַיָּה וְעוֹף כַּיּוֹצֵא בָּהֶן, אַף כָּאן חַיָּה וְעוֹף כַּיּוֹצֵא בָּהֶן!

The Gemara asks: **But why** is the fourfold and fivefold payment limited to oxen and sheep? **Let us derive** otherwise by a verbal analogy of the term **"ox"** in this verse and **"ox" from** a passage dealing with **Shabbat,**[N] where it is stated: "And the seventh day is Sabbath to the Lord your God, you shall not perform any labor, you, your son, and your daughter, and your slave, and your maidservant, and your ox, and your donkey, and all your animals, and the gentile that is within your gates" (Deuteronomy 5:13). **Just as there,** with regard to Shabbat, the *halakha* stated with regard to an ox is not limited to oxen, as **undomesticated animals and fowl are similar to** oxen in that they too are included in this prohibition, as the verse states: "Nor any of your animals," **so too here,** in the case of theft, one can say that **undomesticated animals and fowl are similar to** oxen in that the fourfold or fivefold payment is incurred for their theft.

אֲמַר רָבָא, אָמַר קְרָא: שׁוֹר וָשֶׂה שׁוֹר וָשֶׂה, שְׁנֵי פְּעָמִים; שׁוֹר וָשֶׂה – אִין, מִידֵּי אַחֲרִינָא – לָא.

Rava said: The verse dealing with theft **states "ox" and "sheep," "ox" and "sheep" twice.** This repetition indicates that for **an ox and a sheep, yes,** there is a fourfold or fivefold payment, and **for other items, no,** there is no fourfold or fivefold payment.

אָמְרִי: הֵי מִיַּיתַּר? אִילֵימָא "שׁוֹר" וְ"שֶׂה" דְּסֵיפָא מִיַּיתַּר, דְּנִיכְתּוֹב רַחֲמָנָא: "כִּי יִגְנֹב שׁוֹר אוֹ שֶׂה וּטְבָחוֹ וּמְכָרוֹ חֲמִשָּׁה בָקָר יְשַׁלֵּם תַּחְתָּיו וְאַרְבַּע צֹאן תַּחְתָּיו", אִי כָּתַב רַחֲמָנָא הָכִי, הֲוָה אָמִינָא: בָּעֵי שַׁלּוּמֵי תִּשְׁעָה לְכָל אֶחָד וְאֶחָד!

The Gemara **says,** with regard to Rava's assertion that one of the instances of "ox" and "sheep" is superfluous: **Which** instance of the word "ox" or "sheep" **is the superfluous** one? **If we say** that the instance of **"ox" and "sheep" at the end** of the verse **is superfluous, due to** the following consideration: **Let the Merciful One write: If one steal an ox or a sheep, and slaughter it or sell it, he shall pay five oxen for it and four sheep for it,** without repeating the words "ox" and "sheep," this is not possible. **If the Merciful One had written** the verse **like this, I would say** that the thief is **required to pay nine** animals, five oxen and four sheep, **for each and every** animal stolen.

וְכִי תֵּימָא, הָא כְּתִיב "תַּחְתָּיו" "תַּחְתָּיו", חַד "תַּחְתָּיו" מִיַּיתַּר.

And if you would say that this interpretation is not possible, as the suggestion is that the verse would have **written: For it, for it,** twice, whereas if a payment of nine animals were required for each stolen animal the verse would have written: For it, only once; then **one** mention of: **For it, is superfluous,** to teach us that it is five for an ox and four for a sheep.

הַהוּא מִיבָּעֵי לֵיהּ לִדְרָשָׁה אַחֲרִינָא, דְּתַנְיָא: יָכוֹל גָּנַב שׁוֹר שָׁוֶה מָנֶה יְשַׁלֵּם תַּחְתָּיו נְגִידִין? תַּלְמוּד לוֹמַר: "תַּחְתָּיו" "תַּחְתָּיו"!

The Gemara rejects this: **That** repetition of: For it, **is required for another interpretation,** and cannot teach that it is five for an ox and four for a sheep. **As it is taught** in a *baraita*: One **might** have thought that if one **stole** an expensive **ox worth one hundred dinars he may pay for it with lean,** inferior **animals** [***negidin***].[L] To counter this, **the verse states: "For** the ox" and **"for** the sheep," which indicates that the oxen and sheep used for payment must be similar to the stolen animal in quality. Since one might have erred and understood that the thief is required to pay nine animals, five oxen and four sheep, for each and every animal stolen, that suggested version of the verse is not a possibility. The words "ox" and "sheep" at the end of the verse could not have been omitted, so they are not superfluous.

אֶלָּא "שׁוֹר" וְ"שֶׂה" דְּרֵישָׁא מְיוּתָּר, דְּנִכְתּוֹב רַחֲמָנָא: "כִּי יִגְנֹב אִישׁ וּטְבָחוֹ וּמְכָרוֹ חֲמִשָּׁה בָקָר יְשַׁלֵּם תַּחַת הַשּׁוֹר וְאַרְבַּע צֹאן תַּחַת הַשֶּׂה".

The Gemara suggests: **Rather,** the words **"ox" and "sheep" in the first** part of the verse **are superfluous, due to** the following consideration: **Let the Merciful One write: If a man steal, and slaughter it or sell it, he shall pay five oxen for the ox, and four sheep for the sheep,** without mentioning "ox" or "sheep" at the beginning of the verse.

אִי כָּתַב רַחֲמָנָא הָכִי, הֲוָה אָמִינָא: עַד דְּגָנֵיב תְּרֵי וְטָבַח לְהוּ! "וּטְבָחוֹ" כְּתִיב, לְחַד.

The Gemara objects: It is not possible for the verse to have been written this way, as **if the Merciful One had written** it in **this** manner **I would say:** A thief is not required to pay the fourfold or fivefold payment **unless he steals two** animals, an ox and a sheep, **and slaughters them** both. The Gemara responds: One could not interpret the verse in this manner, as it **is written: "And slaughter it."** The singular pronoun "it" is referring **to** the slaughter of only **one** animal.

NOTES

Let us derive ox and ox from Shabbat – נֵילַף שׁוֹר שׁוֹר מִשַּׁבָּת: The commentaries ask: How can this verbal analogy be suggested? The verse addressing a thief mentions both an ox and a sheep, and it distinguishes between them. Consequently, it is impossible that the term "ox" can be referring to all animals. One answer is that the Gemara is suggesting that one might have argued that "ox" and "sheep" should be interpreted as categories of animals. In other words, stealing not only an ox but any beast of burden would be subject to a fivefold payment, and the theft of other animals that are not used for work, like sheep, would be subject to a fourfold payment (*Penei Yehoshua*).

LANGUAGE

Lean animals [*negidin*] – נְגִידִין: Rashi maintains that *nagad* is Aramaic for the Hebrew *gava*, dying. It is also possible that it means pulling, i.e., animals that cannot walk on their own but must be pulled and dragged along.

וְאֵימָא: עַד דְּגָנֵיב תַּרְוַיְיהוּ וּמְזַבֵּין לְהוּ! ״וּמְכָרוֹ״ כְּתִיב, לְחַד.

The Gemara asks: **But** one could **say** that a thief is not required to pay the fourfold or fivefold payment **unless he steals both** of these animals, an ox and a sheep, **and sells them** both. The Gemara rejects this suggestion in a similar manner: This interpretation is also not possible, as it is **written: "Or sell it,"** which is referring **to** the sale of only **one** animal.

וְאֵימָא, הֲוָה אָמִינָא: עַד דְּגָנֵיב תְּרֵי, וְטָבַח חַד וּמְזַבֵּין חַד! ״אוֹ מְכָרוֹ״ כְּתִיב.

The Gemara further asks: **But** one could **say** a different interpretation: **I would say** that a thief is not required to pay the fourfold or fivefold payment **unless he steals two** animals, an ox and a sheep, **and slaughters one** of them **and sells** the other **one.** The Gemara rejects this suggestion as well: This interpretation is impossible, as it is **written:** "And slaughter it **or sell it.**" The term "or" indicates that only one of these two actions results in paying the penalty.

וְאַכַּתִּי הֲוָה אָמִינָא: עַד דְּגָנֵיב תַּרְוַיְיהוּ, וְטָבַח חַד וּמְשַׁיֵּיר חַד, אוֹ מְזַבֵּין חַד וּמְשַׁיֵּיר חַד!

The Gemara asks: **But still,** had the verse been worded without mentioning an ox or sheep at the start, **I would say:** A thief does not pay the fourfold or fivefold payment **unless he steals two** animals, an ox and a sheep, **and slaughters one** of them **and leaves** the other **one, or sells one and leaves** the other **one.** It is therefore impossible to omit the words "ox" and "sheep" in the beginning of the verse, which means that these words are not superfluous.

אֶלָּא, ״שׁוֹר״ דְּסֵיפָא וְ״שֶׂה״ דְּרֵישָׁא מְיַיתַּר, דְּנִיכְתּוֹב רַחֲמָנָא: ״כִּי יִגְנֹב אִישׁ שׁוֹר וּטְבָחוֹ וּמְכָרוֹ חֲמִשָּׁה בָקָר יְשַׁלֵּם תַּחְתָּיו וְאַרְבַּע צֹאן תַּחַת הַשֶּׂה״, ״שׁוֹר״ דְּסֵיפָא וְ״שֶׂה״ דְּרֵישָׁא לָמָּה לִי? שְׁמַע מִינָּהּ: שׁוֹר וְשֶׂה – אִין, מִידֵּי אַחֲרִינָא – לָא.

The Gemara gives its final explanation of Rava's statement: **Rather, "ox" at the end** of the verse **and "sheep" in the first** part of the verse **are superfluous, due to** the following consideration: **Let the Merciful One write: If a man steal an ox and slaughter it or sell it, he shall pay five oxen for it, and four sheep for a sheep. Why do I** need the word **"ox" at the end** of the verse **and** the word **"sheep" in the first** part of the verse? **Conclude from** these apparently superfluous words that for **an ox and a sheep, yes,** a thief is obligated to pay the fourfold or fivefold payment, but for stealing **other items, no,** he is not.

״אֵין הַגּוֹנֵב אַחַר הַגַּנָּב מְשַׁלֵּם תַּשְׁלוּמֵי כֶפֶל״. אָמַר רַב: לֹא שָׁנוּ אֶלָּא לִפְנֵי יֵאוּשׁ, אֲבָל לְאַחַר יֵאוּשׁ – קְנָאוֹ גַּנָּב רִאשׁוֹן, וְגַנָּב שֵׁנִי מְשַׁלֵּם תַּשְׁלוּמֵי כֶפֶל לַגַּנָּב רִאשׁוֹן.

§ The mishna teaches: **One who steals** an item **after a thief** has already stolen it, i.e., one who steals a stolen item, **does not pay** the **double payment** to the thief or to the prior owner. Rather, he pays the principal amount alone. **Rav says: They taught** this *halakha* **only** in a case where the second thief stole from the first thief **before** the owner's **despair** of recovering his item. **But** if the second thief stole it **after** the owner's **despair, the first thief had acquired** the stolen item for himself as a result of the owner's despair, **and the second thief pays** the **double payment to the first thief,** who at the time of the second theft was its legal owner.

אֲמַר רַב שֵׁשֶׁת, אָמִינָא: כִּי נָיֵים וְשָׁכֵיב רַב אֲמַר לְהָא שְׁמַעְתָּא. דְּתַנְיָא, אָמַר רַבִּי עֲקִיבָא: מִפְּנֵי מָה אָמְרָה תּוֹרָה טָבַח וּמָכַר מְשַׁלֵּם תַּשְׁלוּמֵי אַרְבָּעָה וַחֲמִשָּׁה? מִפְּנֵי שֶׁנִּשְׁתָּרֵשׁ בְּחֵטְא; אֵימַת? אִילֵימָא לִפְנֵי יֵאוּשׁ,

Rav Sheshet said: I say that **when Rav was sleepy and lying down** to rest **he said this *halakha*,** i.e., he did not give it enough thought. This ruling is incorrect, **as it is taught** in a *baraita* that **Rabbi Akiva said: For what reason did the Torah say that** if a thief **slaughtered or sold** a stolen ox or sheep **he pays** the **fourfold or fivefold payment?** It is **because** by selling or slaughtering the animal the thief **becomes** more **deeply entrenched in sin.**[N] Rav Sheshet analyzes Rabbi Akiva's statement: **When** did this sale of the stolen animal take place? **If we say** it occurred **before** the owner's **despair** of recovering his property,

NOTES

The thief becomes more deeply entrenched [*nishtaresh*] in sin – נִשְׁתָּרֵשׁ בְּחֵטְא: Most commentaries follow Rashi's explanation that the term *nishtaresh* is related to the word *shoresh*, meaning root. By slaughtering or selling the animal, the thief strikes roots, as it were, in his sin of theft, by making the animal even more unattainable to its owner. Others explain *nishtaresh* as an Aramaic word, meaning: To achieve gain. By selling the stolen animal, the thief profits further from the theft (Rabbeinu Ḥananel).

מִי אִיכָּא נִשְׁתָּרֵשׁ? אֶלָּא לְאַחַר יֵאוּשׁ. וְאִי סָלְקָא דַּעְתָּךְ יֵאוּשׁ קָנֵי, אַמַּאי מְשַׁלֵּם תַּשְׁלוּמֵי אַרְבָּעָה וַחֲמִשָּׁה? שֶׁלּוֹ הוּא טוֹבֵחַ, שֶׁלּוֹ הוּא מוֹכֵר!

is it possible to say that **there is** any **entrenchment** in sin? The sale does not take effect, as it occurred before the owner despaired, which means that the thief did not in fact deepen his sin by selling the animal. **Rather,** it must be that the sale occurred **after** the owner's **despair. And if it enters your mind** that the owner's **despair** causes the thief to **acquire** the animal, **why does he pay** the **fourfold or fivefold payment?** Since the animal belongs to him after the owner's despair, in effect **he slaughters his own** animal or **sells his own** animal.

אָמְרִי, כִּדְאָמַר רָבָא: מִפְּנֵי שֶׁשָּׁנָה בְּחֵטְא, הָכָא נַמִּי מִפְּנֵי שֶׁשָּׁנָה בְּחֵטְא.

The Sages **say:** It is possible to explain the term: Entrenched in sin, **in accordance with** what **Rava said:** The thief is liable **because he repeated** his **sin,** i.e., he sinned a second time by going through the motions of the sale, regardless of the fact the sale was not legally binding. **Here too,** one can say that the thief is liable **because he repeated** his **sin.**

תָּא שְׁמַע: ״וּטְבָחוֹ אוֹ מְכָרוֹ״ – מַה טְּבִיחָה שֶׁאֵינָהּ חוֹזֶרֶת, אַף מְכִירָה שֶׁאֵינָהּ חוֹזֶרֶת;

The Gemara suggests: **Come** and **hear** a proof from a *baraita*: It is written: "If a man steal an ox or a sheep, **and slaughter it or sell it**" (Exodus 21:37). **Just as slaughter** is an act **that cannot be undone, so too** the **selling** referred to here is an act **that cannot be undone.**[N]

אֵימַת? אִילֵּימָא לִפְנֵי יֵאוּשׁ, אַמַּאי אֵינָהּ חוֹזֶרֶת? אֶלָּא לְאַחַר יֵאוּשׁ; וְאִי סָלְקָא דַּעְתָּךְ קַנְיֵיהּ, אַמַּאי מְשַׁלֵּם אַרְבָּעָה וַחֲמִשָּׁה? שֶׁלּוֹ הוּא טוֹבֵחַ, שֶׁלּוֹ הוּא מוֹכֵר!

The Gemara analyzes the *baraita*: Now, **when** is a sale irreversible? **If we say** this sale occurred **before** the owner's **despair** of recovering his stolen animal, **why can it not be undone?** Since the thief's sale of the animal before the owner's despair is ineffective, the sale is easily undone. **Rather,** the *baraita* must be speaking about a case where the thief sold the animal **after** the owner's **despair. And if it enters your mind** that a thief **acquires** a stolen item after the owner's despair, **why does he pay the fourfold or fivefold payment** for slaughtering or selling the animal at this point? **He slaughters his own** animal or **he sells his own** animal. Apparently, a thief does not acquire the stolen item after the owner's despair.

כִּדְאָמַר רַב נַחְמָן: פְּרָט לְשֶׁהִקְנָה לִשְׁלֹשִׁים יוֹם, הָכָא נַמִּי פְּרָט לְשֶׁהִקְנָה לִשְׁלֹשִׁים יוֹם.

The Gemara rejects this proof: The explanation for this *baraita* **is as Rav Naḥman said** in reference to a different *baraita*. Rav Naḥman said that when that *baraita* speaks of a sale that cannot be undone, this **excludes one who transferred** ownership of the animal to another in a temporary manner, e.g., **for thirty days. Here too,** one can answer in the same way, that it **excludes one who transferred** ownership of the animal **for thirty days.**[H] Accordingly, if one sold the animal permanently, even if the sale was performed before the owner despaired and is therefore not legally binding, he is nevertheless required to pay the fourfold or fivefold payment.

מֵיתִיבֵי: גָּנַב, וּבָא אַחֵר וּגְנָבוֹ – הָרִאשׁוֹן מְשַׁלֵּם תַּשְׁלוּמֵי כֶפֶל, וְהַשֵּׁנִי אֵינוֹ מְשַׁלֵּם אֶלָּא קֶרֶן בִּלְבַד.

The Gemara **raises an objection** from another *baraita*: If one **stole** an animal, **and another** person subsequently **came and stole it** from him,[H] **the first** thief **pays double payment** to the owner, **and the second** thief **pays only the principal** to the first thief. This is because one who steals from a thief does not pay the double payment, as the mishna teaches.

גָּנַב וּמָכַר, וּבָא אַחֵר וּגְנָבוֹ – הָרִאשׁוֹן מְשַׁלֵּם תַּשְׁלוּמֵי אַרְבָּעָה וַחֲמִשָּׁה, וְהַשֵּׁנִי מְשַׁלֵּם תַּשְׁלוּמֵי כֶפֶל; גָּנַב וְטָבַח, וּבָא אַחֵר וּגְנָבוֹ – הָרִאשׁוֹן מְשַׁלֵּם תַּשְׁלוּמֵי אַרְבָּעָה וַחֲמִשָּׁה, וְהַשֵּׁנִי אֵינוֹ מְשַׁלֵּם תַּשְׁלוּמֵי כֶפֶל אֶלָּא קֶרֶן בִּלְבַד.

If one **stole** an animal **and sold it, and another** individual **came and stole it**[H] from the purchaser, **the first** thief **pays the fourfold or fivefold payment** to the owner, **and the second** thief **pays** the **double payment** to the purchaser, who has become the new owner of the animal. If one **stole** an animal **and slaughtered it, and another** person **came and stole** the slaughtered animal,[H] **the first** thief **pays the fourfold or fivefold payment** to the owner, **and the second** thief **does not pay** the **double payment but only the principal,** in accordance with the *halakha* that one who steals from a thief does not pay the double payment.

NOTES

The selling is an act that cannot be undone – מְכִירָה שֶׁאֵינָהּ חוֹזֶרֶת: The conceptual difference between the Gemara's question and its answer is as follows: When the Gemara asks its question, it assumes that a sale that cannot be undone is one that is legally binding, i.e., one that is not reversed automatically due to a faulty nature. According to the Gemara's answer, a sale that cannot be undone is one that is permanent, as a temporary sale is essentially a rental.

HALAKHA

One who transferred ownership of the animal for thirty days – שֶׁהִקְנָה לִשְׁלֹשִׁים יוֹם: If one stole an animal and sold it on the condition that it revert to the thief after thirty days, and the thief was discovered during these thirty days, he does not pay the fourfold or fivefold payment but only the double payment. This is how the Rambam interprets the Gemara here. It is possible that he had a different version of the text (Rambam *Sefer Nezikin, Hilkhot Geneiva* 2:11 and *Maggid Mishne* there; *Tur, Ḥoshen Mishpat* 350).

If one stole an animal and another came and stole it from him – גָּנַב וּבָא אַחֵר וּגְנָבוֹ: A thief who steals from a thief does not pay the double payment to the first thief. This is the *halakha* even if the second thief stole the item after the owner had despaired of recovering the stolen item. Likewise, if the second thief slaughtered or sold the animal that he had stolen from the first thief, he does not pay the fourfold or fivefold payment to the thief. This is because the owner's despair alone does not effect acquisition for the first thief (Rambam *Sefer Nezikin, Hilkhot Geneiva* 1:17; *Tur, Ḥoshen Mishpat* 350).

If one stole an animal and sold it and another came and stole it – גָּנַב וּמָכַר וּבָא אַחֵר וּגְנָבוֹ: In a case where one stole an animal and sold it, and another person stole it from the purchaser, if the owner had despaired of recovering the animal before the first thief sold it, then the first thief pays the owner the fourfold or fivefold payment, and the second thief pays the double payment to the purchaser. If there was no despair on the part of the owner, the second thief pays only the principal amount. This is because the owner's despair together with a change of possession does effect acquisition for the thief (Rambam *Sefer Nezikin, Hilkhot Geneiva* 1:18; *Tur, Ḥoshen Mishpat* 350).

If one stole an animal and slaughtered it and another came and stole it – גָּנַב וְטָבַח וּבָא אַחֵר וּגְנָבוֹ: If one stole an animal and slaughtered it, and another person stole the carcass, then the second thief pays the double payment to the first thief, as the first thief has acquired the meat by virtue of the physical change it has undergone. The first thief pays the fourfold or fivefold payment to the owner (Rambam *Sefer Nezikin, Hilkhot Geneiva* 1:18; *Tur, Ḥoshen Mishpat* 350).

קָתָנֵי מִיהָא מְצִיעֲתָא: גָּנַב וּמָכַר, וּבָא אַחֵר וּגְנָבוֹ – הָרִאשׁוֹן מְשַׁלֵּם תַּשְׁלוּמֵי אַרְבָּעָה וַחֲמִשָּׁה, וְהַשֵּׁנִי מְשַׁלֵּם תַּשְׁלוּמֵי כֶפֶל;

The Gemara analyzes this *baraita*: **In any event,** the *baraita* **teaches** in **the middle clause:** If one **stole** an animal **and sold** it, **and another came and stole it** from the purchaser, **the first** thief **pays the fourfold or fivefold payment** to the owner, **and the second** thief **pays** the **double payment** to the purchaser.

אֵימַת? אִילֵימָא לִפְנֵי יֵאוּשׁ, שֵׁנִי אַמַּאי מְשַׁלֵּם תַּשְׁלוּמֵי כֶפֶל? שִׁינּוּי רְשׁוּת בְּלֹא יֵאוּשׁ מִי אִיכָּא לְמַאן דְּאָמַר דְּקָנֵי?

When did this sale occur? **If we say** it happened **before** the owner's **despair, why does** the second thief **pay** the **double payment** to the purchaser? **Is there anyone who says that a change in possession** of a stolen item, i.e., when it leaves the possession of the thief and enters the possession of another, **without** the additional factor of the owner's **despair,** causes the one who has it to **acquire** the item? There is no such opinion. Therefore, the so-called purchaser of the animal does not become its owner, as the sale is invalid. This should be considered as a case of one who steals from a thief, and consequently there should be no double payment.

אֶלָּא פְּשִׁיטָא לְאַחַר יֵאוּשׁ; וְאִי סָלְקָא דַּעְתָּךְ יֵאוּשׁ קוֹנֶה, אַמַּאי מְשַׁלֵּם תַּשְׁלוּמֵי אַרְבָּעָה וַחֲמִשָּׁה? דִּידֵיהּ הוּא דְּזַבֵּין!

Rather, it is obvious that the sale occurred **after** the owner's **despair. And if it enters your mind** that a thief **acquires** a stolen item after the owner's **despair, why** should the first thief **pay** the **fourfold or fivefold payment?** After all, **it is his own** animal **that he sold,** having acquired it immediately upon the owner's despair.

וְתוּ, דְּקָתָנֵי רֵישָׁא: גָּנַב, וּבָא אַחֵר וּגְנָבוֹ – רִאשׁוֹן מְשַׁלֵּם תַּשְׁלוּמֵי כֶפֶל, וְהַשֵּׁנִי אֵין מְשַׁלֵּם אֶלָּא קֶרֶן;

And furthermore, consider **that** which the *baraita* **teaches** in **the first clause:** If one **stole** an animal, **and another** subsequently **came and stole it** from him, **the first** thief **pays** the **double payment** to the owner, **and the second** thief **pays only the principal** to the first thief.

מִכְּדִי לְאַחַר יֵאוּשׁ קָיְימִינַן, וְאִי סָלְקָא דַּעְתָּךְ יֵאוּשׁ קוֹנֶה, שֵׁנִי אַמַּאי אֵינוֹ מְשַׁלֵּם אֶלָּא קֶרֶן? אֶלָּא לָאו שְׁמַע מִינָּהּ: יֵאוּשׁ לָא קָנֵי, וְקַשְׁיָא לְרַב!

Now, in this *baraita* **we are dealing with** a situation **after** the owner's **despair,** as the Gemara just established. **And if it enters your mind** that the owner's **despair** causes the thief to **acquire** the item, **why does** the **second** thief **pay only the principal?** After the owner has despaired of recovering his item, the thief becomes the owner of the item, and the second thief should have to pay him double payment for stealing his property. **Rather,** must one **not conclude from** the *baraita* that the owner's **despair does not** cause the thief to **acquire** the item? **And** this presents **a difficulty to** the opinion of **Rav.**

אֲמַר רָבָא: וְתִסְבְּרָא, הָא מְתָרַצְתָּא הִיא? אֶלָּא דְּקָתָנֵי סֵיפָא: גָּנַב וְטָבַח וּבָא אַחֵר וּגְנָבוֹ – רִאשׁוֹן מְשַׁלֵּם תַּשְׁלוּמֵי אַרְבָּעָה וַחֲמִשָּׁה, וְשֵׁנִי אֵינוֹ מְשַׁלֵּם אֶלָּא קֶרֶן; וּמִי אִיכָּא לְמַאן דְּאָמַר שִׁינּוּי מַעֲשֶׂה לָא קָנֵי?

Rava said: And can **you understand** that the text of **this** *baraita* **is accurate? But** consider **that** which **it teaches** in **the last clause:** If one **stole** an animal **and slaughtered** it, **and another came and stole** the slaughtered animal, the **first** thief **pays** the **fourfold or fivefold payment** to the owner, **and the second** thief **pays only the principal** to the first thief. **And is there anyone who says that** a physical **change** brought about by **an action does not** cause the thief to **acquire** the item? There is no such opinion; the thief certainly becomes the owner of the animal after slaughtering it. Consequently, the second thief should have to pay the double payment to the thief for stealing his slaughtered animal. It must therefore be concluded that the text of the *baraita* has been corrupted and must be reformulated.

אֶלָּא, לְעוֹלָם כּוּלָּהּ לִפְנֵי יֵאוּשׁ, וְאֵיפוּךְ סֵיפָא לִמְצִיעֲתָא וּמְצִיעֲתָא לְסֵיפָא, וְאֵימָא הָכִי: גָּנַב וּמָכַר, וּבָא אַחֵר וּגְנָבוֹ – הָרִאשׁוֹן מְשַׁלֵּם תַּשְׁלוּמֵי אַרְבָּעָה וַחֲמִשָּׁה, וְהַשֵּׁנִי אֵינוֹ מְשַׁלֵּם אֶלָּא קֶרֶן, דְּשִׁינּוּי רְשׁוּת בְּלֹא יֵאוּשׁ לָא קָנֵי.

Rather, actually the entire *baraita* is referring to the stage **before** the owner's **despair. And** you must **reverse** the *halakha* stated in **the last clause with** that stated in **the middle clause, and** reverse the *halakha* stated in **the middle clause with** that stated in **the last clause, and say like this:** If one **stole** an animal **and sold** it, **and another came and stole it** from the purchaser, **the first** thief **pays** the **fourfold or fivefold payment** to the owner, **and the second** thief **pays only the principal** to the purchaser, **as a change in possession without** the additional factor of owner's **despair does not** cause one to **acquire** the item.

גָּנַב וְטָבַח וּבָא אַחֵר וּגְנָבוֹ – הָרִאשׁוֹן מְשַׁלֵּם תַּשְׁלוּמֵי אַרְבָּעָה וַחֲמִשָּׁה, וְהַשֵּׁנִי מְשַׁלֵּם תַּשְׁלוּמֵי כֶפֶל, דְּקַנְיֵיהּ בְּשִׁינּוּי מַעֲשֶׂה.

If one **stole** an animal **and slaughtered** it, **and another came and stole** the slaughtered animal, **the first** thief **pays** the **fourfold or fivefold payment** to the owner, **and the second** thief **pays** the **double payment** to the first thief, **as** the first thief **acquired** it through the physical **change** brought about by **an action,** i.e., slaughter.

רַב פַּפָּא אֲמַר: לְעוֹלָם לָא תֵּיפוּךְ, סֵיפָא בֵּית שַׁמַּאי הִיא, דְּאָמְרִי: שִׁינּוּי בִּמְקוֹמָהּ עוֹמֵד.

Rav Pappa said: Actually, do not reverse the middle and last clauses of the *baraita*.[N] With regard to the difficult **last clause, it is** in accordance with the opinion of **Beit Shammai, who say:** Even if an item has undergone a physical **change, it remains in its place,** i.e., a stolen item remains the property of the owner. A thief never attains ownership of it, even if it undergoes a physical change.

אִי הָכִי, קַשְׁיָא רֵישָׁא וּמְצִיעֲתָא לְרַב!

The Gemara asks: **If so,** if the *baraita* is not reversed, and if it is referring to the stage after the owner's despair, then **the first clause and the middle clause** of the *baraita* present **a difficulty to** the opinion **of Rav,** who maintains that after the owner's despair the item belongs entirely to the thief.

אָמַר רַב זְבִיד: לְעוֹלָם כּוּלָּהּ לִפְנֵי יֵאוּשׁ, וְהָכָא בְּמַאי עָסְקִינַן – שֶׁנִּתְיָיאֲשׁוּ הַבְּעָלִים בְּלוֹקֵחַ וְלֹא נִתְיָאֲשׁוּ בְּגַנָּב, דַּהֲוָה לֵיהּ יֵאוּשׁ וְשִׁינּוּי רְשׁוּת.

Rav Zevid said: Actually, the entire *baraita* is dealing with the stage **before** the owner's **despair. And with what are we dealing here,** in the middle clause of the *baraita*? We are dealing with a case **where the owners despaired** of recovering the item when it was already **in** the possession of the **purchaser, but they had not** yet **despaired** when the item was **in** the possession of the **thief.** The purchaser is considered the owner **because** after the despair occurred, **there were** two factors in play, both the owner's **despair and a change in possession.**[H] The combination of these two factors effects acquisition of the item on behalf of the purchaser.

וְלָא תֵּימָא מִשּׁוּם דִּבְעֵינַן יֵאוּשׁ וְשִׁינּוּי רְשׁוּת, אֶלָּא אֲפִילּוּ בְּיֵאוּשׁ לְחוּדֵיהּ נָמֵי קָנֵי גַּבֵּי גַּנָּב.

Rav Zevid continues: **And do not say** that in the middle clause the reason the owner's item is acquired by another is only **because we require** two factors, i.e., the owner's **despair and change of possession. Rather, even** in a case **of** the owner's **despair by itself,** the item **is acquired by the thief,** in accordance with Rav's opinion that despair alone effects acquisition on behalf of the thief.

אֶלָּא דְּלָא מַשְׁכַּחַתְּ דִּמְשַׁלְּמִי תַּרְוַיְיהוּ גַּנָּב רִאשׁוֹן וְגַנָּב שֵׁנִי אֶלָּא בְּהָכִי.

Nevertheless, the *baraita* chose a case in which both of these factors are present **because you will not find a case in which both of them, the first thief and the second thief, pay** a penalty **except in such** a case. The first thief pays the fourfold or fivefold payment, and the second thief pays the double payment. Had the owner despaired before the sale, the first thief would have been considered the owner and would therefore be exempt from the additional payment.

אִיתְּמַר: הַמּוֹכֵר לִפְנֵי יֵאוּשׁ, רַב נַחְמָן אָמַר: חַיָּיב, רַב שֵׁשֶׁת אָמַר: פָּטוּר.

§ **It was stated:** With regard to a thief **who sells** a stolen animal **before** the owner's **despair,**[H] **Rav Naḥman says:** He is **liable** to pay the fourfold or fivefold payment, despite the fact that the sale is invalid. **Rav Sheshet says:** He is **exempt** from this payment.

רַב נַחְמָן אָמַר חַיָּיב, "וּמְכָרוֹ" אָמַר רַחֲמָנָא, וְהָא זַבֵּין, לָא שְׁנָא לִפְנֵי יֵאוּשׁ לָא שְׁנָא לְאַחַר יֵאוּשׁ. רַב שֵׁשֶׁת אָמַר פָּטוּר, חִיּוּבֵיהּ לְאַחַר יֵאוּשׁ הוּא, דְּאַהֲנוּ מַעֲשָׂיו, אֲבָל לִפְנֵי יֵאוּשׁ דְּלָא אַהֲנוּ מַעֲשָׂיו – לָא מִיחַיַּיב, דּוּמְיָא דִּטְבִיחָה בָּעֵינַן דְּאַהֲנוּ מַעֲשָׂיו.

The two *amora'im* explain the reasons for their respective rulings. **Rav Naḥman says:** He is **liable,** because **the Merciful One states** with regard to the fourfold or fivefold payment: "And slaughter it **or sell it"** (Exodus 21:37), **and he has sold it.** There **is no difference** if the sale occurs **before despair,** and there **is no difference** if it takes place **after despair. Rav Sheshet says:** He is **exempt,** as **his liability is** in effect only if he sells the animal **after** the owner's **despair, when his action,** i.e., the sale, **is effective. But** if he sells it **before** the owner's **despair, when his action is not effective,** he **is not liable,** as **we require** that the sale be **similar to the slaughter,** as they are mentioned together, and **when** he slaughters the animal **his action is effective.**

NOTES

Actually do not reverse the ***baraita*** **– לְעוֹלָם לָא תֵּיפוּךְ:** The early commentaries discuss whether Rav Pappa meant that the *baraita* should now be interpreted as dealing with a situation after the owner's despair, as the Gemara had initially assumed (Rashi), or that even according to Rava, who interpreted the *baraita* as referring to a situation before the owner's despair, there is no need to reverse the middle and last clauses of the *baraita*. These two interpretations of Rav Pappa are dependent upon textual variants of the Gemara (see Ra'avad).

HALAKHA

The owner's despair and a change in possession – יֵאוּשׁ וְשִׁינּוּי רְשׁוּת: The combination of the owner's despair of recovering his stolen item and a change in possession of the item effects acquisition. Consequently, one who buys a stolen item from a thief does not have to return it to its owner. The authorities discuss whether the owner's despair must precede the sale for this *halakha* to apply. Likewise (see 115a), they discuss the circumstances under which the purchaser is required to pay monetary restitution to the owner (Rambam *Sefer Nezikin, Hilkhot Geneiva* 5:3 and *Hilkhot Gezeila VaAveda* 2:3; *Shulḥan Arukh, Ḥoshen Mishpat* 353:3, 361:4, 362:3).

A thief who sells a stolen animal before the owner's despair – הַמּוֹכֵר לִפְנֵי יֵאוּשׁ: If a thief sells or slaughters a stolen animal before the owner despairs of recovering it, he must pay the fourfold or fivefold payment. The *halakha* is in accordance with the opinion of Rav Naḥman, whose rulings are authoritative in monetary matters and who concurs with Rabbi Yoḥanan in this matter (Rambam *Sefer Nezikin, Hilkhot Geneiva* 1:16; *Tur, Ḥoshen Mishpat* 350).

אָמַר רַב שֵׁשֶׁת: מְנָא אָמֵינָא לַהּ? דְּתַנְיָא, אָמַר רַבִּי עֲקִיבָא: מִפְּנֵי מָה אָמְרָה תּוֹרָה טָבַח וּמָכַר מְשַׁלֵּם אַרְבָּעָה וַחֲמִשָּׁה? מִפְּנֵי שֶׁנִּשְׁתָּרֵשׁ בְּחֵטְא.

Rav Sheshet said: From where do I say he is exempt? **As it is taught** in a *baraita* that **Rabbi Akiva said: For what** reason **did the Torah say that** a thief **who slaughtered or sold** a stolen animal **pays the fourfold or fivefold payment?** It is **because he has become entrenched in sin** by slaughtering or selling the animal he stole.

אֵימַת? אִילֵימָא לִפְנֵי יֵאוּשׁ, מִי אִיכָּא נִשְׁתָּרֵשׁ? אֶלָּא לָאו לְאַחַר יֵאוּשׁ הוּא! אָמַר רָבָא: מִפְּנֵי שֶׁשָּׁנָה בְּחֵטְא.

Rav Sheshet analyzes the *baraita*: **When** did this sale, referred to by Rabbi Akiva, occur? **If we say** that it happened **before** the owner's **despair, is** it possible that **there** is any **entrenchment** in sin here? A sale before the owner's despair is invalid, which means there is no deepening of his earlier sin. **Rather, is it not** the case that this **is** referring to a sale **after** the owner's **despair? Rava said:** This is not a proof, as one can explain that the thief is entrenched in sin **because he repeated** his **sin,** i.e. sinned a second time, by his act of sale, regardless of the fact that the sale is invalid.

תָּא שְׁמַע: "וּטְבָחוֹ וּמְכָרוֹ" – מָה טְבִיחָה שֶׁאֵינָהּ חוֹזֶרֶת, אַף מְכִירָה שֶׁאֵינָהּ חוֹזֶרֶת; אֵימַת? אִילֵימָא לִפְנֵי יֵאוּשׁ, אַמַּאי אֵינָהּ חוֹזֶרֶת? אֶלָּא לְאַחַר יֵאוּשׁ, וּשְׁמַע מִינָּהּ: חִיּוּבָא לְאַחַר יֵאוּשׁ הוּא! תַּרְגְּמָהּ רַב נַחְמָן: פְּרָט לְשֶׁהִקְנָה לוֹ לִשְׁלֹשִׁים יוֹם.

The Gemara suggests: **Come** and **hear** a proof for the opinion of Rav Sheshet from a different *baraita*: It is written: **"And slaughter it or sell it"** (Exodus 21:37). **Just as slaughter** is an act **that cannot be undone, so too** the **selling** referred to here is an act **that cannot be undone.** The Gemara analyzes this *baraita*: **When** did this sale take place? **If we say** that it happened **before** the owner's **despair** of recovering his stolen item, **why can it not be undone?** The thief's sale of the animal is invalid before the owner's despair, and therefore the sale is easily undone. **Rather,** it must be referring to a sale that took place **after** the owner's **despair. And** one can **conclude from** the *baraita* that there is **liability** to pay the fourfold or fivefold payment only if the animal is sold **after** the owner's **despair. Rav Naḥman** rejected this proof, as he **interpreted** that *baraita* as serving to **exclude one who transferred** ownership of the animal temporarily, e.g., **for thirty days.**

וְאַף רַבִּי אֶלְעָזָר סָבַר: חִיּוּבֵיהּ לְאַחַר יֵאוּשׁ הוּא, דְּאָמַר רַבִּי אֶלְעָזָר:

The Gemara adds: **And Rabbi Elazar also holds** that **the liability** of a thief to pay the fourfold or fivefold payment applies if he sells it **after** the owner's **despair** of recovering his stolen animal, **as Rabbi Elazar says:**

Perek **VII**
Daf **68** Amud **b**

HALAKHA

An ordinary case of theft is assumed to result in the owner's despair – סְתָם גְּנֵיבָה יֵאוּשׁ בְּעָלִים הוּא: When an item is stolen, it is ordinarily assumed that the owner has despaired of recovering it. Some commentaries write that in light of this assumption, one who buys stolen goods from a thief does not have to return them to the prior owner, as the buyer has fully acquired the goods through the combination of the owner's despair and the change in possession of the goods that occurred when he bought them. Nevertheless, it is the accepted custom to return stolen items in any event, and one may not deviate from this practice (Rambam *Sefer Nezikin, Hilkhot Gezeila VaAveda* 6:3; *Shulḥan Arukh, Ḥoshen Mishpat* 368:1, and in the comment of Rema).

תֵּדַע שֶׁסְּתָם גְּנֵיבָה יֵאוּשׁ בְּעָלִים הוּא,

Know that an ordinary case of **theft is** assumed to result in **the owner's despair**[H] of recovering the stolen item. In other words, in the absence of evidence to the contrary, one may assume that the victim of theft has despaired of recovering his item.

שֶׁהֲרֵי אָמְרָה תּוֹרָה טָבַח וּמָכַר מְשַׁלֵּם תַּשְׁלוּמֵי אַרְבָּעָה וַחֲמִשָּׁה; וְדִלְמָא לָא אִיָּיאַשׁ! אֶלָּא לָאו מִשּׁוּם דְּאָמְרִינַן: סְתָם גְּנֵיבָה יֵאוּשׁ בְּעָלִים הִיא.

The reason is **that the Torah stated** that if a thief **slaughtered or sold** the animal he had stolen, **he pays** the **fourfold or fivefold payment. But** why is this so? **Perhaps** the owner **did not** yet **despair** at the time the thief sold the animal, in which case the sale is invalid, and there should be no fourfold or fivefold payment. **Rather, is it not because we say that an ordinary** case of **theft is** assumed to result in **the owner's despair** of recovering the stolen item? This concludes the statement of Rabbi Elazar, which clearly indicates that there is no fourfold or fivefold payment if the animal is sold before the owner's despair.

וְדִלְמָא אַף עַל גַּב דְּלָא אִיָּיאַשׁ!

The Gemara asks a question with regard to Rabbi Elazar's assumption: **But perhaps** the Torah obligates the thief to pay the fourfold or fivefold payment **even if** the owner has **not** yet **despaired** at the time of the sale, despite the fact that the sale is invalid, as Rav Naḥman stated.

אָמְרִי: לָא סָלְקָא דַּעְתָּךְ, דּוּמְיָא דִּטְבִיחָה, מַה טְּבִיחָה דְּאַהֲנוּ מַעֲשָׂיו, אַף מְכִירָה דְּאַהֲנוּ מַעֲשָׂיו, וְאִי לִפְנֵי יֵאוּשׁ – מַאי אַהֲנוּ?

In response to this question the Sages **say:** This **cannot enter your mind,** as Rabbi Elazar maintains that the juxtaposition of slaughtering and selling in the verse that states: "And slaughter it or sell it," teaches that the thief's sale of the animal is **similar to** his **slaughter** of it. **Just as slaughter** is a matter in **which his action was effective, so too,** the case of **selling** the animal is one in **which his action was effective,** i.e., the sale is valid. **And if** the sale occurred **before** the owner's **despair,** in **what** sense were his actions **effective?**

וְדִלְמָא דְּשָׁמְעִינֵיהּ דְּאִיַּאַשׁ! אָמְרִי: לָא סָלְקָא דַּעְתָּךְ, דּוּמְיָא דִּטְבִיחָה, מַה טְּבִיחָה לְאַלְתַּר, אַף מְכִירָה לְאַלְתַּר.

The Gemara asks another question with regard to Rabbi Elazar's reasoning: **But perhaps** the Torah requires the fourfold or fivefold payment only in the specific case **where** the animal is sold after **we heard that** the owner **despaired** of its recovery. The Sages respond to this and **say:** This **cannot enter your mind,** since, as explained above, the thief's sale of the animal must be **similar to** his **slaughter** of it. Therefore, **just as** the thief is liable to pay the fourfold or fivefold payment for **slaughtering** the animal even if he does so **immediately, so too,** the *halakha* that he pays the fourfold or fivefold payment for **selling** it applies even if he does so **immediately,** before it is known that the owner has despaired of recovering the animal.

אָמַר לוֹ רַבִּי יוֹחָנָן: גְּנֵיבָה בְּנֶפֶשׁ תּוֹכִיחַ, שֶׁאֵין יֵאוּשׁ בְּעָלִים, וְחַיָּיב! מִכְּלָל דְּסָבַר רַבִּי יוֹחָנָן: לִפְנֵי יֵאוּשׁ – חַיָּיב.

Rabbi Yoḥanan said to Rabbi Elazar: The case of **stealing a human being,**[H] i.e., kidnapping, **proves** that your reasoning is incorrect. The Torah states: "And he who steals a man and sells him or if he is found in his hand, he shall be put to death" (Exodus 21:16). In this case **there is no owner's despair,** as no one ever despairs of his own freedom. Consequently, the thief's sale of the person he kidnapped is invalid, **and** yet the Torah states that he is **liable** to receive the death penalty for selling him. One can learn **by inference** from this question **that Rabbi Yoḥanan holds** that if the thief sells the stolen animal **before** the owner's **despair** he is **liable** to pay the fourfold or fivefold payment.

לְאַחַר יֵאוּשׁ מַאי? רַבִּי יוֹחָנָן אָמַר: חַיָּיב, וְרֵישׁ לָקִישׁ אָמַר: פָּטוּר.

§ The Gemara asks: If the thief sells the animal **after** the owner's **despair, what** is the *halakha*?[H] **Rabbi Yoḥanan says:** He is **liable.**[N] **And Reish Lakish says:** He is **exempt.**

רַבִּי יוֹחָנָן אָמַר חַיָּיב, חִיּוּבֵיהּ בֵּין לִפְנֵי יֵאוּשׁ בֵּין לְאַחַר יֵאוּשׁ; רֵישׁ לָקִישׁ אָמַר פָּטוּר, חִיּוּבֵיהּ לִפְנֵי יֵאוּשׁ הוּא, אֲבָל לְאַחַר יֵאוּשׁ – קָנָה, שֶׁלּוֹ הוּא טוֹבֵחַ וְשֶׁלּוֹ הוּא מוֹכֵר.

The Gemara elaborates: **Rabbi Yoḥanan says:** He is **liable,** as the thief's **liability** applies **whether** the animal is sold **before** the owner's **despair or after** his **despair. Reish Lakish says:** He is **exempt,** as the thief's **liability is** in effect only if he sells the animal **before** the owner's **despair, but after** the owner's **despair** there is no liability, because the thief has **acquired** the animal by virtue of the owner's despair, **and** therefore it is **his own** animal that **he slaughters or his own** animal that **he sells.**

אֵיתִיבֵיהּ רַבִּי יוֹחָנָן לְרֵישׁ לָקִישׁ: גָּנַב וְהִקְדִּישׁ וְאַחַר כָּךְ טָבַח – מְשַׁלֵּם תַּשְׁלוּמֵי כֶפֶל וְאֵינוֹ מְשַׁלֵּם תַּשְׁלוּמֵי אַרְבָּעָה וַחֲמִשָּׁה;

Rabbi Yoḥanan raised an objection to the opinion of **Reish Lakish** from a *baraita*: If one **stole** an animal **and consecrated** it, **and subsequently slaughtered** it,[H] **he pays** the **double payment** to the owner of the animal, **but he does not pay** the **fourfold or fivefold payment.** The Torah states: "The one whom the judges convict shall pay double to his neighbor" (Exodus 22:8). The word "neighbor" excludes the case of one who steals a consecrated item from the Temple treasury. Since there is no double payment to the Temple treasury there can be no fourfold or fivefold payment either, as the fourfold or fivefold payment is considered an addition to, not a replacement of, of the double payment (see 75a). Therefore, a thief does not pay the fourfold or fivefold payment to the Temple treasury for slaughtering one of its animals.

אֵימַת? אִילֵימָא לִפְנֵי יֵאוּשׁ, מִי קָדוֹשׁ? "אִישׁ כִּי יַקְדִּשׁ אֶת בֵּיתוֹ קֹדֶשׁ" אָמַר רַחֲמָנָא, מַה בֵּיתוֹ שֶׁלּוֹ, אַף כֹּל שֶׁלּוֹ!

The Gemara analyzes the *baraita*: **When** did the events described in the *baraita* occur? **If we say** they happened **before** the owner's **despair, is** the animal **consecrated** at all? A thief cannot consecrate a stolen item before the owner despairs of recovering it, as **the Merciful One states** in the Torah: "And **when a man shall sanctify his house to be holy unto the Lord**" (Leviticus 27:14), from which it is derived: **Just as one's house belongs to him, so too, anything** that one consecrates must **belong to him,**[H] and therefore a thief cannot consecrate a stolen item.

HALAKHA

Stealing a human being – גְּנֵיבָה בְּנֶפֶשׁ: One who kidnaps a Jew, takes him into his own domain, forces him to work for him, and then sells him to another is liable to receive the punishment of death by strangulation (Rambam *Sefer Nezikin, Hilkhot Geneiva* 9:1–2).

If he sells it after the owner's despair, what is the *halakha* – לְאַחַר יֵאוּשׁ מַאי: If one steals an animal and slaughters it or sells it he pays the fourfold or fivefold payment, whether this occurs before the owner despaired of recovering it or afterward. The *halakha* is in accordance with the opinion of Rabbi Yoḥanan and Rav Naḥman (Rambam *Sefer Nezikin, Hilkhot Geneiva* 1:16; *Tur, Ḥoshen Mishpat* 350).

If one stole an animal and consecrated it and subsequently slaughtered it – גָּנַב וְהִקְדִּישׁ וְאַחַר כָּךְ טָבַח: If one stole an animal, consecrated it, and subsequently slaughtered or sold it, he pays the double payment, but not the fourfold or fivefold payment. This applies when he consecrated the animal after the owner despaired of recovery. If he consecrated it before the owner's despair, the animal is not consecrated, and if he subsequently slaughters or sells it he pays the fourfold or fivefold payment to the owner (Rambam *Sefer Nezikin, Hilkhot Geneiva* 2:6; *Tur, Ḥoshen Mishpat* 350).

Just as one's house belongs to him so too anything that one consecrates must belong to him – מַה בֵּיתוֹ שֶׁלּוֹ אַף כֹּל שֶׁלּוֹ: One cannot consecrate an item that does not belong to him (Rambam *Sefer Hafla'a, Hilkhot Arakhin VaḤaramim* 6:21).

NOTES

If he sells it after the owner's despair…Rabbi Yoḥanan says he is liable – לְאַחַר יֵאוּשׁ...רַבִּי יוֹחָנָן אָמַר חַיָּיב: Rashi explains that Rabbi Yoḥanan maintains that the owner's despair does not effect acquisition for the thief, as if it did so, the thief would not be liable because he would thereafter be slaughtering or selling his own animal. Since despair does not effect acquisition for the thief, it is more logical that the Torah requires fourfold or fivefold payment for selling the animal after the owner's despair, when the sale would be valid, than before his despair. Others explain that in general, Rabbi Yoḥanan does hold that the owner's despair effects acquisition for the thief. Nevertheless, he maintains, based on a scriptural derivation, that if a thief slaughters or sells a stolen animal after the owner's despair he pays the fourfold or fivefold payment as a penalty for his sinful acts (see *Tosefot Rabbeinu Peretz*).

אֶלָּא פְּשִׁיטָא לְאַחַר יֵאוּשׁ; וְטַעְמָא דְּהִקְדִּישׁ הוּא דְּאֵינוֹ מְשַׁלֵּם תַּשְׁלוּמֵי אַרְבָּעָה וַחֲמִשָּׁה, דְּכִי קָא טָבַח – דְּהֶקְדֵּשׁ קָא טָבַח, אֲבָל לֹא הִקְדִּישׁ – טָבַח מְשַׁלֵּם תַּשְׁלוּמֵי אַרְבָּעָה וַחֲמִשָּׁה; וְאִי סָלְקָא דַּעְתָּךְ יֵאוּשׁ קוֹנֶה, אַמַּאי מְשַׁלֵּם? שֶׁלּוֹ הוּא טוֹבֵחַ, שֶׁלּוֹ הוּא מוֹכֵר!

Rather, it is **obvious** that the *baraita* is dealing with events that occurred **after** the owner's **despair. And** yet **the** only **reason that he does not pay the fourfold or fivefold payment is that he consecrated** the animal, on the grounds **that when he slaughtered** it **he slaughtered consecrated** property. **But if he did not consecrate** the animal before **he slaughtered** it **he would pay the fourfold or fivefold payment. And if it enters your mind that** the owner's **despair** serves to **acquire** the animal for the thief, **why** would he have to **pay?** At that point it is **his own** animal that **he slaughters or his own** animal that **he sells.**

אֲמַר לֵיהּ: הָכָא בְּמַאי עָסְקִינַן – כְּגוֹן שֶׁהִקְדִּישׁוּהוּ בְּעָלִים בְּיַד גַּנָּב.

Reish Lakish **said to** Rabbi Yoḥanan: **With what are we dealing here?** The *baraita* is referring to a case that occurred before the owner's despair, and it is not the thief who consecrated the animal, as he cannot do so. Rather, we are dealing with a case **where the owner consecrated the animal** while it was **in the thief's possession.**

וּמִי קָדוֹשׁ? וְהָאָמַר רַבִּי יוֹחָנָן: גָּזַל וְלֹא נִתְיָיאֲשׁוּ הַבְּעָלִים – שְׁנֵיהֶן אֵינָן יְכוֹלִין לְהַקְדִּישׁ, זֶה לְפִי שֶׁאֵינוֹ שֶׁלּוֹ, וְזֶה לְפִי שֶׁאֵינוֹ בִּרְשׁוּתוֹ! אָמְרִי: הוּא דְּאָמַר כִּצְנוּעִין,

The Gemara asks: **And is** the animal **consecrated** in this situation? **But didn't Rabbi Yoḥanan say:** If one **stole** an item **and the owner has not** yet **despaired** of recovering it, **neither of them is able to consecrate it.**[H] **This** one, the thief, cannot consecrate the item, **because it does not belong to him; and that** one, the owner, cannot consecrate it, **because it is not in his possession.** The Sages **state** an answer on behalf of Reish Lakish: **He stated** his opinion **in accordance with** the opinion of **the pious ones** [*tzenuin*],[L] who acted not in accordance with the opinion of Rabbi Yoḥanan.

דִּתְנַן: הַצְּנוּעִין מַנִּיחִין אֶת הַמָּעוֹת, וְאוֹמְרִים: "כָּל הַנִּלְקָט מִזֶּה יְהֵא מְחוּלָּל עַל הַמָּעוֹת הָאֵלּוּ".

As we learned in a mishna (*Ma'aser Sheni* 5:1): **The pious ones would set aside** some **coins**[H] **and say: Anything that was picked from this** vine by passersby **shall be desacralized onto these coins.** This mishna is referring to a grapevine in its fourth year after planting. The grapes on this vine must be either eaten in Jerusalem or redeemed with money that is then taken to Jerusalem and spent on food. The fruit may not be eaten outside Jerusalem without being redeemed. The pious ones were concerned that a passerby might help himself to some of their grapes, thereby transgressing a prohibition. Therefore, they would redeem any of their grapes that might be picked and eaten by passersby. Evidently, these pious ones were of the opinion that the owner of a stolen item can redeem it despite the fact that it is no longer in his possession. Likewise, they would say, contrary to the opinion of Rabbi Yoḥanan, that an owner of a stolen item can consecrate it even though it is no longer in his possession.

וַהֲרֵי חָזְרָה קֶרֶן לַבְּעָלִים!

The Gemara asks a question with regard to Reish Lakish's explanation of the *baraita*, that it is discussing a case where the owner of the animal consecrated it after it was stolen: **But the principal** amount, i.e., the stolen animal itself, **has returned to the owner.** By consecrating the animal, the owner has exercised his ownership of it, and it is therefore considered to have been returned to him at that point. The thief should therefore not be required to pay the double payment, as a thief is liable for double payment only when the stolen item is in his possession at the time of the trial, as it states: "The theft shall be found in his hand" (Exodus 22:3).

כְּשֶׁעָמַד בַּדִּין.

The Gemara answers: The *baraita* is discussing a case **where** the thief **stood in judgment** and was found guilty of theft before the owner consecrated the animal. Consequently, the liability to pay the double payment preceded the owner's consecration of his property.

הֵיכִי דָּמֵי? אִי דְּאָמְרִי "צֵא תֵּן לוֹ", מַאי אִירְיָא הִקְדִּישׁ? אֲפִילּוּ לֹא הִקְדִּישׁ נַמִּי לָא לִיחַיְּיבֵיהּ!

The Gemara raises a difficulty with regard to this answer: **What are the circumstances** of this trial of the thief? **If** it refers to a situation **where** the members of the court **say** to him: **Go out** and **give** the animal back **to** its owner, **why** does the *baraita* say that the thief is exempt from the fourfold or fivefold payment **specifically** because the owner **consecrated** the animal before it was slaughtered? **Even if he did not consecrate it** the thief **should also not be liable** to pay the fourfold or fivefold payment.

HALAKHA

If one stole an item and the owner has not yet despaired neither of them is able to consecrate it – גָּזַל וְלֹא נִתְיָיאֲשׁוּ הַבְּעָלִים שְׁנֵיהֶן אֵינָן יְכוֹלִין לְהַקְדִּישׁ: If one stole an item and the owner has not yet despaired of recovering it, the owner cannot consecrate it because it is not in his possession, and the thief cannot consecrate it because it does not belong to him (Rambam *Sefer Hafla'a, Hilkhot Arakhin VaḤaramim* 6:24).

The pious ones would set aside some coins, etc. – הַצְּנוּעִין מַנִּיחִין אֶת הַמָּעוֹת וכו׳: With regard to fourth-year fruits during the Sabbatical Year, when it is permitted for everyone to take fruit from trees, the tree should be demarcated so that people will know that it is fourth-year fruit and requires redemption. The pious ones would set aside coins and say: Anything that was picked from this vine by passersby shall be desacralized onto these coins (Rambam *Sefer Zera'im, Hilkhot Ma'aser Sheni VeNeta Revai* 9:7).

LANGUAGE

Pious ones [*tzenuin*] – צְנוּעִין: Although the primary meaning of the root *tzadi, nun, ayin* is to be modest or hidden from sight, and people who act modestly are called *tzenuin*. Apparently, in this context the use of the term is influenced by the Aramaic meaning of the same root, which denotes possession of wisdom and understanding. Consequently, the reference is to individuals who are exceptional in their wisdom or fear of God.

דְּאָמַר רָבָא: ״צֵא תֵּן לוֹ״, טָבַח וּמָכַר – פָּטוּר, מַאי טַעֲמָא?

The Gemara elaborates. **As Rava says:** If the court tells a thief: **Go out** and **give** the stolen animal back **to** the owner[NH] and instead the thief **slaughtered or sold** it, he is **exempt** from the fourfold or fivefold payment. **What is the reason** for this?

כֵּיוָן דְּפַסְקוּהּ לְמִילְּתֵיהּ וְטָבַח וּמָכַר הֲוָה לֵיהּ גַּזְלָן, וְגַזְלָן אֵינוֹ מְשַׁלֵּם תַּשְׁלוּמֵי אַרְבָּעָה וַחֲמִשָּׁה;

Since the court **has issued a definitive ruling in** this **matter, and he** later **slaughtered or sold** the animal, **he is considered a robber, and a robber does not pay** the **fourfold or fivefold payment.** The difference between a thief, concerning whom the Torah prescribes the double payment and the fourfold or fivefold payment, and a robber, who does not incur these obligations, is that a thief acts stealthily, whereas a robber brazenly uses force to take an item from its owner. Once a court has obligated a thief to make restitution and he has defied this sentence, he is considered a robber, and therefore the fourfold or fivefold payment and its atonement are not applicable to him.

Perek **VII**
Daf **69** Amud **a**

״חַיָּיב אַתָּה לִיתֵּן לוֹ״, טָבַח וּמָכַר – מְשַׁלֵּם תַּשְׁלוּמֵי אַרְבָּעָה וַחֲמִשָּׁה, מַאי טַעֲמָא? כֵּיוָן דְּלָא פַּסְקָה מִילְּתָא אַכַּתִּי גַּנָּב הוּא!

Rava continues: But if the court says to the thief only: **You are obligated to give** the stolen animal back **to** its owner,[H] without actually ordering him to pay, and **he** subsequently **slaughtered or sold** the animal, **he pays the fourfold or fivefold payment. What is the reason** for this? **Since** the court **has not issued a definitive ruling** in this **matter, he is still** considered **a thief** rather than a robber.

לָא צְרִיכָא, דְּאָמְרִי לֵיהּ ״חַיָּיב אַתָּה לִיתֵּן לוֹ״.

The Gemara answers: **No,** this is not a challenge to the ruling of Reish Lakish. It is **necessary** for the *baraita* to state the *halakha* in a case **where they say to him** only: **You are obligated to give** the stolen animal back **to** its owner. Consequently, he remains categorized as a thief.

גּוּפָא, אָמַר רַבִּי יוֹחָנָן: גָּזַל וְלֹא נִתְיָיאֲשׁוּ הַבְּעָלִים – שְׁנֵיהֶם אֵינָן יְכוֹלִים לְהַקְדִּישׁ, זֶה לְפִי שֶׁאֵינוֹ שֶׁלּוֹ, וְזֶה לְפִי שֶׁאֵינוֹ בִּרְשׁוּתוֹ. וּמִי אָמַר רַבִּי יוֹחָנָן הָכִי? וְהָאָמַר רַבִּי יוֹחָנָן: הֲלָכָה כִּסְתָם מִשְׁנָה,

§ The Gemara returns to **the** matter **itself. Rabbi Yoḥanan says:** If one **stole** an item **and the owner has not** yet **despaired** of recovering it, **neither of them is able to consecrate** it. **This** one, the thief, cannot consecrate it **because it does not belong to him, and that** one, the owner, cannot consecrate it **because it is not in his possession.** The Gemara asks: **And did Rabbi Yoḥanan** actually **say this? But doesn't Rabbi Yoḥanan say:** The *halakha* is invariably in accordance with the ruling of **an unattributed mishna,** i.e., a mishna that states a *halakha* without citing it in the name of a particular Sage?

וּתְנַן: כֶּרֶם רְבָעִי הָיוּ מְצַיְּינִין אוֹתוֹ בְּקוֹזוֹת אֲדָמָה. סִימָנָא כִּי אֲדָמָה, מָה אֲדָמָה אִיכָּא הֲנָאָה מִינַּהּ, אַף הַאי נַמִּי כִּי מִפָּרְקָא שָׁרֵי לְאִיתְהַנּוֹיֵי מִינַּהּ;

And there is a mishna of this kind (*Ma'aser Sheni* 5:1) that contradicts Rabbi Yoḥanan's statement, as **we learned** in a mishna: With regard to **a vineyard in its fourth year, they would demarcate it with clods of earth** [*bikzozot*][NL] placed around it on the ground, to alert people that they may not eat or derive any benefit from its grapes without redeeming them.[H] The Gemara interrupts its quotation of the mishna to explain: This particular **distinguishing mark** of earth is used because a vineyard in its fourth year is **like earth: Just as** with regard to **earth there is** permission to derive **benefit from it** through its cultivation, **so too,** with **this** fruit, **when it has been redeemed** by means of coins, it is likewise **permitted to benefit from it.**

NOTES

Go out and give the stolen animal back to the owner, etc. – צֵא תֵּן לוֹ וכו׳: Once the court has issued a definitive ruling, the animal is considered to be no more than a deposit the owner has given to the thief for safeguarding, and therefore he is deemed responsible for it (Ra'avad).

HALAKHA

Go out and give the stolen animal back to the owner – צֵא תֵּן לוֹ: If a thief stands trial and the judges rule that he must return what he stole, and the thief subsequently slaughters or sells the animal, he is exempt from the fourfold or fivefold payment (Rambam *Sefer Nezikin*, *Hilkhot Geneiva* 2:15).

HALAKHA

You are obligated to give it back to its owner – חַיָּיב אַתָּה לִיתֵּן לוֹ: With regard to a thief who was told by the judges: You are obligated to return what you stole to the owner, and he subsequently sold the animal, he is obligated in the fourfold or fivefold payment. The reason is that the judges' ruling was not definitive, and therefore he is still considered a thief (Rambam *Sefer Nezikin*, *Hilkhot Geneiva* 2:15).

A fourth-year vineyard in the Sabbatical Year – כֶּרֶם רְבָעִי בִּשְׁנַת שְׁמִיטָּה: If one has a fourth-year grapevine in the Sabbatical Year, when everyone is permitted to pick grapes, he should demarcate it with clods of earth so that people should know not to eat the grapes without desacralizing them first. If the grapevine was within its first three years at the time of the Sabbatical Year, the owner should demarcate it with potsherd to publicize that one may not eat these grapes. The pious ones would set aside coins for their fourth-year vines during the Sabbatical Year and say: Any fourth-year fruit picked from these trees shall be desacralized onto these coins. The Ramban does not accept the opinion of the pious ones (Rambam *Sefer Zera'im*, *Hilkhot Ma'aser Sheni VeNeta Revai* 9:7).

NOTES

With regard to a vineyard in its fourth year they would demarcate it with clods of earth – כֶּרֶם רְבָעִי הָיוּ מְצַיְּינִין אוֹתוֹ בְּקוֹזוֹת אֲדָמָה: The commentaries ask: Why does this mishna discuss the demarcation of fourth-year fruit before that of *orla*, which chronologically precedes the fourth year? One answer is that the mishna sought to juxtapose *orla*, which is absolutely prohibited, without any possibility of redemption, to graves, which are similarly prohibited in absolute terms (*Tosefot Rabbeinu Peretz*). Others suggest that the three topics follow a logical progression: Fourth-year fruit is forbidden only for consumption; *orla* is forbidden for both consumption and deriving benefit; and finally a grave also imparts ritual impurity (*Naḥalat Moshe*). Yet others answer simply that this mishna appears in *Ma'aser Sheni*, which discusses the *halakhot* of fourth-year produce, and therefore it is natural that the *tanna* began his discussion of demarcations with fourth-year fruit (*Tosefot HaRosh*).

LANGUAGE

Clods of earth [*kezozot*] – קוֹזוֹת: Apparently from the root *kuf*, *zayin*, *zayin*, akin to the root *kuf*, *tzadi*, *tzadi*, meaning to cut up, alluding to the fact that clods of earth are chunks of earth that have been separated from one another. Some commentaries explain that this refers to pieces of red earth that are easily distinguishable from ordinary earth, and therefore people who see them will realize that they may not eat from the vineyard (*Arukh*).

וְשֶׁל עָרְלָה – בַּחֲרָסִית. סִימָנָא כַּחֲרָסִית, מַה חֲרָסִית שֶׁאֵין הֲנָאָה מִינָּהּ, אַף הַאי דְּלֵית בֵּיהּ הֲנָאָה מִינֵּיהּ;

The Gemara resumes its citation from the mishna: **And** a grapevine **of *orla* is** demarcated **with potsherds** [***ḥarsit***][N] placed around it, to alert people that its grapes may not be eaten nor may any benefit be derived from them at all (see Leviticus 19:23). The Gemara explains: This particular **distinguishing mark** is used because *orla* is **like potsherds: Just as no benefit** is derived **from** potsherd, **so too, no benefit** may be derived **from this** *orla*.

וְשֶׁל קְבָרוֹת – בְּסִיד. סִימָנָא דְּחִיוָּר כַּעֲצָמוֹת; וּמְמַחֶה וְשׁוֹפֵךְ. כִּי הֵיכִי דְּנִיחֲוַור טְפֵי;

The mishna continues: **And** an area **of graves** is demarcated **with lime,**[H] to notify people that the demarcated area is ritually impure and will impart impurity to those who pass over it. The Gemara explains: The reason this particular **distinguishing mark** is used is **that** lime is **white, like bones.** The mishna further states: **And** one **dissolves** the lime in water **and pours** it out around the gravesite. The Gemara explains: This is performed **in order that** the lime **should be whiter** than in its non-dissolved form.

אָמַר רַבָּן שִׁמְעוֹן בֶּן גַּמְלִיאֵל: בַּמֶּה דְּבָרִים אֲמוּרִים – בַּשְּׁבִיעִית. דְּהֶפְקֵר נִינְהוּ,

The Gemara resumes the citation from the mishna: **Rabban Shimon ben Gamliel said: In what case is this statement,** that vineyards of the fourth year and of *orla* require demarcation, **said? During the Sabbatical** Year. The Gemara explains: The reason is **that** all fruit that grows during that year may be taken by anyone (see Leviticus 25:5–6), as in that year all fruit is considered to be **ownerless** property.

אֲבָל בִּשְׁאָר שְׁנֵי שָׁבוּעַ – הַלְעִיטֵהוּ לָרָשָׁע וְיָמוּת;

The mishna continues: **But during the other years of** the Sabbatical **cycle,** when anyone who takes the grapes of another is guilty of theft, there is no requirement to demarcate these vineyards. This is in accordance with the adage: **Feed it to the wicked man and let him die.** That is, one is not required to take precautions to protect the wicked from the consequences of their own sins. Here too, there is no obligation to warn a thief that the grapes he is stealing are prohibited.

וְהַצְּנוּעִין מַנִּיחִין אֶת הַמָּעוֹת, וְאוֹמְרִים: ״כָּל הַנִּלְקָט מִזֶּה מְחוּלָּל עַל הַמָּעוֹת הַלָּלוּ״!

The mishna continues: **But the pious ones would set aside** some **coins**[N] **and say: Anything that was picked from this** vine by passersby **shall be desacralized onto these coins.** These pious ones maintain that the owner can desacralize the grapes despite the fact that they are no longer in his possession. Similarly, contrary to the opinion of Rabbi Yoḥanan, they would claim that an owner can consecrate a stolen item even though it is no longer in his possession. Since this opinion is cited in the mishna without being attributed to any particular Sage, Rabbi Yoḥanan should have accepted this ruling.

וְכִי תֵּימָא: מַאן תְּנָא צְנוּעִין – רַבָּן שִׁמְעוֹן בֶּן גַּמְלִיאֵל, וְרַבִּי יוֹחָנָן כִּסְתַם יְחִידָאָה לָא אָמַר.

And if you would say: Who is the *tanna* that **taught** this practice of the **pious ones** in the mishna? It is **Rabban Shimon ben Gamliel, and Rabbi Yoḥanan did not say** his principle that the *halakha* is always in accordance with **an unattributed** mishna when it follows **an individual** opinion; this suggestion does not alleviate the difficulty.

וְהָאָמַר רַבָּה בַּר בַּר חָנָה אָמַר רַבִּי יוֹחָנָן: כָּל מָקוֹם שֶׁשָּׁנָה רַבָּן שִׁמְעוֹן בֶּן גַּמְלִיאֵל בְּמִשְׁנָתֵנוּ – הֲלָכָה כְּמוֹתוֹ, חוּץ מֵעָרֵב וְצַיְדָּן וּרְאָיָה אַחֲרוֹנָה!

The Gemara explains: **But doesn't Rabba bar bar Ḥana say** that **Rabbi Yoḥanan says: Wherever Rabban Shimon ben Gamliel taught** a statement **in** the corpus of **our Mishna, the *halakha* is in accordance with his** opinion, **except for** the case of the responsibility of the **guarantor** (see *Bava Batra* 173b), and the incident that occurred in the city of **Tzaidan** (see *Gittin* 74a), **and** the dispute with regard to **evidence** in the **final** disagreement[N] (see *Sanhedrin* 31a). Consequently, even if the opinion of the pious ones was cited by Rabban Shimon ben Gamliel, Rabbi Yoḥanan should have accepted it as authoritative.

NOTES

Potsherds [*ḥarsit*] – חֲרָסִית: Some commentaries explain that *ḥarsit* refers to broken pieces of pottery, as translated here (Rashi; Meiri). Others maintain that *ḥarsit* is pottery that has been ground up into dust, while others say the term refers to a kind of earth that is infertile and unusable for agriculture (*Tosafot*; Rabbeinu Tam; Rashba). Similarly, the *ge'onim* define it as clay-like earth from which bricks and earthenware are made.

The Rambam in his Commentary on the Mishna states that it refers to burnt clay. He also provides an explanation as to why this particular substance is used for *orla*, rather than the clods used for the fourth-year fruit: Since *orla* is a more serious prohibition than fourth-year produce, it is marked with a substance that is more permanent and less likely to dissolve over time. The Jerusalem Talmud explains that *ḥarsit* has a lighter color than clods of dirt, and the lime used to mark graves is lighter still.

But the pious ones would set aside some coins – וְהַצְּנוּעִין מַנִּיחִין אֶת הַמָּעוֹת: The early commentaries discuss whether the pious ones did this in the Sabbatical Year, to protect honest people who were fully entitled to pick grapes from any vine, or if they did so even during other years, when those picking the grapes would be thieves. Some write that as these people were pious, they did not mind if passersby occasionally took some grapes, and therefore those who did so were not really thieves. Consequently, the pious ones assisted them by redeeming the grapes on their behalf (Meiri).

A guarantor, Tzaidan, and the evidence in the final disagreement – עָרֵב וְצַיְדָּן וּרְאָיָה אַחֲרוֹנָה: These three *halakhot* are the only cases in which Rabbi Yoḥanan holds that the *halakha* is not in accordance with the opinion of Rabban Shimon ben Gamliel in a mishna. The issue of under what circumstances the creditor can collect from the guarantor is a dispute between the Sages and Rabban Shimon ben Gamliel (see *Bava Batra* 103b). The reference to Tzaidan concerns an incident recorded in tractate *Gittin* (74a). The last issue is the subject of a dispute between the Sages and Rabban Shimon ben Gamliel with regard to evidence brought by a litigant after a judgment has already been rendered (see *Sanhedrin* 31a).

HALAKHA

And an area of graves is demarcated with lime – וְשֶׁל קְבָרוֹת בְּסִיד: If one comes across a grave, a corpse, or anything that conveys ritual impurity to those who pass over it, he must place a distinguishing mark at that spot, to alert others to the source of impurity. The site is demarcated by dissolving lime in water and pouring the mixture over the place of impurity (Rambam *Sefer Tahara, Hilkhot Tumat Met* 8:9).

אָמְרִי: לָא תֵּימָא "כָּל הַנִּלְקָט מִזֶּה", אֶלָּא אֵימָא: "כָּל הַמִּתְלַקֵּט מִזֶּה".

The Sages **say,** in explanation of the opinion of Rabbi Yoḥanan: When quoting the declaration of the pious ones, **do not say** in the past tense: **Anything that was picked from this** vine by passersby shall be desacralized onto these coins. **Rather, say: Anything that will be picked from this** vine[N] shall be desacralized onto these coins. In other words, the desacralizing is performed before the fruit is picked, while it is still in the full possession of the owner of the vine.

וּמִי אֲמַר רַבִּי יוֹחָנָן הָכִי? וְהָאָמַר רַבִּי יוֹחָנָן: צְנוּעִין וְרַבִּי דּוֹסָא אָמְרוּ דָּבָר אֶחָד, וְרַבִּי דּוֹסָא "נִלְקָט" קָאָמַר.

The Gemara asks: **And did Rabbi Yoḥanan** actually **say such** a ruling? Could Rabbi Yoḥanan agree to this reformulation of the declaration of the pious ones? **But doesn't Rabbi Yoḥanan say: The pious ones and Rabbi Dosa said the same thing,** i.e., their opinions are equivalent? **And Rabbi Dosa says** that this declaration is formulated in the past tense, as: Anything **that was picked.**

דְּתַנְיָא, רַבִּי יְהוּדָה אוֹמֵר: שַׁחֲרִית בַּעַל הַבַּיִת עוֹמֵד וְאוֹמֵר: "כָּל שֶׁיִּלְקְטוּ עֲנִיִּים הַיּוֹם יְהֵא הֶפְקֵר".

As it is taught in a *baraita* that **Rabbi Yehuda says:** In the **morning the homeowner,** i.e., the owner of a field, **stands and says: Anything that the poor will pick today** that is not rightfully theirs **shall** hereby **be** considered **ownerless** property.[N] The poor are entitled to glean leftover grain from a field after it is harvested (Leviticus 23:22). Yet there are many *halakhot* involved in determining what produce they are entitled to take, and not all poor people are learned enough to know these *halakhot*. Consequently, there will inevitably be poor people who will take a certain amount of grain to which they are not entitled. For this reason, the owner of the field should relinquish, in advance, ownership over whatever the poor might unlawfully take.

רַבִּי דּוֹסָא אוֹמֵר: לְעִיתּוֹתֵי עֶרֶב אוֹמֵר: "כָּל שֶׁלִּקְטוּ עֲנִיִּים יְהֵא הֶפְקֵר"!

Rabbi Dosa says: This is not the correct practice. Rather, **toward evening**[N] the owner should **say: Anything that the poor picked** today that is not rightfully theirs **shall** hereby **be** considered **ownerless** property. Since Rabbi Yoḥanan stated that the opinions of the pious ones and Rabbi Dosa are the same, this indicates that the declaration of the pious ones was in the past tense, which means that they permitted redemption of fourth-year produce after it was already stolen. If so, the question remains: Why did Rabbi Yoḥanan not accept the ruling of the pious ones as authoritative?

אֵיפּוּךְ דְּרַבִּי יְהוּדָה לְרַבִּי דּוֹסָא, וְרַבִּי דּוֹסָא לְרַבִּי יְהוּדָה. אַמַּאי אָפְכַתְּ מַתְנִיתָא? אַפְכָהּ לְרַבִּי יוֹחָנָן, וְאֵימָא: צְנוּעִין וְרַבִּי יְהוּדָה אָמְרוּ דָּבָר אֶחָד!

The Gemara answers: **Reverse** the opinion **of Rabbi Yehuda with** that of **Rabbi Dosa, and** that **of Rabbi Dosa with** that of **Rabbi Yehuda.** According to this new version of the *baraita*, Rabbi Dosa does not permit the owner of an item to exercise any control over it after it has been stolen from him. The Gemara asks: **Why do you reverse the *baraita*** to avoid a contradiction between the statements of Rabbi Yoḥanan? It is better to **reverse** the statement of **Rabbi Yoḥanan** himself, **and say** that he actually stated: **The pious ones and Rabbi Yehuda said the same thing,** and leave the *baraita* intact.

אָמְרִי: לָא סַגְיָא דְּלָא מִתְהַפְכַת מַתְנִיתָא, דִּבְהָא מַתְנִיתִין קָתָנֵי דְּאִית לֵיהּ לְרַבִּי יְהוּדָה בְּרֵירָה, וּשְׁמַעִינַן לֵיהּ לְרַבִּי יְהוּדָה בְּעָלְמָא דְּלֵית לֵיהּ בְּרֵירָה; דִּתְנַן:

The Gemara **says: There is no alternative, as** one **cannot** do otherwise than **to reverse the *baraita*,** as that would mean **that in this *baraita* it teaches that Rabbi Yehuda holds** that there is a principle of retroactive **designation.**[NB] **And we have heard** elsewhere **that Rabbi Yehuda generally does not accept** the principle of retroactive **designation, as we learned** in a mishna (*Demai* 7:4):

NOTES

Anything that will be picked from this vine, etc. – כָּל הַמִּתְלַקֵּט מִזֶּה וכו׳: According to this formulation, the desacralizing of the grapes occurs when they are still attached to the vine. The commentaries ask: If desacralizing can be performed while the fruit is still attached, why does the owner not simply desacralize all the grapes of the vineyard at this time, as he will have to do this at some point anyway? *Tosafot* answer that the owner may wish to bring his fruit to Jerusalem rather than desacralize it. Some commentaries, following the Jerusalem Talmud, rule that it is in fact not possible to desacralize grapes that are attached to the vine (Rambam *Sefer Zera'im, Hilkhot Ma'aser Sheni VeNeta Revai* 9:2).

Anything that the poor will pick today shall be ownerless property – כָּל שֶׁיִּלְקְטוּ עֲנִיִּים הַיּוֹם יְהֵא הֶפְקֵר: The Sages determined that when the Torah (Leviticus 19:9) decrees that missed stalks of grain must be left for the poor to glean, this applies only if one or two stalks escape the sickle's cut; if there are three or more they belong to the owner of the field (*Pe'a* 6:5). If the owner is concerned that there may be poor people who do not know this *halakha*, he can issue the declaration of relinquishment of ownership described here in the Gemara to enable them to avoid transgressing.

Toward evening – לְעִיתּוֹתֵי עֶרֶב: The commentaries note that Rabbi Dosa agrees that the owner could just as well make this declaration in the morning, by saying: Whatever the poor people will pick today that is beyond their allowance shall be deemed ownerless as soon as it is picked. The reason Rabbi Dosa suggested that one should issue this declaration in the evening is that if the poor would become aware that the owner relinquished everything they will pick during the day, they might deliberately take more than the amount to which they are entitled (*Tosafot*).

It teaches that Rabbi Yehuda holds that there is a principle of retroactive designation – קָתָנֵי דְּאִית לֵיהּ לְרַבִּי יְהוּדָה בְּרֵירָה: This conclusion is derived from the fact that the owner relinquishes the produce that will be picked in the future, and these items are unidentifiable at the time of the declaration. Consequently, the declaration would be effective only if one accepts the principle of retroactive designation (Rashi).

BACKGROUND

Retroactive designation – בְּרֵירָה: The Sages disagreed with regard to the validity of the principle that an item that was not explicitly designated initially for a certain purpose may retroactively be considered as though it had been designated for that purpose from the outset. This could apply, for example, in a case where one declares that the tithe from his granary will consist of the last tenth remaining after the rest of the produce has been consumed. If the principle of retroactive designation is accepted, his separation of the tithe is valid, as although the tithe he designated did not exist as a distinct, separate entity when he issued his statement, the tithe is retroactively considered that remaining tenth from the outset. There is a dispute among the Sages whether the principle of retroactive designation is accepted as *halakha*. In practice, the principle is generally accepted with regard to questions involving rabbinic law but not concerning matters of Torah law.

הַלּוֹקֵחַ יַיִן מִבֵּין הַכּוּתִים אוֹמֵר: ״שְׁנֵי לוּגִּין שֶׁאֲנִי עָתִיד לְהַפְרִישׁ הֲרֵי הֵן תְּרוּמָה, עֲשָׂרָה – מַעֲשֵׂר רִאשׁוֹן, תִּשְׁעָה – מַעֲשֵׂר שֵׁנִי״, וּמֵיחֵל וְשׁוֹתֶה מִיָּד, דִּבְרֵי רַבִּי מֵאִיר,

In the case of **one who purchases wine**[H] **from among the Samaritans** [*Kutim*],[BN] if there is reason to suspect that *teruma* and tithes were not separated, and he cannot separate them before the start of Shabbat,[N] he acts as follows. If there are one hundred *log* of wine in the barrels, he **says: Two *log* that I will separate in the future are *teruma*,** as the mandated average measure of *teruma* is one-fiftieth; **ten** *log* are **first tithe;** and a tenth of the remainder, **nine** *log,* are **second tithe.**[N] **And he desacralizes**[N] the second tithe that he will separate in the future by transferring its sanctity onto money, **and he may drink** the wine **immediately,** relying on the separation that he will perform later. This is **the statement of Rabbi Meir.**

רַבִּי יְהוּדָה וְרַבִּי יוֹסֵי וְרַבִּי שִׁמְעוֹן אוֹסְרִין.

Rabbi Yehuda, Rabbi Yosei, and Rabbi Shimon prohibit one from doing so. The objection of these three Sages is presumably that this arrangement relies on the principle of retroactive designation, as at the time of the declaration the identity of the particular portions of wine that will be *teruma* and tithes is unknown, and these Sages do not accept this principle. It is apparent from this mishna that Rabbi Yehuda does not accept retroactive designation, and therefore he cannot be the one who said that the owner of the field may issue his declaration of relinquishment in the morning.

אָמְרִי: סוֹף סוֹף אַמַּאי קָא אֲפַכְתְּ לָהּ לְמַתְנִיתִין – מִשּׁוּם דְּקַשְׁיָא דְּרַבִּי יְהוּדָה אַדְּרַבִּי יְהוּדָה, הָשְׁתָּא נַמִּי קַשְׁיָא דְּרַבִּי יוֹחָנָן אַדְּרַבִּי יוֹחָנָן;

The Gemara **says: Ultimately, why do you reverse the *baraita*** that contains the opinions of Rabbi Yehuda and Rabbi Dosa? It is **because** there is **a difficulty** due to the contradiction between one statement **of Rabbi Yehuda** and another statement **of Rabbi Yehuda. Now too,** although you have reversed the *baraita*, a similar problem remains, as there is **a difficulty** due to the contradiction between one statement **of Rabbi Yoḥanan** and another statement **of Rabbi Yoḥanan.**

דְּאָמְרַתְּ לְרַבִּי יוֹחָנָן: לָא תֵּימָא ״כָּל הַנִּלְקָט״ אֶלָּא אֵימָא ״כָּל הַמִּתְלַקֵּט״, אַלְמָא אִית לֵיהּ בְּרֵירָה. וְהָא רַבִּי יוֹחָנָן לֵית לֵיהּ בְּרֵירָה,

As you said, according to the opinion of **Rabbi Yoḥanan: Do not say** that **anything that was picked** from this vine by passersby shall be desacralized onto these coins. **Rather, say** that **anything that will be picked from this** vine shall be desacralized onto these coins. **Apparently,** Rabbi Yoḥanan here **accepts** the principle of retroactive **designation. But** it is established that **Rabbi Yoḥanan does not accept** the principle of retroactive **designation.**

HALAKHA

One who purchases wine, etc. – הַלּוֹקֵחַ יַיִן וכו׳: If one has one hundred *log* of wine that is completely untithed and says: Two *log* that I will later separate from this wine shall be *teruma*, ten *log* shall be first tithe and nine *log* shall be second tithe, he must actually separate the *teruma* and tithes before he may drink the wine, in accordance with the opinion of Rabbi Yosei and Rabbi Yehuda (Rambam *Sefer Zera'im, Hilkhot Ma'aser* 7:1).

BACKGROUND

Samaritans [*Kutim*] – כּוּתִים: *Kutim* is the name given to those peoples who were exiled to Eretz Yisrael by Sennacherib, king of Assyria, in order to replace the exiles from the kingdom of Israel. They settled in Samaria [*Shomron*] and were therefore also known as Samaritans [*Shomronim*]. These immigrants eventually took upon themselves several of the Torah's mitzvot (see II Kings, chapter 17). Relations between the Samaritans and the Jews deteriorated at the beginning of the Second Temple period, during the time of Ezra and Nehemiah.

The Samaritans later established a center of worship on Mount Gerizim, claiming that the sanctity of the mountain is established in the book of Deuteronomy. Several generations of Sages recognized Samaritans as Jewish, going so far as to declare them more punctilious in their observance of their selected mitzvot than the Jews themselves. Later, as the Samaritans continued to distance themselves from the Jewish people in virtually every regard, they were ultimately accorded the legal status of gentiles. The community of Samaritans in modern-day Israel numbers roughly seven hundred individuals. They reside in two locations, Mount Gerizim and Holon, and enjoy cordial relations with both Jews and Arabs.

NOTES

From among the Samaritans – מִבֵּין הַכּוּתִים: The early commentaries discuss why this *halakha* was taught specifically with regard to wine purchased from Samaritans, as opposed to the topic of the tractate, *demai*, doubtfully tithed produce, which could have been purchased from any individual who is not meticulous about tithing [*am ha'aretz*]. They answer that several notable *halakhot* are conveyed through using the specific example of Samaritans: One *halakha* is that although the Samaritans were known to be meticulous about tithing their produce, they did not refrain from selling untithed produce to others, and therefore one who purchased produce from a Samaritan would have to take care of this matter himself. Another point is that when purchasing produce from an *am ha'aretz* there is no requirement to separate *teruma*, as it is assumed that even those who are not meticulous about tithing at least separate *teruma*; this assumption is not necessarily true of Samaritans, as the mishna indicates. Furthermore, as wine purchased from Samaritans is considered produce that is definitely not tithed, the declaration described here would have to take place before twilight Friday afternoon, whereas doubtfully tithed produce can be tithed during twilight (Rashba).

The commentaries note that this mishna was taught before the Sages declared that the Samaritans should be regarded as gentiles with regard to all halakhic matters. After that decision was taken, it became prohibited to drink their wine altogether, just as it is prohibited to drink the wine of a gentile (Meiri).

Before Shabbat – לִפְנֵי שַׁבָּת: It is prohibited by rabbinic law to separate tithes on Shabbat, as this has the appearance of preparing an item that was unfit to be eaten before Shabbat. Furthermore, the separation of tithes is similar to consecration, which is prohibited on Shabbat because it resembles commerce.

Ten are first tithe, nine are second tithe – עֲשָׂרָה מַעֲשֵׂר רִאשׁוֹן תִּשְׁעָה מַעֲשֵׂר שֵׁנִי: Although both tithes are a tenth of the produce, the second tithe is only 9 percent of the total, as after removing ten *log* for the first tithe there are only ninety *log* left. In reality, the second tithe is slightly less than 9 percent and the first is slightly less than 10 percent, since after separation of *teruma* only 98 percent remains and after the first tithe is removed there is 88.2 percent left. The mishna does not speak in terms of these precise calculations.

He desacralizes [*meiḥel*] – מֵיחֵל: This translation, which is in accordance with Rashi's interpretation, assumes a derivation from the root, *ḥet, lamed, lamed,* meaning secular. He explains that the desacralizing should be performed before Shabbat, as any steps that can be taken to permit the consumption of the wine should be performed in advance. Many early commentaries disagree with this interpretation, maintaining that redemption of second tithe cannot be undertaken until the second tithe has already been specifically designated. They therefore explain that the term means: To dilute a drink, from the root *mem, heh, lamed* (Rabbeinu Tam; Rav Hai Gaon). The Rambam gives a third explanation for the word: To start, from the root *tav, ḥet, lamed,* so that this phrase in the mishna means that one may begin to drink immediately.

דְּאָמַר רַב אַסִּי אָמַר רַבִּי יוֹחָנָן: הָאַחִין שֶׁחָלְקוּ – לָקוֹחוֹת הֵן, וּמַחֲזִירִין זֶה לָזֶה בַּיּוֹבֵל!

As Rav Asi says that **Rabbi Yoḥanan says: Brothers who divided** property[H] received as an inheritance **are** considered **purchasers**[N] from each other, **and** as purchasers of land **they must return** the portions **to each other in the Jubilee** Year,[B] at which point they may redistribute the property. This demonstrates that Rabbi Yoḥanan does not hold that it is retroactively clarified that each brother's portion was designated for him directly upon their father's death, but rather all the land was considered joint property until the brothers traded or bought their respective portions from each other at the time of the distribution of the estate.

אֶלָּא, לְעוֹלָם "כָּל הַנִּלְקָט".

In light of this objection, the Gemara retracts its previous assertion that Rabbi Yoḥanan reformulated the declaration of the pious ones. **Rather,** the pious ones **actually** declared in the past tense: **Anything that was picked** from this vine by passersby shall be desacralized onto these coins, i.e., the desacralizing took place after the grapes were stolen. If so, the question remains: Why did Rabbi Yoḥanan not accept the opinion of the pious ones, but instead ruled that the owner of an item cannot consecrate it after it has been stolen?

וְרַבִּי יוֹחָנָן סְתָמָא אַחֲרִינָא אַשְׁכַּח, דִּתְנַן: אֵין הַגּוֹנֵב אַחַר הַגַּנָּב מְשַׁלֵּם תַּשְׁלוּמֵי כֶפֶל; אַמַּאי? בִּשְׁלָמָא לַגַּנָּב רִאשׁוֹן לֹא מְשַׁלֵּם – "וְגֻנַּב מִבֵּית הָאִישׁ" וְלֹא מִבֵּית הַגַּנָּב, אֶלָּא לַבְּעָלִים נְשַׁלֵּם!

The Gemara answers: **Rabbi Yoḥanan found a different unattributed** mishna, which contradicts the opinion of the pious ones. **As we learned** in the mishna here (62b): **One who steals** an item **after a thief** has already stolen it, i.e., one who steals a stolen item, **does not pay** the **double payment** to the thief or to the prior owner. **Why** not? **Granted** that **he does not pay to the first thief, as** the verse states: **"And it was stolen from the house of the man;** if the thief shall be found he shall pay double" (Exodus 22:6), which indicates that the double payment applies in the case of an item "stolen from the house of the man," i.e., from the owner's jurisdiction, but **not** to an item stolen from **the thief's house. But let him pay** the double payment **to the owner,** as it presumably still belonged to the owner when the second thief stole it.

אֶלָּא לָאו שְׁמַע מִינָּהּ: זֶה לְפִי שֶׁאֵינוֹ שֶׁלּוֹ, וְזֶה לְפִי שֶׁאֵינוֹ בִּרְשׁוּתוֹ.

Rather, must one **not conclude from** this that a stolen item is not under the full jurisdiction of either the owner or the thief? It is not under the jurisdiction of **this** one, the first thief, **because it does not belong to him, and** it is not under the jurisdiction of **that** one, the owner, **because it is not in his possession.** Therefore, neither of them can consecrate the stolen item.

וּמַאי חָזֵית דְּאָזֵיל בָּתַר הַהִיא סְתָמָא? לִיעֲבֵיד כִּי הַאי סְתָמָא דִּצְנוּעִין!

The Gemara asks: Granted that this unattributed mishna disagrees with the mishna that cites the pious ones, **but what did you see** that led you to **follow that unattributed** mishna, the one that discusses the double payment? **Let** Rabbi Yoḥanan **act,** i.e., rule, **in accordance with this unattributed** mishna, which states the practice **of the pious ones.** On what basis did he choose one mishna over the other?

מִשּׁוּם דִּמְסַיַּיע לֵיהּ קְרָא: "וְאִישׁ כִּי יַקְדִּשׁ אֶת בֵּיתוֹ קֹדֶשׁ לַה'", מַה בֵּיתוֹ בִּרְשׁוּתוֹ, אַף כֹּל בִּרְשׁוּתוֹ.

The Gemara answers: Rabbi Yoḥanan followed the mishna that discusses the double payment **because** there is **a verse** that **supports it: "And when a man shall sanctify his house to be holy to the Lord"** (Leviticus 27:14), from which it is derived: **Just as one's house is in his possession, so too anything** that one consecrates must **be in his possession,** excluding items that have been stolen from him.

HALAKHA

Brothers who divided property – הָאַחִין שֶׁחָלְקוּ: Brothers who divided between them the property they inherited from their father are considered purchasers, and they must return the property to each other in the Jubilee Year. Nevertheless, the original division of property is not voided at that time (Rambam *Sefer Zera'im, Hilkhot Shemitta VeYovel* 11:20).

BACKGROUND

Jubilee Year – יוֹבֵל: The Jubilee Year occurred once every fifty years up to the end of the First Temple era. In the Jubilee Year, all immovable property that was purchased during those fifty years returns to its original owner. In the case of brothers who divided their father's estate, according to the opinion that they are deemed purchasers from one another they must redistribute the estate in the Jubilee Year.

NOTES

Brothers who divided property are considered purchasers – הָאַחִין שֶׁחָלְקוּ לָקוֹחוֹת הֵן: Since there is no retroactive clarification according to Rabbi Yoḥanan, all the possessions of the deceased are considered the joint property of the heirs, and the division of portions among the heirs is categorized as a sale. For this reason the portions must be returned to joint ownership in the Jubilee Year. The Rambam writes that after the portions have been returned to joint ownership, each heir takes back the portion he had taken originally; a totally new division of the property is not undertaken (Rambam *Sefer Zera'im, Hilkhot Shemitta VeYovel* 11:20). Others disagree with this ruling.

אֲמַר אַבַּיֵי: אִי לָאו דַּאֲמַר רַבִּי יוֹחָנָן: צְנוּעִין וְרַבִּי דּוֹסָא אָמְרוּ דָּבָר אֶחָד, הֲוָה אָמֵינָא: צְנוּעִין אִית לְהוּ דְּרַבִּי דּוֹסָא, וְרַבִּי דּוֹסָא לֵית לֵיהּ דִּצְנוּעִין.

§ **Abaye said: If Rabbi Yoḥanan had not said** that **the pious ones and Rabbi Dosa said the same thing,** i.e., their rulings are identical, **I would say** that **the pious ones accept** the opinion **of Rabbi Dosa,**[N] **but Rabbi Dosa does not accept** the opinion **of the pious ones.**

צְנוּעִין אִית לְהוּ דְּרַבִּי דּוֹסָא; וּמַה בְּגַנָּב עֲבַדוּ רַבָּנַן תַּקַּנְתָּא, עֲנִיִּים צְרִיכָא לְמֵימַר? רַבִּי דּוֹסָא לֵית לֵיהּ דִּצְנוּעִין; עֲנִיִּים הוּא דַּעֲבַדוּ לְהוּ רַבָּנַן תַּקַּנְתָּא, אֲבָל גַּנָּב לָא עֲבַדוּ לֵיהּ רַבָּנַן תַּקַּנְתָּא.

Abaye elaborates: **The pious ones accept** the opinion **of Rabbi Dosa,** for the following reason: **And if the Sages instituted an ordinance for** the sake of **a thief,** to prevent him from eating unredeemed fourth-year grapes, by allowing the owner to desacralize produce that is no longer in his possession, does it **need to be said** that they did so for the sake of innocent **poor people,** as Rabbi Dosa claimed? Conversely, **Rabbi Dosa does not accept** the opinion **of the pious ones,** as he says: It is for the sake of **poor people that the Sages instituted an ordinance; but the Sages did not institute an ordinance for** the sake of **a thief,** in line with the aforementioned principle: Feed it to the wicked man and let him die.

אֲמַר רָבָא: אִי לָאו דְּאָמַר רַבִּי יוֹחָנָן: צְנוּעִין וְרַבִּי דּוֹסָא אָמְרוּ דָּבָר אֶחָד, הֲוָה אָמֵינָא: מַאן תְּנָא צְנוּעִין? רַבִּי מֵאִיר הִיא;

In a similar vein, **Rava said: If Rabbi Yoḥanan had not said** that **the pious ones and Rabbi Dosa said the same thing, I would say** that there is a fundamental difference between the cases of fourth-year produce and gleanings taken by the poor, as one could claim: **Who** is the *tanna* who **taught** the ruling of the **pious ones? It is Rabbi Meir.**

לָאו אָמַר רַבִּי מֵאִיר מַעֲשֵׂר מָמוֹן גָּבוֹהַּ הוּא, וַאֲפִילּוּ הָכִי לְעִנְיַן פִּדְיָיה אוֹקְמֵיהּ רַחֲמָנָא בִּרְשׁוּתֵיהּ, דִּכְתִיב: ״וְאִם גָּאֹל יִגְאַל אִישׁ מִמַּעַשְׂרוֹ חֲמִשִׁתוֹ יֹסֵף עָלָיו״,

Doesn't Rabbi Meir say that second **tithe is property** belonging to the **Most High,**[H] rather than the possession of the one who separated it from his produce, **and even so, with regard to redemption** of the second tithe **the Merciful One establishes it in his possession? As it is written** concerning the second tithe: **"And if a man will redeem any of his tithe, he shall add to it its fifth part"** (Leviticus 27:31).

קַרְיֵיהּ רַחֲמָנָא ״מַעַשְׂרוֹ״ וּמוֹסִיף חוֹמֶשׁ.

Although according to the opinion of Rabbi Meir, second tithe does not belong to the owner of the produce from which it was separated, nevertheless, with regard to redemption **the Merciful One** does distinguish between a stranger and one who separated it from his produce, as the Torah **refers to** the second tithe as **"his tithe" and** thereby decrees that **he,** the owner of the crop from which it is separated, can redeem it by **adding one-fifth**[N] to its value, but no one else can do so. This indicates that although second-tithe produce is not in fact owned by the person, the Torah treats him as the owner of the produce.

כֶּרֶם רְבָעִי נַמִי גָּמַר ״קֹדֶשׁ״ ״קֹדֶשׁ״ מִמַּעֲשֵׂר, כְּתִיב הָכָא: ״קֹדֶשׁ הִלּוּלִים״, וּכְתִיב גַּבֵּי מַעֲשֵׂר: ״וְכָל מַעְשַׂר הָאָרֶץ מִזֶּרַע הָאָרֶץ מִפְּרִי הָעֵץ לַה׳ הוּא קֹדֶשׁ״,

With regard to **a fourth-year vineyard as well,** the Sages **derive** many of its *halakhot* **from** a verbal analogy between **second tithe** and fourth-year fruit, based on the use of the word **"holy"** in the context of fourth-year fruit and **"holy"** in the context of second tithe. **It is written here,** concerning fourth-year fruit trees: "And in the fourth year all its fruit shall be **holy, for giving praise** to the Lord" (Leviticus 19:24), **and it is written with regard to second tithe: "And all the tithe of the land, whether of the seed of the land or of the fruit of the tree, is the Lord's; it is holy"** (Leviticus 27:30).

מַה ״קֹדֶשׁ״ דִּכְתִיב גַּבֵּי מַעֲשֵׂר, אַף עַל גַּב דְּמָמוֹן גָּבוֹהַּ הוּא – לְעִנְיַן פִּדְיָיה אוֹקְמֵיהּ רַחֲמָנָא בִּרְשׁוּתֵיהּ, אַף הַאי ״קֹדֶשׁ״ נַמִי דִּכְתִיב גַּבֵּי כֶּרֶם רְבָעִי, אַף עַל גַּב דְּלָאו מָמוֹן דִּידֵיהּ הוּא – לְעִנְיַן אַחוּלֵי אוֹקְמֵיהּ רַחֲמָנָא בִּרְשׁוּתֵיהּ,

From this analogy it is derived: **Just as** in the case of the term **"holy" that is written in connection to** second **tithe, even though it is property** belonging to the **Most High, with regard to redemption the Merciful One establishes it in** the **jurisdiction** of the one who separated it, **so too** in the context of the word **"holy" that is written in connection to** the **fourth-year vineyard, even though it is not his property,** as it belongs to the Most High, **with regard to desacralizing the Merciful One establishes it in** the vineyard owner's **jurisdiction.**

דְּהָא כִּי אִיתֵיהּ בִּרְשׁוּתֵיהּ נַמִי הָא לָאו דִּידֵיהּ הוּא וְהָא מָצֵי מַחֵיל, מִשּׁוּם הָכִי מָצֵי מַחֵיל.

The effect of this determination is **that** even **when** the fruit **is in his jurisdiction it is not his** property, **and yet he is able to desacralize it.** And **due to that** reason the owner of the vineyard **is able to desacralize** the fruit even after a thief has taken it. Even in normal circumstances when one desacralizes his fourth-year fruit he is desacralizing fruit that does not belong to him. Consequently, there is no novelty in the ruling that one can desacralize fruit even after it has been taken by a thief.

NOTES

I would say the pious ones accept the opinion of Rabbi Dosa, etc. – **הֲוָה אָמֵינָא צְנוּעִין אִית לְהוּ דְּרַבִּי דּוֹסָא וכו׳**: According to the reasoning suggested by Abaye, it is only due to the ordinance instituted by the Sages that owners may redeem or relinquish their produce after it has been taken by thieves; without this special allowance it would not have been possible for them to do so. Consequently, this does not contradict Rabbi Yoḥanan's ruling that an owner may not ordinarily consecrate an item after it has been stolen. When Rabbi Yoḥanan himself associated Rabbi Dosa's opinion with that of the pious ones, he indicated that both opinions are based not on a rabbinical ordinance, but on general halakhic principles. If so, this contradicts his ruling that an owner is not considered to have jurisdiction over an item after it is stolen from him.

It is not clear if Abaye, as well as Rava, intended to disagree with Rabbi Yoḥanan or merely to raise a theoretical alternative possibility. This ambiguity apparently underlies the dispute between the Rambam and the Ramban as to whether the *halakha* is in accordance with the opinion of the pious ones or with that of Rabbi Yoḥanan (*Ḥazon Ish*).

The Merciful One refers to the second tithe as his tithe and he can redeem it by adding one-fifth – **קַרְיֵיהּ רַחֲמָנָא מַעַשְׂרוֹ וּמוֹסִיף חוֹמֶשׁ**: The commentaries note that even without mentioning the extra fifth, the Gemara could have proven that the original owner is considered the owner of the second tithe from the fact that he alone can redeem the second-tithe produce, while others cannot do so without his permission. *Tosafot* explain that the *halakha* that he alone can redeem the produce is merely due to the fact that it is in his jurisdiction, whereas the addition of one-fifth is a sign that the produce had fully belonged to him.

HALAKHA

Second tithe is property belonging to the Most High – **מַעֲשֵׂר מָמוֹן גָּבוֹהַּ הוּא**: Second-tithe produce is considered the property of God, in accordance with the opinion of Rabbi Meir (Rambam *Sefer Zera'im, Hilkhot Ma'aser Sheni VeNeta Revai* 3:17).

אֲבָל גַּבֵּי לֶקֶט, כֵּיוָן דְּמָמוֹנָא דִּידֵיהּ, כִּי אִיתֵיהּ בִּרְשׁוּתֵיהּ הוּא דְּמָצֵי מַפְקַר לֵיהּ, כִּי לֵיתֵיהּ בִּרְשׁוּתֵיהּ לָא מָצֵי מַפְקַר לֵיהּ.

But with regard to gleanings of the poor, **since** the extra sheaves that the poor people inadvertently take **are the property of** the owner of the field, it may be claimed that only **when** those sheaves **are in his possession,** i.e., they have not been taken by anyone else, **can he relinquish** his **ownership of** them, whereas **when** they are **no** longer **in his possession he cannot relinquish** his **ownership of** them. Consequently, the pious ones, who permitted redemption of fourth-year produce after it had been stolen, would not necessarily agree with Rabbi Dosa, who allowed the relinquishment of stolen sheaves.

אֲמַר רָבִינָא: אִי לָאו דַּאֲמַר רַבִּי יוֹחָנָן: צְנוּעִין וְרַבִּי דּוֹסָא אָמְרוּ דָּבָר אֶחָד, הֲוָה אָמֵינָא: מַאן תְּנָא צְנוּעִין? רַבִּי דּוֹסָא הִיא, כִּי הֵיכִי דְּלָא תִּקְשֵׁי סְתַם מִשְׁנָה לְרַבִּי יוֹחָנָן, וְרַבִּי יוֹחָנָן

In a similar vein, **Ravina said: If Rabbi Yoḥanan had not said** that **the pious ones and Rabbi Dosa said the same thing, I would say: Who is the** *tanna* who **taught** the opinion of the **pious ones? It is Rabbi Dosa.** I would have said this **so that an unattributed mishna should not** present **a difficulty to** the opinion of **Rabbi Yoḥanan. And** the reason why this would have resolved the difficulty is that **Rabbi Yoḥanan**

Perek **VII**
Daf **70** Amud **a**

כִּסְתַם יְחִידָאָה לָא אֲמַר.

did not say to apply his principle, that the *halakha* is always in accordance with **an unattributed** mishna, in a case where the mishna expresses the opinion of **an individual** Sage. According to this interpretation Rabbi Yoḥanan does not rule in accordance with the mishna, due to the fact that it represents the opinion of an individual Sage, Rabbi Dosa. Rather, he follows the majority opinion. Yet now that Rabbi Yoḥanan said that the pious ones and Rabbi Dosa said the same thing, it cannot be claimed that they are one and the same Sage. Consequently, the ruling of the mishna is evidently accepted by at least two Sages, and therefore the difficulty from the mishna cannot be resolved by assigning it to a single Sage.

אָמְרִי נְהַרְדְּעֵי: לָא כָּתְבִינַן אוֹרַכְתָּא אַמִּטַּלְטְלֵי. אֲמַר רַב אַשִׁי לְאַמֵימָר: מַאי טַעְמָא? אֲמַר לֵיהּ: מִשּׁוּם דְּרַבִּי יוֹחָנָן,

§ The Sages **of Neharde'a**[P] **say: One cannot write a document of authorization** [*orakhta*][L] to assign another to collect a debt or a deposit **of movable property** on his behalf. **Rav Ashi said to Ameimar: What is the reason** for this *halakha*? Ameimar **said to him:** It is **due to** a principle stated **by Rabbi Yoḥanan.**

דְּאָמַר רַבִּי יוֹחָנָן: גָּזַל וְלֹא נִתְיָיאֲשׁוּ הַבְּעָלִים – שְׁנֵיהֶם אֵינָן יְכוֹלִין לְהַקְדִּישׁ, זֶה לְפִי שֶׁאֵינוֹ שֶׁלּוֹ, וְזֶה לְפִי שֶׁאֵינוֹ בִּרְשׁוּתוֹ.

As Rabbi Yoḥanan says: If one **stole** an item **and the owners have not** yet **despaired** of recovering it, **neither of them is able to consecrate** it: **This** one, the thief, cannot consecrate the item **because it does not belong to him, and that** one, the owner, cannot consecrate it **because it is not in his possession.** The granting of authority to collect a debt involves the transfer of ownership of the item or money from the owner to the collector; otherwise the debtor could refuse to convey it to the collector. In the case of movable property, as it is being held by another, it is not in the possession of the owner; just as the owner cannot consecrate this item he cannot transfer ownership of it.

PERSONALITIES

The Sages of Neharde'a – נְהַרְדְּעֵי: It is explained in tractate *Sanhedrin* (17b) that this anonymous attribution is referring to Rav Ḥama, and it may be assumed that this is the meaning here as well. A fourth-generation *amora* in Babylonia, Rav Ḥama apparently lived a long life, as he is depicted as engaging in discussions with Sages of previous generations. Since he was the head of the yeshiva in Neharde'a for over twenty years, some of his *halakhot* are cited as the opinion of the Sages of Neharde'a, without further identification.

LANGUAGE

Document of authorization [*orakhta*] – אוֹרַכְתָּא: In most sources the word is as it appears here, *orakhta*, and this is the version favored by Rabbeinu Tam in his *Sefer HaYashar*. It refers to a document through which one gives permission to another party to take action pertaining to the principal's property. Some sources have instead the word *adrakhta*. This document, also known as *hardafa*, entitles one to pursue [*lirdof*] and seize money owed to him. It is a legal document drafted by the court, authorizing a creditor to locate and take possession of any property belonging to a debtor in repayment of the debt.

איכָּא דְּאָמְרִי, אָמְרִי נְהַרְדְּעֵי: לָא כָּתְבִינַן אוֹרַכְתָּא אַמִּטַּלְטְלֵי דִּכְפַרֵיהּ. טַעֲמָא דִּכְפַרֵיהּ, דְּמֶיחֱזֵי כְּשִׁיקְרָא, אֲבָל לָא כְּפַרֵיהּ – כָּתְבִינַן.

There are those **who state** a different version of this *halakha*. The Sages **of Neharde'a say: One cannot write a document of authorization for** the collection of **movable property that** the bailee or debtor **has denied** owing.[NH] The Gemara infers: According to this version, the only **reason** the document cannot be written is **that** the bailee or debtor **has denied** owing the item, **as** a document written under these circumstances **has the appearance of falsehood,**[N] since the purported owner is transferring ownership of an item over which his own ownership is in doubt. **But** it can be inferred that **if** the bailee or debtor **did not deny** owing the item, **one can write** a document of authorization.

וְאָמְרִי נְהַרְדְּעֵי: אוֹרַכְתָּא דְּלָא כְּתִיב בֵּיהּ "זִיל דּוּן וּזְכֵי וְאַפֵּיק לְנַפְשָׁךְ" – לֵית בֵּיהּ מְשָׁשָׁא. מַאי טַעְמָא? מִשּׁוּם דְּאָמַר לֵיהּ הָאֵיךְ: "לָאו בַּעַל דְּבָרִים דִּידִי אַתְּ".

And the Sages **of Neharde'a state** another *halakha* with regard to this kind of document: **A document of authorization in which it is not written: Go** and **take legal action** against so-and-so **and take possession** of the owed property[H] **and collect it** from him **for yourself, has no substance,** i.e., it is not a valid document. **What is the reason** for this? It is **because the other** party, the bailee or debtor, **can say** to the collector who presents a document without this clause: **I am not legally answerable to you;** I am willing to deal only with the person to whom the item is owed. To avoid this situation, the authorization document must transfer actual ownership of the item to the collector, who is now claiming it for himself.

אֲמַר אַבַּיֵי: וְאִי כְּתִיב בֵּיהּ לְמֶחֱצָה לִשְׁלִישׁ וְלִרְבִיעַ – מִיגּוֹ דְּמִשְׁתַּעֵי דִּינָא אַפַּלְגָּא, מִשְׁתַּעֵי דִּינָא אַכּוּלָּהּ.

Abaye said: And if it is written in the document that the owner transferred ownership **of** only **half** of the item to the collector, **or a third or a quarter** of it, this is sufficient. The reason is that **since** the bailee or debtor must **relate** to the **judgment,** i.e., engage in litigation with the collector, **over the half**[H] or third or quarter of the item that has been transferred to the collector, he must **relate** to the **judgment concerning all of it.**

NOTES

For the collection of movable property that the bailee or debtor has denied owing – אַמִּטַּלְטְלֵי דִּכְפַרֵיהּ: The reason an authorization cannot be issued in this case is that the ownership of the item to be collected is in dispute, and therefore a document attesting to the transfer of ownership from the purported owner to the one collecting the item has the appearance of falsehood. According to this version, the statement of the Sages of Neharde'a is unrelated to Rabbi Yoḥanan's *halakha*, and consequently one may authorize another in writing to collect an item, as Rabbi Yoḥanan's ruling about an item not in one's possession was issued only with regard to consecration, for which there is a direct basis in the Torah for the requirement that the one consecrating an item must possess it (Rashba). According to other early commentaries, Rabbi Yoḥanan's *halakha* does apply to other forms of transfer of ownership, including the case of selling an item that one owns but is not in his possession.

It has the appearance of falsehood – דְּמֶיחֱזֵי כְּשִׁיקְרָא: This concept is mentioned several times in the Talmud. According to this principle, a document may not be written and signed by witnesses if it is not accurate at the time, even if it will become correct at a later date. It should be noted that in several places the Gemara rejects this principle (see *Sefer HaYashar*).

HALAKHA

A document of authorization for the collection of movable property that the bailee or debtor has denied owing – אוֹרַכְתָּא אַמִּטַּלְטְלֵי דִּכְפַרֵיהּ: If one claims that he owns movable property or money that is currently in the possession of another, and the latter denies that he owes it to him, the claimant may not write a document of authorization to enable a third party to collect the item, because this document has the appearance of falsehood. This ruling is in accordance with the second version of the statement of the Sages of Neharde'a, following the principle that the *halakha* is generally in accordance with the second version of a statement presented by the Gemara. Later, the *ge'onim* instituted that an authorization may be issued to collect a debt even if the party who supposedly owes the money has denied the claim. This applies only with regard to debts recorded in a promissory note, not for loans by oral agreement. Others maintain that one may issue an authorization to collect loans by oral agreement even if the payee has denied owing the money, as they claim that the concept of appearance of falsehood does not apply in this case (Rambam *Sefer Kinyan, Hilkhot Sheluḥin VeShutafin* 3:6; *Shulḥan Arukh, Ḥoshen Mishpat* 123:1).

Go and take legal action against so-and-so and take possession of the owed property – זִיל דּוּן וּזְכֵי: If one has real estate entrusted to another, or if he has movable property that another is safeguarding, and he wishes to appoint an agent to take legal action and remove the property from the holder's possession, he may write a document of authorization so that the agent can do so. The document must contain a clause in which the owner transfers ownership of the property in question to the agent and says to him: Take legal action and take possession of the property and remove it from his possession for yourself. If the owner does not write this, the party holding the item in question can say to the agent that he is unwilling to engage in legal proceedings with him or with anyone other than the owner of the item (Rambam *Sefer Kinyan, Hilkhot Sheluḥin VeShutafin* 3:1; *Shulḥan Arukh, Ḥoshen Mishpat* 122:4).

Since the bailee or debtor must relate to the judgment over half – מִיגּוֹ דְּמִשְׁתַּעֵי דִּינָא אַפַּלְגָּא: If one authorizes another to collect a third or a quarter of a debt owed to him, the agent may engage in legal action for the entire sum, in accordance with the opinion of Abaye. Some say that this *halakha* applies only if the owner of the item actually transfers ownership of the item to the collector, whereas if he merely tells him: A hundred dinars of that which so-and-so owes me shall be yours, the agent may engage in legal action only for the specified amount (Rambam *Sefer Kinyan, Hilkhot Sheluḥin VeShutafin* 3:2 and Ra'avad there; *Shulḥan Arukh, Ḥoshen Mishpat* 122:5).

אָמַר אַמֵימָר: אִי תָּפַס לָא מַפְּקִינַן מִינֵּיהּ. רַב אַשִׁי אָמַר: בֵּיוָן דִּכְתַבְיהּ לֵיהּ: "כָּל דְּמִתְעַנֵּי מִן דִּינָא קַבִּילִית עֲלַי" – שָׁלִיחַ שַׁוְיֵהּ.

Ameimar said: If the collector who is empowered by the authorization **seized** the item[N] he collected and kept it for himself, the court **does not take it away from him,** as the owner transferred ownership of the item to him in the document of authorization, as explained above. **Rav Ashi** disagreed with Ameimar and **said:**[N] **Since** the owner **wrote to** the collector: **I accept upon myself anything that develops as a result of** this **legal process,**[HN] **he has** in effect **rendered** the collector **an agent**[H] to act on his behalf, and therefore the agent cannot seize the item for himself.

וְאִיכָּא דְּאָמַר: שׁוּתָּפָא שַׁוְיֵהּ. לְמַאי נָפְקָא מִינָּהּ? לְמִיתְפַּס פַּלְגָא. וְהִלְכְתָא: שָׁלִיחַ שַׁוְיֵהּ.

And there is another opinion **that states:** The owner **renders the** collector **a partner** in the collected item, transferring ownership of half of it to him while maintaining ownership over the other half. The Gemara asks: **What is the** practical **difference** between this opinion and that of Rav Ashi? The Gemara answers: The difference is whether the collector has the power **to seize half** of the collected item for himself. If he is merely an agent of the owner, he cannot seize anything; if he is a partner he can seize up to half. The Gemara concludes: **And the *halakha* is** that the owner **renders** the collector his **agent,** and therefore this agent may not seize any portion of the collected item for himself.

מתני׳ גָּנַב עַל פִּי שְׁנַיִם, וְטָבַח וּמָכַר עַל פִּיהֶם אוֹ עַל פִּי שְׁנַיִם אֲחֵרִים – מְשַׁלֵּם תַּשְׁלוּמֵי אַרְבָּעָה וַחֲמִשָּׁה.

MISHNA The mishna lists a series of cases in which a thief is required to pay the fourfold or fivefold penalty. If one **stole** an animal, as established **based on** the testimony of **two** witnesses,[H] **and he** subsequently **slaughtered** the animal **or sold** it, also **based on** the testimony of the same witnesses, **or based on** the testimony of **two other** witnesses, **he pays** the **fourfold or fivefold payment.**

גָּנַב וּמָכַר בְּשַׁבָּת, גָּנַב וּמָכַר לַעֲבוֹדָה זָרָה, גָּנַב וְטָבַח בְּיוֹם הַכִּפּוּרִים,

If one **stole** an animal **and sold it on Shabbat,**[HN] or if **he stole** it **and sold it for idol worship,** or if **he stole** it **and slaughtered** it **on Yom Kippur,** he pays the fourfold or fivefold payment. Although his sale or slaughter in these circumstances involved a sin, he is not liable to receive the death penalty for the sale and must consequently pay the fourfold or fivefold payment.

HALAKHA

Anything that develops as a result of this legal process, etc. – כָּל דְּמִתְעַנֵּי מִן דִּינָא וכו׳: All expenses incurred by an agent who received authorization for the process of legal action and collection of a debt must be reimbursed by the owner, in accordance with the formula stated in a document of authorization: Anything you spend in this legal process shall be incumbent upon me to pay. This *halakha* is in accordance with the opinion of Rav Ashi. Even if one did not write this formulation in the document he is obligated to reimburse the collector for all of his expenses (Rambam *Sefer Kinyan, Hilkhot Sheluḥin VeShutafin* 3:1; *Shulḥan Arukh, Ḥoshen Mishpat* 122:6, and *Shakh* there).

He has rendered the collector an agent – שָׁלִיחַ שַׁוְיֵהּ: Even if it is written in the document of authorization: Go and take legal action and take possession of the item for yourself, and the owner and collector performed an act of acquisition by which the owner transferred ownership of the item to the collector, this collector is considered no more than an agent acting on the owner's behalf. Consequently, he may not seize any part of the item for himself (Rambam *Sefer Kinyan, Hilkhot Sheluḥin VeShutafin*, 3:1; *Shulḥan Arukh, Ḥoshen Mishpat* 122:6, and in the comment of Rema).

If one stole an animal, based on the testimony of two witnesses, etc. – גָּנַב עַל פִּי שְׁנַיִם וכו׳: If two witnesses testified that one stole an ox or sheep, and they or two other witnesses testified that he subsequently slaughtered or sold it, he pays the fourfold or fivefold payment (Rambam *Sefer Nezikin, Hilkhot Geneiva* 3:7; *Tur, Ḥoshen Mishpat* 350).

If one stole an animal and sold it on Shabbat – גָּנַב וּמָכַר בְּשַׁבָּת: If one stole an animal and sold it on Shabbat, or if he sold it for idol worship, or if he stole an animal and sold it or slaughtered it on Yom Kippur, he pays the fourfold or fivefold payment, as these transactions are not punishable by death (Rambam *Sefer Nezikin, Hilkhot Geneiva* 3:5; *Tur, Ḥoshen Mishpat* 350).

NOTES

If the collector seized the item – אִי תָּפַס: Rashi writes two interpretations of this phrase, concerning the issue of who seizes the item from whom. In the explanation he prefers, for which he cites the *ge'onim*, the Gemara means that the collector seizes what he collected or part of it for himself, when he claims he is owed money by the one who sent him. According to Rashi's other interpretation, the Gemara is referring to the collector's seizure of the item from the one holding it. The Gemara states that if he seizes the item against the other's will the seizure is effective, even if the document empowering him as collector did not state the required wording: Go take legal action and take possession of the claimed property and collect it from him for yourself.

Rav Ashi said, etc. – רַב אַשִׁי אָמַר וכו׳: Some commentaries maintain that Rav Ashi disagrees with the entire principle laid down by the Sages of Neharde'a, as he holds that a collector can act as an ordinary agent on behalf of the owner of the item, rather than requiring that its ownership be transferred to the collector (Ba'al HaMaor). Most early commentaries disagree with this interpretation, claiming that Rav Ashi accepts the basic principle of the Sages of Neharde'a. His disagreement is only with the opinion of Ameimar, who allows the collector to seize the item for himself. Rav Ashi maintains that if the owner wrote in the document: I accept upon myself anything that develops as a result of this legal process, the collector may not seize the item for himself, as in that case he is acting as an ordinary agent (see Rashi and Meiri).

I accept upon myself anything that develops [*mitannei*] as a result of this legal process – כָּל דְּמִתְעַנֵּי מִן דִּינָא קַבִּילִית עֲלַי: Most early commentaries understand this phrase and the word *mitannei* to mean that the owner accepts upon himself to provide any answer [*ma'aneh*] that may come about through the legal process of collecting the item, i.e., to engage in the actual discussions in court. Others explain that the owner accepts upon himself all expenses that may be involved in the collection (see Rambam and Meiri).

If one stole an animal and sold it on Shabbat, etc. – גָּנַב וּמָכַר בְּשַׁבָּת וכו׳: The mishna here is very precise, as in each case the same basic principle is applied: Even if the thief transgresses a ritual prohibition in the course of slaughtering or selling the animal, provided that the prohibition is not severe enough to incur the death penalty he is obligated to pay the fourfold or fivefold payment. Therefore, the mishna mentions one who sells an animal on Shabbat, as commercial transactions on Shabbat do not render one liable to receive the death penalty. It does not mention one who slaughters on Shabbat, an act that would incur the death penalty. Likewise, the mishna lists selling the animal for idolatry, which is not a capital offense, but does not mention slaughtering it for idolatry, which is a capital offense. Finally, it cites the case of one who slaughters the animal on Yom Kippur; he is liable to receive excision from the World-to-Come [*karet*] but not the death penalty.

גנב משל אביו וטבח ומכר ואחר כך מת אביו, גנב וטבח ואחר כך הקדיש – משלם תשלומי ארבעה וחמשה.

If one **stole** an animal **of his father's and** then **slaughtered** it **or sold it**,[H] **and afterward his father died** and he inherited his father's estate either on his own or in partnership with his brothers, or if **he stole** an animal **and slaughtered** it **and afterward he consecrated** it,[H] he **pays the fourfold or fivefold payment.**

גנב וטבח לרפואה או לכלבים, השוחט ונמצאת טריפה, השוחט חולין בעזרה – משלם תשלומי ארבעה וחמשה;

In the case of one who **stole** an animal **and slaughtered it,** not for the purpose of eating its meat, but to use it **for medicinal purposes**[H] **or to** feed the meat to **dogs,** and likewise a thief **who slaughters** the animal to eat its meat **but it was found to be an animal with a condition that will cause it to die within twelve months** [*tereifa*],[HN] or a thief **who slaughters a non-sacred** animal **in the** Temple **courtyard,**[HB] he **pays the fourfold or fivefold payment.**

רבי שמעון פוטר בשני אלו.

Rabbi Shimon exempts the thief from the fourfold or fivefold payment **in these** last **two** cases, as he maintains that the legal status of an act of slaughter that is not fit for accomplishing its full ritual purpose is not considered an act of slaughter.

גמ׳ לימא, מתניתין דלא כרבי עקיבא,

GEMARA The mishna teaches that if two witnesses testify about the theft of an animal and two others testify about its slaughter or sale, the thief pays the fourfold or fivefold payment. The Gemara suggests: **Let us say that the mishna is not in accordance with** the opinion of **Rabbi Akiva,** in his exposition of the verse: "Based on the testimony of two witnesses or on the testimony of three witnesses shall a matter be established" (Deuteronomy 19:15).

דאי רבי עקיבא, האמר: "דבר" – ולא חצי דבר!

The Gemara elaborates: **As, if** it is in accordance with the opinion of **Rabbi Akiva,** the thief would be exempt from the fourfold or fivefold payment, as **doesn't** Rabbi Akiva **say** that this verse teaches that witnesses' testimony must refer to an entire **matter, and not part of a matter?** In the case discussed by the mishna the second set of witnesses testifies only that this man slaughtered or sold an ox or sheep, not that he stole it, and therefore their testimony alone would not render the thief liable to pay anything.

דתניא, אמר רבי יוסי: כשהלך אבא חלפתא אצל רבי יוחנן בן נורי ללמוד תורה, ואמרי לה: רבי יוחנן בן נורי אצל אבא

As it is taught in the *Tosefta* (*Bava Batra* 2:4) that **Rabbi Yosei said: When father Ḥalafta**[P] **went to study Torah with Rabbi Yoḥanan ben Nuri, and some say** that he said: When **Rabbi Yoḥanan ben Nuri** went to study **Torah with father**

HALAKHA

If one stole an animal of his father's and then slaughtered or sold it, etc. – גנב משל אביו וטבח ומכר וכו׳: If one stole an animal from his father and slaughtered or sold it while his father was still alive, he pays the fourfold or fivefold payment (Rambam *Sefer Nezikin, Hilkhot Geneiva* 2:6; *Tur, Ḥoshen Mishpat* 350).

He stole an animal and slaughtered it and afterward he consecrated it – גנב וטבח ואחר כך הקדיש: If one stole an animal and slaughtered it and afterward consecrated it, he pays the fourfold or fivefold payment (Rambam *Sefer Nezikin, Hilkhot Geneiva* 2:6; *Tur, Ḥoshen Mishpat* 350).

If one stole an animal and slaughtered it to use it for medicinal purposes, etc. – גנב וטבח לרפואה וכו׳: If one stole an animal and slaughtered it for medicinal purposes or to feed it to the dogs, he pays the fourfold or fivefold payment (Rambam *Sefer Nezikin, Hilkhot Geneiva* 2:8; *Tur, Ḥoshen Mishpat* 350).

A thief who slaughters the animal to eat its meat but it was found to be a *tereifa* – השוחט ונמצאת טריפה: If one steals an animal and slaughters it, and it was found to be a *tereifa*, he pays the fourfold or fivefold payment (Rambam *Sefer Nezikin, Hilkhot Geneiva* 2:8; *Tur, Ḥoshen Mishpat* 350).

A thief who slaughters a non-sacred animal in the Temple courtyard – השוחט חולין בעזרה: If one stole an animal and slaughtered it as a non-sacred animal in the Temple courtyard, he pays the fourfold or fivefold payment (Rambam *Sefer Nezikin, Hilkhot Geneiva* 2:8; *Tur, Ḥoshen Mishpat* 350).

BACKGROUND

Non-sacred animals in the courtyard – חולין בעזרה: It is prohibited to bring non-sacred animals into the Temple courtyard. One who slaughters non-sacred animals in the courtyard receives lashes of rebelliousness by rabbinic law. He may not derive benefit from the animal. Most commentaries agree that this is not a Torah prohibition.

NOTES

A thief who slaughters the animal to eat its meat but it was found to be a *tereifa* – השוחט ונמצאת טריפה: Rabbi Shimon consistently maintains throughout the Talmud that an act of slaughter, even if performed according to halakhic standards, is not considered a valid slaughter for purposes other than eating the meat of the animal if it does not result in the meat being rendered permitted for consumption. Rabbi Shimon agrees that it is a valid slaughter in those cases where a thief slaughters an animal for medicinal purposes or for feeding to dogs, because these acts of slaughter, albeit not intended to produce meat for human consumption, do technically permit the meat to be eaten; the use to which the meat is put after slaughter is irrelevant.

PERSONALITIES

Rabbi Ḥalafta – רבי חלפתא: A third-generation *tanna*, Rabbi Ḥalafta was a native of the city of Tzippori, where he served as the presiding rabbi. In his youth he saw the Temple and he knew the Sages who lived in that generation. He lived a long life, and studied in the yeshiva in Yavne and was a colleague of Rabbi Akiva. Rabbi Ḥalafta is mentioned in the Mishna, and some opinions and anecdotes attributed to him appear in various *baraitot*. His foremost disciple was his son, the *tanna* Rabbi Yosei, who often cites his statements and mentions him many times, invariably referring to him reverently as father Ḥalafta.

חֲלַפְתָּא, אָמַר לוֹ.

Ḥalafta, he said to him the following in the course of their discussion of the *halakhot* of possession.

הֲרֵי שֶׁאֲכָלָהּ שָׁנָה רִאשׁוֹנָה בִּפְנֵי שְׁנַיִם, שְׁנִיָּה בִּפְנֵי שְׁנַיִם, שְׁלִישִׁית בִּפְנֵי שְׁנַיִם, מַהוּ?

If one has been in possession of real estate for three years, this serves as proof of his claim that he is the legal owner. One who is able to prove uninterrupted possession for the necessary period is not required to produce documentary evidence of his legal title to the property. Rabbi Yoḥanan ben Nuri or father Ḥalafta asked: **If one** harvested **and ate**[N] the produce of a field that he claims as his own the **first year**[H] of the three years required for establishing possession of the land **in the presence of two** witnesses, and subsequently ate the produce of the **second** year **in the presence of two** other witnesses, and finally ate the produce of the **third** year **in the presence of** yet **two** other witnesses, **what is** the *halakha*? Can the three testimonies combine to establish full testimony that he ate the produce of three years, thereby confirming his ownership of the field?

אָמַר לוֹ: הֲרֵי זוֹ חֲזָקָה; אָמַר לוֹ: אַף אֲנִי אוֹמֵר כֵּן, אֶלָּא שֶׁרַבִּי עֲקִיבָא חוֹלֵק בַּדָּבָר, שֶׁהָיָה רַבִּי עֲקִיבָא אוֹמֵר: "דָּבָר" – וְלֹא חֲצִי דָבָר!

Rabbi Ḥalafta **said to** Rabbi Yoḥanan ben Nuri, or vice versa: **This** is considered to establish **presumptive ownership** by the one who ate the produce. The other Sage **said to him: I too say** that this is **so, but Rabbi Akiva disputes** this **matter, as Rabbi Akiva would say:** The Torah requires that witnesses must testify with regard to a complete **matter and not part of a matter.** Since there must be testimony concerning consumption of the produce over three years, and each set of witnesses establishes only that it took place for one year, their separate testimonies do not combine. If so, the mishna is apparently not in accordance with the opinion of Rabbi Akiva.

אֲמַר אַבַּיֵי: אֲפִילּוּ תֵּימָא רַבִּי עֲקִיבָא, מִי לָא מוֹדֶה רַבִּי עֲקִיבָא בִּשְׁנַיִם אוֹמְרִים קִידֵּשׁ וּשְׁנַיִם אוֹמְרִים בָּעַל,

The Gemara rejects this assertion. **Abaye said: You** can **even say** that the mishna is in accordance with the opinion of **Rabbi Akiva. Doesn't Rabbi Akiva concede** that **in** a case where **two** witnesses **say:** So-and-so **betrothed**[N] a certain woman, **and two** other witnesses **say:** Someone else subsequently **engaged in sexual intercourse** with that same woman, this is proof that the act of intercourse was adulterous?

דְּאַף עַל גַּב דְּעֵדֵי בִיאָה צְרִיכִי לְעֵדֵי קִדּוּשִׁין, כֵּיוָן דְּעֵדֵי קִדּוּשִׁין לָא צְרִיכִי לְעֵדֵי בִיאָה – "דָּבָר" קָרֵינָא בֵּיהּ?

The reason for this is **that even though the witnesses** testifying about the **intercourse require the witnesses** who testify about the **betrothal,** i.e., the testimony of the second set of witnesses is meaningless without the testimony of the first witnesses, nevertheless, **since the witnesses** testifying about the **betrothal do not require the witnesses** who testify about the **intercourse,** i.e., their testimony by itself establishes a halakhic status, **we call** the testimony of each pair a complete **matter.**

הָכָא נַמִי, אַף עַל גַּב דְּעֵדֵי טְבִיחָה צְרִיכִי לְעֵדֵי גְנֵיבָה, כֵּיוָן דְּעֵדֵי גְנֵיבָה לָא צְרִיכִי לְעֵדֵי טְבִיחָה – "דָּבָר" קָרֵינָא בֵּיהּ.

Here too, the same logic applies in the case of a thief who steals an animal and subsequently slaughters or sells it: **Even though the witnesses** who testify about the **slaughter require the** testimony of the **witnesses** about the **theft** in order for their testimony to have any halakhic significance, **since the witnesses** testifying about the **theft do not require the** testimony of the **witnesses** who testify about the **slaughter,** as their testimony alone establishes that person as a thief who is liable to pay the double payment, **we call** the testimony of each pair a complete **matter.**

וְרַבָּנַן, הַאי "דָּבָר" וְלֹא חֲצִי דָבָר, לְמַעוּטֵי מַאי? לְמַעוּטֵי: אֶחָד אוֹמֵר אַחַת בְּגַבָּהּ, וְאֶחָד אוֹמֵר אַחַת בִּכְרֵיסָהּ.

The Gemara asks: **And** according to the opinion of **the Rabbis,** who disagree with Rabbi Akiva that the Torah stipulates that testimony must be about a **matter and not half of a matter,** the term "matter" (Deuteronomy 19:15) serves **to exclude what?** The Gemara answers: It serves **to exclude** a case involving testimony that a girl has reached majority, in which **one** witness **says** that he saw **one** hair on **her** lower **back,**[NH] **and one** witness **says** that he saw **one** hair on **her** lower **abdomen.**[B] A girl is considered to have reached maturity when she has two pubic hairs. In this case, two witnesses separately testify that they have each seen one hair, and therefore each testimony is halakhically meaningless on its own. The Rabbis derive from the verse that these testimonies do not combine.

NOTES

If one ate – הֲרֵי שֶׁאֲכָלָהּ: In tractate *Bava Batra* (28a) it is explained that if one uses a field for three years, unchallenged, his claim of possession is accepted. This use is often referred to by the Gemara as eating its produce. The *tanna'im* in this *baraita* disagree over whether the same set of witnesses must attest to all three years of use.

Two witnesses say so-and-so betrothed, etc. – שְׁנַיִם אוֹמְרִים קִידֵּשׁ וכו׳: The commentaries disagree over the precise details of this case. Some claim that two witnesses attest to the fact that a certain man has betrothed this woman, after which two other witnesses testify that another man engaged in intercourse with her. The issue before the court is whether the woman and the second man are liable to receive punishment for adultery (Rashi; Ri Migash).

The Rashba questions this explanation, claiming that it is dissimilar to the case of the mishna. He explains that it is referring to a case where two witnesses testify that the woman has been betrothed, which is the first step of the marriage process, while a second set of witnesses testifies that the husband has consummated the marriage through sexual intercourse. The issue is whether the woman is fully married or only betrothed, with all the halakhic implications that this distinction entails.

One witness says that he saw one hair on her back – אֶחָד אוֹמֵר אַחַת בְּגַבָּהּ: The attainment of majority is determined, for both boys and girls, through the growth of two pubic hairs. When necessary, the person in question would be examined by those of their own sex (see *Nidda* 48b and *Mishkenot Ya'akov, Even HaEzer* 42). In this case, one witness testifies to the existence of a one hair in one particular spot, while the other testifies about one hair in a different location.

HALAKHA

If one ate the produce the first year, etc. – הֲרֵי שֶׁאֲכָלָהּ שָׁנָה רִאשׁוֹנָה וכו׳: If two witnesses testify that one has eaten the produce of a field over the course of a year, and two other witnesses testify the same concerning the following year, and two other witnesses testify the same with regard to the third year, all these testimonies combine and he has established presumptive ownership of the field, in accordance with the opinion of the Rabbis (Rambam *Sefer Shofetim, Hilkhot Edut* 21:7; *Tur, Ḥoshen Mishpat* 38).

One witness says that he saw one hair on her back – אֶחָד אוֹמֵר אַחַת בְּגַבָּהּ: If one witness testifies to the existence of a single pubic hair, and another testifies that the child has a second one, this does not constitute a full testimony that establishes that the child in question has reached majority (Rambam *Sefer Shofetim, Hilkhot Edut* 4:7; *Shulḥan Arukh, Ḥoshen Mishpat* 30:13).

BACKGROUND

One hair on her back…and one on her lower abdomen – אַחַת בְּגַבָּהּ...וְאַחַת בִּכְרֵיסָהּ: Since the two hairs that testify to a person's majority are pubic hairs, the terms back and abdomen are understood as euphemisms for various regions in the pubic area. It is also possible that the terms refer to the witnesses' position relative to the girl when they saw the hairs.

HALAKHA

Two witnesses say one hair, etc. – שְׁנַיִם אוֹמְרִים אֶחָד וכו׳: If two witnesses testify to the existence of a single pubic hair on a child, and two other witnesses testify to the existence of a second hair, this is not proof that the child is of age, as each set of witnesses is testifying about half a matter (Rambam *Sefer Shofetim, Hilkhot Edut* 4:7; *Shulḥan Arukh, Ḥoshen Mishpat* 122:6).

הַאי חֲצִי דָבָר וַחֲצִי עֵדוּת הוּא!

The Gemara raises a difficulty: In **this** case each testimony is obviously invalid, as it is **half a matter and** also **half a testimony.** Not only does each testimony refer to one hair, which is half a matter, it is submitted by one witness, which is half a testimony. Consequently, it is obvious that the girl is not considered of age in this case.

אֶלָּא לְמַעוּטֵי: שְׁנַיִם אוֹמְרִים אֶחָד בְּגַבָּהּ וּשְׁנַיִם אוֹמְרִים אֶחָד בִּכְרֵיסָהּ; הָנֵי אָמְרִי קְטַנָּה הִיא, וְהָנֵי אָמְרִי קְטַנָּה הִיא.

The Gemara therefore rejects this explanation. **Rather,** the Rabbis maintain that the term "matter" serves **to exclude** a case in which **two** witnesses **say** that they saw **one** hair on a girl's **back, and two** other witnesses **say** that they saw **one** hair[H] **on her** lower **abdomen.** In this case the testimony of either set of witnesses concerns only one hair, and therefore **these** witnesses **are** essentially **saying** that **she is** still **a minor and those** witnesses **are saying** that **she is** still **a minor.**[N] Therefore, each testimony concerns only half of a matter.

״גָּנַב וּמָכַר בְּשַׁבָּת״ [וכו׳]. וְהָתַנְיָא: פָּטוּר!

§ The mishna teaches: If one **stole** an animal **and sold** it **on Shabbat,** he pays the fourfold or fivefold payment. The Gemara asks: **But isn't it taught** in a *baraita* that in this case he is **exempt** from the fourfold or fivefold payment?

אֲמַר רָמִי בַּר חָמָא: כִּי תַּנְיָא הַהִיא דְּפָטוּר – בְּאוֹמֵר לוֹ ״עֲקוֹץ לְךָ תְּאֵינָה מִתְּאֵינָתִי וְתִיקַנֵי לִי גְּנֵיבוּתִיךְ״.

Rami bar Ḥama said: When it is taught in **that** *baraita* **that** he is **exempt,** this is referring to a case **where** the purchaser **says to** the thief: **Pick off a fig**[N] **for yourself from my fig tree** on Shabbat, **and** through performing this act **your stolen** animal shall be **acquired by me.** Since the act of acquisition of the animal involved the type of Shabbat desecration for which one is liable to receive the death penalty, the thief is exempt from the monetary obligations he would ordinarily incur from this act, i.e., the fourfold or fivefold payment to the animal's prior owner. This is in accordance with the principle that one who commits two or more transgressions by means of a single act, both of which entail punishment, is exempt from the lesser punishment.

אָמְרִי: וְכֵיוָן דְּכִי תָּבַע לֵיהּ קַמָּן בְּדִינָא, לָא אָמְרִינַן לֵיהּ ״זִיל שַׁלֵּים״, דְּמִחַיַּיב בְּנַפְשׁוֹ הוּא, הָא מְכִירָה נַמִי לָאו מְכִירָה הִיא!

The Sages **say,** questioning this explanation of the *baraita*: **But since, if** the purchaser **would bring a legal claim against** the thief **before us,** to force him to deliver the animal acquired by means of picking the fig, the court **would not say to** the thief: **Go** and **pay** him the animal you owe him, **because** the thief **is liable to** receive the **death** penalty for his desecration of Shabbat, this shows that **the sale is not** a valid **sale** at all. Therefore, the *baraita* would not call this exchange a sale and this interpretation of the *baraita* cannot be correct.

אֶלָּא אֲמַר רַב פַּפָּא: בְּאוֹמֵר לוֹ ״זְרוֹק גְּנֵיבוּתִיךְ לַחֲצֵרִי וְתִיקַנֵי לִי גְּנֵיבוּתִיךְ״.

Rather, Rav Pappa said: The *baraita* is discussing a case **where** the purchaser **said to** the thief: **Throw your stolen** animal from the public domain **into my** enclosed **courtyard, and your stolen** animal **will** thereby **be acquired by me.** One can acquire an item if it is placed on his property. In this case, when the thief places the animal on the purchaser's property he moves it from the public domain into the private domain, which is a desecration of Shabbat that entails the death penalty. Consequently, he is exempt from the fourfold or fivefold payment.

NOTES

Those witnesses are saying that she is still a minor – הָנֵי אָמְרִי קְטַנָּה הִיא: Although each account is a valid testimony, it is considered half a matter since each set of witnesses testifies about a matter of no halakhic significance by itself. The difference between this case and that of three sets of witnesses who testify to one's use of a field for one year each, which is not considered half a matter in the opinion of the Rabbis, is not immediately evident, and the early commentaries offer several explanations.

Some say that the distinction lies in the fact that in the case of the three years, each testimony has halakhic ramifications by itself, as if it is discovered that the one using the field is not the owner he will have to pay the owner for all the produce that he ate during any particular year, on the basis of the testimony of the corresponding set of witnesses. Each testimony is therefore an independent, complete matter in that sense (Rif; Rabbeinu Tam in *Sefer HaYashar*; Rashba).

Alternatively, in the case of the three years, each set of witnesses testifies concerning all the required information about a given year, and consequently their testimony is considered a complete matter. By contrast, in the case of the two hairs, each set of witnesses testifies only to a part of the required information about the girl (*Tosafot*).

Yet others suggest that in the case of the field, each set of witnesses testifies that a particular individual has made use of a field as if it were his own. It is merely necessary that this testimony be extended over time, for three years. By contrast, in the case of the hairs, each testimony by itself indicates that the girl is not of age, which is the opposite of the conclusion that would be reached if the testimonies were combined (Ramban, in *Milḥamot Hashem*).

Pick off a fig, etc. – עֲקוֹץ לְךָ תְּאֵינָה וכו׳: The early commentaries dispute the exact legal mechanism of this act of acquisition: Some claim that the taking of the fig constitutes a symbolic exchange between the thief and the purchaser (Rabbeinu Tam). Others state that the animal was already located on the purchaser's property, and the thief stipulated that the sale would take effect when the purchaser picks one of the figs (*Tosefot Rabbeinu Peretz*).

כמאן? כרבי עקיבא, דאמר: קלוטה כמי שהונחה דמיא.

The Gemara asks: If this is the correct explanation of the *baraita*, **in accordance with whose** opinion is the *baraita* taught? It is **in accordance with** the opinion of **Rabbi Akiva, who says:** An item **in the airspace** of a certain area **is considered** as though it were **at rest**[N] in that area.

דאי כרבנן, כיון דמטיא לחצר ביתו קנה, לענין שבת לא מחייב עד דמטיא לארעא!

As, if the *baraita* is **in accordance with** the opinion of **the Rabbis,** who hold that an item in the airspace of a certain area is not considered as though it were at rest in that area, **once** the animal **reaches**[N] **the** airspace **of the courtyard** of the purchaser's **house** he has acquired it, as one can acquire items that are in the airspace of his courtyard just like those on its ground, whereas **with regard to** moving an item from one domain to another on **Shabbat** the thief **is not liable**[H] for Shabbat desecration **until it reaches the ground.** Since the thief's monetary liability is not simultaneous with his incurring of the death penalty, he would not be exempt from payment.

באומר "לא תיקני לי גניבותיך עד שתנוח".

The Gemara answers: It is possible that the *baraita* is in accordance with the opinion of the Rabbis as well, as one can explain that it is speaking of a case **in which** the purchaser **says** to the thief: **Your stolen** animal **shall not be acquired by me until it rests** on the ground.[H] In that case, the acquisition of the animal and the Shabbat desecration are simultaneous.

רבא אמר: לעולם כרמי בר חמא; אתנן אסרה תורה ואפילו בא על אמו, ואי תבעה ליה קמן בדינא, מי אמרינן ליה "קום הב לה אתנן"?

Rava said: Actually, it is possible to explain the ***baraita*** **as Rami bar Ḥama** did, that the animal was acquired through the picking of a fig on Shabbat. And the objection raised earlier, that this act should not be considered a sale at all, is incorrect. This can be demonstrated by the fact that the **Torah prohibits** one to bring as an offering an animal given as the **payment** to a prostitute[H] for services rendered (Deuteronomy 23:19). **And** this prohibition applies **even** if the man in question **engaged in intercourse with his own mother,** which is a capital offense. **But if she** would bring **a legal claim before us, demanding** the payment of the animal that was agreed upon as her fee, **would we say to him: Arise and pay her** the animal? The court would not say this, as the monetary liability was incurred simultaneously with the commission of a capital crime.

אלא אף על גב דכי קא תבעה ליה בדינא, לא אמרינן ליה "זיל הב לה", כיון דכי יהיב לה הוי אתנן. הכא נמי, אף על גב דלענין תשלומין אי תבע בדינא קמן, לא אמרינן ליה "זיל שלים",

Rather, one must say that **even though if she** brings **a legal claim** against **him demanding** the payment of the animal that was agreed upon as her fee **we do not say to him: Go and pay her,** nevertheless, **since if** he does **give it to her it is** considered **payment** to a prostitute, it cannot be used as an offering. **Here too,** in the case of the acquisition of the animal through picking a fig, **even though with regard to payment, if** the purchaser would bring **a legal claim before us** against the thief, **seeking** to force him to deliver the animal, **we would not say to him: Go pay,**

NOTES

An item in airspace is considered at rest – קלוטה כמי שהונחה דמיא: One of the primary categories of prohibited labor on Shabbat is transferring an item from the private domain to the public domain or vice versa. This labor consists of removing an item from one of these domains and laying it to rest in the other domain. According to the opinion of Rabbi Akiva, if an item is thrown from the public domain into a private domain, even if it has not yet come to rest in the private domain, and even if it never comes to rest there at all but continues on to a different domain, once it has entered the airspace of the private domain it is considered as if it had landed there.

Once it reaches, etc. – כיון דמטיא וכו׳: The halakhic principle that one who becomes liable to capital punishment is exempt from monetary payments applies only when the two liabilities are incurred simultaneously. If the monetary liability preceded the liability for capital punishment there is no exemption from payment.

HALAKHA

With regard to Shabbat the thief is not liable – לענין שבת לא מחייב: If one throws an item from one private domain to another, with it passing through a public domain in between, even though the item was in the airspace of the public domain at one point, he is exempt from punishment for Shabbat desecration, in accordance with the opinion of the Rabbis. Rabbi Akiva's principle that an item in airspace is considered as if it were at rest is not accepted as *halakha* (Rambam *Sefer Zemanim, Hilkhot Shabbat* 13:16).

Until it rests on the ground – עד שתנוח: If a thief performs a prohibited act of labor on Shabbat concomitant with his sale of a stolen animal, he is exempt from the fourfold or fivefold payment. An example of this is if the thief says to the purchaser: I am throwing an animal into your courtyard but it will not be acquired by you until it lands in your courtyard. Once the animal lands in the courtyard, the one who threw it has transferred an item from one domain to another, which is a Shabbat desecration and a capital offense. Since the acquisition takes effect at that same moment, he is exempt from the fourfold or fivefold payment. Similarly, if the purchaser says to the thief: Pick a fig from my fig tree and I will thereby acquire your animal, the thief is exempt from paying the fourfold or fivefold payment, as picking the fig is an act of Shabbat desecration for which one is liable to receive the death penalty, and the sale of the animal occurs at the same moment (Rambam *Sefer Nezikin, Hilkhot Geneiva* 3:5; *Tur, Ḥoshen Mishpat* 350).

The Torah prohibits one to bring as an offering an animal given as payment to a prostitute, etc. – אתנן אסרה תורה וכו׳: If one says to a woman with whom sexual intercourse is prohibited to him: Take this item as payment for a sexual act, the item is considered payment to a prostitute and may not be used as an offering. There is no difference in this regard whether the intercourse between the two is forbidden as an ordinary prohibition by Torah law or is a capital offense. An animal given to an unmarried woman who is not related to him, or to one's own wife during her menstrual period, as payment for intercourse, is not included in this *halakha* (Rambam *Sefer Avoda, Hilkhot Issurei Mizbe'aḥ* 4:8).

אֲפִילּוּ הָכִי, כֵּיוָן דְּקָא מַקְנֵי לֵיהּ בְּהָכִי – הָוְיָא מְכִירָה.

and **even so, since** the thief **transfers ownership to** the purchaser **in this** manner, **it is** considered a valid **sale,** and he is required to pay the fourfold or fivefold payment.

״גָּנַב וְטָבַח בְּיוֹם הַכִּפּוּרִים״ וכו׳. אָמְרִי: אַמַּאי? נְהִי דִּקְטָלָא לֵיכָּא, מַלְקוּת מִיהָא אִיכָּא, וְקַיְימָא לָן דְּאֵינוֹ לוֹקֶה וּמְשַׁלֵּם!

§ The mishna teaches: If one **stole** an animal **and slaughtered** it **on Yom Kippur** he pays the fourfold or fivefold payment. The Sages **say,** questioning this ruling: **Why** is he liable to pay it? **Although there is no** penalty of **execution** for slaughtering on Yom Kippur, **nevertheless there is** the penalty of **lashes;**[N] **and we maintain that** one **is not** sentenced to be **flogged and** obligated to **pay** for the same act.[H]

אָמְרִי: הָא מַנִּי? רַבִּי מֵאִיר הִיא, דְּאָמַר: לוֹקֶה וּמְשַׁלֵּם.

The Sages **say** in response: In accordance with **whose** opinion **is this** mishna taught? **It is** taught in accordance with the opinion of **Rabbi Meir, who says:** One is sentenced to be **flogged and** obligated to **pay** for the same action.

אִי רַבִּי מֵאִיר, אֲפִילּוּ טָבַח בְּשַׁבָּת! וְכִי תֵּימָא, לוֹקֶה וּמְשַׁלֵּם אִית לֵיהּ, מֵת וּמְשַׁלֵּם לֵית לֵיהּ;

The Gemara asks: **If** the mishna is in accordance with the opinion of **Rabbi Meir,** then **even** if he **slaughtered** the animal **on Shabbat,** which is a capital offense, he should be obligated to pay the fourfold or fivefold payment, whereas the mishna (74b) states that in this case he is exempt. **And if you would say** that Rabbi Meir **holds** that one is sentenced to be **flogged and** obligated to **pay** for the same act, but **he does not hold** that one is sentenced to the **death** penalty **and** obligated to **pay** for the same act, this is incorrect.

וְלָא? וְהָתַנְיָא: גָּנַב וְטָבַח בְּשַׁבָּת, גָּנַב וְטָבַח לַעֲבוֹדָה זָרָה, גָּנַב שׁוֹר הַנִּסְקָל וּטְבָחוֹ – מְשַׁלֵּם אַרְבָּעָה וַחֲמִשָּׁה, דִּבְרֵי רַבִּי מֵאִיר, וַחֲכָמִים פּוֹטְרִין!

And is it correct to say that Rabbi Meir does **not** maintain that one can be sentenced to the death penalty and to pay for the same act? **But isn't it taught** in a *baraita*: If one **stole** an animal **and slaughtered** it **on Shabbat,**[H] or if **he stole** an animal **and slaughtered** it **for idol worship,** or if **he stole an ox that is** sentenced to be **stoned,** from which it is prohibited to derive any benefit, **and he slaughtered it,** he **pays** the **fourfold or fivefold** payment; **this is the statement of Rabbi Meir. And the Rabbis exempt** him from this payment. Apparently Rabbi Meir maintains that one can be held liable for monetary payment and for capital punishment for the same act, e.g., slaughtering on Shabbat or slaughtering for idol worship.

אָמְרִי: בַּר מִינָּהּ דְּהַהִיא, דְּהָא אִתְּמַר עֲלָהּ: אָמַר רַבִּי יַעֲקֹב אָמַר רַבִּי יוֹחָנָן, וְאָמְרִי לַהּ אָמַר רַבִּי יִרְמְיָה אָמַר רַבִּי שִׁמְעוֹן בֶּן לָקִישׁ, רַבִּי אָבִין וְרַבִּי אֶלְעָא וְכָל חֲבוּרָתָא מִשְּׁמֵיהּ דְּרַבִּי יוֹחָנָן אָמְרִי: בְּטוֹבֵחַ עַל יְדֵי אַחֵר.

The Sages **say** in response: Stand **apart from this** *baraita*, i.e., this *baraita* should not be understood in a straightforward manner, **as it was stated concerning it: Rabbi Ya'akov says** that **Rabbi Yoḥanan says, and some say** it was **Rabbi Yirmeya** who **says** that **Rabbi Shimon ben Lakish says,** and **Rabbi Avin and Rabbi Ela and the entire group**[B] of disciples of Rabbi Yoḥanan also **say in the name of Rabbi Yoḥanan:** The *baraita* is speaking **of** a thief who **slaughters** the stolen animal **through** the agency **of another**[H] person, i.e., he instructed another to slaughter it, and that agent did so on Shabbat or for idolatrous purposes. The thief pays the fourfold or fivefold payment because he himself did not commit a capital offense.

וְכִי זֶה חוֹטֵא וְזֶה מִתְחַיֵּיב?!

The Gemara asks: How can it be that a thief is liable to pay the fourfold or fivefold payment if another person slaughters the stolen animal for him? **But is it so that this one sins**[N] **and that** one **becomes liable?**

אָמַר רָבָא: שָׁאנֵי הָכָא, דְּאָמַר קְרָא: ״וּטְבָחוֹ וּמְכָרוֹ״, מַה מְּכִירָה עַל יְדֵי אַחֵר, אַף טְבִיחָה עַל יְדֵי אַחֵר.

The Gemara provides several reasons why in the case of fourfold or fivefold payment it is possible for the thief to be liable for another's actions. **Rava said:** It **is different here, as the verse states: "And slaughter it or sell it"** (Exodus 21:37), thereby juxtaposing the two acts of slaughtering and selling. It is derived that **just as** there is liability for the fourfold or fivefold payment through **selling,** which by definition is performed **by means of another** party, **so too,** there is liability for **slaughtering** when it is performed **by means of another** party.

NOTES

Nevertheless there is the penalty of lashes – מַלְקוּת מִיהָא אִיכָּא: As with most other prohibitions that are not subject to capital punishment, if one slaughtered an animal on Yom Kippur (see Leviticus 16:29) after having been warned about the consequences of his actions, he is punished with lashes. One cannot be sentenced to receive lashes and to pay a monetary payment for the same act.

But is it so that this one sins, etc. – וְכִי זֶה חוֹטֵא וכו׳: There exists a principle that there is no agency for transgression, i.e., one is not held criminally responsible for transgressions that an agent or anyone else commits on his behalf; the agent is held liable.

HALAKHA

One is not sentenced to be flogged and obligated to pay for the same act – אֵינוֹ לוֹקֶה וּמְשַׁלֵּם: One cannot be flogged and have to pay money for a single action. Therefore, if one steals an animal and slaughters it on Yom Kippur he is exempt from paying the fourfold or fivefold payment, as he is liable to a receive lashes for desecrating Yom Kippur (Rambam *Sefer Nezikin*, *Hilkhot Geneiva* 3:1 and *Hilkhot Ḥovel UMazik* 4:9; *Sefer Nashim*, *Hilkhot Na'ara Betula* 1:11; *Sefer Zera'im*, *Hilkhot Terumot* 6:6; *Tur*, *Ḥoshen Mishpat* 350).

If one stole an animal and slaughtered it on Shabbat, etc. – גָּנַב וְטָבַח בְּשַׁבָּת וכו׳: If one stole an animal and slaughtered it on Shabbat or slaughtered it for idol worship, he does not pay the fourfold or fivefold payment, because these acts of slaughter are capital offenses (Rambam *Sefer Nezikin*, *Hilkhot Geneiva* 3:3; *Tur*, *Ḥoshen Mishpat* 350).

A thief who slaughters the stolen animal through the agency of another, etc. – בְּטוֹבֵחַ עַל יְדֵי אַחֵר וכו׳: According to the *Tur*, the Rambam holds that that if a thief appointed an agent to slaughter a stolen animal for him on Shabbat and the agent did so, then the thief pays the fourfold or fivefold payment. This is because he is not liable to receive the death penalty for this act of slaughter. By contrast, the Rosh maintains that he is exempt, on the grounds that an act of slaughter performed on Shabbat does not render the animal's meat fit to be eaten, in accordance with the opinion of Rabbi Yoḥanan HaSandlar. The *Baḥ* notes that although with regard to the *halakhot* of Shabbat the Rosh does not himself rule in accordance with the opinion of Rabbi Yoḥanan HaSandlar, with regard to monetary matters he accepts the lenient opinion and exempts the thief from payment (Rambam *Sefer Nezikin*, *Hilkhot Geneiva* 3:6; *Tur*, *Ḥoshen Mishpat* 350).

BACKGROUND

The group – חֲבוּרָתָא: This term is used mostly by the Sages of Eretz Yisrael and usually corresponds to the term: The Rabbis, which appears in the Babylonian Talmud, in reference to a group of Sages located in a particular place. This term apparently had a more precise meaning in certain contexts, specifically a group of Sages who studied on a regular basis in a particular yeshiva, in contrast to others who occasionally attended the sessions of that yeshiva.

דְּבֵי רַבִּי יִשְׁמָעֵאל תָּנָא: "אוֹ" – לְרַבּוֹת אֶת הַשָּׁלִיחַ. דְּבֵי חִזְקִיָּה תָּנָא: "תַּחַת" – לְרַבּוֹת אֶת הַשָּׁלִיחַ.

The school of Rabbi Yishmael teaches: The word **"or"** in the phrase: "And slaughter it or sell it," serves **to include** a case in which **the agent**[H] slaughters or sells the animal at the behest of the thief. **The school of Ḥizkiyya teaches:** The separate word **"for"** [*taḥat*] in the phrase: "He shall pay five oxen for an ox, and four sheep for a sheep," which could have been avoided by using the mere prefix of the letter *beit*, serves **to include** a case in which **the agent** slaughters the animal on behalf of the thief.

מַתְקִיף לָהּ מָר זוּטְרָא: כִּי אִיכָּא מִידֵי, דְּאִילּוּ עָבֵיד אִיהוּ לָא מִיחַיַּיב, וְעָבֵיד שָׁלִיחַ וּמִיחַיַּיב?

Mar Zutra objects to this explanation of the *baraita*: **Is there anything** with regard to **which if** one **performs** it **himself** he is **not liable, and** if his **agent performs** it on his behalf one is **liable?** How is it possible for an agent to have more power than the one who appointed him? Can it be that if the thief himself slaughtered the animal on Shabbat he would be exempt, whereas if he has it slaughtered by another he is liable?

אֲמַר לֵיהּ רַב אַשִׁי: הָתָם לָאו מִשּׁוּם דְּלָא מִיחַיַּיב הוּא, אֶלָּא דְּקָם לֵיהּ בִּדְרַבָּה מִינֵּיהּ.

Rav Ashi said to him: There, in the case of the thief who slaughters a stolen animal on Shabbat, **it is not because he is not liable** that he does not pay the fourfold or fivefold payment; **rather,** he is liable but he is excused from payment **because he receives the greater of** the two punishments,[N] i.e., execution, for desecrating Shabbat. When he appoints an agent he has no liability for desecrating Shabbat, and therefore he pays for the slaughter.

וְאִי בְּטוֹבֵחַ עַל יְדֵי אַחֵר, מַאי טַעֲמָא דְּרַבָּנַן דְּפָטְרִי?

The Gemara asks: **But if the** *baraita* is speaking **about** a thief who **slaughters through** the agency of **another** person, **what is the reason of the Rabbis, who exempt** the thief from payment? The thief did not himself do any act for which he is liable to receive the death penalty.

אָמְרִי: מַאן חֲכָמִים? רַבִּי שִׁמְעוֹן, דְּאָמַר: שְׁחִיטָה שֶׁאֵינָהּ רְאוּיָה לֹא שְׁמָהּ שְׁחִיטָה.

The Sages **say** in explanation: **Who are these Rabbis** of the *baraita*? It is **Rabbi Shimon, who said:** The legal status of an act of **slaughter that is not fit**[H] for accomplishing its full ritual purpose **is not considered** an act of **slaughter.** Since slaughtering on Shabbat or slaughtering for idolatrous purposes does not render the meat fit for consumption, Rabbi Shimon rules that there is no liability for the fourfold or fivefold payment.

אָמְרִי: בִּשְׁלָמָא עֲבוֹדָה זָרָה וְשׁוֹר הַנִּסְקָל – שְׁחִיטָה שֶׁאֵינָהּ רְאוּיָה הִיא, אֶלָּא שַׁבָּת – שְׁחִיטָה רְאוּיָה הִיא, דִּתְנַן: הַשּׁוֹחֵט בְּשַׁבָּת וּבְיוֹם הַכִּפּוּרִים, אַף עַל פִּי שֶׁמִּתְחַיֵּיב בְּנַפְשׁוֹ – שְׁחִיטָתוֹ כְּשֵׁרָה!

The Sages **say,** questioning this explanation: **Granted,** slaughtering for **idol worship and** slaughtering **an ox that is** sentenced to be **stoned are** cases of **slaughter that is not fit,** as in both of these cases it is prohibited to derive any benefit from the animal's flesh. **But** slaughtering on **Shabbat is a fit slaughter. As we learned** in a mishna (*Ḥullin* 14a): In the case of **one who slaughters** an animal **on Shabbat**[H] **or on Yom Kippur, although he is liable to** receive the **death** penalty for desecrating Shabbat, **his slaughter is valid** and the meat may be eaten.

אָמְרִי: סָבַר לָהּ כְּרַבִּי יוֹחָנָן הַסַּנְדְּלָר;

The Sages say in response: Rabbi Shimon **holds in accordance with** the opinion of **Rabbi Yoḥanan HaSandlar,**[P] who disagrees with that mishna and prohibits eating the meat of an animal slaughtered on Shabbat.

דִּתְנַן: הַמְבַשֵּׁל בְּשַׁבָּת, בְּשׁוֹגֵג – יֹאכַל, בְּמֵזִיד – לֹא יֹאכַל, דִּבְרֵי רַבִּי מֵאִיר; רַבִּי יְהוּדָה אוֹמֵר: בְּשׁוֹגֵג – יֹאכַל בְּמוֹצָאֵי שַׁבָּת, בְּמֵזִיד – לֹא יֹאכַל עוֹלָמִית;

As we learned in a mishna (*Terumot* 2:3): In the case of **one who cooks** food **on Shabbat,**[H] if he acted **unwittingly he may eat** the food, but if he acted **intentionally he may not eat** it; this is **the statement of Rabbi Meir. Rabbi Yehuda**[N] **says:** If he acted **unwittingly he may eat** the food only **upon the conclusion of Shabbat,** and if he acted **intentionally he may not eat** it **ever,** although others may partake of it.

HALAKHA

To include the agent – לְרַבּוֹת אֶת הַשָּׁלִיחַ: If a thief appointed an agent to sell or slaughter a stolen animal, the thief is obligated to pay the fourfold or fivefold payment (Rambam *Sefer Nezikin, Hilkhot Geneiva* 2:10; *Tur, Ḥoshen Mishpat* 350).

Slaughter that is not fit – שְׁחִיטָה שֶׁאֵינָהּ רְאוּיָה: The legal status of an act of slaughter that is not fit for accomplishing its full ritual purpose is nevertheless considered an act of slaughter for some purposes. The *halakha* is not in accordance with the opinion of Rabbi Shimon (Rambam *Sefer Kedusha, Hilkhot Sheḥita* 12:6).

One who slaughters an animal on Shabbat, etc. – הַשּׁוֹחֵט בְּשַׁבָּת וכו׳: If one slaughters an animal on Shabbat or Yom Kippur, the slaughter is valid and the meat may be eaten, even though slaughter on Shabbat entails a capital offense and slaughter on Yom Kippur is punishable by lashes and *karet*. This is the *halakha* even if he desecrated these holy days deliberately and in public. Although meat of an animal slaughtered by a public Shabbat desecrater may not be eaten, this individual is categorized as a public Shabbat desecrater only after the act of slaughter (Rambam *Sefer Kedusha, Hilkhot Sheḥita* 1:29; *Shulḥan Arukh, Yoreh De'a* 11:2 and *Taz* and *Shakh* there).

One who cooks food on Shabbat – הַמְבַשֵּׁל בְּשַׁבָּת: With regard to one who cooks or performs any other act of labor that is a primary category of prohibited labor on Shabbat, if he did so deliberately he may not derive benefit from his action ever, although others may benefit from it immediately after Shabbat. If he desecrated Shabbat unwittingly, he may derive benefit from the action after Shabbat. The *halakha* is in accordance with the opinion of Rabbi Yehuda. Some authorities rule in accordance with the opinion of Rabbi Meir that after Shabbat even the one who performed the act of labor may derive benefit from a prohibited labor performed unwittingly on Shabbat, while others may derive benefit even on Shabbat (see *Tosafot*). This lenient opinion with regard to unwitting violation may be followed in exigent circumstances (Rambam *Sefer Zemanim, Hilkhot Shabbat* 6:23; *Shulḥan Arukh, Oraḥ Ḥayyim* 318:1 and *Mishna Berura* there, citing Gra).

NOTES

He receives the greater of the punishments – דְּקָם לֵיהּ בִּדְרַבָּה מִינֵּיהּ: Rav Ashi holds that the halakhic principle that one receives the greater punishment and is exempt from monetary payment does not actually remove the monetary obligation from the offending party. Rather, it merely prevents the court from enforcing payment, because it is empowered to impose only one punishment on a person for any given act. If a case arises in which the offending party has not incurred the death penalty, as in the Gemara here, and where the thief's agent commits the transgression, then the obligation to pay is enforced upon the thief.

Rabbi Meir, Rabbi Yehuda, etc. – רַבִּי מֵאִיר רַבִּי יְהוּדָה וכו׳: The commentaries present the opinions of the Sages in simplified form: The status of food cooked intentionally on Shabbat according to Rabbi Meir is equivalent to the status of food cooked unwittingly according to Rabbi Yehuda, while food cooked intentionally on Shabbat according to Rabbi Yehuda is equivalent to food cooked unwittingly according to Rabbi Yoḥanan HaSandlar (Rashba).

PERSONALITIES

Rabbi Yoḥanan HaSandlar – רַבִּי יוֹחָנָן הַסַּנְדְּלָר: A disciple of Rabbi Akiva, Rabbi Yoḥanan HaSandlar was a great-grandson of Hillel the Elder. During the period when Hadrian persecuted the Jewish community in Eretz Yisrael, Rabbi Yoḥanan HaSandlar fled with the intention of going to Babylonia to study under Rabbi Yehuda ben Beteira. When he reached Sidon he found that he could not bear to leave Eretz Yisrael and he returned there.

BACKGROUND

Entrance to the house of the *Nasi* – פִּיתְחָא דְּבֵי נְשִׂיאָה: It was the custom of the *amora'im* of Eretz Yisrael to use the house of the *Nasi* as a base for imparting significant Torah rulings to the masses.

רַבִּי יוֹחָנָן הַסַּנְדְּלָר אוֹמֵר: בְּשׁוֹגֵג – יֵאָכֵל לְמוֹצָאֵי שַׁבָּת לַאֲחֵרִים וְלֹא לוֹ, בְּמֵזִיד – לֹא יֵאָכֵל עוֹלָמִית, לֹא לוֹ וְלֹא לַאֲחֵרִים.

Rabbi Yoḥanan HaSandlar says: If he cooked the food **unwittingly it may be eaten upon the conclusion of Shabbat by others** only, **but not by him;** and if he acted **intentionally it may not be eaten ever, neither by him nor by others.** Slaughter, like cooking, is a desecration of Shabbat that entails the death penalty. It follows that Rabbi Yoḥanan HaSandlar maintains that the meat of an animal intentionally slaughtered on Shabbat may never be eaten. If so, this is a slaughter that does not render the meat fit for consumption, and therefore according to the opinion of Rabbi Shimon there is no fourfold or fivefold payment.

מַאי טַעֲמָא דְּרַבִּי יוֹחָנָן הַסַּנְדְּלָר? כִּדְדָרֵישׁ רַבִּי חִיָּיא אַפִּיתְחָא דְּבֵי נְשִׂיאָה: ״וּשְׁמַרְתֶּם אֶת הַשַּׁבָּת כִּי קֹדֶשׁ הוּא לָכֶם״, מַה קֹּדֶשׁ אָסוּר בַּאֲכִילָה – אַף מַעֲשֵׂה שַׁבָּת אֲסוּרִין בַּאֲכִילָה.

The Gemara asks: **What is the reason for** the opinion of **Rabbi Yoḥanan HaSandlar?** The Gemara explains: This is **as Rabbi Ḥiyya taught at the entrance to the house of the *Nasi*.**[B] It is written: **"And you shall observe Shabbat, for it is holy** [*kodesh*] **to you;** one who profanes it shall be put to death" (Exodus 31:14). **Just as it is prohibited to eat a sacred** item consecrated to the Temple [*kodesh*], **so too is it prohibited to eat** food produced though **action** that desecrates **Shabbat.**

אִי מַה קֹּדֶשׁ אָסוּר בַּהֲנָאָה, אַף מַעֲשֵׂה שַׁבָּת אָסוּר בַּהֲנָאָה! תַּלְמוּד לוֹמַר: ״לָכֶם״, שֶׁלָּכֶם יְהֵא.

The Gemara asks: **If** so, perhaps the analogy should be extended: **Just as it is prohibited to derive benefit** from **a sacred** item, **so too** should it be **prohibited to derive benefit** from a product of **an action** that desecrates **Shabbat.** The Gemara answers: **The verse states:** "It is holy **to you"** (Exodus 31:14), indicating that **it shall be yours** for deriving benefit. Although food cooked on Shabbat may not be eaten, it is permitted to benefit from it in other ways.

יָכוֹל אֲפִילּוּ בְּשׁוֹגֵג? תַּלְמוּד לוֹמַר: ״מְחַלְלֶיהָ מוֹת יוּמָת״, בְּמֵזִיד אָמַרְתִּי לָךְ וְלֹא בְּשׁוֹגֵג.

The Gemara further asks: Based on the analogy between a sacred item and the product of an action that desecrates Shabbat, one **might** have thought that **even** if the action were performed **unwittingly** it should be prohibited to consume the product, like a sacred item. To counter this, **the verse states: "One who profanes it shall be put to death"** (Exodus 31:14), indicating that it is **with regard to** one who desecrates Shabbat **intentionally** that **I said** this analogy **to you,** as the verse clearly is referring to one who is liable to receive the death penalty, **but not** one who desecrates Shabbat **unwittingly,** who is not executed.

פְּלִיגִי בָּהּ רַב אַחָא וְרָבִינָא, חַד אֲמַר: מַעֲשֵׂה שַׁבָּת דְּאוֹרַיְיתָא, וְחַד אֲמַר: מַעֲשֵׂה שַׁבָּת דְּרַבָּנַן.

The Gemara comments: **Rav Aḥa and Ravina disagree with regard to** this matter. **One said** that the product of **an action** that constitutes a desecration of **Shabbat** is forbidden **by Torah law, and one said** that the product of **an action** that constitutes a desecration of **Shabbat** is forbidden **by rabbinic** law.

מַאן דְּאָמַר דְּאוֹרַיְיתָא, כְּדַאֲמָרַן; וּמַאן דְּאָמַר דְּרַבָּנַן, אָמַר קְרָא: ״קֹדֶשׁ הוּא״, הוּא קֹדֶשׁ וְאֵין מַעֲשָׂיו קֹדֶשׁ.

The Gemara elaborates: **The one who says** it is forbidden **by Torah law** explains **as we said,** that the prohibition is based on the verse as interpreted by Rabbi Ḥiyya. **And the one who says** it is forbidden **by rabbinic law** would say that **the verse states: "It is holy,"** from which he infers: **It,** the day itself, **is holy but** the products of its prohibited **actions are not holy,** and therefore they are not compared to sacred items and may be eaten by Torah law.

בִּשְׁלָמָא לְמַאן דַּאֲמַר דְּאוֹרַיְיתָא, אַמְּטוּ

The Gemara asks: **Granted, according to the one who said** that products of a prohibited act are prohibited **by Torah law, it is for**

Perek **VII**
Daf **71** Amud **b**

לְהָכִי פָּטְרִי רַבָּנַן, אֶלָּא לְמַאן דְּאָמַר דְּרַבָּנַן, אַמַּאי פָּטְרִי רַבָּנַן?

this reason that **the Rabbis exempt** the thief from the fourfold or fivefold payment when he slaughters the animal on Shabbat, as slaughter on Shabbat does not render the meat permitted for consumption. **But according to the one who says** that the product of a prohibited act on Shabbat may be eaten by Torah law but is forbidden **by rabbinic law, why do the Rabbis exempt** the thief when he appoints an agent to slaughter the animal for him and the agent performs this action on Shabbat?

אַשְּׁאָרָא, אַעֲבוֹדָה זָרָה וְשׁוֹר הַנִּסְקָל.

The Gemara answers: When the Rabbis exempt him from the fourfold or fivefold payment, they are not referring to the case where the thief's agent slaughters the animal on Shabbat. Rather, they were speaking **of the rest** of the cases listed in the *baraita*, namely, an agent who slaughters the animal **for idol worship and** one who slaughters **an ox that is** sentenced to be **stoned.**

וְרַבִּי מֵאִיר, אַמַּאי מְחַיֵּיב שׁוֹחֵט לַעֲבוֹדָה זָרָה?

The Gemara asks another question with regard to the interpretation of the *baraita* presented above: **And** with regard to **Rabbi Meir,** granted he maintains that the legal status of an act of slaughter not fit for accomplishing its full ritual purpose is nevertheless considered an act of slaughter. But **why** is the thief **liable** to pay the fourfold or fivefold payment when his agent **slaughters** the animal **for idol worship?**

כֵּיוָן דִּשְׁחַט בָּהּ פּוּרְתָּא אַסְרַהּ, אִידָּךְ אִיסּוּרֵי הֲנָאָה הוּא, וְלָא דְּמָרֵיהּ קָא טָבַח וְלָא דִּידֵיהּ קָא טָבַח!

Once he slaughtered the animal **a bit**, at the very start of the act of slaughter, **he has prohibited** the animal, with regard to deriving benefit, as an animal sacrificed to idolatry. When he slaughters **the other** part **it is** already **prohibited** with regard to **deriving benefit,** which means that it is **not** an animal that belongs **to its owner** that he **slaughters, and** it is **not** an animal that belongs **to him** that he **slaughters.** Since deriving benefit from the animal is prohibited, it has no value; therefore, there is no ownership.

אָמַר רָבָא: בְּאוֹמֵר ״בִּגְמַר זְבִיחָה הוּא עוֹבְדָהּ״.

Rava said: This is referring **to one who says** prior to the slaughter that only **with the completion of the slaughter** does **he worship** the idolatry. Therefore, the prohibition does not take effect until that stage, which is also when the liability to pay the fourfold or fivefold payment is incurred.

שׁוֹר הַנִּסְקָל אִיסּוּרֵי הֲנָאָה נִינְהוּ, לָאו דְּמָרֵיהּ קָא טָבַח וְלָאו דִּידֵיהּ קָא טָבַח!

The Gemara raises a question with regard to another of the cases of the *baraita*: **An ox that is** sentenced to be **stoned is an item from which** deriving **benefit is prohibited.** Consequently, when a thief or his agent slaughters this animal, it is **not** an animal that belongs **to its owner** that he **slaughters, and** it is **not** an animal that belongs **to him** that he **slaughters.** Why does Rabbi Meir obligate him to pay the fourfold or fivefold payment?

אָמַר רָבָא: הָכָא בְּמַאי עָסְקִינַן – כְּגוֹן שֶׁמְּסָרוֹ לְשׁוֹמֵר, וְהִזִּיק בְּבֵית שׁוֹמֵר וְהוּעַד בְּבֵית שׁוֹמֵר וְנִגְמַר דִּינוֹ בְּבֵית שׁוֹמֵר. וְרַבִּי מֵאִיר סָבַר לַהּ כְּרַבִּי יַעֲקֹב, וְסָבַר לַהּ כְּרַבִּי שִׁמְעוֹן;

Rava said: With what are we dealing here? This is a case **where** the owners **entrusted** the ox **to a bailee and** the ox fatally **injured** someone while **in the bailee's house, and it was forewarned** while **in the bailee's house,**[N] **and it was sentenced** to be stoned while **in the bailee's house,**[N] and the thief then stole it from the bailee's house and slaughtered it. Rava continues: **And Rabbi Meir holds in accordance with** the opinion of **Rabbi Ya'akov, and he** also **holds in accordance with** the opinion of **Rabbi Shimon.**

סָבַר לַהּ כְּרַבִּי יַעֲקֹב, דְּאָמַר: אַף מִשֶּׁנִּגְמַר דִּינוֹ – הֶחֱזִירוֹ שׁוֹמֵר לַבְּעָלִים מוּחְזָר.

He holds in accordance with the opinion of **Rabbi Ya'akov, who says: Even after** the ox **was sentenced**[H] to be stoned, if the **bailee returned it to its owners** before it was killed, **it is** considered **returned.** Although the ox is now worthless, as no benefit may be derived from it, since the bailee returned a physically intact ox, the owner has no claim against him.

וְסָבַר לַהּ כְּרַבִּי שִׁמְעוֹן, דְּאָמַר: דָּבָר הַגּוֹרֵם לְמָמוֹן כְּמָמוֹן דָּמֵי.

And Rabbi Meir also **holds in accordance with** the opinion of **Rabbi Shimon, who says: An item whose** elimination **causes financial loss**[N] **is considered** to have **monetary** value. With regard to an item that is otherwise worthless, if its elimination causes monetary loss due to the fact that it must be replaced, it is considered to be of value. In this case, although the ox is worthless in and of itself, when the thief slaughters it he prevents the bailee from returning it intact to the owner and causes him to be obligated to pay the owner the value of the ox before it was sentenced to be stoned. Consequently, the thief must reimburse the bailee, as the ox effectively has value for that bailee.

NOTES

And it was forewarned while in the bailee's house – וְהוּעַד בְּבֵית שׁוֹמֵר: The issue of whether the ox was forewarned is not relevant here, as the same *halakha* applies to any ox that killed someone, and some versions of the text omit the mention of forewarning. It may have been added due to the similarity of this case to others; see, e.g., 40a.

And it was sentenced to be stoned while in the bailee's house – וְנִגְמַר דִּינוֹ בְּבֵית שׁוֹמֵר: In this case, where the animal gored and killed someone while the bailee was safeguarding it, the court would normally put the ox to death, and the bailee would have to reimburse the ox's owner. Rabbi Ya'akov maintains that if the bailee hastens to return the ox intact before its execution he is exempt from any further payment. By stealing the ox from him, the thief has brought about a situation in which the bailee will have no other recourse than to pay for the ox in full.

An item whose elimination causes financial loss – דָּבָר הַגּוֹרֵם לְמָמוֹן: Rabbi Shimon maintains that if one steals or destroys an item and thereby causes financial loss to another person, he must make financial restitution to the party who suffered the loss, even if the item is intrinsically worthless or does not belong to the injured party; or both. In the case discussed here, although the ox is considered worthless and ownerless after its sentencing, because the thief causes a monetary loss to the bailee, Rabbi Shimon would require the thief to pay restitution to him.

The commentaries ask: Why did the Gemara invoke Rabbi Shimon here, by asserting that Rabbi Meir, the *tanna* presently under discussion, would have to agree with that Sage's ruling? The Gemara could have omitted any reference to Rabbi Shimon, as it is known that Rabbi Meir maintains that one is liable for indirect damage. For example, if one destroys a promissory note, Rabbi Meir holds him responsible for the note's full value, despite the fact that the destroyed paper is itself virtually worthless. *Tosafot* answer that in the case of the promissory note, the money to which it refers is worth something, as a debt can be transferred, sold, or traded to anyone. By contrast, an ox sentenced to death is of no worth to anyone except the bailee, who can use it to exempt himself from monetary payment to the ox's owner (see *Shita Mekubbetzet*).

HALAKHA

Even after it was sentenced – אַף מִשֶּׁנִּגְמַר דִּינוֹ: If an ox, while in the care of a bailee, killed a person and was sentenced to be killed, the bailee may not exempt himself from payment by returning the now-worthless ox to the owner. The *halakha* is not in accordance with the opinion of Rabbi Ya'akov (Rambam *Sefer Nezikin*, *Hilkhot Nizkei Mamon* 11:9).

דִּתְנַן, רַבִּי שִׁמְעוֹן אוֹמֵר: קָדָשִׁים שֶׁחַיָּיב בְּאַחֲרָיוּתָן – חַיָּיב, אַלְמָא דָּבָר הַגּוֹרֵם לְמָמוֹן כְּמָמוֹן דָּמֵי.

As we learned in a mishna (74b): **Rabbi Shimon says:** In the case of **sacrificial** animals **for which** the owner **bears** financial **responsibility**[HN] to replace any of them with another animal if it is lost or it dies, the thief is **obligated** to pay the fourfold or fivefold payment if he slaughters the animal. Although one is generally not liable to pay the double payment for stealing consecrated items, Rabbi Shimon maintains that this case is different, since as a result of the animal's theft the owner sustains a loss by being required to substitute another animal for it. Since the animal's loss has financial ramifications for the owner apart from any inherent value it has, it has value for him. **Apparently,** Rabbi Shimon holds that **an item whose** elimination **causes financial** loss **is considered** to have **monetary** value.

אֲמַר רַב כָּהֲנָא: אֲמַרִיתָא לִשְׁמַעְתָּא קַמֵּיהּ דְּרַב זְבִיד מִנְּהַרְדְּעָא: מִי מָצֵית מוֹקְמַתְּ מַתְנִיתִין כְּרַבִּי מֵאִיר וְלָא כְּרַבִּי שִׁמְעוֹן? וְהָא קָתָנֵי סֵיפָא: רַבִּי שִׁמְעוֹן פּוֹטֵר בִּשְׁנֵי אֵלּוּ, מִכְּלָל דְּבְכוּלָּהּ מַתְנִיתִין מוֹדֶה!

Rav Kahana said: I recited this *halakha*, according to which the mishna follows the opinion of Rabbi Meir, **in front of Rav Zevid of Neharde'a,** and I asked him: Is it correct to say that **you can establish the mishna in accordance with** the opinion of **Rabbi Meir, and not in accordance with** the opinion of **Rabbi Shimon? But isn't it taught** in **the last clause** of the mishna: **Rabbi Shimon exempts** the thief from the fourfold or fivefold payment **in these** last **two** cases. One can learn **by inference that in all the** rest of the cases in the **mishna,** apart from these two, Rabbi Shimon **concedes** that the thief pays the fourfold or fivefold payment.

אֲמַר לֵיהּ: לָא, מִכְּלָל דְּמוֹדֶה בְּטָבַח וּמָכַר לִרְפוּאָה וְלִכְלָבִים.

Rav Zevid **said to him: No;** that is not the correct inference from the mishna. Rather, **by inference** one can learn only **that** Rabbi Shimon **concedes** that the thief pays the fourfold or fivefold payment in the cases mentioned immediately prior to this one, specifically **in** a case where the thief **slaughtered or sold** the animal in order that it should be used **for medicinal purposes or for** feeding to **dogs.** Therefore, it can be correct to establish the mishna in accordance with the opinion of Rabbi Meir and not in accordance with the opinion of Rabbi Shimon.

״גָּנַב מִשֶּׁל אָבִיו וְטָבַח וּמָכַר״ וכו׳. בְּעָא מִינֵּיהּ רָבָא מֵרַב נַחְמָן: גָּנַב שׁוֹר שֶׁל שְׁנֵי שׁוּתָּפִין וּטְבָחוֹ, וְהוֹדָה לְאֶחָד מֵהֶן, מַהוּ?

§ The mishna teaches: If one **stole** an animal **of his father's and** then **slaughtered or sold** it, and afterward his father died, he pays the fourfold or fivefold payment to his father's other heirs. **Rava raised a dilemma before Rav Naḥman:** If one **stole an ox** belonging **to two partners and slaughtered it, and** subsequently **admitted** the theft **to one of** the partners,[N] which means that he is exempt from paying the fourfold or fivefold payment to that partner, in accordance with the principle that one who admits his own guilt is exempt from fines, **what is** the *halakha* with regard to payment to the other partner?

HALAKHA

Sacrificial animals for which the owner bears financial responsibility – קָדָשִׁים שֶׁחַיָּיב בְּאַחֲרָיוּתָן: If one steals a sacrificial animal from its owner and slaughters it or sells it, he is exempt from the fourfold or fivefold payment, even if the offering was of the type that the owner is obligated to replace. The *halakha* is not in accordance with the opinion of Rabbi Shimon (Rambam *Sefer Nezikin, Hilkhot Geneiva* 2:1).

NOTES

Sacrificial animals for which the owner bears financial responsibility – קָדָשִׁים שֶׁחַיָּיב בְּאַחֲרָיוּתָן: There are differences between various categories of offerings: Some are usually obligatory, e.g., the sin-offering, while others are usually brought voluntarily. With regard to obligatory offerings, until the animal has been sacrificed the obligation to bring the offering to the Temple remains in force. If an animal designated for an offering of this kind was lost before it was sacrificed it would have to be replaced with another animal.

With regard to a voluntary offering, responsibility to replace it depends on the wording of the individual's vow. If he merely said: This particular animal shall be a burnt-offering, he is not obligated to replace it if it becomes lost or it dies. If he said: I hereby accept upon myself that I will bring a burnt-offering, and then designated a specific animal for that offering and the animal was lost or died, he would have to replace it. If one steals an animal that had been designated to be a burnt-offering and must be replaced if lost, then even though a sacrificial animal is no longer considered to belong to its previous owner but to the Temple treasury, since its theft causes him a financial loss it is considered his property for the purposes of this *halakha*. Consequently, the thief is obligated to pay him the double payment or, if he slaughtered or sold it, the fourfold or fivefold payment.

And subsequently admitted to one of the partners, etc. – וְהוֹדָה לְאֶחָד מֵהֶן וכו׳: The commentaries ask: How it is possible for one to concede that he has stolen an animal without admitting that he has stolen it from both of its owners (Rid)? One suggestion is that the thief admitted to one partner in the presence of the court that he stole the animal, but later, when confronted by the second partner in a different court, he denied the theft (*Baḥ*). Alternatively, the Gemara is referring to a case where the thief claims that he is himself the second partner of the animal. In other words, he tells the first partner: I admit to stealing an animal, half of which you own, and I am the owner of the other half. In this manner, he admits only to having stolen half the animal (Rid). Another possibility raised by the Rid is that when the Gemara says that the thief admitted the theft to one partner, this means that he not only admitted the theft to the partner but had already reimbursed him for the theft before he came to court.

״חֲמִשָּׁה בָקָר״ אָמַר רַחֲמָנָא – וְלֹא חֲמִשָּׁה חֲצָאֵי בָקָר, אוֹ דִּלְמָא ״חֲמִשָּׁה בָקָר״ אָמַר רַחֲמָנָא – וַאֲפִילּוּ חֲמִשָּׁה חֲצָאֵי בָקָר? אֲמַר לֵיהּ: ״חֲמִשָּׁה בָקָר״ אָמַר רַחֲמָנָא – וְלֹא חֲמִשָּׁה חֲצָאֵי בָקָר.

The Gemara explains the sides of the dilemma: **The Merciful One states** in the Torah: "He shall pay **five oxen** for an ox" (Exodus 21:37), which indicates five full oxen, **but not five half-oxen. Or** perhaps when **the Merciful One states "five oxen,"** this means that **even five half-oxen** must be paid in a case of this kind. Rav Naḥman **said to** Rava: **The Merciful One states: "Five oxen,"** which means five full oxen, **but not five half-oxen.**

אֵיתִיבֵיהּ: גָּנַב מִשֶּׁל אָבִיו וְטָבַח וּמָכַר, וְאַחַר כָּךְ מֵת אָבִיו – מְשַׁלֵּם תַּשְׁלוּמֵי אַרְבָּעָה וַחֲמִשָּׁה; וְהָא הָכָא, כֵּיוָן דְּמֵת אָבִיו – כְּמוֹ שֶׁקָּדַם וְהוֹדָה לְאֶחָד מֵהֶן דָּמֵי, וְקָתָנֵי: מְשַׁלֵּם תַּשְׁלוּמֵי אַרְבָּעָה וַחֲמִשָּׁה!

Rava **raised an objection to him** from the mishna: If one **stole** an animal **of his father's** and then **slaughtered or sold** it, **and afterward his father died, he pays the fourfold or fivefold payment. But here, since his father died** and the thief has inherited part of the stolen animal himself, it is **similar to** the case of one who stole from two partners **and went ahead and admitted** the theft **to one of them,** i.e., to himself. In the case of the mishna he is exempt from paying the portion of the fine that is for himself, **and** yet the mishna **teaches** that **he pays** the other heirs their portion of **the fourfold or fivefold payment.**

אֲמַר לֵיהּ: הָכָא בְּמַאי עָסְקִינַן – כְּגוֹן שֶׁעָמַד אָבִיו בַּדִּין.

Rav Naḥman **said to** Rava: **With what are we dealing here? With** a case **where his father stood** against his son the thief **in** his **trial,** and the son was convicted for the theft and slaughter of his father's animal. In this case, the liability to pay the fourfold or fivefold payment was established before the father's death, and at that time the payment was five full oxen.

אֲבָל לֹא עָמַד בַּדִּין, מַאי? אֵינוֹ מְשַׁלֵּם תַּשְׁלוּמֵי אַרְבָּעָה וַחֲמִשָּׁה? אִי הָכִי, אַדְּתָנֵי סֵיפָא: גָּנַב מִשֶּׁל אָבִיו וּמֵת וְאַחַר כָּךְ טָבַח וּמָכַר אֵינוֹ מְשַׁלֵּם תַּשְׁלוּמֵי אַרְבָּעָה וַחֲמִשָּׁה – נִיפְלוֹג בְּדִידֵיהּ: בַּמֶּה דְּבָרִים אֲמוּרִים – כְּשֶׁעָמַד בַּדִּין, אֲבָל לֹא עָמַד בַּדִּין – אֵינוֹ מְשַׁלֵּם תַּשְׁלוּמֵי אַרְבָּעָה וַחֲמִשָּׁה!

Rava asked him: **And** if the thief had **not** yet **stood trial** before the father's death, **what** would be the *halakha*, according to your opinion? Would he **not** be required to **pay the fourfold or fivefold payment? If so, rather than teaching in the latter clause** of the mishna (74b): If one **stole his father's** animal **and** the father **died, and afterward he slaughtered or sold** it, **he does not pay the fourfold or fivefold payment;** let the mishna **make a distinction within the same** type of case, as follows: **In what** case **is this statement,** i.e., that the thief is required to pay the fourfold or fivefold payment, **said?** It is **when** the thief **stood trial** in his father's lifetime; **but** if he **did not stand trial** in his father's lifetime **he does not pay the fourfold or fivefold payment.**

אֲמַר לֵיהּ: הָכִי נַמִי, אַיְּידֵי דְּנָסֵיב רֵישָׁא: גָּנַב מִשֶּׁל אָבִיו וְטָבַח וּמָכַר וְאַחַר כָּךְ מֵת אָבִיו – נְסֵיב סֵיפָא נַמִי: גָּנַב מִשֶּׁל אָבִיו וּמֵת אָבִיו וְאַחַר כָּךְ טָבַח וּמָכַר.

Rav Naḥman **said to him: Indeed,** the mishna could have mentioned that case. However, **since** the *tanna* of the mishna has to **cite the first clause,** which discusses one who **stole** an animal **of his father's and slaughtered or sold** it, **and afterward his father died, he cites the latter clause as well,** by means of a similar case: If one **stole his father's** animal **and his father died, and afterward he slaughtered or sold** the animal.

לְצַפְרָא אֲמַר לֵיהּ: ״חֲמִשָּׁה בָקָר״ אָמַר רַחֲמָנָא – וַאֲפִילּוּ חֲמִשָּׁה חֲצָאֵי בָקָר. וְהַאי דְּלָא אֲמַרִי לָךְ בְּאוּרְתָּא,

This discussion between Rava and Rav Naḥman occurred in the evening. **On the** following **morning,** Rav Naḥman retracted his statement and **said to** Rava: **The Merciful One states: "Five oxen,"** and this means that **even five half-oxen**[H] are included. Rav Naḥman explained his change of mind: **And the reason that I did not say** this **to you last night**

HALAKHA

Even five half-oxen – וַאֲפִילּוּ חֲמִשָּׁה חֲצָאֵי בָקָר: In a case where one steals an ox or a sheep that belongs to two partners and then slaughters it or sells it, if he admitted the theft in court to one of the partners, but denied the theft to the second partner, and witnesses subsequently testify that he had stolen the animal, he pays the value of five half-oxen or four half-sheep to the second partner, in accordance with the second ruling of Rav Naḥman (Rambam *Sefer Nezikin, Hilkhot Geneiva* 3:10; *Tur, Ḥoshen Mishpat* 350).

Perek **VII**
Daf **72** Amud **a**

דְּלָא אֲכַלִי בִּשְׂרָא דְּתוֹרָא.

is because I had not eaten ox meat.[N] In other words, I was fasting yesterday and was unable to concentrate properly.

NOTES

Is because I had not eaten ox meat – דְּלָא אֲכַלִי בִּשְׂרָא דְּתוֹרָא: Rashi explains that this is a figure of speech that means: I did not think the matter through sufficiently (see Ya'avetz). Others suggest that Rav Naḥman mentioned ox meat in allusion to the verse: "Five oxen for an ox" (Exodus 21:37). Yet others read this statement literally: Rav Naḥman excused his incorrect answer on the grounds that he had not eaten anything that day and had therefore been weak and not fully alert (*Tosafot*). *Eshel Avraham* explains that he meant he had not partaken of nutritious food on the previous day, and therefore was not as mentally alert as usual (see *Tanya* 1:7).

וְאֶלָּא מַאי שְׁנָא רֵישָׁא וּמַאי שְׁנָא סֵיפָא?

Rava responded to him: **But** if the Torah requires even a partial payment of the fourfold or fivefold payment, **what is different in the first clause,** in which the son must pay, **and what is different** in the **latter clause,** where he is exempt?

אֲמַר לֵיהּ: רֵישָׁא קָרֵינָא בֵּיהּ ״וּטְבָחוֹ״ כּוּלּוֹ בְּאִיסּוּרָא, סֵיפָא לָא קָרֵינָא בֵּיהּ ״וּטְבָחוֹ״ כּוּלּוֹ בְּאִיסּוּרָא.

Rav Naḥman **said to him: In the first clause,** where the father's animal was stolen and slaughtered in his lifetime, **I read about** this case the verse: "If a man steal an ox or a sheep, **and slaughter it**" (Exodus 21:37), which indicates that the thief slaughtered the ox or the sheep **entirely in a prohibited** manner.[N] **In the latter clause,** where the animal was slaughtered after the father's death, **I do not read about** this case the verse: **"And slaughter it,"** which describes a slaughter that was performed **entirely in a prohibited** manner, because the animal already partially belonged to him, and his own portion of the ox was slaughtered in a permitted manner.

״הַשּׁוֹחֵט וְנִמְצֵאת טְרֵיפָה״ וכו׳. אֲמַר לֵיהּ רַב חֲבִיבִי מְחוֹזְנָאָה לְרַב אַשִׁי: שְׁמַע מִינָּהּ אֵינָהּ לִשְׁחִיטָה אֶלָּא לְבַסּוֹף,

§ The mishna teaches: A thief **who slaughters** the animal **but it was found to be a *tereifa*,** and likewise a thief who slaughters a non-sacred animal in the Temple courtyard, pays the fourfold or fivefold payment. **Rav Ḥavivi of Meḥoza said to Rav Ashi: Conclude from** the mishna that the act **of slaughtering** is considered to have been performed **only at the end** of the slaughtering process.[N]

דְּאִי יֶשְׁנָהּ לִשְׁחִיטָה מִתְּחִילָּה וְעַד סוֹף, כֵּיוָן דִּשְׁחַט בָּהּ פּוּרְתָּא – אַסְרַהּ, אִידָּךְ לָא דְּמָרֵיהּ קָא טָבַח!

Rav Ḥavivi of Meḥoza explains: **As, if** you say that the act **of slaughtering** lasts **from beginning to end,** i.e., the halakhic ramifications of slaughtering are in effect throughout the process, one could raise a question with regard to the case of one who slaughters a non-sacred animal in the Temple courtyard: **Once he slaughtered** the animal **a bit,** at the very start of the act of slaughter, **he has prohibited** the animal, with regard to deriving benefit, as a non-sacred animal slaughtered in the Temple courtyard. When he slaughters **the other** part, it is already prohibited with regard to deriving benefit, which means that it is **not** an animal that belongs **to its owner** that he **slaughters.** Since deriving benefit from the animal is prohibited, it has no value; therefore, there is no ownership.

אֲמַר לֵיהּ רַב הוּנָא בְּרֵיהּ דְּרָבָא: כִּי קָא מִחַיַּיב – אַהַהוּא פּוּרְתָּא. אֲמַר לֵיהּ רַב אַשִׁי: לָא תִּידְחֵי, ״וּטְבָחוֹ״ כּוּלּוֹ בָּעֵינַן, וְלֵיכָּא.

Rav Huna, son of Rava, said to Rav Ḥavivi in response: It is possible to explain the mishna even if one maintains that the halakhic ramifications of slaughtering are in effect throughout the slaughter. As, **when does** the thief **become obligated** to pay the fourfold or fivefold payment? It is **when** he performs **that** first **bit** of slaughter in the beginning, before the animal becomes forbidden. **Rav Ashi said to** Rav Huna: **Do not dismiss** Rav Ḥavivi's objection with this explanation. The verse: "If a man steal an ox or a sheep, **and slaughter it**" (Exodus 21:37), indicates that to impose liability to pay the fourfold or fivefold payment **we require** that the thief slaughtered it **completely, and** after having slaughtered it just a bit **there is no** complete slaughter yet.

אֶלָּא קַשְׁיָא! אֲמַר לֵיהּ, הָכִי אֲמַר רַב גַּמְדָּא מִשְּׁמֵיהּ דְּרָבָא: כְּגוֹן שֶׁשָּׁחַט מִקְצָת סִימָנִין בַּחוּץ וּגְמָרָן בִּפְנִים.

Rav Huna said to Rav Ashi: **But** if you are correct, the mishna **is difficult** according to the one who maintains that the halakhic ramifications of slaughtering are in effect throughout the slaughter. Rav Ashi **said to** Rav Huna: **This is what Rav Gamda said in the name of Rava,** concerning this question: The mishna is discussing a case **where** the thief **slaughtered,** i.e., severed, **part** of the **two organs that must be severed in ritual slaughter,** i.e., the trachea and the esophagus [***simanin***], **outside** the Temple, and **finished** slaughtering **them inside** the Temple. Therefore, the animal became prohibited with regard to deriving benefit only at the final stage of slaughter, concomitant with the liability to pay the fourfold or fivefold payment.

אִיכָּא דְּמַתְנֵי לַהּ אַהָא, אָמַר רַבִּי שִׁמְעוֹן מִשּׁוּם דְּרַבִּי לֵוִי סָבָא: אֵינָהּ לִשְׁחִיטָה אֶלָּא לְבַסּוֹף, וְרַבִּי יוֹחָנָן אָמַר: יֶשְׁנָהּ לִשְׁחִיטָה מִתְּחִילָּה וְעַד סוֹף. אֲמַר לֵיהּ רַב חֲבִיבִי מְחוֹזְנָאָה לְרַב אַשִׁי: לֵימָא קָסָבַר רַבִּי יוֹחָנָן חוּלִּין שֶׁנִּשְׁחֲטוּ בָּעֲזָרָה לָאו דְּאוֹרַיְיתָא,

There are those who teach that the preceding exchange took place **with regard to** the following dispute: **Rabbi Shimon** ben Lakish **says in the name of Rabbi Levi the Elder:** The act of slaughtering is considered to have been **performed only at the end** of the slaughtering process. **And Rabbi Yoḥanan says:** The act **of slaughtering lasts from beginning to end.**[H] **Rav Ḥavivi of Meḥoza said to Rav Ashi: Shall we say that Rabbi Yoḥanan holds** that the prohibition against deriving benefit from **non-sacred** animals **that were slaughtered in the Temple courtyard**[H] **is not by Torah law?**

NOTES

And slaughter it entirely in a prohibited manner – וּטְבָחוֹ כּוּלּוֹ בְּאִיסּוּרָא: The verse could have stated: "And slaughter." The direct object: "It," indicates that this is referring to slaughter of the ox that is performed entirely in a prohibited manner. The early commentaries point out that in a parallel case of theft not involving slaughter the thief would be obligated in the double payment despite the fact that at the time of the theft he was already a partial owner of the stolen animal, as the Torah does not use a similar expression with regard to the double payment (*Tosafot*; Rabbeinu Yehonatan).

Slaughtering is considered to have been performed only at the end of the slaughtering process – אֵינָהּ לִשְׁחִיטָה אֶלָּא לְבַסּוֹף: The early commentaries write that this dispute involves only those cases where the Torah specifically mentions slaughtering. With regard to sacrificing an animal for idol worship, where the slaughter is merely a manifestation of the prohibition, the animal is rendered forbidden as soon as the act of slaughter begins, as even this minute deed constitutes an act of idolatry (Ra'avad).

HALAKHA

The act of slaughtering lasts from beginning to end – יֶשְׁנָהּ לִשְׁחִיטָה מִתְּחִילָּה וְעַד סוֹף: Slaughter performed by a gentile is invalid. Therefore, if a gentile begins the act of slaughter and a Jew completes it, or vice versa, the slaughter is invalid, as the act of slaughtering lasts from beginning to end. Similarly, if one begins the slaughter of a sacrificial animal outside the Temple courtyard and the process is completed inside the courtyard, or if an offering that must be slaughtered in the north side of the courtyard was partially slaughtered on the south side and the slaughter was completed in the north, the offering is invalid. The *halakha* is in accordance with the opinion of Rabbi Yoḥanan (Rambam *Sefer Kedusha*, *Hilkhot Sheḥita* 4:13 and *Sefer Avoda*, *Hilkhot Pesulei HaMukdashin* 1:18).

Non-sacred animals that were slaughtered in the Temple courtyard – חוּלִּין שֶׁנִּשְׁחֲטוּ בָּעֲזָרָה: It is prohibited by rabbinic law to derive benefit from a non-sacred animal that has been slaughtered in the Temple courtyard (Rambam *Sefer Kedusha*, *Hilkhot Sheḥita* 2:3).

דְּאִי סָלְקָא דַּעְתָּךְ דְּאוֹרָיְיתָא, מִכִּי שָׁחֵיט לָהּ פּוּרְתָּא – אַסְרַהּ, אִידָּךְ – לָאו דְּמָרָה קָא טָבַח!

As, if it enters your mind that it is prohibited **by Torah law** the mishna here would be difficult, for **as soon as he slaughtered** the animal **a bit,** at the very start of the act of slaughter, **he has prohibited** the animal, with regard to deriving benefit, as a non-sacred animal slaughtered in the Temple courtyard. When he slaughters **the other** part it is already prohibited with regard to deriving benefit, which means that it is **not** an animal that belongs **to its owner** that he **slaughters.**

אֲמַר לֵיהּ רַב אַחָא בְּרֵיהּ דְּרָבָא: כִּי קָא מְחַיֵּיב – נָמֵי אַהַהוּא פּוּרְתָּא. אֲמַר לֵיהּ רַב אַשִׁי: לָא תִּידְחֵיהּ, ״וּטְבָחוֹ״ כּוּלּוֹ בָּעֵינַן, וְלֵיכָּא.

Rav Aḥa, son of Rava, said to Rav Ḥavivi: It is possible to explain the mishna even according to the opinion that the halakhic ramifications of slaughtering are in effect throughout the slaughter, and even if one maintains that it is prohibited by Torah law to benefit from a non-sacred animal slaughtered in the Temple. As, **when does** the thief **become obligated** to pay the fourfold or fivefold payment **as well?** It is **when** he performs **that** first **bit** of slaughter in the beginning, before the animal becomes forbidden. **Rav Ashi said to** Rav Huna: **Do not dismiss** Rav Ḥavivi's suggestion with this explanation. The verse: "If a man steal an ox or a sheep, **and slaughter it**" (Exodus 21:37), indicates that in order to impose liability to pay the fourfold or fivefold payment **we require** that the thief slaughtered it **completely, and** after having slaughtered it just a bit **there is no** complete slaughter yet.

אֶלָּא קַשְׁיָא! אֲמַר לֵיהּ, הָכִי אָמַר רַב גַּמְדָּא מִשְּׁמֵיהּ דְּרָבָא: כִּי קָא מְחַיֵּיב – כְּגוֹן שֶׁשָּׁחַט מִקְצָת סִימָנִין בַּחוּץ וּגְמָרָן בִּפְנִים.

Rav Huna said to Rav Ashi: **But** if you are correct, the mishna **is difficult.** Rav Ashi **said to** Rav Huna: **This is what Rav Gamda said in the name of Rava: When** does the mishna state that the thief **is obligated** to pay the fourfold or fivefold payment? It is in a case **where** the thief **slaughtered part** of the ***simanim*** **outside** the Temple, **and finished** slaughtering **them inside** the Temple. Therefore, the animal became prohibited with regard to deriving benefit only at the final stage of slaughter, concomitant with the liability to pay the fourfold or fivefold payment.

מַתְנִי׳ גָּנַב עַל פִּי שְׁנַיִם וְטָבַח וּמָכַר עַל פִּיהֶן, וְנִמְצְאוּ זוֹמְמִים – מְשַׁלְּמִין הַכֹּל.

MISHNA If one **stole** an ox or a sheep, as established **based on** the testimony of **two** witnesses,[HB] **and he** subsequently **slaughtered** the animal **or sold** it, also **based on** the testimony of the same witnesses, **and** these witnesses **were found** to be **conspiring** witnesses,[N] these witnesses **pay everything,** i.e., not only the principal amount but also the fourfold or fivefold payment. This is in accordance with the Torah's decree with regard to conspiring witnesses: "You shall do to him as he had conspired to do to his brother" (Deuteronomy 19:19). Since these witnesses attempted to obligate the alleged thief to pay the fourfold or fivefold payment, they themselves must pay that full amount.

NOTES

And they were found to be conspiring witnesses – וְנִמְצְאוּ זוֹמְמִים: As the Gemara establishes, this must be referring to a case where the witnesses testified about the theft of the animal and its slaughter or sale at the same time, and that the testimonies about both matters were disqualified together. The reason is that if the testimony concerning the theft was disqualified first, the testimony concerning the slaughter or sale would be of no consequence, and therefore the witnesses would not be subject to the punishment of conspiring witnesses for the testimony about the slaughter or sale. These witnesses would pay only the double payment.

HALAKHA

One stole based on the testimony of two witnesses, etc. – גָּנַב עַל פִּי שְׁנַיִם וכו׳: If two witnesses testify that one stole an animal and slaughtered or sold it, and the witnesses were found to be conspiring witnesses, they pay everything, including the fourfold or fivefold payment (Rambam *Sefer Shofetim, Hilkhot Edut* 21:6).

BACKGROUND

Conspiring witnesses – עֵדִים זוֹמְמִים: When two sets of witnesses provide contradictory testimony, both testimonies are completely discarded, as it is impossible to determine which is true. Nevertheless, the Torah writes: "If an unrighteous witness rise up against any man to bear untrue witness against him, then…the judges shall inquire diligently; and, behold, if the witness is a false witness and has testified falsely against his brother, then you shall do to him as he conspired to do to his brother" (Deuteronomy 19:16–19). This demonstrates that there are situations in which it is possible to rule on which of two contradictory testimonies is true and which is false. The Sages concluded that this situation arises when a first set of witnesses testifies that they witnessed an event, and a second set testifies that the first set could not possibly have witnessed that event, as they were in a different place when the event purportedly occurred. In this case only the second testimony is definitively accepted while the first is rejected. The first witnesses, who are known as conspiring witnesses, receive the same punishment they conspired to impose upon the victim of their testimony, whether it is corporal or monetary punishment, or even the death penalty.

גָּנַב עַל פִּי שְׁנַיִם וְטָבַח וּמָכַר עַל פִּי שְׁנַיִם אֲחֵרִים, אֵלּוּ וְאֵלּוּ נִמְצְאוּ זוֹמְמִין – הָרִאשׁוֹנִים מְשַׁלְּמִין תַּשְׁלוּמֵי כֶפֶל, וְאַחֲרוֹנִים מְשַׁלְּמִין תַּשְׁלוּמֵי שְׁלֹשָׁה;

With regard to one who **stole** an ox or a sheep, as established **based on** the testimony of **two** witnesses, **and he** subsequently **slaughtered** the animal **or sold** it, **based on** the testimony of **two other** witnesses,[H] if both **these** witnesses **and those** witnesses **were found** to be **conspiring** witnesses, **the first** set of witnesses, who testified about the theft of the animal, **pay** the alleged thief the **double payment,**[N] which is what they had conspired to cause him to pay. **And the last** set of witnesses, who attested to the slaughter or sale of the animal, **pay** the alleged thief a twofold payment for a sheep or **a threefold payment** for an ox, which they had conspired to cause him to pay over and above the double payment.

נִמְצְאוּ אַחֲרוֹנִים זוֹמְמִין – הוּא מְשַׁלֵּם תַּשְׁלוּמֵי כֶפֶל, וְהֵן מְשַׁלְּמִין תַּשְׁלוּמֵי שְׁלֹשָׁה;

If only the witnesses in the **last** set **were found** to be **conspiring** witnesses,[H] while the testimony about the theft remains intact, the thief **pays** the **double payment** to the animal's owner **and** the second set of witnesses **pay** the alleged thief the twofold or **threefold payment,** the amount over and above the double payment, which is what they had conspired to cause him to pay.

אֶחָד מִן אַחֲרוֹנִים זוֹמְמִין – בָּטְלָה עֵדוּת שְׁנִיָּה; אֶחָד מִן הָרִאשׁוֹנִים זוֹמְמִין – בָּטְלָה כָּל הָעֵדוּת, שֶׁאִם אֵין גְּנֵיבָה, אֵין טְבִיחָה וְאֵין מְכִירָה.

If only **one** individual **from the last** set of witnesses was found to be **a conspiring** witness,[H] **the second testimony** is **nullified,**[N] as it was not submitted by two valid witnesses, whereas the first testimony remains intact. If **one** individual **from the first** set of witnesses is found to be **a conspiring** witness,[H] **the entire testimony** concerning the thief is **nullified.** The reason is **that if there is no theft** established by reliable testimony **there is no** liability for **slaughtering** the animal **and there is no** liability for **selling** it.

גמ׳ אִיתְּמַר: עֵד זוֹמֵם, אַבַּיֵּי אָמַר: לְמַפְרֵעַ הוּא נִפְסָל, רָבָא אָמַר: מִכָּאן וּלְהַבָּא הוּא נִפְסָל.

GEMARA One who is rendered a conspiring witness is barred from providing testimony in the future. The Gemara cites a fundamental dispute with regard to this disqualification. **It was stated** concerning **a conspiring witness: Abaye says: He is disqualified retroactively,** from when he provided his testimony. Any testimony he may have provided after that point in time is retroactively nullified. **Rava says: He is disqualified** only **from that point forward,** i.e., from when he was established to be a conspiring witness, but not retroactively from when he provided his testimony.

אַבַּיֵּי אָמַר לְמַפְרֵעַ הוּא נִפְסָל, מֵהַהוּא שַׁעְתָּא דְּאַסְהֵיד הֲוָה לֵיהּ רָשָׁע, וְהַתּוֹרָה אָמְרָה: ״אַל תָּשֶׁת...רָשָׁע...עֵד״;

The Gemara explains the reasons for the two opinions: **Abaye says he is disqualified retroactively** because it is **from that time when he testified** that **he is** considered **a wicked man, and the Torah said: "Do not put** your hand with **the wicked** to be an unrighteous **witness"** (Exodus 23:1), which is interpreted to mean: Do not allow a wicked man to serve as a witness.

רָבָא אָמַר מִכָּאן וּלְהַבָּא הוּא נִפְסָל, עֵד זוֹמֵם חִידּוּשׁ הוּא, דְּהָא תְּרֵי וּתְרֵי נִינְהוּ, מַאי חָזֵית דְּצַיֵּית לְהָנֵי? צַיֵּית לְהָנֵי,

Rava says that **he is disqualified** only **from that point forward** because the disqualification of **a conspiring witness is a novelty,**[N] i.e., it is not based on logic. The reason is **that this** is a case of **two** witnesses **against two** other witnesses, in which case neither testimony should be accepted. **What did you see that** causes **you to listen to** the second set of witnesses, who testify that the first set were not at the scene of the purported event? You could instead **listen to** the first set of witnesses, who testify to the event, and disbelieve the second set. Yet the Torah teaches that the second set of witnesses is always deemed credible and the first set is subjected to punishment as conspiring witnesses.

הִלְכָּךְ אֵין לְךָ בּוֹ אֶלָּא מִשְּׁעַת חִידּוּשׁ וְאֵילָךְ.

Therefore, as the disqualification of the conspiring witnesses is an anomaly, **you have** the right to disqualify them **only from the time of the novelty and onward,** i.e., this counterintuitive disqualification is not applied retroactively.

אִיכָּא דְּאָמְרִי: רָבָא נַמִי כְּאַבַּיֵּי סְבִירָא לֵיהּ, דְּאָמַר לְמַפְרֵעַ הוּא נִפְסָל, וְהָכָא הַיְינוּ טַעְמֵיהּ דְּרָבָא,

There are those **who say** that **Rava also holds like Abaye, who says** that by rights a conspiring witness **should be disqualified retroactively** from when he provided his testimony, **and here this is Rava's reason** for not disqualifying him retroactively:

HALAKHA

And he slaughtered or sold it based on the testimony of two other witnesses – וְטָבַח וּמָכַר עַל פִּי שְׁנַיִם אֲחֵרִים: If two witnesses testify that one stole an animal and two others testify that he slaughtered or sold it, and both sets of witnesses were found to be conspiring witnesses, those who testified to the theft pay the double payment to the one they accused, while those who testified concerning the slaughter or sale pay him the remaining twofold or threefold payment (Rambam *Sefer Shofetim, Hilkhot Edut* 21:6).

The witnesses in the last set were found to be conspiring witnesses – נִמְצְאוּ אַחֲרוֹנִים זוֹמְמִין: If two witnesses testify that one stole an animal and two others testify that he sold or slaughtered it, and the witnesses in the second set are found to be conspiring witnesses, the thief pays the double payment and the second set of witnesses pay the thief the remainder of the fourfold or fivefold payment, i.e., a twofold or threefold payment (Rambam *Sefer Shofetim, Hilkhot Edut* 21:6).

One from the last set was found to be a conspiring witness, etc. – אֶחָד מִן אַחֲרוֹנִים זוֹמְמִין וכו׳: If two witnesses testify that one stole an animal and two others testify that he slaughtered it, and one of those testifying about the slaughter is found to be a conspiring witness, the second testimony is nullified (Rambam *Sefer Shofetim, Hilkhot Edut* 21:6).

One from the first set is found to be a conspiring witness, etc. – אֶחָד מִן הָרִאשׁוֹנִים זוֹמְמִין וכו׳: If two witnesses testify that someone stole an animal and two others testify that he slaughtered it, and one witness from the first set of witnesses is found to be a conspiring witness, the entire testimony is nullified. The reason is that if there is no established theft there can be no liability for selling or slaughtering (Rambam *Sefer Shofetim, Hilkhot Edut* 21:6).

NOTES

The first set pay the double payment – הָרִאשׁוֹנִים מְשַׁלְּמִין תַּשְׁלוּמֵי כֶפֶל: The Jerusalem Talmud discusses a case where the witnesses concerning the slaughter testified first, and their account was rejected as irrelevant, due to the lack of testimony concerning the theft. Later, witnesses arrived to testify about the theft, and they were informed that their testimony would be joined with the first testimony, concerning the slaughter. In this case, as the testimony concerning the theft led to the imposition of the entire payment, if the witnesses in the second set are found to be conspiring witnesses, they pay the full sum.

The second testimony is nullified – בָּטְלָה עֵדוּת שְׁנִיָּה: The witness who was rendered a conspiring witness is not subject to monetary punishment, as conspiring witnesses are subject to punishment only if all the members of that set of witnesses are found to be conspiring witnesses (Rashi).

The disqualification of a conspiring witness is a novelty – עֵד זוֹמֵם חִידּוּשׁ הוּא: The novelty of the *halakha* of a conspiring witness is twofold: First, the first witnesses are not merely suspected of lying but are treated as definite false witnesses. Second, the court does not suspect the second set of witnesses of falsehood, despite the fact that the first witnesses deny their account (*Tosafot*).

מִשּׁוּם פְּסֵידָא דְּלָקוֹחוֹת.

It is **due to** the potential monetary **loss for purchasers,** whose acquisitions had been validated by these witnesses between the time of the witnesses' first testimony and when they were rendered conspiring witnesses. If the disqualification of the witnesses were applied retroactively, as by right it should, all these transactions would be nullified, which would cause a loss to these purchasers.

מַאי בֵּינַיְיהוּ? דְּאַסְהִידוּ בֵּיהּ תְּרֵי לְחַד וּתְרֵי לְחַד, אִי נַמִּי דְּפָסְלִינְהוּ בְּגַזְלָנוּתָא.

The Gemara asks: **What is** the practical difference **between** these two explanations of Rava's opinion? After all, according to both explanations Rava did not apply the disqualification of conspiring witnesses retroactively. The Gemara explains that there is a difference in a case **where two** witnesses **testify about one** of the witnesses that he was not at the scene of the supposed crime, **and two** other witnesses testify **about** the other **one**[N] witness in a similar manner. **Alternatively,** there is a practical difference between the two explanations in a case where two witnesses **disqualified** the first set of witnesses **by** testifying that they had once committed **robbery** and are therefore unfit to give testimony.

לְהַךְ לִישָּׁנָא דְּאָמְרַתְּ מִשּׁוּם חִידּוּשׁ – לֵיכָּא, לְהַךְ לִישָּׁנָא דְּאָמְרַתְּ מִשּׁוּם פְּסֵידָא דְּלָקוֹחוֹת – אִיכָּא.

The Gemara elaborates: **According to this version** in **which you say** that Rava's rejection of retroactive disqualification was **because** it is **a novelty,** in these two circumstances **there is no** novelty, and therefore he would agree that the disqualification should be retroactive. **According to that version** in **which you say** that Rava's concern was **due to** a potential **loss for purchasers,** in these two circumstances **there is** a concern for a potential loss for purchasers. Consequently, in these circumstances as well Rava would reject retroactive disqualification.

אֲמַר רַבִּי יִרְמְיָה מִדִּפְתִּי: עֲבַד רַב פָּפָּא עוּבְדָא כְּוָותֵיהּ דְּרָבָא. רַב אָשֵׁי אָמַר: הִלְכְתָא כְּוָותֵיהּ דְּאַבַּיֵי. וְהִלְכְתָא כְּוָותֵיהּ דְּאַבַּיֵי בְּיַע״ל קג״ם.

Rabbi Yirmeya of Difti related: Rav Pappa once **took action,** i.e., ruled in a case, **in accordance with** the opinion **of Rava,** and rejected retroactive disqualification of conspiring witnesses. **Rav Ashi said: The *halakha* is in accordance with** the opinion **of Abaye**[H] with regard to retroactive disqualification of conspiring witnesses. The Gemara provides a principle: **And** in disputes between Abaye and Rava the *halakha* is in accordance with the opinion of Rava, except for six cases in which **the *halakha*** is **in accordance with** the opinion **of Abaye.** They are: **In** the cases represented by the mnemonic ***yod-ayin-lamed kuf-gimmel-mem.*** These *halakhot* are the following: Unknown despair [*ye'ush*]; conspiring witness [*eidim*] who are disqualified retroactively; a side post [*leḥi*] standing alone; betrothal [*kiddushin*] that is not given to consummation; revealing intent with a bill of divorce [*get*]; and an apostate [*mumar*] who sins rebelliously.

תְּנַן: גָּנַב עַל פִּי שְׁנַיִם וְטָבַח וּמָכַר עַל פִּיהֶם, וְנִמְצְאוּ זוֹמְמִין – מְשַׁלְּמִין אֶת הַכֹּל;

The Gemara asks a question with regard to Abaye's opinion from that which **we learned** in the mishna: If one **stole** an ox or a sheep, as established **based on** the testimony of **two** witnesses, **and** he **slaughtered** the animal **or sold** it, also **based on** the testimony of the same witnesses, **and** these witnesses **were found** to be **conspiring witnesses,** these conspiring witnesses **pay everything,** including the fourfold or fivefold payment.

מַאי לָאו שֶׁהֵעִידוּ עַל הַגְּנֵיבָה וְחָזְרוּ וְהֵעִידוּ עַל הַטְּבִיחָה, וְהוּזַמּוּ עַל הַגְּנֵיבָה וְחָזְרוּ וְהוּזַמּוּ עַל הַטְּבִיחָה.

The Gemara explains the question: **What, is it not** referring to a case in **which** the events occurred in the following sequence: The witnesses **testified concerning the theft** of the animal, **and then testified concerning the** animal's **slaughter. And** subsequently **they were rendered conspiring witnesses** for their testimony **concerning the theft, and then they were rendered conspiring witnesses** for their testimony **concerning the slaughter.**

NOTES

Two about one, etc. – תְּרֵי לְחַד וכו׳: In this case, there are a total of four witnesses who undermine the testimony of the first pair of witnesses, two for each witness, and the Gemara indicates that disqualification of the first pair of witnesses one at a time is not considered a novelty. *Tosafot* ask: There is a principle with regard to testimony that no greater credibility is granted to a larger set of witnesses than to a small set. If so, the fact that the united testimony of the first set of witnesses is deemed not credible due to the testimony of the other two sets is a novelty. They explain that this refers to a situation where the first two witnesses described the event from different vantage points and were not even aware of each other's existence. In this case they are not considered a single set of witnesses, but two separate witnesses whose testimonies happen to correspond in such a manner that they can join to form a single valid testimony. Since they are considered individual witnesses, it is reasonable to say that each one's testimony can be negated by two other witnesses.

HALAKHA

The *halakha* is in accordance with the opinion of Abaye – הִלְכְתָא כְּוָותֵיהּ דְּאַבַּיֵי: A conspiring witness is disqualified by Torah law from providing testimony in the future, even if the case in which he conspired involved a monetary issue and he pays the monetary penalty involved. This disqualification goes into effect from the time he provides his testimony in court, in accordance with the opinion of Abaye (Rambam *Sefer Shofetim*, *Hilkhot Edut* 10:4; *Shulḥan Arukh*, *Ḥoshen Mishpat* 34:8).

BACKGROUND

Testimony that was partially invalidated is entirely invalidated – עֵדוּת שֶׁבָּטְלָה מִקְצָתָהּ בָּטְלָה כּוּלָּהּ: If witnesses were disqualified with regard to part of their testimony, some Sages maintain that this invalidates all the testimony they presented, as they have been proven to lack the integrity required for giving testimony. Others hold that it invalidates the rest of the testimony only if it was given concomitantly, as indicated in the Gemara, in which case all the testimony is considered a single testimony. Some authorities distinguish between conspiring witnesses, who are entirely disqualified, and contradicted witnesses, who are not necessarily disqualified but whose testimony cannot be accepted on this matter. The testimony of these witnesses with regard to other matters remains valid.

וְאִי סָלְקָא דַּעְתָּךְ לְמַפְרֵעַ הוּא נִפְסָל, הָנֵי כֵּיוָן דְּאִיתַּזַּמוּ לְהוּ אַגְּנֵיבָה, אִיגַּלַּאי מִילְּתָא לְמַפְרֵעַ דְּכִי אַסְהֲדוּ אַטְּבִיחָה פְּסוּלִין הֲווּ, אַמַּאי מְשַׁלְּמִין אַטְּבִיחָה?

And if it enters your mind to say, in accordance with the opinion of Abaye, that a conspiring witness **is disqualified retroactively** from the time he provided his testimony, then with regard to **these** witnesses, **once they are rendered conspiring witnesses concerning the theft, the matter becomes clarified retroactively that when they testified concerning the slaughter they were disqualified** to serve as witnesses. Consequently, that testimony should be rejected. **Why,** then, **must they pay** the fourfold or fivefold payment for their testimony **concerning** the animal's **slaughter?**

אָמְרִי: הָכָא בְּמַאי עָסְקִינַן – כְּגוֹן שֶׁהוּזְמוּ עַל הַטְּבִיחָה תְּחִילָּה.

The Sages **say** in response: **With what are we dealing here?** We are dealing with a case **where** the events did not happen in this sequence. Rather, the witnesses were **first rendered conspiring witnesses** with regard to their testimony **concerning** the animal's **slaughter,** and only afterward were they rendered conspiring witnesses with regard to the theft.

אָמְרִי: סוֹף סוֹף, כִּי הָדְרִי מִיתַּזְמִי אַגְּנֵיבָה – אִיגַּלַּאי מִילְּתָא דְּכִי אַסְהֲדוּ אַטְּבִיחָה פְּסוּלִין הָווּ, אַמַּאי מְשַׁלְּמִי אַטְּבִיחָה?

The Sages **say,** in rejection of this answer: **Ultimately, when** they **are subsequently rendered conspiring witnesses** with regard to their testimony **concerning the theft, the matter becomes clarified retroactively that when they testified concerning the slaughter they were disqualified** from providing testimony. **Why,** then, **must they pay** the fourfold or fivefold payment for their testimony **concerning the** animal's **slaughter?**

וְהִלְכְתָא: שֶׁהֵעִידוּ בְּבַת אַחַת וְהוּזְמוּ.

The Gemara gives its final answer: **And the *halakha*** is in accordance with the opinion of Abaye, since the mishna can be explained as discussing a case **where** the witnesses **testified** concerning the theft of the animal and its slaughter **at the same time, and** afterward **they were rendered conspiring witnesses** with regard to testimony about both matters. Therefore, even if the disqualification of these witnesses is established retroactively, they were not disqualified when they provided their single testimony concerning the theft and the slaughter.

לֵימָא כְּתַנָּאֵי: הָיוּ שְׁנַיִם מְעִידִין אוֹתוֹ שֶׁגָּנַב וְהֵן מְעִידִין אוֹתוֹ שֶׁטָּבַח, וְהוּזְמוּ עַל הַגְּנֵיבָה – עֵדוּת שֶׁבָּטְלָה מִקְצָתָהּ בָּטְלָה כּוּלָּהּ;

The Gemara proposes: **Let us say** that the dispute between Abaye and Rava is **parallel to** a dispute between ***tanna'im.*** As it is taught in a *baraita*: In a case where **there were two** witnesses **testifying against** someone, claiming **that** he **stole** an animal, **and they** subsequently **testify against him that** he **slaughtered** the animal, **and they were rendered conspiring witnesses** only with regard to their testimony **concerning the theft,** the *halakha* is in accordance with the principle that **testimony that was partially invalidated is entirely invalidated.** In other words, the testimony concerning the slaughter of the animal is null and void, as there is no longer any testimony that the animal was ever stolen. Therefore, the witnesses pay the double payment for having attempted to cause the alleged thief to pay that amount, while the accused is entirely exempt.

הוּזְמוּ עַל הַטְּבִיחָה – הוּא מְשַׁלֵּם תַּשְׁלוּמֵי כֶּפֶל, וְהֵן מְשַׁלְּמִין תַּשְׁלוּמֵי שְׁלֹשָׁה;

But **if they were rendered conspiring witnesses** only with regard to their testimony **concerning the slaughter,** their testimony about the theft remains valid. Consequently, the thief **pays** the **double payment, and** the witnesses **pay** a twofold or **threefold payment** for having attempted to cause the thief to pay this amount, which is the fine for slaughter or sale beyond his double payment.

אָמַר רַבִּי יוֹסֵי: בַּמֶּה דְּבָרִים אֲמוּרִים – בִּשְׁתֵּי עֵדְיוֹת, אֲבָל בְּעֵדוּת אַחַת – עֵדוּת שֶׁבָּטְלָה מִקְצָתָהּ בָּטְלָה כּוּלָּהּ.

The *baraita* continues: **Rabbi Yosei said: In what** case **is this statement said?** It is said when the theft and the slaughter were established **by two** separate **testimonies. But** if these matters were established **by one** single **testimony,** then even if they were rendered conspiring witnesses with regard to the testimony concerning the slaughter, the *halakha* is in accordance with the principle that **testimony that was partially invalidated is entirely invalidated.**[B] When the testimony concerning the slaughter is invalidated the testimony concerning the theft is likewise negated, and the alleged thief is not required to pay the double payment. This concludes the *baraita*.

מַאי "בִּשְׁתֵּי עֵדְיוֹת", וּמַאי "בְּעֵדוּת אַחַת"? אִילֵימָא "בִּשְׁתֵּי עֵדְיוֹת" – בִּשְׁתֵּי עֵדְיוֹת מַמָּשׁ בִּשְׁתֵּי כִתּוֹת, "בְּעֵדוּת אַחַת" – בְּכַת אַחַת בָּזֶה אַחַר זֶה,

The Gemara analyzes Rabbi Yosei's statement. **What** did Rabbi Yosei mean when he said: **By two** separate **testimonies, and what** did he mean when he said: **By one** single **testimony? If we say** that the phrase: **By two** separate **testimonies,** means **literally by two** separate testimonies, i.e., **by two** separate **sets** of witnesses, one of which testifies concerning the theft while the other testifies concerning the slaughter, this would mean that the expression: **By one** single **testimony,** means **by one set** of witnesses that testifies to both the theft and the slaughter, **one** matter **after the other.**

וְאָמַר רַבִּי יוֹסֵי: בְּעֵדוּת אַחַת, בְּכַת אַחַת בָּזֶה אַחַר זֶה, כִּי מַסְהֲדִי אַגְּנֵיבָה וַהֲדַר מַסְהֲדִי אַטְּבִיחָה, כִּי מִתַּזְמִי אַטְּבִיחָה – עֵדוּת שֶׁבָּטְלָה מִקְצָתָהּ בָּטְלָה כּוּלָּהּ וְאִיתַּזְמוּ לְהוּ אַגְּנֵיבָה, מֵהֵיכָא תֵּיתֵי הַךְ?

And if so, when **Rabbi Yosei** then **says** that the facts are established **by one testimony,** he meant **one set** of witnesses testifying about both matters, **one** matter **after the other,** i.e., **that they testify concerning the theft and then testify concerning the slaughter.** Therefore, **when they are rendered conspiring witnesses** only **with regard to the slaughter,** the *halakha* is determined in accordance with the principle that **testimony that was partially invalidated is entirely invalidated. And** consequently Rabbi Yosei would maintain that **they are** considered to have been **rendered conspiring witnesses concerning the theft** as well. The Gemara asks: **From where would this be derived?** Why should the earlier testimony about the theft be negated by their status as conspiring witnesses from the later testimony concerning the slaughter?

אֶלָּא לָאו "בִּשְׁתֵּי עֵדְיוֹת" – בְּעֵדוּת אַחַת כְּעֵין שְׁתֵּי עֵדְיוֹת, וּמַאי נִינְהוּ? כַּת אַחַת בָּזֶה אַחַר זֶה, אֲבָל בְּעֵדוּת אַחַת בְּבַת אַחַת – לָא.

Rather, is it **not** the case that when Rabbi Yosei said: **By two testimonies,** he meant: **By a single testimony** that is **similar to two testimonies. And what is that?** It is **one set** of witnesses who testify about both the theft and the slaughter, **one** matter **after the other,** at two separate times. **But** if these matters were established **by one** single **testimony,** when the witnesses testified about both matters **at the same time,** Rabbi Yosei concedes that these are **not** considered two separate testimonies, despite the fact that they refer to two different events.

וְסַבְרוּהָ, דְּכוּלֵּי עָלְמָא – תּוֹךְ כְּדֵי דִיבּוּר כְּדִיבּוּר דָּמֵי;

The Gemara continues to analyze the dispute between Rabbi Yosei and the Rabbis: The *amora'im* discussing this matter **assumed that** according to **everyone,** i.e., both Rabbi Yosei and the Rabbis, if a witness pauses briefly in his testimony and then continues to testify, it is considered one long testimony. This is in accordance with the principle that the legal status of a pause or retraction **within** the time required **for speaking** a short phrase **is like** that of continuous **speech.**[HB] Therefore, the two testimonies, the one concerning the theft and the one concerning the slaughter, are considered a single testimony.

מַאי לָאו בְּהָא קָמִיפַּלְגִי, דְּרַבָּנַן סָבְרִי: מִכָּאן וּלְהַבָּא הוּא נִפְסָל, וְכֵיוָן דְּמֵהַהִיא שַׁעְתָּא קָא מִיתַּזְמִי, אַטְּבִיחָה דְּקָא מִיתַּזְמִי – אִיתַּזּוּם, אַגְּנֵיבָה דְּלָא מִיתַּזְמִי – לָא אִיתַּזּוּם;

The Gemara asks with regard to the above: **What, is it not with regard to this** that Rabbi Yosei and the Rabbis **disagree? As the Rabbis maintain,** like Rava, **that** a conspiring witness **is disqualified from here on,** i.e., from when he is rendered a conspiring witness. **And since** it was only **from that time,** when the other witnesses testify about them, **that** they **are rendered conspiring witnesses,** it is only with regard to their testimony **concerning** the animal's **slaughter that they are rendered conspiring witnesses,** whereas **concerning the theft** itself **they are not rendered conspiring witnesses.**

HALAKHA

The legal status of a pause or retraction within the time required for speaking a short phrase is like that of continuous speech – תּוֹךְ כְּדֵי דִיבּוּר כְּדִיבּוּר דָּמֵי: If one issues a statement and within the time it takes to say: Peace be upon you my rabbi, he retracts or changes an aspect of his declaration, the second statement overrides the first. There are certain exceptions to this principle: Blasphemy, verbal acceptance of a false deity, betrothal of a woman, and divorce of one's wife. In all these cases there is no possibility of retraction after the original statement, even within the aforementioned time frame (Rambam *Sefer Hafla'a, Hilkhot Shevuot* 2:18 and *Sefer Shofetim, Hilkhot Edut* 20:3; *Shulḥan Arukh, Yoreh De'a* 234:31–33, 340:24 and *Ḥoshen Mishpat* 29:1, 281:7).

BACKGROUND

The legal status of a pause or retraction within the time required for speaking a short phrase is like that of continuous speech – תּוֹךְ כְּדֵי דִיבּוּר כְּדִיבּוּר דָּמֵי: A pause that is not considered to be an interruption in continuous speech is defined as one that is no longer than the time it takes to say: Peace be upon you my rabbi. The Ramban states, citing Rabbeinu Tam, that the Sages instituted this *halakha* so that if one encounters his teacher when he wishes to retract a statement he just made, he can greet him first and subsequently issue his retraction. The Ran does not accept this explanation, as it indicates that this *halakha* is by rabbinic law, whereas in various cases, e.g., vows, this time period applies even with regard to matters of Torah law. He therefore explains that a person generally intends to allow himself to change his mind within a short period after speaking.

NOTES

They are rendered conspiring witnesses concerning the theft as well – אִיתַּזַמּוּ לְהוּ נַמִי אַגְּנֵיבָה: Rashi points out that the Gemara does not mean they have the actual status of conspiring witnesses concerning the theft. Rather, the Gemara means that their testimony about the theft is invalid because it is considered a single testimony together with the testimony concerning the slaughter.

רַבִּי יוֹסֵי סָבַר: לְמַפְרֵעַ הוּא נִפְסָל, וְכֵיוָן דְּמִיָּד כִּי אַסְהִידוּ הוּא דְּמִיפַּסְלִי, אִי אִיתַּזַמּוּ לְהוּ אַטְּבִיחָה – אִיתַּזַמּוּ לְהוּ נַמִי אַגְּנֵיבָה, דְּהָא תּוֹךְ כְּדֵי דִיבּוּר כְּדִיבּוּר דָּמֵי?

And **Rabbi Yosei holds,** like Abaye, **that** a conspiring witness **is disqualified retroactively,** from when he provided his testimony. **And** consequently, **since they are disqualified immediately when they testify, if they are rendered conspiring witnesses concerning the slaughter they are rendered conspiring witnesses concerning the theft as well,**[N] as the legal status of a pause or retraction **within** the time required **for speaking** a short phrase **is like** that of continuous **speech,** i.e., the two testimonies are considered one unit.

אָמְרִי: אִי תּוֹךְ כְּדֵי דִיבּוּר כְּדִיבּוּר דָּמֵי, דְּכוּלֵּי עָלְמָא – לְמַפְרֵעַ הוּא נִפְסָל. אֶלָּא הָכָא בְּתוֹךְ כְּדֵי דִיבּוּר כְּדִיבּוּר דָּמֵי קָא מִיפַּלְגִי, רַבָּנַן סָבְרִי: תּוֹךְ כְּדֵי דִיבּוּר

The Sages **say,** in rejection of this opinion: **If** it were accepted that the legal status of a pause or retraction **within** the time required **for speaking** a short phrase **is like** that of continuous **speech, everyone** would agree that the witnesses are **disqualified retroactively,** and their testimony with regard to the theft would also be negated. **But here they disagree** about that very issue, i.e., whether the legal status of a pause or retraction **within** the time required **for speaking** a short phrase **is like** that of continuous **speech. The Rabbis maintain that** if the pause is **within** the time required **for speaking** a short phrase, then the two aspects of the testimony provided by the witnesses

Perek **VII**
Daf **73** Amud **b**

לָאו כְּדִיבּוּר דָּמֵי, וְרַבִּי יוֹסֵי סָבַר תּוֹךְ כְּדֵי דִיבּוּר כְּדִיבּוּר דָּמֵי.

are not like one testimony of continuous **speech,** but are considered separate testimonies, and therefore the testimony concerning the theft remains valid. **And Rabbi Yosei maintains that** the legal status of a pause **within** the time required **for speaking** a short phrase **is like** that of continuous **speech,** and therefore the testimony about the theft is disqualified together with the testimony concerning the slaughter.

וְסָבַר רַבִּי יוֹסֵי תּוֹךְ כְּדֵי דִיבּוּר כְּדִיבּוּר דָּמֵי? וְהָתְנַן: ״הֲרֵי זוֹ תְּמוּרַת עוֹלָה תְּמוּרַת שְׁלָמִים״ – הֲרֵי זוֹ תְּמוּרַת עוֹלָה, דִּבְרֵי רַבִּי מֵאִיר;

The Gemara asks: **But does Rabbi Yosei** really **maintain** that the legal status of a statement interrupted or retracted **within** the time **required for speaking** a short phrase **is like** that of continuous **speech? But didn't we learn** otherwise in a mishna (*Temura* 25b): If one designates an animal by saying: **This animal is hereby a substitute**[B] **for a burnt-offering, a substitute for a peace-offering,**[H] he has issued two contradictory statements and therefore **this** animal is considered **a substitute for a burnt-offering,** i.e., only the first part of his statement is accepted. This is **the statement of Rabbi Meir.**

BACKGROUND

Substitution – תְּמוּרָה: The possibility of substitution is mentioned in the Torah (Leviticus 27:10), and tractate *Temura* focuses on its *halakhot*. The main features of this concept are as follows: The Torah renders it prohibited to substitute any animal, whether whole or blemished, for an animal designated as an offering. One who does so violates a prohibition and is liable to receive the punishment of lashes. Nevertheless, despite the fact that substituting an animal for an offering is prohibited, if an act of substitution is performed, the second animal does acquire a measure of sanctity, while the animal initially designated as an offering also remains sacred. All animals can be used as substitutes, whether they are whole or blemished, and the animal designated as a substitute can never be worked or redeemed. The fate of the substitute varies with the particular type of offering. In some instances, such as a substitute for a sin-offering, the animal is left to die. In other cases, such as that of a guilt-offering, the animal is put out to graze until it becomes blemished. Lastly, some substitutes, e.g., that of a peace-offering, are consecrated in addition to the original offering.

HALAKHA

This animal is hereby a substitute for a burnt-offering, a substitute for a peace-offering – תְּמוּרַת עוֹלָה תְּמוּרַת שְׁלָמִים: In a case where one says: This animal is hereby a substitute for a burnt-offering and a substitute for a peace-offering, if his intention from the outset was that the animal should be a substitute for both types of offerings, his statement stands. The *halakha* is in accordance with the opinion of Rabbi Yosei, as his rulings are followed in his disputes with Rabbi Meir (Rambam *Sefer Korbanot, Hilkhot Temura* 2:4).

רַבִּי יוֹסֵי אוֹמֵר: אִם לְכָךְ נִתְכַּוֵּין מִתְּחִילָּה, הוֹאִיל וְאִי אֶפְשָׁר לִקְרוֹת שְׁנֵי שֵׁמוֹת כְּאֶחָד – דְּבָרָיו קַיָּימִין; וְאִם אָמַר ״תְּמוּרַת עוֹלָה״ וְנִמְלַךְ וְאָמַר ״תְּמוּרַת שְׁלָמִים״ – הֲרֵי זוֹ תְּמוּרַת עוֹלָה;

Rabbi Yosei says: If he intended this outcome **from the outset,** that the animal should serve both as the substitute of a burnt-offering and as the substitute of a peace-offering, **since it is impossible** for one **to call it** by **two names at once,** i.e., the only way he can make his intent known is by issuing these two apparently contradictory declarations consecutively, **his statement stands,**[N] and the animal has the status of both a substitute for a burnt-offering and a substitute for a peace-offering. **But if he said:** This animal is **a substitute for a burnt-offering and** then **changed his mind and said: A substitute for a peace-offering, it is a substitute for a burnt-offering.**

וְהָוֵינַן בָּהּ: נִמְלַךְ – פְּשִׁיטָא!

And we discussed this ruling: If he **changed his mind** before saying: A substitute for a peace-offering, it is **obvious** that he cannot remove the status he already applied to the animal, and the animal certainly remains a substitute for a burnt-offering. Rabbi Yosei would not have issued such an obvious ruling.

וַאֲמַר רַב פָּפָּא: נִמְלַךְ בְּתוֹךְ כְּדֵי דִיבּוּר קָאָמְרִינַן!

And Rav Pappa said in response to this question: **We are speaking** of a case where the individual **changed his mind within the time required for speaking**[H] a short phrase. Rabbi Yosei holds that when one adds to a statement after a pause, even if the addition was made within a short time, it is considered a separate statement, which does not reverse the initial declaration. This contradicts the explanation given for the *baraita* cited above, according to which Rabbi Yosei maintains that when one adds to an existing statement within the time required for speaking a short phrase it is considered continuous speech.

אָמְרִי: תְּרֵי תּוֹךְ כְּדֵי דִיבּוּר הָוֵי, חַד כְּדֵי שְׁאֵילַת תַּלְמִיד לְרַב, וְחַד כְּדֵי שְׁאֵילַת הָרַב לְתַלְמִיד. כִּי לֵית לֵיהּ לְרַבִּי יוֹסֵי – כְּדֵי שְׁאֵילַת תַּלְמִיד לְרַב ״שָׁלוֹם עָלֶיךָ רַבִּי וּמוֹרִי״, דִּנְפִישׁ, כְּדֵי שְׁאֵילַת הָרַב לְתַלְמִיד ״שָׁלוֹם עָלֶיךָ״ – אִית לֵיהּ.

The Sages **say** in response: **There are two** time frames that are referred to as being **within the time required for speaking**[H] a short phrase. **One is the time required for a student to greet a rabbi,**[N] **and the other one is the time required for the rabbi to greet a student. When does Rabbi Yosei hold** that a statement added within the time required for speaking a short phrase is **not** considered continuous speech? When the words are added **within the time required for a student to greet his rabbi** using the phrase: **Peace be upon you, my rabbi and teacher, as** that **is a long** pause. By contrast, if the statement is added **within the** shorter **time** frame **required for the rabbi to greet his student: Peace be upon you,** Rabbi Yosei **is of** the opinion **that** the added words constitute speech that is continuous with the original statement.

אָמַר רָבָא: עֵדִים שֶׁהוּכְחֲשׁוּ וּלְבַסּוֹף הוּזְמוּ – נֶהֱרָגִין, דְּהַכְחָשָׁה תְּחִילַּת הֲזָמָה הִיא, אֶלָּא שֶׁלֹּא נִגְמְרָה.

§ **Rava says: Witnesses** to a capital crime **who were** first **contradicted** by two other witnesses, and **ultimately they,** the first set of witnesses, **were rendered conspiring witnesses,**[H] **are killed,** in accordance with the punishment for conspiring witnesses involved in a capital case, despite the fact that their testimony was already disqualified prior to the discovery of their conspiracy. The reason is that the **contradiction** of testimony **is the start of determining that** testimony is **conspiring** testimony, **only** the process **has not** yet **been completed** at the time of the contradiction.

NOTES

His statement stands – דְּבָרָיו קַיָּימִין: This animal is treated in the following manner: It is put out to pasture until it develops a blemish, at which point it may be sold. Half of the proceeds from the sale are used to procure a burnt-offering while the other half goes toward the purchase of a peace-offering (Rashi).

The time required for a student to greet a rabbi, etc. – שְׁאֵילַת תַּלְמִיד לְרַב וכו׳: Some claim that the statement quoted in the Gemara: Peace be upon you, my rabbi and teacher, is exact, i.e., the maximum amount of pause is the time required for the recitation of these four Hebrew words. Others maintain that the maximum pause is actually the amount of time required to say just the three Hebrew words: Peace be upon you, my rabbi.

Some early commentaries cite the following reason for this particular choice of time measurement. When one is engaged in an activity or is speaking and his rabbi or student suddenly passes by, it is considered appropriate for him to stop what he is doing to deliver these words of greeting. Since this is not considered an interruption, it may be inferred that any pause of comparable length is likewise not an interruption (Rabbeinu Tam, *Sefer HaYashar*). Others maintain that these words are merely a random example of a short period of time, during which is it acceptable for an average person to retract or alter what he has just said (Ran on *Nedarim* 87a).

HALAKHA

He changed his mind within the time required for speaking – נִמְלַךְ בְּתוֹךְ כְּדֵי דִיבּוּר: In the case mentioned above, if his initial intent was to say merely: A substitute for a burnt-offering, and afterward he changed his mind and said: A substitute for a peace-offering, even if he retracted his first statement within the time required for speaking a short phrase, the first expression is binding, and the animal is considered a substitute only for a burnt-offering. The *halakha* is in accordance with the opinion of Rabbi Yosei, as stated in tractate *Temura* (25b), that one cannot retract a statement of consecration. The Rosh rules that any change of heart that occurs within the time required for speaking a short phrase is considered a continuation of the original speech and consequently a valid retraction, except with regard to statements concerning idol worship, blasphemy, betrothal, and divorce (Rambam *Sefer Korbanot, Hilkhot Temura* 2:4 and *Sefer Avoda, Hilkhot Ma'aseh HaKorbanot* 15:1).

Within the time required for speaking – תּוֹךְ כְּדֵי דִיבּוּר: The time during which one's additional words are considered a continuation of his previous statement is the amount of time that it takes a student to greet his rabbi, by saying: Peace be upon you, my rabbi (Rambam *Sefer HaMadda, Hilkhot Talmud Torah* 5:5; *Sefer Hafla'a, Hilkhot Shevuot* 2:17–19; and *Sefer Shofetim, Hilkhot Edut* 20:3; *Shulḥan Arukh, Yoreh De'a* 242:16).

Were first contradicted and ultimately they were rendered conspiring witnesses – הוּכְחֲשׁוּ וּלְבַסּוֹף הוּזְמוּ: Witnesses who were first contradicted by other witnesses and subsequently rendered conspiring witnesses are subject to the punishment of conspiring witnesses, as the contradiction of testimony is the start of determining that testimony is conspiring testimony, in accordance with the opinion of Rava (Rambam *Sefer Shofetim, Hilkhot Edut* 18:4; *Tur, Ḥoshen Mishpat* 38).

אֲמַר רָבָא: מְנָא אָמֵינָא לָהּ? דְּתַנְיָא: "מְעִידַנִי בְּאִישׁ פְּלוֹנִי שֶׁסִּימֵּא אֶת עֵין עַבְדּוֹ וְהִפִּיל אֶת שִׁינּוֹ", שֶׁהֲרֵי הָרַב אוֹמֵר כֵּן, וְנִמְצְאוּ זוֹמְמִין – מְשַׁלְּמִין דְּמֵי עַיִן לָעֶבֶד;

Rava said: From where do I say that this is so? As it is taught in a *baraita* (*Tosefta, Makkot* 1:3) that if witnesses say: **We testify with regard to so-and-so that he blinded his** Canaanite **slave's eye and** afterward **knocked out his tooth,**[B] and therefore the master is obligated to pay him compensation for the value of his tooth, **as that is what the master says,**[N] i.e., this testimony is advantageous to the master, **and** subsequently **they were found** to be **conspiring witnesses, they pay** the **value of an eye to the slave.**

הֵיכִי דָּמֵי? אִילֵימָא כִּדְקָתָנֵי, דְּלֵיכָּא כַּת אַחֲרִינָא, מְשַׁלְּמִין דְּמֵי עַיִן לָעֶבֶד? בָּתַר דְּמַפְּקִי לֵיהּ לְחֵירוּת, דְּמֵי עֵינוֹ קָבָעֵי שַׁלּוּמֵי?!

Rava explains that the *baraita* as written is problematic: **What are the circumstances** of this case? **If we say that** it is exactly **as it is taught** in the *baraita*, i.e., **that there is no other set** of witnesses other than those whose statement is quoted in the *baraita* and the opposing set of witnesses who establish them as conspiring witnesses, several problems arise: First, why should they **pay the value of an eye to the slave? After emancipating him** by testifying that his master has blinded him, should **they be required to pay** him the **value of his eye?**

וְעוֹד, דְּמֵי כּוּלֵּיהּ עֶבֶד לְרַב בָּעֵי לְשַׁלּוּמֵי! וְעוֹד, "שֶׁהֲרֵי הָרַב אוֹמֵר כֵּן", הָרַב מִי נִיחָא לֵיהּ?

And furthermore, they should be required to pay the **value of the entire slave to the master,** as they intended to cause him to lose ownership of his slave through their false testimony. **And furthermore,** why does the *baraita* say: **As that is what the master says,** i.e., this testimony is advantageous to the master. **Is it** really **satisfactory to the master** that his slave be emancipated as a result of this testimony?

אֶלָּא לָאו כְּגוֹן דְּאָתוּ בֵּי תְּרֵי וְאָמְרִי: הִפִּיל אֶת שִׁינּוֹ סִימֵּא אֶת עֵינוֹ, דְּבָעֵי מֵיתֵיב לֵיהּ הָרַב דְּמֵי עֵינוֹ, וְאָתוּ בֵּי תְּרֵי מְצִיעָאֵי וְאָמְרִי: עֵינוֹ וַהֲדַר שִׁינּוֹ, דְּלָא בָּעֵי לְמֵיתַב לֵיהּ אֶלָּא דְּמֵי שִׁינּוֹ, דְּקָא מַכְחֲשִׁי לֵיהּ קַמָּאֵי לִמְצִיעָאֵי;

Rather, it must be that this case involves another, competing, testimony that is not mentioned in the *baraita*. **Is it not** correct to say that the *baraita* is dealing with a case **where** prior to the testimonies mentioned in the *baraita* **two** other witnesses **came and said:** The master first **knocked out** the slave's **tooth** and then **blinded his eye, in** which case **the master is required** to emancipate the slave and also **to give him** the **value of his eye; and then an intermediate** set of **two** witnesses **came and said** the testimony quoted in the *baraita*, that first the master blinded the slave's **eye and then** knocked out **his tooth?** According to this account the master would still be required to emancipate the slave, but **he would be required to give him only** the **value of his tooth,** which is much less than the value of an eye. **In** this case the testimony of **the first** set of witnesses **contradicts** the testimony of **the intermediate ones.**

וְהַיְינוּ "שֶׁהֲרֵי הָרַב אוֹמֵר כֵּן", דְּנִיחָא לֵיהּ בְּמַאי דְּקָאָמְרִי;

And this is the meaning of the clause: **As that is what the master says,** i.e., this testimony is advantageous to the master. It means **that what** the intermediate witnesses **say,** i.e., that he owes the value of a tooth, **is satisfactory to him,** as according to the claim of the first set, he owes the value of an eye. Since there are now contradictory testimonies, the testimony stating the claim of a loss of lesser value is accepted, and in that case the master would have to pay the slave only for the value of his tooth, in addition to emancipating him. This judgment corresponds exactly to the testimony of the intermediate set of witnesses.

וְקָתָנֵי: וְנִמְצְאוּ זוֹמְמִין מְצִיעָאֵי – מְשַׁלְּמִין דְּמֵי עַיִן לָעֶבֶד,

And the *baraita* subsequently **teaches: And** then **the intermediate** set of witnesses **were found to be conspiring witnesses,** as a third set of witnesses testified that the intermediate set was not at the scene of the incident at all. Therefore, the intermediate set of witnesses **pays** the **value of an eye to the slave** less the value of a tooth, as this is the amount of monetary damage the slave stood to incur as a result of their testimony.

שְׁמַע מִינָּהּ: הַכְחָשָׁה תְּחִילַּת הֲזָמָה הִיא.

Rava concludes his proof: **Learn from** the *baraita* that the **contradiction** of testimony **is the start of determining that** testimony is **conspiring** testimony. Although the testimony of the intermediate set of witnesses had already been contradicted before it was shown to be conspiring testimony, nevertheless, they can still be established as conspiring witness at that later stage, which means that they must pay an amount equivalent to the loss they were attempting to cause through their testimony.

BACKGROUND

He blinded his slave's eye and knocked out his tooth – סִימֵּא אֶת עֵין עַבְדּוֹ וְהִפִּיל אֶת שִׁינּוֹ: The Torah states that a Canaanite slave remains the permanent property of his owner and he may not release him (Leviticus 25:46). Nevertheless, if the owner caused certain types of injuries to his slave, e.g., blinding him in one eye or knocking out a tooth, the slave is automatically emancipated. There are twenty-four limbs whose loss causes a slave to be emancipated. These are enumerated in tractates *Nega'im* (6:7) and *Kiddushin* (25a).

NOTES

As that is what the master says – שֶׁהֲרֵי הָרַב אוֹמֵר כֵּן: If a master both blinds an eye and knocks out a tooth of his Canaanite slave, the slave gains his freedom as a result of the first injury (see Exodus 21:26–27). Subsequently, as a freeman, he receives monetary compensation for the second injury. The value of an eye is substantially greater than that of a tooth. Therefore, the master would prefer the testimony of the witnesses who say that he caused damage to his eye first, rather than those who claim the reverse.

אֲמַר אַבַּיֵי: לָא,

Abaye said: No. There is another possible interpretation for the *baraita*, which answers the questions raised above and yet does not serve as proof for Rava's opinion. According to this interpretation, the contradictory testimony was given after, not before, the testimony mentioned in the *baraita*.

דַּאֲפַכִינְהוּ וְאַזְמִינְהוּ.

It is possible that the *baraita* is discussing a case **where** a second set of witnesses both **reversed** the order of events, by testifying that the tooth was knocked out before the blinding of the eye, **and** at the same time **rendered** the first set witnesses **as conspiring witnesses,** by testifying that those original witnesses were not at the scene of the supposed events they claimed to have witnessed. It can be argued, albeit in a far-fetched manner, that the testimony of the first set of witnesses is considered to be to the master's advantage even at this stage, because he knows what really happened, as reflected in the testimony of the later witnesses. Accordingly, Rava maintains that there are a total of three sets of witnesses in the case of the *baraita*, while Abaye says that there are only two sets.

מִמַּאי?

Abaye elaborates: **From where** do I say that my interpretation of the *baraita* is correct?

Perek **VII**
Daf **74** Amud **a**

מִדְּסֵיפָא בְּמֵיפַךְ וַהֲזָמָה רֵישָׁא נַמִי בְּמֵיפַךְ וַהֲזָמָה,

From the fact that **the latter clause** of the *baraita* states a ruling **with regard to** a case in which the second set of witnesses both **reverses** the order of events **and renders** the first pair **as conspiring witnesses,** it may be inferred that **the first case as well,** in parallel fashion, states a ruling **with regard to** a case in which the second set of witnesses both **reverses** the order of events **and renders** the first pair **as conspiring witnesses.**

דְּקָתָנֵי סֵיפָא: "מְעִידַנוּ אֶת אִישׁ פְּלוֹנִי שֶׁהִפִּיל אֶת שֵׁן עַבְדּוֹ וְסִימֵּא אֶת עֵינוֹ", שֶׁהֲרֵי הָעֶבֶד אוֹמֵר כֵּן, וְנִמְצְאוּ זוֹמְמִין – מְשַׁלְּמִין דְּמֵי עַיִן לָרַב;

This is **as it teaches** in **the latter clause** of the *baraita*, that if witnesses say: **We testify** with regard to **so-and-so that he knocked out his** Canaanite **slave's tooth and** afterward **blinded his eye,** which requires the master to emancipate him and compensate him for the value of his eye, **as that is what the slave says,** i.e., this testimony is advantageous to the slave, **and** subsequently **they were found** to be **conspiring witnesses, they pay the value of an eye to the master.**

הֵיכִי דָּמֵי? אִי דְּלָא קָא מוֹדוּ לְהוּ בַּתְרָאֵי בַּחֲבָלָא כְּלָל, דְּמֵי כּוּלֵּיהּ עֶבֶד לָרַב בָּעֵי שַׁלּוּמֵי לֵיהּ!

Abaye analyzes this clause of the *baraita*: **What are the circumstances** of this case? **If** it is speaking of a situation **where the latter** set of witnesses, who attested that the first set of witnesses were conspiring witnesses, **do not concede that** there was any **injury at all** inflicted on the slave by his master, then there is no testimony to confirm that those injuries were inflicted other than that given by the witnesses who were shown to be conspiring witnesses. Consequently, **they should be required to pay the entire value of the slave to the master,** as this is the amount of monetary damage the master stood to incur as a result of their false testimony.

אֶלָּא פְּשִׁיטָא, דְּקָא מוֹדוּ כּוּלְּהוּ בַּחֲבָלָא,

Rather, it is obvious that all of them, i.e., both the first set of witnesses and the latter set, **concede with regard to the injury** inflicted on the slave by the master. They both agree that the master both blinded the slave's eye and knocked out his tooth and therefore is obligated to emancipate him. They disagree concerning only the order of events. The first set of witnesses said that the tooth injury occurred first and the eye injury occurred afterward. Consequently, they sought to require the master to emancipate the slave and compensate him for the eye injury.

וְדָקָא אַפְכִינַן וְאַזְמִינְהוּ.

And the second set of witnesses **reversed** the order of events in their testimony, saying that the eye injury took place first, **and** in the same testimony, **they rendered** the first pair **conspiring witnesses,**[N] by testifying that they were not present when the events occurred. Since the latter clause of the *baraita* must be interpreted in this manner, it stands to reason that the first case should be explained similarly.

וְהֵיכִי דָּמֵי? אִי דְּקָא מְאַחֲרֵי אַחוּרֵי הָנֵי בַּתְרָאֵי – אַכַּתִּי דְּמֵי עֶבֶד לָרַב בָּעֵי שַׁלּוּמֵי,

The Gemara analyzes Abaye's interpretation of the *baraita*: **And what are the circumstances** of the case? The second set of witnesses, who are deemed credible, have established that the injuries did not take place on the date reported by the first set of witnesses. According to their testimony, when did the injuries take place? **If the latter** witnesses **postdated** the events, by testifying that the injuries were actually inflicted at a later stage than that mentioned by the first set of witnesses, the first set of witnesses should **still be required to pay the** full **value of a slave to the master.**

דְּכִי מְחַיְּיבִי לֵיהּ לְגַבְרָא, אַכַּתִּי גַּבְרָא לָאו בַּר חִיּוּבָא הוּא! אֶלָּא דְּקָא מְקַדְּמֵי קַדּוּמֵי הָנֵי בַּתְרָאֵי.

The reason the first set of witnesses should be liable is **that when they** sought to **impose liability upon the man,** i.e., the master, this **man was not yet** burdened with any **liability.** When the first set of witnesses testified about the injuries, the master was not yet obligated to emancipate his slave or pay damages. Therefore, these conspiring witnesses should be required to pay these sums, which they had sought to impose on the master. **Rather,** it must be that **the latter** set of witnesses **predated** the time of the injuries, by testifying that they were inflicted at an earlier date than that attested to by the first set of witnesses.

וְאִי דְּלָא עָמַד בַּדִּין – אַכַּתִּי דְּמֵי כּוּלֵּיהּ עֶבֶד לָרַב בָּעֵי שַׁלּוּמֵי לֵיהּ, דְּאַכַּתִּי גַּבְרָא לָא מִיחַיַּיב!

The Gemara continues to analyze the case: **And if** the *baraita* is referring to a case **where** the master **had not** yet **stood trial** for having injured his slave when the first set of witnesses submitted their testimony, those witnesses **should still be required to pay the entire value of the slave**[H] **to the master,** as at the time of their testimony **the man,** i.e., the master, was **not yet liable.**[N] The first set of witnesses sought to render the master liable at a time when he was exempt from liability, and therefore they should be obligated to pay him the full value of the slave.

אֶלָּא דְּעָמַד בַּדִּין.

Rather, it must be **that** the master **had** already **stood trial**[H] for having inflicted these injuries, and had been sentenced by the court to emancipate the slave for the first injury and pay him for the second injury. Then, the master evaded payment, and was subsequently brought before another court, where witnesses testified that the first court had established liability for knocking out the tooth first and then blinding the slave's eye. This testimony was subsequently rendered conspiring testimony by a second set of witnesses, who testified both that the first set of witnesses was not at the scene of the first trial and that the results of the trial were actually reversed, i.e., the master's liability was for blinding the eye first and then for knocking out the tooth. Since the first set of witnesses, who were rendered conspiring witnesses, sought to increase the master's liability payment from that of the value of a tooth to that of an eye, they must pay the value of an eye to the master.

אֲמַר לֵיהּ רַב אַחָא בְּרֵיהּ דְּרַב אִיקָא לְרַב אַשִׁי: דּוּקְיָא דְּרָבָא מֵהֵיכָא? אִילֵימָא מֵרֵישָׁא, רֵישָׁא מִי קָא מִתְכַּחֲשִׁי מְצִיעָאֵי?

Rava sought to infer from this *baraita* to his opinion that contradiction of testimony is the start of determining that testimony is conspiring testimony. **Rav Aḥa, son of Rav Ika, said to Rav Ashi: From which** case in the *baraita* **is the inference of Rava? If we say** that his inference is **from the first clause,** this is difficult. In the case of **the first clause,** if it involves three sets of witnesses, as claimed by Rava, **is the intermediate** set of witnesses **contradicted** and rejected before they are established as conspiring witnesses? The first set of witnesses testified that the eye injury took place after the tooth injury, whereas the intermediate set of witnesses reversed the order. If so, the intermediate set of witnesses sought to lower the master's payment from the value of an eye to that of a tooth.

NOTES

And they reversed and they rendered the first pair conspiring witnesses – וְדָקָא אַפְכִינַן וְאַזְמִינְהוּ: It is impossible to explain this latter clause of the *baraita* as involving three sets of witnesses in a manner parallel to Rava's explanation of the first clause. The hypothetical case would be as follows: A first set of witnesses testifies that the master initially inflicted an eye injury and then a tooth injury, which means that the master must emancipate the slave and compensate him for the value of his tooth. An intermediate set testifies that the tooth injury preceded the eye injury, requiring the master to emancipate the slave and to compensate him for the value of his eye. Since the testimony of the intermediate set of witnesses contradicts that of the first set, the testimony that results in the master's paying for the injury of lesser monetary value would be accepted, which in this case is the version that the eye injury occurred first. If so, the testimony of the intermediate set of witnesses had no effect at all on the judgment as it stood after the testimony of the first set. Ultimately, a third set of witnesses arrives and testifies that the intermediate set were not at the scene of the purported events, rendering them conspiring witnesses.

The problem with this interpretation is that there is a principle that conspiring witnesses are not punished if their testimony did not lead to a verdict in court. Since in this case the testimony of the intermediate set of witnesses had no effect on the judgment, they would not incur any punishment at all, even if they were rendered conspiring witnesses. Rava would agree that the case of the latter clause of the *baraita* involves merely two sets of witnesses, with the second set both contradicting the first set and rendering the first set conspiring witnesses. Abaye's argument is that since the latter clause of the *baraita* must be interpreted in this fashion, it is reasonable to assume that the first clause should be interpreted in a similar manner (Rashi).

As the man was not yet liable – דְּאַכַּתִּי גַּבְרָא לָא מִיחַיַּיב: Although the actions for which the master must pay compensation had already occurred before the testimony, the Gemara states that he has no liability as of yet. Rashi explains that this is because one who admits that he has performed an act that is punishable by a fine is not required to pay that fine. As long as no testimony has been submitted against the guilty party he can avoid liability by admitting his guilt. Others explain that unlike in the case of debts and monetary obligations, one is not considered to owe the fine at all, even after he has committed the punishable act. Since a fine by definition is not commensurate with one's actions, he is liable to pay the fine only when a court sentences him to do so (*Tosafot*).

HALAKHA

Should still be required to pay the entire value of the slave, etc. – אַכַּתִּי דְּמֵי כּוּלֵּיהּ עֶבֶד וכו׳: Two witnesses testify that a man committed murder on a particular day in a particular place. Subsequently, two other witnesses render the first set conspiring witnesses, by testifying that those witnesses were in a different place at the time of the purported crime. Even if the second set of witnesses add that the accused did in fact commit the murder on a different day, the conspiring witnesses are liable to receive court-imposed capital punishment, even if that different day is earlier than the day claimed by the conspiring witnesses. The reason is that at the time they submitted their testimony the accused had not yet been convicted (Rambam *Sefer Shofetim, Hilkhot Edut* 19:2).

That the master had already stood trial – דְּעָמַד בַּדִּין: Two witnesses testify that a certain person was convicted of a capital crime by a particular court on a particular day, and subsequently other witnesses render the first set of witnesses conspiring witnesses, i.e., they testify that those witnesses were in a different place at the time of the purported conviction. If the second set of witnesses adds that the accused was convicted on a previous day, the conspiring witnesses are not punished. The reason is that the accused was already a convicted man at the time when these witnesses submitted their testimony (Rambam *Sefer Shofetim, Hilkhot Edut* 19:2).

כֵּיוָן דְּאִי לָא מִתַּזְמִי – סַהֲדוּתָא כְּוָותַיְיהוּ קָא קַיְימָא, דְּדִינָא כְּוָותַיְיהוּ פָּסְקִינַן, דְּיֵשׁ בִּכְלַל מָאתַיִם מָנֶה,

Rav Aḥa continues: **Since if** the second set of witnesses **would not have been rendered conspiring witnesses, the testimony would** have been **established in accordance with** their statement, **as the judgment would have been decided in accordance with** their testimony. The reason their testimony would have determined the ruling is **that one hundred dinars is subsumed within two hundred,** i.e., testimony concerning a large sum includes testimony concerning a smaller sum.

הִלְכָּךְ קַמָּאֵי הוּא דְּקָא מִתְכַּחֲשִׁי, מְצִיעָאֵי לָא מִתְכַּחֲשִׁי מִידֵּי!

Rav Aḥa continues: **Therefore, it is the first** set of witnesses, who testified that the eye injury occurred last, **whose** testimony would be considered **contradicted** and rejected, whereas the testimony of **the intermediate** set of witnesses would **not** be considered **contradicted at all,** as it is accepted in full. If so, this is not a case of witnesses who were rejected due to contradiction and then subsequently rendered conspiring witnesses.

אֲמַר לֵיהּ, רָבָא סָבַר: מִדְּרֵישָׁא בְּשָׁלֹשׁ כִּיתּוֹת, סֵיפָא נַמִּי בְּשָׁלֹשׁ, וְדָיֵיק מִסֵּיפָא,

Rav Ashi **said to** Rav Aḥa in response: **Rava maintains** that **from** the fact **that** the ruling of **the first clause** of the *baraita* is stated **with regard to** a case involving **three sets** of witnesses, it is logical to assume that the ruling of **the latter clause is also** stated **with regard to** a case involving **three** sets of witnesses, **and** Rava **infers** his ruling **from the latter clause.**

כְּגוֹן דְּאָתוּ בֵּי תְּרֵי וְאָמְרִי: הִפִּיל אֶת שִׁינּוֹ וְסִימֵּא עֵינוֹ, וּפָסְקִינֵיהּ לְדִינָא אַפּוּמַיְיהוּ,

Rava explains that the latter clause is referring to a case **where two** witnesses, i.e., the ones mentioned in the *baraita,* **come and say:** The master **knocked out** the slave's **tooth and** afterward **blinded his eye, and** the court **ruled** its **judgment in accordance with their statement,** obligating the master to emancipate his slave and compensate him for the value of his eye.

וְאָתוּ בֵּי תְּרֵי אַחֲרִינֵי וְאָמְרִי: סִימֵּא אֶת עֵינוֹ וְהִפִּיל אֶת שִׁינּוֹ, דְּקָא מַכְחֲשִׁי לְהוּ לְהָנֵי קַמָּאֵי, וְנִמְצְאוּ זוֹמְמִין – קַמָּאֵי מְשַׁלְּמִין דְּמֵי עַיִן לָרַב;

And subsequently **two other** witnesses, who were not mentioned in the *baraita,* **come and say** that the events were reversed: First the master **blinded his** slave's **eye and** then **he knocked out his tooth,** so **that they contradict** the testimony of **those first** witnesses. At this point the master is obligated to emancipate his slave and pay him only the value of his tooth, as this much was required of him according to both sets of witnesses. **And** then the first pair **were found to be conspiring witnesses.** Therefore, as the *baraita* states, **the first** set of witnesses **pays** the **value of an eye to the master,** less the value of a tooth.

וְאִי סָלְקָא דַּעְתָּךְ הַכְחָשָׁה לָאו תְּחִילַּת הֲזָמָה הִיא, אַמַּאי מְשַׁלְּמִי? הָא אִתְכַּחֲשׁוּ לְהוּ מֵעִיקָּרָא! אֶלָּא שְׁמַע מִינָּהּ: הַכְחָשָׁה תְּחִילַּת הֲזָמָה הִיא.

Rava reaches his conclusion based on the following reasoning: **And if it enters your mind that** the **contradiction** of testimony **is not the start of determining that** testimony is **conspiring** testimony, and witnesses who were first contradicted and then rendered conspiring witnesses are not punished as conspiring witnesses, **why must** these witnesses **pay? They were** already **contradicted from the outset,** before they were shown to be conspiring witnesses. **Rather, conclude from** the latter clause of the *baraita* that the **contradiction** of testimony **is the start of determining that** testimony is **conspiring** testimony.[B]

וְאַבַּיֵי אָמַר לָךְ: בִּשְׁלָמָא רֵישָׁא לָא סַגִּי דְּלָא שָׁלֹשׁ כִּיתּוֹת, שֶׁהֲרֵי קָתָנֵי: "הָרַב אוֹמֵר כֵּן",

And how could **Abaye,** who disagrees with Rava, refute this proof? He could **say to you: Granted, it is impossible** to interpret **the first clause without** the supposition **that** there are **three sets** of witnesses involved. The reason is **that** it **is taught** with regard to that first clause: **As that is what the master says,** i.e., this testimony is satisfactory to the master. The only testimony recorded in the *baraita* is that the master blinded the slave's eye and then knocked out his tooth. Why would this be considered satisfactory to the master? It must therefore be assumed that this testimony was preceded by another one that was even less advantageous to the master. That testimony confirmed the injuries but placed the eye injury after the tooth injury, which involves greater liability for the master. Finally, a third set of witnesses must have arrived and rendered the intermediate set as conspiring witnesses, so that there are a total of three sets of witnesses.

BACKGROUND

Contradictory testimony and determining conspiring testimony – הַכְחָשָׁה וַהֲזָמָה: There are several differences between these two forms of disqualifying the testimony of witnesses. A pair of witnesses are rendered conspiring witnesses if a second pair testifies that they could not have witnessed the events in question because they were not in the place where the incident purportedly transpired. Witnesses who are rendered conspiring witnesses receive the same punishment they sought to have imposed on the individual concerning whom they testified. In a case concerning contradictory testimony, two other witnesses simply state a different version of events. Although the first pair of witnesses is suspected of lying, they are not disqualified from testifying in other cases, and they receive no punishment. In this case, the testimony of each pair of witnesses carries equal weight; consequently, the two testimonies neutralize one another.

אֶלָּא סֵיפָא לָמָּה לִי שָׁלֹשׁ כִּיתּוֹת – "שֶׁהֲרֵי הָעֶבֶד אוֹמֵר כֵּן"?

But with regard to **the latter clause, why do I** need to explain it as referring to **three sets** of witnesses? If you say that it is because the *baraita* states concerning this case: **As that is what the slave says,** i.e., this testimony is satisfactory to the slave, this does not prove that there is another testimony, not mentioned in the *baraita*, that is less favorable to the slave than this one.

עֶבֶד כָּל דְּהוּ מֵימַר אָמַר, דְּנִיחָא לֵיהּ דְּנֵיפּוֹק לְחֵירוּת.

The reason is **that a slave would say anything,** i.e., any form of testimony would be favorable to him, **as it is satisfactory for him that he should be emancipated.** The court's acceptance of testimony confirming either order of events would result in his emancipation from slavery, and therefore both testimonies are satisfactory to him. Although there is a compelling reason to posit the existence of three sets of witnesses in the first clause, there is no justification to do so in the second clause, and therefore it should be explained as did Abaye, as discussing only two sets of witnesses.

מַתְקִיף לַהּ רַבִּי זֵירָא, אֵימָא: "סִימֵּא אֶת עֵינוֹ"

Rabbi Zeira objects to the basic assumption of the *baraita* that when a master inflicts two injuries upon his Canaanite slave he must indemnify the slave for the second injury. One can **say** instead that if the master **blinded his** slave's **eye,**

Perek **VII**
Daf **74** Amud **b**

NOTES

With regard to your claim the verse states, etc. – עָלֶיךָ אָמַר קְרָא וכו׳: The commentaries note that a Canaanite slave does not become emancipated as soon as his master inflicts an injury on one of his extremities. Rather, it is only upon the pronouncement of the court's judgment that the slave is emancipated. In light of this *halakha* it is difficult to understand why the master is obligated to compensate the slave for the second injury. After all, at the time this injury was inflicted he was still a slave, and a master does not incur monetary liability for injuring his slave (Rashba). The Rashba explains that once the court passes judgment the slave is considered emancipated retroactively.

נֵיפּוֹק בְּעֵינוֹ, הִפִּיל אֶת שִׁינּוֹ – נֵיפּוֹק בְּשִׁינּוֹ, סִימֵּא אֶת עֵינוֹ וְהִפִּיל אֶת שִׁינּוֹ – נֵיפּוֹק בְּעֵינוֹ וְשִׁינּוֹ!

the slave **should go** free **on account of his eye,** and if he **knocked out his tooth** he **should go** free **on account of his tooth,** and if the master both **blinded his eye and knocked out his tooth,** the slave **should go** free **on account of** both **his eye and his tooth,** without the master having to pay damages for the loss of his tooth.

אֲמַר אַבַּיֵי: עָלֶיךָ אָמַר קְרָא: "תַּחַת עֵינוֹ" – וְלֹא תַּחַת עֵינוֹ וְשִׁינּוֹ, "תַּחַת שִׁינּוֹ" – וְלֹא תַּחַת שִׁינּוֹ וְעֵינוֹ.

Abaye said to him in response: **With regard to your** claim, **the verse states:**[N] "And if a man smites the eye of his slave or the eye of his maidservant and destroys it, he shall let him go free for his eye's sake" (Exodus 21:26). The phrase **"for his eye's sake"** indicates: **But not for the sake of** both **his eye and his tooth.**[H] The same can be inferred from the subsequent verse: "And if he smites out his bondman's tooth or his bondwoman's tooth, he shall let him go free for his tooth's sake" (Exodus 21:27). The phrase **"for his tooth's sake"** indicates: **But not for the sake of** both **his eye and his tooth.**

אֲמַר רַב אִידִי בַּר אָבִין, אַף אֲנַן נַמִי תְּנֵינָא: גָּנַב עַל פִּי שְׁנַיִם וְטָבַח וּמָכַר עַל פִּיהֶם, וְנִמְצְאוּ זוֹמְמִין – מְשַׁלְּמִין לוֹ אֶת הַכֹּל;

The Gemara returns to Rava's opinion that the contradiction of testimony is the start of determining that testimony is conspiring testimony. **Rav Idi bar Avin said: We too** can **learn** from the mishna that Rava's claim is correct, as it teaches (72b): If one **stole** an ox or a sheep, as established **based on** the testimony of **two** witnesses, **and he** subsequently **slaughtered** the animal **or sold** it, also **based on** the testimony of the same witnesses, **and** these witnesses **were found** to be **conspiring witnesses,** these conspiring witnesses **must pay everything,** i.e., not only the principal amount but also the fourfold or fivefold payment.

מַאי לָאו דְּהֵעִידוּ עַל הַגְּנֵיבָה וְחָזְרוּ וְהֵעִידוּ עַל הַטְּבִיחָה, וְהוּזְמוּ עַל הַגְּנֵיבָה וְחָזְרוּ וְהוּזְמוּ עַל הַטְּבִיחָה;

What, is it not referring to a case **where they testified concerning the theft and then testified concerning the slaughter, and they were** subsequently **rendered conspiring witnesses with regard to the theft and then were rendered conspiring witnesses with regard to the slaughter?**

HALAKHA

But not for the sake of both his eye and his tooth – וְלֹא תַּחַת עֵינוֹ וְשִׁינּוֹ: If one intentionally strikes his Canaanite slave and in doing so causes the loss or loss of function of one of his twenty-four extremities, as enumerated in tractates *Nega'im* (6:7) and *Kiddushin* (25a), the slave is immediately emancipated. If his former master injures him a second time, he must pay him damages for that second injury (Rambam *Sefer Kinyan, Hilkhot Avadim* 5:14 and Ra'avad and *Kesef Mishne* there, and *Sefer Nezikin, Hilkhot Ḥovel UMazik* 4:11; *Shulḥan Arukh, Yoreh De'a* 267:39).

וְהָא כֵּיוָן שֶׁהוּזְמוּ עַל דִּגְנֵיבָה, לְגַבֵּי טְבִיחָה הָוֵה לְהוּ מוּכְחָשִׁין, וְקָתָנֵי: מְשַׁלְּמִין לוֹ אֶת הַכֹּל. וְאִי סָלְקָא דַּעְתָּךְ הַכְחָשָׁה לָאו תְּחִילַּת הֲזָמָה הִיא, אַטְּבִיחָה אַמַּאי מְשַׁלְּמִין? אֶלָּא לָאו שְׁמַע מִינָּהּ: הַכְחָשָׁה תְּחִילַּת הֲזָמָה הִיא!

Rav Idi bar Avin states his inference: **But once they were rendered conspiring witnesses with regard to the theft,** their testimony **with regard to the slaughter** is in effect **contradicted,** i.e., nullified, as testimony concerning the slaughter of an animal without prior testimony establishing that the animal was stolen is meaningless. **And** yet the mishna **teaches** that the witnesses **must pay everything. And if it enters your mind** that the **contradiction** of testimony **is not the start of determining that** testimony is **conspiring** testimony, **why should they pay** a fine **for** lying about the **slaughter?** Their testimony concerning the slaughter was rendered irrelevant before it was established as conspiring testimony. **Rather,** must one **not conclude from** this mishna that the **contradiction** of testimony **is the start of determining that** testimony is **conspiring** testimony?

אָמְרִי: הָכָא בְּמַאי עָסְקִינַן – כְּגוֹן שֶׁהוּזְמוּ עַל הַטְּבִיחָה תְּחִילָּה.

The Sages **say** in refutation of this inference: **With what are we dealing here?** We are dealing with a case **where** the witnesses were **rendered conspiring witnesses with regard to the slaughter first,** before they were rendered conspiring witnesses in their testimony concerning the theft itself. In this case, the testimony concerning the slaughter was not rendered irrelevant before it was rendered conspiring testimony.

וּבִפְלוּגְתָּא, עֵדִים שֶׁהוּכְחֲשׁוּ וּלְבַסּוֹף הוּזְמוּ – רַבִּי יוֹחָנָן וְרַבִּי אֶלְעָזָר, חַד אָמַר: נֶהֱרָגִין, וְחַד אָמַר אֵין נֶהֱרָגִין.

And this is a matter **in the dispute** between other *amora'im*, before Rava and Abaye discussed it. As it was stated: With regard to **witnesses** to a capital crime **who were** first **contradicted** by two other witnesses **and ultimately were rendered conspiring witnesses,** this is a matter of dispute between **Rabbi Yoḥanan and Rabbi Elazar. One said:** These witnesses **are killed,** like all conspiring witnesses in a capital case, as the contradiction of testimony is the start of determining that testimony is conspiring testimony, **and one said: They are not killed.**

תִּסְתַּיֵּים דְּרַבִּי אֶלְעָזָר הוּא דְּאָמַר אֵין נֶהֱרָגִין, דְּאָמַר רַבִּי אֶלְעָזָר: עֵדִים שֶׁהוּכְחֲשׁוּ בְּנֶפֶשׁ – לוֹקִין,

The Gemara suggests: **It may be concluded** that **it is Rabbi Elazar who says they are not killed. As Rabbi Elazar says: Witnesses who were contradicted in** a case involving the taking of **a life,** i.e., a capital case, **are flogged**[NH] for violating the prohibition: "You shall not bear false witness against your neighbor" (Exodus 20:13).

וְאִי סָלְקָא דַּעְתָּךְ רַבִּי אֶלְעָזָר הוּא דְּאָמַר נֶהֱרָגִין, אַמַּאי לוֹקִין? הָוֵה לֵיהּ לָאו שֶׁנִּיתַּן לְאַזְהָרַת מִיתַת בֵּית דִּין, וְכׇל לָאו שֶׁנִּיתַּן לְאַזְהָרַת מִיתַת בֵּית דִּין אֵין לוֹקִין עָלָיו!

And if it enters your mind that **it is Rabbi Elazar who says** that witnesses to a capital crime who were first contradicted and ultimately found to be conspiring witnesses **are killed, why are they flogged** in this case? There is always the possibility that they might be rendered conspiring witnesses, which would render them liable to receive court-imposed capital punishment. Consequently, this is a case of **a prohibition given as warning** of liability **for court**-imposed **capital punishment, and** there is a principle that **one is not flogged for** violating **any prohibition given as warning** of liability **for court**-imposed **capital punishment.**[NH]

NOTES

Witnesses who were contradicted in a case involving taking a life are flogged – עֵדִים שֶׁהוּכְחֲשׁוּ בְּנֶפֶשׁ לוֹקִין: The standard punishment for violating a prohibition is flogging. Nevertheless, this does not apply to violations that do not involve an action. Since it is generally established that speaking does not constitute an action, why does Rabbi Elazar call for flogging in the case of false witnesses? Rashi explains that the Torah (Deuteronomy 25:1) indicates that the punishment of flogging is imposed in cases of conspiring testimony where it is impossible to "do to him as he had conspired to do to his brother" (Deuteronomy 19:19). The Gemara in tractate *Makkot* (2b) explains that this principle applies to all cases in which a witness is shown beyond doubt to have lied in his testimony (see Ra'avad).

Any prohibition given as warning of liability for court-imposed capital punishment – כׇּל לָאו שֶׁנִּיתַּן לְאַזְהָרַת מִיתַת בֵּית דִּין: Although the violation of a prohibition is usually punished with lashes, if a transgression of this kind could lead to capital punishment, lashes are not administered. This is how the concept is applied by the Gemara here. *Tosafot* point out that elsewhere this principle is presented in a different manner: With regard to any prohibition that involves capital punishment, even if this can occur only in certain limited cases, the punishment of lashes is never applied to this prohibition in any situation at all. They further explain that the prohibition of: "You shall not bear false witness against your neighbor" (Exodus 20:13), is an exception, as the Gemara derives that there is sometimes a punishment of lashes for its violation (see *Makkot* 2b).

HALAKHA

Witnesses who were contradicted in a case involving taking a life are flogged – עֵדִים שֶׁהוּכְחֲשׁוּ בְּנֶפֶשׁ לוֹקִין: Witnesses in a capital case who were contradicted but were not rendered conspiring witnesses are not flogged, even if they testify that someone had been murdered and the supposed victim subsequently appears in court. The reason is that providing false testimony is a transgression that can be subject to the punishment of court-imposed capital punishment, and such a transgression can never result in the punishment of lashes. Nevertheless, the court may punish him with lashes for rebelliousness to the extent that they see fit. The *halakha* is in accordance with the opinion of Rabbi Yoḥanan and Rava, who maintain that the contradiction of testimony is the start of determining that testimony is conspiring testimony. Consequently, if the false witnesses are subsequently rendered conspiring witnesses they are sentenced to death, which is why this is a prohibition whose transgression can result in court-imposed capital punishment (Rambam *Sefer Shofetim, Hilkhot Sanhedrin* 18:6 and *Kesef Mishne* there).

Any prohibition given as warning of liability for court-imposed capital punishment – כׇּל לָאו שֶׁנִּיתַּן לְאַזְהָרַת מִיתַת בֵּית דִּין: One is not flogged for transgressing any prohibition that can lead to court-imposed capital punishment (Rambam *Sefer Shofetim, Hilkhot Sanhedrin* 18:2).

אֶלָּא לָאו שְׁמַע מִינָּהּ: רַבִּי אֶלְעָזָר הוּא דְּאָמַר אֵין נֶהֱרָגִין, תִּסְתַּיֵּים.

Rather, isn't it correct to **conclude from** this statement that **it is Rabbi Elazar who says** that witnesses to a capital crime who were first contradicted and ultimately were found to be conspiring witnesses **are not killed?** The Gemara affirms: **It may be concluded** that this is so.

לוֹקִין? תְּרֵי וּתְרֵי נִינְהוּ, מַאי חָזֵית דְּסָמְכַתְּ אַהָנֵי? סְמוֹךְ אַהָנֵי!

The Gemara asks a question with regard to Rabbi Elazar's opinion that witnesses who were contradicted in a capital case are flogged. Why **are** they **flogged** simply because their testimony was contradicted? **They are two** witnesses, **and** they are contradicted by **two** other witnesses. **What did you see** in the testimony of the second set of witnesses **that** leads **you** to **rely on those** witnesses to the extent that the first set of witnesses is flogged? You could just as well **rely on these** witnesses, i.e., the first witnesses. How can the court ever determine with certainty that a given testimony is false based merely on contradictory testimony?

אֲמַר אַבַּיֵי: בְּבָא הָרוּג בְּרַגְלָיו.

Abaye said: The contradiction to which Rabbi Elazar is referring involves a case **where** the witnesses testified that they saw a certain person murdered, and subsequently the individual who was allegedly **killed came** to the court **on his feet,** conclusively disproving their testimony.

מתני׳ גָּנַב עַל פִּי שְׁנַיִם, וְטָבַח וּמָכַר עַל פִּי עֵד אֶחָד אוֹ עַל פִּי עַצְמוֹ – מְשַׁלֵּם תַּשְׁלוּמֵי כֶפֶל וְאֵינוֹ מְשַׁלֵּם תַּשְׁלוּמֵי אַרְבָּעָה וַחֲמִשָּׁה.

MISHNA If one **stole** an ox or a sheep, as established **based on** the testimony of **two** witnesses, **and he** subsequently **slaughtered**[H] **or sold** the stolen animal, as established **based on** the testimony of **one witness or based on his own** admission, i.e., he himself admitted that he performed these acts, without there being any witness testimony, **he pays** the **double payment, but he does not pay** the **fourfold or fivefold payment.**

גָּנַב וְטָבַח בְּשַׁבָּת, גָּנַב וְטָבַח לַעֲבוֹדָה זָרָה, גָּנַב מִשֶּׁל אָבִיו וּמֵת אָבִיו וְאַחַר כָּךְ טָבַח וּמָכַר, גָּנַב וְהִקְדִּישׁ וְאַחַר כָּךְ טָבַח וּמָכַר – מְשַׁלֵּם תַּשְׁלוּמֵי כֶפֶל וְאֵינוֹ מְשַׁלֵּם תַּשְׁלוּמֵי אַרְבָּעָה וַחֲמִשָּׁה;

If one **stole** an animal **and slaughtered** it **on Shabbat,**[H] which is a capital offense, or if **he stole** an animal **and slaughtered** it **for the** purpose of **idol worship,** or if **he stole his father's** animal **and** subsequently **his father died,**[H] **and afterward he slaughtered or sold** it, or if **he stole** an animal **and** subsequently **he consecrated** it[H] as an offering **and afterward he slaughtered or sold** it, in all these cases the thief **pays** the **double payment, but he does not pay** the **fourfold or fivefold payment.**

רַבִּי שִׁמְעוֹן אוֹמֵר: קֳדָשִׁים שֶׁחַיָּיב בְּאַחֲרָיוּתָם – מְשַׁלֵּם תַּשְׁלוּמֵי אַרְבָּעָה וַחֲמִשָּׁה, שֶׁאֵין חַיָּיב בְּאַחֲרָיוּתָם – פָּטוּר.

Rabbi Shimon says: In the case of **sacrificial** animals **for which** the owner **bears** financial **responsibility** to replace with another animal if one of the original animals that one stole is lost or dies, the thief is obligated to **pay** the **fourfold or fivefold payment** if he slaughters one of the animals. If it is a sacrificial animal **for which** the owner **bears no** financial **responsibility,** the thief **is exempt** from the fourfold or fivefold payment.

גמ׳ עַל פִּי עֵד אֶחָד, פְּשִׁיטָא!

GEMARA The mishna teaches that if the fact that the thief slaughtered or sold the animal was established **based on** the testimony of **one witness,** he is exempt from the fourfold of fivefold payment. The Gemara asks: Isn't this **obvious?**

אָמְרִי: הָא קָא מַשְׁמַע לָן, עַל פִּי עַצְמוֹ דּוּמְיָא דְּעַל פִּי עֵד אֶחָד, מָה עַל פִּי [עֵד] אֶחָד – כִּי אָתֵי עֵד אֶחָד מִצְטָרֵף בַּהֲדֵיהּ מִיחַיַּיב, עַל פִּי עַצְמוֹ נַמִי – כִּי אָתוּ עֵדִים מִיחַיַּיב;

The Sages **say** in response: By stating this case, the mishna **teaches us this** *halakha*: The case of the thief slaughtering the animal established **based on** the testimony of **one witness is similar to** a case where it is established **based on his own** admission. **Just as** in the case where the slaughter is established **based on** the testimony of **one witness, if one** other **witness comes** and corroborates the testimony of the first, he **joins together with** the first witness and together their testimony is rendered a valid testimony of two, and the thief **becomes obligated** to pay the fourfold or fivefold payment, **so too,** where the slaughter is established **based on his own** admission, **if witnesses come** after his admission he **becomes obligated** to pay the fourfold or fivefold payment.

HALAKHA

If one stole based on the testimony of two and he slaughtered, etc. – **גָּנַב עַל פִּי שְׁנַיִם וְטָבַח וכו׳**: If two witnesses testify that someone stole an animal and a single witness testifies that the thief slaughtered or sold the animal, or if the thief himself admits that he slaughtered or sold the animal, the thief is liable to pay the double payment, but he is exempt from paying the fourfold or fivefold payment (Rambam *Sefer Nezikin, Hilkhot Geneiva* 3:7; *Tur, Ḥoshen Mishpat* 350).

If one stole an animal and slaughtered it on Shabbat – **גָּנַב וְטָבַח בְּשַׁבָּת**: If one stole an animal and slaughtered it on Shabbat, or if he slaughtered it for idol worship, he is exempt from paying the fourfold or fivefold payment, even if he committed the Shabbat or idol worship offenses unwittingly (Rambam *Sefer Nezikin, Hilkhot Geneiva* 3:3; *Tur, Ḥoshen Mishpat* 350).

Stole his father's animal and subsequently his father died, etc. – **גָּנַב מִשֶּׁל אָבִיו וּמֵת אָבִיו וכו׳**: If one stole an animal belonging to his father and subsequently his father died, and afterward the thief sold or slaughtered the stolen animal, he pays the double payment, but he is exempt from paying the fourfold or fivefold payment (Rambam *Sefer Nezikin, Hilkhot Geneiva* 2:6; *Tur, Ḥoshen Mishpat* 350).

If he stole an animal and subsequently he consecrated it, etc. – **גָּנַב וְהִקְדִּישׁ וכו׳**: If one stole an animal and, after the owner despaired of retrieving it, the thief consecrated it and then slaughtered or sold it, he pays the double payment, but he does not pay the fourfold or fivefold payment (Rambam *Sefer Nezikin, Hilkhot Geneiva* 2:6).

לְאַפּוּקֵי מִדְּרַב הוּנָא אָמַר רַב, דְּאָמַר רַב הוּנָא אָמַר רַב: מוֹדֶה בִּקְנָס וְאַחַר כָּךְ בָּאוּ עֵדִים – פָּטוּר.

The Gemara comments: This interpretation of the mishna serves to **exclude** that **which Rav Huna says that Rav says. As Rav Huna says** that **Rav says:** One who **admits** he is liable **to pay a fine is exempt** from payment, even if **afterward witnesses come**[H] and testify to his liability.

גּוּפָא, אָמַר רַב הוּנָא אָמַר רַב: מוֹדֶה בִּקְנָס וְאַחַר כָּךְ בָּאוּ עֵדִים – פָּטוּר. אֵיתִיבֵיהּ רַב חִסְדָּא לְרַב הוּנָא: מַעֲשֶׂה בְּרַבָּן גַּמְלִיאֵל שֶׁסִּימֵּא אֶת עֵין טָבִי עַבְדּוֹ, וְהָיָה שָׂמֵחַ שִׂמְחָה גְּדוֹלָה;

Since Rav Huna's *halakha* was mentioned, the Gemara discusses in detail **the matter itself. Rav Huna says** that **Rav says:** One who **admits** he is liable **to pay a fine is exempt** from payment, even if **afterward witnesses come** and testify to his liability. **Rav Ḥisda raised an objection to Rav Huna** from a *baraita*: There was **an incident involving Rabban Gamliel,**[P] **who blinded the eye of his** Canaanite **slave Tavi,**[P] **and he experienced great joy**[N] as a result. Rabban Gamliel had long wanted to emancipate Tavi, but it is generally prohibited to emancipate a Canaanite slave. The injury provided a fortuitous opportunity for Rabban Gamliel to emancipate his slave, as blinding the eye of one's slave results in his emancipation (see Exodus 21:27).

מְצָאוֹ לְרַבִּי יְהוֹשֻׁעַ, אָמַר לוֹ: אִי אַתָּה יוֹדֵעַ שֶׁטָּבִי עַבְדִּי יָצָא לְחֵירוּת? אָמַר לוֹ: לָמָּה? אָמַר לוֹ: שֶׁסִּמֵּיתִי אֶת עֵינוֹ, אָמַר לוֹ: אֵין בִּדְבָרֶיךָ כְּלוּם, שֶׁכְּבָר אֵין לוֹ עֵדִים;

Rabban Gamliel **encountered Rabbi Yehoshua**[P] and **said to him: Do you know that my slave Tavi was emancipated?** Rabbi Yehoshua **said to him: Why?** What circumstances enabled you to emancipate him? Rabban Gamliel **said to him:** I was able to do so, **as I blinded his eye.** Rabbi Yehoshua **said to** Rabban Gamliel: **Your statement is nothing,** and is not grounds for his emancipation, **as he has no witnesses**[N] who can testify that you did this to him. The principle is that one does not pay a fine based on his own admission. One pays a fine only based on the testimony of witnesses. The requirement to emancipate one's slave after injuring his eye is a type of fine.

HALAKHA

One who admits that he is liable to pay a fine…even if afterward witnesses come – מוֹדֶה בִּקְנָס וְאַחַר כָּךְ בָּאוּ עֵדִים: With regard to one who admits that he has committed an act for which he is obligated to pay a fine, and afterward witnesses come and testify that he committed that act, if his admission was submitted in the presence of a court the perpetrator is exempt from paying the fine. If the admission was made outside of a court the perpetrator must pay the fine, in accordance with the opinion of Rav (Rambam *Sefer Nezikin, Hilkhot Geneiva* 3:8).

NOTES

And he experienced great joy – וְהָיָה שָׂמֵחַ שִׂמְחָה גְּדוֹלָה: It is evident from the story that Rabban Gamliel injured Tavi accidentally. Some commentaries note that this understanding presents a difficulty, as a master's obligation to emancipate his slave in the event of injury applies only to deliberate injuries, as stated in tractate *Kiddushin* (24b). However, a dissenting opinion is presented there (Ya'avetz).

As he has no witnesses – שֶׁכְּבָר אֵין לוֹ עֵדִים: There is a dispute between the early commentaries with regard to one who has committed an act for which he is obligated to pay a fine, in a case where there are no witnesses but the perpetrator himself is aware of his offense. Some say that although the court cannot impose a fine in the absence of testimony, nevertheless the offender has a moral obligation to pay it. Other commentaries disagree with this opinion. It has been claimed that the case of Rabban Gamliel apparently proves that there is no obligation, legal or moral, to pay a fine if there are no witnesses (Rashba). The reason is that if there was only a moral obligation for Rabban Gamliel to emancipate his slave, his happiness would have been warranted, just as if he were obligated by the court to do so.

PERSONALITIES

Rabban Gamliel – רַבָּן גַּמְלִיאֵל: Rabban Gamliel served as *Nasi* of the Sanhedrin and was one of the most important *tanna'im* in the period following the destruction of the Temple. His father, Rabban Shimon ben Gamliel, also served as *Nasi* of the Sanhedrin and was one of the leaders of the nation during the Great Revolt. At the time of the destruction of the Temple, Rabban Yoḥanan ben Zakkai brought Rabban Gamliel to Yavne, to study Torah in safety, away from Jerusalem. After the death of Rabban Yoḥanan ben Zakkai he succeeded him as *Nasi* of the Sanhedrin.

During the period when Rabban Gamliel was the *Nasi*, the city of Yavne became a spiritual center in which different enactments and *halakhot* were established for future generations. Consequently, Rabban Gamliel is also known as Rabban Gamliel of Yavne. The great Sages of his time were his disciples: His brother-in-law, Rabbi Eliezer; Rabbi Yehoshua; Rabbi Akiva; and Rabbi Elazar ben Azarya. This was a remarkable group of Sages that had no equal for many subsequent generations.

Rabban Gamliel wanted to create a spiritual center in Eretz Yisrael that would unite the entire Jewish people, as the Temple had done in its time. As part of this endeavor he tried to raise the stature of the office of the *Nasi* and establish the Sanhedrin as a locus of power. His stern and uncompromising leadership eventually led his friends to dismiss him from office for a period of time and appoint Rabbi Elazar ben Azarya in his place (see *Berakhot* 27b). Ultimately, they all understood that his intentions were only for the good of the nation, and he was quickly restored to his previous position.

There are not many *halakhot* in which Rabban Gamliel's name is mentioned, but in his time and under his tutelage some of the most important decisions affecting the spiritual history of the Jewish people took shape, e.g., the final decision to act in accordance with the opinion of Beit Hillel, the rejection of Rabbi Eliezer's opinion in particular matters, and the establishment of a fixed formula for the *Amida* prayer. In those *halakhot* that were transmitted in his name one can see his general approach to *halakha*, which was to draw consistent conclusions based on the principles he espoused without compromising those principles. It is known that two sons of Rabban Gamliel became Sages: Rabban Shimon ben Gamliel II, who served as the *Nasi* of the Sanhedrin after his father, and Rabbi Ḥanina ben Gamliel.

Tavi – טָבִי: Rabban Gamliel's slave Tavi is the most well-known Canaanite slave mentioned in the Talmud. Rabban Gamliel was very fond of Tavi and appreciated his fine character and extensive Torah knowledge. For this reason, when Rabban Gamliel thought that he had finally found a way to emancipate him he was filled with joy. Some later authorities ponder why Rabban Gamliel was so happy when Tavi was blinded, as it is prohibited to cause bodily injury even to a slave (see 92b). They explain that Tavi agreed to be maimed in order to gain his freedom, and as a result there was no prohibition involved (*Beit Yitzḥak, Yoreh De'a* 2:101). Other later authorities insist that Rabban Gamliel did not do this intentionally, as he did not want to violate the Torah's prohibition against emancipating a Canaanite slave (*Sefer HaMikna* on *Kiddushin* 24b).

Although Tavi remained in the service of Rabban Gamliel due to the prohibition against emancipating Canaanite slaves, Rabban Gamliel treated him like a member of his family, and even mourned him when he died. The Sages said about Tavi: There were many who were worthy to be ordained, like Tavi, the slave of Rabban Gamliel. Due to their lineage, they did not achieve that status.

Rabbi Yehoshua – רַבִּי יְהוֹשֻׁעַ: This is Rabbi Yehoshua ben Ḥananya the Levite, one of the leading Sages in the generation following the destruction of the Second Temple. He served as one of the Levite singers in the Temple. After its destruction, he was among the students who followed their primary teacher, Rabban Yoḥanan ben Zakkai, to Yavne. Rabbi Yehoshua lived a life of poverty, working as a blacksmith, and was recognized by all as one of the leading Torah authorities. While he disagreed with Rabban Gamliel's rulings on several occasions, he ultimately accepted the authority of the *Nasi*. After Rabban Gamliel's death, he served as a leader of the Sages.

הָא יֵשׁ לוֹ עֵדִים – חַיָּיב. וְשָׁמְעִינַן מִינַּהּ: מוֹדֶה בִּקְנָס וְאַחַר כָּךְ בָּאוּ עֵדִים – חַיָּיב!

The Gemara infers from the *baraita*: **But** if Tavi **had witnesses** who could testify with regard to the injury, Rabban Gamliel would be **obligated** to emancipate him, even if they testify after Rabban Gamliel's admission. **And we can learn from** this that one who **admits** that he is liable **to** pay **a fine is liable,** even if **afterward witnesses come** and testify with regard to his liability.

אֲמַר לֵיהּ: שָׁאנֵי רַבָּן גַּמְלִיאֵל, דְּלָא בִּפְנֵי בֵית דִּין אוֹדִי. וְהָא רַבִּי יְהוֹשֻׁעַ אַב בֵּית דִּין הֲוָה!

Rav Huna **said to** Rav Ḥisda: This case involving **Rabban Gamliel is different, as he admitted** to his actions when he was **not in the presence of a court.**[HB] An admission not in the presence of a court does not exempt the perpetrator from paying the relevant fine. The Gemara challenges: **But Rabbi Yehoshua was the president of the court,** so it is likely that the encounter took place in court.

HALAKHA

As he admitted when he was not in the presence of a court – דְּלָא בִּפְנֵי בֵית דִּין אוֹדִי: The requirement to emancipate one's slave after injuring him, although a type of fine, is applicable even in the absence of ordained judges, despite the fact that in general fines cannot be collected in Jewish courts under those circumstances. Therefore, if witnesses testify that they witnessed an injury of this kind the master may no longer retain ownership of the slave. The reason is that if the claimant seizes the payment of a fine he is allowed to keep it, and a slave is by definition in possession of his own body. Some authorities rule that the slave's owner should be excommunicated until he agrees to write a bill of manumission for the injured slave (Ra'avad). The Rema adds that these *halakhot* apply if the master admits that he has inflicted an injury on his slave.

The later commentaries disagree as to the circumstances of the Rema's ruling. Some say that he is referring to a case where witnesses testify with regard to the injury after the master's admission, and the reason he is required to emancipate the slave is that an admission in court in the absence of ordained judges is not considered a valid admission. Others maintain that this ruling applies even if witnesses do not testify, in accordance with the principle that the admission of a litigant is similar to the testimony of witnesses (Rambam *Sefer Kinyan, Hilkhot Avadim* 5:17; *Shulḥan Arukh, Yoreh De'a* 267:40 and *Shakh* and *Beur HaGra* there).

BACKGROUND

Not in the presence of a court – לָא בִּפְנֵי בֵית דִּין: An admission made outside a courtroom does not have the legal status of an admission, as outside the court one might make a statement that he does not intend to make in court, or he may try to fend off a claim by bluffing and obfuscating outside the court (see *Sanhedrin* 29a). Moreover, one generally does not reveal his claims until he reaches the court itself (*Bava Batra* 31a).

Perek **VII**
Daf **75** Amud **a**

שֶׁלֹּא בְּבֵית דִּין הֲוָה קָאֵי.

The Gemara answers: Nevertheless, Rabbi Yehoshua **was not** present **in court** when Rabban Gamliel encountered him.

וְהָתַנְיָא: אָמַר לוֹ: אֵין בִּדְבָרֶיךָ כְּלוּם, שֶׁכְּבָר הוֹדֵיתָ;

The Gemara asks a question from a different source: **But isn't it taught** in a *baraita* that Rabbi Yehoshua **said to** Rabban Gamliel: **Your statement is nothing, as you have already admitted** to inflicting the injury yourself? This indicates that even if witnesses would subsequently testify about the injury, Rabban Gamliel would not emancipate Tavi.

מַאי לָאו תַּנָּאֵי הִיא, הַאי תַּנָּא דְּאָמַר ״שֶׁכְּבָר אֵין לְךָ עֵדִים״ סָבַר: מוֹדֶה בִּקְנָס וְאַחַר כָּךְ בָּאוּ עֵדִים – חַיָּיב, וְהַאי תַּנָּא דְּאָמַר ״שֶׁכְּבָר הוֹדֵיתָ״ סָבַר: מוֹדֶה בִּקְנָס וְאַחַר כָּךְ בָּאוּ עֵדִים – פָּטוּר?

The Gemara suggests: **What, is it not** the case that the difference between these two *baraitot* is a dispute between *tanna'im*? **This** *tanna* of the first *baraita*, **who says** that Rabbi Yehoshua's statement was: **As you have no witnesses, holds** that one who **admits** that he is liable **to** pay **a fine is liable** to pay the fine if **afterward witnesses come** and testify to his liability. **And that** *tanna* of the second *baraita*, **who says** that Rabbi Yehoshua's statement was: **As you have already admitted, holds** that one who **admits** that he is liable **to** pay **a fine is exempt** from payment, even if **afterward witnesses come** and testify to his liability.

לָא, דְּכוּלֵּי עָלְמָא – מוֹדֶה בִּקְנָס וְאַחַר כָּךְ בָּאוּ עֵדִים פָּטוּר, וּבְהָא קָמִיפַּלְגִי: הַאי תַּנָּא דְּאָמַר ״שֶׁכְּבָר אֵין לְךָ עֵדִים״ סָבַר: חוּץ לְבֵית דִּין הֲוָה, וְהָךְ תַּנָּא דְּאָמַר ״שֶׁכְּבָר הוֹדֵיתָ״ סָבַר: בְּבֵית דִּין הֲוָה.

The Gemara rejects this suggestion: **No;** it is possible to understand the *baraitot* differently. **Everyone agrees** that one who **admits** he is liable **to** pay **a fine is exempt,** even if **afterward witnesses come** and testify to his liability. **And they disagree with regard to** the following: **This** *tanna*, **who says** that Rabbi Yehoshua said: **As you have no witnesses, holds that** Rabbi Yehoshua **was outside the court** when Rabban Gamliel encountered him, and therefore his admission is disregarded. **And that** *tanna*, **who says** that Rabbi Yehoshua said: **As you have already admitted, holds** that Rabbi Yehoshua **was in the court** when Rabban Gamliel met him, so Rabban Gamliel's admission is a valid admission.

אִיתְּמַר: מוֹדֶה בִּקְנָס וְאַחַר כָּךְ בָּאוּ עֵדִים – רַב אָמַר: פָּטוּר, וּשְׁמוּאֵל אָמַר: חַיָּיב.

The Gemara analyzes in detail the dispute alluded to above: **It was stated** with regard to one who **admits** that he is liable **to** pay **a fine, and afterward witnesses come** and testify to his liability, that **Rav says** he is **exempt, and Shmuel says** he is **liable.**

אֲמַר רָבָא בַּר אֲהִילַאי: מַאי טַעֲמָא דְּרַב? "אִם הִמָּצֵא" – בְּעֵדִים, "תִּמָּצֵא" – בְּדַיָּינִין, פְּרָט לְמַרְשִׁיעַ אֶת עַצְמוֹ,

Rava bar Ahilai said: What is the reason for the ruling of **Rav?** With regard to theft, which is subject to a fine of double payment, the Torah states: "If the theft shall be found in his possession alive, whether it is an ox, or a donkey, or a sheep, he shall pay double" (Exodus 22:3). The verb for "shall be found" is doubled, as the verse states "*himmatze timmatze*." Rav derives from the repetition that there are two matters that are found: The double payment is imposed only **if it is found** [*himmatze*], i.e., it is revealed that he stole the item, **through** the testimony of **witnesses,** and the theft **is found** [*timmatze*], as determined **through judges.** This **excludes one who incriminates himself** through his own admission.

לָמָּה לִי? מֵ"אֲשֶׁר יַרְשִׁיעֻן" נָפְקָא! אֶלָּא שְׁמַע מִינָּהּ: מוֹדֶה בִּקְנָס וְאַחַר כָּךְ בָּאוּ עֵדִים – פָּטוּר.

Rav asks: But **why do I need** the Torah to teach this here? This principle is already **derived from** a different source: **"The one whom the judges convict** shall pay double to his neighbor" (Exodus 22:8), which indicates that self-incrimination is insufficient to render one liable for double payment. **Rather, conclude from** the fact that there are two verses to serve as the source for this principle that one who **admits** he is liable **to pay a fine is exempt** from paying even if **afterward witnesses come** and testify to his liability. The second verse teaches this additional novelty.

וּשְׁמוּאֵל אָמַר לָךְ: הַהוּא מִבָּעֵי לֵיהּ לְגַנָּב עַצְמוֹ, כִּדְתָנָא דְּבֵי חִזְקִיָּה.

And Shmuel would explain the double expression differently. He could have **said to you: That** verse **is necessary to** teach that a **thief himself** must pay double payment, i.e., the double payment is imposed not only upon a bailee who takes a false oath that the article entrusted to him was stolen, but it is also imposed upon a thief, **as the school of Ḥizkiyya taught** earlier in this chapter (63b).

אֵיתִיבֵיהּ רַב לִשְׁמוּאֵל: רָאָה עֵדִים שֶׁמְּמַשְׁמְשִׁים וּבָאִים, וְאָמַר "גָּנַבְתִּי, אֲבָל לֹא טָבַחְתִּי וְלֹא מָכַרְתִּי" – אֵינוֹ מְשַׁלֵּם אֶלָּא קֶרֶן! אֲמַר לֵיהּ: הָכָא בְּמַאי עָסְקִינַן – כְּגוֹן שֶׁחָזְרוּ עֵדִים לַאֲחוֹרֵיהֶם.

Rav raised an objection to Shmuel from the following *baraita*: If a thief **saw witnesses who were approaching** with the intent to testify against him, **and** at that point **he said:** I admit that **I stole** an animal, **but I did not slaughter or sell** it, **he pays only the principal.** This indicates that even if those witnesses subsequently testify, the thief remains exempt from the double payment as well as the fourfold or fivefold payment. Shmuel **said to him** in response: **With what are we dealing here** in this *baraita*? With a case **where the witnesses returned back,**[N] i.e., ultimately they did not testify.

וְהָא מִדְּתָנֵי סֵיפָא, רַבִּי אֶלְעָזָר בְּרַבִּי שִׁמְעוֹן אוֹמֵר: יָבוֹאוּ עֵדִים וְיָעִידוּ – מִכְּלָל דְּתַנָּא קַמָּא סָבַר: לָא!

Rav raised an objection: **But** this interpretation is impossible, as can be seen **from** the fact **that the latter clause** of the *baraita* **teaches: Rabbi Elazar, son of Rabbi Shimon, says: Let the witnesses come and testify.** This means that their testimony will be accepted and the thief will be required to pay the relevant fines. **By inference** it may be deduced **that the first *tanna*** holds that **no,** there is no point in the witnesses testifying, as the thief will be exempt in any case.

אֲמַר לֵיהּ שְׁמוּאֵל: לָאו אִיכָּא רַבִּי אֶלְעָזָר בְּרַבִּי שִׁמְעוֹן דְּקָאֵי כְּוָותִי? אֲנָא דַּאֲמַרִי כְּרַבִּי אֶלְעָזָר בְּרַבִּי שִׁמְעוֹן

Shmuel said to Rav: **Isn't there** the opinion of **Rabbi Elazar, son of Rabbi Shimon, which stands in accordance with my** opinion? When I said that one who admits that he is liable to pay a fine and afterward witnesses testified that he committed that act is deemed liable, **I said** this ruling **in accordance with** the opinion of **Rabbi Elazar, son of Rabbi Shimon.**

לִשְׁמוּאֵל וַדַּאי תַּנָּאֵי הִיא. לְרַב מִי לֵימָא תַּנָּאֵי הִיא?

The Gemara comments: **According to Shmuel,** his opinion on this matter **is certainly** subject to a dispute between ***tanna'im***, as he himself was forced to admit that his opinion is in accordance only with the opinion of Rabbi Elazar, son of Rabbi Shimon, not that of the first *tanna* of the *baraita*. But **according to Rav, shall we say** that his opinion too **is** necessarily subject to this dispute between ***tanna'im***?

NOTES

Where the witnesses returned back – **כְּגוֹן שֶׁחָזְרוּ עֵדִים לַאֲחוֹרֵיהֶם:** If the witnesses did not testify at all, the *baraita* would be stating the obvious by teaching that the thief pays no fine. Shmuel interprets the *baraita* as referring to a case where the witnesses testify only that the thief slaughtered or sold the animal. Consequently, the *baraita* teaches that the thief, on the basis of his self-admission, is exempt from the double payment, and furthermore he is exempt from the fourfold or fivefold payment, as this fine is not imposed in the absence of an obligation to pay a double payment (Ra'avad).

HALAKHA

But if he says, I did not steal anything, etc. – **אֲבָל אָמַר לֹא גָּנַבְתִּי וכו׳**: If one says in court: I did not steal anything, and witnesses testify that he did in fact steal an animal, and subsequently he admits that he did steal it and that he slaughtered or sold it, and finally witnesses testify that the thief slaughtered or sold the animal, the thief must pay the fourfold or fivefold payment despite his admission. The reason is that through his admission he sought to exempt himself from any payment whatsoever. This *halakha* is in accordance with the opinion of Rav Hamnuna (Rambam *Sefer Nezikin*, *Hilkhot Geneiva* 3:9; *Tur*, *Ḥoshen Mishpat* 348).

LANGUAGE

I have gotten the better [*kipaḥti*] – **קִפַּחְתִּי**: The root *kuf*, *peh*, *ḥet* is apparently Aramaic in origin. Its basic meaning is to hit or break an object. It is a common term in the Gemara for defeating, overcoming, robbing, or physically assaulting another person.

PERSONALITIES

The elders of the school of Rav – **סָבֵי דְּבֵי רַב**: The Gemara in tractate *Sanhedrin* (17b) states that the expression: They say in the school of Rav, refers specifically to Rav Hamnuna (Rashi). *Tosafot* maintain that the Gemara there is referring to Rav Huna, and not to Rav Hamnuna. Apparently, Rav's academy continued to function after his death, as Rav Hamnuna outlived him, and Rav's most noteworthy disciples became the chief spokesmen of this group of Sages.

אָמַר לָךְ רַב: אֲנָא דַּאֲמַרִי אֲפִילּוּ לְרַבִּי אֶלְעָזָר בְּרַבִּי שִׁמְעוֹן; עַד כָּאן לָא קָאָמַר רַבִּי אֶלְעָזָר בְּרַבִּי שִׁמְעוֹן הָתָם – אֶלָּא מִשּׁוּם דְּקָא מוֹדֵי מֵחֲמַת בִּיעֲתוּתָא דְּעֵדִים, אֲבָל הָכָא דְּמוֹדֶה מֵעַצְמוֹ, אֲפִילּוּ רַבִּי אֶלְעָזָר בְּרַבִּי שִׁמְעוֹן מוֹדֶה.

The Gemara explains: Rav could have **said to you: I say** my opinion in accordance with the rulings of both *tanna'im* of the *baraita*, **even according to** the opinion of **Rabbi Elazar, son of Rabbi Shimon. Rabbi Elazar, son of Rabbi Shimon, says** that the testimony of the witnesses obligates the thief to pay a fine even after his admission **only there,** in that specific case, **because** the thief **admitted** his guilt solely **due to** his **fear** of the impending testimony **of the witnesses. But here,** in an ordinary case of admission, **where** there is no impending testimony to incriminate him, and **he admits** his guilt **of his own** volition, **even Rabbi Elazar, son of Rabbi Shimon,** would **concede** that the thief is exempt from payment even if witnesses subsequently testify that he is liable.

אָמַר רַב הַמְנוּנָא: מִסְתַּבְּרָא מִילְּתֵיהּ דְּרַב בְּאוֹמֵר ״גָּנַבְתִּי״ וּבָאוּ עֵדִים שֶׁגָּנַב – פָּטוּר, שֶׁהֲרֵי חִיֵּיב עַצְמוֹ בְּקֶרֶן.

Rav Hamnuna said: Rav's statement is more **reasonable** in a case **where** the thief **says: I stole** an item, **and** subsequently **witnesses came** and testified **that he stole** that item. In that case it is logical that the thief is **exempt** from paying the fine despite the witnesses' testimony, because he at least **obligated himself to pay the principal** amount via his admission.

אֲבָל אָמַר ״לֹא גָּנַבְתִּי״ וּבָאוּ עֵדִים שֶׁגָּנַב, וְחָזַר וְאָמַר ״טָבַחְתִּי וּמָכַרְתִּי״ וּבָאוּ עֵדִים שֶׁטָּבַח וּמָכַר – חַיָּיב, שֶׁהֲרֵי פָּטַר עַצְמוֹ מִכְּלוּם.

But if he says: I did not steal anything,[H] **and witnesses came** and testified **that he did steal** an animal, **and subsequently** the thief **says:** Yes, I did steal the animal, and **I** also **slaughtered** it, **or** I also **sold** it, **and witnesses came** and testified **that he slaughtered or sold** it, he is **liable** to pay the fourfold or fivefold payment. The reason he is liable is **that** through his admission he sought to **exempt himself from any** payment whatsoever. In order for an admission to exempt the perpetrator from a fine, it must include an admission that he is liable to pay some payment.

אָמַר רָבָא: [קִפַּחְתִּי] לְסָבֵי דְּבֵי רַב, דְּהָא רַבָּן גַּמְלִיאֵל פּוֹטֵר עַצְמוֹ מִכְּלוּם הֲוָה, וְקָאָמַר לֵיהּ רַב חִסְדָּא לְרַב הוּנָא וְלָא קָא מְשַׁנֵּי לֵיהּ.

Rava said: In this case **I have gotten the better** [*kipaḥti*][L] **of the elders of the school of Rav,**[P] which is a reference to Rav Hamnuna. The reason is **that** in the *baraita* that discusses **Rabban Gamliel** injuring his slave, he **was** seeking to **exempt himself from any payment** whatsoever through his admission, **and** yet earlier in the Gemara it was said that **Rav Ḥisda stated** this *baraita* **to Rav Huna** to challenge Rav Huna's opinion, **and** Rav Huna **did not answer him** that Rabban Gamliel's case was different because his admission served to exempt him entirely.

אִיתְּמַר נַמִי, אָמַר רַבִּי חִיָּיא בַּר אַבָּא אָמַר רַבִּי יוֹחָנָן: ״גָּנַבְתִּי״ וּבָאוּ עֵדִים שֶׁגָּנַב – פָּטוּר, שֶׁהֲרֵי חִיֵּיב עַצְמוֹ בְּקֶרֶן, אֲבָל אָמַר לֹא גָּנַב וּבָאוּ עֵדִים שֶׁגָּנַב, וְחָזַר וְאָמַר ״טָבַחְתִּי וּמָכַרְתִּי״ וּבָאוּ עֵדִים שֶׁטָּבַח וּמָכַר – חַיָּיב, שֶׁהֲרֵי פָּטַר עַצְמוֹ מִכְּלוּם.

The Gemara notes: **It was also stated** that **Rabbi Ḥiyya bar Abba says** that **Rabbi Yoḥanan says** the same opinion as Rav Hamnuna. If a thief says: **I stole** an item, **and witnesses came** and testified **that he stole** that item, the thief is **exempt** from paying the fine despite the witnesses' testimony, because he at least **obligates himself,** through his admission, **to** pay **the principal. But if he says: I did not steal** anything, **and witnesses came** and testified **that he did steal** an animal, **and subsequently** the thief **says:** Yes, I did steal the animal, and **I** also **slaughtered** it, **or** I also **sold** it, and then **witnesses came** and testified **that he slaughtered or sold** it, he is **liable** to pay the fourfold or fivefold payment, **as** through his admission **he** was seeking to **exempt himself from any** payment whatsoever.

אָמַר רַב אַשִׁי: מַתְנִיתִין וּבָרַיְיתָא נַמִי דַּיְקָא; מַתְנִיתִין, דִּתְנַן: גָּנַב עַל פִּי שְׁנַיִם, וְטָבַח וּמָכַר עַל פִּי עֵד אֶחָד אוֹ עַל פִּי עַצְמוֹ – מְשַׁלֵּם תַּשְׁלוּמֵי כֶפֶל וְאֵינוֹ מְשַׁלֵּם תַּשְׁלוּמֵי אַרְבָּעָה וַחֲמִשָּׁה;

Rav Ashi said: There is **a mishna and a *baraita*** that are **also precisely** formulated in accordance with this opinion. **The mishna** is **as we learned** (74b): If one **stole** an ox or a sheep, as established **based on** the testimony of **two** witnesses, **and he** subsequently **slaughtered or sold** the stolen animal, as established **based on** the testimony of **one witness or based on his own** admission, **he pays the double payment, but he does not pay** the **fourfold or fivefold payment.**

לָמָּה לִי דְּתָנֵי גָּנַב עַל פִּי שְׁנַיִם? לִיתְנֵי: גָּנַב וְטָבַח [וּמָכַר] עַל פִּי עֵד אֶחָד אוֹ עַל פִּי עַצְמוֹ – אֵינוֹ מְשַׁלֵּם אֶלָּא הַקֶּרֶן!

Why do I need the mishna to **teach** in the beginning of this case: If one **stole** an ox or a sheep, as established **based on** the testimony of **two witnesses? Let** the mishna **teach** the case more simply: If one **stole** an animal **and** then **slaughtered or sold** it, as established **based on** the testimony of **one witness or based on his own** admission, **he pays only the principal.** This would serve to teach the same principle in a less complicated manner, without the need for two additional witnesses.

אֶלָּא לָאו הָא קָא מַשְׁמַע לָן: גָּנַב עַל פִּי שְׁנַיִם וְטָבַח עַל פִּי עֵד אֶחָד אוֹ עַל פִּי עַצְמוֹ, הוּא דְּלָא מְחַיֵּיב עַצְמוֹ בְּקֶרֶן,

Rather, is it not correct to say that by citing the more complicated case, **this** is what the mishna **teaches us: It is** only in this case, where it is established that the thief **stole** an animal **based on** the testimony of **two** witnesses, **and** it is established that **he slaughtered** or sold it **based on** the testimony of **one witness or based on his own** admission, and **where he does not obligate himself** through his admission **to pay the principal,** that he is obligated to pay the fine.

הוּא דְּאָמְרִינַן עַל פִּי עַצְמוֹ דּוּמְיָא דְּעַל פִּי עֵד אֶחָד, מָה עַל פִּי עֵד אֶחָד – כִּי אָתֵי עֵד אֶחָד מִצְטָרֵף בַּהֲדֵיהּ מִחַיֵּיב, עַל פִּי עַצְמוֹ נַמִּי – כִּי אָתוּ עֵדִים מִחַיֵּיב

The Gemara elaborates: In other words, it is only in **that** case, where the theft is established based on the testimony of two witnesses, **that we say** that liability **based on his own** admission **is similar to the** testimony **of one witness,** in that **just as when** the slaughter is established **based on** the testimony of **one witness,** if **one** other **witness** later **comes he joins together with** the first witness and together their testimony is rendered a valid testimony of two witnesses and the thief **becomes liable** to pay, so **too,** in a case when the slaughter is established **based on his own** admission, **if witnesses** subsequently **come** and testify, he **becomes liable** to pay the fine, as his admission would not have rendered him liable to pay any payment.

אֲבָל גָּנַב וְטָבַח וּמָכַר עַל פִּי עֵד אֶחָד אוֹ עַל פִּי עַצְמוֹ, דְּחַיֵּיב עַצְמוֹ בְּקֶרֶן – לָא אָמְרִינַן עַל פִּי עַצְמוֹ דּוּמְיָא דְּעַל פִּי עֵד אֶחָד.

But if it is established that the thief **stole** an animal **and slaughtered or sold** it, all **based on** the testimony of **one witness or based on his own** admission, in **which** case through his admission **he obligates himself to** pay **the principal** amount, **we do not say** that when witnesses testify subsequent **to his own** admission it is similar to when they arrive subsequent **to the** testimony **of one witness,** and he is liable to pay the fine in both cases. Rather, since in this case his admission would have rendered him liable to pay the principal due to the fact that the theft was not established based on the testimony of two witnesses, it is considered a proper admission, which exempts him from paying the fine.

בָּרַיְיתָא, דְּתַנְיָא: רָאָה עֵדִים שֶׁמְּמַשְׁמְשִׁין וּבָאִין, וְאָמַר ״גָּנַבְתִּי, אֲבָל לֹא טָבַחְתִּי וְלֹא מָכַרְתִּי״ – אֵינוֹ מְשַׁלֵּם אֶלָּא קֶרֶן; לָמָּה לִי לְמִיתְנָא: וְאָמַר ״גָּנַבְתִּי, אֲבָל לֹא טָבַחְתִּי וְלֹא מָכַרְתִּי״? נִיתְנֵי אוֹ ״גָּנַבְתִּי״ אוֹ ״טָבַחְתִּי וּמָכַרְתִּי״!

The *baraita* that supports Rav Hamnuna's opinion is the one cited earlier, **as it is taught:** If a thief **saw witnesses who were approaching** with the intent to testify against him, **and** at that point he **said:** I admit that **I stole** an animal, **but I did not slaughter or sell** it, **he pays only the principal. Why do I** need the *baraita* **to teach: And** the thief **said:** I admit that **I stole** an animal **but I did not slaughter or sell it? Let it teach** a simpler case, in which the thief said **either: I stole** the animal, **or: I slaughtered** it, **or: I sold** it.

אֶלָּא הָא קָא מַשְׁמַע לָן: טַעֲמָא דְּאָמַר ״גָּנַבְתִּי״ הוּא, דְּחַיֵּיב עַצְמוֹ בְּקֶרֶן – דְּפָטוּר, אֲבָל אָמַר ״לֹא גָּנַבְתִּי״ וּבָאוּ עֵדִים שֶׁגָּנַב, וְחָזַר וְאָמַר ״טָבַחְתִּי וּמָכַרְתִּי״ וּבָאוּ עֵדִים שֶׁטָּבַח וּמָכַר, דְּלָא חַיֵּיב עַצְמוֹ בְּקֶרֶן – חַיָּיב; אַלְמָא הוֹדָאָה דִּטְבִיחָה לָאו הוֹדָאָה הִיא.

Rather, by choosing the more complicated case, **this** is what the *baraita* **teaches us: The** only **reason that** the thief **is exempt** from payment **is that he says: I stole** the animal, **as** in that case **he obligated himself to** pay **the principal. But if he says: I did not steal, and witnesses came** and testified **that he did steal** an animal, **and subsequently he** changed his claim and **says: I slaughtered** it, **or: I sold** it, **and** then **witnesses came** and confirmed **that he slaughtered or sold** it, in which case the thief **did not obligate himself to pay the principal** or any other payment, he would be **liable** to pay the fourfold or fivefold payment. **Apparently, an admission to** the **slaughter** of a stolen animal **is not** considered a valid **admission,** as such an admission does not obligate the perpetrator to pay a fine.

אָמְרִי: לָא, הִיא גּוּפָהּ קָא מַשְׁמַע לָן, דְּכֵיוָן דְּאָמַר ״גָּנַבְתִּי״, אַף עַל גַּב דְּאָמַר ״לֹא טָבַחְתִּי וְלֹא מָכַרְתִּי״ וּבָאוּ עֵדִים שֶׁטָּבַח וּמָכַר – פָּטוּר, מַאי טַעְמָא?

The Gemara **says,** in rejection of this second proof: **No,** it is possible to explain the reason the *tanna* of the *baraita* chose to present this case in a different manner, as it **teaches us this** *halakha* **itself: That once** the thief **says: I stole** the animal, **even if he** also **says: I did not slaughter or sell** it, **and** later **witnesses came** and testified **that he slaughtered or sold it,** he is **exempt** from paying the fourfold or fivefold payment. **What is the reason** for this exemption?

HALAKHA

If two witnesses testify that someone stole an animal, etc. – **הָיוּ שְׁנַיִם מְעִידִין שֶׁגָּנַב וכו׳**: In a case where two witnesses testify that someone stole an animal and two others testify that he slaughtered it, and the two witnesses testifying to the theft were rendered conspiring witnesses, the entire testimony is nullified. If only the second set of witnesses, i.e., those testifying to the slaughter, were rendered conspiring witnesses, the thief pays the double payment for the theft, and the witnesses who testified falsely concerning the slaughter pay the thief a threefold payment for an ox, as this is the amount they sought to cause him to pay beyond what he owed (Rambam *Sefer Shofetim*, *Hilkhot Edut* 21:6).

תַּשְׁלוּמֵי (אַרְבַּע) חֲמִשָּׁה אֲמַר רַחֲמָנָא, וְלֹא תַּשְׁלוּמֵי אַרְבָּעָה וְלֹא תַּשְׁלוּמֵי שְׁלֹשָׁה.

The reason is that **the Merciful One states** in the Torah that there is **a payment of four** sheep for a sheep and **five** oxen for an ox (see Exodus 21:37). This indicates that a thief can be rendered liable to pay, respectively, a fourfold or fivefold payment, **but not a fourfold payment** for an ox, **nor a threefold payment** for a sheep. In other words, one should not view the fines as independent of each other, that if the thief is found with the animal he pays as a fine the double payment, and if he slaughtered or sold it he pays a different fine, i.e., the fourfold or fivefold payment. Rather, the fourfold or fivefold payment comprises the principal, the double payment, and an additional two or three times the principal. By admitting to his act of theft, the thief exempts himself from the double payment, and the remaining fine for slaughtering a sheep would be a threefold payment, or a fourfold payment for an ox, which are not mandated by the Torah.

לֵימָא כְּתַנָּאֵי: הָיוּ שְׁנַיִם מְעִידִין שֶׁגָּנַב, וְהָיוּ שְׁנַיִם מְעִידִים אוֹתוֹ שֶׁטָּבַח וּמָכַר, הוּזְמוּ עֵדֵי גְנֵיבָה – עֵדוּת שֶׁבָּטְלָה מִקְצָתָהּ בָּטְלָה כּוּלָּהּ.

The Gemara proposes: **Let us say** that the opinion of Rav Hamnuna and Rabbi Yoḥanan is the **subject of** a dispute **between *tanna'im*.** As it is taught in a *baraita*: If **two** witnesses **testify that** someone **stole** an animal,[H] **and two** others **testify** against **him that he slaughtered or sold** the animal, and the **witnesses** who had testified concerning the **theft were rendered conspiring witnesses,** the thief is exempt from all payment, as **testimony that was partially invalidated is entirely invalidated.** If the testimony concerning the theft was undermined, the testimony concerning the slaughter or sale is thereby rendered irrelevant. Consequently, the alleged thief is exempt from any payment.

הוּזְמוּ עֵדֵי טְבִיחָה – הוּא מְשַׁלֵּם תַּשְׁלוּמֵי כֶפֶל, וְהֵן מְשַׁלְּמִין תַּשְׁלוּמֵי שְׁלֹשָׁה; מִשּׁוּם סוּמָכוֹס אָמְרוּ: הֵן מְשַׁלְּמִין תַּשְׁלוּמֵי כֶפֶל, וְהוּא מְשַׁלֵּם תַּשְׁלוּמֵי שְׁלֹשָׁה לְפַר וּשְׁנַיִם לְאַיִל;

If **the witnesses** who testified concerning **the slaughter** or sale **were rendered conspiring witnesses,** but the testimony concerning the theft remains credible, the thief **pays** the **double payment, and** the conspiring witnesses **pay a threefold payment,** as that is the loss they sought to impose on the thief. The Sages **said in the name of Sumakhos:** The witnesses **pay** the **double payment, and** the thief **pays a threefold payment for an ox and a twofold** payment **for a ram.** This concludes the *baraita*.

אַהַיָּיא קָאֵי סוּמָכוֹס? אִילֵּימָא אַרֵישָׁא – לֵית לֵיהּ לְסוּמָכוֹס עֵדוּת שֶׁבָּטְלָה מִקְצָתָהּ בָּטְלָה כּוּלָּהּ?

The Gemara analyzes the statement of Sumakhos: **To which** clause in the *baraita* **is Sumakhos referring? If we say** that he is referring **to the first clause,** in which the testimony concerning the theft is invalidated, this is impossible. **Doesn't Sumakhos** accept the principle that **testimony that was partially invalidated is entirely invalidated,** in this case rendering the testimony concerning the slaughter or sale irrelevant if there is no testimony concerning the theft?

וְאֶלָּא אַסֵּיפָא – שַׁפִּיר קָאָמְרִי רַבָּנַן: הוּא מְשַׁלֵּם תַּשְׁלוּמֵי כֶפֶל, וְהֵם מְשַׁלְּמִין תַּשְׁלוּמֵי שְׁלֹשָׁה!

But rather, he must be referring **to the latter clause** of the *baraita*, in which the testimony concerning the slaughter or sale is invalidated. This, too, is impossible, as in this case **the Rabbis,** i.e., the first *tanna* of the *baraita*, **say well,** i.e., what they state is reasonable, **and** the thief **pays** the **double payment and** the witnesses **pay a threefold payment.** On what basis would Sumakhos dispute this ruling?

אֶלָּא מִילְּתָא אַחֲרִיתִי אִיכָּא בֵּינַיְיהוּ, כְּגוֹן דַּאֲתוֹ בֵּי תְרֵי אָמְרִי לֵיהּ ״גְּנַבְתָּ״, אֲמַר לְהוּ ״אִין, גְּנַבְתִּי וְטָבַחְתִּי וּמָכַרְתִּי, מִיהוּ לֹא בִּפְנֵיכֶם גְּנַבְתִּי״, וְאַיְיתִי סָהֲדֵי וְאַזְמִינְהוּ דְּלָא בְּאַפַּיְיהוּ גְּנַב, וְאַיְיתִי בַּעַל הַבַּיִת סָהֲדֵי וְאַסְהִידוּ בֵּיהּ דִּגְנַב וְטָבַח וּמָכַר;

Rather, it must be that Sumakhos is referring to a different case entirely, one that is not mentioned explicitly in the *baraita*, and **a different matter is** at the core of the dispute **between them.** Sumakhos is referring to a case **where two** people **come** and **say to** the thief: **You stole** an animal. The thief **said to them** in reply: **Yes, I did steal** the animal, **and** moreover, **I slaughtered** it, **or: I sold** it. **But I did not steal** it **in your presence,** and your testimony that you saw me steal it is false. **And** subsequently the thief **brought** new **witnesses who rendered** the original witnesses **conspiring witnesses,** by testifying that they were in a different place at the time they claimed that the theft occurred, thereby proving **that** the thief **did not steal in their presence. And** finally, **the owner** of the animal **brought** other **witnesses who testified that** the thief **stole** the animal **and slaughtered or sold** it.

וּבְהוֹדָאַת טְבִיחָה קָמִיפַּלְגִי,

And Sumakhos and the Rabbis **disagree over** whether **an admission to** the **slaughter** of a stolen animal is a valid admission, even though it does not lead to liability to pay any payment. Both parties to the dispute agree that the admission of a perpetrator only in response to the testimony of witnesses is not a valid admission.

דְּרַבָּנַן סָבְרִי: אַף עַל גַּב דְּהוֹדָאָה דִּגְנֵיבָה מֵחֲמַת עֵדִים הוּא דְּקָא מוֹדֶה – הוֹדָאָה דִּטְבִיחָה הוֹדָאָה הִיא, וּפָטוּר;

The dispute between them is **that the Rabbis maintain that even though** the thief's **admission concerning** the **theft** itself is not a valid admission because it is **due** only **to the witnesses** who have testified against him that **he admits** his guilt, nevertheless, his **admission concerning** the **slaughter** of the animal **is** a valid **admission,** despite the fact it does not render the thief liable to pay a fine, **and** he is therefore **exempt** from the fourfold or fivefold payment. The conspiring witnesses must pay the double payment to the thief, since this is the amount of financial damage they sought to impose on him, while the thief pays the double payment to the owner, as valid witnesses ultimately testified that he stole the animal.

וְסוּמָכוֹס סָבַר: כֵּיוָן דְּהוֹדָאָה דִּגְנֵיבָה מֵחֲמַת עֵדִים הוּא דְּקָא מוֹדֶה – דִּטְבִיחָה לָאו הוֹדָאָה,

And Sumakhos maintains that **since** the **admission concerning** the **theft** itself is not a valid admission because it was **due** only **to** the testimony of the **witnesses that he admits** his guilt,[N] so too, the admission **concerning** the **slaughter is not** a valid **admission,** because it does not obligate him to pay a fine, as stated by Rav Hamnuna and Rabbi Yoḥanan.

וְהָנָךְ עֵדִים קַמָּאֵי דְּאַזְּכִינְהוּ מְשַׁלְּמִין תַּשְׁלוּמֵי כֶפֶל, וְהוּא מְשַׁלֵּם שְׁלֹשָׁה לַפָּר וּשְׁנַיִם לָאַיִל.

And consequently, **those first witnesses** to the theft, **who were rendered conspiring witnesses, pay** the **double payment,** as that is the amount of financial damage they sought to impose on him, **and** the thief **pays** the double payment to the owner of the animal, as valid witnesses ultimately testified that he stole it, and since his admission is invalid he must pay an additional **threefold** payment, for a total of a fivefold payment **for an ox, or a twofold** payment, for a total of a fourfold payment, **for a ram.** If this is their dispute, Sumakhos is in agreement with the opinion of Rav Hamnuna and Rabbi Yoḥanan, while the Rabbis disagree with this opinion.

אֲמַר רַב אַחָא בְּרֵיהּ דְּרַב אִיקָא: לָא, דְּכוּלֵּי עָלְמָא – הוֹדָאָה דִּטְבִיחָה לָאו הוֹדָאָה הִיא.

Rav Aḥa, son of Rav Ika, said: No; it is possible to explain the *baraita* differently, as follows: **Everyone,** i.e., both Sumakhos and the Rabbis, maintains that **an admission concerning** the **slaughter** of a stolen animal **is not** a valid **admission,** as it does not render the perpetrator liable to pay any payment.

אֶלָּא בְּעֵדוּת שֶׁאִי אַתָּה יָכוֹל לַהֲזִימָּהּ קָמִיפַּלְגִי; כְּגוֹן דַּאֲתוֹ סָהֲדֵי וְאָמְרִי לֵיהּ "גָּנַבְתָּ", וַאֲמַר לְהוּ "גָּנַבְתִּי וְטָבַחְתִּי וּמָכַרְתִּי, מִיהוּ לֹא בִּפְנֵיכֶם גָּנַבְתִּי אֶלָּא בִּפְנֵי פְּלוֹנִי וּפְלוֹנִי", וְאַיְיתֵי סָהֲדֵי וְאַזְמִינְהוּ דְּלָא בְּאַפַּיְיהוּ גְּנַב, וַאֲתוֹ פְּלוֹנִי וּפְלוֹנִי וְאַסְהִידוּ בֵּיהּ דְּגָנַב וְטָבַח וּמָכַר;

Rather, they disagree over the concept of **testimony that you cannot render conspiratory** testimony.[H] Sumakhos and the Rabbis disagree with regard to a case **where witnesses come and say to** the thief: **You stole** an animal. **And** the thief **said to them** in response: **I did steal** an animal, **and** moreover, **I slaughtered** it, or: **I sold** it. **But** you are false witnesses, as **it was not in your presence that I stole** the animal, **but in the presence of so-and-so and so-and-so. And** the thief subsequently **brought witnesses who established** the first set of witnesses **as conspiring witnesses** by testifying that the thief **did not steal** the animal **in their presence. And** finally, **so-and-so and so-and-so,** the two people mentioned by the thief, **came and testified against** the thief, saying that **he stole** the animal **and** also **slaughtered or sold** it.

וּבְהָא קָמִיפַּלְגִי, דְּרַבָּנַן סָבְרִי: הָוְיָא לַהּ עֵדוּת שֶׁאִי אַתָּה יָכוֹל לַהֲזִימָּהּ, וְכָל עֵדוּת שֶׁאִי אַתָּה יָכוֹל לַהֲזִימָּהּ לָא הָוְיָא עֵדוּת;

And it is **with regard to this** point that **they disagree, that the Rabbis maintain** that the testimony of so-and-so and so-and-so is **testimony that you cannot render conspiratory** testimony, as the thief himself admits that their testimony is true. **And any testimony that you cannot render conspiratory** testimony **is not** considered valid **testimony.** Their testimony is therefore discounted, which leaves only the thief's statement. The thief pays the money he admitted he owes, i.e., the principal of the theft, but he is exempt from paying a fine. Meanwhile, the first witnesses, who had been rendered conspiring witnesses, pay the thief the double payment.

NOTES

It was due only to the witnesses that he admits his guilt – מֵחֲמַת עֵדִים הוּא דְּקָא מוֹדֶה: Although the thief knows that these witnesses are lying, a fact that he ultimately proves in court, he is nevertheless unnerved by their testimony, because at the time of his admission he is not certain that he will succeed in falsifying their account (Meiri; Rashba, citing Rabbeinu Ḥananel). Others offer a different explanation: Although the thief knows that these witnesses are lying about having seen him, he is also aware that there are other witnesses who did see him steal, and he is daunted by the prospect of their coming to testify against him (see Rashba).

HALAKHA

Testimony that you cannot render conspiratory testimony – עֵדוּת שֶׁאִי אַתָּה יָכוֹל לַהֲזִימָּהּ: With regard to testimony that cannot possibly lead to the punishment designated for conspiring witnesses, e.g., in a case where witnesses fail to pinpoint a time and place when the events took place, such testimony is rendered invalid and therefore inadmissible in capital cases. Others maintain that such testimony is invalid even with regard to monetary cases (Rambam *Sefer Shofetim, Hilkhot Edut* 20:7 and *Sefer Nezikin, Hilkhot Rotze'aḥ UShmirat HaNefesh* 2:9; see *Shulḥan Arukh, Ḥoshen Mishpat* 33:16 and *Shakh* there).

וְסוּמָכוֹס סָבַר: עֵדוּת שֶׁאִי אַתָּה יָכוֹל לַהֲזִימָהּ הָוְיָא עֵדוּת.

And Sumakhos maintains that **testimony that you cannot render conspiratory** testimony **is** nevertheless considered valid **testimony.** Therefore, the testimony of so-and-so and so-and-so is valid, and the thief must pay the fourfold or fivefold payment. Sumakhos states that the thief pays a threefold payment for an ox and a twofold payment for a ram. The reason is that the thief receives a double payment from the first, conspiring witnesses, which he gives to the owner of the animal, along with the remainder of the payment. This amounts to a threefold payment for an ox and twofold payment for a ram that he is required to pay from his own funds.

וְהָא קַיְימָא לָן, דְּעֵדוּת שֶׁאִי אַתָּה יָכוֹל לַהֲזִימָהּ לָא הָוְיָא עֵדוּת! הָנֵי מִילֵּי הֵיכָא דְּלָא יָדְעִי בְּאֵיזֶה יוֹם בְּאֵיזֶה שָׁעָה, דְּלֵיכָּא לְעֵדוּת כְּלָל, אֲבָל הָכָא סִיּוּעֵי הוּא דְּקָא מְסַיְּיעִי לֵיהּ.

The Gemara asks: **But do we not maintain** as an accepted principle **that testimony that you cannot render conspiratory** testimony **is not** valid **testimony?** It is not reasonable to suggest that Sumakhos would disagree with that principle. The Gemara answers: **This** statement **applies** in a case **where** witnesses say **that they do not know on which day** or **at which time** of day the events in question occurred, in which case no one could ever say to them: You were in a different place at that time, thereby rendering them conspiring witnesses. With regard to such a case one can say **that** in effect **there is no testimony at all**, as the vague statement of the witnesses does not allow them to be prosecuted as conspiring witnesses. **But here** the thief is **supporting** their testimony, which renders it more credible.

אָמַר מָר: הֵן מְשַׁלְּמִין תַּשְׁלוּמֵי כֶפֶל. מִדְּקָא מוֹדֶה דְּגָנַב, קֶרֶן בָּעֵי שַׁלּוּמֵי! אָמַר רַבִּי אֶלְעָזָר מִשְּׁמֵיהּ דְּרַב, תְּנֵי:

The Master said in the *baraita* that the Sages stated in the name of Sumakhos: The witnesses **pay** the **double payment.** The Gemara asks: **From** the fact **that the thief admits that he stole** the animal, **he is required to pay the principal** amount regardless of any subsequent testimony provided by witnesses. Why, then, should the conspiring witnesses be required to pay a double payment, which includes the principal amount? **Rabbi Elazar says in the name of Rav: Teach** the *baraita* differently, and instead say that Sumakhos said that the witnesses are liable for

תַּשְׁלוּם דְּכֶפֶל.

the **payment of** the extra part of the **double payment,** i.e., the amount that exceeds the principal.

״גָּנַב וְהִקְדִּישׁ וְאַחַר כָּךְ טָבַח וּמָכַר״ כו׳. אָמְרִי: בִּשְׁלָמָא אַטְּבִיחָה לָא מִחַיַּיב, דְּכִי קָא טָבַח – דְּהֶקְדֵּשׁ קָא טָבַח וְלָא דְּמָרֵיהּ קָא טָבַח.

§ The mishna teaches: If one **stole** an animal **and** subsequently **he consecrated it** as an offering, **and afterward he slaughtered or sold** it, the thief pays the double payment but he does not pay the fourfold or fivefold payment. The Sages **say: Granted, he is not liable** to pay the fourfold or fivefold payment **for the slaughter** of the animal, **as when he slaughtered** it, **he slaughtered** an animal **belonging to the Temple** treasury, **and he did not slaughter** the animal **belonging to its owner.**

אֶלָּא אַהֶקְדֵּשׁ לִיחַיַּיב, מַה לִּי מְכָרוֹ לְהֶדְיוֹט מַה לִּי מְכָרוֹ לַשָּׁמַיִם!

But let him be liable to pay the fourfold or fivefold payment **for** having **consecrated** the animal in the first place, as **what** difference **is it to me** if **he sold** the animal **to an ordinary** person, and **what** difference **is it to me** if **he sold it to Heaven** by consecrating it? Consecration should be considered tantamount to a sale, as in either case ownership of the animal is transferred to another party.

הָא מַנִּי? רַבִּי שִׁמְעוֹן הִיא, דְּאָמַר: קֳדָשִׁים שֶׁחַיָּיב בְּאַחֲרָיוּתָן בִּרְשׁוּתֵיהּ דְּמָרֵיהּ קַיְימִי.

The Gemara answers: In accordance with **whose** opinion **is this** mishna taught? **It is** in accordance with the opinion of **Rabbi Shimon, who says** that **sacrificial** animals **for which** the owner **bears** financial **responsibility** to replace with another animal if one of the original animals is lost or dies **are** considered **to be in the possession of their owner**[N] (see 74b). The mishna is referring a case where the thief consecrated the animal in such a manner that he is obligated to replace it if it is lost or damaged before being sacrificed. One consequence of this potential financial loss is that the animal is considered to be in the thief's possession even after he consecrated it. Therefore, the animal's consecration is not tantamount to a sale to another party.

NOTES

To be in the possession of their owner – **בִּרְשׁוּתֵיהּ דְּמָרֵיהּ קַיְימִי**: When a thief consecrates a stolen animal, the act of consecration is not considered a proper sale. Nevertheless, the animal is considered to have been removed from the owner's jurisdiction to a certain extent, and if the thief subsequently slaughters the animal, he is not liable to pay the fourfold or fivefold payment (Rashi). The same reasoning applies to the other answers given by the Gemara in the ensuing discussion.

הָא מִדְּסֵיפָא רַבִּי שִׁמְעוֹן, הֲוֵי רֵישָׁא לָאו רַבִּי שִׁמְעוֹן!

The Gemara rejects this answer: **But from** the fact that **the latter clause** of the mishna is in accordance with the opinion of **Rabbi Shimon,** it follows that **the first clause** of the mishna, which is stated before his opinion is introduced, **is not** in accordance with the opinion of **Rabbi Shimon.**

אֶלָּא הָכָא בְּמַאי עָסְקִינַן – בְּקָדָשִׁים קַלִּים, וְאַלִּיבָּא דְּרַבִּי יוֹסֵי הַגְּלִילִי, דְּאָמַר: קָדָשִׁים קַלִּים מָמוֹן בְּעָלִים הוּא, וּבִרְשׁוּתֵיהּ קָיְימִי.

Rather, with what are we dealing here in the mishna? We are dealing **with** a case where the thief consecrated the animal as **an offering of lesser sanctity,**[B] and the mishna is **in accordance with** the opinion of **Rabbi Yosei HaGelili, who says** that **an offering of lesser sanctity is the property of** its putative **owner, and is** considered **in his possession.** Therefore, its consecration is not tantamount to a sale to another party.

אֲבָל קָדְשֵׁי קָדָשִׁים מַאי? מְשַׁלֵּם תַּשְׁלוּמֵי אַרְבָּעָה וַחֲמִשָּׁה? אַדְּתָנֵי רֵישָׁא: גָּנַב וְטָבַח וְאַחַר כָּךְ הִקְדִּישׁ – מְשַׁלֵּם תַּשְׁלוּמֵי אַרְבָּעָה וַחֲמִשָּׁה, לִיפְלוֹג וְלִיתְנֵי בְּדִידַהּ.

The Gemara rejects this answer as well: **But what** would be the *halakha* had the thief consecrated the animal as **an offering of the most sacred order?** Would he have to **pay the fourfold or fivefold payment?** If so, **rather than teaching** the following in **the earlier clause** of the mishna (70a), in the case that stands in opposition to this one: If **he stole** an animal **and slaughtered** it **and afterward he consecrated** it, **he must pay** the **fourfold or fivefold payment, let** the *tanna* **distinguish and teach** the opposing *halakha* **within** the same category **itself.**

בַּמֶּה דְּבָרִים אֲמוּרִים – בְּקָדָשִׁים קַלִּים, אֲבָל בְּקָדְשֵׁי קָדָשִׁים – מְשַׁלֵּם תַּשְׁלוּמֵי אַרְבָּעָה וַחֲמִשָּׁה!

The Gemara elaborates: The *tanna* could have taught: **In what case is this statement,** that the thief is exempt if he consecrated the stolen animal and then slaughtered or sold it, **said?** It is said only if he consecrated the animal **as an offering of lesser sanctity; but** if he consecrated it **as an offering of the most sacred order he pays** the **fourfold or fivefold payment,** as the consecration itself would be tantamount to a sale to another party.

אֶלָּא, לְעוֹלָם לָא שְׁנָא קָדְשֵׁי קָדָשִׁים וְלָא שְׁנָא קָדָשִׁים קַלִּים. וּדְקַשְׁיָא לָךְ: מָה לִי מְכָרוֹ לְהֶדְיוֹט מָה לִי מְכָרוֹ לַשָּׁמַיִם! מְכָרוֹ לְהֶדְיוֹט – מֵעִיקָּרָא תּוֹרָא דִּרְאוּבֵן וְהַשְׁתָּא תּוֹרָא דְּשִׁמְעוֹן, מְכָרוֹ לַשָּׁמַיִם – מֵעִיקָּרָא תּוֹרָא דִּרְאוּבֵן וְהַשְׁתָּא תּוֹרָא דִּרְאוּבֵן.

Rather, the Gemara states that **actually there is no difference** whether the thief consecrates the animal as **an offering of the most sacred order** and **there is no difference** whether he consecrates it as **an offering of lesser sanctity. And as** for the matter that presented **a difficulty for you,** namely: **What** difference **is it to me** if **he sold** the animal **to an ordinary** person and **what** difference **is it to me** if **he sold it to Heaven** by consecration, one can answer as follows: If someone, e.g., Reuven, **sold** an ox **to an ordinary** person, e.g., Shimon, **at the outset** it was **Reuven's ox and now,** after the sale, **it is Shimon's ox.** By contrast, if **he sold it to Heaven,** i.e., he consecrated it as an offering, it is not considered to have been transferred into the possession of another party, as **at the outset** it was **Reuven's ox and now,** after consecration, **it is** still **Reuven's ox.**[N]

"רַבִּי שִׁמְעוֹן אוֹמֵר" וכו׳. אָמְרִי: נְהִי דִּסְבַר רַבִּי שִׁמְעוֹן: מָה לִי מְכָרוֹ לְהֶדְיוֹט מָה לִי מְכָרוֹ לַשָּׁמַיִם, אִיפְּכָא מִיבַּעֵי לֵיהּ.

§ The mishna teaches: **Rabbi Shimon says:** In the case of sacrificial animals for which the owner bears financial responsibility to replace with another animal if one of the original animals that one stole is lost or dies, the thief is obligated to pay the fourfold or fivefold payment if he slaughters one of the animals. If it is a sacrificial animal for which the owner bears no financial responsibility, the thief is exempt from the fourfold or fivefold payment. At this stage the Gemara assumes that Rabbi Shimon requires the fourfold or fivefold payment as a fine for the act of consecration itself rather than for the act of slaughtering the animal. The Gemara **says: Although Rabbi Shimon holds** that there is a logic of: **What** difference **is it to me** if **he sold** the animal **to an ordinary** person and **what** difference **is it to me** if **he sold it to Heaven** via consecration, nevertheless, he **should have** said **the opposite.**

קָדָשִׁים שֶׁחַיָּיב בְּאַחֲרָיוּתָן – פָּטוּר, דְּאַכַּתִּי לָא נְפַק מֵרְשׁוּתֵיהּ,

The Gemara elaborates: He should have said that if they are **sacrificial** animals **for which one bears** financial **responsibility,** the thief is **exempt** from paying the fourfold or fivefold payment. In other words, if the thief stole a non-sacred animal and subsequently consecrated it as an offering in such a manner that he bears responsibility to replace it, he should be exempt from the fourfold or fivefold payment for the act of consecration. The reason is **that** the animal **has not yet left his possession,** and therefore this act of consecration should not be considered a sale.

BACKGROUND

An offering of lesser sanctity – קָדָשִׁים קַלִּים: The offerings sacrificed in the Temple are divided into two main categories: Offerings of the most sacred order and offerings of lesser sanctity. Offerings of the most sacred order include offerings sacrificed on Yom Kippur, communal sin-offerings, burnt-offerings, and sin-offerings. The offerings of lesser sanctity include peace-offerings, animal tithes, and the Paschal offering. One of the primary differences between the two types of offerings is that offerings of the most sacred order are slaughtered only in the north of the Temple courtyard, whereas offerings of lesser sanctity may be slaughtered anywhere in the courtyard.

NOTES

At the outset it was Reuven's ox and now it is still Reuven's ox – מֵעִיקָּרָא תּוֹרָא דִּרְאוּבֵן וְהַשְׁתָּא תּוֹרָא דִּרְאוּבֵן: The commentaries note that this concept, that a sacrificial animal is still referred to as belonging to the one who consecrated it, applies only to animals consecrated for offerings. If one consecrates the value of an item or animal to the Temple treasury, or consecrates an item or sum of money for any purpose other than sacrifice, it is considered to have completely left his jurisdiction at that point (*Tosafot*). Therefore, if a thief consecrates a stolen animal in the latter manner he is obligated to pay the fourfold or fivefold payment as if he had sold it.

קָדָשִׁים שֶׁאֵינוֹ חַיָּיב בְּאַחֲרָיוּתָן – חַיָּיב, דְּמַפְּקֵי לֵיהּ מֵרְשׁוּתֵיהּ!

By contrast, if they are **sacrificial** animals **for which one does not bear** financial **responsibility,** the thief should be **liable** to pay the fourfold or fivefold payment. If the thief stole a non-sacred animal and then consecrated it as an offering in such a way that he does not bear responsibility to replace it, he should be liable to pay the fourfold or fivefold payment for the act of consecration, **as he has** thereby **removed** the animal **from his possession.**

אָמְרִי: רַבִּי שִׁמְעוֹן אַמִּילְּתָא אַחֲרִיתִי קָאֵי,

The Sages **say** in response: **Rabbi Shimon** is not discussing the issue of whether the consecration of an animal is tantamount to its sale. Rather, **he is referring to a different matter,** one that is not explicitly mentioned in the mishna.

וְהָכִי קָתָנֵי: אֵין הַגּוֹנֵב אַחַר הַגַּנָּב מְשַׁלֵּם תַּשְׁלוּמֵי אַרְבָּעָה וַחֲמִשָּׁה, וְכֵן גּוֹנֵב הֶקְדֵּשׁ מִבֵּית בְּעָלִים – פָּטוּר,

And this is what the mishna **is teaching: One who steals** an animal **after a thief** has already stolen it, i.e., he steals it from the thief, does not pay the double payment, and if he slaughtered or sold the animal he **does not pay** the **fourfold or fivefold payment. And similarly, one who steals consecrated** property **from the house of** its **owner**[H] is exempt from the double payment, and if it was a sacrificial animal and the thief slaughtered or sold it, **he is exempt** from the fourfold or fivefold payment.

מַאי טַעְמָא? ״וְגֻנַּב מִבֵּית הָאִישׁ״ – וְלֹא מִבֵּית הֶקְדֵּשׁ;

What is the reason for this last ruling? The reason is as it is written: "If a man gives his neighbor money or vessels to safeguard **and it was stolen from the house of the man,** if the thief shall be found he shall pay double" (Exodus 22:6). The phrase "from the house of the man" indicates that a thief is obligated to pay the double payment only when they are stolen from a person, **but not** if the item in question was stolen **out of** the **house of the Temple** treasury.

רַבִּי שִׁמְעוֹן אוֹמֵר: קָדָשִׁים שֶׁחַיָּיב בְּאַחֲרָיוּתָן – חַיָּיב, מַאי טַעְמָא? קָרֵינָא בֵּיהּ ״וְגֻנַּב מִבֵּית הָאִישׁ״. וְשֶׁאֵינוֹ חַיָּיב בְּאַחֲרָיוּתָן – פָּטוּר, דְּלָא קָרֵינַן בֵּיהּ ״וְגֻנַּב מִבֵּית הָאִישׁ״.

Rabbi Shimon says: If the stolen items were **sacrificial** animals **for which** the owner **bears** financial **responsibility,** the thief who steals them **is liable** to pay the double payment, as well as the fourfold or fivefold payment if he slaughters or sells them. **What is the reason** for this? Since the owner must replace the animals, **one applies** to this case the phrase **"and it was stolen from the house of the man."** **But** if the stolen animals are those for **which** the owner **does not bear** financial **responsibility,** the thief is **exempt** from the double payment and from the fourfold and fivefold payment, **as one does not apply** to this case the phrase **"and it was stolen from the house of the man."**

מִכְּדֵי שָׁמְעִינַן לֵיהּ לְרַבִּי שִׁמְעוֹן, דְּאָמַר: שְׁחִיטָה שֶׁאֵינָהּ רְאוּיָה לֹא שְׁמָהּ שְׁחִיטָה, קָדָשִׁים נַמִי שְׁחִיטָה שֶׁאֵינָהּ רְאוּיָה הִיא!

Now, we have heard elsewhere **concerning Rabbi Shimon that he said:** An act of **slaughter that is not fit** for accomplishing its full ritual purpose **is not considered** an act of **slaughter** at all. And if the thief slaughtered the **sacrificial** animal he stole, this **is also** an act of **slaughter that is not fit** for accomplishing its full ritual purpose, as it does not render the animal's meat fit for consumption, in light of the *halakha* that it is prohibited to eat a sacrificial animal slaughtered outside the Temple.

כִּי אֲתָא רַב דִּימִי אָמַר רַבִּי יוֹחָנָן: בְּשׁוֹחֵט תְּמִימִים מִבִּפְנִים לְשֵׁם בְּעָלִים.

When Rav Dimi came from Eretz Yisrael, he said that **Rabbi Yoḥanan says:** This is referring to a case **where** the thief **slaughters** the animal, **unblemished, inside** the Temple,[B] **for the sake of** its **owner.** In this case, its meat may be eaten.

HALAKHA

One who steals consecrated property from the house of its owner – גּוֹנֵב הֶקְדֵּשׁ מִבֵּית בְּעָלִים: One who steals consecrated property pays only the principal value of the stolen item. This is also the *halakha* in the case of one who steals a sacrificial animal from its owner's house, regardless of whether the animal was designated as an offering of lesser sanctity or an offering of the most sacred order, and regardless of whether it was an animal concerning which the owner bears responsibility to replace it if lost. In all these cases the thief is exempt from the double payment and from the fourfold or fivefold payment. This *halakha* is not in accordance with the opinion of Rabbi Shimon, who distinguishes between animals for which the owner bears responsibility and those for which he does not (Rambam *Sefer Nezikin, Hilkhot Geneiva* 2:1).

BACKGROUND

Unblemished inside the Temple – תְּמִימִים בִּפְנִים: A blemished animal cannot be used as an offering and therefore its consecration as an offering is invalid. Consequently, if one slaughtered a blemished animal outside the Temple it may be eaten without being redeemed, as its consecration as an offering did not take effect. By contrast, if the animal was consecrated for Temple maintenance one may not slaughter it without it first being redeemed.

וַהֲרֵי חָזְרָה קֶרֶן לַבְּעָלִים! אָמַר רַבִּי יִצְחָק בַּר אָבִין: שֶׁנִּשְׁפַּךְ הַדָּם.

The Gemara asks: **But** by slaughtering and sacrificing the sacrificial animal on behalf of the owner, it is as though the **principal,** i.e., the animal itself, has been **returned to the owner,** and the fourfold or fivefold payment should no longer apply. The owner had designated the animal as his offering, and it was in fact used for that purpose. **Rabbi Yitzḥak bar Avin said** in response: This is referring to a situation **where the** animal's **blood was spilled** before it could be sprinkled on the altar. Consequently, the owner did not achieve atonement through this offering, which is why it is not considered as though the animal has been returned to the owner.

כִּי אֲתָא רָבִין אָמַר רַבִּי יוֹחָנָן: בְּשׁוֹחֵט תְּמִימִים בִּפְנִים שֶׁלֹּא לְשֵׁם בְּעָלִים.

When Ravin came from Eretz Yisrael, he cited a different version of this answer, and said that **Rabbi Yoḥanan says:** This is referring to a case **where** the thief **slaughters** the animal, **unblemished, inside** the Temple, but **not for the sake of** its **owner.**[H] The *halakha* in this case is that the animal's meat may be eaten but the owner has not fulfilled his obligation with this offering. In such a case, the slaughter of the animal does render its meat fit for consumption. Yet, it is not considered as though the animal has been returned to the owner.

HALAKHA

Slaughters the animal unblemished, inside the Temple but not for the sake of its owner – שׁוֹחֵט תְּמִימִים בִּפְנִים שֶׁלֹּא לְשֵׁם בְּעָלִים: Any offering that was slaughtered for the sake of someone other than its owner is valid. Despite this, the owner has not fulfilled his obligation through this offering. The exceptions to this principle are sin-offerings and Paschal offerings, which are entirely invalid if slaughtered not for the sake of the owner (Rambam *Sefer Avoda*, *Hilkhot Pesulei HaMukdashin* 15:1).

Perek **VII**
Daf **76** Amud **b**

וְרֵישׁ לָקִישׁ אָמַר: בְּשׁוֹחֵט בַּעֲלֵי מוּמִין בַּחוּץ.

And Reish Lakish says yet another explanation as to why the principal has not been returned to the owner: This is referring to a case **where** the thief **slaughters blemished** animals **outside** the Temple. A blemished animal may be slaughtered outside the Temple and its meat may be eaten, provided that it is redeemed with money.

תָּהֵי בָּהּ רַבִּי אֶלְעָזָר לְרַבִּי יוֹחָנָן, שְׁחִיטָה מַתֶּרֶת? וַהֲלֹא זְרִיקָה מַתֶּרֶת!

Rabbi Elazar wondered about this discussion: **According to** the explanations attributed to **Rabbi Yoḥanan,** which are based on the assumption that this is referring to slaughtering a sacrificial animal inside the Temple, is it the **slaughtering** of the animal that **renders** it **permitted** for consumption? **But isn't it** the **sprinkling**[B] of the blood that **renders** it **permitted?** It is prohibited to eat sacrificial meat immediately after the slaughter; only after the sprinkling of the blood is it permitted to consume the meat. As the slaughter itself does not render the animal's meat permitted, there should be no liability to pay the fourfold or fivefold payment.

לְרֵישׁ לָקִישׁ, שְׁחִיטָה מַתֶּרֶת? וַהֲלֹא פְּדִיָּיה מַתֶּרֶת!

Rabbi Elazar continues: And **according to** the explanation of **Reish Lakish,** who states that the case is referring to the slaughter of a consecrated blemished animal outside the Temple, is it the **slaughtering** of the animal that **renders** it **permitted** for consumption? **But isn't it** the **redemption** of the animal that **renders it permitted?** Since the thief slaughtered a sacrificial animal, it is prohibited to eat its meat until its sanctity is removed by redeeming it with money. Once again, the slaughter itself does not render the meat permitted, and here too, there should be no liability to pay the fourfold or fivefold payment.

אִישְׁתְּמִיטְתֵיהּ הָא דְּרַבִּי שִׁמְעוֹן: כׇּל הָעוֹמֵד לִזְרוֹק כְּזָרוּק דָּמֵי, וְכׇל הָעוֹמֵד לִפְדּוֹת כְּפָדוּי דָּמֵי.

The Gemara comments: Apparently, **this** following statement **of Rabbi Shimon escaped** Rabbi Elazar, who asked these questions. Rabbi Shimon holds that **any** blood **that is ready to be sprinkled is considered** as though it had already been **sprinkled, and** likewise, **any** animal **that is ready to be redeemed is considered** as if it had already been **redeemed.**[N]

BACKGROUND

Sprinkling – זְרִיקָה:

Priests sprinkling blood on the altar

NOTES

And any animal that is ready to be redeemed is considered as if it had already been redeemed – וְכׇל הָעוֹמֵד לִפְדּוֹת כְּפָדוּי דָּמֵי: All sacrificial animals that are blemished are considered ready for redemption, as one may not sacrifice them in their current state and there is no alternative but to redeem them (Rashi). Moreover, it is a mitzva to redeem blemished sacrificial animals (see Rashba).

HALAKHA

Leftover – נוֹתָר: Leftover sacrificial meat is susceptible to contracting ritual impurity, despite the fact that it is prohibited to derive benefit from it. This *halakha* is not in accordance with the opinion of Rabbi Shimon (Rambam *Sefer Tahara*, *Hilkhot Tumat Okhalin* 1:25).

כָּל הָעוֹמֵד לִזְרוֹק כִּזָרוּק דָּמֵי, דְּתַנְיָא, רַבִּי שִׁמְעוֹן אוֹמֵר: יֵשׁ נוֹתָר שֶׁהוּא מְטַמֵּא טוּמְאַת אוֹכָלִין, וְיֵשׁ נוֹתָר שֶׁאֵינוֹ מְטַמֵּא טוּמְאַת אוֹכָלִין,

The Gemara proves that Rabbi Shimon maintains these two opinions. Rabbi Shimon holds that **any blood that is ready to be sprinkled is considered** as though it had already been **sprinkled, as it is taught** in a *baraita* that **Rabbi Shimon says: There are** cases involving **leftover** sacrificial meat **after the time allotted for its consumption** [*notar*],[HN] in **which** the meat is susceptible to **contracting ritual impurity of food, and there are** cases of **leftover** sacrificial meat in which the meat **is not** susceptible to **contracting ritual impurity of food.**[N]

כֵּיצַד? לָן לִפְנֵי זְרִיקָה – אֵינוֹ מְטַמֵּא טוּמְאַת אוֹכָלִין, לְאַחַר זְרִיקָה – מְטַמֵּא טוּמְאַת אוֹכָלִין;

How so? If sacrificial meat was disqualified due to the fact that it **remained overnight,** i.e., after the allotted time for that offering, **before** the **sprinkling** of its blood, it **is not** susceptible to **contracting ritual impurity of food,** as it was never fit for consumption. According to Rabbi Shimon, for an item to be susceptible to contracting ritual impurity of food it must have been permitted for consumption or benefit, either at present or at some point in the past. Sacrificial meat may not be consumed before the sprinkling of its blood, nor may it be consumed if it had been left over after a specific period of time, in most cases overnight. If it was disqualified by being left overnight before its blood had been sprinkled, there was never a time when the meat was permitted. By contrast, if the meat was disqualified by being left over **after** the **sprinkling** of the blood, it **is** susceptible to **contracting ritual impurity of food,** as it was permitted for consumption at some point after the sprinkling of the blood.

וְקַיְימָא לַן, מַאי "לִפְנֵי זְרִיקָה" – קוֹדֶם שֶׁנִּרְאָה לִזְרִיקָה, "לְאַחַר זְרִיקָה" – לְאַחַר שֶׁנִּרְאָה לִזְרִיקָה;

And we maintain, as a result of a discussion recorded in tractate *Menaḥot* (101b): **What** is the meaning of: **Before** the **sprinkling** of the blood? It means **before** the blood **became fit for sprinkling.** And what is meant by: **After** the **sprinkling** of the blood? This means **after** the blood **became fit for sprinkling,** i.e., immediately subsequent to the slaughter.

קוֹדֶם שֶׁנִּרְאָה לִזְרִיקָה לָן מַאי הִיא? דְּלָא הֲוָיא שְׁהוּת בַּיּוֹם לְמִזְרְקֵיהּ, דְּשַׁחֲטֵיהּ סָמוּךְ לִשְׁקִיעַת הַחַמָּה, וְאֵינוֹ מְטַמֵּא טוּמְאַת אוֹכָלִין;

The Gemara elaborates: **What is** the case in which the meat **remained overnight before** the blood **became fit for sprinkling?** Since the blood is fit for sprinkling almost immediately after the animal's slaughter, how is it possible for the meat to become *notar* before that stage? The Gemara answers: This is referring to a case **where there was not enough time in the day to sprinkle** the blood, **as he slaughtered** the offering **immediately prior to sunset.** The blood was never fit for sprinkling, as the act of sprinkling must be performed before sunset. **And** in this case the meat is **not** susceptible to **contracting ritual impurity of food,** as there was never a time when it was permitted for consumption.

לְאַחַר שֶׁנִּרְאָה לִזְרִיקָה לָן – דַּהֲוָיא שְׁהוּת בַּיּוֹם לְמִזְרְקֵיהּ, מְטַמֵּא טוּמְאַת אוֹכָלִין; אַלְמָא: כָּל הָעוֹמֵד לִזְרוֹק כִּזָרוּק דָּמֵי.

What is the case where the meat **remained overnight after** the blood **became fit for sprinkling?** It was **when there was** enough **time** remaining **in the day** after the slaughter **to sprinkle** the blood, and therefore the meat **is** susceptible to **contracting ritual impurity of food.** The Gemara states its conclusion: **Evidently,** Rabbi Shimon maintains that **any blood that is ready to be sprinkled is considered** as though it had already been **sprinkled.**

וְכָל הָעוֹמֵד לִפְדּוֹת כִּפְדוּי דָּמֵי, דְּתַנְיָא, רַבִּי שִׁמְעוֹן אוֹמֵר:

And Rabbi Shimon holds that **any** animal **that is ready to be redeemed is considered** as though it is already **redeemed, as it is taught** in a *baraita* that **Rabbi Shimon says:**

NOTES

Leftover [*notar*] – נוֹתָר: With regard to any offering whose meat is eaten, the Torah stipulates a set time for its consumption. For example, in the cases of a thanks-offering and a sin-offering, the meat may be eaten until the morning after its sacrifice. The meat of a peace-offering may be eaten for two days and the intervening night. After the allotted time for eating has passed, the leftover meat is referred to as *notar* and may not be eaten, nor may any benefit be derived from it. One who eats *notar* is liable to receive the punishment of *karet*, excision from the World-to-Come.

Is not susceptible to contracting ritual impurity of food – שֶׁאֵינוֹ מְטַמֵּא טוּמְאַת אוֹכָלִין: Food is rendered ritually impure upon coming into contact with an impure person or item. This is the *halakha* only if the food is edible. Rabbi Shimon adds that for food to be susceptible to contracting ritual impurity it must not only be edible, but it must also be fit for consumption according to certain halakhic criteria. It is not required that it be fit for a Jew to eat, but it must at least be halakhically permitted for a Jew to give it to a gentile to eat. This excludes food from which it is prohibited to derive any benefit. Nevertheless, Rabbi Shimon concedes that even if it is currently prohibited to derive benefit from a particular food, if deriving benefit from it had been permitted at some point in the past it is susceptible to ritual impurity.

Perek **VII**
Daf **77** Amud **a**

פָּרָה מְטַמֵּא טוּמְאַת אוֹכָלִין, הוֹאִיל וְהָיְתָה לָהּ שְׁעַת הַכּוֹשֶׁר;

The meat of the red **heifer**[N] is susceptible to **contracting ritual impurity of food,**[NH] despite the fact that it is prohibited to derive benefit from such meat, **since it had a time when it was fit** for consumption.

NOTES

Red heifer – **פָּרָה**: The red heifer, whose ashes are mixed with springwater and used for the purification of people or vessels that became ritually impure by contracting impurity imparted by a corpse, is not slaughtered inside the Temple and does not have the status of an offering. It is slaughtered and its blood is sprinkled seven times toward the Temple, after which the body of the animal is wholly burned on a pyre of wood. The entire ritual, along with the *halakhot* concerning impurity imparted by a corpse and the subsequent purification process, is described in Numbers 19:1–20.

The meat of the red heifer is susceptible to contracting ritual impurity of food – **פָּרָה מְטַמֵּא טוּמְאַת אוֹכָלִין**: *Tosafot* cite a difficulty raised by Rashi on *Ḥullin* 81b: The meat of the red heifer is impure in its own right (see Numbers 19:7–10), even if it does not come into contact with a different source of impurity. If this is the case, what does it matter whether it can also contract ritual impurity of food? Rashi's answer, based on the fact that ritual impurity can be contracted by food only if it is larger than an egg-bulk, is that there is a difference in the following case: A piece of meat of the red heifer, smaller than the size of an egg-bulk, is wrapped up in dough that is also less than an egg-bulk, but the two items together exceed the size of an egg-bulk. If the heifer's meat is considered food, it combines with the dough to form the minimum size necessary for contracting impurity, and the dough would be rendered impure. If the meat does not have the status of food, the minimum size is not reached and the dough remains pure.

HALAKHA

The meat of the red heifer is susceptible to contracting ritual impurity of food – **פָּרָה מְטַמֵּא טוּמְאַת אוֹכָלִין**: The meat of the red heifer can contract ritual impurity of food only if someone intended to eat it. The *halakha* is not in accordance with the opinion of Rabbi Shimon, but rather in accordance with the dissenting ruling of the Rabbis (Rambam *Sefer Tahara, Hilkhot She'ar Avot HaTumot* 3:3, *Hilkhot Tumat Okhalin* 1:25 and *Mishne LaMelekh* there).

Perek **VII**
Daf **77** Amud **b**

וְאָמַר רֵישׁ לָקִישׁ: אוֹמֵר הָיָה רַבִּי שִׁמְעוֹן: פָּרָה נִפְדֵּית עַל גַּבֵּי מַעֲרַכְתָּהּ; אַלְמָא: כׇּל הָעוֹמֵד לִפְדּוֹת כְּפָדוּי דָּמֵי.

And Reish Lakish says, in explanation of Rabbi Shimon's statement: **Rabbi Shimon would say** that the red **heifer can be redeemed**[H] with money even when it has already been slaughtered **upon its pyre,** i.e., for the sake of purification. For this reason Rabbi Shimon claimed that the meat had a time when it was fit for consumption, as it can be rendered permitted for consumption through redemption. The Gemara states its conclusion: **Evidently,** Rabbi Shimon holds that **any** animal **that is ready to be redeemed is considered** as though it has already been **redeemed.**

בִּשְׁלָמָא רַבִּי יוֹחָנָן לָא אָמַר כְּרַבִּי שִׁמְעוֹן בֶּן לָקִישׁ, דְּקָא בָּעֵי לְאוֹקְמַהּ לְמַתְנִיתִין אֲפִילּוּ בִּתְמִימִין, אֶלָּא רֵישׁ לָקִישׁ מַאי טַעְמָא לָא אָמַר כְּרַבִּי יוֹחָנָן?

The Gemara discusses the relative merits of the answers provided by Rabbi Yoḥanan and Reish Lakish: **Granted, Rabbi Yoḥanan did not state** an answer **in accordance with** that of **Rabbi Shimon ben Lakish,** i.e., Reish Lakish, that the mishna is referring to a blemished animal, **because he wants to interpret the mishna** as dealing with all kinds of sacrificial animals, **even with unblemished** ones. **But what is the reason** that **Reish Lakish did not state** an answer **in accordance with** that of **Rabbi Yoḥanan?**

אָמַר לָךְ: ״וּטְבָחוֹ וּמְכָרוֹ״ – כׇּל הֵיכָא דְּאִיתֵיהּ בִּמְכִירָה אִיתֵיהּ בִּטְבִיחָה, וְכׇל הֵיכָא דְּלֵיתֵיהּ בִּמְכִירָה לֵיתֵיהּ בִּטְבִיחָה; וְהָנֵי קָדָשִׁים, הוֹאִיל דְּכִי מְזַבֵּין קָדָשִׁים לָא הָוְיָא מְכִירָה – לֵיתְנְהוּ בִּטְבִיחָה.

Reish Lakish could have **said to you** that the verse states: "If a man steals an ox or a sheep, **and slaughters it or sells it**" (Exodus 21:37). This verse compares slaughtering to selling, thereby indicating that **anywhere that** the fourfold or fivefold payment **is** applicable **for the sale** of a particular animal **it is** likewise applicable **for** its **slaughter, and anywhere that** the fourfold or fivefold payment **is not** applicable **for the sale** of an animal **it is not** applicable **for** its **slaughter** either. **And** with regard to **this** case of **sacrificial** animals, **since when one sells sacrificial** animals **it is not** a valid **sale,** and no fourfold or fivefold payment is incurred, so too, **there is no** fourfold or fivefold payment for their **slaughter.**

HALAKHA

The red heifer can be redeemed, etc. – **פָּרָה נִפְדֵּית וכו׳**: A red heifer that was slaughtered with the intent that it should be used for non-sacred purposes can be redeemed and eaten. It may not be used for ritual purification. If it was slaughtered upon its pyre, it cannot be redeemed. The *halakha* is not in accordance with the opinion of Rabbi Shimon (Rambam *Sefer Tahara, Hilkhot Para Aduma* 1:9).

וְאָזְדוּ לְטַעֲמַיְיהוּ, דְּאִתְּמַר: הַמּוֹכֵר טְרֵיפָה, לְדִבְרֵי רַבִּי שִׁמְעוֹן – רַבִּי יוֹחָנָן אָמַר: חַיָּיב, וְרֵישׁ לָקִישׁ אָמַר: פָּטוּר;

And these two Sages **follow their** own lines of **reasoning. As it was stated: According to the statement of Rabbi Shimon** that an act of slaughter that is not fit for accomplishing its full ritual purpose is not considered an act of slaughter at all and does not entail liability to pay the fourfold or fivefold payment, in the case of a thief who **sells** a stolen **animal with a wound that will cause it to die within twelve months [*tereifa*],**[B] **Rabbi Yoḥanan says:** The thief is **liable** to pay the fourfold or fivefold payment if he sells the animal rather than slaughters it. **And Reish Lakish says:** He is **exempt.**

רַבִּי יוֹחָנָן אָמַר חַיָּיב, אַף עַל גַּב דְּלֵיתֵיהּ בִּטְבִיחָה אִיתֵיהּ בִּמְכִירָה; וְרֵישׁ לָקִישׁ אָמַר פָּטוּר, כֵּיוָן דְּלֵיתֵיהּ בִּטְבִיחָה לֵיתֵיהּ בִּמְכִירָה.

The Gemara elaborates: **Rabbi Yoḥanan says** that he is **liable,** as **even though** the fourfold or fivefold payment **is not** applicable **for the slaughter** of a *tereifa* according to the opinion of Rabbi Shimon, as its meat may not be eaten, nevertheless, **it is** applicable **for** its **sale. And Reish Lakish says** that the thief is **exempt,** as, **since** the fourfold or fivefold payment **is not** applicable **for the slaughter** of a *tereifa* according to Rabbi Shimon, **it is not** applicable **for its sale** either.

אֵיתִיבֵיהּ רַבִּי יוֹחָנָן לְרַבִּי שִׁמְעוֹן בֶּן לָקִישׁ: גָּנַב כִּלְאַיִם וּטְבָחָהּ, טְרֵיפָה וּמְכָרָהּ – מְשַׁלֵּם תַּשְׁלוּמֵי אַרְבָּעָה וַחֲמִשָּׁה; מַאי לָאו רַבִּי שִׁמְעוֹן הִיא? אַלְמָא: אַף עַל גַּב דְּלֵיתֵיהּ בִּטְבִיחָה אִיתֵיהּ בִּמְכִירָה!

Rabbi Yoḥanan raised an objection to the opinion of **Rabbi Shimon ben Lakish** from the following *baraita*: If one **stole** an animal of **diverse kinds,**[BH] e.g., a sheep-goat hybrid, **and slaughtered it,** or if he stole **a *tereifa* and sold it, he pays** the **fourfold or fivefold payment. What, is it not** correct to say that this *baraita*, which mentions the case of selling a stolen *tereifa* but not slaughtering it, **is** in accordance with the opinion of **Rabbi Shimon? Apparently,** according to Rabbi Shimon, **even though** the fourfold or fivefold payment **is not** applicable **for the slaughter** of a *tereifa*, **it is** nevertheless applicable **for** its **sale.**

אֲמַר לֵיהּ: לָא, רַבָּנַן.

Reish Lakish **said to** Rabbi Yoḥanan in response: **No;** this *baraita* is not taught in accordance with the opinion of Rabbi Shimon. Rather, it follows the opinion of **the Rabbis,** who disagree with Rabbi Shimon and maintain that a thief is liable for the fourfold or fivefold payment for slaughtering an animal even if the act of slaughter does not render its meat fit for consumption, as in the case of a *tereifa*.

אִי רַבָּנַן, טְרֵיפָה בִּמְכִירָה אִיתָא, בִּזְבִיחָה לֵיתָא?!

The Gemara asks: **If** the *baraita* reflects the opinion of **the Rabbis,** why does it mention the sale of a *tereifa* but not its slaughter? According to the opinion of the Rabbis, is the fourfold or fivefold payment applicable **for the sale of a *tereifa*** while **it is not** applicable **for** its **slaughter?** This is certainly not the case.

וְאֶלָּא מַאי, רַבִּי שִׁמְעוֹן? כִּלְאַיִם בִּטְבִיחָה אִיתָא, בִּמְכִירָה לֵיתָא?!

The Gemara responds with a counter-question: **Rather, what** would you say, that the *baraita* reflects the opinion of **Rabbi Shimon?** The same difficulty could be raised in the case of **diverse kinds,** as the *baraita* mentions the animal's slaughter but not its sale: Is the fourfold of fivefold payment applicable **for the slaughter** of an animal of diverse kinds, while **it is not** applicable **for** its **sale?** There is certainly no difference between slaughtering and selling in this case.

אֶלָּא, תְּנָא טְבִיחָה וְהוּא הַדִּין לִמְכִירָה, אֵימָא לְרַבָּנַן נַמִי: תְּנָא מְכִירָה וְהוּא הַדִּין לִטְבִיחָה.

Rather, one cannot make such inferences from the *baraita*, as it **teaches** liability with regard to the **slaughter** of diverse kinds, **and the same is true** with regard **to** its **sale.** If so, one can **say** the same **for** the opinion of **the Rabbis as well:** The *baraita* **teaches** liability with regard to the **sale** of a *tereifa*, **and the same is true** with regard **to** its **slaughter.** Once the *baraita* is interpreted in accordance with the opinion of the Rabbis and not that of Rabbi Shimon, it has no bearing on the dispute between Rabbi Yoḥanan and Reish Lakish.

וְרַבִּי יוֹחָנָן אָמַר לָךְ: הַאי מַאי? אִי אָמְרַתְּ בִּשְׁלָמָא רַבִּי שִׁמְעוֹן, אַיְּידֵי דִּתְנָא טְרֵיפָה בַּחֲדָא תְּנָא כִּלְאַיִם בַּחֲדָא.

And Rabbi Yoḥanan could say **to you: What is this** comparison? **Granted, if you say** that the *baraita* reflects the opinion of **Rabbi Shimon,** and that is why it referred specifically to the sale of a *tereifa*, the *baraita* can be explained: **Since it** necessarily **taught** the case of ***tereifa* in** only **one** manner, that of selling, it maintained the same style of presentation and **taught** the case of **diverse kinds in** only **one** manner, that of slaughtering.

BACKGROUND

Tereifa – טְרֵיפָה: Generally speaking, a *tereifa* is an animal that is suffering from a wound that will cause it to die within twelve months. The Torah renders it prohibited to eat an animal that has been injured or is stricken with a disease of this nature, although the actual source for this prohibition is a matter of dispute. Some authorities cite Exodus 22:30: "You shall not eat any flesh that is torn of animals in the field," while others suggest that this *halakha* originates from Deuteronomy 14:21: "You shall not eat of any animal carcass." According to the *Minḥat Ḥinnukh* and others, both verses together serve as the source for the prohibition.

Diverse kinds – כִּלְאַיִם: The *halakhot* concerning diverse kinds of animals include two separate prohibitions. The first is the prohibition against the crossbreeding of animals from different species. The second is the prohibition against working a team of animals comprising different species: "You shall not plow with an ox and a donkey together" (Deuteronomy 22:10). If different species of animals were crossbred, the offspring are called *kilayim*.

HALAKHA

If one stole an animal of diverse kinds, etc. – גָּנַב כִּלְאַיִם וכו׳: If one steals a sheep-goat hybrid or a *tereifa* and slaughters or sells it, he must pay the fourfold or fivefold payment, in accordance with the opinion of the Rabbis (Rambam *Sefer Nezikin*, *Hilkhot Geneiva* 2:9; *Tur*, *Ḥoshen Mishpat* 350).

אֶלָּא אִי אָמְרַתְּ רַבָּנַן, נְעָרְבִינְהוּ וְנִיתְנִינְהוּ: גָּנַב כִּלְאַיִם וּטְרֵיפָה, טְבָחָן וּמְכָרָן – מְשַׁלֵּם תַּשְׁלוּמֵי אַרְבָּעָה וַחֲמִשָּׁה! קַשְׁיָא.

But if you say that the *baraita* is in accordance with the opinion of **the Rabbis,** there is no reason for it to present just one scenario in either case. Rather, **let the** *baraita* **combine them and teach them** in a single sentence: **If one stole** an animal of **diverse kinds or a** ***tereifa*** and then **slaughtered or sold** either one of **them, he pays** the **fourfold or fivefold payment.** The Gemara concludes: This is **difficult** according to the opinion of Reish Lakish.

כִּלְאַיִם – ״שֶׂה״ כְּתִיב, וְאָמַר רָבָא: זֶה בָּנָה אָב, כָּל מָקוֹם שֶׁנֶּאֱמַר ״שֶׂה״ אֵינוֹ אֶלָּא לְהוֹצִיא אֶת הַכִּלְאַיִם!

§ The *baraita* teaches that a thief is liable to pay the fourfold or fivefold payment in the case of an animal of **diverse kinds.** The Gemara asks: It is **written** in the Torah: "If a man steals an ox or a **sheep** [*seh*]" (Exodus 21:37),[L] **and Rava says,** concerning the verse: "These are the animals that you may eat: The ox, the *seh* of a sheep, and the *seh* of a goat" (Deuteronomy 14:4), that **this** verse **establishes a paradigm** for other cases: **Wherever** the word ***seh*** **is stated** in the Torah, **it** serves **to exclude only** an animal of **diverse kinds.** The Hebrew word *seh* denotes either a sheep or a goat. A hybrid, which is neither a sheep nor a goat, does not qualify as a *seh*. Why, then, is the fourfold or fivefold payment applicable to one who stole this kind of animal?

שָׁאנֵי הָכָא, דְּאָמַר קְרָא ״אוֹ״ – לְרַבּוֹת אֶת הַכִּלְאַיִם.

The Gemara answers: **It is different here,** in the case of the fourfold or fivefold payment, **as the verse states "or"** (Exodus 21:37), a term that could have been avoided, as explained earlier (67b). This extra word serves **to include** an animal of **diverse kinds,** i.e., the sheep-goat hybrid.

וְכָל ״אוֹ״ לְרַבּוֹת הוּא? וְהָתַנְיָא: ״שׁוֹר אוֹ כֶשֶׂב״ – פְּרָט לְכִלְאַיִם, ״אוֹ עֵז״ – פְּרָט לְנִדְמֶה!

The Gemara asks: **And** does **every** instance of the word **"or"** serve **to include** diverse kinds? **But isn't it taught** in a *baraita*: It is written: "When a bull or a sheep or a goat is born, it shall be seven days under its mother and from the eighth day onward it may be accepted as a fire-offering to the Lord" (Leviticus 22:27). The phrase **"a bull or a sheep"** serves to **exclude diverse kinds,**[H] i.e., an animal of diverse kinds may not be brought as an offering. The phrase **"or a goat"** serves to **exclude** an animal that **resembles** another,[HB] i.e., a sheep that is the offspring of two sheep but that looks like a goat, or vice versa.

אֲמַר רָבָא: הָכָא מֵעִנְיָינֵיהּ דִּקְרָא, וְהָכָא מֵעִנְיָינֵיהּ דִּקְרָא; הָכָא גַּבֵּי גְּנֵיבָה דִּכְתִיב ״שׁוֹר אוֹ שֶׂה״, שֶׁאִי אַתָּה יָכוֹל לְהוֹצִיא כִּלְאַיִם מִבֵּינֵיהֶם – ״אוֹ״ לְרַבּוֹת כִּלְאַיִם; גַּבֵּי קֳדָשִׁים דִּכְתִיב כֶּשֶׂב וָעֵז, שֶׁאַתָּה יָכוֹל לְהוֹצִיא כִּלְאַיִם מִבֵּינֵיהֶם – ״אוֹ״ לְמַעֵט הוּא.

Rava said in response: The derivation from the word "or" depends on the verse in question. **Here,** it is interpreted **based on the context of the verse, and there,** it is also interpreted **based on the context of the verse. Here, with regard to theft,** the reason the word "or" serves as an inclusion is **that it is written: "An ox or a sheep,"** which are two animals **from which you cannot produce diverse kinds,**[BN] as they cannot procreate together, and therefore the word **"or"** serves **to include** an animal of **diverse kinds.** By contrast, **with regard to sacrificial** animals, the reason the word "or" serves as an exclusion is **that it is written "sheep" and "goat,"** which are two animals **from which you can produce diverse kinds.** Consequently, the word **"or"** serves **to exclude** diverse kinds.

LANGUAGE

Seh – **שֶׂה**: Both a goat and a sheep can be referred to in the Bible by the Hebrew word *seh*. For lack of a corresponding English word, many Bible translations render *seh* as a sheep, which often leads to confusion and inaccuracies.

HALAKHA

To exclude diverse kinds – פְּרָט לְכִלְאַיִם: A hybrid animal that is the product of the union of a sheep and a goat is unfit for sacrifice on the altar (Rambam *Sefer Avoda, Hilkhot Issurei Mizbe'aḥ* 3:4).

To exclude an animal that resembles another – פְּרָט לְנִדְמֶה: An animal that looks like a different species is unfit for sacrifice on the altar, even if it is not a hybrid. For example, if a ewe gave birth to a lamb that looks like a goat, or a she-goat produced a kid that looks like a sheep, it is unfit for sacrifice on the altar due to its resemblance to a different species (Rambam *Sefer Avoda, Hilkhot Issurei Mizbe'aḥ* 3:5).

BACKGROUND

An animal that resembles another – נִדְמֶה: Sometimes an animal is born with a defect that causes it to look like a member of a different species. Occasionally the animal is entirely similar to another type, especially in the case of goats and sheep, which are closely related biologically. It is also possible for an animal to be born lacking a trait characteristic of its kind, or possessing a trait characteristic of another kind, and this causes it to resemble a different type of animal, e.g., when a lamb is born without its customary fat-tail, or with horns that are uncharacteristic of a sheep, it resembles a goat.

You cannot produce diverse kinds – אִי אַתָּה יָכוֹל לְהוֹצִיא כִּלְאַיִם: Sheep and goats belong to the subfamily Caprinae, whereas oxen belong to the subfamily Bovinae. Because they belong to different subfamilies, and also due to the size difference between them, it is impossible to crossbreed oxen and sheep.

NOTES

From which you cannot produce diverse kinds – שֶׁאִי אַתָּה יָכוֹל לְהוֹצִיא כִּלְאַיִם מִבֵּינֵיהֶם: The significance of the word "or" is that the Torah could have used the prefix *vav*, which means: And, to include two or more items. In the verse pertaining to the fourfold or fivefold payment, had the Torah stated: An ox and a sheep, one would not have included diverse kinds, as no hybrid can be produced from these two animals. The use of the word "or" serves to teach that a sheep-goat hybrid should be included in this *halakha*. By contrast, with regard to sacrificial animals, where the Torah states: A sheep or a goat, had the verse stated: A sheep and a goat, it would have been assumed that diverse kinds are also included in this category, as these animals can produce a hybrid. Yet the term "or" teaches the contrary, that diverse kinds are excluded.

NOTES

If it is referring to animal tithe – אִי לְמַעֲשֵׂר: The early commentaries raise an obvious question: This verse does not mention the word *seh* at all. How, then, could Rava's principle possibly apply to it? Rashi explains that the suggestion is that Rava's *halakha* applies to the plural word *tzon* just as it applies to the singular *seh*.

הָא גַּבֵּי קֳדָשִׁים נַמִּי נֶאֱמַר ״שׁוֹר אוֹ כֶשֶׂב״ שֶׁאֵין אַתָּה יָכוֹל לְהוֹצִיא כִּלְאַיִם מִבֵּינֵיהֶם, וּנְרַבֵּי! מִדְּסֵיפָא לְמַעֵט, רֵישָׁא נַמִּי לְמַעֵט. אַדְּרַבָּה, מִדְּרֵישָׁא לְרַבּוֹת, סֵיפָא נַמִּי לְרַבּוֹת!

The Gemara asks: **But with regard to sacrificial** animals **it is also stated** in the first part of the verse: **"A bull or a sheep"** (Leviticus 22:27), which are two animals **from which you cannot produce diverse kinds. And** accordingly, **let us include** an animal of diverse kinds as being fit for sacrifice on the altar on that account. The Gemara answers: **From** the fact **that the latter clause** of the verse: "Or a goat," serves **to exclude** a type of animal from being fit for sacrifice on the altar, it may be inferred that the **first clause:** "A bull or a sheep," also serves **to exclude** a type of animal from being fit for sacrifice on the altar. The Gemara asks: **On the contrary,** one could equally argue that **from** the fact **that the first clause** of the verse serves **to include** a type of animal as being fit for sacrifice on the altar, the **latter clause also** serves **to include** a type of animal as being fit for sacrifice on the altar.

הַאי מַאי? אִי אָמְרַתְּ בִּשְׁלָמָא לְמַעֵט – הוּא דְּאִיצְטְרִיךְ תְּרֵי מִיעוּטֵי, דְּאַף עַל גַּב דְּאִימַּעַט כִּלְאַיִם אִיצְטְרִיךְ לְמַעוּטֵי נִדְמֶה. אֶלָּא אִי אָמְרַתְּ לְרַבּוֹת, תְּרֵי רִיבּוּיֵי לָמָּה? הָשְׁתָּא כִּלְאַיִם אִירַבֵּי לֵיהּ, נִדְמֶה מִבָּעְיָא?

The Gemara rejects this argument: **What** is **this** comparison? **Granted, if you say** that both expressions serve **to exclude** types of animals from being fit for sacrifice on the altar, **this is** why **two exclusions were necessary:** One exclusion is referring to diverse kinds and the other is referring to an animal that resembles another species, **as even though** an animal of **diverse kinds is excluded, it** was still **necessary to exclude** an animal that **resembles** another. **But if you say** that both phrases serve **to include** types of animals as being fit for sacrifice on the altar, **why are two inclusions** required? **Now that** an animal of **diverse kinds has been included,** in the first inclusion, is it **necessary** to say that an animal that **resembles** another is also included? There is more justification for including an animal that resembles another, whose parentage is entirely of one species, than for including an animal of diverse kinds.

אֶלָּא הָא דְּאָמַר רָבָא: זֶה בָּנָה אָב, כָּל מָקוֹם שֶׁנֶּאֱמַר ״שֶׂה״ אֵינוֹ אֶלָּא לְהוֹצִיא אֶת הַכִּלְאַיִם, לְמַאי הִלְכְתָא? אִי לְקָדָשִׁים – בְּהֶדְיָא כְּתִיב בְּהוּ ״שׁוֹר אוֹ כֶשֶׂב״ פְּרָט לְכִלְאַיִם,

The Gemara has established that when the Torah uses the word *seh* (Exodus 21:37) in the context of theft it does not serve to exclude animals of diverse kinds. The Gemara asks: **If so,** what is meant by **this** statement **that Rava says** with regard to the verse: "The ox, the *seh* of a sheep, and the *seh* of a goat" (Deuteronomy 14:4), that **this establishes a paradigm** for other cases, teaching that **wherever** the word ***seh* is stated** in the Torah, **it** serves **to exclude only** an animal of **diverse kinds. With regard to what *halakha*** did Rava state this principle? **If** this principle is referring **to the *halakha*** concerning **sacrificial** animals, **it is written explicitly with regard to them: "A bull or a sheep"** (Leviticus 22:27), which, as taught in the aforementioned *baraita*, serves to **exclude diverse kinds.**

אִי לְמַעֲשֵׂר – ״תַּחַת״ ״תַּחַת״ יָלֵיף מִקָּדָשִׁים,

If this principle is referring **to** the *halakha* concerning **animal tithe,**[NH] concerning which it is written: "And all the tithe of the herd or the flock [*tzon*], any one that passes under the rod, the tenth shall be sacred unto the Lord" (Leviticus 27:32), this principle is not necessary either. The reason is that the exclusion of diverse kinds can be **derived** by means of a verbal analogy **from** the term **"under"** in this verse, and the word **"under"** in a verse that deals with **sacrificial** animals: "When a bull, or a sheep, or a goat is born, it shall be seven days under its mother" (Leviticus 22:27). This verbal analogy, from which many *halakhot* of animal tithe are derived, indicates that diverse kinds are not subject to animal tithe, just as they cannot be used for an offering.

HALAKHA

Diverse kinds with regard to animal tithe – כִּלְאַיִם לְמַעֲשֵׂר: All of one's animals must be placed in a pen for tithing, including those with blemishes or those that are disqualified from serving as an offering for some other reason. One should not place an animal of diverse kinds, including a sheep-goat hybrid, in a pen for tithing (Rambam *Sefer Korbanot, Hilkhot Bekhorot* 6:13).

אִי לִבְכוֹר – הַעֲבָרָה הַעֲבָרָה יָלֵיף מִמַּעֲשֵׂר!

If this principle is referring **to firstborn** animals, concerning which it is written: "However, the firstborn among animals, which is born as a firstling to the Lord, no man shall sanctify it; whether it be ox or *seh*, it is the Lord's" (Leviticus 27:26), it is not necessary in that context either. The reason is that this can be **derived** by a verbal analogy between the term **passing**, in the verse: "And you shall cause to pass to the Lord all that open the womb" (Exodus 13:12), and the same term **passing**, **from** a verse concerning **animal tithe:** "And all the tithe of the herd or the flock, any one that passes under the rod, the tenth shall be sacred unto the Lord" (Leviticus 27:32). This verbal analogy teaches that if the firstborn of a ewe or a she-goat is an animal of diverse kinds it is not considered a firstborn with regard to the *halakhot* of firstborn animals, which means that Rava's principle is not necessary here.

אִי נַמִי, נִדְמֶה אָמְרַתְּ לָא, דִּכְתִיב "אַךְ בְּכוֹר שׁוֹר" – עַד שֶׁיְּהֵא הוּא שׁוֹר וּבְכוֹרוֹ שׁוֹר, כִּלְאַיִם מִבַּעְיָא?

Alternatively, you must **say** that an animal that **resembles** another is **not** subject to the *halakhot* of a firstborn,[H] **as it is written: "But the firstborn of a bull,** or the firstborn of a sheep, or the firstborn of a goat, you shall not redeem; they are holy" (Numbers 18:17). This indicates that the *halakhot* of the firstborn are not applicable **unless** the fathering animal **is a bull and its firstborn is also a bull.** This excludes an animal that resembles another species, rather than its father. Once it is established that an animal that resembles another is not subject to the *halakhot* of a firstborn, is it **necessary** for the Torah to state the same with regard to **diverse kinds?** Since it is evident that firstborn status does not apply to diverse kinds, Rava's principle is not required here either.

אֶלָּא, כִּי אִיתְּמַר דְּרָבָא – לְעִנְיַן פֶּטֶר חֲמוֹר, כִּדְתְנַן: אֵין פּוֹדִין לֹא בְּעֵגֶל וְלֹא בְּחַיָּה, וְלֹא בִּשְׁחוּטָה וְלֹא בִּטְרֵיפָה, וְלֹא בְּכִלְאַיִם וְלֹא בְּכוֹי.

Rather, Rava's principle **was stated with regard to** the redemption of a **firstborn donkey,**[H] concerning which it is written: "And every firstborn of a donkey you shall redeem with a *seh*" (Exodus 13:13), **as we learned** in a mishna (*Bekhorot* 12a): **One may not redeem** a firstborn donkey **neither with a calf, nor with a non-domesticated animal, nor with a slaughtered** animal, **nor with a** *tereifa* animal, **nor with diverse kinds,** i.e., a sheep-goat hybrid, **nor with a** ***koy.***[B] Rava's principle is referring to the source for the prohibition against using an animal of diverse kinds for the redemption of a firstborn donkey.

וּלְרַבִּי אֶלְעָזָר דְּמַתִּיר בְּכִלְאַיִם, דִּתְנַן: רַבִּי אֶלְעָזָר מַתִּיר בְּכִלְאַיִם מִפְּנֵי שֶׁהוּא שֶׂה, לְמַאי הִלְכְתָא?

The Gemara asks: **But** what about **according to** the opinion of **Rabbi Elazar, who** disagrees with this ruling and **permits** the use of an animal of **diverse kinds** for the redemption of a firstborn donkey? **As we learned** in the same mishna: **Rabbi Elazar permits diverse kinds** for use in the redemption of a firstborn donkey **because it is** considered **a** ***seh.*** Accordingly, **with regard to what** ***halakha*** is Rava's principle relevant?

אָמַר לָךְ רַבִּי אֶלְעָזָר: כִּי אִיתְּמַר דְּרָבָא – לְטָמֵא שֶׁנּוֹלַד מִן הַטָּהוֹר וְעִיבּוּרוֹ מִן הַטָּמֵא. וּדְלָא כְּרַבִּי יְהוֹשֻׁעַ, דְּאִי רַבִּי יְהוֹשֻׁעַ, מִ"שֵּׂה כְשָׂבִים וְשֵׂה עִזִּים" נָפְקָא לֵיהּ, עַד שֶׁיְּהֵא אָבִיו כֶּבֶשׂ וְאִמּוֹ כִּבְשָׂה.

Rabbi Elazar could have **said to you:** Rava's principle **was stated with regard to a non-kosher** animal **that was born from a kosher** mother, **whose impregnation was from a non-kosher** animal. Rava is saying that this animal is not kosher. **And** this is **not in accordance with** the opinion of **Rabbi Yehoshua, as, if** it were in accordance with the opinion of **Rabbi Yehoshua,** although he would agree with this *halakha*, **he derives** this *halakha* (see *Bekhorot* 7a) **from** the phrase: **"The** ***seh*** **of sheep [*kevasim*], and the** ***seh*** **of goats [*izzim*]"** (Deuteronomy 14:4). The plural forms "*kevasim*" and "*izzim*" indicate that a lamb is not kosher **unless** both **its father is a sheep and its mother is a ewe,** and the same *halakha* applies to a kid.

וּטְהוֹרָה מִטְּמֵאָה מִי מִיעַבְּרָא? אִין, דְּקַיְימָא לַן

The Gemara asks with regard to the case under discussion: **But can a kosher** animal **become impregnated by a non-kosher** animal in the first place?[B] Is it even possible for this to occur? Why did Rabbi Yehoshua and Rava have to find a biblical source to deem this offspring as non-kosher? The Gemara answers: **Yes,** it is possible. **As we maintain** elsewhere (*Bekhorot* 7a)

HALAKHA

An animal that resembles another is not subject to the ***halakhot*** **of a firstborn – נִדְמֶה לִבְכוֹר:** With regard to a ewe that gives birth to an offspring that resembles a goat, or a goat that gives birth to an animal that resembles a sheep, the *halakhot* pertaining to firstborn animals do not apply to such offspring (Rambam *Sefer Korbanot, Hilkhot Bekhorot* 2:6; *Shulḥan Arukh, Yoreh De'a* 315:5).

Diverse kinds with regard to the redemption of a firstborn donkey – כִּלְאַיִם לְעִנְיַן פֶּטֶר חֲמוֹר: One may not redeem a firstborn donkey with any animal other than a sheep or a goat, and an animal of diverse kinds may not be used for this purpose (Rambam *Sefer Zera'im, Hilkhot Bikkurim* 12:8).

BACKGROUND

Koy **– כּוֹי:** Many problems arise in trying to identify the *koy*. It is mentioned numerous times in the Mishna and the Gemara, not because it is a common animal, but rather, because it is useful in discussions that explore the application and limits of the *halakhot* concerning domestic animals versus wild animals. As early as the mishnaic period, the Sages disagreed with regard to the identification of the *koy*. Some maintain that it is a hybrid born to a goat and a deer or another kosher wild animal.

According to many researchers, the *koy* is identified as the water buffalo. There are allusions to this identification in some medieval rabbinic sources. Others reject this idea and claim that water buffalo did not live in Eretz Yisrael during the time of the Mishna, when the *koy* was first mentioned. Others maintain that the *koy* is the mouflon, a subspecies of wild sheep, although there are a number of opinions as to the specific subspecies of mouflon it may be. There is also uncertainty with regard to both the origin of the term *koy* and its proper vocalization.

Water buffalo

Mouflon

Offspring of a kosher animal and a non-kosher animal – וָלָד שֶׁל טְהוֹרָה וּטְמֵאָה: All kosher animals belong to the order Artiodactyla, also called cloven-hoofed or even-toed, whereas most non-kosher animals are so dissimilar to this group that crossbreeding is impossible. Even camels and pigs, which are part of the order Artiodactyla, belong to different families, and therefore crossbreeding between kosher and non-kosher animals in general is not possible.

דְּאִיעַבַּר מִקָּלוּט כְּרַבִּי שִׁמְעוֹן.

that the mother animal **became impregnated from** an animal with **non-cloven** hooves[B] that was born from a kosher mother and father. This is **in accordance with** the opinion of **Rabbi Shimon,** who maintains that the offspring resulting from this, which does not have cloven hooves, is not kosher. Since the animal's father is not kosher according to the opinion of Rabbi Shimon, the offspring is also not kosher, in accordance with Rava's principle.

בָּעֵי רָבָא: ״הֲרֵי עָלַי עוֹלָה״ וְהִפְרִישׁ שׁוֹר, וּבָא אַחֵר וְגָנַב, מִי פָּטַר גַּנָּב נַפְשֵׁיהּ בְּכֶבֶשׂ לְרַבָּנַן, בְּעוֹלַת הָעוֹף לְרַבִּי אֶלְעָזָר בֶּן עֲזַרְיָה? דִּתְנַן: ״הֲרֵי עָלַי עוֹלָה״ – יָבִיא כֶּבֶשׂ, רַבִּי אֶלְעָזָר בֶּן עֲזַרְיָה אוֹמֵר: יָבִיא תּוֹר אוֹ בֶּן יוֹנָה,

Rava raises a dilemma: With regard to one who says: **It is** incumbent **upon me** to bring **a burnt-offering,**[H] **and he** subsequently **set aside a bull** for this purpose, **and another** person **came and stole** the bull, **can the thief exempt himself** from liability[N] **by** repaying the owner with **a sheep, according to** the opinion of **the Rabbis, or** by repaying him with a bird to be used as **a bird burnt-offering, according to** the opinion of **Rabbi Elazar ben Azarya?** This is **as we learned** in a mishna (*Menaḥot* 107a): If one says: **It is** incumbent **upon me** to bring **a burnt-offering, he must bring** a bull or **a sheep** as a burnt-offering to fulfill his vow. **Rabbi Elazar ben Azarya says: He may** even **bring a turtledove or a young pigeon** as a burnt-offering.

מַאי? מִי אָמְרִינַן שֵׁם עוֹלָה קַבֵּיל עִילָּוֵיהּ, אוֹ דִּלְמָא מָצֵי אָמַר לֵיהּ: אֲנָא מִצְוָה מִן הַמּוּבְחָר בָּעֵינָא לְמֶיעֱבַד?

Rava elaborates: **What** is the *halakha* in this case? **Do we say** that he **accepted upon himself** to sacrifice an animal with the **status of a burnt-offering,**[N] in which case any animal that fulfills this requirement will suffice? If so, the thief may compensate the owner with a sheep or bird, as the owner can sacrifice that animal as a burnt-offering. **Or perhaps** the owner **can say to** the thief: **I want to perform** the **mitzva** in **the optimal manner,** which is by sacrificing a bull. Therefore, you must pay me back with a bull.

בָּתַר דְּאִיבַּעְיָא הֲדַר פְּשַׁט: גַּנָּב פָּטַר עַצְמוֹ בְּכֶבֶשׂ לְרַבָּנַן, בְּעוֹלַת הָעוֹף לְרַבִּי אֶלְעָזָר בֶּן עֲזַרְיָה.

After he raised the dilemma, Rava himself **subsequently resolved** it: The **thief can exempt himself** from liability by repaying the owner **with a sheep,**[H] **according to** the opinion of **the Rabbis,** or **by** repaying him with a bird to be used as **a bird burnt-offering, according to** the opinion of **Rabbi Elazar ben Azarya.**

רַב אַחָא בְּרֵיהּ דְּרַב אִיקָא מַתְנֵי לָהּ בְּהֶדְיָא, אָמַר רָבָא: ״הֲרֵי עָלַי עוֹלָה״ וְהִפְרִישׁ שׁוֹר, וּבָא אַחֵר וּגְנָבוֹ – פָּטַר עַצְמוֹ בְּכֶבֶשׂ לְרַבָּנַן, וּבְעוֹלַת הָעוֹף לְרַבִּי אֶלְעָזָר בֶּן עֲזַרְיָה.

Rav Aḥa, son of Rav Ika, teaches this *halakha* **explicitly,** i.e., without the question-and-answer format: **Rava says:** With regard to one who says: **It is** incumbent **upon me** to bring **a burnt-offering, and he** subsequently **set aside a bull** for this purpose, **and another** person **came and stole** the bull, the thief can **exempt himself** from liability **by** repaying the owner with **a sheep, according to** the opinion of **the Rabbis, or by** repaying him with a bird to be used as **a bird burnt-offering, according to** the opinion of **Rabbi Elazar ben Azarya.**

BACKGROUND

An animal with non-cloven hooves – קָלוּט: Sometimes an offspring of two cloven-hoofed animals is born with a birth defect of non-cloven hooves. This offspring lacks one of the two signs of a kosher animal, despite the fact that genetically it is certainly a kosher species.

HALAKHA

It is incumbent upon me to bring a burnt-offering – הֲרֵי עָלַי עוֹלָה: With regard to one who says: It is incumbent upon me to bring a burnt-offering, without specifying what kind of burnt-offering he intends, if it is the usual practice in that place to refer even to bird-offerings simply as burnt-offerings, he may bring a turtledove or a young pigeon. If the local practice is to refer specifically to a cattle burnt-offering when they mention a burnt-offering, he must bring a bull (Rambam *Sefer Avoda, Hilkhot Ma'aseh HaKorbanot* 16:3).

Exempt himself from liability with a sheep, etc. – פָּטַר עַצְמוֹ בְּכֶבֶשׂ וכו׳: If one said: I undertake to bring a burnt-offering, and he subsequently designated a bull for this purpose, and afterward the bull was stolen from him, he may fulfill his vow with a sheep, as indicated by Rava's statement. This *halakha* is in accordance with the opinion of the Rabbis, who disagree with Rabbi Elazar ben Azarya. The Rambam does not discuss the liability of the thief in this case, which is the primary issue addressed by Rava. It is possible that he had a different version of the Gemara (Rambam *Sefer Avoda, Hilkhot Ma'aseh HaKorbanot* 16:7).

NOTES

Can the thief exempt himself from liability, etc. – מִי פָּטַר גַּנָּב נַפְשֵׁיהּ וכו׳: Rashi explains that the question here concerns only the thief's obligation to the owner. With regard to the thief's liability to the Temple treasury, he is not required to pay compensation, as the Gemara establishes earlier (76a) that the phrase: "And it was stolen from the house of the man" (Exodus 22:6), indicates that payment is demanded from the thief only in that situation, not if it was stolen from the Temple treasury. Others point out that if the animal is still intact, the thief is obligated to give it back to the Temple to be sacrificed; moreover, if he had eaten that animal's meat he would have to pay its full price to the Temple (Ra'avad).

Accepted upon himself to sacrifice an animal with the status of a burnt-offering – שֵׁם עוֹלָה קַבֵּיל עִילָּוֵיהּ: According to several commentaries, Rava's question is based on the opinion of Rabbi Shimon (76a), who maintains that a sacrificial animal for which the owner bears financial responsibility to replace with another animal if the original is lost or dies is considered in the possession of its owner. Therefore, the thief has stolen an animal from its owner, and the Gemara is discussing how to calculate the owner's loss. According to the dissenting opinion of the Rabbis, the thief is considered to have stolen the animal from the Temple treasury, and therefore the owner's intention is irrelevant (see Rashi; *Shiltei HaGibborim, Bava Batra* 6a).

מתני׳ מְכָרוֹ חוּץ מֵאֶחָד מִמֵּאָה שֶׁבּוֹ, אוֹ שֶׁהָיְתָה לוֹ בּוֹ שׁוּתָּפוּת, הַשּׁוֹחֵט וְנִתְנַבְּלָה בְּיָדוֹ, הַנּוֹחֵר, וְהַמְעַקֵּר – מְשַׁלֵּם תַּשְׁלוּמֵי כֶפֶל וְאֵינוֹ מְשַׁלֵּם תַּשְׁלוּמֵי אַרְבָּעָה וַחֲמִשָּׁה.

MISHNA If a thief **sold** a stolen animal in a partial fashion, e.g., **except for** one **one-hundredth of it,**[N] which he kept for himself; **or if he had a partnership in** owning the animal[H] before stealing it; or in the case of a thief **who slaughtered** the stolen animal **and it became non-kosher** meat **in his hand**[H] because he slaughtered it improperly; or in the case of a thief **who ripped open** the animal rather than slaughtering it halakhically; **or** in the case of a thief **who tore loose** the gullet or windpipe of the animal as he slaughtered it, rendering the slaughter invalid, in all these cases **he pays** the **double payment but does not pay** the **fourfold or fivefold payment.** The fourfold or fivefold payment applies only if the animal is entirely sold or if it is slaughtered in accordance with the halakhic definition of animal slaughter.

גמ׳ מַאי חוּץ מֵאֶחָד מִמֵּאָה שֶׁבּוֹ? אָמַר רַב: חוּץ מִדָּבָר הַנִּיתָּר עִמּוֹ בִּשְׁחִיטָה, וְלֵוִי אָמַר: חוּץ מִגִּיזּוֹתֶיהָ; וְכֵן תַּנְיָא בְּמַתְנִיתָא: חוּץ מִגִּיזּוֹתֶיהָ.

GEMARA **What** does the mishna mean when it states that the thief sold the animal **except for** one **one-hundredth**[H] **of it?** Which part of the animal must the thief keep for himself for him to be exempt from the fourfold or fivefold payment? **Rav says:** The mishna means that he sold it **except for some** part of the animal **that becomes permitted through** its **slaughter.** This does not apply to horns or a sheep's fleece, which do not require slaughter in order to be used. **And Levi says:** The mishna's statement applies even if the thief sold the entire animal **except for its fleece. And it is likewise taught in a** ***baraita*****:** The thief is exempt even if he sells the whole animal **except for its fleece.**

מֵיתִיבֵי: מְכָרָהּ חוּץ מִיָּדָהּ חוּץ מֵרַגְלָהּ, חוּץ מִקַּרְנָהּ, חוּץ מִגִּיזּוֹתֶיהָ – אֵינוֹ מְשַׁלֵּם תַּשְׁלוּמֵי אַרְבָּעָה וַחֲמִשָּׁה; רַבִּי אוֹמֵר: דָּבָר הַמְעַכֵּב בִּשְׁחִיטָה – אֵינוֹ מְשַׁלֵּם תַּשְׁלוּמֵי אַרְבָּעָה וַחֲמִשָּׁה,

The Gemara **raises an objection** to the opinion of Rav from a *baraita*: If the thief **sold** the whole animal **except for its foreleg,** or **except for its hind leg,** or **except for its horn,** or **except for its fleece, he does not pay** the **fourfold or fivefold payment. Rabbi** Yehuda HaNasi **says:** If the thief sells the animal except for some **part** of it whose absence **invalidates its slaughter,**[N] **he does not pay** the **fourfold or fivefold payment.**

וְשֶׁאֵינוֹ מְעַכֵּב בִּשְׁחִיטָה – מְשַׁלֵּם תַּשְׁלוּמֵי אַרְבָּעָה וַחֲמִשָּׁה.

Rabbi Yehuda HaNasi continues: But if he leaves out from the sale a part of the animal whose absence **does not invalidate the slaughter, he pays** the **fourfold or fivefold payment.** If an animal is missing one of its vital organs, e.g., its liver, one of its intestines, its gullet, or its windpipe, it is considered already dead and its slaughter at this stage would be invalid. For the thief to be exempt from the fourfold or fivefold payment on the grounds of an incomplete sale, he must retain one of these organs for himself.

רַבִּי שִׁמְעוֹן בֶּן אֶלְעָזָר אוֹמֵר: חוּץ מִקַּרְנָהּ – אֵינוֹ מְשַׁלֵּם תַּשְׁלוּמֵי אַרְבָּעָה וַחֲמִשָּׁה, חוּץ מִגִּיזּוֹתֶיהָ – מְשַׁלֵּם תַּשְׁלוּמֵי אַרְבָּעָה וַחֲמִשָּׁה;

The *baraita* continues: **Rabbi Shimon ben Elazar says:** If the thief sells the whole animal **except for its horn, he does not pay** the **fourfold or fivefold payment.** If he sells the whole animal **except for its fleece, he does pay** the **fourfold or fivefold payment.**

NOTES

Except for one one-hundredth of it – חוּץ מֵאֶחָד מִמֵּאָה שֶׁבּוֹ: The reference to one one-hundredth is not meant to be exact. Rather, it refers to any portion of the animal at all (Rabbeinu Ḥananel; Rabbeinu Barukh).

In the Jerusalem Talmud a question is raised with regard to a thief who sells part of the stolen animal to one individual and the remainder to another. The conclusion there is that if there is a part that is not sold to either party it is considered a significant withholding, and therefore the thief is exempt from the fourfold or fivefold payment.

A part whose absence invalidates its slaughter – דָּבָר הַמְעַכֵּב בִּשְׁחִיטָה: Even if an animal has a grievous wound, which renders it prohibited for consumption as a *tereifa*, slaughtering it still has halakhic ramifications, as the body of the animal would not be considered a carcass, which renders items that touch it ritually impure. Rashi explains that by contrast, if the animal is missing a vital organ and is in the process of dying, it is already considered a carcass, even if it shows signs of life. Slaughter would no longer accomplish anything, and it would not be included in the term: "And slaughters it" (Exodus 21:37).

HALAKHA

He had a partnership in the animal – הָיְתָה לוֹ בּוֹ שׁוּתָּפוּת: If one steals and sells an ox or sheep in which he held partial ownership, he is exempt from paying the fourfold or fivefold payment to the other partners (Rambam *Sefer Nezikin*, *Hilkhot Geneiva* 2:13; *Tur*, *Ḥoshen Mishpat* 350).

Who slaughtered and it became non-kosher meat in his hand, etc. – הַשּׁוֹחֵט וְנִתְנַבְּלָה בְּיָדוֹ וכו׳: If one stole an ox or a sheep and it became non-kosher meat in the process of his slaughtering it, or if he ripped open the animal or tore loose its gullet or windpipe, he pays the double payment but not the fourfold or fivefold payment (Rambam *Sefer Nezikin*, *Hilkhot Geneiva* 2:8; *Tur*, *Ḥoshen Mishpat* 350).

Except for one one-hundredth, etc. – חוּץ מֵאֶחָד מִמֵּאָה וכו׳: With regard to one who stole an animal and sold it apart from one one-hundredth of it, or excluding its foreleg or its hind leg, or any part of the animal that is rendered permitted for consumption through its slaughter, he is exempt from the fourfold or fivefold payment. If he sold the entire animal except for its fleece or its horns, which are not rendered permitted through its slaughter, he pays the fourfold or fivefold payment. This is in accordance with the opinion of Rav, as well as that of Rabbi Shimon ben Elazar in the second *baraita*. The Rosh maintains that even if he sells the entire animal apart from its horns or fleece he is exempt from paying the fourfold or fivefold payment, in accordance with the opinion of the Rabbis in the *baraita* (Rambam *Sefer Nezikin*, *Hilkhot Geneiva* 2:11; *Tur*, *Ḥoshen Mishpat* 350).

בשלמא ללוי – כתנא קמא, אלא לרב כמאן?

The Gemara explains the objection from this *baraita*: **Granted, according to** the opinion of **Levi** this *baraita* does not present a difficulty, as his ruling is exactly **like** that of **the first** *tanna*. **But according to** the opinion of **Rav** it does present a difficulty, as in accordance with **whose** opinion does his ruling accord? None of the three opinions expressed in the *baraita* correlate with that of Rav.

אמרי: רב דאמר כי האי תנא; דתניא, רבי שמעון בן אלעזר אומר: מכרה חוץ מידה וחוץ מרגלה – אינו משלם תשלומי ארבעה וחמשה, חוץ מקרנה חוץ מגיזותיה – משלם תשלומי ארבעה וחמשה.

The Sages **say** in response: **Rav says** his opinion **in accordance with** the opinion of **this** *tanna*, **as it is taught** in another *baraita*: **Rabbi Shimon ben Elazar says:** If the thief **sold** the entire animal **except for its foreleg or except for its hind leg, he does not pay the fourfold or fivefold payment.** If he sold the entire animal **except for its horn** or **except for its fleece, he does pay** the **fourfold or fivefold payment.**

במאי קמיפלגי? תנא קמא סבר: ״וטבחו״ כולו בעינן, ״ומכרו״ כולו בעינן;

The Gemara analyzes the four opinions of the *tanna'im* presented in these *baraitot*. **With regard to what** principle **do they disagree? The first** *tanna* **holds** that when the Torah states: "If a man steals an ox or a sheep, and slaughters it or sells it, he shall pay five oxen for an ox and four sheep for a sheep" (Exodus 21:37), the term **"and slaughters it"** indicates that **we require** him to slaughter **all of it** for him to incur liability to pay the fourfold or fivefold payment. Likewise, the term **"or sells it"** teaches that **we require** him to sell **all of it,** not leaving any portion at all for himself, even the fleece.

ורבי סבר: ״וטבחו״ – מידי דהוי בטביחה, לאפוקי מידי דלא הויא בטביחה, ״ומכרו״ דומיא דטביחה;

And Rabbi Yehuda HaNasi **holds** that the term **"and slaughters it"** is referring to **parts** of the animal **that are** affected **by** its **slaughter,** which serves **to exclude parts** of the animal **that are not** affected **by** its **slaughter.** When the Torah immediately adds the term **"or sells it,"** this indicates that selling is **similar to slaughter.** Consequently, if the sale excludes the animal's fleece or horns, i.e., those parts that are not affected by slaughter, there is still fourfold or fivefold payment.

ורבי שמעון בן אלעזר סבר: קרנא דלא למגזא קיימא – הוי שיור, ואינו משלם תשלום ארבעה וחמשה, גיזותיה דלמיגז קיימי – לא הוי שיור, ומשלם תשלום ארבעה וחמשה;

And Rabbi Shimon ben Elazar holds, according to the first version of his opinion, that **the** animal's **horn, which is not meant to be cut off** in the animal's lifetime, **is** considered a significant **withholding** if the thief keeps that part for himself, **and he does not pay the fourfold or fivefold payment.** By contrast, **fleece, which is meant to be cut off** in the animal's lifetime, **is not** considered a significant **withholding** if the thief keeps it for himself, **and** therefore **he must pay the fourfold or fivefold payment.**

ואידך תנא דבי רבי שמעון בן אלעזר סבר: ידיו ורגליו דצריכי טביחה – הוי שיור, ולא משלם תשלומי ארבעה וחמשה, קרניה וגיזותיה דלא צריכי טביחה – לא הוי שיור.

And the other *tanna* **of the school of Rabbi Shimon ben Elazar holds** that the animal's **forelegs and hind legs, which require slaughter** for them to be put to their usual use, i.e., for eating, **are** considered a significant **withholding** if the thief keeps one of them for himself, **and** consequently **he does not pay the fourfold or fivefold payment.** By contrast, **its horns and its fleece, which do not require slaughter** in order to be used, **are not** considered a significant **withholding** if the thief keeps them for himself.

קשיא דרבי שמעון בן אלעזר אדרבי שמעון בן אלעזר! תרי תנאי ואליבא דרבי שמעון בן אלעזר.

The Gemara asks: This presents **a difficulty,** as there is a contradiction between one statement **of Rabbi Shimon ben Elazar and** another opinion presented in the name **of Rabbi Shimon ben Elazar.** The Gemara answers: The two rulings represent the reports of **two** *tanna'im,* **and** they disagree **with regard to** the opinion **of Rabbi Shimon ben Elazar.**

תנו רבנן: הגונב הקיטעת ואת החיגרת ואת הסומא, וכן הגונב בהמת השותפין – חייב, ושותפים שגנבו – פטורים. והתניא: שותפין שגנבו – חייבין!

The Sages taught in a *baraita*: **One who steals** an animal that is **missing a limb,**[H] **or** that is **lame, or** that is **blind,** and he subsequently sold it, **and similarly, one who steals an animal** belonging to several **partners**[H] and he subsequently sold it, is **liable** to pay the fourfold or fivefold payment. **But** several **partners who stole** an animal together and sell it are **exempt** from the fourfold or fivefold payment. The Gemara asks: **But isn't it taught** in another *baraita* to the contrary, that several **partners who stole** an animal together and sell it are **liable** to pay the fourfold or fivefold payment?

HALAKHA

One who steals an animal that is missing a limb, etc. – **הגונב הקיטעת וכו׳**: If one steals and sells an animal that is missing a limb or is lame or blind, he must pay the fourfold or fivefold payment (Rambam *Sefer Nezikin, Hilkhot Geneiva* 2:9; *Tur, Ḥoshen Mishpat* 350).

One who steals an animal belonging to several partners – **הגונב בהמת השותפין**: If one steals an animal that belongs to several partners and subsequently slaughters or sells it, he is liable to pay the fourfold or fivefold payment (Rambam *Sefer Nezikin, Hilkhot Geneiva* 2:9; *Tur, Ḥoshen Mishpat* 350).

אמר רב נחמן, לא קשיא: כאן בשותף שגנב מחבירו, כאן בשותף שגנב מעלמא.

The Gemara resolves the contradiction: **Rav Naḥman said** that this is **not difficult. Here,** where the *baraita* states that he is exempt, it is referring **to one partner who stole** an animal **from another** partner. **There,** where the *baraita* states that he is liable, it is dealing **with a partner, who,** together with other thieves, **stole** an animal **from** someone else **outside** their group.

איתיביה רבא לרב נחמן: יכול שותף שגנב מחבירו, ושותפים שגנבו יהו חייבין? תלמוד לומר: "וטבחו" – כולו בעינן, וליכא!

Rava raised an objection to Rav Naḥman from another *baraita*: One **might** have thought that **a partner who stole** an animal **from another** partner and slaughtered it, **and** likewise **partners who** jointly **stole**[N] an animal and one of them slaughtered it, **should be liable** to pay the fourfold or fivefold payment. To counter this, **the verse states: "And slaughters it,"** which indicates that **we require** liability for slaughtering **all of it, and** in these cases **it is not** so. One who steals an animal that he partly owns is not liable for slaughtering his own portion. Likewise, when several partners steal an animal, the one who slaughters it is not liable for slaughtering the portions of his fellow thieves.

אלא אמר רב נחמן, לא קשיא: כאן בשותף שטבח לדעת חבירו, כאן בשותף שטבח שלא לדעת חבירו.

Rather, Rav Naḥman said a different resolution of the contradiction: This is **not difficult.** Both *baraitot* are speaking of partners who together stole an animal from someone else. **Here,** where the *baraita* states that the thief is liable, it is referring **to a partner who slaughtered** the animal **with the knowledge** and consent of **another** partner.[H] In such a case the one slaughtering is acting as the agent of the partner as well and is fully liable for the slaughter. **There,** where the *baraita* states that the thief is exempt, it is speaking **of a partner who slaughtered** the animal **without the knowledge of another** partner in the theft. Consequently, the one slaughtering is acting solely on his own and is not liable for the slaughter of his partner's share, which is why he is exempt from any payment.

בעי רבי ירמיה: מכרה חוץ משלשים יום, חוץ ממלאכתה, חוץ מעוברה, מהו?

§ **Rabbi Yirmeya raises** several **dilemmas:** If the thief **sold** the animal **except for thirty days,** i.e., the thief reserved the right to use the animal himself for thirty days before the sale takes effect, what is the *halakha*? If he sold it **except for its work,**[H] i.e., he stipulated with the buyer that any work the animal performs would be for the thief's own benefit and profit, what is the *halakha*? If he stole a pregnant animal and sold it **except for its fetus, what is the** *halakha*?

אליבא דמאן דאמר עובר ירך אמו הוא – לא תבעי לך, דהא שייר בה. כי תבעי לך – אליבא דמאן דאמר דעובר לאו ירך אמו, מאי? מימר אמרינן: כיון דמחובר בה הוי שיור, או דלמא: כיון דלמפרש מינה קאי לא הוי שיור?

The Gemara elaborates on the last dilemma: **According to the one who says that a fetus is** considered as **its mother's thigh,**[H] i.e., a part of its mother, **you should not raise the dilemma, as** it is clear that the thief, by retaining the fetus, **has withheld** part of the animal. **When you should raise the dilemma,** it is **according** to the opinion of **the one who says that a fetus is not** considered as **its mother's thigh,** i.e., it has the status of an independent being. **What** is the *halakha* in this case? **Do we say that since it is** in fact **attached** to the mother, if the thief keeps the fetus for himself **it is** considered a significant **withholding? Or perhaps, since it stands to become detached from** the mother **it is not** considered a significant **withholding?**

איכא דאמרי: כיון דלאו ירך אמו הוא לא הוי שיור, או דלמא: כיון דצריך לאישתרויי בהדה בשחיטה, כמאן דשייר בגופה דמי? תיקו.

There are those **who state** a different analysis of this dilemma: **Since** a fetus is **not** considered as **its mother's thigh, it is not** considered a significant **withholding, or perhaps,** since it **needs** its mother **to be rendered permitted** for consumption **through** the mother's **slaughter, it is considered as though** the thief **has withheld a part of the** mother's **body.** The Gemara concludes: All these dilemmas **shall stand** unresolved.

בעי רב פפא: גנבה, קטעה ומכרה, מהו? מי אמרינן: מאי דגנב הא לא זבין, או דלמא: מה דזבין הא לא שייר? תיקו.

Rav Pappa raises a dilemma: If one **stole** an animal, **severed** one of its limbs, **and** then **sold it,**[H] **what is** the *halakha*? **Do we say** that the essential factor is that part of **what he stole he has not sold,** as the missing limb was not sold, and therefore he is exempt from the fourfold or fivefold payment? **Or perhaps** the essential factor is that with regard to that **which he sold he has not withheld** any part for himself. Once again, the Gemara states that this dilemma **shall stand** unresolved.

NOTES

And partners who stole, etc. – **ושותפים שגנבו וכו׳**: If one person steals an animal and another slaughters it, there is no fourfold or fivefold payment, unless the second person slaughtered it on behalf of the thief, in which case he serves as his agent and the thief is liable to pay the fourfold or fivefold payment, as the Gemara explained earlier in the chapter (71a). Consequently, if several thieves jointly steal an animal, and one of them slaughters it, the one who slaughters would theoretically be liable to pay the fourfold or fivefold payment only for his own portion of the animal, but not for his partners' shares. Since he is not liable for a portion of the animal, he is not liable at all, as the term: "And slaughters it" (Exodus 21:37), indicates that the slaughter must be one for which the thief is entirely liable (Rashi).

HALAKHA

A partner who slaughtered with the knowledge of another partner – **שותף שטבח לדעת חבירו**: If several people join together and steal an ox or a sheep, and one of them slaughters or sells the animal with the consent of the others, they all share liability to pay the fourfold or fivefold payment. If he did so without their consent, they are exempt from the fourfold or fivefold payment, although they must still pay double payment, in accordance with the opinion of Rav Naḥman (Rambam *Sefer Nezikin*, *Hilkhot Geneiva* 2:14; *Tur*, *Ḥoshen Mishpat* 350).

Sold it except for thirty days, except for its work – **מכרה חוץ משלשים יום חוץ ממלאכתה**: If one stole an animal and sold it excluding the first thirty days, or excluding its work, the court does not require him to pay the fourfold or fivefold payment. Nevertheless, if the animal's prior owner seized payment from the thief the court does not force him to repay it. This is the Rambam's standard halakhic ruling with regard to unresolved dilemmas involving monetary issues in the Gemara: The defendant is not required to pay, but if the claimant seizes money from him he may keep it. The Ra'avad and the Rosh, for different reasons, disagree with this opinion and rule that seizure of payment is not effective in these cases. Rather, the claimant must return the seized money (Rambam *Sefer Nezikin*, *Hilkhot Geneiva* 2:12; *Tur*, *Ḥoshen Mishpat* 350).

A fetus is considered as its mother's thigh – **עובר ירך אמו הוא**: A fetus is considered part of its mother's body and is rendered permitted for consumption through the slaughter of its mother. If a thief sold a stolen animal apart from its fetus he is exempt from paying the fourfold or fivefold payment (Rambam *Sefer Nezikin*, *Hilkhot Nizkei Mamon* 11:12 and *Sefer Kedusha*, *Hilkhot Ma'akhalot Assurot* 5:14; *Shulḥan Arukh*, *Yoreh De'a* 13:2).

If one stole an animal, severed one of its limbs and sold it, etc. – **גנבה קטעה ומכרה וכו׳**: If one steals an animal, severs one of its limbs, and then sells it, the court will not require him to pay the fourfold or fivefold payment. Nevertheless, if the animal's prior owner seizes payment from the thief, he is not forced to return it. The Ra'avad and the Rosh, as mentioned earlier, dispute this ruling (Rambam *Sefer Nezikin*, *Hilkhot Geneiva* 2:12; *Tur*, *Ḥoshen Mishpat* 350).

תנו רבנן: גנב ונתן לאחר וטבח, גנב ונתן לאחר ומכר,

§ **The Sages taught** in a *baraita*: If one **stole** an animal **and gave it to another and** that person **slaughtered it** for him, or if **he stole** an animal **and gave it to another and** that person **sold it** for him, the thief is liable to pay the fourfold or fivefold payment, as performing these actions through an agent is equivalent to performing them by oneself.

Perek **VII**
Daf **79** Amud **a**

גנב והקדיש, גנב והקיף, גנב והחליף, גנב ונתן במתנה, גנב ופרע חובו, גנב ופרע בהקיפו, גנב ושלח סבלונות בבית חמיו – משלם תשלומי ארבעה וחמשה.

The *baraita* continues: If **he stole** an animal **and consecrated** it, or if he **stole** an animal **and sold** it **on credit,**[H] i.e., without receiving any money for it at the time, or if **he stole** an animal **and exchanged** it for another item, or if **he stole** an animal **and gave it** to another **as a gift,** or if **he stole** an animal **and** used it to **repay his debt,** or if **he stole** an animal and used it to **pay** for an item **he** purchased on **credit,** or if **he stole** an animal **and sent it in** the form of **presents** to his betrothed **in his father-in-law's house,** in all of these cases **he pays** the **fourfold or fivefold payment,** as these acts are all considered forms of selling. This concludes the *baraita*.

מאי קא משמע לן? אשמעינן רישא גנב ונתן לאחר וטבח, דיש שליח לדבר עבירה; אף על גב דבכל התורה כולה אין שליח לדבר עבירה – הכא יש שליח לדבר עבירה,

The Gemara asks: **What is this** *baraita* **teaching us?** All of the *halakhot* it states are obvious. The Gemara answers: **The first clause teaches us,** through the case of one who **stole** an animal **and gave it to another and** that person **slaughtered** or sold it on his behalf, **that** in this case **there is agency for transgression. Even though in the entire Torah** there is a principle that **there is no agency for transgression,**[H] **here there is agency for transgression.**[H] The Torah's principle is that a transgression committed by an agent who was appointed by another person is not considered the act of the one who appointed the agent, but the independent act of the agent himself. The case discussed by this *baraita* is an exception to the rule, as here, the agent's slaughter or sale of the animal is legally considered the action of the thief.

מאי טעמא? "וטבחו ומכרו" – מה מכירה דלא אפשר דלאו על ידי אחר, אף טביחה על ידי אחר מחייב;

What is the reason that this case is an exception to the principle? It is because the verse states: **"And slaughters it or sells it"** (Exodus 21:37), which juxtaposes the two acts of slaughtering and selling. This teaches that **just as** one becomes liable for **selling, which** by definition **is impossible without another** party, i.e., the buyer, **so too one becomes liable** for **slaughtering** even when it is **by means of another** party, i.e., when the thief instructs another person to slaughter the animal on his behalf.

ואשמעינן סיפא גנב והקדיש, מה לי מכרו להדיוט, מה לי מכרו לשמים.

And the latter clause of the *baraita* **teaches us** a novelty in the case of one who **stole** an animal **and consecrated** it. The novelty is that this is considered a sale despite the fact that there is no purchaser. This is due to the following argument: **What** difference **is it to me** if **he sold** the animal **to an ordinary** person,[HN] and **what** difference **is it to me** if **he sold it to Heaven** by consecrating it? If the animal changes ownership, it is considered a sale, and it does not matter if the new owner is an ordinary person or the Temple treasury.

HALAKHA

If one stole and sold it on credit, etc. – **גנב והקיף וכו׳**: If one stole an animal and gave it away as a gift, or sold it on credit, or exchanged it for another item, or used it to pay back a loan or money he owed as a result of purchasing an item on credit, or sent it as a present to his betrothed, he must pay the fourfold or fivefold payment (Rambam *Sefer Nezikin*, *Hilkhot Geneiva* 2:10; *Tur*, *Hoshen Mishpat* 350).

There is no agency for transgression – **אין שליח לדבר עבירה**: In almost all areas of *halakha* there is a principle that there is no agency for transgression. In other words, if one sent another to perform a transgression on his behalf, it is the agent who is responsible for committing the transgression, not the one who appointed him. There are three exceptions to this principle, each of which is derived from a biblical verse: Misuse of consecrated property, misappropriation of an item under one's trust, and a thief who sells or slaughters a stolen animal (Rambam *Sefer Avoda*, *Hilkhot Me'ila* 7:2 and *Sefer Nezikin*, *Hilkhot Gezeila VaAveda* 3:11).

Here there is agency for transgression – **הכא יש שליח לדבר עבירה**: If one steals an ox or sheep and instructs an agent to sell it or slaughter it, and the agent then does so, the thief is obligated to pay the fourfold or fivefold payment (Rambam *Sefer Nezikin*, *Hilkhot Geneiva* 2:10; *Tur*, *Hoshen Mishpat* 350).

What difference is it to me if he sold the animal to an ordinary person, etc. – **מה לי מכרו להדיוט וכו׳**: If one stole an ox or sheep and consecrated it to the Temple treasury, he must pay the fourfold or fivefold payment, as this is equivalent to selling it to an ordinary person (Rambam *Sefer Nezikin*, *Hilkhot Geneiva* 2:6 and Ra'avad there).

NOTES

What difference is it to me if he sold the animal to an ordinary person, etc. – **מה לי מכרו להדיוט**: The early commentaries ask: The statement of the Gemara here apparently contradicts the earlier claim (76a) that if a thief consecrates a stolen animal, this is not considered a sale, and the thief is not liable to pay the fourfold or fivefold payment. The reason for that ruling is stated by the Gemara there: At the outset it was Reuven's ox and now, after consecration, it is still Reuven's ox. Some answer that previously the Gemara was discussing the consecration of an animal as an offering, in which case it is appropriate to say that the ox still belongs to Reuven, because it is sacrificed upon the altar for his sake and in his name. Here, the Gemara is referring to consecration of an animal for the purpose of using its value for Temple maintenance. Consequently, Reuven no longer has any connection to his ox after its consecration (*Tosafot*; Ra'avad). Others state that the two statements in the Gemara are in fact contradictory, and the ruling of this *baraita* is rejected (Ramah; Meiri).

מתני׳ גָּנַב בִּרְשׁוּת הַבְּעָלִים וְטָבַח וּמָכַר חוּץ מֵרְשׁוּתָם, אוֹ שֶׁגָּנַב חוּץ מֵרְשׁוּתָם וְטָבַח וּמָכַר בִּרְשׁוּתָם, אוֹ שֶׁגָּנַב וְטָבַח וּמָכַר חוּץ מֵרְשׁוּתָם – מְשַׁלֵּם תַּשְׁלוּמֵי אַרְבָּעָה וַחֲמִשָּׁה. אֲבָל גָּנַב וְטָבַח וּמָכַר בִּרְשׁוּתָם – פָּטוּר.

MISHNA If one **stole** an animal **in** its **owner's domain,**[H] i.e., he took hold of it or established control over it but had not yet removed it from the owner's premises, **and** then **he slaughtered** it **or sold** it **outside** of the owner's **domain; or if he stole** an animal **outside** of the owner's **domain and slaughtered** it **or sold** it **in** the owner's **domain; or** if **he stole** an animal **and slaughtered** it **or sold** it, and all of this occurred **outside** the owner's **domain,** in all of these cases, **he must pay** the **fourfold or fivefold payment. But if he stole** it **and slaughtered or sold** it, and all of this occurred **in** the owner's **domain,**[H] he is **exempt** from any of the fines for theft, as it is not considered theft until the stolen object is actually removed from the owner's premises.

הָיָה מוֹשְׁכוֹ וְיוֹצֵא, וּמֵת בִּרְשׁוּת הַבְּעָלִים – פָּטוּר, הִגְבִּיהוֹ אוֹ הוֹצִיאוֹ מֵרְשׁוּת בְּעָלִים וּמֵת – חַיָּיב.

If the thief **was** in the process of **leading** the animal **and leaving**[H] the owner's premises, **and it died** while it was still **in the owner's domain,** the thief is **exempt** from all fines. **If he lifted it up or led it out of the owner's domain and** then the animal **died,** he is **liable** for his theft. For an act to be considered theft, the thief must acquire the item by pulling it or moving it, which are ineffective forms of acquisition on the owner's premises; or by lifting it up, which is effective even when performed in the owner's domain.

נְתָנוֹ לִבְכוֹרוֹת בְּנוֹ אוֹ לְבַעַל חוֹב, לְשׁוֹמֵר חִנָּם, לְשׁוֹאֵל, לְנוֹשֵׂא שָׂכָר וּלְשׁוֹכֵר, וְהָיָה מוֹשְׁכוֹ וּמֵת בִּרְשׁוּת הַבְּעָלִים – פָּטוּר, הִגְבִּיהוֹ אוֹ שֶׁהוֹצִיאוֹ מֵרְשׁוּת הַבְּעָלִים וּמֵת – חַיָּיב.

If the thief **gave** the animal as payment **for the redemption of his firstborn son,**[H] **or** as payment **to a creditor,** or conveyed it for safeguarding **to an unpaid bailee,** or lent it **to a borrower,** or conveyed it for safeguarding **to a paid bailee, or** leased it **to a renter, and he was leading out** the animal **and it died in the owner's domain,** the thief is **exempt** from all fines. If that individual, following the thief's instructions, **lifted up** the animal **or led it out of the owner's domain, and it** subsequently **died,** the thief is **liable**[N] for the theft. The thief is liable for instructing another to remove the animal for the purposes of payment of a debt, safekeeping, borrowing, or rental, as this is tantamount to the thief taking it with his own hands.

גמ׳ בָּעֵי אַמֵּימָר: תִּיקְּנוּ מְשִׁיכָה בְּשׁוֹמְרִים אוֹ לֹא?

GEMARA Ameimar raises a dilemma: Did the Sages **institute** the requirement of **pulling**[H] or leading an animal **with regard to bailees, or not?** When an animal or other item is purchased, the parties to the sale are not bound by the deal until the purchaser performs an act of acquisition, one of which is pulling the animal or leads it along. Did the Sages institute an ordinance that the same applies to bailees? In other words, does the bailee's obligation to safeguard the animal or item begin as soon as he consents to watch it, or only after he has taken the animal and moved it even minimally?

אֲמַר רַב יֵימָר, תָּא שְׁמַע: נְתָנוֹ לִבְכוֹרוֹת בְּנוֹ אוֹ לְבַעַל חוֹבוֹ, לְשׁוֹמֵר חִנָּם וּלְשׁוֹאֵל, לְנוֹשֵׂא שָׂכָר וּלְשׁוֹכֵר, הָיָה מוֹשְׁכוֹ וְיוֹצֵא וּמֵת בִּרְשׁוּת הַבְּעָלִים – פָּטוּר; מַאי לָאו שׁוֹמֵר? וּשְׁמַע מִינָּהּ: תִּיקְּנוּ מְשִׁיכָה בְּשׁוֹמְרִין.

Rav Yeimar said: Come and hear a proof from the mishna: If the thief **gave** the animal as payment **for the redemption of his firstborn son,**[B] **or** as payment **to a creditor,** or conveyed it for safeguarding **to an unpaid bailee,** or lent it **to a borrower,** or conveyed it for safeguarding **to a paid bailee, or** rented it **to a renter, and he was leading out** the animal **and it died in the owner's domain,** the thief is **exempt** from payment. **What, is it not** talking about the **bailee** leading out the animal, when it states that the thief is exempt? **And** if so, **conclude from** this mishna that the Sages **instituted** the requirement of **pulling with regard to bailees.** If the bailee's obligation begins immediately upon his consent to watch over the item, it would be considered stolen by the thief at that stage, even before the bailee moves it.

אֲמַר לֵיהּ: לָא, גַּנָּב.

Ameimar **said to** Rav Yeimar: **No,** this is not necessarily the correct interpretation of the mishna. The mishna may mean that the owner gave the animal to his creditor or to a bailee, and subsequently a thief came to steal it from the house of the creditor or the bailee, and it was the **thief** who was leading the animal out of those premises when it died.

HALAKHA

If one stole an animal in its owner's domain, etc. – גָּנַב בִּרְשׁוּת הַבְּעָלִים וכו׳: If one stole an animal in the domain of its owner and then removed it from the owner's premises and slaughtered or sold it, or if he stole it when it was outside the owner's domain and subsequently slaughtered or sold it inside the owner's premises, he must pay the fourfold or fivefold payment (Rambam *Sefer Nezikin, Hilkhot Geneiva* 2:18).

If he stole it and slaughtered or sold it in the owner's domain – גָּנַב וְטָבַח וּמָכַר בִּרְשׁוּתָם: If one took hold of an animal without removing it from the owner's premises, and slaughtered or sold it there, he is exempt from the double, fourfold, and fivefold payment (Rambam *Sefer Nezikin, Hilkhot Geneiva* 2:16).

If he was leading it and leaving, etc. – הָיָה מוֹשְׁכוֹ וְיוֹצֵא וכו׳: With regard to one who stole an animal and was leading it out of the owner's premises when it died, if he did not remove it from the owner's premises and he did not lift up the animal, he is exempt from the double payment. If he did remove it from the owner's premises, or if he lifted it up even inside the owner's premises, he is liable to pay the double payment (Rambam *Sefer Nezikin, Hilkhot Geneiva* 2:16).

If he gave it as payment for the redemption of his firstborn son, etc. – נְתָנוֹ לִבְכוֹרוֹת בְּנוֹ וכו׳: With regard to one who stole an animal and gave it, while it was still in the owner's domain, to a priest for the redemption of his firstborn son, or to his creditor as payment, or for safeguarding to a bailee, and the individual to whom the thief gave the animal was in the process of removing it from the owner's premises when it died, that individual is exempt from paying for the animal. If that person lifted up the animal or removed it from the owner's premises, he is liable. According to this ruling of the Rambam, the thief is exempt from paying any compensation, as he himself did not remove the animal from the owner's premises (Rambam *Sefer Nezikin, Hilkhot Geneiva* 2:16).

Acquiring an animal by pulling – קִנְיַן מְשִׁיכָה בִּבְהֵמָה: An animal is acquired if it is pulled along, or if it is ridden. Likewise, it is acquired if it responds to being called, or if the one acquiring it causes it to run before him by striking it. Once it raises its foreleg and hind leg in response to being struck, it is acquired. Pulling is sufficient for one to acquire an animal in the presence of the owner. By contrast, in the owner's absence it has to be made clear that the method of pulling is being employed as an act of acquisition (Rambam *Sefer Kinyan, Hilkhot Mekhira* 2:6; *Shulḥan Arukh, Ḥoshen Mishpat* 197:3).

NOTES

If he lifted up the animal or led it out of the owner's domain and it died, the thief is liable – הִגְבִּיהוֹ אוֹ שֶׁהוֹצִיאוֹ מֵרְשׁוּת הַבְּעָלִים וּמֵת חַיָּיב: The thief is liable if someone else, at his behest, took the animal from the owner. How does this accord with the principle that there is no agency for transgression, i.e., that when an agent is sent to commit a transgression on behalf of another, the agent alone is culpable for his own actions? The commentaries explain that here the Gemara is addressing a case where the agent, whether he is collecting the animal as a debt payment, taking it to safeguard as a bailee, or borrowing it, does not realize that he is committing a transgression. Rather, he is under the mistaken impression that the animal belongs to the thief. The principle that there is no agency for transgression does not apply in such cases (*Tosafot*).

BACKGROUND

For the redemption of his firstborn son – בִּכוֹרוֹת בְּנוֹ: The Torah requires a father to redeem his son with five silver coins, which are given to a priest when the child is over thirty days old (see Numbers 18:16). A child may also be redeemed with the equivalent in value of five silver coins (*Shevuot* 4b). Even in a case where an animal is not the equivalent in value to five silver coins, if the priest accepts it as redemption of a firstborn, it is valid (*Kiddushin* 8a).

HALAKHA

The Sages instituted the requirement of pulling with regard to bailees – תִּיקְּנוּ מְשִׁיכָה בְּשׁוֹמְרִין: The act of pulling an item, which effects acquisition, is likewise effective in the case of bailees. In other words, the two sides can renege on the deal and the bailee is not yet responsible for the item as long as the bailee has not pulled it or performed some other act of acquisition for the item. *Tosafot* and the Rosh say that the bailee's responsibility begins before he pulls the item, as soon as he agrees to watch it, or when he says to the owner: You may leave it with me, and the owner stops watching it (Rambam *Sefer Kinyan*, *Hilkhot Sekhirut* 2:8; *Shulḥan Arukh*, *Ḥoshen Mishpat* 291:5, 307:2).

הָא תְּנָא לֵיהּ רֵישָׁא! תְּנָא גַּנָּב שֶׁגָּנַב מִבֵּית הַבְּעָלִים, וּתְנָא גַּנָּב שֶׁגָּנַב מִבֵּית שׁוֹמֵר.

Rav Yeimar asked: How can that clause of the mishna refer to an animal that died as the thief was leading it out? The mishna already **taught this** *halakha* **in the first clause.** Ameimar answered: Nevertheless, it is possible that the mishna **taught** this *halakha* concerning **a thief who stole** an animal **from its owner's house, and** then **taught** it again with regard to **a thief who stole** an animal **from a bailee's house.**

אֲמַר לֵיהּ רַב אַשִׁי: לָא תִּדְחֲיֵיהּ, מָה לִּי גַּנָּב שֶׁגָּנַב מִבֵּית שׁוֹמֵר, מָה לִּי גַּנָּב שֶׁגָּנַב מִבֵּית בְּעָלִים!

Rav Ashi said to Ameimar: **Do not reject** Rav Yeimar's argument by means of this alternative interpretation of the mishna. It is not reasonable to assert that the mishna taught this *halakha* twice, as what difference **is it to me** if the **thief stole** it **from the bailee's house** and **what** difference **is it to me** if the **thief stole** it **from the owner's house?** There is no halakhic distinction between these two cases. Therefore, the mishna would not have discussed both of them.

אֶלָּא לָאו שׁוֹמֵר, וּשְׁמַע מִינָּהּ: תִּיקְּנוּ מְשִׁיכָה בְּשׁוֹמְרִין, שְׁמַע מִינָּהּ. אִיתְּמַר נַמִי, אָמַר רַבִּי אֶלְעָזָר: כְּדֶרֶךְ שֶׁתִּיקְּנוּ מְשִׁיכָה בְּלָקוֹחוֹת, כָּךְ תִּיקְּנוּ מְשִׁיכָה בְּשׁוֹמְרִין.

Rather, is it not more reasonable to say that the mishna should be interpreted as meaning that the **bailee** was leading the animal out of the owner's house at the behest of the thief, as Rav Yeimar claimed? **And** therefore, one should **conclude from** the mishna that the Sages **instituted** the requirement of **pulling with regard to bailees.**[H] The Gemara affirms: **Conclude from** the mishna that they did. **It was also stated** explicitly that **Rabbi Elazar says: Just as** the Sages **instituted** the requirement of **pulling with regard to purchasers, so too** they **instituted** the requirement of **pulling with regard to bailees.**

תַּנְיָא נַמִי הָכִי: כְּדֶרֶךְ שֶׁתִּיקְּנוּ מְשִׁיכָה בְּלָקוֹחוֹת, כָּךְ תִּיקְּנוּ מְשִׁיכָה בְּשׁוֹמְרִין; וּכְשֵׁם שֶׁהַקַּרְקַע נִקְנֵית בְּכֶסֶף, בִּשְׁטָר וּבַחֲזָקָה, כָּךְ שְׂכִירוּת נִקְנֵית בְּכֶסֶף, בִּשְׁטָר וּבַחֲזָקָה.

This is also taught in a *baraita*: **Just as** the Sages **instituted** the requirement of **pulling with regard to purchasers, so too** they **instituted** the requirement of **pulling with regard to bailees. And just as land is acquired by** the payment of **money, by** the writing of **a deed** of sale, **or by** the purchaser **taking possession** of the land through working it, **so too a rental** deal is finalized **by** the payment of **money, by** the writing of **a deed** of rent, **or by** the renter **taking possession** of the land. This concludes the *baraita*.

שְׂכִירוּת דְּמַאי? אִילֵימָא

The Gemara asks: When the *baraita* speaks of rental, it is referring to **rental of what** kind of property? **If we say**

Perek **VII**
Daf **79** Amud **b**

NOTES

Is movable property subject to the writing of a deed – מְטַלְטְלֵי בְּנֵי שְׁטָרָא נִינְהוּ: A deed of sale is not one of the ways through which movable property is acquired. The transfer of a deed is entirely ineffectual as a method of acquisition with regard to movable property (see Rashi and Rashba).

שְׂכִירוּת דְּמִטַּלְטְלִין – מִטַּלְטְלֵי בְּנֵי שְׁטָרָא נִינְהוּ? אֲמַר רַב חִסְדָּא: שְׂכִירוּת דְּקַרְקַע.

it is speaking of **the rental of movable property, is movable property** subject to the writing of **a deed?**[N] Rather, **Rav Ḥisda said:** It is referring to **the rental of land.**[H]

אָמַר רַבִּי אֶלְעָזָר: רָאוּהוּ שֶׁהִטְמִין בְּחוֹרָשִׁין וְטָבַח וּמָכַר – מְשַׁלֵּם תַּשְׁלוּמֵי אַרְבָּעָה וַחֲמִשָּׁה. אַמַּאי? הָא לֹא מָשַׁךְ! אָמַר רַב חִסְדָּא: שֶׁהִכִּישָׁהּ בְּמַקֵּל.

§ **Rabbi Elazar says:** If people **saw** a thief **who was hiding in the woods**[H] near a herd of grazing animals, **and** that individual emerged and **slaughtered or sold** one of the animals from the herd, **he pays the fourfold or fivefold payment.** The Gemara asks: **Why** is the thief liable to the fourfold or fivefold payment? **But he did not pull** the animal. Rabbi Elazar is apparently describing a case where the thief emerged from the forest and slaughtered one of the animals without first moving it, and there is no fourfold or fivefold payment unless the thief first steals the animal. **Rav Ḥisda says:** This is referring to a case **where he hit** the animal **with a stick,** causing it to move.

HALAKHA

Rental of land – שְׂכִירוּת דְּקַרְקַע: Just as land is purchased by means of money, through the writing of a deed, or by taking possession, so too a rental agreement is finalized by means of money, through the writing a deed, or by taking possession (Rambam *Sefer Kinyan*, *Hilkhot Mekhira* 1:18; *Shulḥan Arukh*, *Ḥoshen Mishpat* 195:9, 315:1).

If they saw a thief who was hiding in the woods – רָאוּהוּ שֶׁהִטְמִין בְּחוֹרָשִׁין: In a case where a herd is grazing in a forest, if someone strikes one of the animals to move it over to a hidden place between trees, he is liable to pay the double payment of a thief. If he subsequently slaughtered it or sold it, he is liable to pay the fourfold or fivefold payment (Rambam *Sefer Nezikin*, *Hilkhot Geneiva* 2:17; *Tur*, *Ḥoshen Mishpat* 350).

אמרי: וכיון דראוהו, גזלן הוא! כיון דקא מטמרי מינייהו, גנב הוא.

With regard to Rabbi Elazar's statement, the Sages **say: But since** people **saw him** doing all this, **he is a robber,** not a thief, and the fourfold or fivefold payment applies only to thieves. A thief is one who sneaks into a house or other private property; one who commits his act brazenly, in public, is classified as a robber. The Gemara answers: **Since he was hiding from them, he is** considered **a thief,** despite the fact that they saw him.

ואלא גזלן היכי דמי? אמר רבי אבהו: כגון בניהו בן יהוידע, שנאמר: "ויגזל את החנית מיד המצרי ויהרגהו בחניתו".

The Gemara asks: **But if so, what are the circumstances of a robber?**[H] **Rabbi Abbahu said:** Robbers are **like** the case of **Benaiah ben Jehoiada, as it is stated** concerning him: "He slew an Egyptian, a goodly man; and the Egyptian had a spear in his hand; but he went down to him with a staff, **and he robbed the spear out of the Egyptian's hand, and slew him with his own spear**" (II Samuel 23:21).

רבי יוחנן אמר: כגון בעלי שכם, שנאמר: "וישימו לו בעלי שכם מארבים על ראשי ההרים ויגזלו [את] כל אשר יעבר עליהם בדרך".

Rabbi Yoḥanan said: A different example of a robber is a case **like** that of **the men of Shechem, as it is stated: "And the men of Shechem set ambushers for him on the tops of the mountains, and they robbed all that came along that way by them"** (Judges 9:25).

ורבי אבהו מאי טעמא לא אמר מהאי? אמר לך: כיון דמטמרי איטמורי, לא גזלני נינהו. ורבי יוחנן: הא דקא מטמרי, דלא ניחזינהו אינשי וניערקו מינייהו.

The Gemara asks: **And what is the reason** that **Rabbi Abbahu did not say** the example **from this** verse, which discusses the men of Shechem? He could have **said to you: Since** the men of Shechem **were hiding** in ambush, **they are not** considered **robbers**[N] but thieves. And how would **Rabbi Yoḥanan** respond to this claim? **This** fact **that they were hiding** was not because they were hesitant to steal in view of the public. Rather, they acted in this manner **so that** the travelers **should not see them** in advance **and flee from them.**

שאלו תלמידיו את רבן יוחנן בן זכאי: מפני מה החמירה תורה בגנב יותר מגזלן? אמר להן: זה השוה כבוד עבד לכבוד קונו, וזה לא השוה כבוד עבד לכבוד קונו,

§ The Gemara concludes its discussion of theft with several aggadic statements. **His students asked Rabban Yoḥanan ben Zakkai: For what reason was the Torah stricter with a thief than with a robber?** Only a thief is required to pay the double, fourfold, or fivefold payment, not a robber. Rabban Yoḥanan ben Zakkai **said to them** in response: **This one,** the robber, **equated the honor of** the **servant to the honor of his Master, and that one,** the thief, **did not equate the honor of** the **servant to the honor of his Master.** The robber fears neither God nor people, as he is not afraid to rob in public. The thief does not fear God but he does fear other people, which demonstrates that he is more concerned about humans than God.

כביכול, עשה עין של מטה כאילו אינה רואה ואוזן של מטה כאילו אינה שומעת, שנאמר: "הוי המעמיקים מה' לסתר עצה והיה במחשך מעשיהם" וגו', וכתיב: "ויאמרו לא יראה יה ולא יבין אלהי יעקב", וכתיב: "כי [אמרו] עזב ה' את הארץ ואין ה' ראה".

As it were, the thief **establishes the eye below,** i.e., God's eye, **as though it does not see, and the ear below,** i.e., God's ear, **as though it does not hear.** The Gemara cites verses that describe people who imagine that God does not see their actions, **as it is stated: "Woe to them who seek deeply to hide their counsel from the Lord, and their works are in the dark,** and they say: Who sees us, and who knows us?" (Isaiah 29:15). **And it is written: "And they say: The Lord will not see, neither will the God of Jacob give heed"** (Psalms 94:7). **And it is written: "For they say: The Lord has forsaken the land, and the Lord does not see"** (Ezekiel 9:9).

תניא אמר רבי מאיר: משלו כשל משום רבן גמליאל, למה הדבר דומה? לשני בני אדם שהיו בעיר ועשו משתה, אחד זימן את בני העיר ולא זימן את בני המלך, ואחד לא זימן את בני העיר ולא זימן את בני המלך, איזה מהן עונשו מרובה? הוי אומר: זה שזימן את בני העיר ולא זימן את בני המלך.

It is taught in a *baraita* that **Rabbi Meir said:** To illustrate the severity of a thief over a robber, as per Rabban Yoḥanan ben Zakkai's explanation, **they stated a parable in the name of Rabban Gamliel. To what is this matter comparable? To two people who were** living **in the** same **city, and** both of them **prepared a feast. One** of them **invited the people of the city** to his feast **but he did not invite the king's sons. And the other did not invite the people of the city and** also **did not invite the king's sons. Which of them** deserves **a greater punishment? You must say** that it is **this one who invited the people of the city but did not invite the king's sons.** Likewise, both the thief and the robber show disdain for God, but the robber does not display more respect for people.

HALAKHA

What are the circumstances of a robber, etc. – **גזלן היכי דמי וכו׳**: A thief is defined as one who takes another person's possessions stealthily, without his knowledge. Even in a case where the owner is aware that his money is being stolen, if the perpetrator does not act in public but waits in hiding, he is called a thief. A robber is defined as one who takes another's possessions by force. Examples of robbery include grabbing money from another's hand, entering another's property uninvited and taking property from there, taking animals or servants by force and using them for one's own purposes, and entering the field of another and eating its produce (Rambam *Sefer Nezikin*, *Hilkhot Geneiva* 1:3 and *Hilkhot Gezeila VaAveda* 1:3 and *Leḥem Mishne* there; *Shulḥan Arukh*, *Ḥoshen Mishpat* 348:3, 359:7 and *Beur HaGra* there).

NOTES

They are not robbers – **לא גזלני נינהו**: The commentaries wonder how it is possible to assert that the men of Shechem were not robbers, when the verse in Judges (9:25) explicitly states: "And they robbed all that came along" (Ra'avad). Some explain that since they took money by force, an act that resembles robbery externally, the verse refers to this as robbing. Nevertheless, since they lay hidden in ambush, the *halakha* categorizes them as thieves. A similar claim appears elsewhere in the Gemara (57a) with regard to an armed bandit who hides as he lies in wait (*Torat Ḥayyim*).

אָמַר רַבִּי מֵאִיר: בֹּא וּרְאֵה כַּמָּה גָּדוֹל כֹּחַ שֶׁל מְלָאכָה, שׁוֹר שֶׁבִּיטְּלוֹ מִמְּלַאכְתּוֹ – חֲמִשָּׁה, שֶׂה שֶׁלֹּא בִּיטְּלוֹ מִמְּלַאכְתּוֹ – אַרְבָּעָה.

The Gemara discusses why there is a fourfold payment for a sheep but a fivefold payment for an ox. **Rabbi Meir said: Come and see how great the power of labor is.** The theft of **an ox, which** was forced **by** the thief **to cease its labor,** leads to **a fivefold** payment; whereas the theft of **a sheep, which** was **not** forced **by** the thief **to cease its labor,** as a sheep performs no labor, leads to only **a fourfold** payment.

אָמַר רַבָּן יוֹחָנָן בֶּן זַכַּאי: בֹּא וּרְאֵה כַּמָּה גָּדוֹל כְּבוֹד הַבְּרִיּוֹת, שׁוֹר שֶׁהָלַךְ בְּרַגְלָיו – חֲמִשָּׁה, שֶׂה שֶׁהִרְכִּיבוֹ עַל כְּתֵיפוֹ – אַרְבָּעָה.

Rabban Yoḥanan ben Zakkai said: Come and see how great human dignity is. The theft of **an ox, which walked** on its own **legs** as the thief stole it, leads to **a fivefold** payment, whereas the theft of **a sheep, which** the thief **carried on his shoulder** as he walked, thereby causing himself embarrassment, leads to only **a fourfold** payment.

מתני׳ אֵין מְגַדְּלִין בְּהֵמָה דַּקָּה בְּאֶרֶץ יִשְׂרָאֵל, אֲבָל מְגַדְּלִין בְּסוּרְיָא וּבַמִּדְבָּרוֹת שֶׁל אֶרֶץ יִשְׂרָאֵל.

MISHNA One may not raise small domesticated animals,[BH] i.e., sheep and goats, **in** settled areas of **Eretz Yisrael,**[N] as they graze on people's crops. **But one may raise** them **in Syria,** despite the fact that with regard to many other *halakhot* Syria is treated like Eretz Yisrael, **and in the wilderness**[B] **of Eretz Yisrael.**

אֵין מְגַדְּלִין תַּרְנְגוֹלִין בִּירוּשָׁלַיִם – מִפְּנֵי הַקֳּדָשִׁים, וְלֹא כֹּהֲנִים בְּאֶרֶץ יִשְׂרָאֵל מִפְּנֵי הַטֳּהָרוֹת.

One may not raise chickens in Jerusalem,[H] **due to the sacrificial meat** that is common there. There is a concern that chickens will pick up garbage that imparts ritual impurity and bring it into contact with sacrificial meat, thereby rendering it ritually impure. **And priests may not** raise chickens anywhere **in Eretz Yisrael,**[N] **because of the** many foods in a priest's possession that must be kept **ritually pure,** e.g., *teruma*.

אֵין מְגַדְּלִין חֲזִירִין בְּכָל מָקוֹם. לֹא יְגַדֵּל אָדָם אֶת הַכֶּלֶב אֶלָּא אִם כֵּן הָיָה קָשׁוּר בְּשַׁלְשֶׁלֶת. אֵין פּוֹרְסִין נִישׁוּבִים לַיּוֹנִים אֶלָּא אִם כֵּן הָיָה רָחוֹק מִן הַיִּשּׁוּב שְׁלֹשִׁים רִיס.

Furthermore, **one may not raise pigs**[HN] **anywhere,** and **a person may not raise a dog**[H] **unless it is tied with chains. One may spread out traps** [*nishovim*][HL] **for pigeons only if** this was performed **at a distance of** at least **thirty *ris*,** which is 8,000 cubits, **from** any **settled area,** to ensure that privately owned pigeons are not caught in the traps.

גמ׳ תָּנוּ רַבָּנַן: אֵין מְגַדְּלִין בְּהֵמָה דַּקָּה בְּאֶרֶץ יִשְׂרָאֵל, אֲבָל מְגַדְּלִין בְּחוּרָשִׁין שֶׁל אֶרֶץ יִשְׂרָאֵל, בְּסוּרְיָא – אֲפִילּוּ בַּיִּשּׁוּב, וְאֵין צָרִיךְ לוֹמַר בְּחוּצָה לָאָרֶץ.

GEMARA The Sages taught in a *baraita*: **One may not raise small domesticated animals,** i.e., sheep and goats, in settled areas **of Eretz Yisrael. But one may raise** them **in the forests of Eretz Yisrael. In Syria,** it is permitted to do so **even in a settled area. And, needless to say,** it is permitted to do so **outside of Eretz** Yisrael.

BACKGROUND

Small domesticated animals – בְּהֵמָה דַּקָּה: The term: Small domesticated animals, refers to sheep and goats. They cause great environmental damage to forested areas, eating up all the soft vegetation. They can even destroy entire forests, leading to extensive soil depletion. Since the location in question is Eretz Yisrael, where settlement constitutes a mitzva, and there is not an abundance of natural grassland, there is ample reason to prohibit raising these animals there.

Wilderness – מִדְבָּרוֹת: A wilderness [*midbar*], in both biblical and mishnaic Hebrew, does not refer to an entirely desolate region where nothing grows, but to an area that is uninhabited due to sparse rainfall, lack of water supply, or other reasons. A wilderness of this kind has vegetation that is suitable for grazing, especially for sheep and goats. There are several such areas in Eretz Yisrael that are full of greenery during the rainy season and for a short while thereafter, which serve as grazing land. The root of the word *midbar*, which is *dalet*, *beit*, *reish*, can refer to leading animals for grazing.

HALAKHA

One may not raise small domesticated animals, etc. – אֵין מְגַדְּלִין בְּהֵמָה דַּקָּה וכו׳: The Sages prohibited raising small domesticated animals in Eretz Yisrael, even in one's house. This prohibition applies in areas where there are fields and vineyards. In regions where there are only forests and wilderness, it is permitted. In Syria, one may raise small domesticated animals in all locations, despite the fact that with regard to many *halakhot*, Syria is treated like Eretz Yisrael (Rambam *Sefer Nezikin*, *Hilkhot Nizkei Mamon* 5:2; *Shulḥan Arukh*, *Ḥoshen Mishpat* 409:1; see *Pe'at HaShulḥan* 1:47).

One may not raise chickens in Jerusalem – אֵין מְגַדְּלִין תַּרְנְגוֹלִין בִּירוּשָׁלַיִם: One may not raise chickens in Jerusalem, due to the abundance of sacrificial food found there. Likewise, priests may not raise chickens anywhere in Eretz Yisrael, because of the sacred foods they eat that must be kept ritually pure (Rambam *Sefer Avoda*, *Hilkhot Beit HaBeḥira* 7:14).

One may not raise pigs – אֵין מְגַדְּלִין חֲזִירִין: By rabbinic law, it is prohibited to raise pigs anywhere, even in order to use their fat for greasing hides, and all the more so for trade (Rambam *Sefer Nezikin*, *Hilkhot Nizkei Mamon* 5:9; *Shulḥan Arukh*, *Ḥoshen Mishpat* 409:2).

A person may not raise a dog – לֹא יְגַדֵּל אָדָם אֶת הַכֶּלֶב: One may not raise a dog unless it is restrained by a chain, per the Gemara on 83a (Rambam *Sefer Nezikin*, *Hilkhot Nizkei Mamon* 5:9; *Shulḥan Arukh*, *Ḥoshen Mishpat* 409:3).

One may spread out traps…only, etc. – אֵין פּוֹרְסִין נִישׁוּבִים...אֶלָּא וכו׳: By rabbinic law, it is prohibited to trap pigeons in an inhabited area. One may not lay out traps for pigeons unless he distances himself four *mil* from inhabited areas; see 83a (Rambam *Sefer Nezikin*, *Hilkhot Gezeila VaAveda* 6:8; *Tur*, *Ḥoshen Mishpat* 370).

LANGUAGE

Traps [*nishovim*] – נִישׁוּבִים: The source of this word is apparently the Aramaic *nishba*, a net. Here the term refers to nets spread out by trappers, typically to catch birds, but occasionally for larger animals as well.

NOTES

Small domesticated animals in Eretz Yisrael – בְּהֵמָה דַּקָּה בְּאֶרֶץ יִשְׂרָאֵל: Rashi explains that small animals tend to wander off, with or without the shepherd's knowledge, and graze on other people's land, thereby damaging their crops. Although this concern applies outside of Eretz Yisrael, as well, the Sages did not impose their decree there. Rather, they left it up to the injured party, in such cases, to sue the offender for damages. By contrast, in Eretz Yisrael, the Sages wanted to avoid any damage to agricultural fields in order to bolster and enhance the settlement of the land.

Others explain this distinction differently: Because most fields in Eretz Yisrael are owned by Jews, the Sages decreed that extra precautions should be taken to avoid damaging the fields. There is a halakhic difference between these two interpretations: According to the first explanation, which refers to the settlement of Eretz Yisrael, the prohibition applies even in times and places where the land is owned by gentiles (*Kaftor VaFeraḥ*). By contrast, according to the second explanation, the prohibition does not apply unless the land is owned by Jews (see *Tur*).

Priests in Eretz Yisrael – כֹּהֲנִים בְּאֶרֶץ יִשְׂרָאֵל: Priests possess *teruma*, which they must safeguard against ritual contamination. Therefore, it is prohibited for them to raise chickens, which might peck on an item that can impart ritual impurity and thereby bring it into contact with the *teruma*. The mishna applies this prohibition only to priests, although there were also non-priests in Eretz Yisrael who voluntarily followed the strictures of *teruma* and kept all their food in a state of ritual purity. The Sages did not impose their ordinance on these individuals because even if their food did become contaminated, this would not be considered a transgression (Meiri).

One may not raise pigs – אֵין מְגַדְּלִין חֲזִירִין: Rambam's Commentary on the Mishna states that the prohibition applies equally to all non-kosher animals; pigs are mentioned specifically only because this is the most common case. The Mishna (*Shevi'it* 7:3) teaches that it is prohibited to engage in business dealings that involve any non-kosher animal. Other commentaries claim that the rabbinic ordinance against raising pigs is in addition to the general prohibition against business dealings involving non-kosher animals (Meiri). Alternatively, the general prohibition against dealing in non-kosher animals applies only when they are sold for food, not if they are being raised for their pelts or other by-products. In the case of pigs, the Sages prohibited raising them even for purposes unrelated to food (Rabbeinu Tam in *Tosafot* on 82b; see the Jerusalem Talmud).

תניא אידך: אין מגדלין בהמה דקה בארץ ישראל, אבל מגדלין במדבר שביהודה ובמדבר שבכספר עכו. ואף על פי שאמרו אין מגדלין בהמה דקה, אבל מגדלין בהמה גסה, לפי שאין גוזרין גזרה על הצבור אלא אם כן רוב צבור יכולין לעמוד בה;

It is taught in another *baraita*: **One may not raise small domesticated animals in** settled areas of **Eretz Yisrael. But one may raise** them **in the wilderness that is in Judea**[B] **and in the wilderness that is on the border near Akko.**[B] **And even though** the Sages **said that one may not raise small domesticated animals, nevertheless, one may raise large, domesticated animals,** i.e., cattle, **because** the Sages **issue a decree upon the public only**[H] **if a majority of the public is able to abide by it.**

בהמה דקה אפשר להביא מחוצה לארץ, בהמה גסה אי אפשר להביא מחוצה לארץ.

This difference is that it is **possible** for someone **to bring small domesticated animals from outside of Eretz** Yisrael in the event that they are needed. But it is **not possible** for someone **to bring large, domesticated animals from outside of Eretz** Yisrael whenever he needs one, since there is a constant need for them as beasts of burden. Therefore, the Sages did not issue a decree with regard to these types of animals.

ואף על פי שאמרו אין מגדלין בהמה דקה, אבל משהה הוא קודם לרגל שלשים יום, וקודם משתה בנו שלשים יום, ובלבד שלא ישהה את האחרונה שלשים יום;

The *baraita* continues: **And even though they said that one may not raise small domesticated animals, however, one may keep** these animals on his premises for **thirty days before a pilgrimage Festival, and thirty days before the** wedding **feast of one's son,** when many animals are needed for food, **provided that he does not leave the last** one, i.e., the animal which he purchased immediately before the Festival, for **thirty days.**

דסלקא דעתך אמינא, דאי נפק ליה רגל, ומכי זבנה עד השתא אכתי לא מלו ליה תלתין יומין, לא נימא: תלתין משרא שרי ליה לשהויי. אלא כיון דנפק ליה רגל לא מבעי ליה לשהויי.

The Gemara clarifies the final line of the *baraita*: The *baraita* needs to state this ruling as it might **enter your mind to say that if the pilgrimage Festival has passed and thirty days have not yet elapsed from** the time **when he bought** the animal **until now,** he may keep the animal until thirty days have elapsed. To counter this, the *baraita* teaches that **we do not say: It is permitted to keep** it for a total of **thirty days. Rather, once the pilgrimage Festival has passed, he should not keep it** any longer.

BACKGROUND

The wilderness that is in Judea – מִדְבָּר שֶׁבִּיהוּדָה: This refers to the area spreading from the eastern slopes of Jerusalem all the way down to the Dead Sea. This area was used for grazing flocks since the days of King David.

The wilderness that is on the border near Akko – מִדְבָּר שֶׁבִּכְסַפַר עַכּוֹ: There are several variant readings of the name of this place, such as: The wilderness of the village of Amiko. The reference is apparently to the sandy areas of the Zevulun Valley, which are not suited for ordinary agricultural activity but do have extensive vegetative growth during the rainy season.

HALAKHA

The Sages issue a decree upon the public only, etc. – אין גוזרין גזרה על הצבור אלא: The court may not issue a decree for the public unless a majority can abide by it (Rambam *Sefer Shofetim, Hilkhot Mamrim* 2:5 and *Sefer Zemanim, Hilkhot Ta'anit* 1:5).

Perek **VII**
Daf **80** Amud **a**

והטבח לוקח ושוחט, לוקח ושוהה, ובלבד שלא ישהה העגונה שבהן שלשים יום.

The *baraita* continues: **And a butcher may buy**[H] small domesticated animals **and slaughter** them, and again **buy** small domesticated animals **and keep** them for a while, **provided that he does not keep the last one of them** that he bought beyond **thirty days.**

שאלו תלמידיו את רבן גמליאל: מהו לגדל? אמר להן: מותר. והתנן: אין מגדלין!

His students asked Rabban Gamliel: What is the *halakha* **with regard to raising** small domesticated animals in Eretz Yisrael? Rabban Gamliel **said to them: It is permitted.** The Gemara interrupts its citation of the *baraita* to pose a question: How could Rabban Gamliel say this? **But didn't we learn in the mishna: One may not raise** small domesticated animals in Eretz Yisrael?

אלא הכי קא בעו מיניה: מהו לשהות? אמר להן: מותר, ובלבד שלא תצא ותרעה בעדר, אלא קושרה בכרעי המטה.

Rather, the text of the *baraita* must be emended, and **they** actually **raised this dilemma before him: What is the** *halakha* **with regard to keeping** them for a while?[N] The Gemara resumes the quotation of the *baraita*: Rabban Gamliel **said to them:** It is **permitted, provided that** the animal **does not go out and graze among the flock. Rather,** one should **tie it to the legs of the bed** in his house.

HALAKHA

And a butcher may buy, etc. – וְהַטַּבָּח לוֹקֵחַ וכו׳: Although it is prohibited to raise small animals in Eretz Yisrael, it is permitted to keep them for thirty days prior to a Festival or a wedding feast. Similarly, a butcher may buy animals in bulk, keep them, and slaughter them one at a time. The Rambam rules in this manner because he maintains that Rabban Gamliel disagrees with the opinion of the first *tanna*, and the *halakha* is in accordance with the opinion of Rabban Gamliel (*Leḥem Mishne*). In all these cases, one may not allow the animal that is kept to go out and graze; rather, it must be kept indoors so that it does not cause damage to other people's crops (Rambam *Sefer Nezikin, Hilkhot Nizkei Mamon* 5:7; *Tur, Ḥoshen Mishpat* 409).

NOTES

What is the *halakha* with regard to keeping them for a while – מַהוּ לְשַׁהוֹת: Rashi explains that Rabban Gamliel was asked whether one may keep the animals for an extended time even if they are not needed for a pilgrimage festival. In permitting one to keep them under certain circumstances, Rabban Gamliel dissents from the *baraita* cited previously. By contrast, according to *Tosafot*, Rabban Gamliel's opinion does not differ from that expressed in the *baraita*; he permits keeping the animals only within the time frame allotted there, and even then only in his house (*Tosafot*).

תָּנוּ רַבָּנַן: מַעֲשֶׂה בְּחָסִיד אֶחָד שֶׁהָיָה גּוֹנֵחַ מִלִּבּוֹ, וְשָׁאֲלוּ לָרוֹפְאִים, וְאָמְרוּ: אֵין לוֹ תַּקָּנָה עַד שֶׁיִּנַק חָלָב רוֹתֵחַ מִשַּׁחֲרִית לְשַׁחֲרִית; וְהֵבִיאוּ לוֹ עֵז וְקָשְׁרוּ לוֹ בְּכַרְעֵי הַמִּטָּה, וְהָיָה יוֹנֵק מִמֶּנָּה מִשַּׁחֲרִית לְשַׁחֲרִית.

The Sages taught in a *baraita*: There was **an incident involving a certain pious man who was groaning,** i.e., suffering, **due to** a pain **in his heart.**[B] Those caring for the man **asked the physicians** what to do for him, **and they said: There is no other remedy for him but that he should suckle warm milk every morning. And they brought him a she-goat and tied it to the leg of the bed for him, and he would suckle** milk **from it every morning.**

לְיָמִים נִכְנְסוּ חֲבֵירָיו לְבַקְּרוֹ, כֵּיוָן שֶׁרָאוּ אוֹתָהּ הָעֵז קְשׁוּרָה בְּכַרְעֵי הַמִּטָּה חָזְרוּ לַאֲחוֹרֵיהֶם, וְאָמְרוּ: לִסְטִים מְזוּיָּין בְּבֵיתוֹ שֶׁל זֶה, וְאָנוּ נִכְנָסִין אֶצְלוֹ?

Days later, his friends came in to visit him. When they saw that she-goat tied to the legs of the bed, they turned back, saying: There **is an armed bandit in this** man's **house, and we are going in to visit him?** They referred to the goat in this manner because small animals habitually graze on the vegetation of others, thereby stealing their crops.

יָשְׁבוּ וּבָדְקוּ וְלֹא מָצְאוּ בּוֹ אֶלָּא אוֹתוֹ עָוֹן שֶׁל אוֹתָהּ הָעֵז. וְאַף הוּא בִּשְׁעַת מִיתָתוֹ אָמַר: יוֹדֵעַ אֲנִי שֶׁאֵין בִּי עָוֹן אֶלָּא עֲוֹן אוֹתָהּ הָעֵז, שֶׁעָבַרְתִּי עַל דִּבְרֵי חֲבֵרַי.

His friends **sat down and investigated** this pious man's behavior, **and they could not find** any sin attributable **to him except that sin**[N] of keeping **that she-goat** in his house. That man **himself also said at the time of his death: I know** for a fact **that I have no sin** attributable **to me except** the **sin of** keeping **that she-goat** in my house, **as I transgressed the statement of my colleagues,** the Sages.

אָמַר רַבִּי יִשְׁמָעֵאל: מִבַּעֲלֵי בָתִּים שֶׁבַּגָּלִיל הָעֶלְיוֹן הָיוּ בֵּית אַבָּא, וּמִפְּנֵי מָה חָרְבוּ? שֶׁהָיוּ מַרְעִין בְּחוֹרָשִׁין, וְדָנִין דִּינֵי מָמוֹנוֹת בְּיָחִיד. וְאַף עַל פִּי שֶׁהָיוּ לָהֶם חוֹרָשִׁים סָמוּךְ לְבָתֵּיהֶם, שָׂדֶה קְטַנָּה הָיְתָה וּמַעֲבִירִין דֶּרֶךְ עָלֶיהָ.

Rabbi Yishmael said: The members of my **father's family were among the wealthy property holders in the upper Galilee. And for what reason were they destroyed?** It was due to the fact **that they would graze** flocks **in the forests,** and also because they would **judge** cases of **monetary law by means of a single judge.**[N] **And even though there were forests close to their houses,** and therefore there should have been no problem for them to take their animals to graze in these forests, **there was a small,** private **field and they would convey** the animals **on a path through it.**

תָּנוּ רַבָּנַן: רוֹעֶה שֶׁעָשָׂה תְּשׁוּבָה, אֵין מְחַיְּיבִין אוֹתוֹ לִמְכּוֹר מִיָּד, אֶלָּא מוֹכֵר עַל יַד עַל יָד. וְכֵן גֵּר שֶׁנָּפְלוּ לוֹ כְּלָבִים וַחֲזִירִים בִּירוּשָּׁתוֹ, אֵין מְחַיְּיבִין אוֹתוֹ לִמְכּוֹר מִיָּד, אֶלָּא מוֹכֵר עַל יַד עַל יָד.

§ **The Sages taught** in a *baraita*: If there is **a shepherd** of small domesticated animals **who repented,**[NH] the court **does not obligate him to sell** all his animals **immediately.**[N] **Rather, he may sell** them **gradually. And likewise,** in the case of **a convert who came into** possession[H] **of dogs and pigs** (see 83a) as part of **his inheritance,** the court **does not obligate him to sell** all of them **immediately. Rather, he may sell** them **gradually.**

וְכֵן מִי שֶׁנָּדַר לִיקַּח בַּיִת וְלִיקַּח אִשָּׁה בְּאֶרֶץ יִשְׂרָאֵל, אֵין מְחַיְּיבִין אוֹתוֹ לִיקַּח מִיָּד, עַד שֶׁיִּמְצָא אֶת הַהוֹגֶנֶת לוֹ;

And similarly, with regard to **one who vowed to purchase a house**[H] **or to marry a woman in Eretz Yisrael,** the court **does not obligate him to acquire** the first house or marry the first woman he sees **immediately** upon his arrival in Eretz Yisrael. Instead, he may wait **until he finds** the house or wife **appropriate for him.**

וּמַעֲשֶׂה בְּאִשָּׁה אַחַת שֶׁהָיָה בְּנָהּ מֵיצֵר לָהּ, וְקָפְצָה וְנִשְׁבְּעָה: ״כׇּל מִי שֶׁיָּבֹא אֵינִי מַחֲזִירַתּוּ״, וְקָפְצוּ עָלֶיהָ בְּנֵי אָדָם שֶׁאֵינָן מְהוּגָּנִין, וּכְשֶׁבָּא הַדָּבָר אֵצֶל חֲכָמִים, אָמְרוּ: לֹא נִתְכַּוְּונָה זוֹ אֶלָּא לְהָגוּן לָהּ.

And there was an incident involving a certain unmarried **woman who had a son who was distressing her, and she jumped up and took an oath**[H] impulsively: **Any man who comes** to marry me and will discipline my son, **I will not turn him away. And unworthy men jumped** at the opportunity to marry **her. And when the matter came before the Sages, they said:** She need not marry one of these men, as **this** woman's **intention** in her oath was certainly **to** marry **only** a man **who is appropriate for her.**

BACKGROUND

Groaning due to a pain in his heart – גּוֹנֵחַ מִלִּבּוֹ: There are several different explanations of the exact nature of this man's illness. The most likely is that of Rabbeinu Ḥananel, who writes that this individual had a disease of the lungs, perhaps tuberculosis, which caused him to suffer chest pains as well as to cough up sputum and blood. In ancient times, drinking milk was recommended as a treatment or amelioration for diseases of the lung.

NOTES

Except that sin – אֶלָּא אוֹתוֹ עָוֹן: The commentaries explain that although it is permitted to transgress any Torah prohibition in order to save a life, with very few exceptions, the Sages did not approve of the pious man's conduct because he had violated a rabbinic enactment, and rabbinic enactments are in some respects treated even more stringently than Torah prohibitions (see *Eiruvin* 21b); and because keeping small domesticated animals causes a loss to others (Meiri). Others explain that the pious man's illness was not life-threatening, and therefore he should not have transgressed the prohibition against raising small animals (Maharsha). Alternatively, those who accepted upon themselves pious practices would not transgress any prohibitions, even to save their lives (see *Shabbat* 121b).

Cases of monetary law by means of a single judge – דִּינֵי מָמוֹנוֹת בְּיָחִיד: Although the Sages permitted an expert judge to hear cases by himself, this practice is discouraged, as stated in *Avot* (4:7): Do not judge cases alone, as there is only One who judges alone, i.e., God.

A shepherd of small animals who repented – רוֹעֶה שֶׁעָשָׂה תְּשׁוּבָה: The *baraita* is not referring to a shepherd who tends to other people's animals for a salary, as how could he be expected to sell any of the animals in his care? Rather, the *baraita* deals with one who shepherds his own flock. The Sages declared that shepherds are not permitted to give testimony in court because they are almost certainly guilty of theft, as their animals or those in their care graze and cause damage to crops belonging to others. Like any other person whose testimony is inadmissible due to theft or other dishonest practices, a shepherd must repent before he can be acceptable as a witness.

The court does not obligate him to sell all his animals immediately, etc. – אֵין מְחַיְּיבִין אוֹתוֹ לִמְכּוֹר מִיָּד וכו׳: The reason for this leniency is that the Sages wanted to encourage repentance. If harsh compliance measures were mandated, many people would be dissuaded from repenting. Similarly, in cases of vows, if a strict interpretation of the vow were enforced, people would refrain from vowing to perform mitzvot (Rabbeinu Yehonatan of Lunel).

HALAKHA

A shepherd who repented – רוֹעֶה שֶׁעָשָׂה תְּשׁוּבָה: A shepherd of small domesticated animals in Eretz Yisrael who wishes to repent and abandon this practice is not required to sell all his animals at once. Rather, he may sell them off gradually (Rambam *Sefer Nezikin, Hilkhot Nizkei Mamon* 5:10; *Tur, Ḥoshen Mishpat* 409).

A convert who came into possession, etc. – גֵּר שֶׁנָּפְלוּ לוֹ וכו׳: If one received an inheritance of dogs, he is not required to sell them all immediately but may sell them off gradually (Rambam *Sefer Nezikin, Hilkhot Nizkei Mamon* 5:10; *Shulḥan Arukh, Ḥoshen Mishpat* 409:4).

One who vowed to purchase a house, etc. – מִי שֶׁנָּדַר לִיקַּח בַּיִת וכו׳: If one vowed that he would purchase a house in Eretz Yisrael, or that he would marry, or that he would travel with a caravan or go out to sea, and he did not delineate a specific time for the fulfillment of his vow, he is not required to do so immediately. Instead, he may wait until the appropriate circumstances arise to fulfill his vow (Rambam *Sefer Hafla'a, Hilkhot Nedarim* 8:13; *Shulḥan Arukh, Yoreh De'a* 219:1).

And she jumped up and took an oath – וְקָפְצָה וְנִשְׁבְּעָה: There was once an incident involving a woman who vowed that she would marry whoever proposed to her, and unworthy men jumped at the opportunity to do so. The Sages ruled that her intent in her vow was specifically to marry a man appropriate for her (Rambam *Sefer Hafla'a, Hilkhot Nedarim* 8:13).

כְּשֵׁם שֶׁאָמְרוּ אֵין מְגַדְּלִין בְּהֵמָה דַּקָּה, כָּךְ אָמְרוּ אֵין מְגַדְּלִין חַיָּה דַּקָּה; רַבִּי יִשְׁמָעֵאל אוֹמֵר: מְגַדְּלִין כְּלָבִים כּוּפְרִין, וַחֲתוּלִים, וְקוֹפִין, וְחוּלְדוֹת סְנָאִים, מִפְּנֵי שֶׁעֲשׂוּיִים לְנַקֵּר אֶת הַבַּיִת.

The *baraita* continues: **Just as** the Sages **said** that **one may not raise small domesticated animals,** i.e., sheep and goats, **so** too **they said** that **one may not raise small undomesticated animals.**[H] **Rabbi Yishmael says: One may raise village dogs,**[B] **cats, monkeys, and genets,**[B] **because they serve to clean the house** of mice and other vermin.

מַאי חוּלְדוֹת סְנָאִים? אֲמַר רַב יְהוּדָה: שַׁרְצָא חַרְצָא; וְאִיכָּא דְּאָמְרִי: חַרְזָא, דִּקְטִינֵי שָׁקֵיהּ וְרָעֲיָא בֵּינֵי וַורְדִּינֵי. וּמַאי שַׁרְצָא – דְּמִתְּתַאי שָׁקֵיהּ.

The Gemara asks: **What are these genets? Rav Yehuda said:** These are known in Aramaic as ***shartza ḥartza.* And there are those who say** that in Aramaic this animal is called ***ḥarza.*** This creature **has short thighs and it grazes among the thorn bushes. And what** is the reason that they are called ***shartza,*** a term that generally refers to creeping creatures that slither [*shoretz*] rather than walk? It is **because its thighs are** so **short** that it appears to slither instead of walking on legs.

אָמַר רַב יְהוּדָה אָמַר רַב: עָשִׂינוּ עַצְמֵנוּ בְּבָבֶל כְּאֶרֶץ יִשְׂרָאֵל לִבְהֵמָה דַּקָּה. אֲמַר לֵיהּ רַב אַדָּא בַּר אַהֲבָה לְרַב הוּנָא: דִּידָךְ מַאי?

§ **Rav Yehuda says** that **Rav says: We in Babylonia have rendered ourselves**[H] **like** the residents of **Eretz Yisrael**[N] with regard **to** the prohibition of the Sages against raising **small domesticated animals. Rav Adda bar Ahava said to Rav Huna: What of your** sheep and goats? How can you raise these animals in Babylonia?

אֲמַר לֵיהּ: דִּידָן קָא מִינַטְרָא לְהוּ חוּבָה. אֲמַר לֵיהּ: חוּבָה תִּקְבְּרִינְהוּ לִבְנָהּ! כּוּלָּהּ שְׁנֵיהּ דְּרַב אַדָּא בַּר אַהֲבָה לָא אִקַּיַּים זַרְעָא לְרַב הוּנָא מֵחוּבָה. אִיכָּא דְּאָמְרִי, אָמַר רַב הוּנָא אָמַר רַב: עָשִׂינוּ עַצְמֵנוּ בְּבָבֶל כְּאֶרֶץ יִשְׂרָאֵל לִבְהֵמָה דַּקָּה, מִכִּי אֲתָא רַב לְבָבֶל.

Rav Huna **said to him: Ḥova,**[L] my wife, **watches** the animals to ensure that they do not graze on land belonging to others. Rav Adda bar Ahava cursed Rav Huna and **said to him: May Ḥova bury her son!**[N] In **all the years of Rav Adda bar Ahava, no children of Rav Huna from Ḥova survived,** due to this curse. **There are** those **who say** a different version of the above statement: **Rav Huna says** that **Rav says: We in Babylonia rendered ourselves like** those of **Eretz Yisrael** with regard **to** raising **small domesticated animals,** from the time **when Rav came to Babylonia.**[N]

רַב וּשְׁמוּאֵל וְרַב אַסִי אִיקְּלְעוּ לְבֵי שְׁבוּעַ הַבֵּן, וְאָמְרִי לָהּ לְבֵי יֵשׁוּעַ הַבֵּן, רַב לָא עָיֵיל קַמֵּיהּ דִּשְׁמוּאֵל,

§ **Rav and Shmuel and Rav Asi** once **happened to be** present at **a house** where a celebration was being held marking the passage **of a week of** a newborn **son,** i.e., a circumcision. **And some say it was a house** where a celebration was being held marking the **redemption of** a firstborn **son. Rav would not enter before Shmuel,** for reasons the Gemara will explain;

HALAKHA

One may not raise small undomesticated animals – אֵין מְגַדְּלִין חַיָּה דַּקָּה: It is prohibited to raise small wild animals in Eretz Yisrael (Rambam *Sefer Nezikin, Hilkhot Nizkei Mamon* 5:2).

We in Babylonia have rendered ourselves, etc. – עָשִׂינוּ עַצְמֵנוּ בְּבָבֶל וכו׳: The Sages established Babylonia as equivalent to Eretz Yisrael with regard to the prohibition against raising small domesticated animals, because in those days most of the fields and vineyards in Babylonia belonged to Jews (Rambam *Sefer Nezikin, Hilkhot Nizkei Mamon* 5:8; see *Tur, Ḥoshen Mishpat* 409).

LANGUAGE

Ḥova – חוּבָה: The name Ḥuba appears in I Chronicles 7:34, although there it refers to a man. It is likely derived from the root *ḥet, beit, beit,* meaning love. If so, it is comparable to the Modern Hebrew name Ahuva, meaning beloved.

NOTES

We in Babylonia have rendered ourselves like Eretz Yisrael, etc. – עָשִׂינוּ עַצְמֵנוּ בְּבָבֶל כְּאֶרֶץ יִשְׂרָאֵל וכו׳: The reason for this stringency is that there was a large, permanent Jewish settlement in Babylonia. Consequently, it was appropriate to take measures against encroaching on other people's fields there (Rashi). Moreover, in some areas of Babylonia the majority of the fields belonged to Jews (Meiri).

May Ḥova bury her son – חוּבָה תִּקְבְּרִינְהוּ לִבְנָהּ: The basic interpretation of Rav Adda's statement is that he cursed Ḥova for transgressing an enactment of the Sages. Some explain that this was actually a rhetorical question: Does Ḥova bury all her children that she has so much time on her hands to devote to tending the flocks (Rabbeinu Ḥananel)? Alternatively, Rav Adda meant as follows: Isn't Ḥova concerned that she will end up burying her children as a punishment for flouting the Sages' decree (*Tosafot*)?

From when Rav came to Babylonia – מִכִּי אֲתָא רַב לְבָבֶל: Some explain that the situation in Babylonia changed when Rav arrived there and established his great yeshiva, as many Jews from other lands flocked to that academy. As a result, the area soon had an overwhelmingly Jewish population (Rashi). Alternatively, when Rav came, he taught the populace that due to the status of Babylonia as a major Jewish population center, the prohibition against raising small domesticated animals applies there as in Eretz Yisrael (Rashi; Rabbeinu Tam; *Tosafot*).

BACKGROUND

Village [*kufri*] dog – כֶּלֶב כּוּפְרִי: The *kufri* is a breed of dog whose name is derived from the word *kefar,* meaning village. The term refers to a dog raised in villages. The mishna in *Kilayim* (1:6) indicates that this kind of dog is similar to a fox, and it is therefore likely, in accordance with the explanation of the *Arukh* and others, that it was a small dog similar in form to a jackal or a fox. These kinds of dogs were used to hunt mice, cats, and the like, and they may also have served as pets. Rambam's Commentary on the Mishna refers to a breed identified by some scholars today as the saluki, a hound whose ancestors date back thousands of years.

Top: Male saluki
Bottom: Egyptian engraving of a dog with features of a saluki

Genets – חוּלְדוֹת סְנָאִים: From the description of the Gemara, this animal could possibly be identified as the common genet, *Genetta genetta.* This creature, which is biologically similar to the mongoose, is the size of a small cat and has a long tail and very short legs. The basic color of its fur is light brown, but it is extensively spotted with black blotches and rings. This animal usually lives in forested mountains, as its flexile body allows it to climb easily on trees and rocks. The genet feeds on small animals, such as birds and small rodents. Due to its great dexterity in catching mice, it was often kept in houses.

Common genet

שְׁמוּאֵל לָא עָיֵיל קַמֵּיהּ דְּרַב אַסִי, רַב אַסִי לָא עָיֵיל קַמֵּיהּ דְּרַב. אָמְרִי: מַאן נִתְרָח? נִתְרָח שְׁמוּאֵל, וְנֵיתֵי רַב וְרַב אַסִי.

Shmuel would not enter before Rav Asi, as he considered Rav Asi to be greater than he; and **Rav Asi would not enter before Rav,** as Rav was his teacher. **They said: Which** of us **should stay behind** and let the other two come in before him? They decided: **Let Shmuel stay behind, and let Rav and Rav Asi come** inside in that order. Afterward, Shmuel himself would enter.

וְנִתְרָח רַב אוֹ רַב אַסִי! רַב, מִילְּתָא בְּעָלְמָא הוּא דַּעֲבַד לֵיהּ לִשְׁמוּאֵל, מִשּׁוּם הַהוּא מַעֲשֶׂה דְּלָטְיֵיהּ אַדְבְּרֵיהּ רַב עֲלֵיהּ.

The Gemara asks: **And** why didn't they decide to **let Rav or Rav Asi stay behind?** The Gemara explains: It was **a mere gesture that Rav performed for Shmuel** in initially stating that Shmuel should precede him, as Rav did not really feel that Shmuel was superior to him. Rather, **on account of that incident** in **which** he inadvertently **cursed** Shmuel,[N] **Rav took upon himself** to treat Shmuel with deference.

אַדְּהָכִי וְהָכִי אֲתָא שׁוּנָרָא קְטַעֵיהּ לִידָא דְּיָנוֹקָא. נְפַק רַב וְדָרַשׁ: חָתוּל – מוּתָּר לְהוֹרְגוֹ, וְאָסוּר לְקַיְּימוֹ, וְאֵין בּוֹ מִשּׁוּם גָּזֵל, וְאֵין בּוֹ מִשּׁוּם הָשֵׁב אֲבֵידָה לַבְּעָלִים.

In the meantime, while all this was going on, **a cat** [*shunara*][L] **came and severed the hand of the baby. Rav emerged** from the house **and taught:** With regard to **a cat, it is permitted to kill it**[NH] even if it is privately owned; **and it is prohibited to maintain it** in one's possession; **and it is not subject to** the prohibition against **theft** if one takes it from its owner; and, in the case of a lost cat, **it is not subject to** the obligation of **returning a lost item to its owner.**

וְכֵיוָן דְּאָמְרַתְּ "מוּתָּר לְהוֹרְגוֹ", מַאי נִיהוּ תּוּ "אָסוּר לְקַיְּימוֹ"? מַהוּ דְּתֵימָא "מוּתָּר לְהוֹרְגוֹ" – אִיסּוּרָא לֵיכָּא, קָא מַשְׁמַע לַן.

The Gemara asks a question with regard to Rav's statement: **And since you said** that **it is permitted to kill it, what is** the need to state **further** that **it is prohibited to maintain it** in one's possession? If a cat is considered such a dangerous animal that it is permitted to kill it, of course one cannot keep it in his possession. The Gemara answers: **Lest you say** that although Rav ruled that **it is permitted to kill it,** he concedes that **there is no prohibition** in keeping it, Rav therefore **teaches us** that it is also prohibited to keep it in one's possession.

אָמְרִי: וְכֵיוָן דְּאָמְרַתְּ "אֵין בּוֹ מִשּׁוּם גָּזֵל", מַאי נִיהוּ תּוּ "אֵין בּוֹ מִשּׁוּם הָשֵׁב אֲבֵידָה לַבְּעָלִים"? אָמַר רָבִינָא: לְעוֹרוֹ.

The Sages say, further questioning Rav's statement: **And since you said** that **it is not subject to** the prohibition against **theft** if one takes it from its owner, **what is** the need to state **further** that **it is not subject to** the obligation of **returning a lost item to its owner** in the case of a lost cat? If one may actively steal a cat, certainly there is no obligation to return it when found. **Ravina said** in response: Rav was referring **to its hide.**[N]

מֵיתִיבֵי, רַבִּי שִׁמְעוֹן בֶּן אֶלְעָזָר אוֹמֵר: מְגַדְּלִין כְּלָבִים כּוּפְרִין, וַחֲתוּלִין, וְקוֹפִין, וְחוּלְדּוֹת סְנָאִים, מִפְּנֵי שֶׁעֲשׂוּיִין לְנַקֵּר אֶת הַבַּיִת! לָא קַשְׁיָא: הָא בְּאוּכָּמָא, הָא בְּחִיוּוֹרָא.

The Gemara **raises an objection** from a *baraita* against Rav's ruling that it is prohibited to keep a cat. **Rabbi Shimon ben Elazar says: One may raise village dogs, cats, monkeys, and genets, because they serve to clean the house** of mice and other vermin. The Gemara resolves the apparent contradiction: It is **not difficult. This** ruling in the *baraita* is stated **with regard to a black** cat, which is harmless, whereas **that** ruling of Rav is stated **with regard to a white cat,**[B] which is dangerous.

וְהָא מַעֲשֶׂה דְּרַב – אוּכָּמָא הֲוָה! הָתָם אוּכָּמָא בַּר חִיוָּרָא הֲוָה. וְהָא מִבַּעְיָא בָּעֲיָא לֵיהּ רָבִינָא;

The Gemara raises a difficulty against this answer: **But in the incident of Rav it was a black** cat. Since this cat severed the baby's hand, it was obviously a vicious, dangerous animal. The Gemara answers: **There it was a black cat,** but it was **the offspring of a white** one. The offspring of a white cat is dangerous, even if it itself is black. The Gemara further objects: **But didn't Ravina raise this** very issue **as a dilemma?**

דְּבָעֵי רָבִינָא: אוּכָּמָא בַּר חִיוָּרָא, מַהוּ? כִּי קָמִבַּעְיָא לֵיהּ לְרָבִינָא – בְּאוּכָּמָא בַּר חִיוָּרָא בַּר אוּכָּמָא, מַעֲשֶׂה דְּרַב – בְּאוּכָּמָא בַּר חִיוָּרָא בַּר חִיוָּרָא הֲוָה.

As Ravina raised a dilemma: What is the *halakha* with regard to a **black** cat that is **the offspring of a white** one? Is it also dangerous like its parent? The Gemara answers: **When Ravina raised the dilemma,** it was **with regard to a black** cat that is **the offspring of a white** cat that itself is **the offspring of a black** cat. By contrast, in **the incident with Rav** it was **a black** cat that was **the offspring of a white** one, which was itself **the offspring of a white** cat. That animal is definitely dangerous.

NOTES

That incident in which he inadvertently cursed Shmuel – הַהוּא מַעֲשֶׂה דְּלָטְיֵיהּ: This incident is related in *Shabbat* 108a. When Rav arrived in Babylonia, Shmuel prepared a medicinal treatment and gave it to him without his knowledge. Since it caused him severe discomfort, Rav, not realizing that the treatment was meant to heal his stomach ailment, cursed whoever it was who had brought this pain upon him. When Rav found out that it was Shmuel, and that he had acted for his own good, he sought to appease him by honoring him at all times.

It is permitted to kill it – מוּתָּר לְהוֹרְגוֹ: The commentaries raise a contradiction against this ruling from the Gemara in *Sanhedrin* 15b, where Reish Lakish states that one may not kill a privately owned dangerous animal unless it has actually killed a person. *Tosafot* answer that the Gemara in *Sanhedrin* is referring to animals that are restrained by a leash, as this is the normal way of raising dangerous animals. Here, the Gemara is referring to cats that roam free. Another answer suggested by *Tosafot* is that people are accustomed to being careful in the vicinity of known dangerous animals, whereas they are not so cautious around cats. In practice, this renders cats more of a menace to humans. Alternatively, Rav sought to strengthen the force of his edict against raising cats by declaring that it was permitted to kill them (Rabbeinu Yeshaya, cited in *Shita Mekubbetzet*).

Rav was referring to its hide – לְעוֹרוֹ: The commentaries explain that if one finds a dead cat, he may keep its hide for himself. Although the cat obviously no longer poses a danger, he need not return it to its owner (*Tosafot*).

LANGUAGE

Cat [*shunara*] – שׁוּנָרָא: Some linguists maintain that the Aramaic word *shunara* is derived from the Greek σαίνουρος, *sainouros*, meaning one that waves its tail and ingratiates itself.

HALAKHA

With regard to a cat, it is permitted to kill it, etc. – חָתוּל מוּתָּר לְהוֹרְגוֹ וכו׳: It is prohibited to raise a dangerous cat, which is capable of killing or harming an infant. There is no prohibition against taking this cat from its owner by force, nor is there a mitzva to return it to its owner. Whoever finds a lost cat of this kind may keep it, and its hide belongs to the finder (Rambam *Sefer Nezikin, Hilkhot Gezeila VaAveda* 15:17; *Shulḥan Arukh, Ḥoshen Mishpat* 266:4).

BACKGROUND

This is stated with regard to a black cat, that is stated with regard to a white cat – הָא בְּאוּכָּמָא הָא בְּחִיוּוֹרָא: The distinction between various cats is not dependent on the color of their fur per se, but on the different types of cats. In the talmudic period, cats were not yet fully domesticated. The cats referred to in the Talmud were wild cats, which lived in the vicinity of human dwellings. White, or pale, cats were apparently genetically closer to wild cats, perhaps *Felis libyca* or *Felis caracal*. Therefore, Rav declared that these cats should be considered animals of prey for all purposes. Even a black cat born from a white parent, a hybrid, was considered dangerous due the characteristics inherited from its wild ancestors.

(חב״ד בי״ח בח״ן סִימָן) אָמַר רַבִּי אַחָא בַּר פַּפָּא מִשּׁוּם רַבִּי אַבָּא בַּר פַּפָּא מִשּׁוּם רַבִּי אַדָּא בַּר פַּפָּא, וְאָמְרִי לָהּ: אָמַר רַבִּי אַבָּא בַּר פַּפָּא מִשּׁוּם רַבִּי חִיָּיא בַּר פַּפָּא מִשּׁוּם רַבִּי אַחָא בַּר פַּפָּא, וְאָמְרִי לָהּ: אָמַר רַבִּי אַבָּא בַּר פַּפָּא מִשּׁוּם רַבִּי אַחָא בַּר פַּפָּא מִשּׁוּם רַבִּי חֲנִינָא בַּר פַּפָּא.

§ The Gemara provides **a mnemonic** device for the distinguishing letters in the various names of the sons of Rav Pappa in the ensuing list: ***Ḥet beit dalet, beit yod ḥet, beit ḥet nun.*** **Rabbi Aḥa bar Pappa says** the following three statements **in the name of Rabbi Abba bar Pappa,** who said them **in the name of Rabbi Adda bar Pappa. And some say Rabbi Abba bar Pappa says** them **in the name of Rabbi Ḥiyya bar Pappa,** who said them **in the name of Rabbi Aḥa bar Pappa. And some say Rabbi Abba bar Pappa says** them **in the name of Rabbi Aḥa bar Pappa,** who said them **in the name of Rabbi Ḥanina bar Pappa.**[P]

מַתְרִיעִין עַל הַחִיכּוּךְ בְּשַׁבָּת, וְדֶלֶת הַנִּנְעֶלֶת לֹא בִּמְהֵרָה תִּפָּתַח, וְהַלּוֹקֵחַ בַּיִת בְּאֶרֶץ יִשְׂרָאֵל – כּוֹתְבִין עָלָיו אוֹנוֹ אֲפִילּוּ בְּשַׁבָּת.

The three statements are as follows: The court **sounds the alarm**[N] **on Shabbat over** a breakout of **sores;**[H] **and a door that is locked will not be opened quickly; and** with regard to **one who purchases a house in Eretz Yisrael, one writes a bill of sale for** this transaction **even on Shabbat.**

מֵיתִיבֵי: וּשְׁאָר פּוּרְעָנִיּוֹת הַמִּתְרַגְּשׁוֹת וּבָאוֹת עַל הַצִּבּוּר, כְּגוֹן חִיכּוּךְ, חָגָב, זְבוּב, צִירְעָה, וְיַתּוּשׁ, וְשִׁילּוּחַ נְחָשִׁים וְעַקְרַבִּים – לֹא הָיוּ מַתְרִיעִין אֶלָּא צוֹעֲקִים!

The Gemara **raises an objection** from a *baraita*: After explaining how the public engages in prayer when there is a drought, the *baraita* teaches: **And** with regard to **all other types of calamities that break out upon the community,** other than drought, **such as sores,** a plague of **locusts, flies, hornets,**[H] **or mosquitoes,**[B] **or infestations of snakes or scorpions,**[B] the court **would not sound the alarm** on Shabbat, **but** the people would **cry out.** This indicates that it is not proper to sound the alarm on Shabbat for an epidemic of sores.

לָא קַשְׁיָא: כָּאן בְּלַח, כָּאן בְּיָבֵשׁ; דְּאָמַר רַבִּי יְהוֹשֻׁעַ בֶּן לֵוִי: שְׁחִין שֶׁהֵבִיא הַקָּדוֹשׁ בָּרוּךְ הוּא עַל הַמִּצְרִים – לַח מִבַּחוּץ וְיָבֵשׁ מִבִּפְנִים, שֶׁנֶּאֱמַר: ״וַיְהִי שְׁחִין אֲבַעְבֻּעֹת פּוֹרֵחַ בָּאָדָם וּבַבְּהֵמָה״.

The Gemara answers: This is **not difficult. Here** it is referring **to moist** sores; whereas **there** it is referring **to dry** sores,[N] which are more dangerous than moist ones. **As Rabbi Yehoshua ben Levi says: The boils that the Holy One, Blessed be He, brought upon the Egyptians** were **moist on the outside and dry on the inside, as it is stated: "And it became a boil breaking out with oozing upon man and upon beast"** (Exodus 9:10). The phrase "breaking out" is referring to the exterior of the wound. Since the verse specifies that the outside was oozing with secretions, it can be inferred that the inside was dry. This indicates that the sores can be of either type.

PERSONALITIES

Sons of Rav Pappa – בְּנֵי רַב פַּפָּא: Five sons of Rav Pappa are mentioned here as the possible source of this statement. They must be the children of someone other than the *amora* who was called Rav Pappa, as they are given the title Rabbi, which was granted only to those living in Eretz Yisrael; in Rav Pappa's time, there was no ordination of Rabbis in Babylonia.

NOTES

The court sounds the alarm, etc. – מַתְרִיעִין וכו׳: These three *halakhot* are apparently unrelated. Nevertheless, it has been noted that they have a common theme: The importance of taking advantage of an opportunity that presents itself, without delay. Accordingly, it is permitted to sound the alarm on Shabbat in a case of danger as perhaps that moment is a time of grace, when prayer is most efficacious. A door that is locked, as the Gemara later explains, is referring to an opportunity for ordination, which may not present itself again. Finally, with regard to purchasing a home in Eretz Yisrael, if the sale is not finalized at the first opportunity the seller may change his mind (Maharatz Ḥayyut).

Here it is referring to moist sores whereas there it is referring to dry sores – כָּאן בְּלַח כָּאן בְּיָבֵשׁ: There is a disagreement among the early authorities as to which *baraita* is referring to which circumstance. Rashi explains that the dry sores are the more dangerous ones, for which the court would sound the alarm on Shabbat, and the Rambam and Meiri explain it in the opposite manner.

HALAKHA

The court sounds the alarm on Shabbat over a breakout of sores – מַתְרִיעִין עַל הַחִיכּוּךְ בְּשַׁבָּת: If a majority of the community suffers from moist sores, it is appropriate to fast and sound the alarm. If it is an affliction of dry sores, they only cry out in prayer. Later commentaries note that the Rambam, who does not mention Shabbat in this context, apparently did not have the word Shabbat in his text of the Gemara (Rambam *Sefer Zemanim, Hilkhot Ta'anit* 2:13; *Shulḥan Arukh, Oraḥ Ḥayyim* 576:5).

Flies, hornets, etc. – זְבוּב צִירְעָה וכו׳: If there is an infestation of flies, mosquitoes, or other kinds of pests that cause large-scale problems, including snakes and scorpions, the community cries out in prayer, but not they do not fast or sound the alarm. Some commentaries write that if these infestations are deadly, they should fast (Ra'avad; *Tur*), and this is the ruling in the *Shulḥan Arukh* as well (Rambam *Sefer Zemanim, Hilkhot Ta'anit* 2:9; *Shulḥan Arukh, Oraḥ Ḥayyim* 576:7).

BACKGROUND

Flies, hornets, or mosquitoes – זְבוּב צִירְעָה וְיַתּוּשׁ: In general, these insects are not considered to be dangerous to humans and they are prevalent in populated areas. It is puzzling that prayers were needed to avert these common pests. Possibly the fly mentioned here is a reference to the tsetse fly, which spreads sleeping sickness in central Africa. This can lead to coma and even death, and it kills some 250,000 to 300,000 people every year. Similarly, the mosquito that is mentioned may refer to the mosquito of the genus *Anopheles*, which is responsible for 300 million cases of malaria each year, and causes between one and three million deaths a year. As for hornets, they are capable of stinging repeatedly and can kill even people who are not allergic to wasp venom, if they are stung thirty times or more.

Infestations of snakes or scorpions – שִׁילּוּחַ נְחָשִׁים וְעַקְרַבִּים: This refers to a significant increase in the population of snakes or scorpions, which causes them to expand beyond their natural habitat into populated areas. The increase in numbers causes the chances of a person encountering one of these creatures to increase accordingly. In addition, these animals often become more aggressive in these situations. Population increases often occur in years when there is an abundance of prey to feed on; breeding is more intense and the rate of mortality lower. Sometimes crowding alone causes animals to become more violent, and warm weather can also lead to a change in behavior.

״וְדֶלֶת הַנִּנְעֶלֶת לֹא בִּמְהֵרָה תִּפָּתַח״, מַאי הִיא? מָר זוּטְרָא אֲמַר: סְמִיכָה. רַב אַשִׁי אֲמַר: כׇּל הַמְּרִיעִין לוֹ לֹא בִּמְהֵרָה מְטִיבִין לוֹ. רַב אַחָא מִדִּיפְתִּי אֲמַר: לְעוֹלָם אֵין מְטִיבִין לוֹ. וְלָא הִיא, רַב אַחָא מִדִּיפְתִּי מִילְּתָא דְּנַפְשֵׁיהּ הוּא דַּאֲמַר.

The Gemara analyzes the second of the three statements: **And a door that is locked will not be opened quickly.** This is clearly a metaphor, but to **what is it** referring? **Mar Zutra**[P] **said:** It is a metaphor for rabbinic **ordination.**[B] If one meets with resistance in his quest to receive ordination, he should take it as a sign that this opportunity will not soon open up for him again. **Rav Ashi said:** It means that **anyone who is treated poorly will not soon be treated well. Rav Aḥa of Difti said: He will never be treated well.** The Gemara comments: **But that is not so; Rav Aḥa of Difti was saying** only **a matter** that reflected what had occurred **to him.**[N]

״וְהַלּוֹקֵחַ בַּיִת בְּאֶרֶץ יִשְׂרָאֵל – כּוֹתְבִין עָלָיו אוֹנוֹ אֲפִילּוּ בְּשַׁבָּת״. בְּשַׁבָּת סָלְקָא דַּעְתָּךְ?

The Gemara turns its attention to the third statement: **And with** regard to **one who purchases a house in Eretz Yisrael,**[H] **one writes a bill of sale for** this transaction **even on Shabbat.** The Gemara asks: Can it **enter your mind** that one may write this bill of sale **on Shabbat?** Writing on Shabbat is a prohibited labor for which one is liable to receive the death penalty.

אֶלָּא כִּדְאָמַר רָבָא הָתָם: אוֹמֵר לְגוֹי וְעוֹשֶׂה, הָכִי נַמִי – אוֹמֵר לְגוֹי וְעוֹשֶׂה. וְאַף עַל גַּב דַּאֲמִירָה לְגוֹי שְׁבוּת הִיא, מִשּׁוּם יִשּׁוּב אֶרֶץ יִשְׂרָאֵל לֹא גָּזְרוּ בֵּיהּ רַבָּנַן.

The Gemara explains: **Rather,** this is **as Rava said there,** with regard to a similar issue, that one **tells a gentile**[N] to do it, **and he does** so. **Here, too,** it is referring to a situation where he **tells a gentile** to write a bill of sale for the house, **and he does** it. **And even though telling a gentile** to perform an action that is prohibited for a Jew on Shabbat **is** generally a violation of **a rabbinic decree,** as the Sages prohibited telling a gentile to perform prohibited labor on behalf of a Jew on Shabbat, here **the Sages did not** impose this **decree, due to** the mitzva of **settling Eretz Yisrael.**

אָמַר רַבִּי שְׁמוּאֵל בַּר נַחְמָנִי אָמַר רַבִּי יוֹנָתָן: הַלּוֹקֵחַ עִיר בְּאֶרֶץ יִשְׂרָאֵל, כּוֹפִין אוֹתוֹ לִיקַּח לָהּ דֶּרֶךְ מֵאַרְבַּע רוּחוֹתֶיהָ, מִשּׁוּם יִשּׁוּב אֶרֶץ יִשְׂרָאֵל.

Rabbi Shmuel bar Naḥmani says that **Rabbi Yonatan says:** With regard to **one who purchases a city in Eretz Yisrael,**[H] the court **forces him to purchase a path to** the city **from** all **four of its sides, due to** the importance of **settling Eretz Yisrael.**

תָּנוּ רַבָּנַן, עֲשָׂרָה תְּנָאִין הִתְנָה יְהוֹשֻׁעַ:

§ **The Sages taught** in a *baraita*: **Joshua stipulated ten conditions** when he apportioned Eretz Yisrael among the tribes:

PERSONALITIES

Mar Zutra – מָר זוּטְרָא: This Sage is mentioned several times in the Talmud. No halakhic rulings are cited in his name, but stories are recorded about his good deeds and in praise of his humility and his careful treatment of the money and dignity of others. The title *Mar*, meaning Master, which precedes his name, indicates that he was a member of the family of the Exilarch. This is also evident from an account that he was carried on a palanquin when he attended the lecture that was given by the Exilarch or another member of his family on a Festival. Some claim that he was himself the Exilarch.

BACKGROUND

Ordination – סְמִיכָה: In the time of the Sages, the process of ordination ensured that great rabbis received and transmitted the Torah of their teachers and continued the chain begun by Moses, who ordained Joshua and transmitted the leadership to him. This ordination required three Elders except in turbulent periods of Jewish history, when even an individual Sage could ordain his disciples. The Romans, who understood the importance of ordination to the continuity of Jewish tradition, prohibited it on pain of death, and thereafter it became increasingly difficult to find opportunities to ordain disciples. Mar Zutra explains that these doors of opportunity to ordain disciples could easily be locked for significant periods; therefore, the Sages should utilize them to convene and ordain their disciples.

NOTES

A matter that reflected what had occurred to him, etc. – מִילְּתָא דְּנַפְשֵׁיהּ וכו׳: This refers to the following episode: The Sages once decided to appoint Rav Aḥa head of the yeshiva. Then, another Sage arrived before him, rallied the other Sages, and became the head of the yeshiva instead of Rav Aḥa. Rav Aḥa never received a second opportunity (*Bava Batra* 123b; see *Tosafot*).

One tells a gentile, etc. – אוֹמֵר לְגוֹי וכו׳: The early commentaries discuss whether one should conclude from here that Shabbat desecration by means of a gentile is permitted whenever it serves to fulfill a mitzva, or whether settling Eretz Yisrael is considered a more urgent mitzva than others (*Tosafot*). There is also a discussion as to whether Shabbat desecration is permitted by means of a gentile in order to perform a mitzva that applies by rabbinic law. Yet another issue that arises in this context is whether it is permitted to ask a gentile to perform an act that would violate only a rabbinic prohibition even if it were done by a Jew.

HALAKHA

One who purchases a house in Eretz Yisrael – הַלּוֹקֵחַ בַּיִת בְּאֶרֶץ יִשְׂרָאֵל: If one purchases a house from a gentile in Eretz Yisrael, it is permitted for him to instruct a gentile to write the deed of sale even on Shabbat. This is because the prohibition against instructing a gentile to perform a prohibited labor on Shabbat is a rabbinical enactment, and this enactment does not apply with regard to the important mitzva of settling Eretz Yisrael (Rambam *Sefer Zemanim, Hilkhot Shabbat* 6:11; *Shulḥan Arukh, Oraḥ Ḥayyim* 306:11).

One who purchases a city in Eretz Yisrael – הַלּוֹקֵחַ עִיר בְּאֶרֶץ יִשְׂרָאֵל: If one purchases a city in Eretz Yisrael, the court compels him to acquire paths to the city from all four of its sides, to enhance the settlement of Eretz Yisrael (Rambam *Sefer Kinyan, Hilkhot Shekhenim* 6:2).

שֶׁיְּהוּ מַרְעִין בֶּחוֹרָשִׁין, וּמְלַקְּטִין עֵצִים בִּשְׂדוֹתֵיהֶם, וּמְלַקְּטִים עֲשָׂבִים בְּכָל מָקוֹם חוּץ מִתִּלְתָּן, וְקוֹטְמִים נְטִיעוֹת בְּכָל מָקוֹם חוּץ מִגְּרוֹפִיּוֹת שֶׁל זַיִת, וּמַעְיָן הַיּוֹצֵא בַּתְּחִילָּה בְּנֵי הָעִיר מִסְתַּפְּקִין מִמֶּנּוּ, וּמְחַכִּין בְּיַמָּה שֶׁל טְבֶרְיָא וּבִלְבַד שֶׁלֹּא יִפְרוֹס קֶלַע וְיַעֲמִיד אֶת הַסְּפִינָה,

The conditions are **that** people **shall** have the right to **graze** their animals **in forests,**[N] even on private property; **and** that **they** shall have the right to **gather wood from** each other's **fields,** to be used as animal fodder; **and** that **they** shall have the right to **gather** wild **vegetation** for animal fodder in any place **except for** a field of **fenugreek; and** that **they** shall have the right to **pluck off a shoot anywhere** for propagation and planting, **except for olive shoots; and** that **the people of the city** shall have the right to **take supplies** of water from a spring on private property, even **from a spring that emerges for the first time;**[N] **and** that **they** shall have the right to **fish in the Sea of Tiberias,** i.e., the Sea of Galilee, **provided that** the fisherman **does not build an** underwater **fence**[B] to catch fish, thereby **causing an impediment to boats.**[B]

וְנִפְנִין לַאֲחוֹרֵי הַגָּדֵר וַאֲפִילּוּ בְּשָׂדֶה מְלֵיאָה כַּרְכּוֹם, וּמְהַלְּכִים בִּשְׁבִילֵי הָרְשׁוּת עַד שֶׁתֵּרֵד רְבִיעָה שְׁנִיָּה, וּמִסְתַּלְּקִין לְצִידֵּי הַדְּרָכִים מִפְּנֵי יְתֵידוֹת הַדְּרָכִים, וְהַתּוֹעֶה בֵּין הַכְּרָמִים מְפַסֵּיג וְעוֹלֶה מְפַסֵּיג וְיוֹרֵד, וּמֵת מִצְוָה קוֹנֶה מְקוֹמוֹ.

The *baraita* continues the list of Joshua's ten conditions: **And** people shall have the right to **relieve themselves** outdoors **behind a fence, even in a field** that is **full of saffron** [*karkom*];[L] **and they** shall have the right to **walk in permitted paths,** i.e., those paths that cut through a private field, throughout the summer **until the second rainfall,** when crops begin to sprout; **and they** shall have the right to **veer off to the sides of the roads** onto private property **because of hard protrusions** [*yeteidot*][L] **of the road; and one who becomes lost among the vineyards** shall have the right to **cut down branches and enter** an area of the vineyard, or **cut down branches and exit** an area of the vineyard, until he finds his way back to the road; **and** that **a corpse with no one to bury it** [*met mitzva*] **acquires its place** and is buried where it was found.

״שֶׁיְּהוּ מַרְעִין בֶּחוֹרָשִׁין״. אָמַר רַב פָּפָּא: לָא אֲמַרַן אֶלָּא דַּקָּה בְּגַסָּה, אֲבָל דַּקָּה בְּדַקָּה וְגַסָּה בְּגַסָּה – לָא, וְכׇל שֶׁכֵּן גַּסָּה בְּדַקָּה דְּלָא.

The first condition mentioned in the *baraita* is **that** people shall have the right to **graze** their animals **in forests. Rav Pappa said: We said** this **only** with regard to **small** domesticated animals, i.e., sheep or goats, that graze **in** a forest of **large** trees.[H] Small animals grazing in a forest of this kind would not destroy it. **But** in the case of **small** animals grazing **in** a forest with **small** growth, or **large** animals, e.g., oxen, grazing **in** a forest of **large** trees, these practices are **not** permitted, as in either of these scenarios the practice would destroy the forest. **And, all the more so,** it is understood **that large** animals grazing **in** a forest with **small** growth is **not** permitted.

״וּמְלַקְּטִין עֵצִים מִשְּׂדוֹתֵיהֶם״. לָא אֲמַרַן אֶלָּא בְּהִיזְמֵי וְהִיגֵי, אֲבָל בִּשְׁאָר עֵצִים – לָא; וַאֲפִילּוּ בְּהִיזְמֵי וְהִיגֵי – לָא אֲמַרַן אֶלָּא בִּמְחוּבָּרִין, אֲבָל בְּתְלוּשִׁין – לָא;

The Gemara discusses the next condition mentioned in the *baraita*: **And** that **they** shall have the right to **gather wood from** each other's **fields,**[H] to be used as animal fodder. The Gemara comments: **We said** this **only with regard to** twigs of **thorns and shrubs,** as the field's owner does not care about these. **But** with regard to **other** types of **wood,** it is **not** permitted. **And even with regard to** twigs of **thorns**[B] **and shrubs,**[B] **we said** this **only when** they are **attached** to the ground. **But when** they have been **detached** by the owner it is **not** permitted, as he has already claimed them for himself.

LANGUAGE

Saffron [*karkom*] – כַּרְכּוֹם: The earliest source for this word is apparently the Sanskrit *kunkuma*, which was adopted into many other languages with an *n* to *r* shift, leading to forms such as *karkom*, or *crocus* in Latin.

Hard protrusion [*yeteida*] – יְתֵידָה: Some explain that when a well-traversed road dries out in the summertime, it is full of depressions and protrusions, which are called *yeteidot*, literally meaning pegs. Alternatively, actual pegs were inserted in places where the road was wet, so that travelers could step on them and avoid treading in the mud.

HALAKHA

We said this only with regard to small animals in a forest of large trees – לָא אֲמַרַן אֶלָּא דַּקָּה בְּגַסָּה: One of the conditions that Joshua stipulated, upon the entry of the tribes into Eretz Yisrael, is that people may graze their animals in forests. It is permitted to graze only small animals, and only in a forest with large trees (Rambam *Sefer Nezikin, Hilkhot Nizkei Mamon* 5:3; *Tur, Ḥoshen Mishpat* 274).

And they shall have the right to gather wood from each other's fields – וּמְלַקְּטִין עֵצִים מִשְּׂדוֹתֵיהֶם: Joshua stipulated that people shall have the right to gather wood from the fields of others. This *halakha* applies only to inferior kinds of wood, e.g., thorn bushes, and only if they are still moist and attached to the ground. Furthermore, it is permitted to merely cut them off, but not to uproot them (Rambam *Sefer Nezikin, Hilkhot Nizkei Mamon* 5:3; *Tur, Ḥoshen Mishpat* 274).

NOTES

Graze their animals in forests [*ḥorashin*] – מַרְעִין בֶּחוֹרָשִׁין: Most commentaries translate *ḥorashin* as forests. Alternatively, it might refer to plowed fields; one may allow his animals to graze in such fields provided that crops have not yet been sown there (*Shita Mekubbetzet*).

A spring that emerges for the first time – מַעְיָן הַיּוֹצֵא בַּתְּחִילָּה: Some explain that this refers to a spring that flows inside a city. Joshua stipulated that only the residents of that city may draw its water, not people from elsewhere, despite the fact that the source of the spring is outside the city (*Ge'onim*; Rambam). Others maintain that this is an expansion of rights, not a limitation. In other words, anyone may take water from a spring located on private property, provided that they do not cause damage to the property (Rashi; Rabbeinu Yehonatan of Lunel; Meiri). Some commentaries distinguish between a spring that emerges naturally and a water source produced by digging. If the spring was dug out, the water belongs exclusively to the owner (*Tosafot*).

BACKGROUND

Build a fence [*kela*] – יִפְרוֹס קֶלַע: Some explain that a *kela* is not a fence but a kind of fishing net, i.e., a small, round net with a weight on the bottom, which is thrown onto a large fish or a swarm of smaller fish.

Causing an impediment to boats – יַעֲמִיד אֶת הַסְּפִינָה: Some commentaries interpret this phrase differently and explain that it is common for fishermen, especially in the Sea of Galilee, to stop their boats in the water and throw out a large, durable net that surrounds the fish from all sides. Afterward the fishermen will join forces to draw up the net with its fish. This practice can yield a large catch and was therefore prohibited, as the depletion would impinge on the welfare of those living close to the sea, who depended on fishing for their livelihood.

Thorns – הִיזְמֵי: This probably refers to the restharrow, *Ononis antiquorum* L., of the Papilinaceae or legume family. It is a thorny bush about 20–55 cm high, which is commonly found in fields and alongside streams. Its leaves are usually in clusters of three, and its side branches are thorny and tend to spread out.

Spiny restharrow

Shrubs – הִיגֵי: This is apparently the common camel thorn, *Alhagi maurorum*, a thorny plant with plain, rounded leaves. It usually reaches 30 cm high, but there are some that reach a height of 1 m. It can be found in fields and salt flats.

Camel thorn

NOTES

Fenugreek that sprouted, etc. – **תִּלְתָּן שֶׁעָלְתָה וכו׳**: Rashi writes that since the other vegetation is harmful to the fenugreek, the owner will certainly uproot it himself, without the *halakha* mandating that he do so. Others explain that when different kinds of vegetation sprout together of their own accord, there is no prohibition against allowing them to grow mingled together unless the combination is beneficial to the owner of the field. Since wild vegetation is harmful to fenugreek, its removal is not required by *halakha* at all (*Tosafot*).

וַאֲפִילּוּ בִּמְחוּבָּרִין – לָא אֲמַרַן אֶלָּא בְּלַח, אֲבָל בְּיָבֵשִׁים – לָא. וּבִלְבַד שֶׁלֹּא יְשָׁרֵשׁ.

And even when they are **attached we said** this **only when** the twigs are still **moist, but when** they are completely **dry** it is **not** permitted, as the owner requires these for firewood. Moreover, it is permitted only **provided that one does not uproot** the thorn bush or shrub from the ground, but it is prohibited to pull them out with their roots.

״וּמְלַקְּטִין עֲשָׂבִים בְּכׇל מָקוֹם, חוּץ מִשְּׂדֵה תִּלְתָּן״. לְמֵימְרָא דְּתִלְתָּן מַעֲלוּ לַהּ עֲשָׂבִים? וּרְמִינְהִי: תִּלְתָּן שֶׁעָלְתָה עִם מִינֵי עֲשָׂבִים – אֵין מְחַיְּיבִין אוֹתוֹ לַעֲקוֹר!

The Gemara further discusses Joshua's conditions: **And that they** shall have the right to **gather** wild **vegetation**[H] for animal fodder in any place **except for** a field of **fenugreek.**[B] The Gemara asks: Is this **to say that** wild **vegetation is good for fenugreek,** and therefore the owner wants it to be left in his field? The Gemara **raises a contradiction** from a mishna that deals with diverse kinds (*Kilayim* 2:5): With regard to **fenugreek that sprouted**[N] **alongside** various **types of** wild **vegetation,**[H] **one is not required to uproot** the vegetation. Although it is generally prohibited to grow different species of vegetables together in one patch, if the species have a negative impact on each other's growth, it is not prohibited. In this case the wild vegetation may be left alongside the fenugreek because it is harmful to it, and the *halakhot* of diverse kinds do not apply in a case of this kind.

אָמַר רַב יִרְמְיָה: לָא קַשְׁיָא, כָּאן לְזֶרַע, כָּאן לְזִירִין; לְזֶרַע – קָשׁוּ לַהּ עֲשָׂבִים, דְּמַכְחֲשִׁי לַהּ; לְזִירִין – מַעֲלֵי לַהּ, דְּכִי קָיְימִי בֵּינֵי עֲשָׂבִים מִירַכְּבָא.

Rav Yirmeya said: This is **not difficult. Here,** the mishna is referring to a case where the fenugreek was planted **for** its **seeds; there,** the *baraita* that lists Joshua's conditions is referring to fenugreek planted **for** its **stalks.** When it is planted **for** its **seeds,** wild **vegetation is bad for it, as it weakens** the fenugreek and lowers its yield. But when it is planted **for** its **stalks,** wild vegetation is **good for it, as when it is situated among vegetation it climbs on it** and thereby grows to a larger size.

HALAKHA

And they shall have the right to gather wild vegetation – **וּמְלַקְּטִין עֲשָׂבִים**: Another of Joshua's stipulations is that people shall have the right to gather wild vegetation from any field except for a field of fenugreek that was planted for animal consumption. This ruling is in accordance with the Gemara's second answer with regard to the apparent contradiction to the mishna. Some commentaries write that if the fenugreek was planted for its stalks, it is also prohibited (*Tur*), a ruling that takes into account the Gemara's first answer as well (Rambam *Sefer Nezikin, Hilkhot Nizkei Mamon* 5:3; *Tur, Ḥoshen Mishpat* 274).

Fenugreek that sprouted alongside various types of wild vegetation – **תִּלְתָּן שֶׁעָלְתָה עִם מִינֵי עֲשָׂבִים**: In a case where wild vegetation grew in a field and the owner of the field is not interested in keeping it, he is not obligated to uproot it on account of the prohibition of diverse kinds. The same applies to fenugreek sown for human consumption, if wild vegetation sprouted in its midst. How can it be determined if a particular fenugreek field is sown for human consumption? If it is sown in rows, it is for human consumption; if it is sown haphazardly, it is for animal fodder. This *halakha* is in accordance with the explanation of Rav Pappa (Rambam *Sefer Zera'im, Hilkhot Kilayim* 2:7–10; *Shulḥan Arukh, Yoreh De'a* 296:9).

BACKGROUND

Fenugreek – **תִּלְתָּן**: This is Greek hay, or *Trigonella foenum-graecum*, a low plant of less than 1 m tall, of the Fabaceae family. It has hollow, hairy, light green leaves that are clustered in sets of three, and white flowers. It produces thin pods of up to 15 cm, that contain flat seeds of up to around 5 mm. Fenugreek is usually cultivated for its seeds, which can be eaten or used in the preparation of many different spices. Its young branches are also edible as a spice, after cooking. In many countries fenugreek is also used as animal fodder and as fertilizer.

Fenugreek stalks, seeds, and pods

אִיבָּעֵית אֵימָא: כָּאן לְאָדָם, כָּאן לִבְהֵמָה, דְּכֵיוָן דְּלִבְהֵמָה הוּא דְּזַרְעָהּ, עֲשָׂבִים נַמִּי מִיבָּעֵי לָהּ. וּמְנָא יָדְעִינַן? אֲמַר רַב פַּפָּא: שָׁארֵיה מְשַׁארֵי – לְאָדָם, לָא שָׁארֵיה מְשָׁארֵי – לִבְהֵמָה.

If you wish, say instead another answer: Here, the mishna is referring to a case where the fenugreek was planted **for human** consumption; and **there,** the *baraita* is referring to fenugreek planted **for animal** consumption. **Since** the owner **sowed** the fenugreek **for animal** consumption, the wild **vegetation is also required by him,** as this too can be used for animal fodder. **And how can we know** if a particular fenugreek field was planted for human or animal consumption, and thereby know whether the vegetation may be picked and taken? **Rav Pappa said:** If he planted it **in rows** [***mesharei***],[L] it is **for human** consumption; if he did **not** plant **in rows** but planted haphazardly, it is **for animal** consumption.

״וְקוֹטְמִין נְטִיעָה בְּכָל מָקוֹם, חוּץ מִגְּרוֹפִיּוֹת שֶׁל זַיִת״. פֵּירְשׁוּ רַבִּי תַּנְחוּם וְרַבִּי בְּרַיִיס מִשּׁוּם זָקֵן אֶחָד: בַּזַּיִת – כְּבֵיצָה, בַּקָּנִים וּבַגְּפָנִים – מִן הַפְּקָק וּלְמַעְלָה, וּשְׁאָר כָּל הָאִילָנוֹת – מִן אוּבּוֹ שֶׁל אִילָן וְלֹא מִן חוּדּוֹ שֶׁל אִילָן,

The *baraita* teaches: **And** that **they** shall have the right to **pluck off a shoot**[H] **anywhere** for propagation and planting, **except for olive shoots,** as this would cause damage to the olive tree. **Rabbi Tanḥum and Rabbi Berayes explained** this **in the name of a certain elder: With regard to olive** trees, one must distance himself by **the size of an egg**[N] from the trunk before detaching a shoot; in the case **of reeds and grape vines,** he may take shoots only **from the** place of the first **knot and above.**[B] **And** with regard to **all other trees,**[H] shoots may be taken only **from the thick** part **of the tree,**[N] where there are many branches growing, **but not from the thin** part of the tree.

מִן חָדָשׁ שֶׁאֵינוֹ עוֹשֶׂה פֵּירוֹת וְלֹא מִן יָשָׁן שֶׁהוּא עוֹשֶׂה פֵּירוֹת, מִמָּקוֹם שֶׁאֵינוֹ רוֹאֶה אֶת הַחַמָּה

Furthermore, one may take **from a new** branch,[B] **which does not** yet **produce fruit, but not from old** branches, **which do produce fruit;** and one may take **from a place that does not face the sun,**[B]

LANGUAGE

Rows [*mesharei*] – מְשָׁארֵי: *Mesharei* is the Aramaic word for a garden bed in which seeds are sown in a straight line and in a delineated area, so that there is enough space between the plants for one to tend to them as they grow.

HALAKHA

And they may pluck off a shoot – וְקוֹטְמִין נְטִיעָה: Joshua stipulated that one may pluck off shoots for propagation and planting, with the exception of olive shoots, which may be plucked off only up to the size of an egg. Some commentaries maintain that one may cut off a branch only if he leaves part of it, the size of an egg, attached to the trunk (*Tur*). In the case of bamboo and grape vines, only branches above the lowest knot may be plucked off (Rambam *Sefer Nezikin*, *Hilkhot Nizkei Mamon* 5:3; *Tur*, *Ḥoshen Mishpat* 274).

And all other trees – וּשְׁאָר כָּל הָאִילָנוֹת: When one plucks a branch from any tree other than an olive tree and a grapevine, he may take a branch only from the middle of the tree, not from the thin part, and only from the young, soft branches (*Tur*). Furthermore, it is permitted to take only branches that do not yet bear fruit. Finally, one may not take branches that are directly exposed to the sun (Rambam *Sefer Nezikin*, *Hilkhot Nizkei Mamon* 5:3).

NOTES

With regard to olive trees, by the size of an egg – בַּזַּיִת כְּבֵיצָה: Rashi explains that when cutting off a twig, one must leave the size of an egg of the twig attached to the trunk, rather than cutting it all the way down. Others explain that only a small portion of the twig, the size of an egg, may be severed from the tree (Rabbeinu Ḥananel; see Rambam). Alternatively, the Gemara means that one should not cut off part of a branch unless it is fully mature and thick, so that it can continue to grow after being trimmed; the minimum thickness of a mature branch is that of the size of an egg (*Ge'onim*).

The thick part of the tree [*ubbo*] – אוּבּוֹ: There are several variations of this term. Rashi reads *ibbo* and explains that the reference is to young, soft branches. Rashi also cites another reading, *ḥovo*. He explains that this is related to *maḥbo*, a hiding place. In this context it refers to the thick part of the tree, where many branches obscure the trunk.

BACKGROUND

From the place of the first knot and above – מִן הַפְּקָק וּלְמַעְלָה: A knot is a place on a grapevine or other plant where there is a potential for branch growth. When a vine is cut above the knot, new branches will sprout from the knot. However, if a vine is cut beneath the knot, it will no longer sprout new branches from the place where it was cut.

New branch, etc. – חָדָשׁ וכו׳: With regard to many trees, their fruit will not grow on a new branch that has sprouted in the current year, even if it is very large. Consequently, cutting off a new branch does not cause an immediate loss.

That does not face the sun – שֶׁאֵינוֹ רוֹאֶה אֶת הַחַמָּה: In many kinds of trees the main growth occurs on the side facing the sun. Additionally, more fruits grow on that side and they ripen faster. Therefore, one who takes a branch from the sunny side of a tree will cause a loss to the tree's owner.

Perek **VII**
Daf **81** Amud **b**

HALAKHA

A spring that emerges for the first time, etc. – מַעְיָן הַיּוֹצֵא תְּחִילָּה וכו׳: One of Joshua's stipulations was that the inhabitants of a city in which a new spring emerges shall have the right to use its waters, to the exclusion of all other places. This applies even if the source of the spring is outside the city (Rambam *Sefer Nezikin, Hilkhot Nizkei Mamon* 5:3; *Tur, Ḥoshen Mishpat* 274).

And they shall have the right to fish in the Sea of Tiberias – וּמְחַכִּין בְּיַמָּהּ שֶׁל טְבֶרְיָא: Joshua stipulated that all have the right to fish in the Sea of Galilee, provided that they fish only with hooks. One may not build an underwater fence, nor may he stop his boat in the middle of the sea and fish there. These latter activities are permitted only to the tribes in whose portion the Sea of Tiberias is located. This is the Rambam's opinion; others maintain that building a fence is prohibited even for them, so as not to interfere with the passage of boats (*Tur*). All agree that they have the exclusive right to use fishing nets (Rambam *Sefer Nezikin, Hilkhot Nizkei Mamon* 5:3; *Tur, Ḥoshen Mishpat* 274).

And they shall have the right to relieve themselves behind a fence – וְנִפְנִין לַאֲחוֹרֵי הַגָּדֵר: Another stipulation of Joshua is that one shall have the right to relieve himself behind a fence in a field, even if the field is sown with spices, and he may use stones that he finds in the field to clean himself afterward (Rambam *Sefer Nezikin, Hilkhot Nizkei Mamon* 5:3; *Tur, Ḥoshen Mishpat* 274).

And even on Shabbat – וַאֲפִילּוּ בְּשַׁבָּת: A stone that has vegetative growth on it may be taken on Shabbat for the purpose of cleaning after relieving oneself. Although in general the use of a stone is prohibited on Shabbat by rabbinic law as a form of the labor of uprooting vegetation, it is permitted here due to the importance of human dignity (*Shulḥan Arukh, Oraḥ Ḥayyim* 312:3 and *Mishna Berura* there).

BACKGROUND

Traps – מִכְמָרוֹת: Some explain that here the Gemara is referring to fish traps that resemble woven wicker baskets, from which fish are unable to escape. Apparently, this form of fishing is permitted because the fish enter by themselves, and the fisherman does not perform any direct action to facilitate a large catch.

NOTES

In the countryside [*negev*] – בַּנֶּגֶב: Although the term *negev* usually refers to the southern part of Eretz Yisrael, here Rashi explains that it means farmland in the countryside. It is called *negev*, or parched, because it consists of large, open spaces exposed to the sun.

To take a stone out of a wall – לִיטּוֹל הֵימֶנּוּ צְרוֹר: Some explain that this stipulation was necessary because saffron is valuable and requires a sturdy wall to keep out intruders. Nevertheless, it is permitted to compromise the sturdiness of the wall by taking out stones to use for this purpose (Rabbeinu Yehonatan of Lunel). Others explain that the Gemara is referring to a stone lodged in the ground amongst the saffron. Despite the risk that one might uproot some saffron plants while removing the stone, it is permitted to do so (*Shita Mekubbetzet*).

And even on Shabbat – וַאֲפִילּוּ בְּשַׁבָּת: According to those who maintain that this is referring to taking a stone from a wall, the Gemara is saying that performing this action on Shabbat does not constitute the prohibited labor of demolishing a structure. The commentaries add that this is the *halakha* only if the stone is not fixed into the wall with mortar (Ra'avad). According to those who explain that the case involves taking a stone from the ground, the Gemara means that this is permitted despite the fact that stones are generally considered set aside [*muktze*] and may not be handled on Shabbat. In this particular case it is permitted, due to the importance of human dignity (see *Shabbat* 81a–b).

וְלֹא מִמָּקוֹם שֶׁהוּא רוֹאֶה אֶת הַחַמָּה, שֶׁנֶּאֱמַר "וּמִמֶּגֶד תְּבוּאֹת שָׁמֶשׁ".

but not from a place that faces the sun, where the fruits grow copiously, **as it is stated: "And for the precious things of the fruits of the sun"** (Deuteronomy 33:14).

"וּמַעְיָן הַיּוֹצֵא תְּחִילָּה בְּנֵי הָעִיר מִסְתַּפְּקִין מִמֶּנּוּ". אָמַר רַבָּה בַּר רַב הוּנָא: וְנוֹתֵן לוֹ דָּמִים. וְלֵית הִלְכְתָא כְּוָותֵיהּ.

The *baraita* further states: **And the people of the city** shall have the right to **take supplies** of water from a spring on private property, even **from a spring that emerges for the first time.**[H] **Rabba bar Rav Huna says: And** although one may draw water from that spring, **he** must **give money to** reimburse the owner of the property. The Gemara concludes: **But the *halakha* is not in accordance with his** opinion, as the water may be taken without payment.

"וּמְחַכִּין בְּיַמָּהּ שֶׁל טְבֶרְיָא, וּבִלְבַד שֶׁלֹּא יִפְרוֹס קֶלַע וְיַעֲמִיד אֶת הַסְּפִינָה". אֲבָל צָד הוּא בְּרְשָׁתוֹת וּבְמִכְמָרוֹת. תָּנוּ רַבָּנַן: בָּרִאשׁוֹנָה הִתְנוּ שְׁבָטִים זֶה עִם זֶה שֶׁלֹּא יִפְרוֹס קְלִיעָה וְיַעֲמִיד אֶת הַסְּפִינָה, אֲבָל צָד הוּא בְּרְשָׁתוֹת וּבְמִכְמָרוֹת.

The next of Joshua's conditions is: And that **they** shall have the right to **fish in the Sea of Tiberias,**[H] **provided that** the fisherman **does not build an** underwater **fence** to catch fish, thereby **causing an impediment to boats.** The Gemara comments: **But one may fish with nets and with traps. The Sages taught** in a *baraita*: **Initially, the tribes stipulated with each other that one may not build** an underwater **fence** to catch fish, thereby **causing an impediment to boats, but one may fish with nets and with traps.**[B]

תָּנוּ רַבָּנַן: יַמָּהּ שֶׁל טְבֶרְיָא בְּחֶלְקוֹ שֶׁל נַפְתָּלִי הָיְתָה; וְלֹא עוֹד, אֶלָּא שֶׁנָּטַל מְלֹא חֶבֶל חֵרֶם בִּדְרוֹמָהּ, לְקַיֵּים מַה שֶּׁנֶּאֱמַר: "יָם וְדָרוֹם יְרָשָׁה".

The Sages taught in a *baraita*: **The Sea of Tiberias was** located **in the portion of** the tribe of **Naphtali. Moreover,** the tribe of Naphtali **received** in addition a small stretch of land equal to **the full** length of the **rope of** a fish **trap.** This stretch of land was located **to the south** of the sea, where the members of this tribe could spread out their fishing nets, **to fulfill that which is stated:** "And of Naphtali he said: O Naphtali, satisfied with favor, and full with the blessing of the Lord; **possess the sea and the south"** (Deuteronomy 33:23).

תַּנְיָא, רַבִּי שִׁמְעוֹן בֶּן אֶלְעָזָר אוֹמֵר: תְּלוּשִׁין שֶׁבֶּהָרִים – בְּחֶזְקַת כׇּל הַשְּׁבָטִים הֵן עוֹמְדִים, וּמְחוּבָּרִים – בְּחֶזְקַת אוֹתוֹ הַשֵּׁבֶט.

It is taught in a *baraita*: **Rabbi Shimon ben Elazar says: Detached** items **that are** found **in the mountains** at the time of conquest **are** considered to be **in the possession of all the tribes** equally, as spoils of war; **but** that which is **attached,** e.g., trees, **are** considered to be **in the** sole **possession of that tribe** that would receive the land where the tree was found.

וְאֵין לְךָ כׇּל שֵׁבֶט וְשֵׁבֶט מִיִּשְׂרָאֵל שֶׁאֵין לוֹ בָּהָר וּבַשְּׁפֵלָה וּבַנֶּגֶב וּבָעֵמֶק, שֶׁנֶּאֱמַר: "פְּנוּ וּסְעוּ לָכֶם וּבֹאוּ הַר הָאֱמֹרִי וְאֶל כׇּל שְׁכֵנָיו בָּעֲרָבָה בָהָר בַּשְּׁפֵלָה וּבַנֶּגֶב וּבְחוֹף הַיָּם" וגו׳; וְכֵן אַתָּה מוֹצֵא בִּכְנַעֲנִים וּבִפְרִיזִּים וּבָאֱמוֹרִיִּים שֶׁלִּפְנֵיהֶם, שֶׁנֶּאֱמַר: "וְאֶל כׇּל שְׁכֵנָיו", אַלְמָא, שְׁכֵנָיו הָכִי הָווּ.

The *baraita* adds: **And you do not have a single tribe of Israel that did not have** in its portion at least some land **in the mountains, and some in the lowland, and some in the countryside,**[N] **and some in the valley, as it is stated: "Turn and take your journey, and go to the hill-country of the Amorites and to all their neighbors, in the Arabah, in the hill-country, and in the lowland, and in the countryside, and by the seashore"** (Deuteronomy 1:7). **And you find similarly with regard to the Canaanites and Perizzites and Amorites who** inhabited the land **before** the Jews, **as it stated** in the above verse: "The Amorites **and to all their neighbors." Apparently,** the Amorites and **their neighbors** all **had this** variety of types of land in their respective territories.

"וְנִפְנִין לַאֲחוֹרֵי הַגָּדֵר, וַאֲפִילּוּ בְּשָׂדֶה שֶׁהִיא מְלֵאָה כַּרְכּוֹם". אֲמַר רַב אַחָא בַּר יַעֲקֹב: לָא נִצְרְכָה, אֶלָּא לִיטּוֹל הֵימֶנּוּ צְרוֹר. אֲמַר רַב חִסְדָּא: וַאֲפִילּוּ בְּשַׁבָּת. מָר זוּטְרָא חֲסִידָא שָׁקֵיל וּמְהַדַּר, וַאֲמַר לֵיהּ לְשַׁמָּעֵיהּ (לְמָחָר): זִיל שִׁירְקֵיהּ.

§ The Gemara discusses the next of Joshua's conditions: **And** people shall have the right to **relieve themselves** outdoors **behind a fence,**[H] **even in a field** that is **full of saffron. Rav Aḥa bar Ya'akov said:** It goes without saying that one may relieve himself when necessary; this stipulation **is necessary only** to permit the one relieving himself **to take a stone out of** a wall[N] in the field with which to clean himself. **Rav Ḥisda said: And** it is permitted to remove a stone from a wall for this purpose **even on Shabbat.**[HN] **Mar Zutra the Pious would take** a stone in this manner on Shabbat **and replace** it in the wall, **and say to his attendant** after Shabbat: **Go and plaster it over,** so that it would fit securely back in the wall.

״וּמְהַלְּכִין בִּשְׁבִילֵי הָרְשׁוּת עַד שֶׁתֵּרֵד רְבִיעָה שְׁנִיָּה״. אָמַר רַב פַּפָּא: וְהַאי דִּידַן אֲפִילּוּ טַל קָשֵׁי לָהּ.

The *baraita* further states: **And they** shall have the right to **walk in permitted paths,**[H] i.e., those paths that cut through a private field, throughout the summer **until the second rainfall,** when crops begin to sprout. **Rav Pappa said:** And with regard to **these** fields that we have in Babylonia, **even dew** that settled the previous night **is bad for them.**[B] Even after a night of dew, the field is sufficiently moistened that trampling on it will cause damage, and therefore this condition does not apply if there was dew the previous night.

״וּמִסְתַּלְּקִין לְצִידֵּי הַדְּרָכִים מִפְּנֵי יְתֵידוֹת הַדְּרָכִים״. שְׁמוּאֵל וְרַב יְהוּדָה הָווּ שָׁקְלִי וְאָזְלִי בְּאוֹרְחָא, הֲוָה מִסְתַּלֵּק שְׁמוּאֵל לְצִידֵּי הַדְּרָכִים; אֲמַר לֵיהּ רַב יְהוּדָה: תְּנָאִין שֶׁהִתְנָה יְהוֹשֻׁעַ, אֲפִילּוּ בְּבָבֶל? אֲמַר לֵיהּ, שֶׁאֲנִי אוֹמֵר: אֲפִילּוּ בְּחוּצָה לָאָרֶץ.

The next item on the list of conditions is: **And they** shall have the right to **veer off to the sides of the roads**[H] onto private property **because of hard protrusions of the road.** The Gemara relates: **Shmuel and Rav Yehuda,** who lived in Babylonia, **were** once **walking along the road,** and **Shmuel veered off to the sides of the road** onto private property. **Rav Yehuda said to him:** Do the **conditions that Joshua stipulated** apply **even in Babylonia?** Shmuel **said to him:** Indeed so, **as I say** that they apply **even outside of** Eretz Yisrael.[H]

רַבִּי וְרַבִּי חִיָּיא הָווּ שָׁקְלִי וְאָזְלִי בְּאוֹרְחָא, אִסְתַּלְּקוּ לְצִידֵּי הַדְּרָכִים; הֲוָה קָא מַפְסִיעַ וְאָזֵיל רַבִּי יְהוּדָה בֶּן קְנוֹסָא קַמַּיְיהוּ, אֲמַר לֵיהּ רַבִּי לְרַבִּי חִיָּיא: מִי הוּא זֶה שֶׁמַּרְאֶה גְּדוּלָּה בְּפָנֵינוּ?

Rabbi Yehuda HaNasi **and Rabbi Ḥiyya were** once **walking along the road,** and **they veered off to the sides of the road. Rabbi Yehuda ben Kanosa**[P] **was taking broad steps** on the road, to avoid the protrusions without going off to the side of the road, **while walking in front of them. Rabbi** Yehuda HaNasi **said to Rabbi Ḥiyya: Who is this** man **who is showing off** his supposed **greatness in our presence?**[N] By acting more stringently than required by *halakha,* he is displaying insolence.

אֲמַר לֵיהּ רַבִּי חִיָּיא: שֶׁמָּא רַבִּי יְהוּדָה בֶּן קְנוֹסָא תַּלְמִידִי הוּא, וְכׇל מַעֲשָׂיו לְשֵׁם שָׁמַיִם. כִּי מָטוּ לְגַבֵּיהּ, חַזְיֵיהּ, אֲמַר לֵיהּ: אִי לָאו יְהוּדָה בֶּן קְנוֹסָא אַתְּ, גְּזַרְתִּינְהוּ לְשָׁקָךְ בְּגִיזְרָא דְפַרְזְלָא.

Rabbi Ḥiyya said to Rabbi Yehuda HaNasi: **Perhaps it is my student Rabbi Yehuda ben Kanosa. And** if so, **all of his actions are** undertaken **for the sake of Heaven;** he is not acting out of haughtiness. **When they reached him** and Rabbi Yehuda HaNasi **saw him, he said to him: If you were not Yehuda ben Kanosa I would have cut off your legs with iron shears,**[N] i.e., I would have excommunicated you for your impudence.

״הַתּוֹעֶה בֵּין הַכְּרָמִים, מְפַסֵּיג וְיוֹרֵד מְפַסֵּיג וְעוֹלֶה״. תָּנוּ רַבָּנַן: הָרוֹאֶה חֲבֵירוֹ תּוֹעֶה בֵּין הַכְּרָמִים, מְפַסֵּיג וְעוֹלֶה מְפַסֵּיג וְיוֹרֵד עַד שֶׁמַּעֲלֵהוּ לָעִיר אוֹ לַדֶּרֶךְ; וְכֵן הוּא שֶׁתּוֹעֶה בֵּין הַכְּרָמִים, מְפַסֵּיג וְעוֹלֶה מְפַסֵּיג וְיוֹרֵד עַד שֶׁיַּעֲלֶה לָעִיר אוֹ לַדֶּרֶךְ.

The *baraita* further teaches: **And one who becomes lost among the vineyards**[H] shall have the right to **cut down** [*mefaseig*][L] **branches and enter** an area of the vineyard, or **cut down branches and exit** an area of the vineyard, until he finds his way back to the road. **The Sages taught** in a *baraita* that this stipulation extends further: With regard to **one who sees another** person **lost among the vineyards, he may cut down branches and enter** an area of the vineyard, or **cut down branches and exit** an area of the vineyard **until he** reaches him and **brings him** back **up to the city or to the road. And similarly,** if **he** himself is the one **who is lost among the vineyards, he may cut down branches and enter** an area of the vineyard, or **cut down branches and exit** an area of the vineyard **until he comes** back **up to the city or to the road.**

BACKGROUND

Even dew is bad for them – אֲפִילּוּ טַל קָשֵׁי לָהּ: Rav Pappa is referring to the fields of Babylonia. The ground in that country is often damp, due to its flat terrain and the large concentration of water there. With the further dampness of the dew the soil becomes especially wet, and anyone who walked on it would leave significant depressions in the ground, which would interfere with the growth of crops there. The ground in Eretz Yisrael, by contrast, is usually dry, and therefore, in the absence of regular rainfall, walking on it does not leave deep imprints.

PERSONALITIES

Rabbi Yehuda ben Kanosa – רַבִּי יְהוּדָה בֶּן קְנוֹסָא: Also known as Rabbi Yehuda ben Nakosa, Rabbi Yehuda ben Kanosa was a *tanna* from the last generation of *tanna'im*. He was apparently a younger contemporary of Rabbi Yehuda HaNasi, from whom he studied Torah, like many others of that period. He also received and transmitted statements of other Sages from the preceding generation. Rabbi Yehuda ben Nakosa is cited in several places in both the Babylonian Talmud and the Jerusalem Talmud. It is related that he successfully engaged in debates with heretics.

NOTES

Who is this who is showing off his supposed greatness in our presence – מִי הוּא זֶה שֶׁמַּרְאֶה גְּדוּלָּה בְּפָנֵינוּ: The commentaries write that one should not act in an overly stringent manner in the presence of his master. The reason is that this belittles his master who acts less stringently, as it implies that he is less righteous than his disciple (Meiri).

With iron shears – בְּגִיזְרָא דְפַרְזְלָא: Most commentaries explain that this is a figure of speech, referring to excommunication. Since an excommunicated person is not permitted to interact with other people, it is as though his feet have been cut off (*Shita Mekubbetzet*). Alternatively, Rabbi Yehuda HaNasi is saying that he would have presented so many questions and refutations to Rabbi Yehuda ben Kanosa that he would have been unable to stand (*Arukh*). This is similar to the English expression: You have no leg to stand on. Others interpret the phrase literally (see *Arukh*). The commentaries write that the conclusion to be drawn from this incident is that one should not adopt a halakhic stringency in the presence of a person who is superior to oneself in Torah knowledge, when that person does not follow the stringency himself (Meiri).

LANGUAGE

Cut down [*mefaseig*] – מְפַסֵּיג: From the root *peh, samekh, gimmel,* which is related in meaning to the similar root *peh, samekh, kuf,* meaning to open up or to spread apart. In this context, it means that one separates the vine branches that block his way, and in doing so one is likely to break some of them or spoil the arrangement of the vines.

HALAKHA

And they shall have the right to walk on permitted paths, etc. – וּמְהַלְּכִין בִּשְׁבִילֵי הָרְשׁוּת וכו׳: King Solomon instituted an ordinance that it is permitted for travelers to traverse paths in private fields until the second rainfall. In Babylonia, it is prohibited to use such paths after dew has fallen (Rambam *Sefer Nezikin, Hilkhot Nizkei Mamon* 5:4; *Ḥoshen Mishpat* 274).

And they shall have the right to veer off to the sides of the roads – וּמִסְתַּלְּקִין לְצִידֵּי הַדְּרָכִים: Joshua stipulated that when there is mud, or ditches filled with water, in the public thoroughfare, it is permitted for travelers to veer off the road and walk on its sides, despite the fact that this land is private property. Some commentaries maintain that this is permitted even if the sides of the road are sown with crops (Rambam *Sefer Nezikin, Hilkhot Nizkei Mamon* 5:3; *Tur, Ḥoshen Mishpat* 274).

Even outside of Eretz Yisrael – אֲפִילּוּ בְּחוּצָה לָאָרֶץ: These stipulations of Joshua apply in all Jewish settlements, even outside Eretz Yisrael (Rambam *Sefer Nezikin, Hilkhot Nizkei Mamon* 5:5; *Shulḥan Arukh, Ḥoshen Mishpat* 274:1, and in the comment of Rema).

One who becomes lost among the vineyards – הַתּוֹעֶה בֵּין הַכְּרָמִים: One of Joshua's ordinances was that anyone who is lost in a vineyard shall have the right to cut down branches until he finds his way out. The commentaries add that he must reimburse the owner of the vineyard for any loss incurred (Rambam *Sefer Nezikin, Hilkhot Nizkei Mamon* 5:3; *Tur, Ḥoshen Mishpat* 274).

מַאי "וְכֵן"? מַהוּ דְּתֵימָא: חֲבֵירוֹ הוּא דְּיָדַע לְהֵיכָא מְסַלֵּק דְּנִיפְסוֹג, אֲבָל הוּא דְּלָא יָדַע לְהֵיכָא קָא סָלֵיק – לָא נִיפְסוֹג, נְהַדְרֵיהּ נְהֲדַר בֵּי מֵיצְרֵי, קָא מַשְׁמַע לָן.

The Gemara asks a question with regard to this *baraita*: **What** is the point of the clause that begins with: **And similarly?** It is obvious that a lost individual himself has the same right to cut down branches as one who assists him to find his way out. The Gemara answers: That is taught **lest you say** that it is only **another** person who is permitted to cut down branches, **as,** having seen the lost party, **he knows** exactly **where he is going** to rescue the other and help him leave the vineyard, and **that** is why **he may cut down branches; but** with regard to the lost person himself, **who does not know where he is going,** one might have said that **he may not cut down branches** but must **go** all the way **back to the boundary** of the vineyard. The *baraita* therefore **teaches us** that one who is lost may cut down branches in his quest to find his own way to the nearby town or road.

הָא דְּאוֹרַיְיתָא הוּא, דְּתַנְיָא: הֲשָׁבַת גּוּפוֹ מִנַּיִין? תַּלְמוּד לוֹמַר: "וַהֲשֵׁבוֹתוֹ"!

The Gemara asks a further question: Why was it necessary for Joshua to stipulate that one may find his way out in this manner? After all, **this** *halakha* applies **by Torah law.** When one is lost, whoever can assist in helping him find his way must do so by Torah law, **as it is taught** in a *baraita*: There is a mitzva to return lost items to their owner. **From where** is it derived that the requirement applies even to **returning his body,**[H] i.e., helping a lost person find his way? **The verse states: "And you shall restore it** to him" (Deuteronomy 22:2), which can also be translated as: And you shall restore himself to him. If this is required by Torah law, why did Joshua stipulate a condition to this effect?

דְּאוֹרַיְיתָא הוּא דְּקָאֵי בֵּי מֵיצְרֵי, אֲתָא הוּא תַּקֵּין דִּמְפַסֵּיג וְעוֹלֶה מְפַסֵּיג וְיוֹרֵד.

The Gemara answers: **By Torah law** one is required only to walk in a roundabout path **along the boundaries,** without damaging another's vines by cutting off branches. Joshua **came and instituted** the stipulation **that one may** go even further and **cut off branches and ascend** or **cut off branches and descend,** thereby leaving through the most direct route.

"וּמֵת מִצְוָה קָנָה מְקוֹמוֹ". וּרְמִינְהִי: הַמּוֹצֵא מֵת מוּטָּל בְּאִיסְרַטְיָא – מְפַנֵּהוּ לִימִין אִיסְרַטְיָא אוֹ לִשְׂמֹאל אִיסְרַטְיָא, שְׂדֵה בּוּר וּשְׂדֵה נִיר – מְפַנֵּהוּ לִשְׂדֵה בּוּר,

The Gemara addresses the last stipulation in the *baraita*: **And** that **a corpse with no one to bury it** [*met mitzva*] **acquires its place**[H] and is buried where it was found. The Gemara **raises a contradiction** from a *baraita*: **One who finds a corpse laid out on a main street** [*isratya*][L] **evacuates it** for burial either **to the right of the street or to the left of the street,** but it may not be buried under the main street itself. If one can move the corpse either to **a fallow field or** to **a plowed field, he evacuates it to the fallow field.**

שְׂדֵה נִיר וּשְׂדֵה זֶרַע – מְפַנֵּהוּ לִשְׂדֵה נִיר; הָיוּ שְׁתֵּיהֶן בּוּרוֹת, שְׁתֵּיהֶן נִירוֹת, שְׁתֵּיהֶן זְרוּעוֹת – מְפַנֵּהוּ לְמָקוֹם שֶׁיִּרְצֶה!

If the choice is between **a plowed field and a sown field, he evacuates it to the plowed field.** If **both** fields **were fallow,** or if **both** were **plowed,** or if **both were sown, he evacuates it to any side where he wishes** to move it. According to this *baraita*, a *met mitzva* is not necessarily buried where it is found. It may be moved elsewhere.

אֲמַר רַב בֵּיבָי: בַּמּוּטָּל עַל הַמֵּיצַר, מִתּוֹךְ שֶׁנִּיתָּן לְפַנּוֹתוֹ, מְפַנֵּהוּ לְכָל מָקוֹם שֶׁיִּרְצֶה.

Rav Beivai said: The ruling of this *baraita* is stated **with regard to** a corpse **laid out on the pathway.**[N] Were the corpse buried there, it would prohibit passage by priests. **Since permission was** already **granted to evacuate it** from there, **one may evacuate it to any place he wishes.** If, however, the corpse was in a field, it would be prohibited to move it.

אָמְרִי: עֲשָׂרָה? הָנֵי חַד סְרֵי הָוְיָין! מְהַלְּכִין בִּשְׁבִילֵי הָרְשׁוּת שְׁלֹמֹה אֲמָרָהּ;

§ The Gemara returns to the opening statement of the *baraita*, that Joshua stipulated ten conditions. The Gemara **says:** Are there really only **ten? These** conditions enumerated in the *baraita* **are** actually **eleven.** The Gemara answers: The condition that **one may walk in permitted paths** that cut through a private field in the summer was not instituted by Joshua; rather, King **Solomon said it.**

HALAKHA

Returning his body – הֲשָׁבַת גּוּפוֹ: If one sees another in a situation of danger he must rescue him, or hire others to save him. If he neglects to do so he has violated the injunction of the verse (Leviticus 19:16): "Neither shall you stand idly by the blood of your neighbor," as well as the verse (Deuteronomy 22:2): "And you shall restore it to him" (Rambam *Sefer Nezikin, Hilkhot Rotze'aḥ* 1:14; *Shulḥan Arukh, Ḥoshen Mishpat* 426:1 and *Sma* there).

A corpse with no one to bury it acquires its place – מֵת מִצְוָה קָנָה מְקוֹמוֹ: Joshua instituted a stipulation that a corpse found anywhere acquires its place, i.e., it should be buried where it was found, even in a field of saffron. If the corpse is lying on a boundary or in a place where it would impart impurity to the public traversing there, it should be buried on the side of the road. If it was found between a fallow field and a plowed field, it is buried in the fallow field; if it was between a plowed field and a sown field it is buried in the plowed field. If the fields on both sides of the road were similar, one should bury it in the one closer to where the corpse was found. The commentaries note that nowadays, when there is concern that a grave in an open field would be treated with disrespect, it is proper to remove the corpse for burial in a cemetery (Rambam *Sefer Nezikin, Hilkhot Nizkei Mamon* 5:3 and *Sefer Tahara, Hilkhot Tumat Met* 8:7; *Shulḥan Arukh, Yoreh De'a* 364:3 and *Shakh* there).

LANGUAGE

Main street [*isratya*] – אִיסְרַטְיָא: From the Greek στράτα, *strata*, and the Latin strata, meaning street or road.

NOTES

A corpse laid out on the pathway – בַּמּוּטָּל עַל הַמֵּיצַר: Rashi explains that the corpse is found stretched out over the entire width of the road. It is impossible to bury the body exactly where it is found, as this would impart ritual impurity to all those who would travel on that road. Others explain that this phrase means: In the boundaries. In other words, if the corpse is found within the boundaries of a municipal area, it should be brought to a proper place of burial, e.g., a cemetery, or if there is none nearby, to the adjacent fields (Meiri).

כִּדְתַנְיָא: הֲרֵי שֶׁכָּלוּ פֵּירוֹתָיו מִן הַשָּׂדֶה, וְאֵינוֹ מַנִּיחַ בְּנֵי אָדָם לִיכָּנֵס בְּתוֹךְ שָׂדֵהוּ, מָה הַבְּרִיּוֹת אוֹמְרוֹת עָלָיו – מַה הֲנָאָה יֵשׁ לִפְלוֹנִי, וּמָה הַבְּרִיּוֹת מַזִּיקוֹת לוֹ! עָלָיו הַכָּתוּב אוֹמֵר "מִהְיוֹת טוֹב אַל תִּקָּרֵי רַע". וּמִי כְּתִיב "מִהְיוֹת טוֹב אַל תִּקָּרֵי רַע"? אִין, כְּתִיב כִּי הַאי גַּוְונָא: "אַל תִּמְנַע טוֹב מִבְּעָלָיו בִּהְיוֹת לְאֵל יָדְךָ לַעֲשׂוֹת".

As it is taught in a *baraita*: If one's **produce was completely** harvested **from the field, but he does not allow people to enter into his field** to shorten their route, **what do people say about him?** They say: **What benefit does so-and-so have** by denying entry into his field? **And what harm are people causing him** by traversing his field? **Concerning him, the verse says: Do not be called wicked** by refraining **from being good.** The Gemara asks: **Is it really written: Do not be called wicked** by refraining **from being good?** There is no such verse in the Bible. The Gemara answers: **Yes,** an idea **like this** is found in the Bible, albeit in a slightly different form, as **it is written like this: "Withhold not good from him to whom it is due, when it is in the power of your hand to do it"** (Proverbs 3:27).

וְתוּ לֵיכָּא? וְהָא אִיכָּא דְּרַבִּי יְהוּדָה! דְּתַנְיָא, רַבִּי יְהוּדָה אוֹמֵר: בִּשְׁעַת הוֹצָאַת זְבָלִים, אָדָם מוֹצִיא זִבְלוֹ לִרְשׁוּת הָרַבִּים וְצוֹבְרוֹ כׇּל שְׁלֹשִׁים, כְּדֵי שֶׁיְּהֵא נִישּׁוֹף בְּרַגְלֵי אָדָם וּבְרַגְלֵי בְהֵמָה, שֶׁעַל מְנָת כֵּן הִנְחִיל יְהוֹשֻׁעַ לְיִשְׂרָאֵל אֶת הָאָרֶץ!

The Gemara further questions the statement of the *baraita* that Joshua instituted ten stipulations: **And is there nothing more** that Joshua instituted? **But there is** also the stipulation mentioned **by Rabbi Yehuda. As it is taught** in a *baraita*: **Rabbi Yehuda says: During the time of manure removal, a person may remove his manure**[H] from his property **into the public thoroughfare and pile it up** there for **a full thirty** days, **so that it should be trodden by the feet of people and by the feet of animals,** thereby improving its quality, as it was **on this condition** that **Joshua apportioned Eretz** Yisrael **to the Jewish people.**

וְהָא אִיכָּא דְּרַבִּי יִשְׁמָעֵאל בְּנוֹ שֶׁל רַבִּי יוֹחָנָן בֶּן בְּרוֹקָה! דְּתַנְיָא, רַבִּי יִשְׁמָעֵאל בְּנוֹ שֶׁל רַבִּי יוֹחָנָן בֶּן בְּרוֹקָה אוֹמֵר: תְּנַאי בֵּית דִּין הוּא, שֶׁיְּהֵא זֶה יוֹרֵד לְתוֹךְ שְׂדֵה חֲבֵירוֹ וְקוֹצֵץ שׁוֹכוֹ שֶׁל חֲבֵירוֹ לְהַצִּיל נְחִיל שֶׁלּוֹ, וְנוֹתֵן לוֹ דְּמֵי שׁוֹכוֹ שֶׁל חֲבֵירוֹ;

The Gemara continues this line of questioning: **And** furthermore, **there are** the stipulations mentioned **by Rabbi Yishmael, son of Rabbi Yoḥanan ben Beroka, as it is taught** in a *baraita*: **Rabbi Yishmael, son of Rabbi Yoḥanan ben Beroka, says: It is a stipulation of the court,** i.e., it is an automatic right even when not explicitly granted, **that this** owner of a bee colony **may enter the field of another and chop off**[H] **the other's branch** in order **to save his bee colony, and** afterward **he gives him the value of the other's** severed **branch.** That is, if a beekeeper finds that one of his colonies has relocated to a tree in a neighboring field, he may bring it back to his own property together with the branch, provided that he later reimburses the owner of the tree.

וּתְנַאי בֵּית דִּין הוּא, שֶׁיְּהֵא זֶה שׁוֹפֵךְ יֵינוֹ וּמַצִּיל דּוּבְשָׁנוֹ שֶׁל חֲבֵירוֹ, וְנוֹטֵל דְּמֵי יֵינוֹ מִתּוֹךְ דּוּבְשָׁנוֹ שֶׁל חֲבֵירוֹ; וּתְנַאי בֵּית דִּין הוּא, שֶׁיְּהֵא זֶה מְפָרֵק אֶת עֵצָיו וְטוֹעֵן פִּשְׁתָּנוֹ שֶׁל חֲבֵירוֹ, וְנוֹטֵל דְּמֵי עֵצָיו מִתּוֹךְ פִּשְׁתָּנוֹ שֶׁל חֲבֵירוֹ, שֶׁעַל מְנָת כֵּן הִנְחִיל יְהוֹשֻׁעַ לְיִשְׂרָאֵל אֶת הָאָרֶץ!

The *baraita* continues: **And it is** also **a stipulation of the court that this** bearer of wine **pours out his wine**[H] from his barrel **and** uses the barrel **to save another's** spilling **honey,** which is more valuable than the wine, **and** then **he takes the value of his wine from the** saved **honey of the other,** as reimbursement. **And it is** likewise **a stipulation of the court that this** owner of wood **unloads his wood** from his donkey **and loads another's flax,** which is more valuable than wood, if the load of flax is stranded on the road due to a mishap, **and** later **he takes the value of his wood from the** saved **flax of that other** individual. Once again, the reason is that it was **on this condition** that **Joshua apportioned Eretz** Yisrael **to the Jewish people.**

בִּיחִידָאֵי לָא קָאָמְרִינַן.

The Gemara explains why the stipulations mentioned by Rabbi Yehuda and Rabbi Yishmael are omitted by the earlier *baraita*: In the *baraita*, **we are not speaking of individual** opinions, but only of those that are accepted by all the Sages.

HALAKHA

A person may remove his manure – אָדָם מוֹצִיא זִבְלוֹ: During the time of year when people put out their manure into the public thoroughfare, it is permitted to do so, for it to be trampled by the people and animals that walk there. Nevertheless, one is liable for any damage caused by his manure. If another person takes the manure from there for himself, it is considered theft (Rambam *Sefer Nezikin, Hilkhot Nizkei Mamon* 13:15 and *Hilkhot Gezeila VaAveda* 6:5; *Shulḥan Arukh, Ḥoshen Mishpat* 414:2).

One may enter the field of another and chop off, etc. – יוֹרֵד לְתוֹךְ שְׂדֵה חֲבֵירוֹ וְקוֹצֵץ וכו׳: In a case of bees from a bee colony that set up a hive on the property of another, some say that it is permitted for the owner of the bees to cut off the branch upon which the beehive is situated and reimburse the other for the loss involved, as the *halakha* is in accordance with the opinion of Rabbi Yishmael, son of Rabbi Yoḥanan ben Beroka (*Tur*, citing Rosh). Others disagree and maintain that although it is permitted for him to enter the neighboring field to save his bee colony, it is not permitted for him to chop off the branch upon which the hive is located (Rambam *Sefer Nezikin, Hilkhot Gezeila VaAveda* 6:14; *Shulḥan Arukh, Ḥoshen Mishpat* 274:1, and in the comment of Rema).

Pours out his wine, etc. – שׁוֹפֵךְ יֵינוֹ וכו׳: If one was carrying a barrel of wine and encountered a leaking barrel of honey, and he spilled out his wine to use the barrel to save the honey, the owner of the wine is not reimbursed for his loss, as he may claim only a worker's wage for the actions that he performed. If the owner of the wine stipulated beforehand with the owner of the honey, or in the presence of a court, that he wishes to be paid for his wine, he is entitled to reimbursement. If the owner of the honey agrees to reimburse the owner of the wine, the latter is obligated to spill out his wine to save the honey. The *halakha* is the same in any similar case, e.g., a load of wood and flax. This *halakha* is in accordance with the opinion of Rabbi Yishmael, son of Rabbi Yoḥanan ben Beroka (*Tur*, citing Rosh). Others (Rif; Ramah) disagree with this ruling (Rambam *Sefer Nezikin, Hilkhot Gezeila VaAveda* 12:6; *Tur, Ḥoshen Mishpat* 274; *Shulḥan Arukh, Ḥoshen Mishpat* 264:5).

HALAKHA

A tree that leans into the field of another – **אִילָן הַנּוֹטֶה לְתוֹךְ שְׂדֵה חֲבֵירוֹ**: With regard to one who has a tree that is situated close to the boundary of a neighbor's field or that leans over into his field, although he should have distanced the tree to prevent these situations, nevertheless he brings the first fruits of that tree to the Temple and recites the declaration, as it is on this condition that Joshua apportioned Eretz Yisrael to the tribes (Rambam *Sefer Zera'im, Hilkhot Bikkurim* 2:11).

That they read on Shabbat in the afternoon, etc. – **שֶׁקּוֹרִין בְּמִנְחָה בְּשַׁבָּת וכו׳**: Moses instituted that the Torah be publicly read on Shabbat mornings, Mondays, and Thursdays. Ezra further instituted that it be read on Shabbat in the afternoon as well. He also instituted that on this occasion and on Mondays and Thursdays three people be called to read, and a total of at least ten verses be read (Rambam *Sefer Ahava, Hilkhot Tefilla* 12:1).

And judge every Monday and Thursday – **וְדָנִין בְּשֵׁנִי וּבַחֲמִישִׁי**: Ezra instituted an ordinance that the courts convene on Mondays and Thursdays, as on these days people from the countryside would come to town to hear the reading of the Torah. Nowadays there is no need for the court to convene specifically on these days (*Tur, Ḥoshen Mishpat* 5).

One does laundry on Thursday – **מְכַבְּסִים בַּחֲמִישִׁי בְּשַׁבָּת**: Ezra instituted that laundry be done on Thursday, in honor of Shabbat. Accordingly, it is improper to wear the same shirt, without laundering, on successive *Shabbatot* (Rambam *Sefer Zemanim, Hilkhot Shabbat* 30:3; *Shulḥan Arukh, Oraḥ Ḥayyim* 242:1 and *Mishna Berura* there).

PERSONALITIES

Rav Geviha from Bei Katil – **רַב גְּבִיהָה מִבֵּי כָּתִיל**: Rav Geviha was from the fifth and sixth generations of Babylonian *amora'im*. Apparently he lived a long life, as he studied from the great *amora* Rava, and in the following generation he was a respected scholar who often spoke at important public events. Rav Geviha was a colleague of Rav Ashi, whom he outlived and with whom he would often debate halakhic issues. In the *Iggeret of Rav Sherira Gaon* it is related that Rav Geviha served as head of the yeshiva in Pumbedita from the year 429 CE until his death in 434 CE.

Rabbi Berayes – **רַבִּי בְּרָיֵיס**: Rabbi Berayes was an *amora* of Eretz Yisrael, apparently from the third generation of *amora'im*. Rabbi Berayes cites several Sages who preceded him, including some late *tanna'im*. There are several different versions of his name: Berayes, Beraim, Birayim. It is likely that his is a Greek name, perhaps related to the Greek word **Βορέας**, *boreas*, meaning a north wind.

וְהָא כִּי אֲתָא רַבִּי אָבִין אָמַר רַבִּי יוֹחָנָן: אֶחָד אִילָן הַנּוֹטֶה לְתוֹךְ שְׂדֵה חֲבֵירוֹ, וְאֶחָד אִילָן הַסָּמוּךְ לְמֵצַר – מֵבִיא וְקוֹרֵא, שֶׁעַל מְנָת כֵּן הִנְחִיל יְהוֹשֻׁעַ לְיִשְׂרָאֵל אֶת הָאָרֶץ!

The Gemara further questions the number of Joshua's stipulations: **But when Rabbi Avin came** from Eretz Yisrael he said that **Rabbi Yoḥanan says:** With regard to **both a tree that leans**[N] **into the field of another**[H] **and a tree that is close to a boundary** with another field, the owner of the tree **brings** the first fruits of the tree **and recites** the accompanying declaration, as described in Deuteronomy 26:5–10, **as it was on this condition that Joshua apportioned Eretz Yisrael to the Jewish people.** This is an additional stipulation by Joshua, which means that there are more than ten.

אֶלָּא מַאן תְּנָא עֲשָׂרָה תְּנָאִין שֶׁהִתְנָה יְהוֹשֻׁעַ? רַבִּי יְהוֹשֻׁעַ בֶּן לֵוִי הוּא. רַב גְּבִיהָה מִבֵּי כָּתִיל מַתְנֵי לָהּ בְּהֶדְיָא: רַבִּי תַּנְחוּם וְרַבִּי בְּרָיֵיס אָמְרִי מִשּׁוּם זָקֵן אֶחָד, וּמַנּוּ? רַבִּי יְהוֹשֻׁעַ בֶּן לֵוִי: עֲשָׂרָה תְּנָאִין הִתְנָה יְהוֹשֻׁעַ.

The Gemara answers: **Rather, who** is the one who **taught** the *baraita* that deals with the **ten conditions that Joshua stipulated? It is Rabbi Yehoshua ben Levi**, an *amora*. Therefore, Rabbi Yoḥanan, another *amora*, can disagree with it. **Rav Geviha from Bei Katil**[P] **teaches** this **explicitly** in his version of the *baraita*: **Rabbi Tanḥum and Rabbi Berayes**[P] **say in the name of a certain elder, and who is that** elder? It **is Rabbi Yehoshua ben Levi: Joshua stipulated ten conditions.**

עֲשָׂרָה תַּקָּנוֹת תִּיקֵּן עֶזְרָא: שֶׁקּוֹרִין בְּמִנְחָה בְּשַׁבָּת, וְקוֹרִין בְּשֵׁנִי וּבַחֲמִישִׁי, וְדָנִין בְּשֵׁנִי וּבַחֲמִישִׁי, וּמְכַבְּסִים בַּחֲמִישִׁי בְּשַׁבָּת, וְאוֹכְלִין שׁוּם בְּעֶרֶב שַׁבָּת, וְשֶׁתְּהֵא אִשָּׁה מַשְׁכֶּמֶת וְאוֹפָה, וְשֶׁתְּהֵא אִשָּׁה חוֹגֶרֶת בְּסִינָר, וְשֶׁתְּהֵא אִשָּׁה חוֹפֶפֶת וְטוֹבֶלֶת, וְשֶׁיְּהוּ רוֹכְלִין מַחֲזִירִין בָּעֲיָירוֹת, וְתִיקֵּן טְבִילָה לְבַעֲלֵי קְרָיִין.

§ The Sages taught that **Ezra** the Scribe **instituted ten ordinances:** He instituted **that** communities **read** the Torah **on Shabbat in the afternoon;**[H] **and** they also **read** the Torah **on** every **Monday and Thursday;** and the courts convene and **judge** every **Monday and Thursday;**[HN] **and one does laundry on Thursday;**[HN] **and one eats garlic on Shabbat eve. And** Ezra further instituted **that a woman should rise early and bake**[N] bread on those days when she wants to bake; **and that a woman should don a breechcloth; and that a woman should** first **comb** her hair **and** only then **immerse** in a ritual bath after being ritually impure; **and that peddlers** of cosmetics and perfumes **should travel around through** all **the towns. And** Ezra further **instituted** the requirement of **immersion for those who experienced a seminal emission.**

״שֶׁיְּהוּ קוֹרִאין בְּמִנְחָה בְּשַׁבָּת״ – מִשּׁוּם יוֹשְׁבֵי קְרָנוֹת.

The Gemara analyzes these ordinances, the first of which is **that** communities **shall read** the Torah **on Shabbat afternoon.** This Gemara explains that this ordinance was instituted **due to those who sit** idly on street **corners,**[N] who do not attend the synagogue during the week.

NOTES

A tree that leans, etc. – **אִילָן הַנּוֹטֶה וכו׳**: The verse states: "The choicest first fruits of your land you shall bring into the house of the Lord your God" (Exodus 23:19), which indicates that the fruits must have grown completely in "your land" (*Bikkurim* 1:1). In the cases mentioned here, some branches of the tree are located above the land of another, or the tree itself is planted too close to the land of a neighbor, which is prohibited by rabbinic law because the tree's roots might harm the fertility of the neighbor's land. Nevertheless, the owner of the tree brings its first fruits to the Temple, because Joshua stipulated that people not be particular with each other in these matters.

And judge every Monday and Thursday – **וְדָנִין בְּשֵׁנִי וּבַחֲמִישִׁי**: Elsewhere in the Talmud (*Ketubot* 3a) it is stated that before Ezra's time the courts used to convene every weekday. If so, how was Ezra's ordinance an improvement on that situation (*Tosafot*)? Rabbeinu Tam explains that prior to Ezra's ordinance the courts would sit in session every day only in the large cities, whereas Ezra instituted that on Mondays and Thursdays they convene even in small towns. Alternatively, before Ezra's time the courts would meet haphazardly, whenever it was necessary to hear a case. Ezra instituted an ordinance that there be set times when the courts would convene (Rashba).

One does laundry on Thursday – **מְכַבְּסִים בַּחֲמִישִׁי בְּשַׁבָּת**: This day was chosen so that people would be free on Friday to devote their time to Shabbat preparations (Rabbeinu Yehonatan of Lunel; Meiri).

Rise early and bake – **מַשְׁכֶּמֶת וְאוֹפָה**: Rashi explains that this is referring to those days when she normally bakes. Alternatively, the reference is specifically to Friday mornings; a woman should bake bread on Friday morning for the whole week, so that poor people, who would collect bread from people's houses, would have enough to eat all week (Rabbeinu Yehonatan of Lunel). This interpretation is stated explicitly in the Jerusalem Talmud.

Due to those who sit on street corners – **מִשּׁוּם יוֹשְׁבֵי קְרָנוֹת**: Rashi explains that this refers to store owners who are unable to attend the synagogue during the week, due to their busy work schedule. Since they do not hear the Torah readings on Monday and Thursday, Ezra instituted that there be a reading on Shabbat afternoon, when even these individuals would be able to come and hear it. Others explain that the reference here is to unlearned idlers, who would congregate on street corners on Shabbat afternoon and engage in idle socializing. Ezra instituted the extra Torah reading so that these people would go to the synagogue instead and hear the words of the Torah (*Shita Mekubbetzet*; Meiri).

״וְשֶׁיְּהוּ קוֹרְאִין בְּשֵׁנִי וּבַחֲמִישִׁי״ – עֶזְרָא תִּיקֵּן? וְהָא מֵעִיקָּרָא הֲוָה מִיתַּקְנָא! דְּתַנְיָא: ״וַיֵּלְכוּ שְׁלֹשֶׁת יָמִים בַּמִּדְבָּר וְלֹא מָצְאוּ מָיִם״, דּוֹרְשֵׁי רְשׁוּמוֹת אָמְרוּ: אֵין מַיִם אֶלָּא תּוֹרָה, שֶׁנֶּאֱמַר: ״הוֹי כׇּל צָמֵא לְכוּ לַמַּיִם״,

The Gemara discusses the second of Ezra's ordinances: **And that they should read** the Torah **on** every **Monday and Thursday.** The Gemara asks: **Did Ezra institute** this practice? **But it was instituted from the beginning,** i.e., long before his time. **As it is taught** in a *baraita* with regard to the verse: "And Moses led Israel onward from the Red Sea, and they went out into the wilderness of Shur; **and they went three days in the wilderness, and found no water**" (Exodus 15:22). **Those who interpret verses** metaphorically **said** that **water** here is referring to **nothing other than Torah, as it is stated** metaphorically, concerning those who desire wisdom: **"Ho, everyone who thirsts, come for water"** (Isaiah 55:1).

כֵּיוָן שֶׁהָלְכוּ שְׁלֹשֶׁת יָמִים בְּלֹא תּוֹרָה נִלְאוּ, עָמְדוּ נְבִיאִים שֶׁבֵּינֵיהֶם וְתִיקְּנוּ לָהֶם שֶׁיְּהוּ קוֹרִין בְּשַׁבָּת וּמַפְסִיקִין בְּאֶחָד בְּשַׁבָּת, וְקוֹרִין בְּשֵׁנִי וּמַפְסִיקִין שְׁלִישִׁי וּרְבִיעִי, וְקוֹרִין בַּחֲמִישִׁי וּמַפְסִיקִין עֶרֶב שַׁבָּת, כְּדֵי שֶׁלֹּא יָלִינוּ שְׁלֹשָׁה יָמִים בְּלֹא תּוֹרָה!

The *baraita* continues: The verse means that **since** the Jews **traveled for three days without** hearing any **Torah they became weary,** and therefore the **prophets among them arose and instituted for them that they should read** from the Torah each **Shabbat, and pause** on **Sunday, and read** again on **Monday, and pause** on **Tuesday and Wednesday, and read** again on **Thursday, and pause** on **Shabbat eve, so they would not tarry three days without** hearing the **Torah.** Evidently this practice predates Ezra.

מֵעִיקָּרָא תִּקְּנוּ חַד גַּבְרָא תְּלָתָא פְּסוּקֵי, אִי נַמִּי תְּלָתָא גַּבְרֵי תְּלָתָא פְּסוּקֵי, כְּנֶגֶד כֹּהֲנִים לְוִיִּם וְיִשְׂרְאֵלִים, אֲתָא הוּא תִּיקֵּן תְּלָתָא גַּבְרֵי וַעֲשָׂרָה פְּסוּקֵי, כְּנֶגֶד עֲשָׂרָה בַּטְלָנִין.

The Gemara answers: **Initially they instituted** that **one man** read **three verses;** or **alternatively,** that **three men** read **three verses.** Either way, the number three **corresponds to** the three types of Jews: **Priests, Levites, and Israelites.** Ezra later **came** and **instituted** that **three men** always read, **and** that **ten verses** altogether be read by them, **corresponding to the ten idlers** in a city, i.e., the ten men who are paid to spend their time dealing with synagogue and communal matters.

״וְדָנִין בְּשֵׁנִי וּבַחֲמִישִׁי״ – דִּשְׁכִיחִי, דְּאָתוּ לְמִקְרָא בְּסִיפְרָא.

The next ordinance of Ezra is: **And** the courts convene and **judge** every **Monday and Thursday.** The Gemara explains that the reason for this ordinance is **that** many people are **found** in a city on these days, **as they come** from the countryside **for the reading of the** holy **book,** the Torah, which is performed on Mondays and Thursdays, as stated above.

״וְשֶׁיְּהוּ מְכַבְּסִין בַּחֲמִישִׁי בְּשַׁבָּת״ – מִשּׁוּם כְּבוֹד שַׁבָּת.

The *baraita* teaches: **And that one should do laundry on Thursday.** This was instituted **due to** the need to have clean garments in **deference to Shabbat.**

״וְשֶׁיְּהוּ אוֹכְלִין שׁוּם בְּעֶרֶב שַׁבָּת״ – מִשּׁוּם עוֹנָה, דִּכְתִיב: ״אֲשֶׁר פִּרְיוֹ יִתֵּן בְּעִתּוֹ״, וְאָמַר רַבִּי יְהוּדָה, וְאִיתֵּימָא רַב נַחְמָן, וְאִיתֵּימָא רַב כָּהֲנָא, וְאִיתֵּימָא רַבִּי יוֹחָנָן: זֶה הַמְשַׁמֵּשׁ מִטָּתוֹ מֵעֶרֶב שַׁבָּת לְעֶרֶב שַׁבָּת.

The Gemara explains the next listed ordinance: **And that one should eat garlic**[B] **Shabbat eve.** This is **due to** the fact that garlic enhances sexual potency, and Friday night is an appropriate time for **conjugal relations. As it is written** concerning the righteous: "And he shall be like a tree planted by streams of water, **who brings forth his fruit in his season**" (Psalms 1:3); **and Rabbi Yehuda says, and some say** it was **Rav Naḥman, and some say** it was **Rav Kahana, and some say** it was **Rabbi Yoḥanan** who said: **This** is referring **to one who engages in sexual intercourse**[H] **every Shabbat eve.**

תָּנוּ רַבָּנַן: חֲמִשָּׁה דְּבָרִים נֶאֶמְרוּ בְּשׁוּם: מַשְׂבִּיעַ, וּמַשְׁחִין, וּמַצְהִיל פָּנִים, וּמַרְבֶּה הַזֶּרַע, וְהוֹרֵג כִּנִּים שֶׁבִּבְנֵי מֵעַיִים; וְיֵשׁ אוֹמְרִים: מַכְנִיס אַהֲבָה וּמוֹצִיא אֶת הַקִּנְאָה.

The Sages taught in a *baraita* that **five matters were stated with regard to garlic: It satisfies; it warms** the body; **it causes** one's **countenance to shine; it increases** one's **sperm, and it kills lice that are in the intestines. And some say** that it also **instills love** into those who eat it **and removes jealousy** from them.

BACKGROUND

Garlic – שׁוּם: Garlic is not only a seasoning and an appetizer, but a food that provides many health benefits. The role of garlic in killing intestinal worms has long been known, and recent studies have shown its benefits with regard to several other health issues as well. Due to the large amount of protein it contains, up to 20 percent of the weight of a dried garlic clove, it is also satisfying and causes a general feeling of warmth in the body.

HALAKHA

This is referring to one who engages in sexual intercourse, etc. – זֶה הַמְשַׁמֵּשׁ מִטָּתוֹ וכו׳: The prescribed frequency of sexual intercourse for Torah scholars is once a week (see *Ketubot* 62b). It is proper for Torah scholars to engage in intercourse each Friday night. Kabbalistic reasons have been suggested for this practice (Rambam *Sefer Nashim, Hilkhot Ishut* 14:1; *Shulḥan Arukh, Oraḥ Ḥayyim* 240:1 and *Even HaEzer* 76:2).

LANGUAGE

Breechcloth [*sinar*] – סִינָר: The source of this word is not known for certain. Some maintain that it is from the Greek **ζωνάριον**, *zonarion*, which is a diminutive form of a term that means, among other things, a belt or girdle. The *sinar* referred to by the Sages is apparently a kind of undergarment.

"וְשֶׁתְּהֵא אִשָּׁה מַשְׁכֶּמֶת וְאוֹפָה" – כְּדֵי שֶׁתְּהֵא פַּת מְצוּיָה לַעֲנִיִּים.

The next ordinance is: **And that a woman should rise early**[H] **and bake** bread on those days when she bakes. This Gemara explains that this was instituted **so that bread should be available for poor people,** who go begging for bread in the mornings.

"וְשֶׁתְּהֵא אִשָּׁה חוֹגֶרֶת בְּסִינָר" – מִשּׁוּם צְנִיעוּתָא.

The *baraita* further teaches: **And that a woman should don a breechcloth** [***sinar***].[LHN] This ordinance was instituted **due to** reasons of **modesty.**

"וְשֶׁתְּהֵא אִשָּׁה חוֹפֶפֶת וְטוֹבֶלֶת" – דְּאוֹרַיְיתָא הִיא!

The *baraita* adds: **And that a woman should** first **comb** her hair[HN] **and** only then **immerse** in a ritual bath. This is to ensure that there is no dirt or other substance in the hair that would invalidate the immersion. The Gemara questions this: **This is** required **by Torah law,** Ezra did not institute this.

דְּתַנְיָא: "וְרָחַץ אֶת בְּשָׂרוֹ בַּמַּיִם" – שֶׁלֹּא יְהֵא דָּבָר חוֹצֵץ בֵּין בְּשָׂרוֹ לַמַּיִם, "אֶת בְּשָׂרוֹ" – אֶת הַטָּפֵל לִבְשָׂרוֹ, וּמַאי נִיהוּ? שֵׂעָר!

As it is taught in a *baraita,* concerning a verse that discusses one who must undergo ritual immersion: **"And he shall bathe his flesh** [***et besaro***] **in water"** (Leviticus 14:9). This verse teaches **that no substance should interpose between his flesh and the water.** When the verse states this in the expanded form of **"*et* his flesh,"** using the term "*et*," this teaches that the water must come into contact even with **that which is subordinate to his flesh. And what is that?** It is one's **hair.** Accordingly, the Torah itself states that there may not be any interposing substance in the hair at the time of immersion. What, then, did Ezra add?

אָמְרִי: דְּאוֹרַיְיתָא – לְעַיּוּנֵי דִּלְמָא מִיקְטַר, אִי נַמִי מָאוּס מִידֵי, מִשּׁוּם חֲצִיצָה,

The Sages **say** in response: **By Torah law** one is required **to inspect**[H] his or her hair before immersion, as **perhaps** some hairs are **knotted** together,[H] preventing contact with water at that spot, **or** perhaps there is some **repulsive substance** in his hair. One must perform this inspection **because** these would constitute **an interposition.**

HALAKHA

That a woman should rise early – שֶׁתְּהֵא אִשָּׁה מַשְׁכֶּמֶת: Ezra instituted that women should rise early and bake bread, so that bread would be available for the poor early in the morning (Rambam *Sefer Nashim, Hilkhot Ishut* 21:5).

That a woman should don a breechcloth – שֶׁתְּהֵא אִשָּׁה חוֹגֶרֶת בְּסִינָר: Ezra instituted that every woman should always don a breechcloth in her house, for reasons of modesty (Rambam *Sefer Nashim, Hilkhot Ishut* 24:13).

That a woman should first comb her hair – שֶׁתְּהֵא אִשָּׁה חוֹפֶפֶת: Before immersing in a ritual bath, a woman must scrub every place on her body where there is a concentration of hair, and she must comb the hair on her head (Rambam *Sefer Tahara, Hilkhot Mikvaot* 2:16; *Shulḥan Arukh, Yoreh De'a* 199:1).

To inspect – לְעַיּוּנֵי: Before immersing in a ritual bath, a woman must inspect and clean herself to ensure that there is no repulsive substance on her body that would constitute an interposition between herself and the water. Nowadays the accepted custom is that nothing at all be on the woman's body during immersion, including a substance that is not repulsive and whose presence on her body she does not mind (Rambam *Sefer Tahara, Hilkhot Mikvaot* 1:12; *Shulḥan Arukh, Yoreh De'a* 198:1, 199:1).

Perhaps some hairs are knotted together, etc. – דִּלְמָא מִיקְטַר וכו׳: In a case where a single hair became tangled and knotted, if the woman is bothered by its presence it constitutes an interposition. If she does not mind it, the knotted hair is not considered an interposition unless most of the hairs are in this condition (Rambam *Sefer Tahara, Hilkhot Mikvaot* 2:15; *Shulḥan Arukh, Yoreh De'a* 198:5).

NOTES

Don a breechcloth [*sinar*] – חוֹגֶרֶת בְּסִינָר: Rashi explains that a *sinar* is a type of undergarment worn for reasons of modesty. Others explain that *sinar* is a kind of apron that is worn over the main garments, more like a modern apron, in order to keep one's clothes clean while doing housework (Meiri). The Gemara associates the *sinar* with modesty because without an apron the woman would fold up the bottom of her skirt to keep it from becoming soiled as she works (see also Jerusalem Talmud, *Megilla* 4:1).

Comb [*ḥofefet*] her hair – חוֹפֶפֶת: Rashi explains that *ḥofefet* means combing. Others maintain that this term refers to washing (Rid). As for combing the hair, the Rid writes that this is what the Gemara means when it says later that inspecting the hair for knots is required by Torah law. Alternatively, *ḥofefet* means rubbing, i.e., scrubbing (*Arukh*). Some commentaries contend that *ḥofefet* applies only to the hair on the head; and the Sages said that prior to immersion in the ritual bath, it is proper for one to wash any area on the body where there are folds in the skin, in which unnoticed dirt can collect (*Tosafot*, citing Rabbeinu Tam). The practice of women nowadays to bathe their bodies in hot water before immersion is a custom, and is not due to a rabbinic decree.

וַאֲתָא אִיהוּ תִּיקֵּן חֲפִיפָה.

And Ezra **came** and added to the Torah's minimal obligation. He **instituted** the requirement of **combing** the hair even when it is known that it is not knotted and contains no repulsive substance.

״וְשֶׁיְּהוּ רוֹכְלִין מְחַזְּרִין בָּעֲיָירוֹת״ – מִשּׁוּם תַּכְשִׁיטֵי נָשִׁים, כְּדֵי שֶׁלֹּא יִתְגַּנּוּ עַל בַּעֲלֵיהֶם.

The Gemara discusses the next of Ezra's ordinances: **And that peddlers should**[N] **circulate**[H] **through all the towns.** This Gemara explains that this is **because** peddlers supply **women's cosmetics,**[B] and therefore Ezra instituted this practice **so that** women **should not become unattractive to their husbands.**

״וְתִיקֵּן טְבִילָה לְבַעֲלֵי קְרָיין״ – דְּאוֹרַיְיתָא הוּא, דִּכְתִיב: ״וְאִישׁ כִּי תֵצֵא מִמֶּנּוּ שִׁכְבַת זָרַע וְרָחַץ אֶת בְּשָׂרוֹ בַּמַּיִם״! דְּאוֹרַיְיתָא הוּא לִתְרוּמָה וְקָדָשִׁים, אֲתָא הוּא תִּיקֵּן אֲפִילּוּ לְדִבְרֵי תוֹרָה.

The Gemara analyzes the last of the ten ordinances: **And he instituted** the requirement of **immersion**[N] **for those who experienced a seminal emission.** The Gemara asks: But this **is required by Torah law,**[H] **as it is written: "And if the flow of seed go out from a man, then he shall bathe** all his flesh in water" (Leviticus 15:16). The Gemara answers: **By Torah law** immersion **is** required only if one wishes to partake **of *teruma* or sacrificial** meat. Ezra **came** and further **instituted** that immersion is necessary **even for** reciting or studying **matters of Torah.**[H]

עֲשָׂרָה דְּבָרִים נֶאֶמְרוּ בִּירוּשָׁלַיִם: אֵין הַבַּיִת חָלוּט בָּהּ, וְאֵינָהּ מְבִיאָה עֶגְלָה עֲרוּפָה, וְאֵינָהּ נַעֲשֵׂית עִיר הַנִּדַּחַת,

§ The mishna teaches that one may not raise chickens in Jerusalem. The Gemara cites a *baraita* that contains a list of other *halakhot* that are unique to Jerusalem. **Ten matters were stated**[N] **with regard to Jerusalem:**[H] **A house** situated in Jerusalem **does not** become **irredeemable**[H] one year after its sale. Those who sell houses in other walled cities have the right to buy back their property for one year after the transaction. If they fail to do so, the house becomes the permanent possession of the buyer (see Leviticus 25:29–30). This *halakha* does not apply to houses in Jerusalem. **And its Elders do not bring a heifer whose neck is broken**[HB] as required when a murder victim is found near a city and the murderer is unknown (see Deuteronomy 21:1–9); **and it cannot become an idolatrous city** (see Deuteronomy 13:13–19).[HB]

NOTES

And that peddlers should, etc. – וְשֶׁיְּהוּ רוֹכְלִין וכו׳: Ezra instituted that peddlers be permitted to circulate through all cities to sell their wares, without opposition from local store owners (Meiri).

And he instituted the requirement of immersion, etc. – וְתִיקֵּן טְבִילָה וכו׳: By Torah law one who is ritually impure is not prohibited to studying Torah. Ezra instituted the requirement of immersion prior to Torah study in this particular case of a seminal emission in order to foster purity and sanctity. The Gemara (*Berakhot* 22a) teaches that this requirement was subsequently annulled, and therefore it is now permitted to study Torah or pray after a seminal emission even without immersion.

Several explanations are suggested as to how the requirement of immersion before Torah study was nullified in this case, since a later court generally may not annul an ordinance instituted by an earlier and greater court. Some contend that the later court did not accept the accuracy of the claim that Ezra instituted this ordinance in the first place; others say that Ezra himself intended the ordinance to be temporary and subject to annulment at a future time (*Tosafot*). Alternatively, the ordinance never gained wide acceptance, and under such circumstances an ordinance is subject to annulment. Some note that the wording of the *baraita*, which introduces only this ordinance with the phrase: And he instituted, indicates that in this case, by contrast to the other ordinances, Ezra alone was the initiator, as the other authorities of his time did not agree to this requirement (*Shita Mekubbetzet*).

Ten matters were stated, etc. – עֲשָׂרָה דְּבָרִים נֶאֶמְרוּ וכו׳: The early commentaries cite *Avot deRabbi Natan*, chapter 35, which provides a different version of this list that has several other *halakhot*, including: Human remains may not be passed through Jerusalem; no graves are permitted inside the city except for those that were already there since antiquity, e.g., those of the Davidic kings; and some maintain that the *halakha* of the rebellious son (Deuteronomy 21:18–21) does not apply in Jerusalem.

BACKGROUND

Women's cosmetics – תַּכְשִׁיטֵי נָשִׁים: Here the reference is specifically to certain kinds of soaps, perfumes, and depilatories. These were the main products sold by traveling peddlers.

A heifer whose neck is broken – עֶגְלָה עֲרוּפָה: When a murder victim's corpse is found outside a town and it is not known who caused his death, the following procedure is carried out (Deuteronomy 21:1–9): First, judges who are members of the Great Sanhedrin come to measure the distance between the corpse and the nearest town, to determine which town must perform the rite of the heifer whose neck is broken. This measurement is carried out even if it is obvious which town is closest to the corpse. Afterward, the Elders of that town bring a heifer that has never been used for any labor, and they break its neck in a riverbed that is not tilled. The Elders wash their hands and make a statement absolving themselves of guilt. If the murderer is discovered before the heifer has been killed, the rite is not performed.

Idolatrous city – עִיר הַנִּדַּחַת: This is a city in which the majority of inhabitants worship idolatry (Deuteronomy 13:13–19). The city is judged by the Great Sanhedrin, the court of seventy-one. The Sanhedrin has the authority to send an army to subdue the city. Afterward, courts are convened and each of the city's adult inhabitants is judged. Those found guilty of idol worship are beheaded rather than stoned, which is the usual punishment for idolatry. The innocent are not slain. All the property in the city, including that of the righteous, is destroyed, and all its buildings are razed. It remains in ruins forever.

HALAKHA

That peddlers should circulate, etc. – שֶׁיְּהוּ רוֹכְלִין מְחַזְּרִין וכו׳: The inhabitants of a city may not prevent traveling peddlers from selling their wares in their city, as Ezra instituted an ordinance that they be permitted to do so, to ensure that cosmetics and perfumes be readily available to Jewish women (Rambam *Sefer Kinyan*, *Hilkhot Shekhenim* 6:9; *Shulḥan Arukh*, *Ḥoshen Mishpat* 156:6).

Is required by Torah law – דְּאוֹרַיְיתָא הוּא: Any man who has experienced a seminal emission, and men and women who engaged in sexual intercourse, and one who touches semen, are ritually impure by Torah law, and they require immersion in a ritual bath for their purification (Rambam *Sefer Tahara*, *Hilkhot Avot HaTuma* 5:15).

For matters of Torah – לְדִבְרֵי תוֹרָה: By Torah law one who is ritually impure is not barred from studying Torah. Ezra instituted that one who is impure due to experiencing a seminal emission is prohibited from studying Torah, reciting *Shema*, or praying before he immerses in water. Nevertheless, this ordinance was subsequently abolished by the Sages, who restored the original *halakha* that these people do not require immersion before studying Torah. Nevertheless, pious men follow Ezra's edict and immerse themselves in this situation (Rambam *Sefer Ahava*, *Hilkhot Keriat Shema* 4:8; *Shulḥan Arukh*, *Oraḥ Ḥayyim* 88:1).

Ten matters were stated with regard to Jerusalem – עֲשָׂרָה דְּבָרִים נֶאֶמְרוּ בִּירוּשָׁלַיִם: The Sages instituted several ordinances with regard to conduct in Jerusalem and the Temple: A corpse may not be left overnight in Jerusalem; human remains may not be passed through the city; houses may not be leased there; a gentile may not be given a place to live there, even if he is not an idolater; burial grounds are not allowed there, except for graves that have been there since antiquity; gardens and orchards may not be planted in the capital; one may not plow or sow there; one may not sustain trees there, except for the rose garden that was there since the times of the early prophets; dung heaps are not allowed in Jerusalem; kilns are not allowed there; one may not build balconies or other projections over a public thoroughfare in the city; and finally, chickens may not be raised there (Rambam *Sefer Avoda*, *Hilkhot Beit HaBeḥira* 7:14).

A house in Jerusalem does not become irredeemable – אֵין הַבַּיִת חָלוּט בָּהּ: One who sold a house in Jerusalem has the right to repurchase it, even if he has not done so within a year of its sale (Rambam *Sefer Avoda*, *Hilkhot Beit HaBeḥira* 7:14 and *Sefer Zera'im*, *Hilkhot Shemitta VeYovel* 12:12).

Its Elders do not bring a heifer whose neck is broken – אֵינָהּ מְבִיאָה עֶגְלָה עֲרוּפָה: If a murder victim is found near Jerusalem, the Elders of the city do not bring a heifer whose neck is broken, as Jerusalem was not apportioned to any of the tribes (Rambam *Sefer Nezikin*, *Hilkhot Rotze'aḥ UShmirat HaNefesh* 9:4).

It cannot become an idolatrous city – אֵינָהּ נַעֲשֵׂית עִיר הַנִּדַּחַת: Jerusalem cannot be treated as an idolatrous city, even if all the conditions for an idolatrous city have been met there, as Jerusalem was not apportioned to any of the tribes (Rambam *Sefer HaMadda*, *Hilkhot Avoda Zara* 4:4).

וְאֵינָהּ מִטַּמְּאָה בִּנְגָעִים, וְאֵין מוֹצִיאִין בָּהּ זִיזִין וּגְזוּזְטְרָאוֹת, וְאֵין עוֹשִׂין בָּהּ אַשְׁפָּתוֹת, וְאֵין עוֹשִׂין בָּהּ כִּבְשׁוֹנוֹת, וְאֵין עוֹשִׂין בָּהּ גַּנּוֹת וּפַרְדֵּסוֹת חוּץ מִגַּנּוֹת וְוַרְדִּין שֶׁהָיוּ מִימוֹת נְבִיאִים הָרִאשׁוֹנִים, וְאֵין מְגַדְּלִים בָּהּ תַּרְנְגוֹלִין, וְאֵין מְלִינִין בָּהּ אֶת הַמֵּת.

The *baraita* continues its list: **And** a house in Jerusalem **cannot become ritually impure** with the impurity **of leprous sores;**[H] **and one may not build out projections or balconies** [*gezuztraot*][L] from houses that are **in it; and one may not establish garbage dumps** in Jerusalem; **and one may not build kilns in it; and one may not plant gardens and orchards** [*pardesot*][L] **in it, except for** the **rose gardens**[N] **that were** already there **from the times of the early prophets; and one may not raise chickens in it;** and finally, **one may not leave a corpse overnight in** Jerusalem.

״אֵין הַבַּיִת חָלוּט בָּהּ״ – דִּכְתִיב: ״וְקָם הַבַּיִת...אֲשֶׁר לוֹ חוֹמָה לַצְּמִיתֻת לַקֹּנֶה אֹתוֹ לְדֹרֹתָיו״, וְקָסָבַר: לֹא נִתְחַלְּקָה יְרוּשָׁלַיִם לִשְׁבָטִים.

The Gemara discusses these ten *halakhot* pertaining to Jerusalem, one by one: **A house** situated **in** it does **not** become **irredeemable** one year after its sale. The reason is **that it is written:** "And if it is not redeemed within the space of a full year, then **the house** that is in the **walled** city **shall be made sure in perpetuity to him who bought it, throughout his generations"** (Leviticus 25:30). **And** the *tanna* who taught this *baraita* **maintains** that **Jerusalem was not apportioned to** any single one of **the tribes** of Israel; rather, it is considered common property. Since no one has ancestral ownership of any house in Jerusalem, its houses cannot be sold permanently.

״וְאֵינָהּ מְבִיאָה עֶגְלָה עֲרוּפָה״ – דִּכְתִיב: ״כִּי יִמָּצֵא חָלָל בָּאֲדָמָה אֲשֶׁר ה׳ אֱלֹהֶיךָ נֹתֵן לְךָ לְרִשְׁתָּהּ״, וִירוּשָׁלַיִם לֹא נִתְחַלְּקָה לִשְׁבָטִים.

The Gemara analyzes the next *halakha*: **And** its inhabitants do **not bring a heifer whose neck is broken.** The reason is **that it is written: "If one is found slain in the land that the Lord your God gives you to possess it"** (Deuteronomy 21:1). **And,** again, the *tanna* who taught this *baraita* **maintains** that **Jerusalem was not apportioned to** any one of **the tribes**[B] of Israel. Therefore, it is not included in the description: "The land that the Lord your God gives you to possess it."

״וְאֵינָהּ נַעֲשֵׂית עִיר הַנִּדַּחַת״ – דִּכְתִיב: ״עָרֶיךָ״, וִירוּשָׁלַיִם לֹא נִתְחַלְּקָה לִשְׁבָטִים.

The *baraita* states: **And** it **cannot become an idolatrous city.** The reason is **that it is written,** in the introduction of the passage dealing with the *halakha* of an idolatrous city: "If you shall hear tell concerning one of **your cities,** which the Lord your God gives you to dwell there" (Deuteronomy 13:13). **And** the *tanna* who taught this *baraita* maintains that **Jerusalem was not apportioned to** any one of **the tribes** of Israel. It is therefore not included in the description "one of your cities, which the Lord your God gives you to dwell there."

״וְאֵינָהּ מִטַּמְּאָה בִּנְגָעִים״ – דִּכְתִיב: ״וְנָתַתִּי נֶגַע צָרַעַת בְּבֵית אֶרֶץ אֲחֻזַּתְכֶם״, וִירוּשָׁלַיִם לֹא נִתְחַלְּקָה לִשְׁבָטִים.

The *baraita* further teaches: **And** a house in Jerusalem does **not become ritually impure** with the impurity **of leprous sores.** The reason is **that it is written: "And I put the plague of leprosy**[B] **in a house of the land of your possession"** (Leviticus 14:34). **And** the *tanna* who taught this *baraita* maintains that **Jerusalem was not apportioned to** any one of **the tribes** of Israel. It is therefore not included in the description "a house of the land of your possession."

״וְאֵין מוֹצִיאִין בָּהּ זִיזִין וּגְזוּזְטְרָאוֹת״ – מִפְּנֵי אֹהֶל הַטּוּמְאָה, וּמִשּׁוּם דְּלָא לִיתַּזְּקוּ עוֹלֵי רְגָלִים.

The Gemara discusses the next *halakha*: **And one may not build out projections or balconies** from houses that are **in** Jerusalem. The Gemara provides two reasons for this prohibition. First, it is **due to** the danger of contracting **ritual impurity** by being in **the** same **tent** as a corpse, i.e., under the same roof, in which case the impurity spreads to all items under the roof. If even a small part of a corpse is under a balcony, everyone who passes under that balcony is rendered impure. Many people come to Jerusalem to sacrifice offerings, and they must maintain a state of ritual purity. The other reason is **so that those** great crowds of **pilgrims not be injured** by colliding with the projections.

״וְאֵין עוֹשִׂין בָּהּ אַשְׁפָּתוֹת״ – מִשּׁוּם שְׁקָצִים.

The next *halakha* pertaining to Jerusalem is: **And one may not establish garbage dumps in it.** The Gemara explains that the reason is **due to** the **repugnant creatures** that are attracted to such heaps and impart ritual impurity upon their death.

״וְאֵין עוֹשִׂין בָּהּ כִּבְשׁוֹנוֹת״ – מִשּׁוּם קוּטְרָא.

The *baraita* states: **And one may not build kilns in** Jerusalem. The reason is **due to the** unsightly **smoke** produced by kilns. The Sages sought to preserve the beauty of Jerusalem and the Temple.

HALAKHA

A house in Jerusalem cannot become ritually impure with the impurity of leprous sores – אֵינָהּ מִטַּמְּאָה בִּנְגָעִים: The houses of Jerusalem cannot become ritually impure with the impurity of leprous sores, as Jerusalem was not apportioned to any of the tribes (Rambam *Sefer Tahara, Hilkhot Tumat Tzara'at* 14:11).

LANGUAGE

Balconies [*gezuztraot*] – גְּזוּזְטְרָאוֹת: From the Greek ἐξώστρα, *exostra*, meaning a balcony or area that protrudes from a building.

Orchards [*pardesot*] – פַּרְדֵּסוֹת: This word, which is found in the Bible (Song of Songs 4:13; Ecclesiastes 2:5), may stem from the Old Persian word paridaia, meaning a pleasure garden. It was borrowed by many languages and used in ways both closely and distantly related to its original meaning, including the English word paradise.

NOTES

Rose gardens – גַּנּוֹת וְוַרְדִּין: Rashi writes that roses are a necessary ingredient of the Temple incense. Others disagree (see Meiri).

BACKGROUND

Jerusalem was not apportioned to any one of the tribes – יְרוּשָׁלַיִם לֹא נִתְחַלְּקָה לִשְׁבָטִים: There are different opinions among the *tanna'im* with regard to the status of Jerusalem. Some maintain that Jerusalem itself was divided between the tribes of Judah and Benjamin, and therefore it is subject to the *halakhot* of a heifer whose neck is broken and can be an idolatrous city. Others maintain that the division between Judah and Benjamin referred only to the area of the Temple, whereas the rest of Jerusalem was never divided and belonged to all the tribes. This is the opinion of the *baraita*.

Leprosy [*tzara'at*] – צָרַעַת: The term *tzara'at* used in the Torah, traditionally rendered as leprosy, is not necessarily the medical equivalent of that disease. In the Torah, the term refers to symptoms that cause severe ritual impurity. The *halakhot* governing these symptoms are articulated at length in Leviticus, chapters 13–15, and in the Mishna in tractate *Nega'im*. *Tzara'at* can be leprosy of the skin, of the hair, of articles of clothing, and of houses. When a symptom appears, it is examined by a priest, and only a priest is authorized to determine whether to quarantine the affected person for a certain period or to declare immediately that the symptom is or is not leprosy. Leprosy is one of the primary sources of ritual impurity, and it is particularly severe in that it imparts ritual impurity to objects found in the same enclosure with it, like the impurity imparted by a corpse. One afflicted with leprosy is sent out of the Israelite settlement and must live alone until his affliction is cured. A cured leper undergoes special rites outside the city and a purification ceremony in the Temple itself. He is obligated to bring certain offerings as part of his purification.

״וְאֵין עוֹשִׂין בָּהּ גִּנּוֹת וּפַרְדֵּסִין״ – מִשּׁוּם סִירְחָא.

The *baraita* teaches: **And one may not plant gardens and orchards in it.** This is **due to the odor** emitted by these places, either from discarded weeds or from fertilizer.

״וְאֵין מְגַדְּלִין בָּהּ תַּרְנְגוֹלִין״ – מִשּׁוּם קֳדָשִׁים.

The next *halakha* on the list is: **And one may not raise chickens in** Jerusalem. The Gemara explains that this is **due to the sacrificial** meat that is consumed in Jerusalem. Since chickens peck in the garbage, they are likely to pick up items that impart ritual impurity and bring them into contact with the consecrated food, which may not be eaten in an impure state.

״וְאֵין מְלִינִין בָּהּ אֶת הַמֵּת״ – גְּמָרָא.

The Gemara discusses the last *halakha*: **And one may not leave a corpse overnight in it.** The Gemara notes that this prohibition is **a tradition;**[N] there is no known explanation for it.

״אֵין מְגַדְּלִין חֲזִירִים בְּכָל מָקוֹם״. תָּנוּ רַבָּנַן: כְּשֶׁצָּרוּ בֵּית חַשְׁמוֹנַאי זֶה עַל זֶה, הָיָה הוּרְקָנוּס מִבִּפְנִים וְאַרִיסְטוֹבְלוּס מִבַּחוּץ, וּבְכָל יוֹם הָיוּ מְשַׁלְשִׁים לָהֶם בְּקוּפָּה דִּינָרִין, וְהָיוּ מַעֲלִים לָהֶם תְּמִידִים.

§ The mishna teaches that **one may not raise pigs**[N] **anywhere. The Sages taught** in a *baraita* the background for this *halakha*: **When** the members of **the house of Hasmonean** monarchy **were at war with each other,**[B] **Hyrcanus,** one of the parties to this war, **was inside** the besieged Jerusalem, **while** his brother **Aristobulus,** the other contender to the throne, was **on the outside. And every day** the people inside **would lower down money in a box** from the Temple walls, to purchase sheep to sacrifice, **and** those on other side **would** take the money and **send up** sheep **to them** over the wall for the **daily offerings.**

הָיָה שָׁם זָקֵן אֶחָד שֶׁהָיָה מַכִּיר בְּחָכְמַת יְוָנִית, אָמַר לָהֶם: כָּל זְמַן שֶׁעוֹסְקִין בַּעֲבוֹדָה אֵין נִמְסָרִים בְּיֶדְכֶם. לְמָחָר שִׁלְשְׁלוּ דִּינָרִין בְּקוּפָּה, וְהֶעֱלוּ לָהֶם חֲזִיר. כֵּיוָן שֶׁהִגִּיעַ לַחֲצִי הַחוֹמָה נָעַץ צִפָּרְנָיו בַּחוֹמָה, וְנִזְדַּעְזְעָה אֶרֶץ יִשְׂרָאֵל אַרְבַּע מֵאוֹת פַּרְסָה עַל אַרְבַּע מֵאוֹת פַּרְסָה.

There was a certain elder there who was familiar with Greek wisdom, and **he said** to those besieging Jerusalem: **As long as they occupy themselves with the Temple service, they will not be delivered into your hands. The next day they lowered down money in a box** as usual, **but** this time **they sent up to them a pig. When the pig reached to the midpoint of the** Temple **wall it stuck its hooves into the wall, and Eretz Yisrael quaked** over an area of **four hundred parasangs by four hundred parasangs.**

בְּאוֹתָהּ שָׁעָה אָמְרוּ: אָרוּר הָאִישׁ שֶׁיְּגַדֵּל חֲזִירִים, וְאָרוּר הָאָדָם שֶׁיְּלַמֵּד אֶת בְּנוֹ חָכְמַת יְוָנִית. וְעַל אוֹתָהּ שָׁעָה שָׁנִינוּ: מַעֲשֶׂה שֶׁבָּא עוֹמֶר מִגַּנּוֹת הַצְּרִיפִין, וּשְׁתֵּי הַלֶּחֶם מִבִּקְעַת עֵין סוֹכֵר.

At that time the Sages **said: Cursed be the man who raises pigs,**[H] **and cursed be the man who teaches his son Greek wisdom.**[NB] **And** it was **concerning that time** of siege **that we learned** in a mishna: There was **an incident** in which the barley for the ***omer* offering came from the gardens of Tzerifin,**[B] far from Jerusalem, **and** the wheat for **the two loaves** of *Shavuot* was brought **from the valley of Ein Sokher.**[B] Barley and wheat could not be brought from any nearer because the besiegers had destroyed all the produce around Jerusalem. This concludes the *baraita*.

וְחָכְמַת יְוָנִית מִי אֲסִירָא? וְהָתַנְיָא, אָמַר רַבִּי: בְּאֶרֶץ יִשְׂרָאֵל

The Gemara asks a question with regard to this *baraita*: **And is it** really **prohibited** to study **Greek wisdom? But isn't it taught** in a *baraita*: **Rabbi** Yehuda HaNasi **said: In Eretz Yisrael,**

NOTES

Tradition – גְּמָרָא: Rashi explains that it is simply a tradition that this *halakha* applies to Jerusalem, for reasons unknown. Other commentaries note that there is a Torah prohibition against leaving a dead body overnight without burial (see Deuteronomy 21:23). Why, then, is it stated here that this *halakha* is unique to Jerusalem and that its origin is a mystery? They answer that generally it is permitted to delay a funeral for a day or so if the deceased will thereby receive greater honor, e.g., when relatives will take some time to arrive to attend the funeral. In Jerusalem even this is prohibited (*Shita Mekubbetzet*). Possibly the reason for this practice is based, like several of the other prohibitions listed here, on the desire to limit as much as possible any source of ritual impurity in Jerusalem.

One may not raise pigs – אֵין מְגַדְּלִין חֲזִירִים: The commentaries ask: There is a general *halakha* that one may not conduct business dealings with non-kosher food (see *Shevi'it* 7:3); if so, why are pigs specified here? Some explain that if a non-kosher animal is raised for a purpose other than food, e.g., for industrial use of its hide or fat, this is generally permitted, whereas in the case of pigs, this too is prohibited (*Tosafot*). Others write that although other non-kosher animals may not be raised *ab initio*, if one happened to come into possession of them, e.g., through a gift or inheritance, they may be sold for profit. In the case of pigs, however, even this is not allowed (Ra'avad; Rashba). Yet others suggest that an edict of excommunication was decreed against those who raise pigs, which does not apply to those who raise other non-kosher animals (Meiri).

Cursed be the man who teaches his son Greek wisdom – אָרוּר הָאָדָם שֶׁיְּלַמֵּד אֶת בְּנוֹ חָכְמַת יְוָנִית: This prohibition is mentioned elsewhere (*Sota* 49a) in connection with Titus's siege of Jerusalem, which occurred several centuries after the Hasmonean fraternal conflict described here. The commentaries explain that the original decree did not gain widespread acceptance in Hasmonean times, and it was therefore necessary to issue the decree once again in later times. Alternatively, there was initially a curse placed on those who teach their children the ways of Greek wisdom; in the days of Titus an actual prohibition was decreed.

HALAKHA

Cursed be the man who raises pigs – אָרוּר הָאִישׁ שֶׁיְּגַדֵּל חֲזִירִים: The Sages said: Cursed be the man who raises pigs, because they cause extensive damage to their surroundings. The prohibition applies even to raising them in order to use their fat for processing hides (Rambam *Sefer Nezikin, Hilkhot Nizkei Mamon* 5:9; *Shulḥan Arukh, Ḥoshen Mishpat* 409:2).

BACKGROUND

When the members of the house of the Hasmonean monarchy were at war with each other – כְּשֶׁצָּרוּ בֵּית חַשְׁמוֹנַאי זֶה עַל זֶה: Before her death, Queen Shlomzion, Salome Alexandra, bequeathed the throne to her firstborn son, Hyrcanus II. His brother, Aristobulus II, rebelled against him and took control of the country. After some time Hyrcanus returned and, with the assistance and encouragement of Herod's father Antipater, gathered a militia that succeeded in defeating Aristobulus's army, forcing him to take refuge in the fortified Jerusalem. During the course of Hyrcanus's siege of the city, in the year 65 CE, the besieged inhabitants sought sheep for the daily offerings of the Temple from beyond the walls of Jerusalem and paid for them with large sums of money. This incident is recounted by Josephus in *Antiquities of the Jews* 14:2. There he relates that the besieged inhabitants sought sheep for the Paschal offering and promised the exorbitant sum of one thousand drachmas per animal. Josephus also states that as a divine punishment for not honoring the pledge to provide animals for the offering and for causing an interruption in the daily sacrificial service, there was a tremendous storm in Eretz Yisrael, which destroyed almost all of the crops of that year. It is perhaps in reference to this calamity that the Gemara states that Eretz Yisrael quaked over an area of four hundred parasangs by four hundred parasangs.

Greek wisdom – חָכְמַת יְוָנִית: As indicated by various sources, the term Greek wisdom apparently refers to knowledge of Greek culture, meaning its poetry, literature, and the like. The language generally used by the Jews during the Second Temple period for everyday speech was Koine Greek, which was spoken by the gentiles living among them. Very few Jews were conversant in classical Greek and its culture, a fact that enabled those few who were to communicate with one another through allusions that could not be understood by most listeners.

The gardens of Tzerifin – גַּנּוֹת הַצְּרִיפִין: The name of this place is preserved in the Arab village Sarafand Al-Amar. The village was located east of modern Rishon LeTzion, along the Ramla–Jaffa road.

Ein Sokher – עֵין סוֹכֵר: The accepted identification of Ein Sokher is the valley called in Arabic سهل عسكر, *sahl 'askar*. It is located southwest of Mount Ebal, and the main road from Shechem to Jerusalem runs through it. The name is apparently derived from a deep well [*ein*] located in a neighboring village.

לָשׁוֹן סוּרְסִי לָמָּה? אוֹ לְשׁוֹן הַקֹּדֶשׁ אוֹ לָשׁוֹן יְוָנִית! וְאָמַר רַבִּי יוֹסֵי: בְּבָבֶל לָשׁוֹן אֲרַמִּי לָמָּה? אוֹ לְשׁוֹן הַקֹּדֶשׁ אוֹ לָשׁוֹן פַּרְסִי! אָמְרִי: לָשׁוֹן יְוָנִי לְחוּד, חָכְמַת יְוָנִית לְחוּד.

why would one speak the **Syriac** [*Sursi*][L] **language?** One should speak **either the sacred tongue,** Hebrew, **or the Greek language.**[B] **And Rabbi Yosei said** similarly: In **Babylonia, why** would one speak the **Aramaic language?** One should speak **either the sacred tongue or the Persian language.**[B] At any rate, Rabbi Yehuda HaNasi's statement indicates that there is nothing wrong with learning and speaking Greek. The Sages **say** in response: **The Greek language** is **discrete, and Greek wisdom** is **discrete.** In other words, these are two separate issues; only Greek wisdom is prohibited, not the Greek language.

וְחָכְמַת יְוָנִית מִי אֲסִירָא? וְהָאָמַר רַב יְהוּדָה אָמַר שְׁמוּאֵל מִשּׁוּם רַבָּן שִׁמְעוֹן בֶּן גַּמְלִיאֵל: ״עֵינִי עוֹלְלָה לְנַפְשִׁי מִכֹּל בְּנוֹת עִירִי״ – אֶלֶף יְלָדִים הָיוּ בְּבֵית אַבָּא, חֲמֵשׁ מֵאוֹת מֵהֶם לָמְדוּ תּוֹרָה, חֲמֵשׁ מֵאוֹת לָמְדוּ חָכְמַת יְוָנִית, וְלֹא נִשְׁתַּיֵּיר מֵהֶם אֶלָּא אֲנִי כָּאן וּבֶן אֲחִי אַבָּא בְּעַסְיָא!

The Gemara further pursues this line of inquiry: **And is Greek wisdom** itself actually **prohibited? But doesn't Rav Yehuda say** that **Shmuel says in the name of Rabban Shimon ben Gamliel:** It is written: **"My eye affected my soul, because of all the daughters of my city"** (Lamentations 3:51). Rabban Shimon ben Gamliel applied this verse to a personal tragedy: **There were a thousand children in the household of** my **father,** Rabban Gamliel; **five hundred of them studied** the **Torah, and five hundred of them studied Greek wisdom.** All of them were killed by the Romans; **and the only** ones that **remain of them are I,** who is **here, and the son of** my **father's brother,** who is **in Asia Minor** [**Asya**].[L] Rabban Shimon ben Gamliel's statement indicates that it is permitted to study Greek wisdom.

אָמְרִי: שָׁאנֵי בֵּית רַבָּן גַּמְלִיאֵל, שֶׁהָיוּ קְרוֹבִים לַמַּלְכוּת; וְכִדְתַנְיָא: הַמְסַפֵּר קוֹמִי הֲרֵי זֶה מִדַּרְכֵי הָאֱמוֹרִי. אַבְטוֹלְמוֹס בַּר רְאוּבֵן הִתִּירוּ לוֹ לְסַפֵּר קוֹמִי, מִפְּנֵי שֶׁהוּא קָרוֹב לַמַּלְכוּת; שֶׁל בֵּית רַבָּן גַּמְלִיאֵל הִתִּירוּ לָהֶם לְסַפֵּר בְּחָכְמַת יְוָנִית, מִפְּנֵי שֶׁקְּרוֹבִים לַמַּלְכוּת.

The Sages **say** in response: **The household of Rabban Gamliel is different, as they** held **close** ties **with the government.** Since knowledge of Greek wisdom was crucial for the members of this family, the Sages exempted them from the general decree, **as it is taught** in a *baraita*: With regard to **one who cuts his hair** in the fashion of ***komi*,**[LH] a certain haircut favored by the Romans, **this is** considered one **of the ways of the Amorites,**[N] i.e., a gentile practice prohibited by the Torah (Leviticus 18:3). Despite this, the Sages **permitted Avtolmos bar Reuven**[P] **to cut his hair** in the fashion of ***komi*, because he** had **close** ties **with the government.**[H] Likewise, **they permitted** the members **of the household of Rabban Gamliel to discuss** matters **of Greek wisdom, because they** had **close** ties **with the government.**

LANGUAGE

Syriac [*Sursi*] – סוּרְסִי: This is an altered form of the Greek Σύρος, *Suros*, meaning Syrian. It refers to Middle Aramaic, which was used primarily in the Middle East.

Asia Minor [Asya] – עַסְיָא: From the Greek Ἀσία, *Asia*, which is also the appellation for the region known as Asia Minor. Part of Asia Minor was a Roman province known as Asia. It seems that when using this term, the Sages were referring to a specific district, perhaps Cilicia, located in that region.

***Komi* – קוֹמִי:** From the Greek κόμη, *komē*, meaning hair or locks of hair. It is unknown for certain what exactly the *komi* haircut looked like; apparently it involved cutting off the hair evenly around the head, without leaving over any noticeable hair on the temples.

BACKGROUND

Greek language – לָשׁוֹן יְוָנִית: The Greeks were known for their superior culture and literature, which spawned genres such as comedy, tragedy, and legends told in dramatic verse. Moreover, they also established rhetorical conventions and methods of debate. These, as well as Greek philosophy, form the basis of Greek wisdom, which the Gemara proscribes unless needed for political reasons, to curry favor with the rulers. By contrast, the Greek language itself is simply the platform used for all these cultural advances; the language itself is not problematic and even has positive aspects, as it is stated: "God enlarge Japheth" (Genesis 9:27). This verse is traditionally interpreted as a reference to Greece, an indication that the Greek language was popular because of its innate beauty (see Rabbi Ovadya Bartenura on *Shekalim* 3:2).

Persian language – לָשׁוֹן פַּרְסִי: Most of the Jews in the Persian kingdom lived in the geographic area of Babylonia. They spoke the language of native Babylonians, which was Aramaic, although they apparently spoke a unique Jewish dialect. The official language of the kingdom was Persian, in which few Jews were proficient. Rabbi Yosei is saying that it is preferable to speak either the authentic Jewish language, Hebrew, or the official government language, Persian, as opposed to the local dialect.

HALAKHA

One who cuts his hair in the fashion of *komi* – הַמְסַפֵּר קוֹמִי: It is prohibited to shave off one's hair from ear to ear and leave the back part of the hair uncut, in the fashion of the gentiles (Rambam *Sefer HaMadda*, *Hilkhot Avoda Zara* 11:1; *Shulḥan Arukh*, *Yoreh De'a* 178:1).

Close ties with the government – קָרוֹב לַמַּלְכוּת: If a Jew maintains close ties with the government and must meet with gentile kings, and it is embarrassing for him to appear different from them, he is allowed to dress and wear his hair in accordance with their fashion (Rambam *Sefer HaMadda*, *Hilkhot Avoda Zara* 11:3; *Shulḥan Arukh*, *Yoreh De'a* 178:2).

NOTES

The ways of the Amorites – דַּרְכֵי הָאֱמוֹרִי: It is prohibited for a Jew to adopt customs that are unique to gentiles. This is true even if the custom has no connection to idolatry but is based on some superstition or is performed by the people of a certain nation as an expression of their national identity. This is derived from the verse: "Like the actions of the land of Egypt, where you dwelt, you shall not do; and like the actions of the land of Canaan, to which I bring you, you shall not do, nor shall you walk in their statutes" (Leviticus 18:3). The early commentaries ask: If wearing one's hair in the fashion of *komi* is prohibited by Torah law, how could the Sages permit Avtolmos to do so? Some say that the specifics of this prohibition are not delineated by the Torah, and therefore the Sages had the authority to define what does and does not constitute a violation (*Kesef Mishne*). Others similarly explain that when the Sages decreed that certain actions are prohibited as ways of the Amorites, they stipulated at the outset that this does not apply in the case of one who maintains close ties to the government (*Tosafot*). Alternatively, the Torah's prohibition applies only when one adopts a gentile custom out of a desire to resemble them. When it is done for some tangible benefit, it is permitted (Maharik).

PERSONALITIES

Avtolmos bar Reuven – אַבְטוֹלְמוֹס בַּר רְאוּבֵן: It is not known in what period this man lived. Some identify him with the Avtolmos who was one of Rabbi Yosei's teachers. It is possible that Avtolmos maintained ties with Rabbi Reuven Iztrobili. It is related that Rabbi Reuven Iztrobili, a fourth-generation *tanna*, would dress and cut his hair in the gentile fashion in order to better mix with government officials and prevail upon them to annul anti-Jewish edicts (see *Me'ila* 17a). Avtolmos bar Reuven apparently fulfilled a similar role of unofficial contact with government officials.

״לֹא יְגַדֵּל אָדָם אֶת הַכֶּלֶב אֶלָּא אִם כֵּן קָשׁוּר בְּשַׁלְשְׁלָאוֹת״ כו׳. תָּנוּ רַבָּנַן: לֹא יְגַדֵּל אָדָם אֶת הַכֶּלֶב אֶלָּא אִם כֵּן קָשׁוּר בְּשַׁלְשֶׁלֶת, אֲבָל מְגַדֵּל הוּא בְּעִיר הַסְּמוּכָה לַסְּפָר, וְקוֹשְׁרוֹ בַּיּוֹם וּמַתִּירוֹ בַּלַּיְלָה.

§ The mishna teaches: **A person may not raise a dog unless it is tied with chains. The Sages taught** in a *baraita*: **A person may not raise a dog unless it is tied with a chain. But he may raise** a dog **in a city that is close to the border**[HB] of the country, **and** in that case he should **tie it during the day but may release it at night.**

תַּנְיָא, רַבִּי אֱלִיעֶזֶר הַגָּדוֹל אוֹמֵר: הַמְגַדֵּל כְּלָבִים כִּמְגַדֵּל חֲזִירִים. לְמַאי נָפְקָא מִינָּהּ? לְמֵיקַם עֲלֵיהּ בְּ״אָרוּר״.

It is taught in a *baraita* that **Rabbi Eliezer the Great says: One who raises dogs is like one who raises pigs.** The Gemara asks: **What is the** practical **significance** of this statement? Since both are prohibited, what is the point of this comparison? The Gemara answers: The significance is with regard **to determining when one is liable** to be **cursed**[H] **for it.** Rabbi Eliezer is saying that the same curse meted out to one who raises pigs also applies to one who raises dogs.

אָמַר רַב יוֹסֵף בַּר מִנְיוּמֵי אָמַר רַב נַחְמָן: בָּבֶל כְּעִיר הַסְּמוּכָה לַסְּפָר דָּמֵי. תַּרְגְּמָהּ: נְהַרְדְּעָא.

Rav Yosef bar Minyumi says that **Rav Naḥman says: Babylonia is** considered **like a city close to the border,** and therefore it is permitted to raise dogs there. The Gemara qualifies this statement, and in this context, Babylonia is **interpreted** as referring only to **Neharde'a,**[B] a city that was close to the border.

דָּרֵישׁ רַבִּי דּוֹסְתַּאי דְּמִן בִּירִי: ״וּבְנֻחֹה יֹאמַר שׁוּבָה ה׳ רִבְבוֹת אַלְפֵי יִשְׂרָאֵל״ – לְלַמֶּדְךָ, שֶׁאֵין שְׁכִינָה שׁוֹרָה עַל יִשְׂרָאֵל פָּחוֹת מִשְּׁנֵי אֲלָפִים וּשְׁנֵי רְבָבוֹת; חָסֵר אַחַת, וְהָיְתָה אִשָּׁה מְעוּבֶּרֶת בֵּינֵיהֶם וּרְאוּיָה לְהַשְׁלִים, וְנָבַח בָּהּ כֶּלֶב וְהִפִּילָה, נִמְצָא זֶה גּוֹרֵם לַשְּׁכִינָה שֶׁתִּסְתַּלֵּק מִיִּשְׂרָאֵל.

With regard to raising dogs, **Rabbi Dostai from Biri expounded:** It is written in connection to the Ark of the Covenant: **"And when it rested, he said: Return, O Lord, to the myriads of the thousands of Israel"** (Numbers 10:36). This verse serves **to teach you that the Divine Presence does not rest upon the Jewish people** if they number **fewer than two thousand and two myriads,**[N] where one myriad is equal to ten thousand. The plural form of "myriads" and "thousands" indicates at least two of each. If they are **lacking one** individual from this total, **and there was a pregnant woman among them, who was fit to complete** the number by giving birth, **and a dog barked at her and she miscarried** as a result of the fright, **this** owner of the dog **is found** to have **caused the Divine Presence to depart from the Jewish people.**

הַהִיא אִיתְּתָא דַּעֲלַת לְמֵיפָא בְּהַהוּא בֵּיתָא, נְבַח בָּהּ כַּלְבָּא, אֲמַר לָהּ מָרֵיהּ: לָא תִּיסְתְּפִי מִינֵּיהּ, שְׁקוּלֵי נִיבֵיהּ. אֲמַרָה לֵיהּ: שְׁקִילִי טֵיבוּתִיךְ וְשַׁדְיָא אַחִיזְרֵי, כְּבָר נָד וָלָד.

There was **a certain woman who entered a certain building to bake. A dog barked at her. Its owner said to her: Do not be afraid of it; its canine teeth**[B] **have been removed. She said to him:** It is too late for your reassurances. **Take your favors and throw them on the thorns!** I have felt that **the baby has already moved** from its place in the womb and will not be born alive.

HALAKHA

In a city that is close to the border – בְּעִיר הַסְּמוּכָה לַסְּפָר: It is permitted to raise dogs in a city that is close to the border of a country. These dogs should be restrained by day but may be let loose at night. Some commentaries write that when Jews dwell among gentiles and it is dangerous for them to remain unprotected, it is permitted to own a dog (Rema). In any event, a vicious dog should be tied and restrained, to prevent it from injuring anyone, and so that innocent people will not be frightened of it, as occurred in the incident related by the Gemara (Rambam *Sefer Nezikin, Hilkhot Nizkei Mamon* 5:9; *Shulḥan Arukh, Ḥoshen Mishpat* 409:3 and *Sma* and *Beur HaGra* there).

To determining when one is liable to be cursed – לְמֵיקַם עֲלֵיהּ בְּאָרוּר: One who raises dogs where it is not permitted to do so is subject to the same curse of the Sages that applies to one who raises pigs (Rambam *Sefer Nezikin, Hilkhot Nizkei Mamon* 5:9).

NOTES

Two thousand and two myriads – שְׁנֵי אֲלָפִים וּשְׁנֵי רְבָבוֹת: There is an allusion to this idea in the Torah, as the number of Levites counted in the census in the wilderness was twenty-two thousand (see Numbers 3:39), and the Levites by themselves were worthy of having the Divine Presence rest upon them (Rabbeinu Yeshaya, cited in *Shita Mekubbetzet*). The commentaries note that elsewhere (*Sanhedrin* 39a) the Sages teach that the Divine Presence dwells among any gathering of ten Jews, which apparently contradicts the Gemara here. *Tosafot* explain that the minimum of twenty-two thousand Jews is required for the manifest expression of the Divine Presence, through prophecy or in the Tabernacle or Temple.

BACKGROUND

Close to the border – סְמוּכָה לַסְּפָר: In a city close to the border, particularly if relations with the neighboring country are hostile, not only is there a threat of military attack in a time of war but there is also a constant threat of cross-border incidents of theft by those who seek to take advantage of the fact that they cannot easily be pursued across the border. As a protection against these thieves and plunderers in these places, permission was granted to raise dogs, which alert their owners against intruders and safeguard their property.

Neharde'a – נְהַרְדְּעָא: A city on the Euphrates, near the Malka River, and one of the oldest Jewish communities in Babylonia. According to tradition, Jews lived in Neharde'a as early as the First Temple period, in the sixth century BCE, from the exile of King Jehoiachin of Judea.

Neharde'a was one of the most important Jewish communities in Babylonia. It was a center of Torah learning from an early period, and its yeshiva was the oldest in Babylonia. Many of the greatest *tanna'im* visited Neharde'a, including Rabbi Akiva, who intercalated the calendar there. In Rav's time, the first half of the third century CE, the yeshiva of Neharde'a was headed by Rav Sheila, followed by Shmuel.

Since the city lay near the border between the Roman and Persian Empires, it frequently suffered in the wars between the two, and Pappa ben Nazer Odonathus, king of Tadmor, destroyed it completely in 259 CE. Later, however, Jews resettled there, and many Torah scholars remained in Neharde'a even after its yeshiva relocated to Meḥoza and Pumbedita.

Its canine teeth – נִיבֵיהּ: This refers to the four long, sharp teeth in various animals' mouths. They protrude farther and are stronger in predatory animals. A dog that has lost these teeth is no longer able to harm people seriously with its bite.

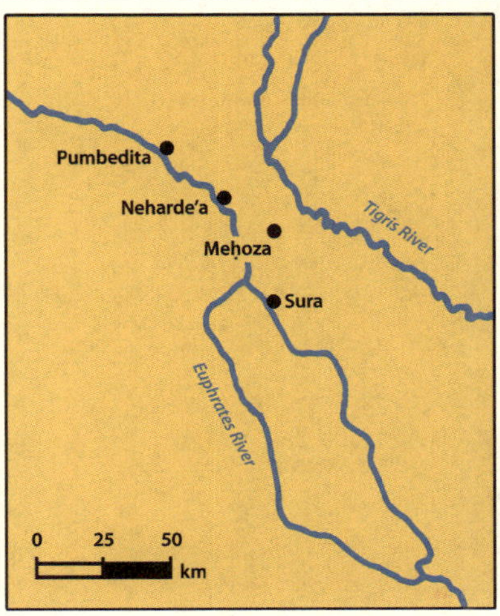

Location of Neharde'a

Male baboon displaying his canine teeth

"אין פורסין נישבין ליונים" וכו'. ומי אזלי כולי האי? והתנן: מרחיקין את השובך מן העיר חמשים אמה! אמר אביי: מישט שייטי טובא, כרסייהו בחמשים אמה מליא.

§ The mishna teaches: **One may spread out traps for pigeons only** if this was performed at a distance of at least thirty *ris*, which is eight thousand cubits, from any settled area, to ensure that privately owned pigeons are not caught in the traps. The Gemara asks: **And do** pigeons really **travel that** far from their established places? **But didn't we learn** in a mishna (*Bava Batra* 23a): **One must distance a dovecote**[H] **fifty cubits from the city,** so that the pigeons that settle in the cotes do not eat the crops that grow in the gardens of the city. This shows that the range of a pigeon is only fifty cubits, whereas four *mil* is eight thousand cubits. **Abaye said:** Pigeons **fly**[B] much **more** than fifty cubits away from their cotes, but **their stomachs become full** from the food they find **within fifty cubits,** and therefore they do not eat any more beyond that range.

ומישט שלשים ריס ותו לא? והתניא: בישוב – אפילו מאה מיל לא יפרוס! רב יוסף אמר: בישוב כרמים. רבה אמר: בישוב שובכין.

The Gemara asks: **And** with regard to **flying,** is their range only **thirty** ***ris*** **and no more? But isn't it taught** in a *baraita*: **In a settled area, one may not spread out** a trap for pigeons **even** at a distance of **one hundred** ***mil*** from the settlement? This indicates that a privately owned pigeon might be trapped even one hundred *mil* away from a settled area. Why, then, does the mishna permit trapping beyond four *mil*? **Rav Yosef said:** The *baraita* is not talking about an ordinary city but **about a settled area** where **vineyards** are grown.[H] Since the pigeons rest in the vineyards as they travel, they are able to traverse great distances. **Rabba stated** a different answer: The *baraita* is dealing **with a settled area** where there are many **dovecotes**[H] in which they can rest from their flight.

ותיפוק ליה משום שובכין גופייהו! איבעית אימא: בדגוי, ואיבעית אימא: בדהפקר, ואיבעית אימא: בדידיה.

The Gemara asks: If there are many dovecotes along the way, **let** the *tanna* **derive** the prohibition against setting pigeon traps **due to the dovecotes themselves.** Since the mishna teaches that it is prohibited to trap pigeons within four *mil* of privately owned dovecotes, it should be irrelevant that there is a city one hundred *mil* away. The Gemara answers: **If you wish, say** that the *baraita* is dealing with dovecotes **that** belong **to a gentile,**[N] and the prohibition against trapping pigeons from private dovecotes applies only to birds owned by Jews. **Or if you wish, say** that the *baraita* is dealing **with** abandoned dovecotes **that** are **ownerless. Or if you wish, say** that it is referring to dovecotes **that are his,** i.e., they belong to the same individual who is setting the pigeon trap.

הדרן עלך מרובה

HALAKHA

One must distance a dovecote, etc. – מרחיקין את השובך וכו': If one wishes to set up a dovecote he must distance it fifty cubits from a city (Rambam *Sefer Nezikin, Hilkhot Gezeila VaAveda* 6:9; *Shulḥan Arukh, Ḥoshen Mishpat* 155:24).

A settled area where vineyards are grown – בישוב כרמים: If there is a settled area where vineyards are grown, even if it is one hundred *mil* long, one may not spread out traps for pigeons there, as pigeons belonging to the owners of the vineyards might become trapped in them. The commentaries write that one may spread out traps for pigeons only if he distances himself four *mil* from the city, in the direction of the wilderness. In a place where there are vineyards one may not spread out these traps even one hundred *mil* away, as pigeons travel very far by way of the vineyards (Rambam *Sefer Nezikin, Hilkhot Gezeila VaAveda* 6:8; *Tur, Ḥoshen Mishpat* 370).

In a settled area where there are many dovecotes, etc. – בישוב שובכין וכו': One may not spread out a net for trapping doves in a place where there are dovecotes, even if the dovecotes belong to the one setting the net, or they belong to a gentile, or they are ownerless, and even if he distances himself one hundred *mil* from the city. The reason for this is because pigeons owned by others travel and perch in these dovecotes and may be trapped by the nets (Rambam *Sefer Nezikin, Hilkhot Gezeila VaAveda* 6:8).

BACKGROUND

Pigeons fly – מישט שייטי: Pigeons are capable of flying great distances. Carrier pigeons can cover distances of 750 kilometers in a single day. They collect their food from the ground, and if the food they eat, which is mainly seeds, is available, they will take that which is nearby and will not wander off to search for food elsewhere.

NOTES

Dovecotes that belong to a gentile – בדגוי: Although it is prohibited to steal from a gentile, pigeons raised in a dovecote, even by Jews, are strictly speaking not considered the property of their putative owners. The Sages decreed, for the sake of peace and harmony, that people should not take pigeons raised by others, but technically this is not considered theft. In a place where gentiles themselves do not consider these actions criminal, this decree was not applied to doves owned by them (see also *Shita Mekubbetzet*).

Summary of **Perek VII**

With regard to the liabilities of a thief, one must distinguish between the basic monetary obligation of reimbursement on the one hand and the fines imposed by the Torah on the other. A different set of regulations applies to the collection of fines than to ordinary monetary compensation. For instance, a fine may be imposed only by a court composed of judges who have received proper ordination. Furthermore, a fine is waived if the perpetrator of the act engendering the fine admits his liability without having been incriminated by witnesses.

The double payment applies to the theft of any item, with the exception of land, slaves, and bonds, whereas the fourfold or fivefold payment is prescribed only for slaughtering or selling a stolen sheep or ox, respectively.

Additionally, the double payment applies not only to a thief, but also to a bailee who embezzles the item or money entrusted to him and subsequently takes a false oath in court that it was stolen by someone else.

There are certain specific requirements that must be met for the fourfold or fivefold payment to be imposed. For instance, this fine does not apply in the case of an animal of diverse kinds, nor when the slaughter is not carried out according to halakhic requirements, and likewise it does not apply when the animal is sold in an incomplete manner. Moreover, the fine is not imposed when the stolen animal was fully acquired by the thief before the slaughter or sale.

The last section of the chapter dealt with various sets of ancient ordinances that were instituted in biblical times by Joshua and Ezra. A further list of regulations instituted by the Sages that apply specifically to Jerusalem is also discussed.

Image **Credits**

My Notes

תלמוד בבלי

— מהדורת נאה —

בבא קמא חלק ה

Steinsaltz Center

KOREN

ease note that the number ranges that appear at the bottom of each daf of the Vilna pages
dicate the corresponding pages of the Koren Talmud Bavli translation and commentary.

תלמוד בבלי

הוצאת קורן ירושלים

— מהדורת נאה —

מסכת בבא קמא
דף סב: עד דף פג.

COMMENTARY BY

Rabbi Adin Even-Israel Steinsaltz

EDITOR-IN-CHIEF

Rabbi Dr Tzvi Hersh Weinreb

EXECUTIVE EDITOR

Rabbi Joshua Schreier

STEINSALTZ CENTER
KOREN PUBLISHERS JERUSALEM

עז א מיי' פ"ו מהל' חובל ומזיק הל' יא טוש"ע ח"מ סי' שפד סעי' ב:
עח ב ג מיי' פי"ד מהל' נזקי ממון הל' יג סמג עשין סט טוש"ע ח"מ סי' תיח סעי' יב:
עט ד מיי' שם טוש"ע א"ח סי' תרעא סעי' ו:
פ ה מיי' פ"ד מהל' חנוכה הלכה ז סמג עשין מד סי' ה טוש"ע שם:
א ו ז מיי' פ"א מהל' גניבה הל' ו:
ב ח ט מיי' שם הל' יז סמג עשין מא טוח"מ סי' שנ:
ג י מיי' פ"ד שם הל' א סמג שם טוח"מ סי' שנב:
ד כ ל מיי' שם פ"ב הל' א והל' ב טוח"מ סי' שנ:

מתני' *גץ שֶׁיָּצָא מִתַּחַת הַפַּטִּישׁ וְהִזִּיק — חַיָּיב. *גָּמָל שֶׁהָיָה טָעוּן פִּשְׁתָּן וְעָבַר בִּרְשׁוּת הָרַבִּים, וְנִכְנַס פִּשְׁתָּנוֹ לְתוֹךְ הַחֲנוּת, וְדָלְקוּ בְּנֵרוֹ שֶׁל חֶנְוָנִי וְהִדְלִיק אֶת הַבִּירָה — בַּעַל גָּמָל חַיָּיב, הִנִּיחַ חֶנְוָנִי נֵרוֹ מִבַּחוּץ — הַחֶנְוָנִי חַיָּיב; *רַבִּי יְהוּדָה אוֹמֵר: בְּנֵר חֲנוּכָּה — פָּטוּר.§ גמ' *אָמַר רָבִינָא מִשְּׁמֵיהּ דְּרָבָא, ש"מ מִדְּרַבִּי יְהוּדָה: נֵר חֲנוּכָּה מִצְוָה לְהַנִּיחָהּ בְּתוֹךְ עֲשָׂרָה, דְּאִי סָלְקָא דַּעְתָּךְ לְמַעְלָה מֵעֲשָׂרָה, אַמַּאי אָמַר ר' יְהוּדָה: נֵר חֲנוּכָּה — פָּטוּר? לֵימָא לֵיהּ: הֲוָה *לֵיהּ לְאַנּוֹחָהּ לְמַעְלָה מִגָּמָל וְרוֹכְבוֹ! אֶלָּא לָאו ש"מ: מִצְוָה לְהַנִּיחָהּ בְּתוֹךְ עֲשָׂרָה. אָמְרִי: לָא, לְעוֹלָם אֵימָא לָךְ אֲפִי' לְמַעְלָה מֵעֲשָׂרָה; מַאי אָמְרַתְּ, אִבְּעֵי לָךְ לְאַנּוֹחָהּ לְמַעְלָה מִגָּמָל וְרוֹכְבוֹ? כֵּיוָן דְּבְמִצְוָה קָא עָסֵיק, כּוּלֵּי הַאי לָא אַטְרַחוּהּ רַבָּנַן. *אָמַר רַב כָּהֲנָא דָּרַשׁ רַב נָתָן בַּר מַנְיוּמֵי מִשְּׁמֵיהּ דְּרַבִּי תַּנְחוּם: נֵר חֲנוּכָּה שֶׁהִנִּיחָהּ לְמַעְלָה מֵעֶשְׂרִים אַמָּה — פְּסוּלָה, כְּסוּכָּה וּכְמָבוֹי.§

הדרן עלך הכונם

מְרוּבָּה מִדַּת תַּשְׁלוּמֵי כֶפֶל מִמִּדַּת תַּשְׁלוּמֵי אַרְבָּעָה וַחֲמִשָּׁה, שֶׁמִּדַּת תַּשְׁלוּמֵי כֶפֶל נוֹהֶגֶת בֵּין בְּדָבָר שֶׁיֵּשׁ בּוֹ רוּחַ חַיִּים וּבֵין בְּדָבָר שֶׁאֵין בּוֹ רוּחַ חַיִּים, וּמִדַּת תַּשְׁלוּמֵי אַרְבָּעָה וַחֲמִשָּׁה אֵינָהּ נוֹהֶגֶת אֶלָּא בְּשׁוֹר וָשֶׂה בִּלְבַד, שֶׁנֶּאֱמַר: "כִּי יִגְנֹב אִישׁ שׁוֹר אוֹ שֶׂה וּטְבָחוֹ אוֹ מְכָרוֹ" וגו'. *אֵין הַגּוֹנֵב אַחַר הַגַּנָּב מְשַׁלֵּם תַּשְׁלוּמֵי כֶפֶל, וְלֹא הַטּוֹבֵחַ וְלֹא הַמּוֹכֵר אַחַר הַגַּנָּב מְשַׁלֵּם תַּשְׁלוּמֵי אַרְבָּעָה וַחֲמִשָּׁה.§ גמ' וְאִילּוּ מִדַּת תַּשְׁלוּמֵי כֶפֶל נוֹהֶגֶת בֵּין בְּגַנָּב בֵּין בְּטוֹעֵן טַעֲנַת גַּנָּב, וּמִדַּת תַּשְׁלוּמֵי אַרְבָּעָה וַחֲמִשָּׁה אֵינָהּ נוֹהֶגֶת אֶלָּא בְּגַנָּב בִּלְבַד — לָא קָתָנֵי; מְסַיֵּיע לֵיהּ לְרַבִּי חִיָּיא בַּר אַבָּא, *דְּא"ר חִיָּיא בַּר אַבָּא א"ר יוֹחָנָן: הַטּוֹעֵן טַעֲנַת גַּנָּב בְּפִקָּדוֹן — מְשַׁלֵּם תַּשְׁלוּמֵי כֶפֶל, טָבַח וּמָכַר — מְשַׁלֵּם תַּשְׁלוּמֵי אַרְבָּעָה וַחֲמִשָּׁה. אִיכָּא דְּאָמְרִי: לֵימָא מְסַיֵּיע לֵיהּ לְרַבִּי חִיָּיא בַּר אַבָּא, דְּא"ר חִיָּיא בַּר אַבָּא א"ר יוֹחָנָן: הַטּוֹעֵן טַעֲנַת גַּנָּב בְּפִקָּדוֹן — מְשַׁלֵּם תַּשְׁלוּמֵי כֶפֶל, טָבַח וּמָכַר — מְשַׁלֵּם תַּשְׁלוּמֵי אַרְבָּעָה וַחֲמִשָּׁה? מִי קָתָנֵי "אֵין בֵּין"? "מְרוּבָּה" קָתָנֵי, *תְּנָא וְשַׁיֵּיר.§ "שֶׁמִּדַּת תַּשְׁלוּמֵי כֶפֶל נוֹהֶגֶת" כו'.§ מנה"מ? דת"ר: *"עַל כָּל דְּבַר פֶּשַׁע" כְּלָל, "עַל שׁוֹר עַל חֲמוֹר עַל שֶׂה וְעַל שַׂלְמָה" — פְּרָט, "עַל כָּל אֲבֵדָה" — חָזַר וְכָלַל, כְּלָל וּפְרָט וּכְלָל אִי אַתָּה דָּן אֶלָּא כְּעֵין הַפְּרָט, מָה הַפְּרָט מְפוֹרָשׁ דָּבָר הַמִּטַּלְטֵל וְגוּפוֹ מָמוֹן, אַף כָּל דָּבָר הַמִּטַּלְטֵל וְגוּפוֹ מָמוֹן, *יָצְאוּ קַרְקָעוֹת — שֶׁאֵינָן מִטַּלְטְלִין, יָצְאוּ עֲבָדִים — שֶׁהוּקְּשׁוּ לְקַרְקָעוֹת, יָצְאוּ שְׁטָרוֹת — שֶׁאַף עַל פִּי שֶׁמִּטַּלְטְלִין אֵין גּוּפָן מָמוֹן, יָצָא הֶקְדֵּשׁ — "רֵעֵהוּ" כְּתִיב. אִי מָה הַפְּרָט מְפוֹרָשׁ דָּבָר שֶׁנִּבְלָתוֹ מְטַמֵּא בְּמַגָּע וּבְמַשָּׂא, אַף כָּל דָּבָר שֶׁנִּבְלָתוֹ מְטַמֵּא בְּמַגָּע וּבְמַשָּׂא, אֲבָל עוֹפוֹת לָא! וּמִי מָצֵית אָמְרַתְּ הָכִי? וְהָא "שַׂלְמָה" כְּתִיב! אָמְרִי: אֲנַן בְּבַעֲלֵי חַיִּים קָאָמְרִינַן, אֵימָא: בְּבַעֲלֵי חַיִּים, דָּבָר שֶׁנִּבְלָתוֹ מְטַמֵּא בְּמַגָּע וּבְמַשָּׂא — אִין, דָּבָר שֶׁאֵין נִבְלָתוֹ מְטַמֵּא בְּמַגָּע וּבְמַשָּׂא — לָא,

דְּהָא

מתני' גיץ. אשטנציי"ל. גמ' למעלה מעשרים אמה. לא חזו לה אינשי ולא מפרסם ניסא, ואנן לפרסומי ניסא בעינן.

הדרן עלך הכונם

מְרוּבָּה. אין הגונב אחר הגנב כו'. דכתיב: "וגונב מבית האיש" ולא מבית הגנב. גמ' בטוען טענת גנב. גנב הוא וגנבו. ודרשינן לקמן בשמעתין דחייבו רחמנא כפילא אם נשבע ונמצא שקרן. לא קתני. אלמא נהגי ד' וה' בטוען טענת גנב אם טבח ומכר. מי קתני אין בין. דהוי דווקא, ולא שייר מידי. קתני. קצת דברים שזו מרובה על זו, ושייר. שהוקשו לקרקעות. דכתיב: "והתנחלתם אותם" וגו' (ויקרא כה). אין גופן ממון. אלא גורמין לגבות ממון.

דהא

פסולה כסוכה וכמבוי. תימה: דהוה ליה למימר "ימעט", כדאמרי' בריש מסכת סוכה (דף ב.): מבוי דרבנן תני תקנתא! וי"ל: משום דבעי למימר כסוכה, נקט לשון "פסולה". אי נמי: לפי שהיה צריך להאריך בלשון, ולומר: יכבה וימעט ויחזור וידליק. דלמעט כמו שהיא מודלקת לא סגי, כדאמרינן בפ' "במה מדליקין" (שבת דף כג:): הדליקה בפנים והוציאה בחוץ — לא עשה ולא כלום. והכא נמי לא שנא.

הדרן עלך הכונם

מרובה. מי קתני אין בין כו'. משמע הכא היכא דתני "אין בין" לא שייך למימר "תנא ושייר". והקשה הר"י מאורלינ"ש מהא דתנן בפ"ק דמגילה (ד' ח. ושם ד"ה אין): אין בין נדרים לנדבות אלא שהנדרים חייב באחריותן ונדבות אינו חייב באחריותן. ואכתי, הא איכא שהנדבה באה מן המעשר ונדר שהוא דבר שבחובה אין בא אלא מן החולין, כדתנן ב"התודה" (מנחות ד' פא.)! וי"ל: דהתם לא בא לשנות כל ענין שנדר ונדבה חלוקים זה מזה, אלא בא לומר שאין חיוב הבאה בזה יותר מבזה אלא אחריות, אבל לענין "בל תאחר" זה וזה שוין. וכן "אין בין שבת ליום הכפורים" — לא איירי לכל דברים שביניהם, כגון איסור אכילה. וכן "אין בין יו"ט לשבת אלא אוכל נפש בלבד" — לא איירי בחומר שבשניהם כגון לאו ומיתה, אלא בדבר האסור או מותר לעשות בהן. ועוד י"ל: דהך משנה דמגילה שנויה במסכת קנים (פ"א מ"א) גבי עולת העוף, ועולה בין נדר בין נדבה אין באה מן המעשר כיון דאין בה אכילת אדם, כדדרש בסיפרי בפ' "עשר תעשר": ת"ל "ואכלת ושמחת" שמחה שיש בה אכילה, יצאו עולות שאין עמהן אכילה. ואין להאריך כאן יותר*.

מרובה קתני תנא ושייר. לשון ראשון דמייתי סייעתא לא בעי למימר דשייר, דסבר ההוא לישנא דכיון דקתני "מרובה" — אין לומר שייר, כמו ב"אין בין". וכן משמע הלשון, דקאמר ללישנא בתרא: מי קתני "אין בין"? "מרובה" קתני! משמע שתחילה היה סבור ד"מרובה" הוי כמו "אין בין". וא"ת: ומאי שייר דהאי שייר? וי"ל: דשייר טענת גנב באבידה. דדריש לקמן רבי יוחנן דמשלם כפל, ואי טעין טענת גנב בפקדון לא משלם ארבעה וחמשה בטבח ומכר — הכי נמי טוען טענת גנב באבידה. ועוד: שמשייר שותף שגנב מחבירו, ושותפין שגנבו לא משלם ארבעה וחמשה, כדאמר לקמן בפירקין (ד' עח:). ועוד יש מפרשים דאין לחוש הכא אם א"ט משייר כי אם דבר אחד, כיון דלא נחת למניינא, אלא דגלי לן שיש ריבוי בכפל מארבעה וחמשה.

יצאו קרקעות כו'. וא"ת: כיון דאמעיטי משבועה, כדאמרינן בפרק "הזהב" (ב"מ ד' נז:), תיפוק ליה דאין בהם כפל בטוען טענת גנב, דלא משלם אלא בשבועה, כדאמרינן לקמן בשמעתין. וליכא למימר דאצטריך לקופץ ונשבע, דב"הגוזל" קמא" (לקמן ד' קו.) מוכח דלא משלם אא"כ ב"ד משביעין אותו! וי"ל: דאצטריך להיכא דנשבע ע"י גלגול, כדתנן (קדושין ד' כו.): זוקקין הנכסים שיש להם אחריות עם הנכסים כו' לישבע עליהן. ומיהו, לפי מאי דמסקינן לקמן: האי "כל" ריבוי הוא, מדלא כתיב הני פרטי גבי "כסף" ו"כלים", וס"ל דכפל ושבועה הכל אחד ניחא, דליכא אלא חד קרא לתרוייהו. וא"ת: וגניבה בקרקע היכי שייכא? וי"ל: במשיג גבול. א"נ: במחובר לקרקע, כי ההיא די' גפנים טעונות, וטוען שגנבו לו ה', ונמצא שהוא גנבם (שבועות ד' מג:). יצאו שטרות. ואם תאמר: למה לי קרא למעט מכפל? והא אפי' אבדו בידים לא משלם קרן למאן דלא דאין דינא דגרמי, ואפי' מאן דדאין לא הוו אלא מדרבנן כדפריבית בסוף ["הספינה"] (ד' נד: ד"ה "ממור")! וי"ל: כיון דאי איתיה לשטר — בעין חייב להחזיר (משלם), סלקא דעתך דכשמחזיר [משלם] (מחזיר) הכפל עמו. ר"מ

רעהו

[ב"ב מו. שבת כח:]
לעיל כב. שבת כח:
לעיל ל.
[שבת כח:]
[תו"כ לך]
שבת כח:
שמות כא
[לקמן סט ועי' תוס' לעיל סז: ד"ה אין]
[לקמן סג: קו:]
שמות כב
ב"מ נז: שבועו' מב:
[לקמן קיז:]
[סוכה נב. וש"נ]
[עי' תוס' חגיגה ח. ד"ה אמאי ותוס' תענית יג: ד"ה מאין]

גליון הש"ס

מתני' החנוני חייב. עיין לעיל דף כז ע"ב תוס' ד"ה ה"ג אמאי:

תורה אור

דְּהָא כָּל חַד וְחַד כְּלָל וּפְרָט בְּאַפֵּי נַפְשֵׁיהּ דָּרְשִׁינַן לֵיהּ, אֲבָל עוֹפוֹת לָא! א"כ, נִכְתּוֹב רַחֲמָנָא חַד פְּרָטָא. הֵי נִכְתּוֹב רַחֲמָנָא? אִי כְּתַב רַחֲמָנָא "שׁוֹר", הֲוָה אָמִינָא: קָרֵב לְגַבֵּי מִזְבֵּחַ — אִין, שֶׁאֵין קָרֵב לְגַבֵּי מִזְבֵּחַ — לָא, וְאִי כְּתַב רַחֲמָנָא "חֲמוֹר", הֲוָה אָמִינָא: קָדוֹשׁ בִּבְכוֹרָה — אִין, שֶׁאֵין קָדוֹשׁ בִּבְכוֹרָה — לָא! אָמְרִי: א"כ, נִכְתּוֹב רַחֲמָנָא "שׁוֹר" וַ"חֲמוֹר", "שֶׂה" לָמָּה לִי? ש"מ: לְאַתּוּיֵי עוֹפוֹת. וְאֵימָא: לְאַתּוּיֵי עוֹפוֹת טְהוֹרִים, דּוּמְיָא דְּשֶׂה, דִּמְטַמֵּא בְּגָדִים אַבֵּית הַבְּלִיעָה, אֲבָל עוֹפוֹת טְמֵאִים דְּלֵית בְּהוּ טוּמְאָה, דְּלָא מְטַמְּאֵי בְּגָדִים אַבֵּית הַבְּלִיעָה — לָא! "כָּל" רִיבּוּיָא הוּא. וְכָל הֵיכָא דִּכְתַב "כָּל" רִיבּוּיָא הוּא? וְהָא גַּבֵּי מַעֲשֵׂר דִּכְתִיב "כל", וְקָא דָּרְשִׁינַן לֵיהּ בִּכְלָל וּפְרָט! דִּתְנְיָא*: (דברים יד) °"וְנָתַתָּה הַכֶּסֶף בְּכֹל אֲשֶׁר תְּאַוֶּה נַפְשְׁךָ" — כְּלָל, "בַּבָּקָר וּבַצֹּאן וּבַיַּיִן וּבַשֵּׁכָר" — פְּרָט, "וּבְכֹל אֲשֶׁר תִּשְׁאָלְךָ נַפְשֶׁךָ" — חָזַר וְכָלַל, כְּלָל וּפְרָט וּכְלָל אִי אַתָּה דָּן אֶלָּא כְּעֵין הַפְּרָט, מָה הַפְּרָט מְפוֹרָשׁ פְּרִי מִפְּרִי וְגִידּוּלֵי קַרְקַע, אַף כָּל פְּרִי מִפְּרִי וְגִידּוּלֵי קַרְקַע! אָמְרִי: "בְּכֹל" — כְּלָלָא, "כָּל" — רִיבּוּיָא הוּא. וְאִיבָּעֵית אֵימָא: "כָּל" — כְּלָלָא הוּא, מִידֵּי "כָּל" דְּהָכָא — רִיבּוּיָא הוּא; מִכְּדֵי כְּתִיב מֵעִיקָּרָא כְּלָל וּפְרָט וּכְלָל, דִּכְתִיב: (שמות כב) *°"כִּי יִתֵּן אִישׁ אֶל רֵעֵהוּ" — כְּלָל, "כֶּסֶף אוֹ כֵלִים" — פְּרָט, "לִשְׁמוֹר" — הֲדַר וְכָלַל, וְאִי סָלְקָא דַּעְתָּךְ הַאי "עַל כָּל דְּבַר פֶּשַׁע" נַמִי לִכְלָל וּפְרָט הוּא דַּאֲתָא, נִכְתּוֹב רַחֲמָנָא לְהָנֵי פְּרָטֵי גַּבֵּי הָאֵיךְ כְּלָל וּפְרָט, "עַל כָּל דְּבַר פֶּשַׁע" לָמָּה לִי? ש"מ רִיבּוּיָא הוּא. הָשְׁתָּא דְּאָמְרַתְּ "כָּל" רִיבּוּיָא, כָּל הָנֵי פְּרָטֵי לָמָּה לִי? חַד לְמַעוּטֵי קַרְקַע, וְחַד לְמַעוּטֵי עֲבָדִים, וְחַד לְמַעוּטֵי שְׁטָרוֹת, "שַׂלְמָה" — לְמַעוּטֵי דָּבָר שֶׁאֵינוֹ מְסוּיָּים, "עַל כָּל אֲבֵידָה" — לְכִדְר' חִיָּיא בַּר אַבָּא, *דְּאָמַר ר' חִיָּיא בַּר אַבָּא אָמַר ר' יוֹחָנָן: הַטּוֹעֵן טַעֲנַת גַּנָּב בַּאֲבֵידָה

דהא כל חד וחד כלל ופרט באנפיה נפשיה דרשינן ליה. כלומר: היכא דאיכא פרטי יתירי – כל חד וחד מרבי כעין דידיה, ולא דרשינן כולהו בהדדי דליהוי כעין הפרט. ד"שלמה" – לרבות בעלי חיים שאין נבלתן מטמאה, כדאמר לקמן. כדתני דבי חזקיה: שדי "שור" בין "המצא" ל"תמצא" כו', שדי "חמור" בין "המצא" ל"תמצא". אלמא: כל חד וחד באפי נפשיה מדריש. **א"כ.** דכעין הפרט בכל לדדין הוא דמייתי – לא נכתוב אלא חד מהני פרטי דבעלי חיים, ומתרבי כעין הפרט כל שנבלתו מטמאה. ומדכתב פרטי יתירי – תנהו ענין לרבות שאר בעלי חיים. **קדוש בבכורה.** כעין שור ושה הוא דמתרבי מכעין הפרט ד"חמור", דדמי ליה בתלת לדדין: בעלי חיים, ובבכורה, ונבלתו מטמאה. אבל גדי וחיל, דלא דמי ליה אלא בתרתי – לא. להכי כתב "שור", דאם אינו ענין לו – תנהו ענין לשאינו קדוש בבכורה, דדמי מיהת בתרתי לפרטא: ב"ח ונבלתו מטמא, ולעולם עופות לא. ה"ג: א"כ לכתוב רחמנא שור וחמור שה למה לי לאתויי עופות. **ואימא** טהורין. דדמי לפרטא קצת, דיש טומאה בנבלתם קצת, לטמא בבית הבליעה. **אבל עופות טמאים לא.** דלית בהו טומאה, כדאיתא בחולין (ד' ק:): יכול תהא נבלת עוף טמא מטמא בגדים אבית הבליעה – ת"ל: "נבלה וטרפה לא יאכל לטמאה בה" מי שאיסורו משום בל תאכל נבילה וטריפה, יצא זה שאין איסורו משום בל תאכל נבילה וטריפה, אלא משום בל תאכל טמא. **פרי מפרי.** ולד מולד, וגפן מחרצן. למעוטי מים ומלח וכמיהין ופטריות. **גידולי קרקע.** למעוטי דגים. **מכדי כתיב.** בראש הפרשה כלל ופרט: "כי יתן איש", ודרשינן ליה בפרק "הזהב" לענין שבועת שומרין, למימר דאין נשבעין אלא על כעין הפרט, שמטלטל וגופו ממון. **ואי ס"ד האי על כל דבר פשע.** דאתא, לענין כפל למידרשיה בכלל ופרט אתא, ולא מתרבי לכפל אלא כעין הפרט – לכתבינהו להני פרטי בקרא קמא, ולדרוש כל חד באפי נפשיה כדקאמרת, דהא בקרא קמא נמי כפילא כתיב. אלא ש"מ: האי כללא דקרא בתרא ריבויא הוא, ולענין כפל [לא] דרשינן כלל ופרט, וקרא קמא דכתיב ביה כלל ופרט – לענין שבועה הוא דאתא, כדכתיב בתריה: "ונקרב בעל הבית" וגו'. **שלמה.** יש לה סימנים, כדאמרינן ב"אלו מציאות" (ב"מ דף כח.): מה שלמה מיוחדת שיש לה סימנים כו'. **למעוטי דבר שאינו מסויים.** שאין לבעלים סימן בו, שפטור מכפל.

---

*__רעהו__ אמר רחמנא. ולא הקדש. תימה לר"י: ומאי איצטריך "רעהו" למעוטי הקדש מכפל בטוען טענת גנב? הא ליכא שבועה בהקדש! ולמסקנא דנפיק כפל ושבועה מחד קרא — א"ש. וא"ת: דלקמן נפקא לן בפרקין (ד' עו.) למעט הקדש מ"וגונב מבית האיש" ולא מבית הקדש! וי"ל: דהתם נמי לא מ"איש" קדריש, דגבי הקדש נמי שייך לשון איש. ולא משום דכתיב (שמות טו) "ה' איש מלחמה", אלא משום דבכל דבר שהוא לשון זכר שייך לשון איש, ואשה על לשון נקבה, כגון "אשה אל אחותה" בקרשים (שם כו). אלא התם ה"פ: מבית איש דשייך ביה "רעהו" כדכתיב, ולא מבית הקדש. ואגב דגבי גנב *איצטריך למנקט האי לישנא למידרש: ולא מבית הגנב — נקט ליה נמי לענין הקדש*.

דהא כל חד וחד דרשינן כלל ופרט באפי נפשיה. וא"ת: והא לקמן גבי "ונתת הכסף" דרשינן כולהו פרטי באחת, ובפרק קמא דקדושין (ד' יז. ושם) גבי הענקה! וי"ל: כיון דכתיב "על" אכל פרטא, כדכתיב "על שור על חמור על שה על שלמה" — ש"מ למידרש כל חד וחד פרטא באפי נפשיה. אי נמי: ע"כ אית לן למידרש כל חד פרטא באפי נפשיה ולמעט עופות, דאי לאו הכי — לשתוק מכולהו פרטי, ולכתוב "שלמה" לחודיה ותו לא — דמ"שלמה" אתי כל מילי, בין בעלי חיים בין אינם ב"ח, מכלל ופרט וכלל, דמשום דהוו ב"ח לא גריעי. והשתא בתחילה כשהקשה: ואימא מה הפרט מפורש דבר שנבלתו מטמאה כו', הו"מ למפרך קושיא אחריתי, לפי מה שסובר דאמרינן מה הפרט מפורש דבר המטלטל וגופו ממון: לא לכתוב אלא "שלמה" לחודיה ולשתוק מכל שאר פרטי. אלא הא עדיפא ליה למיפרך, שמקשה דאפי' מה שאמר אין אמת.

דלא מטמא נבלתו. כדממעט להו בתורת כהנים ובזבחים בפ' "חטאת [העוף]" (ד' סט:).

למה לי. למהדר למכתב כללא אחרינא? אלא לאו ש"מ "כל" ריבויא הוא. לפי מאי דמסיק השתא (כל ריבויא הוא השתא) נפיק מקרא דהכא כפל ושבועה. וא"ת: ל"ל דכתב רחמנא כל הני פרטי? לא לכתוב אלא "כסף", ומינה שמעינן דבר המטלטל וגופו ממון מכלל ופרט וכלל! וכי תימא שלא הייתי דורשו לכלל ופרט משום דאיצטריך, כדדרשינן בשבועות (דף לט: ושם ד"ה מה): מה כלים שנים — והא ע"כ כלל ופרט דרשינן ליה ב"הזהב" (ב"מ דף נז: ושם ד"ה כי) לענין שבועה, דאין נשבעין על הקרקעות ועל עבדים ושטרות. וכפל ושבועה הכל אחד, מדקאמר: לכתבינהו להנך פרטי התם. והיכי הוה מצי למכתבינהו? א"כ הייתי ממעט עופות טמאים משבועה! אלא ע"כ אם תמעטם מכפל — ג"כ משבועה תמעטם. ועוד: אי הוה כתיב להו התם — לא הוה דרשינן להו גבי כפל אלא גבי שבועה, אלא פשיטא לן דהני קראי קיימי אכפל ושבועה! וי"ל: "כסף או כלים" איצטריך *לכדדרשינן בשבועות: מה כלים שנים כו'. והא דדרשינן ליה בפ' "הזהב" (שם) לכללי ופרטי וכללי — אילו לא נאמר קאמר, כלומר: אילו לא נאמר "על כל דבר פשע" היינו דורשין מיעוט קרקעות ועבדים ושטרות מקרא ד"כי יתן", אבל השתא דכתיב "על כל דבר פשע" — אייתר ליה "כסף או כלים" למה כלים שנים. ולפי מה שפירשתי דכפל ושבועה הכל אחד, כי היכי דדרשינן לענין שבועה מה כלים שנים — הכי נמי לענין כפל, וכן הא דממעטינן דבר שאינו מסויים — הוי *בין לענין שבועה בין לענין כפל, ואפי' היכא דנשבע על ידי גלגול בדבר שאינו מסויים — פטור הוא מכפל.

אלא כל ריבויא. אע"ג דבברייתא (לעיל) דריש להו כלל ופרט וכלל — לאו משום דדריש לקרא הכי, אלא מאיזה טעם שיהיה מרבינן כל דבר המטלטל וגופו ממון, ולפי שדרשה זו שגורה בגמרא נקט בענין זה.

חד למעוטי קרקעות. שטרות הוה ליה למעוטי בריש, דדמי טפי למעוטי, כדמוכח לקמן בפ' בתרא (ד' קיז:) דלמאן דדריש ריבויי ומיעוטי לא הוה ממעט אלא שטרות.

וחד למעוטי עבדים. אע"ג דלעיל ילפינן עבדים מדאתקוש לקרקעות, הכא כיון דכתיב "כל" ריבויא — בעי לכל חד מיעוט באפי נפשיה.

דבר שאינו מסויים. פירש הקונטרס: דבר שאין לבעלים סימן בו. וקשה: מה לי יש בו סימן, מה לי אין בו סימן? ומפרש ריב"א: כגון ההיא דתנן ב"שבועות הדיינין" (שבועות ד' מג: ושם ד"ה על): אין נשבעין אלא על דבר שבמדה שבמשקל ושבמנין, לאפוקי "בית מלא מסרתי לך" "כיס מלא", והלה אומר: "מה שהנחת אתה נוטל". אבל זה אומר: עד הזיז, וזה אומר: עד החלון — חייב. ומנא ליה הא סברא אי לא משום דדרשינן מ"שלמה". ועוד היינו יכולין לפרש דבר המסויים כי ההיא דפרק "הזהב" (ב"מ ד' מז.): מה נעל דבר מסויים כו', ◦לאפוקי חצי רימון וחצי אגוז דלא. וכן אמרינן לקמן (דף סד:) גבי דרשה ד"המצא תמצא" דאמר: שדי "חמור" בין "המצא תמצא", למעוטי דבר שאינו מסויים, היינו חצי רימון וחצי אגוז, דממעט להו מכפל. ודבר שבמדה ושבמשקל ושבמנין דמצרכי גבי חיוב שבועה — תיפוק ליה ממשמעות ד"כי הוא זה". ויש ספרים ◦דגרסי לקמן: לאתויי דבר שאינו מסויים. ואין נראה, דמהיכא הוה ס"ד למעוטי, דאיצטריך קרא לאתויי? דאף על גב דממעטינן ליה לענין טוען טענת גנב מכפל, בגנב עצמו מהיכא אתי? אלא "למעוטי" גרס, ואף על פי שנתמעט מגנב עצמו בפסוק הראשון — אין למעט בכך בפסוק האחרון עד שימעט הכתוב בהדיא, דהא קרקעות עבדים ושטרות איצטריך למעוטי ולא ילפינן מהדדי.

והעדים

לעיל נד: נזיר לה: ערכין כז:
ב"מ נז: שבועות מג.
לעיל נז. לקמן קז:
שייך לעיל:
[לקמן סט:]
[ועיין תוספות בכורות יח. ד"ה וגונב]
ס"א ל"ג
עיין בר"מ
עיין רש"א

גליון הש"ס

תום' ד"ה דבר וכו' לאפוקי חלי רימון. עי' שבת דף לג ע"ב תום' ד"ה אמאי: **בא"ד** דגרסי לקמן לאתויי דבר שאינו מסויים. עיין בהרא"ש פ"ק דקדושין סי' כ':

בַּאֲבֵידָה מְשַׁלֵּם תַּשְׁלוּמֵי כֶפֶל, שֶׁנֶּאֱמַר: °"עַל כָּל אֲבֵידָה אֲשֶׁר יֹאמַר". תְּנַן הָתָם: *[א]"הֵיכָן פִּקְדוֹנִי? אָמַר לֵיהּ: אָבַד. מַשְׁבִּיעֲךָ אֲנִי, וְאָמַר: אָמֵן, וְהָעֵדִים מְעִידִים אוֹתוֹ שֶׁאֲכָלוֹ — מְשַׁלֵּם אֶת הַקֶּרֶן. [ב]הוֹדָה עַל פִּי עַצְמוֹ — מְשַׁלֵּם קֶרֶן וְחוֹמֶשׁ וְאָשָׁם; [ג]הֵיכָן פִּקְדוֹנִי? אָמַר לוֹ: נִגְנַב. מַשְׁבִּיעֲךָ אֲנִי, וְאָמַר: אָמֵן, וְהָעֵדִים מְעִידִים אוֹתוֹ שֶׁגְּנָבוֹ — מְשַׁלֵּם תַּשְׁלוּמֵי כֶפֶל. [ד]הוֹדָה מֵעַצְמוֹ — מְשַׁלֵּם קֶרֶן וְחוֹמֶשׁ וְאָשָׁם. קָתָנֵי מִיהָא בְּטוֹעֵן טַעֲנַת גַּנָּב דִּמְשַׁלֵּם תַּשְׁלוּמֵי כֶפֶל, [ה]אֲבָל בְּטוֹעֵן טַעֲנַת אָבַד — לֹא מְשַׁלֵּם תַּשְׁלוּמֵי כֶפֶל. [ו]וַאֲפִי' טוֹעֵן טַעֲנַת גַּנָּב, בִּשְׁבוּעָה הוּא דִּמְשַׁלֵּם תַּשְׁלוּמֵי כֶפֶל, אֲבָל שֶׁלֹּא בִּשְׁבוּעָה אֵינוֹ מְשַׁלֵּם תַּשְׁלוּמֵי כֶפֶל. מְנָהָנֵי מִילֵּי? דְּתָנוּ רַבָּנַן: °"אִם יִמָּצֵא הַגַּנָּב" — בְּטוֹעֵן טַעֲנַת גַּנָּב הַכָּתוּב מְדַבֵּר; אַתָּה אוֹמֵר: בְּטוֹעֵן טַעֲנַת גַּנָּב, אוֹ אֵינוֹ אֶלָּא בְּגַנָּב עַצְמוֹ? כְּשֶׁהוּא אוֹמֵר: "אִם לֹא יִמָּצֵא הַגַּנָּב" (א) — בְּטוֹעֵן טַעֲנַת גַּנָּב הַכָּתוּב מְדַבֵּר. תַּנְיָא אִידָךְ: "אִם יִמָּצֵא הַגַּנָּב" — בְּגַנָּב עַצְמוֹ הַכָּתוּב מְדַבֵּר; אַתָּה אוֹמֵר: בְּגַנָּב עַצְמוֹ, אוֹ אֵינוֹ אֶלָּא בְּטוֹעֵן טַעֲנַת גַּנָּב? כְּשֶׁהוּא אוֹמֵר: "אִם לֹא יִמָּצֵא הַגַּנָּב" — הֲרֵי טוֹעֵן טַעֲנַת גַּנָּב אָמוּר, הָא מָה אֲנִי מְקַיֵּים "אִם יִמָּצֵא הַגַּנָּב"? בְּגַנָּב עַצְמוֹ הַכָּתוּב מְדַבֵּר. דְּכוּלֵּי עָלְמָא מִיהַת: "אִם לֹא יִמָּצֵא הַגַּנָּב" — בְּטוֹעֵן טַעֲנַת גַּנָּב כְּתִיב, מַאי מַשְׁמַע? אָמַר רָבָא: "אִם לֹא יִמָּצֵא" כְּמָה שֶׁאָמַר, אֶלָּא שֶׁהוּא עַצְמוֹ גְּנָבוֹ — יְשַׁלֵּם שְׁנַיִם. וּמְנָלַן דְּבִשְׁבוּעָה? דְּתַנְיָא: *°"וְנִקְרַב בַּעַל הַבַּיִת אֶל הָאֱלֹהִים" — [ז]לִשְׁבוּעָה; אַתָּה אוֹמֵר: לִשְׁבוּעָה, אוֹ אֵינוֹ אֶלָּא לְדִין? נֶאֱמַר שְׁלִיחוּת יָד לְמַטָּה וְנֶאֱמַר שְׁלִיחוּת יָד לְמַעְלָה, מַה לְּהַלָּן לִשְׁבוּעָה, אַף כָּאן לִשְׁבוּעָה. בִּשְׁלָמָא לְמַאן דְּאָמַר חַד בְּגַנָּב וְחַד בְּטוֹעֵן טַעֲנַת גַּנָּב — הַיְינוּ דִּכְתִיבִי תְּרֵי קְרָאֵי, אֶלָּא לְמַאן דְּאָמַר תַּרְוַיְיהוּ בְּטוֹעֵן טַעֲנַת גַּנָּב, תְּרֵי קְרָאֵי לָמָּה לִי? אָמְרִי: חַד לְמַעוֹטֵי טַעֲנַת אָבַד. וּלְמַאן דְּאָמַר חַד בְּגַנָּב וְחַד בְּטוֹעֵן טַעֲנַת גַּנָּב, דְּלָא מַיְּיתַר, לְמַעוֹטֵי טַעֲנַת אָבַד מְנָא לֵיהּ? מִ"גַּנָּב" "הַגַּנָּב", וּלְמַאן דְּאָמַר תַּרְוַיְיהוּ בְּטוֹעֵן טַעֲנַת גַּנָּב, דְּמִיעֵט לֵיהּ טוֹעֵן טַעֲנַת אָבַד, "גַּנָּב" "הַגַּנָּב" מַאי דָּרֵישׁ בֵּיהּ? אָמַר לָךְ: מִבְּעֵי לֵיהּ לְכִדְרַבִּי חִיָּיא בַּר אַבָּא אָמַר רַבִּי יוֹחָנָן, *דְּאָמַר רַבִּי חִיָּיא בַּר אַבָּא אָמַר רַבִּי יוֹחָנָן: הַטּוֹעֵן טַעֲנַת גַּנָּב בְּפִקָּדוֹן — מְשַׁלֵּם תַּשְׁלוּמֵי כֶפֶל, טָבַח וּמָכַר — מְשַׁלֵּם תַּשְׁלוּמֵי אַרְבָּעָה וַחֲמִשָּׁה. לְמַאן דְּאָמַר חַד בְּגַנָּב וְחַד בְּטוֹעֵן טַעֲנַת גַּנָּב, דְּהַאי "גַּנָּב" "הַגַּנָּב" אַפְּקֵיהּ לְמַעוֹטֵי טַעֲנַת אָבַד, דְּר' חִיָּיא בַּר אַבָּא מְנָא לֵיהּ? אָמַר לָךְ: הֶקֵּישָׁא הוּא, *וְאֵין מְשִׁיבִין עַל הֶקֵּישָׁא. בִּשְׁלָמָא לְמַאן דְּאָמַר חַד בְּגַנָּב וְחַד בְּטוֹעֵן טַעֲנַת גַּנָּב — שַׁפִּיר, אֶלָּא לְמַאן דְּאָמַר תַּרְוַיְיהוּ בְּטוֹעֵן טַעֲנַת גַּנָּב, גַּנָּב עַצְמוֹ מְנָא לֵיהּ? וְכִי תֵּימָא: לֵיתֵי בְּק"ו מִטּוֹעֵן טַעֲנַת גַּנָּב — דַּיּוֹ לַבָּא מִן הַדִּין לִהְיוֹת כַּנִּדּוֹן, מַה לְּהַלָּן בִּשְׁבוּעָה, אַף כָּאן בִּשְׁבוּעָה! נָפְקָא לֵיהּ מִדְּתָנָא דְּבֵי חִזְקִיָּה, *דְּתָנָא דְּבֵי חִזְקִיָּה: יֹאמַר שׁוֹר וּגְנֵיבָה, וְהַכֹּל בִּכְלָל! אִילּוּ כָּךְ, הָיִיתִי אוֹמֵר: מָה הַפְּרָט מְפוֹרָשׁ קָרֵב לְגַבֵּי מִזְבֵּחַ, אַף כָּל קָרֵב לְגַבֵּי מִזְבֵּחַ, מַה יֵּשׁ לְךָ לְהָבִיא? שֶׂה, כְּשֶׁהוּא

והעדים מעידים אותו שאכלו. אכלו נקט לרבותא, אף על פי שאבדו מן העולם — פטור מן הכפל בטענת אבד. וסיפא נקט שנגנבו לרבותא, דאע"פ שהוא בעין — חייב כפל, כיון שטוען טענת גנב. הוי אומר בטוען טענת גנב דבר הכתוב. דבא זה ולימד על זה. מגנב הגנב. ד"הגנב" משמע המיוחד, כמו "העולה" — עולה ראשונה (פסחים דף נט:), "הירך" — המיומנת שבירך (חולין דף צא.). ואידך (ב) הגנב לכדר' חייא בר אבא. אע"ג דהאי דריש לריבוי והאי למיעוט — אין לחוש, דהכל לפי סברת הדרש.

בַּאֲבֵידָה. מוֹצֵא אֲבֵידָה שֶׁטּוֹעֵן: נִגְנְבָה הֵימֶנִּי לְאַחַר שֶׁמְּצָאתִיהָ. שֶׁנֶּאֱמַר עַל כָּל אֲבֵידָה וגו'. וּבְטוֹעֵן טַעֲנַת גַּנָּב מוֹקְמִינַן לֵיהּ לְהַאי קְרָא, לְקַמָּן בְּמַתְנִיתִין. תְּנַן הָתָם. בְּ"הַגּוֹזֵל עֵצִים". מְשַׁלֵּם אֶת הַקֶּרֶן. דְּאֵין כֶּפֶל אֶלָּא בְּטַעֲנַת גַּנָּב. הוֹדָה מֵעַצְמוֹ מְשַׁלֵּם קֶרֶן וְחוֹמֶשׁ וְאָשָׁם. דִּכְתִיב (ויקרא ה): "אוֹ מִכֹּל אֲשֶׁר יִשָּׁבַע עָלָיו לַשֶּׁקֶר" וגו', וְזֶהוּ אֲשַׁם גְּזֵילוֹת, וְאֵינוֹ בָּא אֶלָּא עַל הוֹדָאַת פִּיו. דְּאַע"פ דְּלָא כְּתַב בְּהַהִיא פָּרָשָׁה הוֹדָאָה – כְּתַב רַחֲמָנָא בַּאֲשַׁם גֵּזֶל הַגֵּר בְּפָרָשַׁת נָשֹׂא: "וְהִתְוַדּוּ אֶת חַטָּאתָם" וגו'. וְחוֹמֶשׁ נַמִי אֵינוֹ בְּלֹא אָשָׁם. טַעֲנַת אֲבֵדָה. אָבַד הֵימֶנּוּ. בִּשְׁבוּעָה. לְאַחַר שֶׁנִּשְׁבַּע לַשֶּׁקֶר, כִּדְקָתָנֵי מַשְׁבִּיעֲךָ אֲנִי. בְּטוֹעֵן טַעֲנַת גַּנָּב. בְּבַעַל הַבַּיִת שֶׁטּוֹעֵן טַעֲנַת גַּנָּב בְּפִקָּדוֹן זֶה, כִּדְכְתִיב: "וְגוּנַּב מִבֵּית הָאִישׁ" וגו' הַכָּתוּב מְדַבֵּר, וְקָאָמַר דְּאִם יִמָּצֵא שֶׁהוּא גַּנָּב שֶׁיְּשַׁלֵּם שְׁנַיִם. אוֹ אֵינוֹ אֶלָּא בְּגַנָּב עַצְמוֹ. שֶׁבַּעַל הַבַּיִת אֱמֶת טָעַן, וְנִמְצָא הַגַּנָּב שֶׁגְּנָבוֹ. כְּשֶׁהוּא אוֹמֵר אִם לֹא יִמָּצֵא הַגַּנָּב. וּלְקַמֵּיהּ מוֹקְמִינַן לָהּ בְּטוֹעֵן טַעֲנַת גַּנָּב, שֶׁנִּמְצָא הוּא בְּעַצְמוֹ *גַּנָּב, הֲוֵי אוֹמֵר דְּהַאי קְרָא דִּלְעֵיל נַמִי כְּשֶׁנִּמְצָא בַּעַל הַבַּיִת שַׁקְרָן קָאָמַר. וּלְקַמֵּיהּ פָּרְכִינַן: תְּרֵי קְרָאֵי לָמָּה לִי! בְּגַנָּב עַצְמוֹ. מַגִּיד הַכָּתוּב שֶׁגַּנָּב מְשַׁלֵּם כֶּפֶל. אוֹ אֵינוֹ אֶלָּא בְּטוֹעֵן טַעֲנַת גַּנָּב קָאָמַר. דְּכִי נִמְצָא הוּא גַּנָּב – מְשַׁלֵּם כֶּפֶל. ה"ג: כְּשֶׁהוּא אוֹמֵר אִם לֹא יִמָּצֵא הַגַּנָּב הֲרֵי טוֹעֵן טַעֲנַת גַּנָּב אָמוּר הָא מָה אֲנִי מְקַיֵּים כו'. אִם לֹא יִמָּצֵא כְּמוֹ שֶׁאָמַר. שֶׁטּוֹעֵן נִגְנְבָה, כִּדְכְתִיב: "וְגוּנַּב מִבֵּית הָאִישׁ". אֶלָּא הוּא עַצְמוֹ גְּנָבוֹ. "וְנִקְרַב בַּעַל הַבַּיִת", כְּלוֹמַר: וְהוּא כְּבָר נִשְׁבַּע בְּדָבָר שֶׁלֹּא שָׁלַח יָדוֹ, מַה כְּתִיב אַחֲרָיו – "עַל כָּל דְּבַר פֶּשַׁע וגו' יְשַׁלֵּם שְׁנַיִם". וּמִמַּאי. דְּהַאי "וְנִקְרַב בַּעַל הַבַּיִת" לִשְׁבוּעָה קָאָמַר. לִשְׁבוּעָה. שֶׁכֵּיוָן שֶׁטּוֹעֵן "וְגוּנַּב מִבֵּית הָאִישׁ" – יִשָּׁבַע שֶׁנִּגְנְבָה, וְיִפָּטֵר. אוֹ אֵינוֹ אֶלָּא לְדִין. *לְפֵרָעוֹן, דְּשׁוֹמֵר חִנָּם שֶׁטּוֹעֵן נִגְנְבָה יְשַׁלֵּם. דְּהַאי קְרָא בְּשׁוֹמֵר חִנָּם כְּתִיב, כִּדְאָמְרִי' בְּ"הַשּׁוֹאֵל" (ב"מ דף צד:). שְׁלִיחוּת יָד לְמַטָּה. בְּשׁוֹמֵר שָׂכָר, "שְׁבוּעַת ה' תִּהְיֶה בֵּין שְׁנֵיהֶם אִם לֹא שָׁלַח" וגו'. שְׁלִיחוּת יָד לְמַעְלָה. "וְנִקְרַב בַּעַל הַבַּיִת אֶל הָאֱלֹהִים אִם לֹא שָׁלַח יָדוֹ". לְמַעוֹטֵי טַעֲנַת אָבַד. אִם טָעַן נֶאֶבְדָה הֵימֶנּוּ, וְעֵדִים מְעִידִים שֶׁגְּנָבוֹ – פָּטוּר מִכֶּפֶל, אֲפִילּוּ נִשְׁבַּע. מְשַׁלֵּם תַּשְׁלוּמֵי אַרְבָּעָה וַחֲמִשָּׁה. כְּגַנָּב עַצְמוֹ, דְּנָפְקָא לֵיהּ מִ"גַּנָּב" "הַגַּנָּב". הֶקֵּישָׁא הוּא. כֵּיוָן דִּסְמִיכִי לַהֲדָדֵי הָנֵי קְרָאֵי אִיתַּקַּשׁ גַּנָּב וְטוֹעֵן טַעֲנַת גַּנָּב לַהֲדָדֵי: מַה גַּנָּב מְשַׁלֵּם תַּשְׁלוּמֵי אַרְבָּעָה וַחֲמִשָּׁה אִם טָבַח וּמָכַר – אַף טוֹעֵן טַעֲנַת גַּנָּב מְשַׁלֵּם אַרְבָּעָה וַחֲמִשָּׁה. וְאַע"ג דְּאִיכָּא לְמִיפְרַךְ: מַה לְּגַנָּב עַצְמוֹ שֶׁכֵּן חַיָּיב כֶּפֶל בְּלֹא שְׁבוּעָה, תֹּאמַר בְּטוֹעֵן טַעֲנַת גַּנָּב שֶׁצָּרִיךְ שְׁבוּעָה – אֵין מְשִׁיבִין עַל הַהֶיקֵּשׁ, כִּדְאָמְרִינַן לְהָא מִילְּתָא בְּ"הַגּוֹזֵל עֵצִים" (לקמן דף קח.). וְאִיכָּא דְּאָמְרִי: הֶקֵּישָׁא – כִּדְמְפָרֵשׁ הָתָם: הוֹאִיל וְגַנָּב מְשַׁלֵּם כֶּפֶל, וְטוֹעֵן טַעֲנַת גַּנָּב מְשַׁלֵּם כֶּפֶל, מַה גַּנָּב טָבַח וּמָכַר מְשַׁלֵּם תַּשְׁלוּמֵי אַרְבָּעָה וַחֲמִשָּׁה – אַף טוֹעֵן טַעֲנַת גַּנָּב טָבַח וּמָכַר מְשַׁלֵּם אַרְבָּעָה וַחֲמִשָּׁה. וְלָאו מִילְּתָא הִיא, דְּהַאי מַה מָּצִינוּ בִּנְיַן אָב הוּא. וְלָא הֶקֵּישָׁא. אֶלָּא סְמִיכוּת הַמִּקְרָאוֹת קָרֵי הֶיקֵּשׁ, וְהָכִי נַמִי שָׁמְעִינַן הָתָם. הָנִיחָא לְמ"ד חַד בְּגַנָּב וְחַד בְּטוֹעֵן [טַעֲנַת גַּנָּב] שַׁפִּיר. נָפְקָא לֵיהּ גַּנָּב מֵהָכָא, אֶלָּא לְמ"ד כו'. מִדְּתָנָא דְּבֵי חִזְקִיָּה. דְּדָרֵישׁ קְרָא אַחֲרִינָא דְּמִשְׁתָּעֵי בְּגַנָּב עַצְמוֹ: "אִם הִמָּצֵא תִמָּצֵא בְיָדוֹ הַגְּנֵבָה" וגו'. וְהַאי דְּנָקַט דְּרָשָׁה וְלָא נָקַט קְרָא – מִשּׁוּם דְּמִקְּרָא לָא נָפְקָא לַן בְּהֶדְיָא אֶלָּא בַּעֲלֵי חַיִּים, כִּדְכְתִיב: "מִשּׁוֹר וְעַד חֲמוֹר עַד שֶׂה חַיִּים" וּמִדְּרָשָׁה מְרַבֵּה לְהוּ תַּנָּא דְּבֵי חִזְקִיָּה לְכוּלְּהוּ. יֹאמַר שׁוֹר וּגְנֵיבָה וְהַכֹּל בִּכְלָל. דִּמְרַבִּינַן כָּל כְּעֵין הַפְּרָט – דָּבָר הַמִּטַּלְטֵל וְגוּפוֹ מָמוֹן, חֲמוֹר וָשֶׂה לָמָּה לִי? וּמְשַׁנֵּי: אִילּוּ כֵּן וכו'. וּלְקַמֵּיהּ מְפָרֵשׁ מַאי קָאָמַר, הָא לָאו כְּלָל וּפְרָט וּכְלָל הוּא דְּקָדָרֵישׁ לֵיהּ כְּעֵין הַפְּרָט. אַף כָּל קָרֵב. וְלָא מְתַרְבֵּי מִכְּעֵין הַפְּרָט אֶלָּא הַקָּרֵב לַמִּזְבֵּחַ. לְהָכִי כְּתַב "שֶׂה", דְּלָא תֵּימָא "כֹּל" לְאֵתוּיֵי קָרֵב לַמִּזְבֵּחַ קָאָתֵי, דְּמַה יֵּשׁ לְךָ לְהָבִיא שֶׁקָּרֵב לַמִּזְבֵּחַ וְלֹא נִכְתַּב בְּפֵירוּשׁ – שֶׂה, כְּשֶׁהוּא אוֹמֵר "שֶׂה" – הֲרֵי שֶׂה אָמוּר, הָא מָה אֲנִי מְקַיֵּים גְּנֵיבָה שֶׁאֲנִי דּוֹרֵשׁ בִּכְעֵין הַפְּרָט. לְרַבּוֹת

תורה אור: שמות כב; שם; שם

עין משפט נר מצוה

ה א מיי' פ"ד מהל' גניבה הל' ג ועיין במ"מ טוח"מ סי' שנב:

ו ב מיי' פ"א מהל' שבועות הל' ח ט סמג לאוין רמ:

ז ג מיי' פ"ד מהל' גניבה הלכה א טוח"מ שם:

ח ד מיי' פ"א מהל' שבועות הל' ט י יא סמג שם:

ט ה מיי' פ"ד הלכות גניבה הלכה ג טוח"מ שם:

י ו מיי' שם הלכה א טוח"מ שם:

יא ז מיי' פ"א מהל' שכירות הל' ב סמג עשין פט טוש"ע ח"מ סי' רנא סעיף א:

הגהות הב"ח

(א) גמ' אם לא ימצא הגנב הוי אומר בטוען טענת גנב: (ב) תוס' ד"ה ואידך גנב הגנב כו':

מסורת הש"ס

לקמן קו. קח: שבועות

[נ"ל גנבו יעב"ץ]

ב"מ מא:

[לקמן קו:] לעיל סב:

[לקמן קו: מנחות פב:]

ע' רש"א וברי"מ

[לקמן עט.]

לרבות שאר דברים. כל הני. אילו כן. לשון תשובת שאילה הן. אף כל קדוש בבכורה. ולא מתרבי מדרשא אלא חמור, הלכך מה היה לך להביא שלא נכתב – חמור. להכי כתב חמור, דע"כ כלל ופרט(ג) לשאר דברים אתי. והכל בכלל. "חיים", דמשמע לרבות כל בעלי חיים, למה לי? מי כתיב שור. ברישא, והדר "גניבה", דהוה ליה פרט וכלל, דנימא הכל בכלל דנעשה כלל מוסיף על הפרט? "גניבה" ו"שור" כתיב, דהוה ליה כלל ופרט, ושור – אין, מידי אחרינא – לא! וכי תימא אילו נאמר קאמר. אילו נאמר "שור" ברישא והדר "גניבה", לא היה צריך לכתוב יותר, ולמה לא נכתב כן. אילו נאמר שור וגניבה. בתמיה: הא ודאי ה"ל פרט וכלל, ושפיר קשיא לי', ומאי "אילו כן" קמהדר ליה? אלא כדכתיב קאמרי. בתמי': גניבה ושור, הא הוה ליה כלל ופרט, ומאי "הכל בכלל" דקא קשי' לי', ומאי "מה הפרט מפורש" דמהדר ליה? הא כלל ופרט לא מרבי מידי! אחיים סמיך. "גניבה", דה"ל כללא קמא, סמיך ליה א"חיים", דהוי כללא בתרא, ודריש בכלל ופרט וכלל. וסיפא דקתני: ויאמר גניבה שור ושה וחמור והכל בכלל. הואיל וא"חיים" סמיך ליה מאי קשיא לי'? הא טפי לא כתיבו! "אם המצא תמצא" קשיא ליה, כדאמר במסקנא. ומיהו, אפסקיה גמרא למילתי' דרבא בפרכי אחריתי, ולא שבק לאסוקיה למילתי'. והא לא דמי כללא בתרא. דלא קייל אלא בעלי חיים, לכללא קמא, דמשמע כל דבר. הא תנא דבי רבי ישמעאל. בשילהי "אלו טריפות". והכי קא קשיא ליה. לתנא דבי חזקיה, בסיפא דמילתא. אם המצא תמצא. דמשמע ריבויי, למה לי? והשת' קא מפרש לה רבא לכולא מתני'. הכל בכלל. דמתרבי כל כעין הפרט, דבר המטלטל וגופו ממון. הא מה אני מקיים גניבה. דדרשינן בכלל ופרט, לרבות כל דבר. יאמר גניבה ושור ושה וחמור וחיים והכל בכלל. "אם המצא" ל"ל? ומשני: אילו כן הייתי אומר אף כל ב"ח. להכי איצטריך "אם המצא תמצא" למימר דלאו מ"גניבה" ו"חיים" דרשינהו לכלל, אלא מ"אם המצא תמצא", ושדינהו לכל הני פרטי בינייהו, כדמפרש לקמן. הדר פריך תנא דבי חזקיה: מה יש לך להביא שאר ב"ח כשהוא אומר חיים הרי בעלי חיים אמור. כלומר מקרא בהדיא נפקי, ולאו מכלל ופרט. הלכך, מה אני מקיים כלל ופרט – לרבות כל דבר, ואכתי "המצא תמצא" למה לי? והכי מסקנא דתנא דבי חזקיה.

[בעלי חיים]

בחים ל: ח: חולין סו. [כריתות כא.]

כשהוא אומר "שה" – הרי שה אמור, הא מה אני מקיים "גניבה"? לרבות כל דבר. יאמר "שור" "שה" ו"גניבה", והכל בכלל! אילו כך, הייתי אומר: מה הפרט מפורש דבר הקדוש בבכורה, אף כל דבר הקדוש בבכורה, מה יש לך להביא? חמור, כשהוא אומר "חמור" – הרי חמור אמור, הא מה אני מקיים "גניבה"? לרבות כל דבר. יאמר "שור" ו"חמור" "שה" ו"גניבה", והכל בכלל! אילו כך, הייתי אומר: מה הפרט מפורש בעלי חיים, אף כל ב"ח, מה יש לך להביא? שאר בעלי חיים, כשהוא אומר "חיים" – הרי *חיים אמור, הא מה אני מקיים "גניבה"? לרבות כל דבר. אמר מר: יאמר "שור" ו"גניבה". מי כתיב "שור" ו"גניבה"? "גניבה" ו"שור" הוא דכתיב! וכי תימא "אילו נאמר" קאמר, אילו נאמר "שור" ו"גניבה" – ומי מצית אמרת מה הפרט מפורש? הוה "שור" – פרט, ו"גניבה" – כלל, פרט וכלל – נעשה כלל מוסיף על הפרט, ואיתרבו להו כל מילי! אלא כדכתיב קאמרי, "גניבה" ו"שור" – מי מצית אמרת "הכל בכלל" או "מה הפרט מפורש"? הוה ליה "גניבה" – כלל, ו"שור" – פרט, כלל ופרט – אין בכלל אלא מה שבפרט, שור – אין, מידי אחרינא – לא! אמר רבא: תנא א"חיים" קא סמיך ליה, וכלל ופרט וכלל קא"ל. והא לא דמי כללא בתרא לכללא קמא! הא תנא *דבי רבי ישמעאל הוא, דכה"ג דריש כללי ופרטי. והכי קא קשיא ליה: "אם המצא תמצא" למה לי? יאמר שור וגניבה וחיים, והכל בכלל! אילו כן, הייתי אומר: מה הפרט מפורש – דבר הקרב לגבי מזבח, אף כל הקרב לגבי מזבח, מה יש (א) להביא? שה, כשהוא אומר "שה" – הרי שה אמור, הא מה אני מקיים "גניבה"? לרבות כל דבר. יאמר גניבה ושור ושה וחיים, והכל בכלל! אילו כן, הייתי אומר: מה הפרט מפורש דבר הקדוש בבכורה, אף כל דבר הקדוש בבכורה, מה יש לך להביא? חמור, [כשהוא אומר "חמור"] – הרי חמור אמור, הא מה אני מקיים "גניבה"? לרבות כל דבר. יאמר גניבה ושור ושה וחמור וחיים, והכל בכלל! אילו כן, הייתי אומר: מה הפרט מפורש בעלי חיים, אף כל ב"ח, מה יש לך להביא? שאר ב"ח, כשהוא אומר "חיים" – הרי (ב) חיים אמור, הא מה אני מקיים "גניבה"? לרבות כל דבר, "אם המצא תמצא" ל"ל?

אי

לאמה לי? והכי מסקנא דתנא דבי חזקיה.

אי

כשהוא אומר שה כו'. אף על גב ד"חמור" כתיב ברישא, נקט כי האי גוונא, משום דהכי מסיק מילתיה שפיר. **יאמר** גניבה ושור וחיים והכל בכלל. שאל הר"ר אשר מלוני"ל את ר"י היכי ס"ד דמ"גניבה" "שור" ו"חיים" מרבינן כל דבר? ולא (ד) יהיה אלא פרט וכלל, דלא הוה מרבינן מיניה אלא ב"ח והשתא בעי לרבויי בכלל ופרט וכלל טפי ממאי דמשמע כללא בתרא! והשיב לו ר"י: כיון דלא מסיק אכתי אדעתיה לד קדושה בבכורות וקרב לגבי מזבח, א"כ, אם נאמר: מה הפרט מפורש בעלי חיים – נמצא שאין כלום בכלל בתרא ד"חיים" יותר מכעין הפרט. והואיל וכן הוא אית לן למימר ד"חיים" כלל הוא, להיות משמע כל דבר כמו "גניבה", באם אינו ענין לחיים ממש תניהו לענין כל דבר. או נפרש "חיים" לשון חשיבות, כמו "אחייה לקרן כעין שגנב" דלקמן. ולהכי קאמר והכל בכלל, דאם לא בא לרבות מכעין הפרט אלא בעלי חיים – לא יכתוב שום פרט אלא "גניבה" ו"חיים", וליהוי "גניבה" כלל ו"חיים" פרט, ונ"מ בעלי חיים. והא דפריך: הא לא דמיא כללא בתרא לכללא קמא, אע"ג [דפרישית] ד"חיים" משמע כל דבר, כמו כלל ד"גניבה" – מ"מ הואיל ומשמעות פשט שלהן אין שוה – אין לעשות כלל ופרט וכלל מהם. ומשני: ה"א קרב לגבי מזבח – אין, וכלל חיים כמשמעותיה, ומכעין הפרט אנו ממעטינן שאר ב"ח שאין קריבין לגבי מזבח, כמו בכל מקום דכעין הפרט אתא למעוטי מכללא בתרא. והכל מתיישב (ה) כפי' ר"י. אך האחרון, דקאמר: יאמר "גניבה" "שור" ו"שה" ו"חמור" ו"חיים" והכל בכלל, דכיון דמכח פרטי בעי למימר שיהיה הכל בכלל, מאי קמשני: אילו כן הייתי אומר מה הפרט מפורש בעלי חיים? והא מכח פרטות בא לרבות אפי' לאו בעלי חיים! ואור"י: דהמתרץ לא הבין דברי המקשן, וחוזר ומקשה לו אותה קושיא עצמה ומפרש דבריו. ואין נראה, דאין זו סוגיית הגמ', אלא תנא אחד הוא שואל ומשיב לעצמו. לכך נראה לפרש, דהתנא לרווחא דמילתא בא לפרש, דאפילו תאמר שאין חילוק בין ב"ח לשאין בעלי חיים, ולא ממעטינן מ"חיים" דלאו ב"ח – אפ"ה מפרטא ד"שור" לא תרבה כל דבר המטלטל וגופו ממון, ותקשה לך: "המצא תמצא" ל"ל? דהא לא מרבינן מפרטא ד"שור" אלא דבר הקרב לגבי מזבח. ומסיק: ויאמר "גניבה" ו"שור" ו"חמור" "שה" ו"חיים" והכל בכלל, וא"כ "המצא תמצא" למה לי? ומשני: אילו כן הייתי אומר: מה הפרט מפורש ב"ח. עתה שאין מוצא טעם אחר מחלק בין בעלי חיים לשאין בעלי חיים, אבל בתחלה שהיו לו טעמים אחרים – לא חושש אם לא נחלק. והשתא איצטריך "המצא תמצא" לרבות שאין בעלי חיים. ופריך: מה יש לך להביא בעלי חיים, כשהוא אומר "חיים" – הרי חיים אמור, ולמה לי כל הני פרטי? הא מה אני מקיים "גניבה", פירוש כלל ופרט וכלל – לרבות כל דבר. ועוד שאלו: דאמאי הוצרך לומר "מה הפרט מפורש ב"ח", ה"ל למימר: אילו כן הייתי אומר מה הפרט מפורש דבר שנבלתו מטמא – לאתויי עופות טהורים, ולא הוי מצי לאקשויי תו: כשהוא אומר "חיים" הרי חיים אמור כו', ושפיר איצטריך "המצא תמצא"! ואור"י: דסובר זה התנא שאין לנו לתלות זה הדבר בגלל טומאה, *כיון שטומאה חלוקה יותר מדאי, שזה במגע ובמשא וזה בבית הבליעה דוקא. ועוד שאלו: למה ליה לרבא למימר ד"אם המצא תמצא" קא קשיא ליה, ולריך להפוך דברי הברייתא ולומר "גניבה" ו"שור"? לימא דחזקיה אתא לפרושי למה כל הני פרטי, וא"אם המצא תמצא" סמיך, וכבני מערבא ס"ל, דאמרי בשני כללות הסמוכי' זה לזה הטל פרט ביניהם ודונם בכלל ופרט. וה"ק: יאמר "המצא" ו"שור" ו"גניבה", והכל בכללו! אבל "המצא תמצא" לא חשיב להו שני כללות, דדברה תורה כלשון בני אדם. ומשני דמ"שור" לחודיה ועם שני כללות לא אתי. ומסיק: ויאמר "המצא" ו"שור" ו"חמור" ו"שה" ו"גניבה" והכל בכלל, אילו כן הייתי אומר מה הפרט מפורש ב"ח. והשתא מסיים שפיר כשהוא אומר "חיים" – הרי חיים אמור, הא מה אני מקיים כלל ופרט – לרבות כל דבר, והוי אתי מסקנא דברייתא שפיר. דלפי מה שמפרש רבא ד"המצא תמצא" קא קשיא ליה אין מתרץ בברייתא עצמה כלום, וגם מה שמזכיר "שור" קודם ל"גניבה" – הוה אתי נמי שפיר! והשיב לו ר"י: חדא, דאין לומר *דברה תורה כלשון בני אדם אלא במקום שאי אפשר לומר בע"א, ואין להאריך כאן בזה. ועוד: דא"כ היאך היה יכול לומר: אילו כן הייתי אומר מה הפרט מפורש קרב לגבי מזבח וקדוש בבכורה? הא ע"כ כיון דסבר האי תנא דשני כללות הסמוכים זה לזה בריבה ומיעט וריבה דיינינן ליה – א"כ משני כללות הוה מרבינן כל דבר, דהא ליכא למימר הטל פרט ביניהם כבני מערבא, דא"כ תקשה ליה: "שה" למה לי, כדפריך בסמוך.

אי

(א) גמ' מה יש לך להביא שה: (ב) שם כשהוא אומר חיים הרי בעלי חיים: (ג) רש"י ד"ה אף כל וכו' כלל ופרט וכלל לשאר: (ד) תוס' ד"ה יאמר וכו' ולא יהא אלא פרט: (ה) בא"ד מתיישב לפי' ר"י וכו' למימר שיהיה הכל בכלל חיים מאי קמשני וכו' והא מכח פרטות בא לרבות בכלל חיים אפילו לאו:

וא"כ אינו יכול לומר הכל השוה שבהם. הסתק מחילופי גרסאות

[illegible] דלא הי' לריך לומ' בכה וכו' דמבעי' ליה כדתניא יכול וכו' ולימוד המצא המצא או תמצא תמצא לא משמע ליה כדפירשו התוספות לקמן. הסתק מחילופי גרסאות:

תורה אור

אִי הָכִי, שַׁפִּיר קַשְׁיָא לֵיהּ! מִשּׁוּם דְּאִית לֵיהּ פִּירְכָא: לְרַבּוֹת כָּל דָּבָר מֵהֵיכָא קָמַיְיתֵי לֵיהּ? מִכְּלָל בַּתְרָא; כְּלָלָא גּוּפֵיהּ "חַיִּים" כְּתִיב בֵּיהּ, כְּלָל וּפְרָט וּכְלָל מַאי קָא מְהַנֵּי לֵיהּ? אִי לְאַתּוּיֵי כָּל דָּבָר – הָא "חַיִּים" כְּתִיב, בַּעֲלֵי חַיִּים – אִין, מִידֵּי אַחֲרִינָא – לָא! מִשּׁוּם הָכָא אִיצְטְרִיךְ "אִם הִמָּצֵא". אָמְרִי: וְהָא שְׁנֵי כְּלָלוֹת דִּסְמִיכֵי אַהֲדָדֵי נִינְהוּ! אָמַר רָבִינָא, *כִּדְאָמְרִי בְּמַעְרְבָא: כָּל מָקוֹם שֶׁאַתָּה מוֹצֵא שְׁנֵי כְּלָלוֹת הַסְּמוּכִים זֶה לָזֶה – הַטֵּל פְּרָט בֵּינֵיהֶם וְדוּנֵם בִּכְלָל וּפְרָט; שְׁדִי "שׁוֹר" בֵּין "הִמָּצֵא" לְ"תִמָּצֵא", לְאַתּוּיֵי מַאי? אִי לְאַתּוּיֵי ב"ח, מֵ"חַיִּים" נָפְקָא! אֶלָּא לְאַתּוּיֵי דָּבָר שֶׁאֵין בַּעֲלֵי חַיִּים, וּדְרוֹשׁ הָכִי: מָה הַפְּרָט מְפוֹרָשׁ – דָּבָר הַמִּטַּלְטֵל וְגוּפוֹ מָמוֹן, אַף כָּל דָּבָר הַמִּטַּלְטֵל וְגוּפוֹ מָמוֹן. וְתוּ, שְׁדִי "חֲמוֹר" בֵּין "הִמָּצֵא" לְ"תִמָּצֵא", לְאַתּוּיֵי מַאי? אִי לְאַתּוּיֵי דָּבָר שֶׁאֵין בַּעֲלֵי חַיִּים, מִ"שּׁוֹר" נָפְקָא! אֶלָּא לְאַתּוּיֵי דָּבָר מְסוּיָּים, א"ה "שֶׂה" לָמָּה לִי? אֶלָּא, רִיבָּה וּמִיעֵט וְרִיבָּה הוּא, כִּדְתָנָא דְּבֵי רַבִּי יִשְׁמָעֵאל, *דְּתָנָא דְּבֵי ר' יִשְׁמָעֵאל: "בַּמַּיִם" "בַּמַּיִם" ב' פְּעָמִים, אֵין זֶה כְּלָל וּפְרָט, אֶלָּא *רִיבָּה וּמִיעֵט וְרִיבָּה – רִיבָּה הַכֹּל. מַאי רַבֵּי, רַבֵּי כָּל מִילֵּי? אִי הָכִי, כָּל הָנֵי פְּרָטֵי לָמָּה לִי? חַד לְמַעוּטֵי קַרְקַע, וְחַד לְמַעוּטֵי עֲבָדִים, וְחַד לְמַעוּטֵי שְׁטָרוֹת, "גְּנֵיבָה" וְ"חַיִּים" – לְכִדְרַב, דְּאָמַר: אַחֲיֵיהּ לְקֶרֶן כְּעֵין שֶׁגָּנַב. וּלְמ"ד חַד בְּגַנָּב וְחַד בְּטוֹעֵן טַעֲנַת גַּנָּב, וְגַנָּב עַצְמוֹ נָפְקָא לֵיהּ מֵ"אִם יִמָּצֵא הַגַּנָּב", הַאי "אִם הִמָּצֵא תִמָּצֵא" מַאי דָּרֵישׁ בֵּיהּ? מִבָּעֵי לֵיהּ לְכִדְרַבָּא בַּר אֲהִילַאי, *דְּאָמַר רַבָּא בַּר אֲהִילַאי: מַאי טַעְמָא דְּרַב, דְּאָמַר: מוֹדֶה בִּקְנָס וְאַחַר כָּךְ בָּאוּ עֵדִים פָּטוּר? דִּכְתִיב: "אִם הִמָּצֵא תִמָּצֵא", "אִם הִמָּצֵא" – בְּעֵדִים, "תִמָּצֵא" – בְּדַיָּינִים, פְּרָט לְמַרְשִׁיעַ אֶת עַצְמוֹ. וּלְמ"ד תַּרְוַיְיהוּ בְּטוֹעֵן טַעֲנַת גַּנָּב, דְּהַאי "אִם הִמָּצֵא תִמָּצֵא" מַפֵּיק לֵיהּ לְגַנָּב עַצְמוֹ, מַרְשִׁיעַ עַצְמוֹ מְנָלַן? °מֵ"אֲשֶׁר יַרְשִׁיעֻן אֱלֹהִים" – וְלֹא הַמַּרְשִׁיעַ אֶת עַצְמוֹ. וּלְמ"ד חַד בְּגַנָּב וְחַד בְּטוֹעֵן טַעֲנַת גַּנָּב, דְּאַיְיתֵי לֵיהּ מֵ"הִמָּצֵא תִמָּצֵא" לְמַרְשִׁיעַ אֶת עַצְמוֹ, הַאי "אֲשֶׁר יַרְשִׁיעֻן" מַאי דָּרֵישׁ בֵּיהּ? אָמַר לָךְ: הַהוּא מִיבָּעֵי לֵיהּ לְמוֹדֶה בִּקְנָס דְּפָטוּר. וּמ"ד תַּרְוַיְיהוּ בְּטוֹעֵן טַעֲנַת גַּנָּב, קָסָבַר: מוֹדֶה בִּקְנָס וְאח"כ בָּאוּ עֵדִים – חַיָּיב. וּלְמ"ד חַד בְּגַנָּב וְחַד בְּטוֹעֵן טַעֲנַת גַּנָּב, דְּנָפְקָא לֵיהּ גַּנָּב מֵהָתָם, בִּשְׁלָמָא "אִם הִמָּצֵא תִמָּצֵא" לְכִדְרַבָּא בַּר אֲהִילַאי, אֲבָל כָּל הָנֵי פְּרָטֵי לָמָּה לִי? כִּדְתָנָא דְּבֵי רַבִּי יִשְׁמָעֵאל, *דְּתָנָא דְּבֵי רַבִּי יִשְׁמָעֵאל: כָּל פָּרָשָׁה שֶׁנֶּאֶמְרָה וְנִשְׁנֵית, לֹא נִשְׁנֵית אֶלָּא לְדָבָר שֶׁנִּתְחַדֵּשׁ בָּהּ. וְאֵימָא: גַּנָּב עַצְמוֹ בִּשְׁבוּעָה! לָא ס"ד, דְּתַנְיָא, רַבִּי יַעֲקֹב אוֹמֵר: "שְׁנַיִם יְשַׁלֵּם" – אשֶׁלֹּא בִּשְׁבוּעָה; אַתָּה אוֹמֵר: שֶׁלֹּא בִּשְׁבוּעָה, אוֹ אֵינוֹ אֶלָּא בִּשְׁבוּעָה? אָמַרְתָּ: לֹא כָּךְ הָיָה. מַאי "לֹא כָּךְ הָיָה"? אָמַר אַבַּיֵי: לָא לִכְתּוֹב רַחֲמָנָא "שְׁנַיִם יְשַׁלֵּם" בְּגַנָּב, וְלֵיתֵי בְּק"ו מִטּוֹעֵן טַעֲנַת גַּנָּב: וּמַה טּוֹעֵן טַעֲנַת גַּנָּב דְּבְהֶיתֵּירָא אֲתָא לִידֵיהּ – אָמַר קְרָא לִישַׁלֵּם תְּרֵי, גַּנָּב עַצְמוֹ דְּבְאִיסּוּרָא אֲתָא לִידֵיהּ, לֹא כָּל שֶׁכֵּן? אֶלָּא "שְׁנַיִם יְשַׁלֵּם" דִּכְתַב רַחֲמָנָא בְּגַנָּב עַצְמוֹ לָמָּה לִי? דַּאֲפִילּוּ שֶׁלֹּא בִּשְׁבוּעָה. וְהַאי "אִם הִמָּצֵא" לְהָכִי הוּא דַּאֲתָא? הָא מִיבָּעֵי לֵיהּ *לְכִדְתַנְיָא: "יָדוֹ", אֵין

שמות כב

אִי הָכִי שַׁפִּיר קָא קַשְׁיָא לֵיהּ. וּמַאי תְּשׁוּבָה יֵשׁ בַּדָּבָר? ה"ג: לְרַבּוֹת כָּל דָּבָר **מֵהֵיכָא** מַיְיתֵי לָהּ מִכְּלָל בַּתְרָא **כְּלָלָא גּוּפָא** חַיִּים כְּתִיב בֵּיהּ. כְּלוֹמַר: אִיצְטְרִיךְ "אִם הִמָּצֵא תִמָּצֵא". דְּאִי מִ"גְּנֵיבָה" וְ"חַיִּים" דָּרַשְׁתְּ לִכְלָל, אִיכָּא לְמִיפְרַךְ: שְׁאָר דְּבָרִים מֵהֵיכָא מַיְיתֵית לְהוּ – מִכְּלָלָא בַּתְרָא "אַף כָּל", כְּלָלָא גּוּפֵיהּ חַיִּים כְּתִיב בֵּיהּ! דְּכָל הֵיכָא דְּדָרְשִׁינַן כְּלָל וּפְרָט וּכְלָל, "אַף כָּל" מִכְּלָלָא בַּתְרָא מִידְרַשׁ. דִּכְלָלָא קַמָּא לְמַעוּטֵי הוּא דְּאָתֵי, דִּבְלָאו אִיהוּ הָוֵי פְּרָט וּכְלָל, דְּאִיתְרַבּוּ כָּל מִילֵּי, וּמְהַנֵּי כְּלָלָא קַמָּא לְמַעוּטֵי מַאי דְּלָא דָּמֵי לֵיהּ לִפְרָטָא. וּכְלָלָא בַּתְרָא לְרַבּוּיֵי אָתֵי, דְּאִי לָאו אִיהוּ – ה"ל כְּלָל וּפְרָט, וְאֵין בַּכְּלָל אֶלָּא מַה שֶּׁבַּפְּרָט. הִלְכָּךְ לָא דָּרְשִׁינַן מִינֵּיהּ אֶלָּא בַּעֲלֵי חַיִּים, וּבָטֵיל לֵיהּ כְּלָל וּפְרָט. דְּאע"ג דְּדָרֵישׁ תַּנָּא דְּבֵי ר' יִשְׁמָעֵאל בְּעָלְמָא כְּלָלָא דְּלָא דָּמֵי (לֵיהּ פְּרָטָא) – הָנֵי מִילֵּי לְרַבּוּיֵי מִידֵּי דְּהָוֵי בִּכְלָלָא בַּתְרָא. **לְהָכִי אִיצְטְרִיךְ אִם הִמָּצֵא תִמָּצֵא.** לְמִידְרַשׁ כְּלָלֵי מִינֵּיהּ, כִּדְמְפָרֵשׁ וְאָזֵיל. **וְהָא תְּרֵי** כְּלָלֵי דִּסְמִיכֵי נִינְהוּ. "הִמָּצֵא" "תִמָּצֵא", וְהֵיכִי מָצֵי לְמִדְרַשׁ מִינַּיְיהוּ כְּלָל וּפְרָט וּכְלָל? הַטֵּל פְּרָט. הַכָּתוּב בְּלִיךְ, בֵּינֵיהֶן. **אֶלָּא לְאַתּוּיֵי דָּבָר הַמְסוּיָּים.** אִין, אֲבָל דָּבָר שֶׁאֵינוֹ מְסוּיָּם – לָא. וּמֵרִיבּוּיָא דָּרְשִׁינַן לָהּ, וְלָא מִמַּשְׁמָעוּתָא. דְּיֵשׁ בְּהֵמוֹת הַרְבֵּה שֶׁאֵין בָּהֶן סִימָן, דְּאִי מִמַּשְׁמָעוּתָא דִּקְרָא נָפְקָא – תֵּיפּ"ק מִכְּעֵין הַפְּרָט דְּשׁוֹר. ה"ג: **דְּתָנָא דְּבֵי** ר' יִשְׁמָעֵאל בַּמַּיִם בַּמַּיִם ב' פְּעָמִים. וְלָא גָּרַס "כָּל מָקוֹם שֶׁנֶּאֱמַר בַּמַּיִם בַּמַּיִם". "תֹּאכְלוּ כֹּל אֲשֶׁר בַּמַּיִם" "כֹּל אֲשֶׁר לוֹ סְנַפִּיר וְקַשְׂקֶשֶׂת בַּמַּיִם", הוֹאִיל וּכְלָלִים סְמוּכִים הֵם, וְהַפְּרָט אֵינוֹ בֵּינֵיהֶן, אֶלָּא אַחֲרֵיהֶם כְּתִיב: "בַּיַּמִּים וּבַנְּחָלִים", דְּמַשְׁמַע דְּיַמִּים וּנְחָלִים הוּא דְּבָעֵינַן סְנַפִּיר וְקַשְׂקֶשֶׂת, אֲבָל שִׁיחִין וּמְעָרוֹת לָא – אֵין זֶה נִדְרָשׁ בִּכְלָל וּפְרָט, דְּלָא לִיתְרַבֵּי אֶלָּא כְּעֵין הַפְּרָט. אֶלָּא בְּרִיבָּה וּמִיעֵט וְרִיבָּה, וְאִתְרַבֵּי כָּל מִילֵּי, אֶלָּא דְּמִיעוּט מְהַנֵּי לְמַעוּטֵי פּוּרְתָּא, חֲדָא מִילְּתָא וְתוּ לָא. חַד לְמַעוּטֵי קַרְקַע כו'. וְעַד הַשְׁתָּא לָא מָצֵי לְתָרוֹצֵי הָכִי. דְּכִי הֲוָה דָּיְינִינַן לְהוּ בִּכְלָל וּפְרָט – לָא הֲוָה מִתְרַבֵּי כְּעֵין הַפְּרָט אֶלָּא דָּבָר הַמִּטַּלְטֵל וְגוּפוֹ מָמוֹן, וּמִתְּפִילָּא הֲוֵי מְמַעֲטֵי כָּל הָנֵי. **אַחֲיֵיהּ לְקֶרֶן** כְּעֵין שֶׁגָּנַב. לְקַמָּן הִיא בִּשְׁמַעְתִּין, דְּאִם גָּנַב בְּהֵמָה וְהוּכְחֲשָׁה אוֹ הוּזְלָה – מְשַׁלֵּם כִּשְׁעַת הַגְּנֵיבָה, דִּכְתִיב: "חַיִּים" – הַחֲיֵיהוּ לְקֶרֶן שֶׁל גְּנֵיבָה שֶׁיְּהֵא שָׁלֵם. מ"ט דְּרַב. לְקַמֵּיהּ הִיא בְּהַאי פִּירְקָא. **אִם הִמָּצֵא בְּעֵדִים.** אִם תְּחִלָּה פִּמָּצֵא בְּעֵדִים – תִּמָּצֵא הַכֶּפֶל שֶׁהוּא קְנָס, בְּדַיָּינִין. **פְּרָט לְמַרְשִׁיעַ אֶת עַצְמוֹ.** אע"פ שֶׁבָּאוּ עֵדִים אַחֲרֵי כֵן, אֵין מְשַׁלֵּם כֶּפֶל. **הַהוּא מִיבָּעֵי לֵיהּ** לְמוֹדֶה בִּקְנָס דְּפָטוּר. אִם לֹא בָּאוּ עֵדִים אַחֲרֵי כֵן, וְאַיְּיתַר לֵיהּ "אִם הִמָּצֵא תִמָּצֵא" לִפְטוֹר אֲפִילּוּ בָּאוּ עֵדִים. דְּאִי לָא כְּתִיב אֶלָּא חַד קְרָא – הֲוָה מוֹקְמִינַן לֵיהּ בְּלֹא בָּאוּ עֵדִים. **כָּל הָנֵי פְּרָטֵי לָמָּה** לִי. אִי לְמַעוּטֵי קַרְקָעוֹת וַעֲבָדִים וּשְׁטָרוֹת כִּדְאָמְרַן – הָא אִימְעִיטוּ לְהוּ לְהָנָךְ מֵהָנָךְ פְּרָטֵי דִּכְתִיבִי בְּ"עַל כָּל דְּבַר פֶּשַׁע". **שֶׁנִּתְחַדֵּשׁ בָּהּ.** "אִם הִמָּצֵא" בְּעֵדִים "תִמָּצֵא" בְּדַיָּינִין, פְּרָט לְמוֹדֶה בִּקְנָס. **וְאֵימָא גַּנָּב עַצְמוֹ.** לֹא יְשַׁלֵּם כֶּפֶל עַד שֶׁיִּשָּׁבַע לַשֶּׁקֶר, הוֹאִיל וּמִקְרָאֵי דִּלְעֵיל נָפְקָא לָן גַּנָּב עַצְמוֹ. בְּחוּשָׁה

אִי הכי שפיר קשיא ליה. ומשני: משום דלית ליה פירכא, אע"ג דהאי פירכא ליתא בברייתא — היינו משום דלא חש לפרשה.

מהיכא קמייתי ליה מכללא בתרא כללא גופי' חיים כתיב ביה. גם זה שאל ה"ר אשר מלוני"ל את ר"י, דאכתי תקשה: "המצא תמצא" ל"ל? דהא כיון דלא מצי לרבויי בכלל ופרט וכלל טפי אלא בעלי חיים, משום דכללא גופיה "חיים" כתיב ביה, א"כ ע"כ "חיים" לכללא לא אתיא, דאי כללא — אמאי איצטריך כל הנהו פרטי? לא לכתוב אלא "גניבה" ו"חיים" והוה מרבינן נמי כל בעלי חיים. אלמא, לאו כללא הוא אלא פרטא, ומפרט ד"חיים" לחוד נרבה כל ב"ח, ומכל הני פרטי נרבה כל דבר. והכי איתא בסמוך: אי לאתויי בעלי חיים — מ"חיים" נפקא! והשיב ר"י: דלקמן ודאי דאיכא כללא ופרטא וכללא, כדאמר: שדי "שור" בין "המצא תמצא" — קאמר שפיר דמכעין הפרט ד"שור" מרבינן אפילו דלאו ב"ח, דכל ב"ח מפרטא ד"חיים" נפקא. אבל הכא, בלא "המצא תמצא", אי "חיים" לא הוי כלל — היכי מתרבו דלאו ב"ח מפרטי, כיון דליכא כלל בתרא לרבויי מיניה כעין הפרט? והואיל שאין לרבות מהן כלום אם נעשה "חיים" פרט — ע"כ צריכין אנו לעשות מ"חיים" כלל, ויבואו הפרטות למעט מן הכלל, ונאמר: מה הפרט מפורש דבר שנבלתו מטמאה, ונמעט מהם עופות טמאים. ואע"ג דהאי תנא אין נראה לו לתפוס לד טומאה — היינו דוקא לפי מה שהיה יכול לתפוס לד ב"ח, ורוצה לעשות כלל ד"חיים" כמו כלל ד"גניבה". אבל השתא דמסיק דמ"חיים" לא משמע אלא ב"ח, ואין יכול לתפוס לד ב"ח, דא"כ פרטי למה לי — ע"כ היה צריך לתפוס לד טומאה. להכי איצטריך "המצא תמצא" לרבות כל דבר, כדמסיק.

למעוטי דבר שאין מסוים. אית ספרים דגרסי "לאתויי", ולעיל (דף סג. ד"ה דבר) מפורש.

אי הכי שה ל"ל. ° ה"מ לאקשויי: "שור ושה" ל"ל? *דמכעין הפרט ד"חיים" לחוד מרבינן כל דבר, אפילו דלאו ב"ח. ולפי שהגמרא התחיל דבריו בשור שהוא ראשון נקט הכי, אבל באמת הוא ששניהם מיותרים.

יב א מיי' פ"א מהל' גניבה הלכה ז סמג עשין עא:

שבועות ה. [חולין זבחים מג. בכורות ע"ש]

ס"א ל"ג ומוס' שבנא ה דלא דמי ליה לכללא כ ומהרש"ש הגיה דלא לפרטי ה"מ כו' ו דדריש בעלמא כללא דמי להדדי לפרטי כל לכלל ופרט וכלל לומר מה הפרט עכ"ל

שבועות דף ה. חולין דף סז. בכורות נא.

[עי' תוס' שבועות ה. דתנא]

לקמן עה.

[עיין בהרא"ש ריש קידושין סי' ב']

דאל"כ כללא בתרא למה לי לרבות כעין הפרט הא בפרט עצמו משמע כל. הגהות מחילופי גרסאות

סוטה ג. שבועות [מנחות י.]

גיטין ד' עז. ב"מ י:

גליון הש"ס
תוס' ד"ה אי הכי שה למה לי ה"מ לאקשויי. עיין תשובת מהר"י אלדיבי סי' קלה:

אֵין לִי אֶלָּא יָדוֹ, גַּגּוֹ חֲצֵירוֹ וְקַרְפֵּיפוֹ מִנַּיִן? ת"ל: °"אִם הִמָּצֵא תִמָּצֵא", מ"מ! א"כ, לֵימָא קְרָא אוֹ "הִמָּצֵא הִמָּצֵא" אוֹ "תִּמָּצֵא תִמָּצֵא", מִדְּשַׁנֵּי קְרָא ש"מ תַּרְתֵּי.§ גּוּפָא, אָמַר רַב: [א]קֶרֶן — כְּעֵין שֶׁגָּנַב, תַּשְׁלוּמֵי כֶפֶל [ב]וְתַשְׁלוּמֵי אַרְבָּעָה וַחֲמִשָּׁה — כִּשְׁעַת הַעֲמָדָה בַּדִּין. מַאי טַעֲמָא דְּרַב? אָמַר קְרָא "גְּנֵיבָה" וְ"חַיִּים", אַמַּאי קָאָמַר רַחֲמָנָא "חַיִּים" בִּגְנֵיבָה? אַהֲדְרֵיהּ לְקֶרֶן כְּעֵין שֶׁגָּנַב. °אָמַר רַב שֵׁשֶׁת, אָמִינָא: *כִּי נָיֵים וְשָׁכֵיב רַב אֲמַר לְהָא שְׁמַעְתָּא; דְּתַנְיָא: [ג]כְּחוּשָׁה וְהִשְׁמִינָה — מְשַׁלֵּם תַּשְׁלוּמֵי כֶפֶל וְתַשְׁלוּמֵי אַרְבָּעָה וַחֲמִשָּׁה כְּעֵין שֶׁגָּנַב! אָמְרִי: מִשּׁוּם [ד]דְּא"ל: אֲנָא פְּטֵימְנָא וְאַתְּ שָׁקְלַתְּ? ת"ש: [ה]שְׁמֵינָה וְהִכְחִישָׁה — מְשַׁלֵּם תַּשְׁלוּמֵי כֶפֶל וְתַשְׁלוּמֵי אַרְבָּעָה וַחֲמִשָּׁה כְּעֵין שֶׁגָּנַב! הָתָם נַמִי, מִשּׁוּם דְּאָמְרִינַן לֵיהּ: מַה לִּי קַטְלָהּ כּוּלָּהּ מַה לִּי קַטְלָהּ פַּלְגָא, כִּי קָאָמַר רַב — [ו]בְּיוֹקְרָא וְזוֹלָא הוּא דְּקָאָמַר. הֵיכִי דָּמֵי? אִילֵימָא דְּמֵעִיקָּרָא שָׁוְיָא זוּזָא וּלְבַסּוֹף שָׁוְיָא ד' זוּזֵי, קֶרֶן — כְּעֵין שֶׁגָּנַב; לֵימָא פְּלִיגָא דְּרַב אַדְּרַבָּה, *דְּאָמַר *רַבָּה: הַאי [ז]מַאן דִּגְזַל חָבִיתָא דְּחַמְרָא מֵחַבְרֵיהּ, מֵעִיקָּרָא שָׁוְיָא זוּזָא וּלְבַסּוֹף שָׁוְיָא ד' זוּזֵי, תַּבְרָהּ אוֹ שַׁתְיָהּ — מְשַׁלֵּם ד', אִיתְּבַר מִמֵּילָא — מְשַׁלֵּם זוּזָא? אָמְרִי: [ח]כִּי קָאָמַר רַב, כְּגוֹן דְּמֵעִיקָּרָא שָׁוְיָא ד' וּלְבַסּוֹף שָׁוְיָא זוּזָא, קֶרֶן — כְּעֵין שֶׁגָּנַב, [ט]תַּשְׁלוּמֵי כֶפֶל וְתַשְׁלוּמֵי אַרְבָּעָה וַחֲמִשָּׁה — כִּשְׁעַת הַעֲמָדָה בַּדִּין. תָּנֵי רַבִּי חֲנִינָא לְסִיּוּעֵיהּ לְרַב:* בעה"ב שֶׁטָּעַן טַעֲנַת גַּנָּב בְּפִקָּדוֹן, וְנִשְׁבַּע וְהוֹדָה וּבָאוּ עֵדִים, אִם עַד שֶׁלֹּא בָּאוּ עֵדִים הוֹדָה — [י]מְשַׁלֵּם קֶרֶן וְחוֹמֶשׁ וְאָשָׁם, וְאִם מִשֶּׁבָּאוּ עֵדִים הוֹדָה — [כ]מְשַׁלֵּם תַּשְׁלוּמֵי כֶפֶל וְאָשָׁם, וְחוּמְשׁוֹ עוֹלֶה לוֹ בִּכְפֵילוֹ, דִּבְרֵי רַבִּי יַעֲקֹב; וַחֲכָמִים

שמות כב — תורה אור

רש"י

כְּחוּשָׁה וְהִשְׁמִינָה כו'. הַגַּנָּב פִּטְּמָהּ. וְקַשְׁיָא לְרַב, דְּאָמַר תַּשְׁלוּמֵי ד' וְה' כִּשְׁעַת הַעֲמָדָה בַּדִּין. וְקס"ד בֵּין שְׁבָחָהּ בֵּין הַכְחָשָׁהּ הַגַּנָּב בְּיָדַיִם. וּמְשַׁנֵּי: מִשּׁוּם דְּא"ל כו'. אֲבָל שְׁבָחָהּ בְּדָמִים, שֶׁהוּקְרוּ בְּהֵמוֹת בַּשּׁוּק אוֹ שֶׁנִּתְפַּטְּמָה מֵאֵלֶיהָ — מְשַׁלֵּם כֶּפֶל כִּי הָשְׁתָּא. וְהִכְחִישָׁהּ. הַגַּנָּב הִכְחִישָׁהּ בְּיָדַיִם, בְּטוֹרַח מְלָאכָה אוֹ בְּמַקֵּל. מַה לִּי קַטְלָהּ פַּלְגָא. הִלְכָּךְ מֵהַהִיא שַׁעְתָּא דְּאַכְחָשָׁהּ אַתְחֲלָה לָהּ טְבִיחָה. וּלְבַסּוֹף שָׁוְיָא ד'. בְּשָׁעָה שֶׁאֲבָדָהּ מִן הָעוֹלָם. תַּבְרָהּ. בְּיָדַיִם אוֹ שַׁתְיָהּ — מְשַׁלֵּם ד'. וּבְ"הַמַּפְקִיד" (ב"מ דף מג.) מְפָרֵשׁ טַעְמָא, דְּכָל כַּמָּה דְּאִיתֵיהּ בְּעֵינָא — בִּרְשׁוּתָא דְּמָרָהּ קַיְימָא, דְּהָא בָּעֵי לְאַהֲדוּרָהּ, הִלְכָּךְ בִּרְשׁוּתָא דְּמָרָהּ הוּקְרָה, וְהַהִיא שַׁעְתָּא דְּתַבְרָהּ וְשַׁתְיָהּ הוּא דְּקָא גָּזֵיל לָהּ. אֲבָל אִיתְּבַר מִמֵּילָא, אַמַּאי מְחַיְּיבַתְּ לֵיהּ — אַהַהִיא שַׁעְתָּא דְּגַזְלָהּ, וְהַהִיא שַׁעְתָּא זוּזָא הוּא דְּשָׁוְיָא. וְגַבֵּי טְבִיחָה וּמְכִירָה הָוֵי כִּי תַּבְרָהּ אוֹ שַׁתְיָהּ. מְשַׁלֵּם קֶרֶן וְחוֹמֶשׁ וְאָשָׁם. מִשּׁוּם שְׁבוּעָה, וְאֵין כָּאן כֶּפֶל — דְּמוֹדֶה בִּקְנָס פָּטוּר. וְאִם מִשֶּׁבָּאוּ עֵדִים. וְנִתְחַיֵּיב בְּכֶפֶל, הוֹדָה. מְשַׁלֵּם כֶּפֶל וְאָשָׁם וְחוֹמֶשׁ עוֹלֶה לוֹ בְּתוֹךְ הַכֶּפֶל. שֶׁהֲרֵי חוֹמֶשׁ לַבְּעָלִים הוּא, וְהוּא שָׁקַל. וְע"כ הָא דְּר' יַעֲקֹב כְּשֶׁשָּׁוִין כְּאֶחָד הַחוֹמֶשׁ וְהַכֶּפֶל קָמַיְירֵי, דְּאִי הֲוָה כְּפֵילָא טְפֵי מֵחוּמְשָׁא — לָאו חוּמְשָׁא הָוֵי, וְלָא מִיפְּטַר לֵיהּ עַד דִּמְשַׁלֵּם חוֹמֶשׁ, דְּחוֹמֶשׁ כַּפָּרָה דִּשְׁבוּעָה הוּא.

תוספות

אין לי אלא בידו. פי': שגנבו בידו ממש. גגו חלירו — כלומר שהכישה במקל מחלירו של בעה"ב ונכנסה לגגו חלירו וקרפיפו. ואילטריך לרבויי חלר, לאשמועינן דחלר קונה אף לחובתו. דלא תימא כשליח דמיא, ואין שליח לדבר עבירה. קמ"ל דקונה, כדמפרש בפ"ק דב"מ (דף י:) דיש שליח לדבר עבירה היכא דשליח לאו בר חיובא הוא, וכן מוכח התם כדפרישית.

ליכתוב או אם המצא המצא או תמצא תמצא. משמע דאורחיה דקרא ליכתוב ב' פעמים תיבה אחת, וכן ב"החובל" (לקמן פה.) גבי "ורפא ירפא". וקשה: *דבריש "היו בודקין" (סנהדרין דף מ: ושם ד"ה מדהוה) קאמר גבי גז"ש ד"היטב היטב" דמופנה, מדה"ל למכתב או "דרוש תדרוש" או "חקור תחקור", מדשני קרא בדבוריה ב"היטב" כו'. משמע דאי הוה כתב הכי — לא הוה מופנה. ואמאי? אכתי הוה מופנה, מדהוי ליה למיכתב או "דרוש דרוש" או "תחקור תחקור"! וי"ל: דאין ה"נ, אלא משום דאין יורד לאותה סברא, וניחא ליה למנקט כפל לשון השגור בכמה מקומות, כמו "העניק תעניק" "נתון תתן" (דברים טו).

גופא אמר רב קרן כעין שגנב. במסקנא דמילתא אמרינן דרב איירי לענין יוקרא וזולא. וא"ת: ומאי קמ"ל? מתניתין היא בריש "הגוזל קמא" (לקמן דף צג:): כל הגזלנין משלמין כשעת הגזילה. ואע"ג דמתני' משמע דלענין שינוי איירי, כגון עלים ועשאן כלים, והתם (דף צו:) נמי קאמר בגמ': כל הגזלנים משלמים כשעת הגזילה — לאתויי דר' אלעאי, גזל טלה ונעשה איל — נעשה שינוי בידו וקנאו. מ"מ לענין יוקרא וזולא נמי איירי, כדמוכח בסוף "המפקיד" (ב"מ דף מג.) דמייתי לה איוקרא וזולא. וכן פרק "כל שעה" (פסחים דף לב.) גבי אוכל תרומה, דקאמר: היכא דמעיקרא שויא ד' ולבסוף שויא זוזא — לא תבעי לך, דודאי לפי דמים משלם, דלא גרע מגזלן, דתנן: כל הגזלנים משלמים כשעת הגזילה! וי"ל: דעיקר רב לא אתא לאשמועינן אלא תשלומי כפל ותשלומי ארבעה וחמשה כשעת העמדה בדין. והא דקאמר מ"ט דרב — אתשלומי כפל ותשלומי ד' וה' קא בעי. וה"פ: אמר קרא גניבה וחיים, אחייה לקרן כעין שגנב, ומשמע ליה דוקא לקרן, ולא תשלומי ד' וה'. וא"ת: ב"הגוזל קמא" (לקמן דף קה.) דאמר רבא גזל שלש אגודות בג' פרוטות, והוזלו ועמדו על ב', והחזיר לו ב' — חייב להחזיר לו אחת. ותנא תונא: גזל חמץ ועבר עליו הפסח. אמאי לא מייתי ראיה ממתני' ד"כל הגזלנים משלמין כשעת הגזילה", כיון דלענין יוקרא וזולא נמי איירי? וי"ל: דממתניתין ד"כל הגזלנים" לא מצי מייתי, דהתם אם איתא לגזילה בעין — הויא בת השבה, ולהכי כי ליתא נמי בעין — משלם כשעת הגזילה. אבל גבי אגודה, דאם איתא בעין — לא הויא בת השבה, דהשתא לא שויא פרוטה — הוה אמינא דכי ליתא נמי לא משלם. אבל מההיא ד"חמץ ועבר עליו הפסח" מייתי שפיר, דאילו הוי בעין לא שוי מידי — אפ"ה היכא דליתא בעין משלם כדמעיקרא. ובפרק "כל שעה" (פסחים דף לב.) הוי מצי לאתויי מההוא ד"גזל חמץ" דמשלם כדמעיקרא, אלא דניחא ליה להביא ההיא ד"כל הגזלנים", שהיא שנויה תחילה. ועוד אור"י: דמ"גזל חמץ" לא מצי למידק כלל דלפי דמים משלם היכא דמעיקרא שויא ד' ולבסוף שויא זוזא, דה"א דגבי חמץ כי ליתא בעין בעי לשלומי ליה חמץ מעליא כאותה חתיכה שגזל, דלפי מדה משלם, אבל לא כדמים של שעת הגזילה.

דתניא כחושה והשמינה כו'. תימה: היכי ס"ד דרב ששת שדבר רב בכחושה והשמינה, דא"כ היה מגרע כחו של קרן, וממילתיה דרב משמע שבא ליפות כחו של קרן ולגרע כח כפל וד' וה', דקאמר: אחייה לקרן דוקא כעין שגנב, ו"אחייה" משמע לשון יפוי כח! וי"ל ד"אחייה" אין לשון יפוי אלא לשון תשלומים, וכל דבר שמשלים החסרון שגנב או גזל קרי "אחייה". וכן משמע בסוף שמעתין דקאמר: *טלאים כדמעיקרא [משלם], כפל ד' וה' כשל עכשיו. משמע אפי' מעיקרא שויא זוזא ולבסוף ד', דומיא דטלה ונעשה איל — משלם כפל כי השתא, לפי' ר"י דלקמן. ושם אפרש בע"ה. ומיהו ר"ת פי' בע"א לקמן, דלגרע כח הכפל קאמר רב כשעת העמדה בדין, ולא ליפות.

אנא מפטימנא ואת שקלת. משמע דכשנתפטמה מאליה הוי כשעת העמדה בדין. ולפי זה הוה מצי לאוקמי מילתיה דרב כשנתפטמה מאליה, ולא הוה צריך לאוקמיה ביוקרא וזולא. ומיהו, לפי האמת, אפי' כשנתפטמה מאליה — משלם כפל ד' וה' כעין שגנב, כמו בטלה ונעשה איל, דאמר לקמן דמשלם כפל ד' וה' כעין שגנב, ואפי' שינוי לא קני, משום דאמר ליה: אטו תורא גנבי מינך? דיכרא גנבי מינך? הכא נמי כשנתפטמה מאליה, מצי אמר ליה: אטו שמינה גנבי מינך? ודוקא ביוקרא וזולא הוא דקאמר רב כפל ד' וה' כשעת העמדה בדין, דלא שייך למימר: אטו יוקרא גנבי מינך. וטעמא אפרש לקמן בע"ה גבי הא דקאמר: טלאים כדמעיקרא, דמים כשל עכשיו.

מה לי קטלה כולה מ"ל קטלה פלגא. פ"ה: משום דהכחשה אתחלה דטביחה היא. וקשה לר"י: דלא שייכא הכחשה לטביחה מידי, כיון שאם היה הורגה כולה בענין זה לא היה בה דין ד' וה'! אלא הכי פריך: מה לי קטלה כולה — דאין הולכין בתר הדמים דהשתא, דקנאה בשינוי ואינה של נגנב, אלא בתר מעיקרא שהיתה שלו, וה"ה בקטלה פלגא. ולפי זה ה"ה בהוכחשה ממילא, דמשלם כדמעיקרא, דמה לי מתה כולה מה לי מתה פלגא — ודאי מתה כולה מאליה יש לחייבו כדמעיקרא, שהיתה של נגנב, ולא בתר השתא. וכי קא משני ומוקי מילתא דרב ביוקרא וזולא — לא הוה מצי לאוקמי בכחשה דממילא. ועוד אר"י דמצי לפרש בע"א: מ"ל קטלה כולה מ"ל קטלה פלגא, כלומר: אפי' למ"ד אין לשחיטה אלא לבסוף, ולא מחייב ד' וה' עד משהו אחרון — אפ"ה לא אזלינן בתר חשיבותא דההיא שעתא כפי מה שהוא שוה במשהו אחרון, אלא כפי מה ששוה קודס שחיטה. א"כ, כי קטלה פלגא נמי, דהיינו הכחישה — לא אזלינן בתר השתא, אלא בתר מעיקרא. ולפי טעם זה ה"מ לאוקמיה מילתי' דרב בהוכחשה ממילא.

כפילא

עין משפט נר מצוה

יג א מיי' פ"א מהל' גניבה הל' יד סמג עשין עא טוש"ע ח"מ סי' שנד סעיף ג:

יד ב מיי' שם סמג שם טוש"ע שם:

טו ג מיי' שם הלכה יג סמג שם טוש"ע ח"מ שם סעיף ד:

טז ד טוש"ע שם בהג"ה ובסעי' א:

יז ה מיי' שם טוש"ע שם סעי' ד:

יח ו טוש"ע שם ס"ג:

[ע' בתוס' פסחים מח: ד"ה א"כ ותוס' מנחות יז: ד"ה לכתוב ותוס' כתובות לט: ד"ה אין]

יט ז מיי' שם הלכה יד ופ"ג מהל' גזילה הל' א סמג שם טוש"ע ח"מ שם סעי' ג וסי' שסב סעי' י:

כ ח מיי' פ"א מהלכות גניבה הלי"ד ופ"ג מהלכות גזילה ה"ב סמג שם טוש"ע ח"מ סי' שנד ס"ג וסי' שסב סעי' יא:

כא ט מיי' פ"א מהל' גניבה הל' יד סמג שם טוח"מ סי' שנד:

כב י מיי' פ"א מהל' שבועות הלכה ח והל' ט ופ"ז שם הל' א והל' ב סמג לאוין רמח:

כג כ מיי' פ"ד מהל' גניבה הלכה א סמג עשין עא טוח"מ סי' שנב:

מסורת הש"ס

[יבמות כב: ושם נסמן]

[תוספות ב"מ מג: ד"ה אלא הגי' רבא]

[לקמן קז. שבועות לז:]

[ג' רש"א טלאים כדמעיקרא דמים כשל עכשיו משמע כו' וכן הוא גי' הר"ש ע"ש]

גליון הש"ס

גמרא אמר רב ששת אמינא כי נייס. לעיל דף מז ע"ב וש"נ:

תוס' ד"ה לכתוב וכו' וכן בהחובל גבי ורפא ירפא. וכן תענית ג ע"א מנחות יז ע"ב:

וַחֲכָמִים אוֹמְרִים: א°"בְּרֹאשׁוֹ וַחֲמִישִׁתוֹ" — מָמוֹן הַמִּשְׁתַּלֵּם בְּרֹאשׁ מוֹסִיף חוֹמֶשׁ, מָמוֹן שֶׁאֵין מִשְׁתַּלֵּם בְּרֹאשׁ אֵין מוֹסִיף חוֹמֶשׁ; ר"ש בֶּן יוֹחַאי אוֹמֵר: אֵין חוֹמֶשׁ וְאָשָׁם מִשְׁתַּלֵּם בְּמָקוֹם שֶׁיֵּשׁ כֶּפֶל. קָתָנֵי מִיהַת: חוּמְשׁוֹ עוֹלֶה לוֹ בִּכְפֵילוֹ, דִּבְרֵי רַבִּי יַעֲקֹב; ה"ד? אִילֵימָא דְּמֵעִיקָּרָא שַׁוְיָא ד' וּלְבַסּוֹף שַׁוְיָא אַרְבָּעָה, חוּמְשׁוֹ עוֹלֶה לוֹ בִּכְפֵילוֹ? כְּפֵילָא אַרְבָּעָה וְחוּמְשָׁא זוּזָא! אֶלָּא לָאו דְּמֵעִיקָּרָא שַׁוְיָא אַרְבָּעָה וּלְבַסּוֹף שַׁוְיָא זוּזָא, דִּכְפֵילָא זוּזָא וְחוּמְשֵׁיהּ זוּזָא, אַלְמָא: קֶרֶן — כְּעֵין שֶׁגָּנַב, תַּשְׁלוּמֵי כֶפֶל וְתַשְׁלוּמֵי ד' וְה' — כִּשְׁעַת הַעֲמָדָה בַּדִּין! אָמַר רָבָא: לְעוֹלָם דְּמֵעִיקָּרָא שַׁוְיָא אַרְבָּעָה וְהַשְׁתָּא נַמִי שַׁוְיָא אַרְבָּעָה, וּדְקָא קַשְׁיָא: כְּפֵילָא ד' וְחוּמְשֵׁיהּ זוּזָא! הב"ע — כְּגוֹן שֶׁנִּשְׁבַּע וְחָזַר וְנִשְׁבַּע אַרְבַּע פְּעָמִים וְהוֹדָה, וְהַתּוֹרָה אָמְרָה "וַחֲמִשִׁתָיו", *בהַתּוֹרָה רִיבְּתָה חֲמִישִׁיּוֹת הַרְבֵּה בְּקֶרֶן אַחַת. אָמַר מָר, וַחֲכָמִים אוֹמְרִים: "בְּרֹאשׁוֹ וַחֲמִישִׁתוֹ" — מָמוֹן הַמִּשְׁתַּלֵּם בְּרֹאשׁ מוֹסִיף חוֹמֶשׁ, מָמוֹן שֶׁאֵין מִשְׁתַּלֵּם בְּרֹאשׁ אֵין מוֹסִיף חוֹמֶשׁ. אֲבָל אָשָׁם מַיְיתֵי. מַאי שְׁנָא חוֹמֶשׁ דְּלָא מְשַׁלֵּם — דִּכְתִיב: "בְּרֹאשׁוֹ וַחֲמִישִׁתוֹ", אָשָׁם נַמִי לָא מְשַׁלֵּם, דְּהָא כְּתִיב: "בְּרֹאשׁוֹ וַחֲמִישִׁתוֹ וְאֶת אֲשָׁמוֹ"! אָמְרִי לָךְ רַבָּנַן: "אֶת" פַּסְקֵיהּ קְרָא. וְר"ש בֶּן יוֹחַאי? "וְאֶת" עַרְבֵיהּ קְרָא. וְרַבָּנַן אָמְרִי לָךְ: לָא לִיכְתּוֹב רַחֲמָנָא לָא וָי"ו וְלָא "אֶת". וְר"ש בֶּן יוֹחַאי אָמַר לָךְ: "אֶת" לָא סַגְיָא דְּלָא כְּתַב, לְאַפְסוֹקֵי בֵּין מָמוֹן גָּבוֹהַּ לְמָמוֹן הֶדְיוֹט, הִלְכָּךְ אֲתָא וָי"ו עַרְבֵיהּ קְרָא. *אָמַר רַבִּי אִילְעָא: גגָּנַב טָלֶה וְנַעֲשָׂה אַיִל, עֵגֶל וְנַעֲשָׂה שׁוֹר — נַעֲשָׂה שִׁינּוּי בְּיָדוֹ וּקְנָאוֹ, טָבַח וּמָכַר — שֶׁלּוֹ הוּא טוֹבֵחַ, שֶׁלּוֹ הוּא מוֹכֵר. אֵיתִיבֵיהּ רַבִּי חֲנִינָא לְר' אִילְעָא: דגָּנַב טָלֶה וְנַעֲשָׂה אַיִל, עֵגֶל וְנַעֲשָׂה שׁוֹר — מְשַׁלֵּם תַּשְׁלוּמֵי כֶפֶל וְתַשְׁלוּמֵי אַרְבָּעָה וַחֲמִשָּׁה כְּעֵין שֶׁגָּנַב; וְאִי ס"ד קַנְיֵיהּ בְּשִׁינּוּי, אַמַּאי מְשַׁלֵּם? שֶׁלּוֹ הוּא טוֹבֵחַ, שֶׁלּוֹ הוּא מוֹכֵר! אֲמַר לֵיהּ: וְאֶלָּא מַאי, שִׁינּוּי לָא קָנֵי? אַמַּאי מְשַׁלֵּם כְּעֵין שֶׁגָּנַב? לְשַׁלֵּם כִּי הַשְׁתָּא! אֲמַר לֵיהּ: כִּי הַשְׁתָּא הַיְינוּ טַעְמָא דְּלָא מְשַׁלֵּם, מִשּׁוּם דְּא"ל: תּוֹרָא גְּנַבִי מִמָּךְ?! דִּיכְרָא גְּנַבִי מִמָּךְ?! א"ל: *רַחֲמָנָא נִיצְּלָן מֵהַאי דַּעְתָּא! אֲמַר לֵיהּ: אַדְּרַבָּה, רַחֲמָנָא נִיצְּלָן מִדַּעְתָּא דִּידָךְ! § מַתְקִיף לָהּ רַבִּי זֵירָא: וְנִיקְנִינְהוּ בְּשִׁינּוּי הַשֵּׁם! אָמַר רָבָא: השׁוֹר בֶּן יוֹמוֹ קָרוּי שׁוֹר, אַיִל בֶּן יוֹמוֹ קָרוּי אַיִל; שׁוֹר בֶּן יוֹמוֹ קָרוּי שׁוֹר, דִּכְתִיב: °"שׁוֹר אוֹ כֶשֶׂב אוֹ עֵז כִּי יִוָּלֵד"; אַיִל בֶּן יוֹמוֹ קָרוּי אַיִל, דִּכְתִיב: °"וְאֵילֵי צֹאנְךָ לֹא אָכָלְתִּי", אֵילִים הוּא דְּלָא אֲכַל, כְּבָשִׂים אֲכַל? אֶלָּא לָאו ש"מ: אַיִל בֶּן יוֹמוֹ קָרוּי אַיִל. מ"מ קַשְׁיָא! א"ר שֵׁשֶׁת: הָא מַנִּי? ב"ש הִיא, *דְּאָמְרִי: שִׁינּוּי בִּמְקוֹמוֹ (א) עוֹמֶדֶת, וְלָא קָנֵי; דְּתַנְיָא: *נָתַן לָהּ בְּאֶתְנַנָּהּ וחִטִּין וַעֲשָׂאָן סוֹלֶת, זֵיתִים וַעֲשָׂאָן שֶׁמֶן, עֲנָבִים וַעֲשָׂאָן יַיִן, תָּנֵי חֲדָא: אָסוּר, וְתָנֵי חֲדָא: זמוּתָּר; וְאָמַר רַב יוֹסֵף, תָּנֵי גּוּרְיוֹן דְּמֵאַסְפּוֹרַק: ב"ש אוֹסְרִין, וּבֵית הִלֵּל מַתִּירִין. מַאי טַעְמָא דְּבֵית שַׁמַּאי? דִּכְתִיב: "גַּם" — לְרַבּוֹת שִׁינּוּיֵיהֶם. וּבֵית הִלֵּל? "הֵם" — וְלֹא שִׁינּוּיֵיהֶם. וּבֵית שַׁמַּאי? הַהוּא, הֵם

רש"י

וַחכ"א מָמוֹן הַמִּשְׁתַּלֵּם בְּרֹאשׁ. שֶׁאֵינוֹ מְשַׁלֵּם אֶלָּא קֶרֶן. "וְהֵשִׁיב אֶת אֲשָׁמוֹ" – הַיְינוּ קֶרֶן, שֶׁהוּא אָשֵׁם וְחוֹטֵא עָלָיו. וּבִקְרָא אַחֲרִינָא כְּתִיב הָתָם: "וְאֶת אֲשָׁמוֹ יָבִיא לַה'" וגו'. וְשֶׁאֵינוֹ מִשְׁתַּלֵּם בְּרֹאשׁ. כִּי הָכָא, דְּאִיכָּא כֶּפֶל – לָא שַׁיָּיךְ בָּהּ דִּין חוֹמֶשׁ כְּלָל. וַאֲפִי' לָא שָׁוִין חוּמְשָׁא וּכְפֵילָא – פָּטוּר. וְר"ש אָשָׁם קָאָתֵי לַאֲסוּפֵי לִפְטוּרָא. כְּפֵילָא ד' וְחוּמְשָׁא זוּזָא. וְכֵיוָן דְּאֵינָן שָׁוִין – לָא חוֹמֶשׁ מִקְרֵי, וְלָא סָלֵיק לֵיהּ. דִּכְפֵילָא זוּזָא וְחוּמְשָׁא זוּזָא. דְּחוֹמֶשׁ בָּתַר קַרְנָא שָׁיְימִינַן, וְקֶרֶן מְשַׁלֵּם כְּעֵין שֶׁגָּנַב. נִמְצָא קֶרֶן ד' וְחוּמְשׁוֹ מוֹסִיף עָלָיו מִבַּחוּץ זוּזָא, וּכְפֵילָא זוּזָא. וְכֶפֶל כִּשְׁעַת הַעֲמָדָה בַּדִּין. וְהַיְינוּ כְּרַב, דְּאִי לָאו קֶרֶן כְּעֵין שֶׁגָּנַב – לָא הָוֵי זוּזָא חוֹמֶשׁ, וְאִי כֶּפֶל כְּעֵין שֶׁגָּנַב – הָוֵי ד'. אֶלָּא ש"מ כְּרַב. וְרַבָּנַן אָמְרִי לָךְ. אִי לְעַרְבִינְהוּ קָבָּעֵי, לָא לִיכְתּוֹב לָא וָי"ו וְלָא "אֶת". לְאַפְסוּקֵי בֵּין מָמוֹן גָּבוֹהַּ. אָשָׁם. לְמָמוֹן הֶדְיוֹט. חוֹמֶשׁ, דְּלָאו אוֹרַח אַרְעָא לַעֲרוּבִינְהוּ לַהֲדָיָא. נַעֲשָׂה שִׁינּוּי בְּיָדוֹ וּקְנָאוֹ. בְּשִׁינּוּי לְהָא מִילְּתָא, דְּאִם טָבַח וּמָכַר – שֶׁלּוֹ הוּא טוֹבֵחַ וכו' וּפָטוּר מִד' וְה'. אֲבָל קֶרֶן וְכֶפֶל מְשַׁלֵּם, קֶרֶן כִּי הָשְׁתָּא, וְכֶפֶל כְּעֵין שֶׁגָּנַב אוֹ כִּשְׁעַת הַעֲמָדָה בַּדִּין. כְּעֵין שֶׁגָּנַב. לְקַמָּן אוֹתְבִינַן לְרַב מֵהָא דְּקָאמַר תַּשְׁלוּמֵי כֶפֶל ד' וְה' כִּשְׁעַת הַעֲמָדָה בַּדִּין. וּלְרַבָּה דְּאָמַר תַּבְרָהּ אוֹ שֶׁתְיָיהּ מְשַׁלֵּם ד' [כִּדְהָשְׁתָּא] – לֵיכָּא לְאוֹתוּבֵי, דְּיָכוֹל לְשַׁנּוּיֵי דְּהַךְ מַתְנִיתָא כֶּפֶל ד' וְה' דַּוְקָא נָקַט, אֲבָל קֶרֶן – הֵיכָא *דְּאַשְׁכַּח כִּי הָשְׁתָּא מְשַׁלֵּם. תּוֹרָא גְּנַבִי מִינָּךְ. בִּתְמִיָּה. וְנִקְנִינְהוּ בְּשִׁינּוּי הַשֵּׁם. נְהִי דְּשֶׁבַח דְּגוּפֵיהּ לָם הָוֵי שִׁינּוּי, דְּמִמֵּילָא קָשָׁבַח וְאָזֵיל, וּמִיהָ בִּשְׁמָא וַדַּאי אִישְׁתַּנֵּי. מ"מ קַשְׁיָא. לְר' אִילְעָא. שִׁינּוּי בִּמְקוֹמוֹ עוֹמֵד. אַע"ג דְּאִישְׁתַּנֵּי, לָא נָפֵיק מֵרְשׁוּת בְּעָלִים. תָּנֵי חֲדָא אָסוּר. לְקָרְבָּן. עַד

תוספות

כפילא ארבע וחומשא זוזא. לפי מה שפ"ה דחומשא עולה לו בכפילא, שמשלם את הכפל ונפטר בכך מן החומש — קשה קצת, מה בכך אי כפילא ארבע וחומשא זוזא? ומיהו, בקונט' פי' דלית ליה כפרה בחומש, כיון שאין ניכר, ומובלע בתוך הכפל. ואי הוה מפרש דחומשו עולה לו בכפילו, שמשלם את החומש ועולה לו לכפל — הוה ניחא, דהוה פריך שפיר. אבל לשון "בכפילו" לא משמע הכי. ובתוספתא נמי גרסי': וחומשו עולה לו מתוך כפילו. וריב"א מפרש: דאלשון ברייתא קפריך, דמשמע דחומשו עולה בכל כפילו.

אלמא קרן כעין שגנב. תימה: אמאי לא דחי כגון דמעיקרא שוי' זוזא ולבסוף שוי' ד', וכפילא זוזא כעין שגנב דלא כרב, וחומשא זוזא כשעת העמדה בדין, כדאמר דתברה או שתייה משלם ד'! וי"ל: דליכא למימר הכי כלל, דמהיכא תיתי דקרן יהא כשעת העמדה בדין וכפל ד' וה' יהי' כעין שגנב? דאין לחלק בין כפל ד' וה' לקרן אם לא מכח הפסוק, ובזה אין לנו שום פסוק. ורב נמי דמחלק — היינו משום דקרא קדריש. ועוד: דבלאו הכי דחי שפיר, ונוח לו כפי האמת, ובאותו ענין שהיה המסייע אומר שאין להעמידה.

ואי אמרת שינוי קונה. פירוש, כי האי דטלה ונעשה איל. אבל הא פשיטא דשינוי קני, כדאמר בסמוך דשינוי קונה לב"ה.

איל בן יומו קרוי איל. מיהו, ודאי לענין קרבן אמרינן *דאיל בן שתי שנים מדכתיב במקום אחר "כבש בן שנתו" (ויקרא יב).

הא מני בית שמאי היא. האי שנויא ליתא לרבה, דאית ליה בריש "הגוזל קמא" (לקמן דף צד.) דוקא לגבוה אסרי ב"ש, משום דמאיס. וא"ת: היכי מדמה ליה, דמה ענין אתנן אצל שינוי? וי"ל: דקסבר דאי שינוי קונה — א"כ ראוי הוא להתיר שינוי באתנן, דחשיב כאחר, ואין זה אותו שבא לידה בתורת אתנן, וממאיס נמי לא מאיס.

הן ולא שינוייהם. תימה: דבסמוך נפקא ליה לרבה דשינוי קונה מקרא אחרינא, דכתיב "אשר גזל" — כעין שגזל יחזיר! ועוד קשה: דרב חסדא קאמר *דשינוי אין קונה, דדריש "אשר גזל" מ"מ, וב"הגוזל קמא" (צד:) קאמר רבי יוחנן: דבר תורה גזילה המשתנית — חוזרת בעיניה, מדכתיב "והשיב את הגזילה" מ"מ. וכי פליגי אבית הלל? ונראה לר"י דלקמן איירי בשינוי החוזר לברייתו, והכי מייתי בריש "הגוזל קמא" מלתיה דר' יוחנן. ורבה דבסמוך סבר דאפי' שינוי החוזר לברייתו נמי קני. וצריכי תרי קראי, דאי לאו אלא חד קרא הוה מוקמינן ליה בשינוי שאין חוזר. והא דמייתי רבה סיוע לדבריו ממתניתין ד"הגוזל עצים" (לקמן ד' צג:) — משום דמיירי בשינוי חוזר לברייתו, כדמוקי לי' התם בריש פרקין (שם) בעצים משופים ולמר טווי. והיא דלא הספיק ליתן לו עד שצבעו — נראה לרבה דאיירי נמי בשינוי החוזר, שיכול להעבירו ע"י לפון, כדאמר בריש "הגוזל" (שם). ואע"פ דלר' יוחנן מיירי בשינוי שאינו חוזר, ומוקי לה בקלא אילן דלא עבר לה — לרבה נראה לו דוחק להעמידה בקלא אילן (דלא עבר), ולהכי מייתי מיניה סייעתא. הם

עין משפט נר מצוה

כד א מיי' פ"ד מהל' גניבה הלכה א והלכה ו:

כה ב מיי' פ"ז מהל' שבועות הלכה טו ופ"ז מהל' גזילה הלכה יב והל' יג:

כו ג ד מיי' פ"א מהל' גניבה הל' יג ופ"ב מהל' גזילה ואבידה הלכה יד טוח"מ סי' שנג:

כז ה מיי' פ"ד מהל' איסורי מזבח הלכה טו והל' יח סמג לאוין שיו:

הגהות הב"ח

(א) גמ' שינוי במקומו עומד כצ"ל:

גליון הש"ס

גמ' שור בן יומו קרוי שור. עי' מנחות לא ע"ב ותוס' שם ד"ה ת"ל: שם חיטין ועשאן סולת. עיין בספר יראים לרא"ם סי' ר"ז:

מסורת הש"ס

ויקרא ה

לקמן קח.

נ"ל דאשכח

[מגילה ב: ע"ז נב.]

לקמן נו:

[שבת פד: כתובות מה:]

ויקרא כב

בראשית לא

[לקמן סח.]

לקמן נג: תמורה ל:

[פרה פ"א מ"ג]

[לקמן סז. ע"ש]

"הֵם" וְלֹא וְלָדוֹתֵיהֶם הוּא דַּאֲתָא. וּבֵית הִלֵּל: תַּרְתֵּי שְׁמָעַת מִינָּהּ: "הֵם" – וְלֹא שִׁינּוּיֵיהֶם, [א]"הֵם" – וְלֹא וְלָדוֹתֵיהֶם. [א] וּבֵית הִלֵּל, הָכְתִיב "גַּם"! "גַּם" לְבֵית הִלֵּל קַשְׁיָא. עַד כָּאן לָא פְּלִיגִי, אֶלָּא דְּמָר סָבַר: שִׁינּוּי קוֹנֶה, וּמ"ס: אֵין שִׁינּוּי קוֹנֶה, אֲבָל לְעִנְיַן שַׁלּוּמֵי – כ"ע כִּדְמֵעִיקָּרָא מְשַׁלֵּם, דְּקָתָנֵי: מְשַׁלֵּם תַּשְׁלוּמֵי כֶפֶל וְתַשְׁלוּמֵי אַרְבָּעָה וַחֲמִשָּׁה כְּעֵין שֶׁגָּנַב; לֵימָא, תֶּיהֱוֵי תְּיוּבְתָּא דְּרַב, דְּאָמַר רַב: קֶרֶן – כְּעֵין שֶׁגָּנַב מְשַׁלֵּם, תַּשְׁלוּמֵי כֶפֶל וְתַשְׁלוּמֵי ד' וְה' – כִּשְׁעַת הַעֲמָדָה בַּדִּין? אָמַר רָבָא: טְלָאִים – כִּדְמֵעִיקָּרָא, דָּמִים – כְּשֶׁל עַכְשָׁיו. אָמַר רַבָּה: [ב]שִׁינּוּי קוֹנֶה כְּתִיבָא וְתָנֵינָא; כְּתִיבָא: ○"וְהֵשִׁיב אֶת הַגְּזֵלָה אֲשֶׁר גָּזָל" – *מַה ת"ל "אֲשֶׁר גָּזָל"? אִם כְּעֵין שֶׁגָּזַל – יַחֲזִיר, וְאִם לָאו – דָּמִים בְּעָלְמָא בָּעֵי שַׁלּוּמֵי; תָּנֵינָא: *הַגּוֹזֵל עֵצִים וַעֲשָׂאָן כֵּלִים, צֶמֶר וַעֲשָׂאָן בְּגָדִים – מְשַׁלֵּם כִּשְׁעַת הַגְּזֵילָה; א"נ: לֹא *הִסְפִּיק לִיתְּנוֹ לוֹ עַד שֶׁצְּבָעוֹ – פָּטוּר; אַלְמָא: שִׁינּוּי קוֹנֶה. יֵאוּשׁ – אָמְרִי רַבָּנַן דְּנִיקְנֵי, מִיהוּ לָא יָדְעִינַן אִי דְּאוֹרַיְיתָא אִי דְּרַבָּנַן; אִי דְּאוֹרַיְיתָא, מִידֵּי דַּהֲוָה אַמּוֹצֵא אֲבֵידָה, מוֹצֵא אֲבֵידָה לָאו כֵּיוָן דְּמִיָּאֵשׁ מָרֵיהּ מִינָּהּ מִקַּמֵּי דְּתֵיתֵי לִידֵיהּ קָנֵי לֵיהּ, הַאי נָמֵי כֵּיוָן דְּמִיָּאֵשׁ מָרֵיהּ קָנֵי לֵיהּ, אַלְמָא קָנֵי; אוֹ דִּלְמָא לָא דָּמְיָא לַאֲבֵידָה, אֲבֵידָה הוּא דְּכִי אָתַאי לִידֵיהּ – בְּהֶתֵּירָא אַתְיָא לִידֵיהּ, אֲבָל הַאי, כֵּיוָן דִּבְאִיסּוּרָא אֲתַאי לִידֵיהּ – מִדְּרַבָּנַן הוּא, דְּאָמוּר רַבָּנַן נִיקְנֵי מִפְּנֵי תַּקָּנַת הַשָּׁבִים. וְרַב יוֹסֵף אָמַר: [ג]יֵאוּשׁ אֵינוֹ קוֹנֶה, וַאֲפִילּוּ מִדְּרַבָּנַן.§ אֵיתִיבֵיהּ רַב יוֹסֵף לְרַבָּה: *גָּזַל חָמֵץ וְעָבַר עָלָיו הַפֶּסַח, אוֹמֵר

תורה אור: ויקרא ה

רש"י

עַד כָּאן לָא פְּלִיגִי. ר' אֶלְעָא וְר' חֲנִינָא. אֲבָל לְעִנְיַן שַׁלּוּמֵי. כְּגוֹן כֶּפֶל לְר' אֶלְעָא, וְד' וְה' לְר' חֲנִינָא. א"נ: בְּיוֹקְרָא וְזוּלָא בְּלֹא שִׁינּוּי, דְּכוּלֵּי עָלְמָא כִּדְמֵעִיקָּרָא מְשַׁלֵּם, דְּקָתָנֵי: כְּעֵין שֶׁגָּנַב. לֵימָא תֶּיהֱוֵי תְּיוּבְתָּא דְּרַב. דְּאָמַר לְעֵיל: כִּשְׁעַת הַעֲמָדָה בַּדִּין כְּשֶׁהוּזְלָה, וְכ"ש כְּשֶׁהוּקְרָה. דְּהָתָם אֲפִי' קֶרֶן מְחַיֵּיב לֵיהּ רַב כִּי הַשְׁתָּא, דְּהָא כְּרַבָּה ס"ל דְּאָמַר: תְּבָרָהּ אוֹ שַׁחְיֵיהּ מְשַׁלֵּם ד'. טְלָאִים כִּדְמֵעִיקָּרָא. כְּלוֹמַר, בָּא לְשַׁלֵּם טְלָאִים – כִּדְמֵעִיקָּרָא סַגֵּי, דְּטָלֶה גָּנַב וְטָלֶה מְשַׁלֵּם. שִׁינּוּי קוֹנֶה. הֵיכָא דְּשַׁנֵּי לְהוּ בְּיָדַיִם – פְּשִׁיטָא לֵיהּ דְּמִדְּאוֹרַיְיתָא וַדַּאי קָנֵה, וְכִי מַהְדַּר – לָא בָּעֵי לְאַהְדְּרִינְהוּ בְּעֵינַיְיהוּ, אֶלָּא דָּמִים מְשַׁלֵּם, כְּגוֹן צֶמֶר וַעֲשָׂאוֹ בְּגָדִים, דְּהָא כְּתִיבָא בְּהֶדְיָא, וְתָנֵינָא כו'. אֲבָל יֵאוּשׁ מְסַפְּקָא לֵיהּ, הָא דַּאֲמוּר רַבָּנַן קָנֵי – אִי דְּאוֹרַיְיתָא אִי דְּרַבָּנַן. לֹא הִסְפִּיק לִיתְּנוֹ לוֹ. לְרֵאשִׁית הַגֵּז לַכֹּהֵן. עַד שֶׁצְּבָעוֹ פָּטוּר. מֵרֵאשִׁית הַגֵּז, דְּקַנְיֵיהּ בְּשִׁינּוּי. וַאֲפִילּוּ דָּמִים לֹא מְשַׁלֵּם, דְּאֵין כֹּהֵן יָכוֹל לְהַזְמִינוֹ בַּדִּין, דְּיָכוֹל לוֹמַר: לְאַחֵר אֶתְּנֶנּוּ. אֲבָל קוֹדֶם שֶׁצְּבָעוֹ – ●מִי שֶׁחֲטָפוֹ זָכָה בּוֹ. יֵאוּשׁ. שֶׁנִּתְיָיאֲשׁוּ הַבְּעָלִים, אָמוּר רַבָּנַן דְּנִקְנֵי, וְדַיּוֹ אִם מְשַׁלֵּם דָּמָיו. מוֹצֵא אֲבֵדָה לָאו כֵּיוָן דְּמִיָּאֵשׁ לֵיהּ מָרֵיהּ. מִקַּמֵּי דְּתֵיתֵי לִידֵיהּ קָנֵי לָהּ. אִם נִתְיָיאֲשׁוּ בְּעָלִים קוֹדֶם שֶׁמְּצָאָהּ – זֶה קָנָה, דְּתַנְיָא בְּ"אֵלּוּ מְצִיאוֹת" (ב"מ דף כב:): מִנַּיִן לַאֲבֵידָה שֶׁשְּׁטָפָהּ נָהָר, הוֹאִיל וְנִתְיָיאֲשׁוּ הַבְּעָלִים שֶׁהִיא מוּתֶּרֶת – ת"ל: "אֲשֶׁר תֹּאבַד מִמֶּנּוּ" שֶׁאֲבוּדָה מִמֶּנּוּ וּמְצוּיָה לְשְׁאָר בְּנֵי אָדָם, יָצְתָה זוֹ. אַלְמָא: קָנֵי. וְהָכָא בִּגְזֵילָה דְּאָתֵי לִידֵיהּ מִקַּמֵּי יֵאוּשׁ וַהֲדַר אַיְּאוּשׁ – סַגֵּי לֵיהּ בְּדָמִים. מִשּׁוּם תַּקָּנַת הַשָּׁבִים. שֶׁלֹּא יְהֵא צָרִיךְ לַחֲזוֹר וְלִטְרוֹחַ אַחַר הַגְּזֵילָה עַצְמָהּ. אֵינוֹ קוֹנֶה. וְהִיא עַצְמָהּ יְשַׁלֵּם.

[לקמן סז. לח: קיב.] | לקמן נג: | שם וחולין קלה. [לקמן לד:] | לקמן נו:

תוספות

הם ולא ולדותיהם. משמע הכא דטפי מסתבר לאסור חטין ועשאן סולת יותר מולדותיהם. ותימה: דבפ' "כל הצלמים" (ע"ז דף מז. ושם ד"ה הכא) משמע איפכא, גבי יש שינוי לנעבד או לא, דבעי למימר דמשתחוה לחטין — קמחן מותר למנחות, ואע"ג דאמרינן בעיברו ולבסוף נרבעו דברי הכל אסורים, דהתם מעיקרא בהמה והשתא בהמה (א) ובבא הוא דאחידה באפה, הכא מעיקרא חטין והשתא קמח. ואין לומר דהא דשרינן ולד אתנן — היינו בנותן לה ואח"כ עיברה, דהא משמע בפ' "כל האסורין" (תמורה דף ל: ושם ד"ה דניחא) דדומיא דולד (ב) הנרבעת שרינן ולד אתנן! וי"ל: דהתם ודאי יש להתיר יותר חטין שנשתנה שנעשה סולת מולד נרבעת, דהיא וולדה נרבעו, (ג) ובבא בעלמא דאחידה באפה. אבל גבי אתנן — עיקר דעתה משום קמח, וגבי בהמה — עיקר דעתה אפרה ולא אולד.

טלאים כדמעיקרא. נראה לר"י דה"פ: דלענין טלה ונעשה איל, או כחושה ונתפטמה או איפכא, לשלם כפל נמי, וכן ד' וה' — כדמעיקרא, כמו קרן. אבל דמים, דהיינו יוקרא וזולא — כשל עכשיו, שמין אותו טלה של שעת גניבה לפי גדלותו או קטנותו שהיה בשעת גניבה לפי יוקרא וזולא דהשתא, וטעמא דטלאים — משום דא"ל: "תורא גנבי ממך"? והוא הדין כחושה והשמינה, דא"ל: "שמינה גנבי ממך"? אבל לגבי דמים — אין שייך למימר "יוקרא גנבי מינך"? ובלישנא דקרא נמי גוף לאן ובקר נזכרים בפסוק, ודרשי' מינה (לקמן דף סז:) שאם גנב שור שוה מנה לא ישלם תחתיו ה' נגידים, דכתיב "תחתיו" דמשמע תחת גוף השור, ומשום דלשון גוף השור נזכר בפסוק, משום הכי אמרינן טלאים כדמעיקרא. ואע"פ שעל שעת טביחה בא ד' וה', מ"מ כמו כן שעת גניבה גרמה לו, שאם אין גניבה — אין טביחה ומכירה. אבל דמים, שכל עיקרם תלוים בשומת ב"ד, וגם אין נזכרין בפסוק — סברא הוא דמוקמינן בהו אחייה לקרן דוקא כעין שגנב, ולא ד' וה', אלא כשעת העמדה בדין, שב"ד שמין אותה באותה שעה. ור"ת מפרש: דאין חילוק בין טלאים ליוקרא וזולא, וה"פ: טלאים שדבר בהן הברייתא, דהיינו טלה ונעשה איל שנשתנו למעליותא — כדמעיקרא, וה"ה ביוקרא וזולא, דמעיקרא שוין זוזא ולבסוף ארבעה, דהיינו כדמעיקרא, דלהחמיר על ד' וה' לא אמר רב. "דמים" פי': דמים דאיירי בהו רב, כגון דמעיקרא שוים ארבעה ולבסוף שוים זוזא, דנשתנו לגריעותא — בההיא קאמר רב כשל עכשיו.

וה"ה בטלאים, כגון שמינה והכחישה דהוי כשל עכשיו. והא דאמר לעיל: שמינה והכחישה כעין שגנב — צ"ל דוקא בהכחישה בידים.

לא הספיק ליתנו עד שצבעו פטור. אפי' כשגזז שיעור חמשה רחילות יחד, שחל עליו חיוב ראשית הגז — פטור כשצבעו, כדאשכחן בריש "הגוזל קמא" (לקמן דף צג. ושם) גבי פיאה דמלותה בקמה, וכשנשתנית, למ"ד שינוי קונה — פטור. וא"ת: הא דמייתי התם: גזז ראשון (ד) ולבעו פטור, מאי איריא ראשון ראשון? אפי' הכל יחד נמי! וי"ל: דהתם אפי' לבע מקלת והניח מקלת פטור אפי' מה שלא לבע, שלא חל עליו חיוב ראשית הגז, כיון שאין מצטרף. אבל הכא, שגזז כשיעור תחילה ונתחייב לכהן — דוקא לבעו כולו פטור, אבל הניח מקלת — מה שהניח חייב, אע"פ שאין בו שיעור, שכבר נתחייב.

עד שצבעו. אין לפרש שלבע חלקו של כהן מה שהפריש לו מן הגיזה, דלא שייכא ביה הפרשה כמו גבי תרומה דהפרשה שייכא ביה. [אבל] הפרשת ראשית הגז אין כלום מה שמפריש לבד אחד, וכאילו לא הפרישו. **מוצא** אבידה לאו כיון דאייאש מרה מינה כו'. אור"י: דנפקא לן דיאוש קונה באבידה מהא דאמר ב"אלו מציאות" (ב"מ דף כז. ושם): (ה) מה שמלה מיוחדת שיש לה סימנין ויש לה תובעים, פי': ע"י שיש לה סימנין יש לה תובעים, שאין הבעלים מתייאשין כיון שיש בהם סימן. ולא כמו שפ"ה שם שיש לה תובעין — שאינה של הפקר, דשמלה דבר הנעשה בידי אדם הוא. דהא ל"ל קרא להכי? פשיטא דשל הפקר פטור, דלמי ישיב? וקשה לר"ת: למ"ד סימנין לאו דאורייתא, א"כ בין בדבר שיש בו סימן בין בדבר שאין בו סימן אין מחזיר לבעלים מן התורה אלא ע"י עדים, ואי מתייאש מדבר שאין בו סימן — כך מתייאש מדבר שיש בו סימן, דזה וזה אין מחזיר לבעלים אלא ע"י עדים, וא"כ לא יחזיר אבידה לעולם! ומירץ: דאע"ג דסימן לאו דאורייתא, ואין מחזיר כ"א בעדים — מ"מ אין מתייאש מדבר שיש בו סימן, ששואל לבני אדם: ראיתם טלית שלי שאבדתי, שהיה בו כך וכך סימנין? אבל כשאין בה סימנין — מתייאש, שאין יודע מה לשאול, ואין סבור למצוא עדים לעולם. וא"ת: א"כ, מה דוחק לשנויי התם למ"ד סימנין לאו דאורייתא: סימנין כדי נסבא? הא איכא למימר דלא נקט סימן אלא לומר דע"י כך יש לה תובעין! וי"ל: דאי לאו דסימנין דאורייתא לא היה לו כלל להזכירם, ולא הוה ליה למימר טפי, אלא: מה שמלה מיוחדת שיש לה תובעים, וממילא ידעינן דמשום סימנים הוא.

הכא נמי כיון דמייאש כו'. אע"פ שאין יאוש מועיל באבידה בתר דאתי לידיה, כדקאמר: לאו כיון דמייאש מרה מינה מקמי דאתי לידיה קני ליה, וכדאמר ב"אלו מציאות" (ב"מ דף כא:) בהדיא, מ"מ בעי למילף שפיר דיאוש קני בגזל בתר דאתי לידיה. דבמציאה נמי, נהי שלא היה קונה לענין זה שלא יצטרך להשיב ולהפטר לגמרי, הואיל וכבר נתחייב בהשבה, מ"מ היה קונה לענין זה שלא יתחייב לשלם כי אם דמים, כמו לגבי גזל.

כיון דבאיסורא אתי לידיה. מכאן משמע שיאוש (ו) אין כהפקר גמור, דא"כ — אפי' בתר דאתא לידיה באיסורא יוכל לקנות מן ההפקר. והא דאמר ב"השולח" (גיטין דף לט:): "נתייאשתי מפלוני עבדי" דלא בעי גט שחרור אי אמרי' המפקיר עבדו יצא לחירות ואין צריך גט שחרור, לא משום דכי מתייאש הרי הוא מפקירו, דאי יאוש הוי הפקר — א"כ אפי' אתא לידיה באיסורא, כיון שמפקיר זכה בהן. אלא התם היינו טעמא: דכי היכי דבהפקר אין צריך גט שחרור, לפי שאין רשות לרבו עליו — ה"נ כשנתייאש אין לרבו רשות עליו.

אילימא

[ע"ש ומי' עוד לח. ובשמואל לא מיבעיא וכו']

עין משפט נר מצוה

כח א מיי' פ"ד מהל' איסורי מזבח הלכה יד סמג לאוין שטז:

כט ב מיי' פ"א מהל' גניבה הלכה יב ופ"ב מהל' גזילה הלכה א סמג עשין עא טוש"ע ח"מ סי' שנג סעיף א וסי' שם סעיף א וסעי' ה וסי' שסא סעיף ד וסי' שסב סעיף א:

ל ג מיי' פ"א מהל' גניבה הלכה יב ופ"ב מהל' גזילה הלכה א וסמג שם טוש"ע ח"מ סי' שנג סעיף ב וסי' שסא סעיף א ועיין בטור ובב"י ריש סי' שנג:

הגהות הב"ח

(א) תוס' ד"ה הם כו' ובבא הוא כו' כצ"ל: (ב) בא"ד דנרבעת כו' דאתנן כו' כצ"ל: (ג) שם ובבא בעלמא הוא דאחידה. כצ"ל: (ד) ד"ה לא כו'. ראשון ראשון ולבעו כצ"ל: (ה) ד"ה מוצא כו' דאמר באלו מציאות כו'. וע"ש דבירושלמי נפקא לן יאוש מאשר תאבד ממנו: (ו) ד"ה כיון כו' איט כהפקר גמור כצ"ל:

גליון הש"ס

רש"י ד"ה עד שלבעו וכו' מי שחטפו זכה בו. עיין תוס' ב"מ דף ו ע"א ד"ה והא הכא:

הגהות מהר"ב רנשבורג

א] גמ' וב"ה הכתיב גם גם לב"ה קשיא. הא דלא קאמר דאתיא לאתנן אסרה תורה ואפי' בא על אמו כדלקמן דף ע ע"ב מתרץ בשו"ת מהר"ם בר ברוך הקלריס ס"ם ח' דף ו ע"א דלהא לא איצטריך דנפקא לן מג"ש תועבה תועבה מעריות עכ"ל ועיין לקמן דף ע ע"ב תוס' ד"ה אתנן וכו' וגם בב"מ דף נא ע"א תוס' ד"ה אתנן:

אומר לו "הרי שלך לפניך". והאי כיון דמטא עידן איסורא ודאי מייאש, ואי ס"ד יאוש קנה, אמאי אומר לו "הרי שלך לפניך"? דמי מעליא בעי שלומי ליה! א"ל: כי קאמינא אנא — זה מתייאש וזה רוצה לקנות, האי — זה מתייאש וזה אינו רוצה לקנות. איתיבי' אביי *לרבה: °"קרבנו" — *אולא הגזול; היכי דמי? אילימא לפני יאוש, למה לי קרא? פשיטא! אלא לאו לאחר יאוש, ש"מ: יאוש לא קני! אמר ליה *רבא: וליטעמיך, הא דתניא: °ב"משכבו" — ולא הגזול, ה"ד? אילימא דגזל עמרא ועבדיה משכב, מי איכא למ"ד שינוי מעשה לא קני? אלא מאי אית לך למימר — גדגזל משכב דחבריה, ה"נ דגזל קרבן דחבריה.§ איתיביה אביי לרב יוסף: *דעורות של בעל הבית — מחשבה מטמאתן, הושל עבדן — אין מחשבה מטמאתן, ושל גנב — מחשבה מטמאתן, זשל גזלן — אין מחשבה מטמאתן; רבי שמעון אומר, חילוף הדברים: של גזלן — מחשבה מטמאתן, ושל גנב — אין מחשבה מטמאתן, לפי שלא נתייאשו הבעלים; וש"מ: יאוש קנה! א"ל: הכא במאי עסקינן — כגון שקיצען. מתקיף לה רבה בר רב חנן: והלא עיצבא שנו כאן, ועיצבא אין צריכה קיצוע. *דתנן: חכל מקום שאין חסרון מלאכה — מחשבה מטמאתו, יש חסרון מלאכה — אין מחשבה מטמאתו, חוץ מן העיצבא! אלא *אמר רבא: האי מילתא קשי בה רבה לרב יוסף עשרין ותרתין שנין, ולא איפרקה עד דיתיב רב יוסף ברישא ופרקה: טשינוי השם כשינוי מעשה דמי; שינוי מעשה מאי טעמא? התם מעיקרא עצים השתא כלים, שינוי השם נמי — מעיקרא קרו ליה משכא והשתא אברזין. והרי מריש, דאיכא שינוי השם, °דמעיקרא כשורא °והשתא טללא, ותנן: *יעל המריש הגזול שבנאו בבירה — שנוטל דמיו, מפני תקנת השבים; טעמא מפני תקנת השבים, הא

אומר לו. לגזול. הרי שלך לפניך. בעין, כמות שהוא. דהיזק שאינו ניכר הוא. קרבנו. "אם עולה קרבנו" (ויקרא א). ולא הגזול. דגזול לאו לרצון אתי. קס"ד דגזל בהמת חולין ואייתי, ה"ד? אי נימא כו'. וליטעמיך. דס"ד דגזל חולין ואקדשינהו. הא דתניא. גבי זב. משכבו. "איש אשר יגע במשכבו" (שם טו). גזירת הכתוב להוציא את המשכב הגזול, שאינו נעשה אב הטומאה לטמא אדם. מי איכא למ"ד. חד מהני אמוראי שינוי לא קני? הא ביאוש הוא דפליגי! דגזל קרבן דחבריה. שהקדיש חבירו. ולעולם לפני יאוש, ואיצטריך לאשמועינן דאינו עולה לרצון כלל, ואפי' לבעלים הראשונים, ואע"ג דלא הוה יאוש. ל"א: דגזל קרבן דחבריה. הלכך, אפי' לאחר יאוש לא קנייה, דקרבן אינו נגזל, דכל היכא דאיתיה — בי גזא דרחמנא איתיה. מחשבה מטמאתן. בעל הבית אינו עשוי למוכרן, ועושה מהן מטות ודולבקאות וקטבלאות. ומשחשב עליהן לדבר שראוי לו, בלא חסרון מלאכה — מקבלין טומאה מיד. ושל עבדן. העשוי למכור — אין מחשבתו מטמאתו, דעביד דממליך ומזבין, והלוקח יעשה מהם מנעלים, ועדיין לא נגמרה מלאכתן לכך. של גנב מחשבתו מטמאתם. דקננהו ביאוש. דקסבר: סתם גניבה יאוש בעלים היא, דלא ידע למאן לתבעו. ושל גזלן אין מחשבה מטמאתן. ואע"פ שחישב עליהן לדבר שאין בו חסרון מלאכה, כגון לכיסוי חבילות סוסים ופרדים כמו שעושין מעורות דובין. מ"ט — דסתם גזילות ליכא יאוש, דכיון דידע מאן שקליה, אזיל ותבע ליה לדינא. חילוף הדברים. סתם גזילה איכא יאוש, דכיון דלעיניה גזלה מיניה — איניש אלמא הוא. אבל סתם גניבה — ליכא יאוש, דסבר משכחנא ליה לגנב. שקיצען. דרומי"ר בלע"ז. דאיכא תרתי — שינוי מעשה ויאוש. ולעולם יאוש גרידא לא קני. והלא עיצבא שנו כאן. שחשב עליהן לעילבא = דולבקי שאוכלין עליו, וכעין שולחן הוא. ועיצבא אינה צריכה קיצוע. דבלאו קילוע נמי מטמאה, דהא חזיא למילתיה, שהקילוע אינו עשוי אלא לייפות. ומנא תימרא דבעילבא קעסיק – דתנן גבי דההיא במס' כלים: כל מקום שאין חסרון מלאכה כו'. חוץ מן העיצבא. שאע"פ שמחסר קילוע מחשבה מטמאתה. אברזין. הוא עילבא בלשון ארמי. אבל יאוש גרידא לא קני. דמעיקרא כשורא. קודם שניתן בבנין. והשתא טללא. גג. לאחר שנתנו בבירה, ונותן עליו תקרת נסרים ועלייה. על המריש. קורה. ותקנות קחשיב ואזיל במס' גיטין.

צלעות

אילימא לפני יאוש ל"ל קרא פשיטא. דאפילו קדשינהו אינו קדוש, דגזל ולא נתייאשו — הבעלים שניהן אין יכולין להקדיש. שמע מינה דיאוש לא קני. דאי קני — א"כ חשיב שפיר קרבנו. ולא מיפסיל משום מצוה הבאה בעבירה, הואיל והוא קנוי לו קודם שהקדישו, כמו שאפרש לקמן (דף סז. ד"ה אמר עולא) בע"ה. אבל אי לא קני ביאוש — מיפסיל. ומ"מ קדוש הוא, *אע"ג דאכתי לא ידע טעמא דשינוי השם, דקאמר לקמן מעיקרא חולין והשתא הקדש, (א) מ"מ יש כאן יאוש ושינוי רשות *באותן קרבנות דאין [הגזלן] חייב באחריותן. מי איכא למ"ד שינוי מעשה לא קני. ולא בעי לאוקמיה כב"ש, דאמר שינוי במקומו עומד. אף על גב דאיכא נמי תנאי דסברי הכי ב"הגוזל קמא" (לקמן דף צג:), מ"מ הלכה כב"ה דשינוי קונה. והתם נמי דחי רבא דכולהו תנאי מלו סברי כב"ה, ובכל הגמרא סובר כן. ולא בעי לאוקמי בשינוי החוזר לברייתו, דאיכא למ"ד דלא קני. דרב יוסף לא פליג עליה דרבה אלא ביאוש לחודיה, אבל שינוי מעשה — אפי' בחוזר לברייתו, דאיירי ביה רבה כדפרישית לעיל, לא פליג עליה. דגזל משכב דחבריה. משמע מתוך פ"ה שר"ל: משכב גמור של חבירו, אם גזלו — אין מטמא משכב, דגזירת הכתוב הוא. וזהו תימה. ועוד קשה לרשב"ס: דבטהרות (פ"ז מ"ו) גבי גנבים שנכנסו לבית, תנן: המשכבות ומושבות טהורים, ואם יש עמהם גוי או אשה — הכל טמא, כי שמא נדה היא וגוי כזב לכל דבריו. משמע שמטמא משכב ומושב שאין שלו! ומיהו, יש לדחות: דהתם מדרבנן. ועוד קשה: דהתם (בתורת כהנים פרשת מצורע) מייתי עלה פלוגתא דר"ש ורבנן דגנב וגזלן דבסמוך, והכי איתא התם: "משכבו" ולא הגזול, יכול שאני מוציא אף הגנוב — ת"ל "טמא". [ר' שמעון אומר: "במשכבו" ולא הגנוב, יכול שאני מוציא את הגזול — ת"ל "טמא"]. אמרו לו: ומה ראית לרבות את זה ולהוציא את זה? אחר שריבה הכתוב ומיעט, מרבה אני את אלו שנתייאשו הבעלים ממנו כו'. ומדמייתי עלה פלוגתא דר"ש ורבנן — משמע דהוי טעם משום דאין מחשבה מטמאתו, כי ההיא דבסמוך דאין יחוד של גזלן יחוד! ומפרש ר"י: דגזל משכב דחבריה — שגזל עורות של בעל הבית, שאינן מחוסרין אלא יחוד, ואין צריך שום תיקון, ואין חסר רק מחשבה, והוי שפיר דומיא דגזל קרבן דחבריה. שאם היה גוזל בהמה של חולין שמחוסרת קדושה — זה היה כמו מחוסר מעשה גמור, כעין עמרא ועבדיה משכב. אבל גזל או גנב משכב גמור דחבריה — מטמא משכב לכ"ע. ואע"ג דהך "משכבו ולא הגזול" איירי קודם יאוש, והך ד"קרבנו ולא הגזול" איירי אף בתר יאוש — אין להקפיד, אע"ג דאין דומה זה לזה. דגזל קרבן דחבריה. תימה: ל"ל קרא? דאי בחטאת, הא אפי' הוא עצמו אם אכל חלב אתמול, והפריש קרבן — אין מתכפר באותו קרבן על חלב שאכל היום. ואי בעולה ושלמים — הא אמרי' בפסחים (דף פט:): המוכר עולתו ושלמיו לא עשה ולא כלום! והיה נראה לאוקמי בפסח, שיכול למנות אחרים עמו על פסחו ולמוכרו, כדמוכח התם. אבל קשה: דהאי קרא בעולה כתיב, אם לא שיעמיד בפסח ב"אם אינו ענין"! ואין לומר שבא הכתוב לפסול הקרבן, דהא אמרינן לקמן (דף עו.) גבי גנב, שאם שחט תמימים לפנים לשם בעלים — *יחזרו קרן לבעלים. כגון שקיצען. ומועיל עם היאוש. אבל לחודיה לא קני, דלאו שינוי מעשה הוא. ועיצבא אינה צריכה קיצוע. ומיהו, היכא דחשיב עליה לקולעה, אמרינן בפ' "דם חטאת" (זבחים דף לד.) דטהורה עד שיקליענה. מ"מ דייק הכא שפיר, דכיון דראויה להשתמש בלא קילוע — אין קילוע שלה חשוב שינוי מעשה כלל. כל שאין בו חסרון מלאכה מחשבה מטמאתה. וא"ת: בלאו ההוא דעילבא, אמאי לא פריך ליה מהכא דמחשבה מועלת, אלמא יאוש קני! וי"ל: דלמא הך דהכא איירי בבעל הבית. שינוי השם כשינוי מעשה דמי. לאו כשינוי מעשה ממש. דשינוי מעשה לחודיה קני, כדמוכח לעיל, ולקמן (דף סח.) גבי גנב וטבח ובא אחר וגנבו, דפריך: ושינוי מעשה מי איכא למ"ד דלא קני? אבל שינוי השם גרידא לא קני בלא יאוש או שינוי מעשה.

הא

לא א מיי' פ"ה מהל' איסורי מזבח הלכה ז סמג לאוין שיח שיט ועי' בכ"מ:

לב ב ג מיי' פכ"ד מהל' כלים הלכה ז:

לג ד ה מיי' שם הל' ו:

מש"ה אצטריך קרא להורות שאינו עולה משום מצוה הבאה בעבירה. הועתק מחילופי גרסאות

דאף אם יאוש כדי לא קני הועיל למכרה או להקדישה ועי' לקמן סז: בתו' ד"ה רבא ולקמן קיא: הועתק מחילופי גרסאות

לד ו ז מיי' שם הלכה ז:

לה ח מיי' שם הלכה ו:

לו ט מיי' פ"א מהל' גניבה הלכה יג ופ"ב מהל' גזילה ואבידה הל' יד סמג עשין עא טוש"ע ח"מ סי' שנג סעיף א וסי' שם סעיף י בהג"ה:

לז י מיי' פ"א מהל' גזילה ואבידה הלכה ה סמג עשין עג טוש"ע ח"מ סי' שם סעיף א:

הגהות הב"ח

(א) תוד"ה ש"מ כו' מ"מ יש כאן יאוש כו'. עי' תוס' לקמן סו: ע"ג ד"ה והשתא.

גליון הש"ס

גמ' דמעיקרא כשורא. תרגום של קורתי (בראשית יט ח) שריתי: שם והשתא טללא. על שם שעושה צל תרגום של בצל (שם) בטללי:

ויקרא א | שם טו | תורה אור

ל"ל לרבא רש"ל | [לקמן סז:] | [עי' תוס' לקמן סז: ד"ה רבא] | לקמן קיח. כלים פכ"ו מ"ח | כלים פכ"ו מ"ח | [כתובות מב:] | [לקמן קה. גיטין נה. [עדיי' פרק ז מ"ט]] | ל"ל חזרה רש"ל

הא לאו הכי הדרא בעיניה! אמר רב יוסף: מריש שמו עליו, דתניא: °"צלעות הבית" — אלו המלטמין, "והעובים" — אלו המרישות. רבי זירא אמר: אשינוי החוזר לברייתו — בשינוי השם לא הוי שינוי. ושינוי השם שאינו חוזר לברייתו מי הוי *שינוי? והרי צינור, דמעיקרא קציצתא והשתא צינורא, ותניא:* בצינור שחקקו ולבסוף קבעו — פוסל את המקוה, קבעו ולבסוף חקקו — אינו פוסל את המקוה; ואי אמרת שינוי השם מילתא היא, אפי' קבעו ולבסוף חקקו נמי ליפסל! *שאני שאיבה, גדמדרבנן היא. אי הכי, אפילו דרישא נמי! התם איכא תורת כלי עליו בתלוש, הכא אין תורת כלי עליו בתלוש. מיתיבי: *דהגנב, והגזלן, והאנס — הקדישן הקדש, ותרומתן תרומה, ומעשרותן מעשר! אמרי: התם איכא שינוי השם, דמעיקרא טיבלא והשתא תרומה, הקדש — מעיקרא חולין והשתא הקדש. אמר רב חסדא א"ר יונתן: מניין לשנוי שהוא קונה? שנאמר: °"והשיב את הגזלה", *מה ת"ל "אשר גזל"? אם כעין שגזל — יחזיר, ואם לאו — דמים בעלמא בעי שלומי. האי "אשר גזל" מיבעי *הלמעוטי גזל אביו, שאינו מוסיף חומש על גזל אביו! א"כ, *ניכתוב רחמנא "והשיב את גזילו", "אשר גזל" למה לי למכתב? ש"מ תרתי. ואיכא דאמרי, אמר רב חסדא א"ר יונתן: מניין לשנויי *שאינו קונה? שנאמר: "והשיב את הגזילה", מ"מ. והא כתיב: "אשר גזל"! ההוא מיבעי ליה: *על גזילו שלו מוסיף חומש, ואין מוסיף חומש על גזל אביו.§ אמר עולא: מניין ליאוש שאינו קונה? שנאמר: °"והבאתם גזול את הפסח ואת החולה", *גזול דומיא דפסח, מה פסח דלית ליה תקנתא כלל, אף

רש"י

צלעות הבית והעובים. קרא כתיב גבי בית עולמים. המלטמים. המלטי, כדאמרינן ב"השותפין" (ב"ב דף ו.) שנותנים נסרים סביב פתחי חלונות ופתחין, ובמקום חורי קיבוע הקורות. אלמא: בתר הכי קרי להו נמי מרישות. היינו טעמא דלא מקנייא בשינוי השם — משום דחוזר לברייתו הוא, אם יסתר הוי כשורא כדמעיקרא. ⊕ אבל אברזין — תו לא מקרי משכא. דמעיקרא קציצתא. שקודם שחקקו נקרא קלילת עץ בעלמא. ולבסוף קבעו. והמשיך בו מי גשמים או מי נהר למקוה — פסלו משום מים שאובין. קבעו ולבסוף חקקו. לאו כלי הוא, אלא ארעא סמיכתא היא. שאיבה. מה שמקוה נפסל בג' לוגין מים שאובין — מדרבנן הוא. אנס. חמסן, דיהיב דמי. הקדישן הקדש. ואסור ליהנות. ותרומתן. אסור לזרים. אלמא: קני ליה לגזילה ביאוש. על גזל אביו. ב"הגוזל" (לקמן ד' קד:) מפרש לה: אפילו נשבע אביו לשקר. אבל אקרן מחייב ליה קרא, כדאמרינן התם. את גזילו. ומילא אימעוט גזל אביו.

ה"ג

תוספות

הא לאו הכי הדרא בעיניה. וקשה מריש, כיון שבנאו בבירה — מתייאשים הבעלים ממנו. וא"ת: דמשמע דלא מקשה אלא לרב יוסף. אדרבה, כ"ש דקשה לרבה טפי, דלדידיה יאוש גרידא קני! ולמאי דמשני דמריש שמו עליו — אכתי תקשה לרבה, דמהכא משמע דיאוש לא קנה! ונראה לפרש דבלא יאוש איירי, ולהכי פריך לרב יוסף: א"א בשלמא דשינוי השם לא כלום הוא — שפיר, אלא אי אמרת דשינוי השם קטן עם יאוש קני — א"כ שינוי השם גדול כי האי דמריש — יש לו לקנותו בפני עצמו. וכן משמע לעיל דשינוי השם חשוב גרידא קני, דפריך גבי גנב טלה ונעשה איל — ונקניה בשינוי השם, דהוי שינוי השם חשוב. ועוד יש לומר: דבכל מקום הוי שינוי השם גרידא קני לרב יוסף בלא יאוש, ולכך יש להועיל לו במריש בלא יאוש. דמה שצריך יאוש בעורות — לאו משום קנין, דקנין הוי משום שינוי השם לחודיה, והיאוש אין צריך אלא כדי שיועיל מחשבת יחודו לשוייה אברזין, דאם לאו היאוש — אין כאן שינוי השם. וכן בהקדש בעי עמו יאוש, שאם אין יאוש — אין שם הקדש חל עליו, ואין כאן שינוי השם. וכן שינוי רשות, אם אין יאוש — אין שינוי רשות. אבל מריש — בלא יאוש נמי איכא שינוי השם, ויש לו להועיל בפני עצמו. וכן גבי טלה ונעשה איל, דאמרי' לעיל: וניקני בשינוי השם. **צנור** שחקקו ולבסוף קבעו פוסל את המקוה. כשיש לו לבזבז מד' רוחותיו איירי, שאם הוא פרוץ אפי' מרוח אחד — לא היה פוסל המקוה, כדמוכח במסכת מקוואות (פ"ד מ"ד), דדוקא טבלא שיש לה לבזבז פוסל. והר"י מסימפונ"ט פירש דאפילו פרוץ משני רוחות איירי, כדרך צנור, וכגון שחטטו לקבל צרורות שלא יעכבו את הגשמים, כי ההיא דפ"ד דמקואות (מ"ג): החוטט בצנור לקבל צרורות, בשל עץ — בכל שהוא, ובשל חרס — ברביעית. וא"ת: א"כ, מאי קאמר מעיקרא קלינתא והשתא צנור, דמשמע דאפי' קבע תחילה יש לפסול המקוה, לפי שמשתנה שמו ע"י חקיקה? והלא אין משתנה שמו ע"י חטיטה שעושה לקבל צרורות, דאותה היא שגורמת לפסול את המקוה! וי"ל: כיון שמשתנה שמו ע"י *חטיטה — יש לחשבו כתלוש, והחטיטה שעושה כאילו עושה אותה בתלוש. **שאני** שאיבה דרבנן. מפורש בפרק "המוכר [את] הבית" (ב"ב ד' סו. ושם ד"ה מכלל). **הגנב** והגזלן. ב"הגוזל בתרא" (לקמן קיד.) פריך: אי רבנן — קשה גזלן, אי רבי שמעון — קשה גנב. ומשני לה שפיר. **מעיקרא** טיבלא. ואע"ג דשינוי החוזר לברייתו על ידי שאלה, כדאמרינן ב"האשה רבה" (יבמות ד' פח.) ובסוף "הנודר מן הירק" (נדרים ד' נט.) — מ"מ לא חשיב להו שינוי החוזר לברייתו, כיון דלא שכיחא. **מעיקרא** חולין והשתא הקדש. בקדשים שאין חייב באחריות — לא הוה צריך ליתן טעם זה, דיש כאן שינוי רשות. אלא בעי לאוקומי אפי' בחטאת ובאשם. ואע"ג דמעיקרא תורא דראובן והשתא תורא דראובן (א) — מכל מקום שינוי השם יש כאן. **אמר** עולא מניין ליאוש שאין קונה. משמע הכא דסבר עולא דיאוש לא קני. וכן ב"הניזקין" (גיטין ד' נה. ושם ד"ה מאי) דאמר עולא: דבר תורה, בין נודע בין לא נודע — אין מכפרת, מ"ט — יאוש כדי לא קני. וקשה לר"ת: דב"הגוזל בתרא" (לקמן ד' קיד.) גבי פלוגתא דרבי שמעון ורבנן דגנב וגזלן, קאמר עולא: מחלוקת בסתם, אבל בידוע — ד"ה יאוש קני! ואור"ת: דבכל מקום יאוש קונה, רק לענין קרבן משום דהוי מצוה הבאה בעבירה. ומביא ראיה מההיא ד"הניזקין" (גיטין ד' נה: ושם) דפריך התם לעולא מההיא דגנב והקדיש ואח"כ טבח ומכר — משלם תשלומי כפל ואין משלם ד' וה', ותני עלה: כה"ג בחוץ ענוש כרת, ואי אמרת יאוש לא קני — כרת מאי עבידתיה? והשתא בלאו הכיא דתני עלה הוה ליה למפרך מגופה, דאי יאוש לא קני — אם כן אין לו כח להקדיש, ואמאי פטור מד' וה'? הא לא טבח דהקדש! אלא ודאי לכל מילי מודה עולא דיאוש קני, רק לענין הקרבה, ולהכי פריך מדתני עלה דבחוץ ענוש כרת — אלמא ראוי לפתח אוהל מועד. ועוד מייתי ראיה ר"ת מריש "לולב הגזול" (סוכה ד' ל. ושם), דפסלינן לולב הגזול אפי' בי"ט שני. ומפרש רבי יוחנן: משום מצוה הבאה בעבירה, שנאמר "והבאתם גזול את הפסח" — גזול דומיא דפסח, בין לפני יאוש בין לאחר יאוש. בשלמא לפני יאוש — דלאו דידיה היא, אלא לאחר יאוש — הא קנייה ביאוש! מ"ט לאו? לאו משום מצוה הבאה בעבירה. משמע דסבר בכל דוכתי דיאוש קני, רק לענין מצוה. וקשה לר"י לפי': דאם כן, מאי פריך לעיל אביי לרבה מ"קרבנו" ולא הגזול? דלמא בקרבנו מודה רבה כמו עולא! וכ"ת דסבר אביי אין חילוק, כמ"ד בסוכה (שם) מתוך שיוצא בשאול יוצא בגזול, דלית ליה טעמא דמצוה הבאה בעבירה — הא ע"כ אית ליה. דאי לאו הכי, כי אמרת נמי יאוש לא קני — תקשה ליה: אמאי אסור להקריבו, כיון דשם הקדש חל עליו, כדאמר דהוי יאוש ושינוי השם? אלא ודאי משום דהוי מצוה הבאה בעבירה. ועוד, בההיא דגיטין (ד' נה: ושם), דבעי רבא: כי אוקמוה רבנן ברשותיה משעת גניבה או משעת הקדישה, ומאי נ"מ — לגיזותיה וולדותיה. ואליבא דעולא בעי לה, כדמוכח סוגיא דהתם. ואי בעלמא קני — הא ע"כ משעת יאוש גיזותיה וולדות דידיה הוו! ע"כ נראה לר"י דבכל מקום לעולא יאוש לא קני. וההיא ד"הגוזל בתרא" (לקמן ד' קיד.) הוי יאוש ושינוי השם, דמעיקרא משכא והשתא אברזין. ואע"ג דגבי קרבן נמי הוי יאוש ושינוי השם, כדאמר לעיל דמעיקרא חולין והשתא הקדש, מכל מקום כיון דאין קנוי לו אלא מחמת שהקדיש ולא (ב) היו לו קנוי קודם — פסליה רחמנא להקרבה משום מצוה הבאה בעבירה, *כדמוכח בפרק "לולב הגזול" (סוכה ד' ל. ושם) דאמר להו רב להנהו אוונכרי: כי זבניתו אסא מן הגוים לגזוז אינהו כו'. ופריך: ולקנינהו בשינוי השם! משמע דאי קנו ליה — תו לא הוי מצוה הבאה בעבירה. ודוחק לומר דסבר כרבי יצחק בר נחמני דלא חייש התם למצוה הבאה בעבירה. ועוד אמר התם (ד' לא.): האי כשורא דמטללתא עבדו ביה רבנן תקנתא מפני תקנת השבים. וסוכה לא בעינן משלכם, ולא מיפסל אלא משום מצוה הבאה בעבירה. וכי קנייה בתקנתא דרבנן — לא חשיב מצוה הבאה בעבירה, כ"ש אי קנה קנין גמור. והא דאמר בריש "הגוזל קמא" (לקמן ד' צד.): הרי שגזל סאה חטין טחנה לשה אפאה והרים ממנה חלה כיצד מברך אין זה מברך אלא מנאץ, ודאי ליה התם דמאי סבר בעלמא דשינוי קונה, והכא משום מצוה הבאה בעבירה אע"ג דקנה קודם לכן, לענין ברכה, להזכיר שם שמים עליו — ראוי להחמיר יותר. אי נמי: התם דחוי בעלמא הוא. והשתא לעיל פריך אביי שפיר מ"קרבנו" ולא הגזול, דאי יאוש קנה — אמאי מיפסל? הא לא חשיב מצוה הבאה בעבירה, כיון דקודם שהקדישה קנאה! אלא ודאי יאוש גרידא לא קני, אלא מחמת שהקדישה, דה"ל יאוש ושינוי רשות, או יאוש ושינוי השם כדמסיק לבסוף. ולכך מפסל, משום דה"ל מצוה הבאה בעבירה. וב"הניזקין" (גיטין ד' נה: ושם) נמי, אי לא דתני עלה לא מצי פריך לעולא, דאע"ג דיאוש לא קני — שפיר חל הקדש, משום דה"ל יאוש ושינוי השם. ואדרבה, מגופה דברייתא הוי סייעתא לעולא, דאי יאוש קני — כי לא הקדיש נמי פטור מד' וה', דשלו הוא טובח ושלו הוא מוכר, כדפריך מינה לקמן (ד' סח:) רבי יוחנן לריש לקיש דאמר יאוש קני. ואדרבה, תימה דלא פריך מינה לרב יהודה, דפליג התם

עין משפט נר מצוה

לח א מיי' פ"א מהל' גניבה הלי"ג ופ"ב מהל' גזילה ואבידה הל' י סמג עשין עא עג טוש"ע ח"מ סי' שנ"ג סעי' א וסי' שם ס"ה:

לט ב מיי' פ"ו מהל' מקואות הל' ו סמג עשין רמח טוש"ע י"ד סי' רא סעי' לד וסעי' לו: [רב אלפס ב"ב פ"ד דף ק"ל ובשבועות פ"ב ד' רל"א]

ס"א ושינוי השם מילתא היא והרי וכו' מהרש"ל וכן הגיה הה"ג מוה' שכנא

מ ג מיי' שם פ"ד הל' ב סמג שם:

מא ד מיי' פ"ד מהל' תרומות הל' יא:

מב ה מיי' פ"ז מהל' גזלה הל' ג סמג עשין עג:

מסורת הש"ס

ב"ב סו: [תוספתא מקואות פ"ד]

[ב"ב סו:]

לקמן קיז. [תוספתא תרומות פ"א]

ויקרא ה

לקמן קד:

[לקמן לג:]

תמורה ו.

מלאכי א

סוכה ל. [ע' תוספות לקמן קיז: ד"ה גזל]

נ"ל חקיקה

תורה אור

יחזקאל מא

לקמן קיב. [לעיל סו. וש"נ]

גי' רש"ל כך נכתוב רחמנא והשיב את גזילו והשיב את הגזילה אשר גזל ל"ל

הגהות הב"ח

(א) תוס' ד"ה מעיקרא חולין וכו' תורה דראובן. נ"ב לקמן דף ש ע"א. (ב) ד"ה אמר וכו' ולא היה קנוי לו קודם שהקדישו:

גליון הש"ס

רש"י ד"ה אבל אברזין. עי' סוכה דף ל ע"ב תוס' ד"ה ולקנייה:

ומיהו אם היה קנוי לו קודם ההקדש לא הוי חשיב מצוה הבאה בעבירה כדמוכח כו' כן הגי' מהרש"ל וכן הוא בתוס' גיטין

אַף גָּזוּל דְּלֵית לֵיהּ תַּקַּנְתָּא, לָא שְׁנָא לִפְנֵי יֵאוּשׁ וְלָא שְׁנָא אַחַר יֵאוּשׁ. רָבָא אָמַר, מֵהָכָא: "קָרְבָּנוֹ" – *"וְלֹא הַגָּזוּל; אֵימַת? אִילֵימָא לִפְנֵי יֵאוּשׁ, פְּשִׁיטָא, לָמָּה לִי קְרָא? אֶלָּא לָאו לְאַחַר יֵאוּשׁ, וש"מ: יֵאוּשׁ לָא קָנֵי, ש"מ. וְהָא רָבָא הוּא דְּאָמַר דְּגָזַל קָרְבַּן דְּחַבְרֵיהּ! אִיבָּעֵית אֵימָא: הֲדַר בֵּיהּ, וְאִיבָּעֵית אֵימָא: *חַד מִינַּיְיהוּ (א) רַב פַּפָּא אֲמָרָהּ.§ "וּמִדַּת תַּשְׁלוּמֵי אַרְבָּעָה וַחֲמִשָּׁה" וכו'.§ וְאַמַּאי? נֵילַף "שׁוֹר" "שׁוֹר" מִשַּׁבָּת, מַה לְּהַלָּן חַיָּה וְעוֹף כַּיּוֹצֵא בָּהֶן, אַף כָּאן חַיָּה וְעוֹף כַּיּוֹצֵא בָּהֶן! אָמַר רָבָא, אָמַר קְרָא: °"שׁוֹר וָשֶׂה, שׁוֹר וָשֶׂה, שְׁנֵי פְּעָמִים; שׁוֹר וָשֶׂה – אִין, מִידֵּי אַחֲרִינָא – לָא. אָמְרִי: הֵי מְיַיתַּר? אִילֵימָא "שׁוֹר" וְ"שֶׂה" דְּסֵיפָא מְיַיתַּר, דְּנִיכְתּוֹב רַחֲמָנָא: "כִּי יִגְנֹב שׁוֹר אוֹ שֶׂה וּטְבָחוֹ וּמְכָרוֹ חֲמִשָּׁה בָקָר יְשַׁלֵּם תַּחְתָּיו וְאַרְבַּע צֹאן תַּחְתָּיו", אִי כָּתַב רַחֲמָנָא הָכִי, הֲוָה אָמִינָא: בָּעֵי שַׁלּוּמֵי תִּשְׁעָה לְכָל אֶחָד וְאֶחָד! וְכִי תֵּימָא, הָא כְּתִיב "תַּחְתָּיו" "תַּחְתָּיו", חַד "תַּחְתָּיו" מְיַיתַּר. הַהוּא מִיבָּעֵי לֵיהּ לִדְרָשָׁה אַחֲרִינָא, דְּתַנְיָא: יָכוֹל גָּנַב שׁוֹר שָׁוֶה מָנֶה יְשַׁלֵּם תַּחְתָּיו נְגִידִין? ת"ל: "תַּחְתָּיו" "תַּחְתָּיו"! אֶלָּא "שׁוֹר" וְ"שֶׂה" דְּרֵישָׁא מְיוּתָּר, דְּנִכְתּוֹב רַחֲמָנָא: "כִּי יִגְנֹב אִישׁ וּטְבָחוֹ וּמְכָרוֹ חֲמִשָּׁה בָקָר יְשַׁלֵּם תַּחַת הַשּׁוֹר וְאַרְבַּע צֹאן תַּחַת הַשֶּׂה". אִי כָּתַב רַחֲמָנָא הָכִי, הֲוָה אָמִינָא: עַד דְּגָנֵיב תְּרֵי וְטָבַח לְהוּ! "וּטְבָחוֹ" כְּתִיב, לְחַד. וְאֵימָא: עַד דְּגָנֵיב תַּרְוַיְיהוּ וּמְזַבֵּין לְהוּ! "וּמְכָרוֹ" כְּתִיב, לְחַד. וְאֵימָא, הֲוָה אָמִינָא: עַד דְּגָנֵיב תְּרֵי, וְטָבַח חַד וּמְזַבֵּין חַד! "אוֹ מְכָרוֹ" כְּתִיב. וְאַכַּתִּי הֲוָה אָמִינָא: עַד דְּגָנֵיב תַּרְוַיְיהוּ, וְטָבַח חַד וּמְשַׁיֵּיר חַד, אוֹ מְזַבֵּין חַד וּמְשַׁיֵּיר חַד! אֶלָּא, "שׁוֹר" דְּסֵיפָא וְ"שֶׂה" דְּרֵישָׁא מְיַיתַּר, דְּנִיכְתּוֹב רַחֲמָנָא: "כִּי יִגְנֹב אִישׁ שׁוֹר וּטְבָחוֹ וּמְכָרוֹ חֲמִשָּׁה בָקָר יְשַׁלֵּם תַּחְתָּיו וְאַרְבַּע צֹאן תַּחַת הַשֶּׂה", "שׁוֹר" דְּסֵיפָא וְ"שֶׂה" דְּרֵישָׁא לָמָּה לִי? שְׁמַע מִינָּהּ: שׁוֹר וָשֶׂה – אִין, מִידֵּי אַחֲרִינָא – לָא.§ "אֵין הַגּוֹנֵב אַחַר הַגַּנָּב מְשַׁלֵּם תַּשְׁלוּמֵי כֶפֶל".§ אָמַר רַב: לֹא שָׁנוּ אֶלָּא לִפְנֵי יֵאוּשׁ, אֲבָל לְאַחַר יֵאוּשׁ – קְנָאוֹ גַּנָּב רִאשׁוֹן, וְגַנָּב שֵׁנִי מְשַׁלֵּם תַּשְׁלוּמֵי כֶפֶל לְגַנָּב רִאשׁוֹן. *אָמַר רַב שֵׁשֶׁת, אָמִינָא: כִּי נָיֵים וְשָׁכֵיב רַב אֲמַר לְהָא שְׁמַעְתָּא; דְּתַנְיָא, אָמַר ר' עֲקִיבָא: מִפְּנֵי מָה אָמְרָה תּוֹרָה טָבַח וּמָכַר מְשַׁלֵּם תַּשְׁלוּמֵי אַרְבָּעָה וַחֲמִשָּׁה? מִפְּנֵי שֶׁנִּשְׁתָּרֵשׁ בַּחֵטְא; אֵימַת? אִילֵימָא לִפְנֵי יֵאוּשׁ,

מִי

ה"ג: וְכ"ת הָא כְּתִיב תַּחְתָּיו תַּחְתָּיו חַד תַּחְתָּיו מְיַיתַּר כו'. וְכ"ת: הָא כְּתִיב תְּרֵי זִימְנֵי "תַּחְתָּיו" דְּמִישְׁתַּמְּעֵי חַד אַ"שׁוֹר" וְחַד אַ"שֶׂה", דְּאִי תַּרְוַיְיהוּ אַחַד קָיְימִי – הָכִי אִיבָּעֵי לֵיהּ לְמִיכְתַּב "ה' בָּקָר וְד' צֹאן יְשַׁלֵּם תַּחְתָּיו" – לָאו מִילְּתָא הִיא, דְּאִיכָּא לְמֵימַר חַד "תַּחְתָּיו" אִיַּיתַּר לִדְרָשָׁה אַחֲרִינָא, וְאַכַּתִּי תִּשְׁעָה מִשְׁתַּמְּעֵי בֵּין אַשּׁוֹר בֵּין אַשֶּׂה. נְגִידִים. גְּוִיעִים. כִּדְמְתַרְגְּמִינַן "וַיִּגְוַע" – וְאִיתְנְגִיד (בראשית כ). כְּלוֹמַר: כְּחוּשִׁין וּקְרוֹבִין לָמוּת. ה"א עַד דְּגָנַב תַּרְתֵּי וְטָבַח לְחַד וּמְזַבֵּין לְחַד. לְהָכִי אִצְטְרִיךְ "שׁוֹר אוֹ שֶׂה" דְּרֵישָׁא, לְמֵימַר דְּאע"ג דְּחַד הוּא דְּגָנַב – מְחַיֵּיב. אוֹ מְכָרוֹ כְּתִיב. דְּמַשְׁמַע אוֹ טְבִיחָה אוֹ מְכִירָה, דְּהָא כְּתִיב "אוֹ" לְחַלֵּק. וְאֵימָא עַד דְּגָנַב תַּרְתֵּי. כִּדְכְתִיב בְּסֵיפָא: "תַּחַת הַשּׁוֹר" "תַּחַת הַשֶּׂה", וּלְהָכִי אִצְטְרִיךְ "שׁוֹר אוֹ שֶׂה" דְּרֵישָׁא. שֶׁנִּשְׁתָּרֵשׁ. עָשָׂה שָׁרָשִׁין. כְּלוֹמַר: נִתְחַזֵּק בַּחֵטְא, שֶׁקְּנָאוֹ וּמְהַנּוּ מַעֲשָׂיו. אִילֵימָא לִפְנֵי יֵאוּשׁ. מְכָרוֹ.

מִי

הָתָם אָעוּלָּא, וְסָבַר דְּיֵאוּשׁ כְּדֵי הֲוֵי יֵאוּשׁ. וְלִיכָּא לְשַׁנּוּיֵי כִּדְמְשַׁנֵּי לְקַמָּן לְרִ"ל לְקִישׁ כְּגוֹן שֶׁהִקְדִּישׁוּ בְּעָלִים בְּיַד גַּנָּב – דְּאִם כֵּן מַאי פָּרִיךְ הָתָם לְעוּלָּא: כָּרֵת מַאי עֲבִידְתֵּיהּ? הָא מִתְחַיֵּיב כָּרֵת שַׁפִּיר, דְּרָאוּי לְפֶתַח אֹהֶל מוֹעֵד, כֵּיוָן שֶׁהִקְדִּישׁוּ בְּעָלִים! וי"ל: דְּהָמ"ל "וּלְטַעְמִיךְ". אִי נָמֵי: דְּרַב יְהוּדָה נָמֵי אִית לֵיהּ דְּיֵאוּשׁ לָא קָנֵי.

וְטַעְמָא דְּרַב יְהוּדָה דְּאָמַר בֵּין נוֹדַעַת בֵּין לֹא נוֹדַעַת מְכַפֶּרֶת – מִשּׁוּם דְּלָא חָיְישׁ לְטַעְמָא דְּמִצְוָה הַבָּאָה בַּעֲבֵירָה. וְלָא גָּרְסִינַן הָתָם "מַאי טַעְמָא קָסָבַר יֵאוּשׁ כְּדֵי קָנֵי". וּבְסוּכָּה (ד' ל. וְשָׁם), דְּקָאָמַר: אֶלָּא לְאַחַר יֵאוּשׁ הָא קַנְיֵיהּ בְּיֵאוּשׁ – ה"פ: הָא קַנְיֵיהּ בְּיֵאוּשׁ וְשִׁינּוּי הַשֵּׁם. וּמַה שֶּׁאֵין מַזְכִּיר אֶלָּא יֵאוּשׁ – מִשּׁוּם דְּע"י יֵאוּשׁ שֶׁקּוֹדֵם לָכֵן קָנָאָה בְּשִׁינּוּי הַשֵּׁם. וְאִית סְפָרִים דְּלָא גָּרְסִי "בְּיֵאוּשׁ", אֶלָּא: הָא קַנְיֵיהּ. וְתֵדַע, דְּהָא הָתָם ר' יוֹחָנָן קָאָמַר לֵיהּ, וְר' יוֹחָנָן אִית לֵיהּ דְּיֵאוּשׁ לָא קָנֵי. דְּאָמַר לְקַמָּן: חֵיוּבֵיהּ בֵּין לִפְנֵי יֵאוּשׁ בֵּין לְאַחַר יֵאוּשׁ, וְאִי סָבַר דְּיֵאוּשׁ קָנֵי – אַמַּאי חַיָּיב לְאַחַר יֵאוּשׁ? שֶׁלּוֹ הוּא טוֹבֵחַ וְשֶׁלּוֹ הוּא מוֹכֵר! וּבְ"הַגּוֹזֵל בַּתְרָא" קָאָמַר רַבִּי יוֹחָנָן מִשְּׁמֵיהּ דְּרַבִּי יַנַּאי דְּשִׁינּוּי רְשׁוּת וְאַחַר כָּךְ יֵאוּשׁ לָא קָנֵי. ור"ת הִקְשָׁה: דְּבְּ"הַגּוֹזֵל בַּתְרָא" (לְקַמָּן ד' קיד.) מַשְׁמַע דִּלְעוּלָּא יֵאוּשׁ כְּדֵי קָנֵי. דְּפָרִיךְ מִמַּתְנִיתִין דְּ"נָטְלוּ מוֹכְסִים חֲמוֹרוֹ וְנָתְנוּ לוֹ חֲמוֹר אַחֵר הֲרֵי זֶה שֶׁלּוֹ". וְקָאָמַר: בִּשְׁלָמָא לְעוּלָּא – בְּיָדוּעַ וְדִבְרֵי הַכֹּל. וְנָתְנוּ לוֹ חֲמוֹר אַחֵר חָשֵׁיב לֵיהּ הָתָם יֵאוּשׁ כְּדֵי, דְּקָאָמַר הָתָם, תָּנָא: וְאִם נָטַל – מַחֲזִיר לַבְּעָלִים הָרִאשׁוֹנִים. וּמְפָרֵשׁ דְּקָסָבַר יֵאוּשׁ כְּדֵי לָא קָנֵי. וְטַעְמָא נִרְאֶה דְּלָא חָשֵׁיב לֵיהּ שִׁינּוּי רְשׁוּת, מִשּׁוּם דְּע"כ נוֹתְנִים לוֹ! וְתֵירֵץ ר"י: דִּבְרַיְיתָא ע"כ לָא אַיְירֵי כְּמַתְנִי', דְּהָא בְּמַתְנִיתִין קָתָנֵי: הֲרֵי הוּא שֶׁלּוֹ, וּבְרַיְיתָא קָתָנֵי: מַחֲזִיר לַבְּעָלִים הָרִאשׁוֹנִים. וְעוֹד: דְּאִ"כ דְּמַתְנִיתִין קַיְימָא – תִּקְשֵׁי מִבְּרַיְיתָא לְרַבָּה, דְּאָמַר יֵאוּשׁ כְּדֵי קָנֵי. אֶלָּא בְּרַיְיתָא אַיְירֵי שֶׁהַבְּעָלִים עוֹמְדִים, וְלָא נִתְיָיאֲשׁוּ עֲדַיִין כְּשֶׁנְּתָנוּ לָזֶה. אע"ג דִּלְבַסּוֹף אַחַר דְּאָתָא לִידֵיהּ נִתְיָיאֲשׁוּ – לָא קָנֵי, דְּשִׁינּוּי רְשׁוּת דְּקוֹדֶם יֵאוּשׁ לָא קָנֵי, כִּדְמַשְׁמַע לְקַמָּן. וְיֵאוּשׁ גְּרֵידָא נָמֵי לָא קָנֵי, אֲפִי' לְרַבָּה – כֵּיוָן דְּבְאִיסּוּרָא אָתָא לִידֵיהּ, וְצָרִיךְ לְהַחֲזִיר הַדָּמִים. אֲבָל מַתְנִיתִין אַיְירֵי לְעוּלָּא בְּיָדוּעַ שֶׁנִּתְיָיאֵשׁ מִקַּמֵּי דְּאָתָא לִידֵיהּ, וְכִי אָתָא לִידֵיהּ – הָוֵה לֵיהּ יֵאוּשׁ וְשִׁינּוּי רְשׁוּת.

אף גָּזוּל דְּלֵית לֵיהּ תַּקַּנְתָּא. אע"ג דְּאָמַר לְעֵיל (דף סה:) גָּנַב טָלֶה וְנַעֲשָׂה אַיִל נַעֲשָׂה שִׁינּוּי בְּיָדוֹ וּקְנָאוֹ, מ"מ כְּמוֹ שֶׁהוּא לֵית לֵיהּ תַּקַּנְתָּא. **רבא** אמר מהכא קרבנו ולא הגזול. רָבָא גָּרְסִינַן, וְלָא רַבָּה. מִדְּקָאָמַר: חַד מִינַּיְיהוּ רַב פַּפָּא אָמַר, וְלָא הָיוּ טוֹעִים אֶלָּא בֵּין רַב פַּפָּא *לְרָבָא שֶׁהָיָה רַבּוֹ, וּפְעָמִים כְּשֶׁהָיָה אוֹמֵר רַב פַּפָּא דְּבָרִים בִּסְתָם הָיוּ סְבוּרִים שֶׁדִּבְרֵי רָבָא הֵן. אֲבָל בֵּין דִּבְרֵי רַב פַּפָּא לְדִבְרֵי רַבָּה לָא הָיוּ יְכוֹלִין לִטְעוֹת. וּלְעֵיל (דף סו:) גָּרַס: אָמַר לֵיהּ רָבָא מִשְׁכְּנוֹ וְלָא הַגָּזוּל כו', אע"ג דְּרַבָּה הֲוָה בַּר פְּלוּגְתֵּיהּ דְּרַב יוֹסֵף, וּלְרַבָּה הִקְשָׁה אַבַּיֵּי – צָרִיךְ לוֹמַר דְּרַבָּה עַצְמוֹ לָא הֵשִׁיב לוֹ כְּלוּם, אֶלָּא רָבָא הֵשִׁיב לוֹ, מִדְּפָרִיךְ הָכָא: וְהָא רָבָא הוּא דְּאָמַר דְּגָזַל קָרְבַּן דְּחַבְרֵיהּ, וְקָאָמַר דְּחַד מִינַּיְיהוּ רַב פַּפָּא אֲמָרָהּ. וְכֵן מַשְׁמַע, דִּבְכָל הַסְּפָרִים גָּרַס לְעֵיל: אָמַר לֵיהּ רָבָא. וְאִי רַבָּה הֱשִׁיבוֹ – הֲוָה לֵיהּ לְמֵימַר, "אָמַר לֵיהּ" וְלָא הָיָה צָרִיךְ לְהַזְכִּיר רַבָּה, כֵּיוָן דְּמַקְשֶׁה לְרַבָּה. וְכֵן מַשְׁמַע בְּ"הַנִּיזָּקִין" (גיטין דף נה: וְשָׁם) דְּרָבָא אִית לֵיהּ דְּיֵאוּשׁ כְּדֵי לָא קָנֵי. דְּבָעֵי רָבָא: כִּי אוֹקְמוּהָ רַבָּנַן בִּרְשׁוּתֵיהּ – מִשְּׁעַת גְּנֵיבָה אוֹ מִשְּׁעַת הֶקְדֵּשׁ, לְמַאי נ"מ כו'. וְאִי יֵאוּשׁ קָנֵי – לְכָל הַפָּחוֹת מִשְּׁעַת יֵאוּשׁ כְּבָר הוּא בִּרְשׁוּתֵיהּ. וּבְפֶרֶק בַּתְרָא (דף קיא: וְשָׁם) קָאָמַר רָבָא: לְעוֹלָם רְשׁוּת יוֹרֵשׁ לָאו כִּרְשׁוּת לוֹקֵחַ דָּמֵי, מַשְׁמַע הָתָם דְּאִית לֵיהּ דְּיֵאוּשׁ לָא קָנֵי, וְהָתָם רָבָא דְּהוּא בַּר פְּלוּגְתֵּיהּ דְּרָמֵי בַּר חָמָא. וְהָא דְּאָמַר רָבָא בְּפֶרֶק "אֵלּוּ מְצִיאוֹת" (ב"מ דף כו:) גַּבֵּי מְצִיאָה: נְטָלָהּ לִפְנֵי יֵאוּשׁ עַל מְנָת לְגָזְלָהּ – עוֹבֵר בְּכוּלָּן, וְאע"ג דְּאַהַדְרֵיהּ בָּתַר יֵאוּשׁ – מַתָּנָה בְּעָלְמָא הוּא דְּיָהֵיב לֵיהּ. אע"ג דְּיֵאוּשׁ לָא קָנֵי, מ"מ כֵּיוָן דְּהוֹעִיל יֵאוּשׁ לְמוֹכְרָהּ אוֹ לְהַקְדִּישָׁהּ – חָשֵׁיב גַּזְלָן. **שור** וְשֶׂה שְׁנֵי פְּעָמִים. וא"ת: וְ"שֶׂה" דִּכְתִיב ב' פְּעָמִים לָמָּה לִי? הָא בְּשַׁבָּת לָא כְּתִיב שֶׂה! °וי"ל: דְּאִי לָא כְּתִיב "שֶׂה" שְׁנֵי פְּעָמִים הֲוָה אָמִינָא שֶׁבָּא "שׁוֹר" לְמַעוּטֵי שְׁאָר מִילֵּי מִדִּין שׁוֹר, דְּלָא הֲווּ בְּתַשְׁלוּמִין ה', וְלוּקְמֵיהּ אַדִּין שֶׂה – לְהָכִי כְּתִיב "שֶׂה" לְמַעוּטֵי לְגַמְרֵי.

חמשה בָקָר יְשַׁלֵּם תַּחְתָּיו. וּמִסְבָּרָא הֲוָה יָדַעְנָא דְ"חֲמִשָּׁה בָקָר" קַיְימָא אַ"שׁוֹר", וְ"אַרְבַּע צֹאן" קַיְימֵי אַ"שֶׂה". **אין** הגונב כו'. בַּגְּמָרָא (דף סט:) דָּרֵישׁ לַהּ מִ"וְּגֻנַּב מִבֵּית הָאִישׁ" וְלֹא מִבֵּית הַגַּנָּב. וּלְמַאן דְּמוֹקֵי חַד בְּגַנָּב וְחַד בְּטוֹעֵן טַעֲנַת גַּנָּב ה"ש. אֲבָל לְמַאן דְּמוֹקֵי תַּרְוַיְיהוּ לְטוֹעֵן טַעֲנַת גַּנָּב – לָא שַׁיָּיךְ כְּלָל לְמִדְרַשׁ הָכִי. וְצָרִיךְ לוֹמַר דִּלְדִידֵיהּ נָפְקָא לֵיהּ לְמַעוּטֵי גַּנָּב אַחַר הַגַּנָּב מִקְּרָא אַחֲרִינָא.

דתניא אמר רבי עקיבא כו'. מִכָּל הָנְהוּ דְּפָרִיךְ הָכָא לְרַב *ה"מ לְמִפְרַךְ לְעֵיל לְרַבָּה, וּמֵהָנְהוּ דְּפָרִיךְ לְעֵיל לְרַבָּה ה"מ לְמִפְרַךְ לְרַב. אֶלָּא דְּרַבָּה דְּאַיְירֵי בְּגַזְלָן – פָּרִיךְ לֵיהּ מִמִּילֵּי דְגַזְלָן, וּלְרַב דְּמַיְירֵי בְּגַנָּב – נִיחָא לֵיהּ לְמִיפְרַךְ מִמִּילֵּי דְגַנָּב, אע"פ שֶׁאֵין סְבָרָא לְחַלֵּק. וְעוֹד: דִּכְמוֹ שֶׁהוּקְשׁוּ בְּבֵית הַמִּדְרָשׁ נִקְבְּעוּ בַּגְּמָרָא, וּלְתַרְוַיְיהוּ הֲוָה מָצֵי לְמִפְרַךְ מֵהַהִיא דְּגַנָּב וְהִקְדִּישׁ, דְּפָרִיךְ מִינַּהּ לְקַמָּן לְרַבִּי יוֹחָנָן לְרִישׁ לָקִישׁ.

אִי

הגהות הב"ח

(א) גמ' רב פפא אמרה. נ"ב משום דמלך בתר אביי ורבא כ"כ תוס' בשבועות דף כו ע"א וכה"ג כתבו תוס' בפ' במה מדליקין ד' כז ע"ב:

גליון הש"ס

תוס' ד"ה שור כו' וי"ל דאי לא כתיב. עיין תשובת מהר"י אדריבי סי' שלה:

[ע' תוס' בכורות נד: ד"ה חלא ותוס' שבועות כו. ד"ה חלא]

עיין בת"ח

מסורת הש"ס

[לעיל סו:]

[שבת כז. שבועות כ בכורות נד:]

[יבמות כד: וש"נ]

תורה אור

שמות כא

מִי אִיכָּא נִשְׁתָּרֵשׁ? אֶלָּא לְאַחַר יֵאוּשׁ; וְאִי ס"ד יֵאוּשׁ קָנֵי, אַמַּאי מְשַׁלֵּם תַּשְׁלוּמֵי אַרְבָּעָה וַחֲמִשָּׁה? שֶׁלּוֹ הוּא טוֹבֵחַ, שֶׁלּוֹ הוּא מוֹכֵר! אָמְרִי, כִּדְאָמַר רָבָא: מִפְּנֵי שֶׁשָּׁנָה בְּחֵטְא, הָכָא נַמִי מִפְּנֵי שֶׁשָּׁנָה בְּחֵטְא. ת"ש: °"וּטְבָחוֹ אוֹ מְכָרוֹ" — *מַה טְּבִיחָה שֶׁאֵינָהּ חוֹזֶרֶת, אַף מְכִירָה שֶׁאֵינָהּ חוֹזֶרֶת; אֵימַת? אִילֵימָא לִפְנֵי יֵאוּשׁ, אַמַּאי אֵינָהּ חוֹזֶרֶת? אֶלָּא לְאַחַר יֵאוּשׁ; וְאִי ס"ד קַנְיֵיהּ, אַמַּאי מְשַׁלֵּם ד' וְה'? שֶׁלּוֹ הוּא טוֹבֵחַ, שֶׁלּוֹ הוּא מוֹכֵר! כִּדְאָמַר רַב נַחְמָן: אפְּרָט לְשֶׁהִקְנָה לִשְׁלֹשִׁים יוֹם, הָכָא נַמִי פְּרָט לְשֶׁהִקְנָה לִשְׁלֹשִׁים יוֹם. מֵיתִיבֵי: גָּנַב, וּבָא אַחֵר וּגְנָבוֹ — הָרִאשׁוֹן מְשַׁלֵּם תַּשְׁלוּמֵי כֶפֶל, וְהַשֵּׁנִי אֵינוֹ מְשַׁלֵּם אֶלָּא קֶרֶן בִּלְבַד; גָּנַב וּמָכַר, וּבָא אַחֵר וּגְנָבוֹ — הָרִאשׁוֹן מְשַׁלֵּם תַּשְׁלוּמֵי אַרְבָּעָה וַחֲמִשָּׁה, וְהַשֵּׁנִי מְשַׁלֵּם תַּשְׁלוּמֵי כֶפֶל; גָּנַב וְטָבַח, וּבָא אַחֵר וּגְנָבוֹ — הָרִאשׁוֹן מְשַׁלֵּם תַּשְׁלוּמֵי ד' וְה', וְהַשֵּׁנִי אֵינוֹ מְשַׁלֵּם תַּשְׁלוּמֵי כֶפֶל אֶלָּא קֶרֶן בִּלְבַד. קָתָנֵי מִיהָא מְצִיעֲתָא: בגָּנַב וּמָכַר, וּבָא אַחֵר וּגְנָבוֹ — הָרִאשׁוֹן מְשַׁלֵּם תַּשְׁלוּמֵי ד' וה', וְהַשֵּׁנִי מְשַׁלֵּם תַּשְׁלוּמֵי כֶפֶל; אֵימַת? אִילֵימָא לִפְנֵי יֵאוּשׁ, שֵׁנִי אַמַּאי מְשַׁלֵּם תַּשְׁלוּמֵי כֶפֶל? שִׁינּוּי רְשׁוּת בְּלֹא יֵאוּשׁ מִי אִיכָּא לְמ"ד דְּקָנֵי? אֶלָּא פְּשִׁיטָא גלְאַחַר יֵאוּשׁ; וְאִי ס"ד יֵאוּשׁ קוֹנֶה, אַמַּאי מְשַׁלֵּם תַּשְׁלוּמֵי ד' וְה'? דִּידֵיהּ הוּא דְּזַבֵּין! וְתוּ, דְּקָתָנֵי רֵישָׁא: גָּנַב, וּבָא אַחֵר וּגְנָבוֹ — רִאשׁוֹן מְשַׁלֵּם תַּשְׁלוּמֵי כֶפֶל, וְהַשֵּׁנִי אֵין מְשַׁלֵּם אֶלָּא קֶרֶן; מִכְּדִי לְאַחַר יֵאוּשׁ קָיְימִינַן, וְאִי ס"ד יֵאוּשׁ קוֹנֶה, שֵׁנִי אַמַּאי אֵינוֹ מְשַׁלֵּם אֶלָּא קֶרֶן? אֶלָּא לָאו דש"מ: יֵאוּשׁ לָא קָנֵי, וְקַשְׁיָא לְרַב! אָמַר רָבָא: וְתִסְבְּרָא, הָא מְתָרַצְתָּא הִיא? אֶלָּא דְּקָתָנֵי סֵיפָא: גָּנַב וְטָבַח וּבָא אַחֵר וּגְנָבוֹ — רִאשׁוֹן מְשַׁלֵּם תַּשְׁלוּמֵי אַרְבָּעָה וַחֲמִשָּׁה, וְשֵׁנִי אֵינוֹ מְשַׁלֵּם אֶלָּא קֶרֶן; וּמִי אִיכָּא לְמ"ד שִׁינּוּי מַעֲשֶׂה לָא קָנֵי? אֶלָּא, לְעוֹלָם כּוּלָּהּ לִפְנֵי יֵאוּשׁ, וְאֵיפוּךְ סֵיפָא לִמְצִיעֲתָא וּמְצִיעֲתָא לְסֵיפָא, וְאֵימָא הָכִי: הגָּנַב וּמָכַר, וּבָא אַחֵר וּגְנָבוֹ — הָרִאשׁוֹן מְשַׁלֵּם תַּשְׁלוּמֵי אַרְבָּעָה וַחֲמִשָּׁה, וְהַשֵּׁנִי אֵינוֹ מְשַׁלֵּם אֶלָּא קֶרֶן, ודְּשִׁינּוּי רְשׁוּת בְּלֹא יֵאוּשׁ לָא קָנֵי; זגָּנַב וְטָבַח וּבָא אַחֵר וּגְנָבוֹ — הָרִאשׁוֹן מְשַׁלֵּם תַּשְׁלוּמֵי אַרְבָּעָה וַחֲמִשָּׁה, וְהַשֵּׁנִי מְשַׁלֵּם תַּשְׁלוּמֵי כֶפֶל, דְּקַנְיֵיהּ בְּשִׁינּוּי מַעֲשֶׂה. רַב פַּפָּא אָמַר: לְעוֹלָם לָא תֵּיפוּךְ, סֵיפָא *ב"ש הִיא, דְּאָמְרִי: שִׁינּוּי (א) בִּמְקוֹמָהּ עוֹמֵד. אִי הָכִי, קַשְׁיָא רֵישָׁא וּמְצִיעֲתָא לְרַב! א"ר זְבִיד: לְעוֹלָם כּוּלָּהּ לִפְנֵי יֵאוּשׁ, וְהב"ע — שֶׁנִּתְיָיאֲשׁוּ הַבְּעָלִים בְּלוֹקֵחַ וְלֹא נִתְיָיאֲשׁוּ בְּגַנָּב, [א] דַּהֲוָ"ל יֵאוּשׁ (וְשִׁינּוּי רְשׁוּת). וְלָא תֵּימָא מִשּׁוּם דְּבָעֵינַן יֵאוּשׁ וְשִׁינּוּי רְשׁוּת, אֶלָּא אֲפִילּוּ בְּיֵאוּשׁ לְחוּדֵיהּ נַמִי קָנֵי גַּבֵּי גַּנָּב. אֶלָּא דְּלָא מַשְׁכַּחַתְּ דִּמְשַׁלְּמִי תַּרְוַיְיהוּ גַּנָּב רִאשׁוֹן וְגַנָּב שֵׁנִי אֶלָּא בְּהָכִי.§ אִיתְּמַר: הַמּוֹכֵר לִפְנֵי יֵאוּשׁ, רַב נַחְמָן אָמַר: חחַיָּיב, רַב שֵׁשֶׁת אָמַר: פָּטוּר. רַב נַחְמָן אָמַר חַיָּיב, "וּמְכָרוֹ" אָמַר רַחֲמָנָא, וְהָא זַבֵּין, לָא שְׁנָא לִפְנֵי יֵאוּשׁ לָא שְׁנָא לְאַחַר יֵאוּשׁ; רַב שֵׁשֶׁת אָמַר פָּטוּר, חִיּוּבֵיהּ לְאַחַר יֵאוּשׁ הוּא, דְּאַהֲנוּ מַעֲשָׂיו, אֲבָל לִפְנֵי יֵאוּשׁ דְּלָא אַהֲנוּ מַעֲשָׂיו — לָא מִיחַיַּיב, דּוּמְיָא דִּטְבִיחָה בָּעֵינַן דְּאַהֲנוּ מַעֲשָׂיו. א"ר שֵׁשֶׁת: מְנָא אָמִינָא לָהּ? דְּתַנְיָא, א"ר עֲקִיבָא: מִפְּנֵי מָה אָמְרָה תּוֹרָה טָבַח וּמָכַר מְשַׁלֵּם ד' וְה'? מִפְּנֵי שֶׁנִּשְׁתָּרֵשׁ בְּחֵטְא; אֵימַת? אִילֵימָא לִפְנֵי יֵאוּשׁ, מִי אִיכָּא נִשְׁתָּרֵשׁ? אֶלָּא לָאו לְאַחַר יֵאוּשׁ הוּא! אָמַר רָבָא: מִפְּנֵי שֶׁשָּׁנָה בְּחֵטְא. ת"ש: "וּטְבָחוֹ וּמְכָרוֹ" — מַה טְּבִיחָה שֶׁאֵינָהּ חוֹזֶרֶת, אַף מְכִירָה שֶׁאֵינָהּ חוֹזֶרֶת; אֵימַת? אִילֵימָא לִפְנֵי יֵאוּשׁ, אַמַּאי אֵינָהּ חוֹזֶרֶת? אֶלָּא לְאַחַר יֵאוּשׁ, וש"מ: חִיּוּבָא לְאַחַר יֵאוּשׁ הוּא! תַּרְגְּמָהּ רַב נַחְמָן: פְּרָט לְשֶׁהִקְנָה לוֹ לִשְׁלֹשִׁים יוֹם. וְאַף ר' אֶלְעָזָר סָבַר: חִיּוּבֵיהּ לְאַחַר יֵאוּשׁ הוּא, דְּאָמַר ר' אֶלְעָזָר:

תֵּדַע

תורה אור: שמות כא

רש"י

מִי אִיכָּא נִשְׁתָּרֵשׁ. הָא לָא אַהֲנוּ מַעֲשָׂיו. דְּשִׁינּוּי רְשׁוּת שֶׁשִּׁינָּהוּ מֵרְשׁוּתוֹ לִרְשׁוּת לוֹקֵחַ בְּלֹא יֵאוּשׁ – לֵיכָּא לְמ"ד דְּקָנֵי. לְאַחַר יֵאוּשׁ. דְּאַהֲנוּ מַעֲשָׂיו. דְּהַשְׁתָּא קָנֵי לוֹקֵחַ בְּתַרְתֵּי – יֵאוּשׁ וְשִׁינּוּי רְשׁוּת. וְאִי ס"ד יֵאוּשׁ. גְּרֵידָא קָנְיָא גַּנָּב, אַמַּאי מְשַׁלֵּם אַרְבָּעָה וַחֲמִשָּׁה? הָא דְּמֵי בְּעָלְמָא הוּא דְּאִית לְהוּ לַבְּעָלִים גַּבֵּיהּ, וְשֶׁלּוֹ טָבַח וּמָכַר. כִּדְאָמַר רָבָא. לְקַמָּן בִּשְׁמַעְתִּין. שֶׁשָּׁנָה בְּחֵטְא. וּלְעוֹלָם לִפְנֵי יֵאוּשׁ, וְאַע"פ דְּלָא אַהֲנוּ מַעֲשָׂיו מְחַיֵּיב. שֶׁאֵינָהּ חוֹזֶרֶת. קס"ד דְּה"ק: דְּלָא מְחַיֵּיב אֶלָּא הֵיכָא דִּמְכִירָתוֹ מְכִירָה גְּמוּרָה, וְקַנְיֵיהּ לוֹקֵחַ. אַמַּאי אֵינָהּ חוֹזֶרֶת. שִׁינּוּי רְשׁוּת בְּלֹא יֵאוּשׁ מִי קָנֵי? לְאַחַר יֵאוּשׁ. דְּכִי מָטָא בְּיַד לוֹקֵחַ אִיכָּא תַּרְתֵּי, יֵאוּשׁ וְשִׁינּוּי רְשׁוּת, וְקַנְיֵיהּ. וְאִי ס"ד קַנְיֵיהּ. גַּנָּב בְּיֵאוּשׁ גְּרֵידָא, אַמַּאי מְשַׁלֵּם כו'? כִּדְאָמַר רַב נַחְמָן. לְקַמָּן בִּשְׁמַעְתִּין. פְּרָט לְשֶׁהִקְנָה לוֹ לִשְׁלֹשִׁים יוֹם. כְּלוֹמַר: לְעוֹלָם לִפְנֵי יֵאוּשׁ, וְהַאי "אֵינָהּ חוֹזֶרֶת" דְּקָתָנֵי – לָא לְמַעוּטֵי הֵיכָא דְּלָא אַהֲנוּ מַעֲשָׂיו, דְּאַע"ג דְּלָא אַהֲנוּ חַיְּיבֵיהּ רַחֲמָנָא, הוֹאִיל וְשָׁנָה בְּחֵטְא. אֶלָּא לְמַעוּטֵי הֵיכָא דְּלֹא מָכַר גַּנָּב לַלּוֹקֵחַ אֶלָּא לַעֲשׂוֹת בָּהּ מְלָאכָה שְׁלֹשִׁים יוֹם, דְּהוּא כִּשְׂכִירוּת בְּעָלְמָא. וְשֵׁנִי אֵינוֹ מְשַׁלֵּם אֶלָּא קֶרֶן. לְגַנָּב רִאשׁוֹן, דִּכְתִיב: "וְגוּנַּב מִבֵּית הָאִישׁ". גָּנַב וּמָכַר. קַנְיֵיהּ לוֹקֵחַ בְּשִׁינּוּי רְשׁוּת, הִלְכָּךְ (רִאשׁוֹן מְשַׁלֵּם ד' וְה') שֵׁנִי מְשַׁלֵּם כֶּפֶל לַלּוֹקֵחַ. וְשֵׁנִי אֵינוֹ מְשַׁלֵּם אֶלָּא קֶרֶן. וּלְקַמָּן פָּרֵיךְ: אַמַּאי לָא מְשַׁלֵּם כֶּפֶל? הָא קַנְיֵיהּ גַּנָּב רִאשׁוֹן בְּשִׁינּוּי מַעֲשֶׂה! אֵימַת. מְכָרָהּ? אִילֵימָא לִפְנֵי יֵאוּשׁ – הַשֵּׁנִי אַמַּאי מְשַׁלֵּם כֶּפֶל? אֶלָּא פְּשִׁיטָא לְאַחַר יֵאוּשׁ. דְּאִיכָּא תַּרְתֵּי בְּיַד לוֹקֵחַ. וְאִי ס"ד כו'. וְאִי קַשְׁיָא: הָא יָכוֹל לְתָרוּצַהּ כְּגוֹן שֶׁנִּתְיָיאֲשׁוּ בְּעָלִים לְאַחַר מְכִירַת גַּנָּב, דְּקוֹנֶה לוֹקֵחַ, וּבְיַד גַּנָּב לָא הָיָה יֵאוּשׁ לְקָנוֹתָהּ – ה"נ מְשַׁנֵּי לֵיהּ לְקַמָּן. מִכְּדִי לְאַחַר יֵאוּשׁ קָיְימִינַן. דְּע"כ הָכִי מוֹקְמַתְּ לָהּ מִשּׁוּם מְצִיעֲתָא. אֶלָּא כּוּלָּהּ לִפְנֵי יֵאוּשׁ. וּמש"ה רֵישָׁא שֵׁנִי פָּטוּר מִכֶּפֶל. וְאֵיפוּךְ סֵיפָא לִמְצִיעֲתָא כו'. וְתָנֵי בִּמְצִיעֲתָא: שֵׁנִי אֵין מְשַׁלֵּם אֶלָּא קֶרֶן. דְּלָא קַנְיֵיהּ לוֹקֵחַ בְּשִׁינּוּי רְשׁוּת בְּלֹא יֵאוּשׁ. א"ה. דִּלְאַחַר יֵאוּשׁ מוֹקְמַתְּ לָהּ, קַשְׁיָא רֵישָׁא וּמְצִיעֲתָא לְרַב. א"ר זְבִיד כּוּלָּהּ לִפְנֵי יֵאוּשׁ. וְאַפּוּכֵי נַמִי לָא תַּפְכָהּ. וְסֵיפָא כִּדְאוֹקִימְנָא כְּב"ש, וּמְצִיעֲתָא דְּקָתָנֵי: שֵׁנִי מְשַׁלֵּם כֶּפֶל – כְּגוֹן שֶׁנִּתְיָיאֲשׁוּ הַבְּעָלִים לְאַחַר מְכִירָה וְלֹא נִתְיָיאֲשׁוּ בְּיַד גַּנָּב. וּלְהָכִי רִאשׁוֹן מְשַׁלֵּם ד' וְה' – דְּלָא הָוֵי יֵאוּשׁ גַּבֵּי' דְּלִיקַנְיֵיהּ. וְרֵישָׁא נַמִי, לְפִיכָךְ שֵׁנִי פָּטוּר מִכֶּפֶל. וְלָא תֵּימָא. הָא דְּנָקַט מַתְנִי' חִיּוּבָא דְּשֵׁנִי גַּבֵּי לוֹקֵחַ, וְלָא נָקַט לָהּ לְחִיּוּב דְּשֵׁנִי גַּבֵּי רִאשׁוֹן, וְתוֹקְמָהּ נַמִי בִּלְאַחַר יֵאוּשׁ כִּדְמְשַׁנֵּי בְּלוֹקֵחַ – מִשּׁוּם דְּבָעֵי יֵאוּשׁ וְשִׁינּוּי רְשׁוּת. אֶלָּא בְּיֵאוּשׁ לְחוּדֵיהּ נַמִי קָנֵי כְּרַב, וְאִם גְּנָבָהּ מֵרִאשׁוֹן לְאַחַר יֵאוּשׁ – מְשַׁלֵּם לוֹ כֶּפֶל. אֶלָּא. לְהָכִי נָקַט תַּנָּא לְכוּלֵּיהּ מִלְּתָא בִּדְלֵיכָּא יֵאוּשׁ גַּבֵּי גַּנָּב – מִשּׁוּם דְּלָא מַשְׁכַּחַתְּ לָהּ דִּמְשַׁלְּמִי תַּרְוַויְהוּ, הַאי תַּשְׁלוּמֵי ד' וְה' וְהַאי כֶּפֶל. אֶלָּא בְּהָכִי. דְּאִי הָוֵי יֵאוּשׁ בְּיַד גַּנָּב – לָא מִיחַיֵּיב קַמָּא בִּמְכִירָתוֹ ד' וְה'. וְכֵיוָן דִּמְצִיעֲתָא לָא סַגִּי (ב) לָהּ אֶלָּא לִפְנֵי יֵאוּשׁ – תָּנָא נַמִי לְרֵישָׁא בְּלִפְנֵי יֵאוּשׁ וּפְטָרוֹ מִכֶּפֶל. חִיּוּבָא לְאַחַר יֵאוּשׁ הוּא דְּאַהֲנוּ מַעֲשָׂיו. מִשֶּׁקְּנָאוֹ לוֹקֵחַ. וּתְלָאָה אֲמוֹרָאֵי נִינְהוּ. רַב סָבַר: יֵאוּשׁ קָנֵי. הִלְכָּךְ לָא מִיחַיֵּיב אֶלָּא בְּלִפְנֵי יֵאוּשׁ, דְּאִי לְאַחַר יֵאוּשׁ – שֶׁלּוֹ הוּא טוֹבֵחַ וּמוֹכֵר. וְרַב נַחְמָן וְרַב שֵׁשֶׁת סָבְרִי: יֵאוּשׁ גְּרֵידָא לָא קָנֵי, וּמִשּׁוּם הָכִי לְאַחַר יֵאוּשׁ מִיחַיֵּיב. וּמִיהוּ בְּהָא פְּלִיגִי, דְּרַב נַחְמָן לָא בָּעֵי אַהֲנוּ מַעֲשָׂיו, הִלְכָּךְ אֲפִילּוּ לִפְנֵי יֵאוּשׁ גְּרֵידָא נַמִי חַיָּיב. וְרַב שֵׁשֶׁת בָּעֵי מְכִירָה גְּמוּרָה. נִשְׁתָּרֵשׁ. עָשָׂה שָׁרָשִׁין. מַשְׁמַע דְּאַהֲנוּ מַעֲשָׂיו.

תֵּדַע

תוספות

אִי הכי קשה מציעתא לרב. דאין להופכו, כיון דברייתא לא מוכחא מידי שצריך לתרלה ולהפכה.

מַה טביחה דאהנו מעשיו. משמע דסבר ר"א דשינוי קונה, דאהנו מעשיו משמע: לאפוקי מרשות בעלים, דומיא דאהנו מעשיו דמכירה. וקשה לפי' רשב"ם, דמפרש בפ"ק (ד' יא.) אהא דאמר עולא א"ר אלעזר: שמין לגנב ולגזלן — דהיינו לענין פחת נבילה דהוי דנגזל, משום דלא קני לה גזלן בשינוי. וי"ל: דדוקא בשינוי שאין הגזלן עושה בידים לא קני, כגון שמתה הבהמה. אבל שינוי שעושה הגזלן בידים, כגון טביחה, מודה ר"א דקני. א"נ, אהנו מעשיו דטביחה — היינו שמחסרה מן הבעלים, ולאו דקני ליה, ולא הוי כאהנו מעשיו דמכירה.

מה

[מכילתא משפטים פ' יב]

ס"א ל"ג

[לעיל סה:]

מהרכ"ש מ"ז

מג א מיי' פ"ב מהל' גניבה הל' יא טוח"מ סי' שנ:

[שייך לע"ב]

מד ב ג מיי' שם פ"א הל' יח טוח"מ שם:

מה ד מיי' שם הל' יז טוח"מ שם:

מו ה מיי' שם הל' יח טוח"מ שם:

מז ו מיי' שם ופ"ה שם הלכה ג ועיין בהשגות ובמ"מ ופ"ב מהלכות גזילה הלכה א טוש"ע ח"מ סימן שנג סעי' ג וסי' שסא סעי' ד וסי' שסב סעי' ג' טוח"מ סי' שנ:

מח ז מיי' פ"א מהל' גניבה הלכה יח טוח"מ סי' שנ:

[וע' תוס' ב"מ נו: ד"ה זיל שליס]

מט ח מיי' פ"א מהל' גניבה הל' יז טוח"מ שם:

הגהות הב"ח

(א) גמ' שינוי במקומו עומד כצ"ל: (ב) רש"י ד"ה אלא כו' לא סגי דלאו לפני יאוש כצ"ל:

הגהות הגר"א

[א] גמ' (דהוי ליה יאוש ושינוי רשות) תא"מ:

תדע ^אשסתם גניבה יאוש בעלים הוא, שהרי אמרה תורה טבח ומכר משלם תשלומי ארבעה וחמשה; ודלמא לא איאש! אלא לאו משום דאמרי': סתם גניבה יאוש בעלים היא. ודלמא אף על גב דלא איאש! אמרי: לא סלקא דעתך, דומיא דטביחה, מה טביחה דאהנו מעשיו, אף מכירה דאהנו מעשיו, ואי לפני יאוש — מאי אהנו? °ודלמא דשמעיניה דאייאש! אמרי: לא סלקא דעתך, דומיא דטביחה, מה טביחה לאלתר, אף מכירה לאלתר. א"ל ר' יוחנן: גניבה בנפש תוכיח, שאין יאוש בעלים, ^בוחייב! מכלל דסבר רבי יוחנן: לפני יאוש — חייב. לאחר יאוש מאי? ר' יוחנן אמר: ^גחייב, וריש לקיש אמר: פטור. רבי יוחנן אמר חייב, חיוביה בין לפני יאוש בין לאחר יאוש; ריש לקיש אמר פטור, חיוביה לפני יאוש הוא, אבל לאחר יאוש — קנה, ושלו הוא טובח ושלו הוא מוכר. *איתיביה ר' יוחנן לריש לקיש: ^דגנב והקדיש ואחר כך טבח — משלם תשלומי כפל ואינו משלם תשלומי ארבעה וחמשה; אימת? אילימא לפני יאוש, מי קדוש? °"איש כי יקדיש את ביתו קדש" אמר רחמנא, *^המה ביתו שלו, אף כל שלו! אלא פשיטא לאחר יאוש; וטעמא דהקדיש הוא דאינו משלם תשלומי ארבעה וחמשה, דכי קא טבח — דהקדש קא טבח, אבל לא הקדיש — טבח משלם תשלומי ארבעה וחמשה; ואי סלקא דעתך יאוש קונה, אמאי משלם? שלו הוא טובח, שלו הוא מוכר! א"ל: הכא במאי עסקינן — כגון שהקדישוהו בעלים ביד גנב. ומי קדוש? *והאמר ר' יוחנן: ^וגזל ולא נתייאשו הבעלים — שניהן אינן יכולין להקדיש, זה לפי שאינו שלו, וזה לפי שאינו ברשותו! אמרי: הוא דאמר כצנועין, דתנן: *^זהצנועין מניחין את המעות, ואומרים: "כל הנלקט מזה יהא מחולל על המעות האלו". והרי חזרה קרן לבעלים! כשעמד בדין. היכי דמי? אי דאמרי "צא תן לו", מאי איריא הקדיש? אפילו לא הקדיש נמי לא ליחייביה! *דאמר רבא: ^ח"צא תן לו", טבח ומכר — פטור, מ"ט? כיון דפסקוה למילתיה וטבח ומכר הוה ליה גזלן, וגזלן אינו משלם תשלומי ארבעה וחמשה;

חייב

ויקרא כז

תורה אור

רש"י

תדע שסתם גניבה. מיד מתייאשין, ואם מכרן גנב לאחר – מיד קנה, דאיכא תרתי: יאוש ושינוי רשות. ומנאי – שהרי אמרה תורה גנב ומכר משלם ד' וה', והא דלמא לא איאוש מריה, ולאו מכירה היא? **אלא לאו משום דסתם גניבה יאוש בעלים היא.** אלמא, מדיליף ר' אלעזר טעמא מהאי – ש"מ כרב ששת ס"ל, דאי שמעינא ליה למריה בהדיא דלא איאש – פטור המוכר מד' וה'. **ודלמא.** חייביה רחמנא ואע"ג דלא איאוש! לר"א פריך, דיליף מהכא יאוש לסתם גניבה. **ודלמא דשמעיניה דאייאש.** בהכי משתעי קרא, אבל סתם גניבה לא תילף מינה. **גניבה בנפש.** הגונב נפש ומכרו אין כאן יאוש, שאין אדם מתייאש על עצמו. ורחמנא חייביה, אע"ג דלא אהנו מעשיו. **לאחר יאוש מאי.** מי ס"ל יאוש גרידא קני, כרב, ושלו טובח ומוכר. או דלמא: יאוש לא קני, וכ"ש דלאחר יאוש מחייב – דאהנו מעשיו. **גנב והקדיש** משלם כפל. לבעלים. **ואינו משלם ד' וה'.** דהא כי טבח – דהקדש טבח, ו"רעהו" אמר רחמנא, "ישלם שנים לרעהו" ולא להקדש. וכיון דפטריה מכפל – תו לא מחייב בטביחה ומכירה, דתשלומי ארבעה וחמשה אמר רחמנא ולא שלשה וארבעה, וכי מדלית כפל מינייהו הוו ליה שלשה וארבעה. "מה ביתו שלו אף כל שלו" גרסי'. **שהקדישו בעלים.** ולעולם לפני יאוש. **הוא דאמר.** ר"ל, דתרלה כשהקדישוהו בעלים. סבר לה כצנועין. דאמרינן לקמן (ד' סט.) בכרם רבעי: הצנועים מניחין כו'. בני אדם חסידים שרוצין לסלק ידי כל אדם מן העבירה, כשיש להן כרם רבעי וחוששין שמא אוכלין ממנו עוברי דרכים בלא פדיון. מניחין מעות ואומרים כל הנלקט מזה. כל מה שלקטו בני אדם היום מכאן – יהא מחולל. אלמא, אע"ג דליתיה ברשותייהו – מיפרק, ותפיס להו למעות בקדושה. **והרי חזרה קרן לבעלים.** אי כשהקדישו בעלים, כפל אמאי משלם? הרי חוזרה קרן לידם, דאקדשוה כל היכא דאיתיה. וכפל לא מחייב אלא כשנמצאת ביד גנב שבאו עדים, כדכתיב: "אם המצא תמצא בידו". **כשעמד בדין.** שבאו עדים קודם שהקדישוהו בעלים.

בקזוזות

תוספות

מה טביחה לאלתר אף מכירה לאלתר. וא"ת: והא ממש לאלתר קודם ידיעת בעלים אי אפשר להיות דומיא דטביחה, דה"ל יאוש שלא מדעת, וקיימא לן כאביי דלא הוי יאוש! וי"ל: דטביחה נמי, אין דרך לטבוח לאלתר עד שיבוא לביתו, ובתוך כך מסתמא יודעין הבעלים.

גניבה בנפש תוכיח. וא"ת: גניבה בנפש שאני, דלא איתקש לטביחה! וי"ל: דהכא נמי לא איתקש לטביחה, אלא בלא היקישא יליף לה מטביחה, ולהכי קאמר ר' יוחנן דאדרבה אית לן למילף מכירה ממכירה. **רבי** יוחנן סבר חיוביה בין לפני יאוש בין לאחר יאוש. תימה: דלכאורה קי"ל כרבה דיאוש כדי קני, וקי"ל כר' יוחנן לגבי ר"ל דחיוביה אף לאחר יאוש ואמאי חייב אחר יאוש כיון דיאוש קני שלו הוא טובח ושלו הוא מוכר! וי"ל: דאפשר דלא קי"ל לא כרבה ולא כר' יוחנן, דכמה אמוראי נחלקו בשני אלו הדברים.

הוא דאמר כצנועין. וא"ת: והא צנועים מחללין אף אחר יאוש, דהא סתם גניבה הוי יאוש בעלים כרבנן דר"ש,* א"כ קסברי צנועין דיאוש לא קני. ור"ל מודה דאין יכול להקדיש אחר היאוש, דסבר יאוש קונה! וכ"ת דהוי יאוש שלא מדעת, שאינם יודעים אם לקטו אם לאו — הא גבי תמרי דזיקא אמרי' ב"אלו מציאות" (ב"מ ד' כב: ושם*) כיון דשכיחי דנתרי — חשיב יאוש מדעת! וי"ל: דהכא לא שכיח כולי האי שילקטו, שיראים מן הבעלים, ולא דמי לתמרי דזיקא, וחשיב יאוש שלא מדעת. ואפי' למ"ד יאוש שלא מדעת הוי יאוש — איכא למימר דצנועין סברי כר"ש, דאמר דסתם גניבה לא הוי יאוש בעלים. וא"ת: והיכי מדמי הקדש לחילול, שכמו שיכול לחלל מה שביד חבירו כן יכול להקדיש? והלא אע"פ שאין יכול להקדיש פירות של חבירו — יכול לחלל הקדש של חבירו, כדמשמע בריש "האשה רבה" (יבמות ד' פח.), דקאמר: אי קדושת דמים — משום דבידו לפדותו ואי קדושת הגוף, אי דידיה כו'. משמע דבקדושת דמים אין חילוק בין דידיה לחבריה! וי"ל: דלא דמי, דהקדש מאחר שהוקדש — יצא מרשות בעלים, וכמו שהבעלים יכולין לפדותו כמו כן אחר. אבל כרם רבעי — *הבעלים זכאים לאוכלה בירושלים. וא"ת: אכתי הרי יכול לחלל מעשר שני של חבירו, דאמרינן בפרק "האיש מקדש" (קדושין דף נה: ושם): אין לוקחין בהמה טמאה עבדים וקרקעות ממעות מעשר שני, ואם לקח — יאכל כנגדן בירושלים. ופריך: אמאי? יחזרו דמים למקומן. ומשני: כשברח. אלמא: מחללין מעות שביד המוכר! וי"ל: דהתם הוי כמו גזלן, דאי לא ברח — הוי המקח חוזר בו, והוי כמו גזל ולא נתייאשו הבעלים, וכלנועין דהכא. אי נמי: התם קנסא בעלמא, וכן משמע התם מתוך הסוגיא. ומיהו, בפרק "לולב הגזול" (סוכה ד' לט. ושם) משמע שיכול אדם לחלל [דמי] פירות שביעית של חבירו שלא מדעתו, דתניא: אין מוסרין דמי פירות שביעית לעם הארץ יותר ממזון שלש סעודות, ואם מסר — אומר: הרי מעות הללו מחוללין על פירות שיש לי בתוך ביתי, ובא ואוכלן בתורת שביעית. וי"ל: דאפקינהו רבנן מרשות עם הארץ כדי שלא יהא נכשל, ואוקמינהו ברשות זה שיכול לחלל, דהפקר ב"ד הפקר. ומיהו קשה: דבפ"ק דבכורות (דף יא. ושם ד"ה הפודה) משמע דהפודה פטר חמור של חבירו פדיונו פדוי, ואפילו שלא מדעתו, מדבעי ליה: פדיונו פדוי לפודה, או דלמא פדיונו פדוי לבעלים. ואי מדעת בעלים — דומה היה דפדיונו פדוי לבעלים! ויש לומר: דפטר חמור לא דמי לכרם רבעי, דכיון דאסור בהנאה הוי כמו הקדש לענין זה שיכול כל אדם לפדותו. ולא ממש הוי כהקדש, דבהקדש פשיטא לן דפדיונו פדוי לפודה, ובפטר חמור מסקינן דפדוי לבעלים. ומיהו: דבר תימה, דהיכי מדמי הקדש כלל לחילול? דלמה לא יוכל לחלל נטע רבעי ומעשר שני של חבירו שלא מדעתו, כיון דזכות הוא לו, דזכין לאדם שלא בפניו! דהא דמבעי לן ב"אין בין המודר" (נדרים ד' לו:): התורם משלו על של חבירו צריך דעת בעלים או לאו — היינו טעמא כדקאמר התם, דדלמא ניחא ליה למעבד מצוה בממוניה. אבל הכא — וכי אין טוב להם למלקטים שיאכלו אותם הבעלים ממה שיאכלו בלא חילול? [וע' תוס' קדושין נו. ד"ה מתקיף].

חייב

עין משפט נר מצוה

נ א מיי' פכ"ד מהל' כלים הל' ז ופ"ו מהל' גזילה הלכה ג טוש"ע ח"מ סי' שסח בהג"ה:

נא ב מיי' פ"ט מהל' גניבה הל' א סמג לאוין קנד:

נב ג מיי' שם פ"א הל' טז סמג עשין עא טוח"מ סי' שנ:

נג ד מיי' שם פ"ב הל' ו סמג שם:

נד ה מיי' פ"ו מהל' ערכין הל' כא סמג עשין קלב:

נה ו מיי' שם הלכה כד סמג שם טוש"ע ח"מ סי' שנד סעי' ז וטוש"ע י"ד סי' רנח ס"ו:

נו ז מיי' פ"ט מהל' מעשר שני הלכה ז וע"ש בכ"מ:

נז ח מיי' פ"ב מהל' גניבה הל' טו:

גליון הש"ס

גמ' ודלמא דשמעיניה דאייאש. עי' לקמן דף קיד ע"א תוס' ד"ה רבה אומר:

[לקמן קיד.] [ד"ה מאחר] אע"ג דממון גבוה הוא מ"מ הבעלים כו'. העתק מחילופי גרסאות

יטין נה: [לקמן עד:] | לקמן סט: ב"מ ו. ע"ז ס... חולין קלט. תמורה ט. כ... ערכין כא. ע"ש] | [לקמן סט. ע. קדושין נ... ב"מ ז.] | מעשר שני פ"ה מ"א | לקמן קו:

א"חייב אתה ליתן לו", טבח ומכר – משלם תשלומי ארבעה וחמשה, מ"ט? כיון דלא (א) פסקה מילתא אכתי גנב הוא! לא צריכא, דאמרי ליה "חייב אתה ליתן לו". § גופא, *אמר רבי יוחנן: גזל ולא נתייאשו הבעלים – שניהם אינן יכולים להקדיש, זה לפי שאינו שלו, וזה לפי שאינו ברשותו. ומי אמר ר' יוחנן הכי? *והא"ר יוחנן: הלכה כסתם משנה, *ותנן: בכרם רבעי היו מציינין אותו בקזוזות אדמה. סימנא כי אדמה, מה אדמה איכא הנאה מינה, אף האי נמי כי מפרקא שרי לאיתהנויי מינה; גושל ערלה – בחרסית. סימנא כחרסית, מה חרסית שאין הנאה מינה, אף האי דלית ביה הנאה מיניה; דושל קברות – בסיד. סימנא דחיור כעצמות; הוממחה ושופך. כי היכי דניחוור טפי; אמר רבן שמעון בן גמליאל: ובד"א – בשביעית. דהפקר נינהו, אבל בשאר שני שבוע – הלעיטהו לרשע וימות; זוהצנועין מניחין את המעות, ואומרים: "כל הנלקט מזה מחולל על המעות הללו"! וכי תימא: מאן תנא צנועין – רשב"ג, (ורבי יוחנן כסתם יחידאה לא אמר). והאמר רבה בר בר חנה אמר רבי יוחנן: *כל מקום ששנה רשב"ג במשנתנו – הלכה כמותו, חוץ מערב וצידן וראיה אחרונה! אמרי: לא תימא "כל הנלקט מזה", אלא אימא: "כל המתלקט מזה". ומי א"ר יוחנן הכי? והא"ר יוחנן: צנועין ורבי דוסא אמרו דבר אחד, ורבי דוסא "נלקט" קאמר: דתניא, *רבי יהודה אומר: שחרית בעל הבית עומד ואומר: "כל שילקטו עניים היום יהא הפקר", רבי דוסא אומר: לעיתותי ערב אומר: "כל שלקטו עניים יהא הפקר"! איפוך דר' יהודה לר' דוסא, ורבי דוסא לרבי יהודה. אמאי אפכת מתניתא? אפכה לרבי יוחנן, ואימא: צנועין ורבי יהודה אמרו דבר אחד! אמרי: לא סגיא דלא מתהפכת מתניתא, דבהא *מתניתין קתני דאית ליה לרבי יהודה ברירה, ושמעינן ליה לרבי יהודה בעלמא *דלית ליה ברירה; *דתנן:

הלוקח

רש"י

בקזוזות. מוט"ש. נותן פיסת רגבים סביבות הגבולים להודיע שהוא כרם רבעי, ואסור בלא פדיון. דאיכא הנאה מיניה. לאחר זמן, בחרישה וזריעה וקלירה. אף האי נמי איכא הנאה מיניה. בפדיון. חרסית. כתותי רעפים, טיילו"ש בלע"ז. וממחה ושופך. ממחה את הסיד במים, ושופך סביבות הקבר. בד"א. דעבדינן להו היכירא לעוברים ושבים. בשביעית. שהוא הפקר, ובהיתר הן באין לאכול. אבל בשאר שני שבוע. שהן באים לגזול, יניחם ויאכלו דבר האסור, והלעיטהו לרשע וימות. כל הנלקט כו'. אלמא: אע"ג דליתיה ברשותיה – מפריק, ותופס פדיונו. וכי תימא צנועין. לאו סתמא היא, אלא רשב"ג מסיים ואזיל ליה למילתיה. ערב. בגט "פשוט". צידן. ב"מי שאחזו קורדייקוס". וראיה. בפרק שני דסנהדרין. המתלקט. שעתידין ללקוט. רבי דוסא. לענין לקט קמיירי, דקיימא לן: שני שבולין – לקט, שלש – אינו לקט, ואין כל העניים בקיאין בהלכה, לפיכך צריך בעל הבית להפקיר. דאית ליה לר' יהודה ברירה. דקאמר: כל שילקוט. וכי לקיט אמרינן הוברר שזה הפקר, ואע"פ שאין בעל הבית יודע בשחרית, דשמא לא ילקטו יותר על דינם. הלוקח

תוספות

חייב אתה ליתן לו כו'. משמע ד"חייב אתה ליתן לו". לא הוי גמר דין, עד שיאמר "לא תן לו". והא דאמר בפרק קמא דסנהדרין (ד' ו: ושם ד"ה נגמר): נגמר הדין אי אתה רשאי לבצוע, ומפרש היכי דמי גמר דין – "פלוני אתה זכאי", "פלוני אתה חייב". *אע"ג דלא הוי גמר דין ממש, כיון שקרוב הדין לגמור – אסור להטעות את הזכאי. [ועי' תוס' ב"מ יז. ד"ה חייב].

כרם רבעי כו'. ק"ק, דלא נקט ערלה תחלה.

חרסית. פירש הקונטרס: כתותי רעפים. וקשה: דבפרק "כסוי הדם" (חולין דף פח. ושם ד"ה חרסית) חשיב חרסית ולבינה כתושה.

מה חרסית דלית ביה הנאה. תימה לר"י: דבסוף "כסוי הדם" (שם:) אומר דאין מכסים אלא בדבר שזורעים בו ומצמיח, ומשמע התם דמכסין בחרסית! ותירץ ר"ת: דחרסית זורעים בו ומצמיח, אבל אין מוציאה *כדי נפילה, לכך קרי דלית ביה הנאה. ואפילו מוציאה יותר מכדי נפילה, הואיל ופירותיה מועטים – חשיב לית בה הנאה.

והצנועין מניחין את המעות כו'. אי שביעית נוהג בכרם רבעי, כדמשמע [דאמילתיה] דת"ק [קאי], צריך לומר דצנועין אשאר שני שבוע קיימי. דאי אשביעית, כיון שהיו זוכים מן ההפקר – לא היו יכולים לחלל.

כל הנלקט מזה יהא מחולל. תימה: מתי היו אומרים? דלמה שמלקטים אחר אמירה – לא היה מועיל. ואם כן, וכי בכל שעה היו אומרים כן בלי הפסק? וכ"ת שבכל ערב היו אומרים כן, כמו גבי עניים בסמוך – מ"מ לא היתה תקנה למה שאכלו קודם אמירה! ואור"י: ד"כל הנלקט" – לאו דוקא ממש אחר לקיטה, אלא מניח מעות בעוד שלא נלקט, ואומר: כרם רבעי זה לכשיהיה נלקט יהיה מחולל אחר הלקיטה. והא דקאמר ר' דוסא לעיתותי ערב – אפילו מן השחרית היה יכול לעשות כן כמו שפירשתי. אלא עצה טובה קמ"ל, שלא יתפקרו עניים ללקט הרבה, כיון שהפקיר. אי נמי: לעיתותי ערב דוקא, אבל שחרית – גזרינן שמא לא יפריש, דלאחר לקיטה יחול ההפקר. וא"ת: וכיון שיש חילול במחובר לקרקע, כדמשמע בסמוך, למה היו הצנועים דוחקים? למה לא היו מחללים כל הכרם בבת אחת? וי"ל: דשמא היו רוצים להוליך שאר הפירות לירושלים, לפיכך לא היו רוצים לחלל הכל בבת אחת. אי נמי: לפי שלא היה מועיל חילול למה שיגדל אחרי כן. וא"ת: כי קאמר "כל המתלקט" הא לא היה מועיל למה שגדל אחר כך! וי"ל: דמ"מ מה שהיו יכולין לתקן היו מתקנים. ועוד: דשמא היה בטל ברוב. א] ואע"ג דדבר שיש לו מתירין אפילו באלף לא בטיל – מכל מקום מדאורייתא בטיל.

אימא כל המתלקט. משמע דחל פדיון במחובר לקרקע, שהרי קודם לקיטה היה מתחלל. שהרי אחר שנלקט, שבא לרשות אחרים – אין לבעלים כח בהן לחלל. ותימה: דבתוספתא משמע דאין חילול במחובר, דתניא בסוף מעשר שני: כרם רבעי, ב"ש אומרים: אין פודין אותם ענבים אלא יין, וב"ה אומרים: ענבים ויין. והכל מודים שאין פודין במחובר לקרקע. ונראה דטעמא דילפינן קדש קדש ממעשר! ויש לומר: דהתם לא הוי טעמא אלא משום דמחובר אין דמיו ידועין, ולכך אין פודין אפילו על פי שלשה, והיינו נמי טעמא דב"ש.

כל שלקטו עניים היום יהא הפקר. תקנה עושה לעניים לפוטרם מן המעשר כשמלקטין יותר מדינם, כגון ג' שבולים, ואוכלין בלא מעשר. לפי שלקט שכחה ופאה פטורים מן המעשר, לכך אומר בעה"ב: כל שלקטו יהיה הפקר, כדי שיפטור הכל ממעשר, דהפקר פטור ממעשר. וצריך לומר דבעל הבית אין מתייאש, דאם היה מתייאש, וחשיב יאוש מדעת כמו תמרי דזיקא, וא"כ למ"ד יאוש כדי קני – תקשה ליה: מה מועיל הפקר לפוטרו מן המעשר? והלא כבר זכו בהן עניים בתורת גזל על ידי יאוש! ומיהו, זה אין להקשות: אם בעל הבית מתייאש, למה צריך להפקיר כדי לפוטרו מן המעשר, והלא יאוש חשוב הוא כהפקר לפוטרו מן המעשר, כדמוכח ב"אלו מציאות" (ב"מ ד' כא:)! ועוד: דלמה לא יועיל כל שלקטו לכ"ע? דאטו מי גרע מיאוש? דהא לא דמי יאוש דהכא דגבי גזלן, ליאוש דמציאה. דאי יאוש קני בכל ענין, אפילו אם אין הגזילה ברשות הגזלן בשעת יאוש – אם כן יאוש דהכא לא הוי אלא כלפי דידיה, והוי כמתנה בעלמא, ואין לו לפטור מן המעשר. ואפילו את"ל דלא קני אא"כ הגזילה ברשות הגזלן, אבל אם היא ברשות הרבים בשעת יאוש כל המחזיק בה זכה בה. אי נמי, למ"ד יאוש כדי לא קני כלל וכל המחזיק בה זכה בה – *מ"מ אין זה יאוש פוטר מן המעשר. דנהי דנגזל אין יכול לתבוע מן המחזיק בה אחר יאוש, כדאמרינן ב"הגוזל בתרא" (לקמן ד' קיא:) דדוקא גזל ולא נתייאשו הבעלים ובא אחר ואכלו – רצה מזה גובה רצה מזה גובה, אבל אחר יאוש – אין יכול לגבות כלום מן השני. מ"מ, כיון שכל אדם אסור להחזיק בה, מפני שהיא צריכה לגזלן ליפטר *מן הנגזל, ואם כבר זכה בה אחר – לכל הפחות חייב לשלם דמים לגזלן, כדאמר לעיל, דאפילו למ"ד יאוש לא קני חייב גנב שני לשלם קרן לגנב ראשון – לא חשיב כהפקר לפטור מן המעשר. דטעמא דהפקר פטור מן המעשר – משום דכתיב "ובא הלוי כי אין לו חלק ונחלה עמך" יצא לקט ושכחה ופאה שיש לו חלק ונחלה עמך. והכא אין לו חלק בה, שאסור לזכות בה, ואם זכה – חייב לשלם לכל הפחות דמים. והיינו טעמא דהפקר. ועוד: דבסתמא אין מתייאש אלא לגבי עניים, ואין מועיל לפטור מן המעשר עד שיהיה הפקר לעניים ולעשירים כשמיטה.

הלוקח

עין משפט נר מצוה

נח א מיי' פ"ב מהל' גניבה הל' טו:

נט ב ג מיי' פ"ט מהל' מעשר שני הל' ז:

עיין ר"מ

ס ד ה מיי' פ"ח מהל' טומאת מת הל' ט:

סא ו ז מיי' פ"ט מהל' מעשר שני הלכה ז:

מעשר שני פ"ה מ"א

יותר מכדי גי' ר"מ [בפי' הברטנורא ותוי"ט וכן בפי' הר"ש איתא כדי נפילה ופירוש של כדי נפילה פי' רש"י ב"מ קה. זרע שמפזרים במפולת יד]

רש"א

[תוספת' פאה פ"ב]

נ"ל מתניתא

[נ"ל דתניא וכ"כ תוספו' ביומא ובחולין ובעירובין]

וא"כ הוי הפקר לכל. העתק מחולפי גרסאות

שהרי מחויב לשלם לנגזל. העתק מח"ג

מסורת הש"ס

ב"מ ז. קדושין נב. [לעיל סח: לקמן ע.]

[שבת מו. וש"נ]

הר"מ מ"ז

גיטין לח. עה. כתובות עז. ב"מ לח: ב"ב קעד. סנהדרין לא: [בכורות כז.]

[עירובין לז. וש"נ]

הגהות הב"ח

(א) גמ' דלא פסקה למילתא כצ"ל:

הגהות מהר"ב רנשבורג

א] תוד"ה כל הנלקט וכו'. ואע"ג דדבר שיש לו מתירין וכו'. עי' שיטה מקובצת שמביא עוד למידי דלא ניכר לא הוי דבר שיש לו מתירין.

*הַלּוֹקֵחַ יַיִן מִבֵּין הַכּוּתִים אוֹמֵר: "שְׁנֵי לוּגִּין שֶׁאֲנִי עָתִיד לְהַפְרִישׁ הֲרֵי הֵן תְּרוּמָה, עֲשָׂרָה – מַעֲשֵׂר רִאשׁוֹן, ט' – מַעֲשֵׂר שֵׁנִי", וּמֵיחֵל וְשׁוֹתֶה מִיָּד, דִּבְרֵי ר"מ, ר' יְהוּדָה וְר' יוֹסֵי וְר"ש [א]אוֹסְרִין. אָמְרִי: סוֹף סוֹף אַמַּאי קָא אַפְכַתְּ לָהּ לְמַתְנִיתִין – מִשּׁוּם דְּקַשְׁיָא דְּר' יְהוּדָה אַדְּר' יְהוּדָה, הַשְׁתָּא נַמִי קַשְׁיָא דְּר' יוֹחָנָן אַדְּרַבִּי יוֹחָנָן; דְּאָמְרַתְּ לְר' יוֹחָנָן: לָא תֵּימָא "כָּל הַנִּלְקָט" אֶלָּא אֵימָא "כָּל הַמִּתְלַקֵּט", אַלְמָא אִית לֵיהּ בְּרֵירָה. וְהָא רַבִּי יוֹחָנָן לֵית לֵיהּ בְּרֵירָה, *דְּאָמַר רַב אַסִּי א"ר יוֹחָנָן: הָאַחִין [ב]שֶׁחָלְקוּ – לָקוֹחוֹת הֵן, וּמַחֲזִירִין זֶה לָזֶה בַּיּוֹבֵל! אֶלָּא, לְעוֹלָם "כָּל הַנִּלְקָט", וְרַבִּי יוֹחָנָן סְתָמָא אַחֲרִינָא אַשְׁכַּח, דִּתְנַן: *אֵין הַגּוֹנֵב אַחַר הַגַּנָּב מְשַׁלֵּם תַּשְׁלוּמֵי כֶפֶל; אַמַּאי? בִּשְׁלָמָא לַגַּנָּב רִאשׁוֹן לֹא מְשַׁלֵּם – °"וְגוּנַּב מִבֵּית הָאִישׁ" (שמות כב) וְלֹא מִבֵּית הַגַּנָּב, אֶלָּא לַבְּעָלִים נְשַׁלֵּם! אֶלָּא לָאו ש"מ: זֶה לְפִי שֶׁאֵינוֹ שֶׁלּוֹ, וְזֶה לְפִי שֶׁאֵינוֹ בִּרְשׁוּתוֹ. וּמַאי חָזֵית דְּאָזֵיל בָּתַר הַהִיא סְתָמָא? לִיעֲבִיד כִּי הַאי סְתָמָא דִּצְנוּעִין! מִשּׁוּם דִּמְסַיֵּיעַ לֵיהּ קְרָא: °"וְאִישׁ כִּי יַקְדִּישׁ אֶת בֵּיתוֹ קֹדֶשׁ לַה'" (ויקרא כז), *מַה בֵּיתוֹ בִּרְשׁוּתוֹ, אַף כֹּל בִּרְשׁוּתוֹ. אָמַר אַבַּיֵי: אִי לָאו דְּא"ר יוֹחָנָן: צְנוּעִין וְרַבִּי דוֹסָא אָמְרוּ דָּבָר אֶחָד, הֲוָה אָמִינָא: צְנוּעִין אִית לְהוּ דְּרַבִּי דוֹסָא, וְרַבִּי דוֹסָא לֵית לֵיהּ דִּצְנוּעִין. צְנוּעִין אִית לְהוּ דְּרַבִּי דוֹסָא; וּמָה בְּגַנָּב עֲבַדוּ רַבָּנַן תַּקַּנְתָּא, עֲנִיִּים צְרִיכָא לְמֵימַר? ר' דוֹסָא לֵית לֵיהּ דִּצְנוּעִין; עֲנִיִּים הוּא דַּעֲבַדוּ לְהוּ רַבָּנַן תַּקַּנְתָּא, אֲבָל גַּנָּב לָא עֲבַדוּ לֵיהּ רַבָּנַן תַּקַּנְתָּא. אָמַר רָבָא: אִי לָאו דְּא"ר יוֹחָנָן: צְנוּעִין וְרַבִּי דוֹסָא אָמְרוּ דָּבָר אֶחָד, הֲוָה אָמִינָא: מַאן תְּנָא צְנוּעִין? ר"מ הִיא; לָאו *אָמַר ר"מ [ג]מַעֲשֵׂר מָמוֹן גָּבוֹהַּ הוּא, וַאֲפִילּוּ הָכִי לְעִנְיַן פְּדִיָּיה אוֹקְמֵיהּ רַחֲמָנָא בִּרְשׁוּתֵיהּ, דִּכְתִיב: °"וְאִם גָּאֹל יִגְאַל אִישׁ מִמַּעַשְׂרוֹ חֲמִשִׁיתוֹ יֹסֵף עָלָיו" (ויקרא כז), קַרְיֵיהּ רַחֲמָנָא "מַעַשְׂרוֹ" וּמוֹסִיף חוֹמֶשׁ. כֶּרֶם רְבָעִי נַמִי גָּמַר "קֹדֶשׁ" "קֹדֶשׁ" מִמַּעֲשֵׂר, כְּתִיב הָכָא: °"קֹדֶשׁ הִלּוּלִים" (שם יט), וּכְתִיב גַּבֵּי מַעֲשֵׂר: °"וְכָל מַעְשַׂר הָאָרֶץ מִזֶּרַע הָאָרֶץ מִפְּרִי הָעֵץ לַה' הוּא קֹדֶשׁ" (שם כז), מַה "קֹדֶשׁ" דִּכְתִיב גַּבֵּי מַעֲשֵׂר, אע"ג דְּמָמוֹן גָּבוֹהַּ הוּא – לְעִנְיַן פְּדִיָּיה אוֹקְמֵיהּ רַחֲמָנָא בִּרְשׁוּתֵיהּ, אַף הַאי "קֹדֶשׁ" נַמִי דִּכְתִיב גַּבֵּי כֶּרֶם רְבָעִי, אע"ג דְּלָאו מָמוֹן דִּידֵיהּ הוּא – לְעִנְיַן אַחוּלֵי אוֹקְמֵיהּ רַחֲמָנָא בִּרְשׁוּתֵיהּ, דְּהָא כִּי אִיתֵיהּ בִּרְשׁוּתֵיהּ נַמִי הָא לָאו דִּידֵיהּ הוּא וְהָא מָצֵי מַחֵיל, מִשּׁוּם הָכִי מָצֵי מַחֵיל. אֲבָל גַּבֵּי לֶקֶט, כֵּיוָן דְּמָמוֹנָא דִּידֵיהּ, כִּי אִיתֵיהּ בִּרְשׁוּתֵיהּ הוּא דְּמָצֵי מַפְקַר לֵיהּ, כִּי לֵיתֵיהּ בִּרְשׁוּתֵיהּ לָא מָצֵי מַפְקַר לֵיהּ. אָמַר רָבִינָא: אִי לָאו דְּא"ר יוֹחָנָן: צְנוּעִין וְרַבִּי דוֹסָא אָמְרוּ דָּבָר אֶחָד, הֲוָה אָמִינָא: מַאן תְּנָא צְנוּעִין? רַבִּי דוֹסָא הִיא, כִּי הֵיכִי דְּלָא תִּקְשֵׁי סְתָם מִשְׁנָה לְרַבִּי יוֹחָנָן, וְרַבִּי יוֹחָנָן

כִּסְתָם

רש"י

הלוקח יין מבין הכותים. בערב שבת בין השמשות, כדתניא בתוספתא, וקדש עליו היום ואין לו מה לשתות בשבת, ואין לו פנאי להפריש. שני לוגין. ממאה. מיחל. מוליא מעשר שני לחולין על מעות שיש לו בבית. דמה שיש לו פנאי לתקן – יתקן. דהא באמירה בעלמא סגי, כדאמרי' לקמן. אוסרין. דלית להו ברירה, לומר: מן החולין הוא שותה, ותרומה ומעשר ראשון נותרין בנוד. לקוחות הן. ולא אמרינן: הוברר הדבר שזה חלק המגיע לכל אחד, וירושה לא קאמר רחמנא דתיהדר. אלא אמרינן: חלקו של זה היה ראוי לזה, והחליפו, והרי הוא כמקח, וחוזרין ומחליפין ביובל. אלא לעולם כל הנלקט. אמרו צנועין ורבי דוסא. ודקא קשיא סתם משנה דצנועין לרבי יוחנן. ר' יוחנן סתמא אחרינא אשכח. ואי קשיא: והא לא סגיא דלא מתהפכא מתני' – משום ברירה לא תיפוך, דאית ליה לרבי יהודה ברירה, וטעמא דלוקח יין קתני התם – משום שמא יבקע הנוד, ולא משום ברירה. מה ביתו ברשותו. הכי גרסינן הכא. מאן תנא צנועין רבי מאיר. דאמר בקדושין: מעשר ממון גבוה הוא, דכל היכא דאיתיה למעשר לאו דידיה הוא אלא דגבוה הוא, ולענין פדייה אוקמיה ברשותו דמחייב ליה חומשא, ואי לאו דידיה הוא – לא הוה יהיב חומש, שאין מוסיף חומש אלא בעלים, דכתיב: "ממעשרו". הכא נמי בכרם רבעי, אע"ג דלאו דידיה הוא, "קדש" "קדש" ממעשר יליף, אבל לקט והקדש בעלמא לא, אבל השתא דאמר רבי יוחנן: צנועין ורבי דוסא אמרו דבר אחד – ש"מ טעמייהו משום דלא בעי ברשותו ואפילו במילתא דעלמא, דכל כמה דלא אייאוש – יכול להפקיר ולהקדיש ולחלל.

אורכתא

תוספות

הלוקח יין מן הכותים. הכל מפורש בפרק "כל הגט" (גיטין דף כה. ושם).

אלא לעולם כל הנלקט. הקשה רבינו טוביה: תקשה דרבי יוחנן אדרבי יוחנן. דלית ליה לרבי יוחנן ברירה, והאמר רבי יוחנן הלכה כסתם משנה, וסתם מתניתין ב"הלוקח" כר"מ, דאית ליה ברירה. ואע"ג דבסתמא דצנועים לית ליה ברירה, מ"מ תקשה: מאי אולמיה דהאי סתמא מהאי סתמא? ושמא רבי יוחנן היכא שמתנה בפירוש — לא קאמר ר' יוחנן דאין ברירה. ובריש "כל הגט" (שם) דקאמר רבי יוחנן: אף אחרון אינו פוסל משום דאין ברירה — שאני התם, דכתיב "וכתב לה" דמשמע שיהיה צריך שיהיה מבורר בשעת כתיבה, כמו שמפורש בריש "כל הגט".

ה"א צנועים אית להו דר' דוסא. ולא מן הדין, דגזל ולא נתייאשו הבעלים שניהן אין יכולין להקדיש ולחלל ולהפקיר. אלא מחמת תקנה הוא דאוקמי רבנן ברשותיה לחלל ולהפקיר, שלא יכשלו עניים וגנב. ורבי דוסא לית ליה דצנועין, דבעניים עבוד רבנן תקנה, ולא בגנב. אבל השתא דקאמר ר' יוחנן צנועין ור' דוסא אמרו דבר אחד — א"כ סובר הוא דלא מחמת תקנה, אלא מן הדין. ולא בעי למימר דלענין ברירה דוקא קאמרי דבר אחד, דתרוייהו לית להו ברירה — שהרי "דבר אחד" משמע ממש דבר אחד. וקשה: דבפרק "העור והרוטב" (חולין דף קכד:) אמר רבי יוחנן: ר' ישמעאל ורבי דוסא בן הרכינס אמרו דבר אחד, דלאו ממש דבר אחד, דבמגע דוקא אמרו דבר אחד, אבל במשא פליגי. דהתם תנן: שני חלאי זיתים מטמאים במשא ולא במגע, דברי רבי ישמעאל. ובההיא דרבי דוסא תנן במסכת אהלות בפרק ג' (משנה א): כל המטמאין באהל שנחלקו והכניסן לבית, רבי דוסא בן הרכינס מטהר וחכמים מטמאין. כיצד? הנוגע בשני חלאי זיתים מן הנבילה, או נושאן כו'. משמע דר' דוסא בן הרכינס מטהר במגע ובמשא! ויש לומר: כיון דבמגע אמרו דבר אחד — אין חושש, אע"ג דלא שוו במשא. ועוד אומר ר"י: דלגמרי מצית למימר דסבר רבי דוסא כרבי ישמעאל. והא דלרבי ישמעאל מלטרפים — היינו במרודד, ור' דוסא איירי במפוזר לגמרי, דלגבי משא בעי נושא והוא דנישא, שיהא מחובר יחד, כדקאמר עולא בההיא שמעתא.

ואוקי עולא כרבי דוסא ולא כרבנן, דבלאו הכי פליגי בה תנאי דעולא, *ומה שיכול לתרץ אלידיה מתרץ. אי נמי: עולא מוקי פלוגתייהו במרודד, ואתי כרבנן, ולית ליה דאמרו דבר אחד.

קרייה רחמנא מעשרו ומוסיף חומש. תימה לר"י: דבלא חומש יכול לדקדק דאוקמיה רחמנא ברשותיה, מכיון שיכול לפדותו ואין שום אדם יכול לעכב עליו. אבל אחר — אין יכול לפדות בע"כ! וי"ל: דהא מה שהוא יכול לפדותו ולא אחר — היינו לפי שהוא בידו, אבל כשהוא ביד אחרים, כמו כרם רבעי דלעיל — אז לא יוכל לפדותו. אבל השתא, דאשכחן שיהיה חשוב כ"כ שלו שמוסיף חומש, ואחר אפילו כשפודה מדעתו אין מוסיף חומש — ש"מ דלגמרי אוקמיה רחמנא ברשותיה, ואפילו הוא ברשות אחרים.

קדש קדש יליף ממעשר. תימה: דל"ל למידרש בפרק "כילד מברכין" (ברכות ד' לה. ושם ד"ה אחליה) מדכתיב "קדש הלולים", אחליה והדר אכליה. פירוש: כרם רבעי טעון חילול? תיפוק ליה מ"קדש" "קדש" דמעשר! וי"ל: דאי לאו דאשכחן ביה פדיון הוה ילפינן "קדש" "קדש" משביעית, שאין לו פדיון כלל. ואין להקשות כלל: למה לי "קדש", תיפוק ליה מ"הלולים" — דגזירה שוה ד"קדש" אצטריך למימר דיש לו חומש, כדאמר בפ' ב' דקדושין (ד' נד: ושם ד"ה גמר). ורבינו חיים תירץ: דאי לאו "הלולים", מגזירה שוה לא הוה ידעינן שצריך חילול (א) *בשביעית, שאין מעשר שני נוהג בשביעית. והביא ראיה מירושלמי דמעשר שני פ"ה, דקאמר: מה דאת אמרת אין מעשר שני נוהג בשביעית, דכוותיה אין נטע רבעי בשביעית וכו'. ודייק התם שגם שלישית וששית שאין בהם מעשר שני לא יהיה בהן נטע רבעי. אמר רבי יוסי: שלישית וששית יש בהם מעשרות, ושביעית אין בה מעשר כל עיקר. אבל לקט דממון דידיה הוא. לא הוה צריך למימר אלא דגבי לקט ליכא קרא, אלא לרווחא דמילתיה נקטיה, דאפי' איכא קרא — לא דמי אהדדי.

כבסתם

עין משפט נר מצוה

סב א מיי' פ"ז מהל' מעשר הל' א סמג עשין קלה:

סג ב מיי' פי"א מהל' שמיטה ויובל הל' כ:

סד ג מיי' פ"ג מהל' מעשר שני הל' יז סמג לאוין רסד:

הגהות הב"ח

(א) תוד"ה קדש וכו' שצריך חילול בשלישית שאין מעשר שני נוהג בשלישית והביא ראיה:

ועולא ס"ל כר"א והא דמקשי התם על עולא ולא משני דס"ל כר' דוסא לז"א ומה שיכול לתרץ כו'. העתק מחילופי גרסאות

מסורת הש"ס

דמאי פ"ז מ"ד סוכה [...] יומא כה: עירובין [...] מעילה כב. חולין [...] [גיטין כה. כח. תו[...] דדמאי פ"ח]

ביצה לז: בכורות נב: [גיטין כה. מח.]

לעיל סב:

[לעיל סח: ע"ש ב"מ ו. [...] סג. חולין קלט. תמורה [...] כט: ערכין כח.]

קידושין כד. [...]

[...] בכל כתוס' ברכות [...] שני' בשלישית [...] וציין [...]

כסתם יחידאה לא אמר. *אמרי נהרדעי: לא כתבינן אורכתא אמטלטלי. אמר רב אשי לאמימר: מאי טעמא? אמר ליה: משום דרבי יוחנן, *דא"ר יוחנן: גזל ולא נתייאשו הבעלים — שניהם אינן יכולין להקדיש, זה לפי שאינו שלו, וזה לפי שאינו ברשותו. איכא דאמרי, אמרי נהרדעי: [א] לא כתבינן אורכתא אמטלטלי דכפריה. טעמא דכפריה, דמיחזי כשיקרא, אבל לא כפריה — כתבינן. ואמרי נהרדעי: [ב] אורכתא דלא כתיב ביה "זיל דון וזכי ואפיק לנפשך" — לית ביה מששא. מ"ט? [ג] משום דא"ל האיך: "לאו בעל דברים דידי את". אמר אביי: [ד] ואי כתיב ביה למחצה לשליש ולרביע — מיגו דמשתעי דינא אפלגא, משתעי דינא אכולה. אמר אמימר: אי תפס לא מפקינן מיניה. רב אשי אמר: [ה] כיון דכתביה ליה: "כל דמתעני מן דינא קבילית עלי" — שליח שויה. ואיכא דאמר: שותפא שויה. למאי נפקא מינה? למיתפס פלגא. (א) [ו] ◉ והלכתא: שליח שויה.§

מתני' [ז] גנב ע"פ שנים, וטבח ומכר על פיהם או על פי שנים אחרים — משלם תשלומי ארבעה וחמשה. [ח] גנב ומכר בשבת, גנב ומכר לע"ז, [ט] גנב וטבח ביום הכפורים, [י] גנב משל אביו וטבח ומכר ואח"כ מת אביו, [כ] גנב וטבח ואחר כך הקדיש — משלם תשלומי ארבעה וחמשה. [ל] גנב וטבח לרפואה או לכלבים, [מ] השוחט ונמצאת טריפה, [נ] השוחט חולין בעזרה — משלם תשלומי ארבעה וחמשה; רבי שמעון פוטר בשני אלו.§ **גמ'** לימא, מתניתין דלא כרבי עקיבא, דאי ר' עקיבא, האמר: "דבר" — ולא חצי דבר! דתניא, *אמר רבי יוסי: כשהלך אבא חלפתא אצל ר' יוחנן בן נורי ללמוד תורה, ואמרי לה: רבי יוחנן בן נורי אצל אבא חלפתא

חלפתא

רש"י

אורכתא. הרשאה. **משום דר' יוחנן.** דהואיל ואינו ברשות הבעלים אינו יכול להקנותו לשליח, הלכך אם אחד — יכול לחזור ולתבוע מיד הנאמן. **דכפריה.** אם תבעיה מפקיד לנאמן בבית דין וכפר בו. **דמיחזי.** דחתמינן אשיקרא, דיהיב ליה לשליח מידי דלית ליה גבי האיך. **דאמר ליה האיך.** נאמן לשליח: לאו בעל דברים דידי את. **ואי כתב בה למחצה ולשליש.** דון וזכי לנפשך, והמותר שלי. **מיגו דמשתעי.** נאמן דינא בהדי שליח אפלגא על כרחיה, דלא מצי למימר ליה "לאו בעל דברים דידי את" — משתעי אכולה. **ואי תפס.** שליח משל נאמן. **לא מפקינן מיניה.** אף על גב דלא כתיב ביה "אפיק לנפשך". ל"א: ואי תפס שליח ממון שהוציא ועיכבו לעצמו — לא מפקינן מיניה. כך מצאתי כתוב בתשובות הגאונים, וזה עיקר. **רב אשי** פליג עליה דאמימר. **כיון דכתיב** קבילית עלאי. אלמא שליח שוייה, הלכך אי תפיס — מפקינן מיניה. וללישנא קמא נמי, אי תפס משל נאמן — מפקינן מיניה, דהא שליח בעלמא הוא, והוי כתופס לבעל חוב. **למיתפס פלגא.** ממון שהביא, אם רוצה לעכב חציו. ה"ג: והלכתא שליח שוייה ולא שקיל מידי. **מתני'** **על פי שנים.** כלומר, שנים מעידין אותו שגנב. **גנב ומכר בשבת.** אבל טבח — קם ליה בדרבה מיניה. **וטבח ביום הכפורים.** דאין זדונו אלא כרת. **וטבח ומכר ואחר כך מת אביו.** אבל מת אביו ואח"כ טבח ומכר — תנא בסיפא דפטור, שהרי ירש את אביו ושלו הוא טובח ומוכר. **בשני אלו.** בטריפה ובחולין בעזרה. דקא סבר רבי שמעון: שחיטה שאינה ראויה לא שמה שחיטה. אבל לרפואה ולכלבים — שחיטה ראויה היא, דאי בעי מצי אכיל מיניה. **גמ'** **דבר ולא חצי דבר.** "על פי שנים עדים יקום דבר", והני עדי טביחה דקתני במתני' "או על פי שנים עדים אחרים" — חצי דבר קמסהדי, דאי לאו עדי גניבה איכא למימר דידיה קא טבח.

חלפתא

תוספות

כסתם יחידאה לא אמר. תימה: דבכמה מקומות משמע דאמר אפילו כסתם יחידאה. דבסוף "המוציא" (שבת דף פא:) פריך: והאמר רבי יוחנן הלכה כסתם משנה, ותנן: נזיר חופף ומפספס אבל לא סורק, ואע"ג דבפ' "ג' מינים" (נזיר ד' מב. ושם) מוקמינן ליה כר"ש. ובפרק "החולץ" (יבמות דף מב:) גבי "אחת בתולות", דפריך נמי: והאמר ר' יוחנן הלכה כסתם משנה, אע"ג דאתי כרבי מאיר. וכן בכמה מקומות! וי"ל דה"פ: ה"א מאן תנא לנוטעים ר' דוסא כי היכי דלא תקשה סתם משנה לרבי יוחנן. כלומר, דלא תקשה: מאי אולמיה האי סתמא מהאי סתמא. דכיון דאיכא למימר דיחידאה היא — לא חשיבא כי ההיא סתם משנה דאתי כרבים. וא"ת: והא האי סתמא נמי ד"אין הגונב אחר הגנב" יחידאה היא, דהיינו רבי יהודה בר פלוגתיה דרבי דוסא, דאמר: "כל שילקטו" דוקא ולא "כל מה שלקטו"! ויש לומר: דדלמא רבי יהודה "כל שלקטו" נמי שרי, ולא נקט "כל שילקטו" אלא לרבותא, דאע"ג דלא שרי אלא על ידי ברירה. ועי"ל דה"ק: ה"א דכסתמא יחידאה לא אמר, כי היכי דלא תקשה ליה סתם משנה אבל השתא שהוצרכו לעשות תירוץ אחר — לא נאמר יותר, אלא אפי' (ב) משנה יחידאה נמי אמר. **לא** כתבינן אורכתא אמטלטלי. דוקא אמטלטלין דגזליה, אבל אמטלטלין דפקדון — כתבינן, דהא תלי טעמא בהקדש, ויש כח לאדם להקדיש פקדון שיש לו ביד חבירו, כדמוכח ב"המוכר את הספינה" (ב"ב דף פח.) גבי ההוא גברא דאייתי קרי לפומבדיתא, אתו כ"ע שקלי חדא חדא, אמר: "הרי הן מוקדשין לשמים", ומשמע התם דאי לא קילו דמייהו הוו קדשי. ועוד, דלעיל אמר: אין הגונב אחר הגנב משלם כפל משום דאין בעלים יכולין להקדיש. וגונב מבית הנפקד משלם כפל לבעלים, כדתניא בהמפקיד (ב"מ דף לג:). ועיקר קרא בגונב מבית שומר כתיב. **אמטלטלין** דכפריה. כתב ר"ח דהאידנא נהגו לכתוב אורכתא אפילו אמטלטלי דכפריה, וטעמא לא ידענא. ור"ת מפרש דטעמא דהלכתא כלישנא בתרא, דסוגיא דגמרא כוותיה. דבשבועות (דף לג: ושם*) דייק: טעמא ד"משביע (ג) עליכם דאיש פלוני כהן הוא", הא "מנה לפלוני ביד פלוני" — חייבין. והא קתני סיפא: עד שישמעו מפי התובע! אמר שמואל: בבא בהרשאה. והא אמרי נהרדעי: לא כתבינן אורכתא אמטלטלי! הני מילי (ד) דכפריה, אבל לא כפריה כתבינן. וכן בפרק "יש בכור" (בכורות דף מט.). וכיון דהלכתא כלישנא בתרא, אם כן אפילו כפריה — כתבינן, דהא לישנא בתרא מפרש טעמא דלא כתבינן אמטלטלין דכפריה משום דמיחזי כשיקרא, ולמיחזא כשיקרא לא חיישינן, כדמסיק ב"הכותב" (כתובות דף פה.) ובפרק "כל הגט" (גיטין דף כו:) דליתא לדרב פפי דאמר: האי אשרתא דדייני דמיכתבא מקמי דלסהדו סהדי אחתימות ידייהו פסולה משום דמיחזי כשיקרא. וא"ת: כיון דלא חיישינן למיחזי כשיקרא, אם כן בשבועות (דף לג:) ובבכורות (דף מט.) כי פריך מנהרדעי דאמרי לא כתבינן — הוה ליה למימר דליתא! וי"ל: דאורחא דגמרא למיפרך ממילתא אע"ג דליתא, דבפרק ב' דכתובות (ד' כא:) נמי פריך מדרב פפי אמילתיה דרב הונא וחוזר בה מחמת זה ומגיה דברים, אע"ג דאמר ב"הכותב" (כתובות ד' פה.) דליתיה. ומיהו, לפי המפרש התם דהא דקאמר "ליתא" לא קאי ארב פפי, אלא כלומר: ליתא לקושיא, דאין קושיא, דבקיום שטרות דוקא חיישינן למיחזי כשיקרא דבית דין, אבל בשאר מילי לא מדרב נחמן — אין זה ראיה משום דפריך מדרב פפי. וא"ת: וללישנא קמא דנהרדעי, מאי הוה משני אמתניתין דשבועות ודבכורות? ומיהו אמתניתין דשבועות מצי לאוקמי *בקרקעות, וכמ"ד נשבעין, אבל בההיא דבכורות דאיירי בפדיון בכור — ליכא לאוקמי כמ"ד פודין בקרקעות, דהא קתני בההיא משנה דאין פודין! ויש לומר: דאיכא לאוקמינה שהאחד חייב לחבירו ושואל, מדרבי נתן. אי נמי, שנתן לו במעמד שלשתן. ומיהו בההיא דבכורות צריך לדקדק אם יכול ליתן במעמד שלשתן, כיון דהוא עצמו לא היה יכול להוציא מידו. כמו שבכתובה אין יכולה ליתן במעמד שלשתן כיון דלא ניתנה לגבות מחיים, כמו שמפורש ב"החובל" (לקמן ד' פט.). ואין לתמוה על מה שאנו נוהגין לכתוב הרשאה אפי' במלוה אע"פ שאין אדם יכול להקנות הלואתו לחבירו, כדמוכח ב"מי שמת" (ב"ב ד' קמח.) שדוחק למצוא ד"הלואתו לפלוני" איתא בבריא, ולא מצי לאשכוחי אלא הואיל ויורש יורשה, אי נמי במעמד שלשתן, משמע דבשום ענין לא מצי מקני ליה. דכיון דקי"ל כ"איכא דאמרי", ולהך לישנא אמטלטלין דגזילה נמי כתבינן אורכתא אע"פ שאין יכול להקנותו כמו שאין יכול להקדיש, דקיימא לן כרבי יוחנן דגזל ולא נתייאשו הבעלים שניהם אין יכולין להקדיש, כדמשמע בפ"ק דב"מ (ד' ז. ע"ש) דפריך מיניה לרב, ומשמע נמי התם דסבר סתמא דגמרא דאם המטלטלין לא היה נגזל יכול להקדיש. ה"ה הלואה, אע"פ שאין יכול להקנותה — כתבינן הרשאה. וטעמא, דלהאי לישנא מסקינן דשליח שויה, ועשו תקנה לענין שליחות כאילו היה קונה קנין גמור. ויש סמך למנהג ב"הגוזל *(בתרא)" (לקמן ד' קד:) דרב פפא הוה מסיק זוזי בי חוזאי, אקנינהו לרב שמואל בר יהודה אגב אסיפא דביתיה, כי אתא נפק לאפיה עד תווך, ו"מסיק" משמע לשון הלואה. ויש לדחוק ד"מסיק" — בעיסקא מיירי, שלא ניתן להוצאה. ועוד דב"הזהב" (ב"מ ד' מו.) וב"המוכר את הספינה" (ב"ב ד' עז:) ל"ג ו"מסיק", אלא: "הוה ליה זוזי בי חוזאי" בכל הספרים. ואין לדקדק מההיא דבכורות (ד' מט.) גבי פדיון הבן שיכול להרשות אע"פ שניתן לכהן ע"מ להוציא דלא מסקי אדעתייהו שימות תוך שלשים — אלמא יכול להרשות במלוה. דהתם ע"כ לאו ע"מ להוציא נתנו לו, דקיימא לן כשמואל דאמר התם בסמוך להאי שמעתא (שם) דפודה בנו בתוך שלשים ◉ ונתאכלו המעות דאין בנו פדוי.

מסורת הש"ס

שבועות לג: בכורות מט.

קדושין נב. ב"מ ז. לעיל סח: סט.

ב"ב נו: [תוספתא דב"ב פ"ב]

[ד"ה היכא]

עיין רש"א

נ"ל קמא

עין משפט נר מצוה

סה א מיי' פ"ג מהל' שלוחין הל' ו ועיין בהשגות ובמ"מ סמג עשין פב טוח"מ וש"ע סי' קכג סעיף א [רב אלפס כאן ובפ' הגוזל עלים דף מ:]

סו ב ג מיי' שם הל' א סמג שם טוש"ע ח"מ סי' קכב סעיף ד:

סז ד מיי' שם הל' ב טוש"ע שם סעיף ה:

סח ה מיי' שם הלכה א טוש"ע שם סעיף ו:

סט ו מיי' שם טוש"ע שם בהג"ה:

ע ז מיי' פ"א מהלכות גניבה הלכה ו ופ"ג הל' ז טוח"מ סי' שנ:

עא ח מיי' שם פ"ג הל' ה טוח"מ שם:

עב ט מיי' שם הל' ב טור ח"מ שם:

עג י כ מיי' שם פ"ב הל' ו טוח"מ שם:

עד ל נ מיי' שם הל' ט טוח"מ שם:

הגהות הב"ח

(א) גמ' למיתפס פלגא (והלכתא שליח שויה). תא"מ ונ"ב עיין באשר"י כתב דלא גרסי' ליה: (ב) תום' ד"ה כסתם וכו' כסתם משנה דיחידאה: (ג) ד"ה אמטלטלין וכו' טעמא דמשביע אני עליכם: (ד) בא"ד ה"מ היכא דכפריה אבל:

גליון הש"ס

גמ' והלכתא שליח שויה. עיין ב"ב דף קכז ע"א תוס' ד"ה מדלרש: **תום'** ד"ה אמטלטלין וכו' בסה"ד ונתאכלו המעות דאין בנו פדוי. ועיין ב"ב דף קכז ע"א תוספות ד"ה מדלרש:

חֲלַפְתָּא, אָמַר לוֹ: הֲרֵי שֶׁאֲכָלָהּ שָׁנָה רִאשׁוֹנָה בִּפְנֵי שְׁנַיִם, שְׁנִיָּה בִּפְנֵי שְׁנַיִם, שְׁלִישִׁית בִּפְנֵי שְׁנַיִם, מַהוּ? אָמַר לוֹ: הֲרֵי זוֹ חֲזָקָה; אָמַר לוֹ: אַף אֲנִי אוֹמֵר כֵּן, אֶלָּא שֶׁרַבִּי עֲקִיבָא חוֹלֵק בַּדָּבָר, שֶׁהָיָה *רַבִּי עֲקִיבָא אוֹמֵר: °"דָּבָר" – וְלֹא חֲצִי דָּבָר! אָמַר אַבַּיֵי: אֲפִילּוּ תֵּימָא רַבִּי עֲקִיבָא, מִי לָא מוֹדֶה רַבִּי עֲקִיבָא בִּשְׁנַיִם אוֹמְרִים קִידֵּשׁ וּשְׁנַיִם אוֹמְרִים בָּעַל, דְּאע"ג דְּעֵדֵי בִיאָה צְרִיכִי לְעֵדֵי קִדּוּשִׁין, כֵּיוָן דְּעֵדֵי קִדּוּשִׁין לָא צְרִיכִי לְעֵדֵי בִיאָה – "דָּבָר" קָרֵינָא בֵּיהּ? ה"נ, אע"ג דְּעֵדֵי טְבִיחָה צְרִיכִי לְעֵדֵי גְנֵיבָה, כֵּיוָן דְּעֵדֵי גְנֵיבָה לָא צְרִיכִי לְעֵדֵי טְבִיחָה – "דָּבָר" קָרֵינָא בֵּיהּ. וְרַבָּנַן, הַאי "דָּבָר" וְלֹא חֲצִי דָּבָר, לְמַעוּטֵי מַאי? *אלְמַעוּטֵי: *אֶחָד אוֹמֵר אֶחָד בִּגְבָּהּ, וְאֶחָד אוֹמֵר אֶחָד בִּכְרֵיסָהּ. הַאי חֲצִי דָבָר וַחֲצִי עֵדוּת הוּא! באֶלָּא לְמַעוּטֵי שְׁנַיִם אוֹמְרִים אֶחָד בִּגְבָּהּ וּשְׁנַיִם אוֹמְרִים אֶחָד בִּכְרֵיסָהּ; הָנֵי אָמְרִי קְטַנָּה הִיא, וְהָנֵי אָמְרִי קְטַנָּה הִיא.§ "גָּנַב וּמָכַר בְּשַׁבָּת [וכו']"§ וְהָתַנְיָא: פָּטוּר! אָמַר רָמִי בַּר חָמָא: כִּי תַּנְיָא הַהִיא דְּפָטוּר – גבְּאוֹמֵר לוֹ "עֲקוֹץ (לְךָ) תְּאֵנָה מִתְּאֵינָתִי וְתִיקְנֵי לִי גְּנֵיבוּתִיךְ". אָמְרִי: וְכֵיוָן דְּכִי תָּבַע לֵיהּ קַמָּן בְּדִינָא, לָא אָמְרִינַן לֵיהּ "זִיל שַׁלֵּים", דְּמִחַיֵּיב בְּנַפְשׁוֹ הוּא, הָא מְכִירָה נַמִי לָאו מְכִירָה הִיא! אֶלָּא אָמַר רַב פַּפָּא: דבְּאוֹמֵר לוֹ "זְרוֹק גְּנֵיבוּתִיךְ לַחֲצֵרִי וְתִיקְנֵי לִי גְּנֵיבוּתִיךְ". כְּמַאן? כְּר"ע דְּאָמַר: *קְלוּטָה כְּמִי שֶׁהוּנְחָה דָּמְיָא. דְּאִי כְּרַבָּנַן, כֵּיוָן דְּמָטְיָא לַחֲצַר בֵּיתוֹ קָנֵה, לְעִנְיַן שַׁבָּת לָא מִחַיַּיב עַד דְּמָטְיָא לְאַרְעָא! הבְּאוֹמֵר "לָא תִּיקְנֵי לִי גְּנֵיבוּתִיךְ עַד שֶׁתָּנוּחַ". רָבָא אָמַר: לְעוֹלָם כְּרָמִי בַּר חָמָא; *ואֶתְנָן אָסְרָה תּוֹרָה וַאֲפִילּוּ בָּא עַל אִמּוֹ, וְאִי תָּבְעָה לֵיהּ קַמָּן בְּדִינָא, מִי אָמְרִינַן לֵיהּ "קוּם הַב לָהּ אֶתְנָן"? אֶלָּא אע"ג דְּכִי קָא תָּבְעָה לֵיהּ בְּדִינָא, לָא אָמְרִינַן לֵיהּ "זִיל הַב לָהּ", כֵּיוָן דְּכִי יָהֵיב לָהּ הָוֵי אֶתְנָן. הָכָא נַמִי, אע"ג דִּלְעִנְיַן תַּשְׁלוּמִין אִי תָּבַע בְּדִינָא קַמָּן, לָא אָמְרִינַן לֵיהּ "זִיל שַׁלֵּים", אֲפִילּוּ

חֲלַפְתָּא. שֵׁם אָבִיו שֶׁל רַבִּי יוֹסֵי. בִּשְׁנַיִם אוֹמְרִים קִידֵּשׁ. פְּלוֹנִי אֶת הָאִשָּׁה בְּנִיסָן. וּשְׁנַיִם אוֹמְרִים בָּעַל. אִישׁ אַחֵר בְּאִיָּיר. דְּאע"ג דְּעֵדֵי בִיאָה. הַבָּאִים לַהֲמִית צְרִיכִין לְעֵדוּת קִדּוּשִׁין, דְּאִי לָא קִידְּשָׁהּ אִיכָּא לְמֵימַר פְּנוּיָה הִיא. כֵּיוָן דְּעֵדֵי קִדּוּשִׁין לֹא צְרִיכִין לְעֵדֵי בִיאָה. דִּבְלָאו נִינְהוּ שָׁווּ לָהּ קַמָּאֵי אֵשֶׁת אִישׁ לֵיאָסֵר עַל כָּל הָעוֹלָם. דָּבָר הוּא. אַף עֵדוּת שֶׁל בִּיאָה קַיָּים, וְנֶהֱרֶגֶת. הָכָא נַמִי כו'. עֵדֵי גְנֵיבָה חַיְּיבוּ לֵיהּ כְּפֵילָא בְּלָאו עֵדֵי טְבִיחָה. אֲבָל הָנֵי דְּעֵדוּת חֲזָקָה – שְׁלָשְׁתָּן הַכִּיתּוֹת צְרִיכוֹת זוֹ לָזוֹ. לְמַעוּטֵי אֶחָד אוֹמֵר אַחַת בִּגְבָּהּ וכו'. וְקָאָתוּ לְשַׁוְּיָהּ גְּדוֹלָה לְעִנְיַן עוֹנָשִׁין, אוֹ לְעִנְיַן שֶׁיְּהוּ קִידּוּשֶׁיהָ קִדּוּשִׁין. בִּגְבָּהּ. שֵׂעָר רָאִיתִי בְּקִשְׁרֵי אֶצְבְּעוֹתֶיהָ. חֲצִי דָּבָר. שֵׂעָר אֶחָד. וַחֲצִי עֵדוּת. עַד אֶחָד יֵשׁ לַשֵּׂעָר, וּפְשִׁיטָא דְּלָאו עֵדוּת הִיא. אַכַּתִּי קְטַנָּה הִיא כו'. הִלְכָּךְ לָא מִצְטָרְפִין. אֲבָל לְגַבֵּי חֲזָקָה – כּוּלָּן מְעִידִין שֶׁהָיָה מוּחְזָק בָּהּ. עֲקוֹץ תְּאֵנָה. "לְקוֹט תְּאֵנִים מִתְּאֵינָתִי בִּדְמֵי הַגְּנֵיבָה בְּשַׁבָּת". וְכֵן עָשָׂה וְנִתְחַיֵּיב מִיתָה. וְהָא אִי תָּבַע לֵיהּ. בַּעַל הַתְּאֵינָה לַלּוֹקֵט. בְּדִינָא. לוֹמַר: הַחֲזֵר לִי תְּאֵנִים שֶׁלִּקַּטְתָּ, אוֹ תֵּן לִי מַה שֶּׁמָּכַרְתָּ לִי בִּדְמֵיהֶן. לָא אָמְרִינַן. לַגַּנָּב: זִיל שַׁלֵּים, אִשְׁתַּכַּח דְּלָאו מְכִירָה הוּא (*וְאַמַּאי מְשַׁלֵּם ד' וה'?). זְרוֹק גְּנֵיבָה לַחֲצֵרִי. בְּשַׁבָּת, וַאֲנִי אֶתֵּן לְךָ מָעוֹת. וְכֵן עָשָׂה – קְנָאָהּ לוֹקֵחַ, וְזֶה נִתְחַיֵּיב מִיתָה. כְּרַבִּי עֲקִיבָא דְּאָמַר. בְּ"הַזּוֹרֵק" (שבת דף צז.). קְלוּטָה כְּמִי שֶׁהוּנְחָה. הַזּוֹרֵק מֵרְשׁוּת לִרְשׁוּת, כֵּיוָן שֶׁקְּלָטָהּ הָאֲוִיר – נִתְחַיֵּיב מִשּׁוּם שַׁבָּת. נִמְצָא חִיּוּב שַׁבָּת וְחִיּוּב מְכִירָה בָּאִין כְּאֶחָד, שֶׁאֲוִיר חָצֵר קָנָה לַלּוֹקֵחַ. דְּכֵיוָן דְּסוֹפוֹ לָנוּחַ – כְּמוּנָּח דָּמֵי. אָסְרָה תּוֹרָה. לְהָבִיא לְבֵית הַמִּקְדָּשׁ לְכָל נֶדֶר. וַאֲפִילּוּ בָּא עַל אִמּוֹ. וְנָתַן לָהּ טָלֶה בְּאֶתְנַנָּהּ – אָסוּר. וְאַף עַל גַּב דְּאִי לָא הֲוָה יָהֵיב לָהּ נִיהֲלָהּ *וְהוֹאִיל תָּבְעָה לֵיהּ בְּדִינָא – לָא אָמְרִינַן לֵיהּ: קַיֵּים לָהּ תְּנָאָהּ, דְּהָא מִתְחַיֵּיב בְּנַפְשֵׁיהּ הוּא. אֲפִילּוּ

דאף על גב דעדי ביאה צריכין לעדי קדושין. פירוש: כל זמן שלא הוחזקה באשת איש.

למעוטי שנים אומרים אחד בגבה כו'. ולא דמי לשנה ראשונה בפני שנים כו', דהתם ראו כל מה שהיו יכולין לראות באותה שנה. ורב אלפס פירש: משום דהתם מהני סהדותייהו לענין פירות שאכל בשנה ראשונה, שחייב לשלם אם לא ימצא יותר עדים. וטעם ראשון נראה לר"י עיקר. דתנן בפרק "התקבל" (גיטין דף סג:): האשה שאמרה "התקבל לי גיטי" צריכה שתי כיתי עדים, שנים שיאמרו "בפנינו אמרה", ושנים שיאמרו "בפנינו קבל וקרע". אלמא לא חשיב כי האי גוונא חצי דבר אע"ג דצריכי אלו לאלו. דאפי' למאן דאמר שליח נאמן כשגט בידו ולא צריכי עדי אמירה לעדי קבלה, מ"מ כיון שצריך שנראה הגט בידו — חצי דבר הוא. אלא ע"כ משום שכל כת רואה כל מה שיכולה [לראות] באותה שעה, ואתיא מתניתין [דגיטין] כרבנן.

באומר לו עקוץ תאינה מתאינתי כו'. וא"ת: והיכי דמי? אי דקיימא גניבה בחצירו של לוקח בשעת עקירה, מאי פריך עלה: וכיון דאי קתבע ליה כו' מכירה נמי לא הוי מכירה? נהי דמחייב בנפשו, מכל מקום קנייה ליה חצירו ללוקח! ואלא דליתא בחצירו של לוקח, דל חיוב שבת מהכא — לאו מכירה היא, דהא קי"ל כרב נחמן דאמר *פירות לא עבדי חליפין! ומיהו לפר"ת ניחא, דמפרש דהא דפירי לא עבדי חליפין היינו בתורת קנין סודר, שמחזיר לו הסודר ולא יהיב לו אלא לקנין בעלמא, אבל במכוין להקנות זה תחת זה שוה בשוה בתורת דמים — קני. ואומר ר"י: דהכא לא דייק אלא אלשון מכר, דאפי' קאי בחצר הלוקח, כיון דלא אמר "זיל שלים" — אין זו מכירה אלא מתנה. ואף על גב דבתשלומי ארבעה וחמשה מתחייב על המתנה כמו על המכר כדאמרינן לקמן, מ"מ "גנב ומכר בשבת" קתני, ואין זו מכירה, וכך לן "עקוץ תאינה מתאינתי" כמו "עקוץ תאינה מתאינתיך".

כמאן כרבי עקיבא דאמר קלוטה כמי שהונחה דמיא. ואם תאמר לרבי עקיבא נמי, כיון דמטא לאויר חצירו — חייב לענין שבת, דרשות היחיד עולה עד לרקיע, ולענין קנין לא קני באויר עד דמטי לתוך המחילות. כדמוכח בגיטין ב"הזורק" (דף עט. ושם) גבי הוא מלמעלה והיא מלמטה כיון שיצא מרשות הגג מגורשת, ומוקי לה כגון שמחילות התחתונות עודפות על העליונות! וי"ל: דהכא איירי שזרק לחצר דרך פתח או דרך חלון, ולא מעל מחילת החצר. וא"ת: ומ"ש דבגיטין נקט רבי והכא נקט רבי עקיבא? וי"ל: דהכא נקט רבי עקיבא משום דאיירי בסתם חצר שאין מקורה. דרבי לא אמר קלוטה כמי שהונחה דמיא אלא ברה"י מקורה, כדאמרינן בריש שבת (דף ה. ושם*) דאמר: ביתא כמאן דמליא דמיא. אבל רבי עקיבא אית ליה אפילו ברשות הרבים שאין מקורה. ובגיטין נקט רבי משום דאוקמא כשמחילות התחתונות עודפות. דלרבי עקיבא לא מצי למינקט, דלדידיה אפי' בלא מחילות כלל כמו ברה"ר אית ליה כמי שהונחה דמיא, בריש שבת. וס"ד דלרבי אפילו במחילות בלא קרוי אמרינן כמאן דמליא דמיא. אי נמי, למאי דבעי לאוקמי כרבי איירי בחצר מקורה. לענין שבת לא מחייב עד דניחה בחצר. וא"ת: וכיון שהקנין בא בין עקירה להנחה — אית לן למימר: קם ליה בדרבה מיניה, כדאמרינן בריש "אלו נערות" (כתובות דף לא. ושם*) דאמר רבי אבין: זרק חץ מתחילת ד' לסוף ד' וקרע שיראין בהליכתו — פטור, עקירה לורך הנחה הוא! ולפי מה שמפרש רבינו תם דאי אפשר לניסוך בלא הגבהה, ורבי ירמיה דאמר ב"הניזקין" (גיטין דף נב: ושם*) גבי מנסך: משעת הגבהה קני, מתחייב בנפשו לא הוי עד שעת ניסוך — לית ליה הגבהה לורך ניסוך, הוא הדין דלית ליה עקירה לורך הנחה — אתי שפיר, דפריך הכא אליבא דרבי ירמיה. ונראה לר"י: דהוי מצי לשנויי דעקירה לורך הנחה הוא, אלא לדברי המקשן שלא היה סובר טעם זה משיב ליה דמשכחת ליה שפיר באומר "לא תקנה גניבותיך עד שתנוח".

אתנן אסרה תורה ואפילו בא על אמו. תימה: דמנ"ל הא? וי"מ: משום דאמר ב"הבא על יבמתו" (יבמות דף נט: ושם) דאתנן כלב ומחיר זונה מותרין מדכתיב "גם שניהם" ולא ארבעה, ומדמיעט אתנן כלב שהוא במיתה — ש"מ באשה כה"ג הוי אתנן. ואין נראה פירוש זה, דאטו מי כתיב "ולא ארבעה"? "שניהם" כתיב, ונאמר: שניהם ולא שלשה, ולא אתא למעוטי אלא מחיר זונה! ונראה לפרש: משום דעיקר אתנן בעריות הוא דכתיב, כדמוכח בפ' "כל האסורים" (תמורה דף כט. ושם) דזונה דגבי אתנן בחייבי כריתות משתעי. וא"ת: דלמא כי אסר הכתוב אתנן — כגון שאמר לה אדם אחר "הא לך טלה זה ושכבי עם בנך", דההוא לא מחייב מיתה, ושייך אתנן כה"ג כדתנן בפרק "כל האסורים" (שם דף כט. ושם:*) האומר "הא לך טלה זה ותלין שפחתך אצל עבדי" ר"מ אומר: אינו אתנן, וחכמים אומרים: הרי זה אתנן. ואפילו ר"מ לא קאמר אלא משום דשפחה בעבד שריא, כדמפרש התם דיש לו אשה ובניס רבו מוסר לו שפחה כנענית! ותירץ ר"י: דפשטי' דקרא ד"לא תביא אתנן זונה" משמע בסתם אתנן, שהבועל הוא הנותן אתנן. [ועי' תוס' בכורות נו: ד"ה זונה]. אילו תבעה ליה כו'. אע"ג דמוקמיה בע"ז (דף סג. ושם) דקאי אתנן באסרה — מטעם זה לא היה נאסר, ולא חשיב אתנן אלא מתנה בעלמא. ועיקר טעמא דאתנן כדמסיק הכא — משום

עין משפטנר מצוה

עה א ב מיי' פ"ד מהל' עדות הלכה ז סמג עשין קט טוש"ע ח"מ סי' ל סעיף יג:

עו ג טוח"מ סימן שנ:

עז ד ה מיי' פ"ג מהל' גניבה הלכה ה טור ח"מ שם:

עח ו מיי' פ"ד מהל' איסורי מזבח הל' ח סמג לאוין שטז:

גליון הש"ס

גמ' דבר ולא חצי דבר. עיין הוריות דף ד ע"א תוס' ד"ה קרי: רש"י ד"ה בדינא לומר החזר לי תאינים. עיין סנהדרין דף עב ע"א וצ"ע:

מסורת הש"ס

דברים יט — תורה אור

ב"ב נו: סנהדרין ל.

[ב"ב נו: סנהדרין ל: פו.]

[וע' נדה נב: ובפרש"י להתם]

רש"ל מ"ז

[ב"מ מז.]

ש"א ואמאי קתני מכר לאו מכירה היא

שבת ד.: לז. גיטין עט

בנ"י והיא אילו

ב"מ נח.

[ב"ה לא]

[ד"ה שעקירה]

[ד"ה מנסך]

ד"ה כגון

אֲפִילּוּ הָכִי, כֵּיוָן דְּקָא מַקְנֵי לֵיהּ בְּהָכִי — הָוְיָא מְכִירָה.§ "גָּנַב וְטָבַח בְּיוֹם הַכִּפּוּרִים" וכו'.§ אָמְרִי: אַמַּאי? נְהִי דִּקְטָלָא לֵיכָּא, מַלְקוֹת מִיהָא אִיכָּא, [א]וְקַיְ"ל דְּאֵינוֹ לוֹקֶה וּמְשַׁלֵּם! אָמְרִי: הָא מַנִּי? ר"מ הִיא, דְּאָמַר: *לוֹקֶה וּמְשַׁלֵּם. אִי ר"מ, אֲפִילּוּ טָבַח בְּשַׁבָּת! וְכִי תֵּימָא, לוֹקֶה וּמְשַׁלֵּם אִית לֵיהּ, מֵת וּמְשַׁלֵּם לֵית לֵיהּ; וְלָא? וְהָתַנְיָא: גָּנַב וְטָבַח בְּשַׁבָּת, גָּנַב וְטָבַח לַעֲ"ז, גָּנַב שׁוֹר הַנִּסְקָל וּטְבָחוֹ — מְשַׁלֵּם אַרְבָּעָה וַחֲמִשָּׁה, דִּבְרֵי ר"מ, וַחֲכָמִים [ב]פּוֹטְרִין! אָמְרִי: בַּר מִינַּהּ דְּהַהִיא, דְּהָא אִתְּמַר עֲלָהּ: א"ר יַעֲקֹב א"ר יוֹחָנָן, וְאָמְרִי לָהּ א"ר יִרְמְיָה אָמַר רַבִּי שִׁמְעוֹן בֶּן לָקִישׁ, רַבִּי אָבִין וְרַבִּי אֶלְעָא וְכָל חֲבוּרָתָא מִשְּׁמֵיהּ דְּרַבִּי יוֹחָנָן אָמְרִי: [ג]בְּטוֹבֵחַ ע"י אַחֵר. וְכִי זֶה חוֹטֵא וְזֶה מִתְחַיֵּיב?! אָמַר רָבָא: שָׁאנֵי הָכָא, דְּאָמַר קְרָא: °"וּטְבָחוֹ *וּמְכָרוֹ", *מַה מְּכִירָה ע"י אַחֵר, אַף טְבִיחָה ע"י אַחֵר. דְּבֵי ר' יִשְׁמָעֵאל תָּנָא: "אוֹ" — [ד]לְרַבּוֹת אֶת הַשָּׁלִיחַ. דְּבֵי חִזְקִיָּה תָּנָא: "תַּחַת" — לְרַבּוֹת אֶת הַשָּׁלִיחַ. *מַתְקִיף לָהּ מָר זוּטְרָא: מִי אִיכָּא מִידֵי, דְּאִילּוּ עָבֵיד אִיהוּ לָא מִיחַיַּיב, וְעָבֵיד שָׁלִיחַ וּמִיחַיַּיב? א"ל רַב אַשִׁי: הָתָם לָאו מִשּׁוּם דְּלָא מִיחַיַּיב הוּא, אֶלָּא דְּקָם לֵיהּ בִּדְרַבָּה מִינֵּיהּ. וְאִי בְּטוֹבֵחַ עַל יְדֵי אַחֵר, מ"ט דְּרַבָּנַן דְּפָטְרִי? אָמְרִי: *מַאן חֲכָמִים? ר"ש דְּאָמַר: *[ה]שְׁחִיטָה שֶׁאֵינָהּ רְאוּיָה לָא שְׁמָהּ שְׁחִיטָה. אָמְרִי: בִּשְׁלָמָא ע"ז וְשׁוֹר הַנִּסְקָל — שְׁחִיטָה שֶׁאֵינָהּ רְאוּיָה הִיא, אֶלָּא שַׁבָּת — שְׁחִיטָה רְאוּיָה הִיא, דִּתְנַן:* [ו]הַשּׁוֹחֵט בְּשַׁבָּת וּבְיוֹם הַכִּפּוּרִים, אע"פ שֶׁמִּתְחַיֵּיב בְּנַפְשׁוֹ — שְׁחִיטָתוֹ כְּשֵׁרָה! אָמְרִי: סָבַר לָהּ כְּרַבִּי יוֹחָנָן הַסַּנְדְּלָר; דִּתְנַן:* הַמְבַשֵּׁל בְּשַׁבָּת, בְּשׁוֹגֵג — יֹאכַל, בְּמֵזִיד — לֹא יֹאכַל, דִּבְרֵי ר"מ; רַבִּי יְהוּדָה אוֹמֵר: [ז]בְּשׁוֹגֵג — יֹאכַל בְּמוֹצָאֵי שַׁבָּת, בְּמֵזִיד — לֹא יֹאכַל עוֹלָמִית; רַבִּי יוֹחָנָן הַסַּנְדְּלָר אוֹמֵר: בְּשׁוֹגֵג — יֵאָכֵל לְמוֹצָאֵי שַׁבָּת לַאֲחֵרִים וְלֹא לוֹ, בְּמֵזִיד — לֹא יֵאָכֵל עוֹלָמִית, לֹא לוֹ וְלֹא לַאֲחֵרִים. מ"ט דְּר' יוֹחָנָן הַסַּנְדְּלָר? כִּדְדָרֵישׁ רַבִּי חִיָּיא אַפִּיתְחָא דְּבֵי נְשִׂיאָה: °"וּשְׁמַרְתֶּם אֶת הַשַּׁבָּת כִּי קֹדֶשׁ הִיא לָכֶם", מַה קֹּדֶשׁ אָסוּר בַּאֲכִילָה — אַף מַעֲשֵׂה שַׁבָּת אֲסוּרִין בַּאֲכִילָה. אִי מַה קֹּדֶשׁ אָסוּר בַּהֲנָאָה, אַף מַעֲשֵׂה שַׁבָּת אָסוּר בַּהֲנָאָה! ת"ל: "לָכֶם", שֶׁלָּכֶם יְהֵא. יָכוֹל אֲפִילּוּ בְּשׁוֹגֵג? ת"ל: °"מְחַלְלֶיהָ מוֹת יוּמָת", בְּמֵזִיד אֲמַרְתִּי לָךְ וְלֹא בְּשׁוֹגֵג. פְּלִיגִי בָּהּ רַב אַחָא וְרָבִינָא, חַד אָמַר: מַעֲשֵׂה שַׁבָּת דְּאוֹרַיְיתָא, וְחַד אָמַר: מַעֲשֵׂה שַׁבָּת דְּרַבָּנַן. מ"ד דְּאוֹרַיְיתָא, כְּדַאֲמָרַן; וּמ"ד דְּרַבָּנַן, אָמַר קְרָא: "קֹדֶשׁ הוּא", הוּא קֹדֶשׁ *[ח]וְאֵין מַעֲשָׂיו קֹדֶשׁ. בִּשְׁלָמָא לְמ"ד דְּאוֹרַיְית' אַמְּטוּ לְהָכִי

רש"י

אֲפִי' הָכִי. כִּי יָהֵיב לָהּ – חָיֵיל עֲלֵיהּ דְּטָלֶה אִיסּוּר אֶתְנָן. הָכָא נַמִי כו'. מַלְקוֹת אִיכָּא. מִשּׁוּם לָאו. ר' מֵאִיר הִיא. בְּמַסֶּכֶת מַכּוֹת (דף ד.): "מְעִידִים אָנוּ בִּפְלוֹנִי שֶׁחַיָּיב לַחֲבֵירוֹ מָאתַיִם זוּז" וְנִמְצְאוּ זוֹמְמִין – לוֹקִין וּמְשַׁלְּמִין, שֶׁלֹּא הַשֵּׁם הַמְבִיאָן לִידֵי מַכּוֹת מְבִיאָן לִידֵי תַּשְׁלוּמִין. גָּנַב וְטָבַח בְּשַׁבָּת. וְאַע"ג דְּאִיכָּא חִיּוּב מִיתָה. גָּנַב שׁוֹר הַנִּסְקָל. אַע"ג דְּאִיסּוּרֵי הֲנָאָה הוּא – חַיָּיב, וּכְדְתָנֵי לְקַמָּן טַעְמָא. וְכִי. שָׁלִיחַ חוֹטֵא וְשׁוֹלֵחַ מִתְחַיֵּיב בְּתַשְׁלוּמֵי ד' וה'? וְהָא קַיְימָא לָן דְּאֵין שָׁלִיחַ לִדְבַר עֲבֵירָה! בְּמַסֶּכֶת קִדּוּשִׁין (דף מב:). אֵין מְכִירָה אֶלָּא בִּשְׁנַיִם, מוֹכֵר וְלוֹקֵחַ. הָתָם. כִּי עָבֵיד אִיהוּ *דְּפָטְרָא לֵיהּ – לָאו מִשּׁוּם דְּלָא מִיחַיַּיב, אֶלָּא מִשּׁוּם דְּקָם לֵיהּ בִּדְרַבָּה מִינֵּיהּ. ר"ש דְּאָמַר שְׁחִיטָה שֶׁאֵינָהּ רְאוּיָה כו'. כְּדִתְנַן בְּפִרְקִין: רַבִּי שִׁמְעוֹן פּוֹטֵר בִּשְׁנֵי אֵלּוּ. בִּשְׁלָמָא ע"ז וְשׁוֹר הַנִּסְקָל. אִיסּוּרֵי הֲנָאָה נִינְהוּ, דְּאָמַר בְּמַסֶּכֶת ע"ז (דף נד.): אע"פ שֶׁאָמְרוּ הַמִּשְׁתַּחֲוֶה לְבֶהֱמַת חֲבֵירוֹ – לֹא אֲסָרָהּ, עָשָׂה בָּהּ מַעֲשֶׂה – אֲסָרָהּ. בְּשׁוֹגֵג יֹאכַל. אֲפִי' הוּא עַצְמוֹ, וַאֲפִילּוּ בּוֹ בַּיּוֹם. בְּמֵזִיד לֹא יֹאכַל. בּוֹ בַּיּוֹם, וְהוּא הַדִּין לַאֲחֵרִים. וְאַיְּידֵי דְּתָנָא רֵישָׁא בְּדִידֵיהּ, תָּנָא נַמִי סֵיפָא בְּדִידֵיהּ. וְהָכִי אִיבָּעֵי לָן לְפָרוּשֵׁי בְּ"הַכֹּל שׁוֹחֲטִין". רַבִּי יְהוּדָה אוֹמֵר בְּשׁוֹגֵג יֹאכַל. הוּא בְּעַצְמוֹ לְמוֹצָאֵי שַׁבָּת. וּבוֹ בַּיּוֹם לֹא הוּא וְלֹא אֲחֵרִים. וְאַיְּידֵי דְּבָעֵי לְמִיתְנָא סֵיפָא בְּדִידֵיהּ תָּנָא נַמִי בְּרֵישָׁא בְּדִידֵיהּ. בְּמֵזִיד לֹא יֹאכַל. הוּא עוֹלָמִית. אֲבָל אֲחֵרִים אוֹכְלִים. בִּדְר' יוֹחָנָן הַסַּנְדְּלָר גָּרְסִינַן יֵאָכֵל. יָכוֹל אֲפִי' בְּשׁוֹגֵג. יֵאָסֵר בַּאֲכִילָה. בְּמֵזִיד אֲמַרְתִּי לָךְ. "קוֹדֶשׁ הוּא" – הֵיכָא דְּשַׁיָּיךְ דִּין מִיתָה וְלֹא בְּשׁוֹגֵג. מַעֲשֵׂה שַׁבָּת דְּאוֹרַיְיתָא. אֲסוּרִין בַּאֲכִילָה. לְהָכִי

תוספות

משום דקא יהיב לה הוי אתנן, פי': כיון שצריך לתת לה, לצאת ידי שמים — אפי' לא היה עומד בצבירה חשיב אתנן, ולא מתנה. ה"נ הויא מכירה. וכן משמע ב"השוכר את הפועלים" (ב"מ דף צא. ושם) דחייב ליתן לצאת ידי שמים. דאמר התם: החוסם את הפרה ודש בה — לוקה ומשלם ד' קבים לפרה וג' קבים לחמור. ופריך: והא קיימא לן דאין לוקה ומשלם! ומשני רבא: אתנן אסרה תורה אפי' בא על אמו. וא"ת: דבפרק "בן סורר ומורה" (סנהדרין דף עב. ושם*) אמרינן: רבא איגניבו ליה [דיכרי] במחתרת, אהדרינהו ניהליה ולא קבלינהו, הואיל ונפק מפומיה דרב דבדמים קנינהו. ואם היו חייבין לצאת ידי שמים — אמאי לא קבלינהו? וי"ל: שהם לא היו מחזירים אלא משום שהיו סבורים שחייבין להחזיר מן הדין.

והא קי"ל דאין לוקה ומשלם. הכי נמי פריך אמתניתין ד"אלו נערות" (כתובות דף לב. ושם*). ותימה: דהא בקנס משמע דמודו כולי עלמא דלוקה ומשלם, דילפינן ממוציא שם רע, כדמוכח בפ"ק דמכות (דף ד. ושם) דהוי גמרינן בכל דוכתין ממוציא שם רע — אי לאו דאיכא למפרך: מה למוציא שם רע שכן קנס ו"כדי רשעתו", נוקי בשאר ממון דלאו קנס! ודוחק לומר דרבנן פליגי אדרבי מאיר, וסברי עדים זוממים קנסא הוא, ו"כדי רשעתו" בעדים זוממים כתיב למימרא דאפי' בקנס משום רשעה אחת אתה מחייבו ואי אתה מחייבו משום שתי רשעיות. וי"ל: דודאי אי לאו דאיכא למפרך מה למוציא שם רע שכן קנס — הוה ילפינן בכל דוכתא דלוקה ומשלם, והוה דרשינן "כדי רשעתו" לדרשה אחרת, כדדרשינן ב"אלו נערות". אבל השתא, דאיכא למפרך, ומוקמי "כדי רשעתו" דאין לוקה ומשלם — מהשתא ילפינן בכל דוכתין מהתם דאין עדים זוממים לוקין ומשלמין, אפילו בקנס, דבכל ענין אמרה תורה דאין עדים זוממים לוקין ומשלמין, אפי' בשעה שהעידו שקר טבחו ומכרו דהוי קנס. ומעדים זוממין ילפינן טפי ממוציא ש"ר, דעיקר מלקות כתיב בהן, ומלאו דחסימה דסמיך ליה ילפינן לכל המלקיות. **בטובח** ע"י אחר. ואם תאמר: ולרבה דאמר בפרק "אלו נערות" (כתובות דף לד: ושם*) דלרבי מאיר חידוש הוא שחדשה תורה בקנס, דאף ע"ג דמקטל משלם, היכי הוה משני מתני'? דאי כר"מ — אפי' טובח בשבת נמי! וי"ל: דהוה מוקים מתני' בדלא אתרו ביה, וכרבי יוחנן, דאמר: חייבי מלקיות שוגגין חייבין בתשלומין. והכי משני רבה התם מתניתין ד"אלו נערות". **או** לרבות את השליח. ומאן דמצריך "או" לחלק, דריש מ"תחת" לרבות את השליח. **בשלמא** ע"ז ושור הנסקל שחיטה שאין ראויה היא. הך סוגיא אתיא כמ"ד ב"השוחט" (חולין דף מ.): אדם אוסר דבר שאין שלו בעשה בה מעשה, דפלוגתא דתנאי היא. וא"ת: והא אמר התם דאפילו למ"ד אדם אוסר — הני מילי גוי, אבל ישראל — לצעורי קמכוין, ואכתי שחיטה ראויה היא! וי"ל: (א) כשנתן רשות לשליח לשחוט כרצונו, ואפי' לע"ז. דאין שייך לומר לצעורי בעלים קמכוין, שהשליח סבור שהוא של גנב. מפורש בפרק "הניזקין" (גיטין דף נג: ושם*). **המבשל** בשבת. **מה** קדש אסור אף מעשה שבת אסורים. וא"ת: ולא ליכתוב לא "קדש" ולא "לכם" ואנא ידענא דאסירי, מ"לא תאכל כל תועבה" — כל שתעבתי לך הרי הוא בבל תאכל! וי"ל: דאי מהתם ה"א אפי' שוגג, להכי איצטריך למיכתב הכא ולסמכיה ל"מחלליה", לומר: במזיד אמרתי לך ולא בשוגג. **היא** קדש ואין מעשיה קדש. ולא סגי דלא ליכתוב לא "היא" ולא "קדש", דמ"כל שתעבתי לך" הוה אסרינן באכילה. והכי איתא בהדיא בפרק "כל הבשר" (חולין דף קטו. ושם*). ***אלא** למ"ד דרבנן אמאי פטרי רבנן. הוה מצי למימר דלא דרשי "או" ו"תחת" לרבות את השליח. אלא דלא ניחא ליה למימר דפליגי בשליח. ואם תאמר: והא משמע לקמן דאפי' בדרבנן פטרינן שחיטה שאין ראויה, דהא בעי למימר אליבא דמתני' דקסבר ר' יוחנן דחולין שנשחטו בעזרה לאו דאורייתא, וקתני: רבי שמעון פוטר בשני אלו! וי"ל: דעל כרחך לא בעי למימר דלאו דאורייתא אלא לת"ק. דבפרק "כיסוי הדם" (חולין דף פה: ושם) דייקינן בהדיא דסבר רבי שמעון חולין שנשחטו בעזרה דאורייתא, מדתנן בפרק בתרא דתמורה (דף לג:): רבי שמעון אומר: חולין שנשחטו בעזרה ישרפו, וכן חיה. וכי דייק התם ממתניתין דתמורה — הוא הדין דהוה מצי למידק ממתניתין, דקתני: רבי שמעון פוטר בשני אלו.

כיון

עין משפט נר מצוה

עט א מיי' פ"ג מהל' גניבה הלכה א ופ"א מהלכות נערה הלכה יא ופי"ח מהלכות סנהדרין הלכה ב ופ"י מהלכות תרומות הל' ו ופ"ד מהל' חובל הלכה ט טוח"מ סי' שנ:

פ ב מיי' פ"ג מהלכות גניבה הלכה ג סמג עשין עא טוח"מ סי' שנ טוש"ע ח"מ סי' שנח:

[ד"ה ולא]

פא ג ד מיי' שם הל' ו טוח"מ סי' שנ:

פב ה מיי' פי"ב מהל' שחיטה הל' ו ועיין בלח"מ ופי"ד הל' י ופ"ב מהל' גניבה הל' ח סמג עשין סד עא טוש"ע י"ד סי' טז סעיף ט וסי' כח סעיף יז וטוח"מ סי' שנ:

[ד"ה לאין]

[כתובות לג: קדושין מג. לקמן עט.]

פג ו מיי' פ"א מהל' שחיטה הלכה כט סמג עשין סג טוש"ע י"ד סי' יא סעיף ב:

פד ז ח מיי' פ"ו מהל' שבת הלכה כג סמג לאוין סה טוש"ע א"ח סי' שיח סעיף א:

הגהות הב"ח

(א) תום' ד"ה בשלמא וכו' וי"ל דמיירי כשנתן:

כתובות לד. חולין יד.

שבת לח. ביצה יז: תרומות פ"ב מ"ג כתובות לד. גיטין נג: ע"ש חולין טו. [תוספתא דשבת פ"ג]

[ד"ה ור"מ] [כתובות לד. חולין קטו.]

[ד"ה המבשל]

[ד"ה היא]

מסורת הש"ס

תורה אור

כתובות לג: ב"מ נא. וש"נ

נ"ל דפטרינן יעב"ץ

ש"ל או מכרו וכ"ל בכתובות

שמות כא

כתובות שכ

ערכין פג. וש"נ

חולין פ. פח. פה: כתובות ל. קדושין נז. לקמן עו.

שמות לא

שם

דש היא היא קדש ואין מעשיה כל"ב

עין משפט
נר מצוה

פה א מיי' פ"ג מהל' גניבה הל' י טוח"מ סי' שנ:

הגהות הב"ח
(א) רש"י ד"ה חייב לשלם כפל ד' וה' דאע"ג:

גליון הש"ס
גמ' ואפילו חמשה חצאי בקר. עיין לעיל דף מ ע"א תוספות ד"ה כופר שלם:

מסורת הש"ס

תורה אור

להכי פטרי רבנן, אלא למ"ד דרבנן, אמאי פטרי רבנן? אשארא, אע"ז ושור הנסקל. ורבי מאיר, אמאי מחייב שוחט לע"ז? כיון דשחט בה פורתא אסרה, אידך איסורי הנאה הוא, ולא דמריה קא טבח (ולא דידיה קא טבח)! אמר רבא: *באומר "בגמר זביחה הוא עובדה". שור הנסקל איסורי הנאה נינהו, לאו דמריה קא טבח (ולאו דידיה קא טבח)! אמר רבא: הכא במאי עסקינן — כגון שמסרו לשומר, והזיק בבית שומר והועד בבית שומר ונגמר דינו בבית שומר.* ור"מ סבר לה כרבי יעקב, וס"ל כר' שמעון; סבר לה כרבי יעקב, דאמר:* אף משנגמר דינו — החזירו שומר לבעלים מוחזר. וסבר לה כרבי שמעון, דאמר: *דבר הגורם לממון כממון דמי. דתנן, *ר"ש אומר: קדשים שחייב באחריותן — חייב, אלמא דבר הגורם לממון כממון דמי. אמר רב כהנא: אמריתא לשמעתא קמיה דרב זביד מנהרדעא: מי מצית מוקמת מתניתין כר"מ ולא כר"ש? והא קתני סיפא: רבי שמעון פוטר בשני אלו, מכלל דבכולה מתניתין מודה! א"ל: לא, מכלל דמודה בטבח ומכר לרפואה ולכלבים.§ "גנב משל אביו וטבח ומכר" וכו'.§ בעא מיניה רבא מרב נחמן: גנב שור של שני שותפין וטבחו, והודה לאחד מהן, מהו? "חמשה בקר" אמר רחמנא — ולא חמשה חצאי בקר, או דלמא "חמשה בקר" אמר רחמנא — ואפילו חמשה חצאי בקר? א"ל: "חמשה בקר" אמר רחמנא — ולא חמשה חצאי בקר. איתיביה: גנב משל אביו וטבח ומכר, ואח"כ מת אביו — משלם תשלומי ארבעה וחמשה; והא הכא, כיון דמת אביו — כמו שקדם והודה לאחד מהן דמי, וקתני: משלם תשלומי ארבעה וחמשה! א"ל: הכא במאי עסקינן — *כגון שעמד אביו בדין. אבל לא עמד בדין, מאי? אינו משלם תשלומי ארבעה וחמשה? אי הכי, אדתני סיפא: גנב משל אביו ומת ואח"כ טבח ומכר אינו משלם תשלומי ארבעה וחמשה — ניפלוג בדידיה: במה דברים אמורים — כשעמד בדין, אבל לא עמד בדין — אינו משלם תשלומי ארבעה וחמשה! א"ל: הכי נמי, איידי דנסיב רישא: גנב משל אביו וטבח ומכר ואח"כ מת אביו — נסיב סיפא נמי: גנב משל אביו ומת אביו ואח"כ טבח ומכר. לצפרא א"ל: "חמשה בקר" אמר רחמנא — **ואפי' חמשה חצאי בקר. והאי דלא אמרי לך באורתא, דלא

שמות כא

להכי פטרי רבנן. דשחיטה שאינה ראויה היא, וכדברי ר' שמעון. כיון דשחיט בה פורתא איתסרא. משום זבחי מתים. דקא סלקא דעתך ישנה לשחיטה מתחילה ועד סוף, ומתחילתה נאסרה משום זבחי מתים. ולענין תשלומין ד' וה' – "וטבחו" כולו בעינן, כדאמרינן לקמן. כי גמר לה – לאו דמריה קטבח, שכבר איבדה ממנו קודם שחיטה ונאסרה עליו, והוה ליה כמו שהשליכה לאור קודם שחיטה, דמשלם קרן וכפל ותו לא. בגמר זביחה הוא עובדה. לע"ז הוא עובד בגמר זביחה, ולא בתחילה. שמסרו בעליו לשומר. קודם שהזיק, והזיק בבית שומר כו'. דר' יעקב. בשילהי "שור שנגח ד' וה'". מוחזר. ואומר לו: הרי שלך לפניך. נמצאת שאע"פ שאינו שוה כלום – גורם לממון הוא, דכל זמן שהוא קיים – שומר פוטר את עצמו בו, ואם יאבד ישלם דמיו. קדשים שחייב באחריותן. גנב שגנב קדשים מבית בעלים, אם קיבלם בעליו עליו באחריות, כגון דאמר "הרי עלי עולה" והפריש זו. חייב. לשלם כפל. (א) דאע"ג דלאו דידיה הוה אלא דהקדש, כיון דגורם לממון הוא, דאי מית בידו בעי לשלומי – כדידיה דמיא. מי מצית מוקמת למתניתין. ד"גנב וטבח ביום הכפורים" כרבי מאיר לחודיה, דאמר: לוקה ומשלם? והא מדקתני כו'. לרפואה ולכלבים. ואיצטריך לאשמועינן, אע"ג דלרבי שמעון שחיטה שאינה ראויה לא שמה שחיטה – הך שחיטה ראויה קא חשיב לה. אבל ביום הכפורים פליג, משום דאין לוקה ומשלם. והודה לאחד מהן. על חלקו, ומודה בקנס פטור. מהו. לחייבו לשלם לחבירו את חלקו, כשיבאו עדים.
דלא

כיון ששחט בה פורתא אסרה. ואפילו למ"ד אין לשחיטה אלא בסוף — נאסרת בפורתא קמא, שהאיסור תלוי במעשה ולא בשחיטה, כדקאמרינן ב"השוחט" (חולין דף מ.): אע"ג שאמר המשתחוה לבהמת חבירו — לא אסרה, עשה בה מעשה — אסרה. ואההוא פורתא לא מחייב בתשלומי ד' וה', ואפילו למ"ד ישנה לשחיטה מתחילה ועד סוף, כדאמרינן לקמן דבעינן "וטבחו" כוליה באיסורא. איסורי הנאה ולא דמריה קשחיט. וא"ת: ולמה לי טעמא דלא דמריה קשחיט? תיפוק ליה דאין זה טביחה, דמתתך בעפר בעלמא הוא. כדאמרינן ב"השוחט" (שם) גבי השוחט חטאת בשבת בחוץ לע"ז חייב שלשה חטאות. ופריך: אשחוטי חוץ לא ליחייב, מתתך בעפר הוא, דאסרה בשחיטה פורתא לע"ז! ויש לומר: דהתם נמי לא פריך אלא משום דבעי ראויה לפתח אהל מועד, וכיון דנאסרה בשחיטה פורתא — תו לא חזי לפתח אהל מועד. ואם תאמר: ומה בכך דלאו דמרה קטבח? הא כל טובח נמי לאו דמריה קטבח, דמכי שחט בה פורתא — קנייה בשינוי מעשה! ויש לומר: דלא חשיב שינוי מעשה לקנות בכך. ואם תאמר: ומ"ט דרבי מאיר דמחייב הכא? והא בפרק "כיסוי הדם" (חולין דף פה. ושם*) מפרש טעמא דר' מאיר דלא בעי שחיטה ראויה משום דגמר שחיטה משחוטי חוץ, דדנין שחיטה משחיטה ואין דנין שחיטה מטביחה, מ"טבוח טבח והכן". אבל הכא, דכתיב "וטבחו" — אדרבה, אית לן למילף טפי טביחה מטביחה ממאי דנילף טביחה משחיטה! וי"ל: דהכא איכא למימר דנין שחיטה דעבירה משחיטה דעבירה, שאסור לו לגנוב ולשחוט משחוטי חוץ, ואין דנין טביחה מ"טבוח טבח והכן" שהיא שחיטת היתר. והא דלא משני הכי בפרק "כיסוי הדם" (שם) — משום דבשוחט אותו ואת בנו פעמים ששוחט את הטריפה קודם שהוא (שוחט השנית) שחיטת היתר. ועי"ל: דדנין דבר הנאמר בסיני מדבר הנאמר בסיני, אבל "וטבוח טבח" לא נאמר בסיני. והא דלא משני התם הכי — משום דאית ליה שינויי אחריני. ומיהו קשה, בריש פ' ב' דיבמות (דף יז:) אמר: דנין "אחים" מ"אחים" ואין דנין "אחים" מ"אחיך" אע"ג ד"שנים עשר עבדיך אחים אנחנו" לא נאמר בסיני! וי"ל: כיון דילפינן ככר בחד דוכתא דשמה שחיטה, כגון באותו ואת בנו, משום דהוי שחיטה משחיטה — קסבר רבי מאיר יש לנו לומר בכל מקום, ולהכי בתשלומי ארבעה וחמשה נמי שמה שחיטה. וליכא למימר לאדרבה, נילף בתשלומי ארבעה וחמשה טביחה מטביחה — דשחיטה שאין ראויה לא שמה שחיטה, ונימא הוא הדין באותו ואת בנו. דהא כיון דאיכא למימר הכי והכי, סברא דדנין דבר הנאמר בסיני מדבר הנאמר בסיני.

וסבר לה כרבי שמעון דאמר דבר הגורם לממון כממון דמי. תימה: דל"ל למימר דסבר כרבי שמעון? לימא דר' מאיר לטעמיה, דדאין דינא דגרמי, דכל שכן דמחייב בדבר הגורם לממון. דהא אמר ב"הגוזל קמא" (לקמן דף צח:): אימור דאמר ר' שמעון דכממון דמי — דבר שעיקרו ממון, דבר שאין עיקרו ממון, כגון שורף שטרותיו של חבירו — מי שמעת ליה? אם כן רבי מאיר דמחייב בשורף שטרותיו, כדאמרינן התם (לקמן דף צח: ושם) דמאן דדאין דינא דגרמי מגבי ביה דמי שטרא מעליא — כ"ש דמחייב בדבר הגורם לממון! וי"ל: דאיכא נמי סברא למימר איפכא, דע"כ לא מחייב רבי מאיר אלא בדינא דגרמי, כגון בשורף שטרות של חבירו וכיוצא בו, שראוי השטר לכל העולם למכור ולגבות בו, וכן במסכך גפנו על גבי תבואתו של חבירו — ראויה התבואה לכל העולם. אבל דבר הגורם לממון, כמו שור הנסקל וקדשים שחייב באחריותן, אינו ראוי אלא לזה שיפטר בו עצמו — לא יחייב רבי מאיר. להכי קאמר דסבר לה כרבי שמעון. וי"מ דלהכי קאמר דסבר לה כרבי שמעון: משום דרבי שמעון קאמר בהדיא דחייב ארבעה וחמשה בדבר הגורם לממון. אבל ממאי דמחייב רבי מאיר בדינא דגרמי — אין להוכיח שיחייב ארבעה וחמשה בדבר הגורם לממון. וריב"א מפרש: דבדינא דגרמי לא מחייב רבי מאיר אלא מדרבנן, כדמוכח בסוף "הכונס" (לעיל דף סב.) [ע' תוס' לעיל נד. ד"ה חמור]. מכלל דבכולה מתניתין מודה. קצת קשה: דמה דיוק הוא זה? אליבא דמ"ד (לקמן דף עה.): מודה בקנס ואחר כך באו עדים פטור מיבעי ליה. טבח והודה לאחד מהם מהו. דע"כ כשיש עדים בדבר מיירי, דאי באין עדים — בהודאה לא יתחייב בשום ענין.

דלא

[כתובות לז. וש"נ]
ונגנב מבית שומר כו'
לעיל מה. לקמן [כתובות לז.]
[פסחים כט: וש"נ]
לקמן עד:
[ד"ה דנין]
עי' תוס' כתובות לח: ד"ה בגר
עי' תוס' ב"מ נו. ד"ה נשאל]

דְּלָא אֲכַלִי בִּשְׂרָא דְּתוֹרָא. וְאֶלָּא מַאי שְׁנָא רֵישָׁא וּמַאי שְׁנָא סֵיפָא? א"ל: רֵישָׁא קָרֵינָא בֵּיהּ "וּטְבָחוֹ" כּוּלּוֹ בְּאִיסּוּרָא, סֵיפָא לָא קָרֵינָא בֵּיהּ "וּטְבָחוֹ" כּוּלּוֹ בְּאִיסּוּרָא.§ "הַשּׁוֹחֵט וְנִמְצֵאת טְרֵיפָה" וכו'.§ א"ל רַב חֲבִיבִי מְחוֹזְנָאָה לְרַב אַשִׁי: ש"מ *אֵינָהּ לִשְׁחִיטָה אֶלָּא לְבַסּוֹף, דְּאִי יֶשְׁנָהּ לִשְׁחִיטָה מִתְּחִילָּה וְעַד סוֹף, כֵּיוָן דִּשְׁחַט בָּהּ פּוּרְתָּא — אֲסַרָהּ, אִידָּךְ לָא דְּמָרֵיהּ קָא טָבַח! א"ל רַב הוּנָא בְּרֵיהּ דְּרָבָא: כִּי קָא מְחַיֵּיב — אַהַהוּא פּוּרְתָּא. א"ל רַב אַשִׁי: לָא תִּידְחֵי, "וּטְבָחוֹ" כּוּלּוֹ בָּעֵינַן, וְלֵיכָּא. אֶלָּא קַשְׁיָא! א"ל, הָכִי אֲמַר רַב גַּמְדָּא מִשְּׁמֵיהּ דְּרָבָא: כְּגוֹן שֶׁשָּׁחַט מִקְצָת סִימָנִין בַּחוּץ וּגְמָרָן בִּפְנִים. אִיכָּא דְּמַתְנֵי לָהּ אַהָא, *א"ר שִׁמְעוֹן מִשּׁוּם דְּרַבִּי לֵוִי סָבָא: אֵינָהּ לִשְׁחִיטָה אֶלָּא לְבַסּוֹף, וְר' יוֹחָנָן אָמַר: יֶשְׁנָהּ לִשְׁחִיטָה מִתְּחִילָּה וְעַד סוֹף. א"ל רַב חֲבִיבִי מְחוֹזְנָאָה לְרַב אַשִׁי: לֵימָא קָסָבַר רַבִּי יוֹחָנָן [א]חוּלִּין שֶׁנִּשְׁחֲטוּ בָּעֲזָרָה לָאו דְּאוֹרַיְיתָא, דְּאִי

רש"י

דְּלָא אֲכַלִי בִּשְׂרָא דְּתוֹרָא. לֹא דִּקְדַּקְתִּי טַעֲמוֹ שֶׁל דָּבָר. וּמַאי שְׁנָא סֵיפָא. כֵּיוָן דְּרֵישָׁא אֲפִי' לֹא עָמַד בַּדִּין [קָאָמַר רַחֲמָנָא] דַּחֲמִשָּׁה בָּקָר וַאֲפִי' חֲמִשָּׁה חֲצָאֵי בָקָר, סֵיפָא כְּשֶׁמֵּת אָבִיו וְאַחַר כָּךְ טָבַח וּמָכַר לָמָּה לֹא יְשַׁלֵּם לְאֶחָיו אֶת חֶלְקָם? וּטְבָחוֹ. כּוּלּוֹ מַשְׁמַע. ש"מ. מִדְּקָתָנֵי מַתְנִיתִין: הַשּׁוֹחֵט חוּלִּין בָּעֲזָרָה – חַיָּיב. אֵינָהּ לִשְׁחִיטָה אֶלָּא לְבַסּוֹף. הִלְכָּךְ, כָּל כַּמָּה דְּטָבַח – דְּמָרֵיהּ קָא טָבַח, וּבִגְמַר שְׁחִיטָה הוּא דְּמִיתְּסַר בַּהֲנָאָה. כְּגוֹן שֶׁשָּׁחַט מִיעוּט סִימָנִין בַּחוּץ וּגְמָרָן בִּפְנִים. אוֹ הִשְׁלִימָן לָרוֹב, דִּבִגְמַר טְבִיחָה הוּא דְּאִיתְּסַרָא, וְעַד הַשְׁתָּא דְּמָרֵיהּ קָא טָבַח. אֵינָהּ לִשְׁחִיטָה. אֵין שְׁחִיטָה נִקְרֵאת אֶלָּא לְבַסּוֹף. וְנָפְקָא מִינָּהּ לְעִנְיַן הַמְחַשֵּׁב בְּקָדָשִׁים חוּץ לִמְקוֹמָם, אוֹ חוּץ לִזְמַנָּן, אוֹ מְחַשֵּׁב שֶׁלֹּא לִשְׁמָן – אֵינָהּ מַחֲשָׁבָה אא"כ חִישֵּׁב בְּסוֹף שְׁחִיטָה. מִתְּחִילָּה וְעַד סוֹף. וְכָל כַּמָּה דְּחָשֵׁיב הָוְיָא מַחֲשָׁבָה. חוּלִּין שֶׁנִּשְׁחֲטוּ בָּעֲזָרָה. פְּלוּגְתָּא הִיא בְּמַסֶּכֶת קִדּוּשִׁין (דף נח.), אִי דְּאוֹרַיְיתָא הִיא אִי דְּרַבָּנַן. דְּאִי

תוספות

דלא אכלי בשרא דתורא. שרוי בתענית היה. סיפא לא קרינא ביה וטבחו כולו באיסורא. משמע: אבל כפל — מחייב, אע"ג דלא עמד בדין. ואפי' ארבעה וחמשה הוה מחייב, אי לאו דבעינן וטבחו כולו באיסורא. ורישא נמי קתני: חייב בארבעה וחמשה, ואע"ג דאיירי בלא עמד בדין, כמו בסיפא — דאין חילוק בין רישא לסיפא, אלא דברישא טבח ואח"כ מת אביו, ובסיפא מת אביו ואח"כ טבח. ולמאי דס"ל מעיקרא לרב נחמן ולא חמשה חצאי בקר — לא מוקי כשעמד בדין אלא משום דלא ליהוי ה' חצאי בקר. אם כן משמע כל הסוגיא דאדם מוריש קנס לבניו. והקשה ריב"א: דבריש "נערה שנתפתתה" (כתובות דף מב: ושם) אמרינן: כי קאמרינן ממונא הוי להורישו לבניו — בשאר קנסות. והתם הוי פי' משום שעמד בדין, אבל לא עמד בדין — משמע כולה שמעתא דלא מצי להוריש! וי"ל: דרבא ורב נחמן דהכא לית להו סוגיא דהתם, דס"ל דיכול להוריש בשאר קנסות אע"ג שלא עמד בדין. דנהי דקנס של אונס ופיתוי אין יכול להוריש בשום ענין, כדקתני במתני' — דהתם היינו משום דאותו דבר שהקנס יוצא ממנו, דהיינו הבת, אין יכול להורישו לבניו כדאמרינן התם: אותם לבניכם, ולא בנותיכם לבניכם. אבל ממון דהכא, שהכפל ד' וה' יוצאין ממנו, דהיינו בהמה — הוא מוריש לבניו, לפיכך זה הקנס מוריש לבניו. ועוד נראה לר"י: דרבא ורב נחמן דהכא לא פליגי אסוגיא דרבה ואביי דפרק "נערה" (שם.), דמיירי הכא כולה מתניתין כשעמד בדין, ואמרו ליה "חייב אתה ליתן לו", דכה"ג אדם מוריש לבניו קנס כיון דא"ל "חייב אתה ליתן לו". ולא שייך השתא למפרך ארישא: ליפלוג בדידיה, בטבח ומכר בחיי אביו, בין עמד בדין ללא עמד. דניחא ליה למתני כולה בעמד בדין, דתו לא הוי קנס, דאפ"ה בסיפא מת אביו ואח"כ טבח — דפטור, משום דבעינן וטבחו כולו באיסורא וליכא. וחידוש זה אינו יכול להשמיענו אלא במת אביו ואח"כ טבח ומכר. אבל מעיקרא, דסבירא ליה חמשה בקר אמר רחמנא ולא חמשה חצאי בקר, והיינו טעמא דמפטר בסיפא — פריך שפיר, דליפלוג וליתני בדידיה: במה דברים אמורים — כשעמד בדין ואמר לו "לא תן לו", אבל לא עמד בדין, פירוש שלא אמר לו "לא תן לו", אלא "חייב אתה ליתן לו", וטבח ומכר ואח"כ מת אביו — פטור מטעם ולא ה' חצאי בקר. *דהיינו טעמא דסיפא, דסיפא נמי איירי בלא עמד בדין בחיי אביו, שלא אמר לו "לא תן לו", אלא "חייב אתה לו". אם כן בחנם נקט בסיפא מת אביו ואחר כך טבח, דבזה הענין אפי' טבח ואחר כך מת נמי. וקצת נראה דוחק פירוש זה, דמאחר דמועלת העמדה בדין ד"חייב אתה ליתן לו" לענין שחשוב כאילו זכה, שיכול להוריש לבניו — אם כן גם לענין זה תועיל שיחשוב כאילו נתחייב לאביו ה' בקר שלמים, שמכח האב הוא מתחייב לשלם לאחיו, ולא מכחם. ור"י הלבן מפרש דבכל קנס אדם מוריש לבניו. *והיא דפרק "נערה" (שם) — לענין קרבן שבועה איירי, כמו שמוכח תחילת הסוגיא דלענין קרבן שבועה שאל אביי לרבה, ועל זה השיבו: כי קאמינא ממון הוי לרבי שמעון — להתחייב עליו קרבן שבועה להורישו לבניו, שאם מת ותבעוהו אחר מיתת אביהם קנס שהיית חייב לאבינו, והעמידך בדין ונתחייבת לו בדין, וכפר ונשבע ואחר כך הודה, הואיל ואגלאי מילתא דבשעת שנפל ליד היורשים כבר היה ממון אצל אביהם, שהרי כבר עמד עליו בדין ונתחייב לו ולא היה יכול להודות ולהפטר מהן — אם כן לגבי דידהו אין עקרו קנס, וה"ל דומיא דפקדון דקרא, ומתחייב עליה קרבן שבועה. אבל אם לא עמד בדין, אע"פ שהיורש יורשו — מכל מקום אין דומיא דפקדון, ולא מחייב בטענתו קרבן שבועה, אפי' העמידוהו בדין ונתחייב להו בדין, ואחר כך, עתה כשתבעוהו כפר ונשבע והודה, שהרי עיקרו קנס. והא דקאמר בתר הכי דאיצטריך קרא "וכיחש" לעמדה בדין ובגרה ואחר כך מתה, דהתם כי קא ירית מינה קא ירית — *מכל מקום אין דומיא דפקדון, אע"פ שע"י ירושה בא ליד האב עכשיו, הואיל ותחילתו קנס לגבי דידה ודידיה — *אפי' מתה אחר שבגרה עיקרו קנס מיקרי לגבי האב, ולא מתחייב קרבן שבועה. ואם תאמר: בפרק "אלו נערות" (שם דף לח: ושם ד"ה יש), דקבעי: יש בגר בקבר ופקע אב, או אין בגר ולא פקע אב. ולמאי פקע אב כשיש בגר בקבר? נהי דאין לו מכחו — יהיה לו מכח ירושה שיורש את בתו, כיון דקנס נמי בר ירושה הוא! ויש לומר: דהתם אין יכול לזכות מכחה, שהבת לא היתה ראויה לזכות בו מעולם.* ואם תאמר: וכי בעי מעיקרא: יש בגר בקבר ודבנה הוי. היאך יכול להיות של בנה? הלא אינה יכולה להורישה, כדקאמר בבעיא בתרייתא: יש בגר בקבר ופקע אב! ויש לומר: דבעיא קמייתא הויא בבושת ופגם, דהוי ממונא, ומורשת שפיר לבנה. אע"ג דבושת ופגם איתקש לקנס, כדתנן בפרק "נערה" (שם דף מא:): לא הספיקה לעמוד בדין עד שמת האב — הרי הן של עצמה. משמע דאבושת ופגם נמי קאי, מדקתני "הרי הן" לשון רבים — היינו דוקא לענין גביית האב איתקוש לקנס, כדכתיב "ונתן האיש השוכב עמה לאבי הנערה חמשים" וגו', ודרשינן: הנאת שכיבה נ', מכלל דאיכא בושת ופגם. ואית דדריש "תחת אשר עינה" — מכלל דאיכא בושת ופגם. אבל הכא, נהי דמפטר המאנס מן הקנס — לפי שאין יכולה להוריש, שלא זכתה בו, מבושת ופגם דהוי ממונא — לא מפטר. דאי ישנה לשחיטה מתחילה ועד סוף מכי שחיט פורתא כו'. ממאי דחייב רחמנא אחולין בעזרה ואשחוטי חוץ לא מצי למפרך: אי ישנה לשחיטה מתחילה ועד סוף — מכי שחטה פורתא אסרה, ואידך מחתך עפר בעלמא הוא. אע"ג דליכא למימר דמחייב אההוא פורתא כמו שאפרש בסמוך. דכיון דאין שם פסול אחר אלא דשחוטי חוץ לבדו — איכא למימר דבהכי חייב רחמנא. אבל כשיש פסול אחר עמו — אז יש לפטור, אפילו למ"ד ישנה לשחיטה מתחילה ועד סוף, כיון דבסוף שחיטה הוי כמחתך עפר בעלמא. כי קמחייב אההוא פורתא מחייב. תימה: כיון דסוף השחיטה פוסלת — אין לו להתחייב אפורתא קמא אפילו למ"ד ישנה לשחיטה מתחילה ועד סוף, כדמשמע בפ' ב' דחולין (דף כט:), דפריך מההיא דאירע בה פסול בשחיטה, בין קודם פסולה בין לאחר פסולה — אין מטמאה בגדים, בהוצאתה; קודם פסולה — מטמאה בגדים, לאחר פסולה — אין מטמאה בגדים. ואי אמרת ישנה לשחיטה מתחילה ועד סוף — ניפלוג נמי בשחיטתה! ומשני: נתקלקלה בשחיטה קאמרת, כיון דנתקלקלה בשחיטה לבסוף — איגלאי מילתא למפרע דמעיקרא לאו שחיטה היא כלל. ואותו קלקול מפ' ר"ת דלאו דוקא נתקלקלה בגוף השחיטה, כגון נוחר ומעקר, אלא אפי' נתקלקלה ע"י מלאכה שעשה בשעת שחיטה. דומיא דאירע בה פסול בהוצאתה, דמיירי בפסול מלאכה. דאי לאו הכי, אכתי תקשה לו: ניפלוג נמי בשחיטתה בפסול מלאכה! אלמא משמע התם, דאפי' למ"ד ישנה לשחיטה מתחילה ועד סוף, כשאירע פסול באמצע — אין תחילת השחיטה שחיטה! וי"ל: דהכא נמי ה"מ לאקשויי ליה, אלא בלאו הכי מסלק ליה שפיר. לימא קסבר רבי יוחנן חולין שנשחטו בעזרה לאו דאורייתא. ותקשה דידיה אדידיה, דאיהו גופיה אמר בפרק "האיש מקדש" (קדושין דף נז:): חולין שנשחטו בעזרה — דאורייתא, ויליף לה מקרא.

דאי

רש"ל

פסחים סג. חולין כט: [לו. קכת. זבחים ל.]

[חולין כט: וע"ל ר"ש בן לקיש]

אעפ"כ יליף מוכחש לפטור מקרבן שבועה. העתק מחילופי גרסאות

פו א מיי' פ"ב מהלכות גניבה הלכה ח ופ"ב מהלכות שחיטה הל' ג וע"ש בכ"מ:

אבל כפל משלם שהרי עמד בדין וא"ל חייב אתה ליתן ויכול להוריש לבניו. העתק מחילופי גרסאות

אפי' לא עמד בדין וא"כ סוגיא דהכא איירי בלא עמד בדין. העתק מחילופי גרסאות

שקודם שבגרה לאחר העמדה בדין היתה שלו בתורת קנסא ומשבגרה היא שלה ע"י קנס. העתק מהג"ל

שהרי מתה כשהיא נערה. העתק מהג"ל

דְּאִי ס"ד דְּאוֹרַיְיתָא, מִכִּי שָׁחֵיט לָהּ פּוּרְתָּא — אֲסָרָהּ, אִידָּךְ — לָאו דְּמָרָהּ קָא טָבַח! א"ל רַב אַחָא בְּרֵיהּ דְּרָבָא: כִּי קָא מְחַיֵּיב — נַמִי אַהַהוּא פּוּרְתָּא. א"ל רַב אַשִׁי: לָא תִּידְחֵיהּ, "וּטְבָחוֹ" כּוּלּוֹ בָּעֵינַן, וְלֵיכָּא. אֶלָּא קַשְׁיָא! א"ל, הָכִי אֲמַר רַב גַּמְדָּא מִשְּׁמֵיהּ דְּרָבָא: כִּי קָא מְחַיֵּיב — כְּגוֹן שֶׁשָּׁחַט מִקְצָת סִימָנִין בַּחוּץ וּגְמָרָן בִּפְנִים.§

מתני' גָּנַב עַל פִּי שְׁנַיִם וְטָבַח וּמָכַר עַל פִּיהֶן, וְנִמְצְאוּ זוֹמְמִים — [א]מְשַׁלְּמִין הַכֹּל. גָּנַב עַל פִּי שְׁנַיִם וְטָבַח וּמָכַר עַל פִּי שְׁנַיִם אֲחֵרִים, אֵלּוּ וְאֵלּוּ נִמְצְאוּ זוֹמְמִין — [ב]הָרִאשׁוֹנִים מְשַׁלְּמִין תַּשְׁלוּמֵי כֶפֶל, וַאֲחֵרוֹנִים מְשַׁלְּמִין תַּשְׁלוּמֵי ג'; נִמְצְאוּ אַחֲרוֹנִים זוֹמְמִין — [ג]הוּא מְשַׁלֵּם תַּשְׁלוּמֵי כֶפֶל, וְהֵן מְשַׁלְּמִין תַּשְׁלוּמֵי ג'; אֶחָד מִן אַחֲרוֹנִים זוֹמְמִין — בָּטְלָה עֵדוּת שְׁנִיָּה; אֶחָד מִן הָרִאשׁוֹנִים זוֹמְמִין — [ד]בָּטְלָה כָּל הָעֵדוּת, שֶׁאִם אֵין גְּנֵיבָה, אֵין טְבִיחָה וְאֵין מְכִירָה.§

גמ' אִיתְּמַר: *עֵד זוֹמֵם, אַבַּיֵי אָמַר: [ה]לְמַפְרֵעַ הוּא נִפְסָל, רָבָא אָמַר: מִכָּאן וּלְהַבָּא הוּא נִפְסָל. אַבַּיֵי אָמַר לְמַפְרֵעַ הוּא נִפְסָל, מֵהַהוּא שַׁעְתָּא דְּאַסְהֵיד הֲוָה לֵיהּ רָשָׁע, וְהַתּוֹרָה אָמְרָה: °"אַל תָּשֶׁת רָשָׁע עֵד"; רָבָא אָמַר מִכָּאן וּלְהַבָּא הוּא נִפְסָל, עֵד זוֹמֵם חִידּוּשׁ הוּא, דְּהָא תְּרֵי וּתְרֵי נִינְהוּ, מַאי חָזֵית דְּצַיֵּית לְהָנֵי? צַיֵּית לְהָנֵי, הִלְכָּךְ אֵין לְךָ בּוֹ אֶלָּא מִשְּׁעַת חִידּוּשׁ וְאֵילָךְ. אִיכָּא דְּאָמְרִי: רָבָא נַמִי כְּאַבַּיֵי סְבִירָא לֵיהּ, דְּאָמַר לְמַפְרֵעַ הוּא נִפְסָל, וְהָכָא הַיְינוּ טַעְמֵיהּ דְּרָבָא, מִשּׁוּם

(תורה אור: שמות כג)

רש"י: דְּאִי ס"ד דְּאוֹרַיְיתָא. הֵיכִי מְתָרֵץ רַבִּי יוֹחָנָן לְמַתְנִי'? הָא בְּפוּרְתָּא קָא מִתַּסְרָא לָהּ! כִּי קָא מְחַיֵּיב. בְּתַשְׁלוּמִין. אַהַהוּא פּוּרְתָּא. מְחַיֵּיב, דְּכִי הֵיכִי דְּהָוֵי שְׁחִיטָה לְעִנְיַן חוּלִּין בָּעֲזָרָה בִּתְחִילָּתָהּ – הָוֵי נַמִי טְבִיחָה לְעִנְיַן תַּשְׁלוּמִין. וּגְמָרָן בִּפְנִים. דְּאִיכָּא "וּטְבָחוֹ" כּוּלּוֹ, קוֹדֶם שֶׁנֶּאֶסְרָה בַּהֲנָאָה. **מתני'** מְשַׁלְּמִין לוֹ אֶת הַכֹּל. וּבַגְּמָ' מוֹקֵי לָהּ כְּשֶׁהוּזְמוּ תְּחִלָּה עַל הַטְּבִיחָה. וְהָאַחֲרוֹנִים מְשַׁלְּמִים ג'. לַשּׁוֹר. וּכְגוֹן שֶׁהוּזְמוּ אַחֲרוֹנִים תְּחִילָּה, דְּאִי עֵדֵי גְנֵיבָה הוּזְמוּ תְּחִילָּה – בָּטְלָה לָהּ עֵדוּת טְבִיחָה, דְּדִלְמָא בְּעָלִים מְכָרוּהוּ לוֹ, וְכִי מִיתַּזְמִי – אַמַּאי מְשַׁלְּמִי? בָּטְלָה עֵדוּת שְׁנִיָּה. וְהוּא מְשַׁלֵּם כֶּפֶל מִשּׁוּם רִאשׁוֹנִים. וְהֵן פְּטוּרִין, דְּאֵין עֵדִים מְשַׁלְּמִין מָמוֹן עַד שֶׁיּוּזְמוּ שְׁנֵיהֶן. בָּטְלָה כָּל הָעֵדוּת. וְהוּא פָּטוּר וְהֵן פְּטוּרִין. וַאֲפִי' חָזְרוּ וְהוּזְמוּ אַחֲרוֹנִים אַחֲרֵי כֵן – אֵין מְשַׁלְּמִין, שֶׁהֲרֵי בָּטְלָה עֵדוּתָן כְּבָר וְהוּכְחֲשׁוּ, דְּכֵיוָן דְּלֹא גָּנַב – לֹא טָבַח. וְאַהָכִי לָא מִחַיְּיבוּ אֶלָּא אַ"עִמָּנוּ הֱיִיתֶם" שֶׁסָּתְרוּ גּוּפָהּ שֶׁל עֵדוּת. וְכ"שׁ אִם הוּזְמוּ שְׁנַיִם הָרִאשׁוֹנִים תְּחִילָּה, שֶׁעֵדוּת שְׁנִיָּה בְּטֵלָה. אֶלָּא שֶׁבִּזְמַן שֶׁלֹּא הוּזְמוּ אֶלָּא אֶחָד – בָּטְלוּ שְׁתֵּיהֶן, אֲבָל כְּשֶׁהוּזְמוּ שְׁנֵיהֶם – לֹא בָּטְלָה עֵדוּת רִאשׁוֹנָה, אֶלָּא מְשַׁלְּמִין כֶּפֶל. **גמ'** לְמַפְרֵעַ נִפְסָל. הֵעִיד בְּנִיסָן וְהוּזַם עַל עֵדוּת זוֹ בְּאִיָּיר – כָּל הָעֵדְיוֹת שֶׁהֵעִיד בֵּינְתַיִם פְּסוּלוֹת, דְּמִשָּׁעָה שֶׁהֵעִיד עֵדוּת זוֹ נִפְסָל. מִכָּאן וּלְהַבָּא. מִשֶּׁהוּזַם. אַל תָּשֶׁת. יָדְךָ עִם רָשָׁע.

פְּסֵידָא

(סנהדרין כז.)

תוספות: **דאי** ס"ד דאורייתא מכי שחיט בה כו'. משמע דאי הוה מדרבנן — חשיב דמרה שפיר. ומתוך כך היה נראה לדקדק דתקרובת ע"ז אסורה בהנאה דאורייתא, מדקאמר לעיל: ור"מ שוחט לע"ז אמאי מחייב? כיון דשחט פורתא אסרה, אידך — לא דמרה קטבח. ואי דרבנן — הוה חשיב שפיר דמרה. ומיהו, יש לדחות: דתקרובת ע"ז ⊕אפי' לא אסורה בהנאה אלא מדרבנן — חשיב ליה שפיר לאו דידיה, כיון דאסרו חכמים בכל הנאות, דאפילו קידש בו אין האשה מקודשת, כדתנן בתוספתא דקדושין (פ"ד): המקדש ביין נסך (ובע"ז) בעורות לבובים כו', אע"פ שקדש בדמיהן — אינה מקודשת. אבל חולין בעזרה, אי הוי דרבנן וקידש בו את האשה — מקודשת, לכך חשיב דמריה. דבסוף "האיש מקדש" (קדושין דף נח.) קתני גבי חולין שנשחטו בעזרה: רבי שמעון אומר מקודשת. ופריך: אלמא קסבר רבי שמעון חולין שנשחטו בעזרה לאו דאורייתא כו'. ומיהו, איסור אכילה דהויא — ודאי דאורייתא. יש לדקדק משמעתין דלעיל, דפטרי רבנן שוחט לע"ז משום שחיטה שאין ראויה, ואי איסור אכילה לא הויא אלא מדרבנן — לא היה נחשב בכך שחיטה שאינה ראויה, כמו מעשה דשבת למאן דאמר דרבנן. וא"ל דאי אסור באכילה דאורייתא — היינו על כרחך משום דהוקשו למת, מהאי טעמא נמי תיאסר בהנאה כמת! וי"ל: כיון דכתיב "ויאכלו זבחי מתים" — לאכילה איתקוש ולא להנאה. **רבא** אמר מכאן ולהבא הוא נפסל. תימה: [דבריש] "חזקת הבתים" (ב"ב דף לא. ושם*) אמר: זה אומר של אבותי, (א) וזה אומר של אבותי — האי אייתי סהדי דאבהתיה היא ואכלה שני חזקה, והאי אייתי סהדי דאכלה שני חזקה. אמר רב נחמן: אוקי אכילתא בהדי אכילתא, ואוקי ארעא בחזקת אבהתיה. אמר ליה רבא: והא עדות מוכחשת היא! והשתא אמאי הוי מוכחשת? הא רבא אית ליה הכא מכאן ולהבא הוא נפסל, ואית לן למימר לדידיה: אאכילה דאיתכחוש — איתכחוש, ואאבהתא דלא איתכחוש — לא איתכחוש. מידי דהוי אשנים מעידים אותו שגנב וטבח והוזמו אטביחה, דלרבא דאמר מכאן ולהבא הוא נפסל, אע"ג דתוך כדי דיבור כדיבור *דמי, כיון דמההיא שעתא דקא מתזמי הוא דפסלי, אטביחה דקמיתזמו — איתזום, אגניבה דלא איתזום — לא איתזום, כדמוכח לקמן. ולהאי טעמא דמפרש משום חידוש — ניחא. *אבל טעמא דהוי משום פסידא דלקוחות — קשה, דאין נראה דנקט לקוחות דוקא, מדלא קאמר איכא בינייהו כל עדות שאין לענין לקוחות! וי"ל: דלמאי דמחלק התם בין אותו עדות לעדות אחרת — ניחא, דכיון דהוחזקו משקרים על אותה קרקע — תו לא מהימני עלה. אבל הכא, אע"פ שהוחזקו משקרים על הטביחה — לא הוחזקו משקרים על הגניבה, דלא חשיב ליה כאותה עדות. **אין** לך בו אלא משעת חידושו ואילך. אין להקשות: מנא ליה דמהימני המזימין לפוסלן? נימא דאין לך לרבויי אלא חידושו "ועשיתם לו כאשר זמם", אבל אין נפסלין! דודאי כיון דמשלמין ממון ונהרגים — כ"ש נפסלין, דלא המניינהו רחמנא לאלאין. אבל קשה, דלרב חסדא דאמר "בחזקת הבתים" (ב"ב שם:): שתי כיתי עדים המכחישות זו את זו — בהדי סהדי שקרי למה לי, אם כן אין חידוש מה שנפסלין, אדרבה: מה שהמזימין כשרים הוי חידוש לרב חסדא. והתם בעי למימר דרבא כרב חסדא! וי"ל: דלמאי דבעי למימר התם דרבא כרב חסדא — לא הוי טעמא דרבא משום חידוש, אלא משום פסידא דלקוחות, ומסקנא דהתם דמוקי לה כרב הונא, דאמר: זו באה בפני עצמה כו' — הוי חידוש מה שנפסלין קמאי. והא דמשני רבא בפרק "כל הנשבעין" (שבועות דף מז. ושם) אליבא דרב חסדא מתניתין דראש השנה — לאו משום דס"ל כוותיה. ועי"ל: דלרב חסדא נמי הוי חידוש מה שנפסלין ודאי. והאי דחשיב להו סהדי שקרי בשתי כיתי עדים — אינו אלא מספיקא, ואם היו שנים מן השוק מעידין "פלוני לוה מפלוני מנה" ואחת משתי כיתי עדים הללו המכחישות זו את זו אומרת "לא לוה" — לא הייתי מוציא ממון מספק. ואלו המזימים פסולים לגמרי, אפי' להחזיק הממון על פיהן. הלכך חידוש הוא, ולגבי הכי אין לך בו אלא משעת חידוש ואילך, לאושבם כודאי פסולין. *ולפי זה הוה מצי למימר דאיכא בינייהו כל שטרי מלוה ומקח הבאין להוציא, דלטעמא דפסידא דלקוחות — נאמנים להוציא, אלא דלא חשיב אלא מילתא דאיכא בינייהו בין לרב הונא בין לרב חסדא. ואם תאמר: ולמה הוי חידוש כלל? והלא מן הדין יש להאמין בתראי, במיגו דאי בעו הוו פסלי לקמאי בגזלנותא. ובשתי כיתי עדים המכחישות זו את זו — ליהמני בתראי במיגו, בין לרב הונא בין לרב חסדא! ואור"י: דלא שייך מיגו אלא באדם אחד, אבל בשני בני אדם — לא שייך מיגו, דאין דעת שניהם שוה, ומה שירלה לטעון זה לא יטעון זה. ועוד נראה: דקלא דמי האי מיגו למיגו במקום עדים — שהרי יש עדים כנגד האי מיגו להכחישם. ואע"פ שיש כמו כן עדים עם המיגו — אין בכך כלום. [*ועוד]: דלא עדיף מיגו מעדים, שאם היו עדים מסייעים לאלו — לא היה להם כח להכחיש את אלו, דהא תרי כמאה, וכ"ש מיגו. והא דאמר בפ"ב דכתובות (דף יח: ושם): שנים החתומים על השטר ואמרו קטנים או אנוסים היינו כו', אם אין כתב ידם יוצא ממקום אחר — הרי אלו נאמנים. האי לאו מיגו הוא, שאין השטר מתקיים אלא על פיהם, והפה שאסר הוא הפה שהתיר, כדאמרינן התם בההוא פירקא (דף כב:): מנין להפה שאסור הוא הפה שהתיר. ופריך: הא למ"ל קרא? סברא הוא. ובשנים החתומים על השטר ומתו ובאו ב' מן השוק ואמרו קטנים או אנוסים או פסולי עדות היו, דאמר התם דאי כתב ידם יוצא ממקום אחר אין נאמנים, אלא הוו תרי ותרי — צ"ל דפסולי עדות דקאמר היינו קרובים, דאי גזלנים — הוי אלו נאמנים אפילו היו בפנינו. ועוד יש תירוצים אחרים, ואין להאריך כאן. **מכאן** ולהבא הוא נפסל. נראה שאם לא נראה השטר עד לאחר הזמה, אף על פי שזמנו מוקדם להזמה — מודה רבא דלא מסגחינן בהו, דמי יודע שמא אחר הזמה כתבו אלו המזימים זה השטר, והקדימו זמנו. והא דאמר דאין נפסל למפרע — היינו בשטר שנראה קודם הזמה.

משום

עין משפט נר מצוה

פז א ב ג ד מיי' פכ"א מהל' עדות הל' ו:

פח ה מיי' פי"ו מהל' עדות הלכה ד סמג לאוין ריד טור ש"ע ח"מ סי' לח סעיף ח:

הגהות הב"ח

(א) תוס' ד"ה רבא וכו' זה אומר של אבותי ואכלתיה שני חזקה וזה אומר של אבותי ואכלתיה שני חזקה האי אייתי סהדי:

גליון הש"ס

תוס' ד"ה דאי וכו' אפי' לא אסורה בנאה אלא מדרבנן. עיין חולין דף קטז ע"א תד"ה חדא מתרתי:

[ד"ה א"ל]

כוונתם לייסב דלא לימא ההוא דח"ה איירי דהעידו תוך כדי דיבור. העתק מחילופי גרסאות

דדוקא גבי הזמה אמ... מכאן ולהבא דחדוש ... גבי הכחשה. הע... מחילופי גרסאות

מפעת העדות עד הז... במוכחשים והוו כ... פסולין. העתק מהג"ל

גי' ת"ח וכן הוא בת... פרק ח"ה

מִשּׁוּם פְּסֵידָא דְּלָקוֹחוֹת. מַאי בֵּינַיְיהוּ? *דְּאַסְהִידוּ בֵּיהּ תְּרֵי לְחַד וּתְרֵי לְחַד, אִי נַמִּי דְּפָסְלִינְהוּ בְּגַזְלָנוּתָא, לְהַךְ לִישָּׁנָא דְּאָמְרַתְּ מִשּׁוּם חִידּוּשׁ — לֵיכָּא, לְהַךְ לִישָּׁנָא דְּאָמְרַתְּ מִשּׁוּם פְּסֵידָא דְּלָקוֹחוֹת — אִיכָּא. אָמַר רַבִּי יִרְמְיָה מִדִּפְתִּי: עֲבַד רַב פַּפָּא עוּבְדָא כְּוָותֵיהּ דְּרָבָא. רַב אַשִׁי אָמַר: הִלְכְתָא כְּוָותֵיהּ דְּאַבַּיֵי. *וְהִלְכְתָא כְּוָותֵיהּ דְּאַבַּיֵי בְּיַע"ל קג"ם.§ תְּנַן: גָּנַב עַל פִּי שְׁנַיִם וְטָבַח וּמָכַר עַל פִּיהֶם, וְנִמְצְאוּ זוֹמְמִין — מְשַׁלְּמִין אֶת הַכֹּל; מַאי לָאו שֶׁהֵעִידוּ עַל הַגְּנֵיבָה וְחָזְרוּ וְהֵעִידוּ עַל הַטְּבִיחָה, וְהוּזְמוּ עַל הַגְּנֵיבָה וְחָזְרוּ וְהוּזְמוּ עַל הַטְּבִיחָה. וְאִי סָלְקָא דַּעְתָּךְ לְמַפְרֵעַ הוּא נִפְסָל, הָנֵי כֵּיוָן דְּאִיתַּזְמוּ לְהוּ אַגְּנֵיבָה, אִיגְלַאי מִילְּתָא לְמַפְרֵעַ דְּכִי אַסְהֲדוּ אַטְּבִיחָה פְּסוּלִין הֲווּ, אַמַּאי מְשַׁלְּמִין אַטְּבִיחָה? אָמְרִי: הָכָא בְּמַאי עָסְקִינַן — כְּגוֹן שֶׁהוּזְמוּ עַל הַטְּבִיחָה תְּחִילָּה. אָמְרִי: סוֹף סוֹף, כִּי הָדְרִי מִיתַּזְמִי אַגְּנֵיבָה — אִיגְלַאי מִילְּתָא דְּכִי אַסְהֲדוּ אַטְּבִיחָה פְּסוּלִין הָווּ, אַמַּאי מְשַׁלְּמִי אַטְּבִיחָה? וְהִלְכְתָא: שֶׁהֵעִידוּ בְּבַת אַחַת וְהוּזְמוּ. לֵימָא כְּתַנָּאֵי: הָיוּ שְׁנַיִם מְעִידִין אוֹתוֹ שֶׁגָּנַב וְהֵן מְעִידִין אוֹתוֹ שֶׁטָּבַח, וְהוּזְמוּ עַל הַגְּנֵיבָה — עֵדוּת שֶׁבָּטְלָה מִקְצָתָהּ בָּטְלָה כּוּלָּהּ; הוּזְמוּ עַל הַטְּבִיחָה — הוּא מְשַׁלֵּם תַּשְׁלוּמֵי כֶפֶל, וְהֵן מְשַׁלְּמִין תַּשְׁלוּמֵי שְׁלֹשָׁה; א"ר יוֹסֵי: בד"א — בִּשְׁתֵּי עֵדִיּוֹת, אֲבָל בְּעֵדוּת אַחַת — עֵדוּת שֶׁבָּטְלָה מִקְצָתָהּ בָּטְלָה כּוּלָּהּ. מַאי "בִּשְׁתֵּי עֵדִיּוֹת", וּמַאי "בְּעֵדוּת אַחַת"? אִילֵימָא "בִּשְׁתֵּי עֵדִיּוֹת" — בִּשְׁתֵּי עֵדִיּוֹת מַמָּשׁ בִּשְׁתֵּי כִּתּוֹת, "בְּעֵדוּת אַחַת" — בְּכַת אַחַת בָּזֶה אַחַר זֶה, וְא"ר יוֹסֵי: בְּעֵדוּת אַחַת, בְּכַת אַחַת בָּזֶה אַחַר זֶה, כִּי מַסְהֲדִי אַגְּנֵיבָה וַהֲדַר מַסְהֲדִי אַטְּבִיחָה, כִּי מִתַּזְמִי אַטְּבִיחָה — [א]עֵדוּת שֶׁבָּטְלָה מִקְצָתָהּ בָּטְלָה כּוּלָּהּ וְאִיתַּזְמוּ לְהוּ אַגְּנֵיבָה, מֵהֵיכָא תֵּיתֵי הַךְ? אֶלָּא לָאו "בִּשְׁתֵּי עֵדִיּוֹת" — בְּעֵדוּת אַחַת כְּעֵין שְׁתֵּי עֵדִיּוֹת, וּמַאי נִינְהוּ? כַּת אַחַת בָּזֶה אַחַר זֶה, אֲבָל בְּעֵדוּת אַחַת בְּבַת אַחַת — לָא. וְסַבְרוּהָ, דְּכוּלֵּי עָלְמָא — *[ב]תּוֹךְ כְּדֵי דִיבּוּר כְּדִיבּוּר דָּמֵי; מַאי לָאו בְּהָא קָמִיפַּלְגִי, דְּרַבָּנַן סָבְרִי: מִכָּאן וּלְהַבָּא הוּא נִפְסָל, וְכֵיוָן דְּמֵהַהִיא שַׁעְתָּא קָא מִיתַּזְמִי, אַטְּבִיחָה דְּקָא מִיתַּזְמִי — אִיתַּזּוּם, אַגְּנֵיבָה דְּלָא מִיתַּזְמִי — לָא אִיתַּזּוּם; ר' יוֹסֵי סָבַר: לְמַפְרֵעַ הוּא נִפְסָל, וְכֵיוָן דְּמִיָּד כִּי אַסְהִידוּ הוּא דְּמִיפַּסְלִי, כִּי אִיתַּזְמוּ לְהוּ אַטְּבִיחָה — אִיתַּזְמוּ לְהוּ נַמִּי אַגְּנֵיבָה, דְּהָא תּוֹךְ כְּדֵי דִיבּוּר כְּדִיבּוּר דָּמֵי? אָמְרִי: אִי תּוֹךְ כְּדֵי דִיבּוּר כְּדִיבּוּר דָּמֵי, דְּכוּלֵּי עָלְמָא — לְמַפְרֵעַ הוּא נִפְסָל. אֶלָּא הָכָא בְּתוֹךְ כְּדֵי דִיבּוּר כְּדִיבּוּר דָּמֵי קָא מִיפַּלְגִי, רַבָּנַן סָבְרִי: תּוֹךְ כְּדֵי דִיבּוּר לָאו

רש"י

פְּסֵידָא דְּלָקוֹחוֹת. שֶׁחֲתָמוּהוּ עַל שְׁטַר מְכִירָה בֵּינְתַיִם. מַאי בֵּינַיְיהוּ. בֵּין הָנֵי תַּרְתֵּי לִישָּׁנָא דְּרָבָא. תְּרֵי לְחַד. עִמָּנוּ הֱיִיתֶם, וּתְרֵי אֲחֵרִינֵי לְחַד דְּלֵיכָּא חִידּוּשָׁא. בְּגַזְלָנוּתָא. שֶׁלֹּא הֱזִימוּהוּ, אֶלָּא הֵעִידוּ שְׁנַיִם עַל אֵלּוּ שֶׁהֵן גַּזְלָנִין. וְהָכָא לֵיכָּא לְמֵימַר סְמוֹךְ אַהָנֵי, דְּהָא מִילְּתָא אַחֲרִיתָא הִיא. יע"ל קג"ם. סִימָנֵי שְׁמוּעוֹת הֵן, וְזוֹ אֶחָד מֵהֶן: עֵד זוֹמֵם. פְּסוּלִין הֲווּ. וְאֵין עֵדוּתָן עֵדוּת. אַמַּאי. מְשַׁלְּמִי עַל הַטְּבִיחָה. כִּי הָדְרִי מִיתַּזְמִי אַגְּנֵיבָה. כְּשֶׁחוֹזְרִין וְנִיזּוֹמִין עַל הַגְּנֵיבָה אִיגְּלַאי מִילְּתָא כו'. ה"ג: וְהִלְכְתָא שֶׁהֵעִידוּ בְּבַת אַחַת וְהוּזְמוּ. וְלָא גָּרְסִינַן: וְהוּזְמוּ בְּבַת אַחַת. דְּכֵיוָן דְּהֵעִידוּ בְּבַת אַחַת — לֵיכָּא לְמֵימַר בִּשְׁעַת עֵדוּת טְבִיחָה פְּסוּלִין הָווּ, וַאֲפִילּוּ אִי אָמְרִינַן לְמַפְרֵעַ נִפְסָל — דְּהָא תּוֹךְ כְּדֵי דִיבּוּר הֲוָה. וַהֲזָמָה לָא אִיכְפַּת לָן אִי בְּבַת אַחַת אִי בָּזֶה אַחַר זֶה, וּבִלְבַד שֶׁיָּזּוֹמוּ עַל הַטְּבִיחָה תְּחִילָּה. הָיוּ שְׁנַיִם מְעִידִים אוֹתוֹ שֶׁגָּנַב וְהֵן. עַצְמָם מְעִידִים אוֹתוֹ שֶׁטָּבַח. בָּטְלָה כּוּלָּהּ. וּמְשַׁלְּמִי כֶּפֶל. וְהוּא פָּטוּר, דְּכֵיוָן דְּלֹא גָּנַב — לֹא טָבַח, וַאֲפִילּוּ חָזְרוּ וְהוּזְמוּ עַל הַטְּבִיחָה — *פְּטוּרִין. הוּזְמוּ עַל הַטְּבִיחָה. וְלֹא עַל הַגְּנֵיבָה. בַּמֶּה דְּבָרִים אֲמוּרִים. דְּהוּא מְשַׁלֵּם כֶּפֶל וְלֹא בָּטַל עֵדוּת גְּנֵיבָה — בִּשְׁתֵּי עֵדִיּוֹת. בְּכַת אַחַת בָּזֶה אַחַר זֶה. שֶׁהֵעִידוּ הַיּוֹם עַל הַגְּנֵיבָה, וְאָמְרוּ: בְּאֶחָד בְּשַׁבָּת גָּנַב. וּלְמָחָר עַל הַטְּבִיחָה, וְאָמְרוּ: בְּשֵׁנִי בְּשַׁבָּת טָבַח. וְא"ר יוֹסֵי. דְּכִי אָמְרִי לְהוּ סָהֲדֵי: עִמָּנוּ הֱיִיתֶם בְּיוֹם שֵׁנִי — הוּזְמוּ אַף עַל הַגְּנֵיבָה שֶׁבְּיוֹם רִאשׁוֹן, מֵהֵיכָא תֵּיתֵי הַאי? וּמַאי נִינְהוּ כו' אֲבָל בְּעֵדוּת אַחַת בְּבַת אַחַת. שֶׁהֵעִידוּ עַל שְׁתֵּיהֶן זוֹ בְּתוֹךְ כְּדֵי דִיבּוּר שֶׁל זוֹ, וְאָמְרוּ: בְּאֶחָד בְּשַׁבָּת גָּנַב וּבְשֵׁנִי בְּשַׁבָּת טָבַח, וְהוּזְמוּ עַל שֵׁנִי בְּשַׁבָּת. וְאַע"ג דְּאַאֶחָד בְּשַׁבָּת לָא אִיתַּזּוּם, מִיהוּ אִיגְּלַאי מִלְּתָא דְּכִי אַסְהוּד פְּסוּלִין הָווּ, דְּקָסָבַר ר' יוֹסֵי לְמַפְרֵעַ הוּא נִפְסָל, וּבָטְלָה כָּל עֵדוּת אוֹתָהּ שָׁעָה, שֶׁכּוּלָּהּ עֵדוּת אַחַת הִיא. כְּדֵי דִיבּוּר. לְקַמָּן מְפָרֵשׁ. מִכָּאן וּלְהַבָּא. מִיּוֹם שֶׁהוּזְמוּ, וְלֹא מִיּוֹם שֶׁהֵעִידוּ. אַגְּנֵיבָה דְּלָא מִיתַּזְמִי לָא אִיתַּזּוּם. וְאַע"ג דְּבַהֲדֵי אַסְהִידוּ לֵיהּ, הָא לָא אַתְחִיל פְּסוּלַיְיהוּ מֵהַהִיא שַׁעְתָּא, דְּיֵימָא: אַע"ג דְּאַאֶחָד בְּשַׁבָּת לָא אִיתַּזּוּס, מִיהוּ שְׁעַת עֵדוּתָן שְׁעַת פַּסְלוּת הָיְתָה. אִיתַּזְמוּ לְהוּ [נַמִּי] אַגְּנֵיבָה. הַאי אִיתַּזְמוּ — לָאו הֲזָמָה דַּוְקָא (*נָקַט) לְשַׁלֵּם מָמוֹן, אֶלָּא אִיפַּסְלוּ לְהוּ אַגְּנֵיבָה מִשּׁוּם פְּסוּל עֵדוּת. לָאו

תוספות

משום פסידא דלקוחות. י"מ דהא דחיישינן לפסידא דלקוחות — היינו דוקא היכא דאיכא עדי מסירה, דידעי שהשטר אמת. ואין נראה, דא"כ איכא בינייהו טובא היכא דאין עדים אלא החתומים על השטר. **דאסהידו** ביה תרי בחד ותרי בחד. משמע לפי שיש שני מזימים על כל אחד ואחד לא הוי חידוש. ותימה: מה בכך? הרי תרי כמאה הוו! ונראה לפרש; דאסהידו ביה תרי בחד — כגון שאין הניזומין מסייע אחד לחבירו. שאין האחד יודע כלום בעדותו של חבירו, שראה אחד מחלון זה ואחד מחלון זה, או בהודאה אחר הודאה, ואלו שנים מזימים את שניהם, שכך שוים אלו כמו אחרים. ולא נקט האי לישנא אלא משום דמשתמע מיניה שאין המוזמין מסייעין זה את זה. **אי** נמי דפסלינהו בגזלנותא. והא דאמרי' בפרק "זה בורר" (סנהדרין דף כו:) דההיא מתנה דהוו חתים עליה תרי גזלנין, סבר רב פפא בר שמואל לאכשוריה משום דהא לא אכריזנא עלייהו. ומסיק, דגזלן דאורייתא לא בעי הכרזה, ולא חיישינן לפסידא דמקבל מתנה. אע"ג דפסידא דלקוחות לאו דוקא, דה"ה דיש לחוש לפסידא דמקבל מתנה — מ"מ פסלינן לההיא מתנה, דמיירי שכבר העידו עליהן בב"ד קודם שחתמו בשטר מתנה, או לא נראית ההיא שטר מתנה עד אחר שנודע פסולן בב"ד, ואע"ג דזמנה קודם — יש לחוש שמא הקדימו, כדפרישית לעיל. *ומיהו, ההוא עובדא דפרק "זה בורר" (שם דף כז.) דחד אמר קמאי דידי גנב כו' — לדיני נפשות פשיטא שיש לפוסלו למפרע. והוי מצי למימר איכא בינייהו לענין דיני נפשות, או לאסור אשה לבעלה, ולענין גיטין וקדושין, ועדות החדש, דלטעמא דחידוש — אין לפוסלן למפרע, ולטעמא דפסידא דלקוחות — פוסלין למפרע לכל אלו. אלא דדחיק לאשכוחי דאיכא בינייהו לענין ממון. **והוזמו** על הגניבה וחזרו והוזמו על הטביחה. וא"ת: אפי' למאן דאמר מכאן ולהבא הוא נפסל תקשה, דמכל מקום אם אין גניבה — אין טביחה ומכירה, וכשחזרו והוזמו על הטביחה — אמאי משלמין? וי"ל משום דקסבר הכחשה תחילת הזמה היא. **שהעידו** בבת אחת והוזמו. דכיון שהעידו בבת אחת — ליכא למימר בשעת עדות טביחה פסולין היו, אע"ג דלמפרע הוא נפסל, דכיון שהעידו בבת אחת — כשרים היו כשהעידו על הטביחה, כיון שהיו יכולין לחזור בהן על העדות של גניבה, דתוך כדי דיבור הוה. ועל מה שפירש בקונטרס דלא גרסינן "והוזמו בבת אחת", דבהזמה לא איכפת לן אי בבת אחת אי בזה אחר זה היא, ובלבד שהוזמו על הטביחה תחילה. וקשה לר"י: דמה מרויח בקונט' בהזמת טביחה תחילה? דאי משום שאם הוזמו על הגניבה תחילה הוו מוכחשים על הטביחה, ואנן אליביה דאביי מסיקנן, דס"ל לקמן דהכחשה לאו תחילת הזמה היא — א"כ גם כשהוזמו על הטביחה תחילה הוו מוכחשים על הגניבה, מאחר שהעידו בבת אחת, ותוך כדי דיבור כדיבור דמי, כדאמר בסמוך לרבי יוסי דכי העידו בבת אחת והוזמו על הטביחה — בטלה כל העדות משום דתוך כדי דיבור כדיבור דמי! ואם באנו ליישב תירוץ זה לסברת אביי דלקמן, דסבר הכחשה לאו תחילת הזמה היא, צריך לגרוס: והוזמו בבת אחת. אבל אין לחוש, שאין הגמרא חושש עתה ליישב דברי אביי אלא במה שאמר למפרע הוא נפסל, והולך ומתרץ לפי שיטת המקשה הסובר דהכחשה תחילת הזמה היא, כדפרישית לעיל. וכן לקמן, כי משני מתני' לאביי אהא דאמר הכחשה לאו תחילת הזמה היא, ומוקי לה כשהוזמו תחילה על הטביחה — אין חושש לתרץ למאי דאמר אביי למפרע הוא נפסל, כי לפי זה היה צריך להעמידה כגון שהעידו בבת אחת, אלא דדרך הגמרא הוא שאין חושש לתרץ אלא הקושיא שמקשה לו. הרי

עין משפט נר מצוה

פט א מיי' פ"כ מהל' עדות הלכה ג:

צ ב מיי' פ"ח מהלכות אבל הל' ח וע"ש ופ"כ מהלכות שבועות הל' יח ועיין בהשגות ובכ"מ ופ"כ מהל' עדות הל' ג ועיין בהשגות ובכ"מ ופ"ו מהל' נחלות הל' ו ופ"ב מהל' תמורה הל' ד סמג עשין צ קז ולאוין רמא טוש"ע י"ד סי' רלד סעיף לא לב לג וסי' שמ סעיף כד כה וטוש"ע ח"מ סי' כט סעיף א וסי' רפא סעיף ז.

גליון הש"ס

גמ' ביע"ל קג"ס. עיין מג"א סימן שמ ס"ק טו:

מסורת הש"ס

ס"א דאוזמו

[שבועות לב. ב"מ כב: סנהדרין כז.]

ס"א פטור

[דף עב ע"ב ד"ה מכאן]

[ריש פז. נזיר כ: ב"ב ע. מכות ו. שבועות לב. תמורה כה:]

רש"ל מ"ז

עין משפט
נר מצוה

צא א ב מיי' פ"ב מהל' תמורה הל' ד סמג לאוין שמה:
צב ג מיי' פ"ב מהלכות שבועות הלכה טז ופ"כ מהל' עדות הל' ג:
צג ד מיי' פי"ח מהל' עדות הלכה ד סמג עשין קי טוח"מ סי' לח:
צד ה ו מיי' פרק כא מהל' עדות הל' ד:

מסורת הש"ס

זבחים ל. תמורה כו. נדרים סט:

לאו כדיבור דמי, ורבי יוסי סבר תוך כדי דיבור כדיבור דמי. וסבר ר' יוסי תוך כדי דיבור כדיבור דמי? והתנן: "הרי זו תמורת עולה תמורת שלמים" — הרי זו תמורת עולה, דברי ר"מ; ר' יוסי אומר: [א]אם לכך נתכוון מתחילה, הואיל ואי אפשר לקרות שני שמות כאחד — דבריו קיימין; ואם אמר "תמורת עולה" ונמלך ואמר "תמורת שלמים" — הרי זו תמורת עולה; והוינן בה: נמלך — פשיטא! *ואמר רב פפא: [ב]נמלך בתוך כדי דיבור קאמרינן! אמרי: תרי תוך כדי דיבור הוי, חד [ג]כדי שאילת תלמיד לרב, וחד כדי שאילת הרב לתלמיד. כי לית ליה לרבי יוסי — כדי שאילת תלמיד לרב "שלום עליך רבי ומורי", דנפיש, כדי שאילת הרב לתלמיד "שלום עליך" — אית ליה.§ אמר רבא: [ד]עדים שהוכחשו ולבסוף הוזמו — נהרגין, *דהכחשה תחילת הזמה היא, אלא שלא נגמרה. אמר רבא: מנא אמינא לה? *דתניא: "מעידני באיש פלוני שסימא את עין עבדו והפיל את שינו", שהרי הרב אומר כן, ונמצאו זוממין — משלמין דמי עין לעבד; היכי דמי? אילימא כדקתני, דליכא כת אחרינא, משלמין דמי עין לעבד? בתר דמפקי ליה לחירות, דמי עינו קבעי שלומי?! ועוד, [ה]דמי כוליה עבד לרב בעי לשלומי! ועוד, "שהרי הרב אומר כן", הרב מי ניחא ליה? אלא לאו כגון דאתו בי תרי ואמרי: הפיל את שינו סימא את עינו, דבעי מיתיב ליה הרב דמי עינו, ואתו בי תרי מציעאי ואמרי: עינו והדר שינו, דלא בעי למיתב ליה אלא דמי שינו, דקא מכחשי ליה קמאי למציעאי; והיינו "שהרי הרב אומר כן", דניחא ליה במאי דקאמרי; וקתני: ונמצאו זוממין מציעאי — משלמין דמי עין לעבד, שמע מינה: הכחשה תחילת הזמה היא. אמר אביי: לא, דאפכינהו [ו]ואזמינהו. ממאי? מדסיפא

רש"י

לאו כדיבור דמי. והוו ליה שני עדיות. ומשום חדא לא אתכחש אידך, דמשמעות דיבור אחרון נפסלו, ולא משמעות דיבור ראשון. וכחד עדות דמי, והרי פסולין היו באותה שעה. ה"ג: הרי זו תמורת עולה תמורת שלמים ולא גרסינן "ותמורת שלמים". הרי זו תמורת עולה דברי ר"מ. דאית ליה לר"מ "תפוס לשון ראשון". דבריו קיימין. ותרעה עד שתסתאב, ותימכר, ויביא בדמי חציה עולה ובדמי חציה שלמים. שהוכחשו ולבסוף הוזמו נהרגין. וכשנגמר הדין על פיהם קודם שהוכחשו אמרה רבא. שאם לא נגמר הדין עדיין, אפילו הוזמו מתחילה — אין נהרגין, שאין העדים זוממין נהרגין עד שיגמר הדין. והכי מיתוקמא בסיפא דשמעתין: כגון דאתו בי תרי ואמרי הכי, ופסקינהו לדינא אפומייהו. שהוכחשו. שנים אומרים הרג ושנים אומרים לא הרג. ולבסוף הוזמו. שבאת כת שלישית ואמרה "עמנו הייתם" נהרגין. שסימא את עין עבדו. ויצא לחירות, ואח"כ הפיל את שינו, וחייב ליתן לו דמי שינו. שהרי הרב אומר כן. כלומר: דניחא ליה לרב בסהדותא דהני. ולקמן מפרש מאי ניחותא. ש"מ הכחשה תחילת הזמה היא. דאי לאו תחילת הזמה היא, מאחר שבטלה עדותן — מי אית בהו דין הזמה. אמר ליה אביי לא. אי דהוכחשו על ידי כת ראשונה — שוב אין כת שלישית מזימתן. והכא — כשאין שם כת ראשונה אלא הם. ודקשיא לך: דמי עבד לרב בעי לשלומי — הכא כגון שכת שניה אפכינהו ואזמינהו, שאמרו להם: אותו היום שאתם אומרים — עמנו הייתם במקום פלוני, אבל ביום אחר הוה, ואיפכא הוה. דממה נפשך עבד נפיק לחירות. והן משלמין לו דמי עין שרצו להפסידו, וניחא ליה לרב דניפוק בעינו ויתן לו דמי שינו. ואי קשיא: הואיל וראשונים הם, מאי הוי מפסדי ליה? הא לחירות הוי מפקי ליה, ואכתי דמי עבד לרב בעי לשלומי! לקמיה פריך ליה, ומוקמינן לה בשעמד בדין.
מדסיפא

[ע"ש בתמורה דמילתא דרב פפא איה אמשנה הקודמת שם]

[כתובות יט:]

תוספת' דמכות פ"א

תוספות

הרי זו תמורת עולה דברי ר"מ. בפ"ב דזבחים (ד' ל. ושם) אמרי' "הרי זו תמורת עולה ושלמים" מהו? אמר אביי: בהא ודאי מודה ר"מ. וטעמא דאביי כדמפרש בפ' "כילד מעריבין" (תמורה ד' כו. ושם) דטעמא דר"מ משום דהוי כמו תחול זו ואח"כ תחול זו, מדהוה ליה למימר "תמורת עולה ושלמים" ואמר "תמורת עולה תמורת שלמים". אבל רבא פליג עליה, וקאמר דעדיין היא מחלוקת, דקסבר רבא דטעמא של ר"מ משום דדעתו של אדם, אם יכולין שניהם לחול — יחולו, ואם לאו — תפוס לשון ראשון, דדעתיה אקמא. **ונמלך** תוך כדי דיבור כו'. למאי דסבר נמי השתא דרבי יוסי סבר תוך כדי דיבור לאו כדיבור דמי, נראה דכשמתכוין לכך, ואמר היום "תמורת שלמים", ולמחר "תמורת עולה" — דאין דבריו קיימים, והוו כמו דברים שבלב, ודוקא תוך כדי דיבור הוא דמהני, דלענין לפרש דבריו מהני תוך כדי דיבור. **תרי** תוך כדי דיבור הוו. השתא תוך כדי דיבור דתמורה איירי תוך כדי דיבור גדול, וכיון דתוך כדי דיבור קטן אית ליה, ותוך כדי דיבור גדול לית ליה — נראה דתוך כדי דיבור גדול אין מועיל כלום, אפי' לפרש דבריו, דלא הוי אלא כאומר היום "תמורת עולה" ולמחר "תמורת שלמים", דהוו דברים שבלב. וה"פ דברייתא: אם לכך נתכוין תחילה, כלומר שאומר תוך כדי דיבור קטן, שדומה לנתכוין תחילה לכך — דבריו קיימים. ואפי' לא נתכוין נמי, כיון דכדיבור דמי. אבל בנמלך, כלומר שאומר תוך כדי דיבור גדול, שדומה כמו נמלך — הרי זו תמורת עולה, אפי' נתכוין תחילה לשניהם. **כדי** שאילת תלמיד לרב. והא דאמר בפרק "תפלת השחר" (ברכות ד' כז. ושם*): הנותן שלום, והמחזיר שלום לרבו גורם לשכינה שתסתלק מישראל — היינו כשנותן שלום לרבו כמו לחבירו, כמו שאמר ליה "שלום עליך" ולא אמר "רבי". והא דאמר בפ' "ר"ע" (שבת ד' פט.): כלום יש עבד שנותן שלום לרבו! — עבד שאני, שאימת רבו עליו, ובשום ענין אין ליתן לו שלום.

[ד"ה והנותן]

כי לית ליה לרבי יוסי כדי שאילת תלמיד לרב. תימה; דרב אחא מדיפתי, דאמר בפ"ק דמכות (דף ו.) ובפרק "שבועת העדות" (שבועות דף לב. ושם) תוך כדי דיבור — כדי שאילת תלמיד לרב, כמאן? דלרבנן לית להו כלל כדי דיבור, אפי' כדי דיבור קטן, ור' יוסי נמי כתלמיד לרב מודי דלאו כדיבור דמי! וי"ל: דסבר לה כברייתא דמי שאמר הריני נזיר ושמע חבירו ואמר ואני (נזיר דף כא. ושם). וכן הלכתא דתוך כדי דיבור כדיבור דמי. והכי פסקינן הלכתא בנדרים בפרק בתרא (דף פז.) דתוך כדי דבור כדיבור דמי, חוץ ממגדף ועובד ע"ז ומקדש ומגרש, ואפי' בכדי שאילת תלמיד לרב, כריש לקיש וכרב אחא דמכות (דף ו.) וד"שבועת העדות" (שבועות דף לב.). ושיעור כדי שאילת שלום תלמיד לרב, מפרש ר"ת דהיינו טעמא: דכשאדם מעיד עדות, או עוסק במקח וממכר, וחבירו נותן לו שלום או רבו — ע"כ יש לו להשיב ולהפסיק, כדאמר ברכות (ד' ו:): הנותן שלום לחבירו ואין מחזיר — נקרא גזלן, שנאמר "גזילת העני בבתיכם", ולכך תיקנו חכמים שלא יהיה זה חשוב הפסק. וכן מוכח בנזיר (ד' כ:) דקאמר: תוך — לא שבקת רווחא לתלמיד. ומיהו, בפ' בתרא דנדרים (ד' פז.) אין מתיישב טעם זה לענין קריעה, דכסבור שמת וקרע ואח"כ מת, אם מת תוך כדי דיבור — יצא ידי קריעה, ואם לאו — לא יצא ידי קריעה, והתם מאי שייך שיעור זה? *ושמא לענין קריעה הקילו. **אמר** ליה אביי לא דאפכינהו ואזמינהו ממאי מדסיפא כו'. נראה לר"י: דכל סוגיא זו כפי מאי דס"ד השתא דדיוקא דרבא הוי מרישא, אבל לפי האמת — מסקנא דדיוקא דרבא מסיפא, ולא אמר אביי זה מעולם, אלא בני הישיבה היו מתרלים כן אליביה דאביי, לפי מה שהיו סוברים דדיוקא דרבא מרישא. אבל לפי המסקנא (א) דאמר אביי דרישא בשלש כתות כדאוקמא רבא בלא מיפך והזמה, ובסיפא בשתים במיפך והזמה. ולאו דוקא נקט אביי אפכינהו תחילה — דאם כן איתכחשו להו, אלא מעיקרא אזמינהו והדר אפכינהו. א"נ: מעיקרא אפכינהו, ואזמינהו תוך כדי דיבור. ונראה לר"י: דאביי מוקי לה בג' כתות, כדמוכח לקמן, דקאמר: ואביי אמר לך בשלמא רישא לא סגי בלא ג' כתות דקתני "שהרי הרב אומר כן". ואיירי דמציעאי נמי אפכינהו ואזמינהו לקמאי, דהשתא לא איתכחשי מציעאי כלל, וליכא למידק מינה דהכחשה תחילת הזמה היא דמשלמי. וכי קתני נמצאו זוממין מציעאי משלמין דמי עין לעבד — ה"ה דמי עין לקמאי, שהרי היו מחייבין אותם דמי עין לרב משום "כאשר זמם", אלא לפי שלא הוזכרו ראשונים בברייתא לא חש למיתני. ומיהו, אין אנו צריכין כלל להיפוך בתראי למציעאי, דכיון דהוזמו — ממילא קיימא עדות קמאי. ובקונט' פי' דאביי מוקי רישא בב' כתות כמו סיפא. ויש ליישב הא דקתני "שהרי הרב אומר כן", דמעיקרא ודאי דלא ידעינן דאפכינהו, והוה קשה לן מאי "שהרב אומר כן". אבל השתא דאפכינהו — שמח הרב בעדותן של אלו שאין מחייבים אותו כ"א דמי שן, לפי שיודע שיבאו עדים שיחייבו אותו דמי עין. ולפי זה איכא לאוקמי כל סוגיא זו לפי האמת, דרבא לא הביא הרישא אלא לדקדק הימנה דסיפא איירי בשלש כתות כמו רישא, ואביי מהדר ליה: דוק לאידך גיסא, מדסיפא סגי בב' כתות ובמיפך והזמה — רישא נמי סגי בב' כיתות, ואין לך ראיה מסיפא מכח רישא, דאיכא לאוקמי כולה בב' כתות. והא דקאמר לקמן: בשלמא רישא לא סגי בלא שלש כתות — ה"ק: אי נמי לא תתיישב לך "שהרי הרב אומר כן" אי לא מוקמת לה בשלש כתות, מכל מקום סיפא איירי בב' כתות. ואם תאמר: אי בב' כתות מוקמת לה לרישא, אמאי משלמי דמי עין לעבד? תקשה ליה כדפרכינן

ועי' בר"ן בנדרים שם ד"ה והלכתא ובתוס' ב"ב קכט: ד"ה והלכתא

הגהות הב"ח

(א) תוס' ד"ה אמר וכו' לפי המסקנא קאמר אביי דרישא בשלש כיתות וכו' לא סגי דבלאו ג' וכו' תחלת הזמה היא מדמשלמי וכי:

מִדְּסֵיפָא בְּמֵיפַךְ וַהֲזָמָה רֵישָׁא נַמִי בְּמֵיפַךְ וַהֲזָמָה, דְּקָתָנֵי סֵיפָא: "מְעִידֵנוּ אֶת אִישׁ פְּלוֹנִי שֶׁהִפִּיל אֶת שֵׁן עַבְדּוֹ וְסִימֵּא אֶת עֵינוֹ", שֶׁהֲרֵי הָעֶבֶד אוֹמֵר כֵּן, וְנִמְצְאוּ זוֹמְמִין – מְשַׁלְּמִין דְּמֵי עַיִן לָרַב; הֵיכִי דָּמֵי? אִי דְּלָא קָא מוֹדוּ לְהוּ בַּתְרָאֵי בַּחֲבָלָא כְּלָל, דְּמֵי כּוּלֵּיהּ עֶבֶד לָרַב בָּעֵי שַׁלּוּמֵי לֵיהּ! אֶלָּא פְּשִׁיטָא, דְּקָא מוֹדוּ כּוּלְּהוּ בַּחֲבָלָא, וּדְקָא(א) אַפְּכִינַן וְאַזְמִינְהוּ. וְהֵיכִי דָּמֵי? אִי דְּקָא מְאַחֲרֵי אַחוּרֵי הָנֵי בַּתְרָאֵי – [א]אַכַּתִּי דְּמֵי עֶבֶד לָרַב בָּעֵי שַׁלּוּמֵי, דְּכִי מְחַיְּיבִי לֵיהּ לְגַבְרָא, אַכַּתִּי גַּבְרָא לָאו בַּר חִיּוּבָא הוּא! אֶלָּא דְּקָא מְקַדְּמִי קַדּוּמֵי הָנֵי בַּתְרָאֵי. וְאִי דְּלָא עָמַד בַּדִּין – אַכַּתִּי דְּמֵי כּוּלֵּיהּ עֶבֶד לָרַב בָּעֵי שַׁלּוּמֵי לֵיהּ, דְּאַכַּתִּי גַּבְרָא לָא מִיחַיַּיב! אֶלָּא דְּעָמַד בַּדִּין. א"ל רַב אַחָא בְּרֵיהּ דְּרַב אִיקָא לְרַב אַשִׁי: דּוּקְיָא דְּרָבָא מֵהֵיכָא? אִילֵימָא מֵרֵישָׁא, רֵישָׁא מִי קָא מִתְכַּחֲשִׁי מְצִיעָאֵי? כֵּיוָן דְּאִי לָא מִתַּזְמִי – סַהֲדוּתָא כְּוָותַיְיהוּ קָא קַיְימָא, דְּדִינָא כְּוָותַיְיהוּ פָּסְקִינַן, דְּיֵשׁ בִּכְלַל מָאתַיִם מָנֶה, הִלְכָּךְ קַמָּאֵי הוּא דְּקָא מִתְכַּחֲשִׁי, מְצִיעָאֵי לָא מִתְכַּחֲשִׁי מִידֵּי! אָמַר לֵיהּ, רָבָא סָבַר: מִדְּרֵישָׁא בְּשָׁלֹשׁ כִּיתּוֹת, סֵיפָא נַמִי בְּשָׁלֹשׁ, וְדָיֵיק מִסֵּיפָא, כְּגוֹן דְּאָתוּ בֵּי תְּרֵי וְאָמְרִי: הִפִּיל אֶת שִׁינּוֹ וְסִימֵּא עֵינוֹ, וּפָסְקִינֵיהּ לְדִינָא אַפּוּמַיְיהוּ, וְאָתוּ בֵּי תְּרֵי אַחֲרִינֵי וְאָמְרִי: סִימֵּא אֶת עֵינוֹ וְהִפִּיל אֶת שִׁינּוֹ, דְּקָא מַכְחֲשִׁי לְהוּ לְהָנֵי קַמָּאֵי, וְנִמְצְאוּ זוֹמְמִין – קַמָּאֵי מְשַׁלְּמִין דְּמֵי עַיִן לָרַב; וְאִי סָלְקָא דַּעְתָּךְ הַכְחָשָׁה לָאו תְּחִילַּת הֲזָמָה הִיא, אַמַּאי מְשַׁלְּמִי? הָא אִתְכַּחֲשׁוּ לְהוּ מֵעִיקָּרָא! אֶלָּא שְׁמַע מִינַּהּ: הַכְחָשָׁה תְּחִילַּת הֲזָמָה הִיא. וְאַבַּיֵי אָמַר לָךְ: בִּשְׁלָמָא רֵישָׁא לָא סַגִּי דְּלָא שָׁלֹשׁ כִּיתּוֹת, שֶׁהֲרֵי קָתָנֵי: "הָרַב אוֹמֵר כֵּן", אֶלָּא סֵיפָא לָמָּה לִי שָׁלֹשׁ כִּיתּוֹת – "שֶׁהֲרֵי הָעֶבֶד אוֹמֵר כֵּן"? עֶבֶד כׇּל דְּהוּ מֵימַר אָמַר, דְּנִיחָא לֵיהּ דְּנֵיפּוֹק לְחֵירוּת. מַתְקִיף לַהּ ר' זֵירָא, אֵימָא: "סִימֵּא אֶת עֵינוֹ" –
נֵיפּוֹק

מִדְּסֵיפָא. בִּשְׁתֵּי כִּיתּוֹת. לְהָכִי תָּלֵי רֵישָׁא בְּסֵיפָא, דְּרֵישָׁא לָא נִיחָא לַן לְאוֹקְמָהּ בִּשְׁתֵּי כִּיתּוֹת אֶלָּא בְּג׳, מִשּׁוּם דְּקָתָנֵי "שֶׁהֲרֵי הָרַב אוֹמֵר כֵּן", וְאִי דְּלָא אֲתַאי כַּת אַחֲרִיתִי מִקַּמֵּי דִּידְהוּ וַאֲמַרוּ אִיפְּכָא – לָא הֲוָה נִיחָא לֵיהּ בְּהָנֵי, דְּמַפְּקִי לֵיהּ לָעֶבֶד לְחֵירוּת. אֶלָּא מִדְּסֵיפָא מִיתּוֹקְמָא בִּשְׁתֵּי כִּיתּוֹת, וְע"כ בְּמֵיפַךְ וַהֲזָמָה מוֹקְמֵית לֵיהּ – הִלְכָּךְ רֵישָׁא נַמִי אוֹקֵי בְּמֵיפַךְ וַהֲזָמָה. **שֶׁהֲרֵי הָעֶבֶד אוֹמֵר כֵּן.** דְּנִיחָא לֵיהּ דְּמַפְּקִי לֵיהּ לְחֵירוּת, וְיָהֲבֵי לֵיהּ דְּמֵי עַיִן. **בַּתְרָאֵי.** אוֹתָן שֶׁמְּזִימִין. **אִילֵימָא דְּלָא קָמוֹדוּ.** הָנָךְ בַּתְרָאֵי בַּחֲבָלָא דְּעֶבֶד כְּלָל, אֶלָּא דְּקָאָמְרִי: עִמָּנוּ הֱיִיתֶם, וְתוּ לָא מִידֵּי. **כּוּלֵּיהּ עֶבֶד.** בָּעֵי קַמָּאֵי לְשַׁלּוּמֵי. **וְאַפְּכִינְהוּ.** וְאַהֲנוּ לֵיהּ לָרַב לְפוֹטְרוֹ מִדְּמֵי עַיִן שֶׁהֵן מְרוּבִּין מִדְּמֵי שֵׁן, וּמִיהוּ עֶבֶד נָפֵיק לְחֵירוּת. **וְאַזְמִינְהוּ.** וְהָכָא לֵיכָּא לְמֵימַר כִּדְאָמַר רָבָא בְּרֵישָׁא, דַּאֲתַאי כַּת אַחֲרִיתִי מִקַּמֵּי דִּידְהוּ וְאָמְרִי אִיפְּכָא: סִימֵּא אֶת עֵינוֹ וְהִפִּיל אֶת שִׁינּוֹ. דְּאִי אֲתַאי כַּת אַחֲרִיתִי בְּרֵישָׁא, וַהֲדַר אֲמַרִי הָנֵי: הִפִּיל אֶת שִׁינּוֹ וְסִימֵּא אֶת עֵינוֹ, כֵּיוָן דְּלָא אַפּוּמַיְיהוּ פָּסְקִינַן דִּינָא אֶלָּא בָּרִאשׁוֹנִים שֶׁמַּזְקִיקִים אֶת הָרַב לִדְמֵי שֵׁן שֶׁיֶּשְׁנוֹ בִּכְלַל דְּמֵי עַיִן שֶׁל אַחֲרוֹנִים, אֲפִילּוּ נִמְצְאוּ זוֹמְמִין אֵלּוּ הָאַחֲרוֹנִים – לָא הָוֵי מְחַיְּיבוּ, דְּאֵין עֵדִים זוֹמְמִים מִתְחַיְּיבִים עַד שֶׁיִּגָּמֵר הַדִּין עַל פִּיהֶם. הִלְכָּךְ, הַךְ סֵיפָא מוֹכְחָא לְפוּס רִיהֲטָא בִּשְׁתֵּי כִּיתּוֹת, וּמֵיפַךְ וַהֲזָמָה. **וְהֵיכִי דָּמֵי.** בֵּין רֵישָׁא וּבֵין סֵיפָא, כֵּיוָן דְּהַשְׁתָּא מוֹקְמַתְּ לָהּ בְּמֵיפַךְ וַהֲזָמָה וּבִשְׁתֵּי כִּיתּוֹת עֵדִים, הֵיכִי דָּמֵי? **אִי דִּמְאַחֲרֵי אַחוּרֵי הָנֵי בַּתְרָאֵי.** כְּגוֹן דְּאָמְרִי קַמָּאֵי: יוֹם רִאשׁוֹן הֲוָה מַעֲשֶׂה, וַאֲתוּ בַּתְרָאֵי וְאָמְרִי: °יוֹם שֵׁנִי הֲוָה מַעֲשֶׂה, וְאִיפְּכָא הֲוָה. **אַכַּתִּי כּוּלֵּיהּ עֶבֶד** בָּעֵי לְשַׁלּוּמֵי לָרַב. דְּכִי מְחַיְּיבִי לֵיהּ מִיּוֹם רִאשׁוֹן לְהוֹצִיא עַבְדּוֹ לְחֵירוּת – אַכַּתִּי לָא הֲוָה בַּר חִיּוּבָא, דְּהָא בְּיוֹם שֵׁנִי הֲוָה מַעֲשֶׂה. וְאַכַּתִּי כּוּלֵּיהּ עֶבֶד בָּעֵי לְשַׁלּוּמֵי לָרַב, דְּכִי אֲתוּ לְאַסְהוּדֵי לְחִיּוּבֵיהּ לָרַב – אַכַּתִּי לָאו בַּר חִיּוּבָא הוּא. **דִּמְקַדְּמֵי אַקְדּוּמֵי הָנֵי בַּתְרָאֵי.** שֶׁהֵם מוֹדִים דְּקוֹדֶם שֶׁבָּאת כַּת רִאשׁוֹנָה לְהָעִיד נַעֲשָׂה מַעֲשֶׂה. **וְאִי דְּלָא הֶעֱמִידוֹ.** הָעֶבֶד לְרַבּוֹ בַּדִּין קוֹדֶם שֶׁבָּאת כַּת רִאשׁוֹנָה לְהָעִיד – אַכַּתִּי כּוּלֵּי דְּמֵי עֶבֶד בָּעֵי שַׁלּוּמֵי, דְּהָא כּוּלֵּיהּ בָּעֵי אַפְסוּדֵיהּ מִינֵּיהּ. **דְּאַכַּתִּי גַּבְרָא לָא מִיחַיַּיב,** דְּאִי הֲוָה בָּעֵי – הֲוָה אָתָא לְבֵי דִינָא וּמוֹדֶה וּמִפַּטַר, דְּמוֹדֶה בִּקְנָס פָּטוּר, וְחֵירוּת דְּשֵׁן וְעַיִן קְנָסָא הוּא. **כְּשֶׁעָמַד בַּדִּין.** עַל הַחֲבָלוֹת הַלָּלוּ ע"י עֵדִים אֲחֵרִים בְּב"ד אַחֵר, וְחִיְּיבוּהוּ לְהַנִּיחַ הָעֶבֶד, וּבָרַח, דְּהַשְׁתָּא אִי קָאָתֵי בְּעָלִים קַמָּן – הָא לָא מְהַנְּיָא לֵיהּ הוֹדָאָה. וְקָתָבַע לֵיהּ הַאי עֶבֶד: הִפַּלְתָּ אֶת שִׁינִּי, וְסִימֵּתָ אֶת עֵינִי, וְהַעֲמַדְתִּיךָ בַּדִּין וְנִתְחַיַּיבְתָּ לִי דְּמֵי עֵינִי, וְהֵבִיא עֵדִים אֵלּוּ עַל כָּךְ. וַאֲתוּ סָהֲדֵי אַחֲרִינֵי וְאַפְּכִינְהוּ, וַאֲמַרוּ: לָא חַיְּיבִינְהוּ ב"ד אֶלָּא דְּמֵי שֵׁן, וְאַזְמִינְהוּ. הִלְכָּךְ, בֵּין רֵישָׁא וּבֵין סֵיפָא – אַדְּמֵי עֶבֶד לָא מְחַיְּיבֵי, דְּהָא מִבְּ"ד קַמָּא נָפַק עֶבֶד לְחֵירוּת, אֶלָּא שֶׁזֶּה הָיָה מַחֲזִיק בּוֹ. אֲבָל דְּמֵי עַיִן מְשַׁלְּמִי לְעֶבֶד בְּבָבָא דְּרֵישָׁא, דְּהָא מָמוֹנָא דְּעַיִן אִית לֵיהּ גַּבֵּיהּ מִבֵּית דִּין קַמָּא, וְקָבָעוּ הָנֵי לְמִיפְטְרֵיהּ. וּבְסֵיפָא מְשַׁלְּמִי דְּמֵי עַיִן לָרַב – דְּקָא מְחַיְּיבֵי לֵיהּ אַשִּׁקְרָא. וְע"כ בִּדְאַפְּכִינְהוּ מוֹקְמַתְּ לֵיהּ, דְּאִי לָאו הָכִי, כֵּיוָן דְּלֵיכָּא סָהֲדֵי אַבֵּי דִינָא קַמָּא – כּוּלֵּיהּ עֶבֶד בָּעֵי שַׁלּוּמֵי. **דּוּקְיָא דְּרָבָא.** דְּהַכְחָשָׁה תְּחִילַּת הֲזָמָה הִיא, מֵהֵיכָא? **אִילֵימָא מֵרֵישָׁא.** דְּמוֹקֵי לָהּ בְּשָׁלֹשׁ כִּיתּוֹת. סוֹף סוֹף מִי קָא אִיתְכַּחֲשׁוּ דְּתֶיהֱוֵי עֵדוּתָן בְּטֵילָה בְּהַכְחָשָׁה דְּקַמָּאֵי? הָא אִי לָאו מִיתַּזְמִי – דִּינָא כְּוָותַיְיהוּ פָּסְקִינַן, וְיָהֵיב דְּמֵי שֵׁן, דְּיֶשְׁנוֹ בִּכְלַל עֵדוּת הָרִאשׁוֹנִים, וּמִשּׁוּם הָכִי מְהַנְּיָא בְּהֶן תּוֹרַת הֲזָמָה. אֲבָל גַּבֵּי שְׁנַיִם אוֹמְרִים הָרַג וּשְׁנַיִם אוֹמְרִים לֹא הָרַג, דְּאִיתְכַּחוּשׁ קַמָּאֵי וְלָא קָטְלִינַן לֵיהּ – וּלְעוֹלָם אֵימָא לָךְ: כֵּיוָן דִּבְטֵיל סַהֲדוּתַיְיהוּ לָא מְהַנְּיָא בְּהוּ תּוֹרַת הֲזָמָה. **מִדְּרֵישָׁא.** מוֹכְחָא בְּשָׁלֹשׁ כִּיתּוֹת, דְּקָתָנֵי "שֶׁהֲרֵי הָרַב אוֹמֵר כֵּן", אַלְמָא דַּאֲתוּ כַּת אַחֲרִיתִי בְּרֵישָׁא דַּהֲוָה מְחַיֵּיב לֵיהּ דְּמֵי עַיִן. **סֵיפָא נַמִי בְּשָׁלֹשׁ.** כִּיתּוֹת. וְנִהִי דְּלָא אֶפְשָׁר דְּתֶהֱוֵי כַּת אַחֲרִיתִי קוֹדֶמֶת, דְּא"כ דְּקַמָּאֵי אָמְרִי סִימֵּא וַהֲדַר הִפִּיל, וְהָנֵי אָמְרִי הִפִּיל, וַהֲדַר סִימֵּא – לָא מִיגְמַר דִּינָא אַפּוּמַיְיהוּ לְמֵיתַן דְּמֵי עֵינָא אֶלָּא דְּמֵי שֵׁן, וְהָוֵי בִּכְלָלָא דְּתַרְוַיְיהוּ. וְכֵיוָן דְּלָא נִגְמַר הַדִּין עַל פִּיהֶם – לָא מְחַיְּיבֵי הָנֵי מְלִיעָאֵי בַּהֲזָמָה דְּכַת שְׁלִישִׁית. מִיהוּ, הָכִי מוֹקֵי לָהּ – דַּאֲתוּ הָנֵי בֵּי תְּרֵי בְּרֵישָׁא וְאָמְרִי: הִפִּיל וַהֲדַר סִימֵּא, וּפָסְקִינַן לְדִינָא אַפּוּמַיְיהוּ כו׳. **דְּקָא מַכְחֲשֵׁי לְקַמָּאֵי.** וּבָטְלָה עֵדוּתָן, דְּלָא יָהֵיב דָּמִים הַיְּתֵירִים. וְקָתָנֵי דְּכִי נִמְצְאוּ זוֹמְמִים עַל יְדֵי כַּת שְׁלִישִׁית – מְשַׁלְּמִין. **אֶלָּא סֵיפָא לָמָּה לִי.** לְאוֹקְמָהּ בְּדוּחְקָא בְּשָׁלֹשׁ כִּיתּוֹת? הָא בִּתְרֵי סַגְיָא, וּבִדְאַפְּכִינְהוּ וְאַזְמִינְהוּ. וְרֵישָׁא כִּדְמַשְׁמַע – בִּשְׁלֹשָׁה, וּדְלָא בִּדְאַפְּכִינְהוּ. וּמִיהוּ, מִינַּהּ לֵיכָּא לְמֵידַק מִידֵּי.
נֵיפּוֹק

כדפרכינן לעיל: בתר דמפקי ליה לחירות דמי עין בעי לשלומי ליה? ויכולין לומר לטובתו באנו, כדאמר בפ׳ "היו בודקין" (סנהדרין מא.) דיכולין לומר: לאוסרה על בעלה באנו! וי"ל: דלמאי דמוקי לה השתא במיפך והזמה, מסקינן דאיירי כשעמד כבר בדין, ומסתמא כבר נתפרסם הדבר שילא העבד לחירות. והרב בעצמו מודה, כדקתני: שהרב אומר כך, שעמד בדין, וכל עיקר שבאין לדין עכשיו לפי שהעבד תובע דמי עינו ומזמין את הרב לדין, ורבו מודה לו דמי שינו. לכך, כי אתו סהדי — לא אתו אלא לגרע כחו של עבד, שאם יבאו עדים על דמי עינו — לא יהיה ממש בדבריהם, ויודעים הם שיבאו עדים. אבל מעיקרא, לא הוה ידעינן דמיירי כשעמד בדין, אפי׳ הרב מודה כמה פעמים — צריך העבד לעדים, דמודה בקנס פטור, משום הכי פריך שפיר: בתר דמפקי ליה לחירות כו׳. וא"ת: למה דחק אביי לאוקמי לסיפא במיפך והזמה? כיון דבעמד בדין מוקמינן לה, יאמר שהעבד תובעו דמי עינו והרב מודה לו דמי שינו, והביא עבד עדים דהפיל את שינו וסימא את עינו, ובאו עדים והזימום! וי"ל: דודאי ה"ה כך שוה אם מיפך הוה ע"י הודאת הרב כמו על פי עדים, אלא אורחא דמילתא נקט, שאין רגילות הרב להודות כלל אלא כשיש עדים בדבר.

דאכתי גברא לא מחייב. אין הטעם משום דאי הוה בעי הוה אתי לב"ד ומודה ומיפטר, דאפי׳ לשמואל דאמר לקמן (דף עה.): מודה בקנס ואח"כ באו עדים חייב — הכא, כיון דלא עמד בדין — לא חשבינן לגברא בר חיובא לענין קנס, כדפרישית בסוף "המניח" (לעיל לג. ושם: ד"ה איכא) בשמעתין דהוחלט השור.

ונמצאו זוממים קמאי. בהך סיפא הוצרך לומר שהעדים שהוזכרו בברייתא שהוזמו הם היו ראשונים, משום דצריך לומר דפסקינן לדינא אפומייהו. דאין העדים זוממים משלמים עד שיגמר הדין על פיהם, ואם לא שבאו תחילה — לא ה"מ למפסק דינא אפומייהו. אבל ברישא, אע"פ שבאו לסוף פסקינן דינא אפומייהו.

עבד כל דהו מימר אמר. הרבה יש לתמוה: אמאי קאמר כל דהו? דלגמרי באין לסיועיה!
הוה

צה א מיי׳ פי"ט מהל׳ עדות הלכה ב:

הגהות הב"ח
(א) גמ׳ ודקא אפכינהו ואזמינהו:

[ד"ה איכא]

גליון הש"ס
רש"י ד"ה אי דמאחרי כו׳ יום שני הוה. וקשה לי הא בזה לא בעי שלומי דכי העידו היה באמת חייב וזהו בכלל מה דמשני אלא דאקדמי אקדומי וכמ"ש רש"י ד"ה דמקדמי דכל שקודם שבאת כת שניה להעיד נעשה מעשה סגי. והו"ל לרש"י לפרש דמאחרי שאומרים שאחר שהעידו נעשה המעשה וצ"ע:

ניפוק בעינו, הפיל את שינו — ניפוק בשינו, סימא את עינו והפיל את שינו — ניפוק בעינו ושינו! אמר אביי: עליך אמר קרא: "תחת עינו" (שמות כא) — ולא תחת עינו ושינו, "תחת שינו" — ולא תחת שינו ועינו. אמר רב אידי בר אבין, אף אנן נמי תנינא: גנב ע"פ שנים וטבח ומכר על פיהם, ונמצאו זוממין — משלמין לו את הכל; מאי לאו דהעידו על הגניבה וחזרו והעידו על הטביחה, והוזמו על הגניבה וחזרו והוזמו על הטביחה; והא כיון שהוזמו על הגניבה, לגבי טביחה הוה להו מוכחשין, וקתני: משלמין לו את הכל. ואי ס"ד הכחשה לאו תחילת הזמה היא, אטביחה אמאי משלמין? אלא לאו ש"מ: הכחשה תחילת הזמה היא! אמרי: הכא במאי עסקינן — כגון שהוזמו על הטביחה תחילה. ובפלוגתא, עדים שהוכחשו ולבסוף הוזמו — ר' יוחנן ור"א, חד אמר: נהרגין, וחד אמר: אין נהרגין. תסתיים דר"א הוא דאמר אין נהרגין, דאמר ר"א: עדים שהוכחשו בנפש — לוקין, ואי ס"ד ר"א הוא דאמר נהרגין, אמאי לוקין? הוה ליה לאו שניתן לאזהרת מיתת ב"ד, *וכל לאו שניתן לאזהרת מיתת ב"ד ^ב^אין לוקין עליו! אלא לאו ש"מ: ר"א הוא דאמר אין נהרגין, תסתיים. לוקין? תרי ותרי נינהו, מאי חזית דסמכת אהני? סמוך אהני! אמר אביי: בבא הרוג ברגליו.§ **מתני'** ^ג^גנב ע"פ שנים, וטבח ומכר ע"פ עד אחד או ע"פ עצמו — משלם תשלומי כפל ואינו משלם תשלומי ד' וה'. ^ד^גנב וטבח בשבת, גנב וטבח לע"ז, ^ה^גנב משל אביו ומת אביו ואח"כ טבח ומכר, *^ו^גנב והקדיש ואח"כ טבח ומכר — משלם תשלומי כפל ואינו משלם תשלומי ד' וה'; *ר"ש אומר: קדשים שחייב באחריותם — משלם תשלומי ד' וה', שאין חייב באחריותם — פטור.§ **גמ'** על פי עד אחד, פשיטא! אמרי: הא קמ"ל, ע"פ עצמו דומיא דע"פ עד אחד, מה ע"פ [עד] אחד — כי אתי עד אחד מצטרף בהדיה מיחייב, ע"פ עצמו נמי — כי אתו עדים מיחייב; לאפוקי מדרב הונא אמר רב, דאמר רב הונא אמר רב: *^ז^מודה בקנס ואח"כ באו עדים — פטור.§ גופא, אמר רב הונא אמר רב: מודה בקנס ואח"כ באו עדים — פטור.§ איתיביה רב חסדא לרב הונא: מעשה בר"ג שסימא את עין טבי עבדו, והיה שמח שמחה גדולה; מצאו לר' יהושע, אמר לו: אי אתה יודע שטבי עבדי יצא לחירות? אמר לו: למה? א"ל: שסמיתי את עינו, אמר לו: אין בדבריך כלום, [א] שכבר אין לו עדים; הא יש לו עדים — חייב. ושמעינן מינה: מודה בקנס ואח"כ באו עדים — חייב! א"ל: שאני ר"ג, [ב] ^ח^דלא בפני ב"ד אודי. והא ר' יהושע אב בית דין הוה! שלא

רש"י

ניפוק בעינו ובשינו. ולעולם דמי לא ניתב ליה! מאי לאו שהעידו על הגניבה. שגנב באחד בשבת. וחזרו והעידו. שטבח בשני בשבת, והוזמו על יום ראשון בשלישי בשבת. וחזרו והוזמו. ברביעי בשבת על יום שני. וקתני משלמין ד' וה'. ואע"ג דמשלישי בשבת היו מוכחשים על הטביחה, דכיון דלא גנב — לא טבח. על הטביחה תחילה. ונתחייבו בתשלומי שלשה, ועדיין עדות גניבה קיימת. וכשהוזמו ונתחייבו בכפל — הרי חמשה. ובפלוגתא. דאביי ורבא, פליגי נמי ר' יוחנן ור' אלעזר. דאמר ר"א עדים שהוכחשו בנפש. ולא הוזמו. לוקין. משום "לא תענה". ואע"ג דלאו שאין בו מעשה הוא — הא מייתי בהדיא במס' מכות (ד' ב:) דמלקות בעדים זוממין כתיב, מ"והצדיקו [את] הצדיק" [וגו']. ואי ס"ד. לר"א, אם הוזמו אחרי כן — נהרגין, כי לא הוזמו — אמאי לוקין? הוה ליה לאו שניתן לאזהרת [כו']. שלא יעשה כך, שלא ימיתוהו בית דין. ואין לוקין עליו. דמיתת ב"ד הוא עונשו של לאו. מאי חזית דסמכת כו'. בשלמא הזמה — חידוש, גזירת הכתוב הוא. אבל הכחשה — לאו חידוש, [*כשמתכרה] גופה של עדות הוא דכתביה רחמנא. בבא הרוג ברגליו. אותו שאמר עליו שהוא נהרג, בא חי ברגליו לפנינו. **מתני'** משלם תשלומי כפל דהאיכא סהדי אגניבה. ואינו משלם ד' וה'. על הודאת עצמו, דמודה בקנס פטור. וגנב וטבח בשבת. פטור אטביחה, דהוי מתחייב בנפשו. ומת אביו. והוא יורשו, ולא הויא טביחה כולה באיסורא. גנב והקדיש. כי קא טבח — דהקדש טבח, ולא דבעלים. ר"ש אומר כו'. בגמרא מפ' אהייא. **גמ'** ע"פ עד אחד פשיטא. בשלמא ע"פ עצמו — איצטריך לאשמועינן דמודה בקנס פטור, אלא ע"פ עד אחד למה לי? כי אתי עד אחד מצטרף. דהלכה *כר' יהושע בן קרחה, דאמר בסנהדרין (ד' ל.): שומעין דבריו של זה היום, וכשיבא חבירו למחר שומעין את דבריו. כי אתו עדים מחייב. וכי אמרי' דמודה בקנס פטור — היכא דלא באו עדים אחרי כן. טבי. שם העבד. והיה שמח. לפי שעבד כשר היה, והיה מתאוה לשחררו, אלא שהמשחרר עבדו עובר בעשה. שכבר אין לך עדים. ועל פי עצמך לא תשלם קנס. הא יש לו עדים. ואתו בתר הודאה — חייב. שלא

תוספות

הוה ליה לאו שניתן לאזהרת מיתת ב"ד. אבל אי אין נהרגין — לא חשיב לאו שניתן לאזהרת מיתת ב"ד. ותימה לר"י: דבכל גמרא משמע אפי' התרו בו למלקות ולא למיתה, דאע"ג שלעולם לא יבא לידי חיוב מיתה, כיון שלא התרו בו למיתה — חשיב לאו שניתן לאזהרת מיתת ב"ד. ובפרק "מי שהחשיך" (שבת דף קנד. ושם ד"ה בלאו) אמר דאין לוקין על לאו דמחמר משום דהוי לאו שניתן לאזהרת מיתת ב"ד לשאר מלאכות, אע"ג דבמחמר אין בו חיוב מיתה. ובפ"ק דעירובין (דף יז:) אמר דאין לוקין בתחומין דהוי אזהרה נמי להוצאה. ואפי' מאן דפליג נמי לא קאמר אלא משום דמי כתיב "אל יוציא"? "אל יצא" כתיב, אע"פ שאין מיתה בתחומין אפילו למ"ד דאורייתא! ותי' ר"י: דשאני לאו ד"לא תענה" דגלי ביה קרא דלקי מ"והיה אם בן הכות הרשע", כדאמרינן בריש מכות (דף ב. ושם) ובפ"ק דסנהדרין (דף י. ושם*), וכיון דגלי קרא — מוקמינן ליה לקרא במקום שאין יכול לבא לידי חיוב מיתה, כי ההיא דהתם דמעידין שהוא בן גרושה או בן חלוצה, או כמו עדים שהוכחשו בנפש, למ"ד אין נהרגין כשהוזמו לבסוף. אבל למ"ד נהרגין — אין סברא להעמיד בו הפסוק, כיון שיכול לבא לידי חיוב מיתה. וכי פריך התם דת"ל מ"לא תענה", פי': ולמ"ל קרא ד"והיה אם בן הכות הרשע", ומשני: משום דה"ל לאו שאין בו מעשה, הוה מצי לשנויי דהוה לאו שניתן לאזהרת מיתת ב"ד כה"ג בעלמא לא לקי, אלא דבעי לשנויי לכ"ע, אפי' אליבא דר"מ דנפקא ליה אזהרה לעדים זוממים מקרא אחרינא בפ"ק דמכות (ד' ד:). וא"ת: והשתא דמשני משום דה"ל לאו שאין בו מעשה — לא אתי אליבא דר' יהודה דאמר (שם) לאו שאין בו מעשה לוקין עליו! וי"ל: דדחיק טפי לשנויי כר"מ, משום דאיירי התם (שם.) בסיפא גבי מאתים זוז, וגבי מלקות משמע דבבן גרושה או בן חלוצה מודה. א"נ: אתי ההוא שינויא כרבי יהודה, דהא טעמא דרבי יהודה דאמר לאו שאין בו מעשה לוקין עליו — משום דגמר ממוציא ש"ר ומעדים זוממין בבנין אב, ואי לאו דגלי בעדים זוממין מ"והיה אם בן הכות הרשע" — הוה אמרי' בכל דוכתי דלאו שאין בו מעשה אין לוקין עליו. וא"ת: דההיא שינויא היכי אתי אליבא דר"מ? והא לר"מ בלא "והיה אם בין הכות הרשע" ידעינן דלקו עדים זוממין אע"פ שאין בו מעשה, דגמרינן ממוציא ש"ר, כי היכי דגמר בפ"ק דמכות (שם:) ממוציא ש"ר דעדים זוממין לוקין ומשלמין! וי"ל: דאע"ג דגמר ממוציא ש"ר — היינו דוקא לענין שלוקין ומשלמין, משום דאיכא לאוקמי "כדי רשעתו" לדרשה אחריתי, *כדאיתא ב"אלו נערות" (כתובות דף לג.). אבל לענין לאו שאין בו מעשה, דילפינן מ"לעשות" ב"אלו הן הלוקין" (מכות ד' יג:) דבעינן לאו שיש בו מעשה — לא הוה גמרינן ממוציא ש"ר אי לאו דגלי קרא בהדיא. ועוד י"ל: דמוציא ש"ר גופיה לא נפקא לן דלקי אלא מ"והיה אם בן הכות הרשע", כדאמר בכתובות פרק "נערה" (ד' מו.) דגמר "ויסרו" מ"ויסרו" כו'. והא דאמר בפ"ק דמכות (ד' ד:): ורבנן האי "לא תענה" מאי דרשי ביה? ההוא מיבעי ליה לאזהרת עדים זוממין. פי': ולהכי לא לקי אלא ארבעים במעידים על פלוני שחייב מלקות, לא בעי למימר דלא לקי א"לא תענה" משום דהוי לאו שניתן לאזהרת מיתת ב"ד — דהא במעידים עליו שהוא בן גרושה אמרי רבנן דלקי, ובמעידים שחייב לפלוני מאתים זוז אי לאו "כדי רשעתו" היו לוקין ומשלמין. אלא ה"פ: ההוא מבעי ליה לאזהרת עדים זוממין, דמשום "כאשר זמם" לא לקו כשמעידים על פלוני שחייב מלקות, אלא משום "לא תענה", דלא ענש הכתוב אא"כ הזהיר. הלכך, אלאו ד"לא תענה" לא לקי שמונים, פי': שילקו משום עדות שקר שהעידו ומשום "כאשר זמם" ותרוייהו משום לאו אחד. אבל במעידים שחייב מאה זוז, דבלאו קרא ד"לא תענה" היה מתחייב לשלם משום "כאשר זמם", דממון לא בעי אזהרה — התם ודאי אי לאו "כדי רשעתו" הוה לקי מ"לא תענה", וכן במעידים שהוא בן גרושה או בן חלוצה. **כי** **אתא עד אחד מצטרף בהדיה.** למ"ד סנהדרין (ד' ל.) אין עדותן מצטרפת עד שיעידו שניהם כאחד, הוי הכא השני מצטרף בהדיה — היינו שיעידו שניהם (א) בב"ד. משום

עין משפט נר מצוה

צו א מיי' פ"ה מהל' עבדים הל' יד ועיין בהשגות ובכ"מ ופ"ד מהלכות חובל ומזיק הל' יא וע"ש סמג עשין עא פז טור ש"ע י"ד סימן רסז סעיף לט:

צז ב מיי' פי"ח מהלכות סנהדרין הלכה ב:

צח ג מיי' פ"ג מהל' גניבה הלכה ז סמג עשין עא טוח"מ סי' שנ:

צט ד מיי' שם הל' ג סמג שם טוח"מ שם:

ק ה ו מיי' שם פ"ב הלכה ו:

קא ז ח מיי' שם פ"ג הלכה ח סמג שם טוח"מ שם:

הגהות הב"ח

(א) תום' ד"ה כי אתא וכו' שניהם כאחד בב"ד:

הגהות הגר"א

[א] גמ' שכבר אין לו עדים. נ"ב ש"מ דאף לגאת ידי שמים אין צריך בקנס בלא עדים. ירושלמי פ"ג דכתובות. וה"ה לאבק רבית. רשב"א. וכ"י חולק (ועי' בהגר"א יו"ד סימן קסא סק"ז): [ב] שם דלא בפני ב"ד אודי. נ"ב וה"ה האידנא דליכא ב"ד מומחין:

גליון הש"ס

גמ' בבא הרוג ברגליו. כריתות כד ע"א: **מתני'** **וטבח** ומכר ע"פ עד אחד. והא דלא אמרינן דנתחייב שבועה להכחיש העד וא"י לישבע דהא נעשה פסול ע"י שניים שמעידים שגנב. והו"ל חשוד דכנגדו נשבע ונוטל היינו דבקנס אינו צריך לישבע נגד העד כיון דאילו מודה מיפטר וכמ"ש תוס' לעיל דף מה ע"ב ד"ה מודה וכו' דאין סברא לומר וכו': **תד"ה** ה"ל כו' אפי' התרו בו למלקות. עי' סנהדרין דף סג ע"א תד"ה משום:

מסורת הש"ס

שמות כא

[ד"ה משום]

רש"ל ועי' מכות ה.

[שבת קנד. עירובין יז: סנהדרין פו: מכות יג: שבועות ז.]

[לעיל סח: גיטין נה:]

[לעיל עח:]

נראה שיש למחוק כריב"ל ולהגיה במקומו כרבי נתן אך מאחר שמבואר בסנהדרין ל. דריב"ק תנא לרבי נתן נראה לא למחקו מהרש"ל

[לעיל יד:]

[נראה דצ"ל כדפרישית באלו נערות ור"ל בד"ה דאין]

שֶׁלֹּא בְּבֵית דִּין הֲוָה קָאֵי. וְהָתַנְיָא, אָמַר לוֹ: אֵין בִּדְבָרֶיךָ כְּלוּם, שֶׁכְּבָר הוֹדֵיתָ; מַאי לָאו תַּנָּאֵי הִיא, הַאי תַּנָּא דְּאָמַר "שֶׁכְּבָר אֵין לְךָ עֵדִים" סָבַר: מוֹדֶה בִּקְנָס וְאַחַר כָּךְ בָּאוּ עֵדִים — חַיָּיב, וְהַאי תַּנָּא דְּאָמַר "שֶׁכְּבָר הוֹדֵיתָ" סָבַר: מוֹדֶה בִּקְנָס וְאח"כ בָּאוּ עֵדִים — פָּטוּר? לָא, דְּכ"ע — מוֹדֶה בִּקְנָס וְאח"כ בָּאוּ עֵדִים פָּטוּר, וּבְהָא קָמִיפַּלְגִי: הַאי תַּנָּא דְּאָמַר "שֶׁכְּבָר אֵין לְךָ עֵדִים" סָבַר: חוּץ לְב"ד הֲוָה, וְהַךְ תַּנָּא דְּאָמַר "שֶׁכְּבָר הוֹדֵיתָ" סָבַר: בְּבֵית דִּין הֲוָה.§ אִיתְּמַר: מוֹדֶה בִּקְנָס וְאח"כ בָּאוּ עֵדִים — רַב אָמַר: פָּטוּר, וּשְׁמוּאֵל אָמַר: חַיָּיב. *אָמַר רָבָא בַּר אֲהִילַאי: מַאי טַעְמָא דְּרַב? °"אִם הִמָּצֵא" — בְּעֵדִים, "תִּמָּצֵא" — בְּדַיָּינִין, פְּרָט לְמַרְשִׁיעַ אֶת עַצְמוֹ, לָמָּה לִי? °מֵ"אֲשֶׁר יַרְשִׁיעֻן" נָפְקָא! אֶלָּא ש"מ: מוֹדֶה בִּקְנָס וְאח"כ בָּאוּ עֵדִים — פָּטוּר. וּשְׁמוּאֵל אָמַר לָךְ: הַהוּא מִבָּעֵי לֵיהּ לְגַנָּב עַצְמוֹ, *כִּדְתָנָא דְּבֵי חִזְקִיָּה. אֵיתִיבֵיהּ רַב לִשְׁמוּאֵל: *רָאָה עֵדִים שֶׁמְּמַשְׁמְשִׁים וּבָאִים, וְאָמַר "גָּנַבְתִּי, אֲבָל לֹא טָבַחְתִּי וְלֹא מָכַרְתִּי" — אֵינוֹ מְשַׁלֵּם אֶלָּא קֶרֶן! אֲמַר לֵיהּ: הָכָא בְּמַאי עָסְקִינַן — כְּגוֹן שֶׁחָזְרוּ עֵדִים לַאֲחוֹרֵיהֶם. וְהָא מִדְּתָנֵי סֵיפָא, רַבִּי אֶלְעָזָר בְּרַ' שִׁמְעוֹן אוֹמֵר: יָבוֹאוּ עֵדִים וְיָעִידוּ — מִכְּלָל דְּתַנָּא קַמָּא סָבַר: לֹא! אֲמַר לֵיהּ שְׁמוּאֵל: לָאו אִיכָּא ר' אֶלְעָזָר בְּרַ' שִׁמְעוֹן דְּקָאֵי כְּווֹתִי? אֲנָא דַּאֲמַרִי כְּרַ' אֶלְעָזָר בְּרַ' שִׁמְעוֹן. לִשְׁמוּאֵל וַדַּאי תַּנָּאֵי הִיא, לְרַב מִי לֵימָא תַּנָּאֵי הִיא? אָמַר לָךְ רַב: אֲנָא דַּאֲמַרִי אֲפִי' לְרַבִּי אֶלְעָזָר בְּרַ' שִׁמְעוֹן; עַד כָּאן לָא קָאָמַר ר' אֶלְעָזָר בְּרַ' שִׁמְעוֹן הָתָם — אֶלָּא מִשּׁוּם דְּקָא מוֹדֵי מֵחֲמַת בִּיעֲתוּתָא דְּעֵדִים, אֲבָל הָכָא דְּמוֹדֶה מֵעַצְמוֹ, אֲפִי' ר' אֶלְעָזָר בְּרַ' שִׁמְעוֹן מוֹדֶה. אָמַר רַב הַמְנוּנָא: מִסְתַּבְּרָא מִילְּתֵיהּ דְּרַב [א]בְּאוֹמֵר "גָּנַבְתִּי" וּבָאוּ עֵדִים שֶׁגָּנַב — פָּטוּר, שֶׁהֲרֵי חִיֵּיב עַצְמוֹ בְּקֶרֶן. אֲבָל אָמַר "לֹא גָּנַבְתִּי" וּבָאוּ עֵדִים שֶׁגָּנַב, וְחָזַר וְאָמַר "טָבַחְתִּי וּמָכַרְתִּי" וּבָאוּ עֵדִים שֶׁטָּבַח וּמָכַר — חַיָּיב, [ב]שֶׁהֲרֵי פָּטַר עַצְמוֹ מִכְּלוּם. אָמַר (א) רָבָא: [קִפַּחְתִּי] לְסָבֵי דְּבֵי רַב, דְּהָא רַבָּן גַּמְלִיאֵל פּוֹטֵר עַצְמוֹ מִכְּלוּם הֲוָה, וְקָאָמַר לֵיהּ רַב חִסְדָּא לְרַב הוּנָא וְלָא קָא מְשַׁנֵּי לֵיהּ. אִיתְּמַר נַמִי, אָמַר ר' חִיָּיא בַּר אַבָּא אָמַר ר' יוֹחָנָן: "גָּנַבְתִּי" וּבָאוּ עֵדִים שֶׁגָּנַב — פָּטוּר, שֶׁהֲרֵי חִיֵּיב עַצְמוֹ בְּקֶרֶן, אֲבָל אָמַר לֹא (ב) גָּנַב וּבָאוּ עֵדִים שֶׁגָּנַב, וְחָזַר וְאָמַר "טָבַחְתִּי וּמָכַרְתִּי" וּבָאוּ עֵדִים שֶׁטָּבַח וּמָכַר — חַיָּיב, שֶׁהֲרֵי פָּטַר עַצְמוֹ מִכְּלוּם. אָמַר רַב אַשִׁי: מַתְנִיתִין וּבָרַיְיתָא נַמִי דַּיְקָא; מַתְנִיתִין, דִּתְנַן: גָּנַב עַל פִּי שְׁנַיִם, וְטָבַח וּמָכַר ע"פ עֵד אֶחָד אוֹ עַל פִּי עַצְמוֹ — מְשַׁלֵּם תַּשְׁלוּמֵי כֶפֶל וְאֵינוֹ מְשַׁלֵּם תַּשְׁלוּמֵי אַרְבָּעָה וַחֲמִשָּׁה; לָמָּה לִי דְּתָנֵי גָּנַב עַל פִּי שְׁנַיִם? לִיתְנֵי: גָּנַב וְטָבַח [וּמָכַר] עַל פִּי עֵד אֶחָד אוֹ עַל פִּי עַצְמוֹ — אֵינוֹ מְשַׁלֵּם אֶלָּא הַקֶּרֶן! אֶלָּא

רש"י

שֶׁלֹּא בְּבֵית דִּין הֲוָה. לֹא הָיוּ בֵּית דִּין יוֹשְׁבִין, וְלֹא מְקוֹם יְשִׁיבַת ב"ד הֲוָה, אֶלָּא בַּשּׁוּק הוֹדָה לוֹ. שֶׁכְּבָר הוֹדֵיתָ. מַשְׁמַע: אֲפִילּוּ אָתוּ עֵדִים בָּתַר הָכִי – פָּטוּר. תִּמָּצֵא בְּדַיָּינִין פְּרָט לְמַרְשִׁיעַ אֶת עַצְמוֹ. וְהַאי קְרָא לְמ"ל? מֵ"אֲשֶׁר יַרְשִׁיעוּן אֱלֹהִים" נָפְקָא, פְּרָט לְמַרְשִׁיעַ אֶת עַצְמוֹ! אֶלָּא לָאו שְׁמַע מִינָּהּ: חַד לְמוֹדֶה בִּקְנָס וְלֹא *בְּעֵדִים, וְחַד לְמוֹדֶה בִּקְנָס וְאַחֲרֵי כֵן בָּאוּ עֵדִים. מִיבָּעֵי לֵיהּ לְגַנָּב עַצְמוֹ. לְחַיֵּיב כֶּפֶל לְגַנָּב עַצְמוֹ, דְּדָרְשִׁינַן כְּלָל וּפְרָט מֵ"הִמָּצֵא תִמָּצֵא" כִּדְתָנָא דְּבֵי חִזְקִיָּה (ג). גָּנַבְתִּי. וְחִיֵּיב עַצְמוֹ בַּקֶּרֶן. אֲבָל לֹא טָבַחְתִּי וְלֹא מָכַרְתִּי. רְבוּתָא אַשְׁמְעִי', כִּדְאָמְרִינַן לְקַמָּן, דְּאע"ג דְּאַטְבִיחָה לֹא הוֹדָה, וְנִמְצָא שֶׁטָּבַח אוֹ מָכַר, דְּבָאוּ עֵדִים – פָּטוּר. דְּכֵיוָן דְּמִכֶּפֶל אִיפְּטַר לֵיהּ בַּהוֹדָאָה דְּ"גָנַבְתִּי" – תּוּ לָא מִחַיֵּיב אַרְבָּעָה וַחֲמִשָּׁה, דְּכֵיוָן דְּמִדְלִית כֶּפֶל מִינַּיְיהוּ – הָוֵי לֵיהּ תַּשְׁלוּמֵי שְׁלֹשָׁה וְאַרְבָּעָה, וְהָנֵי לָא כְּתִיבִי. וְיָעִידוּ. לְאַחַר שֶׁהוֹדָה, וְיִתְחַיֵּיב קְנָסָא. לִשְׁמוּאֵל וַדַּאי תַּנָּאֵי הִיא. דְּהָא לָא מָצֵי לְמֵימַר דְּתַנָּא קַמָּא קָאֵי כְּוָותֵיהּ, דְּהַשְׁתָּא וּמַה הָכָא דְּשָׁמַע שֶׁמְּמַשְׁמְשִׁין וּבָאִין וּמֵחֲמַת בִּיעֲתוּתַיְיהוּ אוֹדֵי – פָּטַר לֵיהּ, וְאַף ע"ג דַּהֲדַרוּ אָתוּ. כָּל שֶׁכֵּן מוֹדֶה מֵעַצְמוֹ וְאח"כ בָּאוּ. לְרַב מִי לֵימָא. מִי אִיצְטְרִיכָא לֵיהּ לְאוֹקְמֵי מִילְּתֵיהּ כְּתַנָּאֵי, אוֹ דִּלְמָא מָצֵי לְשַׁנּוּיֵי לְרַ' אֶלְעָזָר בַּר ר' שִׁמְעוֹן אַלִּיבֵּיהּ, וּלְמֵימַר דְּשָׁנֵי לֵיהּ לְרַ' אֶלְעָזָר בֵּין רָאָה עֵדִים שֶׁמְּמַשְׁמְשִׁין וּבָאִין לְמוֹדֶה מֵעַצְמוֹ בְּלֹא פַּחַד עֵדִים? מִסְתַּבְּרָא מִילְּתֵיהּ דְּרַב. דְּפָטַר אֲפִילּוּ אִם בָּאוּ עֵדִים. בְּאוֹמֵר גָּנַבְתִּי. דְּחִיֵּיב עַצְמוֹ לְשַׁלֵּם קֶרֶן מִיהָא בַּהוֹדָאָה, הִלְכָּךְ הוֹדָאָה גְּמוּרָה הִיא, וּפָטוּר מִכֶּפֶל וּמֵאַרְבָּעָה וַחֲמִשָּׁה. שֶׁהֲרֵי פָּטַר עַצְמוֹ מִכְּלוּם. בַּהוֹדָאָה דִּטְבִיחָה לֹא הָיָה מְחַיֵּיב עַצְמוֹ בִּכְלוּם, שֶׁהָיָה יוֹדֵעַ שֶׁהַמּוֹדֶה בִּקְנָס פָּטוּר, הִלְכָּךְ – לָאו הוֹדָאָה הִיא, וּמְשַׁלֵּם אִם בָּאוּ עֵדִים. וְלָא אָמְרִינַן מוֹדֶה בִּקְנָס וּבָאוּ עֵדִים פָּטוּר אֶלָּא הֵיכָא דְּאִיכָּא קֶרֶן וּקְנָס, דְּאִיחַיֵּיב לֵיהּ מָמוֹנָא בְּהוֹדָאָתוֹ, וּמִתְכַּוֵּין לְהַחֲזִיר מָמוֹן. (ד) אָמַר רָבָא גָּרְסִינַן. וְלָא גָּרְסִינַן: אֲמַר לֵיהּ קַפַּחְתִּינְהוּ לְסָבֵי דְּבֵי רַב. רַב הַמְנוּנָא קָרֵי סָבֵי דְּבֵי רַב, כִּדְאָמַר בְּפ"ק דְּסַנְהֶדְרִין (דף יז:). [קִפַּחְתִּי]. *יֵשׁ בְּיָדִי תְּשׁוּבָה לְקַפֵּחַ דְּבָרָיו. דְּהָא רַבָּן גַּמְלִיאֵל. בַּהוֹדָאָה שֶׁסִּימֵּא אֶת עֵין עַבְדּוֹ פָּטַר עַצְמוֹ מִכְּלוּם הָיָה, דְּאֵין כָּאן אֶלָּא קְנָס, וְכִי מוֹדֶה – מִפַּטַּר מֵאֵלָיו, וְהָא חָזֵינַן לְעֵיל דְּאוֹתְבֵיהּ רַב חִסְדָּא לְרַב הוּנָא מִינָּהּ מִדּוּקְיָא דְּ"כְבָר אֵין לְךָ עֵדִים", הָא אָתוּ עֵדִים – מִחַיֵּיב. וְלָא שַׁנֵּי לֵיהּ. רַב הוּנָא לְמֵימַר דְּשָׁאנֵי רַבָּן גַּמְלִיאֵל דְּפוֹטֵר עַצְמוֹ מִכְּלוּם הֲוָה, וְכִי הַאי גַּוְונָא צְרִיכָא לֵיהּ לְאוֹקְמֵי בְּחוּץ לְבֵית דִּין, הָא בְּבֵית דִּין – מִיפַּטַר לֵיהּ בְּהַהִיא הוֹדָאָה אַלִּיבָּא דְּרַב. שֶׁהֲרֵי חִיֵּיב עַצְמוֹ בְּקֶרֶן. בְּהוֹדָאָה רִאשׁוֹנָה, הִלְכָּךְ נִפְטָר מִן הַכֶּפֶל. וְכֵיוָן דְּלֵיכָּא כֶּפֶל – תּוּ לָא מִחַיֵּיב בְּאַרְבָּעָה וַחֲמִשָּׁה. שֶׁהֲרֵי פָּטַר עַצְמוֹ מִכְּלוּם. כְּלוֹמַר: אֵין זֶה הוֹדָאָה, שֶׁהֲרֵי אֵינוֹ בָּא לְהָשִׁיב כְּלוּם בְּהוֹדָאָתוֹ, דְּיוֹדֵעַ הוּא דְּמוֹדֶה בִּקְנָס פָּטוּר, הִלְכָּךְ לִפְטוֹר עַצְמוֹ נִתְכַּוֵּין. לָמָּה לִי דְּקָתָנֵי. הָכִי? הוֹאִיל וַאֲתָא לְאַשְׁמוּעִינַן דְּמוֹדֶה בִּקְנָס פָּטוּר – לַשְׁמְעִינַן בֵּין בְּכֶפֶל וּבֵין בְּד' וַחֲמִשָּׁה, וְנִיתְנֵי: גָּנַב וְטָבַח וּמָכַר ע"פ עֵד אֶחָד אוֹ ע"פ עַצְמוֹ – אֵינוֹ מְשַׁלֵּם אֶלָּא קֶרֶן! אֶלָּא לָאו ש"מ: לְהָכִי לָא נְקַט הוֹדָאָה גַּבֵּי קֶרֶן וְכֶפֶל – דְּבָעֵי לְמִיתְנֵי ע"פ עַצְמוֹ דּוּמְיָא דְּעֵד אֶחָד, וּלְמֵימַר דְּאִי הֲדַר אֲתוֹ עֵדִים – חַיָּיב. וְאִי הֲוָה תָּנֵי הוֹדָאָה גַּבֵּי גְּנֵיבָה – תּוּ לָא מִיתְנֵי לֵיהּ ע"פ עַצְמוֹ דּוּמְיָא דְּעֵד אֶחָד, דְּאִ"נ אֲתוֹ עֵדִים פָּטוּר. אֲבָל הַשְׁתָּא דְּלָא אוֹדֵי בַּקֶּרֶן, דִּשְׁנֵי עֵדִים שֶׁהֵעִידוּ עַל הַגְּנֵיבָה חִיְּיבוּהוּ – מִחַיֵּיב אַף בְּאַרְבָּעָה וַחֲמִשָּׁה לְכִי אָתוּ סָהֲדֵי, כְּרַ' יוֹחָנָן. ה"ג

תוספות

משום ביעתותא דעדים קא מודה. והא דאמר בפרק "שבועת העדות" (שבועות ד' לג:) דלרבי אלעזר בר' שמעון לא משכחת לה דמודה מפי עצמו דפטור אלא היכא דליכא עדים כלל — היינו אליבא דשמואל.

אמר ליה רבא (ה) *קפחת לסבי דבי רב. פי' בקונטרס: ליערת תלמידים שבבית המדרש, שאמר דבר שאינו. דהא רב הונא דידע מילתיה דרב גדול ממך אין לו זה החילוק. וקשה: דבכל דוכתי הוי קיפוח לשון נילוח, כמו "לקפחני בהלכות הן באין" בפ' שני דקדושין (ד' נב:) ודנזיר (ד' מט:), וכמו "קפחינהו לתלתא רבנן סמיכי בטעותא" גיטין (ד' כט:)! ורשב"ם פי': דל"ג "אמר ליה רבא" אלא "אמר רבא קפחתי לסבי דבי רב", פירוש: נלחתי את רב המנונא, שהוא סבי דבי רב, והוכחתי לו מכח דברי רב הונא, שהיה יודע דברי רב יותר ממנו, שאין לחלק כמו שחילק. והביא ראיה מפ"ק דסנהדרין (ד' יז: ושם*) דאמר התם: "אמרי בי רב" — רב הונא. ופריך: והאמר רב הונא אמרי בי רב! ומשני: אלא אימא רב המנונא. ולהכי קרי ליה סבי דבי רב. וקשה: חדא, שמוחק כאן בספרים "אמר ליה", ועוד: דאין דרך לומר "איתמר נמי" אחרי שסתר את דבריו. ועוד: דכוותיה דרב המנונא דייק מתני' ובריית', כדאמר בסמוך, ולרב הונא מפקא מתני' מדברי רב! ונראה לפרש: אמר ליה רבא (ו) קפחת לסבי דבי רב. כלומר, אמר ליה רבא לרב המנונא: נלחת את רב הונא שהוא סבי דבי רב, שהוא לא ידע לחלק כאשר חלקת. ובסנהדרין מפרש ר"ת אימא רב המנונא — פירוש: לא תימא "אמר רב הונא אמרי בי רב", אלא: "אמר רב המנונא אמרי בי רב". וכן משמע, דלפי האמת נמי הוי "אמרי בי רב" — רב הונא, דב"הערל" (יבמות ד' פג: ושם*) קאמר: בי רב מני — רב הונא, ורב הונא אין הלכה קאמר. ובקונט' דחק שם לפרש דהא דאמר בסנהדרין אימא רב המנונא — דוקא היכא דמוכח, דהיינו היכא דאיכא "אמר רב הונא: אמרי בי רב" — התם הוי רב המנונא. וקשה: דא"כ כי קאמר בסנהדרין: "שלחו מתם" — רבי יוסי בר חנינא, "מחכו עליה במערבא" — ר' אלעזר. ופריך: הא שלחו מתם לרבי יוסי בר חנינא מוכח כו'. ומשני: אלא איפוך. ה"ל לשנויי: היכא דמוכח — שאני! ועוד: דלא יתכן כלל שיאמר רב הונא משום רב המנונא, שהיה תלמיד תלמידו, כדמשמע בריש "הדר" (עירובין ד' סג.). ואין להאריך כאן בזה.

בריית‍א

הגהות הב"ח

(א) גמ' אמר ליה רבא קפחתינהו לסבי דבי רב: (ב) שם אבל אמר לא גנבתי ובאו: (ג) רש"י ד"ה מבעי ליה וכו' דבי חזקיה. נ"ב לעיל סף דף ס"ג: (ד) ד"ה (אמר רבא גרסי' ולא גרסינן אמר ליה). תא"מ ונ"ב זהו מפי' רשב"ם ואח"כ מה"ד קפחתינהו לסבי דבי רב ליערת והכעסת והריעות לכל בני הישיבה של בית המדרש באמרך לפניהם דבר שאינו ותשובתו בצדו זהו פי' רש"י ולפי זה שפיר גרסי' אמר ליה ואח"כ מה"ד (רב המנונא קרי וכו' דבריו) תא"מ ונ"ב גם זה מפרשב"ם: (ה) תוס' ד"ה אמר ליה רבא קפחתינהו לסבי וכו' שאמרת דבר: (ו) בא"ד ונראה לפרש אמר ליה רבא קפחתינהו לסבי:

קב א ב מיי' פ"ג מהלכות גניבה הל' ט סמג עשין עא:

נ"א קפחתינהו רש"א

[ד"ה אלא]

[ד"ה אמרי]

ל"ל ולא באו עדים

לעיל סד:

לעיל סג:

שבועות מט. [ועי' תוס' כ"ה ד"ה ראה ולקמן ע"ב ד"ה ברייתא]

רש"ל נ"א קפחתינהו לסבי דבי רב ליערת והכעסת לכל בני הישיבה שאמרת בפניהם דבר שאינו תשובתו בצידו ומ"ש בפנים אינו מפי' רש"י ועיין רש"א

שמות כב

שם

קג א מיי' פכ"א מהל' עדות הלכה ו:
קד ב מיי' פ"כ מהל' עדות הלכה ז ופ"ב מהל' רוצח הלכה ט סמג לאוין קסא:

אֶלָּא לָאו הָא קמ"ל: גָּנַב עַל פִּי שְׁנַיִם וְטָבַח עַל פִּי עֵד אֶחָד אוֹ עַל פִּי עַצְמוֹ, (א) הוּא דְּלָא מְחַיֵּיב עַצְמוֹ בְּקֶרֶן — הוּא דְּאָמְרִינַן ע"פ עַצְמוֹ דּוּמְיָא דְּע"פ עֵד אֶחָד, מָה ע"פ עֵד אֶחָד — כִּי אָתֵי עֵד אֶחָד מִצְטָרֵף בַּהֲדֵיהּ מְחַיֵּיב, עַל פִּי עַצְמוֹ נַמִי — כִּי אָתוּ עֵדִים מְחַיֵּיב. אֲבָל גָּנַב וְטָבַח וּמָכַר ע"פ עֵד אֶחָד אוֹ ע"פ עַצְמוֹ, דְּחַיֵּיב עַצְמוֹ בְּקֶרֶן — לָא אָמְרִינַן עַל פִּי עַצְמוֹ דּוּמְיָא דְּעַל פִּי עֵד אֶחָד. בָּרַיְיתָא, דְּתַנְיָא: רָאָה עֵדִים שֶׁמְּמַשְׁמְשִׁין וּבָאִין, וְאָמַר "גָּנַבְתִּי, אֲבָל לֹא טָבַחְתִּי וְלֹא מָכַרְתִּי" — אֵינוֹ מְשַׁלֵּם אֶלָּא קֶרֶן; לָמָּה לִי לְמִיתְנָא: וְאָמַר "גָּנַבְתִּי, אֲבָל לֹא טָבַחְתִּי וְלֹא מָכַרְתִּי"? נִיתְנֵי (ב) אוֹ "גָּנַבְתִּי" אוֹ "טָבַחְתִּי וּמָכַרְתִּי"! אֶלָּא הָא קמ"ל: טַעֲמָא דְּאָמַר "גָּנַבְתִּי" (ג) הוּא, דְּחַיֵּיב עַצְמוֹ בְּקֶרֶן — דְּפָטוּר, אֲבָל אָמַר "לֹא גָּנַבְתִּי" וּבָאוּ עֵדִים שֶׁגָּנַב, וְחָזַר וְאָמַר "טָבַחְתִּי וּמָכַרְתִּי" וּבָאוּ עֵדִים שֶׁטָּבַח וּמָכַר, דְּלֹא חַיֵּיב עַצְמוֹ בְּקֶרֶן — חַיָּיב; אַלְמָא הוֹדָאָה דִּטְבִיחָה לָאו הוֹדָאָה הִיא. אָמְרִי: לָא, הִיא גּוּפָהּ קמ"ל, דְּכֵיוָן דְּאָמַר "גָּנַבְתִּי", אע"ג דְּאָמַר "לֹא טָבַחְתִּי וְלֹא מָכַרְתִּי" וּבָאוּ עֵדִים שֶׁטָּבַח וּמָכַר — פָּטוּר, מַאי טַעְמָא? תַּשְׁלוּמֵי (אַרְבַּע) חֲמִשָּׁה אָמַר רַחֲמָנָא, וְלֹא תַּשְׁלוּמֵי אַרְבָּעָה וְלֹא תַּשְׁלוּמֵי שְׁלֹשָׁה. לֵימָא כְּתַנָּאֵי: [א]הָיוּ שְׁנַיִם מְעִידִין שֶׁגָּנַב, וְהָיוּ שְׁנַיִם מְעִידִים אוֹתוֹ שֶׁטָּבַח וּמָכַר, הוּזְמוּ עֵדֵי גְנֵיבָה — עֵדוּת שֶׁבָּטְלָה מִקְצָתָהּ בָּטְלָה כּוּלָּהּ. הוּזְמוּ עֵדֵי טְבִיחָה — הוּא מְשַׁלֵּם תַּשְׁלוּמֵי כֶפֶל, וְהֵן מְשַׁלְּמִין תַּשְׁלוּמֵי שְׁלֹשָׁה; מִשּׁוּם סוּמָכוֹס אָמְרוּ: הֵן מְשַׁלְּמִין תַּשְׁלוּמֵי כֶפֶל, וְהוּא מְשַׁלֵּם תַּשְׁלוּמֵי שְׁלֹשָׁה לַפָּר וּשְׁנַיִם לָאַיִל; אַהַיָּיא קָאֵי סוּמָכוֹס? אִילֵימָא אַרֵישָׁא — לֵית לֵיהּ לְסוּמָכוֹס עֵדוּת שֶׁבָּטְלָה מִקְצָתָהּ בָּטְלָה כּוּלָּהּ? וְאֶלָּא אַסֵּיפָא — שַׁפִּיר קָאָמְרִי רַבָּנַן: הוּא מְשַׁלֵּם תַּשְׁלוּמֵי כֶפֶל, וְהֵם מְשַׁלְּמִין תַּשְׁלוּמֵי שְׁלֹשָׁה! אֶלָּא מִילְּתָא אַחֲרִיתִי אִיכָּא בֵּינַיְיהוּ, כְּגוֹן דַּאֲתוּ בֵּי תְּרֵי אָמְרִי לֵיהּ "גָּנַבְתָּ", אֲמַר לְהוּ "אִין, גָּנַבְתִּי וְטָבַחְתִּי וּמָכַרְתִּי, מִיהוּ לֹא בִּפְנֵיכֶם גָּנַבְתִּי", וְאַיְיתֵי סָהֲדֵי וְאַזְמִינְהוּ דְּלָא בְּאַפַּיְיהוּ גָּנַב, וְאַיְיתֵי בַּעַל הַבַּיִת סָהֲדֵי וְאַסְהִידוּ בֵּיהּ דְּגָנַב וְטָבַח וּמָכַר; וּבְהוֹדָאַת טְבִיחָה קָמִיפַּלְגִי, דְּרַבָּנַן סָבְרִי: אע"ג דְּהוֹדָאָה דִּגְנֵיבָה מֵחֲמַת עֵדִים הוּא דְּקָא מוֹדֶה — הוֹדָאָה דִּטְבִיחָה הוֹדָאָה הִיא, וּפָטוּר; וְסוּמָכוֹס סָבַר: כֵּיוָן דְּהוֹדָאָה דִּגְנֵיבָה מֵחֲמַת עֵדִים הוּא דְּקָא מוֹדֶה — דִּטְבִיחָה לָאו הוֹדָאָה, וְהָנָךְ עֵדִים קַמָּאֵי דְּאַזְמִינְהוּ מְשַׁלְּמִין תַּשְׁלוּמֵי כֶפֶל, וְהוּא מְשַׁלֵּם שְׁלֹשָׁה לַפָּר וּשְׁנַיִם לָאַיִל. אָמַר רַב אַחָא בְּרֵיהּ דְּרַב אִיקָא: לָא, דְּכוּלֵּי עָלְמָא — הוֹדָאָה דִּטְבִיחָה לָאו הוֹדָאָה הִיא. אֶלָּא בְּעֵדוּת שֶׁאִי אַתָּה יָכוֹל לַהֲזִימָהּ קָמִיפַּלְגִי; כְּגוֹן דַּאֲתוּ סָהֲדֵי וְאָמְרִי לֵיהּ "גָּנַבְתָּ", וַאֲמַר לְהוּ "גָּנַבְתִּי וְטָבַחְתִּי וּמָכַרְתִּי, מִיהוּ לֹא בִּפְנֵיכֶם גָּנַבְתִּי אֶלָּא בִּפְנֵי פְלוֹנִי וּפְלוֹנִי", וְאַיְיתֵי סָהֲדֵי וְאַזְמִינְהוּ דְּלָא בְּאַפַּיְיהוּ גָּנַב, וַאֲתוּ פְּלוֹנִי וּפְלוֹנִי וְאַסְהִידוּ בֵּיהּ דְּגָנַב וְטָבַח וּמָכַר; וּבְהָא קָמִיפַּלְגִי, דְּרַבָּנַן סָבְרִי: הָוְיָא לָהּ עֵדוּת שֶׁאִי אַתָּה יָכוֹל לַהֲזִימָהּ, וְכָל עֵדוּת שֶׁאִי אַתָּה יָכוֹל לַהֲזִימָהּ לָא הָוְיָא עֵדוּת; וְסוּמָכוֹס סָבַר: עֵדוּת שֶׁאִי אַתָּה יָכוֹל לַהֲזִימָהּ הָוְיָא עֵדוּת. וְהָא [ב]קַיְימָא לָן, *דְּעֵדוּת שֶׁאִי אַתָּה יָכוֹל לַהֲזִימָהּ לָא הָוְיָא עֵדוּת! הָנֵי מִילֵּי הֵיכָא דְּלָא יָדְעֵי בְּאֵיזֶה יוֹם בְּאֵיזֶה שָׁעָה, דְּלֵיכָּא לְעֵדוּת כְּלָל, אֲבָל הָכָא סִיּוּעֵי הוּא דְּקָא *מְסַיְּיעִי לֵיהּ. אָמַר מָר: הֵן מְשַׁלְּמִין תַּשְׁלוּמֵי כֶפֶל. מִדְּקָא מוֹדֶה דְּגָנַב, קֶרֶן בָּעֵי שַׁלּוּמֵי! אָמַר רַבִּי אֶלְעָזָר מִשְּׁמֵיהּ דְּרַב, תְּנִי: תַּשְׁלוּם

[סנהדרין מא: עת.]

[ומסייע להו כנ"ל]

ה"ג: אֶלָּא לָאו הָא קמ"ל גָּנַב עַל פִּי שְׁנַיִם וְטָבַח וּמָכַר ע"פ עַצְמוֹ אוֹ ע"פ אֶחָד דְּלֹא חַיֵּיב עַצְמוֹ בְּקֶרֶן הוּא דְּאָמְרִינַן ע"פ עַצְמוֹ כו'. כְּלוֹמַר: בְּכִי הַאי גַּוְונָא הוּא דְּקָאָמַר דּוּמְיָא דְּעֵד אֶחָד לְחַיְּיבֵיהּ כִּי הֲדַר אָתוּ סָהֲדֵי. אֲבָל הֵיכָא דִּגְנֵיבָה (ד) עַצְמוֹ מוֹדֶה — לָא אָמְרִינַן דּוּמְיָא דְּעֵד אֶחָד. נִיתְנֵי גָּנַבְתִּי אוֹ שֶׁאָמַר טָבַחְתִּי וּמָכַרְתִּי. פָּטוּר מִתַּשְׁלוּמֵי ד' וְה'. וְשָׁמְעִינַן מִינָּהּ תַּרְתֵּי, דְּאע"ג דְּלָא הוֹדָה אֶלָּא אַטְּבִיחָה וּפָטַר עַצְמוֹ מִכְּלוּם — הָוְיָא הוֹדָאָה! אֶלָּא מִדְּלָא תָּנֵי הָכִי — ש"מ טַעְמָא דְּאָמַר גָּנַבְתִּי כו'. לֵימָא כְּתַנָּאֵי. הוֹדָאָה דִּטְבִיחָה אִי הוֹדָאָה הָוְיָא בְּלָא הוֹדָאָה דִּגְנֵיבָה, דְּלָא מְחַיֵּיב עַצְמוֹ בְּקֶרֶן, לְפוֹטְרוֹ אִם בָּאוּ עֵדִים אוֹ לָא. בָּטְלָה כּוּלָּהּ. דְּכֵיוָן דְּלָא גָּנַב — לָא טָבַח. וְהָרִאשׁוֹנִים מְשַׁלְּמִין כֶּפֶל, וְהוּא פָּטוּר וְהָאַחֲרוֹנִים פְּטוּרִין. הוּזְמוּ עֵדֵי טְבִיחָה. וְלֹא עֵדֵי גְנֵיבָה. וְהֵן מְשַׁלְּמִין תַּשְׁלוּמֵי שְׁלֹשָׁה. לַגַּנָּב. אִילֵימָא אַרֵישָׁא. דְּהוּזְמוּ עֵדֵי גְנֵיבָה, וְקָאָמַר סוּמָכוֹס: הֵן מְשַׁלְּמִין כֶּפֶל בִּשְׁבִילוֹ לַבְּעָלִים כְּמִשְׁפָּטוֹ, וְהוּא מְשַׁלֵּם שְׁלֹשָׁה מִשּׁוּם טְבִיחָה, דְּעֵדֵי טְבִיחָה לֹא הוּזְמוּ. וְלֵית לֵיהּ לְסוּמָכוֹס כו'. הָא וַדַּאי כֵּיוָן דְּלֹא גָּנַב — לֹא טָבַח. אֶלָּא לָאו עַל כָּרְחִיךְ מִילְּתָא אַחֲרִיתִי. אָמוּר רַבָּנַן דְּקָאֵי סוּמָכוֹס עֲלַהּ, וְלָא מַשְׁכַּחַתְּ דְּתֵיקוּ מִילְּתָא דְּסוּמָכוֹס אַתַּנָּא קַמָּא שַׁפִּיר, אֶלָּא הָכִי: כְּגוֹן דַּאֲתוּ כו'. אִין גָּנַבְתִּי. וְהַךְ הוֹדָאָה דְּגַנָּב לָאו הוֹדָאָה הִיא, דְּהָא מֵחֲמַת הָנֵי עֵדִים דְּקָאָמְרִי לֵיהּ "גָּנַבְתָּ" הוּא דְּמוֹדֶה. אֲבָל הוֹדָאָה דִּטְבִיחָה וּמְכִירָה — לָאו מֵחֲמַת בִּיעֲתוּתַיְיהוּ אוֹדֵי, דְּהָא לָא אָמְרִי לֵיהּ ["טָבַחְתָּ"] אֶלָּא "גָּנַבְתָּ". וְאַיְיתֵי בַּעַל הַבַּיִת סָהֲדֵי. אַחֲרִינֵי, דְּגָנַב וְטָבַח וּמָכַר. וְקָאָמְרִי רַבָּנַן דְּהֵן מְשַׁלְּמִין תַּשְׁלוּמֵי כֶּפֶל לַגַּנָּב, וְהַגַּנָּב לַבְּעָלִים, וְהוּא פָּטוּר מִד' וְה' — דְּהָא אוֹדֵי אַטְּבִיחָה, וְהוֹדָאָה הִיא. וְאע"ג דְּאַיְיתֵי בַּעַל הַבַּיִת סָהֲדֵי דְּגָנַב — פָּטוּר, דְּהוֹדָאָה גְּמוּרָה הִיא, אַף ע"פ שֶׁלֹּא חִיֵּיב עַצְמוֹ בְּקֶרֶן. וְקָאָמַר לְהוּ סוּמָכוֹס: הֵן מְשַׁלְּמִין כֶּפֶל, וְהוּא מְשַׁלֵּם תַּשְׁלוּמֵי שְׁלֹשָׁה. דְּהוֹדָאָה דִּטְבִיחָה — לָאו הוֹדָאָה הִיא, שֶׁהֲרֵי פָּטַר עַצְמוֹ מִכְּלוּם. רַבָּנַן סָבְרִי אע"ג דִּגְנֵיבָה מֵחֲמַת עֵדִים קָא מוֹדֶה. וְאֵינָהּ הוֹדָאָה, וְחַיָּיב לְשַׁלֵּם לַבְּעָלִים אוֹתוֹ כֶּפֶל שֶׁנּוֹטֵל מֵאֵלּוּ. הוֹדָאָה דִּטְבִיחָה. דְּלָאו מֵחֲמַת בִּיעֲתוּתָא אוֹדֵי — מִיהָא הוֹדָאָה הִיא, וּפָטוּר מִד' וְה' אע"ג דְּפָטַר עַצְמוֹ מִכְּלוּם בְּהוֹדָאָה זוֹ, דְּהָא הוֹדָאָה שֶׁ"גָּנַבְתִּי" כְּמַאן דְּאָמַר "לֹא גָּנַבְתִּי" דָּמֵי, דְּמֵחֲמַת קַמָּאֵי אוֹדֵי. וּמַה דִּמְחַיֵּיב בְּקֶרֶן וְכֶפֶל — מִשּׁוּם עֵדוּת הָאַחֲרוֹנִים הוּא, וְלָאו מִשּׁוּם הוֹדָאָתוֹ. לֹא דְּכוּלֵּי עָלְמָא הוֹדָאָה דִּטְבִיחָה. בְּלֹא הוֹדָאָה דִּגְנֵיבָה — לָאו כְּלוּם הִיא לְפוֹטְרוֹ בִּמְקוֹם עֵדִים, כְּרַבִּי יוֹחָנָן, וְאִי הָנֵי סָהֲדֵי בַּתְרָאֵי סַהֲדוּתָא מַעַלְיוּתָא הָוְיָא — לָא הֲוֵי פָּטְרִי לֵיהּ רַבָּנַן. אֶלָּא הָכָא בְּעֵדוּת שֶׁאִי אַתָּה יָכוֹל לַהֲזִימָהּ עָסְקִינַן, וּכְגוֹן דְּהָנֵי עֵדִים אַחֲרוֹנִים הַכְּשֵׁרִים שֶׁהֵבִיא בַּעַל הַבַּיִת לְהָעִיד שֶׁגָּנַב וְטָבַח וּמָכַר — עַל פִּי הַגַּנָּב הֱבִיאָם, שֶׁאָמַר הַגַּנָּב בְּבֵית דִּין: "בִּפְנֵי פְלוֹנִי וּפְלוֹנִי גָּנַבְתִּי", כִּדְמְפָרֵשׁ וְאָזֵיל, וַאֲתוּ פְּלוֹנִי וּפְלוֹנִי כו'. רַבָּנַן פָּטְרִי לֵיהּ לַגַּנָּב מֵאַרְבָּעָה וַחֲמִשָּׁה, אֶלָּא מְשַׁלֵּם לַבְּעָלִים קֶרֶן לְבַדּוֹ, וְהוּא נוֹטֵל כֶּפֶל מִן הָרִאשׁוֹנִים שֶׁרָצוּ לְהַפְסִידוֹ כֶּפֶל. וּקְנָסָא לָא מְשַׁלֵּם, מַאי טַעְמָא — דְּהָנֵי סָהֲדֵי בַּתְרָאֵי אֵינָן עֵדִים, דְּאֵינְךָ יָכוֹל לַהֲזִימָם וּלְקַיֵּים בְּעֵדוּת זוֹ דִּין הֲזָמָה, שֶׁהֲרֵי הוּא הוֹדָה תְּחִלָּה שֶׁבִּפְנֵיהֶם גָּנַב, וְעַל פִּיו בָּאוּ לְהָעִיד, וְלָאו עֵדוּת הִיא. הִלְכָּךְ אַמַּאי מְחַיְּיבַתְּ לֵיהּ — אַהוֹדָאַת פִּיו, עַל פִּי עַצְמוֹ לֹא יְשַׁלֵּם קְנָס. וְאַהָא מִילְּתָא קָאֵי סוּמָכוֹס וְסָבַר: עֵדוּת שֶׁאִי אַתָּה יָכוֹל לַהֲזִימָהּ עֵדוּת הִיא. וְעֵדִים הַמּוּזָּמִין מְשַׁלְּמִין תַּשְׁלוּמֵי כֶפֶל לַבְּעָלִים בִּמְקוֹם גַּנָּב, וְהוּא מְשַׁלֵּם שְׁלֹשָׁה לַפָּר — דְּהָא אֲתוּ סָהֲדֵי דְּטָבַח וּמָכַר. הָנֵי מִילֵּי. דְּלָא הָוְיָא עֵדוּת. הֵיכָא דְּאָמְרִי לָא יָדְעִינַן בְּאֵיזוֹ יוֹם בְּאֵיזוֹ שָׁעָה. דְּאִיכָּא לְמֵימַר דִּלְהָכִי עָבְדִי, דְּמִסְתַּפּוּ דְּלָא לֵיתוּ סָהֲדֵי דְּלַזְמִינְהוּ "וַהֲלֹא בְּאוֹתָהּ שָׁעָה עִמָּנוּ הֱיִיתֶם", וְעֵדִים שַׁקְרָנִים הֵם. אֲבָל הָכָא. דְּהָא דְּאֵין אַתָּה יָכוֹל לַהֲזִימָהּ הַיְינוּ מִשּׁוּם דְּקוּשְׁטָא קָא מַסְהֲדֵי — מִכָּל שֶׁכֵּן דְּעֵדוּתָן עֵדוּת דְּסִיּוּעֵי קָא מְסַיְּיעֵי לְהוּ. הִלְכָּךְ: הַךְ רִאשׁוֹנִים שֶׁהוּזְמוּ — מְשַׁלְּמִים בִּשְׁבִילוֹ כֶּפֶל, וְהוּא מְשַׁלֵּם שְׁלֹשָׁה לְתַשְׁלוּמֵי חֲמִשָּׁה דְּפַר, וּשְׁנַיִם לָאַיִל. דְּעֵדוּת אִיכָּא, וְהוֹדָאָה לֵיכָּא, דְּהוֹדָאָה דִּגְנֵיבָה מֵחֲמַת בִּיעֲתוּתָא דְּקַמָּאֵי אוֹדֵי, וְהוֹדָאָה דִּטְבִיחָה — פּוֹטֵר עַצְמוֹ מִכְּלוּם הֲוָה. תַּשְׁלוּמֵי כֶפֶל. קָאָמַר סוּמָכוֹס בְּכִי הַאי גַּוְונָא דְּקַמָּאֵי מְשַׁלְּמִין כֶּפֶל, דְּמַשְׁמַע קֶרֶן וְכֶפֶל. וְאַמַּאי? כֵּיוָן דְּקָא מוֹדֵי וְאָמַר "גָּנַבְתִּי" — אִיהוּ קֶרֶן קָא בָּעֵי לְשַׁלּוּמֵי! דְּבִשְׁלָמָא קְנָסָא דְּכֶפֶל הָווּ קָא בָּעֵי לְאַפְסוּדֵי בְּעֵדוּת שֶׁקֶר דִּידְהוּ, דְּאַכַּתִּי לֹא עָמַד בַּדִּין, וְאִיכָּא לְמֵימַר דְּמוֹדֶה וּמִיפְּטַר. אֶלָּא קֶרֶן הוּא מִחוּיָּיב וְקָאֵי, וְלָא מַפְסְדֵי לֵיהּ מִידֵּי. תַּשְׁלוּם

ברייתא דתניא ראה עדים כו'. תימה: דאמאי לא הביא מתניתין דפרק בתרא דשבועות (דף מט. וסס*)? דלעיל ודאי ניחא שמביא ברייתא — לפי שצריך לדקדק מסיפא דר"א בר' שמעון דלא מתניא במתני' דשבועות. אבל הכא אין צריך לדקדק כלל מסיפא! וי"ל: דאמתני' דשבועות ידע שפיר דאיכא לדחויי דהיא גופה קמ"ל, כדקאמר בסמוך. אבל ברייתא שמוספת על המשנה, סבור דקמ"ל דהודאה דטביחה לאו הודאה היא.
תשלום

[ד"ה ראה]

הגהות הב"ח

(א) גמ' על פי עצמו דלא מיחייב כצ"ל ותיבת הוא נמחק: (ב) שם ניתני גנבתי כצ"ל ותיבת או נמחק: (ג) שם טעמא דאמר גנבתי דחייב עצמו בקרן הוא דפטור: (ד) רש"י ד"ה ה"ג אלא וכו' אבל היכא דגניבה מחמת עצמו הודה:

קה א מיי' פ"ב מהל' גניבה הלכה א סמג עשין עא:

תַּשְׁלוּם דְּכֶפֶל. מְשַׁלְּמִין אֶת הַכֶּפֶל, וְהוּא מְשַׁלֵּם שְׁלֹשָׁה לְבַד הַקֶּרֶן. כִּי קָא טָבַח דְּהֶקְדֵּשׁ קָא טָבַח. דְּהָא בִּלְאַחַר יֵאוּשׁ קָיְימִינַן, דְּאִי לִפְנֵי יֵאוּשׁ — לָאו קַדְשָׁהּ. וְכֵיוָן דְּאִיָּאוּשׁ קַנְיֵיהּ הֶקְדֵּשׁ בְּיֵאוּשׁ וְשִׁינּוּי רְשׁוּת, הִלְכָּךְ לָאו דְּמָרֵיהּ קְטָבַח. ר"ש הִיא. וּכְגוֹן שֶׁאָמַר "הֲרֵי עָלַי עוֹלָה", וְהִפְרִישׁ גְּנֵיבָה זוֹ לְנִדְרוֹ. דְּכֵיוָן דְּחַיָּיב בְּאַחֲרָיוּתוֹ, וְדָבָר הַגּוֹרֵם לְמָמוֹן הוּא — כְּמָמוֹן דָּמֵי, וְלָאו מְכִירָה הִיא. וּמִיהוּ, לְעִנְיַן טְבִיחָה פָּטוּר, דְּאַע"ג דְּבִרְשׁוּת גַּנָּב קַיְימָא דְּאִם אֲבָדוֹ חַיָּיב בְּאַחֲרָיוּתָם לְהֶקְדֵּשׁ — חָל עָלֶיהָ מִיהָא שֵׁם הֶקְדֵּשׁ לְאַפּוֹקֵי מֵרְשׁוּת מָרָהּ קַמָּא, וְלָאו דְּמָרָהּ קָא טָבַח. בְּקָדָשִׁים קַלִּים. שֶׁהִקְדִּישׁוֹ לִשְׁלָמִים. דְּר' יוֹסֵי הַגְּלִילִי. בְּפ"ק (דף יג:), הִלְכָּךְ לָאו מְכִירָה הִיא. וּמִיהוּ, מֵרְשׁוּת מָרָהּ קַמָּא אַפְּקִינְהוּ שֵׁם הֶקְדֵּשׁ, וְכִי קָא טָבַח — לָאו דְּמָרָהּ קָא טָבַח. ל"א: בִּטְבִיחָה מִשּׁוּם הָכִי לָא מְחַיֵּיב — דְּבִשְׁעַת טְבִיחָה דְּהֶקְדֵּשׁ נִינְהוּ, דְּאָמַר בְּפ"ק דְּכִי אָמַר רַבִּי יוֹסֵי הַגְּלִילִי מָמוֹן בְּעָלִים — מֵחַיִּים, אֲבָל לְאַחַר טְבִיחָה — לָא, אֶלָּא מִשֻּׁלְחַן גָּבוֹהַּ קָא זָכוּ. וְלָא נְהִירָא לִי, דְּהָכִי הַאי שְׁחִיטָה לָא אָמַר ר' יוֹסֵי הַגְּלִילִי דְּמִשֻּׁלְחַן גָּבוֹהַּ קָא זָכוּ, אֶלָּא בְּמִקְדָּשׁ בְּחֶלְקוֹ שֶׁלָּקוּחַ בְּקָדָשִׁים, דְּהָוְיָא הָתָם שְׁחִיטָה וּזְרִיקָה וְהַקְטָרַת חֲלָבִים, אֲבָל בִּשְׁעַת טְבִיחָה — אַכַּתִּי מָמוֹן בְּעָלִים הֵם. אַדְּתָנֵי רֵישָׁא כו'. דְּמַשְׁמַע דְּלָא מָצֵי לְמִיתְנֵי חִיּוּבָא בָּתַר לְהַקְדִּישׁ. לִפְלוֹג וְלִיתְנֵי. בְּסֵיפָא, וּלְאַשְׁמוּעִינַן חִיּוּבָא אֲפִילּוּ הֵיכָא דְּלְהַקְדִּישׁ קוֹדֶם טְבִיחָה. מְכָרוֹ לְהֶדְיוֹט מֵעִיקָּרָא תּוֹרָא דִּרְאוּבֵן. קוֹדֶם שֶׁמְּכָרוֹ קָרוּי הַשּׁוֹר עַל שְׁמוֹ שֶׁל גַּנָּב, וּמִשֶּׁמְּכָרוֹ קָרוּי עַל שֵׁם לוֹקֵחַ. אֲבָל מְכָרוֹ לַשָּׁמַיִם — עֲדַיִין שֵׁם הַמַּקְדִּישׁוֹ עָלָיו, שֶׁקָּרוּי "עוֹלָתוֹ שֶׁל פְּלוֹנִי". אָמְרִי נְהִי דְּסָבַר רַבִּי שִׁמְעוֹן כו'. דְּקָא סָלְקָא דַּעְתָּךְ מִשּׁוּם טְבִיחָה לָא מְחַיֵּיב לֵיהּ ר"ש, *דַּאֲפִילּוּ הִפְרִישׁוֹ לְשֵׁם נֶדֶר הַמּוּטָּל עָלָיו אַחֲרָיוּת — נָפַק מֵרְשׁוּת מָרֵיהּ קַמָּא, וְנַעֲשָׂה זֶה שׁוֹמֵר לַהֶקְדֵּשׁ, וְכִי טָבַח — לָאו דְּמָרֵיהּ קָא טָבַח. וְכִי מְחַיֵּיב לֵיהּ ר"ש — אַשַּׁעְתָּא דְּהֶקְדֵּשׁ קָמְחַיֵּיב לֵיהּ, דְּהָוְיָא מְכִירָה. הִלְכָּךְ מִיבְּעֵי לֵיהּ לְמֵימַר אִיפְּכָא. דְּאַכַּתִּי לָא נָפֵיק מֵרְשׁוּתֵיהּ. הִלְכָּךְ לָאו מְכִירָה הִיא. וְאַטְּבִיחָה נָמֵי לָא מְחַיֵּיב, דְּמֵרְשׁוּת מָרֵיהּ קַמָּא נָפֵיק. שֶׁאֵין חַיָּיב בְּאַחֲרָיוּתָן חַיָּיב. שַׁעְתָּא דְּהֶקְדֵּשׁ דִּמְכִירָה הִיא. אַמִּילְּתָא אַחֲרִיתִי קָאֵי. דְּהֵיכָא דְּלְהַקְדִּישׁ גַּנָּב, בֵּין לְנֶדֶר בֵּין לִנְדָבָה — לָא מְחַיֵּיב לֵיהּ ר"ש; לָאו אַשַּׁעְתָּא דְּהֶקְדֵּשׁ — מִשּׁוּם דַּעֲדַיִין שְׁמוֹ עָלָיו, "נִדְבָתוֹ שֶׁל פְּלוֹנִי". וְלָאו אַטְּבִיחָה — דְּהָא מֵרְשׁוּת מָרֵיהּ קַמָּא נָפַק. אֶלָּא אַגּוֹנֵב הֶקְדֵּשׁ שֶׁהִקְדִּישׁוּהוּ בְּעָלִים קָאֵי, דְּכֵיוָן דְּחַיָּיב בְּעָלִים בְּאַחֲרָיוּת, כִּי קָא טָבַח — דְּמָרֵיהּ קָא טָבַח. דְּדָבָר הַגּוֹרֵם לְמָמוֹן כְּמָמוֹן דָּמֵי. שָׁמְעִינַן לֵיהּ לְרַבִּי שִׁמְעוֹן. דְּמַתְנִי', דְּפָטַר אַטְּבִיחַת טְרֵיפָה. קָדָשִׁים נָמֵי שְׁחִיטָה שֶׁאֵינָהּ רְאוּיָה הִיא. דְּקָדָשִׁים הַנִּשְׁחָטִין בַּחוּץ פְּסוּלִין, וּמַאי טַעְמָא דְּרַבִּי שִׁמְעוֹן דְּאָמַר: קָדָשִׁים שֶׁחַיָּיב בְּאַחֲרָיוּתָן חַיָּיב, דְּמַשְׁמַע שֶׁאִם גָּנַב קָדָשִׁים וּטְבָחָן דְּחַיָּיב בְּתַשְׁלוּמֵי ד' וָה'. וַהֲרֵי חָזְרָה קֶרֶן לַבַּעַל הַבַּיִת. הוֹאִיל וּלְשֵׁם בְּעָלִים נִזְבְּחוּ. שֶׁנִּשְׁפַּךְ הַדָּם. וּמִיהוּ, בִּשְׁעַת שְׁחִיטָה רְאוּיָה הִיא. שֶׁלֹּא לְשֵׁם בְּעָלֵיהֶן. דִּשְׁחִיטָה רְאוּיָה הִיא, דְּקַיְימָא לָן (זבחים ד' ב.): כָּל הַזְּבָחִים שֶׁנִּזְבְּחוּ שֶׁלֹּא לִשְׁמָן — כְּשֵׁרִים. וְקֶרֶן לָא חָזְרָה לַבְּעָלִים, דְּקַיְימָא לָן שֶׁלֹּא עָלוּ לַבְּעָלִים לְשֵׁם חוֹבָה. בְּעָלֵי

תַּשְׁלוּם דְּכֶפֶל.§ "גָּנַב וְהִקְדִּישׁ וְאַחַר כָּךְ טָבַח וּמָכַר" כו'.§ אָמְרִי: בִּשְׁלָמָא אַטְּבִיחָה לָא מְחַיֵּיב, דְּכִי קָא טָבַח — דְּהֶקְדֵּשׁ קָא טָבַח וְלָא דְּמָרֵיהּ קָא טָבַח. אֶלָּא אַהֶקְדֵּשׁ לִיחַיֵּיב, *מַה לִּי מְכָרוֹ לְהֶדְיוֹט מַה לִּי מְכָרוֹ לַשָּׁמַיִם! הָא מַנִּי? ר"ש הִיא, דְּאָמַר: קָדָשִׁים שֶׁחַיָּיב בְּאַחֲרָיוּתָן בִּרְשׁוּתֵיהּ דְּמָרֵיהּ קָיְימִי. הָא מִדְּסֵיפָא ר"ש, הָוֵי רֵישָׁא לָאו ר"ש! אֶלָּא הָכָא בְּמַאי עָסְקִינַן — בְּקָדָשִׁים קַלִּים, *וְאַלִּיבָּא דְּר' יוֹסֵי הַגְּלִילִי, דְּאָמַר: קָדָשִׁים קַלִּים מָמוֹן בְּעָלִים הוּא, וּבִרְשׁוּתֵיהּ קָיְימִי. אֲבָל קָדְשֵׁי קָדָשִׁים מַאי? מְשַׁלֵּם תַּשְׁלוּמֵי ד' וַחֲמִשָּׁה? אַדְּתָנֵי רֵישָׁא: גָּנַב וְטָבַח וְאח"כ הִקְדִּישׁ — מְשַׁלֵּם תַּשְׁלוּמֵי ד' וָה', לִיפְלוֹג וְלִיתְנֵי בְּדִידַהּ: בַּמֶּה דְּבָרִים אֲמוּרִים — בְּקָדָשִׁים קַלִּים, אֲבָל בְּקָדְשֵׁי קָדָשִׁים — מְשַׁלֵּם תַּשְׁלוּמֵי אַרְבָּעָה וַחֲמִשָּׁה! אֶלָּא, לְעוֹלָם לָא שְׁנָא קָדְשֵׁי קָדָשִׁים וְלָא שְׁנָא קָדָשִׁים קַלִּים. וּדְקַשְׁיָא לָךְ: מַה לִּי מְכָרוֹ לְהֶדְיוֹט מַה לִּי מְכָרוֹ לַשָּׁמַיִם! מְכָרוֹ לְהֶדְיוֹט — מֵעִיקָּרָא תּוֹרָא דִּרְאוּבֵן וְהַשְׁתָּא תּוֹרָא דְּשִׁמְעוֹן, מְכָרוֹ לַשָּׁמַיִם — מֵעִיקָּרָא תּוֹרָא דִּרְאוּבֵן וְהַשְׁתָּא תּוֹרָא דִּרְאוּבֵן.§ "רַבִּי שִׁמְעוֹן אוֹמֵר" וכו'.§ אָמְרִי: נְהִי דְּסָבַר ר"ש: מַה לִּי מְכָרוֹ לְהֶדְיוֹט מַה לִּי מְכָרוֹ לַשָּׁמַיִם, אִיפְּכָא מִיבְּעֵי לֵיהּ: קָדָשִׁים שֶׁחַיָּיב בְּאַחֲרָיוּתָן — פָּטוּר, דְּאַכַּתִּי לָא נְפַק מֵרְשׁוּתֵיהּ, קָדָשִׁים שֶׁאֵינוֹ חַיָּיב בְּאַחֲרָיוּתָן — חַיָּיב, דְּמַפְּקֵי לֵיהּ מֵרְשׁוּתֵיהּ! אָמְרִי: ר"ש אַמִּילְּתָא אַחֲרִיתִי קָאֵי, וְהָכִי קָתָנֵי: אֵין הַגּוֹנֵב אַחַר הַגַּנָּב מְשַׁלֵּם תַּשְׁלוּמֵי ד' וָה', [א]וְכֵן גּוֹנֵב הֶקְדֵּשׁ מִבֵּית בְּעָלִים — פָּטוּר, מ"ט? "וְגֻנַּב מִבֵּית הָאִישׁ" — *וְלֹא מִבֵּית הֶקְדֵּשׁ; רַבִּי שִׁמְעוֹן אוֹמֵר: קָדָשִׁים שֶׁחַיָּיב בְּאַחֲרָיוּתָן — חַיָּיב, מַאי טַעְמָא? קָרֵינָא בֵּיהּ "וְגֻנַּב מִבֵּית הָאִישׁ". וְשֶׁאֵינוֹ חַיָּיב בְּאַחֲרָיוּתָן — פָּטוּר, דְּלָא קָרֵינַן בֵּיהּ "וְגֻנַּב מִבֵּית הָאִישׁ". מִכְּדִי שָׁמְעִינַן לֵיהּ לְר"ש, *דְּאָמַר: שְׁחִיטָה שֶׁאֵינָהּ רְאוּיָה לֹא שְׁמָהּ שְׁחִיטָה, קָדָשִׁים נָמֵי שְׁחִיטָה שֶׁאֵינָהּ רְאוּיָה הִיא! כִּי אֲתָא רַב דִּימִי אָמַר ר' יוֹחָנָן: בְּשׁוֹחֵט תְּמִימִים מִבִּפְנִים לְשֵׁם בְּעָלִים. וַהֲרֵי חָזְרָה קֶרֶן לַבְּעָלִים! אָמַר רַבִּי יִצְחָק בַּר אָבִין: שֶׁנִּשְׁפַּךְ הַדָּם. כִּי אֲתָא רָבִין אָמַר רַבִּי יוֹחָנָן: בְּשׁוֹחֵט תְּמִימִים בִּפְנִים שֶׁלֹּא לְשֵׁם בְּעָלִים. וְרֵ'ישׁ

תשלום דכפל. ולעיל (דף סח:) דמוקי ר"ש לקיש מתני' דגנב והקדיש ואח"כ טבח משלם תשלומי כפל כשהקדישו בעלים ביד גנב — לריך לומר נמי תשלום דכפל. **אלא** אהקדש ליחייב. כולה הך סוגיא כר' יוחנן, ודלא כר"ש לקיש דמוקי לה לעיל (דף סח:) כשהקדישו בעלים ביד גנב.

והשתא תורא דשמעון. והא דאמר לקמן: (א) גנב והקדיש חייב ד' וה', דהוי כמוכרו להדיוט — היינו בקדשי בדק הבית, דלא מיקרו על שם בעלים. וקדשי מזבח, אומר ר"י: אע"ג דמיקרו על שם בעלים, ולא הוי הקדש כמכירה, מ"מ למ"ד יאוש לא קני — חשיב כיאוש ושינוי רשות, לענין דחל הקדש אחר יאוש. כדמשמע לעיל (דף סו:) דבעי לאוקומי אביי לרבה דיאוש לא קני מ"קרבנו" ולא הגזול, ואפילו הכי אמר שם דחל הקדש, אע"ג דאכתי לא אסיק אדעתיה דהוי יאוש ושינוי השם, אלא משום דהוי יאוש ושינוי רשות.

ורבי שמעון הא אמר שחיטה שאינה ראויה לא שמה שחיטה. הא לא איצטריך אלא משום מ"ד אין לשחיטה אלא לבסוף. דלמ"ד ישנה לשחיטה מתחילה ועד סוף, מלי למפרך: אפילו סבר ר"ש שחיטה שאינה ראויה שמה שחיטה, אמאי חייב אשחוטי חוץ ד' וה'? הכי שחט ביה פורתא אסרה, ואידך — לאו דמרה קטלה. **שחיטה** שאינה ראויה היא ולא שמה שחיטה. לגבי ארבעה וחמשה, דגמר מ"וטבוח טבח והכן", בר מלגבי לאו דשחוטי חוץ, דהכי חייב רחמנא. וא"ת: ואמאי חשיב ליה שחיטה שאינה ראויה? הא יכול לפדות בשעת פירכוס, דבר העמדה והערכה היא, כדאמרינן בפ"ב דחולין (דף ל.), ואין לך מום גדול יותר משחיטה! ואין סברא לומר דלפי שנפסל שוב אין לו פדיון. דבשלמא פסול שהוא בשריפה, כגון פיגול — אין לו פדייה, משום דמלוה לשורפו, כדאמרינן בפרק "כל שעה" (פסחים ד' כד.): כל שבקדש פסול — באש ישרף. אבל שחיטת חוץ אינה בשריפה אלא בקבורה, כדאמרינן בפרק "עד כמה" (בכורות דף כח.): מי שאינו מומחה וראה את הבכור ונשחט על פיו — הרי זה יקבר. ומיהו, לדברי המפרש דלא חשיב המפרכסת כחיה אלא כגון ישראל בטמאה וגוי בטהורה, דלאו שחיטה היא. דהכא דשחט בה שנים או רוב שנים ועדיין מפרכסת הרי היא כחיה, דבפ"ב דחולין (ד' ל. *ושם) — אין משנה בשום מקום, אלא היינו ההיא ד"הטור והרוטב" (שם ד' קכא.) דשונים ישראל בטמאה כו'. אבל היכא דשחטה כתיקונה לא חשיב מפרכסת כחיה — מתיישב כאן, דשחיטת חוץ לאו בת פדייה היא, כיון דשחיטה גמורה היא להוציא מידי נבילה וגם להתירה באכילה, אם היה לה פדיון. דהכא אליבא דר"ש קיימי, דבין רבי יוחנן ובין ר"ל מודו דקדשי מזבח לר"ש היו בכלל העמדה והערכה, כדאמרינן בפרק בתרא דתמורה (ד' לג:), ולא פליגי אלא אליבא דרבנן. אבל מ"מ קשה לריש לקיש אליבא דרבנן, דקדשי מזבח לא הוי בכלל העמדה והערכה, כדאמר הכא דלא משתמיט בשום מקום לשום תנא שיהיו נפדין! ודוחק לומר דמדרבנן הוא דאין נפדין, לפי שעשה מום זה בידים, כשאר מטיל מום שאין נשחט וניתר על ידי אותו מום. וי"ל: דמום שהוא מחיים חשיב מום לפדות על ידו, אבל מום ° דלאחר מיתה — לא חשיב מום, כדתניא בסוף תמורה (לג.) בהדיא: מתו תמימים — יקברו, בעלי מומים — יפדו, דלא בעי העמדה והערכה, ואפילו הכי תמימים יקברו. **שלא** לשם בעליהן. וה"ה שלא לשמן. אי נמי: ההוא נמי קרי ליה שלא לשם בעליהן, משום שלא עלו לבעלים לשם חובה. ונראה לו דוחק להעמיד בנשפך הדם. ורב דימי דאוקמא כשנשפך הדם — משום דניחא ליה לאוקומא בכל קדשים שחייב באחריותן, [דבשלא] לשם בעליהן לא מתוקמא בפסח וחטאת, דמפסלי שלא לשמן.

ור"ל

[לקמן עט.]

לעיל יב: פסחים לו. סנהדרין קיב:

רש"ל גורס ואפילו

לעיל דף עה. [וש"נ]

שמות כב

בכורות יח. [עי' תוס' לעיל סג. ד"ה לעטן]

[ע"ש בתוספות ד"ה והתקן ועשו שם פה. ד"ה בעינן ותוס' בכורות לב. ד"ה הא לאחר שחיטה]

הגהות הב"ח

(א) תוס' ד"ה והשתא וכו' לקמן. נ"ב תחילת דף עט ועיין בתוס' ד"ה גנב:

גליון הש"ס

תוס' ד"ה שחיטה וכו' דלאחר מיתה לא חשיב מום. עי' בכתב"י ריש מעילה ד"ה כמאן דתנקינן:

וְרֵישׁ לָקִישׁ אָמַר: בְּשׁוֹחֵט בַּעֲלֵי מוּמִין בַּחוּץ. תָּהֵי בָּהּ רַבִּי אֶלְעָזָר: לְר' יוֹחָנָן, שְׁחִיטָה מַתֶּרֶת? וַהֲלֹא זְרִיקָה מַתֶּרֶת! לְרֵישׁ לָקִישׁ, שְׁחִיטָה מַתֶּרֶת? וַהֲלֹא פְּדִיָּיה מַתֶּרֶת! אִישְׁתְּמִיטְתֵיהּ הָא דְּרַבִּי שִׁמְעוֹן: *כָּל הָעוֹמֵד לִזְרוֹק כְּזָרוּק דָּמֵי, וְכָל הָעוֹמֵד לִפְדּוֹת כְּפָדוּי דָּמֵי. כָּל הָעוֹמֵד לִזְרוֹק כְּזָרוּק דָּמֵי, דְּתַנְיָא, *רַבִּי שִׁמְעוֹן אוֹמֵר: יֵשׁ נוֹתָר שֶׁהוּא מְטַמֵּא טוּמְאַת אוֹכָלִין, וְיֵשׁ נוֹתָר שֶׁאֵינוֹ מְטַמֵּא טוּמְאַת אוֹכָלִין, כֵּיצַד? לָן לִפְנֵי זְרִיקָה — אֵינוֹ מְטַמֵּא טוּמְאַת אוֹכָלִין, לְאַחַר זְרִיקָה — מְטַמֵּא טוּמְאַת אוֹכָלִין; וְקַיְימָא לָן, מַאי "לִפְנֵי זְרִיקָה" — קוֹדֶם שֶׁנִּרְאָה לִזְרִיקָה, "לְאַחַר זְרִיקָה" — לְאַחַר שֶׁנִּרְאָה לִזְרִיקָה; קוֹדֶם שֶׁנִּרְאָה לִזְרִיקָה לָן מַאי הִיא? דְּלָא הֲוָיָא שְׁהוּת בַּיּוֹם לְמִזְרְקֵיהּ, דְּשַׁחֲטֵיהּ סָמוּךְ לִשְׁקִיעַת הַחַמָּה, וְאֵינוֹ מְטַמֵּא טוּמְאַת אוֹכָלִין; לְאַחַר שֶׁנִּרְאָה לִזְרִיקָה לָן — דַּהֲוָיָא שְׁהוּת בַּיּוֹם לְמִזְרְקֵיהּ, מְטַמֵּא טוּמְאַת אוֹכָלִין; אַלְמָא: כָּל הָעוֹמֵד לִזְרוֹק כְּזָרוּק דָּמֵי. וְכָל הָעוֹמֵד לִפְדּוֹת כְּפָדוּי דָּמֵי, דְּתַנְיָא, רַבִּי שִׁמְעוֹן אוֹמֵר:

פָּרָה

בַּעֲלֵי מוּמִין. שְׁחִיטָתָן הֶיתֵּר בַּחוּץ. תָּהֵי. לְשׁוֹן מְרִיחַ בְּקַנְקַן, כְּמוֹ: תָּהֵי לֵיהּ אַקַּנְקַנֵּיהּ (ב"ב ד' כב.). כְּלוֹמַר דָּיֵיק לָהּ רַבִּי אֶלְעָזָר, וּפָרֵיךְ לְרַבִּין אַלִּיבָּא דְּרַבִּי יוֹחָנָן: וְכִי שְׁחִיטָתוֹ מַתֶּרֶת? וַהֲלֹא זְרִיקָה מַתֶּרֶת, וּבִשְׁעַת טְבִיחָה שְׁחִיטָה שֶׁאֵינָהּ רְאוּיָה הִיא! אִישְׁתַּמִּיטְתֵיהּ. לְרַבִּי אֶלְעָזָר הָא דְּר' שִׁמְעוֹן כָּל הָעוֹמֵד כו'. וְכָל הָעוֹמֵד לִפְדּוֹת כו'. וּבַעֲלֵי מוּמִין כִּפְדוּיִם דָּמוּ, הוֹאִיל וְסוֹפָן לְכָךְ. וּבְבַעֲלֵי מוּמִין מֵעִיקָּרָן עָסְקִינַן, דְּאִי בְּשֶׁקָּדַם הֶקְדֵּישָׁן אֶת מוּמָן – תּוּ לָא חֲזוּ לְפִדְיוֹן מִשֶּׁנִּשְׁחֲטוּ, דִּשְׁמְעִינַן לֵיהּ לְרַבִּי שִׁמְעוֹן בֶּן לָקִישׁ אַלִּיבָּא דְּר' שִׁמְעוֹן בִּשְׁמַעְתָּא בַּתְרַיְיתָא דְּמַסֶּכֶת תְּמוּרָה (ד' לג:): קָדְשֵׁי מִזְבֵּחַ בִּכְלַל הַעֲמָדָה וְהַעֲרָכָה, וּמִשֶּׁנִּשְׁחֲטָה אֵינָהּ יְכוֹלָה לַעֲמוֹד. אֲבָל בְּבַעַל מוּם מֵעִיקָּרוֹ מוֹדֶה. יֵשׁ נוֹתָר שֶׁמְּטַמֵּא כו'. לְרַבִּי שִׁמְעוֹן אִיסּוּרֵי הֲנָאָה אֵין מְטַמְּאִין טוּמְאַת אוֹכָלִין, דְּדָרֵישׁ מִ"כָּל הָאוֹכֶל אֲשֶׁר יֵאָכֵל": אוֹכֶל שֶׁאַתָּה יָכוֹל לְהַאֲכִילוֹ לַאֲחֵרִים, אוֹ לְגוֹי אוֹ לְיִשְׂרָאֵל – קָרוּי אוֹכֶל, בְּפֶרֶק קַמָּא דִּבְכוֹרוֹת (ד' ט:). וְאִם הָיְתָה לָהּ שְׁעַת הֶיתֵּר הֲנָאָה מִשֶּׁנִּשְׁחֲטָה – יָרְדָה עָלָיו דִּין קַבָּלַת טוּמְאָה, וַאֲפִילּוּ נֶאֱסַר לְאַחַר כֵּן – מְקַבֶּלֶת טוּמְאָה. לָן לִפְנֵי זְרִיקָה. קָדָשִׁים הַנִּפְסָלִין לִהְיוֹת נוֹתָר בְּלַיְלָה אֶחָת, כְּגוֹן תּוֹדָה וְקָדְשֵׁי קָדָשִׁים כּוּלָּן, אִם לֹא נִזְרַק דָּמָן וְלֹא נִיתַּר בַּאֲכִילָה – אֵין מְטַמֵּא טוּמְאַת אוֹכָלִין. וְקַיְימָא לָן. בְּפֶרֶק "הַמְּנָחוֹת וְהַנְּסָכִים", דְּהַאי לִפְנֵי זְרִיקָה – קוֹדֶם שֶׁנִּרְאָה לִזְרִיקָה קָאָמַר, דְּלָא הֲוָה לֵיהּ שְׁהוּת בַּיּוֹם, דְּלָאו עוֹמֵד לִזְרוֹק בַּיּוֹם הֲוָה, דְּלֵיכָּא לְמֵימַר כְּזָרוּק דָּמֵי לְשַׁוּוּיֵהּ אוֹכְלָא. לָן לְאַחַר שֶׁנִּרְאָה לִזְרִיקָה, דַּהֲוֵי שְׁהוּת בַּיּוֹם – אוֹכְלָא הוּא, אַלְמָא: כְּזָרוּק דָּמֵי.

פָּרָה

פסחים דף יג: [מנחות ע... קב: כריתות כד: תמור... כב:]

ור"ל אמר כו'. ריש לקיש לא קאי אסוגיא דידן, דלדידיה לא צריך למימר, דרבי שמעון קאי אמילתא אחריתי. אלא לפי דבריו, דמוקי מתניתין לעיל (ד' סח:) כשהקדישו בעלים ביד גנב — מוקי לה בשוחט בעלי מומין בחוץ. **בשוחט** בעלי מומין בחוץ. פי' בקונטרס: דבבעלי מומין מעיקרא עסקינן. דאי בשקדם הקדשן למומן — תו לא חזו לפדיון משנשחטו, דשמעינן ליה לר"ל אליבא דרבי שמעון בשמעתא בתרייתא דתמורה (ד' לג:) דקדשי מזבח היו בכלל העמדה והערכה, ומשנשחטה אין יכולה לעמוד. ובבעל מום מעיקרו מודה. ורבינו תם מפרש: דבשעת פירכוס, בעודן יכולין לעמוד — בני העמדה והערכה נינהו, כדאמרינן בפ"ב דחולין (ד' ל. ושם). ומיהו, לאותן המפרשים דבשחיטה גמורה אין מועיל פירכוס, כמו שפירשתי לעיל (עמוד א*), צריך לאוקמי בבעל מום מעיקרו, כמו שפי' בקונטרס. **והלא** זריקה מתרת. למאן דמוקי לה כשנשפך הדם פריך. דאי למאן דאמר שלא לשם בעליהן, כיון דנשחט ונזרק בהכשר — שחיטה ראויה היא, בלא טעם כל העומד לזרוק כזרוק דמי. ואף על גב דבפרק "אותו ואת בנו" (חולין ד' פ: ושם*) בעי למימר דכל שחיטת קדשים שחיטה שאין ראויה היא — לא קיימא מסקנא הכי, אלא במסקנא משמע היכא דנזרק הדם לבסוף — שחיטה ראויה היא, אע"פ שלא היה עומד לזרוק, כגון ב"אותו ואת בנו" דהוי מחוסר זמן. דלא אמרינן לרבי שמעון כזרוק דמי אלא במקום שמצוה לזרוק, כדאמר בפרק "המנחות והנסכים" (מנחות דף קא: ושם): בשלמא פרה עומדת לפדותה, פירוש: דאם מצא נאה ממנה מצוה לפדותה, אלא הני מנחות — אין מצוה לפדותן. ובכריתות בפ' "אשם תלוי" (ד' כד:) אמר בהדיא: אימור דאמר רבי שמעון במידי דעומד לזרוק. והכי איתא הגירסא בספרים: אלא אמר רבא, ה"ק רב המנונא: אין מלקות אותו ואת בנו נוהג בקדשים, (א) דכיון דלכל כמה דלא נזרק דם לא משתרי בשר, בעידנא דקא שחיט הויא התראת ספק, ולא שמיה התראה ולא לקי. משמע: למאן דאמר שמה התראה — לקי, אם כן שחיטה ראויה היא היכא דנזרק לבסוף. ובקונטרס פי' התם, דגרס: אין מלקות אותו ואת בנו בקדשים, ולא יותר. ולא משום דהוו התראת ספק, אלא משום דמחוסר זמן הוא, דשחיטה שאינה ראויה היא. וקשה לר"י: אי חשיב מחוסר זמן, ואסור לשוחטו משום אותו ואת בנו — אם כן הוא לוקה משום "לא תשחטו", כיון דאמר רחמנא אותו ואת בנו נוהג בקדשים, וא"א אלא בשחיטה שאין ראויה — בעל כרחך גזירת הכתוב כך היא שהיא כשחיטה הראויה להתחייב עליה. מידי דהוה אשחוטי חוץ, (ב) ואע"ג דלמידי אחרינא חשיב שחיטה שאינה ראויה — לענין שחוטי חוץ מיהא מחייב, כיון שאין האיסור מחמת דבר אחר. ה"נ באותו ואת בנו! וא"ת: ואמאי צריך בפרק בתרא דזבחים (דף קיג:) למעוטי רובע ונרבע דלא מחייב משום שחוטי חוץ, מדכתיב "ואל פתח אהל" כו'? תיפוק ליה דשחיטה שאין ראויה היא מחמת איסור אחר! ודוחק לומר דלרבנן איצטריך קרא ולא לרבי שמעון. ויש שהיו רוצים לתרץ: דאע"ג דבעלמא ילפינן מ"וטבוח טבח והכן" — בשחוטי חוץ גופיה סברא הוא דילפינן מגופייהו. ואין נראה לר"י, דאם כן שוחט טריפת חולין בעזרה אמאי מתיר רבי שמעון בהנאה בספ"ב דקדושין (דף נח. ושם) וב"כיסוי הדם" (חולין דף פה: ושם) משום דהויא שחיטה שאינה ראויה? נילף מגופה, דלעולם שחיטת חולין בעזרה שחיטה שאין ראויה היא, דקסבר רבי שמעון חולין שנשחטו בעזרה דאורייתא! אלא משום דאפילו הכי בעינן שלא יהא בה פסול אחר. **והלא** פדייה מתרת. תימה: מה פריך? דלמא כשנפדית איירי, שהרי יכול לפדות אחר שחיטה, לפי' הקונטרס דאיירי בבעל מום מעיקרו, וכיון דלבסוף נפדה — הויא שחיטה ראויה, כדמוכח בחולין (דף פ: ושם)! ומיהו, לפר"ת דמיירי בהקדישו קודם למומו, אע"ג דבשעת פירכוס היה יכול לפדות — סתמא דמילתא דגנב אין נודע לו שהוא דקדשים עד אחר זמן, שכבר אין מפרכס. אבל לפירוש הקונטרס קשה! מיהו, לפירושו נמי מצי למימר: דסתם גניבה שחיטה וכל מעשיה בסתר, ומיד אחר השחיטה רגילין לאוכלה. וסתמא דמילתא לא נודע לו שהיא דהקדש עד שנאכלה, דתו לא מיפרקא. **כל** העומד לזרוק כזרוק דמי. תימה: דבפרק "אותו ואת בנו" (חולין דף פ. ושם) אמר רבי אושעיא: כולה מתניתין דלא כרבי שמעון כו' עד קדשים בפנים. מכדי שמעינן ליה לרבי שמעון דאמר שחיטה שאינה ראויה לא שמה שחיטה, קדשים נמי שחיטה שאינה ראויה היא, דכל כמה דלא זרק הדם לא משתרי בשר, שני אמאי סופג את הארבעים ופסול? כלומר, דחשבינן ליה לקמא כאילו קטליה, והוה ליה שני כשר גמור. ואמאי חשיב ליה שחיטה שאין ראויה? נהי דלא משתרי בשר אלא בזריקת הדם — הלא משעת שחיטה הוי כזרוק, דכל העומד לזרוק כזרוק דמי! ומפרש רבינו תם: דרבי אושעיא לית ליה כל העומד לזרוק כזרוק דמי, אלא סבירא ליה כתנא קמא דמתניתין דהתם (ד' פא:), דתנן: השוחט ונמצאת טריפה, השוחט פרת חטאת — רבי שמעון פוטר. דלא מחייב משום אותו ואת בנו, דשחיטה שאין ראויה היא, ולית ליה כל העומד לפדות כפדוי דמי. והתם בגמרא פריך עלה מההיא דפרה מטמא טומאת אוכלין, ומשני: פרת חטאת אינה משנה. אבל ר' אושעיא סבר לאדרבה, מתניתין דהתם עיקר, וההיא דפרה ליתא. ועוד י"ל, דקסבר ר' אושעיא: כיון דלא אמרינן כזרוק דמי עד שיתקבל בכוס, כדמשמע בפ"ק דפסחים (דף יג: ושם) דמצוה הוא להמתין מלזרוק עד שתקבל כל דם הנפש — הלכך בגמר השחיטה, שעדיין לא נתקבל כל הדם, לא אמרינן כזרוק דמי. ועי"ל: דקסבר ר' אושעיא דאפילו הוי כזרוק בשעת שחיטה, כיון דבשחיטה לחודה לא משתרי בשר, אלא מחמת דהוי כזרוק — לא הוי דומיא ד"טבוח טבח והכן", ושחיטה שאין ראויה היא. וא"ש, דבריש "המנחות והנסכים" (מנחות דף קא: ושם) פריך ליה לר' אושעיא: מכדי שמעינן ליה לר' שמעון כל העומד לזרוק כזרוק דמי כו'. ומיהו, סוגיא דשמעתין חשיב ליה שפיר שחיטה ראויה, וכן במסקנא דהתם. וכי היכי דפריך התם ארב המנונא הוי מצי למפרך לר' אושעיא, וכי היכי דמתרץ לרב המנונא הוי מצי לתרץ לרבי אושעיא, דהא דלא מוקי מתניתין כרבי שמעון — משום דלרבי שמעון שני אין סופג את הארבעים, דה"ל התראת ספק. ור"ת לא גרס "ושני אמאי סופג את הארבעים ופסול", דשני *כבר נפסל, דשחיטה ראשונה שחיטה ראויה היא כיון דנזרק הדם בהכשר, והוי שני מחוסר זמן. אלא גרסינן: "אמאי סופג את הארבעים" ותו לא. ומן השני דייק, דשחיטה שאינה ראויה היא, ואמאי סופג את הארבעים? הא ה"ל התראת ספק, דשמא לא יזרוק. וכזרוק לא הוי, כיון דאין מצוה לזורקו. ופריך: פשיטא דהכי איתא, דהיאך ילקה דהא התראת ספק היא! ועוד, דאסור לזרוק הדם, ופשיטא דלא תגמר השחיטה! ומשני: קדשים כו'. והשתא ארבי אושעיא לא מצי פריך מידי, אלא לרב המנונא.

פרה

מנחות דף קא: [תוספתא דשוקלין פ"ג]

[ד"ה שחיטה]

[ד"ה דכמה]

גי' ב"י שפיר נפסל

הגהות הב"ח

(א) תום' ד"ה והלא זריקה וכו' נוהג בקדשים מ"ט דכיון דלכל כמה וכו' משמע דלמאן דאמר: (ב) בא"ד דאע"ג דלמידי אחריני:

*פָּרָה מְטַמָּא טוּמְאַת אוֹכָלִין, הוֹאִיל וְהָיְתָה לָהּ שְׁעַת הַכּוֹשֶׁר; וְאָמַר

פָּרָה. אֲדוּמָּה מְטַמְּאָה טוּמְאַת אוֹכְלִין. דַּהֲוָיָא לָהּ שְׁעַת הַכּוֹשֶׁר. לֶאֱכוֹל מִשֶּׁנִּשְׁחֲטָה, וְיָרְדָה לָהּ תּוֹרַת אוֹכֶל. וְאָמַר

פרה מטמא טומאת אוכלין כו'. תימה: דמדקאמר הואיל והיתה לה שעת הכושר — מכלל דהשתא לאו בת פדייה היא, ואמאי? והא אית ליה לר"ש בשבועות (דף יא: ושם) דפרה קדשי בדק הבית היא, ולר"ש אית ליה דקדשי בדק הבית לא היו בכלל העמדה והערכה בההיא שמעתא גופא! ונראה לפרש: דהא דקתני הואיל והיתה לה שעת הכושר — מיירי לאחר הזאה, דאין סברא שתהא בת פדייה אחר שהוזה דמה. ואפ"ה מטמא טומאת אוכלין, הואיל והיתה לה שעת הכושר קודם הזאה. וא"ת: והא כל העומד להזות כמוזה דמי! וי"ל: דקודם קבלה (א) לאו כמוזה דמי, כדפרישית לעיל. הקשה רבינו שמואל בר חיים: למה לי דהיתה לה שעת הכושר? תיפוק ליה דחיבת הקדש מכשרתו ומשויא לה אוכלא, כדדרשינן בפ"ב דחולין (דף לו: ושם) "והבשר" לרבות עצים ולבונה! וכ"ת דפרה לר"ש כיון דקדשי בדק הבית היא לא שייך בה חיבת הקדש, דאפילו בקדשי מזבח לא מהני חיבת הקדש אלא כשקדשו קדושת הגוף בכלי שרת, כדמוכח בריש "המנחות והנסכים" (מנחות דף קב:) ובפ' "כל הפסולין" (זבחים דף לד.) — הא ע"כ שייך בפרה חיבת הקדש אפילו לר"ש, דבריש "המנחות והנסכים" פריך לר"ש: נותר ופרה אמאי מטמא טומאת אוכלין? עפרא בעלמא הוא, דכל העומד לשרוף כשרוף דמי! ומשני: חיבת הקדש מכשרתו. והיינו טעמא, דאע"ג דאין בה קידוש כלי כיון דקדשי בדק הבית היא — מ"מ שייך ביה חיבת הקדש, כיון דחטאת קרייה רחמנא, וכל ענייניה כעין עבודת הגוף, שיש בה הזאה ופסולה שלא לשמה! ותירץ ר"י דאין חיבת הקדש מועלת אלא לשוייה שאין אוכל כאוכל, כגון נותר ופרה שהן חשובים כעפרא, ועצים ולבונה. אבל דבר שהוא אוכל, אלא שאין מקבל טומאה לר"ש משום (ב) אוכל שאין אתה יכול להאכילו לאחרים — לא יועיל חיבת הקדש לעשות האיסור כמותר. והא דמשמע בריש "כל הפסולין" דאוכל בשר שנטמא לפני זריקה ה"א דלא לקי, על ידי דרשה דכל שאין ניתר לטהורים אין חייבין עליו משום טומאה, אי לאו משום דמרבינן מ"והבשר" כמו עצים ולבונה — התם כיון דלא בעי פטור ליה אלא משום דבעי למילף מטומאת הגוף, יש לנו לרבות מ"והבשר" מק"ו דעצים ולבונה. וא"ת: אמאי לא אמר דכל קדשים יקבלו טומאה מחיים, כיון דמלוה לשוחטן, ונימא: כל העומד לשחוט כשחוט דמי! וי"ל: דאפילו נשחט לא אמרינן דכזרוק דמי עד שיקבל בכוס, כ"ש כשעדיין לא נשחט. ומיהו, שעיר המשתלח קשה לר"י, שיטמא מחיים טומאת אוכלין לר"ש, למ"ד (יומא סז.) דשרו (ג) איבריו בהנאה, דכיון שעומד לדחות כדחוי דמי! וי"ל: דכל העומד לעשות לא אמר דכעשוי דמי אלא באוכל האסור להיות כמותר, וקרינן ביה אוכל שאתה יכול להאכילו לאחרים, אבל לא מהני לשאין אוכל כמו כ"ש ליחשב כאוכל, אע"ג דהוה מהני על האוכל כגון נותר ופרה ליחשב כעפרא, אי לאו דמכשר להו חיבת הקדש. מידי דהוה אבן פקועה ודגים שהן מותרין בלא שחיטה, ואפ"ה חיותן מטהרתן לרבנן דפליגי אר' יוסי הגלילי בפ' "בהמה המקשה" (חולין דף עה.). **פרה** מטמא טומאת אוכלין. הקשה בקונטרס בפ' "אותו ואת בנו" (חולין דף פא: ושם): למה לי קבלת טומאה? תיפוק ליה דהיא גופה מטמאה אדם ובגדים! ותירץ דבכה"ג מפרש בכריתות בפ' "דם שחיטה" (דף כא.) כגון (ד) שחיפהו פחות מכביצה בצק, אי משוית לה אוכל — מצטרף בהדי בצק, ומקבל האי בצק טומאה אם יגע בטומאה, ומטמא שאר אוכלים. ואי לאו אוכל הוא — לא מקבל האי בצק טומאה, דלית ביה שיעורא, וכי נגעו ביה אוכלין אחרים — טהורין הן, שאין נוגעין בנבילה אלא בבצק, עכ"ל. ומה שהזכיר נבילה — משום דעלה דכריתות קאמר. ומה שאמר ומקבל האי בצק טומאה אם יגע בטומאה — נראה לר"י דלא דק, דההיא דחיפהו בבצק דכריתות — מיירי כשיש כזית מן הנבילה. ונראה שטמא הבצק מן הנבילה ע"י צרופו לכבילה, כמו שמיטמא ממקום אחר, שהכזית יכול להיות מטמא ומצטרף. ונראה שחזר בו משיטתו שהיה רגיל לפרש בכל מקום, דאוכל פחות מכביצה מקבל טומאה מן התורה, שהרי פירש בהדיא דלא מקבל האי בצק טומאה, דלית ביה שיעורא. ואין לתרץ קושיית הקונטרס דבלא צירוף בצק צריך הוא לטעם של שעת הכושר, משום דלא מצינו שמטמאה אלא מתעסקין, כדתנן במס' פרה (פ"ח מ"ג): השורף פרה ופרים והמשלח את השעיר — מטמא בגדים, והן עצמם אין מטמא בגדים, הרי זה אומר: [מטמאיך] לא טימאוני ואת טמאתני. דמ"מ מטמאה היא אוכלין ומשקין, מאחר שסופה לטמא טומאה חמורה את מתעסקין, ולא בעי לא הכשר מים ולא הכשר שרץ, כדתני דבי ר' ישמעאל בפ' "בא סימן" (נדה דף נא. ושם): מה זרעים שאין סופן לטמא טומאה חמורה צריכין הכשר כו'. ור"י מתרץ: דמה שסופו לטמא טומאה חמורה לא מהני אלא לענין זה דחשבינן ליה כאילו הוכשר במים וכאילו נגע בשרץ, אבל אין מועיל לעשות שאין אוכל כאוכל. הלכך, לר"ש דבעי אוכל שאתה יכול להאכיל לאחרים — מה שסופו לטמא טומאה חמורה לא יעשנו [כאוכל] להאכילו לאחרים, ולכך לא מטמא אלא משום שהיה לה שעת הכושר. וכן מוכח בזבחים בס"פ "טבול יום" (דף קה.), דת"ר: השורף הפרה ופרים, והמשלח השעיר — מטמא בגדים, והם [עצמם] אינם מטמא בגדים אלא מטמא אוכל ומשקה, דברי ר"מ, וחכמים אומרים: פרה ופרים מטמא טומאת אוכלין ומשקין, אבל לא שעיר המשתלח מפני שהוא חי. ופריך: בשלמא ר"מ — כדתנא דבי ר' ישמעאל מה זרעים כו'. אלא לרבנן, אי אית להו דתנא דבי ר' ישמעאל — אפילו שעיר המשתלח נמי, ואי לית להו — פרה ופרים מנליה? ומשני: אין צריכין הכשר טומאה ממקום אחר. פי': נהי דהאי דסופו לטמא טומאה חמורה אין צריכין הכשר טומאה, אבל הכשר אוכל בעי. ומש"ה, שעיר המשתלח דלא חזי לאכילה, שהוא חי — לא מטמא. והשתא פליגי, דר"מ סבר דמה שסופו לטמא טומאה חמורה — מועיל ליחשב אכילה, ורבנן סברי: דפרה ופרים דוקא מטמא, ולא שעיר המשתלח, משום דאינו מועיל ליחשב אוכל. ור"ש סבר: דוקא פרה, הואיל והיתה לה שעת הכושר קרינן ביה אוכל שאתה יכול להאכילו לאחרים, ולא פרים ושעיר המשתלח שלא היתה להן שעת הכושר. וכן מוכח בתוספתא דפרה, דבתר מילתייהו דר"מ ורבנן קתני: ר"ש אומר: פרה מטמא טומאת אוכלין, הואיל והיתה לה שעת הכושר, פרים הנשרפין ושעירים הנשרפין אין מטמאין טומאת אוכלין, הואיל ולא היה להן שעת הכושר. ועוד מייתי ר"י ראייה: דבכמה דוכתי קתני צריכין מחשבה ואין צריכין הכשר, בפ' "דם שחיטה" (כריתות דף כא.) גבי נבלת בהמה טמאה בכל מקום ונבלת העוף בכפרים, ובפ' "בא סימן" (נדה דף נ:) גבי גוזל שנפל לגת, ובריש טהרות גבי נבלת עוף טהור, דאע"פ שאין צריכין הכשר, לפי שסופו לטמא טומאה חמורה — צריכין מחשבה, דלגבי הא [לשווי אוכל] לא מהני מה שסופו לטמא טומאה חמורה. ותימה אי פליג ר"מ אכל הני. ועוד, *דבפ' "ג"ה" (חולין דף קכ.) ובפ' "טבול יום" (זבחים ד' קה:) בעי למידק דההיא דצריכה מחשבה ואין צריכה הכשר דטהרות אתיא כר"מ, מדסיפא ר"מ, דקתני: שחיטה ומליקה מטהרת טריפתה מטומאתה. ומשני: מידי אריא, סיפא ר"מ ורישא רבנן. והיכי הוה בעי לאוכוחי? הא ע"כ צריכה מחשבה אתא דלא כר"מ! ועוד: דב"העור והרוטב" (חולין ד' קכח: ושם) גבי חתך בשר מן אבר מן החי, חתכו ואח"כ חישב עליו — טהור, חישב עליו ואח"כ חתכו — טמא. ומוקמינן לה התם כר"מ. ופריך התם למאן דמוקי לה בשהוכשר, ל"ל הוכשר? הרי מטמא טומאה חמורה אגב אביו! משמע: אע"ג דמוקמינן לה כר"מ — ניחא ליה מה שמועיל לטמא טומאה חמורה אגב אביו לענין דלא בעי הכשר, ולענין מחשבה לא מהני! ואור"י: דיש לחלק בין שעיר המשתלח, דממילא אם היה נשחט הוי חזי לאכילה בלא מחשבה, מה שאין בנבלת עוף טהור ובאבר מן החי שאין סופו לעשות אוכל — מודה ר"מ דבעינן מחשבה. וגרסינן "פרה מטמא", ול"ג "מיטמאה". דלמאי נ"מ קבלת טומאה שלה? אי לטמא אחרים, כיון שהיתה לה שעת הכושר — תורת אוכל יש לה, ובלא קבלת טומאה היא מטמא אחרים משום דסופה לטמא טומאה חמורה. ובתוספתא נמי מוכח דגרסינן "מטמא", ולא "מיטמאה", דקתני: מטמא אוכלין ומשקין. ואי גרסינן "מיטמא" — צ"ל כמו שתירץ רש"י, כשצירפה (ה) פחות מכביצה בצק, שאי אפשר לפרה לטמא בצק. שאין מועיל מה שסופו לטמא טומאה חמורה אלא דהוי כנוגע בשרץ, ואילו נגע בשרץ — לא היה מטמא את הבצק, כיון שבשר פרה הוא פחות מכביצה, לכך צריך קבלת טומאה ממקום אחר כדי שיטמא הבצק. וקשה: דלמאי נ"מ במה שמצטרף לפחות מכביצה? הא בלא"ה אוכל מקבל טומאה בכל שהוא! ואי לענין קבלת טומאה דאורייתא, לשרוף עליו את הקדשים — הניחא אי חיבת הקדש דפרה דאורייתא, אע"פ שאין בה קידוש כלי. אבל אם מדרבנן — ע"כ לא מקבלי טומאה הני אוכלין אלא מדרבנן, דמדאורייתא כשרוף דמי, ועפרא בעלמא נינהו. ועוד מפרש ר"י: מה שמיטמא ע"י קבלת טומאה מן השרץ (ו) ונפסלת בכך, אי לאו דהיתה לה שעת הכושר — לא היתה מקבלת טומאה ולא היתה נפסלת. דאע"ג דקפיד רחמנא בעוסקין בה שיהיו טהורים — לאו משום דהוה מטמאו לה, אלא משום גזירת הכתוב הוא, דאפילו בעוסקין בה בקנה או בפשוטי כלי עץ בעינן שיהיו טהורין. וא"ת: דאי לאפסולי [היא] עצמה — גם האפר יהיה נפסל בנגיעת הטומאה, כדאמר בפרק "חומר בקדש" (חגיגה דף כג. ושם): לא ישא אדם אפר חטאת ומי חטאת ויעבירם בספינה, משום מעשה שהיה! וי"ל: דאי חשיבא אוכל — מקבל טומאה משני ומשלישי, ואי לא — לא. ואין לומר דנ"מ מה שמטמא טומאת אוכלין, דמאחר שנפסל ואין עליה עוד טומאה חמורה — אכתי אשתייר בה טומאת אוכלין. אי נמי, הכי קאמר: אחר שנפסלה, אם נגע בה שרץ — מיטמא טומאת אוכלין, הואיל והיתה לה שעת הכושר. דמה שכבר טמא טומאה חמורה אין מועיל לו, מאחר דהשתא מיהא אין עוד סופו לטמא טומאה חמורה. וראייה מפרק "בהמה המקשה" (חולין דף עג:). ואין להאריך כאן בזה, דלא יתכן לפרש כאן כלל, מדפריך במנחות (דף קב:) כיון דכל העומד לשרוף כשרוף דמי, נותר ופרה אמאי מטמא טומאת אוכלין? ומאי קושיא, והא לאחר שקבלה הפרה טומאה אין עומדת לישרף, דנפסלה ונשתייר בה מגע טומאה. ואפילו לא נגע בה שרץ אלא פעם אחת, מכל מקום — בתחילת נגיעה כבר נפסלה הפרה, ובסוף נגיעה מטמאה טומאת אוכלין, דאז כבר אין עומדת לישרף.

אומר

שבועות יא: חולין פא: מנחות קא: [תוספתא פרה פ"ו]

לא נמצא שם

הגהות הב"ח

(א) תום' ד"ה פרה וכו' וי"ל דקודם קבלה בכוס לאו כמוזה: (ב) בא"ד לר"ש משום דבעי אוכל שאתה יכול כצ"ל: (ג) בא"ד למ"ד דשרו אברים בהנאה דכיון שעומד לדחות לצוק כדחוי דמי וי"ל דלא אמרינן דכל העומד לעשות דכעשוי דמי אלא כצ"ל: (ד) ד"ה פרה וכו' בפרק דם שחיטה כגון בשר שחיפהו כצ"ל: (ה) בא"ד שתירץ רש"י כשצירפה לפחות: (ו) בא"ד מן השרץ נפסלת בכך ואי לאו וכו' משום דגזירת הכתוב:

גליון הש"ס

תום' ד"ה פרה וכו' ועוד דבפ' גיד הנשה דף קכ ובפ' טבול יום דף קה בעי למידק. בפ' גה"נ לא נזכר מזה ובפ' טבול יום מבואר דקאמר דרישא דצריכא מחשב' אתיא כר"מ וקיימא כן במסקנא אלא דמציעתא דמטמא בכבילה רבנן ובהכרח דתו' היה להם גי' אחרת שם:

תורה אור

ואמר ריש לקיש: אומר היה רבי שמעון: פרה נפדית ע"ג מערכתה; אלמא: כל העומד לפדות כפדוי דמי. בשלמא רבי יוחנן לא אמר כרבי שמעון בן לקיש, דקא בעי לאוקמה למתניתין אפילו בתמימין, אלא ריש לקיש מאי טעמא לא אמר כרבי יוחנן? אמר לך: °"וטבחו *ומכרו" — כל היכא דאיתיה במכירה איתיה בטביחה, *וכל היכא דליתיה במכירה ליתיה בטביחה; והני קדשים, הואיל דכי מזבין קדשים לא הויא מכירה — ליתנהו בטביחה. ואזדו לטעמייהו, דאתמר: המוכר טריפה, לדברי ר' שמעון — רבי יוחנן אמר: חייב, וריש לקיש אמר: פטור; רבי יוחנן אמר חייב, אע"ג דליתיה בטביחה איתיה במכירה; וריש לקיש אמר פטור, כיון דליתיה בטביחה ליתיה במכירה. איתיביה רבי יוחנן לר"ש בן לקיש: [א]גנב כלאים וטבחה, טריפה ומכרה — משלם תשלומי ארבעה וחמשה; מאי לאו ר"ש היא? אלמא: אע"ג דליתיה בטביחה איתיה במכירה! אמר ליה: לא, רבנן. אי רבנן, טריפה במכירה איתא, בזביחה ליתא?! ואלא מאי, ר"ש? כלאים בטביחה איתא, במכירה ליתא?! אלא, תנא טביחה והוא הדין למכירה, אימא לרבנן נמי: תנא מכירה והוא הדין לטביחה. ורבי יוחנן אמר לך: האי מאי? אי אמרת בשלמא ר"ש, איידי דתנא טריפה בחדא תנא כלאים בחדא. אלא אי אמרת רבנן, נערבינהו וניתנינהו: גנב כלאים וטריפה, טבחן ומכרן — משלם תשלומי ארבעה וחמשה! קשיא. כלאים — "שה" כתיב, *ואמר רבא: זה בנה אב, כל מקום שנאמר "שה" אינו אלא להוציא את הכלאים! שאני הכא, דאמר קרא "או" — לרבות את הכלאים. וכל "או" לרבות הוא? והתניא: °"שור או כשב" — *[ב]פרט לכלאים, "או עז" — [ג]פרט לנדמה! אמר רבא: הכא מענייניה דקרא, והכא מענייניה דקרא; הכא גבי גניבה דכתיב: "שור או שה", שאי אתה יכול להוציא כלאים מביניהם — "או" לרבות כלאים; גבי קדשים דכתיב כשב ועז, שאתה יכול להוציא כלאים מביניהם — "או" למעט הוא. והא

שמות כא | ויקרא כב

ואמר ריש לקיש. איזו שעת הכושר היתה לה – דאומר היה ר"ש: פרה נפדית אפילו נשחטה על (א) המערכה כמשפט, אם מצא אחרת יפה ממנה, וזהו שעת הכושר שלה. ואע"פ דלא נפדית, אפילו הכי משוי לה אוכלא, הואיל וראויה לפדות. אפילו בתמימין. וכ"ש בבעלי מומין בחוץ, דשינויא דחיקא הוא. לא הויא מכירה. דאין קדשים תמימים יוצאים לחולין, הלכך בבעלי מומין עסקינן, דאיתנהו בתרוייהו. ואזדו לטעמייהו. דאיפליגו בה אי בעינן תרוייהו אי לא. לדברי ר"ש. שפוטר על טביחתה. גנב כלאים. מכבשה ותיש בא. ואע"ג דכתיב גבי טביחה "שה", ואמר רבא לקמן: כל מקום שנאמר "שה" – אין כלאים במשמע – הכא מחייב, דאיתרבי בהדיא כדלקמן. מאי לאו ר"ש היא. מדנקט בטריפה מכירה, ולא נקט טביחה. דתנא טריפה בחדא. דלא מצי לערובי כלאים וטריפה ולמיתני טביחה ומכירה בתרוייהו בהדדי, ואצטריך למיתני טריפה בחדא, במכירה ולא בטביחה. תנא נמי כלאים בחדא. ואף על גב דאיתיה בתרוייהו. ונקט ביה טביחה דפתח ביה קרא ברישא. או. "שור או שה" דאמר בפ' דלעיל (דף סז:) שור דסיפא ושה דרישא מייתר, הלכך "או" נמי מייתר. פרט לכלאים. דפסול לקרבן. נדמה. דאינו דומה לאביו ולא לאמו, שבא מאיל ורחל ודומה לעז. גבי גניבה דכתיב שור או שה. דאי לא הוה כתיב "או" לרבות – לא משתמע כלאים מינייהו, שהרי אין מתעברין זה מזה, שאין עיבורן שוה, דבהמה גסה יולדת לתשעה ודקה לחמשה. הלכך "או" לרבויי אתא, ולא להוציא. דהא בלאו הכי לא אתי כלאים במשמעות דקרא.
להוציא

אומר היה ר"ש פרה נפדית כו'. נרא' שר"ל דאפילו מדרבנן מותר לפדותה. דבספ"ק דשבועות (דף יא:) דייק אמתניתא (תוספתא פ"א) דמסכת פרה, דקתני: שחטה על גב מערכתה אין לה פדייה עולמית — דלא אתי כר"ש, דלר"ש נפדית היא, כדאשכחן הכא. ותימה: דע"כ מה שאין נפדית לרבנן — אין זה מן התורה, דהא בת העמדה והערכה היא כל זמן שמפרכסת, לפי פי' אחד דלעיל (ד' עו.*), ואם כן מנ"ל *לר"ל דר"ש פליג ארבנן? דלמא מודה ר"ש דמדרבנן לאו בת פדייה היא אלא מדאורייתא, ולהכי מטמא טומאת אוכלים — הואיל והיתה לה שעת הכושר! וזה דוחק לומר דאף על גב דמדאורייתא בת פדייה היא, כיון דמדרבנן לאו בת פדייה לא חשיב אוכל שאתה יכול להאכיל לאחרים! וי"ל: דמאן דאסר — אסר אפילו מדאורייתא, כיון ששחט לשמה בהכשר קרבן, ומאן דשרי — שרי אפילו מדרבנן עד שיעשו הזיותיה, כדפרישית לעיל. ואם היינו אומרים דלרבנן פרה קדשי מזבח היא — הוי א"ש. אך אין נראה שיסבור שום תנא דפרה קדשי מזבח היא, מדקא מתמה גמרא בריש "אין מעמידין" (ע"ז ד' כג: ושם): שמע מינה דפרה קדשי מזבח היא? ובכמה מקומות קאמר דחטאת קרייה רחמנא, משמע דקדשי בדק הבית היא. אע"ג דתנן בשקלים (ד' ו) שהיא מתרומת הלשכה — היינו לפי שצריכין לה כהנים העובדים קרבנות חשיב צורך קרבן, ולב ב"ד מתנה עליהן, דאפילו מלמדי הלכות קמילה לכהנים נוטלין שכרן מתרומת הלשכה. ואפילו בלא ב"ד מתנה על הלשכה יכול להיות שבאה ממנה מן התורה הואיל וצורך קרבנות היא. והא דאמר דקדשי בדק הבית היא — לא שתהא קנויה מקדשי בדק הבית, אלא דינה כקדשי בדק הבית, דקדושה קדושת דמים ולא קדושת הגוף כקדשי מזבח. כל היכא דאיתיה במכירה איתיה בטביחה כו'. ומוכר בשבת דחייב, אע"ג דאם טבח פטור — ההיא בהמה איתא בטביחה בחול. זה בנה אב כל מקום שנאמר שה אינו אלא להוציא את הכלאים. בפרק "אותו ואת בנו" (חולין ד' עח: ושם*) פי' בקונטרס דעביד בנין אב מדכתיב "שור שה כשבים ושה עזים". וקשה לר"י: דלקמן אמר דלרבי אליעזר אתאי דרבא לטמא שנולד מן הטהור ועיבורו מן הטמא, דלא כר' יהושע, דאי כר' יהושע מ"שה כשבים" ומ"שה עזים" נפקא, כלומר ולא צריך לבנין אב דרבא. ואדרבה, מההוא קרא הוי בנין אב דרבא! ונראה לר"י: דבנין אב דרבא הוי מ"שה" דפסח, דכתיב (שמות יב) "שה תמים זכר בן שנה יהיה לכם". תדע, דהא מסקינן: כי איתמר דרבא — לענין פטר חמור איתמר, דתנן: אין פודין כו', ובספ"ק דבכורות (ד' יב. ושם) מפיק ליה מ"שה" "שה" דפסח. וא"ת: ומ"ש דהכא קרי ליה בנין אב, ובבכורות קרי ליה ג"ש, דקאמר: נאמר כאן "שה" ונאמר להלן "שה"? ועוד: מ"ש דנקט רבא כלאים טפי מעגל וחיה טריפה ושחוטה? דכל הני נפקא לן דאין פודין פטר חמור מ"שה" דפסח, דקאמר התם: מה להלן פרט לכל השמות הללו! ועוד: אמאי לא פריך: טריפה — "שה" כתיב, כי היכא דפריך: כלאים — "שה" כתיב? ועוד: דלרבי אליעזר, דשרי לפדות בכלאים פטר חמור, אמאי לא שרי בשחוטה וטריפה, כיון דמוקי לה בנין אב לטמא שנולד כו' כדאמרינן לקמן בשמעתין? ועוד: כי בעי לקמן: לרבי אליעזר בנין אב דרבא למאי הלכתא — לימא: למעוטי אחריני אתא, דאין פודין! וכ"ת דטריפה ושחוטה ממשמעותיה ד"שה" נפקא, כמו עגל וחיה, דהא אמר בפרק "הוציאו לו" (יומא ד' מט: ושם*) דפר אפילו שחוט קרוי פר, וכן שה דפסח, אי לאו דכתיב "מהיות משה" מחיותיה דשה! ונראה לר"י דבנין אב דרבא וג"ש דבכורות לאו חדא מילתא היא, דודאי תרוייהו נפקי מ"שה" דפסח. ובנין אב דרבא אתי מיתורא ד"כשבים ומן העזים תקחו", דמשמע עד שיהא אביו כבש ואמו כבשה. ולגופיה לא איצטריך, דמשאר קדשים נפקא, דתניא בסמוך "שור או כשב או עז" פרט לכלאים. אלא ללמוד בעלמא אתי, דכל מקום שנאמר "שה" — אינו אלא להוציא כלאים. ואי לאו בנין אב — מגזירה שוה ד"שה" "שה" לא הוה ממעטינן כלאים, משום דה"א "תפדה" "תפדה" ריבה, כי היכי דלא ממעטינן התם שאינו זכר תמים ובן שנה מג"ש, משום "תפדה תפדה" ריבה. וסברא הוא למעט כולה מגזירה שוה ד"שה" טפי מכלאים, [דאיהו נמי מקרי שה], ומש"ה רבי אליעזר דמוקי בנין אב דרבא לטמא שנולד כו' — שרי בכלאים. ולקמן דקאמר: אי לקדשים בהדיא כתיב בהו — משמע דאי לא הוה כתיב בהדיא הוה אתי ליה שפיר, אע"ג דעיקר בנין אב לא הוה מייתר בפסח אלא משום דבפסח גופיה לא איצטריך, דמקדשים נפקא — כן דרך הגמרא, שעושה כאילו קים ליה ממקום אחר. וה"ק: אי לקדשים, ותאמר דמקרא אחרינא נפקא לן בפסח למעוטי כלאים כו'. וכענין זה יש בריש קדושין (דף ג: ושם*) ובפרק "נערה" (כתובות דף מו:) גבי קידושי הבת לאביה, דקאמר: וכ"ת נילף מבושת ופגם. אע"ג דבושת ופגם גופיה לא קים לן דלאבוה הוא אלא מקדושין, בס"פ "אלו נערות" (שם דף מ: ושם*).

גבי גניבה דכתיב שור או שה שאין אתה יכול להוציא כלאים מביניהם. ואם תאמר: בלאו הכי נמי תמ"ל: גבי גניבה דכתיב "שה" — למעט כלאים כדרבא אתי, או לרבויי! וי"ל: דמילתא דרבא לא איתמר אלא היכא דכתיב "שה" לחוד, אבל הכא כתיב נמי "שור".
והא

קו א מיי' פ"ב מהלכות גניבה הלכה ט טור ח"מ סי' שנ:
קז ב מיי' פ"ג מהלכות איסורי מזבח הלכה ד והלכה יא:
קח ג מיי' שם הלכה ה:

[ד"ה שחיטה]
עיין רש"א ובספר כ"י

הגהות הב"ח
(א) רש"י ד"ה ואמר ריש לקיש וכו' נשחטה על גבי מערכתה:

[או מכרו כל"ל]
[עי' תוס' כתובות לג: ד"ה גנב]
חולין עח.
נדה מא. בכורות יב.
נז. חולין לח:
[ד"ה זה]
[ד"ה שאני]
[ד"ה וכי]

וְהָא גַּבֵּי קָדָשִׁים נַמִּי נֶאֱמַר "שׁוֹר אוֹ כֶשֶׂב" שֶׁאֵין אַתָּה יָכוֹל לְהוֹצִיא כִּלְאַיִם מִבֵּינֵיהֶם, וּנְרַבֵּי! מִדְּסֵיפָא לְמַעֵט, רֵישָׁא נַמִּי לְמַעֵט. אַדְּרַבָּה, מִדְּרֵישָׁא לְרַבּוֹת, סֵיפָא נַמִּי לְרַבּוֹת! הַאי מַאי? אִי אָמְרַתְּ בִּשְׁלָמָא לְמַעֵט — הוּא דְּאִיצְטְרִיךְ תְּרֵי מִיעוּטֵי, דְּאע"ג דְּאִימַּעַט כִּלְאַיִם אִיצְטְרִיךְ לְמַעוּטֵי נִדְמֶה. אֶלָּא אִי אָמְרַתְּ לְרַבּוֹת, תְּרֵי רִיבּוּיֵי לָמָּה? הַשְׁתָּא כִּלְאַיִם אִירַבֵּי לֵיהּ, נִדְמֶה מִבַּעְיָא? *אֶלָּא הָא דְּאָמַר רָבָא: זֶה בָּנָה אָב, כָּל מָקוֹם שֶׁנֶּאֱמַר "שֶׂה" אֵינוֹ אֶלָּא לְהוֹצִיא אֶת הַכִּלְאַיִם, לְמַאי הִלְכְתָא? אִי לְקָדָשִׁים — בְּהֶדְיָא כְּתִיב בְּהוּ: °"שׁוֹר אוֹ כֶשֶׂב" פְּרָט לַכִּלְאַיִם, אִי [א]לְמַעֲשֵׂר — "תַּחַת" "תַּחַת" יָלֵיף מִקָּדָשִׁים, *אִי לִבְכוֹר — הַעֲבָרָה הַעֲבָרָה יָלֵיף מִמַּעֲשֵׂר! אִי נַמִּי, נִדְמֶה אָמְרַתְּ לָא, דִּכְתִיב: °"אַךְ בְּכוֹר שׁוֹר" — *[ב]עַד שֶׁיְּהֵא הוּא שׁוֹר וּבְכוֹרוֹ שׁוֹר, כִּלְאַיִם מִבַּעְיָא? אֶלָּא, כִּי אִיתְּמַר דְּרָבָא — לְעִנְיַן פֶּטֶר חֲמוֹר, כִּדְתְנַן: *[ג]אֵין פּוֹדִין לֹא בְּעֵגֶל וְלֹא בְּחַיָּה, וְלֹא בִּשְׁחוּטָה וְלֹא בִּטְרֵיפָה, וְלֹא בְּכִלְאַיִם וְלֹא בְּכוֹי. וּלְרַבִּי אֶלְעָזָר דְּמַתִּיר בְּכִלְאַיִם, דִּתְנַן: *ר"א מַתִּיר בְּכִלְאַיִם מִפְּנֵי שֶׁהוּא שֶׂה, לְמַאי הִלְכְתָא? אָמַר לָךְ ר"א: כִּי אִיתְּמַר דְּרָבָא — לְטָמֵא שֶׁנּוֹלַד מִן הַטָּהוֹר וְעִיבּוּרוֹ מִן הַטָּמֵא. וּדְלָא כְּרַבִּי יְהוֹשֻׁעַ, דְּאִי ר' יְהוֹשֻׁעַ, מִ"שֵּׂה כְשָׂבִים וְשֵׂה עִזִּים" נָפְקָא לֵיהּ, *עַד שֶׁיְּהֵא אָבִיו כֶּבֶשׂ וְאִמּוֹ כִּבְשָׂה. וּטְהוֹרָה מִטְּמֵאָה מִי מִיעַבְּרָא? אִין, דְּקיי"ל

דְּאִיעַבַּר

ויקרא כב | במדבר יח

רש"י

לְהוֹצִיא כִּלְאַיִם מִבֵּינֵיהֶם. אֵין כִּלְאַיִם בָּאִים מִשְּׁנֵיהֶם. **מִדְּסֵיפָא** לְמַעֵט. "אוֹ" דְּסֵיפָא דִּקְרָא "כֶּשֶׂב אוֹ עֵז" וַדַּאי לְמַעֵט אֲתָא, שֶׁהֲרֵי כִּלְאַיִם בָּאִים מֵהֶם, וּמִמֵּילָא מִשְׁתַּמַּע. (א) לְרַבּוֹת לָא אִיצְטְרִיךְ. וְאִי לְרַבּוֹת נִדְמֶה — כָּל שֶׁכֵּן דְּלָא אִיצְטְרִיךְ, דְּכֵיוָן דְּמֵרֵישָׁא הוּא מִתְרַבֵּי כִּלְאַיִם — כָּל שֶׁכֵּן נִדְמֶה, דְּקִיל. **אִי** לְקָדָשִׁים. לְמֵימְרָא דְּפָסוּל לְקָרְבָּן, דִּכְתִיב בְּהוּ "שֶׂה" בִּנְדָבוֹת בְּפָרָשַׁת נְסָכִים (במדבר טו), "אוֹ לַשֶּׂה בַּכְּבָשִׂים" וגו'. **הָא** בְּהֶדְיָא כְּתִיב בְּהוּ. מֵרִבּוּיָא דְּ"אוֹ כֶשֶׂב" פְּרָט לְכִלְאַיִם דְּפָסוּל. **אִי** לְמַעֲשֵׂר בְּהֵמָה. וְאע"ג דְּלָא כְּתִיב בֵּיהּ "שֶׂה" אֶלָּא "צֹאן" קָאָמַר רָבָא דְּפָסוּל — הָא אָמְרִינַן בִּבְכוֹרוֹת לְעִנְיַן מִילֵּי טוּבָא דְּגָמַר "תַּחַת הַשֵּׁבֶט" מִ"תַּחַת אִמּוֹ", הִלְכָּךְ לְהָא מִלְּתָא יָלֵיף נַמִּי וּפָסוּל. הַעֲבָרָה הַעֲבָרָה. "וְהַעֲבַרְתָּ כָל פֶּטֶר רֶחֶם לַה'" (שמות יג) "וְכָל אֲשֶׁר יַעֲבוֹר" (ויקרא כז). לְעִנְיַן פִּדְיוֹן פֶּטֶר חֲמוֹר. דִּכְתִיב "שֶׂה", וְקָא מַשְׁמְעִינַן רָבָא: טַעְמָא דְּמַתְנִי' דְּקָתָנֵי אֵין פּוֹדִין בְּכִלְאַיִם — מֵהָכָא הוּא. וְלֹא **בְּחַיָּה**. צְבִי וְאַיִל. וְלֹא **בְּשֶׂה שְׁחוּטָה**. דְּלָאו "שֶׂה" קָרֵינָא בֵּהּ. **כִּלְאַיִם**. מִשְּׁנֵי מִינֵי בְּהֵמוֹת. כּוֹי. מִבְּהֵמָה וְחַיָּה. **לְטָמֵא** שֶׁנּוֹלַד מִן הַטָּהוֹר. פָּרָה שֶׁיָּלְדָה סוּס וְאָבִיו סוּס, אוֹ רָחֵל שֶׁיָּלְדָה חֲזִיר וְאָבִיו חֲזִיר — דְּאָסוּר בַּאֲכִילָה, דִּכְתִיב: "זֹאת הַבְּהֵמָה אֲשֶׁר תֹּאכֵלוּ שׁוֹר שֵׂה כְשָׂבִים" (דברים יד). וְכֵיוָן דִּכְתִיב "שֶׂה" — פְּרָט לְכִלְאַיִם כה"ג הוּא. דְּר' יְהוֹשֻׁעַ. בְּפֶרֶק קַמָּא דִּבְכוֹרוֹת (דף ז.). וּטְהוֹרָה מִטְּמֵאָה מִי מִיעַבְּרָא. דְּאִיצְטְרִיךְ לְמַעוּטֵי? וְהָא קַיְימָא לָן בְּפ"ק דִּבְכוֹרוֹת (דף ז.): לְעוֹלָם אֵין מִתְעַבֶּרֶת לֹא טְמֵאָה מִן הַטְּהוֹרָה וְלֹא טְהוֹרָה מִן הַטְּמֵאָה!

דְּאִיעַבַּר

חולין עח: לעיל עז: | [בכורות ה: וש"נ] | ומא מט: ע"ש בכורות יב. | בכורות שם | [בכורות ז.]

תוספות

והא גבי קדשים דכתיב שור או כשב נרבייה. תימה: מה ריבוי לריך? נהי דמשור וכשב לא מלי לרבויי כלאים, מכשב ועז שאתה יכול להוליא כלאים מבינייהו אתי! ואור"י: דאע"ג דאתי כלאים מדסמך כשב לעז, מכל מקום יש למעטם מדסמך שור לכשב, דלאוחרא מקשינן, וכיון דאי לא הוי כתיב שום "או" לא בסיפא ולא ברישא — הייתי ממעט כלאים, יש לי לומר דאתא "או" לרבות. ומשני: מדסיפא למעט, כלומר "או" דכתיב גבי כשב ועז כיולא בו במקום אחר — אית לן למימר למעוטי, הלכך ה"נ דרשינן למעוטי, וה"ה "או" דרישא למעוטי דרשינן ליה ולא לרבויי. ופריך: אדרבה, אימא איפכא, ד"או" ראשון כתיב במקום שכיולא בו במקום אחר ראוי לדרשו לרבות, ודרשי ליה נמי הכא לרבות, וה"ה נמי שני! ומשני כו'. ואם תאמר: ולא ליכתוב אלא ההוא "או" דבין כשב ועז, דמשור וכשב הוה ממעטינן כלאים, ומ"או" דכשב ועז הוה ממעטינן נדמה! וי"ל: דאי לא כתיב אלא חד — אפילו הוה כתיב גבי כשב ועז הוה דרשינן לרבות כלאים, כיון דאי לא כתיב "או" כלל הוה ממעטינן כלאים משור וכשב, כדפרישית לעיל.

השתא כלאים איתרבו כו'. וא"ת: בלא ק"ו דכלאים איכא למפרך, דמה לריך לרבות? דממילא מתרבי כל כמה דלא מעטיה קרא, דהא כי אמר דאתו אוין למעט לריך קרא למעוטי, ואע"ג דממעטינן כלאים לא הוה ממעטינן נדמה אי לאו דמעטיה קרא! וי"ל: דבלא שום קרא הוה מרבינן נדמה שדומה במקלת סימנין, וממעטינן נדמה שאין דומה כלל, דהוה ילפינן ב"תחת" "תחת" ממעשר, ומעשר ב"העברה" "העברה" דבכור, והשתא כי אמר דאתי "או" למעט — ממעט נדמה, אפילו אותו שנדמה במקלת סימנים, וכי אמרי אתא לרבויי — בעי לרבויי נדמה אפילו אותו שאין דומה כלל. ולהכי דייק: השתא כלאים איתרבי, נדמה אפילו אין דומה כלל, מבעיא?

אי למעשר. פירוש דהוי כאילו כתיב ביה "שה" מג"ש דהעברה העברה מבכור דכתיב ביה "שה" (ויקרא כו) "אם שור אם שה". ובקונטרס פי' דבמעשר כתיב "לאן" דהוי כמו שה. ואין נראה. ועוד, בפרק בתרא דבכורות (דף נז.) פריך: אי גמר מעשר "תחת" "תחת" מקדשים — אפי' הנך נמי, פי': יולא דופן ומחוסר זמן ויתום לא יכנסו לדיר להתעשר. ואי לא גמר מקדשים, בשלמא טריפה "כל אשר יעבור" — פרט לטריפה, אלא כלאים מנ"ל? ומאי קושיא? לימא ליה דמבנין אב דרבא נפקא ליה כלאים, כיון דבמעשר כתיב ["לאן"] *כדפירש בקונטרס הכא! ולפי מה שפירשתי ד"אשה" דבכור סמיך — א"ש, דלא מצי למימר התם דיליף מעשר מבכור דמיעט ביה כלאים, דאם כן יולא דופן נמי נמעט במעשר דנילף מבכור.

עד שיהא הוא שור ובכורו שור. אומר ר"י: דבפרק קמא דבכורות (דף ה:) מוקי לה דוקא באין דומה כלל, אבל דומה במקלת סימנין — יליף התם מ"אך" דקדיש בבכור. ולריך למעט נדמה בקדשים ובכור, דאי לא כתיב אלא בקדשים — הוה ילפינן בכור מקדשים, והוה ממעטינן בבכורות אפילו יש בו מקלת סימן. ואי הוה כתיב ריבוי לחודיה בבכורות לרבות נדמה שיש בו מקלת סימן — הוה מרבינן ליה נמי בקדשים, דילפינן מהדדי בג"ש. וכן אי לא הוה כתיב בקדשים כלל אלא בבכור מיעוט וריבוי — הוה ילפינן קדשים מבכור. אבל השתא דכתיב בקדשים, וכתיב נמי מיעוט וריבוי בבכור — ליכא למילף קדשים מבכור, דאם כן לישתוק קרא ממיעוט דקדשים.

לטמא שנולד מן הטהור ועיבורו מן הטמא ודלא כר' יהושע. פי' בקונטרס: דר' יהושע פליג אדר"ש, ושרי גמל הבא מן הפרה שעיברתו משור בסימן אחד של טהרה — מעלה גרה או מפריס פרסה. ודריש: "את זה לא תאכלו את הגמל" — גמל אי אתה אוכל בסימן אחד, אבל אחר אתה אוכל בסימן אחד, ואיזה זה — זה טמא שנולד מן הטהור ועיבורו מן הטהור. יכול אפי' עיבורו מן הטמא? כלומר, כשם שאני מכשיר בו כך אני מכשיר בבנו, אם נתעברה הימנו פרה — ת"ל "שה כשבים" כו'. ועיבורו מן הטמא — לאו דוקא, דלדידיה הוי טהור, אלא דומה לטמא. וכולה סוגיא דבכורות (דף ו: ושם) לא משתמע כפירושו, אלא משמע דמודה ר' יהושע לר"ש דגמל גמור הנולד מפרה ומשור שהוא אסור, ואם יש בו סימן אחד שדומה מקלת לפרה — מותר, ולא קאי כלל אסימנים דקרא (ב) ממעלה גרה או ממפריסי פרסה. והכי איתא התם (שם): רחל שילדה מין עז ועז שילדה מין רחל פטורה מן הבכורה, ואם יש בו מקלת סימנין חייבת. ר"ש אומר: עד שיהא ראשו ורובו דומה לאמו. ועלה דההיא מבעיא ליה לר"ש בגמרא: בן פרה, מי בעי שיהא ראשו ורובו דומה לאמו להתירו באכילה, או אפי' במקלת? ובעי למפשט מדר' יהושע דסבר כר"ש, מדקרי לה "טמא" וקאמר: אבל אתה אוכל בסימן אחד כו', אלמא לא בעי ראשו ורובו להתירו באכילה. ודחי: ודלמא סבר לה כר"ש בחדא ופליג עליה בחדא. ועוד משמע התם *דטעמא דר' יהושע משום דקסבר זה וזה גורם אסור, ולפי זה אפי' טהור שנולד מן הטהור ועיבורו מן הטמא — אסור. והך דשמעתין דמוקי רבא לטמא שנולד מן הטהור ועיבורו מן הטמא — מיירי נמי שדומה קלת לאמו, כההיא דרבי יהושע. שאם היה דומה לגמרי לגמל — אפילו עיבורו מן הטהור היה אסור, דהא ס"ל כר"ש, אוקמא דאיעבר מקלוט וכר"ש. וה"ה דה"מ למנקט טהור שנולד מן הטהור ועיבורו מן הטמא דאסור, כיון ד"שה" להוציא כלאים, ואסור משום זה וזה גורם. אלא משום דנקט במילתיה דר' יהושע "טמא שנולד" — נקט נמי הכי במילתיה דרבא. ובמילתיה דר' יהושע נקט משום דרישא קתני: אבל אתה אוכל בסימן אחד טמא שנולד מן הטהור ועיבורו מן הטהור — להכי נקט בסיפא נמי: יכול שאתה אוכל טמא שנולד מן הטהור ועיבורו מן הטמא. וה"ה אפילו טהור שנולד מן הטהור ועיבורו מן הטמא דאסור, משום זה וזה גורם. והא דקאמר הכא ודלא כר' יהושע — כ"ש דהוי דלא כר"א בר פלוגתיה, דשרי ליה לגמרי. וה"ג: ר' אלעזר, ולא ר' אליעזר.

מי

עין משפט נר מצוה

קט א מיי' פ"ו מהל' בכורות הלכה יד סמג עשין ריב:
קי ב מיי' שם פ"ב הל' ו סמג עשין ריא ולאוין רמג טוש"ע י"ד סימן שטו סעיף ה:
קיא ג מיי' פי"ב מהל' בכורים הלכה ח סמג עשין קמא טוש"ע י"ד סימן שכא סעיף ב:

הגהות הב"ח

(א) רש"י ד"ה מדסיפא וכו' ולרבות לא אלטריך וכו' למרישא הוה מתרבי: (ב) תום' ד"ה לטמא וכו' אמעלה גרה או אמפריסי וכו' איתא התם ת"ר רחל שילדה וכו' לר"ש בגמל בן פרה מי בעי ר' שמעון שיהא ראשו ורובו וכו' וקאמר אבל אחר אתה אוכל:

דה"ל כאלו כתיב שה והכא ליכא לאקשויי תחת תחת יליף שהרי לפי סברא לא גמר מקדשים. העתק מחלופי גרסאות

גליון הש"ס

גמ' אי לבכור העברה. עיין נדה דף מ ע"א תוספות ד"ה גמר לידה:

ועיין בספר פני יהושע

דְּאִיעַבַּר מִקָּלוּט כְּר' שִׁמְעוֹן. בָּעֵי רָבָא: "הֲרֵי עָלַי עוֹלָה" וְהִפְרִישׁ שׁוֹר, וּבָא אַחֵר וְגָנַב, מִי פָּטַר גַּנָּב נַפְשֵׁיהּ בְּכֶבֶשׂ לְרַבָּנַן, בְּעוֹלַת הָעוֹף לְר' אֶלְעָזָר בֶּן עֲזַרְיָה? דִּתְנַן: *[א]"הֲרֵי עָלַי עוֹלָה" – יָבִיא כֶּבֶשׂ, ר"א בֶּן עֲזַרְיָה אוֹמֵר: יָבִיא תּוֹר אוֹ בֶן יוֹנָה, מַאי? מִי אָמְרִינַן שֵׁם עוֹלָה קַבֵּיל עִילָּוֵיהּ, אוֹ דִּלְמָא מָצֵי א"ל: אֲנָא מִצְוָה מִן הַמּוּבְחָר בָּעֵינָא לְמֶיעֱבַד? בָּתַר דְּאִיבַּעְיָא [ג]הֲדַר פְּשַׁט: גַּנָּב פָּטַר עַצְמוֹ בְּכֶבֶשׂ לְרַבָּנַן, בְּעוֹלַת הָעוֹף לְר' אֶלְעָזָר בֶּן עֲזַרְיָה. רַב אַחָא בְּרֵיהּ דְּרַב אִיקָא מַתְנֵי לָהּ בְּהֶדְיָא, אָמַר רָבָא: "הֲרֵי עָלַי עוֹלָה" וְהִפְרִישׁ שׁוֹר, וּבָא אַחֵר וּגְנָבוֹ – פָּטַר עַצְמוֹ בְּכֶבֶשׂ לְרַבָּנַן, וּבְעוֹלַת הָעוֹף לְר' אֶלְעָזָר בֶּן עֲזַרְיָה.§ **מתני'** [ג]מְכָרוֹ חוּץ מֵאֶחָד מִמֵּאָה שֶׁבּוֹ, אוֹ שֶׁהָיְתָה לוֹ בּוֹ שׁוּתָּפוּת, [ד]הַשּׁוֹחֵט וְנִתְנַבְּלָה בְּיָדוֹ, הַנּוֹחֵר, וְהַמְעַקֵּר – מְשַׁלֵּם תַּשְׁלוּמֵי כֶפֶל וְאֵינוֹ מְשַׁלֵּם תַּשְׁלוּמֵי אַרְבָּעָה וַחֲמִשָּׁה.§ **גמ'** מַאי חוּץ מֵאֶחָד מִמֵּאָה שֶׁבּוֹ? אָמַר רַב: [ה]חוּץ מִדָּבָר הַנִּיתָּר עִמּוֹ בִּשְׁחִיטָה, וְלֵוִי אָמַר: חוּץ מִגִּיזּוֹתֶיהָ; וְכֵן תַּנְיָא בְּמַתְנִיתָא: חוּץ מִגִּיזּוֹתֶיהָ. מֵיתִיבֵי: מְכָרָהּ חוּץ מִיָּדָהּ, חוּץ מֵרַגְלָהּ, חוּץ מִקַּרְנָהּ, חוּץ מִגִּיזּוֹתֶיהָ – אֵינוֹ מְשַׁלֵּם תַּשְׁלוּמֵי אַרְבָּעָה וַחֲמִשָּׁה; רַבִּי אוֹמֵר: [ו]דָּבָר הַמְעַכֵּב בִּשְׁחִיטָה – אֵינוֹ מְשַׁלֵּם תַּשְׁלוּמֵי אַרְבָּעָה וַחֲמִשָּׁה, וְשֶׁאֵינוֹ מְעַכֵּב בִּשְׁחִיטָה – מְשַׁלֵּם תַּשְׁלוּמֵי אַרְבָּעָה וַחֲמִשָּׁה. ר"ש בֶּן אֶלְעָזָר אוֹמֵר: חוּץ מִקַּרְנָהּ – אֵינוֹ מְשַׁלֵּם תַּשְׁלוּמֵי אַרְבָּעָה וַחֲמִשָּׁה, חוּץ מִגִּיזּוֹתֶיהָ – מְשַׁלֵּם תַּשְׁלוּמֵי אַרְבָּעָה וַחֲמִשָּׁה; בִּשְׁלָמָא לְלֵוִי – כְּתַנָּא קַמָּא, אֶלָּא לְרַב כְּמַאן? אָמְרִי: רַב דְּאָמַר כִּי הַאי תַּנָּא; דְּתַנְיָא, ר"ש בֶּן אֶלְעָזָר אוֹמֵר: מְכָרָהּ חוּץ מִיָּדָהּ וְחוּץ מֵרַגְלָהּ – אֵינוֹ מְשַׁלֵּם תַּשְׁלוּמֵי אַרְבָּעָה וַחֲמִשָּׁה, [ז]חוּץ מִקַּרְנָהּ חוּץ מִגִּיזּוֹתֶיהָ – מְשַׁלֵּם תַּשְׁלוּמֵי אַרְבָּעָה וַחֲמִשָּׁה. בְּמַאי קָמִיפַּלְגִי? תַּנָּא קַמָּא סָבַר: °"וּטְבָחוֹ" כּוּלּוֹ בָּעֵינַן, "וּמְכָרוֹ" כּוּלּוֹ בָּעֵינַן; וְרַבִּי סָבַר: "וּטְבָחוֹ" – מִידֵי דַּהֲוֵי בִּטְבִיחָה, לְאַפּוֹקֵי מִידֵי דְּלָא הָוְיָא בִּטְבִיחָה, "וּמְכָרוֹ" דּוּמְיָא (א) דִּטְבִיחָה; וְר' שִׁמְעוֹן בֶּן אֶלְעָזָר סָבַר: קַרְנָא דְּלָא לְמִגְזָא קַיְימָא – הָוֵי שִׁיּוּר, וְאֵינוֹ מְשַׁלֵּם תַּשְׁלוּם אַרְבָּעָה וַחֲמִשָּׁה, גִּיזּוֹתֶיהָ דִּלְמֵיגַז קַיְימִי – לָא הָוֵי שִׁיּוּר, וּמְשַׁלֵּם תַּשְׁלוּם אַרְבָּעָה וַחֲמִשָּׁה; וְאִידָךְ תַּנָּא דְּבֵי ר' שִׁמְעוֹן בֶּן אֶלְעָזָר סָבַר: יָדָיו וְרַגְלָיו דִּצְרִיכֵי טְבִיחָה – הָוֵי שִׁיּוּר, וְלָא מְשַׁלֵּם תַּשְׁלוּמֵי אַרְבָּעָה וַחֲמִשָּׁה, קַרְנֶיהָ וְגִיזּוֹתֶיהָ דְּלָא צְרִיכֵי טְבִיחָה – לָא הָוֵי שִׁיּוּר. קַשְׁיָא דְּר' שִׁמְעוֹן בֶּן אֶלְעָזָר אַדְּר' שִׁמְעוֹן בֶּן אֶלְעָזָר! תְּרֵי תַּנָּאֵי וְאַלִּיבָּא דְּר"ש בֶּן אֶלְעָזָר. ת"ר: *[ח]הַגּוֹנֵב הַקִּיטַּעַת וְאֶת הַחִיגֶּרֶת וְאֶת הַסּוּמָא, וְכֵן הַגּוֹנֵב בֶּהֱמַת הַשּׁוּתָּפִין – חַיָּיב, וְשׁוּתָּפִים שֶׁגָּנְבוּ – פְּטוּרִים. וְהָתַנְיָא: *שׁוּתָּפִין שֶׁגָּנְבוּ – חַיָּיבִין! אָמַר רַב נַחְמָן, לָא קַשְׁיָא: כָּאן בְּשׁוּתָּף שֶׁגָּנַב מֵחֲבֵירוֹ, כָּאן בְּשׁוּתָּף שֶׁגָּנַב מֵעָלְמָא. אֵיתִיבֵיהּ רָבָא לְרַב נַחְמָן: יָכוֹל שׁוּתָּף שֶׁגָּנַב מֵחֲבֵירוֹ, וְשׁוּתָּפִין שֶׁגָּנְבוּ יְהוּ חַיָּיבִין? תַּלְמוּד לוֹמַר: "וּטְבָחוֹ" – כּוּלּוֹ בָּעֵינַן, וְלֵיכָּא! אֶלָּא אָמַר רַב נַחְמָן, לָא קַשְׁיָא: [ט]כָּאן בְּשׁוּתָּף שֶׁטָּבַח לְדַעַת חֲבֵירוֹ, כָּאן בְּשׁוּתָּף שֶׁטָּבַח שֶׁלֹּא לְדַעַת חֲבֵירוֹ. [י]בָּעֵי רַבִּי יִרְמְיָה: מְכָרָהּ חוּץ מִשְּׁלֹשִׁים יוֹם, חוּץ מִמְּלַאכְתָּהּ, חוּץ מֵעוּבָּרָהּ, מַהוּ? אַלִּיבָּא דְּמַאן דְּאָמַר *עוּבָּר יֶרֶךְ אִמּוֹ הוּא – לָא תִּבְּעֵי לָךְ, דְּהָא שַׁיֵּיר בָּהּ. כִּי תִּבְּעֵי לָךְ – אַלִּיבָּא דְּמַאן דְּאָמַר עוּבָּר לָאו יֶרֶךְ אִמּוֹ, מַאי? מִימַר אָמְרִינַן: כֵּיוָן דִּמְחוּבָּר בָּהּ הָוֵי שִׁיּוּר, אוֹ דִלְמָא: כֵּיוָן דְּלִמְפְרַשׁ מִינַּהּ קָאֵי לָא הָוֵי שִׁיּוּר? אִיכָּא דְּאָמְרִי: כֵּיוָן דְּלָאו יֶרֶךְ אִמּוֹ הוּא לָא הָוֵי שִׁיּוּר, אוֹ דִלְמָא: כֵּיוָן דִּצְרִיךְ לְאִשְׁתְּרוּיֵי בַּהֲדַהּ בִּשְׁחִיטָה, כְּמַאן דְּשַׁיֵּיר בְּגוּפַהּ דָּמֵי? תֵּיקוּ.§ בָּעֵי רַב פַּפָּא: [כ]גְּנָבָהּ, קְטָעָהּ וּמְכָרָהּ, מַהוּ? מִי אָמְרִינַן: מַאי דִּגְנַב הָא לָא זַבֵּין, אוֹ דִלְמָא: מַה דְּזַבֵּין הָא לָא שַׁיֵּיר? תֵּיקוּ.§ תָּנוּ רַבָּנַן: *[ל]גָּנַב וְנָתַן לְאַחֵר וְטָבַח, גָּנַב וְנָתַן לְאַחֵר וּמָכַר, גָּנַב

רש"י

דְּאִיעַבַּר מִקָּלוּט כְּרַבִּי שִׁמְעוֹן. קָלוּט = פַּרְסוֹתָיו קְלוּטוֹת, וְנוֹלַד מִן הַטָּהוֹר. וְרַבִּי שִׁמְעוֹן קָרֵי לֵיהּ טָמֵא, דְּתַנְיָא בְּכוֹרוֹת (דף ו:), רַבִּי שִׁמְעוֹן אוֹמֵר: "גָּמָל" "גָּמָל" שְׁנֵי פְּעָמִים, אֶחָד גָּמָל הַנּוֹלָד מִן הַגְּמַלָּה וְאֶחָד גָּמָל הַנּוֹלָד מִן הַפָּרָה, וַאֲפִילּוּ עִבַּרְתּוֹ מִן הַטָּהוֹר מִשּׁוֹר גָּמוּר קָאָסַר לֵיהּ ר"ש. וּפָלֵיג עֲלֵיהּ רַבִּי יְהוֹשֻׁעַ הֵיכָא דְּעִבַּרְתּוֹ מִן הַטָּהוֹר, מִשּׁוֹר שֶׁאֵינוֹ קָלוּט, וּמַתִּירוֹ בְּסִימָן אֶחָד שֶׁל טַהֲרָה, אוֹ מַעֲלֶה גֵרָה אוֹ מַפְרִיס פַּרְסָה, וְדוֹרֵשׁ: "אֶת זֶה לֹא תֹאכְלוּ אֶת הַגָּמָל" – זֶה אִי אַתָּה אוֹכֵל בְּסִימָן אֶחָד, אֲבָל יֵשׁ אַחֵר שֶׁאַתָּה אוֹכֵל בְּסִימָן אֶחָד, וְאֵי זֶה – זֶה טָמֵא הַנּוֹלָד מִן הַטָּהוֹר וְעִיבּוּרוֹ מִן הַטָּהוֹר. יָכוֹל אַף עִיבּוּרוֹ מִן הַטָּמֵא, כְּלוֹמַר: יָכוֹל כְּשֵׁם שֶׁאֲנִי מַכְשִׁיר בּוֹ כָּךְ אֲנִי מַכְשִׁיר בְּבְנוֹ, אִם נִתְעַבְּרָה פָּרָה הֵימֶנּוּ – ת"ל: "שֵׂה כְשָׂבִים וְשֵׂה עִזִּים" – עַד שֶׁיְּהֵא נוֹלָד מִשְּׁנֵי כְבָשִׂים, שֶׁיְּהוּ אָבִיו וְאִמּוֹ כְּבָשִׂים. וְהַהִיא פְּסוּלָה דִּבְנוֹ, דְּנָפְקָא לֵיהּ לְר' יְהוֹשֻׁעַ מִ"כְּבָשִׂים" – מַשְׁמַע לֵיהּ לְרַבָּא מִ"שֵּׂה". מִי פָּטַר גַּנָּב נַפְשֵׁיהּ. גַּבֵּי בְּעָלִים. בְּכֶבֶשׂ. דְּאָמַר לֵיהּ: עוֹלָה קָא מְחַיַּיבְתְּ וְעוֹלָה מְשַׁלֵּימְנָא לָךְ, (ב) וְלָא אַפְסַדְתָּךְ תּוּ מִידֵּי, דְּהָא יוֹצֵא בָּהּ אַתָּה יְדֵי נִדְרְךָ. גַּנָּב פָּטַר עַצְמוֹ. דְּאַתַּשְׁלוּמִין דִּבְעָלִים מְחַיֵּיב, וַהֲרֵי הוֹצִיאוֹ יְדֵי נִדְרוֹ. וְאַפְסֵידָא דְּהֶקְדֵּשׁ מִיפְּטַר, דְּ"מִבֵּית הָאִישׁ" כְּתִיב, וְלֹא הֶקְדֵּשׁ. וְאַלִּיבָּא דְּר' שִׁמְעוֹן נָקַט לָהּ, דְּאָמַר קָדָשִׁים שֶׁחַיָּיב בְּאַחֲרָיוּתָן חַיָּיב. פְּלוּגְתַּיְיהוּ דְּרַבָּנַן וְר"א וְטַעֲמַיְיהוּ בְּפֶרֶק בַּתְרָא דִּמְנָחוֹת. **מתני'** אוֹ שֶׁהָיְתָה לוֹ בּוֹ שׁוּתָּפוּת. קוֹדֶם שֶׁגְּנָבוֹ, לָא קָרֵינַן בֵּיהּ: "וּמְכָרוֹ" כּוּלּוֹ בְּאִיסּוּרָא. הַנּוֹחֵר. *קוֹרְעוֹ מִנְּחִירָיו עַד לִבּוֹ. וְהַמְעַקֵּר. עוֹקֵר סִימָנִין. פָּטוּר. וַאֲפִי' לְרַבָּנַן, דְּהָא לָאו שְׁחִיטָה הִיא כְּלָל. **גמ'** מַאי חוּץ מֵאֶחָד מִמֵּאָה. כְּלוֹמַר: מִמַּאי קָאָמְרִינַן דְּאִי שַׁיְּירֵיהּ הָוֵי שִׁיּוּרָא. הַנִּיתָּר עִמּוֹ. כְּגוֹן מִבְּשָׂרוֹ, אֲבָל שִׁיֶּרֶת עוֹרָהּ וְקַרְנֶיהָ וְגִיזּוֹתֶיהָ – לָא הָוֵי שִׁיּוּר. וְלֵוִי אָמַר. אֲפִילּוּ גִּיזּוֹתֶיהָ הָוֵי שִׁיּוּר. הַמְעַכֵּב בִּשְׁחִיטָה. דָּבָר שֶׁאִם נִיטַּל הֵימֶנָּה נַעֲשֵׂית בּוֹ נְבֵלָה מֵחַיִּים, כְּגוֹן וֶושֶׁט אוֹ קָנֶה אוֹ הַיָּרֵךְ *וְחָלָל שֶׁלָּהּ, אוֹ כָּבֵד, אוֹ אֶחָד מִבְּנֵי מֵעַיִים דְּלֹא מַתִּיר לָהּ שְׁחִיטָה. אֲבָל יָדָהּ וְרַגְלָהּ מִן הָאַרְכּוּבָה וּלְמַטָּה – לֹא. וְטַעֲמָא דְּכוּלְּהוּ מְפָרֵשׁ לְקַמָּן. אֶלָּא לְרַב דְּאָמַר כְּמַאן. אִי כְּת"ק – אֲפִי' חוּץ מִגִּיזּוֹתֶיהָ, אִי כְּרַבִּי – אֲפִילּוּ יָדָהּ נַמִי לָא. מִידֵּי דַּהֲוֵי בִּטְבִיחָה. הָוֵי שִׁיּוּר בִּמְכִירָה. וְר"ש בֶּן אֶלְעָזָר. לָא דָּרֵישׁ דּוּמְיָא דִּטְבִיחָה. וּמִיהוּ, גִּיזּוֹתֶיהָ לָא הָוֵי שִׁיּוּר, דִּלְמֵיגַז קָיְימִי. אֶת הַקִּיטַּעַת. אַע"ג דְּלֵיכָּא כּוּלָּהּ חַיָּיב, דְּמַאי דְּגָנַב הָא זַבֵּין כּוּלֵּיהּ. שׁוּתָּף שֶׁגָּנַב מֵחֲבֵירוֹ. פָּטוּר מֵאַרְבָּעָה וַחֲמִשָּׁה, אֲפִי' מֵחֵלֶק חֲבֵירוֹ, דְּלֵיכָּא "וּטְבָחוֹ" כּוּלּוֹ בְּאִיסּוּרָא. שׁוּתָּף שֶׁטָּבַח לְדַעַת חֲבֵירוֹ. מְשַׁלְּמִין בֵּין שְׁנֵיהֶם, דְּאִיכָּא "וּטְבָחוֹ" כּוּלָּהּ בְּחִיּוּבָא. דְּהַטּוֹבֵחַ חַיָּיב עַל חֶלְקוֹ, וַחֲבֵירוֹ נַמִי עֲשָׂאוֹ שָׁלִיחַ, וְהָא רַבִּינַן לְעֵיל (דף עא.) דְּיֵשׁ שָׁלִיחַ לִדְבַר עֲבֵירָה הָכָא, דְּאָמְרִינַן "תַּחַת" לְרַבּוֹת אֶת הַשָּׁלִיחַ. שׁוּתָּף שֶׁטָּבַח שֶׁלֹּא לְדַעַת חֲבֵירוֹ. פָּטוּר, דְּלֵיכָּא "וּטְבָחוֹ" כּוּלּוֹ בְּחִיּוּבָא. דִּבְהַהוּא פַּלְגָּא דְּחַבְרֵיהּ לֹא נַעֲשָׂה שָׁלִיחַ, וַהֲוָה לֵיהּ כְּטוֹבֵחַ וּמוֹכֵר אַחַר הַגַּנָּב, דְּפָטוּר. וְעַל חֶלְקוֹ נַמִי פָּטוּר, הוֹאִיל וְלֵיכָּא "וּטְבָחוֹ" כּוּלּוֹ בְּחִיּוּבָא. וְאַף עַל גַּב דְּאָמְרַן לְעֵיל: "חֲמִשָּׁה בָקָר" וַאֲפִי' חֲמִשָּׁה חֶלְקֵי בָקָר – הָנֵי מִילֵּי הֵיכָא שֶׁגָּנַב בֶּהֱמַת הַשּׁוּתָּפִין וּטְבָחוֹ, וְאַחַר כָּךְ הוֹדָה לְאֶחָד מֵהֶם עַל חֶלְקוֹ, דִּבְשַׁעַת טְבִיחָה הֲוַאי כּוּלֵּיהּ בְּחִיּוּבָא. וְהָכִי אָמְרִינַן בְּ"הַגּוֹזֵל" (לקמן דף קו:) דְּשׁוּתָּף שֶׁטָּבַח שֶׁלֹּא לְדַעַת חֲבֵירוֹ – פָּטוּר. חוּץ מִשְּׁלֹשִׁים יוֹם. אֶעֱשֶׂה בָּהּ מְלַאכְתִּי. חוּץ מִמְּלַאכְתָּהּ. אִם תִּרְצֶה לְשׁוֹחֲטָהּ – שְׁחוֹט מִיָּד, וְאִם תַּעֲשֶׂה בָּהּ מְלָאכָה – הַמְּלָאכָה הִיא שֶׁלִּי, מִי הָוֵי שִׁיּוּר אוֹ לָא? עוּבָּר יֶרֶךְ אִמּוֹ הוּא. פְּלוּגְתָּא בִּתְמוּרָה (ל: לא.). גָּנַב וְנָתַן לְאַחֵר וְטָבַח. לֹא נָתַן בְּמַתָּנָה, דְּא"כ – אֲפִילּוּ לֹא טָבַח מְחַיֵּיב אַנְּתִינָה מִשּׁוּם מְכִירָה, כִּדְקָתָנֵי סֵיפָא. אֶלָּא עֲשָׂאוֹ שָׁלִיחַ לִטְבִיחָה אוֹ לִמְכִירָה.

וְהִקִּיף

תוספות

מי פטר נפשיה כו'. אבל הנודר עצמו פשיטא דמצי פטר נפשיה, אי לא בעי למיעבד מצוה מן המובחר.

גנב

עין משפט נר מצוה

קיב א מיי' פט"ז מהל' מעשה הקרבנות הלכה ג:
קיג ב מיי' שם הלכה ז:
קיד ג מיי' פ"ב מהל' גניבה הלכה יא טור ח"מ סימן שנ סמג עשין עא:
קטו ד מיי' שם הל' ח:
קטז ה ו ז מיי' שם הלכה יא:
קיז ח מיי' שם הל' ט:
קיח ט מיי' שם הי"ד:
קיט י כ מיי' שם הי"ב:
קכ ל מיי' שם הל' י:

הגהות הב"ח

(א) גמ' דומיא לוטבחו וכו' שמעון וכו' דלא למיגז קיימא: (ב) רש"י ד"ה בכבש וכו' משלימנא לך גבי הקדש ולא אפסדתך:

גליון הש"ס

רש"י ד"ה שותף שטבח כו' ואע"ג דאמרן לעיל. עי' רש"י לקמן דף קו ע"ב ד"ה בשותף שטבח וצ"ע:

מסורת הש"ס

מנחות קח. קז. תמורה כ
עי' בשלטי הגבורים פ"ב קנט.
מפרש"י חולין פה ע"ב פרק חונקו (חו"י)
[או מכרו כל"ל]
ס"א או חלל
[תוספתא פ"ז]
[שבת לג: ע"ש לע"ק כ"ח]
[חולין נח. וש"נ]
[תוספתא פ"ז]
תורה אור: שמות כא

גָּנַב וְהִקְדִּישׁ, גָּנַב וְהִקִּיף, גָּנַב וְהֶחֱלִיף, גָּנַב וְנָתַן בְּמַתָּנָה, גָּנַב וּפָרַע (א) חובו, גָּנַב וּפָרַע בְּהֶקֵּיפוֹ, גָּנַב וְשָׁלַח סִבְלוֹנוֹת בְּבֵית חָמִיו — מְשַׁלֵּם תַּשְׁלוּמֵי אַרְבָּעָה וַחֲמִשָּׁה. מַאי קמ"ל? אַשְׁמַעִינַן רֵישָׁא גָּנַב וְנָתַן לְאַחֵר וְטָבַח, דְּיֵשׁ שָׁלִיחַ לִדְבַר עֲבֵירָה; אע"ג דִּבְכָל הַתּוֹרָה כּוּלָּהּ *[א]אֵין שָׁלִיחַ לִדְבַר עֲבֵירָה — [ב]הָכָא יֵשׁ שָׁלִיחַ לִדְבַר עֲבֵירָה, מַאי טַעְמָא? "וּטְבָחוֹ וּמְכָרוֹ" — *מַה מְּכִירָה דְּלָא אֶפְשָׁר דְּלָאו עַל יְדֵי אַחֵר, אַף טְבִיחָה ע"י אַחֵר מְחַיֵּיב; וְאַשְׁמַעִינַן סֵיפָא גָּנַב וְהִקְדִּישׁ, *מַה לִּי מְכָרוֹ לְהֶדְיוֹט, מַה לִּי מְכָרוֹ לַשָּׁמַיִם.§ **מתני'** [ג]גָּנַב בִּרְשׁוּת הַבְּעָלִים וְטָבַח וּמָכַר חוּץ מֵרְשׁוּתָם, אוֹ שֶׁגָּנַב חוּץ מֵרְשׁוּתָם וְטָבַח וּמָכַר בִּרְשׁוּתָם, אוֹ שֶׁגָּנַב וְטָבַח וּמָכַר חוּץ מֵרְשׁוּתָם — מְשַׁלֵּם תַּשְׁלוּמֵי אַרְבָּעָה וַחֲמִשָּׁה. [ד]אֲבָל גָּנַב וְטָבַח וּמָכַר בִּרְשׁוּתָם — פָּטוּר. *[ה]הָיָה מוֹשְׁכוֹ וְיוֹצֵא, וּמֵת בִּרְשׁוּת הַבְּעָלִים — פָּטוּר, הִגְבִּיהוֹ אוֹ הוֹצִיאוֹ מֵרְשׁוּת בְּעָלִים וּמֵת — חַיָּיב. [ו]נְתָנוֹ לְבְכוֹרוֹת בְּנוֹ אוֹ לְבַעַל חוֹב, לְשׁוֹמֵר חִנָּם, לְשׁוֹאֵל, לְנוֹשֵׂא שָׂכָר וּלְשׂוֹכֵר, וְהָיָה מוֹשְׁכוֹ וּמֵת בִּרְשׁוּת הַבְּעָלִים — פָּטוּר, הִגְבִּיהוֹ אוֹ שֶׁהוֹצִיאוֹ מֵרְשׁוּת הַבְּעָלִים וּמֵת — חַיָּיב.§ **גמ'** בָּעֵי אַמֵימָר: תִּיקְּנוּ מְשִׁיכָה בְּשׁוֹמְרִים אוֹ לֹא? אֲמַר רַב יֵימָר, ת"ש: נְתָנוֹ לִבְכוֹרוֹת בְּנוֹ אוֹ לְבַעַל חוֹבוֹ, לְשׁוֹמֵר חִנָּם וּלְשׁוֹאֵל, לְנוֹשֵׂא שָׂכָר וּלְשׂוֹכֵר, הָיָה מוֹשְׁכוֹ וְיוֹצֵא וּמֵת בִּרְשׁוּת הַבְּעָלִים — פָּטוּר; מַאי לָאו [ז]שׁוֹמֵר? וש"מ: תִּיקְּנוּ מְשִׁיכָה בְּשׁוֹמְרִין. אֲמַר לֵיהּ: לָא, גַּנָּב. הָא תְּנָא לֵיהּ רֵישָׁא! תְּנָא גַּנָּב שֶׁגָּנַב מִבֵּית הַבְּעָלִים, וּתְנָא גַּנָּב שֶׁגָּנַב מִבֵּית שׁוֹמֵר. אֲמַר לֵיהּ רַב אַשִׁי: לָא תִּדְחֲיֵיהּ, מַה לִּי גַּנָּב שֶׁגָּנַב מִבֵּית שׁוֹמֵר, מַה לִּי גַּנָּב שֶׁגָּנַב מִבֵּית בְּעָלִים! אֶלָּא לָאו שׁוֹמֵר, וש"מ: תִּיקְּנוּ מְשִׁיכָה בְּשׁוֹמְרִין, ש"מ. *אִיתְּמַר נַמִּי, אָמַר ר' אֶלְעָזָר: כְּדֶרֶךְ שֶׁתִּיקְּנוּ מְשִׁיכָה בְּלָקוֹחוֹת, [ח]כָּךְ תִּיקְּנוּ מְשִׁיכָה בְּשׁוֹמְרִין. תַּנְיָא נַמִּי הָכִי: כְּדֶרֶךְ שֶׁתִּיקְּנוּ מְשִׁיכָה בְּלָקוֹחוֹת, כָּךְ תִּיקְּנוּ מְשִׁיכָה בְּשׁוֹמְרִין; וּכְשֵׁם שֶׁהַקַּרְקַע נִקְנֵית בְּכֶסֶף, בִּשְׁטָר וּבַחֲזָקָה, *[ט]כָּךְ שְׂכִירוּת נִקְנֵית בְּכֶסֶף, בִּשְׁטָר וּבַחֲזָקָה. *שְׂכִירוּת דְּמַאי? אִילֵימָא שְׂכִירוּת [ב"מ לט.] [עי' תוספות קדושין כז. ד"ה ומקומו]

רש"י

והקיף. מכר באמנה ואשראי, ולא קיבל דמים. גנב ופרע בהקיפו. שהקיפו חבירו פרקמטיא באשראי, ופרע לו בהמה זו. **מתני'** (ב) וטבחו ומכרו חוץ מרשותו. כשהוליא מרשותו נעשה עליו גנב (לרב יהודה) וקנאו. או שגנב חוץ מרשותו. קנאו במשיכה מיד, ונעשה גנב עליו. אבל גנב וטבח ומכר ברשותו – פטור, דלא נעשה עליו גנב. היה. גנב מושכו ויוצא פטור *מכלום. הגביהו. אפי' ברשות בעלים, שהרי הגבהה קונה בכל מקום, במסכת קדושין (דף כה:). נתנו. בעליו לבכורות בנו לכהן בה' סלעים של פדיון הבן. ל"א: נתנו גנב לבכורות בנו, ונתנו לו שם במקום שגנבו לשומר חנם ולשואל. היה מושכו. הכהן או בעל חוב או השומר, ומת ברשות בעלים. פטור. הגנב מכלום. ולשון אחרינא עיקר. האי "חייב" אגנב קאי, דמחייב גנב בקנין שלוחיו. דאי בנותנו בעליו – מאי חייב? נהי דשואל מצי למימר חייב באונסין. אלא שאר שומרים מי חייבי במתה כדרכה? ועוד: לגבי כהן ובעל חוב מאי חייב ופטור איכא? הפסיד ולא הפסיד מבעי ליה. **גמ'** תיקנו משיכה בשומרים. שלא יתחייב שומר בשמירה עד שימשוך. מאי לאו. היה מושכו שומר ומת – חייב גנב במשיכת שומר? לא גנב. והכי קאמר: נתן בעל הבית לבכורות בנו כו', ובא גנב לגונבו משם היה מושכו ויוצא כו'.

שכירות

ס"א ל"ג | ס"א מכפל | [לעיל נח. וש"נ] | [לעיל עח. וש"נ] | [לעיל עו.] | כתובות לח:

תוספות

גנב והקדיש משלם ד' וה'. כדמפרש: מה לי מכרו להדיוט מה לי מכרו לשמים. ואיירי בקדשי בדק הבית, דלא שייך למימר "מעיקרא תורא דראובן והשתא תורא דראובן" כמו בקדשי מזבח, שקרבן קרב לכפר על הבעלים, ונשחט לשמו, ושם בעליו עליו. ואין להקשות: אמאי לא פריך לעיל (דף עו.): וליפלוג וליתני בדידיה; בד"א — בקדשי מזבח, אבל בקדשי בדק הבית — משלם תשלומי ארבעה וחמשה. כדפריך לעיל: ולפלוג וליתני בדידיה: בד"א — בקדשים קלים. דלעיל פריך שפיר, דהוי הכל קדשי מזבח, אבל בקדשי בדק הבית — לא בעי לפלוגי, דהתם קדושה דשור ושה דמחיים הוי למזבח. אע"ג דהתם מפליג וקאמר: (ג) טבח ואח"כ הקדיש — משלם ארבעה וחמשה, ואותו הקדש הוי קדשי בדק הבית — התם לא הוי מחיים. ולמ"ד יאוש לא קני — א"ש, שכשמקדיש לאחר יאוש לאו דידיה קמקדיש. ולמ"ד יאוש קני, וחיובו הוה דוקא לפני יאוש, אבל אחר יאוש שלו הוא טובח ושלו הוא מוכר — אפ"ה מחייב אהקדש אע"ג דלא חייל הקדש מקמי יאוש, כי היכי דמחייב במכר ומתנה קודם יאוש אע"ג דלא אהנו מעשיו, שלא חל המכר והמתנה, כיון דאמירתו לגבוה כמסירתו להדיוט בדבר שבידו להקדיש.

אבל גנב וטבח ומכר ברשותו פטור. בשלא הגביהו עסקינן, דבהגביהו הוי קני וחייב, כדלקמן.

או שהוציאו מרשות בעלים כו'. בריש "אלו נערות" (כתובות דף לא: ושם*) פליגי רב אחא ורבינא, חד אמר: שהוציאו לסמטא, אבל לרה"ר לא קני. ודייק מסיפא: הוציאו דומיא דהגביהו, דאתי לרשותיה. ואידך אמר: אפילו הוציאו לרה"ר קנה, ודייק מרישא דמת ברשות בעלים פטור, הא חוץ לרשות — חייב, אפי' הוציאוהו לרה"ר. ונראה דההוא פליג אאביי ורבא דאמרי ב"המוכר את הספינה" (ב"ב דף פד:): משיכה קונה בסמטא, אבל לא ברה"ר. ואין נראה לחלק כלל בין קניית גנב שאין אלא להתחייב באונסין ולשאר קניות, מדדרשינן לעיל (דף סה.) גבי גנב: אין לי אלא ידו, גגו חצירו וקרפיפו מנין. משמע דלא מחייב אלא במקום שראוי לקנות, כי היכי דדרשינן גיטין (דף עז.) "ונתן בידה". ונראה דהלכה כאביי ורבא, מדמייתי מילתייהו ב"המוכר [את] הספינה" (שם) משמע שהם עיקר. ולא שייך כאן כל היכא דפליגי רב אחא ורבינא הלכה כרבינא לקולא.

נתנו לבכורות בנו או לב"ח. אותו לשון שפירש בקונטרס דאבעלים קאי רחוק מאד; חדא: שצריך לפרש לאותו לשון שמת בפשיעה, ולא כי אורחיה. ועוד: דלשון חיוב ופטור לא שייך אבכורות בנו וב"ח. וצריך לדחות, דמשום אחרינא נקט חיוב ופטור. ועוד: דבתוספתא (פ"ז) קתני: הגביהו או נתנו לבכורות בנו — משמע דאגנב קאי, דאי אבעלים — מה צריך הגבהה, והא דידיה הוא! ועוד: דראיה דמייתי ממתני' בגמרא אַבָּעיא דתקנו משיכה בשומרים אי אפשר ליישבה להאי לישנא לפי מה שמפרש בגמ'. ול"א שפירש בקונטרס נתנו הגנב לבכורות בנו — הוא עיקר, דמתחייב הגנב במשיכת הני. וא"ת: ואמאי מחייב במשיכה? והא אין שליח לדבר עבירה! וי"ל: דהכהו לא ידעי דאתי לידיה באיסורא, אלא סבורין שהיה שלו. ובין ללישנא דמפרש בפ"ק דבבא מציעא (דף י: ושם*) טעמא דאין שליח לדבר עבירה משום דשליח בר חיובא הוא, ודברי הרב ודברי התלמיד דברי מי שומעין, ובין ללישנא דאי בעי עביד אי בעי לא עביד — אין שייך לכאן. דהתם אין יודע שהשליח יעבור, אבל כאן יודע הוא שיקח, מאחר שהוא סבור שהוא שלו. ולעיל (עא.) גבי גנב וטבח בשבת, דמוקי לה בטובח על ידי אחר, ופריך: וכי היכן מצינו שזה חוטא וזה מתחייב? הוי מצי למימר דסבור שהוא שלו. אבל משני שפיר, והאמת. אבל ק"ק: היכי יליף "מה מכירה ע"י אחר אף טביחה" כו'? דלמא דוקא כשסבור שהוא שלו, כיון דליכא יתור! [ועיין תוס' קדושין מג: ד"ה אמאי].

תיקנו משיכה בשומרין או לא. הא לא מבעי ליה אי משעת משיכה [או משעת מלאכה] מתחייבים כל חד וחד כדיניה, שומר חנם בפשיעה ושומר שכר בגניבה ואבידה, ושואל באונסין — דפשיטא דמשעת משיכה מתחייבים, דאם לא כן — מאימתי? דב"השואל" (ב"מ דף לח: ושם) תנן: אם אמר לו השואל "שלח" ושלחה ומתה — חייב. ובגמרא אמר: פרה במשיכה. ובשמעתין דשואל קורדום (שם לט.) אמר: אי לאונסים — מ"ש פרה דמשעת שאלה. אלא אור"י: דמבעי ליה בשואל ושוכר, אי מצי משאיל ומשכיר למיהדר ביה אפי' משך, עד שיתחיל במלאכה, או לא. דאיכא למ"ד גבי שואל קורדום מחבירו, ביקע בו — קנאו, לא ביקע בו — לא קנאו, ומצי משאיל הדר ביה. וכן בפרה, עד שיעשה בה מלאכה. ופשיט ליה ממתניתין דנתנו לבכורות בנו, דקתני: הגביהו או שהוציאו מרשות בעלים ומת — חייב. מאי לאו שומר? ומדמחייב גנב אמשיכת שומר — ש"מ דמשיכה גמורה הוא שאין יכול לחזור בו, שאם היה יכול לחזור בו — לא היה מתחייב במשיכתו. ומשני: לא, גנב. שהיה גנב מושכה מבית שומרים, ותנא גנב שגנבו מבית שומרים. ומיירי שלא נתן לבכורות בנו ולבעל חובו לגמרי — דא"כ הוו בעלים ולא שומר, אלא אפותיקי בעלמא עשה להם, שאם לא יפרע עד יום פלוני שיהא קנוי להם. ורב הונא, דאמר בפרק "השואל" דלא ביקע בו מצי משאיל הדר ביה, הוה דחי הכי, ולא חייש לפירכא דבסמוך: מה לי גנב מרשות שומר מה לי גנב מרשות בעלים. וב"האיש מקדש" (קדושין דף מז: ושם) איכא תנא כרב הונא, דאפי' במלוה יכול לחזור כל זמן שלא הוציאו, כ"ש שאילה. וג' מחלוקות בדבר; דלרב הונא לא תקנו משיכה בשומר. ולר"א תקנו, כדקאמר התם:* ופליגא דר"א ולר' אלעזר נמי מדאורייתא יכול לחזור, אלא שחכמים תקנו דלא מצי הדר ביה משעת משיכה. ועוד קאמר התם: ופליגא אדרבי אמי, דאמר ר' אמי: המשאיל קורדום של הקדש לחבירו — מעל, וחבירו מותר לבקע בו לכתחילה. משמע דסבר דקנה מדאורייתא, דאי מדרבנן ומעל משום דמדרבנן אין יכול לחזור ° כמו נתנה לבלן בפרק "הזהב" (ב"מ דף מח. ושם) — א"כ הוי חומרא דאתי לידי קולא, דחבירו מותר לבקע בו לכתחילה.

שהטמין

[ד"ה וברשות] | [עי' ב"מ לט:] | [ד"ה אין] | ב"מ לט.

עין משפט נר מצוה

קכא א מיי' פ"ז מהל' מעילה הלכה ב:
קכב ב מיי' פ"ב מהל' גניבה הלכה י טור ח"מ סימן שנ:
קכג ג מיי' שם הל' יח:
קכד ד ה ו ז מיי' שם הלכה טז ועיין במ"מ:
קכה ח מיי' פ"ב מהל' שכירות הלכה ח סמג עשין פט טוש"ע ח"מ סימן שז סעיף ב:
קכו ט מיי' פ"א מהל' מכירה הלכה יח סמג עשין פב טוש"ע ח"מ סימן קצה סעיף ט וסימן שז סעיף ב וסימן שטו סעיף א:

הגהות הב"ח

(א) גמ' ופרע בחובו: (ב) רש"י ד"ה וטבח ומכר חוץ מרשותו דכשהוליאו חוץ מרשותו: (ג) תוס' ד"ה גנב וכו' מפליג וקאמר גנב וטבח ואח"כ:

גליון הש"ס

תוס' ד"ה תיקנו וכו' כמו נתנה לבלן בפ' הזהב. לענ"ד נראה דזה ל"ל בסוף הדיבור הזה והביאו ראיה דלקולא לא אזלינן בתר קנין דרבנן והיינו מדאמרינן שם גבי בלן דלר"י דמעות קונות ד"ת נתן לספר מעל אף דמדרבנן לא קני ה"נ הכא אם מה"ת ל"ק אף דמדרבנן קני מ"מ לא יהא מותר לבקע בו:

תורה אור

שְׂכִירוּת דִּמְטַּלְטְלִין — מִטַּלְטְלֵי בְּנֵי שְׁטָרָא נִינְהוּ? אָמַר רַב חִסְדָּא: [א]שְׂכִירוּת דְּקַרְקַע.§ אָמַר ר' אֶלְעָזָר: [ב]רָאוּהוּ שֶׁהִטְמִין בְּחוּרְשִׁין וְטָבַח וּמָכַר — מְשַׁלֵּם תַּשְׁלוּמֵי אַרְבָּעָה וַחֲמִשָּׁה. אַמַּאי? הָא לֹא מָשַׁךְ! א"ר חִסְדָּא: [ג]שֶׁהִכִּישָׁהּ בְּמַקֵּל. אָמְרִי: וְכֵיוָן דְּרָאוּהוּ, גַּזְלָן הוּא! *כֵּיוָן דְּקָא מִטַּמְּרִי מִנַּיְיהוּ, גַּנָּב הוּא. וְאֶלָּא גַּזְלָן הֵיכִי דָּמֵי? אָמַר ר' אַבָּהוּ: [ד]כְּגוֹן בְּנָיָהוּ בֶּן יְהוֹיָדָע, שֶׁנֶּאֱמַר: °"וַיִּגְזֹל אֶת הַחֲנִית מִיַּד הַמִּצְרִי וַיַּהַרְגֵהוּ בַּחֲנִיתוֹ". ר' יוֹחָנָן אָמַר: כְּגוֹן בַּעֲלֵי שְׁכֶם, שֶׁנֶּאֱמַר: °"וַיָּשִׂימוּ לוֹ בַעֲלֵי שְׁכֶם מְאָרְבִים עַל רָאשֵׁי הֶהָרִים וַיִּגְזְלוּ [אֵת] כָּל אֲשֶׁר יַעֲבֹר עֲלֵיהֶם בַּדָּרֶךְ". וְר' אַבָּהוּ מַאי טַעֲמָא לָא אֲמַר מֵהַאי? אָמַר לָךְ: כֵּיוָן דְּמִטַּמְּרִי אִיטְמוּרֵי, לָא גַּזְלָנֵי נִינְהוּ. וְר' יוֹחָנָן: הָא דְּקָא מִטַּמְּרִי, דְּלָא נִיחַזְיִנְהוּ אֱינָשֵׁי וְנִיעַרְקוּ מִנַּיְיהוּ. שָׁאֲלוּ תַּלְמִידָיו אֶת רַבָּן יוֹחָנָן בֶּן זַכַּאי: מִפְּנֵי מָה הֶחֱמִירָה תּוֹרָה בְּגַנָּב יוֹתֵר (א) מִגַּזְלָן? אָמַר לָהֶן: זֶה הִשְׁוָה כְּבוֹד עֶבֶד לִכְבוֹד קוֹנוֹ, וְזֶה לֹא הִשְׁוָה כְּבוֹד עֶבֶד לִכְבוֹד קוֹנוֹ, *כִּבְיָכוֹל, עָשָׂה עַיִן שֶׁל מַטָּה כְּאִילּוּ אֵינָהּ רוֹאָה וְאוֹזֶן שֶׁל מַטָּה כְּאִילּוּ אֵינָהּ שׁוֹמַעַת, שֶׁנֶּאֱמַר: °"הוֹי הַמַּעֲמִיקִים מֵה' לַסְתִּיר עֵצָה וְהָיָה בְמַחְשָׁךְ מַעֲשֵׂיהֶם" וגו', וּכְתִיב: °"וַיֹּאמְרוּ לֹא יִרְאֶה יָּהּ וְלֹא יָבִין אֱלֹהֵי יַעֲקֹב", וּכְתִיב: °"כִּי [אָמְרוּ] עָזַב ה' אֶת הָאָרֶץ וְאֵין ה' רוֹאֶה". (תַּנְיָא) אָמַר ר' מֵאִיר: מָשְׁלוּ מָשָׁל מִשּׁוּם רַבָּן גַּמְלִיאֵל, לְמָה הַדָּבָר דּוֹמֶה? לִשְׁנֵי בְנֵי אָדָם שֶׁהָיוּ בָּעִיר וְעָשׂוּ מִשְׁתֶּה, אֶחָד זִימֵּן אֶת בְּנֵי הָעִיר וְלֹא זִימֵּן אֶת בְּנֵי הַמֶּלֶךְ, וְאֶחָד לֹא זִימֵּן אֶת בְּנֵי הָעִיר וְלֹא זִימֵּן אֶת בְּנֵי הַמֶּלֶךְ, אֵיזֶה מֵהֶן עוֹנְשׁוֹ מְרוּבֶּה? הֱוֵי אוֹמֵר: זֶה שֶׁזִּימֵּן אֶת בְּנֵי הָעִיר וְלֹא זִימֵּן אֶת בְּנֵי הַמֶּלֶךְ. אָמַר רַבִּי מֵאִיר: בֹּא וּרְאֵה כַּמָּה גָּדוֹל כֹּחַ שֶׁל מְלָאכָה, שׁוֹר שֶׁבִּיטְּלוֹ מִמְּלַאכְתּוֹ — חֲמִשָּׁה, שֶׂה שֶׁלֹּא בִּיטְּלוֹ מִמְּלַאכְתּוֹ — אַרְבָּעָה. אָמַר רַבָּן יוֹחָנָן בֶּן זַכַּאי: בֹּא וּרְאֵה כַּמָּה גָּדוֹל כְּבוֹד הַבְּרִיּוֹת, שׁוֹר שֶׁהָלַךְ בְּרַגְלָיו — חֲמִשָּׁה, שֶׂה שֶׁהִרְכִּיבוֹ עַל כְּתֵיפוֹ — אַרְבָּעָה.§

מתני' *[ה]אֵין מְגַדְּלִין בְּהֵמָה דַּקָּה בְּא"י, [ו]אֲבָל מְגַדְּלִין בְּסוּרְיָא וּבַמִּדְבָּרוֹת שֶׁל אֶרֶץ יִשְׂרָאֵל. [ז]אֵין מְגַדְּלִין תַּרְנְגוֹלִין בִּירוּשָׁלַיִם — מִפְּנֵי הַקֳּדָשִׁים, [ח]וְלֹא כֹּהֲנִים בְּאֶרֶץ יִשְׂרָאֵל מִפְּנֵי הַטָּהֳרוֹת. *[ט]אֵין מְגַדְּלִין חֲזִירִין בְּכָל מָקוֹם. [י]לֹא יְגַדֵּל אָדָם אֶת הַכֶּלֶב אֶלָּא אִם כֵּן הָיָה קָשׁוּר בְּשַׁלְשֶׁלֶת. *[כ]אֵין פּוֹרְסִין נִישׁוּבִים לַיּוֹנִים אֶלָּא אִם כֵּן הָיָה רָחוֹק מִן הַיִּשּׁוּב ל' רִיס.§

גמ' ת"ר: אֵין מְגַדְּלִין בְּהֵמָה דַּקָּה בְּא"י, אֲבָל מְגַדְּלִין בְּחוּרָשִׁין שֶׁבְּאֶרֶץ יִשְׂרָאֵל, בְּסוּרְיָא — אֲפִילּוּ בַּיִּשּׁוּב, וְאֵין צָרִיךְ לוֹמַר בְּחוּצָה לָאָרֶץ. תַּנְיָא אִידָךְ: אֵין מְגַדְּלִין בְּהֵמָה דַּקָּה בְּאֶרֶץ יִשְׂרָאֵל, אֲבָל מְגַדְּלִין בַּמִּדְבָּר שֶׁבִּיהוּדָה וּבַמִּדְבָּר שֶׁבִּסְפַר עַכּוֹ. וְאַף עַל פִּי שֶׁאָמְרוּ אֵין מְגַדְּלִין בְּהֵמָה דַּקָּה, אֲבָל מְגַדְּלִין בְּהֵמָה גַּסָּה, לְפִי *[ל]שֶׁאֵין גּוֹזְרִין גְּזֵרָה עַל הַצִּבּוּר אֶלָּא אִם כֵּן רוֹב צִבּוּר יְכוֹלִין לַעֲמוֹד בָּהּ; בְּהֵמָה דַּקָּה אֶפְשָׁר לְהָבִיא מִחוּצָה לָאָרֶץ, בְּהֵמָה גַּסָּה אִי אֶפְשָׁר לְהָבִיא מִחוּצָה לָאָרֶץ. וְאַף עַל פִּי שֶׁאָמְרוּ אֵין מְגַדְּלִין בְּהֵמָה דַּקָּה, [מ]אֲבָל *מַשְׁהֶה הוּא קוֹדֶם לָרֶגֶל שְׁלֹשִׁים יוֹם, וְקוֹדֶם מִשְׁתֵּה בְנוֹ ל' יוֹם, וּבִלְבַד שֶׁלֹּא יַשְׁהֶה אֶת הָאַחֲרוֹנָה שְׁלֹשִׁים יוֹם; דְּסד"א, דְּאִי נָפַק לֵיהּ רֶגֶל, וּמִכִּי זַבְנָהּ עַד הַשְׁתָּא אַכַּתִּי לָא מְלוּ לֵיהּ תְּלָתִין יוֹמִין, לָא נֵימָא: תְּלָתִין מִשְׁרָא שָׁרֵי לֵיהּ לְשַׁהוּיֵי. אֶלָּא כֵּיוָן דִּנְפַק לֵיהּ רֶגֶל לָא מִבָּעֵי לֵיהּ לְשַׁהוּיֵי.

וְהַטַּבָּח

רש"י

שְׂכִירוּת דִּמְטַּלְטְלֵי. שֶׁהִשְׂכִּיר לוֹ כֵּלָיו. בְּנֵי שְׁטָרָא נִינְהוּ. בִּתְמִיָּה: הָא לָא מִקְנוּ מִטַּלְטְלִין אֶלָּא בִּמְשִׁיכָה, כִּדְאָמְרִינַן בְּקִדּוּשִׁין (דף כו.)! וְנְהִי נַמֵי דְּמִקְנוּ בְּכַסְפָּא לְעִנְיַן קַבּוּלֵי "מִי שֶׁפָּרַע", מִיהוּ בִּשְׁטָר לָא מִיקְנוּ, מִידֵי דִּדְבָרִים בְּעָלְמָא נִינְהוּ, כִּדְאָמְרִינַן בְּ"הַזָּהָב" (ב"מ דף מט.): דְּבָרִים אֵין בָּהֶם מִשּׁוּם מְחוּסְּרֵי אֲמָנָה. שֶׁהִטְמִין בְּחוּרְשִׁין. שֶׁנִּטְמַן בַּיַּעַר לִגְנוֹב בְּהֵמוֹת הָרוֹעוֹת שָׁם. וְכֵיוָן דְּרָאוּהוּ גַּזְלָן הוּא. וְלָא דּוֹמֶה לְגַנָּב בִּפְנֵי שְׁנַיִם, דְּהָתָם אע"ג דְּחָזוּ לֵיהּ שְׁאָר אֱינָשֵׁי — לָא מִיסְתַּפֵּי מִינַּיְיהוּ, דְּמֵימַר אָמַר: לָא מִינַּיְיהוּ שָׁקֵילְנָא מִידֵּי. אֲבָל חוֹרָשִׁין — מִרְעֶה לַכֹּל הִיא, וְלָא יָדַע דְּמַאן נִיהוּ הַךְ בְּהֵמָה, וְכֵיוָן דְּלָא מִיסְתַּפֵּי מִכּוּלֵּי עָלְמָא — גַּזְלָן הוּא. הֶחְמִירָה תּוֹרָה. לְשַׁלֵּם כֶּפֶל אַרְבָּעָה וַחֲמִשָּׁה. הִשְׁוָה כְּבוֹד עֶבֶד. לֹא יָרֵא מִבְּנֵי אָדָם כְּדֶרֶךְ שֶׁלֹּא יָרֵא מֵהקב"ה. אֲבָל גַּנָּב לֹא הִשְׁוָה עֶבֶד לְקוֹנוֹ, אֶלָּא כִּיבֵּד הָעֶבֶד יוֹתֵר מִקּוֹנוֹ, שֶׁהוּא יָרֵא מִבְּנֵי אָדָם, וּמֵעַיִן שֶׁל מַעְלָה לֹא נִזְהַר. לַסְתִּיר עֵצָה. כְּמוֹ "לְהַסְתִּיר". יוֹעֵץ בְּמִסְתָּרִים לִגְנוֹב לְהָרַע. שֶׂה שֶׁהִרְכִּיבוֹ. הַגַּנָּב עַל כְּתֵיפוֹ, וְזִלְזֵל אֶת עַצְמוֹ בּוֹ — לְפִיכָךְ הֵיקֵל הקב"ה עָלָיו בְּתַשְׁלוּמִין.

מתני' אֵין מְגַדְּלִין בְּהֵמָה דַּקָּה בְּאֶרֶץ יִשְׂרָאֵל. מִשּׁוּם יִשּׁוּב א"י, שֶׁמַּבְעִיר אֶת הַשָּׂדוֹת, וְכָל שְׂדוֹת א"י סְתָמָן דְּיִשְׂרָאֵל. אֲבָל מְגַדְּלִין בְּסוּרְיָא. אֲרַם נוֹבָה. דְּדָוִד כִּיבְּשָׁהּ, וְקָסָבַר דְּלָא שְׁמֵיהּ כִּיבּוּשׁ, וַהֲוָיָא כְּחוּצָה לָאָרֶץ, וּבְחוּצָה לָאָרֶץ מוּתָּר לְגַדֵּל, דְּלָא חָיְישִׁינַן לַיִּשּׁוּב, וְאִם יַפְסִידוּ שְׂדוֹת אֲחֵרִים — יְשַׁלְּמֶנָּה. אֵין מְגַדְּלִין תַּרְנְגוֹלִין בִּירוּשָׁלַיִם. אֲפִי' יִשְׂרָאֵל. מִפְּנֵי הַקֳּדָשִׁים. שֶׁיִּשְׂרָאֵל אוֹכְלִים שָׁם בְּשַׂר שְׁלָמִים וְתוֹדָה וּמַעֲשֵׂר בְּהֵמָה, וְדֶרֶךְ תַּרְנְגוֹלִים לְנַקֵּר בָּאַשְׁפָּה, שֶׁמָּא יָבִיאוּ א] עֶצֶם כַּעֲדָשָׁה מִן הַשֶּׁרֶץ וִיטַמְּאוּ אֶת הַקֳּדָשִׁים. וְלֹא יְגַדְּלוּ כֹּהֲנִים תַּרְנְגוֹלִין. בְּכָל א"י. מִפְּנֵי הַטָּהֳרוֹת. שֶׁהַכֹּהֲנִים אוֹכְלִין תְּרוּמָה הֵן, צְרִיכִין לְהִזָּהֵר בְּטָהֳרָתָן. חֲזִירִין. טַעְמָא מְפָרֵשׁ בַּגְּמָרָא. אֶת הַכֶּלֶב. מִפְּנֵי שֶׁנּוֹשֵׁךְ וּמְנַגֵּחַ, וּמַפֶּלֶת אִשָּׁה מִיִּרְאָתוֹ. נִישׁוּבִים. פַּחִים, שֶׁלֹּא יִלָּכְדוּ בָּהֶן יוֹנֵי בְּנֵי הַיִּשּׁוּב. שְׁלֹשִׁים רִיס. אַרְבַּע מִילִין.

גמ' בְּחוּרְשִׁין. בִּיעָרוֹת כִּדְמְתַרְגְּמִינַן "בַּיַּעַר" — חוּרְשָׁא. בְּהֵמָה גַּסָּה. צְרִיכָה בַּיִּשּׁוּב, לְמַשָּׂאוֹי וְלַחֲרִישָׁה. שֶׁלֹּא יַשְׁהֶה הָאַחֲרוֹנָה שֶׁבָּהֶן שְׁלֹשִׁים יוֹם. לָקַח בְּהֵמוֹת קוֹדֶם לָרֶגֶל שְׁלֹשִׁים יוֹם, וְסָמוּךְ לָרֶגֶל, לֹא יֹאמַר: הֲרֵינִי שׁוֹחֵט אֶת הַמּוּקְדָּמוֹת וּמְאַחֵר אֶת הָאַחֲרוֹנוֹת אַף לְאַחַר הָרֶגֶל, עַד מְלֹאות שְׁלֹשִׁים יוֹם לְמִקְחָן.

וְהַטַּבָּח

תוספות

שהטמין בחורשין. פי': הטמין עלמו. וס"ד שהלך במשאי וטבח הבהמה במקום שהוא, ומש"ה פריך: והא לא משך!

כיון דראוהו גזלן הוא. כלומר, שעושה במקום גלוי, ולא דמי לגונב בבית או בחלר. **ורבי** יוחנן הא דמטמרי כו'. למ"ד ב"הכונס" (לעיל דף נז. ושם) דלר' יוחנן לסטים מזויין, כיון דמטמר מאינשי גנב הוא, אלטריך להאי טעמא. דלמ"ד דגזלן הוא לר' יוחנן — לא לריך להאי טעמא כלל.

מפני מה החמירה תורה כו'. בטוען טענת גנב וטענת גזלן לא שייך האי טעמא כלל.

אין מגדלין בהמה דקה. אפי' בבית קאמר, דלרעות — אפי' בהמה גסה אסור, כדאמרינן ב"זה בורר" (סנהדרין דף כה:): רועה שאמרו — אחד רועה בהמה גסה ואחד רועה בהמה דקה. וא"ת: והא דמסיק התם דרבא מגדלין איתמר, דמגדלי בהמה דקה בארץ ישראל פסולין, בחולה לארץ כשרים, מגדלי בהמה גסה אפי' בא"י כשרים, מאי קמשמע לן — דהא דבחו"ל כשרים? מתני' היא, דאפי' בסוריא שרי, כ"ש בחו"ל! ויש לומר: דודאי לא אלטריך, אלא איידי דאמר דבא"י פסולין, קמסיים דבחו"ל כשרים. ומגדלי בהמה גסה דאפי' בא"י כשרים אלטריך לאשמועינן, דאי ממתניתין, הוה אמינא דאפי' גסה אסור, והא דנקט דקה — לאשמועינן דאפי' דקה שרי בסוריא. ונראה דהא דאמרינן בפ"ק דב"מ (דף ה:) דרועה בהמות של אחרים כשר, דאין אדם חוטא ולא לו — היינו דוקא גסה, שמותר לגדל. אבל דקה בא"י, או בבבל לרב — אין נראה לחלק בין מגדל שלו לשל אחרים, דהא אפי' קשורה בכרעי המטה אסור. ולא כדברי המפרש לקמן דסבר רב הונא שמותר למסור לאשתו כמו שמותר לרועה, ולכך היתה מגטרת להו חובה, דהא כיון דבבל כא"י לבהמה דקה — אין לו לחלק בין על ידי עלמו בין ע"י אחרים. והנהו עיזי דאכלי חושלי בנהרדעא ב"חזקת הבתים" (ב"ב דף לו.) וקאמר: שאני עיזי דמסירי לרועה, אף על גב דנהרדעא היא בבל! שמא לא היו כל כך נזהרים על דברי רב שאמר בבל כא"י לבהמה דקה, שגם רב הונא לא החמיר. וכן משמע דאפי' ע"י אחרים אסור, מדלא מסר ההוא חסיד בהמה לרועה. וכן בעלי בתים שבגליל מסתמא לא היו מרעין בעצמן את לאנן. ורועה שעשה תשובה — מי לא עסקינן שמולא אחרים שירעו לו, ואפי' הכי קאמר: ימכור על יד.

והטבח

עין משפט נר מצוה

קכז א מיי' פ"א מהל' מכירה הלכה יח סמג עשין פב טוש"ע ח"מ סימן קלה סעיף ט וסימן שז סעיף ב וסימן שטו סעיף א:

קכח ב ג מיי' פ"ב מהלכות גניבה הלכה יז:

קכט ד מיי' שם פ"א הלכה ג ועיין בהשגות ובמ"מ ופ"א מהלכות גזילה ואבידה הלכה ג ועיין במ"מ ובל"מ סמג לאוין קנה טוש"ע ח"מ סימן שנט סעיף ז:

קל ה ו מיי' פ"ה מהל' נזקי ממון הלכה ב סמג עשין סו טוש"ע ח"מ סימן תט סעיף א:

קלא ז ח מיי' פ"ז מהלכות בית הבחירה הלכה יד:

קלב ט מיי' פ"ה מהל' נזקי ממון הלכה ט סמג עשין סז טוש"ע ח"מ סימן תט סעיף ב:

קלג מיי' שם טוש"ע שם סעיף ג:

קלד כ מיי' פ"ו מהל' גזילה ואבידה הל' ח סמג עשין עג טור ח"מ סימן שע:

קלה ל מיי' פ"ב מהל' ממרים הלכה ה סמג עשין קיא:

קלו מ מיי' פ"ה מהל' נזקי ממון הלכה ז סמג עשין סו טור ח"מ סימן תט:

הגהות הב"ח

(א) גמ' יותר מגזלן.

מסורת הש"ס

[כעיל נז.]

[עיין פרש"י ביומא ג: ד"ה כביכול]

רש"ל מ"ז

הגה"ת מהר"ב רנשבורג

א] רש"י ד"ה מפני הקדשים הו' עלם כעדשה מלת עלם נמחק:

[תענית כה. תמורה טו:]

[עי' תוספות לקמן פב ד"ה לא]

[ב"ב כג. ועי' רש"י חולין קטז. ותענית י. ד"ה ריסקא משמע דגרס הכא ריסבים]

[ב"ב ס: ע"ז לו. הוריות ג:]

[תוספתא פ"ח]

א וְהַטַּבָּח לוֹקֵחַ וְשׁוֹחֵט, לוֹקֵחַ וְשׁוֹהֶה, וּבִלְבַד שֶׁלֹּא יַשְׁהֶה הָעֲגוּנָה שֶׁבָּהֶן ל' יוֹם.§ *שָׁאֲלוּ תַּלְמִידָיו אֶת ר"ג: מַהוּ לְגַדֵּל? אָמַר לָהֶן: מוּתָּר. וְהָתְנַן: אֵין מְגַדְּלִין! אֶלָּא הָכִי קָא בָּעוּ מִינֵּיהּ: מַהוּ לַשְׁהוֹת? אָמַר לָהֶן: מוּתָּר, ב וּבִלְבַד שֶׁלֹּא תֵּצֵא וְתִרְעֶה בָּעֵדֶר, אֶלָּא קוֹשְׁרָהּ בְּכַרְעֵי הַמִּטָּה.§ *ת"ר: מַעֲשֶׂה בְּחָסִיד אֶחָד שֶׁהָיָה גּוֹנֵחַ מִלִּבּוֹ, וְשָׁאֲלוּ לָרוֹפְאִים, וְאָמְרוּ: אֵין לוֹ תַּקָּנָה עַד שֶׁיִּינַק חָלָב רוֹתֵחַ מִשַּׁחֲרִית לְשַׁחֲרִית; וְהֵבִיאוּ לוֹ עֵז וְקָשְׁרוּ לוֹ בְּכַרְעֵי הַמִּטָּה, וְהָיָה יוֹנֵק מִמֶּנָּה מִשַּׁחֲרִית לְשַׁחֲרִית. לְיָמִים נִכְנְסוּ חֲבֵירָיו לְבַקְּרוֹ, כֵּיוָן שֶׁרָאוּ אוֹתָהּ הָעֵז קְשׁוּרָה בְּכַרְעֵי הַמִּטָּה חָזְרוּ לַאֲחוֹרֵיהֶם, וְאָמְרוּ: לִסְטִים מְזוּיָּין בְּבֵיתוֹ שֶׁל זֶה, וְאָנוּ נִכְנָסִין אֶצְלוֹ? יָשְׁבוּ וּבָדְקוּ וְלֹא מָצְאוּ בּוֹ אֶלָּא אוֹתוֹ עָוֹן שֶׁל אוֹתָהּ הָעֵז. וְאַף הוּא בִּשְׁעַת מִיתָתוֹ אָמַר: יוֹדֵעַ אֲנִי [א] שֶׁאֵין בִּי עָוֹן אֶלָּא עֲוֹן אוֹתָהּ הָעֵז, שֶׁעָבַרְתִּי עַל דִּבְרֵי חֲבֵרַי.§ אָמַר ר' *יִשְׁמָעֵאל: מִבַּעֲלֵי בָתִּים שֶׁבַּגָּלִיל הָעֶלְיוֹן הָיוּ בֵּית אַבָּא, וּמִפְּנֵי מָה חָרְבוּ? שֶׁהָיוּ מַרְעִין בְּחוּרָשִׁין, וְדָנִין דִּינֵי מָמוֹנוֹת בְּיָחִיד. וְאע"פ שֶׁהָיוּ לָהֶם חוּרָשִׁים סָמוּךְ לְבָתֵּיהֶם, שָׂדֶה קְטַנָּה הָיְתָה וּמַעֲבִירִין דֶּרֶךְ עָלֶיהָ. *ג ת"ר: רוֹעֶה שֶׁעָשָׂה תְּשׁוּבָה, אֵין מְחַיְּיבִין אוֹתוֹ לִמְכּוֹר מִיָּד, אֶלָּא מוֹכֵר עַל יַד עַל יָד. ד וְכֵן גֵּר שֶׁנָּפְלוּ לוֹ כְּלָבִים וַחֲזִירִים בִּירוּשָּׁתוֹ, אֵין מְחַיְּיבִין אוֹתוֹ לִמְכּוֹר מִיָּד, אֶלָּא מוֹכֵר עַל יַד עַל יָד. וְכֵן ה מִי שֶׁנָּדַר לִיקַּח בַּיִת וְלִיקַּח אִשָּׁה בְּאֶרֶץ יִשְׂרָאֵל, אֵין מְחַיְּיבִין אוֹתוֹ לִיקַּח מִיָּד, עַד שֶׁיִּמְצָא אֶת הַהוֹגֶנֶת לוֹ; ו וּמַעֲשֶׂה בְּאִשָּׁה אַחַת שֶׁהָיָה בְּנָהּ מֵיצֵר לָהּ, וְקָפְצָה וְנִשְׁבְּעָה: "כָּל מִי שֶׁיָּבֹא אֵינִי מַחֲזִירַתּוּ", וְקָפְצוּ עָלֶיהָ בְּנֵי אָדָם שֶׁאֵינָן מְהוּגָּנִין, וּכְשֶׁבָּא הַדָּבָר אֵצֶל חֲכָמִים, אָמְרוּ: לֹא נִתְכַּוְּונָה זוֹ אֶלָּא לְהָגוּן לָהּ. כְּשֵׁם שֶׁאָמְרוּ אֵין מְגַדְּלִין בְּהֵמָה דַּקָּה, כָּךְ אָמְרוּ ז אֵין מְגַדְּלִין חַיָּה דַּקָּה; *ר' יִשְׁמָעֵאל אוֹמֵר: מְגַדְּלִין כְּלָבִים כּוּפְרִין, וַחֲתוּלִים, וְקוּפִין, וְחוּלְדוֹת סְנָאִים, מִפְּנֵי שֶׁעֲשׂוּיִים לְנַקֵּר אֶת הַבַּיִת. מַאי חוּלְדוֹת סְנָאִים? אָמַר רַב יְהוּדָה: שַׁרְצָא חַרְצָא; וְאִיכָּא דְּאָמְרִי: *חַרְזָא, דִּקְטִינֵי שָׁקֵיהּ וְרָעֲיָא בֵּינֵי וַוְרְדִינֵי. וּמַאי שַׁרְצָא — דְּמִתְּתַאי שָׁקֵיהּ. אָמַר רַב יְהוּדָה אָמַר רַב: ח עָשִׂינוּ עַצְמֵנוּ בְּבָבֶל כְּאֶרֶץ יִשְׂרָאֵל לִבְהֵמָה דַּקָּה. *א"ל רַב אַדָּא בַּר אַהֲבָה לְרַב הוּנָא: דִּידָךְ מַאי? א"ל: דִּידָן קָא מִנְטְרָא לְהוּ חוּבָה. א"ל: חוּבָה תִּקַּבְּרִינְהוּ לִבְנָהּ! כּוּלְּהוּ שְׁנֵיהּ דְּרַב אַדָּא בַּר אַהֲבָה לָא אִקַּיַּים זַרְעָא לְרַב הוּנָא מֵחוּבָה. אִיכָּא דְּאָמְרִי, אָמַר רַב הוּנָא (א) אָמַר רַב: עָשִׂינוּ עַצְמֵנוּ בְּבָבֶל כְּאֶרֶץ יִשְׂרָאֵל לִבְהֵמָה דַּקָּה, *מִכִּי אֲתָא רַב לְבָבֶל. רַב וּשְׁמוּאֵל וְרַב אַסִי אִיקְּלְעוּ לְבֵי שְׁבוּעַ הַבֵּן, וְאָמְרִי לָהּ לְבֵי יֵשׁוּעַ הַבֵּן, רַב לָא עָיֵיל קַמֵּיהּ דִּשְׁמוּאֵל, שְׁמוּאֵל

רש"י

וְהַטַּבָּח. הַמְקַבֵּן אֶת הַבְּהֵמוֹת לְיוֹם הַשּׁוּק. לוֹקֵחַ וְשׁוֹחֵט אוֹ לוֹקֵחַ וְשׁוֹהֶה. עַד יוֹם הַשּׁוּק, שְׁלֹשִׁים יוֹם לְמִקָּחוֹ. וּבִלְבַד שֶׁלֹּא יַשְׁהֶה אֶת הָעֲגוּנָה. הַמְאוּחֶרֶת לְמִקָּחוֹ, שֶׁלָּקַח סָמוּךְ לְעֵת הַשּׁוּק, לֹא יַשְׁהֶה אוֹתָהּ לְאַחַר יוֹם הַשּׁוּק לְהַשְׁלִים שְׁלֹשִׁים יוֹם לְמִקָּחָהּ. הָעֲגוּנָה. מְאוּחֶרֶת, כְּמוֹ "הֲלָהֵן תֵּעָגֵנָה" (רות א) — תְּאַחַרְנָה מִלְּהִנָּשֵׂא. אֶלָּא קוֹשְׁרָהּ. וְרַבָּנַן פְּלִיגֵי עֲלֵיהּ דְּרַבָּן גַּמְלִיאֵל. גּוֹנֵחַ. פלידר"א. צוֹעֵק מִפְּנֵי כְּאֵב הַלֵּב, לֹא הָיָה יָכוֹל לְהָשִׁיב רוּחוֹ. לִסְטִים מְזוּיָּין. רוֹעֶה בִּשְׂדוֹת אֲחֵרִים, וְגוֹזֵל אֶת הָרַבִּים. שֶׁהָיוּ מַרְעִין. בְּהֵמָה דַּקָּה שֶׁלָּהֶן בְּחוּרָשִׁין. וְאע"פ שֶׁהָיוּ חוּרָשִׁין סָמוּךְ לְבָתֵּיהֶם. וְלֹא הָיוּ רוֹעִין בִּשְׂדוֹת אֲחֵרִים. וּמִשּׁוּם חוּרָשִׁין לֵיכָּא גֶּזֶל, דְּאָמַר לְעֵיל: אֲבָל מְגַדְּלִין בְּחוּרָשִׁין, וּלְקַמָּן (דף פא.) נַמִי בְּתַקָּנַת יְהוֹשֻׁעַ תִּיקֵּן שֶׁלֹּא יַקְפִּיד בַּעַל הַיַּעַר עַל כָּךְ — אֲפִי' הָכִי נֶעֶנְשׁוּ, מִפְּנֵי שֶׁשָּׂדֶה קְטַנָּה הָיְתָה בֵּינֵיהֶם, וְשֶׁל אֲחֵרִים הָיְתָה. רוֹעֶה. בְּהֵמוֹת שֶׁלּוֹ. שֶׁעָשָׂה תְּשׁוּבָה. שֶׁלֹּא לְגַדֵּל בְּהֵמָה דַּקָּה עוֹד. כְּלָבִים וַחֲזִירִים. תְּנַן בְּמַתְנִיתִין דְּאָסוּר לְגַדְּלָן. חַיָּה דַּקָּה. זְאֵבִים וְשׁוּעָלִין. כְּלָבִים כּוּפְרִיִּים. קְטַנִּים וְנַנָּסִים הֵם. ל"א: כְּלָבִים גְּדוֹלִים שֶׁל צַיָּידִים, וְאֵין מַזִּיקִין. חוּלְדוֹת סְנָאִין. גְּדֵילוֹת בַּסְּנֶה. לְנַקֵּר אֶת הַבַּיִת. מִן הָעַכְבָּרִים. וַורְדִינֵי = סְנֶה. דִּקְטִינֵי = דַּקִּים. דְּמִתְּתַאי שָׁקֵיהּ. שׁוֹקֶיהָ גּוּלִין. בְּבָבֶל כְּאֶרֶץ יִשְׂרָאֵל. שֶׁמִּיּוֹם גָּלוּת יְכָנְיָה רַבּוּ שָׁם תַּלְמִידִים, וְנִתְיַישְּׁבוּ שָׁם בְּיִשּׁוּב קָבוּעַ. דִּידָךְ מַאי. הֲלֹא יֵשׁ לְךָ בְּהֵמָה דַּקָּה. חוּבָה. שֵׁם אִשְׁתּוֹ. תִּקַּבְּרִינְהוּ לִבְנָהּ. שֶׁאַתָּה סוֹמֵךְ עָלֶיהָ, וְהִיא אֵינָהּ יְכוֹלָה לִשְׁמוֹר. מִכִּי אֲתָא רַב לְבָבֶל. רַבּוּ מִתְיַישְּׁבִין שָׁם מִפְּנֵי יְשִׁיבָתוֹ. לִישָּׁנָא אַחֲרִינָא: הוּא בָּא וְלִמְּדָנוּ לְהִזָּהֵר בְּכָךְ, שֶׁרָאָה שָׁם רוֹב יִשְׂרָאֵל וְיִשּׁוּב קָבוּעַ. שְׁבוּעַ הַבֵּן. בְּרִית מִילָה, עַל שֵׁם שֶׁעָבְרוּ עָלָיו שִׁבְעָה יָמִים. יֵשׁוּעַ הַבֵּן. מִשְׁתֶּה שֶׁעוֹשִׂין לְפִדְיוֹן הַבֵּן בְּכוֹר. ° "יֵשׁוּעַ" מְתַרְגְּמִינַן: פּוּרְקָן, כְּמוֹ פִּדְיוֹן. רַב לָא עָיֵיל קַמֵּיהּ דִּשְׁמוּאֵל. טַעֲמָא אָמְרִינַן לְקַמָּן.

תוספות

והטבח לוקח ושוהה. פי' בקונטרס: עד יום השוק. ובלבד שלא ישהה העגונה שבהם שלשים יום — אותה שלקח באחרונה לא ישלים לה שלשים יום אחר השוק. וקשה: דבתוספתא (פ"ח) גרס "יותר מל' יום", וא"כ לפי התוספתא יכול להשהות אחר יום השוק! ועוד קשה: דלעיל גבי רגל קרי לה אחרונה, והכא קרי לה עגונה! ועוד: שלא הזכיר התנא יום השוק כלל! ונראה לר"י: לפי שהטבח רגיל לקנות כמה בהמות ביחד, ומותר להשהות, ובלבד שאפי' העגונה שבהן, אותה שנשארה יחידה אחר חברותיה — שלא ישהה יותר מל' יום, אף על פי שהיא יחידה. ומיהו, בכל הספרים גרסינן "שלשים יום", ולא גרסינן "יותר".

מהו להשהות קבעו מיניה. אין נ"ל דפליגי רבנן עליה דר"ג כדפי' בקונטרס, דמהו להשהות קודם הרגל קבעו מיניה, ואמר להן מותר. ולאו דוקא נקט קושרה, אלא אורחא דמלתא נקט, שדרכן היה לקשור בהמה דקה לכרעי המטה, כדאמר ב"אלו טריפות" (חולין דף נד:): חבל היוצא מן המטה, עד תשעה טפחים — *טהור, ופירש שם בקונטרס שבכך הוא ראוי לקשור בהמה דקה בכרעי המטה, כדכתי' "אסרו חג בעבותים עד קרנות המזבח" שהיו קושרין הקרבנות בכרעי המטה עד שיביאוהו לקרנות המזבח. אי נמי, נקט "קשרו" לאשמועינן דאפילו בקשורים אסור לגדל כ"א להשהות. ובתוספתא (פ"ח) נמי משמע דאף קודם הרגל לא שרי להשהות אלא בבית, דהכי קתני בהדיא: אבל מגדלים קודם הרגל ל' יום, ולא שתהא יוצאה ורועה בשוק אלא קושרה בכרעי המטה. שאלו לר"ג כו'.

דקטיני שקיה. פי': שוקיו דקין, ולהכי נקרא חרלא שהחרלין ניכר בין השוקים, מתוך שהן דקים ונראין גבוהים. ומשום הכי תנן *בפ"א דאהלות חולדות הסנאים, רבי יוסי אומר: ב"ש מטמא כזית במשא וכעדשה במגע. דמתוך שרגליה גבוהים ודקים מספקא להן שמא לאו היינו חולדה דקרא, ויש לה תורת נבילה, או שמא היינו היא ויש לה תורת שרץ. והאי דמסיים: ומאי שרצא דמתתאי שקיה — ה"ק: ומאי שרצא — חולדה דכתיב בקרא, שאין ספק — דמתתאי שקיה, שהי' רגליה קצרות ושורצת על הארץ. וכן נראה לר"ת.

חובה תקברינהו לבנה. פר"ח: בתמיה, וכי דרכה לקבור בניה? שאין עוסקת לגדלן אלא עוסקת לגדל צאן. והוי כשגגה היוצאת מלפני השליט. ומיהו, בפרק "שני נזירים" (נזיר דף נז: ושם) גבי הקפת הראש אין שייך לפרש כן, דאמר ליה רב אדא בר אהבה לרב הונא: לדידך מאן מקיף להו? אמר ליה: חובה. א"ל: חובה תקברינהו לבנה, ואין שייך לפרש שם אלא לשון קללה. אי נמי, יש לומר: אין ירא שתענש בקבורת בניה?

מכי אתא רב לבבל. פי' בקונטרס: והיו מתישבין שם מפני ישיבתו, והיו רוב שדותיהן מישראל. וכענין זה פי' בפרק קמא דגיטין (דף ו. ושם*): עשינו עצמנו בבבל כארץ ישראל לגיטין מכי אתא רב לבבל — ועשינו בקיאין לשמה מתוך שהרבה ישיבות. וקשה לר"ת: דא"כ מאי פריך התם ממתני' דעכו כארץ ישראל לגיטין, אבל בבל לא? והלא המשניות נשנו קודם דאתא רב לבבל! ומפר"ת התם: מכי אתא רב לבבל — והורה לנו שמימות יכניה והחרש והמסגר שגלו לבבל דינה להיות כארץ ישראל לגיטין, שבקיאין לשמה. וכן כאן, לענין בהמה דקה — שיש שם רוב ישראל. וכן יש בריש "בכל מערבין" (עירובין דף כח.).

לבי ישוע הבן. פ"ה: פדיון הבן. וכן הערוך. וקשה: דאע"ג דמתרגמינן "פדיון" פורקן, מ"מ אין שייך לשון ישועה! ור"ת פי' שנולד שם בן, ועל שם שהולד נושע ונמלט ממעי אמו, כדכתיב "והמליטה זכר" (ישעיה סו) נקט לשון ישועה, והיו רגילין לעשות סעודה.

נפק

עין משפט נר מצוה

קלז א ב מיי' פ"ה מהלכות נזקי ממון הלכה ז סמג עשין סו טוח"מ סי' תט:

קלח ג ד מיי' שם הל' י סמג שם טור וש"ע ח"מ סימן תט סעיף ד:

קלט ה ו מיי' פ"ח מהלכות נדרים הלכה יג סמג לאוין רמב טוש"ע י"ד סימן ריט סעיף א:

קמ ז מיי' פ"ה מהל' נזקי ממון הלכה ב סמג עשין סו טוש"ע ח"מ סימן תט סעיף א ועיין בטור:

קמא ח מיי' שם הלכה ח סמג שם טור ח"מ סימן תט:

[נ"ל טמא וע"ש]

הגהות הב"ח

(א) גמ' אמר ר' הונא עשינו עצמנו כצ"ל ותיבת אמר רב נמחק:

גליון הש"ס

רש"י ד"ה ישוע הבן כו'. ישוע מתרגמינן. נ"ל ויושע מתרגמינן ופרק (שמות יד) ועי' רש"י ע"ז דף ד' ע"א ד"ה להם שוע:

נ"ל בפ"ח דכלאים מ"ה

[לקמן ע"ב איתא ר"ש בן אלעזר וכ"ה בתוספ' פ"ח ובערוך ערך חלד א]

הגהות מהר"ב רנשבורג

[א] גמ' שאין בי עון אלא עון אותה העז. עיין שיטה מקובצת ומהרש"א בח"א כתב בענין אחר ודבריו תמוהים קצת מסוגיא דכתובות דף ס ע"א דגונח יונק בשבת.

מסורת הש"ס

[תוספתא פ"ח]

תמורה טו:

ס"א שמעון שזורי

[תוספתא פ"ח]

ס"א חרצא

נזיר נז:

[גיטין ו.]

[ד"ה מכי]

תורה אור

שְׁמוּאֵל לָא עָיֵיל קַמֵּיהּ דְּרַב אַסִי, רַב אַסִי לָא עָיֵיל קַמֵּיהּ דְּרַב. אָמְרִי: מַאן נִתְרָח? נִתְרָח שְׁמוּאֵל, וְנֵיתֵי רַב וְרַב אַסִי. [א] וְנִתְרָח רַב אוֹ רַב אַסִי! רַב, מִילְּתָא בְּעָלְמָא הוּא דַּעֲבַד לֵיהּ לִשְׁמוּאֵל, מִשּׁוּם הַהוּא מַעֲשֶׂה דְּלָטְיֵיהּ אַדְבְּרֵיהּ רַב עֲלֵיהּ. אַדְּהָכִי וְהָכִי אֲתָא שׁוּנְרָא קְטַעֵיהּ לִידָא דְּיָנוֹקָא. נְפַק רַב וְדָרַשׁ: [א]חָתוּל — מוּתָּר לְהוֹרְגוֹ, וְאָסוּר לְקַיְּימוֹ, וְאֵין בּוֹ מִשּׁוּם גָּזֵל, וְאֵין בּוֹ מִשּׁוּם הָשֵׁב אֲבֵידָה לַבְּעָלִים. וְכֵיוָן דְּאָמְרַתְּ "מוּתָּר לְהוֹרְגוֹ", מַאי נִיהוּ תּוּ "אָסוּר לְקַיְּימוֹ"? מַהוּ דְּתֵימָא: "מוּתָּר לְהוֹרְגוֹ" — אִיסּוּרָא לֵיכָּא, קמ"ל. אָמְרִי: וְכֵיוָן דְּאָמְרַתְּ "אֵין בּוֹ מִשּׁוּם גָּזֵל", מַאי נִיהוּ תּוּ "אֵין בּוֹ מִשּׁוּם הָשֵׁב אֲבֵידָה לַבְּעָלִים"? אָמַר רָבִינָא: [ב]לְעוֹרוֹ. מֵיתִיבֵי, רַבִּי שִׁמְעוֹן בֶּן אֶלְעָזָר אוֹמֵר: מְגַדְּלִין כְּלָבִים כּוֹפְרִין, וַחֲתוּלִין, וְקוֹפִין, וְחוּלְדוֹת סְנָאִים, מִפְּנֵי שֶׁעֲשׂוּיִין לְנַקֵּר אֶת הַבַּיִת! לָא קַשְׁיָא: הָא בְּאוּכָּמָא, הָא בְּחִיוָּרָא. וְהָא מַעֲשֶׂה דְּרַב — אוּכָּמָא הֲוָה! הָתָם אוּכָּמָא בַּר חִיוָּרָא הֲוָה. וְהָא מִבָּעֲיָא בָּעֲיָא לֵיהּ רָבִינָא; דְּבָעֵי רָבִינָא: אוּכָּמָא בַּר חִיוָּרָא, מַהוּ? כִּי קָמִבַּעֲיָא לֵיהּ לְרָבִינָא — בְּאוּכָּמָא בַּר חִיוָּרָא בַּר אוּכָּמָא, מַעֲשֶׂה דְּרַב — בְּאוּכָּמָא בַּר חִיוָּרָא הֲוָה. (חב"ד בי"ח בח"ן סִימָן) אָמַר רַבִּי אַחָא בַּר פַּפָּא מִשּׁוּם רַבִּי אַבָּא בַּר פַּפָּא מִשּׁוּם רַבִּי אַדָּא בַּר פַּפָּא, וְאָמְרִי לָהּ: אָמַר ר' אַבָּא בַּר פַּפָּא מִשּׁוּם רַבִּי חִיָּיא בַּר פַּפָּא מִשּׁוּם רַבִּי אַחָא בַּר פַּפָּא, וְאָמְרִי לָהּ: אָמַר ר' אַבָּא בַּר פַּפָּא מִשּׁוּם רַבִּי אַחָא בַּר פַּפָּא מִשּׁוּם רַבִּי חֲנִינָא בַּר פַּפָּא: [ג]מַתְרִיעִין °עַל הַחִיכּוּךְ בְּשַׁבָּת, וְדֶלֶת הַנִּנְעֶלֶת לֹא בִּמְהֵרָה תִּפָּתַח, וְהַלּוֹקֵחַ בַּיִת בְּאֶרֶץ יִשְׂרָאֵל — כּוֹתְבִין עָלָיו אוֹנוֹ אֲפִילּוּ בְּשַׁבָּת. מֵיתִיבֵי: *[ד]וּשְׁאָר פּוּרְעָנִיּוֹת הַמִּתְרַגְּשׁוֹת וּבָאוֹת עַל הַצִּבּוּר, כְּגוֹן חִיכּוּךְ, חָגָב, זְבוּב, צִירְעָה, וְיַתּוּשׁ, וְשִׁילּוּחַ נְחָשִׁים וְעַקְרַבִּים — לֹא הָיוּ מַתְרִיעִין אֶלָּא צוֹעֲקִים! לָא קַשְׁיָא: [ה]כָּאן בְּלַח, כָּאן בְּיָבֵשׁ; דְּאָמַר רַבִּי יְהוֹשֻׁעַ בֶּן לֵוִי: *שְׁחִין שֶׁהֵבִיא הקב"ה עַל הַמִּצְרִים — לַח מִבַּחוּץ וְיָבֵשׁ מִבִּפְנִים, שֶׁנֶּאֱמַר: °"וַיְהִי שְׁחִין אֲבַעְבּוּעוֹת פּוֹרֵחַ בָּאָדָם וּבַבְּהֵמָה". "וְדֶלֶת הַנִּנְעֶלֶת לֹא בִּמְהֵרָה תִּפָּתַח", מַאי הִיא? מָר זוּטְרָא אָמַר: סְמִיכָה. רַב אַשִׁי אָמַר: *כָּל הַמְּרִיעִין לוֹ לֹא בִּמְהֵרָה מְטִיבִין לוֹ. רַב אַחָא מִדִּיפְתִּי אָמַר: לְעוֹלָם אֵין מְטִיבִין לוֹ. וְלָא הִיא, רַב אַחָא מִדִּיפְתִּי מִילְּתָא דְּנַפְשֵׁיהּ הוּא דַּאֲמַר. [ו]"וְהַלּוֹקֵחַ בַּיִת בְּאֶרֶץ יִשְׂרָאֵל — *כּוֹתְבִין עָלָיו אוֹנוֹ אֲפִילּוּ בְּשַׁבָּת". בְּשַׁבָּת סָלְקָא דַּעְתָּךְ? אֶלָּא כִּדְאָמַר רָבָא הָתָם: *אוֹמֵר לְגוֹי וְעוֹשֶׂה, ה"נ — [ז]אוֹמֵר לְגוֹי וְעוֹשֶׂה. וְאע"ג *דַּאֲמִירָה לְגוֹי שְׁבוּת הִיא, מִשּׁוּם יִשּׁוּב אֶרֶץ יִשְׂרָאֵל לֹא גָּזְרוּ בֵּיהּ רַבָּנַן. אָמַר רַבִּי שְׁמוּאֵל בַּר נַחְמָנִי אָמַר רַבִּי יוֹנָתָן: [ח]הַלּוֹקֵחַ עִיר בְּאֶרֶץ יִשְׂרָאֵל, כּוֹפִין אוֹתוֹ לִיקַּח לָהּ דֶּרֶךְ מֵאַרְבַּע רוּחוֹתֶיהָ, מִשּׁוּם יִשּׁוּב אֶרֶץ יִשְׂרָאֵל.§ ת"ר: *[ט]עֲשָׂרָה תְּנָאִין הִתְנָה יְהוֹשֻׁעַ: שֶׁיְּהוּ

תענית יט.

בכורות מא.

שמות ט

ב"ב יב:

גיטין ח:

[שבת קכט. ביצה כב.]

[שבת קנ. עירובין סז. גיטין ח: ב"מ ל.]

עירובין יז.

רש"י

שְׁמוּאֵל לָא עָיֵיל קַמֵּיהּ דְּרַב אַסִי. שֶׁהָיָה גָּדוֹל מִמֶּנּוּ, וְרַב אַסִי תַּלְמִיד שֶׁל רַב הֲוָה. °**מַאן נִתְרָח.** מִי יִתְאַחֵר מִבַּחוּץ וְיָבֹא אַחֲרוֹנָה יְחִידִי. **נִתְרָח שְׁמוּאֵל.** בַּחוּץ, וְיָבוֹאוּ רַב וְרַב אַסִי, רַב וְאַח"כ תַּלְמִידוֹ. **מִילְּתָא בְּעָלְמָא הוּא דַּעֲבַד לִשְׁמוּאֵל.** שְׁמוּאֵל קָטָן שֶׁבְּכוּלָּן הָיָה, וְזֶה שֶׁאֵין רַב נִכְנָס לְפָנָיו — טֵיבוּתָא וִיקָרָא הוּא דְּקָא עָבַד לֵיהּ מִשּׁוּם מַעֲשֶׂה דְּלַטְיֵיהּ לִשְׁמוּאֵל, בְּ"שְׁמוֹנָה שְׁרָצִים" (שבת דף קח.). **אַדְבְּרֵיהּ עֲלֵיהּ.** הִטְעִינוֹ עָלֵיהּ לִנְהוֹג בּוֹ כָּבוֹד. **אַדְּהָכִי וְהָכִי.** דְּהָווּ מְסָרְבִי, אֲתָא שׁוּנְרָא וּקְטַעֵיהּ לִידָא דְּהַהוּא יָנוֹקָא. **חִיוָּרָא.** מוּעָד לְהַזִּיק אָדָם. **מַתְרִיעִים.** בְּצִבּוּר וּבִתְחִנָּה וּבְשׁוֹפָרוֹת וּבַחֲצוֹצְרוֹת, בְּמַסֶּכֶת תַּעֲנִית. **חִיכּוּךְ.** שְׁחִין, שֶׁמִּתְחַכֵּךְ הָאָדָם עָלֶיהָ. פרוטי"ר בְּלַעַ"ז. **וְדֶלֶת הַנִּנְעֶלֶת.** עַל הָאָדָם מִהְיוֹת מַצְלִיחַ. **לֹא בִּמְהֵרָה תִּפָּתַח.** וְנָפְקָא מִינָּהּ לְאַפּוּשֵׁי בְּרַחֲמֵי. (א) **מִלְּתָא דְּנַפְשֵׁיהּ.** בְּב"ב בְּ"הַשּׁוּתָּפִין" (דף יב:) דְּאִימְנוּהּ לְאוֹתוּבֵיהּ בְּרֵישָׁא, וְלָא אִיסְתַּיְּעָא מִילְּתָא. **וְהַלּוֹקֵחַ בַּיִת.** מִנָּכְרִי. **אוֹנוֹ.** שְׁטַר מְכִירָה. **לֹא הָיוּ מַתְרִיעִין.** בְּשַׁבָּת. **צוֹעֲקִין.** בְּיָחִיד. **יָבֵשׁ.** קָשֶׁה מִלַּח. **אֲבַעְבּוּעוֹת פּוֹרֵחַ.** בְּפִרְיחָתוֹ, דְּהַיְינוּ מִבַּחוּץ — הוּא מְבַעְבֵּעַ, דְּהַיְינוּ לַח. מִכְּלָל דְּבִפְנִים הָוֵי יָבֵשׁ.

תוספות

נפק רב ודרש. לא עתה על זה המעשה תיקן, דהא פריך עלה מברייתא. אלא דרש דמקודם נתקן.

מותר להורגו ואסור לקיימו. והא דאמר ר"ל בפ"ק דסנהדרין (דף טו: ושם) גבי ארי ונמר ודוב וזאב וברדלס ונחש, דאפי' ר"א דאמר כל הקודם להורגו זכה היינו דוקא כשהמיתו, אבל לא המיתו לא — היינו בקשורין בשלשלת, שכן דרך לגדלן, והכא בחתול שאין קשורה. א"נ: מהנהו רגילים בני אדם להזהר, ולא אתי לידי היזק, אבל מחתול אין נזהרין, שאין יודעים אם היא בר אוכמא או בר חיורא, שאין מכירים באבותיהם.

אמר רבינא לעורו. שאם (ב) מצאו מת אין חייב בהשבת העור. °וקצת תימה: כיון דאשמועינן דאין בו משום גזל, למאי איצטריך הך דמותר להורגו? וי"ל: דאין לחוש, כיון דמתחילה קאמר דמותר להורגו.

מתריעין על החיכוך בשבת. ע"כ לאו היינו התרעה בשופר, דשופר בשבת מי איכא? כדדייק בספ"ק דתענית (דף יד. ושם). אלא התרעה בפה ב"עננו", וסבר כמ"ד התם ד"עננו" קרי ליה התרעה. ותימה: דמאי פריך מההיא דבשאר מיני פורעניות, דקתני: לא היו מתריעין על החיכוך אלא צועקים? דילמא ה"ק: לא היו מתריעין בשופר אלא צועקים בפה ב"עננו"! ואין לומר: אע"ג דתרוייהו בפה, התרעה לחוד וצעקה לחוד. דהתם משמע דלמ"ד "עננו" קרי ליה התרעה — חדא היא! וי"ל, דה"פ: מדקאמר שבשבת מתריעין לכל הפחות ב"עננו" — א"כ ראוי לעשות על החיכוך התרעה אפי' בשופר בחול, כיון שהוא דבר גדול כל כך דבשבת צועקים.

על החגב. ל"ג: ועל הגובאי. דהא במתני' ד"סדר תעניות האלו" (תענית יט.) תנן שמתריעין על הארבה ועל החסיל ועל הגובאי. וי"ל: דהתם בפה. ועי"ל: דשפיר גרסינן ליה, והתם בגובאי המזיק לשדות דומיא דארבה *וחסול דקתני התם. וגובאי דהכא — במזיק לבני אדם, דומיא דצרעים ושילוח נחשים. פירוש ר"י.

לעולם אין מטיבין לו. והא דקאמר איהו גופיה בעובדא דידיה: לא במהרה מטיבין לו, בפרק קמא דבבא בתרא (דף יב.) — זה אמר בשעה שהיה סבור עדיין שיחזירו וימנו אותו ראש ישיבה, אבל לבסוף שלא החזירוהו, אמר: לעולם אין מטיבין לו.

אומר לגוי ועושה. דוקא משום מצוה זו דישוב דא"י, אבל לצורך מצוה אחרת לא שרי אמירה לגוי. ואפי' לצורך מילה משמע בפרק "הדר" (עירובין דף סח.) דלא שרי אמירה לגוי באיסורא דאורייתא, גבי ההוא ינוקא דאישתפיך חמימיה, דקאמר: נשייליה לאימיה, אי צריכה — נחים ליה אגב אימיה. משמע דאי לא צריכה אימיה — לא שרי אפילו על ידי גוי. וי"ס שכתוב בהדיא: נחים ליה גוי אגב אימיה. ולכאורה משמע שלפני המילה היה, והיו צריכין לחמימי כדי למולו, ולא שרי אפילו ע"י גוי אלא אגב אימיה כדשריא הכא. והתם בעובדא דלעיל דקאמר (ג) גבי ינוקא אחרינא נימא ליה לגוי דניתי מגו ביתא — ההוא דלעיל איסורא דרבנן הוה להביא דרך חצר שלא עירב. ואפילו איסורא דרבנן אור"י שאין להתיר משום מצוה אחרת על ידי גוי, כגון להביא ספר דרך כרמלית כדי ללמוד בו. דדוקא מילה, דהיא גופא דחי שבת, שרי על ידי גוי איסור דרבנן. ומיהו, בה"ג משמע דאפילו איסורא דאורייתא שרי על ידי גוי לצורך מילה, שפירש דאפי' דניתי גוי מתוך ביתו — דהיא דרך רשות הרבים, דהוי איסורא דאורייתא — שרי על ידי גוי לצורך מילה, כמו הכא משום ישוב ארץ ישראל. ולדבריהם בעובדא בתרא דקאמר: נחים ליה גוי אגב אימיה — לאחר המילה הוה, ולאחר שלשה שכבר נתרפא הולד יפה. ולספרים דל"ג גוי — נוכל לומר דע"י ישראל קאמר, ותוך שבעה דמחללין עליה השבת אם אמרה "צריכה אני", כדאמרינן בפרק "מפנין" (שבת דף קכט. ושם). אבל אין נראה, דעל ידי ישראל הוה אסור להרבות בשביל התינוק, כדאמרינן בפ"ק דחולין (דף טו:). ולפי ה"ג טפי אית לן למישרי על ידי גוי איסורא דאורייתא מאיסורא דרבנן על ידי ישראל, כדמסיק התם אהאי עובדא: ולא שני לך בין שבות דאית ביה מעשה לשבות דלית ביה מעשה? ואמרינן נמי בפרק ר' אליעזר דמילה" (שבת דף קל:): כשם שאין מביאין דרך רשות הרבים — כך אין מביאין דרך גגות חצירות וקרפיפות. והיה נראה מתוך ה"ג להתיר ביום שני אפילו של ר"ה לעשות כל צרכי מילה, אפילו לכרות עצים לעשות ברזל ע"י ישראל, שהרי מת דלא שרי לקבור על ידי גוי כדמוכח בפ"ק דר"ה (דף כ.), אפילו הכי

עין משפט נר מצוה

קמב א ב מיי' פט"ו מהלכות גזלה ואבדה הלכה יז סמג עשין עג טוש"ע ח"מ סימן רסו סעיף ד:

קמג ג מיי' פ"ב מהל' תענית הלכה יג טוש"ע א"ח סימן תקעו סעיף ה:

קמד ד מיי' שם הלכה ט י ועי' בהשגות ובמ"מ טוש"ע שם סעי' ז:

קמה ה מיי' שם הלכה יג טוש"ע שם סעיף ה:

קמו ו ז מיי' פ"ו מהל' שבת הלכה יא [טוש"ע א"ח סימן שו סעיף יא]:

קמז ח מיי' פ"ו מהל' שכנים הלכה ב:

קמח ט מיי' פ"ה מהל' נזקי ממון הלכה ג סמג עשין סו טוש"ע ח"מ סימן רעד סעיף א בהג"ה:

הגהות הב"ח

(א) רש"י ד"ה מלתא דנפשיה נ"ל אחר ד"ה אבעבועות: (ב) תום' ד"ה אמר וכו' שאם מצאו מת: (ג) ד"ה אומר וכו' דקאמר רבה גבי ינוקא:

גליון הש"ס

גמ' על החיכוך בשבת. עי' בכורות דף לח ע"ב תוספות ד"ה וסימניך: **רש"י** ד"ה מאן נתרח מי יתאחר וכן פרחיה גביה גיטין דף סח ע"ב וכן מתרגמא ע"ז דף יח ע"א: **תום'** ד"ה אמר וכו' וקצת תימה. עיין תשו' רשד"ם חי"ד סימן רלב ובתשובת מהר"י אדריבי סימן של"ו:

[נ"ל וחסיל]

הגהות מהר"ב רנשבורג

[א] גמ' ונתרח רב או רב אסי רב מילתא. עיין שיטה מקובצת:

שֶׁיְּהוּ מַרְעִין בֶּחוֹרָשִׁין, וּמְלַקְּטִין עֵצִים בִּשְׂדוֹתֵיהֶם, וּמְלַקְּטִים עֲשָׂבִים בְּכָל מָקוֹם חוּץ מִתִּלְתָּן, וְקוֹטְמִים נְטִיעוֹת בְּכָל מָקוֹם חוּץ מִגְּרוֹפִיּוֹת שֶׁל זַיִת, וּמַעְיָן הַיּוֹצֵא בַּתְּחִילָּה בְּנֵי הָעִיר מִסְתַּפְּקִין מִמֶּנּוּ, וּמְחַכִּין בְּיַמָּהּ שֶׁל טִבֶרְיָא וּבִלְבַד שֶׁלֹּא יִפְרוֹס קֶלַע וְיַעֲמִיד אֶת הַסְּפִינָה, וְנִפְנִין לַאֲחוֹרֵי הַגָּדֵר וַאֲפִילּוּ בְּשָׂדֶה מְלֵיאָה כַּרְכּוֹם, *וּמְהַלְּכִים בִּשְׁבִילֵי הָרְשׁוּת עַד שֶׁתֵּרֵד רְבִיעָה שְׁנִיָּה, וּמִסְתַּלְּקִין לְצִידֵּי הַדְּרָכִים מִפְּנֵי יְתֵידוֹת הַדְּרָכִים, וְהַתּוֹעֶה בֵּין הַכְּרָמִים מְפַסֵּיג וְעוֹלֶה מְפַסֵּיג וְיוֹרֵד, *וּמֵת מִצְוָה קוֹנֶה מְקוֹמוֹ.§ "שֶׁיְּהוּ מַרְעִין בֶּחוֹרָשִׁין". אָמַר רַב פַּפָּא: [א]לָא אֲמָרַן אֶלָּא דַּקָּה בְּגַסָּה, אֲבָל דַּקָּה בְּדַקָּה וְגַסָּה בְּגַסָּה — לָא, וְכָל שֶׁכֵּן גַּסָּה בְּדַקָּה דְּלָא.§ "וּמְלַקְּטִין עֵצִים מִשְּׂדוֹתֵיהֶם". [ב]לָא אֲמָרַן אֶלָּא בְּהִיזְמֵי וְהִיגֵי, אֲבָל בִּשְׁאָר עֵצִים — לָא; וַאֲפִילּוּ בְּהִיזְמֵי וְהִיגֵי — [ג]לָא אֲמָרַן אֶלָּא בִּמְחוּבָּרִין, אֲבָל בִּתְלוּשִׁין — לָא; וַאֲפִי' בִּמְחוּבָּרִין — [ד]לָא אֲמָרַן אֶלָּא בְּלַח, אֲבָל בְּיָבֵשִׁים — לָא. וּבִלְבַד שֶׁלֹּא יְשָׁרֵשׁ.§ "וּמְלַקְּטִין עֲשָׂבִים בְּכָל מָקוֹם, חוּץ מִשְּׂדֵה תִלְתָּן". לְמֵימְרָא דְּתִלְתָּן מַעֲלוּ לָהּ עֲשָׂבִים? וּרְמִינְהִי: *[ה]תִּלְתָּן שֶׁעָלְתָה עִם מִינֵי עֲשָׂבִים — אֵין מְחַיְּיבִין אוֹתוֹ לַעֲקוֹר! אָמַר רַב יִרְמְיָה: לָא קַשְׁיָא, כָּאן לְזֶרַע, כָּאן לְזִירִין; לְזֶרַע — קָשׁוּ לָהּ עֲשָׂבִים, דְּמַכְחֲשִׁי לָהּ; לְזִירִין (א) — מַעֲלֵי לָהּ, דְּכִי קַיְימִי בֵּינֵי עֲשָׂבִים מִירַכְּבָא. אִיבָּעֵית אֵימָא: [ו]כָּאן לְאָדָם, כָּאן לִבְהֵמָה, דְּכֵיוָן דְּלִבְהֵמָה הוּא דְּזַרְעָהּ, עֲשָׂבִים נַמִי מִיבָּעֵי לָהּ. וּמְנָא יָדְעִינַן? א"ר פַּפָּא: [ז]שָׁאֲרִיהּ מְשָׁארֵי — לְאָדָם, לָא שָׁאֲרִיהּ מְשָׁארֵי — לִבְהֵמָה.§ "וְקוֹטְמִין נְטִיעָה בְּכָל מָקוֹם, חוּץ מִגְּרוֹפִיּוֹת שֶׁל זַיִת". פֵּי' ר' תַּנְחוּם וְר' בְּרַיִים מִשּׁוּם זָקֵן אֶחָד: [ח]בְּזַיִת — כְּבֵיצָה, בְּקָנִים ◉וּבִגְפָנִים — מִן הַפְּקָק וּלְמַעְלָה, וּשְׁאָר כָּל הָאִילָנוֹת — מִן אוּבּוֹ שֶׁל אִילָן וְלֹא מִן חוּדּוֹ שֶׁל אִילָן, מִן חָדָשׁ שֶׁאֵינוֹ עוֹשֶׂה פֵּירוֹת וְלֹא מִן יָשָׁן שֶׁהוּא עוֹשֶׂה פֵּירוֹת, מִמָּקוֹם שֶׁאֵינוֹ רוֹאֶה אֶת הַחַמָּה

וְלֹא

שֶׁיְּהוּ מַרְעִין. בְּהֵמוֹת בֶּחוֹרָשִׁין, וְשֶׁלֹּא יַקְפִּיד בַּעַל הַיַּעַר עַל כָּךְ. וּמְלַקְּטִין עֵצִים. מִשְּׂדֵה חֲבֵירוֹ. וְכֵן עֲשָׂבִים ◉לְמַאֲכַל בְּהֵמָה. חוּץ מִשְּׂדֵה תִלְתָּן. דְּמַעֲלוּ לָהּ עֲשָׂבִים הַגְּדֵילוֹת עִמָּהּ, וְהַתּוֹלְשָׁן מַפְסִיד אֶת הַתִּלְתָּן. תִּלְתָּן = מִין (ב) קִטְנִית, וּשְׁמָהּ פנגרי"א. וְקוֹטְמִין נְטִיעוֹת. מִן הָאִילָן. קוֹטֵס בַּד לִיטַּע אוֹ לְהַרְכִּיב, וְלֹא יַקְפִּיד בַּעַל הָאִילָן. חוּץ מִגְּרוֹפִיּוֹת שֶׁל זַיִת. הַקּוֹצֵץ זֵיתָיו לִשְׂרוֹף — מַנִּיחַ שְׁתֵּי גְּרוֹפִיּוֹת = מְלֹא שְׁנֵי אֲגְרוֹפִין, כִּדְאָמַר בְּ"הַמּוֹכֵר אֶת הַסְּפִינָה" (ב"ב דף פ.), וְהֵן מַחֲלִיפוֹת וּמוֹצִיאוֹת בַּדִּין. וּמִשָּׁם אֵין לִקְטוֹס נְטִיעָה, מִפְּנֵי שֶׁמַּפְסִיד אֶת הַגְּרוֹפִיּוֹת. בַּתְּחִילָּה. מְחָדָשׁ. וְכָל שֶׁכֵּן מַעְיָינוֹת יְשָׁנִים שֶׁהָיוּ מִימוֹת יְהוֹשֻׁעַ. וּמְחַכִּין. וּמַטִּילִין חַכָּה לָצוּד דָּגִים. בְּיַמָּהּ שֶׁל טִבֶרְיָא. וְאַע"פ שֶׁבְּחֶלֶק נַפְתָּלִי הָיְתָה כּוּלָּהּ, כִּדְאָמְרִינַן לְקַמָּן. שֶׁלֹּא יִפְרוֹס קֶלַע. דֶּרֶךְ צַיָּידִים לִתְקוֹעַ יְתֵידוֹת וְלַעֲשׂוֹת גִּדְרֵי קָנִים בַּמַּיִם לְהִלָּכֵד שָׁם דָּגִים. וְקוֹרִין לוֹ בִּמְקוֹמֵינוּ גז"ר, וּבְאֶרֶץ אַשְׁכְּנַז קוֹרִין לוֹ ווכ"א. (*שֶׁלֹּא יִפְרוֹס קֶלַע) מִפְּנֵי שֶׁמְּעַכֵּב וּמַעֲמִיד אֶת הַסְּפִינָה. לַאֲחוֹרֵי הַגָּדֵר. לְקַמָּן מְפָרֵשׁ לָהּ: לָא נִצְרְכָה אֶלָּא לִיטּוֹל הֵימֶנָּה צְרוֹר לְקַנֵּחַ, וְאַע"פ שֶׁפּוֹרֵץ אֶת הַגָּדֵר. וּמְהַלְּכִין בִּשְׁבִילֵי הָרְשׁוּת. סְתָם בְּנֵי אָדָם, מִשֶּׁהִכְנִיסוּ תְּבוּאָתָם עַד שְׁעַת הַזְּרִיעָה — מַפְקִירִים שְׂדוֹתֵיהֶם לִיכָּנֵס בָּהֶן כָּל אָדָם לְקַצֵּר אֶת הַדֶּרֶךְ שֶׁלֹּא יַקִּיף, וְהֵן נִקְרָאִין שְׁבִילֵי הָרְשׁוּת לְפִי שֶׁבִּרְשׁוּת עוֹשִׂין. וְהִתְנָה יְהוֹשֻׁעַ שֶׁלֹּא יַקְפִּידוּ עַל כָּךְ*. עַד שֶׁתֵּרֵד רְבִיעָה שְׁנִיָּה. זְמַנָּהּ בְּי"ז בְּמַרְחֶשְׁוָן, כִּדְאָמְרִינַן בְּתַעֲנִית (דף טז.). וּמֵאָז וָהָלְאָה הַזְּרָעִים צוֹמְחוֹת, וְקָשֶׁה לָהּ דְּרִיסַת הָרֶגֶל. וּמִסְתַּלְּקִין לְצִידֵּי הַדְּרָכִים. בְּכָל עֵת, וַאֲפִי' בִּזְמַן שֶׁהַתְּבוּאָה בַּשָּׂדוֹת — הִפְקִיר לְכָל אָדָם לְהִסְתַּלֵּק מִן הַדֶּרֶךְ מִפְּנֵי הַיְּתֵידוֹת, וְלִיכָּנֵס לִגְבוּל שְׂדֵה חֲבֵירוֹ וְלֵילֵךְ עַל הַמֵּיצָר אֵצֶל הַדֶּרֶךְ. מִפְּנֵי יְתֵידוֹת הַדְּרָכִים. בִּימוֹת הַחַמָּה יָבֵשׁ הַטִּיט וְנַעֲשָׂה כִּיתֵידוֹת מְקוֹם דְּרִיסַת הָאָדָם וּבְהֵמָה שֶׁדָּרְסוּ שָׁם בִּימוֹת הַחוֹרֶף וְנַעֲשׂוּ כִּשְׁחִיתוֹת. מְפַסֵּיג. מְנַתֵּק זְמוֹרוֹת הַנּוֹשְׁכוֹת הַמְעַכְּבוֹת אוֹתוֹ, וְעוֹלֶה וְיוֹרֵד עַד שֶׁמּוֹצֵא אֶת הַדֶּרֶךְ. מְקוֹמוֹ. מָקוֹם שֶׁנָּפַל שָׁם בְּעֵת מוֹתוֹ קְנָאוֹ לִקְבוּרָה, וְאֵין בַּעַל הַשָּׂדֶה מְעַכֵּב עָלָיו. דַּקָּה. בְּהֵמָה דַּקָּה בְּיַעַר גַּסָּה, שֶׁאֵינָהּ מְכַלָּה אֶת הָאִילָנוֹת. אֲבָל בִּתְלוּשִׁין. אַחֲרֵי שֶׁטָּרַח עֲלֵיהֶן בַּעַל הַשָּׂדֶה וּתְלָשָׁן — אָסוּר לִיטְּלָן, דְּדַעְתֵּיהּ עֲלַיְיהוּ. יְבֵשִׁין. דַּעְתּוֹ עֲלֵיהֶם לָאוּר. אֵין מְחַיְּיבִין אוֹתוֹ לַעֲקוֹר. הָעֲשָׂבִים מִמֶּנָּה מִשּׁוּם כִּלְאַיִם, לְפִי דִּבְעַל כָּרְחוֹ עָתִיד לִיטְּלוֹ, שֶׁמַּפְסִיד אֶת הַתִּלְתָּן. כָּאן. שֶׁהַתִּלְתָּן עוֹמֶדֶת לִיזָּרַע. כָּאן. שֶׁזְּרָעָהּ לֶאֱכוֹל. הַזִּירִין = טודילי"ש בְּלַעַ"ז. דְּמִירַכְּבָא. מִתְפַּשֶּׁטֶת וְגוֹדֶלֶת עַל הָעֲשָׂבִים, וְנַעֲשִׂין לָהּ סְמִיכָה, כְּעֵין דָּלֶת שֶׁל כֶּרֶם. וּמְנָא יָדְעִינַן. אִם זְרָעָהּ לְאָדָם, דְּשָׁרֵי לֵיהּ לְמִלְקַט מִן הָעֲשָׂבִים בִּתְנָאֵי יְהוֹשֻׁעַ. מְשָׁארֵי. עֲשׂוּיִים כַּעֲרוּגוֹת. בְּזַיִת כְּבֵיצָה. כְּשִׁיעוּר גּוֹבַהּ בֵּיצָה צָרִיךְ לְהַנִּיחַ מִן הַזַּיִת מִלְּמַטָּה, סָמוּךְ לַגֶּזַע. מִן הַפְּקָק וּלְמַעְלָה. מוּתָּר לִקְטוֹס. פְּקָק = קֶשֶׁר. מֵאִיבּוֹ שֶׁל אִילָן. מִפִּרְיוֹ, כְּלוֹמַר: מֵעֲנָפִין הָרַכִּין וְדַקִּין. וְלֹא מֵחוּדּוֹ. מֵעֲנָפִין גְּדוֹלִים וְגַסִּין, כְּאִילָן גָּמוּר. ל"א: מֵחוּדּוֹ שֶׁל אִילָן — מִמַּחֲבוֹאָתוֹ, מָקוֹם שֶׁיֵּשׁ עֲנָפִין הַרְבֵּה, דְּהַיְינוּ בְּאֶמְצַע גָּבְהוֹ. וְלֹא מֵחוּדּוֹ — מִלְּמַעְלָה עָנָף הָאֶמְצָעִי, שֶׁהוּא עֶלְיוֹן וְעִיקַּר הָאִילָן. מִתְּשׁוּבוֹת הַגְּאוֹנִים. מִן הֶחָדָשׁ. בַּד שֶׁגָּדֵל וְנִיתּוֹסֵף בְּשָׁנָה זוֹ, שֶׁעֲדַיִין אֵין עוֹשֶׂה פְּרִי.

וְלֹא

הכי אמר בפ"ק דביצה (דף ו. ושם): ביו"ט שני יתעסקו בו ישראל, אפילו ביו"ט שני של ר"ה — כ"ש מילה דשרי ע"י גוי איסורא דאורייתא בשבת, כדפי' בהלכות גדולות, ושרי נמי ע"י ישראל ביו"ט שני של ר"ה. ומיהו, אין זה ק"ו, דמן הדין הוה ליה למישרי לקבור מת בשבת, אלא לפי שהוא מכוער ומגונה ומתבייש שנקבר בשבת שנעשה באיסור שבת אפילו ע"י גוי. מידי דהוה אההיא דתנן בפרק "השואל" (שבת דף קנא.): עשה גוי ארון וחפר קבר, אם בשביל ישראל — לא יקבר בו עולמית, ולא שרי בכדי שיעשו כמו בתי, מטעם דפרישית. ותדע, דהא במת שריא כרמלית, כדאמרינן ב"המצניע" (שם דף צד:) דגדול כבוד הבריות, א"כ כ"ש דהוה ליה למישרי לקבור ע"י גוי, אלא על כרחך טעמא הוי כדפרישית. וא"ש נמי הא דאמרינן בפ"ב דביצה (דף כב.): אמימר שרא למיכחל עינא אפי' ביו"ט שני של ר"ה. ופריך: והאמר *רבה מת ביו"ט שני יתעסקו בו ישראל, מה שאין כן בביצה. והשתא מאי פריך מביצה? והא נרכי חולה אית לן למשרי טפי אפי' ממת, דבסוף "מפנין" (שבת דף קכט.*) אמר דכל צרכי חולה נעשין על ידי ארמאי בשבת. ומיכחל עינא מדמה התם לחולה שאין בו סכנה, ואומר לגוי ועושה אפי' איסורא דאורייתא, א"כ אית לן למישרי בק"ו ממת אפי' לכתוש סמנין ביום טוב שני של ראש השנה על ידי ישראל! ולמאי דפרישנא אתי שפיר, דליכא ק"ו.

חוץ מגרופיות של זית. פירש בקונטרס: מלא שני אגרופין. ובערוך פירש: מגרופיים — ענפים, וענפי הזית קרויין גרופיים, כמו יחור בתאנה וזמורה בגפנים, שכל אחד יש לו שם לבדו. והביא הא דאמר בבראשית רבה: "ואתה קח לך מכל מאכל אשר יאכל" — זמורות לנטיעות, יחורי לתאנים, גרופיות לזיתים.

ומעין היוצא בתחילה בני העיר מסתפקין [ממנו]. למאי דאמר לקמן דתנאים שהתנה יהושע אפי' בחו"ל, יש לתמוה: הא דאמר בפרק "כל הצלמים" (ע"ז דף מז. ושם): המשתחוה למעין מימיו מהו לנסכים, ופשיט ליה מהא דאמר: מים של רבים אין נאסרים. ומשני: דנבעי מארעיה. והשתא, אכתי של רבים הם מתנאי יהושע! ויש לחלק בין יוצא מאליו לטרח בו וחפרו.

ומחכין בימה של טבריא. כל אדם. ובלבד שלא יפרוש קלע — נמי לכל אדם, ואפי' הבעלים עצמן, כדתניא לקמן שהתנו השבטים זה עם זה. אבל צד הוא במכמורות וברשת — והיינו הבעלים, שהוא שלהם. **אין** מחייבין אותו לעקור. פירש בקונטרס: שע"כ עתיד ליטלם, לפי שמפסידין את התלתן. וקשה לפירושו: ד"אין מחייבין" משמע שאין אסור בהנאתו. ועוד, דאם מתייאש ומתעצל לעוקרו למה לא נחייבנו? דהא איכא איסור כשמתייאש, כדתנן במסכת כלאים (פ"ה מ"ו): הרואה ירק בכרמו, ואמר "לכשאגיע שם אלקטנו" — מותרין, "לכשאחזור אלקטנו" והוסיף מאתים — אסור! ונראה לר"י: דאין מחייבין אותו לעקור — דליכא איסורא, שהרי הוא לא זרעו אלא מאליהן באו. ומשום מקיים בכלאים ליכא, כיון דקשו להו עשבים. ולר"ע איצטריך, דאמר בפרק בתרא דע"ז (דף סד.) ובמכות (דף כא:): המקיים בכלאים לוקה. ולאו מלקות ממש, דלאו שאין בו מעשה הוא, אלא איסורא בעלמא הוא. א"נ, אפי' לרבנן איצטריך, והיכא דניחא ליה — חייבוהו חכמים, שלא יחשדוהו שזרעם. והא דנקט תלתן שעלתה עם מיני עשבים, ולא נקט תלתן שעלו עמו עשבים — רבותא נקט, אפילו שמתכוין לזרוע תחילה שאר זרעים והתלתן עלה מאליו — אפ"ה, כיון דהשתא מיהא לא ניחא ליה בזרעים, מחמת התלתן שעלה — אין מחייבין אותו לעקור. **כאן** לזירין. ◉ההיא ד"חוץ משדה תלתן" — לזירים, דמעלו ליה. וא"ת: כיון דאיכא איסור כלאים, אמאי אסור ללקט? והאמר בפ"ק דמו"ק (דף ו:) שתקנו שיהיו מפקירין כל השדה שיש בו כלאים! וי"ל דהכא בדליכא שיעורא, כדתנן במסכת כלאים (פ"ב מ"א) ומייתי לה ב"המוכר פירות" (ב"ב דף צג.) כל סאה שיש בו רובע ממין אחר — ימעט.

אין

[תענית ו:]

[עירובין יז. סוטה מה: סנהדרין מז:]

רש"ל מוחק זה

[כלאים פ"ב מ"ה]

...ל בערוך פי' שבילי ...שות היינו שבילין שהן ...ות לבני אדם כלומר ...ן מופקרין לרבים אלא ...להם בעלים ועיין בספר ...תח

[נ"ל רבא]

קמט א מיי' פ"ה מהל' נזקי ממון הל' ג סי' א סמג עשין סו טור ח"מ סימן רעד:

קנ ב ג ד מיי' שם סי' ב טוח"מ שם:

קנא ה ו ז מיי' פ"ב מהלכות כלאים הלכה ז והלכה ח והלכה ט והלכה י סמג לאוין רפ טוש"ע י"ד סימן רלז סעיף ט:

קנב ח מיי' פ"ה מהל' נזקי ממון הל' ג סי' ד סמג עשין סו טוח"מ סימן רעד:

הגהות הב"ח

(א) גמ' מעלו לה עשבים דכי: (ב) רש"י ד"ה חוץ משדה וכו' מין קטנית. נ"ב ובמסכת ר"ה דף יב ע"ב פרש"י דהוא מין תבלין:

גליון הש"ם

גמ' ובגפנים מן הפקק ולמעלה. עיין ב"ב דף ט ע"ב תוס' ד"ה בקנים: **רש"י** ד"ה ומלקטין עלים וכו' למאכל בהמה. עיין בב"מ דף קז ע"א תוספות ד"ה הני תחלי: **תום'** ד"ה כאן וכו' ההוא לחוץ משדה תלתן. עיין תשובת מהרשד"ם סימן רלג:

וְלֹא מִמָּקוֹם שֶׁהוּא רוֹאֶה אֶת הַחַמָּה, שֶׁנֶּאֱמַר: °"וּמִמֶּגֶד תְּבוּאוֹת שָׁמֶשׁ". § "וּמַעְיָן הַיּוֹצֵא תְּחִילָּה בְּנֵי הָעִיר מִסְתַּפְּקִין מִמֶּנּוּ". אָמַר רַבָּה בַּר רַב הוּנָא: וְנוֹתֵן לוֹ דָּמִים. וְלֵית הִלְכְתָא כְּוָותֵיהּ. § "וּמְחַכִּין בְּיַמָּהּ שֶׁל טִבֶרְיָא, וּבִלְבַד שֶׁלֹּא יִפְרוֹס קֶלַע וְיַעֲמִיד אֶת הַסְּפִינָה". [א] אֲבָל צָד הוּא בְּרְשָׁתוֹת וּבְמִכְמָרוֹת. ת"ר: *בָּרִאשׁוֹנָה הִתְנוּ שְׁבָטִים זֶה עִם זֶה שֶׁלֹּא יִפְרוֹס קְלִיעָה וְיַעֲמִיד אֶת הַסְּפִינָה, אֲבָל צָד הוּא בְּרְשָׁתוֹת וּבְמִכְמָרוֹת. תָּנוּ רַבָּנַן: יַמָּהּ שֶׁל טִבֶרְיָא בְּחֶלְקוֹ שֶׁל נַפְתָּלִי הָיְתָה; וְלֹא עוֹד, אֶלָּא שֶׁנָּטַל מְלֹא חֶבֶל חֵרֶם בִּדְרוֹמָהּ, לְקַיֵּים מַה שֶּׁנֶּאֱמַר: °"יָם וְדָרוֹם יְרָשָׁה". תַּנְיָא, רַבִּי שִׁמְעוֹן בֶּן אֶלְעָזָר אוֹמֵר: תְּלוּשִׁין שֶׁבֶּהָרִים — בְּחֶזְקַת כָּל הַשְּׁבָטִים הֵן עוֹמְדִים, וּמְחוּבָּרִים — בְּחֶזְקַת אוֹתוֹ הַשֵּׁבֶט. *וְאֵין לְךָ כָּל שֵׁבֶט וְשֵׁבֶט מִיִּשְׂרָאֵל שֶׁאֵין לוֹ בָּהָר וּבַשְּׁפֵלָה וּבַנֶּגֶב וּבָעֵמֶק, שֶׁנֶּאֱמַר: °"פְּנוּ וּסְעוּ לָכֶם וּבֹאוּ הַר הָאֱמוֹרִי וְאֶל כָּל שְׁכֵנָיו בָּעֲרָבָה בָהָר בַּשְּׁפֵלָה וּבַנֶּגֶב וּבְחוֹף הַיָּם" וגו'; וְכֵן אַתָּה מוֹצֵא בַּכְּנַעֲנִים וּבַפְּרִיזִּים (א) וּבָאֱמוֹרִיִּים שֶׁלִּפְנֵיהֶם, שֶׁנֶּאֱמַר: "וְאֶל כָּל שְׁכֵנָיו", אַלְמָא, שְׁכֵנָיו הָכִי הָווּ. § "וְנִפְנִין לַאֲחוֹרֵי הַגָּדֵר, וַאֲפִילּוּ בְּשָׂדֶה שֶׁהִיא מְלֵאָה כַּרְכּוֹם". אָמַר רַב אַחָא בַּר יַעֲקֹב: [א]לֹא נִצְרְכָה, אֶלָּא לִיטּוֹל הֵימֶנּוּ צְרוֹר. אָמַר רַב חִסְדָּא: [ב]וַאֲפִילּוּ בְּשַׁבָּת. מָר זוּטְרָא חֲסִידָא שָׁקֵיל וּמְהַדַּר, וַא"ל לְשַׁמָּעֵיהּ *(לְמָחָר): זִיל שִׁירְקֵיהּ. § "וּמְהַלְּכִין בִּשְׁבִילֵי הָרְשׁוּת עַד שֶׁתֵּרֵד רְבִיעָה שְׁנִיָּה". אָמַר רַב פָּפָּא: [ג]וְהַאי דִּידַן אֲפִילּוּ טַל קָשֵׁי לָהּ. § "וּמְסַלְּקִין לְצִידֵּי הַדְּרָכִים מִפְּנֵי יְתֵידוֹת הַדְּרָכִים". שְׁמוּאֵל וְרַב יְהוּדָה הָווּ שָׁקְלִי וְאָזְלִי בְּאוֹרְחָא, הֲוָה מִסְתַּלֵּק שְׁמוּאֵל לְצִידֵּי הַדְּרָכִים; א"ל רַב יְהוּדָה: תְּנָאִין שֶׁהִתְנָה יְהוֹשֻׁעַ, אֲפִילּוּ בְּבָבֶל? א"ל, שֶׁאֲנִי אוֹמֵר: [ד]אֲפִילּוּ בְּחוּצָה לָאָרֶץ. רַבִּי וְרַבִּי חִיָּיא הָווּ שָׁקְלִי וְאָזְלִי בְּאוֹרְחָא, אִסְתַּלְּקוּ לְצִידֵּי הַדְּרָכִים; הֲוָה קָא מַפְסִיעַ וְאָזֵיל ר' יְהוּדָה בֶּן קְנוֹסָא קַמַּיְיהוּ, א"ל רַבִּי לְרַבִּי חִיָּיא: מִי הוּא זֶה שֶׁמַּרְאֶה גְּדוּלָּה בְּפָנֵינוּ? א"ל ר' חִיָּיא: שֶׁמָּא ר' יְהוּדָה בֶּן קְנוֹסָא תַּלְמִידִי הוּא, וְכָל מַעֲשָׂיו לְשֵׁם שָׁמַיִם. כִּי מָטוּ לְגַבֵּיהּ, חַזְיֵיהּ, א"ל: אִי לָאו יְהוּדָה בֶּן קְנוֹסָא אַתְּ, גְּזַרְתִּינְהוּ לְשָׁקָךְ בְּגִיזְרָא דְּפַרְזְלָא. § [ה]"הַתּוֹעֶה בֵּין הַכְּרָמִים, מְפַסֵּיג וְיוֹרֵד מְפַסֵּיג וְעוֹלֶה". § ת"ר: *הָרוֹאֶה חֲבֵירוֹ תּוֹעֶה בֵּין הַכְּרָמִים, מְפַסֵּיג וְעוֹלֶה מְפַסֵּיג וְיוֹרֵד עַד שֶׁמַּעֲלֵהוּ לָעִיר אוֹ לַדֶּרֶךְ; וְכֵן הוּא שֶׁתּוֹעֶה בֵּין הַכְּרָמִים, מְפַסֵּיג וְעוֹלֶה מְפַסֵּיג וְיוֹרֵד עַד שֶׁיַּעֲלֶה לָעִיר אוֹ לַדֶּרֶךְ. מַאי "וְכֵן"? מַהוּ דְּתֵימָא: חֲבֵירוֹ הוּא דְּיָדַע לְהֵיכָא מְסַלֵּק דְּנִיפְסוֹג, אֲבָל הוּא דְּלָא יָדַע לְהֵיכָא קָא סָלֵיק — לָא נִיפְסוֹג, נְהַדְרֵיהּ נְהַדַּר בֵּי מֵיצְרֵי, קמ"ל. הָא [ו]דְּאוֹרַיְיתָא הוּא, דְּתַנְיָא: *הֲשָׁבַת גּוּפוֹ מִנַּיִין? ת"ל: °"וַהֲשֵׁבֹתוֹ"! דְּאוֹרַיְיתָא הוּא דְּקָאֵי בֵּי מֵיצְרֵי, אֲתָא הוּא תַּקֵּין דִּמְפַסֵּיג וְעוֹלֶה מְפַסֵּיג וְיוֹרֵד. § "וּמֵת מִצְוָה קָנָה מְקוֹמוֹ". וּרְמִינְהִי: *[ז]הַמּוֹצֵא מֵת מוּטָּל בְּאִיסְרַטְיָא — מְפַנֵּהוּ לִימִין אִיסְרַטְיָא אוֹ לִשְׂמֹאל אִיסְרַטְיָא, שָׂדֶה בּוּר וְשָׂדֶה נִיר — מְפַנֵּהוּ לִשְׂדֵה בּוּר, שָׂדֶה נִיר וּשְׂדֵה זֶרַע — מְפַנֵּהוּ לִשְׂדֵה נִיר; הָיוּ שְׁתֵּיהֶן בּוּרוֹת, שְׁתֵּיהֶן נִירוֹת, שְׁתֵּיהֶן זְרוּעוֹת — מְפַנֵּהוּ לְמָקוֹם שֶׁיִּרְצֶה! אָמַר רַב בֵּיבָי: [ח]בְּמוּטָּל עַל הַמֵּיצַר, מִתּוֹךְ שֶׁנִּיתָּן לְפַנּוֹתוֹ, מְפַנֵּהוּ לְכָל מָקוֹם שֶׁיִּרְצֶה. אָמְרִי: עֲשָׂרָה? הָנֵי חַד סְרֵי הָוְיָין! [ט]מְהַלְּכִין בִּשְׁבִילֵי הָרְשׁוּת שְׁלֹמֹה אֲמָרָהּ; כִּדְתַנְיָא: הֲרֵי שֶׁכָּלוּ פֵּירוֹתָיו מִן הַשָּׂדֶה, וְאֵינוֹ מַנִּיחַ בְּנֵי אָדָם לִיכָּנֵס בְּתוֹךְ שָׂדֵהוּ, מָה הַבְּרִיּוֹת אוֹמְרוֹת עָלָיו — מָה הֲנָאָה יֵשׁ לִפְלוֹנִי, וּמָה הַבְּרִיּוֹת מַזִּיקוֹת לוֹ! עָלָיו הַכָּתוּב אוֹמֵר: "מִהְיוֹת טוֹב אַל תִּקְרֵי רַע". וּמִי כְּתִיב "מִהְיוֹת טוֹב אַל תִּקְרֵי רַע"? אִין, כְּתִיב כִּי הַאי גַּוְונָא: °"אַל תִּמְנַע טוֹב מִבְּעָלָיו בִּהְיוֹת לְאֵל יָדְךָ לַעֲשׂוֹת". [י] וְתוּ לֵיכָּא? וְהָא אִיכָּא דְּרַבִּי יְהוּדָה! *דְּתַנְיָא, רַבִּי יְהוּדָה אוֹמֵר: בִּשְׁעַת הוֹצָאַת זְבָלִים, אָדָם מוֹצִיא זִבְלוֹ לרה"ר וְצוֹבְרוֹ כָּל שְׁלֹשִׁים, כְּדֵי שֶׁיְּהֵא נִישּׁוֹף בְּרַגְלֵי אָדָם וּבְרַגְלֵי בְהֵמָה, שֶׁעַל מְנָת כֵּן הִנְחִיל יְהוֹשֻׁעַ לְיִשְׂרָאֵל אֶת הָאָרֶץ! וְהָא אִיכָּא דְּר' יִשְׁמָעֵאל בְּנוֹ שֶׁל ר' יוֹחָנָן בֶּן בְּרוֹקָה! *דְּתַנְיָא, רַבִּי יִשְׁמָעֵאל בְּנוֹ שֶׁל ר' יוֹחָנָן בֶּן בְּרוֹקָה אוֹמֵר: תְּנַאי ב"ד הוּא, שֶׁיְּהֵא זֶה יוֹרֵד לְתוֹךְ שָׂדֶה חֲבֵירוֹ וְקוֹצֵץ שׂוֹכוֹ שֶׁל חֲבֵירוֹ לְהַצִּיל נְחִיל שֶׁלּוֹ, וְנוֹתֵן לוֹ דְּמֵי שׂוֹכוֹ שֶׁל חֲבֵירוֹ; וּתְנַאי ב"ד הוּא, שֶׁיְּהֵא זֶה שׁוֹפֵךְ יֵינוֹ וּמַצִּיל דּוּבְשָׁנוֹ שֶׁל חֲבֵירוֹ, וְנוֹטֵל דְּמֵי יֵינוֹ מִתּוֹךְ דּוּבְשָׁנוֹ שֶׁל חֲבֵירוֹ; וּתְנַאי ב"ד הוּא, שֶׁיְּהֵא זֶה מְפָרֵק אֶת עֵצָיו וְטוֹעֵן פִּשְׁתָּנוֹ שֶׁל חֲבֵירוֹ, וְנוֹטֵל דְּמֵי עֵצָיו מִתּוֹךְ פִּשְׁתָּנוֹ שֶׁל חֲבֵירוֹ, שֶׁעַל מְנָת כֵּן הִנְחִיל יְהוֹשֻׁעַ לְיִשְׂרָאֵל אֶת הָאָרֶץ! [כ] בִּיחִידָאֵי לָא קָאָמְרִינַן.

וְהָא

רש"י

וְלֹא מִמָּקוֹם הָרוֹאֶה אֶת הַחַמָּה. סְבִיבוֹת גְּדָדִין מִבַּחוּץ, מִפְּנֵי שֶׁהוּא עִיקַּר הָאִילָן, שֶׁהַחַמָּה מְבַשֶּׁלֶת שָׁם אֶת הַפְּרִי וּמַמְתִּיקוֹ. מְלֹא חֶבֶל חֵרֶם. מְלֹא חֶבֶל שֶׁל מְצוּדָה הָיָה לוֹ בִּדְרוֹמָהּ מִן הַיַּבָּשָׁה לִמְשׁוֹךְ רִשְׁתּוֹ. חֵרֶם — כְּמוֹ "מְצוֹדִים וַחֲרָמִים" (קהלת ז). בְּחֶזְקַת כָּל הַשְּׁבָטִים. כָּל מִי שֶׁיִּרְצֶה יִטּוֹל, דְּהָא כְּמִטַּלְטְלֵי וּשְׁאָר הַשָּׁלָל וְהַמַּלְקוֹחַ הָיוּ. וְכֵן אַתָּה מוֹצֵא בַּכְּנַעֲנִי. אע"פ שֶׁכָּתוּב כָּאן הַר הָאֱמוֹרִי — אַף כְּנַעֲנִי וּפְרִיזִי כָּךְ הָיוּ לָהֶם. וְיִשְׂרָאֵל שֶׁיָּרְשׁוּ הָיָה לָהֶם לְכָל אֶחָד הַר וּשְׁפֵלָה וָנֶגֶב וְעֵמֶק — (ב) אֶרֶץ שָׂדוֹת וּבְקָעוֹת שֶׁקּוֹרִין כנפיי"ה. לָכֵן נִקְרֵאת נֶגֶב — שֶׁכָּל שָׁעָה הִיא נְגוּבָה, שֶׁאֵין שָׁם צֵל אִילָנוֹת, וְחַמָּה זוֹרַחַת וּמְנַגַּבְתָּהּ. אֲמַר לֵיהּ לְשַׁמָּעֵיהּ. בַּחוֹל. שִׁרְקֵיהּ. טָחֵיהוּ בְּטִיט וְחַבְּרֵהוּ יָפֶה. וְהָא. קַרְקַע דִּידָן. אֲפִילּוּ טַל. יָרַד עָלֶיהָ בַּלַּיְלָה — קָשֶׁה לָהּ דְּרִיסַת הָרֶגֶל מִמָּחֳרָתוֹ. אֲפִילּוּ בְּחוּצָה לָאָרֶץ. וְכ"ש בְּבָבֶל, שֶׁמְּלוּיִין שָׁם שַׁיָּירוֹת וְעוֹבְרִין וְשָׁבִים, וְהוּצְרַךְ לְהַתְנוֹת. מְפַסַּע וְאָזֵיל. מְיַיחֵד לְיָחֵד פְּסִיעוֹת גַּסּוֹת, וְלֹא הָיָה רוֹצֶה לְהִסְתַּלֵּק אֶל מֵגַר הַשָּׂדֶה. גְּדוּלָּתוֹ. שֶׁהוּא מַרְאֶה לָנוּ שֶׁהוּא יְרֵא שָׁמַיִם מְאֹד, וְאֵינוֹ חוֹשֵׁשׁ לִתְנַאי שֶׁהִתְנָה יְהוֹשֻׁעַ, וּמֶחֱזֵי כְּיוּהֲרָא. בְּגִיזְרָא דְּפַרְזְלָא. כְּלוֹמַר: נִידּוּי. מַאי וְכֵן. פְּשִׁיטָא, מַאי שְׁנָא אִיהוּ מֵחַבְרֵיהּ? וַהֲשֵׁבוֹתוֹ. אֶת גּוּפוֹ, מַשְׁמַע שֶׁאִם טָעָה חֲבֵירְךָ — אַתָּה צָרִיךְ לְהַעֲלוֹתוֹ לַדֶּרֶךְ. דְּאוֹרַיְיתָא בֵּי מֵצְרֵי. יַקִּיף סְבִיבוֹת מִגְרֵי הַכְּרָמִים, וְלֹא יַעֲבוֹר בְּתוֹכָם וְיַפְסִידֵם. אִיסְרַטְיָא. רה"ר ט"ז אַמָּה. שָׂדֶה בּוּר. מִכָּאן לָאִיסְרַטְיָא, וּשְׂדֵה נִיר מִכָּאן — מְפַנֵּהוּ לִשְׂדֵה בּוּר. נִיר = חָרוּשׁ וְלֹא זָרוּעַ. מְפַנֵּהוּ. אַלְמָא לֹא קָנָה מְקוֹמוֹ, דְּאִי קָנָה מְקוֹמוֹ מָצֵי בַּעַל הַשָּׂדֶה שֶׁל יָמִין וְשֶׁל שְׂמֹאל לְעַכּוּבֵיהּ. עַל הַמֵּיצַר. מוּטָּל בְּרוֹחַב הַדֶּרֶךְ, וְעוֹבְרִין וּמַאֲהִילִין עָלָיו עוֹשֵׂי טְהָרוֹת, וּמִטַּמְּאוֹת. כָּל שְׁלֹשִׁים יוֹם. שְׁלֹשִׁים יוֹם רַשַּׁאי לְהַנִּיחוֹ שָׁם. דְּר' יִשְׁמָעֵאל בְּנוֹ שֶׁל ר' יוֹחָנָן בֶּן בְּרוֹקָה. בְּפֶרֶק "הַגּוֹזֵל בַּתְרָא". נְחִיל. שֶׁל דְּבוֹרִים, שֶׁהָלְכוּ לִשְׂדֵה חֲבֵירוֹ וְנִתְיַישְּׁבוּ עַל שׂוֹכָתָהּ שֶׁל אִילָן. וְאִם יִטּוֹל אֶחָד אֶחָד הֵן פּוֹרְחוֹת וְאוֹבְדוֹת, מֵאַחַר שֶׁנָּתְנוּ עֵינֵיהֶן בְּאוֹתָהּ שׂוֹכָה — לְפִיכָךְ קוֹצְצָהּ וְנוֹתֵן לוֹ דָּמִים. וּמַצִּיל דּוּבְשָׁנוֹ. זֶה בָּא בְּכַדּוֹ שֶׁל יַיִן וְזֶה בָּא בְּכַדּוֹ שֶׁל דְּבַשׁ. וְנִסְדְּקָה חָבִית שֶׁל דְּבַשׁ. וְכֵן זֶה בָּא בַּחֲבִילַת פִּשְׁתָּן עַל חֲמוֹרוֹ וְזֶה בָּא בַּחֲבִילַת עֵצִים, וּמֵת חֲמוֹרוֹ שֶׁל בַּעַל פִּשְׁתָּן — יְפָרֵק זֶה אֶת עֵצָיו וְטוֹעֲנוֹ. דְּר' יְהוּדָה וּדְרַבִּי יִשְׁמָעֵאל יְחִידָאֵי נִינְהוּ, וּבָרַיְיתָא דַּעֲשָׂרָה תְּנָאִים סְתָמָא הִיא. וְהָא

תוספות

אין לך כל שבט ושבט מישראל (ג) גרסינן. ובפ' "יש נוחלין" (ב"ב דף קכב. ושם) גבי חלוקת העולם (ד) הכא גרסינן: אין לך כל אחד ואחד מישראל. כן נראה לר"ת. ונוטל דמי יינו מתוך דובשנו של חבירו. ע"כ מיירי כשעקל בית הבד כרוך עליה, דאל"כ לימא ליה: מהפקירא קזכינא, כדאמר לקמן בפרק בתרא (דף קטו:). וא"ת: ואמאי נוטל דמי יינו? הא אמר לקמן בפרק בתרא (שם) דאין לו אלא שכרו! ומצי' למימר דהך דר' ישמעאל בנו של רבי יוחנן בן ברוקה פליג, כדאמר בסמוך: ביחידאה לא קאמר. וכן משמע בתוספתא,* דבתר הך דלא יקוץ, קתני הך. אבל אין נראה, דלמה יטול דמי יינו? הלא יכול לומר: אני הייתי דוחק ומציל כיון

עין משפט נר מצוה

קנג א מיי' פ"ה מהל' נזקי ממון הלכה ג סימן ז סמג עשין סו טוח"מ סימן רעד:

קנד ב (מיי' פ"ח מהל' שבת הלכה ג ופ"י ופכ"א) סמג לאוין סה טוש"ע א"ח סימן שיב סעיף ג:

קנה ג מיי' פ"ה מהל' נזקי ממון הלכה ו סמג עשין סו טור ח"מ סימן רעד:

[פ"י ע"ש וצ"ע]

קנו ד מיי' שם הלכה ה סמג שם טור ח"מ שם:

קנז ה מיי' שם הלכה ג סימן ח:

קנח ו מיי' פ"א מהל' רוצח הל' יג סמג לאוין קסה טוש"ע ח"מ סימן תכו:

קנט ז ח מיי' פ"ח מהלכות טומאת מת הלכה ז ופ"ה מהל' נזקי ממון הל' ג סי' י טוש"ע י"ד סימן שסד סעי' ג וטוח"מ סי' רעד:

ס"א אינו וגם רש"ל מ"ז

קס ט מיי' פ"ה מהל' נזקי ממון הלכה ד סמג עשין סו טוח"מ סימן רעד:

[קס י כ] כל זה איתא ברב אלפס ב"ק פ"י דף ד:

הגהות הב"ח

(א) גמ' בכנענים ובפריזים (שלפניהם) תא"מ ונ"ב ס"א אין זה: (ב) רש"י ד"ה וכן אתה וכו' ונגב ועמק הס"ד ואח"כ מה"ד נגב ארץ: (ג) תום' ד"ה אין וכו' מישראל ובפ' כצ"ל ותיבת גרסינן נמחק: (ד) בא"ד העולם גרסי' כצ"ל ותיבת הכא נמחק:

הגהות הגר"א

[א] ובלבד שלא יפרום קלע ויעמיד את הספינה (אבל צד הוא ברשתות ובמכמרות) תא"מ:

מסורת הש"ס

תורה אור — דברים לג — שם — שם א — שם כב — משלי ג

[תוספתא פ"ח] — ב"ב קכב. — תענית ו: — [תוספתא ב"מ פ"ב] — סנהדרין עג. — עירובין יז: — [ברכות ל.] — [תוספתא דב"מ פי' בזול ל. ב"מ קיח:] — לקמן קיז:

וְהָא כִּי אֲתָא וכו'. וּמַתְנִיתָא הָוְיָא תְּיוּבְתָּא, דְּקָתָנֵי עֲשָׂרָה וְתוּ לָא. ור' יוֹחָנָן אָמוֹרָא הוּא, וְקַשְׁיָא לֵיהּ מַתְנִיתָא. רַבִּי יְהוֹשֻׁעַ בֶּן לֵוִי. אָמְרִינְהוּ, וְלָא מַתְנִיתָא. דְּרַבִּי יְהוֹשֻׁעַ בֶּן לֵוִי אָמוֹרָא הֲוָה, וְרַבִּי יוֹחָנָן פָּלֵיג עֲלֵיהּ. וּמְכַבְּסִים. בִּגְדֵיהֶם לִכְבוֹד שַׁבָּת. וְאוֹכְלִים שׁוּם. לְקַמָּן מְפָרֵשׁ טַעְמָא. וְשֶׁתְּהֵא אִשָּׁה מַשְׁכֶּמֶת. בְּיוֹם שֶׁהִיא צְרִיכָה לֶאֱפוֹת, וְאוֹפָה שַׁחֲרִית. כִּדְמְפָרֵשׁ: שֶׁתְּהֵא פַּת מְצוּיָה לַעֲנִיֵּי הַמְחַזֵּר. סִינָר. דּוּגְמַת מִכְנָסַיִם קְטַנִּים. הָאִשָּׁה חוֹפֶפֶת. בְּמַסְרֵק בְּיוֹם טְבִילָתָהּ מִשּׁוּם חֲצִיצָה. לְקַמָּן פָּרֵיךְ: הָא דְּאוֹרַיְיתָא הִיא. רוֹכְלִין. מְבִיאִים בְּשָׂמִים לְנָשִׁים לְהִתְקַשֵּׁט בָּהֶם. מַחֲזִירִין בָּעֲיָירוֹת. וְלֹא יוּכְלוּ בְּנֵי הָעֲיָירוֹת לְעַכֵּב עֲלֵיהֶם. מִשּׁוּם יוֹשְׁבֵי קְרָנוֹת. יוֹשְׁבֵי חֲנֻיּוֹת, כָּל יְמוֹת הַחוֹל עוֹסְקִין בִּסְחוֹרָה וְאֵין קוֹרִין בְּשֵׁנִי וּבַחֲמִישִׁי, תַּקּוּן בְּגִינַיְיהוּ קְרִיאָה יְתֵירָה. רְשׁוּמוֹת. מִקְרָאוֹת. עֲשָׂרָה בַּטְלָנִין. בְּנֵי אָדָם כְּשֵׁרִים, בְּטֵלִין מִמְּלַאכְתָּן לַעֲסוֹק בְּצָרְכֵי צִבּוּר, (ב) וְלָבֹא קוֹדְמִין לְבֵית הַכְּנֶסֶת כְּדֵי שֶׁיִּהְיוּ מְצוּיִין עֲשָׂרָה לְעֵת הַתְּפִלָּה, וּמִתְפַּרְנְסִים מִשֶּׁל צִבּוּר. מִשּׁוּם עוֹנָה. שֶׁמְּלַוַּת עוֹנָה בְּלֵילֵי שַׁבָּת, כִּדְרַב יְהוּדָה. וְהַשּׁוּם מַרְבֶּה אֶת הַזֶּרַע כִּדְלְקַמָּן. מַשְׂחִין. מְחַמֵּם אֶת הַגּוּף. מַכְנִים אֶת הָאַהֲבָה. מִתּוֹךְ שֶׁמְּשַׂמֵּחַ אֶת הַלֵּב. מִשּׁוּם צְנִיעוּתָא. לְהִתְרַחֵק מִן הָעֲבֵירָה. בְּשָׂרוֹ בַּמַּיִם. מַשְׁמַע שֶׁיִּגַּע בְּשָׂרוֹ לַמַּיִם. דְּמָאוּם. מְלוּכְלָךְ. חֲפִיפָה

תורה אור

וְהָא *כִּי אֲתָא ר' אָבִין א"ר יוֹחָנָן: [א]אֶחָד אִילָן הַנּוֹטֶה לְתוֹךְ שְׂדֵה חֲבֵירוֹ, וְאֶחָד אִילָן הַסָּמוּךְ לְמֵצַר, מֵבִיא וְקוֹרֵא שֶׁעַל מְנָת כֵּן הִנְחִיל יְהוֹשֻׁעַ לְיִשְׂרָאֵל אֶת הָאָרֶץ! אֶלָּא מַאן תְּנָא עֲשָׂרָה תְּנָאִין שֶׁהִתְנָה יְהוֹשֻׁעַ? ר' יְהוֹשֻׁעַ בֶּן לֵוִי הוּא, רַב גְּבִיהָה מִבֵּי כָּתִיל מַתְנֵי לָהּ בְּהֶדְיָא: ר' תַּנְחוּם וְר' בְּרַיִים אָמְרִי מִשּׁוּם זָקֵן אֶחָד, וּמַנּוּ ר' יְהוֹשֻׁעַ בֶּן לֵוִי: עֲשָׂרָה תְּנָאִין הִתְנָה יְהוֹשֻׁעַ.§ עֲשָׂרָה תַּקָּנוֹת תִּיקֵּן עֶזְרָא: שֶׁקּוֹרִין בְּמִנְחָה בְּשַׁבָּת, וְקוֹרִין בְּשֵׁנִי וּבַחֲמִישִׁי, וְדָנִין בְּשֵׁנִי וּבַחֲמִישִׁי וּמְכַבְּסִים בַּחֲמִישִׁי בְּשַׁבָּת, וְאוֹכְלִין שׁוּם בְּעֶרֶב שַׁבָּת, וְשֶׁתְּהֵא אִשָּׁה מַשְׁכֶּמֶת וְאוֹפָה וְשֶׁתְּהֵא אִשָּׁה חוֹגֶרֶת בְּסִינָר. וְשֶׁתְּהֵא אִשָּׁה חוֹפֶפֶת וְטוֹבֶלֶת וְשֶׁיְּהוּ רוֹכְלִין מַחֲזִירִין בָּעֲיָירוֹת, *וְתִיקֵּן טְבִילָה לְבַעֲלֵי קְרָיִין.§ "שֶׁיְּהוּ קוֹרְאִין בַּמִּנְחָה בְּשַׁבָּת" — מִשּׁוּם יוֹשְׁבֵי קְרָנוֹת, וְ"שֶׁיְּהוּ קוֹרְאִין בְּשֵׁנִי וּבַחֲמִישִׁי" — עֶזְרָא תִּיקֵּן? וְהָא מֵעִיקָּרָא הֲוָה מִיתַּקְנָא! דְּתַנְיָא: °"וַיֵּלְכוּ שְׁלֹשֶׁת יָמִים בַּמִּדְבָּר וְלֹא מָצְאוּ מָיִם", דּוֹרְשֵׁי רְשׁוּמוֹת אָמְרוּ: *אֵין מַיִם אֶלָּא תּוֹרָה, שֶׁנֶּאֱמַר: °"הוֹי כָּל צָמֵא לְכוּ לַמַּיִם", כֵּיוָן שֶׁהָלְכוּ שְׁלֹשֶׁת יָמִים בְּלֹא תּוֹרָה (א) נִלְאוּ, [ב]עָמְדוּ נְבִיאִים שֶׁבֵּינֵיהֶם וְתִיקְּנוּ לָהֶם שֶׁיְּהוּ קוֹרִין בְּשַׁבָּת וּמַפְסִיקִין בְּאֶחָד בְּשַׁבָּת, וְקוֹרִין בְּשֵׁנִי וּמַפְסִיקִין שְׁלִישִׁי וּרְבִיעִי, וְקוֹרִין בַּחֲמִישִׁי וּמַפְסִיקִין עֶרֶב שַׁבָּת, כְּדֵי שֶׁלֹּא יָלִינוּ ג' יָמִים בְּלֹא תּוֹרָה. [ג]מֵעִיקָּרָא תַּקְּנוּ חַד גַּבְרָא תְּלָתָא פְּסוּקֵי, אִי נַמִּי תְּלָתָא גַּבְרֵי תְּלָתָא פְּסוּקֵי, כְּנֶגֶד כֹּהֲנִים לְוִיִּם וְיִשְׂרְאֵלִים, אֲתָא הוּא תִּיקֵּן תְּלָתָא גַּבְרֵי וַעֲשָׂרָה פְּסוּקֵי, *כְּנֶגֶד עֲשָׂרָה בַּטְלָנִין.§ [ד]"וְדָנִין בְּשֵׁנִי וּבַחֲמִישִׁי" — דִּשְׁכִיחִי, דְּאָתוּ לְמִקְרָא בְּסִיפְרָא.§ [ה]"וְשֶׁיְּהוּ מְכַבְּסִין בַּחֲמִישִׁי בְּשַׁבָּת" — מִשּׁוּם כְּבוֹד שַׁבָּת.§ "וְשֶׁיְּהוּ אוֹכְלִין שׁוּם בְּעֶ"שׁ" — מִשּׁוּם עוֹנָה, דִּכְתִיב: °"אֲשֶׁר פִּרְיוֹ יִתֵּן בְּעִתּוֹ", *וְא"ר יְהוּדָה, וְאִיתֵּימָא רַב נַחְמָן, וְאִיתֵּימָא רַב כָּהֲנָא, וְאִיתֵּימָא ר' יוֹחָנָן: [ו]זֶה הַמְשַׁמֵּשׁ מִטָּתוֹ מֵעֶ"שׁ לְעֶ"שׁ. ת"ר: חֲמִשָּׁה דְּבָרִים נֶאֶמְרוּ בְּשׁוּם: מַשְׂבִּיעַ, וּמַשְׂחִין, וּמַצְהִיל פָּנִים, וּמַרְבֶּה הַזֶּרַע, וְהוֹרֵג כִּנִּים שֶׁבִּבְנֵי מֵעַיִם; וְיֵ"א: מַכְנִיס אַהֲבָה וּמוֹצִיא אֶת הַקִּנְאָה.§ [ז]"וְשֶׁתְּהֵא אִשָּׁה מַשְׁכֶּמֶת וְאוֹפָה" — כְּדֵי שֶׁתְּהֵא פַּת מְצוּיָה לַעֲנִיִּים.§ "וְשֶׁתְּהֵא אִשָּׁה חוֹגֶרֶת בְּסִינָר" — מִשּׁוּם צְנִיעוּתָא.§ [ח]"וְשֶׁתְּהֵא אִשָּׁה חוֹפֶפֶת וְטוֹבֶלֶת" — דְּאוֹרַיְיתָא הִיא! דְּתַנְיָא: °"וְרָחַץ אֶת בְּשָׂרוֹ בַּמַּיִם" — *[ט]שֶׁלֹּא יְהֵא דָּבָר חוֹצֵץ בֵּין בְּשָׂרוֹ לַמַּיִם, "אֶת בְּשָׂרוֹ" — אֶת הַטָּפֵל לִבְשָׂרוֹ, וּמַאי נִיהוּ? שֵׂעָר! אָמְרִי: דְּאוֹרַיְיתָא — לְעִיּוּנֵי [י]דִּלְמָא מִיקְטַר, אִי נַמִּי מָאוּס מִידֵי, מִשּׁוּם חֲצִיצָה, וַאֲתָא

שמות טו | ישעיה נה | תהלים א | ויקרא יד

כיון דאוקמה כשעקל בית הבד כרוך עליה, שיכול להציל ע"י הדחק. ונראה לר"י: דההיא דלקמן — שבעל היין שפך את יינו מדעתו, שיכול לומר בעל הדבש: למה שפכת? אני הייתי דוחק ומציל. אבל הכא איירי שבא בעל הדבש לשפוך את היין, שתנאי ב"ד הוא שאין בעל היין יכול לעכב, אלא שופך יינו של חבירו בע"כ של חבירו, אלא שנותן לו דמי יינו מתוך דובשנו. והשתא הוי כעין ההיא דנחיל של דבורים, שקללו בע"כ להציל נחילו. וכעין זה נמי ההיא דפשתן. והאי דמשני כיחידאה לא קאמר — משום דמסתמא כי היכי דפליגי בההיא דנחיל, כדתנן לקמן בפרק בתרא (דף קיד.) — פליגי נמי באחריני, דחד טעמא הוא.

כדי שלא ילינו ג' ימים בלא תורה. וא"ת: מ"ש שתיקנו שני וחמישי? וי"ל: משום דאמר במדרש:* משה רבינו ע"ה עלה בחמישי לקבל לוחות האחרונות, וירד בשני, ונתרצה לו המקום. ולפי שהיה עת רצון באותה עלייה וירידה — קבעו בשני וחמישי, ולכך נמי נהגו להתענות בב' וה'. ואף ע"פ שעלה בהשכמה, כדכתיב (שמות לד) "ועלית בבקר", שדומה שכל העליות היו בבקר ולא בלילה, ולא תמצא כ"א מ' יום חסירים לילה אחד — אין להקפיד בכך. ולפי סדר עולם נמי כן הוא, דתניא בסדר עולם: נמצא עלה בו' בסיון וירד בי"ז בתמוז ושבר הלוחות, ובי"ח בתמוז עלה ובקש רחמים עליהם, שנאמר "ואתנפל לפני ה' מ' יום" וגו'. ובכ"ט באב נתרצה המקום וירד משה לפסול הלוחות, ועשה עוד מ' יום מל' באב עד י' בתשרי, ונתרצה המקום וירד משה בי' בתשרי והלוחות בידו. באותו יום נתרצה המקום לישראל, שנאמר "ויאמר ה' סלחתי כדברך" לפיכך סליחה וכפרה הוא לדורות. נמצא דמ' יום אחרונים חסירים לילה, שהרי ביום ל' באב עלה בהשכמה וירד ביום הכפורים, אם לא תאמר דעברוה לאלול. והא דכתיב בפרשת עקב "ואנכי עמדתי בהר כימים הראשונים" שהן מ' יום ומ' לילה — הכי קאמר: כימים הראשונים ולא כלילות, דאחרונות היו חסירים לילה אחד. ואף על גב דאיצטריך "כימים" לומר מה הראשונים ברצון אף האחרונים ברצון, אבל האמצעיים בכעס — הו"מ למיכתב "כראשונים" וכתיב "כימים" לומר: כימים ולא כלילות. ואי להך דרשה לחודא אתא ה"ל למיכתב "ואנכי עמדתי בהר מ' יום" ותו לא. וא"ת: ובסוף "כי תשא" כתיב "ויהי שם עם ה' מ' יום ומ' לילה" ובלוחות אחרונות כתיב! וי"ל: דאימים שהתנפל קאי, ולפי שלא פי' מעשה ד"אולי אכפרה בעד חטאתכם" כמה עמד משה בתפלה, מפרש לה הכא. והא דכתיב בתר הכי "ויכתוב על הלוחות" — היינו אחר אותם מ' יום ומ' לילה, דאותם אחרונים היו חסירים לילה. וא"ת: בשלמא לר' יוסי דאמר בשבת פרק "רבי עקיבא" (דף פז:) (ג) דסיון דההיא שתא הוה באחד בשבת — ניחא. דעלה בה' לפי חשבון דאחד מלא ואחד חסר, דיום ל' באב יום ה' הוה. אבל לרבנן, דאמרי דביום ב' הוה ר"ח סיון — נמצא יום ל' באב ביום ו'. אם לא נאמר לרבנן בי"ז בתמוז שרף את העגל ודן החוטאים, ובו ביום עלה, וביום כ"ח באב ירד בהשכמה ופסל לוחות, וכ"ט באב שהיה יום ה' עלה. או נאמר: שכ"ט באב ירד, ובו ביום עלה, ונאמר שהיה אב חסר, כדי שיבא יום הירידה ביוה"כ, כדאמר ב"יש נוחלין" (ב"ב דף קכא.) שבו ניתנו לוחות אחרונות. אבל לפי מדרש תנחומא* שאומר דבי"ז בתמוז ירד ובי"ח בו שרף את העגל ודן את החוטאים, ובי"ט עלה, ונמצא יום עלייה של מ' אחרונים (ד) באה באלול — לא יבא בה', לא לרבנן ולא לר' יוסי, וגם לא תמצא ירידה ביום הכפורים, אם לא נאמר דעברוה לאלול. [ועי' תוס' שבת פט. ד"ה לסוף]. **ודנין** בב' וה'. וא"ת: והלא קודם תקנת עזרא היו בית דין קבועין בכל יום, כדאמר בכתובות (דף ג. ושם*), א"כ מה תיקן עזרא? וכי תיקן שלא יהו קבועין אלא בב' ובה'?! ואומר *ר"ת: שלא היו קבועין תחילה בכל יום אלא בעיר אחת, והוא תיקן בכל עיר ועיר בב' ובה'.

ושתהא אשה חופפת. אור"ת: שלא תיקן חפיפה אלא בראש. וכן משמע, מדקאמר בסמוך: דאורייתא דלמא מקטר. וחפיפה נמי לא שייכא אלא בראש, כדתנן בנזיר (דף מב.): נזיר חופף ומפספס, אבל לא סורק. אבל בשאר הגוף שייך לשון הדחה, כדאמרינן בפרק בתרא דנדה (דף סו: ושם*): לעולם ילמד אדם בתוך ביתו שתהא אשה מדיחה בית קמטיה במים. ומהתם נמי משמע דבשאר הגוף אין צריך הדחה אלא דוקא בית קמטיה. אף על גב דאיכא למימר דבית קמטיה נקט לרבותא, דאע"ג דביאת מים לא בעינן, ראוי לביאת מים בעינן — מכל מקום, מדלא קאמר "אפילו קמטיה" משמע דוקא לקמטיה ולא בשאר הגוף. וההיא דדודי חסרת כו' (שם דף סח.) אף על פי שאין חובה — היתה רגילה לרחוץ, כמו שנוהגין גם עכשיו לרחוץ כל גופה במים חמין. [ועי' תוספות נדה סו: ד"ה אם].

אתא

ב"ב כז: | ברכות כב: | [לעיל ז. ע"ז ה:] | [מגילה כא:] | כתובות סב: [ע"ש] | [פ' תשא וע"ש היטב] | [ד"ה שבתי] | [ד"ה אם] | גי' רש"י

קסא א מיי' פ"ב מהל' בכורים הלכה יא סמג עשין קלט:
קסב ב מיי' פי"ב מהל' תפלה הלכה א סמג עשין כה טוש"ע א"ח סי' רלב סעי' א וסי' קלה סעיף א:
קסג ג מיי' שם סמג שם:
קסד ד סמג עשין כה טוח"מ סי' א וסי' ה:
קסה ה מיי' פ"ל מהל' שבת הלכה ג סמג שם טוש"ע א"ח סי' רמב:
במדרש תנחומא בפסוק וה' המטיר על סדום כ"כ הרוקח
קסו ו מיי' פי"ד מהל' אישות הלכה א סמג לאוין פא טוש"ע אה"ע סי' עו סעיף ב וטוש"ע א"ח סי' רמ סעיף א:
קסז ז מיי' פכ"א שם הלכה ה סמג עשין עה:
קסח ח מיי' פ"ב מהל' מקואות הלכה טז סמג לאוין קיא טוש"ע י"ד סי' קצח סעיף א:
קסט ט מיי' שם פ"א הלכה יב סמג עשין רמח טוש"ע י"ד סי' קצח סעיף א:
קע י מיי' פ"ב שם הלכה טו טוש"ע שם סעיף ה:
עירובין ל: סוכה ו. [וש"נ]

הגהות הב"ח
(א) גמ' בלא תורה מיד נלאו: (ב) רש"י ד"ה עשרה וכו'. בצרכי צבור וקודמין לבא לבית הכנסת: (ג) תוס' ד"ה כדי וכו' פ' ר' עקיבא דר"ח סיון דההיא: (ד) בא"ד מ' אחרונים באחד באלול:

תורה אור

וַאֲתָא אִיהוּ תִּיקֵּן חֲפִיפָה.§ *א"וְשֶׁיְּהוּ רוֹכְלִין מְחַזְּרִין בָּעֲיָירוֹת" — מִשּׁוּם תַּכְשִׁיטֵי נָשִׁים, כְּדֵי שֶׁלֹּא יִתְגַּנּוּ עַל בַּעֲלֵיהֶם.§ "וְתִיקֵּן טְבִילָה לְבַעֲלֵי קְרָיִין" — בדְּאוֹרַיְיתָא הוּא, דִּכְתִיב: °"וְאִישׁ כִּי תֵצֵא מִמֶּנּוּ שִׁכְבַת זָרַע וְרָחַץ* אֶת בְּשָׂרוֹ בַּמַּיִם"! דְּאוֹרַיְיתָא הוּא לִתְרוּמָה וְקָדָשִׁים, אֲתָא הוּא גתִּיקֵּן אֲפִילּוּ לְדִבְרֵי תוֹרָה.§ *עֲשָׂרָה דְּבָרִים דנֶאֶמְרוּ בִּירוּשָׁלַיִם: האֵין הַבַּיִת חָלוּט בָּהּ, ווְאֵינָהּ מְבִיאָה עֶגְלָה עֲרוּפָה, זוְאֵינָהּ נַעֲשֵׂית עִיר הַנִּדַּחַת, חוְאֵינָהּ מִטַּמְּאָה בִּנְגָעִים, טוְאֵין מוֹצִיאִין בָּהּ זִיזִין וּגְזוּזְטְרָאוֹת, יוְאֵין עוֹשִׂין בָּהּ אַשְׁפָּתוֹת, *כוְאֵין עוֹשִׂין בָּהּ כִּבְשׁוֹנוֹת, לוְאֵין עוֹשִׂין בָּהּ גַּנּוֹת וּפַרְדֵּסוֹת חוּץ מִגַּנּוֹת וְוְרָדִין שֶׁהָיוּ מִימוֹת נְבִיאִים הָרִאשׁוֹנִים, מוְאֵין מְגַדְּלִים בָּהּ תַּרְנְגוֹלִין, נוְאֵין מְלִינִין בָּהּ אֶת הַמֵּת. "אֵין הַבַּיִת חָלוּט בָּהּ" — דִּכְתִיב: °"וְקָם הַבַּיִת אֲשֶׁר לוֹ חוֹמָה לַצְּמִיתוּת לַקּוֹנֶה אוֹתוֹ לְדוֹרוֹתָיו", וְקָסָבַר: לֹא נִתְחַלְּקָה יְרוּשָׁלַיִם לִשְׁבָטִים. "וְאֵינָהּ מְבִיאָה עֶגְלָה עֲרוּפָה" — דִּכְתִיב: °"כִּי יִמָּצֵא חָלָל בָּאֲדָמָה אֲשֶׁר ה' אֱלֹהֶיךָ נוֹתֵן לְךָ לְרִשְׁתָּהּ", וִירוּשָׁלַיִם לֹא נִתְחַלְּקָה לִשְׁבָטִים. "וְאֵינָהּ נַעֲשֵׂית עִיר הַנִּדַּחַת" — דִּכְתִיב: °"עָרֶיךָ", וִירוּשָׁלַיִם לֹא נִתְחַלְּקָה לִשְׁבָטִים. "וְאֵינָהּ מִטַּמְּאָה בִּנְגָעִים" — דִּכְתִיב: °"וְנָתַתִּי נֶגַע צָרַעַת בְּבֵית אֶרֶץ אֲחֻזַּתְכֶם", וִירוּשָׁלַיִם לֹא נִתְחַלְּקָה לִשְׁבָטִים. "וְאֵין מוֹצִיאִין בָּהּ זִיזִין וּגְזוּזְטְרָאוֹת" — מִפְּנֵי אֹהֶל הַטּוּמְאָה, וּמִשּׁוּם דְּלָא לִיתַּזְּקוּ עוֹלֵי רְגָלִים. "וְאֵין עוֹשִׂין בָּהּ אַשְׁפָּתוֹת" — מִשּׁוּם שְׁקָצִים. "וְאֵין עוֹשִׂין בָּהּ כִּבְשׁוֹנוֹת" — מִשּׁוּם קוּטְרָא. "וְאֵין עוֹשִׂין בָּהּ גַּנּוֹת וּפַרְדֵּסִין" — מִשּׁוּם סִירְחָא. "וְאֵין מְגַדְּלִין בָּהּ תַּרְנְגוֹלִין" — מִשּׁוּם קָדָשִׁים. "וְאֵין מְלִינִין בָּהּ אֶת הַמֵּת" — גְּמָרָא.§ "אֵין מְגַדְּלִין חֲזִירִים בְּכָל מָקוֹם".

ויקרא טו | שם כה | דברים כא | שם יג | ויקרא יד

*תָּנוּ רַבָּנַן: כְּשֶׁצָּרוּ בֵּית חַשְׁמוֹנַאי זֶה עַל זֶה, הָיָה °הוֹרְקָנוֹס מִבִּפְנִים וַאֲרִיסְטוֹבְּלוֹס מִבַּחוּץ, וּבְכָל יוֹם הָיוּ מְשַׁלְשְׁלִים לָהֶם בְּקוּפָּה דִּינָרִין, וְהָיוּ מַעֲלִין לָהֶם תְּמִידִים. הָיָה שָׁם זָקֵן אֶחָד שֶׁהָיָה מַכִּיר בְּחָכְמַת יְוָונִית, *אָמַר לָהֶם: כָּל זְמַן שֶׁעוֹסְקִין בַּעֲבוֹדָה אֵין נִמְסָרִים בְּיֶדְכֶם. לְמָחָר שִׁילְשְׁלוּ דִּינָרִין בְּקוּפָּה, וְהֶעֱלוּ לָהֶם חֲזִיר. כֵּיוָן שֶׁהִגִּיעַ לַחֲצִי הַחוֹמָה נָעַץ צִפָּרְנָיו בַּחוֹמָה, וְנִזְדַּעְזְעָה אֶרֶץ יִשְׂרָאֵל אַרְבַּע מֵאוֹת פַּרְסָה עַל אַרְבַּע מֵאוֹת פַּרְסָה. בְּאוֹתָהּ שָׁעָה אָמְרוּ: ס"אָרוּר הָאִישׁ שֶׁיְּגַדֵּל חֲזִירִים, וְאָרוּר הָאָדָם שֶׁיְּלַמֵּד אֶת בְּנוֹ חָכְמַת יְוָונִית. וְעַל אוֹתָהּ שָׁעָה שָׁנִינוּ: *מַעֲשֶׂה שֶׁבָּא עוֹמֶר מִגַּנּוֹת הַצְּרִיפִין, וּשְׁתֵּי הַלֶּחֶם מִבִּקְעַת עֵין סוֹכֵר.§ וְחָכְמַת יְוָונִית מִי אֲסִירָא? וְהָתַנְיָא, אָמַר רַבִּי: בְּאֶרֶץ יִשְׂרָאֵל לָשׁוֹן

חֲפִיפָה. בְּמַסְרֵק, לְהַרְחָקָה דְּמִילְּתָא. לְדִבְרֵי תוֹרָה. שֶׁלֹּא יִשְׁנֶה עַד שֶׁיִּטְבּוֹל. אֵין הַבַּיִת חָלוּט בָּהּ. כְּדִין בָּתֵּי עָרֵי חוֹמָה, אֶלָּא גְּאוּלָּה תִּהְיֶה לוֹ אִם יִרְצֶה לִגְאוֹל, וְאִם יַגִּיעַ יוֹבֵל – יוֹצֵא בַּיּוֹבֵל, כְּבָתֵּי עָרֵי חֲצֵרִים. זִיזִין = קוֹרוֹת יוֹצְאִין מִן הַכְּתָלִים. גְּזוּזְטְרָאוֹת = אולדליו"ר בְּלַעַ"ז, עַל פְּנֵי הָעֲלִיָּיה מִבַּחוּץ. כִּבְשׁוֹנוֹת. מִשְׂרְפוֹת סִיד לִקְדֵירוֹת. גִּינַּת וְרָדִין. כָּךְ שְׁמָהּ, וְהִיא הָיְתָה צְרִיכָה לִקְטוֹרֶת. וְהַיְינוּ "כִּיפַּת הַיַּרְדֵּן" כְּרֵיתוֹת (דף ו.), עַל שֵׁם שֶׁדֶּרֶךְ הַוֶּרֶד לִגְדַּל עַל שְׂפַת הַיַּרְדֵּן. אֵין מְלִינִין בָּהּ אֶת הַמֵּת. מֵת בָּהּ אָדָם – בְּאוֹתוֹ הַיּוֹם קוֹבְרִים אוֹתוֹ מִיָּד. עָרֶיךָ. מַשְׁמַע: שֶׁהַתָּה יוֹדֵעַ לְמִי מְיוּחֶדֶת הִיא. אֹהֶל הַטּוּמְאָה. שֶׁמָּא יְהֵא כַּזַּיִת מִן הַמֵּת מוּטָל בָּאָרֶץ, וְהַגְּזוּזְטְרָאוֹת מַאֲהִילוֹת עָלָיו וְעַל אֲנָשִׁים הַרְבֵּה, וְנִמְצֵאתָ מַרְבֶּה אֶת הַטּוּמְאָה. מִשּׁוּם שְׁרָצִים. דַּרְכָּן לִיגְדַּל בָּאַשְׁפָּה. וּמַרְבִּים טוּמְאָה, לְפִי שֶׁמֵּתִים שָׁם, וּמְטַמְּאִים הַקֳּדָשִׁים שֶׁבִּירוּשָׁלַיִם. קוּטְרָא. = עָשָׁן, שֶׁמַּשְׁחִיר אֶת הַחוֹמָה וּגְנַאי הוּא. סַרְחוֹן. עֲשָׂבִים רָעִים הַגְּדֵלִים שָׁם וְזוֹרְקִין בַּחוּץ. וְעוֹד, דֶּרֶךְ גַּנּוֹת לְזַבְּלָן וְיֵשׁ סַרְחוֹן. מִשּׁוּם קָדָשִׁים. שֶׁתַּרְנְגוֹלִין מְנַקְּרִין בָּאַשְׁפָּה וּמְבִיאִים בְּשַׂר שְׁרָצִים בְּפִיהֶם וּמְטַמְּאִין אֶת הַקֳּדָשִׁים. גְּמָרָא. מָסוֹרֶת הִיא בְּיָדֵינוּ וְאֵין טַעַם *לַדָּבָר. הוֹרְקָנוֹס וַאֲרִיסְטוֹבְּלוֹס. אַחִים הָיוּ וּמְרִידִין עַל דְּבַר הַמְּלוּכָה. הָיוּ מְשַׁלְשְׁלִין. אוֹתָם שֶׁבִּפְנִים מוֹרִידִין מֵעַל הַחוֹמָה דִּינָרִין מִתְּרוּמַת הַלִּשְׁכָּה בְּקוּפָּה לְאוֹתָן שֶׁבַּחוּץ לִקְנוֹת תְּמִידִין. נָעַץ צִפָּרְנָיו = תָּקַע, *שֶׁכֵּן דֶּרֶךְ חֲזִיר כְּשֶׁגּוֹרְרִין אוֹתוֹ. וְעַל אוֹתָהּ שָׁעָה שָׁנִינוּ. בִּמְנָחוֹת (דף סד:): מַעֲשֶׂה שֶׁבָּא הָעוֹמֶר, שֶׁהָיָה רָגִיל לָבֹא מִן הַקָּרוֹב לִירוּשָׁלַיִם, אוֹתָהּ שָׁעָה בָּא מִגַּנּוֹת צְרִיפִין רָחוֹק מִירוּשָׁלַיִם, לְפִי שֶׁהֶחֱרִיבוּ בְּנֵי הַמָּצוֹר אֶת תְּבוּאוֹת הַשָּׂדֶה. מִבִּקְעַת עֵין סוֹכֵר. שֵׁם מָקוֹם. לָשׁוֹן

אתא איהו ותיקן אפילו לדברי תורה. לא קיימא לן הכי, אלא כר' יהודה בן בתירא, דאמר: דברי תורה אין מקבלין טומאה כדאמר ב"ראשית הגז" (חולין דף קלו: ושם*) וב"מי שמתו" (ברכות דף כב.): האידנא נהוג עלמא כתלתא סבי. וא"ת: דהיכי אלים ר' יהודה לבטל תקנת עזרא? וי"ל: דדלמא סבר דלא תיקן עזרא דבר זה. אי נמי: התנה שכל מי שרוצה לבטל יבטל, דבכי האי גוונא מותר, כדאמר בריש מועד קטן (דף ג:). אי נמי: לא פשט איסורו ברוב ישראל, כדאמרינן גבי שמן בפ' "אין מעמידין" (ע"ז דף לו.). ואע"ג דמשמע התם דאי דניאל גזר עליו לא היה ר' יהודה נשיאה יכול לבטלו, אע"פ שלא פשט — היינו במילתא דכתיב בקרא, אבל תקנת עזרא לא כתיב בקרא. והא דדריש ב"מי שמתו" (ברכות דף כא:) מדכתיב "והודעת לבניך" וסמיך ליה "יום אשר עמדת", מה להלן בעלי קריין אסורין כו' — אסמכתא היא, דהא עזרא תיקן. והא דאמר ב"מי שמתו" (שם דף יח:) גבי בניהו דתבר גזיזא דברדא ונחת וטבל — לא לדברי תורה, דאכתי עזרא לא הוה, אלא לאכול חולין בטהרה. **ואינה** מביאה עגלה ערופה. וא"ת: מאי אריא משום דלא נתחלקה? תיפוק ליה משום דאית לן למיזל בתר רובא דעלמא, כדאמר ב"לא יחפור" (ב"ב דף כג:)! ואע"ג דאמר התם דיושבת בין ההרים לא אזלינן בתר רובא, וירושלים הרים סביב לה — מכל מקום היו ישראל נכנסין ויוצאין לה לעלות לרגל, ובשאר ימות השנה נמי לשלם נדרים ונדבות, וגם אומות העולם היו באין לה לסחורה, שקרויה "רוכלת עמים"! וי"ל: דמ"מ היו שם מקומות שלא היו מצויים כי אם יושבי ירושלים לבדם. אי נמי, בימי חזקיה, שכל ישראל היו בירושלים ולא היו באין לסחורה. **ואין** מטמא בנגעים דכתיב אחוזתכם וירושלים לא נתחלקה לשבטים. אין לפרש שנתחלקה אלא שנתנו דושנה של יריחו תחתיה, ולפיכך אין מטמא. דבפ"ק דיומא (דף יב.) משמע דלמ"ד לא נתחלקה לא נתחלקה ממש. וא"ת: מנליה דלא נתחלקה ממש? דלמא סבר נתחלקה, אלא שנתנו דושנה של יריחו תחתיה. כמו לר' יהודה דאמר נתחלקה ומטמא, ובית המקדש עצמו אין מטמא אע"ג דנתחלק, אלא משום שנתנו דושנה של יריחו תחתיו, כדאמר התם! וי"ל: דבית המקדש סברא הוא, אע"ג דנתחלק דחזרו וקנו אותו, כדי שיהא לכל ישראל חלק בו. אבל ירושלים אם מתחילה נתחלקה — למה היו חוזרין וקונין אותה? **לא** יגדל אדם חזירין. וא"ת: ת"ל דאסור לעשות סחורה בכל דברים טמאים, כדתנן במסכת שביעית (פ"ז מ"ג): אין עושין סחורה בנבילות וטריפות. ובפ' "כל שעה" (פסחים דף כג. ושם*) נמי אומר: ליידי חיה ועוף שנזדמנו להם מינים טמאים. דוקא נזדמנו, אבל לכתחילה — לא, כדדריש התם: "יהיו" — בהוייתן יהא. ובת"כ נמי דרשינן: "שקץ הוא לכם" — שלא לעשות סחורה בהן! ותירץ ר"ת: דהיינו דוקא בדבר העומד לאכילה, אבל אם מגדלן למשוח עורות בשומנן, או למוכרן לישראל שימשח בהן — שרי. וכל חלב מותר למכור היכא דלא קאי לאכילה. ובירושלמי נמי מפרש בהאי פירקא דסוסים וחמורים שרי לעשות בהן סחורה, משום דסתמן למלאכה. **ואסור** לאדם שילמד בנו חכמת יוונית. וא"ת: והלא בפולמוס של טיטוס גזרו, כדאמרינן בפרק בתרא דסוטה (דף מט.), וטיטוס היה בשעת חורבן, כדאמרינן ב"הניזקין" (גיטין דף נו:) ומלכות בית חשמונאי קדמי טובא, כדאמרינן בפ"ק דע"ז (דף ט.)! וי"ל: דמעיקרא גזרו ולא קבלו מינייהו. א"נ: אי הוה בעי למיקס ב"ארור" — לא היה מיקרי עבריין. אבל לבסוף איכא גזירה דרבנן. ונראה ד"לא יגדל" דמתני' — היא היתה גזירה דפולמוס של טיטוס. **ועל** אותה שעה שנינו מעשה שבא. כו' משנה היא במנחות בפ' "ר' ישמעאל" (דף סד: ושם*). וא"ת: והא בימי מרדכי הוה המעשה, כדאמר התם בגמ' דאתא חרשא אותיב ידיה אגגה כו', אמר להן מרדכי. ותימה גדולה היא אם חיה מרדכי כל כך, דבית חשמונאי לא היה כי אם ר"ם שנים קודם החורבן, כדאמר בפ"ק דע"ז (דף ט.)! ונראה לר"י: דכל אותן שהיו בקיאים ברמזים ובלשונות היו נקראים על שם מרדכי, לפי שהוא היה ראש וחכם להכיר. ואותו מעשה דג' נשים דמייתי התם, נראה שהיה מרדכי ממש, דקאמר: והיינו דתנן (שקלים פרק ה' משנה א'): פתחיה על הקינין. לשון

[ד"ה כרבי] [ד"ה אמר] [ד"ה אמר]

קעא א מיי' פ"ג מהל' שכנים הלכה ט סמג עשין פה טוש"ע ח"מ סי' קנו סעיף ו:
קעב ב מיי' פ"א מהל' מקואות הלכה א סמג עשין רמח:
קעג ג מיי' פ"ד מהלכות קריאת שמע הלכה ח טוש"ע א"ח סי' פח:
קעד ד מיי' פ"ז מהל' בית הבחירה הלכה יד סמג עשין קסד:
קעה ה מיי' שם (ופי"ד מהלכות טומאת צרעת הלכה יא):
קעו ו מיי' פ"ז מהלכות בית הבחירה הלכה יד ופ"ט מהל' רוצח הלכה ד:
קעז ז מיי' פ"ז מהלכות בית הבחירה הלכה יד ופ"ד מהלכות ע"ז הלכה ד:
קעח ח מיי' פ"ז מהל' בית הבחירה הלכה יד ופי"ד מהלכות טומאת צרעת הלכה יא:
קעט ט י כ ל מ נ מיי' פ"ז מהלכות בית הבחירה הלכה יד:
קפ ס מיי' פ"ה מהלכות נזקי ממון הלכה ט טוש"ע ח"מ סי' תט סעי' ב:

ב"ב כב.
[צ"ל במים את כל בשר]
יומא כג. ערכין לב: אדר"נ פ' לה תוספתא נגעים פ"ו]
[חגיגה כו. זבחים לו.]
סוטה מה:
עיין הטעם בזוהר נשא
יומא יב: [מגילה כו.]
ס"א ונוח
סוטה מט: מנחות סד:
[מנחות סד:]
לעז להן בחכמת יוונית רש"ל

גליון הש"ס

גמ' הורקנוס מבפנים. במנחות דף סד ע"ב ובסוטה דף מט ע"ב אי' בהיפך הורקנוס מבחוץ ואריסטובלוס מבפנים

לָשׁוֹן סוּרְסִי לָמָּה? אוֹ לְשׁוֹן הַקֹּדֶשׁ אוֹ לְשׁוֹן יְוָנִית! וְא"ר יוֹסֵי: בָּבֶל לָשׁוֹן אֲרַמִּי לָמָּה? אוֹ לְשׁוֹן הַקֹּדֶשׁ °אוֹ לְשׁוֹן פַּרְסִי! אָמְרִי: לָשׁוֹן יְוָנִי לְחוּד, חָכְמַת יְוָנִית לְחוּד. וְחָכְמַת יְוָנִית מִי אֲסִירָא? *וְהָאָמַר רַב יְהוּדָה אָמַר שְׁמוּאֵל מִשּׁוּם *רשב"ג: °"עֵינִי עוֹלְלָה לְנַפְשִׁי מִכֹּל בְּנוֹת עִירִי" — אֶלֶף יְלָדִים הָיוּ בְּבֵית אַבָּא, חֲמֵשׁ מֵאוֹת מֵהֶם לָמְדוּ תּוֹרָה, חֲמֵשׁ מֵאוֹת לָמְדוּ חָכְמַת יְוָנִית, וְלֹא נִשְׁתַּיֵּיר מֵהֶם אֶלָּא אֲנִי כָּאן וּבֶן אֲחִי אַבָּא בְּעַסְיָא! אָמְרִי: שָׁאנֵי בֵּית רַבָּן גַּמְלִיאֵל, שֶׁהָיוּ קְרוֹבִים לַמַּלְכוּת; וְכִדְתַנְיָא: [א]הַמְסַפֵּר קוֹמִי הֲרֵי זֶה מִדַּרְכֵי הָאֱמוֹרִי. אַבְטוֹלְמוֹס בַּר רְאוּבֵן [ב]הִתִּירוּ לוֹ לְסַפֵּר קוֹמִי, מִפְּנֵי שֶׁהוּא קָרוֹב לַמַּלְכוּת; *שֶׁל בֵּית רַבָּן גַּמְלִיאֵל הִתִּירוּ לָהֶם לְסַפֵּר בְּחָכְמַת יְוָנִית, מִפְּנֵי שֶׁקְּרוֹבִים לַמַּלְכוּת.§ "לֹא יְגַדֵּל אָדָם אֶת הַכֶּלֶב אא"כ קָשׁוּר בְּשַׁלְשְׁלָאוֹת" כו'.§ תָּנוּ רַבָּנַן: [ג]לֹא יְגַדֵּל אָדָם אֶת הַכֶּלֶב אֶלָּא אִם כֵּן קָשׁוּר בְּשַׁלְשֶׁלֶת, [ד]אֲבָל מְגַדֵּל הוּא בְּעִיר הַסְּמוּכָה לַסְּפָר, וְקוֹשְׁרוֹ בַּיּוֹם וּמַתִּירוֹ בַּלַּיְלָה. תַּנְיָא, רַבִּי אֱלִיעֶזֶר הַגָּדוֹל אוֹמֵר: הַמְגַדֵּל כְּלָבִים כִּמְגַדֵּל חֲזִירִים. לְמַאי נָפְקָא מִינָּהּ? [ה]לְמֵיקַם עֲלֵיהּ בְּ"אָרוּר". *אָמַר רַב יוֹסֵף בַּר מַנְיוֹמֵי אָמַר רַב נַחְמָן: בָּבֶל כְּעִיר הַסְּמוּכָה לַסְּפָר דָּמֵי. תַּרְגְּמָהּ: נְהַרְדְּעָא. דָּרֵישׁ ר' דּוֹסְתַּאי דְּמִן בִּירִי: °"וּבְנֻחֹה יֹאמַר שׁוּבָה ה' רִבְבוֹת אַלְפֵי יִשְׂרָאֵל" — *לְלַמֶּדְךָ, שֶׁאֵין שְׁכִינָה שׁוֹרָה עַל יִשְׂרָאֵל פָּחוֹת מִשְּׁנֵי אֲלָפִים וּשְׁנֵי רְבָבוֹת;(א) חָסֵר אַחַת, וְהָיְתָה אִשָּׁה מְעוּבֶּרֶת בֵּינֵיהֶם וּרְאוּיָה לְהַשְׁלִים, וְנָבַח בָּהּ כֶּלֶב וְהִפִּילָה, נִמְצָא זֶה גּוֹרֵם לַשְּׁכִינָה שֶׁתִּסְתַּלֵּק מִיִּשְׂרָאֵל. *הַהִיא אִיתְּתָא דַּעֲלַת לְמֵיפָא בְּהַהוּא בֵּיתָא, נְבַח בָּהּ כַּלְבָּא, אֲמַר לָהּ מָרֵיהּ: לָא תִּיסְתְּפִי מִינֵּיהּ, שְׁקוּלֵי נִיבֵיהּ. אֲמָרָה לֵיהּ: *שְׁקִילֵי טִיבוּתִיךְ וְשַׁדְיָא אַחִיזְרֵי, כְּבָר נָד וָלָד.§ "אֵין פּוֹרְסִין נִשְׁבִּין לְיוֹנִים" וכו'.§ וּמִי אָזְלֵי כּוּלֵּי הַאי? וְהָתְנַן: *[ו]מַרְחִיקִין אֶת הַשּׁוֹבָךְ מִן הָעִיר חֲמִשִּׁים אַמָּה! אָמַר אַבַּיֵי: מֵישָׁט שָׁיְיטֵי טוּבָא, כְּרֵסַיְיהוּ בַּחֲמִשִּׁים אַמָּה מַלְיָא. וּמֵישַׁט שְׁלֹשִׁים רִיס וְתוּ לָא? וְהָתַנְיָא: [ז]בַּיִּשּׁוּב — אֲפִילּוּ מֵאָה מִיל לֹא יִפְרוֹם! רַב יוֹסֵף אָמַר: [ח]בְּיִשּׁוּב כְּרָמִים. רַבָּה אָמַר: בְּיִשּׁוּב שׁוֹבָכִין. וְתִיפּוֹק לֵיהּ מִשּׁוּם שׁוֹבָכִין גּוּפַיְיהוּ! אִיבָּעֵית אֵימָא: [ט]בִּדְגוֹי, וְאִיבָּעֵית אֵימָא: [י]בְּדְהֶפְקֵר, וְאִיבָּעֵית אֵימָא: [כ]בְּדִידֵיהּ.§

הדרן עלך מרובה

רש"י

לָשׁוֹן סוּרְסִי לָמָּה אֶלָּא אוֹ לְשׁוֹן הַקּוֹדֶשׁ אוֹ לָשׁוֹן יְוָנִי. הוּא לָשׁוֹן נָא, וְסוּרְסִי לָשׁוֹן נִלְעָג הוּא. פַּרְסִי. לָשׁוֹן נָאֶה מֵאֲרַמִּי. בְּאֶרֶץ יִשְׂרָאֵל הַסְּמוּכָה לְיָוָן נָקַט יְוָנִי, וּבָבֶל הַסָּמוּךְ לְפָרַס נָקַט לָשׁוֹן פַּרְסִי. חָכְמַת יְוָנִית. בְּנֵי פַּלָּטִין הַקְּרוֹבִים לַמַּלְכוּת מְסַפְּרִין בָּהּ. עֵינִי עוֹלְלָה לְנַפְשִׁי. לָא גָּרְסִינַן "מַאי דִּכְתִיב". כְּלוֹמַר: כָּךְ אָמַר רַבָּן שִׁמְעוֹן: קוֹרֵא אֲנִי עַל עַצְמִי הַמִּקְרָא הַזֶּה, שֶׁיֵּשׁ עָלַי לְעוֹלֵל עֵינַי בִּבְכִי וְדִמְעָה מִכָּל מִשְׁפְּחוֹת הָעִיר. יְלָדִים. בַּחוּרִים. הַמְסַפֵּר קוֹמִי. לְפָנִים בַּמֵּצַח. מִדַּרְכֵי הָאֱמוֹרִי. שֶׁמְּסַפְּרִים מִלִּפְנֵיהֶם וּמְשַׁיְּירִין בְּלוֹרִית מֵאַחֲרֵיהֶן. ל"א: דֶּרֶךְ רוֹמִיִּים לְגַלֵּחַ שֵׂעָר שֶׁלְּמַעְלָה מִן הָאוֹזֶן, בִּתְשׁוּבַת הַגְּאוֹנִים. לַסְּפָר = מַרְקָא, בֵּין יִשְׂרָאֵל לַגּוֹיִים, וּצְרִיכָה שִׁימּוּר. בְּאָרוּר. כִּדְתַנְיָא לְעֵיל: אָרוּר יִשְׂרָאֵל שֶׁיְּגַדֵּל חֲזִירִים. בָּבֶל. שֵׁם הַמְּדִינָה, וְעִיר אַחַת שֶׁבָּהּ נִקְרֵאת נְהַרְדְּעָא, וְאוֹתָהּ הָעִיר סְמוּכָה לַסְּפָר. וְאַשְׁמוּעִינַן רַב נַחְמָן דְּהוֹאִיל וְיֵשׁ בְּבָבֶל יִשּׁוּב קָבוּעַ, וְיִשְׂרָאֵל הַרְבֵּה — מוּתָּר לְגַדֵּל כְּלָבִים בָּעִיר הַסְּמוּכָה לַסְּפָר כְּאִילּוּ הִיא מֵאֶרֶץ יִשְׂרָאֵל. נִיבֵי = ינייד"ש. ל"א: אַרְבַּע שִׁינֵּי הַכֶּלֶב הָאֲרוּכּוֹת שֶׁבָּהֶן נוֹשֵׁךְ, כָּךְ שָׁמַעְתִּי (חולין דף נט.) (בִּבְכוֹרוֹת). שְׁקִילֵי טִיבוּתִיךְ. נְטוּלָה הִיא טוֹבָתְךָ וּמוּטֶּלֶת עַל הַקּוֹצִים (שֶׁלֹּא קָשַׁרְתָּ אֶת הַכֶּלֶב), מַה שֶּׁאַתָּה מְנַחֲמֵנִי — הֶבֶל. כְּבָר נָד. וְנֶעֱקַר מִמְּקוֹמוֹ. מַרְחִיקִין אֶת הַשּׁוֹבָךְ. שֶׁלֹּא יַפְסִידוּ תְּבוּאָה וּפֵירוֹת *שֶׁסְּבִיב הָעִיר. כְּרֵסַיְיהוּ בַּחֲמִשִּׁים מַלְיָא. בַּמֶּה שֶׁהֵן מְלַקְּטוֹת וּמְנַקְּרוֹת בַּקַּרְקַע מְלֵאִין כַּחֲמִשִּׁין אַמָּה, הִלְכָּךְ לְגַבֵּי אֲכִילַת תְּבוּאַת עִיר אֵין לָחוּשׁ בְּיוֹתֵר. בְּיִשּׁוּב כְּרָמִים. שֶׁהוֹלֵךְ מִכֶּרֶם לְכֶרֶם עַד לְמֵרָחוֹק. בְּדִידֵיהּ. שֶׁאוֹתָן שׁוֹבָכִין שֶׁלּוֹ, וּמִשּׁוּם יוֹנֵי שׁוֹבָכִין שֶׁלֹּא יִלָּכְדוּ בַּפַּחִין אֵין לָחוּשׁ — דְּשֶׁלּוֹ הֵן. אֲבָל יֵשׁ לָחוּשׁ לְיוֹנֵי הַיִּשּׁוּב שֶׁבָּאִין דֶּרֶךְ הַשּׁוֹבָכִין לְמֵרָחוֹק.

הדרן עלך מרובה

תוספות

לשון סורסי. נראה דלשון סורסי הוא לשון ארמי, כדאמר (בראשית רבה פ' עה): אל יהי לשון סורסי קל בעיניך, שהרי בתורה ובנביאים ובכתובים חלק לו הכתוב כבוד, תורה — דכתיב: *יגר שהדותא, בנביאים — דכתיב: *כדנן תימרון להון, בכתובים — דניאל ועזרא. ולבן היה מארם נהרים. *ודניאל נמי קורהו לשון סורסי, אף על גב דכתיב ביה: וידברו הכשדים למלך ארמית. והא דנקט הכא בארץ ישראל לשון סורסי, ובבבל נקט לשון ארמי — אור"ת: לפי שמעט משתנה, כעין לשון לעז שמדברים אותו לשון לא במדינה אחת יותר מבאחרת. כי אונקלוס הגר תירגם "עד הגל הזה" — "סהיד דגורא הדין", ולבן קרא ליה "יגר שהדותא". ונ"ל לשון שדיבר לבן הוא לשון סורסי, ועל שם סוריא נקרא סורסי — דסוריא היא ארם נהרים וארם צובה שכבש דוד, ועל שם שקרובה לארץ ישראל ° אין לשון ארמי שלה לא כל כך.

התירו לספר קומי. מתחילה לא גזרו על קרובים למלכות, והוא היה רגיל, כדאשכחן במעילה (דף יז.) שהלך אבטולמוס בן ראובן וסיפר קומי שלא יכירו שהוא יהודי והטעה אותם.

שני אלפים ושני רבבות גרסינן, ולא גרסינן "שני אלפים רבבות", דבמדבר לא היו כי אם ס' ריבוא ושרתה שכינה. ולא שייך כאן הא ד"אחד דיני ממונות" (סנהדרין דף לט.) דכל בי עשרה שכינה שריא — דהכא אנביאים ואמשכן קאמר.

והתניא ובישוב אפילו ק' מיל לא יפרום. ע"כ השתא לא ידע פירוש הברייתא. [וקשה]: דהא משמע דק' מיל לאו דוקא, אלא אפילו אלף לא יפרום, וא"כ האי ישוב היכי דמי? אי קרי העיר ישוב — א"כ לא יפרום בשום מקום, אפילו במדבר, דאפילו המדבר רחוק אלף מיל, דהא אמר דק' מיל לאו דוקא. ואפילו נאמר דק' מיל דוקא — אכתי תקשה רישא לסיפא, דהא רישא קתני דרחוק שלשים ריס מן הישוב פורסין, ובסיפא קתני: אפילו ק' מיל לא יפרום. דהכי תניא בתוספתא בפירקין (פ"ח): אין פורסין נשבים ליונים אא"כ הרחיק מן הישוב שלשים ריס. בד"א — במדבר, אבל בישוב — אפילו ק' מיל לא יפרום. וליכא למימר נמי דס"ד דבישוב של זרעים שייטי טובא, ורישא דברייתא מיירי בישוב עיר, וקרי ליה מדבר משום דליכא זרעים — דא"כ מאי קשה ליה! ונראה לריצב"א: דודאי ס"ד דאיירי בישוב זרעים, וה"פ: ומישט שייטי שלשים ריס ותו לא, אפילו בישוב זרעים? והא מוכחא סיפא דבישוב זרעים שייטי טובא, ואין זה אלא משום אכילה, אלמא דלא מליא כריסה בחמשים אמה! ומשני: דלא איירי בישוב זרעים אלא בישוב כרמים ובישוב שובכין, וקרי מדבר היכא דליכא ישוב כרמים וישוב שובכין. **הדרן עלך מרובה**

מסורת הש"ס

סוטה מט: גיטין נח. [ע"ש]

איכה ג

[תוספתא דסוטה פט"ו]

ס"א אינו

ס"א שבתוך

במדבר י

יבמות סד. [ע"ש]

שבת סג:

[שבת שם וש"נ]

ב"ק כג.

בראשית לא ירמיה י

[עי' בתוס' ב"ב לא: ד"ה לסוריא]

[עי' תוס' ע"ז לב. ד"ה אבל]

[עירובין מה.]

[רש"א]

עין משפט נר מצוה

קפא א מיי' פי"א מהל' ע"ז הלכה א סמג לאוין נ טוש"ע י"ד סי' קעח סעיף א:

קפב ב מיי' שם הלכה ג טוש"ע שם סעיף ב:

קפג ג ד מיי' פ"ה מהל' נזקי ממון הלכה ט סמג עשין סו טוש"ע ח"מ סי' תט סעיף ג:

קפד ה מיי' שם הלכה ט:

קפה ו מיי' פ"ו מהל' גזלה ואבדה הלכה ט סמג עשין עג טוש"ע ח"מ סי' קנה סעיף כד וטוח"מ סי' שע:

קפו ז ח ט י כ מיי' שם הלכה ח סמג שם טוח"מ סי' שע:

הגהות הב"ח

(א) גמ' ושני רבבות הרי שהיו ישראל שני אלפים ושני רבבות חסר אחד והיתה אשה:

גליון הש"ס

גמ' או לשון פרסי. בתוס' ב"ב דף ל ע"ב ד"ה לסוריא הגי' או לשון סורסי: **תוס'** ד"ה לשון וכו' אין לשון ארמי שלה לא כל כך. ועיין ב"ב דף ל ע"ב תוס' ד"ה לסוריא: